The Nonprofit Manager's Resource Directory

Second Edition

Wiley Nonprofit Law, Finance, and Management Series

The Art of Planned Giving: Understanding Donors and the Culture of Giving by Douglas E. White

Beyond Fund Raising: New Strategies for Nonprofit Investment and Innovation by Kay Grace

Budgeting for Not-for-Profit Organizations by David Maddox

Careers in Fund-Raising by Lilya Wagner

The Complete Guide to Fund Raising Management by Stanley Weinstein

The Complete Guide to Nonprofit Management by Smith, Bucklin & Associates

Critical Issues in Fund Raising edited by Dwight Burlingame

Cultivating Diversity in Fund-Raising by Janice Gow Pettey

Faith-Based Management: Leading Organizations That Are Based on More Than Just Mission by Peter Brinckerhoff

Financial and Accounting Guide for Not-for-Profit Organizations, Sixth Edition by Malvern J. Gross, Jr., Richard F. Larkin, John H. McCarthy, PricewaterhouseCoopers LLP

Financial Empowerment: More Money for More Mission by Peter Brinckerhoff

Financial Management for Nonprofit Organizations by Jo Ann Hankin, Alan Seidner, and John Zietlow

The First Legal Answer Book for Fund-Raisers by Bruce R. Hopkins

Fund-Raising Fundamentals: A Guide to Annual Giving for Professionals and Volunteers by James M. Greenfield

Fundraising Cost Effectiveness: A Self-Assessment Workbook by James M. Greenfield

Fund-Raising Regulation: A State-by-State Handbook of Registration Forms, Requirements, and Procedures by Seth Perlman and Betsy Hills Bush

Grantseeker's Budget Toolkit by James A. Quick and Cheryl S. New

Grantseeker's Toolkit: A Comprehensive Guide to Finding Funding by Cheryl S. New and James A. Quick

Grant Winner's Toolkit: Project Management and Evaluation by James A. Quick and Cheryl S. New

High Impact Philanthropy: How Donors, Boards, and Nonprofit Organizations Can Transform Nonprofit Communities by Kay Sprinkel Grace and Alan L. Wendroff

High Performance Nonprofit Organizations: Managing Upstream for Greater Impact by Christine W. Letts, William P. Ryan, and Allen Grossman

Improving the Economy, Efficiency, and Effectiveness of Nonprofits: Conducting Operational Reviews by Rob Reider

Intermediate Sanctions: Curbing Nonprofit Abuse by Bruce R. Hopkins and D. Benson Tesdahl

International Fund Raising for Nonprofits by Thomas Harris

International Guide to Nonprofit Law by Lester A. Salamon and Stefan Toepler & Associates

Joint Ventures Involving Tax-Exempt Organizations, Second Edition by Michael I. Sanders

The Law of Fund-Raising, Second Edition by Bruce R. Hopkins

The Law of Tax-Exempt Healthcare Organizations, Second Edition by Thomas K. Hyatt and Bruce R. Hopkins

The Law of Tax-Exempt Organizations, Seventh Edition by Bruce R. Hopkins

The Legal Answer Book for Nonprofit Organizations by Bruce R. Hopkins

A Legal Guide to Starting and Managing a Nonprofit Organization, Third Edition by Bruce R. Hopkins

The Legislative Labyrinth: A Map for Not-for-Profits, edited by Walter Pidgeon

Managing Affordable Housing: A Practical Guide to Creating Stable Communities by Bennett L. Hecht, Local Initiatives Support Corporation, and James Stockard

Managingnonprofits.org by Bennett L. Hecht and Rey Ramsey

Mission-Based Management: Leading Your Not-for-Profit in the 21st Century, Second Edition by Peter Brinckerhoff

Mission-Based Management: Leading Your Not-for-Profit in the 21st Century, Second Edition, Workbook by Peter Brinckerhoff

Mission-Based Marketing: How Your Not-for-Profit Can Succeed in a More Competitive World by Peter Brinckerhoff

Nonprofit Boards: Roles, Responsibilities, and Performance by Diane J. Duca

Nonprofit Compensation and Benefits Practices by Applied Research and Development Institute International, Inc.

The Nonprofit Counsel by Bruce R. Hopkins

The Nonprofit Guide to the Internet, Second Edition by Michael Johnston

Nonprofit Investment Policies: A Practical Guide to Creation and Implementation by Robert Fry, Jr.

The Nonprofit Law Dictionary by Bruce R. Hopkins

Nonprofit Compensation, Benefits, and Employment Law by David G. Samuels and Howard Pianko

The Nonprofit Handbook, Third Edition: Management by Tracy Daniel Connors

The Nonprofit Handbook, Third Edition: Fund Raising by James M. Greenfield

The Nonprofit Manager's Resource Dictionary, Second Edition by Ronald A. Landskroner

Nonprofit Organizations' Business Forms: Disk Edition by John Wiley & Sons, Inc.

Planned Giving: Management, Marketing, and Law, Second Edition by Ronald R. Jordan and Katelyn L. Quynn

The Private Foundation Answer Book by Bruce Hopkins and Jody Blazek

Private Foundations: Tax Law and Compliance by Bruce R. Hopkins and Jody Blazek

Program-Related Investments: A Technical Manual for Foundations by Christie I. Baxter

Reengineering Your Nonprofit Organization: A Guide to Strategic Transformation by Alceste T. Pappas

Reinventing the Universe: Managing and Financing Institutions of Higher Education by Sandra L. Johnson and Sean C. Rush, PricewaterhouseCoopers LLP

The Second Legal Answer Book for Nonprofit Organizations by Bruce R. Hopkins

The Second Legal Answer Book for Fund Raisers by Bruce R. Hopkins

Social Entrepreneurship: The Art of Mission-Based Venture Development by Peter Brinckerhoff

Special Events: Proven Strategies for Nonprofit Fund Raising by Alan Wendroff

Starting and Managing a Nonprofit Organization: A Legal Guide, Third Edition by Bruce R. Hopkins

Strategic Communications for Nonprofit Organizations: Seven Steps to Creating a Successful Plan by Janel Radtke

Strategic Planning for Nonprofit Organizations: A Practical Guide and Workbook by Michael Allison and Jude Kay, Support Center for Nonprofit Management

Streetsmart Financial Basics for Nonprofit Managers by Thomas A. McLaughlin

A Streetsmart Guide to Nonprofit Mergers and Networks by Thomas A. McLaughlin

Successful Marketing Strategies for Nonprofit Organizations by Barry J. McLeish

Successful Corporate Fund Raising: Effective Strategies for Today's Nonprofits by Scott Sheldon

The Tax Law of Colleges and Universities by Bertrand M. Harding

Tax Planning and Compliance for Tax-Exempt Organizations: Forms, Checklists, Procedures, Third Edition by Jody Blazek

The Universal Benefits of Volunteering: A Practical Workbook for Nonprofit Organizations, Volunteers and Corporations by Walter P. Pidgeon, Jr.

Trade Secrets for Every Nonprofit Manager by Thomas A. McLaughlin

Values-Based Estate Planning: A Step-by-Step Approach to Wealth Transfers for Professional Advisors by Scott Fithian

Also by Peter M. Brinckerhoff:

Faith-Based Management: Leading Organizations That Are Based on More Than Just Mission by Peter Brinckerhoff

Financial Empowerment: More Money for More Mission by Peter Brinckerhoff

Mission-Based Management: Leading Your Not-for-Profit in the 21st Century, Second Edition by Peter Brinckerhoff

Mission-Based Management: Leading Your Not-for-Profit in the 21st Century, Second Edition, Workbook by Peter Brinckerhoff

Mission-Based Marketing: How Your Not-for-Profit Can Succeed in a More Competitive World by Peter Brinckerhoff

Social Entrepreneurship: The Art of Mission-Based Venture Development by Peter Brinckerhoff

The Nonprofit Manager's Resource Directory

Second Edition

Ronald A. Landskroner

John Wiley & Sons, Inc.
New York • Chichester • Weinheim • Brisbane • Singapore • Toronto

Library of Congress Cataloging-in-Publication Data:

Landskroner, Ronald A.
    The nonprofit manager's resource directory / Ronald A. Landskroner.—2nd ed.
        p. cm.—(Wiley nonprofit law, finance, and management series)
    ISBN 0-471-39242-1 (pbk. : alk. paper)
        1. Nonprofit organizations—United States—Management—Information
services—Directories. 2. Nonprofit organizations—United States—Computer network
resources—Directories. 3. Nonprofit organizations—United States—Bibliography. I. Title.
II. Series.

    Z7164.T87 L36 2001
    [HD62.6]
    016.658´048—dc21   2001045384

Dedication

This book is dedicated to my mother, Sadie, and my very good
friend Barbara/Terry for their never-ending love, encouragement, support, and belief in me.
And to the unconditional love and companionship of Pete, Caitlin, and Susie (my kitties)
as well as all the other critters who have touched me.

Contents

BONUS Appendices—Available only on CD-ROM

A.   **The Nonprofit Sector: An Overview**

Organizations

General Resources

Dimensions, Role, Future

Public Policy

Periodicals

Internet Resources

B.   **Accountability and Ethics Organizations and Research Centers**

Organizations

General Resources

Internet Resources

C.   **Assessment and Evaluation**

Organizations

Product and Service Providers

General Resources

Internet Resources

D.   **International Third Sector**

Organizations

    Worldwide

    Country-by-Country Listing

General Resources

Periodicals

E.   **Leadership**

Organizations

Product and Service Providers

General Resources

Periodicals

Internet Sites

    Websites

    E-Mail Discussion Lists

    Online Publications/E-Zines

F.   **Marketing and Communications**

Organizations

Products & Services

   Advertising

   Cause-Related Marketing

   Direct Mail Marketing

   General Marketing

   Internet Marketing & Advertising

   Media

   Membership Development & Renewal

   Public Opinion Research & Surveys

   Promotion, Publicity, and Public Relations

   Publications

   Social Marketing

   Special Events

General Resources

   Communications

   Direct Marketing

   Market Surveys and Focus Groups

   Marketing

   Media

   Membership

   Promotion, Publicity, and Public Relations

   Public Speaking

   Publications and Publishing

   Social Marketing

   Speakers Bureau

   Special Events

   Volunteer Marketing

Periodicals

Internet Sites

   General Marketing

   General Communications

   Direct Mail

   Internet

   Media

   Newsletters

   Online Publications

   Public Opinion

   Public Speaking, Speechmaking, and Speechwriting

   Speechmaking

   E-Zines

   E-Mail Discussion Lists

G.   Organizational Design, Structure, and Development

Organizations
Product and Service Providers
General Resources
Periodicals
Internet Sites
  E-Mail Discussion Lists

H.   Philanthropy

Organizations
Academic and Research Centers
General
  Civil Society
  Corporate Philanthropy
  Donor Research, Charity Screening, and Philanthropic Accountability
  Ethnic Philanthropy
  Foundations and Other Grant-Making Institutions
  Philanthropy Alliances
  Individual and Family Philanthropy
  Women and Philanthropy
  Workplace and Online Philanthropy
  Youth Philanthropy
Product and Service Providers
  Accounting/Tax
  Charitable Funds Management
  Corporate Philanthropy
  Philanthropic Giving
  Software—Fund Accounting
  Software—Grants Management
  Software—Grants Tracking
  Foundations Grant Services
  General Consulting
  Investment Management
  Online Giving
Publications
  General—Tradition, History, and Practice
  Charity Screening
  Civil Society
  Corporate Philanthropy and Nonprofit-Corporate Collaboration
  Foundations
  Individual and Family Philanthropy
  Multicultural Philanthropy
  Religion and Philanthropy
  Social Change Philanthropy
  Wealth and Philanthropy
  Workplace Philanthropy

The Nonprofit Manager's Resource Directory

Second Edition

PART I

Quotations on Philanthropy

QUOTATIONS ON PHILANTHROPY

The world is before you, and you need not take it or leave it as it was before you came in.

—*James Baldwin*

We must be the change we want to see in the world.

—*Mahatma Gandhi*

The work of a garden bears visible fruits—in a world where most of our labours seem suspiciously meaningless.

—*Pat Brown*

Education should not compete with national defense, the trade deficit, drugs or AIDS. Instead, think of it as a solution to those problems.

—*David Kearns, Chairman, Xerox Corporation*

You can only lead others where you yourself are willing to go.

—*Lachlan McLean*

Nothing is so potent as the silent influence of a good example.

—*James Kent*

Some people give time, some money, some their skills and connections, some their life's blood . . . but everyone has something to give.

—*Barbara Bush*

To know and not to do is not to know.

—*Wang Yang Ming*

The more you give, the more you get back.

—*Zen proverb*

Philanthropy is commendable, but it must not cause the philanthropist to overlook the circumstances of economic injustice which make philanthropy necessary.

—*Martin Luther King, Jr.*

Everybody can be great . . . because anybody can serve. You don't have to have a college degree to serve. You don't have to make your subject and verb agree to serve. You only need a heart full of grace. A soul generated by love.

—*Martin Luther King, Jr.*

The quality, not the longevity, of one's life is what is important.

—*Martin Luther King, Jr.*

He who passively accepts evil is as much involved in it as he who helps to perpetrate it.

—*Martin Luther King, Jr.*

All men are caught in an inescapable network of mutuality. Tied in a single garment of destiny.

—*Martin Luther King, Jr.*

Injustice anywhere is a threat to justice everywhere.

—*Martin Luther King, Jr.*

All that is necessary for the triumph of evil is that good men do nothing.

—*Edmund Burke*

If you want one year of prosperity, grow grain.
If you want ten years of prosperity, grow trees.
If you want one hundred years of prosperity, grow people.

—*Chinese proverb*

What is the use of living if it be not to strive for noble causes and to make this muddled world a better place for those who will live in it after we are gone?

—*Winston Churchill*

It is better to light one candle than curse the darkness.

—*Confucius*

No one is useless in this world who lightens the burden of another.

—*Charles Dickens*

What do we live for, if it is not to make life less difficult for each other?

—*George Elliot*

The luxury of doing good surpasses every other personal enjoyment.

—*John Gay*

You give but little when you give of your possessions. It is when you give of yourself that you truly give.

—*Kahlil Gibran*

Each time a man stands up for an ideal, or acts to improve the lot of others, or strikes out against injustice, he sends forth a tiny ripple of hope, and crossing each other from a million different centres of energy and daring, those ripples build a current that can sweep down the mightiest walls of oppression and resistance.

—*Robert F. Kennedy*

The greatest pleasure I know is to do a good action by stealth, and to have it found out by accident.

—*Charles Lamb*

To do something, however small, to make others happier and better, is the highest ambition, the most elevating hope, which can inspire a human being.

—*John Lubbock*

Accomplishment is when you use your extra strength to help someone else, rather than to get to the top first.

—*Donald Ernest Mansell*

There is a destiny that makes men brothers:
None goes his way alone;
All that we send into the lives of others
Comes back into our own.

—*Edwin Markham*

Energy abounds when you volunteer—do it now.

—*Holly Stewart McMahon*

I want to thank and pay tribute to all of our volunteers—those dedicated people who believe in all work and no pay.

—*Robert Orben*

What we have done for ourselves alone dies with us; what we have done for others and the world remains and is immortal.

—*Albert Pike*

The place to improve the world is first in one's own heart and head and hands, and then work outward from there.

—*Robert M. Pirsig, "Zen and the Art of Motorcycle Maintenance"*

You cannot do a kindness too soon, because you never know how soon it will be too late.

—*Proverb*

Do not wait for extraordinary circumstances to do good actions; try to use ordinary situations.

—*Jean Paul Richer*

I do not know what your destiny will be, but the one thing I know: the only ones among you who will really be happy are those who will have sought and found how to serve.

—*Albert Schweitzer*

It is the greatest of all mistakes to do nothing because you can only do a little. Do what you can.

—*Sydney Smith*

I expect to pass through this world but once. Any good thing, therefore, that I can do or any kindness that I can show for any fellow creature, let me do it now. Let me not defer or neglect it, for I shall not pass this way again.

—*Unknown*

People are lonely because they build walls instead of bridges.

—*Unknown*

Man is a special being and, if left to himself in an isolated condition, would be one of the weakest creatures; but associated with his kind, he works wonders.

—*Daniel Webster*

Do all the good you can,
By all the means you can,
In all the ways you can,
In all the places you can,
At all the times you can,
To all the people you can,
As long as ever you can.

—*John Wesley, "Letters of John Wesley"*

There are two ways of spreading light: to be the candle or the mirror that reflects it.

—*Edith Wharton*

No man has ever risen to the stature of spiritual manhood until he has found that it is finer to serve somebody else than it is to serve himself.

—*Woodrow Wilson*

That best portion of a good man's life,
His little, nameless, unremembered acts
of kindness and of love.

—*William Wordsworth*

Charity is a virtue of the heart. Gifts and alms are the expressions, not the essence, of this virtue.

—*Joseph Addison*

People think that if they were rich they would contribute to charities. My experience has been that if you don't start giving away your money when you have very little, you won't do it when you get a lot.

—*Robert Bainum*

It is more difficult to give money away intelligently than it is to earn it in the first place.

—*Andrew Carnegie*

Continually give, continually gain.

—*Chinese proverb*

It is every man's obligation to put back into the world at least the equivalent of what he takes out of it.

—*Albert Einstein*

The act of philanthropy is a spiritual act, an expression of caring for one's fellow human beings. It is a belief in the future and that the future can be good. It is investing in that future. It is helping to make the dream come true.

—*Arthur Frantzreb*

The word philanthropy has its roots in the Greek language meaning "love for mankind." It was never meant to apply only to donors of thousands or millions of dollars.

—*Arthur Frantzreb*

Charity sees the need, not the cause.

—*German proverb*

It is well to give when asked, but it is better to give unasked, through understanding.

—*Kahlil Gibran*

The main problem is not the haves and the have-nots—it's the give-nots.

—*Arnold Glasow*

If you haven't got any charity in your heart, you have the worst kind of heart trouble.

—*Bob Hope*

We make a living by what we get; we make a life by what we give.

—*Norman Kennedy*

Do your givin' while you're livin' . . . then you'll be knowin' where it's goin'.

—*Ann Landers*

He who obtains has little. He who scatters has much.

—*Lao-Tzu*

I will charge thee nothing but the promise that thee will help the next man thee finds in trouble.

—*Mennonite proverb*

To keep a lamp burning, we have to put oil in it.

—*Mother Teresa*

Charity begins at home, but should not end there.

—*Scottish proverb*

He who gives when he is asked has waited too long.

—*Lucius Annaeus Seneca*

By always taking out and never putting in, the bottom is soon reached.

—*Spanish proverb*

True charity is the desire to be useful to others without thought of recompense.

—*Emanuel Swedenborg*

Charity begins at home and generally dies from lack of outdoor exercise.

—*Unknown*

Real charity doesn't care if it's tax deductible or not.

—*Unknown*

If you are not poor enough to take charity, you are rich enough to give it.

—*Unknown*

Charity and pride have different aims, yet both feed the poor.

—*Unknown*

To give away money is an easy matter and in any person's power. But to decide to whom to give it, and how large and when, And for what purpose, and how, is neither in every person's Power nor an easy matter . . .

—*Aristotle*

Spiritual needs are higher than physical needs, but the physical needs of another are my spiritual need.

—*Rabbi Israel Salanter*

The strongest bond of human sympathy, outside of the family relation, should be one uniting all working people, of all nations, and tongues, and kindreds.

—*Abraham Lincoln*

I wondered why somebody didn't do something. Then I realized, I am somebody.

—*Source unknown*

One is not born into the world to do everything but to do something.

—*Thoreau*

I always knew that one day
   I would take this road but yesterday
   I did not know today
   Would be the day.

—*Nagarjuna*

A FUNDRAISER'S PLACE IN HEAVEN

A man knocked at the heavenly gates,
His face was scarred and old.
He stood before the man of fate
For admission to the fold.
"What have you done," St. Peter asked,
"to gain admission here?"
"I've been a fundraiser, Sir," he said,
"For many and many a year."
The Pearly gates swung open wide;
St. Peter rang the bell.
"Come in and choose your harp," he said,
"You've had your share of hell."

—*Author unknown*

The best and most beautiful things in the world cannot be seen or even touched. They must be felt with the heart.

—*Helen Keller*

PART II

Financial Management

ORGANIZATIONS

(See also General Management; Legal Issues; Philanthropy; Resource Development; Strategic Planning)

Accountants for the Public Interest (API)

University of Baltimore, Merrick School of Business, 1420 North Charles Street, Suite 142, Baltimore, MD 21201
Tel: 410-837-6533; FAX: 410-837-6532
E-mail: api36@juno.com (Thomas Lee Woods)

▶ API is a national nonprofit organization through which volunteer accountants donate their time and expertise. API assists small and start-up businesses, nonprofit organizations, charities, and low-income individuals. Incorporated in 1975, API has a rapidly expanding network of affiliates coast to coast that recruit volunteer accountants and screen requests for help. Affiliates offer a variety of accounting programs to their communities, including tax assistance clinics, hotlines for accounting questions, financial management seminars, and direct assistance to small businesses and nonprofit organizations. Accounting volunteers provide assistance in the following areas: (1) *Direct Service* (assisting with tax preparation, preparing for the annual audit, establishing record-keeping systems, setting up or computerizing an accounting system), (2) *Advisory Service* (financial management, budgets/cash flow forecast, loan applications), and (3) *Community Affairs Service* (workshops on a variety of financial topics, serving on a nonprofit's board of directors, advising local governmental agencies on accounting, tax, budget, and other financial issues). API publishes quarterly the *API Account* newsletter as well as informational guides and handbooks dealing with financial accounting and related tax issues for nonprofits, including: *What a Difference Nonprofits Make: A Guide to Accounting Procedures, What a Difference Preparation Makes: A Guide to the Nonprofit Audit, What a Difference Understanding Makes: Guides to Nonprofit Management, Nonprofit Accounting Guide, What a Difference Knowledge Makes: A Guide to Intermediate Sanctions for 501(c)(3) and_501(c)(4) Organizations,* and the *National Directory of Volunteer Accounting Programs* (see separate listings under Publications).

Accounting Aid Society

18145 Mack Avenue, Suite 2026, Detroit, MI 48224-1444
Tel: 313-647-9620; FAX: 313-647-9628
E-mail: info@accountingaidsociety.org;
WWW: http://www.accountingaidsociety.org

▶ The Nonprofit Services Program assists nonprofit agencies in becoming stable, effective, and efficient by applying sound business practices to their organizations. Client organizations represent a cross-section of human service, arts, religious, civic, environmental and public interest organizations; for nonprofit organizations requiring individualized assistance. Accounting Aid Society's AnswerLine for Nonprofit Management is a free service for quick answers to nonprofit management questions. Answers provided by AnswerLine come from research using the *Michigan Nonprofit Management Manual,* along with expert support from our volunteer partners working in the professional community. Offers consultations, seminars, workshops, information, referrals, direct assistance programs, board and leadership training, business planning, accounting services, and financial management. The Accounting Aid Society also publishes the quarterly newsletter *News from Accounting Aid Society.*

American College of Trust and Estate Counsel (ACTEC) *(See also Legal Issues; Resource Development)*

3415 South Sepulveda Boulevard, Suite 330, Los Angeles, California 90034
Tel: 310-398-1888; FAX: 310-572-7280
E-mail: info@actec.org; WWW: http://www.actec.org,
http://www.actec.org/public/ShowResourcesPublic.asp

▶ The American College of Trust and Estate Counsel is a professional association consisting of approximately 2,700 lawyers from throughout the United States. The purposes of ACTEC are to maintain an international association of lawyers skilled and experienced in the preparation of wills and trusts; estate planning; probate procedure and administration of trusts and estates of decedents, minors, and incompetents; to improve and reform probate, trust and tax laws, procedures, and professional responsibility; to bring together qualified lawyers whose character and ability will contribute to the achievement of the purposes of the college; and to cooperate with bar associations and other organizations with similar purposes.

American Council on Gift Annuities (ACGA)

233 McCrea Street, Suite 400, Indianapolis, Indiana 46225
Tel: 317-269-6271; FAX: 317-269-6276
E-mail: acga@iupui.edu (Gloria Kermeen, ACGA Administrator);
WWW: http://www.ncpg.org/acga.html

▶ The ACGA is a qualified nonprofit organization formed in 1927 as the Committee on Gift Annuities for the purpose of providing educational and other services to American charities regarding gift annuities and other forms of planned gifts. One of the primary activities of the Council is the publication of suggested charitable gift annuity rates for use by charities and their donors. The Council retains the services of an actuarial firm to advise and consult on matters pertaining to life expectancies and related matters. Its suggested rates have long been recognized, not only by charities and donors, but also by state insurance departments and the IRS as being actuarially sound and in the best interests of all parties involved.

American Institute of Certified Public Accountants (AICPA)

1211 Avenue of the Americas, New York, NY 10036-8775
Tel: 800-862-4272, 212-596-6200 (General Inquiries);
FAX: 212-596-6213

Harborside Financial Center, 201 Plaza Three, Jersey City, NJ 07311-3881
Tel: 201-938-3000; FAX: 201-938-3329
WWW: http://www.aicpa.org

▶ National professional member organization representing more than 300,000 CPAs in public practice, industry, education, and government. Member services include: *Publications* (timely publications such as the *Journal of Accountancy, The CPA Letter, The Tax Advisor, InfoTech Update,* and *The Practicing CPA* providing up-to-date news on professional and technical trends that affect daily operation), *Technical Information Services* (toll-free hotline for immediate, practical help on problems in accounting, financial reporting, auditing, attestation, etc., exclusive of tax and legal questions), *Practical Technical Publications* (books and subscriptions in print and electronic formats), *Practice Management Resources* (guidance and publications), *Practice Development Aids* (newsletters for distribution to clients), *Library Services* (access to America's most comprehensive accounting library, with online database searches and lending by mail), *Information Retrieval* (online National Automated Accounting Research System [NAARS] with access to thousands of annual reports plus financial reporting practices and trends), *Member Sections* (for members with special interests in tax, personal financial planning, management consulting, and information technology), *Total On-line Tax and Accounting Library* (a subscription service that allows computerized information retrieval through Mead's LEXIS/NEXIS services, including NAARS), *Seminars and Conferences.* AICPA also advocates in federal and state legislative matters affecting tax laws, legal liability, and other critical issues affecting CPAs.

Arts & Business Council Inc.

121West 27th Street, Suite 702, New York, NY 10001
Tel: 212-727-7146; FAX: 212-727-3873
E-mail: info@artsandbusiness.org;
WWW: http://www.artsandbusiness.org/

▶ Since 1965, Arts & Business Council Inc. has been the nation's leading organization working to "keep the arts in business" by promoting mutually beneficial partnerships between corporations and nonprofit arts groups. Through its local and national programs the Council brings expertise, resources, and leadership talent from the business world to the arts community. The Council's flagship program, Business Volunteers for the Arts (BVA), has helped thousands of nonprofit arts organizations since 1975 by sharing their business expertise and talents on a wide range of consulting projects. In 1978, New York City's Arts & Business Council began to make the highly successful BVA model available to local communities across the United States. Those establishing a BVA chapter became licensed affiliates of the Council. The Council now serves as the national headquarters for a growing affiliate network of 23 locations, coordinating training, communication, and program sharing for the network. Find an affiliate near you online at: http://www.artsandbusiness.org/programs/bvausalist.html.

Business Volunteers Unlimited (BVU) *(See also General Management)*

Tower City Center, Suite 950, 50 Public Square,
Cleveland, Ohio, 44113-2204
Tel: 216-736-7711; FAX: 216-736-7710
E-mail: AKorngold@busvol.org (Alice Korngold, President and CEO), DObrien@busvol.org (Denise M. O'Brien, Administrative Manager); WWW: http://www.businessvolunteers.org

▶ BVU has developed a model to engage volunteers from businesses in leadership and volunteer activities. BVU prepares and refers business volunteers for service on nonprofit boards of trustees, involves professionals in providing volunteer management assistance to nonprofits; and channels thousands of employees and their families to a variety of well-organized direct service volunteer activities. By leveraging volunteer assistance from businesses, BVU enhances the leadership and management and expands the staffing capabilities of hundreds of nonprofits, while enabling businesses to build strategic, powerful, and enduring relationships with the local community.

Center for Governmental and Nonprofit Accounting

P.O. Box 6951, Radford University, Radford, VA 24142
Tel: 540-831-5668
E-mail: famenkhi@runet.edu (Dr. Felix Amenkhienan);
WWW: http://www.runet.edu/~actg-web/cgna.html

▶ The Center for Governmental and Nonprofit Accounting (CGNA) at Radford University keeps you ahead of these changes by informing you of current reporting procedures and research issues and providing professional continuing education workshops. CGNA strives to identify, promote, and become a source for the best practice development for nonprofit and governmental organizations. Join us in making this unique center a success. The Center offers quality educational opportunities for professionals. Recently created by the accounting department, the CGNA provides a forum for interaction and idea exchange among faculty, students, and professionals in governmental and nonprofit accounting.

Clearinghouse for Volunteer Accounting Services (CVAS)

27863 Lassen Street, Castaic, CA 91384
Tel: 805-295-8912; FAX: 805-295-8333
E-mail: paulhglass@cpateam.com (Paul H. Glass, President), kelly@greenery.com (Kelly Alblinger, Administrator);
WWW: http://cpateam.com/cvas/index.html

▶ The CVAS matches accountants with community organizations. The Technical Assistance Program provides direct, short-term help to nonprofit organizations throughout California. Whether it's a small problem, a complete breakdown of the internal accounting system, or preparation of financial information for a potential grantor, CVAS volunteers can help. Free services include preparation, creation, and/or consultation regarding accounting systems, budgets, cash flow projections, computers, financial management, financial reports, internal control systems, and tax returns. The CVAS Board Member Placement Program has been designed to match nonprofit organizations throughout California with volunteers who share common interests.

CPAs for the Public Interest (CPAsPI)

222 South Riverside Plaza, Suite 1600, Chicago, IL 60606-6098
Tel: 800-993-0393 (within Illinois), 312-993-0393;
FAX: 312-993-9432
E-mail: communityservice@icpas.org, VanveenS@icpas.org;
WWW: http://www.icpas.org/icpas/cpaspi/cpaspi.htm

▶ CPAsPI provides pro bono volunteer professionals with financial, tax, technical, accounting, and management expertise to community service projects and not-for-profit organizations. Provides volunteer accounting support through short-term accounting assistance, board placement, public issue analysis, workshops, publications, and Chicago school-reform support; volunteers assist new charities by setting up accounting systems, training staff members, advising on budgeting, and monitoring functions; seeks to provide appropriate financial management systems, train personnel to operate and maintain them, and give financial oversight. CPAs for the Public Interest has services to help organizations at any stage of growth improve their money management—services built on unique strength of financial expertise derived from a volunteer pool of professionals with financial, tax, technical, accounting and management skills. CPAsPI's publications bridge the gap between tax and accounting regulations and the needs of community-based non-profit organizations. Publications are designed to assist nonprofit managers, board members, CPAs, and consultants.

Community Accountants

1420 Walnut Street, Suite 411, Philadelphia, PA 19104
Tel: 215-893-9333; FAX: 215-893-9339
E-mail: commacct@libertynet.org;
WWW: http://www.libertynet.org./commacct

▶ Community Accountants offers a variety of ways to work with your nonprofit to improve the financial management of the organization. Assistance is provided through these programs by volunteer accounting professionals. Programs offered include: direct service (volunteers work one on one with qualified nonprofits on a short-term basis to establish a bookkeeping system, review your current system, and/or teach you how to do bookkeeping, set up and instruct you on a payroll system that is easy to operate and understand, assist you with the financial pages of the IRS for Tax-Exempt Status, prepare your 990 Form or prepare your organization for audit and review); Community Accountants on Boards & Committees (matches your organization with an accounting professional for your board or committee); workshops (arranges for a professional to speak to your group in a workshop setting on any financial issue); Nonprofit Hotline: Ask an Accountant (when your organization has an accounting question, call and you will speak to a professional accountant within two days); and publications *(Starting a Nonprofit Organization, A Simplified Manual for Financial Management of Nonprofit Organizations, Tax and Reporting Guide for Nonprofits and Small Businesses, What a Difference Nonprofits Make: A Guide to Accounting Procedures, What a Difference Preparation Makes: A Guide to the Nonprofit Audit).* Community Accountants publishes a quarterly newsletter, *The Community Accountant.*

Financial Accounting Standards Board

401 Merrit 7, P.O. Box 5116, Norwalk, CT 06856-5116
Tel: 800-748-0659 (to order publications), 203-847-0700;
FAX: 203-849-9714
E-mail: tslucas@fasb.org (Timothy Lucas, Director),
sqbielstein@FASB.ORG (Sue Bielstein, Project Manager);
WWW: http://www.rutgers.edu/Accounting/raw/fasb/,
http://www.financeproject.org/

▶ Since 1973 the FASB has been the designated private sector organization empowered to establish financial accounting and reporting standards. The mission of the FASB is to establish and improve standards of financial accounting and reporting for the guidance and education of the public, including issuers, auditors, and users of financial information. About 1,000 corporations, banks, and other organizations are members of the Financial Accounting Foundation. Additionally, about 7,000 public accounting firms and individual CPAs are members through the Accounting Research Association of the AICPA. The FASB publishes a number of publications relating to accounting practice and procedure. They include *Action Alert* (board actions and upcoming meetings), *Summaries/Status* (summaries and status of all FASB statements), *Exposure Drafts* (recent FASB exposure drafts), *Financial Accounting Research System* (FARS—contents, pricing, and downloadable demo), and *FASB Casebook* (FASB cases on recognition and measurement).

National Association of Philanthropic Planners

(NAPP) *(See also Philanthropy; Resource Development)*
4438 Centerview Drive, Suite 208, San Antonio, TX 78228
Tel: 800-342-6215, 210-735-1479; FAX: 210-735-8755
E-mail: info@napp.net; WWW: http://www.napp.net/

▶ NAPP recognizes the need for qualified financial professionals to include philanthropic planning in their practices. NAPP is committed to supporting the philanthropic planning practices of its members through a variety of association programs and benefits. It is the first formally organized group of its kind serving the philanthropic planning practitioner. NAPP publishes a quarterly newsletter, also available online at *http://www.napp.net/newsletters.html,* and holds an annual conference.

National Association of State Boards of Accountancy (NASBA)

645 Fifth Avenue, Suite 901, New York, NY 10022
150 Fourth Avenue North, Suite 700, Nashville, TN 37219
Tel: 615-880-4200; FAX: 615-880-4290
E-mail: communications@nasba.org, CPE@nasba.org (National Registry of CPE Sponsors), CPAEXAM@nasba.org
(CPA Examination Services); WWW:
http://www.nasba.org/webpages.nsf/pages/home

▶ NASBA serves as a forum for the nation's state boards of accountancy, which administer the Uniform CPA Examination, license certified public accountants, and regulate the practice of public accountancy in the United States. NASBA sponsors committee meetings, conferences, programs, and services designed to enhance the effectiveness of its member boards. NASBA offers a variety of publications to the public. In addition, NASBA publishes a monthly newsletter, the *State Board Report,* which highlights current developments affecting regulation of the profession, as well as legal briefs filed on behalf of state boards.

National Center for Nonprofit Law *(See Legal Issues—Support and Advocacy Organizations for full description)*

The National Center on Nonprofit Enterprise (NCNE)
George Mason University, 3401 North Fairfax Drive, Arlington, VA 22201
Tel: 703-993-8187
E-mail: ncne@nationalcne.org, russcargo@attglobal.net (Russ Cargo); WWW: http://www.nationalcne.org/
▶ NCNE is an independent nonprofit organization affiliated with George Mason University. NCNE assists nonprofit organizations that are seeking information and assistance to help them utilize their scarce economic resources wisely. It brings together expertise and knowledge from the academic community, the business world, and the leadership of nonprofit institutions, through a comprehensive program of education, consultation, networking, knowledge base development, and research. NCNE is a central place for nonprofit organizations to access "best thinking" about the critical economic decisions they face in pricing their services, investing their funds, compensating their staff, fund raising, undertaking entrepreneurial initiatives, and in many other areas where efficient use of scarce resources influences how effectively nonprofits can achieve their missions.

National Executive Service Corps *(See General Management—Support and Advocacy Organizations for full description)*

National Society of Accountants
1010 North Fairfax Street, Alexandria, VA 22314-1574
Tel: 800-966-6679, 703-549-6400; FAX: 703-549-2984
E-mail: dgriffin@nsacct.org, jfelski@nsacct.org;
WWW: http://www.nsacct.org/
▶ Professional membership organization for small business accountants, independent tax practitioners, and accountants working with the nonprofit sector. Services include: Business Growth (free tax research via a toll-free hotline number, tax law analysis, a free bimonthly report written for distribution to your clients, all states tax form service, public information brochures, marketing handbooks); Professsional Advancement (self-study courses, seminars and conferences, technical publications), and Practice Management (monthly *National Public Accountant* journal, biweekly *Practitioner* newsletter, and *Membership Directory*).

Nonprofit Facilities Fund (NFF)
Clara Miller, President, 70 West 36th Street, 11th Floor, New York, NY 10018-8007
Tel: 212-868-6710; FAX: 212-268-8653
E-mail: info@nffny.org;
WWW: http://www.calvertgroup.com/foundation/nonprofi.htm
▶ NFF is dedicated to building the capacity of nonprofits to strengthen and manage their assets, including their facilities, through (1) financing programs: below-market-rate loans and capital and predevelopment grants, and (2) technical assistance: training and special educational workshops, publications, and consultancies. NFF was created in 1980 by the New York Community Trust to help New York City nonprofits manage their ballooning operating expenses during the energy crisis. Founded as the Energy Conservation Fund, the organization helped nonprofits remain solvent by providing them with financing and technical assistance. The Energy Conservation Fund broadened its mission and evolved into the Nonprofit Facilities Fund to bolster the capacity of its nonprofit clients to develop and maintain facilities that support their missions and foster their long-term growth, enhancing their ability to serve the needs of their communities. NFF has five offices—New York, San Francisco, Philadelphia, Boston, and Chicago—and serves organizations in other locations through its National Alliances Program.

Nonprofit Financial Center
111 West Washington Street, Suite 1221, Chicago, IL 60602
Tel: 312-606-8250; FAX: 312-606-0241
E-mail: nfcinfo@nonprofitfinancial.org;
WWW: http://www.nonprofitfinancial.org
▶ Founded in 1980 as the Donors Forum Emergency Loan Fund (a project of the Donors Forum of Chicago) in cooperation with Community Renewal Society, NFC is a management support organization specifically focused on nonprofit financial matters. Its purpose is to provide small not-for-profits with access to the working capital, financing, and financial-related technical and management assistance needed to maintain efficient and effective organizations, programs, and projects; offers credit alternatives and technical assistance to nonprofit organizations. Its educational, training, technical, and management assistance is available to any not-for-profit in the state of Illinois without regard to source of support, size, or mission. Services include: consulting (available on-site or through e-mail in a variety of areas—members only); on-site training (to help your entire organization's knowledge base grow—members only); help desk (telephone consulting answers your urgent questions—free to members); NFC loan programs (fill important gaps in the budgets of nonprofits); NFC Institutes (six-session classes that teach in-depth financial skills that you need for success—member discounts available); NFC seminars and workshops ("How to Read Financial Statements," "Learning Quickbooks," and "Do It Right the First Time: Starting a Nonprofit Organization in Illinois"—member discounts); Dear Advocate (an e-mail service in which practicing professionals answer your questions with a quick turnaround time—members only); NFC publications (including their Accounting Software Selection Handbooks and nonprofit start-up guide—member discounts); Quarterly newsletter (NFC Notables keeps you posted on current issues affecting the nonprofit community—free to members); the NFC Web site (contains information and links—includes members-only area); NFC Financial Management Library and Computer Accounting Lab (offers visitors hands-on resources).

Nonprofit Financial Group
P.O. Box 18614, Minneapolis, MN 55418-0614
*Tel: 612)-617-7850 (press *616)*
E-mail: nfg@bbbsmpls.org;
WWW: http://www.kdv.com/nfg/join_nfg.html
▶ The purpose of NFG is to provide opportunities for networking, education, professional maintenance, and improvement for financial managers of nonprofit organizations. Regular meetings are conducted to provide education on topics of current interest; discussion of common issues; current financial management techniques; and governmental, legislative, and regulatory information. Benefits of membership include monthly program meetings with

informed speakers and group discussion; keeping current on accounting standards, laws, and other governmental regulations; updates about continuing education and other resources; networking opportunities; Members Networking Directory; and learning from the experience of peers.

Nonprofit Resource Center, Inc.

7731 Belle Point Drive, Greenbelt, MD 20770
Tel: 301-507-6247; FAX: 301-507-6250
E-mail: questions@nonprofitresource.com;
WWW: http://www.nonprofitresource.com

▶ Founded in 1990 to provide training and consulting services for nonprofit organizations and the accounting and consulting firms that serve the nonprofit community. It also serves as a national resource of information for nonprofit organizations. Presents a series of half-day in-house seminars on the specialized accounting, audit, tax, and financial management issues of tax-exempt, nonprofit organizations; these courses award CPE credit hours. Courses include Current Accounting & Reporting Issues of Nonprofit Organizations, Special Audit Issues Associated with Nonprofit Organizations, Grant Accounting and Administration, Auditing and Reporting Under Circular A-133, Critical Issues in Obtaining and Maintaining Tax-Exempt Status, and The Unrelated Business Income Tax. It can also design a program for improving the performance of any nonprofit organization.

On its Web site you will find a searchable database of businesses that provide important products and services to nonprofit organizations, along with a special membership section for accountants and financial managers of nonprofit organizations and their external CPA firms. Its Online Bookstore, presented in association with Amazon.com, lists some of the best books on nonprofit management.

Nonprofit Risk Management Center

1001 Connecticut Avenue NW, Suite 900, Washington, DC 20036
Tel: 202-785-3891; FAX: 202-833-5747
E-mail: info@nonprofitrisk.org;
WWW: http://www.nonprofitrisk.org

▶ Created in 1990, its mission is to meet the risk management and insurance needs of community-serving organizations nationwide through research, education, and advocacy; the Center's efforts encompass all types of insurance, as well as health maintenance and risk management strategies designed to reduce injuries, illness, and legal violations against their clients, members, or staff; Services include Risk Management Resource Center (a clearinghouse for legal liability, risk management, employee assistance, and insurance information; training (customized as well as comprehensive workshops designed to meet the specific legal liability, insurance, and risk reduction needs of community-serving organizations, including brief presentations on a single topic as part of a multipurpose conference and institutes, day-long comprehensive seminars); research (ongoing program of research into the causes of claims and the effectiveness of measures designed to prevent them; the legal research staff monitors legal developments and produces analyses for law firms, insurers, and others needing assistance); publications (guidebooks; manuals; directories; technical analyses; *Riskfacts,* a library of informative 3- to 4-page "briefs" that answer frequently asked questions on liability, insurance, and risk management subjects; and a newsletter, *Community Risk Management and Insurance* (see separate listing under Periodicals); advocacy

(fosters efforts to change laws and industry practices to improve the legal environment for community-serving programs); support includes policy analyses, consultation networking of advocates, and legislative action kits on key issues; a special initiative addresses health care reform from the perspective of nonprofit organizations as employers; technical assistance (Council of Technical Advisors advises on issues such as child abuse, sexual harassment, wrongful termination, discrimination, negligent hiring, employment status of volunteers, workplace injuries, risk pooling, board liability, informed consent, waivers, special events, volunteer protection); consulting services and risk audits (direct consultation for organizations requiring hands-on assistance with risk management (services include risk management review of an organization's policies and procedures, analysis of legal issues for policy development and litigation, development of materials and videos, staff training in risk-reducing procedures, sponsorship of group insurance plans, and revision of employment practices).

The Center sponsors an annual conference at which its Nonprofit Risk Management Institutes are held.

Not-for-Profit Services Association (NSA)

111 East Wacker Drive, Suite 990, Chicago, IL 60601
Tel: 800-869-0491, ext. 221; FAX: 312-729-9800
E-mail: info@pencormazur.com, jverhuel@pencorllc.com
(Jennifer Ver Huel); WWW: http://www.cpaselect.com/nsa/back.htm,
http://www.cpaselect.com

▶ NSA is a nationwide network of accomplished CPA firms specifically selected for their experience in and commitment to serving the not-for-profit industry. In addition to traditional accounting, auditing, and tax services, NSA members distinguish themselves by providing management and consulting services that meet the increasingly complex needs of not-for-profits.

The association's principal objective is to enable its member firms to enhance their abilities to serve the nonprofit industry. This goal is achieved via conference registration discounts on semiannual conference meetings filled with intensive training; roundtable meetings on a variety of technical, management, and marketing issues; continuing education and training; networking and resource sharing; industry and member surveys; joint ventures; marketing assistance; newsletters and publications; NSA members-only e-mail listserv; member profile on NSA's Web site with a link to each firm's own site; and customized marketing materials. Membership in NSA is granted to select CPA firms on a territorially exclusive basis throughout the United States. This national network of firms results in an extensive collection of expertise available to nonprofit organizations. The NSA membership directory includes a complete listing and profile of member firms, with details on whom to contact for additional information. Publications include *Nonprofit Observer* (a quarterly newsletter for nonprofit organizations distributed by NSA member firms), *Nonprofit Management Survey Report* (details the results of industry surveys conducted by NSA on various practice management topics), and *NSA Members' Bulletin.*

OMG Center for Collaborative Learning

1528 Walnut Street, Suite 805, Philadelphia, PA 19102
Tel: 215-732-2200; FAX: 215-732-8123
WWW: http://www.omgcenter.org/work/orgcap.htm

▶ OMG offers several types of consulting services specifically designed for not-for-profit and public sector organizations that wish to enhance their organizational capacity for financial and performance management. They use a team approach in which indicators and systems are co-developed with the client organization, which means you understand the systems being developed at every step.

United Chart of Accounts

Support Center of Washington, 2001 O Street, NW, Washington, DC 20036
Tel: 202-833-0300, ext. 18; FAX: 202-857-0077, 202/833-0300

E-mail: supportcenter@scw.org, nporta@SCW.ORG (Neil Porta, Director of Consulting); WWW: http://www.ucoa.org/, http://www.scw.org/

▶ Through its Nonprofit Financial Management Consulting practice, the Center promotes the use of simple, standardized accounting methods that take maximum advantage of the limited resources of nonprofits, and provide clear, concise reporting. The Center also provides training in a wide variety of nonprofit accounting functions through its public training program.

PRODUCT AND SERVICE PROVIDERS

General Consulting

BDO Seidman, LLP

Management Consulting Services, Division of Tax Exempt and Governmental Services, 40 Broad Street, Suite 500, Boston, MA 02109-4308
Tel: 617-422-7521
E-mail: Tommclaughlin@aol.com (Thomas A. McLaughlin, Manager); WWW: http://www.bdo.com/
▶ Thomas McLaughlin assists all types of nonprofit clients with strategic, operations, and financial projects. He is nationally recognized as an expert in nonprofit mergers and alliances and financial management.

JMT Consulting Group

2022 Rt. 22, Suite 105, Brewster, NY 10509
Tel: 888-368-2463, 845-278-9262; FAX: 845-278-9266
E-mail: info@jmtconsulting.com, lborkowski@jmtconsulting.com (Linda Borkowski); WWW: http://www.jmtconsulting.com
▶ JMT Consulting has been providing financial and technology services exclusively to nonprofit organizations since 1991. They serve a variety of clients ranging in size from small local organizations to large national organizations located throughout the eastern seaboard. Services include computer system evaluation and training, accounting services, accounting software, and bookkeeping services. JMT also maintains an office in Morrisville, North Carolina.

Chase Manhattan Bank

The Not for Profit Group, 600 Fifth Avenue, 3rd Floor, New York, NY 10020
Tel: 212-332-4014 (Diane M. Genovesi, Vice President); FAX: 212-332-4048
▶ The Chase Manhattan Bank Not for Profit Group was founded to meet the financial needs of not-for-profit organizations. The Group helps health care institutions, performing arts centers, and educational facilities, colleges and universities, social service organizations, and trade groups. Services include cash management, investment management, credit services, and corporate finance.

Nonprofit Resource Center

Zack & Riggs, PC, 7731 Belle Point Drive, Greenbelt, MD 20770
Tel: 800-883-6247, 301-507-6247, 301-507-6244;
FAX: 301-507-6250
E-mail: info@nonprofitresource.com, questions@nonprofitresource.com;
WWW: http://www.nonprofitresource.com
▶ The Nonprofit Resource Center is a national developer of financial management tools and training exclusively for nonprofit organizations, including marketing and strategic plans, operational audits, reorganizations, management information systems evaluations and selections, tax exposure reviews, member surveys, new revenue development, tax planning and reporting, board presentations, staff training, executive searches, and accounting and auditing.

Accounting and Auditing

Altschuler Melvoin & Glasser—Certified Public Accountants and Consultants (See also Tax Compliance and Reporting, Human Resource Management)

30 South Wacker Drive, Suite 2600, Chicago, IL 60606-7494
Tel: 312-207-2800; FAX: 312-207-6172
E-mail: ssilver@amgnet.com (Robert S. Silver, Director, Nonprofit Practice); WWW: http://www.amgnet.com
▶ AM&G's Nonprofit Services Group provides a variety of consulting services that help social service agencies, trade associations, educational institutions, foundations, and other nonprofit agencies establish and maintain a structure that will handle growth effectively and efficiently. Services include audits and tax compliance, financial reporting, government grant compliance, compensation and benefits planning, executive recruiting, and more. The Group specializes in accounting and consulting services that meet the special needs of nonprofits. Services include auditing and financial statement preparation, audits of government grants, single audits, employee retirement plan record keeping, audit and financial statement preparation, executive recruiting, employee benefits and record keeping, and information management.

Aronson, Fetridge & Weigle *(See also Tax Compliance and Reporting, Resource Development)*

700 King Farm Boulevard, Rockville, MD 20850
Phone 301-231-6200; FAX: 301-231-7630
E-mail: info@afwcpa.com; WWW: http://www.afwcpa.com/
▶ AF&W's Nonprofit & Associations Industry Services Group is a team of specialized, innovative CPAs and consultants who understand the unique tax, accounting, systems, and management needs of tax-exempt organizations. Services include accounting, auditing and financial management (efficient, cost-effective audits; value-added management letter recommendations; proactive advice in areas of importance to one's organization; improved internal accounting controls and reporting systems; more effective communication with financial institutions, governmental agencies, and boards of directors); management advisory and computer services (outsourcing services, federal grant and contract services, operational reviews, executive search, compensation and fringe benefit programs, information technology [certified consultants and resellers of the iMIST membership management and fund-raising system and numerous financial accounting applications; AF&W offers an extensive line of technology training courses to all levels

of users], planned giving and fund-raising assistance); tax management (tax planning to assist the organization with obtaining exempt status and identifying and addressing problems concerning continuing tax-exempt status; advice on avoiding or minimizing the impact of unrelated business income taxes on the organization's operations; assistance with the myriad of payroll tax and other compliance issues facing nonprofits; tax considerations for private foundations; state and local tax issues including sales, use, real estate and other local taxes; tax representation and follow-through for inquiries and examinations by the Internal Revenue Service and other taxing authorities; individual tax and financial planning for executives; designing and administering qualified and nonqualified deferred compensation, and other fringe benefit programs)

They keep their clients current on all important issues through periodic seminars on grants and financial management for nonprofits and the most recent regulatory changes, tax advice, and computer system breakthroughs through their quarterly newsletter, *Nonprofit Journal* (subscribe online at: *http://www.afwcpa.com/aisg/npjsubs.html;* an article index is accessible at: *http://www.afwcpa.com/aisg/npjindex.html*).

Blum Shapiro & Company, PC *(See also Software Assistance)*
Not-for-Profit Services Group, 29 South Main Street,
P.O. Box 272000, West Hartford, CT 06127
Tel: 860-561-4000; FAX: 860-521-9241
E-mail: lmb@bshapiro.com (Lori Budnick), jzp@bshapiro.com
(Jessica Powell, Senior Marketing Coordinator);
WWW: http://www.bshapiro.com/pages/industry/nonforpr.html
▶ Blum Shapiro Business Technology Services, LLC, can perform financial statement audits, provide tax services, assist in complying with income tax and financial planning in accounting standards, charitable gifting rules, endowment fund accounting, and other specialized needs. They can also help implement information technology, providing management with access to timely, accurate information. They can assist you in hardware and software selection, manage installation and oversee training of your staff. Clients include independent schools, social service agencies, museums, trade associations, private foundations, and social and country clubs.

Burr Pilger & Mayer
600 California Street, Suite 1300, San Francisco, CA 94108
Tel: 415-421-5757; FAX: 415-288-6288
E-mail: gmahoney@bpminc.com (Geralyne Mahoney, Chair,
Nonprofit Industry Group), roundtable@bpminc.com;
WWW: http://www.bpminc.com,
http://www.bpminc.com/roundtabjcp.htm (Roundtable Series for
Nonprofit Organizations)
▶ Burr Pilger & Mayer is an accounting and consulting firm with offices in San Francisco and Palo Alto. They provide nonprofit organizations with accounting, audit, tax, human resources, and computer consulting services. They also provide consultation on planned giving vehicles, employee benefits, and investment policies and procedures. In cooperation with other area firms (the law firm of Coblentz, Patch, Duffy & Bass, LLP; fund-raising counsel Essex & Drake; executive search firm Loscavio & LoPresto), they also offer over 40 roundtable sessions a year for nonprofit organizations as a service to the community at no cost to the participants. They are a member of CPA Associates International, Inc.

Clark Nuber & Company, CPAs *(See also Tax Compliance)*
10900 NE 4th Street, Suite 1700, Bellevue, WA 98004
Tel: 425-454-4919; FAX: 425-454-4620
E-mail: rfleming@cnuber.com (Robert J. Fleming, Director, Not-for-Profit Services Group); WWW: http://www.cnuber.com/default.asp
▶ Founded in 1952, Clark Nuber & Company's Not-for-Profit Industry Group offers a full range of auditing, accounting, and tax specializing in compliance requirements of government agencies, donors, lending institutions, and, in particular, the requirements of the Single Audit Act of 1984 and OMB Circulars A-128 and A-133. They also provide consulting services for nonprofit organizations.

Services to nonprofits include developing accounting policies and procedures; developing donation, endowment, and gift acceptance policies; developing personnel policies; assisting with the design of the compensation systems; writing business plans; developing cash flow projection spreadsheets; assisting with strategic planning; facilitating board retreats; recruiting and screening financial personnel; applying for not-for-profit status with the IRS; developing benchmarking criteria; consulting on federal and state tax issues; assisting with needs analysis and choice of computer systems and returns; estate planning (family limited liability companies, limited partnerships, annual gifting, qualified Subchapter S trusts, and charitable remainder trusts); providing computer-related assistance; preparing and negotiating indirect cost rate proposals; consulting on MIP, the most complete and advanced Windows fund accounting software on the market; consulting services (strategic, financial, succession, tax, and estate planning, operations and inventory analysis, mergers and acquisitions, state and local taxes, international business transactions, real estate transactions, technology planning, and the special concerns for high-net-worth individuals).

Clifton Gunderson, LLC
1301 W. 22nd Street, Suite 1100, Oak Brook, IL 60523
Tel: 630-573-8600, ext. 604; FAX: 630-573-0798
E-mail: johnquinn@cliftoncpa.com (John Quinn);
WWW: http://www.cliftoncpa.com
▶ Clifton Gunderson specializes in providing assistance to not-for-profit organizations. Their range of services include traditional accounting services as well as nontraditional services in the areas of audit services, donor restrictions, tax services, payroll services, internal accounting controls, and budget preparation. Specific services include unrelated business income tax issues facing not-for-profits; comprehensive reviews of internal accounting controls and recommendations for improvement; assistance with budget preparation and review of variances to budget; assisting with the controllership function; employee benefit planning and administration including pension plans, 401(k) plans, and 403(b) annuity plans; determination of program feasibility by analyzing projected sources and uses of funds; grant writing and fund raising; human resources consulting, including assistance with health insurance plans, flex plans, and accounting and personnel policy manuals; technology consulting and training (Clifton Gunderson is the Wisconsin and Northern Illinois exclusive business partner for Blackbaud).

Condon O'Meara McGinty and Donnelly, LLP, CPAs

(See also Taxes)
300 East 42nd Street, New York, NY 10017-5947
Tel: 212-661-7777; FAX: 212-661-4010
WWW: http://comdcpa.com/

▶ This is an accounting firm dedicated exclusively to servicing nonprofit organizations, private foundations, and exclusive private clubs with a concentration in the New York Metropolitan Area. They currently serve over 200 nonprofit organizations in New York, New Jersey, and Connecticut. Services include tax planning and return preparation (audits, reviews, compilations), internal control reviews, fraud audits, and technology consulting.

Deloitte & Touche LLP *(See also Taxes, Insurance)*

Mary F. Foster, National Industry Director, Not-for-Profit Services Group, Two World Financial Center, New York, NY 10281-1439
Tel: 212-436-2503; FAX: 212-436-5000
WWW: http://www.dttus.com

▶ Deloitte & Touche provides assurance and advisory, tax, and management consulting services through over 28,000 people in more than 100 U.S. cities. The Not-for-Profit Services Group provides assistance with casualty and risk management (actuarial services [analyze loss and loss expense reserves, analyze self-insured liabilities for corporate and public entities, analyze company assets and liabilities relating to loss-sensitive insurance programs], business continuity planning services [analyze losses to help organizations maximize recoveries, develop disaster recovery programs, provide litigation support to maximize subrogation recoveries], risk management services [recommend alternative risk financing methods, conduct feasibility studies and assist in the implementation of alternative risk financing programs, including captives, analyze existing insurance programs, establish loss prevention and control systems]); tax information reporting evaluation (consists of a thorough analysis of tax reporting requirements and an assessment of whether those requirements are being met, followed by an evaluation of information reporting systems; conducted by a team of tax, audit, and consulting professionals with experience in the not-for-profit sector, it will assess, among other items, whether your present practices provide donors with proper tax substantiation information, identify charitable or exempt activities that create reporting obligations, comply with existing payroll tax and withholding laws, reduce the potential risk of exposure to tax penalties, and provide proper trust information to beneficiaries of annuities or charitable remainder trust gifts); and accountability (financial assessments, regulatory assessments, business systems consulting, human resources consulting, compensation, consulting, and other integrated services [legislative tracking services, government contracting services, telecommunications convergence, real estate valuation, relocation and cost containment services, strategy development and implementation]). Deloitte & Touche publishes the *Not-for-Profit Review* newsletter (for clients), available online at *http://www.dttus.com/pub/nfprevue/foreword.htm.*

Desmond & Ahern, Ltd., Certified Public Accountants *(See also Taxes)*

10827 South Western Avenue, Chicago, IL 60643-3299
Tel: 773-779-4720; FAX: 773-779-8310
E-mail: cpa@desmondcpa.com, E-mail: hugh@desmondcpa.com (Hugh Ahern, President); WWW: http://www.desmond-ahern.com

▶ Desmond & Ahern is a nonprofit-focused CPA firm offering fund accounting assistance including automated solutions streamlining audit, tax, and reporting requirements. Services include accounting assistance, accounting and personnel manuals, grant and program compliance audits, strategic tax (UBIT) planning, financial statement audits, tax planning and preparation, technology consulting (including software selection and installation), personnel training, financial analysis, retirement planning, bookkeeping services. Desmond & Ahern also operates an accounting service bureau for smaller nonprofit agencies needing assistance in accounting and business practices. They work closely with these agencies to develop a strong financial infrastructure and help them address reporting, compliance, and internal control issues. They offer seminars and publish the quarterly *Not-for-Profit* newsletter.

Don Chapin & Associates, PA

3901 National Drive, Suite 260, Burtonsville, MD 20866
Tel: 301-421-1330; FAX: 301-384-0838
E-mail: dan@chapin-cpa.com (Dan Sandstrom, Audit Partner); WWW: http://chapin-cpa.com

▶ Serving the needs of the nonprofit community for over 30 years, and with clients ranging in size from small charities to multinational trade groups. Services include audit and assurance (including OMB Circular A-133), UBIT and proxy taxes, information returns, accounting, and business advisory services. Specific services include: OMB Circular A-133 and "Yellow Book" audits, nonfinancial assurance services, unrelated business taxable income, lobbying and the proxy tax, public disclosure and information returns, industry-specific financial accounting and reporting standards, intermediate sanctions, political action committees, fund/cost accounting and allocations, and internal controls.

Eisner's Not-for-Profit Industry Group

Richard A. Eisner & Company, LLP, 575 Madison Avenue, New York, New York 10022
Tel: 212-891-4232, 212-891-4020 (D. Edward Martin, Director, Eisner's Not-for-Profit Industry Group); FAX: 212-355-2414
E-mail: jfloch@eisner.rae.com (Julie Floch), marrigo@eisner.rae.com (Marie Arrigo, Tax Partner, Not-for-Profit Tax Consulting); WWW: http://www.eisnerllp.com

▶ Eisner's Not-for-Profit Industry Group serves organizations that operate in a variety of areas, including social and religious services, charitable support, membership benefits, political action, the arts, education, and medical/scientific research. They provide a variety of levels of assistance drawn from the firm's primary services areas: financial statement assurance, accounting, tax, systems consulting, and business improvement services. Their Not-for-Profit Tax Consulting Services Team offers the following assistance: establishing the entity as a public charity in compliance with not-for-profit governing rules; applying for tax-exempt status with the IRS; tax planning issues as situations arise (e.g., employee compensation, unrelated business income tax, lobbying, etc.); preparation of federal and state tax filings; handling all federal and state tax audits; and registering with appropriate state attorney general's offices. They also assist many not-for-profit organizations with accounting and auditing services and special consulting services, including employee benefit plans, executive search, operations improvement, information technology, and telecommunications services. In addition, they advise on the tax issues for other charitable entities including charitable remainder trusts, charitable lead trusts, donor-advised funds, and supporting organizations.

Their private foundation clients rely on their services for establishing the entity as a private foundation in compliance with not-for-profit governing rules; applying for tax exempt status with the IRS; registering with appropriate state attorney general's offices; tax planning strategies and minimum distribution requirements; issues relating to the excise tax on net investment income; avoiding onerous excise (penalty) taxes; preparation of federal and state filings; and handling all federal and state tax examinations.

D. Edward Martin is director of Eisner's Not-for-Profit Industry Group. His book for attorneys, *Attorney's Handbook of Accounting, Auditing, and Financial Reporting* (published by Matthew Bender), includes a comprehensive chapter on not-for-profit organizations.

Gelman, Rosenberg & Freedman, CPAs

4800 Hampden Lane, Suite 400, Bethesda, MD 20814
Tel: 301-951-9090; FAX: 301-951-3570
E-mail: info@grfcpa.com; WWW: http://www.grfcpa.com,
gmorgan@grfcpa.com (Gina Morgan),
http://www.grfcpa.com/newsletters.htm

▶ GR&F serves more than 325 not-for-profit organizations throughout the United States and around the world. Wherever your mission takes you, GR&F will be there to provide auditing, Circular A-133 compliance, outsourced accounting services, review and compilation, budgeting, strategic planning, internal control evaluation, accounting system design, computer consulting, investment analysis, executive staffing, employee benefits, and pension consulting.

Graham & Cottrill, PA *(See also Taxes, Charitable Giving)*

Certified Public Accountants, 110 East Hillcrest Street, Orlando, FL 32801
Tel: 800-342-2720, 407-843-1681; FAX: 407-423-3156
E-mail: mbatts@nonprofitcpa.com (Michael E Batts, Director—Nonprofit Services Group); WWW: http://www.nonprofitcpa.com

▶ Graham & Cottrill serve hundreds of nonprofit organizations in the areas of auditing, accounting, tax preparation, tax consulting, tax exemption and representation, planned giving, banking relationships, information systems, lobbying for statute changes, and much more. Specific services offered include auditing and accounting; assistance with internal control; tax compliance assessment; tax advisory services; strategic planning and consulting services; tax return preparation; assistance in establishing planned giving programs; representation before the IRS, Department of Revenue, or other taxing authorities; lobbying for state statute changes; government relations; assistance in banking/lending relationships; membership surveys; and other related services.

In order to assist nonprofit executives in tax compliance by the organizations that they operate, Graham & Cottrill have developed audio courses on "The Basics" of tax compliance. To help keep nonprofit executives up to date, they also publish a complimentary newsletter, the *Nonprofit Watchman* and conduct an annual Nonprofit Conference. Both the newsletter and the conference are designed for nonprofit executives who already have an understanding of "The Basics."

Grant Thornton, LLP

160 North Washington Street, Boston, MA 02114
Tel: 617-848-4850, 617-723-7900
E-mail: bleavy@gt.com (Bob Leavy, Managing Partner, NFP Organizations); WWW: http://www.grantthornton.com

▶ Grant Thronton provides a comprehensive range of services to not-for-profit organizations of all types and sizes such as colleges and universities, associations, social service organizations, religious groups, charities, and foundations. Services include auditing; strategic planning; outsourcing advice; taxes (help organizations elect and maintain the most favorable tax-exempt status for their needs, minimize unrelated business income taxes, minimize state and local taxes, and prepare Forms 990, 990-T and others; can also help organizations avoid *intermediate sanction penalties* that could result from noncompliance with Internal Revenue Service rules relating to compensation levels for board members, officers, and trustees); assurance (can employ the latest computer technology to document and evaluate the effectiveness of internal controls, implement Office of Management and Budget Circular A-133, and prepare timely financial statements); management consultants to help not-for-profits improve productivity and operations, design and implement information systems, develop financial plans and budgets, and conduct confidential surveys of membership organizations; technology (reseller of *iMIS*, association management software package, and *Dynamics*, accounting packages; their Association Software professionals can help organizations provide improved member/donor communication and service, and increase organizational efficiency).

To stay abreast of not-for-profit issues, they maintain a National Not-for-Profit Organizations Committee comprising Grant Thornton accountants and management consultants from throughout the firm. Check out their publications for nonprofits at *http://www.gt.com/content/10497.asp.*

Keller Bruner & Company *(See also Charitable Contributions, Taxes; Human Resource Management)*

6701 Democracy Boulevard, Suite 600, Bethesda, MD 20817
Tel: 301-897-3200; FAX: 301-897-2020
E-mail: bbillig@kbcpas.com (Bob Billing, Partner);
WWW: http://www.kbcpas.com/

700 North Fairfax Street, Suite 400, Alexandria, VA 22314
Tel: 703-549-7800; FAX: 703-836-5591
201 Thomas Johnson Drive, Frederick, MD 21702
Tel: 301-663-8600; FAX: 301-663-0525

▶ Not-for-profit Industry Practice Services include financial statement audits; audits in accordance with OMB Circular A-133; tax services; international tax capabilities; simulated IRS audits; analytical reviews; computer consulting services; strategies for marketing, communication, and governance; management consulting services; organizational planning and evaluation; and personnel policy manuals and employee handbooks.

They publish two newsletters for the not-for-profit industry: the *Not-for-Profit Industry Update* and the *Federal Awards Update.* Keller Bruner also gives seminars that focus on management issues pertinent to not-for-profit organizations.

Kern, DeWenter, Viere, Ltd. *(Formerly Brown & Company)*

220 Park Avenue South, P.O. Box 1304, St. Cloud, MN 56302
Tel: 320-251-7010; FAX: 320-251-1784

7100 Northland Circle North, Suite 119, Minneapolis, MN 55428
Tel: 763-537-3011, 763-569-5760 (David A. Brown, Jr., Certified Public Accountant); FAX: 763-537-9682
E-mail: info@kdv.com, dbrown@kdv.com (David A. Brown, Jr., Certified Public Accountant); WWW: http://www.kdv.com/nonprofit.html

▶ KDV currently serves over 100 nonprofits, ranging in size from $75,000 to $17 million. These organizations are funded from a variety of sources, including government grants, public donations, United Way contributions, service fees, memberships, and lawful gambling. KDV has extensive experience auditing nonprofit organizations—specifically, charitable organizations exempt from income tax under Section 501(c)(3) of the Internal Revenue Code and subject to financial reporting requirements under Financial Accounting Standards Board Statement Numbers 116 and 117. They have also built a network of resources, including specialists in planning, law, fund raising, human resources, marketing, and computer technology. KDV publishes a bimonthly newsletter, *Nonprofit Agendas*. The services they provide clients include but are not limited to performing financial and compliance audits; assisting with developing budgets, cash management plans, tax-advantaged giving programs, and employee benefit plans; assisting with developing internal controls; assisting with setting up and changing accounting systems, including computer installations and conversions; providing technical guidance crucial to obtaining and preserving the charitable status of nonprofit organizations; assisting with negotiations with employee bargaining units; preparing information and unrelated business income tax returns of charitable organizations; and providing consultation on a wide variety of issues, including communications with federal, state, and other regulatory agencies relating to compliance audits and year-end reporting. The firm is a member of the American Institute of Certified Public Accountants and the Minnesota Society of Certified Public Accountants.

Lang Group Chartered Consultants & CPAs

7101 Wisconsin Avenue, Suite 900, Bethesda, MD 20814-4805
Tel: 800-990-9908 (990T), 301-654-4900; FAX: 301-654-3567
E-mail: jhecker@langcpa.com; WWW: http://www.langcpa.com

▶ Lang Group has provided financial, A-133, fraud and pension audits, understandable presentations, trusted tax planning, and accurate 990 services to the nonprofit sector for over 50 years. Lang also offers a full range of accounting and management consulting services, including outsourcing, iMIS, budgeting, reengineering, cost allocation, surveys, revenue enhancements, and financial placement.

Services to nonprofits include audits (financial, pension, fraud, indirect cost rate, publication/fulfillment, OMB Circular A-133, tax compliance—IRS Forms 990 and 990T); professional financial recruitment and placement; outsourcing (processing daily transactions, general ledger, data entry, accounts payable and receivable, payroll, reconciliations, cost allocations, budget preparation and administration, monitoring and reporting, financial statement preparation, and human resources management), tax services; tax-exempt organizations (comprehensive tax check-up; tax planning and consultation re: lobbying, charitable gifts, UBIT, intermediate sanctions, intercompany transactions, foundations; preparation of IRS Forms 990 and 990T; state tax returns required for income, sales, use, or property taxes; application for exemption Forms 1023 or 1024; state charitable registration and/or annual filing; group exemption and chapter check-up; review of royalty, affinity, sponsorship contracts; and IRS Private Letter Ruling Requests); and consulting services. (Lang Group is an authorized reseller of iMIS™, the association management software.)

Langan Associates, PC, CPAs and Consultants

1819 L Street NW, Suite 200, Washington, DC 20036
Tel: 202-730-4224; FAX: 202-730-4250
E-mail: langan@langancpa.com, tenenbaA@langancpa.com
(Annie Tenenbaum, Director of Client Services)

2800 Shirlington Road, Suite 700, Alexandria, VA 22206
Tel: 202-730-4200; FAX: 703-379-5649

980 N. Michigan Avenue, PMB 1400, Chicago, IL 60611
Tel: 312-988-4872; FAX: 773-293-4457
E-mail: langan@langancpa.com;
WWW: http://www.langancpa.com,
http://www.langancpa.com/resources/resources.htm,
http://www.langancpa.com/Newsletter/Archives/index.htm

▶ Langan Associates, PC, is an exclusive provider of accounting and consulting services to the not-for-profit industry. The firm employs over 65 professionals and services more than 350 not-for-profit organizations including trade associations and professional societies, as well as public and private education and charitable organizations. They offer one-stop shopping in audit, tax, outsourced accounting (specific functions such as accounts payable or month-end close to full outsourcing), financial recruiting and placement (temp/perm), management and technology consulting (membership surveys, implementation of new pronouncements, efficiency studies, accounting manuals), and are resellers of Solomon IV, Great Plains Dynamics, and MAS-90. They publish the free publication *The Non-Profit & Association Quarterly*.

PricewaterhouseCoopers LLP

Not-for-Profit Industry Services Group, 3110 Fairview Park Drive, Suite 300, Falls Church, VA 22042
Tel: 703-538-7982; WWW: http://www.pwcglobal.com/

▶ PricewaterhouseCooper serves as an advisor to colleges, universities, and other not-for-profit organizations (foundations, performing arts groups, museums, trade and professional organizations, religious groups, membership organizations, and social welfare organizations). Special services to educational institutions and nonprofit organizations include information technology (organization structure and staffing, governance and decision-making processes, funding, technology architecture, IT infrastructure); student services; auxiliary services; facilities management; development operations (gift receipt and acknowledgment, records management, research, stewardship, fund operations, staff support for fund raisers, publications); human resources (streamlining core human resource processes, recruitment and selection, payroll and personnel actions); and research administration.

Raffa & Associates, P.C.

1899 L Street NW, Suite 600, Washington, DC 20036
Tel: 202-822-5000; FAX: 202-822-0669
E-mail: raffa@raffa.com; WWW: http://www.raffa.com

▶ With more than 300 nonprofit clients, Raffa & Associates perform 225 audits and 250 tax returns for nonprofit organizations each year. In addition, they provide a wide range of other tax, computer, and business advisory services. Services include tax return preparation, management consulting, computer services, Internet services, and pension services. IKNOW *(http://www.iknow.org)* is their collection of some of the best online resources of interest to the nonprofit community.

They provide services to the nonprofit community, including audits; tax and consulting services; accounting and MIS outsourcing; compensation and fringe benefit consulting and design; retirement plan development and administration; Internet services; Web design, maintenance, and hosting; e-commerce and secured transactions; authorized dealers for IBM, HP, Dell, Compaq; certified resellers/consultants for Solomon, Great Plains, MAS 90; database design and programming with Web interfacing; board and organizational development; strategic planning; membership development; executive search; and investment counseling.

Reznick, Fedder & Silverman, CPAs

Nonprofit Services Group, 4520 East West Highway, Suite 300, Bethesda, MD 20814-3319
Tel: 301-652-9100; FAX: 301-652-1848
E-mail: cpa@rfs.com, corines@rfs.com;
WWW: http://www.rfs.com

Two Hopkins Plaza, Suite 2100, Baltimore, MD 21201-2911
Tel: 800-694-4376 (Baltimore), 410-783-4900; FAX: 410-727-0460
E-mail: Gary@rfs.com (Gary C. Pokrant, Chairman, Nonprofit Services Group)

▶ Reznick, Fedder & Silverman is a full-service regional public accounting and business consulting firm providing nonprofit organizations the following services: management control (provides advisory services, including operational analysis, strategic planning for short- and long-term organization needs, design and installation of fund accounting and management information software and hardware systems, cash flow and budgeting analysis, and personnel systems and compensation planning); financial planning (provides audited financial statements on a timely basis; also analyze and interpret financial results for financial trends in organizations to pinpoint strengths and weaknesses to achieve their long-range goals and objectives; in addition to basic audit, assists with requirements such as the Single Audit requirements, GAO government auditing standards, and OMB Circular A-133); and tax planning (assists with application to the IRS for securing tax-exempt status, as well as tax issues related to unrelated business taxable income). They publish the *Nonprofit Advisor* newsletter (see separate listing under Periodicals). They also maintain offices in Boston, Atlanta, and Charlotte.

Rubin, Brown, Gornstein & Co. LLP

230 South Bemiston Avenue, St. Louis, MO 63105
Tel: 314-727-8150; FAX: 314-727-9195
E-mail: rbgco@rbgco.com, judy_murphy@rbgco.com (Judy Murphy, Partner, Not-for-Profit Department);
WWW: http://www.rbgco.com/indspec/ind-not.html, http://www.rbgco.com/inknow/menu6.html

▶ RBG & Co.'s Not-for-Profit Department serves a broad spectrum of not-for-profit organizations including art and cultural organizations, associations (trade, business, and fraternal), housing corporations, human service organizations, labor unions, libraries and museums, private schools and other educational organizations, private foundations, and private operating foundations.

Services include audits of financial statements; preparation of Forms 990, 990-T, and 990-PF; preparation of comprehensive management letters; preparation of Forms 1023/1024 for start-up not-for-profit organizations; unit cost reports; single audits of federal programs under OMB Circular A-133; payroll, sales, and use tax issues; calculation of minimum distribution requirements; unrelated business tax issues; budgeting and forecasting; Internal Revenue Service audits; strategic planning; internal control reviews; cash

management/financing assistance; financial analysis and review; and planning and compliance issues for Section 403(b) plans.

RBG & Co. sponsors periodic Not-for-Profit Roundtables, which bring together members of the not-for-profit industry for informal meetings intended to promote an exchange of ideas and discussion of current trends and issues affecting the not-for-profit environment today. In addition, RBG & Co. hosts seminars on a variety of topics.

Rubino & McGeehin, Certified Public Accountants & Consultants

6905 Rockledge Drive, Suite 700, Bethesda, MD 20817-1818
Tel: 301-564-3636, FAX: 301-564-2994
E-mail: mdeboe@rubino.com (Margaret DeBoe, Director, Exempt Organizations Specialty Group), mdeboe@aol.com;
WWW: http://www.rubino.com/, http://www.rubino.com/alert.htm

1675 Broadway, Suite 1800, Denver, CO 80202
Tel: 720-904-9871; FAX: 720-904-9873

▶ Rubino & McGeehin offer a full spectrum of services regularly provided by a certified public accounting firm in the traditional accounting areas: audits, reviews, and compilations of financial statements; tax return preparation and planning; personal financial planning; and personal and business consulting advice. They serve Washington, D.C., Maryland, and Virginia area government contractors, nonprofit organizations, and health care providers.

The Exempt Organizations Specialty Group offers a broad range of services to not-for-profit organizations. Their services range from the yearly financial statement audit and tax return preparation services to assistance with convention planning. The following represent selected services they currently provide to over 200 not-for-profit organizations: general-purpose and OMB Circular A-133 audits; cost allowability and allocability determinations under federal cost principles; indirect cost rate structure and historical cost submissions; accounting system installation, design, and review; preparation of Forms 990, 990-PF, 990-T, and 8734 and various state reports; consultations on private foundation issues; grant application preparation and review; unrelated business taxable income compliance reviews; management system reviews and assistance; financial reporting assistance; IRS recognition of tax-exempt status assistance; budgeting reviews and assistance; placement and staff training services; strategic planning assistance; state and local charitable registration assistance; and reserve policies and investment policies design assistance.

They keep their clients aware of tax law changes and current events in the financial, government contracts, and nonprofit areas in periodic ALERT publications, and quarterly breakfast seminars.

Tate & Tryon, CPAs & Consultants *(See also Tax Compliance and Reporting, Employee Benefits)*
2011 Pennsylvania Avenue NW, Washington, DC 20006
Tel: 202-293-2200, ext. 305; FAX: 202-293-2208
E-mail: mtryon@tatetryon.com (Michael M. Tryon, Partner), ctate@tatetryon.com (Charles Tate, Partner);
WWW: http://www.tatetryon.com/index.shtml

▶ Tate & Tryon is a public accounting/consulting firm providing financial, technology consulting, auditing, and tax services to the not-for-profit community. Services include executive financial information systems, technology planning and needs analysis, software installation and training, financial statement and A-133 audits, strategic tax planning for related organizations, outsourced accounting and CFO duties, cost allocation systems, finance operations analysis, and executive personal financial planning. There are Microsoft Certified Professionals on staff. They work with hundreds of not-for-profit organizations.

Walker & Company, LLP

5100 Wisconsin Avenue NW, Suite 407, Washington, DC 20016
Tel: 202-363-9300; FAX: 202-363-0531
E-mail: cecountee@walkerllp.com (Charles E. Countee);
WWW: http://www.walkerllp.com

▶ Walker & Company, LLP, is a multiservice accounting and consulting firm serving clientele throughout the United States. The firm provides services in the following areas: accounting and auditing (perform audits, reviews, and compilations of financial statements, and assist in the preparation of financial forecasts and projections for government entities, private companies, and nonprofit organizations in accordance with principles and standards established by AICPA, GAO, federal legislation, OMB, and Treasury guidance); information technology services (information technology planning and evaluation, rapid application development, information systems development support, database design and development, financial management system, internal control and computer security reviews); management consulting (advise clients on improvements in financial and administrative management, planning, and control through budgeting, pricing strategies, and more efficient use of organization, staff, and management resources including business process redesign, strategic planning, research and evaluation, financial advisory services, and operations management); and taxation (tax planning and preparation, investment or tax shelter analysis, estate and trust planning, representation before tax authorities, and obtaining tax-exempt status for qualified nonprofit organizations).

Walthall, Drake & Wallace LLP, CPAs

1621 Euclid Avenue, Suite 1300, Cleveland, Ohio 44115-2182
Tel: 216-696-2330; FAX: 216-696-2336
E-mail: t.wallace@walthall.com (Thomas W. Wallace, Jr., CPA);
WWW: http://www.walthall.com/Services.htm

▶ Walthall, Drake & Wallace specialize in providing accounting, auditing, tax, and consulting services to not-for-profit organizations. They are experienced with private and public funding, cost allocation methods, complex financial reporting requirements, government reporting, fund-raising activities, and volunteer services. For not-for-profit organizations that receive government funding either directly or as a subrecipient, they are thoroughly familiar with Government Auditing Standards (GAS) and OMB Circular A-133.

Zack & Riggs, PC, Certified Public Accountants/ Nonprofit Resource Center—Accounting, Auditing, Tax Planning *(See also Governance, Human Resource Management, Marketing and Communications, Strategic Planning, Resource Development)*

7731 Belle Point Drive, Greenbelt, MD 20770
Tel: 800-883-6247, 301-507-6247, 301-507-6244;
FAX: 301-507-6250
E-mail: info@nonprofitresource.com,
questions@nonprofitresource.com;
WWW: http://www.nonprofitresource.com

▶ Zack & Riggs is a full-service accounting and consulting firm; its affiliate, the Nonprofit Resource Center (see Seminars,

Workshops, and Training for full description), is a national developer of financial management tools and training exclusively for nonprofit organizations; this affiliation provides services tailored to your needs, including marketing and strategic plans, operational audits, reorganizations, MIS evaluations and selections, tax exposure reviews, member surveys, new revenue development, tax planning and reporting, board presentations, staff training, executive searches, and accounting and auditing.

They publishes *The Tax-Exempt Organization Alert!* newsletter (see separate listing under Periodicals).

Charitable Giving and Investment Services

(See also Tax Compliance & Reporting; Legal Issues—Tax Reporting and Compliance; Resource Development—Planned Giving and Estate Planning)

Charitable Trust Administrators

1452 Oregon Street, Redding, CA 96001
Tel: 800-246-0490, 530-244-0300; FAX: 530-2440303

▶ Charitable Trust Administrators provide "back office" support, investment management, tax management, accounting, donor-advised funds, educational seminars, educational materials, and research and development.

Fidelity Investments

Fidelity Charitable Gift Fund, 82 Devonshire Street F35A, Boston, MA 02109
Tel: 800-952-4438 (Charitable Gift Fund), 800-682-4438 (donor-advised fund)
WWW: http://www300.charitablegift.org/,
http://www300.charitablegift.org/faqs/index.shtml,
http://www300.charitablegift.org/resource/index.shtml

▶ The *Fidelity* Charitable Gift Fund[SM] offers two programs: a donor-advised fund and a pooled-income fund.

Freeman, Freeman & Smiley, LLP *(See also Legal Issues, Philanthropy)*

3415 Sepulveda Boulevard, Penthouse Suite 1200, Los Angeles, CA 90034-6060
Tel: 310-255-6100
E-mail: sic@ffslaw.com; WWW: http://www.ffslaw.com/

▶ Since its inception in 1976, Freeman, Freeman & Smiley, LLP, has developed a law practice specializing in the areas of estate planning and charitable and nonprofit organization planning.

Their Estate Planning Group is nationally recognized for their expertise in estate planning for highly compensated individuals. In addition to traditional trust planning, they counsel clients in the use of more sophisticated estate planning devices, such as family partnerships, qualified personal residence trusts, business succession planning, and gifting programs.

They assist individuals to achieve their philanthropic objectives through outright and planned giving arrangements. They also provide counsel to nonprofit institutions in developing and operating their fund-raising programs.

Check out their library at *http://www.ffslaw.com/public_htm/library.html.*

Henry & Associates—Charitable Trust and Estate Planning Services (See also Resource Development, Planned Giving)

22 Hyde Park Place, Springfield, IL 62703
Tel: 217-529-1958, 800-879-2098; FAX: 217-529-1959
E-mail: VWHenry@aol.com (Vaughn W. Henry);
WWW: http://gift-estate.com,
http://members.aol.com/crtrust/EstateSvcs.html,
http://members.aol.com/CRTrust/Estate.html

▶ Henry & Associates provide consulting services for nonprofit organizations on how to integrate planned giving into a development program, offering a virtual planned giving department for smaller charities unable to fully staff a new position. They conduct workshops and private seminars for board members, reluctant philanthropists, for-profit advisors, and referral resources to create improved planning partnerships. Articles, case studies, and professional resources on their Web site are available to nonprofit organizations.

They distribute a gift/estate tax calculator. Subscription information for the mailing list addressing CRT planning issues can be found at *http://gift-estate.com/crt.html*, or send an e-mail to *VWHenry@aol.com* and you will be automatically subscribed.

LMNOP

Seminars Software Publications, 523 Fourth Street, Suite 200A, San Rafael, CA 94901
Tel: 415-485-3744; FAX: 415-485-3748
E-mail: lsm@lmnopstuff.com (Lynda S. Moerschbaecher);
WWW: http://www.sfo.com/~lsm/

▶ LMNOP's services include seminars (Financial and Planned Giving Professionals, Just In Cases, The Well-Planned Gift, Every Coin Has Two Sides, Marketing Magic, Bringing Trust/Fund Management In-House, Are You Dying to Make the Government Rich? Don't, Don't You Worry Your Pretty Little Head! (and other slights that make you furious), Charity Begins at Home; consulting (assessment of your planned gift program, charitable organizations, service providers); software (Charitable Docs in a Box); books, audio/video tapes, brochures, and pamphlets.

Leimberg Associates Inc. and Leimberg & LeClair

P.O. Box 601, Bryn Mawr, PA 19010
Tel: 610-527-5216; FAX 610-527-5226
E-mail: info@leimberg.com; WWW: http://www.leimberg.com

▶ They offer software, books, and tapes for estate planning, financial planning, charitable planning, retirement planning, life insurance planning, and business planning.

R & R Newkirk (See also Tax Compliance and Reporting; Resource Development)

8695 South Archer, Suite 10, Willow Springs, IL 60480
Tel: 800-342-2375; FAX: 708-839-9207
E-mail: newkirk2@aol.com; WWW: http://www.rrnewkirk.com

▶ R & R Newkirk has been providing planned gift promotional programs and training since 1967, serving more than 1,400 clients annually in all 50 states and Canada. Its team of writers, editors, tax attorneys, marketing consultants, artists, and design specialists provide planned gift officers the widest range of assistance. Services include newsletters (their newsletter clients are entitled to toll-free access to the editors of *The Charitable Giving Tax Service*); seminars and workshops; staff training; professional advisors; planned gift response booklets, brochures and pamphlets; board presentations; and Charitable Giving Tax Service (a comprehensive, thoroughly indexed reference and resource library that is updated every other month to remain current with developments in the area of planned giving).

Renaissance, Inc.

6100 West 96th Street, Suite 100, Indianapolis, IN 46278
Social Capital Consulting: Tel: 800-843-0050;
FAX: 317-843-5273
Gift Administration: Tel: 800-843-7997; FAX: 317-843-5270
Social Capital Planning: The CRT Registration:
Tel: 800-843-0050
E-mail: info@reninc.com; WWW: http://www.reninc.com/

▶ Renaissance's mission is to help people recognize the existence of, gain control over, and effectively direct their personal social capital. They assist professional advisors with the charitable planning process (education, marketing, gift design, implementation and administration, and final charitable distribution). Services include Social Capital Consulting (assistance to donor advisors in the design and implementation of planned gifts); training (helping donor advisors understand the many types and facets of social capital tools and providing them with the necessary marketing and implementation knowledge to apply it in their practice); legal support services (assisting attorneys in all 50 states with document drafting issues related to planned gift instruments); gift administration (providing continuous care of a gift by ensuring that all trustee and beneficiary needs are met or exceeded through accounting, tax work, compliance, and communication). It hosts the annual National Conference on Social Capital.

Richard Alan Lehrman

777 Arthur Godfrey Road, Fourth Floor, Miami Beach, FL 33140
Tel: 305-534-1323; FAX: 305-531-0314
E-mail: Lehrman@Trustlaw.net, TrustLaw@ABAnet.org,
RickLehrman@ATT.net; WWW: http://www.lawyers.com/trustlaw,
http://www.lawyers.com/trustlaw/weblinks.htm

▶ Lehrman's practice devoted to planning, design, implementation, and administration of trusts and estates, business succession planning, and charitable gift planning. He helps clients plan and administer their estates to avoid or reduce unnecessary estate taxes, gift taxes, generation-skipping transfer taxes, costs of guardianship, costs of probate administration, and losses to creditor claims. He also helps to keep wealth in the family by offering the following services: estate planning design and implementation, will and trust preparation, charitable planned giving planning, business succession planning, trust administration, and estate (probate) administration.

U.S. Trust Corporation (See also Investments)

114 West 47th Street, New York, NY 10036
Tel: 800-US-TRUST, 800-292-1112 (Mark K. Talt, Managing Director), 212-852-3930
E-mail: info@ustrust.com; WWW: http://www.ustrust.com,
http://www.ustrust.com/ser-indv.htm

▶ U.S. Trust Corporation is an investment management company that manages over $86 billion in assets for clients throughout the country. It offers a broad array of financial services, including private banking; fiduciary services; and tax, estate, and financial planning, for affluent individuals and their families. These include trust and estate services, investment management, planning services, private banking, and investment consulting. It maintains offices in the Pacific Northwest, Washington, DC, New York, and Connecticut.

Wachovia Charitable Funds Management (See also
Investments)
100 North Main Street, NC37131, Winston-Salem, NC 27101
Tel: 800-462-7159; FAX: 336-732-6537
WWW: http://www.wachovia.com/trust

▶ Wachovia specializes in planned giving and charitable trusts (charitable remainder trusts, charitable remainder annuity trusts, charitable lead trusts, wealth replacement trusts, pooled income funds, gift annuities) and endowment and foundation services (a full range of gift administration services for private and corporate foundations, as well as charitable remainder trusts, lead trusts, pooled income funds, and gift annuities). They also have a variety of investment funds (Charitable Equity Investment Fund, Charitable Fixed Income Fund, Charitable Intermediate Fixed Income Fund, and Wachovia Prime or Wachovia Money Market cash equivalent funds) managed specifically for the unique needs of nonprofits.

Yellowstone Trust Administration
490 N. 31st Street, Suite 309, Billings, MT 59101
Tel: 800-572-6394; FAX: 406-255-8685
E-mail: yfss@yfss.com; WWW: http://www.yfss.com/,
http://www.yfss.com/crt_qa.html

▶ Yellowstone Trust Administration provides services for charitable trust administration, including CRAT (charitable remainder annuity trust), SCRUT (straight charitable remainder unitrust), NIWOM (net income without makeup charitable remainder trust), NIMCRUT (net income with makeup charitable remainder unitrust), and FLIP trust (starts as a NIMCRUT and flips to a straight trust after a triggering event).

Financial Planning and Solvency

Corporate Alternatives, Inc. (See also General
Management, Strategic Planning)
2707 West Washington Street, Suite C, Springfield, IL 62702
Tel: 217-787-6993; FAX: 217-787-9316
E-mail: corpalt@fgi.net; WWW: http://www.fgi.net/~corpalt

▶ Corporate Alternatives, inc. (CAi) and its President Peter C. Brinckerhoff specialize in helping not-for-profits get more mission for their money by applying business tools to mission outcomes. Since 1982, CAi has helped thousands of organizations become more mission-capable by improving their internal management, marketing, business development, communications, and financial skills. CAi provides a wide range of management consulting services to board and staff members of not-for-profits. These consulting services include board development; new business development; strategic plan development; corporate restructuring; consultation on mergers, acquisitions, and collaborations; and board/staff retreat planning and facilitation. CAi also has a wide variety of publications for not-for-profits for sale, including Peter Brinckerhoff's books, discussion leader guides, sample business plans, and materials for boards. Specialties include management, marketing, organizational development, and training and facilitation.

A list of free mission-based management ideas and business development tools is available on its Web site at *http://www.fgi.net/~corpalt/ideas.htm.*

Grants Administration and Management

Grantmasters, LLC
33 Little Creek Lane, Fredericksburg, VA 22405
Tel: 540-371-9521; FAX: 540-371-9551
E-mail: rheiman@grantmasters.com (Richard S.V. Heiman,
President); WWW: http://www.grantmasters.com,
http://www.grantmasters.com/faqs.htm

▶ Provides alternative solutions for grants administration, project planning and financial services to public broadcasters and other not-for-profits. Services include project development (develop project budgets for submission, in accordance with grantor's established guidelines, establish project scope and process flow, formulate project business plan, establish production plans, develop project cash flow, customize chart of accounts); project financial monitoring (review, monitor, and audit current programs; perform general ledger reconciliation; prepare and review monthly variance reports; develop project forecast; submit all financial and administrative reports to grantors and management; perform close-out of contracted grants); *post project administration* (interface with funders and auditors regarding all aspects of the project, establish and maintain ancillary reporting systems).

Management Concepts Incorporated (See also
Resource Development and Resource Links to Federal Grants)
8230 Leesburg Pike, Suite 800, Vienna, VA 22182
Tel: 703-790-9595; FAX: 703-790-1371
WWW: http://www.managementconcepts.com

▶ Management Concepts publishes newsletters, loose-leaf services, and books in print, on CD-ROMs, and online. Resources in acquisition and contracting, federal financial management, general management, and project management are available in formats designed to meet customer needs. Services offered include training courses (continually updates, and delivers over 250 practical, competency-based, results-oriented courses in: Acquisition & Contracting; Financial Management, Grants and Assistance, Management, Program Management, Project Management); client on-site courses; publications (*Federal Acquisition & Contracting, Federal Financial Management, Grants & Assistance News You Can Use, Management, Project Management*); continuing education credit; college credit; certificate programs; professional certification training (Financial Management, Grants Management, Management, Program Management Practicum, Project Management); and consulting.

News You Can Use is a free service, designed to keep you informed of key events in the federal grants and assistance arena. This online service is periodically updated to reflect important policy, legislative, and regulatory news. Major stories from previous editions are available in the *Grants News You Can Use Archive,* available online at *http://www.managementconcepts.com/grants/nycuarchive.asp.*

Insurance and Risk Management

Aon/Huntington T. Block
1120 20th Street NW, Suite 600, Washington, DC 20036-3406
Tel: 800-424-8830, 202-223-0876; FAX: 202-857-0143/331-8409;
WWW: http://www.aon.com
333 Bush Street, Suite 600, San Francisco, CA 94104-2878
Tel: 415-228-3000; FAX: 415-399-1905

▶ This company offers comprehensive insurance products for directors' and officers' liability, including employment practices liability for a wide cross-section of nonprofit entities, including, but not limited to museums, performing arts organizations, chambers of commerce, foundations, health care clinics, churches, nursing homes, community hospitals, social service organizations, fraternal organizations, country clubs, fund-raising organizations, and trade associations.

For over 25 years it has administered insurance programs to more than 10,000 nonprofit organizations; together with Chubb's Federal Insurance Company, it has created a special directors' and officers' (D&O) liability program, designed to meet the unique needs of nonprofits. This coverage is available to local United Ways, their funded agencies, and other human service organizations that may not receive United Way funding. Highlights include a two-year policy option with premium guarantee subject to loss history review; mismanagement of company funds coverage; employment-related suits coverage (e.g., discrimination, sexual harassment); personal injury and publisher's liability coverage; fiduciary liability (ERISA) coverage option ($100,000 sublimit; additional cost is equal to 10 percent of annual D&O premium); coverage for nonprofit subsidiaries; coverage for all volunteers, employees, board members, and the organization itself; and duty-to-defend coverage.

CAN Insurance Services *(See also Human Resource Management, Benefits)*
California Association of Nonprofits, P.O. Box 1081, Santa Cruz, CA 95061-1081
Tel: 888-427-5222; FAX: 831-458-9486
E-mail: info@caninsurance.com;
WWW: http://www.caninsurance.com

Branch Office, 25500 Hawthorne Boulevard, Suite 1190, Torrance, CA 90505
FAX: 310-465-0918
E-mail: deborah@caninsurance.com (Deborah Connors, Operation Manager)

▶ As a wholly owned subsidiary of the California Association of Nonprofits, CIS is an insurance brokerage that specializes in providing cost-saving insurance programs designed to meet the unique needs of nonprofit organizations. Coverages include health, dental, life, disability, vision, unemployment, flex benefits, and workers' compensation. It publishes the quarterly CIS newsletter, downloadable on the CAN Web site at *http://www.caninsurance.com/can-newsletter.htm.*

Charity First
One Market, Spear Tower, Suite 200, San Francisco, CA 94105
Tel: 800-352-2761, 415-536-9310, 415-536-8514 (Cindy Hawley, Manager); FAX: 415-536-8561
E-mail: Mike_Komar@ajg.com;
WWW: http://www.charityfirst.com/

▶ Since the early 1960s, Charity First has specialized in insuring nonprofit organizations in the western states. Coverages are tailored specifically for nonprofits: volunteers as additional insured, special events, liquor liability, social workers' professional liability, and directors' and officers' liability; participants include a diversity of risks: shelters for the homeless and battered women, AIDS support groups, senior citizens' housing, boys' and girls' clubs, thrift store operations, and more. Charity First underwrites on behalf of two admitted national carriers with Best's ratings of AXI and AXV, permitting reasonable pricing, long-term stability and a comprehensive package of liability and property coverages.

Products and services available include business, auto, crime, directors' and officers' liability, general liability, property, umbrella liability, workers' compensation.

Charity First provides complementary on-site inspections; safety seminars; online risk management information, and a video rental library to all of its members.

Under a special licensing arrangement with the Nonprofit Risk Management Center, Charity First is able to offer the RISK*facts* library (an extensive collection of informative briefs on a wide range of liability, insurance, and risk management topics designed exclusively for nonprofit organizations and created by the Nonprofit Risk Management Center) to its members online, 24 hours a day.

Chubb Group of Insurance Companies
15 Mountain View Road, Warren, NJ 07059
Tel: 800-36-CHUBB, 908-903-2000; FAX: 908-903-2027
WWW: http://cber.chubb.com/products/index-industry.asp#NonProfit

▶ Chubb has been providing not-for-profit organization liability insurance for more than 15 years, and it counts more than 50,000 not-for-profit organizations among its customers. The member insurers of the Chubb Group of Insurance Companies are rated A++ by A.M. Best. This is Best's top rating. They also receive the top ratings from Moody's and Standard & Poor's for financial stability and claim-paying ability.

Coverages include crime insurance (employee theft coverage, including third-party liability; premises coverage; transit coverage; forgery and alteration coverage; computer theft and funds transfer fraud coverage; claims expense; and extortion coverage); directors' and officers' (D&O) liability insurance with built-in employment practices liability insurance (covers all directors, officers, and employees, including staff, volunteers, and committee members—past, present, and future); fiduciary liability insurance (the Chubb Fiduciary Liability policy responds to this increased risk by offering broad coverage in two distinct areas: *breach of fiduciary duty* applies to a trustee acting in a reasonable and prudent manner in accordance with the standards outlined in ERISA, and *employee benefits liability* coverage protects trustees of employee benefit plans from their liability arising out of an error or omission in the administration of such programs); and outside directorship liability (ODL) insurance. Chubb has designed a system to facilitate risk identification, internal communication, and risk transfer.

Costello & Sons Insurance Brokers, Inc.
1752 Lincoln Ave., San Rafael, CA 94901
Tel: 800-949-0640, 415-455-1515; FAX: 415-455-1517
E-mail: dan@costelloandsons.com.;
WWW: http://www.costelloandsons.com/nonprofit/index.shtml

▶ Costello & Sons is an independent insurance agency specializing in nonprofits. They represent a select group of financially sound, and reputable insurance carriers, and place one's policy with the carrier offering the best coverage for the best price.

Coverages include sexual abuse, professional liability, accident insurance, directors' and officers' liability, and a package policy.

The four areas of professional liability offered by nonprofit insurance carriers are social workers' and counselors' professional liability (this coverage protects the agency in the event of a claim or suit arising out of professional activities such as providing advice, referrals, and even the distribution of medicine at the direction of a physician); health care services professional liability (excluding doctors, psychiatrists, and dentists) (many agencies will provide part-time or full-time nursing or therapy facilities as part of the services available to its client population. Therapy facilities may include occupational, vocational, speech, or audiology. Coverage is intended to protect the insured from these and the many other health care-related services. Some carriers will provide additional coverage for independent contractors, and coverage of this nature needs to be scrutinized by a qualified broker); health care services liability (including doctors, psychiatrists, and dentists) (this coverage addresses the medical malpractice issues of doctors, psychiatrists, and dentists. Coverage will typically pick up the prescription of drugs to client population as well as diagnoses and treatment of patient); and liability from referrals (this is a new and emerging liability exposure for many nonprofits. Coverage is typically written on nonprofit agencies that do not employ social workers or counselors. Coverage is intended to pick up claims from referrals made by the insured to nonemployed, independently contracted medical professionals. Exposure can include negligent referral to other counselors, therapists, medical providers, and/or evaluators).

Executive Risk Management Associates

82 Hopemeadow Street, P.O. Box 2002, Simsbury, CT 06070-7683
Tel: 800-677-5442; FAX: 203-651-7703

▶ Executive Risk Management Associates offers Aetna/Executive Risk, an easy-to-buy liability policy specifically written to protect nonprofit officers and directors. Features include: (1) covers all directors, officers, employees, including staff, volunteers, and committee members; (2) pays defense costs on a current basis, rather than reimbursing expenses after settlement or advancing them at insurer's sole option; (3) policy definitions amended to specifically include employment-related matters; (4) entity coverage available to cover lawsuits against the organization itself; (5) prior acts coverage (no retro-date restrictions); (6) noncancelable by the insurer; (7) provides coverage for employment-related claims; (8) discovery option is bilateral; and (9) admitted carrier (no surplus lines taxes).

First Nonprofit Companies

111 North Canal Street, Suite 801, Chicago, IL 60606
Tel: 800-526-4352, 312-930-9500; FAX: (312) 930-0375
WWW: http://www.firstnonprofit.com

▶ Established in 1978, First Nonprofit is an insurance company owned and governed by nonprofits and dedicated to the nonprofit community. First Nonprofit serves nearly 10,000 nonprofit employees in Illinois, Pennsylvania, Michigan, Wisconsin, and Missouri with the First Nonprofit Unemployment Savings Program, LLC. This program is now a part of the First Nonprofit family of companies and allows them to provide direct support to their policyholders.

Products cover comprehensive general liability, professional liability, automobile liability and physical damage, crime, directors' and officers' liability, workers compensation coverage, 403(b) program, unemployment savings program, umbrella liability, and quality health care options. It offers free admission to educational risk management and on-point nonprofit seminars for nonprofit executives and front-line personnel seminars, in addition to educational publications and workshops. Its unemployment program/personnel services provides advice and guidance via a toll-free number as well as materials on personnel matters. It publishes the quarterly newsletter *Advantage*. It plans future growth in Illinois, Pennsylvania, the District of Columbia, Maryland, Indiana, and Minnesota.

Human Services Unemployment Trust (HSUT)

P.O. Box 22657, Santa Barbara, CA 93121
Tel: 888-249-4788 (HSUT); FAX: 805-566-4921
E-mail: info@hsut.org; WWW: http://www.hsut.org

▶ HSUT is an unemployment tax savings program specifically for nonprofits. HSUT is owned by its over 1,800 participating organizations and has assets of $54 million. Elected trustees, who are CEOs or CFOs of member organizations, govern the trust. The sole purpose of HSUT is to provide nonprofits with a safe, cost-effective alternative to paying state unemployment taxes. Organizations opt out of the state unemployment system and make quarterly contributions directly to the Trust. The Trust handles claims payments directly on their behalf. Free annual training seminars on employment law are offered to members.

Insurance Assessments Consultants, PC

44047 Choptank Terrace, Ashburn, VA 22011
Tel: 703-589-1126

▶ Insurance Assessments Consultants is an independent insurance and risk-management consultant. It offers fee-based, unbiased insurance evaluations. Services include objective coverage analysis and preparation of bid specifications.

Irwin Siegel Agency Inc. Insurance Services

25 Lake Louise Marie Road, Rock Hill, NY 12775
Tel: 800-622-8272, 845-796-3400; FAX: 845-796-3661
E-mail: siegel@ISA1.COM;
WWW: http://www.isiegelagency.com/welcome.html

▶ ISA's programs are tailored for organizations in the disabilities, behavioral health care, and community service fields. It has a Risk Management Department, which works with its insureds in a team approach to safeguarding their consumers, employees, equipment, materials, and property. Working with CNA, ISA has established a team of claims specialists trained in defense strategies and claims handling for all of its programs. Package programs include coverage for property, general/professional liability, automobile, crime, and umbrella. Programs and coverage include directors' and officers' legal liability policy, developmental disabilities package, behavioral health care package, residential home care program, community service package, surety bonds, and guardian and care managers' liability coverage. ISA has established a dedicated claims center that will handle only ISA claims with a 24-hour loss report fax.

J.J. Negley Associates, Inc.

Underwriting Managers, 388 Pompton Avenue, P.O. Box 206, Cedar Grove, NJ 07009
Tel: 973-239-9107; FAX: 973-239-6241
E-mail: info@jjnegley.com; WWW: http://www.jjnegley.com

▶ Founded in 1960, J.J. Negley Associates is an underwriting management firm serving the insurance needs of health care and social service providers. J.J. Negley Associates acts as underwriting managers and managing general agents for a number of carriers. Products include professional liability, commercial general liability, directors' and officers' liability/employment practices liability, and real and personal property. Excess liability and umbrella coverage are also available.

Marketing Asssociates Insurance Agency, Inc.

Surplus Services Insurance Agency, Inc., 154 Wells Avenue, Newton, MA 02159
Tel: 800-852-3077 (MA only), 617-964-5340; FAX: 617-965-1843

▶ Marketing Associates assists human service providers, social service agencies, and nonprofit organizations with their insurance needs. Coverage includes occurrence professional liability, limits to $2,000,000/$6,000,000, broad special property forms available, sexual abuse and molestation coverage, umbrellas to $10,000,000, and directors' and officers' liability.

Mel Himes & Associates Insurance Agency, Inc.

1200 Deltona Boulevard, Suite 61, Deltona, Fl 32725
Tel: 800-329-3031; FAX: 407-574-9209
E-mail: mhj@iag.net, mhjmhaia@iyahoo.com;
WWW: http://501c3-insurance.com/

▶ Mel Himes & Associates specialize in insurance programs for 501(c)(3) corporations: religious organizations (churches, synagogues, houses of worship, ministry groups), social services, charities, private schools, and camps. They will analyze your insurance needs from the viewpoint of risk management. Your existing insurance program will be examined and recommendations and cost comparisons will be reviewed with you. Policy packages offered include liability coverage, counseling, sexual misconduct, teacher liability, directors' and officers' liability, property coverage, buildings, contents, equipment, bus–van–auto, and workers' compensation. Other services provided include: insurance review; child sexual abuse Seminar; loss control survey; background checks; personnel manual.

Mel Himes & Associates maintains three locations across Florida and a location in Nashville, Tennessee.

National Insurance Professionals Corporation

1040 NE Hostmark Street, Suite 200, Poulsbo, WA 98370
Tel: 800-ASK-NIPC, 360-697-3611; FAX: 360-697-3688
E-mail: insurance@nipc.com; WWW: http://www.nipc.com

▶ Programs of interest to nonprofits are *social service agencies* (insurance program with professional and general liability coverages specifically designed for nonprofit social service agencies) and *D&O liability* (including employment practices liability for nonprofit corporations). Other coverages include property, auto, and umbrella. The program is available on a nationwide basis to licensed independent agents and brokers. Eligible entities include nonprofit corporations including foundations and benevolent, charitable, professional, and trade organizations.

Nonprofits' Insurance Alliance of California

P.O. Box 8507, Santa Cruz, CA 95061-8507
Tel: 800-359-6422, 831-459-0980; FAX: 831-459-0853
E-mail: pdavis@niac.org (Pamela Davis, President/CEO);
WWW: http://www.niac.org/

▶ Nonprofits' Insurance Alliance of California (NIAC) is a nonprofit public benefit corporation owned by its 1,000+ California nonprofit agency members. It is a liability insurance pool that was established in 1989 exclusively for 501(c)3 tax-exempt nonprofit organizations in California. NIAC also assists these organizations to develop and implement effective loss control and risk management programs. It caters to nonprofits' unique insurance needs with coverages for fund-raising events, volunteers, counselors, social workers, teachers, and others; all cost savings are passed on to members. NIAC is the only insurance entity to qualify as a "charitable risk pool" under federal law. Such a designation confers on NIAC its own 501(c)(3) tax-exempt status.

It provides a full range of coverages including commercial general liability (including coverage for special events, fund raisers, and volunteers); auto physical damage; auto liability/nonowned/hired auto liability; miscellaneous professional liability (for social workers, teachers, counselors, etc.); improper sexual contact coverage; directors' and officers' liability; and volunteers, employee benefits, umbrella, and liquor liability. Through companion programs, nonprofit members of NIAC may also obtain commercial, fidelity, students/volunteer/participant accident, workers' compensation, and foster parent liability.

NIAC offers workshops, printed materials, on-site visits, and telephone conferences to help reduce your chances of a claim; and maintains a lending library of training materials for members. NIAC plans to expand into other states.

North Island Group, Inc.

30 Park Avenue, Manhasset, NY 11030-2444
Tel: 800-892-8892, 516-365-7440

▶ North Island Group is a recognized managing general agency representing local agents and brokers. Its program, based on long experience with nonprofits, includes property/casualty/automobile, professional liability, fund-raising/special events liability, D&O coverage, and more. The program is underwritten by A+-rated licensed carrier. The coverage area includes Long Island, New Jersey, New York City, Pennsylvania, and Rhode Island.

The Novick Group

11300 Rockville Pike, Suite 907, Rockville, MD 20852
Tel: 301-770-0880; FAX: 301-770-6675
E-mail: lou@novickgroup.com (Louis B. Novick, President)

▶ Since 1986, The Novick Group has provided comprehensive and cost-effective insurance services to more than 700 nonprofit clients throughout the United States.

Philadelphia Insurance Companies

One Bala Plaza, Suite 100, Bala Cynwyd, PA 19004
Tel: 800-873-4552, 800-759-4961, 610-617-7900;
FAX: 610-617-7940
E-mail: pottle@aol.com; WWW: http://www.phlyins.com

▶ Philadelphia Insurance Companies offers insurance for nonprofit organizations, human service agencies, foundations, and associations. Coverage includes nonprofit directors' and officers' and employment practices liability for nonprofits, nonprofit professional liability insurance, and social and human services (a package of insurance uniquely designed to fulfill a wide range of special insurance needs for the Non-Profit Social Service Sector as defined under IRS Code 501(c)(3). The benefits of these programs include: fulfilling social responsibility to the board members and other employees; attracting qualified board members and employees by providing coverage benefits; establishing an efficient risk management program with a broad range of coverage options; and protecting your exposure to large lawsuits, whether legitimate or frivolous. Among the features provided are comprehensive property and crime coverage; professional liability for counselors and social workers; general liability for premises, including coverage for employees, volunteers, and special events; directors' and officers' liability up to $5 million; automobile and van liability and physical damage including non-owned and hired coverage; and interest-free monthly premium payments.

Risk Consultants, Inc.

7506 East Independence Boulevard, Charlotte, NC 28227
Tel: 800-727-7475, 704-537-3400; FAX: 704-532-2359
E-mail: info@risknc.com; WWW: http://risknc.com

▶ Risk Consultants was established in 1969 and provides insurance and risk management consulting for nonprofit organizations. Their services normally fall into three categories: The Risk Management Analysis (study of your insurance coverages, loss exposures, and safety procedures to determine if you are "getting the most bang for the buck" out of the current program and where you should consider reducing or restructuring insurance, self-insuring. or adding coverage); marketing (involves preparing insurance specifications that are designed to implement changes recommended by the analysis as well as obtaining bids from several brokers/agents and direct markets to reduce costs. They analyze the results from a coverage and a cost standpoint, serving as your "in-house" expert); Ongoing Consulting Service (after the program is implemented, they often stay on a retainer basis to monitor the program, serve as watchdogs for you, help with claims, advise you of changes in exposures, new techniques, etc., to keep your risk management program as efficient and cost effective as possible). Insurance coverages analyzed include workers' compensation, auto liability, commercial general liability, employment practices, liability, umbrella or excess liability, professional liability, directors' and officers' liability, property and business interruption exposures, and employee benefits.

Seabury & Smith Nonprofit Resources

505 North Brand Boulevard, Suite 1500, Glendale, CA 91203
Tel: 800-831-6002, 818-502-6520; FAX: 818-547-6252
E-mail: info@nonprofitresources.com;
WWW: http://www.nonprofitresources.com/

▶ Seabury & Smith meets the insurance needs of the nonprofit 501(c)(3)s nationwide. Programs and services include unemployment insurance compensation; commercial property and casualty coverage (coverage specialties include commercial packages, general liability, automobile, business interruption, professional liability, employment practices liability, international, umbrella, and kidnap and ransom); customized employee benefit plans (medical insurance, life insurance, disability insurance, retirement plans and administration, cafeteria plans, worksite marketing, third-party administration, plan design services, eligibility and billing services, claims services, and specialized administrative services); directors' and officers' coverage specifically designed to meet the needs of the nonprofits; and workers' compensation insurance.

Szerlip & Co., Inc.

288 Main Street, Millburn, NJ 07041
Tel: 800-922-0209; FAX: 973-467-0725
E-mail: info@szerlip.com;
WWW: http://www.connectworld.net/szerlip/index.html

▶ Szerlip & Co. assists hundreds of social service agencies across the country to acquire better insurance policies at substantially lower costs by understanding its clients' needs and matching them with the most competitive coverages available.

Volunteers Insurance Service® *(See also Volunteerism—Products and Services)*

Association Insurance Management, 216 South Peyton Street, Alexandria, VA 22314-2813
Tel: 800-468-4200, 800-222-8920, 703-739-9300;
FAX: 703-739-0761
E-mail: inbox@simaworld.com;
WWW: http://www.simaworld.com

▶ Volunteers Insurance Service is a nonprofit association formed for the purpose of researching available and feasible insurance for volunteers, compiling underwriting information, maintaining a central insurance library, furnishing information to its members, and designing and administering insurance for volunteers. It offers the *Volunteer Insurance Plan,* providing broad protection to cover possible risks during volunteer service: personal liability, accident medical reimbursement, accidental death, and excess auto liability for less than $7 per year per volunteer, or less if not all coverages are needed. It insures over 2.5 million volunteers and serves 4,700 nonprofit organizations nationwide. Management information is available through the *VIS® Connections newsletter,* and toll-free counsel on risk management topics.

Investment Management

Chase Not For Profit Group *(See General Consulting)*

Fidelity Investments Tax Exempt Services Company *(See also Retirement Plans)*

Fidelity Investments, P.O. Box 770001, Cincinnati, OH 45277-0003
Tel: 800-462-5450

8 Montgomery Street, San Francisco, CA 94105

Fidelity Distributors Corporation, Fidelity Investments Institutional Services Company, Inc., 82 Devonshire Street, Boston, MA 02109

164 Northern Avenue ZS3, Boston, MA 02210
Tel: 800-841-3363/8235, 800-343-0860; FAX: 617-737-7869
WWW: http://wps.fidelity.com/non-profits/,
http://wps.fidelity.com/npsponsors/if/ifmain.htm

▶ Fidelity Investments has been helping to meet the needs of the nation's leading nonprofit institutions for more than 20 years.

Services include comprehensive investment management services for endowment cash, charitable giving, special purpose, and retirement plans; Charitable Advisory Services offers smaller nonprofits the same opportunity to take advantage of its proven investment expertise for endowments, special funds, and operating accounts.

Investment Architects at Advest Inc.

59 Norwood Farms Road, York Harbor, ME 03911
Tel: 800-733-1198, 207-363-1966; FAX: 207-363-8145
WWW: http://www.advest.com,
http://www.advest.com/individual/office.htm
90 State House Square, Hartford, CT 06103

▶ Investment Architects buildings investment solutions for foundations and endowments.

The Investment Fund for Foundations (TIFF)

2405 Ivy Road, Charlottesville, VA 22903
Tel: 804-817-8200; FAX: 804-817-8231
E-mail: info@tiff.org; WWW: http://www.tiff.org,
http://www.tiff.org/pub/pages/publications.html

▶ TIFF is a member-controlled not-for-profit cooperative, open exclusively to 501(c)(3) organizations, founded by a nationwide network of foundations. Its mission is to improve the investment returns of eligible organizations by making available to them (1) a series of multimanager investment vehicles and (2) resources aimed at enhancing fiduciaries' knowledge of investing. TIFF's services are available to all not-for-profit 501(c)(3) organizations. With the exception of David Salem (TIFF's president), all of the cooperative's directors serve as unpaid volunteers. TIFF offers a variety of investment vehicles and educational resources in furtherance of this mission. All TIFF vehicles are open to private foundations, community foundations, and other 501(c)(3) organizations. TIFF is also open to non–U.S.-based charitable organizations and defined benefit pension or planned giving assets of eligible organizations.

Legg Mason's ASAE Association Investment Program

100 Light Street, 27th Floor, Baltimore, MD 21202
Tel: 888-387-5344, 877-LEGGMASON (877-534-4627);
FAX: 410-454-2075
E-mail: rbkirkconnell@leggmason.com (Robert B. Kirkconnell, Director); WWW: www.legmason.com/AIP

▶ Legg Mason's ASAE Association Investment Program is designed to provide advice to more effectively manage the investment process. Their consultants will help you create an investment policy that provides the strategic link between your investment and your mission. Developed in 1992, this program addresses the unique investment needs of not-for-profits. Their services provide the small to mid-sized (portfolios less than $100 million) not-for-profit organization the highest-quality investment consulting services. The three-step approach to investing provides a structure for reaching a consensus by the board of directors on investment policies and measuring progress toward meeting the organization's investment objectives. The Association Investment Program focuses on long-term relationships, advocating a consultative rather than a transaction-oriented approach. The process helps one manage association reserves; foundations and endowments; retirement plans, including 401(k) plans; and insurance trusts.

Loomis, Sayles & Company, LP

One Financial Center, 5th Floor, Boston, MA 02111
Tel: 888-226-9699, 617-482-2450; FAX: 617-443-0185
555 California Street, Suite 3300, San Francisco, CA 94104
Tel: 415-956-2424; FAX: 415-956-2515
WWW: http://www.loomissayles.com

▶ Established in 1926, Loomis, Sayles & Company, LP, is one of the oldest and largest investment management firms in America. Loomis Sayles Investment Trust is a series of institutional mutual funds established primarily for tax-exempt investors such as pension plans, endowments, and foundations, although other institutions and high-net-worth individuals are eligible to invest.

Check out its online glossary at *http://www.loomissayles.com/glossary/index_gloss.html.*

MLD Investment Advisory, Inc.

3980 Howard Hughes Parkway, Suite 300, Las Vegas, NV 89109
Tel: 702-735-5238; FAX: 702-732-4571
E-mail: mld@anv.net; WWW: http://www.managingmoney.com/

▶ MLD manages money for individuals, corporations, pension and profit-sharing plans, trusts, and nonprofit organizations. All accounts are managed on a fully disclosed and discretionary basis. Currently, MLD manages in excess of $14 million dollars for over 100 accounts.

MLD Investment Advisory, Inc., designs and maintains its own "branded" financial products as well as selectively distributing products from other high-quality advisory firms who have particular areas of expertise. MLD manages money on a separate account basis and designs accounts consisting of either managed stocks and bonds or managed mutual fund programs. Asset Manager is MLD's branded managed mutual fund program.

Winslow Management Company

Sixty State Street, 12th Floor, Boston, MA 02109-1803
Tel: 800-255-6201, 617-788-1600, 371-3900; FAX: 617-788-1605
WWW: http://www.winslowgreen.com/

▶ Winslow Management Company is a Boston-based investment management firm established in 1984 that specializes in managing endowments for nonprofit institutions, pension funds, and high-net-worth individuals by investing in publicly traded, environmentally responsible, and environmentally proactive companies. Winslow supports the Social Investment Forum and supports, with Adams, Harkness & Hill, the Business for Social Responsibility and the Social Venture Network.

Retirement Planning and Employee Benefits *(See also Human Resource Management, Benefits)*

Charles W. Cammack Associates, Inc. (CWCA)

Retirement Plan Consulting for Nonprofits, 2 Rector Street, Suite 1511, New York, NY 10006
Tel: 800-438-7771, 212-227-7770; FAX: 212-267-3832
E-mail: cwcainfo@cwcainc.com; WWW: http://www.cwcainc.com

▶ CWCA is an established, nationally recognized retirement and benefits consulting firm specializing in retirement plans for nonprofit organizations, with emphasis on Web-based benefit systems, benefit information management, retirement plans, employee welfare plans, and financial planning. CWCA has over 450 national clients that include health care systems and cultural organizations.

They specialize in Web-based benefit solutions, complex multi-site/multiplan design and implementation, competitive vendor selection (RFP) process, compliance monitoring, and effective employee communication and education. CWCA is a solution partner with several Web-based benefit application providers. They also maintain offices in New Jersey, Washington, and Florida.

Fidelity Investment Tax-Exempt Services Company (FITSCo)

P.O. Box 770001, Cincinnati, OH 45277-0003
Tel: 800-248-4193 (plan sponsors of nonprofit organizations),
800-841-3363/8235, 800-343-0860
WWW: http://wps.fidelity.com/non-profits/,
http://wps.fidelity.com/npsponsors/

▶ The Fidelity Investments Institutional Retirement Group offers retirement services for 401(k), 403(b), and 457 plans available through employers. Clients include education, health care, research, associations, and religious groups. FITSCo is a provider of 403(b)/401(a) retirement savings plans to not-for-profit organizations, including colleges and universities, health care institutions, foundations, and charitable organizations. In addition to providing institutional plans, FITSCo also provides investment management, and administrative and employee services.

Mutual of America

320 Park Avenue, New York, NY 10022
Tel: 800-468-3785, 800-872-5963 (American Life)
Bishop Ranch Business Park, 4000 Executive Parkway, Suite 512,
San Ramon, CA 94583
Tel: 510-244-0500; FAX: 510-244-0525
WWW: http://www.mutualofamerica.com/

▶ Mutual of America and its wholly owned subsidiary, The American Life Insurance Company of New York, provide group and individual variable annuities and related services for the pension, retirement, and long-range savings needs of various organizations and their employees. Through American Life, individual and group life insurance and group disability products are also available. For 50 years, it has provided nonprofit groups with pension and retirement plans. It has over 9,000 not-for-profit clients and a national network of 36 field offices.

Among the products it offers are group annuity contracts for defined contribution, 401(k) and tax-deferred annuity plans, individual annuities for traditional IRA and Roth IRA plans, and, through American Life, variable universal life insurance.

TIAA-CREF Trust Company, FSB

211 North Broadway, Suite 1000, St. Louis, MO 63102
Tel: 800-842-2252, 888-842-9001; FAX: 314-244-5012
E-mail: lbrizendine@tiaa-cref.org (Lyle Brizendine);
WWW: www.tiaa-cref.org, http://www.tiaa-cref.org/a_regional/index.html

▶ For over 80 years TIAA-CREF has been providing benefits for the education and nonprofit research communities. Products offered include retirement plans, SRAs, IRAs, Keoghs, mutual funds, personal annuities, life insurance, long-term care, trust services, and saving for college.

Waddell & Reed Financial, Inc.

6300 Lamar Avenue, Shawnee Mission, KS 66202
Tel: 888-WADDELL (888-923-3355) (customer service),
800-532-2757, 913-236-1880; FAX: 913-236-1880
E-mail: investorrelations@waddell.com (D. Tyler Towery,
Director of Investor Relations);
WWW: http://www.waddell.com/rp/retirement.html,
http://www.waddell.com/awr/locations.html

▶ They offer a complete selection of retirement benefit plan options for nonprofit organizations such as government, religious, educational institutions, charities, and public services. Educational organizations, state and local governments, and private sector 501(c)(3) organizations qualify for these plans. Products offered include simplified employee pension plan, SIMPLE-IRA, 401(k), SIMPLE-401(k), 430(b)(7) TSA, 403(b) TSA, Title I TSA, 457 plan, profit-sharing plan, money purchase plan, and payroll deduction plan.

Tax Compliance and Reporting *(See also Charitable Giving and Investment Services; Human Resource Management—Benefits; Legal Issues)*

The Non-Profit HELP Center

18 North Main Street, Suite 202, Rochester, NH 03867
Tel: 603-335-3384; FAX: 603-335-0438
E-mail: nonprofit@acornworld.net (Paul M. Dolnier, Executive Director); WWW: http://www.help-page-nonprofits.org

16208 NE 12th Avenue, North Miami Beach, FL 33162
Tel: 305-957-9950; FAX: 305-957-9969

▶ The Non-Profit HELP Center provides assistance to help form nonprofit corporations in all 50 states. They can prepare and file the IRS Package Form 1023, maintain contact with your organization until you are approved and get your "IRS Section 501(c)(3) Tax Exempt Status letter" in the mail, and answer any question(s) you may have regarding nonprofit corporations and tax exemption problems.

Philanthropy Tax Institute—Taxes *(See also Charitable Giving and Investments; Legal Issues, Resource Development – Planned Giving)*

13 Arcadia Road, Old Greenwich, CT 06870
Tel: 800-243-9122, 203-637-4311; FAX: 203-637-4572
E-mail: info@taxwisegiving.com;
WWW: http://www.taxwisegiving.com

▶ Philanthropy Tax Institute is a planned giving specialist offering publications, software, and planned giving lectures. Lectures and seminars include:

For Donors, Prospective Donors, Constituents and Alumni Groups, Trustees (Especially Planned Giving and Bequest Committees), and Volunteers

Estate Planning Strategies & Charitable Giving—a two-hour program that covers estate and financial planning objectives: the essentials of wills and trusts; how to save federal estate, gift, and generation-skipping taxes and probate costs; living wills and durable powers of attorney; and how to make charitable gifts that benefit donor, family members, and charities.

Smart Philanthropy Benefits Charities & Donors—a luncheon or dinner talk about well-planned philanthropy and how it affects donors and your institution. Conrad Teitell will also talk informally with important donors (and their advisors).

For Professional Advisors Attorneys, CPAs, Trust Officers, CLUs, Financial Planners

Charitable Contribution Tax Strategies—two- or four-hour programs that makes informed advisors members of your team. They'll be receptive to development officers' proposals when they learn the sophisticated giving techniques that produce tax savings and other benefits from outright and life-income gifts.

For Development Professionals

Three-Day Comprehensive Planned Giving Course—teaches tax techniques for outright, charitable remainder, and charitable lead gifts: how to start, expand, promote, and administer planned giving programs and the basics of estate planning.

One-Day Crash Course—In Your Community is the condensed version of Teitell's three-day planned giving course (described above) that can include your entire staff as well as local attorneys, CPAs, trust officers, CLUs, and financial planners. Co-sponsor with other charitable organizations or planned giving groups. Local banks, firms, and foundations sometimes act as funding sponsors. Fee $13,000 plus travel expenses. Includes 350-page outline for you to reproduce and distribute to the participants.

Publications for development professionals and advisors include: *Taxwise Giving* (a monthly newsletter of taxwise philanthropy), *Deferred Giving* (explanation, specimen agreements, forms), *Planned Giving* (starting, marketing, administering), *Outright Charitable Gifts* (explanation, substantiation, forms), *Portable Planned Giving Manual, Substantiating Charitable Gifts: Compleat Compliance Manual, Charitable Lead Trusts* (explanation, specimen agreements, forms).

Publications for donors include: *Amicus* (a quarterly planned giving publication) and booklets on tax-encouraged giving

Thompson & Thompson, PC *(See also Charitable Giving and Investment Services; Governance; Human Resource Management; Legal Issues)*
39555 Orchard Hill Place, Suite 600, Novi, MI 48375
Tel: 248-348-5772; FAX: 248-449-2963
E-mail: thompson@exlaw.com; WWW: http://www.t-law.com/nonprofit.shtml
▶ Thompson & Thompson is a full-service law firm in representing charities, nonprofit organizations, and their related entities. They assist clients with the organization and restructuring of nonprofit organizations and their affiliated entities, obtaining and defending qualification of tax-exempt status (at both state and federal levels), rendering legal and tax opinions and other transactional matters, and providing a variety of legal and organizational consultation services.

Services offered to their clients include: entity formation (incorporation, limited liability, creation of trusts and foundations, creation of subsidiaries and affiliates, management of subsidiary and affiliate relationships, reorganizations and restructuring of organizations, review, and revision and preparation of governing documents: articles, charter, bylaws, constitution, etc.); employee compensation (Section 403(b) TSA programs, Section 401(a) qualified pension and profit-sharing plans, 401(k) plans, Section 457 nonqualified deferred compensation plans, negotiate and prepare employee compensation and fringe benefit packages, qualify retirement and fringe benefit programs with the IRS, employment and employment termination agreements, and severance packages and agreements); tax-exemption matters (obtain, maintain, and defend tax-exempt status, defend exempt status change or challenge for §501(c)(3) and all other (c) classes, Social Security options for ministers, etc., state property tax exemptions, sales and use tax exemptions, unrelated business income tax [UBIT], lobbying restrictions, and donations to foreign charities); nonprofit organizations (nonprofit purpose analysis and compliance; fund-raising regulatory compliance [charitable solicitation licensing, etc.], advice regarding planned giving programs; liability prevention and limitation for directors, officers, and volunteers; waivers of liability for participants, volunteers, and contractors; and applicability of state workers' compensation and unemployment compensation laws); living trusts and estate planning (last will and testaments, living trusts with federal estate tax planning, general durable financial powers of attorney, health care powers of attorney, living wills, wealth replacement trusts, charitable remainder trusts, special needs trusts, other irrevocable trusts); governance and management (corporate fundamentals, working with volunteers, working with independent contractors, how a board operates, limiting management's liability exposure, basic management principles, executive and board training seminars, conflicts of interest and self-dealing transactions); general tax issues (defense of audits and tax disputes, worker classification status, income tax analysis and opinions, and sales and use tax licensing and compliance).

They also provide a full range of legal assistance to managers of nonprofit organizations. For information relating to a review of the legal status of your organization's tax status, liability exposure, contracts, proprietary rights, and organizational structure, see their page on *Prevent Legal Audits*. For information about services relating to management training and consulting, see their page on *Nonprofit Training Seminar.*

Check out their 501(c) Qualification Package, which includes fees information.

Tax Exempt Debt Financing

CDA Nonprofit Finance, LLC
CBO Financial, Inc., 6475 Camden Avenue, Suite 201, San Jose, CA 95120
Tel: 408-323-1484; FAX: 408-323-1485
E-mail: info@npofinance.com, cmonteith@cbofinancial.com (Cassandra Monteith); WWW: http://www.npofinance.com
▶ CDA provides nonprofit organizations access to the tax-exempt capital markets. It specializes in security low-interest, fixed-rate financing for small to midsize 501(c)(3) organizations.

Software and Technology Consulting

AccountAbility Solutions, Inc.
117 W. Main Street, Suite 23, Woodland, CA 95695
Contact: Mel Schmidt
Tel: 800-381-4872
E-mail: training@accountabilityreports.com;
WWW: www.accountabilityreports.com

▶ AccountAbility schedules classes for CYMAIV Accounting for Windows Monday through Wednesday on the last week of each month. Class size is limited to six preregistered students.

Accountnet, Inc.
157 West 57th Street, Suite 504, New York, NY 10019
Tel: 212-765-6666 (SOLOMON); FAX: 212-977-7120
E-mail: mail@accountnet-nyc.com;
WWW: http://www.accountnet-nyc.com

▶ Accountnet specializes in accounting solutions designed around Solomon Series software. Clients range from *Fortune* 1000 to financial services, health care, and nonprofit organizations. Accountnet consults, sells, and supports the Solomon IV/Windows Accounting System.

Blum Shapiro & Company, PC
Not-for-Profit Services Group, 29 South Main Street, P.O. Box 272000, West Hartford, CT 06127
Tel: 860-561-4000; FAX: 860-521-9241
E-mail: lmb@bshapiro.com (Lori Budnick), jzp@bshapiro.com (Jessica Powell, Senior Marketing Coordinator);
WWW: http://www.bshapiro.com/pages/industry/nonforpr.html

▶ Blum Shapiro Business Technology Services, LLC, can help implement information technology providing management with access to timely, accurate information. They can assist you in hardware and software selection, manage installation, and oversee training of your staff.

Computerworks Accounting Software
2623 E. Foothill, Pasadena, CA 91107
Tel: 626-792-4044; FAX: 626-792-2709
E-mail: computerwrks@earthlink.net, sales@cssoftware.com;
WWW: http://www.cwsoftware.com/,
http://www.cwsoftware.com/my_html/classes.html,
http://www.cwsoftware.com/html/supportbodysupport.html

▶ Computerworks is a full-service consulting firm specializing in financial and accounting software solutions for not-for-profit organizations and governmental agencies. Computerworks has been selling software and training people in computerized accounting since 1981. Consulting services include needs analysis, software and hardware recommendations, software sales (see *Software*), installation and implementation, training (see *Classes*), and ongoing support (see *Support*). They are certified resellers for American Fundware, MAS 90, and CYMA. Their online newsletter, *The Breeze*, is available at *http://www.cwsoftware.com/html/ newsletter.html.*

Hansen & Associates
9027 E. Aster Drive, Scottsdale, AZ 85260
Tel: 602-314-3432
E-mail: HansenAssc@aol.com (Coleen or Bill Hansen)

▶ Established in 1988, Hansen & Associates provides NFP software, installation, training, support, and report writing as well as assisting clients with their chart of accounts to effectively print the reports they want. They work with large and small not-for-profit firms nationwide.

ICON, Inc. (International Computer Operating Networks, Inc.)
1749 Old Meadow Road, Suite 630, McLean, VA 22102
Tel: 800-482-ICON, 703-556-4266; FAX: 703-556-4280
E-mail: training@iconcorp.com (Chuck Annis),
consulting@iconcorp.com; WWW: http://www.iconcorp.com/

▶ ICON is a technology-driven, systems integration corporation specializing in network implementation, accounting systems, and integrated office solutions.

ISG Solutions
2400 Research Boulevard, Suite 350, Rockville, MD 20850
Tel: 877-810-7ISG, 301-519-3776; FAX: 301-519-9699
E-mail: isginfo@isgsolutions.com; WWW: http://isgsolutions.com

▶ ISG Solutions can help your association increase its productivity through the development of software that ranges from simple enhancements to large and complex systems. Its staff of professional consultants can offer unique solutions to your association's unique software requirements. ISG Solutions' *Internet Resource Digest* is a biweekly e-mail newsletter designed to help association and nonprofit professionals keep up with the latest news and Internet resources.

Integrated Financial Systems *(See also Resource Development)*
1800 Diagonal Road, Suite 600, Alexandria, VA 22314
Tel: 800-763-8759
E-mail: dlarkin@ifsweb.com (David A. Larkin, President);
WWW: http://www.ifsweb.com
4860 Cox Road, Suite 200, Glen Allen, VA 23060
200 North Third Street, Suite 1100, Harrisburg, PA 17101

▶ Since its inception in 1991, IFS has provided technology and guidance to over 400 clients. Integrated Financial Systems provides consulting and automation services to the nonprofit industry. There are over 200 software applications catering to the nonprofit industry, ranging from accounting solutions to fund raising to event management. IFS provides the needs analysis up front to help streamline the selection process. They have recommended products such as Blackbaud, iMIS, Quickbooks, MIP, and many others in the marketplace. By understanding the clients NBS (needs, budgets, and staff), it can provide the client with choices and recommendations.

Kerr Consulting & Support
70 N. Skyflower Court, The Woodlands, TX 77381
Tel: 281-364-8783, 877-280-6344; FAX: 281-296-0805
E-mail: Houston@Kerr-Consulting.com; WWW: www.kerr-consulting.com

▶ Since 1987, Kerr Consulting & Support has been providing clients all over the United States with automated business solutions, as well as training and project management techniques. It has provided seminars to various technology companies and state CPA associations to assist them in developing their service organizations and quality consulting practices.

Nonprofit Business Solutions

P.O. Box 140228, Dallas, TX 75214
Tel: 214-395-7813; FAX: 214-800-4825
E-mail: mgcpa@flash.net (Mark Gilbert);
WWW: http://www.npbiz.com

▶ Provides accounting service to organizations. Services include custom implementation and training (on-site training in all accounting modules by consultants who have implemented the product), financial services (review activity account coding for proper classification according to grant awards), and network maintenance (maintain and install Microsoft NT networks).

Software Vendors—Charitable Estate Planning and Planned Giving

(See also Resource Development, Estate Planning and Planned Giving)

Brentmark Software

3505 Lake Lynda Drive, Suite 212, Orlando, FL 32817-8327
Tel: 800-879-6665, 407-306-6160; FAX: 407-306-6107
E-mail: sales@brentmark.com;
WWW: http://www.brentmark.com/brochure.htm

▶ Brentmark® software provides retirement planning products and services for professionals and consumers: estate, financial, and retirement planning software; informational Web sites (*www.rothira.com* and *www.pensionplanners.com*); online calculators (*www.calctools.com*); and online publications (*www.goldbergreports.com*). Software products include Pension & Roth IRA Analyzer, Estate Planning Tools, Estate Planning QuickView, PFP Notebook, Savings Bond Toolkit, Investment Scenario Generator, Roth IRA Conversion Analyzer, Charitable Financial Planner, IRS Factors Calculator, Roth IRA Conversion Calculator, Pension Distributions Calculator, and Minimum Distributions Calculator.

Crescendo Interactive (Comdel, Inc.)

1601 Carmen Drive, Suite 103, Camarillo, CA 93010
Tel: 800-858-9154; FAX: (805) 388-2483
WWW: http://www.crescendosoft.com

▶ Crescendo Interactive is a supplier of planned gift marketing software. It provides a full line of innovative products and services to the planned giving professional that enhance productivity, create dynamic gift proposal presentations, and deliver donor and advisor gift options and explanations. Products include Crescendo Pro for Windows 95/98/2000/NT (the largest selection of gift plans and innovative tools), Crescendo Estate (a professional advisor's ideal planning and presentation tool), Crescendo Lite (a lighter solution for a less complicated need), Crescendo Plus (group presentations made easy), and Crescendo Presents (notebook presentations software). Crescendo offers a full complement of one- to three-day training seminars (Comprehensive, Advanced, Major Gifts, Case Studies, Professionals, Crescendo Plus, Internet Marketing, G.A. Administration, GiftLaw Teleconference, GiftLegacy Teleconference, and Video Education).

It publishes *Crescendo Notes*, a quarterly newsletter with tax tips, model analysis, case studies, and seminar and product announcements. It provides tax updates within approximately 30 days of tax changes. Annual program enhancements (also including updates to the manual) are shipped on CD. A "Rate of the Month Letter" specifying the applicable federal rate is provided on a monthly basis. Also available is *Crescendo e-notes* (a weekly e-mail newsletter update; it includes the Washington Update from GiftLaw.com, the finance update from GiftLegacy.com, a description of the Case of the Week and Article of the Month and News from Crescendo).

Jane Schuck & Associates

10120 Two Notch Road, Suite 2-123, Columbia, SC 29229
Tel: 800-694-7624 (Sales), 803-699-0169 (Support); FAX: 803-699-8080
E-mail: Nicole2@mindspring.com;
WWW: http://www.janeschuck.com

▶ Jane Schuck & Associates is a developer and distributor of software tools for estate planning attorneys, accountants, and charitable foundations. Products include Charitable Financial Planner (gives you fast answers to complex charitable trust calculations or other charitable giving situations. Get accurate answers based on the latest tax tables and variable AFR rates, including capital gains and income tax consequences), EZ Bond (your information source for Savings Bonds "EE," "E," and "S." Reports contain valuations with accruals, issue date, and more); Henson's Transfers (provides you with the complete tools for transfering securities and real assets. Information at your fingertips includes all 3,219 county recorders in the United States, plus transfer agents for over 5,000 corporations, and more); Wallace Pricing (brings you comprehensive security valuations for estate and gift tax and other probate needs). Databases available include 27,000 securities on CD-ROM, plus immediate access to 25 years of pricing data.

LMNOP

523 Fourth Street, Suite 200A, San Rafael, CA 94901
Tel: 415-485-3744; FAX: 415-485-3748
E-mail: lsm@lmnopstuff.com (Lynda S. Moerschbaecher);
WWW: http://www.sfo.com/~lsm/software.html

▶ LMNOP is the distributor of Charitable Docs in a Box. This is a Windows software for drafting charitable gift vehicles, including charitable remainder trusts, lead trusts, charitable gift annuities, pooled income funds, life estate contracts, and deeds of gift, covering almost every drafting situation you will come across, with help screens and an on-screen library of codes, regulations, rulings, announcements, legislation, cover letters, and other resources.

Lackner Group

700 North Bell Ave., Pittsburgh, PA 15106

The Lackner Group, Inc., Development Division, 1732 Lyter Drive, Johnstown, PA 15905
Tel: 800-709-1041, 412-279-2121 (Support): FAX: 412-279-6426
E-mail: sales@lacknergroup.com;
WWW: http://www.lacknergroup.com

▶ The Lackner Group is a software solution provider for estate and trust administration. Lackner's flagship product, *6-in-1*, provides an integrated solution to those who wish to easily produce the Federal 706, Federal 1041, State Death Tax, State Fiduciary Tax, Court Account, and Inventory. In addition to the 6-in-1 system, they also have the Quik product line. The Quik products include estate and fiduciary tax programs at both the federal and state level. They offer current customers the Bonus Pak, a variety of programs and books that extend your Lackner software, including the following: Probate Forms (*www.lacknergroup.com*);

CircCalc (*www.lacknergroup.com*); NumberCruncher *(www.leimberg.com)*; zCalc (*www.zcalc.com*); Wallace Pricing (*www.financialdata.com*); Laser Librarian (*www.laserlib.com*); EZ Bond (*www.janeschuck.com*); Savings Bond Wizard (*www.savingsbonds.gov/sav/savwizar.htm*); Tiger Tables (*www.tigertables.com*); 706/709 Deskbook (*www.ppcinfo.com/prod/706p.htm*); 1041 Deskbook (*www.ppcinfo.com/prod/t41p.htm*); RIA Fiduciary Tax Return (*www.riatax.com/nsp.html#itg*); Quik Tax Pak (*www.lacknergroup.com*); Quik 709 (*www.lacknergroup.com*); Will Tracker (*www.lacknergroup.com*); and Quik Calc (*www.lacknergroup.com*)

Leimberg Associates, Inc.

P.O. Box 601, Bryn Mawr, PA 19010
Tel: 610-527-5216; FAX: 610-527-5226
E-mail: info@leimberg.com; WWW: http://www.leimberg.com

▶ Leimberg Associates is the distributor of the following software packages: Charitable Gift Planner Software (information on this product available at *http://www.leimberg.com/software/charitbleplanning.html);* NumberCruncher for estate planning (*http://www.leimberg.com/software/estateplanning.html*); and Pension and Roth Analyzer for retirement planning (see details about this software product at *http://www.leimberg.com/software/retirementplanning.html*).

PG Calc Incorporated *(See also Resource Development)*

129 Mount Auburn Street, Tel: 888-497-4970 (Sales and Marketing), Cambridge, MA 02138-9941
Tel: 617-497-4970; FAX: 617-497-4974
E-mail: info@pgcalc.com; WWW: http://www.pgcalc.com

▶ PG Calc's Gift Administration Software includes GiftWrap and Pooled Fund Organizer. GiftWrap is a comprehensive planned gift database. Its range of capabilities include the following: stores complete data on planned gift donors, beneficiaries, and prospects; provides summary reports of people, gifts, and payments; produces gift annuity reserve reports for all states; computes FASB 116/117 liabilities for all planned gift types; projects cash flow expectancies for bequests and life income gifts; provides ongoing estimates of the assets backing each gift annuity contract (CashTrac); produces payment checks and supports electronic funds transfer; prints 1099-R tax forms for gift annuitants; direct link with Planned Giving Manager (see separate listing under Resource Development, Products and Services) that speeds data entry of new gifts; maintains information on thousands of people and thousands of gifts; and it is multiuser and can separately handle data for multiple organizations in its single database.

Pooled Fund Organizer (PFORZ) performs all tasks necessary for complete and efficient administration of charitable pooled income funds. PFORZ can administer pooled funds with thousands of participants and can be configured to administer separately any number of individual funds. Includes the following features: maintains all necessary information on fund beneficiaries; automates production of payment checks, K-1 tax forms, and state tax forms for California and Massachusetts; unitizes new gifts; distributes income among fund participants; and creates numerous additional reports.

PG Calc offers a one-day class devoted to understanding and presenting the benefits of charitable lead trusts. This session covers the basics of lead trusts; reviews their gift, estate, generation-skipping, and income tax implications; and includes comprehensive instruction on creating lead trust presentations in Planned Giving Manager.

PhilanthroTec Inc. *(See also Resource Development—Major Gifts, Planned Giving)*

10800 Independence Pointe Parkway, Suite F, Matthews, NC 28105
Tel: 800-332-7832; FAX: 704-845-5528
E-mail: info@ptec.com; WWW: http://www.ptec.com,
http://www.ptec.com/html/about_us.html

▶ PhilanthroTec is a company that specializes in the design, development, and distribution of Intel PC-based computer software for charitable estate planning and planned giving. PhilanthroTec's flagship software product is The Charitable Scenario. Other products include The Remainder Trust Marketing System, which will be of interest to any planned gift professional who specializes in the charitable remainder unitrust, and The Deduction Calculator, which provides sophisticated deduction calculations for all major gifts. It also offers software training seminars.

Practitioners Publishing Company (PPC)

P.O. Box 966, Fort Worth, TX 76101-0966
Tel: 800-323-8724; FAX: 817-877-3694
E-mail: ppc@onramp.net, Customer.Service@ppctx.com;
WWW: http://www.ppcnet.com

▶ Their Estate and Gift Tax Calculator complements the *Guide to Practical Estate Planning and PPC's 706/709 Deskbook.* It calculates the federal gift tax, estate tax, state death tax credit, and total taxes due for a taxpayer and surviving spouse. It also solves complex interrelated computations in determining the marital or charitable deduction when death taxes or other expenses are allocable to marital or charitable bequests. Plus, it helps one determine the charitable deduction for transfers to charitable remainder trusts, pooled income funds, and charitable lead trusts.

Rodriguez, Horii & Choi

777 South Figueroa Street, Suite 3307, Los Angeles, CA 90017
Tel: 213-892-7700; FAX: 213-892-7777
E-mail: al@rhclaw.com (Albert Rodriguez), Dwayne@rhclaw.com (Dwayne Horii), bill@rhclaw.com (Willaim Choi);
WWW: http://www.rhclaw.com/char_ira.shtml

▶ Rodriguez, Horii & Choi is the distributor of The CCF Charitable Family IRASM, a vehicle that enables donors to use their IRAs to provide a steady stream of income for their loved ones after their death while at the same time using the same IRA to establish a philanthropic legacy in perpetuity with the California Community Foundation.

Tiger Tables Software

4529 Pershing Place, St. Louis, Missouri 63108
Tel: 314-552-6187
E-mail: info@tigertables.com, lkatzenstein@thompsoncoburn.com (Lawrence Katzenstein); WWW: http://www.tigertables.com

▶ This company is the developer and distributor of Tiger Tables. St. Louis attorney Larry Katzenstein's Tiger Tables for Windows will calculate a wide variety of actuarial factors. Tiger Tables Actuarial Software will produce almost any actuarial factor ever likely to be needed by a tax lawyer, estate planner, or accountant. Among the most often used factors calculated by Tiger Tables are the following: qualified personal residence trusts; grantor-retained annuity trusts (GRATs); and charitable factors.

ViewPlan Division of CCH Incorporated

4025 West Peterson Avenue, Chicago, IL, 60646-6085
Tel: 888-879-5515; FAX: (773) 866-3608
WWW: http://tax.cch.com/viewplan/product.htm

▶ CCH ViewPlan® software products provide you with all the tools you'll need to accurately calculate and effectively present estate planning concepts. ViewPlan is a combination of five products that are linked directly to CCH estate and financial planning research publications. Products include Vista (ViewPlan's premiere estate planning program, Vista gives you a way to present visually appealing and understandable estate planning proposals for your clients. Vista performs estate calculations quickly and accurately, calculating for all 50 states in addition to the Federal calcs); Beneview™ (a charitable giving program designed to help clients see the value of charitable gifts by using a unique visual approach); CCH ViewPlan: Factuary™ (an analysis tool that demonstates the benefits of various types of "intrafamily wealth transfers" such as GRITs, GRATs, GRUTs, Private Annuities, and SCINs. Calculation results can be presented in graphical, numerical, and report formats); Progeny™ (a planning tool that illustrates the bottom-line benefits of using the generation-skipping exemption); BeneQuick (designed for quick factor calculations for charitable giving. Calculates for charitable remainder and lead unitrusts and annuity trusts for up to five lives, as well as pooled income funds and gift annuities).

Together, ViewPlan and CCH offer an integrated suite of estate planning presentation and research tools. ViewPlan software links directly to CCH estate and financial planning research publications. Complementary CCH research tools include: CCH Financial and Estate Planning; Federal Estate & Gift Tax Reporter; the softcover reference Federal Estate & Gift Taxes Explained; CCH FinEst Calcs; CCH Inheritance, Estate and Gift Tax Reporter; and New York Estates, Wills, and Trusts.

WealthTec

209 Finale Terrace, Silver Spring, MD 20901
Tel: 301-593-9784; FAX: 301-593-9785
E-mail: howard@wealthtec.com (Howard L. Eisenberg,
President); WWW: http://www.wealthtec.com

▶ WealthTec is a firm specializing in the development of high-end financial and estate planning software applications for the experienced professional. Products include AdvancedPro Series™ (comprehensive wealth preservation and transfer system that allows you to create powerful illustrations in the areas of estate planning, charitable planning, retirement distribution planning, and tax planning; it currently consists of a Financial Profile module and *31 Planners*) and ProPrimer Series™ (allows you to create comprehensive cash flow and net worth illustrations, along with baseline wealth transfer and estate liquidity analyses. This system provides you with the diagnostic power you need to help your clients identify weaknesses in their current financial plans).

zCalc, LLC

574 North 550 East, Lindon, UT 84042
Tel: 801-785-1300; FAX: 801-785-1328
Support: support@zcalc.com; Sales: sales@zcalc.com;
WWW: http://www.zcalc.com

▶ Developer and distributor of zCalc Excel Addin and the zCalc Tool Box tax and charitable software calculations for MS Excel Spreadsheets. Applications include estate planning, financial planning, retirement planning, charitable planning, and income tax planning.

Software Vendors—Fund Accounting

AccountMate Software

81 Digital Drive, Novato, CA 94949
Tel: 800-877-8896, 415-883-8873; FAX: 415-883-5863
E-mail: info@accountmate.com; http://www.accountmate.com,
http://www.sourcemate.com

▶ AccountMate is the distributor of Visual AccountMate Fund Accounting. All systems include System Manager; Crystal Reports™; Seagate Software; integrated into the System Manager; Crystal Reports compared to Visual Fox Pro: General Accounting: Accounts Payable, Accounts Receivable, Bank Reconciliation, Consolidated Ledger, Contact Manager, General Ledger, Purchase Order, Sales Order, and Payroll.

Advanced Data Systems

458 Main Street, Bangor, ME 04401-6295
Tel: 800-779-4494, 207-947-4494; FAX: 207-947-0650
E-mail: info@adspro.com; WWW: http://www.adspro.com

Branch Office, 308 Highlander Way, Manchester, NH 03108-5158
Tel: 800-288-8167, 603-621-7463; FAX: 603-621-7466

▶ Advanced Data Systems is a software developer and reseller of accounting information systems, with over 20 years of experience in the PC-based computing industry. Founded in 1980 to serve the technology needs of the state of Maine, they now serve clients throughout New England and across the country.

They provide fund accounting software solutions for the specific needs of nonprofit organizations. Their primary software development efforts are focused on the ADS ProFund Series of Fund Accounting software. ADS ProFund 2000 software and its successor, ADS ProFund for Windows, is in use at hundreds of nonprofit installations nationwide

Products available include ADS ProFund® Series Fund Accounting Solutions (*ADS ProFund 2000, ADS ProFund for Windows*), Solomon IV (the Windows-based accounting information system solution from Solomon Software), and *ADS Non-Profit Plus*—Fund Accounting for Solomon IV.

Also available is a free copy of the booklet *A Consumer's Guide to Fund Accounting Software: Facts to Know & Features to Look for in Choosing the Right System.*

American Fundware, Inc.

1385 South Colorado Boulevard, Suite 400, Denver, CO 80222
Tel: 800-551-4458, 303-756-3030; FAX: 303-756-7074
E-mail: information@fundware.com.;
WWW: http://www.fundware.com,
http://www.fundware.com/Training/index.htm,
http://www.fundware.com/support.htm

▶ American Fundware provides accounting software solutions for not-for-profit and governmental agencies across North America. American Fundware has extensive experience in helping mission-focused organizations manage highly specialized accounting requirements with its family of over 20 software modules written specifically for not-for-profit organizations. Services include Enterprise Services (project-based services that include implementation of Fundware software in combination with a variety of integration services to create an organization-wide software solution); Consulting Services (Fundware consultants are available for specific tasks on an hourly basis); Educational Services (Fundware Classic and Fundware for Windows training classes are available on a regional classroom or on-site basis). Developer of FundWare 7 Enterprise Edition, the first financial solution targeted for the large multiuser not-for-profit organization.

American Fundware also offers e-based seminars right to the convenience of your desktop. E-Talk's live and prerecorded seminars offer the most comprehensive lineup of solutions and trends, plus nonprofit mission financial overviews. For the latest events schedule and topics, go to *http://www.fundware.com/e-talk/index.htm*

Apta Software

5151 East Broadway Boulevard, Suite 800, Tucson, AZ 85711-3783
Tel: 888-949-APTA, 520-663-0250; FAX: 520-663-0251
E-mail: sales@aptasoft.com; WWW: http://www.aptasoft.com
▶ Apta Software is a software development firm specializing in a fully integrated fund accounting package designed to help schools, not-for-profit organizations, and governments. Apta created AptaFund, an integrated suite of software modules for organizations that use fund accounting.

Araize, Inc. (formerly Institutional Data Systems, Inc.) *(See also Resource Development)*

1157 Executive Circle, Suite D, Cary, NC 27511
Tel: 800-322-4371, 919-319-0903; FAX: 919-460-5983
E-mail: sales@araize.com; WWW: http://www.idsnonprofit.com
▶ Since 1985, Araize, Inc., has provided nonprofit organizations with the ability to effectively manage their fiscal responsibilities, while reducing audit costs and increasing accountability to funding sources.

Araize's *FastFund Nonprofit Software* is a fully integrated accounting and financial management system designed by certified public accountants specifically for nonprofit organizations. The basic accounting functions included in FastFund Nonprofit Software include general ledger, budgeting, check writing, bank reconciliation, and a report generator. Additional modules can be added including accounts payable, accounts receivable, allocations, fund raising, payroll, and Medicaid billing.

For a current price list, check out *http://www.idsnonprofit.com/pricelist.htm*. Training, full support, maintenance and enhancements, and consulting services are also available.

Ascend Technologies, Inc. *(See also Resource Development)*

2658 Crosspark Road, Suite 200, Coralville, IA 52241
Tel: 800-624-4692; FAX: 319-626-5491
E-mail: info@ascend-tech.com; WWW: http://www.ascend-tech.com
▶ *Ascend 2000* is an integrated fund raising, fund accounting, and investment management system for educational and nonprofit organizations. Ascend helps organizations exceed their goals by managing all aspects of the development process, including prospect management, gift processing, profile information, special activity codes, matching gifts, pledges, alumni membership, fund accounting, and investment management. *Ascend 2000* links together all of the information in an organization's database so users can quickly access the data they need. Data updates reflect instantly across the entire system so everyone is working with the most current information.

Ascend is a suite of three major components that work seamlessly together. The Executive component allows you to quickly view, enter, and modify biographical and gift information. The second component, SelectPlus, allows you to zero in on prospects and generate reports, donor profiles, mailing labels, and other output. FastTrack speeds and simplifies administration and maintenance and produces comprehensive reports on all aspects of your efforts.

They produce a quarterly newsletter. Contents may include technical tips, support notes, answers to frequently asked questions, fund-raising information, news about Ascend, scheduled conferences, and more.

Axcess Corporation

4635 South Lakeshore Drive, Tempe, AZ 85282
Tel: 800-AXCENTS (800-292-3687), 888-838-3030, 602-838-3030; FAX: 602-345-4109
E-mail: Kendall@Axcent.CC (Kendall Johnson);
WWW: (under construction)
▶ Axcess distributes Axcent Professional, a financial reporting software package for fund accounting and event tracking that helps you comply with monthly governmental, funding organization, and board of director financial reporting requirements. Major features include financial reporting, allocations, extended reporting, import/export, bank reconciliation, cash management, payroll management, and master/client. Specialty features include nonprofit accounting, accounting for government contractors, government agencies, professional client accounting, and corporate ledger. Includes *Financial Reporting Handbook* which illustrates over 80 reports that can be used for any client. A full support program is available. Two months of free telephone support (toll free in continental United States) is provided upon purchase, plus free training classes at their Phoenix training center for the first six months following purchase.

Banccorp Systems, Inc.—Trust Fund Accounting

Broadway & Seymour Company, 1616 South Kentucky Street, Amarillo, TX 79102-2252
P.O. Box 50597, Amarillo, TX 79159-0597
Tel: 800-423-8862, 806-358-7226; FAX: 806-358-3222
▶ Banccorp Systems offers TrustProcessor, a trust fund accounting software package that includes nonprofit trust administration, comprehensive accounting features, extensive reporting capabilities, and customer support. Users include universities, hospitals, community foundations, religious foundations, private family trust foundations, bank trust departments, and trust companies.

Bi-Tech Software Inc., a Sungard Company *(See also Human Resource Management)*

890 Fortress Street, Chico, CA 95973
Tel: 530-891-5281; FAX: 530-891-5011
E-mail: webmaster@bi-tech.com; WWW: http://www.bi-tech.com/
▶ Bi-Tech provides a complete suite of financial and human resources software to a variety of nonprofit organizations, including cities and counties, colleges and universities, government agencies, and school districts. It offers a fully integrated fund accounting package that meets all accounting/management needs of nonprofit institutions, including state and local governments, colleges and universities, research institutions, and special service districts.

IFAS offers the following functions: general ledger, budget preparation and modeling, job/project ledger, accounts payable, encumbrance, purchasing, accounts receivable/cash receipts, bank reconciliation, payroll/personnel, person/entity, fixed assets, stores inventory, human resources.

Bi-Tech offers comprehensive installation and training. Maintenance services include unlimited telephone support (remedial assistance is provided over the modem and most fixes are resolved within a "same-day" time frame), consulting (the licensee may request and receive verbal information regarding the use of the software), support (provides automatic delivery and installation of software updates and enhancements. To view HFS updates on a task-by-task basis, visit the IFAS Insider's *HFS page*); and the Bi-Tech Listserv (available for use by clients and provides a discussion forum for IFAS-related topics. To join the Bi-Tech mailing list, visit the IFAS Insider listserv page. If you don't have a password, contact your client manager).

Blackbaud *(See also Resource Development)*
4401 Belle Oaks Drive, Charleston, SC 29405-8530
Tel: 800-443-9441; FAX: 843-740-5410
E-mail: sales@blackbaud.com;
WWW: http://www.blackbaud.com,
http://www.blackbaud.com/downloads/default.asp
▶ Blackbaud's Accounting for Nonprofits is an integrated software system featuring flexible, user-defined account structures, multiple fiscal year reporting capabilities, and compliance with FAS 117 requirements. The following accounting software packages are available to meet the specialized needs of nonprofits: general ledger (with budget management and project, grant, and endowment management), accounts payable (with purchase orders), accounts receivable, payroll, fixed assets management, miscellaneous cash receipts, school store manager, and student billing. Additional Modules include project, grant, and endowment management (projects, grants, endowments, scholarships, programs, special events, productions, investments, exhibits, and other similar entities); interest income allocation; and budget management.

Intended users include universities, colleges, private schools, hospitals, religious organizations, foundations, health care agencies, museums, youth organizations, performing arts groups, government agencies, social service organizations, and many other types of nonprofit organizations.

Training options include Blackbaud University (offers a variety of classes at its headquarters in Charleston, South Carolina); regional training (offered in more than 30 locations throughout North America); on-site training for organizations that can't afford to have staff members away from the office for several days); computer-based training (employs CD-ROMs to provide a self-paced interactive learning experience. Comprehensive lessons walk users through tasks, and they can demonstrate their proficiency on tests that follow each section. The CDs will serve as a permanent resource for training new employees and helping staff members review concepts when necessary. Download a sample Interactive Workshop lesson).

Captools Company *(See also Investment Management)*
22510 SE 64th Place, Suite 210, Issaquah, WA 98027
Tel: 800-826-8082; FAX: 425-313-5647
E-mail: sales@captools.com; WWW: www.captools.com

▶ Captool portfolio management software is an investment record-keeping, performance measurement, and portfolio management reporting tool designed for professional money managers, for sophisticated individual investors, and for others entrusted with managing investment assets. It features a fund accounting module that enables users to create and manage funds of pooled investments in which a number of participants are the contributors and/or beneficiaries.

Cost Management Associates, Inc.
635-H Chapel Hill Road, Burlington, NC 27215
Tel: 800-747-0906; FAX: 336-228-1627
E-mail: costmaninc@aol.com;
WWW: http://www.costmaninc.com/
▶ Cost Management Associates develops financial and management software for nonprofit professionals and their organizations. They pioneered the development of client-tracking software and database management solutions for nonprofits. When funders want to know exactly how services were delivered, where money was spent, and what results were achieved, their nonprofit software provides you with the answers. Subscribe to its free online newsletter. Check out their Nonprofit Solutions Forum at *http://www.costman-inc.com/Contact/AskGordon.htm*

Cougar Mountain Software
7180 Potomac Drive, Suite D, P.O. Box 6886, Boise, ID 83707
Tel: 800-388-3038, 208-375-4455; FAX: 208-375-4460
E-mail: sales@cougarmtn.com;
WWW: http://www.cougarmtn.com,
http://www.cougarmtn.com/order/orderfund.html
▶ Developer and distributor of FUND Accounting, a fully integrated affordably priced accounting and financial management software package for nonprofit organizations and government agencies. The FUND Accounting package includes six modules: general ledger, budget/forecast, accounts payable, purchase order/encumbrances, check reconciliation, payroll, and LYNX import/export. An add-on package of billing (accounts receivable), inventory, and revenue tracking (order entry) adds the power of complete tracking of contributions, product sales, or service sales. FUND Accounting automatically handles all the complex transactions demanded of a fund accounting system, including interfund transfers, fund balancing, financial reporting, and budgeting. FUND Accounting includes the FASB 116 and 117 reports.

Cougar Mountain offers on-site training, regional training sites, and training at their corporate headquarters. It publishes *Cougar Tracks,* a quarterly publication of Cougar Mountain Software, also available online at *http://www.cougarmtn.com/cougartracks.*

CYMA Systems, Inc.
2330 West University Drive, Suite 7, Tempe, AZ 85281
Tel: 800-292-2962, 480-303-2962; FAX: 480-303-2969
E-mail: info@cyma.com; WWW: http://www.cyma.com
▶ Founded in 1980, CYMA Systems, Inc., is a developer of business accounting software. CYMA offers a full range of general accounting software for DOS, Windows®95, Windows 98, and Windows NT® platforms. The CYMA^IV Not-for-Profit Edition is a fully featured, complete accounting system with advanced not-for-profit functionality. Standard FASB 117–compliant financial state-

ments, unlimited fund and grant tracking, and automatic interfund offset entries are just a few of the features that make CYMA^{IV} NFP useful for small to midsize not-for-profit organizations. CYMA^{IV} NFP has the following modules available: system manager, general ledger, accounts receivable, accounts payable, payroll, bank reconciliation, remote client entry, server version, crystal reports, and F9 financial report writer.

DacEasy
17950 Preston Road, Suite 50, Dallas, TX 75252
Tel: 800-322-3279, 800-DAC-EASY, 972-732-7500; FAX: 972-713-6331
E-mail: dacsales@sage.com; WWW: http://www.us.sage.com,
http://www.us.sage.com/daceasy/support/FAQ/faqhome.htm

▶ Developed and distributed by Sage Software (see separate listing), DacEasy Accounting for DOS and DacEasy Accounting for Windows with Payroll is an entry-level accounting system for small businesses and nonprofits. The core system includes 12 modules: general ledger, accounts payable, accounts receivable, inventory, purchase order, cash management, budgeting, product assembly, billing, fixed assets, graphics, a custom forms designer, and custom report generator. They can be used together as fully integrated modules, or individually, to suit practically any size organization. They are designed to follow generally accepted accounting principles (GAAP); add-ons include payroll, point of sale, order entry, and job costing and estimating. The Windows version includes banking, customers, vendors, invoicing & purchase orders, inventory, general ledger, and employees.

They have created a new Upgrade Information Center where you can get a timeline of all new features added to their DOS products.

The DacAdvisor interactive tutorial and on-line help system provides in-depth information and lists of steps to help as you use the software. It offers a variety of technical support options as well as nationwide hands-on seminars, tutorials, and books.

DataPro Financial Systems, Inc.
P.O. Box 457, 108 South Main Street, Plainwell, MI 49080
Tel: 616-685-9214; FAX: 616-685-5660
E-mail: sales@data-pro.com; WWW: http://www.data-pro.com/default.htm, http://www.data-pro.com/support.htm, http://www.data-pro.com/faq.html

▶ An independent software firm which develops accounting software packages for multiple platforms. DataPro offers financial solutions IBM AS/400 version and PC Windows version. Modules include: general ledger, accounts payable, accounts receivable, payroll.

Donor2
8848 Red Oak Boulevard, Suite B, Charlotte, NC 28217-5518
Tel: 800-548-6708, 704-522-0002; FAX: 704-522-8842
E-mail: sales@mail.donor2.com ; WWW: http://www.donor2.com

▶ Donor2's Fund Accounting software is a comprehensive fund accounting software package that adheres to GAAP (generally accepted accounting principles), including FASB Statements 116 and 117. It has the ability to operate as a stand-alone fund account package or as a fully integrated add-on package to the Donor2 development system. Fund Accounting is designed to meet the accounting needs of nonprofit organizations. Add-on packages are

available for accounts payable, purchase order, accounts receivable, sales order, payroll, and back reconciliation. Fund Accounting is designed for Windows 95/98/NT and is totally menu-driven.

ECHO Management Group *(See also Resource Development)*
1620 Main Street, Box 540, Center Conway, NH 03813-0540
Tel: 800-635-8209, 603-447-5453; FAX: 603-447-2037
E-mail: sales@echoman.com; WWW: http://www.echoman.com

▶ Accounting for Windows is a fund accounting module accounting system designed to handle all of the complexities of health and human service organizations. This system enables users to track revenue and expenses across multiple programs, multiple cost centers, multiple funds, and multiple fiscal years. The system adheres to FASB standards.

ECHO provides a full range of technical support services for all Echo products, including project planning, classroom and on-site training, phone, fax, Internet, and online help. Echo also provides consulting expertise to behavioral health and human service organizations in the areas of accreditation preparation, organization assessment, organization development, and quality management.

ECHO maintains regional offices in New Hampshire, Maryland, Florida, Colorado, and California.

Encore Business Solutions *(See also Resource Development)*
188 Goulet Street, Winnipeg, Manitoba, Canada, R2H 0R8
Tel: 888-898-4330 (Canada and United States), 204-989-4330; FAX: 204-235-2331
E-mail: encore@ebs.ca;
WWW: http://www.ebs.ca/encore_index.htm

▶ Developers of software products written in Dexterity, Encore Business Solutions has provided computer hardware and software consulting, implementation services and technical support since 1990. They offer a full range of business solutions including not-for-profit and cash management.

With application products designed primarily for added value and functionality to the Dynamics and eEnterprise financial suites, Encore has also developed products for the not-for-profit sector, including Interfund Management (fund accounting), Fund Development Management (fund raising), and Commitment Management (encumbrance accounting). The Interfund Management fund accounting module integrates with Great Plains Dynamics/eEnterprise as an add-on, enabling Interfund transfer capability without user intervention.

Executive Data Systems, Inc. *(See also Resource Development)*
1640 Powers Ferry Road, Building 27, Marietta, GA 30067
Tel: 800-272-3374, 770-955-3374; FAX: 770-955-1975
E-mail: sales@execdata.com; WWW: http://www.execdata.com

▶ Supplying nonprofits with software since 1983, their products include fully integrated Fundraising and Fund Accounting software. Designed for Windows 95/98/NT. Financial statements comply with FASB 116 and 117. Fifteen modules are available. Since one size does not fit all, they also offer Non-Profit Starter Kit—donor records, general ledger, accounts payable, and payroll—specifically designed for smaller nonprofits of all types. Free trials are available for all modules. All modules are available for

Windows only and integrate fully. It provides many capabilities unique to nonprofit accounting and reporting: FASB 116 and 117 financial statements; receipts/statements for donors that conform to IRS requirements; financial statements for funds, projects, programs, and grants; automatic distribution of accounts payable invoices to multiple programs/grants; automatic distribution of wages to multiple projects/programs/grants; and improved communication with donors while reducing fund-raising costs.

Donald R. Frey & Company, Inc.

40 North Grand Avenue, Suite 303, Fort Thomas, KY 41075-1765
Tel: 800-659-3739, 859-441-6566; FAX: 859-441-7152
E-mail: drfrey@drfrey.com;
WWW: http://www.drfrey.com/fund.html
▶ Donald R. Frey & Company, Inc., develops and sells specialized software applications, with emphasis on financial, fund accounting, and utility billing software systems for government agencies and not-for-profit organizations. Distributes BUCS (Budgetary Control System), a fully integrated fund accounting system designed to meet the needs of government, nonprofit, and educational agencies. Designed in modules, BUCS allows the user to select the components that fit their specific needs. Basic modules include general ledger (required), accounts payable, cash receipts, billing–accounts receivable, combining reports, budget planning, requisition control, bank/check reconciliation, fixed assets, and data dictionary.

Fund Balance, Inc., a Tyler Technologies Company

(formerly Micro Arizala Systems, Inc.)
2805 South Industrial, Suite 200, P.O. Box 1987, Ann Arbor, MI 48106
Tel: 800-457-3863 (457-FUND), 734-677-0550;
FAX: 734-677-2070
E-mail: Info@Fundbalance.com;
WWW: http://http://www.fundbalance.com,
http://www.fundbalance.com/index.html
▶ Micro Arizala Systems, Inc. (now known as FundBalance, Inc.) was incorporated in 1984 as a software development company specializing in fund accounting software and other applications for state and local governments, and not-for-profit organizations. In April 1999, Micro Arizala Systems, Inc., merged with Tyler Corporation and became FundBalance, Inc.

Products offered include FundBalance32 (software applications for Windows 95 are designed to work with Windows-compatible personal computers, which includes Windows 95, 98, and NT operating systems) and FundBalance Plus (Sexton software applications for DOS, Windows 3.1, and Windows 95 are designed to work with IBM personal computers and other MS-DOS–compatible systems. Modules include accounts payable, accounts receivable, cash receipts, check reconciliation, fixed assets, general ledger, interface builder, lock box, payroll, and purchase order.

Versions are available for DOS and Windows NT, Windows 95, Windows 98, and 2000 environments.

Fund E-Z Development Corporation *(See also Resource Development)*

106 Corporate Park Drive, White Plains, NY 10604
Tel: 914-696-0900; FAX: 914-696-0948
E-mail: sales@fundez.com;
WWW: http://www.fundez.com/main/ma-main.htm,
http://www.fundez.com/demo/de-main5.htm

▶ Fund E-Z is the developer and distributor of FUND E-Z Accounting, a fully integrated fund accounting and fund raising software program designed for use by not-for-profit organizations. It is available for Windows 3.x, Windows 95/98, Windows NT, and DOS. It provides "Student Interactive" training courses designed for new and existing FUND-EZ users and issues chargeable product upgrades approximately every two years. Revisions are issued periodically free of charge to clients registered under FUND-EZ support.

HWA International

2565 Horizon Lake Drive, Suite 110, Memphis, TN 38133
Tel: 800-328-8661, 901-388-6120; FAX: 901-388-557
E-mail: sales@hwainternational.com, bill@hwainternational.com
(Bill Schamroth); WWW: http://www.hwainternational.com/
▶ HWA International was founded in 1974 to develop, market, and support software and computerized management information systems for a wide range of business and professional environments throughout the United States. In the 1980s and 1990s, trust accounting software became its primary focus. Its flagship product is Trust Accounting System. It separates principal from income and tracks tax lots. The product was first developed in 1977 for IBM desktop computers, and has been enhanced every year from suggestions of trust departments across the country. Features include management reporting, accounting and operations reporting, customer statement options, year-end operations, flexibility, custom programming available, security, audit, advanced modules, and capacity and system limits. Also distributes TAMS (Trust Accounting Mini-System), a "lite version of TrustNet" designed for small and start-up deparments.

S. Hellman Company, Inc. *(See also Resource Development)*

386 Park Avenue South, Suite 1914, New York, NY 10016
Tel: 212-689-5010; Fax: 212-684-5428
E-mail: info@shcco.com; WWW: http://www.shcco.com/
▶ Established in 1983, S. Hellman Company (SHC) has provided fund accounting and fund-raising software, as well as evaluation, implementation, and training services exclusively to not-for-profit organizations. Its client base includes social service organizations, research institutions and quasi-governmental agencies, religious institutions, environmental and cultural arts organizations, and foundations. SHC is an authorized reseller and certified consultant for the following not-for-profit software applications: Fund Accounting, FundWare for Windows, and USL Fund SQL.

KMS Software Incorporated *(See also Killion McCabe & Associates) (See also Resource Development)*

790 Coit Central Tower, 12001 North Central Expressway, Suite 790, Dallas, TX 75243-3734
Tel: 800-800-0293, 972-560-7070; FAX: 972-560-7071
E-mail: dthielker@kmainteractive.com (David Thielker, Sales);
WWW: http://www.kmssoftware.com,
http://www.kmssoftware.com/support/Training.htm
▶ Since 1981, KMS Software has been actively involved in designing software specifically for ministry and nonprofit organizations. Its Fund AccountAbility is a fully integrated accounting product designed to provide complete control over funds management. It provides a wide variety of missionary and project support

features for easy tracking source and destination of funding. Fund AccountAbility will help reduce accounting time with simplified charges/allocations, full-detail account statements and funds tracking. It will create individual missionary checks or combined field account checks. In addition, it provides tools for automatic calculations of missionary support requirements and disbursements. KMA interactive provides a full line of technical support for its software products. This includes initial training, choice of training level at your location or in regularly scheduled regional classes as well as those held at the KMAi corporate headquarters and training center. KMAi clients have a wide range of support options available including telephone and Internet access to the professionals who helped design your system. KMAi also provides consulting services training for ministries and other nonprofits who need counsel in information technology and e-commerce solutions planning, development, and administration.

Lynx Software—General Accounting

Granite Plaza at Las Colinas, 7301 North State Highway 161, Suite 280N, Irving, TX 75039
Tel: 877-838-9989, 972-830-9898; FAX: 972-830-9696
E-mail: Marketing@lynx-software.com; WWW: http://www.lynx-software.com/

▶ Lynx Software Systems, Inc. is the provider of the 4Series product line of accounting software systems. These products are designed for banks, trust companies, and not-for-profit institutions throughout the United States and the Caribbean.

Micro Information Products (MIP)

313 East Anderson Lane, Suite 200, Austin, TX 78752-3772
Tel: 800-647-3863, 512-454-5004; FAX: 512-454-1246
E-mail: info@mip.com; WWW: http://www.mip.com

▶ Since 1982, MIP has provided the MIP Fund Accounting System, a microcomputer-based accounting software program specifically designed for nonprofit and governmental organizations. Its NonProfit Series fund accounting software allows nonprofit organizations and governmental agencies to easily track, manage, and report on funds from multiple sources, across multiple budget periods. Created specifically for the complex reporting requirements of nonprofits, the NonProfit Series system includes a wide variety of preformatted reports, including the audit-ready FASB and GASB financial and accounting reports required by funding sources and auditors and financial reports for executive directors, program managers, and board members. NonProfit Series is a fully integrated system that may be used with other third-party products, including donor tracking and fund-raising software. A demonstration of Nonprofit Series may be downloaded from the vendor's Web site or a CD ordered directly from the vendor.

The modules, which operate around the General Ledger, are individually priced and may be purchased separately. Currently available modules are accounts payable, accounts receivable reporting, accounts receivable billing, allocation management, payroll, budget, purchase orders, encumbrances, bank reconciliation, data import/export, safekey (security), fixed assets, nightshift scheduler, and forms designer.

MIP offers Windows fund accounting seminars. The schedule is available at *http://www.mip.com/seminars.htm.* MIP's newsletter, *Fundamentals,* is available online at *http://www.mip.com/inside_mip/fundamentals.htm.*

Mirasoft, Inc.

865F Cotting Lane, Vacaville, CA 95688
Tel: 800-414-FUND (3863), 707-453-8300; FAX: 707-453-8303
E-mail: info@mirasoft-inc.com (General Information);
WWW: http://www.mirasoft-inc.com

▶ Develops and distributes the ForFUND/NP and ForFUND/Gov, Windows-based family of accounting software solutions. ForFUND Accounting is designed specifically for not-for-profit (nonprofit) and government organizations. Features include general ledger, grant/project management, budgeting, cash receipts, purchase orders, encumbrance accounting, accounts payable, bank reconciliation, accounts receivable, fixed assets, and payroll. This software helps you report on grants across multiple fiscal years, generate your FASB 116/117 reports, ensure that your organization and all funds are in balance, handle multiple distributions, and more. ForFUND/NP complies with all generally accepted accounting principles and covers the complete gamut of multifund accounting needs.

Resource Information Associates, Inc.

215 Dexter Road, Eaton Rapids, MI 48827
Tel: 517-663-7139; FAX: 517-663-2166
E-mail: resource@resource-software.com;
WWW: http://www.resource-software.com/rshome.htm

▶ Resource Information Associates is the distributor of Resource Software, financial software for nonprofits, schools, and local government. Includes general ledger/budgeting, accounts payable, accounts receivable, payroll, cash receipts, and purchase order.

Sage Software Inc.

56 Technology, Irvine, CA 92618
Tel: 800-854-3415, 949-753-1222; FAX: 94-753-0374
WWW: http://www.us.sage.com/products/

▶ Founded in 1981 and headquartered in Irvine, California, Sage Software, Inc., develops, markets, and supports accounting software for medium-size companies.

Solomon Software

200 East Hardin Street, P.O. Box 414, Findlay, OH 45840
Tel: 800-4SOLOMON (800-476-5666), 419-424-0422;
FAX: 419-424-3400
E-mail: sales@solomon.com, Clients@solomon.com;
WWW: http://www.solomon.com/

▶ Solomon designs business software for small to midsized organizations. It includes the following financial series/modules: general ledger datasheet, accounts payable datasheet, accounts receivable datasheet, multi-company datasheet, cash manager datasheet, currency manager datasheet, frx advanced financial report writer, financial statement translation, and payroll.

Subscribe to the Solomon Software International News List Server for periodic notice of significant international news related to Solomon Software. Send an e-mail message to: *join-intl-news@intllists.solomon.com,* or register on the Web.

Systems Support Services *(See also Resource Development)*

8848-B Red Oak Boulevard, Charlotte, NC 28217
Tel: 800-548-6708; FAX: 704-522-8842
E-mail sales@donor2.com (Steve Eshleman);
WWW: http://www.donor2.com

▶ Systems Support Services distributes Donor2, which offers a Fund Accounting package that integrates with Donor2 and Donor2 Enterprise (see separate listing under Resource Development, Products and Services), and includes modules such as system manager, general ledger, payroll, accounts payable, bank reconciliation, and others.

USL Financials

501 Church Street NE, Suite 200, Vienna, VA 22180
Tel: 800-800-0768, 703-242-0402; FAX: 703-242-0403
E-mail: info@uslfinancials.com;
WWW: http://www.uslfinancials.com

▶ USL provides client/server accounting software for larger not-for-profit organizations and state and local government agencies. USL Financials provides its clients with turnkey solutions that include needs analysis, customization, conversion, implementation, training, and ongoing technical support. Their Full-Encumbrance Not-For-Profit Accounting Suite includes the following nine modules: general ledger, accounts payable, accounts receivable, purchase order, purchase requisition, job/project cost, inventory control, check reconciliation, and control system. In addition, USL Financials offers integrated partner solutions for financial reporting, budgeting, allocations, and HR/payroll.

Software Vendors—Grants Management

Grants Management Systems (GMS)

10559 Metropolitan Avenue, Kensington, MD 20895
Tel: 800-933-3501, 301-933-3500; FAX: 301-933-3502
E-mail: gms@gmsactg.com, gmsactg@starpower.net
(Liz Collins); WWW: http://www.gmsactg.com

▶ Since 1980, GMS has designed and distributed software specifically for not-for-profit and public organizations administering grants and contracts, activities, and revolving loan funds. Additional services include comprehensive direct technical support; toll-free hotline; training; a monthly newsletter, *News From GMS;* enhancements, and annual users conference, as well as periodic training for statewide or regional meetings.

Software Vendors—Interrelated Estate Tax Calculation

Cammack Computations

P.O. Box 725, Cleburne, TX 76033
Tel: 800-594-5826; FAX: 817-645-8273
E-mail: cammack@inter-est.com (Cecil Cammack);
WWW: http://www.inter-est.com/

▶ Commack is the developer and distributor of Inter-Est, the only commercial program available that is specifically designed to compute the federal estate tax for the purpose of IRS audit situations and the like. It will compute a high percentage of your interrelated federal estate tax problems. Two versions of Inter-Est are offered—one for DOS and one for Windows.

Software Vendors—Tax Compliance and Reporting

TimeValue Software

4 Jenner Street, Suite 100, Irvine, CA 92618
Tel: 800-426-4741; FAX: 949-727-3268
E-mail: info@timevalue.com; WWW: http://www.timevalue.com

▶ TimeValue develops, markets, and supports time value of money, loan, financial, accounting, tax, and payroll software for personal computers and networks. TimeValue Software products are used by over 100,000 financial professionals and firms, including all of the national accounting firms. Their TaxInterest software program provides assistance with calculating tax interest and penalties. It computes interest, refund interest, "hot" interest, GATT interest, and major tax penalties.

VantageSource LLP, a member firm of Andersen Worldwide *(See also Estate Planning and Planned Giving)*

101 Arthur Andersen Parkway, Sarasota, FL 34232
Tel: 800-USA-1040, 941-365-9469; FAX: 941-341-4312
E-mail: aplustax@arthurandersen.com;
WWW: http://aplustax.arthurandersen.com/

▶ Products include A·Plus·Tax 709 Gift Tax (preparing gift tax and generation tax returns), 990 Exempt Organizations (tax software for private foundation and exempt organization tax returns) and A·Plus·Tax Trust Tax Manager.

Services provided include Customer Support (toll-free telephone and e-mail support and extended hours during tax season and prior to major filing deadlines); Proactive E-mail (A·Plus·Tax Customer Support uses proactive e-mails to keep you informed of program issues and tax law changes); Data Conversion (if you switch from another program to A·Plus·Tax, their Data Conversion team will convert the data on the forms and statements of your federal tax returns into A·Plus·Tax); Program Training (contact an A·Plus·Tax Sales Representative for training opportunities); Organizers (printing and collating hundreds of individual files is no fun, especially when you're crunched for time).

Software Vendors—Trust Accounting

HWA International, Inc.

2565 Horizon Lake Drive, Suite 110, Memphis, TN 38133
Tel: 800-328-8661
E-mail: bill@hwainternational.com (Bill Schamroth);
WWW: http://www.hwainternational.com

▶ HWA is an independent, privately held corporation providing trust accounting software since 1977. Over 100 financial institutions throughout the United States, Canada, and the Caribbean use these trust accounting software products. They include bank trust departments, nonprofit organizations, trust companies, family offices, credit unions, guardianship specialists, and CPA and law firms.

SunGard Trust Systems, Inc.

5510 77 Center Drive, P.O. Box 240882, Charlotte, NC 28224-0882
Tel: 800-877-1655, 704-561-8454; FAX: 704-527-9617
E-mail: john.bingham@clt.sungardtrust.com (John Bingham);
WWW: www.sungardtrust.com

▶ Sungard Non-Profit Solutions provides the processing and reporting necessary to automate the management of planned giving trusts and permanent endowments. It provides nonprofit solutions for permanent endowment funds—unrestricted, permanently restricted, temporarily restricted; charitable remainder trusts—NIMCRUT, FLIP, CRUT, CRAT, gift annuity; pooled income funds; charitable lead trusts; donor-advised funds; special gift administration—real estate, mineral management, personal property, art; and integrated custodial services—centralized clearing and reconciliation of assets and income from multiple asset managers. It accounts for gifts, assets, and the donor's wishes with a comprehensive endowment and charitable trust administration system. Sungard Trust Systems integrates your current G/L fund accounting system, fund-raising, and contact management software with the Asset Investment and Management System. It provides for reports, remittances, and tax preparation.

Sungard has two systems, Trustware Series 7 and AutoTrust/Charlotte, both of which are designed for the not-for-profit industry—performing asset management, endowment, and charitable trust accounting. Trustware Series 7 is targeted for larger institutions, foundations, or trust organizations that choose in-house operations, including management information systems (MIS) departments, asset managers, and administrators. Autotrust/Charlotte is Sungard's asset management product targeted for smaller but sophisticated institutions that choose distributed processing.

Zane and Associates

130 West White Horse Pike, Berlin, NJ 08009-2024
Tel: 800-331-2533 (sales only), 856-768-4100 (Support line);
FAX: 856-767-1510
E-mail: Sales@zanenet.com, Support@zanenet.com;
WWW: http://www.zanenet.com

▶ Zane and Associates provides fiduciary accounting for the trust and estate professional. Their programs are written for those who understand trusts and estates, but may not know a lot about computers.

Zane's products are written as individual modules that share a common "Relational" database. This allows one to use any component (accounting, 706, state death tax, fiduciary income tax, calendar or gift tax) individually. Because of the common database, all appropriate information is shared with the other modules. Changes made in one module are automatically reflected in the others.

Its *Fact and Solutions* newsletter is available online at *http://www.zanenet.com/News.htm.*

GENERAL RESOURCES

(See also Governance [Roles and Responsibilities]; Human Resource Management [Compensation and Benefits]; Legal Issues [Charitable Solicitation, Tax Exemption]; Strategic Planning; Resource Development [Deferred and Planned Giving, For-Profit Ventures, Grants])

General/Basics

Activity-Based Management for Service Industries, Government Entities, and Nonprofit Organizations
JAMES A. BRIMSON, JOHN ANTOS (JOHN WILEY & SONS, 1998)

▶ Using case studies, the authors provide the tools that help organizations detect the resources that drive costs, empower workers, bring strategic goals more clearly into focus, and support continuous improvement. The book showcases the tools that will enable organizations to take advantage of ABM techniques designed to gather complete, structured information about their organizations' activities, the starting point for an ABM system. It examines traditional managerial accounting methods and demonstrates why they have become obsolete in a new age of advanced technology and information systems and much more.

ABM will also show you how to calculate the actual cost per activity and thereby identify the way in which an organization uses its resources to meet its goals; identify specific activities and determine how much of each activity is consumed in the final cost objective, whether it be a customer project or service; and plan and control expected activities in order to help organizations put together a cost-effective budget that meets projected workloads and strategic goals. *Softcover, 364 pages, $42.95*

All the Way to the Bank: Smart Money Management for Tomorrow's Nonprofit
SUSAN KENNY STEVENS AND LISA M. ANDERSON (THE STEVENS GROUP—AVAILABLE FROM THE AMHERST H. WILDER FOUNDATION, 1997)

▶ Stabilize and solidify your nonprofit's financial health. Now you can learn the secrets of one of the country's leading nonprofit financial consulting groups. Provides practical tools and techniques to help you make the most of your financial resources. *Softcover, 116 pages, $17*

Coping with Cutbacks: The Nonprofit Guide to Success When Times Are Tight
EMIL ANGELICA AND VINCENT HYMAN (AMHERST H. WILDER FOUNDATION, 1997)

▶ Devolution—the shifting of money and power from federal to local governments—is here, it's real, and it's BIG. Estimates are that cuts to nonprofits may add up to $250 billion by the year 2002. This guide can help you deal with funding problems—in a new way. It shows you how (and why) to shift your thinking from "How do we get more money to keep our nonprofit in business?" to "How do we involve other segments of the community to address community issues?" *Coping with Cutbacks* also includes a list of 185 short-term solutions collected from a variety of nonprofits. These strategies can be put to use right away to help you overcome short-term crises, manage change, and use your resources effectively. *Softcover, 128 pages, $20*

Economics for Nonprofit Managers
DENNIS R. YOUNG AND RICHARD STEINBERG (FOUNDATION CENTER, 1995)

▶ Dennis Young and Richard Steinberg have designed *Economics for Nonprofit Managers* as a complete course in the economic issues faced by decision makers at America's nonprofit organizations. Treating microeconomic analysis as an indispensable skill for the men and women who guide these organizations, they introduce and explain concepts such as opportunity cost, analysis at the margin, market equilibrium, market failure, and cost–benefit analysis. The volume also focuses on issues of particular concern to nonprofits: the economics of fund raising, regulatory environments; the special impact of competition on nonprofit performance; interactions among various sources of revenue, and much more. *Hardcover, 268 pages, $34.95 (plus $4.50 shipping)*

Essential Financial Considerations for Not-for-Profit Organizations: A Guide for Non-Accounting Executives
EDWARD J. MCMILLAN (AMERICAN SOCIETY OF ASSOCIATION EXECUTIVES, 1994)

▶ This extensive reference handbook is written expressly for the nonfinancial executive. McMillan outlines the rules and regulations exclusive to not-for-profits, as well as the nonfinancial executive's role, in simple-to-understand language.

The handbook covers everything a not-for-profit organization needs to know about the crucial areas of financial management (responsibility for internal control, public access to records, and lobbying regulations to unrelated business income tax [UBIT], working with CPA firms, IRS audits, etc.). This extensive reference handbook is written expressly for the nonfinancial executive. It outlines the rules and regulations exclusive to not-for-profits, as well as the nonfinancial executive's role, in simple-to-understand language. *Loose-leaf binder, 88 pages, $72 (Nonmember), $59.95 (Member) (plus $6.25 shipping)*

Financial and Strategic Management for Nonprofit Organizations: A Comprehensive Reference to Legal, Financial, Management, and Operations Rules and Guidelines for Nonprofits, Third Edition
HERRINGTON J. BRYCE (JOSSEY-BASS, 1999)

▶ Provides an encyclopedic account of all the key financial, legal, and managerial issues facing nonprofit executives. Organized into 20 detailed chapters, this comprehensive reference provides a firm grounding in the five fundamental pillars of effective nonprofit management: Mission, Money, Marketing, Management, and

Membership. It then shows managers and trustees how to strengthen operations in each of these vital areas ethically, legally, and efficiently.

Part 1 covers the basic legal tenets controlling the formation and management of the major types of nonprofit organizations, the fundamental legal context in which these are managed, and the personal and organizational consequences of going astray.

Part 2 is strictly about money-raising revenues to finance the organization's mission. Part 2 also has discussions of strategies and issues concerning the soliciting, giving, and receiving of certain types of assets (insurance policies, annuities, stocks, and real estates). Since all funds raised must be invested, even in the short term, Part 2 develops the concept of an endowment.

In Part 3, the concept of endowment management is presented strictly from the investing side. Part 3 has to do with strategies for controlling costs and risks. The text distinguishes among different types of costs and how they can be controlled. The principal instrument for controlling operating and capital costs is the budget. Accordingly, Part 3 begins with budgeting, but it contains new discussions on joint cost allocations—allocating costs where fund raising is done along with some program or educational activity of the nonprofit.

Part 4 is about managing the finances of the organization. It begins with a discussion on the use of financial statements in support of managerial direction and to uncover concerns for which the manager is responsible—if not personally liable.

Part 5 focuses on the managerial task of growing the organization and ensuring its vitality by always searching for new and exciting strategic opportunities and alliances. This begins with a strategic plan based in part on the evaluation of what the organization is, what it has accomplished, and the options before it.

The final chapter of the book is about restructuring the organization—changing the structure and configuration of the organization. These are serious legal actions that bring into play the dissolution plan discussed in Part 1 and the scrutiny of the IRS, the state attorney general, and the Justice Department or Federal Trade Commission. It is about the marriages, divorces, adoptions, conversion, death, and rebirth of an organization. *Hardcover, 816 pages, $49.95*

Financial Empowerment: More Money for More Mission

PETER C. BRINCKERHOFF (JOHN WILEY & SONS, 1998)

▶ In this book you will learn the eight characteristics of financial empowerment and then explore each one in depth. This is a practical guide for getting more funds from current sources, for finding and developing new sources of funds, for keeping more of what you get, and for using your funds to do more mission over the long term. You will learn the eight characteristics of financial empowerment and then explore each one. The author gives you ideas and techniques you can begin using immediately, including: (1) how to estimate cash needs, (2) how to treat your funders like valued customers, (3) how to develop a money-making business, (4) how to make your financial reports into valuable tools, (5) what financing options are available and what to avoid, (6) an empowering budgeting process, (7) how to price your services effectively, (8) when to set up a subsidiary corporation, (9) the role of the CEO in financial empowerment, (10) the role of the board in financial empowerment, (11) specific steps you can begin now to achieve financial empowerment, (12) a sample empowerment plan, (13) how to keep what you earn so you can do more mission, and more. A companion "Discussion Leader's Guide" (see separate listing) is

available for separate purchase. *Casebound, 238 pages, $51.95 (plus 10% for shipping)*

Financial Empowerment Discussion Leader's Guide

PETER C. BRINCKERHOFF (CORPORATE ALTERNATIVES, INC.)

▶ This accompanying guide to *Financial Empowerment: More Money for More Mission* (see separate listing) will help team facilitators bring financial empowerment strategies to life. It includes a chapter-by-chapter list of key ideas, suggested discussion questions, and wrap-up points, as well as "Self-Assessment Worksheets." Pages can be copied for distribution. *Loose-leaf binder, 42 pages, $21.95 (plus 10% for shipping)*

Financial Management for Nonprofit Organizations (Book and Disk)

JoANN HANKIN, ALAN G. SEIDNER, AND JOHN T. ZIETLOW (JOHN WILEY & SONS, 1998)

▶ This cash management and investment handbook for nonprofit managers helps nonprofit managers from diverse backgrounds learn to manage their organization's money. It examines traditional treasury functions including banking and cash flow and explores investment management and strategies for managing excess cash, endowment, and long-term (planned) gifts. It also examines financial management strategies that affect cash flow, including borrowing, risk management, benchmarking, and long-term planning. Addresses the needs of all types and sizes of organizations, from small religious groups and community social service agencies to major cultural institutions and colleges and universities.

It articulates a new perspective: that every nonprofit management decision is a financial one with far-reaching implications. The book includes a Financial Health Survey Tool that begins to uncover the difficult and sensitive questions about the allocation of organizational resources. It transcends traditional financial management texts by introducing the reader to such ideas as using financial management to accomplish mission; financial ratio analysis, which is a method of measuring organizational financial position historically, in the present, and in comparison to other similar organizations; cash management and banking relations; investment policy and practices; risk management for organizational assets—people and property; and financial information management.

The book includes a diskette with spreadsheet solutions to common financial management problems, such as interest rate calculations, basic yield calculations, financial ratios, and more. It is supplemented annually. *Hardcover w/3.5" IBM-compatible disk, 448 pages, $120*

Financial Management for Nonprofits: The Complete Guide to Maximizing Resources and Managing Assets (Book and Disk)

JAE K. SHIM, JOEL G. SIEGEL (IRWIN PROFESSIONAL, 1997)

▶ This is a book/disk package for managers of nonprofit organizations. Coverage includes nonprofit financial and managerial accounting, financial planning and forecasting, financial statement analysis, budgeting, short- and long-term financing, cost accounting, and financial modeling for program analysis. It includes a glossary, many sample tax forms, and brief descriptions of useful computer software. The companion disk contains software for performing break-even and cost–value–profit analysis, financial ratio analysis, and trend analysis. *Financial Management for Nonprofits* covers operational differences between nonprofit and for-profit corporations; accounting practices broken down by specific nonprofit organizations, ways to spot and avoid financial problems, short-

and long-term financing, and improving managerial and department performance. It also provides practical answers to necessary questions nonprofit organizations ask, including "Do we have a profit or loss?" "Do we have sufficient reserves?" "Are we competing successfully?" and "Are we meeting our budget?" Applicable to all nonprofits from colleges and hospitals to charities and religious institutions, this resource uses case studies, examples, and illustrations. *Hardcover, 336 pages, $39.95*

The Financial Responsibilities of Nonprofit Boards: An Overview of Financial Management for Board Members *(See Governance—Roles and Responsibilities for full description)*

Managing a Nonprofit Organization: Staffing, Fundraising, Choosing Trustees, Financing, Marketing, Computerizing, Planning, Succeeding *(See General Management for full description)*

A Practical Guide to NonProfit Financial Management: A Simple Guide for Executives (Manual)
ANDREW S. LANG (ASPEN PUBLISHERS, 1995)

▶ *A Practical Guide to Nonprofit Financial Management* is designed to help nonprofit executives overcome their fear of finance. It will teach managers with little or no financial background the basics of nonprofit accounting and finance. It accomplishes this by: (1) giving you a solid grounding in the principles of nonprofit accounting and shows you step by step how to put them into action; (2) helping you read, understand, and prepare your own financial statements; and (3) explaining how to use financial analysis to plan your organization's future and make the right decisions. It explains the basic terms and concepts in plain, jargon-free language and then shows you, step by step, how one builds on another to form a meaningful, cohesive whole. You will learn: (1) the nine generally accepted accounting principles and the ins and outs of double-entry bookkeeping, (2) how to read a financial statement and use it to determine your organization's financial strength, (3) how to prepare a balance sheet and put a budget together, (4) how to use a break-even analysis to decide whether you can afford a program, (5) how to protect your nonprofit's tax-exempt status and avoid problems with the IRS, (6) how to use internal controls to safeguard your assets and promote efficient operations, and more.

Dozens of charts, guidelines, and sample statements are included, and it is updated annually. *Loose-leaf binder, 250 pages, $153 (plus $4 shipping)*

The Nonprofit Management Handbook: Operating Policies and Procedures *(See General Management for full description)*

A Nonprofit Organization Operating Manual *(See General Management for full description)*

Nonprofit Organizations' Business Forms, Disk Edition *(See General Management for full description)*

Recording Contributions and Preparing Financial Statements for Not-for-Profit Organizations: A Compliance Guide for SFASs 116 and 117
JOHN P. LANGAN (AMERICAN SOCIETY OF ASSOCIATION EXECUTIVES, 1996)

▶ This is a practical implementation tool to assist associations in adopting SFASs 116 and 117. You'll save time by getting the information you need to comply with these new regulations, in a concise, user-friendly format. Includes explanations of major 116 and 117 requirements, plus insights and examples to help association executives who are responsible for implementing these regulations. For each Statement, this guide includes general requirements; results of the FASB field test, including a list of common errors and misconceptions; a case study in which the standard is applied; accounting system changes required under the new Statement; and key terms and definitions. This valuable resource was written specifically for ASAE members and focuses on the reporting characteristics of ASAE's membership. The compliance guide has been reviewed by a nationally recognized expert in association finance. *Softcover, 96 pages, $36 (Nonmember), $30 (Member)*

Starting and Running a Nonprofit Organization, Second Edition *(See also Legal Issues)*
JOAN M. HUMMEL (UNIVERSITY OF MINNESOTA PRESS, 1996)

▶ Revised by the Center for Nonprofit Management, University of St. Thomas, *Starting and Running a Nonprofit Organization* is a book for people who are forming new nonprofits; thinking about converting an informal, grassroots group into tax-exempt status; reorganizing an existing agency; or currently managing a nonprofit. It provides practical and basic how-to information on legal, tax, organizational, and other issues particular to nonprofits.

The book describes, step-by-step, all of the phases of creating and operating a new nonprofit, including incorporation, establishing a board of directors, writing bylaws, obtaining tax-exempt status, creating a strategic plan, budgeting and grant seeking, understanding accounting principles, managing human resources, and creating a community relations plan. The information provided is specific enough to be immediately useful, yet can be generalized to any nonprofit practitioner in any state. Handy checklists and worksheets, as well as a list of sources for assistance and management development and a bibliography on nonprofit management, make *Starting and Running a Nonprofit Organization* a valuable and unique resource. *Softcover, 168 pages, $14.95*

Streetsmart Financial Basics for Nonprofit Managers (Book with software)
THOMAS A. MCLAUGHLIN (JOHN WILEY & SONS, 1995)

▶ This book explains how to use financial information to effectively run nonprofit organizations. The book is organized into four distinct parts—analysis, accounting, operations, and control. It is a practical guide to nonprofit financial management. Cutting through the technical jargon, it shows how to read, interpret, and use financial information to make sound business decisions. Going beyond the basics of bookkeeping and accounting, and using the IRS Form 990 as the basis of discussion, this reference features in-depth coverage of budgeting, operations, cash flow and capital, balance sheets and cost analyses, internal management control, organizational structure, mission management, and the bottom line. It includes more than 50 real-world exhibits and examples (charts, tables, checklists, and instructive sidebars). An IBM-compatible 3.5-inch computer disk provides spreadsheet templates for financial reports, word processing checklists, and sample documents. *Softcover, 256 pages, $29.95*

What a Difference Understanding Makes: Guides to Nonprofit Management

(ACCOUNTANTS FOR THE PUBLIC INTEREST, 1994)

▶ Concise, clear, and easy-to-use, this series of five booklets on separate nonprofit management topics will help any nonprofit understand the basic finance and accounting issues essential to managing an organization These guides include: (1) *Tracking Special Monies* (restricted funds, special event funds, unrelated business income taxes [UBIT], and capital campaigns), (2) *Filing Nonprofit Tax Forms* (IRS Form 990, 990-T and other state and federal forms), (3) *Making Public Disclosures* (federal and state regulations, reporting requirements, and conflict of interest), (4) *Selecting Computer Software* (computers for smaller nonprofits for financial reports—pros and cons), and (5) *Classifying 501(c)'s;* these booklets serve as a valuable resource to explain subjects that can often prove time consuming to learn and difficult to understand, and are intended to help nonprofits round out their financial management skills so that their monies can be better used to serve their communities. *Softcover, 21/17/14/22/21 pages, $25/set ($7.50 each)*

Accounting/Auditing/Reporting

Accounting & Audit Issues of Not-for-Profit Organizations

GERARD M. ZACK (NONPROFIT RESOURCE CENTER, 1999)

▶ This book covers accounting for and auditing contributions, investments, fixed assets, functional expense allocations, SOP 98-2, preparation of financial statements, internal controls, fraud, and specialized NPO audit issues. *$49 (Nonmember), $36 (Member) (includes shipping and handling)*

Accounting and Budgeting in Public and Nonprofit Organizations: A Manager's Guide

C. WILLIAM GARNER (JOSSEY-BASS, 1991)

▶ Provides an explanation of essential accounting and budgeting language and practices/principles to enable managers to better oversee organizational resources, interpret financial reports, and develop accurate, dependable accounting and budgeting systems.

Designed specifically for public and nonprofit organizations, this practical guide will enable managers and executives to answer important questions about the financial operations of their organizations: Is the organization making the most effective use of its resources? Are legal requirements being met? Have plans been made to deal with anticipated changes in revenue? Are expenditures under control? Focusing on the special features of public and nonprofit accounting, such as fund accounting and government accounting standards, the book offers administrators, executives, and board members clear explanations of key concepts and standard accounting practices as well as the practical guidance necessary to ensure financial integrity and a strong future for the organization. Using generally accepted accounting principles as a guide, Garner also demonstrates how organizations can implement new accounting practices in the most beneficial and effective manner. Charts and tables are included. *Hardcover, 252 pages, $47 (plus $4.50 shipping)*

Accounting and Financial Management, Leadership Series

JILL MUEHRCKE, ED. (THE SOCIETY OF NONPROFIT ORGANIZATIONS, 1993) (BOOKLET)

▶ In articles selected from *Nonprofit World,* writers address financial management, accounting, and investment questions for nonprofit leaders. *115 pages, $35 (Nonmember), $25 (Member) (plus $4.50 shipping)*

Accounting and Reporting for Nonprofit Organizations, 2nd Edition

JOHN P. LISTRO (KENDALL-HUNT, 1998)

This book is designed to provide a basic understanding of the accounting principles of all nonprofit organizations in a clear and practical format. *Softcover, 267 pages, $41.95 (plus $4.00 shipping)*

Accounting for Governmental and Nonprofit Entities with City of Smithville Package, 13th Edition

EARL R. WILSON, SUSAN C. KATTELUS, AND LEON E. HAY (MCGRAW-HILL COLLEGE DIVISION, 2001)

▶ This book provides comprehensive and complete coverage of Governmental Accounting Standards Board's new accounting and financial reporting model (Statement No. 34) for state and local governments and provides familiarization with accounting and financial reporting of many other types of entities, including the federal government, colleges and universities, health care entities, and nonprofit organizations. Additional chapters cover such topics as auditing of governmental and nonprofit organizations, budgeting and cost accounting, cash and investment management, and financial analysis of state and local governments. It is intended for readers concerned with the design and interpretation of financial statements and financial reports, this text reflects all major changes to authoritative pronouncements through March 2000 affecting government and nonprofit organizations.

Instructors' supplements will be available on the Web site (*http://www.mhhe.com*) and CD-ROM.

The authors' home pages provide periodic authoritative updates and on-line response to instructor inquiries. Earl Wilson's home page (source for updates and general information): *http://www.missouri.edu/~accterw/book/book.htm;* Susan Kattelus's home page (links to other interesting sites): *http://www.online.emich.edu/~acc_kattelus. Softcover, 864 pages, $95.31*

Accounting and Reporting for Nonprofit Organizations, 2nd Edition

JOHN P. LISTRO (KENDALL-HUNT, 1998)

▶ This book is designed to provide a basic understanding of the accounting principles of all nonprofit organizations in a clear and practical format. *Softcover, 267 pages, $41.95 (plus $4 shipping)*

Accounting for Costs of Activities of Not-for-Profit Organizations and State and Governmental Entities That Include Fund Raising (AICPA, 1998)

▶ The Accounting Standards Executive Committee has issued Statement of Position (SOP) 98-2, *Accounting for Costs of Activities of Not-for-Profit Organizations and State and Local Governmental Entities That Include Fund Raising* (an Amendment to AICPA Audit and Accounting Guides *Health Care Organizations, Not-for-Profit Organizations,* and *Audits of State and Local Governmental Units*) (No. 014887.) SOP 98-2 is effective for years beginning on or after December 15, 1998.

The SOP provides guidance on accounting for activities of all nongovernmental not-for-profit organizations and all state and local governmental entities that solicit contributions. The SOP focuses on joint activities, which are activities that are part of the fund-raising function and have elements of one or more other functions, such as program or management and general. The SOP provides that if the criteria of purpose, audience, and content as defined in the SOP are met, the costs of joint activities that are identifiable with a particular function should be charged to that function and joint costs should be allocated between fund raising and the appropriate program or management and general function. If any of the criteria are not met, all costs of the activity should be reported as fund-raising costs, including costs that otherwise might be considered program or management and general costs if they had been incurred in a different activity, subject to the exception in the following sentence. Costs of goods or services provided in exchange transactions that are part of joint activities, such as costs of direct donor benefits of a special event (for example, a meal), should not be reported as fund raising. In addition, the SOP requires certain financial statement disclosures if joint costs are allocated. *Softcover, $13.00 (Nonmember), $10.50 (Member)*

The Audit Committee: A Key to Financial Accountability for Nonprofit Organizations

SANDRA JOHNSON (NATIONAL CENTER FOR NONPROFIT BOARDS, 1994)

▶ As nonprofit organizations face increasing media and government scrutiny and ever-changing accounting requirements, the role of the audit committee in ensuring financial accountability is more critical than ever before; in addition to reviewing basic responsibilities of the audit committee, this timely booklet suggests how the committee might be chartered, what type of members should serve on the committee, and how often it should meet; equally valuable for organizations that have an audit committee and those considering one. There is a 25 percent discount for NCNB members. *Softcover, 16 pages, $10 (plus $3.50 shipping)*

The Audit Committee: The Board of Trustees of a Not-for-Profit Organization and the Independent Accountant *(See Governance— Roles and Responsibilities for full description)*

Audit Risk Alerts

(American Institute of Certified Public Accountants)

▶ Planning is one of the most important parts of the audit process, and these alerts may be some of the most useful publications available for planning audits. Available are *General Audit Risk Alert* and *Industry Audit Risk Alerts* (ask for *Not-for-Profit Organizations*); they are designed to focus auditors' attention on current economic, regulatory, and professional developments that can have a significant effect on the audits they perform. They can help auditors increase the efficiency of audit planning by giving them concise and relevant information to help them understand how current developments might affect their clients and control audit risk by focusing their attention on important matters that may require special audit consideration. They also highlight important audit reporting issues, recurring peer review problems, and lessons learned from litigation. *General Audit Risk Alert: $20 (Nonmember), $14 (Member) (plus $3 shipping); Industry Audit Risk Alerts: $18.50 (Nonmember), $12.95 (Member)*

Auditing and Reporting Under OMB Circular A-133
(See also Tax Compliance and Reporting, Grants Management)

GERARD M. ZACK (NONPROFIT RESOURCE CENTER, 1999)

▶ Complete coverage of all auditor and auditee requirements associated with audits of organizations that receive federal awards, including compliance requirements, internal control considerations, and reporting issues. *$49 (Nonmember), $36 (Member) (includes shipping and handling)*

Auditing Recipients of Federal Awards: Practical Guidance for Applying OMB Circular A-133, Audits of States, Local Governments, and Non-Profit Organizations *(See also Grants Management, Tax Compliance and Reporting)*

JOSEPH MORAGLIO (AMERICAN INSTITUTE OF CERTIFIED PUBLIC ACCOUNTANTS, 1998)

▶ This book contains comprehensive analyses of, as well as the very latest guidance on, applying the OMB's most recent revisions to its Circulars for performing Single Audits. It integrates the latest developments in professional auditing standards as well as numerous audit checklists and illustrative examples that will help auditors perform audits that comply with regulations.

The guide contains an illustrative case study of the single audit process that includes selecting major programs, evaluating and testing internal control over the eligibility requirements of a federal program, testing of compliance, and reporting. *Softcover, $56.25 (Nonmember), $45.00 (Member)*

Audits of States, Local Governments, and Not-for-Profit Organizations Receiving Federal Awards (SOP 98-3)

(AMERICAN INSTITUTE OF CERTIFIED PUBLIC ACCOUNTANTS)

▶ This book was developed in response to changes imposed by the final revision of OMB Circular A-133, *Audits of States, Local Governments, and Non-Profit Organizations* (62 FR 35277), which was effective for audits of fiscal years beginning after June 30, 1996. The OMB also issued the OMB Circular A-133 Compliance Supplement. Circular A-133 requires both the auditor and auditee to complete and sign a data collection form (form SF-SAC). The Federal Audit Clearinghouse (FAC) has developed an electronic template of the form in both a WordPerfect format and a Microsoft WORD format. The form is also available on the OMB home page. Auditors should contact the FAC at 1-888-222-9907 with questions on the form. This SOP, which was issued March 17, 1998, supersedes SOP 92-9, *Audits of Not-for-Profit Organizations Receiving Federal Awards,* and Part VII of the Audit and Accounting Guide *Audits of State and Local Governmental Units.* The SOP is included as an appendix to the Audit and Accounting Guides, *Audits of State and Local Governmental Units* (No. 012059) and *Not-for-Profit Organizations* (No. 013392). It is also included in the AICPA Technical Practice Aids (No. 005059).

Checklists and Illustrative Financial Statements for Not for Profit Organizations

(AMERICAN INSTITUTE OF CERTIFIED PUBLIC ACCOUNTANTS, 1999)

▶ Be completely prepared for your next not-for-profit organization audit engagement. Developed especially for use in audits of not-for-profit organizations, this nonauthoritative practice aid includes financial statement disclosures that are likely to be encountered in this industry. *Softcover, $33.75 (Nonmember), $27.00 (Member)*

Essential Financial Considerations for Not-for-Profit Organizations: A Guide for Non-Accounting Executives

EDWARD J. MCMILLAN (AMERICAN SOCIETY OF ASSOCIATION EXECUTIVES, 1994)

▶ From responsibility for internal control, public access to records, and lobbying regulations to unrelated business income tax, working with CPA firms, and IRS audits . . . as a not-for-profit organization executive, do you know all you need to know about these crucial areas of financial management? This extensive reference handbook is written expressly for the nonfinancial executive. McMillan outlines the rules and regulations exclusive to not-for-profits, as well as the nonfinancial executive's role, in simple-to-understand language. *Loose-leaf format, 88 pages, $72 (Nonmember), $59.95 (Member)*

Financial and Accounting Guide For Not-for-Profit Organizations, 5th Edition

MALVERN J. GROSS JR., RICHARD F. LARKIN, ROGER S. BRUTTOMESSO, AND JOHN J. MCNALLY (JOHN WILEY & SONS, 1995)

▶ This book provides complete guidance for various types of organizations, tax and compliance reporting requirements, illustrated explanations of diverse types of acceptable statements, and a how-to section on setting up and keeping books using both a simple cash system and the more complicated accrual systems, along with step-by-step procedures and forms plus commentary on computers and accounting software. The revised and updated edition covers SFAS Nos. 116, 117, and 124 as well as a discussion of a new AICPA exposure draft covering consolidated financial statements of affiliated organizations. It alerts readers to proposed new or revised Financial Accounting Standards Board requirements scheduled to take effect over the next few years. It offers more than 100 sample financial statements, worksheets and ledgers, plus easy-to-use checklists on classification of gifts, cost allocations, affiliated organizations, and more. It is supplemented annually (includes 1996 supplement). *Hardcover, 704 pages, $145 (includes shipping)*

Financial Statement Presentation and Disclosure Practices for Not-for-Profit Organizations

(AMERICAN INSTITUTE OF CERTIFIED PUBLIC ACCOUNTANTS, 1999)

▶ This publication utilizes illustrative financial statements and related disclosures for nongovernmental, not-for-profit organizations, other than health care providers, to provide non-authoritative practical guidance. It includes general sample disclosures as well as disclosures primarily related to the statement of financial position, statement of activity, and related statements. There are chapters on financial statements prepared on a basis other than GAAP, information outside the financial statements, and an appendix containing excerpts from certain authoritative pronouncements. *Softcover, $61.25 (Nonmember), $49.00 (Member)*

Governmental and Nonprofit Accounting, 6th Edition

ROBERT J. FREEMAN AND CRAIG D. SHOULDERS (PRENTICE HALL BUSINESS PUBLISHING, 1999)

▶ This is a textbook that deals with financial accounting and reporting concepts, standards, and procedures applicable to state and local governments; the federal government; and nonprofit and governmental universities, hospitals, voluntary health and welfare organizations, and other nonprofit organizations. Completely

updated content includes all GASB standards through GASB Statement 32; the latest FASB and AICPA guidance on accounting and reporting for not-for-profit organizations; the latest revisions of the OMB and AICPA single audit guidance; the latest changes in federal government accounting and reporting; the new pension plan accounting standards; the latest revision of OMB Circular A-133 on single audits, including coverage of the risk-based approach to identifying major federal assistance programs and changes in auditor reports; and coverage of the GASB's proposed new reporting model. *Hardcover, 936 pages, $137.50*

Guide to Audits of Nonprofit Organizations

(PRACTITIONERS PUBLISHING COMPANY)

▶ Presents a practical system for auditing a wide range of nonprofit organizations. This Guide shows you how to follow the unique nonprofit accounting, auditing, and compliance auditing rules. It discusses the new AICPA audit and accounting guide for not-for-profit organizations and SAS No. 82 on fraud. It also includes guidance on compilation and review engagements. Like other audit guides, this Guide contains a complete set of audit programs, confirmation letters, checklists, report examples, and sample financial statements. *NPO Print—$193, CD-ROM—$223, Both Versions—$273*

Guide to Nonprofit Expenses

(PRACTITIONERS PUBLISHING COMPANY)

▶ This new Guide answers all your questions about accounting for and reporting nonprofit expenses. It shows you how to apply the recently issued SOP 98-2, *Accounting for Costs of Activities of Not-for-Profit Organizations and State and Local Governmental Entities That Include Fund Raising* (the Guide contains practical, specific guidance and "real-life" examples that will help you save time in assisting your clients with the SOP). The Guide illustrates numerous functional expense allocations using different methods, and it helps you determine the program and supporting functions your clients should present. It also includes special operating considerations including a discussion of fraud, internal control, and expense ratios, and percentages. *NPE Print—$85, CD-ROM—$116, Both Versions—$166*

Guide to Nonprofit GAAP

(PRACTITIONERS PUBLISHING COMPANY)

▶ Arranged in an easy-to-use topical format, it provides in-depth coverage of the AICPA Audit and Accounting Guide, *Not-for-Profit Organizations,* as well as recent FASB Statements affecting nonprofit organizations. It also discusses, from a not-for-profit's perspective, the generally accepted accounting principles that all entities must follow. It covers all of the FASB Statements, Interpretations, and Technical Bulletins; APB Opinions; ARBs; and relevant AICPA Statements of Position and EITF issues that apply to nonprofit organizations. The Guide contains numerous practical considerations and examples, extensive cross-references to authoritative literature, and a comprehensive disclosure checklist. *NPG Print or CD-ROM—$69 (additional copies, $62 each), Both Versions—$99*

Guide to Preparing Nonprofit Financial Statements

(PRACTITIONERS PUBLISHING COMPANY)

▶ This Guide was specifically designed to address the new AICPA audit and accounting guide, *Not-for-Profit Organizations,* as well as recent FASB statements affecting not-for-profit organizations. It contains complete guidance on all facets of financial statement preparation including drafting forms and sample financial statements. The Guide thoroughly discusses and illustrates the complex accounting and reporting principles appropriate for nonprofit organizations and includes practical application insights and numerous how-to examples. It is not a reporting or procedural guide for audits, compilations, or reviews, but a practical, how-to book meant to save you time and money. *NFS Print—$172, CD-ROM—$202, Both Versions—$252*

Guide to Single Audits

(PRACTITIONERS PUBLISHING COMPANY)

▶ With the rescission of OMB Circular A-128 and issuance of the new OMB Circular A-133, keeping up with single-audit regulations is tougher than ever! The new Circular covers both governments and nonprofit organizations, and *Guide to Single Audits* gives you all the information you need to stay current and conform with the new provisions. Completely updated to cover the Single Audit Act Amendments of 1996, this Guide is a source for all the rules, regulations, and guidelines for single audits of both governments and nonprofit organizations. To save you valuable research time, in-depth guidance is provided on compliance testing, reporting, and audit strategy for the single audit including how to apply the new SAS No. 82, *Consideration of Fraud in a Financial Statement Audit.* In addition, the Guide includes audit programs, engagement checklists and correspondence, and illustrative workpapers. *GSA Print—$176, CD-ROM—$206, Both Versions—$256*

Introduction to Governmental and Not-for-Profit Accounting, 4th Edition

JOSEPH R. RAZEK, GORDON A. HOSCH, AND MARTIN IVES (PRENTICE HALL, 2000)

▶ Covering the essentials of fund accounting, this flexible book introduces the reader to the basic accounting principles at work in both governmental and not-for-profit organizations. This brief book divides most of the chapters into independent sections, which may be covered as separate units. The information on state and local government financial reporting has been updated for coverage of the new financial reporting model, the reporting entity, and financial condition analysis. New examples have been added to more clearly describe the nature of lease accounting. The module on pension trust funds has been rewritten to reflect new GASB pronouncements in a simpler format. New material was added on the measurement of pension costs and other postemployment benefits. This book is for accountants wishing to increase or refresh their knowledge of government and not-for-profit accounting or public budgeting. *Hardcover, 644 pages, $70*

Joint and Indirect Cost Allocations for Governmental and Nonprofit Organizations: How to Prepare and Audit Them

(CONTINUING PROFESSIONAL EDUCATION)

DAVID L. COTTON (AMERICAN INSTITUTE OF CERTIFIED PUBLIC ACCOUNTANTS)

▶ Be prepared to fulfill the new indirect cost audit responsibilities contained in Circular A-133 revisions, the compliance supplement and SOPs 98-2 and 98-3. This course addresses concerns of auditors in firms assisting clients in preparing joint and indirect cost allocations, and performing audits of entities receiving federal grants and contracts. Course highlights include gaining an understanding of indirect cost allocation theory, learning how to recognize and discern different—and optimum—allocation methodologies, examin-

ing joint cost allocation concepts and restrictions, recognizing the most common cost allocation problem areas, assessing the impact of improper allocations, and understanding how to evaluate internal control related to indirect cost allocations. This course will help you meet the special CPE requirements for CPAs auditing government entities and nonprofit organizations. *$149 (Nonmember), $119 (Member)*

Managing Not-for-Profits in the New Accounting and Auditing Environment

(CONTINUING PROFESSIONAL EDUCATION)

CLIFFORD D. BROWN AND JOSEPH A. MCHUGH (AMERICAN INSTITUTE OF CERTIFIED PUBLIC ACCOUNTANTS)

▶ This course enables practicing CPAs to show not-for-profit client–managers how to use new accounting, budgeting, and control techniques to run their organizations more effectively and to evaluate the organizations' performance in the information age. This course draws on real-life situations and recent pronouncements for practical examples of what to do and how to do it. Course highlights include avoiding recurring threats to solvency; planning for endowment growth–split-interest agreements; critical choices in financial statement presentation; reflecting internal control standards in the budgeting process; monitoring operations; the impact of pronouncements on fund raising, investments, and internal controls; and the new emphasis on risk in identifying programs to audit. This course will help you meet the special CPE requirements for CPAs auditing government entities and nonprofit organizations. *$149 (Nonmember), $119.00 (Member)*

Miller Not-for-Profit Organization Audits— Electronic Workpapers and Reference Guide

WARREN RUPPEL (HARCOURT PROFESSIONAL PUBLISHING)

▶ Their experts will take you step-by-step through this specialized audit, cutting out unnecessary tasks that cause confusion and waste time. You'll learn what to do before, during, and after the audit, and will get the very latest on SOP-98-2 on fund raising, SOP-98-3 on receiving federal awards, and other pronouncements critical to a not-for-profit organization audit. You'll also receive a complete collection of checklists, reports, and client letters on an accompanying CD-ROM. Plus, you'll receive the all new workpaper *Managing Miller Engagement System*™. This software creates client binders that organize and manage all your workpapers and client documents. Also available in CD-ROM and combo formats. *Softcover, $189*

Miller Not-for-Profit Reporting

MARY FOSTER, HOWARD BECKER, AND RICHARD TERRANO (HARCOURT PROFESSIONAL PUBLISHING)

▶ This book puts expert analysis and explanation of not-for-profit accounting, external financial reporting, and regulatory reporting right at your fingertips. It is complete, compact, and indispensable. You will not find a more reliable analysis of not-for-profit pronouncements. This book covers it all, including revenue, expenses, assets, liabilities, organizational issues, external financial reporting, note disclosures, cash flows, GAAP transactions, payroll requirements, and more! Their not-for-profit experts translate complicated jargon to make difficult issues absolutely clear. Also included are sample financial statements presenting the net asset class model, the fund accounting model, and specialized organizations. It includes a listing of not-for-profit accounting resources on the Web and a detailed cross-reference to original pronouncements. It is full of analysis and explanation of not-for-profit accounting, financial presentation, and regulatory reporting. Every chapter is cross-referenced to their entire *Miller Reference Series* through IMPRESS. It is available in print and CD-ROM versions. *Softcover, 500 pages, $89 (CD-ROM), $79 (Print)*

Model Accounting and Financial Policies and Procedures Handbook for Not-for-Profit Organizations (Book and CD-ROM)

EDWARD J. MCMILLAN (AMERICAN SOCIETY OF ASSOCIATION EXECUTIVES, 1999)

▶ This is an essential resource for the executive responsible for creating board-approved financial and accounting policies and procedures. It will help you to strengthen your organization's financial procedures while ensuring your board members that they are meeting their fiduciary responsibilities. Streamline this process with more than 100 sample forms and policies that may be customized to fit your organization's needs. What could be easier than having them on CD-ROM, allowing you the option to change them to fit your particular needs? Major topics include internal financial statement formats, a new chart of accounts, an accounting and financial policies and procedures manual, a glossary, and a full index. *Softcover (with CD-ROM), 170 pages, $50 (Nonmember), $42 (Member) (plus $6.25 shipping)*

The NFC Accounting Software Selection Handbook

(See also Software)

▶ The Nonprofit Financial Center has issued a comprehensive booklet that evaluates 26 commercially available general nonprofit and religious organization fund accounting software programs, including their features, costs, and FASB compliance. *The NFC Accounting Software Selection Handbook* will help any nonprofit or religious organization assess its accounting needs and evaluate the various software packages that address those needs.

This practical Handbook includes chapters about accounting system requirements, the software selection process, cost summaries of popular packages for both simple and complex organizations, and evaluation grids that rate each program's features, ease of use, and hardware requirements. *Softcover, $40.00*

Nonprofit Accounting & Audit Disclosure Manual

(WARREN, GORHAM & LAMONT) (ANNUAL)

▶ *Nonprofit Accounting and Auditing Disclosure Manual* is your one-stop reference for expert guidance on all nonprofit disclosure requirements. You get over 600 GAAP and GAAS disclosure requirements and examples for financial statements, auditors' reports, reviews, and compilations. Written for public accountants with nonprofit clients, as well as controllers and financial officers of nonprofit organizations, the Manual incorporates all currently effective pronouncements by major topic, regardless of their date of issue, and includes all disclosure requirements and corresponding reporting examples for financial statements, auditors' reports, reviews, and compilations. It helps you prepare accurate financial statements and auditors' reports and guard against unintentional omissions or oversights by outlining the accepted, prescribed wording for a given circumstance. The Manual is updated annually. *Hardcover, $210*

Nonprofit Accounting and Auditing Update, 1999–2000 Edition (Videocourse)

MODERATED BY W.A. BROADUS JR. (AMERICAN INSTITUTE OF CERTIFIED PUBLIC ACCOUNTANTS)

▶ This timely update covers the most important accounting and auditing pronouncements for not-for-profit organizations issued in the past year, plus new pronouncements likely to come out in the near future. Course highlights include single-audit implementation issues, including handling the Data Collection Form; revised HUD guidance for NPOs; revised OMB Circular A-122 for nonprofit organizations; pending AICPA actions on accounting and auditing issues; FASB proposed guidance on consolidations; FASB guidance on transfer of assets; and copies of key pronouncements covered. W.A. Broadus Jr., CPA, and other experts provide a 120-minute overview of the manual's contents. Receive a free fall updating supplement, which offers an additional two hours of CPE when you choose this option. *Text: $193.00 (Nonmember), $155.00 (Member); 1 VHS Tape/Manual: $253.00 (Nonmember), $202.00 (Member)*

Nonprofit Controller's Manual

CRAIG R. STEVENS, HORTON SORKIN, AND MARTHA L. BENSON, EDS. (WARREN, GORHAM & LAMONT, 2001) (ANNUAL)

▶ This material shows you how to comply with the latest FASB pronouncements and government regulations, including the new rules on accounting for contributions and preparing financial statements. Along with its guidelines for protecting your organization's tax-exempt status, it helps you develop valuable financial management skills. *Nonprofit Controller's Manual* also clarifies tax management, activity-based costing, risk management issues, pensions and deferred compensation, investment plan management, planned giving, information technology, and system issues. This one-volume reference gives you specific financial requirements of nonprofits, including reporting, tax, regulations, internal control, investments, and other issues; operational issues, such as administration requirements and working with the board of directors; and a practical plain-English format with charts, checklists, tables, worked examples, and numerical and statistical comparisons. Coverage includes analysis of unrelated business income taxation; coverage of the new AICPA Audit and Accounting Guide, *Not-for-Profit Organizations;* accounting for investments and contributions; effect of new FASB pronouncements; essential internal control and audit issues; relationships with CPA firms; analysis of unrelated business income taxation; state and local tax requirement; federal grants issues: administrative and audit requirements; cash management and banking relationships; and more. It is updated annually. *Hardcover, $190*

Nonprofit Financial and Accounting Manual

(PRACTITIONERS PUBLISHING COMPANY)

▶ This book leads you through the basic record-keeping processes of a nonprofit organization. Features include record-keeping basics, nonprofit accounting and taxation, the revenue and disbursement cycles, general ledger, payroll; financial statements, federal grant compliance, budgeting, and software selection. This Manual contains dozens of forms, checklists, and worksheets to help with bookkeeping tasks. *NBK Print—$85 (Additional Copies, $72 each), CD-ROM—$115, Both Versions—$165*

Nonprofit GAAP Practice Manual

MARTHA L. BENSON, ROWNA H. JONES, AND ALLAN B. AFTERMAN, EDS. (WARREN, GORHAM & LAMONT)

▶ A quiet revolution has changed the face of not-for-profit accounting. In the past four years alone, the FASB, AICPA, and OMB have all issued major pronouncements that affect nonprofit financial reporting. Nonprofit GAAP Practice Manual keeps you on top of important developments that affect your work and saves you hours of time preparing financial statements. Written in easy-to-understand language, *Nonprofit GAAP Practice Manual* provides fast, accurate answers organized by topic; real examples of not-for-profit standards; step-by-step examples of calculations; alternate accounting approaches; and quarterly updates of changes in the field. It is updated quarterly. *Hardcover, $385*

The Not-for-Profit Accounting Field Guide 1999–2000

RICHARD F. LARKIN AND MARIE DITOMMASO (JOHN WILEY & SONS, 1999)

▶ This is an easy-to-read vest pocket guide to not-for-profit accounting. Here is a quick reference to the unique accounting and financial reporting issues affecting not-for-profit organizations today. Portable and designed to be carried in your briefcase or vest pocket, it is written in the active voice and covers the gamut of fundamental GAAP accounting principles—all in clear and concise language. It presents not-for-profit GAAP accounting principles in an up-to-date, handy reference format and provides complete answers and simple explanations. It includes tables that highlight key aspects of accounting principles and supplements existing comprehensive GAAP guides and other technical reference manuals. It will be updated annually in paperback. *Softcover, 248 pages, $22.95*

Not-for-Profit Organizations Accounting Guide

(AICPA PROFESSIONAL EDUCATION SERVICES)

▶ AICPA's comprehensive text, *Not-for-Profit Organizations*, presents all of the information required to assist nongovernmental not-for-profit organizations in preparing financial statements in conformity with GAAP and to educate independent auditors in auditing and reporting on those financial statements. *$89.50*

Not-for-Profit Organizations—Audit and Accounting Guide

(AMERICAN INSTITUTE OF CERTIFIED PUBLIC ACCOUNTANTS, 1999)

▶ This Audit and Accounting Guide summarizes applicable standards and delivers how-to advice for handling most financial statement issues. *Not-for-Profit Organizations—Audit and Accounting Guide* describes relevant matters, conditions, and procedures unique to this industry and illustrates reports that highlight significant areas of concern for both auditors and accountants. The Guide is effective for financial statements for fiscal years ending on or after December 31, 1996, although earlier application is permitted. The Guide does not supersede the effective dates for FASB Statements 116 and 117.

The Guide addresses some of the unique accounting and internal control areas that are important to a nonprofit, such as the role of management and the governing board; the frequency of governing board meetings; the qualifications of management and governing board members; the governing board members' involvement in the organization's operations; the process of how restricted contributions are identified, evaluated, and accepted; how promises to give are valued and recorded; the process for valuing and recording contributed goods, services, utilities, facilities, and the use of long-lived assets; how compliance with donor restrictions and board designations are monitored; meeting reporting requirements imposed by donors, contractors, and regulators; the procedures in place to ensure conformity with accounting presentation and disclosure principles; how new programs are identified and accounted for. *Softcover, $42.00 (Nonmember), $33.50 (Member)*

Not-for-Profit Organizations Industry Developments—Audit Risk Alert

(AMERICAN INSTITUTE OF CERTIFIED PUBLIC ACCOUNTANTS, 1999)

▶ This Audit Risk Alert provides auditors of financial statements with an overview of recent industry, regulatory, and professional developments that may affect the audits they perform. It has been designed to complement the specific AICPA Audit and Accounting Guide. *Softcover, $18.50 (Nonmember), $12.95 (Member)*

Single Audit Requirements for Nonprofit and Governmental Organizations

W.A. BROADUS, JR. (AMERICAN INSTITUTE OF CERTIFIED PUBLIC ACCOUNTANTS CONTINUING PROFESSIONAL EDUCATION)

▶ This is a course for both the auditor of a not-for-profit organization receiving federal assistance and for the not-for-profit official. You will learn about the requirements of the Single Audit Act Amendments of 1996 and OMB Circular A-133, plus the guidance in the AICPA's SOP 98-3, *Audits of States, Local Governments, and Not-for-Profit Organizations Receiving Federal Awards,* and the 1998 OMB Circular A-133 *Compliance Supplement.* Course highlights include understanding, assessing, and testing internal controls; testing compliance with laws and regulations; audit reporting; administrative responsibilities for nonprofit recipients, subrecipients, and federal and state agencies; and program-specific audits. This course will help you meet the special CPE requirements for CPAs auditing government entities and nonprofit organizations. *Softcover, $193.00 (Nonmember), $155.00 (Member)*

Solving Complex Single Audit Issues for Government and Nonprofit Organizations

(AMERICAN INSTITUTE OF CERTIFIED PUBLIC ACCOUNTANTS CONTINUING PROFESSIONAL EDUCATION) (VIDEOCOURSE)

▶ Through this course, get complete coverage of the Single Audit Act Amendments of 1996 and revised OMB Circular A-133, including hands-on guidance in implementing their new requirements as they affect audits of governmental and not-for-profit entities receiving federal funds. You will gain a thorough understanding of the changes made—including the mandate for risk-based audits—and be able to conduct and/or arrange for an audit that complies with those changes. Course highlights include how to plan audits complying with the new requirements; understanding and assessing internal controls; testing compliance with laws and regulations; preparing audit reports; and identifying high-risk programs for audit. One of the special features is a detailed case study showing you how to determine major federal programs. *Text: $161.00 (Nonmember), $129.00 (Member); 1 100-min. VHS Tape/Manual: $186 (Nonmember), $149 (Member)*

Understanding Nonprofit Financial Statements: A Primer for Board Members

JOHN PAUL DALSIMER (NATIONAL CENTER FOR NONPROFIT BOARDS, 1996) (BOOKLET)

▶ Revised to reflect important changes in FASB guidelines, this booklet clarifies the basics of board financial oversight. The no-nonsense explanations are especially helpful for board members who are new to financial responsibilities or to nonprofit accounting. Topics include financial reports, accounting concepts, financial statements, ratios, SFA Nos. 116 and 117, annual financial statements, and sample statements. It is part of the Nonprofit Governance Series, A 25 percent discount is available to members. *Softcover, 24 pages, $12 (plus $2.50 shipping)*

Unified Financial Reporting for Not-for-Profit Organizations: A Comprehensive Guide to Unifying GAAP, IRS Form 990 and Other Financial Reports Using a Unified Chart of Accounts

RUSSY D. SUMARIWALLA AND WILSON C. LEVIS (JOSSEY-BASS, 2000)

▶ A must-have for every nonprofit organization required to file IRS Form 990, this indispensable guide shows nonprofits how to unify their financial reporting for greater efficiency and accountability. In the face of increasing demands of federal and state regulators, foundations, and other organizations, a three-year collaboration between the IRS and a major charity and civic group developed this definitive guide to nonprofit reporting. It offers step-by-step help for nonprofits faced with the daunting task of filing Form 990 from the ins and outs of creating IRS-compliant budgets to filling out and filing the form. This book shows in clear language how to make sense of and work under GAAP, AICPA, and IRS financial reporting guidelines. It helps nonprofits integrate all of their financial reporting to be in line with Form 990 saving time and ensuring accountability. It is sponsored by CompassPoint Nonprofit Services, formerly known as the Support Center for Nonprofit Management/Nonprofit Development Center.

Nothing can be more important to an organization's health and success than the quality of its financial reporting. This comprehensive guide is for all nonprofits that are required to comply with financial reporting standards set by the IRS and 35 state charity regulators (Form 990), FASB and AICPA (GAAP), grant makers, and the like. It shows how to unify financial reporting requirements without compromising the organization's accuracy and accountability. Much more than a standard accounting manual, this book is a thoughtful guide to improving financial reporting so organizations can focus on the business of fulfilling mission, developing essential programs, and serving communities. Armed with the latest information, the authors discuss a unified chart of accounts, activity-level accounting, cost allocation, and computerization. They also explore ways of unifying internal and external financial reports, including GAAP statements, grant reports, and others. This Guide offers a powerful resource section including information on various appendices program service reporting, government regulation, voluntary standards expert review groups, and more. Much more than a standard accounting manual, *Unified Financial Reporting System for Not-for-Profit Organizations* is a thoughtful guide to improving financial reporting so organizations can focus on the business of fulfilling mission, developing essential programs, and serving communities. *Softcover, 355 pages, $32.95*

Using the AICPA Not-for-Profit Organizations Audit and Accounting Guide (Professional Continuing Education)

CHARLES KIRKLAND (AMERICAN INSTITUTE OF CERTIFIED PUBLIC ACCOUNTANTS)

▶ Based on the *AICPA Audit and Accounting Guide, Not-for-Profit Organizations,* this course offers implementation advice that is uniform, clear, and authoritative. It provides you with expert support in using the Guide as well as guidance for such topics as split-interest agreements and related disclosure requirements. Course highlights include basic financial statements (including SFAS Nos. 116 and 117), cash and cash equivalents, debt and other liabilities, contributions received and agency transactions, property and equipment, and SOP 98-2. This course will help you meet the special CPE requirements for CPAs auditing government entities and nonprofit organizations. *Softcover, $149.00 (Nonmember), $119.00 (Member)*

What a Difference Nonprofits Make: A Guide to Accounting Procedures

(ACCOUNTANTS FOR THE PUBLIC INTEREST, 1994)

▶ Designed for the nonprofit sector, this Guide clarifies accounting procedures in detail, an often complex and confusing business issue. It highlights the differences between for-profit and nonprofit accounting. Contents include tax exemption for nonprofits, maintaining professional standards, working with the board of directors, controls in the nonprofit sector, financial statements for nonprofits, and budgeting in nonprofits. Also included are sample financial statements and federal tax forms. *Softcover, 73 pages, $10 (includes shipping)*

What a Difference Preparation Makes: A Guide to the Nonprofit Audit

(ACCOUNTANTS FOR THE PUBLIC INTEREST, 1992)

▶ This guide provides an in-depth look at the nonprofit audit and addresses complex topics in clear steps for better understanding. Practical guidance is offered to nonprofits in preparing for an audit, accounting information processing for nonprofits, recording and processing transactions, methods of internal control for nonprofits, engaging an auditor, preparing for and participating in the audit, and many money-saving tips to reduce staff time and audit costs. Helpful sample forms include accountant's reports, balance sheets, cash receipts journals, and a request for proposal of audit services. *Softcover, 96 pages, $15 (includes shipping)*

Wiley Not-for-Profit GAAP 2000

RICHARD F. LARKIN AND MARIE DITOMMASO (JOHN WILEY & SONS, 2000)

▶ This book provides extensive coverage of accounting standards affecting not-for-profit organizations. *Wiley Not-for-Profit GAAP 2000* is a comprehensive reference tool that helps not-for-profit organizations and their auditors, accountants, and financial advisors prepare financial statements in accordance with generally accepted accounting principles (GAAP). This annual edition covers FASB Statements, Interpretations, and Technical Bulletins; APB Opinions; ARBs and relevant AICPA Statements of Position; and FASB EITF issues and provides a thorough examination of the authoritative standards for measurement, presentations, and disclosure. *Softcover, 522 pages, $69*

Workpaper Preparation Techniques for Government and Nonprofit Organizations (Videocourse)

RHETT D. HARRELL (AMERICAN INSTITUTE OF CERTIFIED PUBLIC ACCOUNTANTS)

▶ Get guidance from this course on how to prepare workpapers needed to complete a government or not-for-profit audit. The course provides more efficient and effective methods of auditing local government and not-for-profit organizations and reviews how much audit work and documentation is necessary to perform a thorough audit. It references to applicable sections of OMB A-133 and SOP 98-3. It covers the key factors in planning for an audit and details the steps in auditing assets, liabilities, fund equity, revenues, and expenses. Helpful examples of single-audit workpapers are included. Gary A. Hotchkiss, CPA, Frank W. Crawford, CPA, Roger Jones, CPA, and Stephen Langowski, CPA, provide a 120-minute overview of the manual's contents. This course will help you meet the special CPE requirements for CPAs auditing government entities and nonprofit organizations. *Text: $161.00 (Nonmember), $129.00 (Member); 1 VHS Tape/Manual: $211.00 (Nonmember), $169.00 (Member)*

Budgeting and Financial Planning

The Budget-Building Book for Nonprofits: A Step-by-Step Guide for Managers and Boards
MURRAY DROPKIN AND BILL LATOUCHE (JOSSEY-BASS, 1998)

▶ This nuts-and-bolts workbook guides nonprofit executives and boards through the budget cycle, offering practical instruction on completing each step of the process. This one-source budgeting tool kit is specifically designed to give nonprofits everything they need to prepare, approve, and implement their own budgets. It provides smaller nonprofit budgeters and nonfinancial nonprofit managers with a simple, systematic method to create, maintain, and track their budgets. Examples, to-do lists, worksheets, schedules, and other hands-on tools help readers get down to work. *Softcover, 192 pages, $26*

Budgeting and Financial Accountability
BRIAN O'CONNELL (INDEPENDENT SECTOR, 1988) (BOOKLET)

▶ Part eight of a nine-part series on nonprofit management (see Nine-Part Nonprofit Management Series) looks at the need for audits and gives tips on how voluntary organization budgeting differs from that of for-profit enterprises. *20 pages, $5.00 (Member); $3.50 Nonmember) (plus $2.50 shipping)*

Budgeting and Financial Management Handbook for Not-for-Profit Organizations, Revised Edition
EDWARD J. MCMILLAN (AMERICAN SOCIETY OF ASSOCIATION EXECUTIVES, 2000)

▶ Update an obsolete or ineffective budgeting system with a budgeting system that works. McMillan's "Continuous Budgeting" and financial management program is easy to implement and monitor. Also included in this bestseller are sample forms and financial statements, formats for sending budget documents to your approving body, and methods for addressing budget problems. It includes an all-new section that illustrates how to compile a monthly budget. *Softcover, 116 pages, $46 (Nonmember), $38 (Member) (plus $6.25 shipping)*

Budgeting for Not-for-Profit Organizations
DAVID C. MADDOX (JOHN WILEY & SONS, 1999)

▶ A well-functioning budget process is more than a set of procedures—it provides a focus for the organization and management to analyze key financial and strategic issues. This reference addresses the fundamentals of managerial incentives and resource allocation, and practical ways in which these incentives can be managed to serve the strategic goals of the organization by taking an in-depth look at the principles of budgeting for not-for-profit organizations—higher education, charities and foundations, religious organizations, and hospitals and health care organizations. *Hardcover, 288 pages, $85.00*

Building and Managing an Asset Base: Information and Advice for Nonprofit Organizations—New Directions for Philanthropic Fundraising #14
JIMMIE R. ALFORD (JOSSEY-BASS, 1996)
SPONSORED BY THE INDIANA CENTER ON PHILANTHROPY

▶ For any nonprofit organization, building and managing an asset base is a continual process that demands hard work and creative leadership rather than mere luck. The authors of this volume—nonprofit directors and fund raisers, as well as accountants, lawyers, and consultants who assist nonprofits—offer insightful, practical recommendations and real-world examples of how to build and manage an asset base. Learn how any organization can develop a planned and deferred giving program and successfully present that program to potential donors. Get expert advice on the technical side of building and managing assets with updates on tax issues and investment strategies for maximizing income from endowment growth. Discover how to work effectively with intermediary agents such as trust and private banking officers, legal counselors, and community trusts to secure planned and major gift support. *Softcover, 130 pages, $25.00*

Financial Planning for Nonprofit Organizations
JODY BLAZEK (JOHN WILEY & SONS, 1996)

▶ *Financial Planning for Nonprofit Organizations* provides practical, proven strategies to safeguard your nonprofit organization's financial future. It coaches you in the essentials of financial planning and supplies easy-to-use tools and techniques for the financial management of nonprofits of every size and type. You will learn how to fine-tune investing and budgeting practices to make the very most of those hard-won contributor dollars, manage and maximize precious resources to fulfill the organization's mission, and achieve the best possible year-end results without endangering its long-term financial picture or tax-exempt status. Blazek leads you step-by-step through the major areas of financial planning, including general administration (tracking, reporting, and financial analysis); the roles and responsibilities of staff, board members, and professional advisors; developing and implementing budgets; asset and resource management; and internal controls to prevent waste and fraud.

You'll explore a variety of tested budgeting strategies, learn accounting and financial reporting techniques, understand how to use a businesslike approach to managing working capital, and discover more efficient methods for interpreting and using financial information. Blazek also supplies useful worksheets, forms, and checklists that make it easier to manage your organization's financial resources. *Softcover, 275 pages, $59.99*

Handbook of Budgeting for Nonprofit Organizations
JAE K. SHIM, JOEL C. SIEGEL & ABRAHAM J. SIMON (PRENTICE HALL BUSINESS & PROFESSIONAL PUBLISHING, 1996)

▶ This all-inclusive Handbook details practical budget strategies and techniques. It shows you how to develop a sound budget to make reliable estimates of income, set realistic financial targets, control costs through variance analysis, spot problems and take corrective steps at once, establish realistic prices for services, plan and schedule activities efficiently, discover key factors affecting your operation, measure performance of people and programs, and communicate your goals to employees, donors, government agencies, and the public. It includes scores of examples, case histories, illustrations, checklists, exhibits, practical applications, statistical data, and more. It also provides assistance with computer applications that save time and ensure accuracy in preparing your budgets, financial modeling tips that predict income and expenses, forecasting techniques most suitable for your operation, "what-if" techniques and risk analysis that prevent surprises, budgeting your programs and services to use resources most advantageously, financial analysis and presentations that impress donors, cash flow appraisal, and cost reduction programs. Also included are forecasting models, flow charts of the budget process, typical budget forms and reports, and sample computer printouts. There is also a Lotus 1-2-3 diskette featuring several budgeting templates you can use at once to develop your spreadsheet programs. *Hardcover, 528 pages, $79.95 (plus $9.75 shipping)*

Saving Money in Nonprofit Organizations: More than 100 Money-Saving Ideas, Tips, and Strategies for Reducing Expenses WITHOUT Cutting Your Budget

GREGORY J. DABEL (JOSSEY-BASS, 1998)

▶ A straightforward, no-nonsense guide to streamlining expenses without sacrificing valuable programs and services. This nuts-and-bolts resource will help you find ways to effectively balance your budget; minimize spending through 30 general money-saving principles and opportunities; maximize your organization's various assets; save money on personnel costs without firing anyone; reduce office equipment and supply costs; negotiate the best possible price with vendors; decrease travel, insurance, and tax expenses; develop long- and short-term strategies for expense reduction; and create an action plan as well as a cost-saving team. *Softcover, 128 pages, $23.95*

Charitable Contributions (Estate Planning, Planned Giving, Trusts)

(See also Resource Development—Planned and Deferred Giving; Philanthropy)

The Charitable ESOP: A Nonprofit's Guide to Using Gifts of Privately Held Stock

(THE NATIONAL CENTER FOR EMPLOYEE OWNERSHIP)

▶ This booklet explains to nonprofit organizations how donors who own closely held companies can use an ESOP in conjunction with charitable giving. Employee stock ownership plans (ESOPs) enable charitable organizations to turn gifts of privately held stock into cash. The ESOP can serve as a tax-deductible private stock market for business owners and their families. Professional fund raisers can inform their present and potential donor base of business owners about the ESOP option. They will be assisting departing small-business owners in the vitally important task of succession and estate planning, while potentially increasing both the size of the contributions they receive and the number of donors. *Softcover, 33 pages, $8 or $4.25 each if 10 or more are ordered*

Charitable Lead Trusts: Explanation, Specimen Agreements, Forms *(See also Resource Development)*

CONRAD TEITELL (PHILANTHROPY TAX INSTITUTE/TAXWISE GIVING)

▶ This publication details the income, gift, estate, and capital gains tax implications for all types of lead trusts. It explains the Internal Revenue Code, published revenue rulings, letter rulings, and Treasury regulations and provides the definitive explanation of charitable lead annuity trusts, charitable lead unitrusts, nonstatutory charitable lead trusts, reversions to donor, remainders to grandchildren and others, inter vivos and testamentary, charitable lead trusts created by corporations, opportunities to seize, and pitfalls. It is supplemented and revised annually. *Loose-leaf binder, $175 (plus $7 shipping)*

Deferred Giving: Explanation, Specimen Agreements, Forms *(See also Resource Development)*

CONRAD TEITELL (PHILANTHROPY TAX INSTITUTE/TAXWISE GIVING)

▶ For maximum tax benefits, agreements must meet numerous complex technical requirements; omit a key phrase or include a few prohibited words and the IRS can disallow the income, gift, or estate tax charitable deduction as well as other unpleasant tax consequences. The claim for the charitable deduction must be substantiated in great detail, with the amount and type of income received under each plan properly reported on federal tax returns by both donors and charitable organizations. Correct tax reporting greatly reduces the possibility of expensive, time-consuming audits and penalties. Teitell points out the pitfalls and builds on IRS specimens to give you workable documents. This two-volume set explains income, gift, estate, and capital gains tax implications for all types of deferred gifts; provides simplified forms, instructions, and tables for computing charitable deductions for all deferred gifts; includes a comprehensive explanation of wills, estate planning, life insurance, gifts, and specimen SEC disclosure statement for a pooled income fund; provides specimen agreements for all types of lifetime and testamentary trusts; includes specimen forms for reporting to the federal government. Supplemented and revised annually. *Loose-leaf binder, 2-volume set, $275 (plus $9 shipping)*

Guide to Nonprofit Contributions

(PRACTITIONERS PUBLISHING COMPANY)

▶ This Guide contains practical and clear guidance that takes you step-by-step through the process of determining whether a transaction is a contribution, exchange, or agency transaction. You'll find guidance on recording and valuing in-kind gifts and contributed services. This Guide also covers special contribution operating considerations such as substantiation and disclosure requirements, internal control, and fraud. You'll also get straightforward answers to your clients' most difficult accounting questions. *NPC Print—$85, CD-ROM—$115, Both Versions—$165*

Employee Benefits

(See also Accounting and Auditing)

2001 Retirement Plans for Not-for-Profit Organizations (Book or CD-ROM)

ANDREW DZAMBA (HARCOURT BRACE PROFESSIONAL PUBLISHING)

▶ This resource delivers all the help you need to select, create, and administer a compliant, effective retirement plan. From 401(k)s to profit-sharing plans—everything you need is in one easy-to-use volume. You'll get the very latest on key court cases that affect plan structures, updates on cash balance plans, hot tips on automatic plan administration and employee self-service technologies, and more. It includes a CD-ROM containing sample plan documents, including tax-sheltered annuity adoption agreements, defined contribution plan documents, a SIMPLE 401(k) defined contribution plan, a defined benefit pension plan, and more. It contains all the plans, options, and help you need to select, create, and administer a compliant, effective retirement plan. It provides resources for selecting, creating, amending, and administering the perfect pension plan for your organization. Key features include the newest laws and rule changes for retirement plans; the latest on the Employee Retirement and Income Security Act 401(k) plan for nonprofits; tax-sheltered annuities: 403(b) plans; 457 plans: the local government employee retirement plan; profit-sharing plans; cutting-edge "hybrid" plans; tips on how to cope with IRS scrutiny; and other cutting-edge retirement ideas. *$91.00*

For-Profit Ventures

(See also Resource Development)

Developing Affordable Housing: A Practical Guide for Nonprofit Organizations, 2nd Edition
BENNETT L. HECHT (JOHN WILEY & SONS, 1999)

▶ Taking you step-by-step through the entire development process, *Developing Affordable Housing* covers all the bases, from putting together the development team to determining project feasibility to obtaining site control. Along with details on using Hope 6 funds for neighborhood revitalization programs, it contains a new chapter on joint ventures that includes specifics on limited liability corporations (LLCs). Packed with numerous checklists, step-by-step procedures, sample contracts, and model documents, *Developing Affordable Housing* provides information on raising capital—loans, grants, equity, public housing funds; property development—deposit and escrow, closing and recording costs, settlements, tenancies, risk of loss, purchaser inspection; prepurchase considerations—applying for financing and operating subsidies, determining ownership entity, interviewing management companies, developing plans for renting or selling units; settling on acquisition—title insurance, the settlement agent, property location survey, governmental regulations, building permits; and financing and taxation—Low-Income Housing Tax Credit (LIHTC), Fannie Mae and Freddie Mac, tax-exempt bonds. It is supplemented annually to keep readers up-to-date on changes in the law, additional programs, developments in funding and financing, and recent trends in the nonprofit sector and real estate market. *Hardcover, 690 pages, $95*

Enterprise (for-Profit) Endeavors, Leadership Series *(see Resource Development—for-Profit Ventures, for full description)*

Legal Aspects of Program-Related Investments *(See Legal Issues—Investment for full description)*

Managing for Profit in the Nonprofit World *(See General Management—Publications for full description)*

The Nonprofit Entrepreneur: Creating Ventures to Earn Income *(See Resource Development—for-Profit Ventures for full description)*

Partnerships and Joint Ventures Involving Tax-Exempt Organizations *(See Legal Issues—for-Profit Ventures/Investments for full description)*

Something Ventured, Something Gained: A Business Development Guide for Nonprofit Organizations *(See Resource Development—for-Profit Ventures for full description)*

Fund Accounting/Grants Management

Federal Grants Management Handbook
SUSAN LAUSCHER, ED. (GRANTS MANAGEMENT ADVISORY SERVICE/THOMPSON PUBLISHING GROUP)

▶ This two-volume handbook cuts through the jargon to provide practical advice and straightforward answers to help grants managers comply with complex administrative requirements for federal grants. It is a reference tool that covers regulations, executive orders, and administrative and court decisions affecting federal grants management.

The Handbook explains everything from setting up financial management systems to purchasing procedures to record keeping and reporting to audits. You learn how to comply with a wide array of laws and directives, such as nondiscrimination, environmental impact, lobbying restrictions, and much more. It includes every government-wide directive that affects the federal grants administration process and is thoroughly indexed and cross-referenced for ease of use. Plus, new sections have been added in 1998 to cover various aspects of electronic grants management, including federal interagency initiatives, cross-servicing payment and reporting systems, and the electronic rule-making process. Subscriptions include monthly updates to the loose-leaf handbook and a *Current Developments* newsletter for timely coverage of key issues and events. It is published in cooperation with the Grants Management Advisory Service.

Also available are 23 separate Federal Agency Reference chapters, which include detailed information about each federal agency's grant programs, agency- and program-specific regulatory citations, and key grants personnel.

A one-year subscription to the print version of the *Federal Grants Management Handbook* includes a two-volume manual with monthly newsletters and update pages. A one-year subscription to the online version of the *Federal Grants Management Handbook* gives you online access to the entire manual, the newsletter archive, updates, special reports, and annotated links. All components of the online Handbook are searchable, cross-references are hyperlinked, and you'll have a choice of newsletter delivery options. *Loose-leaf binder or online version, $269*

Grant Accounting & Administration
GERARD M. ZACK (NONPROFIT RESOURCE CENTER, 1999)

▶ This book offers a comprehensive explanation of the cost principles of OMB Circular A-122 and the administrative rules of OMB Circular A-110. Also covered is the preparation of indirect cost rate proposals. *$49 (Nonmember), $36 (Member) (includes shipping & handling)*

Online Guide to Federal Program Compliance and Audits (Thompson Publishing Group) (Online Service)

▶ The *Online Guide to Federal Program Compliance and Audits* is the most comprehensive source of federal grant compliance information and audit guidance available. Continually updated to reflect changes to program rules and audit guidance, the site pulls together all of the information independent auditors must have to perform a thorough audit and grantees need to prepare for an audit as well as to monitor sub-recipients. Developed by the editor of the *Single Audit Information Service* and the *Federal Grants Management Handbook,* the *Online Guide* is the one-stop shop for the most current federal grant rules and audit guidance. The fully searchable *Online Guide* provides instant access to the *Federal Register, Code of Federal Regulations,* statutes, OMB circulars, and the current *Catalog of Federal Domestic Assistance* numbers and titles. It offers the following features for finding the most current compliance information and audit guidance for federal assistance programs: keyword searching of federal assistance programs, custom audit guidance, the *Federal Register,* Public Laws, and the *Code of Federal Regulations;* faster, more frequent updating; hypertext links to guidance documents and federal agencies; and a huge array of other audit-related online resources. Optional e-mail alerts bring the latest single-audit, grants management, and other news right to your desktop. *$319 per year (discounted, multiuser site licenses are also available)*

Single Audit Information Service

SUSAN PERNA-DAMON, ED. (THOMPSON PUBLISHING GROUP) (HANDBOOK)

▶ A comprehensive support system for arranging and conducting single audits, this periodic reference service covers developments affecting organizations receiving federal assistance as well as those performing the audits. Included are up-to-date information and practical guidance for single audits of state and local governments as well as the single-audit requirements for colleges, universities, and nonprofit agencies.

Detailed analytical sections review every aspect of single-audit law and policy. An index, logically designed tabs, and extensive cross-references make access to specific information quick and easy. The 500-page reference section is a compendium of primary-source documents: laws, OMB circulars, GAO guidance, and federal agency implementing regulations.

Subscription includes monthly updates to the loose-leaf handbook and a monthly newsletter covering recent developments. Summary of Contents: Audit Requirements; Arranging for Audits; Performing the Audit; Content and Use of the Single Audit Report; Audit Follow-Up; Technical Assistance Materials. *$298*

Techniques for Monitoring Federal Subawards

(THOMPSON PUBLISHING GROUP)

▶ *Techniques for Monitoring Federal Subawards* helps federal grant recipients and subrecipients understand and participate in the monitoring process. It discusses the variety of compliance monitoring tools that grant recipients can use and provides practical guidance for executing them. Written by the editors of the Single Audit Information Service (see separate listing), this new publication explains such issues as the roles and responsibilities of the grantees and subrecipients; how to structure subaward agreements—and what provisions to include in those agreements; how to determine the most cost-effective monitoring methods for particular subrecipients; how pass-through entities and subrecipients should communicate during and after the monitoring visit; and what auditors will look for in grantees' monitoring activities of grantees. Included are samples of actual agreements used by grantees and checklists and excerpts from relevant Office of Management and Budget circulars. *Softcover, 120 pages, $79*

Insurance, Risk Management, and Liability

(See also Legal Issues)

Avoiding Crash Course: Auto Liability, Insurance and Safety for Nonprofits (Booklet)

CHARLES TREMPER (NONPROFIT RISK MANAGEMENT CENTER, 1994)

▶ Chances are one in three that you will be seriously injured in a traffic accident in your lifetime. Yet most accidents are avoidable and can be prevented. This book gives commonsense tips for avoiding accidents and decreasing the likelihood of injury when an accident occurs. Also included is a sample accident report form, information on what to do after an accident, and ways to establish

guidelines limiting vehicle use. Auto accidents are one of the most frequent sources of insurance claims against nonprofits; if your employees or volunteers drive, your organization can be liable even if you don't own the vehicle. It explains your potential liability, describes insurance options, and provides postaccident procedures. Forms and checklists are included. *Softcover, 44 pages, $4.50 (plus $3.50 shipping)*

Beyond the Myths About Disabilities and Risks: Myths About Individuals with Disabilities

(NONPROFIT RISK MANAGEMENT CENTER)

▶ To counteract misconceptions about the risks of involving people with disabilities, the Nonprofit Risk Management Center has created a pamphlet, *Beyond the Myths about Disabilities and Risks.* The pamphlet identifies common risk assumptions that volunteer administrators may have and examines strategies to safely accommodate people with disabilities. *First copy free; 10 copies for $5.00; 100 copies for $35.00*

Board Liability: Guide for Nonprofit Directors

DANIEL L. KURTZ (MOYER BELL, 1988)

▶ This is the authoritative guide to avoiding liability, geared for boards of directors of nonprofit institutions and their lawyers. It provides an in-depth examination of board responsibilities, emphasizing care, loyalty, and obedience. *Softcover, 196 pages, $12.95*

Child Abuse Prevention Primer for Your Organization (Booklet)

(NONPROFIT RISK MANAGEMENT CENTER, 1995)

▶ Without careful planning and effective risk management, children may become victims in programs designed to serve them. The *Child Abuse Prevention Primer* offers insights on best practices protecting the youthful participants in your program. This timely resource builds on a factual foundation with practical insights on the four Ps of child abuse prevention in a volunteer or nonprofit organization: Personnel, Program, Premises, and Participants. It includes references for dozens of abuse-prevention books, videos, and other tools. *Softcover, 85 pages, $7.50 (plus $3 shipping)*

D&O: What You Need to Know

(NONPROFIT RISK MANAGEMENT CENTER, 1998)

▶ This brand new resource on nonprofit directors' and officers' liability insurance describes important subtleties in nonprofit D&O coverage. If you're considering the first-time purchase of D&O coverage or you want to make sure that your current policy provides the coverage you need, this book will be invaluable. The text outlines risk management strategies, provides an overview of the emergence of nonprofit D&O coverage, and offers useful insight on the D&O application, coverage elements, and policy nuances. This book concludes with tips on reading an insurance policy, purchasing coverage, and answers to common questions about nonprofit D&O insurance. *Softcover, 76 pages, $15*

Directors and Officers Liability Insurance and Indemnification

JOHN A. EDIE (COUNCIL ON FOUNDATIONS, 1993)

▶ This revised edition discusses risks, how they can be minimized, what to look for in a good directors' and officers' liability insurance policy, and the effect of new state immunity statutes. It answers such questions as "What are the real risks and how can they be minimized?" "What should one look for in a good D&O policy?" "How much coverage is needed?" It is designed for the non-lawyer board member as a basic introduction to this topic. *Softcover, 38 pages, $25 (Nonmember); $15 (Member) (plus $2 shipping)*

Leaving Nothing to Chance: Achieving Board Accountability Through Risk Management
(NONPROFIT RISK MANAGEMENT CENTER, 1998)

▶ Risk management plays a fundamental role in the governance of a nonprofit, and every board is both responsible for the overall well-being of the organization and accountable to its constituencies. This new booklet outlines 10 steps for achieving board accountability through risk management, including formulating risk management policies; creating models for safe volunteer and staff activities, organizing a risk management committee; establishing sound financial management policies, ensuring proper management of the board's activities; and seeking expert help from trustworthy sources. *Softcover, 34 pages, $12*

Mission Accomplished: A Practical Guide to Risk Management for Nonprofits, 2nd Edition
(NONPROFIT RISK MANAGEMENT CENTER, 1999)

▶ A new section in the second edition of this popular Center publication addresses electronic risk management issues. Preventing misuse of Internet and e-mail privileges by employees and volunteers, protecting children on the Internet, limiting access to private or privileged information, protecting the organization's software and equipment from damaging computer viruses, and preventing the loss of valuable information through equipment failure are just a few of the issues addressed in this new section. In addition, this book explains the risk management process and helps you begin to integrate risk management techniques and strategies into your nonprofit's operations. *Softcover, 82 pages, $25.00*

More Than a Matter of Trust: Managing the Risks of Mentoring
(NONPROFIT RISK MANAGEMENT CENTER, 1998)

▶ Trust is a critical element in an effective mentoring relationship and has a devastating effect whenever that trust is broken. This book will help your organization avoid breaching that trust. This publication explores 10 keys to managing the risks of mentoring programs. It discusses the importance of understanding your clientele, selecting personnel, establishing program boundaries and the need for quality supervision. Gain practical insight into the effective management of mentoring programs. *Softcover, 59 pages, $15*

Nonprofit CARES (Computer Assisted Risk Evaluation System) (Software)
(NONPROFIT RISK MANAGEMENT CENTER)

▶ CARES™ is an assessment tool on CD-ROM that will help you examine your management and operational practices in depth. You'll build a detailed report with practical recommendations on how to make your organization safer and more secure without sacrificing your mission. CARES™ will guide you through a series of modules, each focusing on a different category of risk facing your nonprofit. The program starts with an *Introduction to Risk Management*, which provides the foundation you need to start a risk management program. CARES™ continues with modules on Employment Practices, Harm to Clients, Transportation, Contracts, and Special Events. Detailed information, including a Demo, Tour, and FAQ is available at *http://www.nonprofitrisk.org/cares/cares.htm. $89*

State Liability Laws for Charitable Organizations and Volunteers (See Legal Issues—Insurance, Liability & Risk Management for full description)

Investments

Nonprofit Investment Policies: Practical Steps for Growing Charitable Funds
ROBERT P. FRY JR. (JOHN WILEY & SONS, 1998)

▶ This guide is designed to help nonprofit organizations understand, develop, implement, and monitor their investment policies. By presenting the fundamentals of investing, from the Prudent Man Rule to portfolio management, it will help nonprofit managers with little or no financial background understand these underlying concepts. Brief overviews of relevant exempt organization and securities law will ensure that nonprofits are in compliance with all regulations.

Covering every element of investment strategy for nonprofits, the book explains investing legal concerns, the investment environment, the internal organization of an efficient charity, how to get started in investment, how to use investment successes as a fundraising tool, and much more.

The book includes an exploration of the unique characteristics of nonprofit resources, including endowment management, planned gifts, and socially responsible investing; a full examination of the legal issues involved in nonprofit investment—the tools officers and directors of charities need to protect themselves from investment liability in an increasingly litigious world; case studies from the real world of nonprofit investment showing successful policies in action—and failures that display policy pitfalls to avoid; advice on finding and hiring outside advisors, plus an explanation of the essentials of investment accounting and performance reporting; and tables and checklists to guide nonprofit managers in fiscal decision making. *Hardcover, 302 pages, $55*

The PRI Index: 500 Foundation Charitable Loans and Investments
CRYSTAL MANDLER, ED. (THE FOUNDATION CENTER, 1997)

▶ This volume features crucial facts on loans and other charitable investments made by the growing community of foundations that make program-related investments (PRIs). Listings of some 500 recent PRIs made by 125 foundations include funder name and state; recipient name, city, and state (or country); PRI amount; year of authorization or payment; and a description of the project funded. Four indexes guide PRI seekers to records by foundation location, subject/type of support, recipient name, and recipient location. Any nonprofit interested in pursuing this grant alternative should not miss this informative volume. *Softcover, 65 pages, $75*

Program-Related Investments: A Technical Manual for Foundations
CHRISTINE I. BAXTER (JOHN WILEY & SONS, 1997)

▶ Program-related investments (PRIs) are a hybrid grant/loan made by foundations to charities. Instead of simply giving away money, foundations make loans to, or otherwise invest in, grantees. Because the strategies, procedures, and administration of PRI loans are significantly different than those for grant making, this book presents all the information needed to establish and monitor PRIs. The raw materials in this book are invaluable, and the additional context, commentary, and insight made by the author clearly explain the whys and hows behind the documents. It is supplemented annually. *Hardcover, 448 pages, $135.00*

Software

(See also Products and Services)

CTS Guide to Selecting Software for Non-Profit Organizations and Trade Associations

(COMPUTER TRAINING SERVICES)

▶ CTS compares all the major features of software vendors' packages for nonprofit organizations and trade associations with each other, feature by feature. Then it compares those features to your needs. The *CTS Guide* gives you an in-depth analysis of two to three pages on each system. You read all about the software packages: what modules are available, operating systems/network options, minimum hardware required, types/sizes of target entities, ease of installation, updated windows releases, pricing, technical support, vendor/dealer training, year vendor started in business, number of installations, programming language(s) used, and source code availability. Tables categorize the software packages by the following criteria: functional area, platform (Windows, DOS, UNIX...), organization size; and organization type. It includes a section with tips and guidelines for selecting the best software package, written by an expert in that area: Fund Accounting & Reporting, Membership Management, Fund Raising/Alumni Development, Meeting & Conference Management, Grant Management, Religious Organization Management, Publication Management, and School & University Accounting. *Softcover, $99 (plus $5 shipping and handling)*

A Guide to Purchasing Fund Accounting Software

(M.I.P. FUND ACCOUNTING)

▶ Free

The NFC Accounting Software Selection Handbook

(NONPROFIT FINANCIAL CENTER)

▶ This is a comprehensive booklet that evaluates 26 commercially available general nonprofit and religious organization fund accounting software programs, including their features, costs, and FASB compliance. The *NFC Accounting Software Selection Handbook* will help any nonprofit or religious organization assess its accounting needs and evaluate the various software packages that address those needs. This practical Handbook includes chapters about accounting system requirements, the software selection process, cost summaries of popular packages for both simple and complex organizations, and evaluation grids that rate each program's features, ease of use, and hardware requirements. *$40.00*

Strategic Planning

Nonprofit Mergers and Alliances: A Strategic Planning Guide

THOMAS A. MCLAUGHLIN (JOHN WILEY & SONS, 1998)

▶ Mergers are no longer just for Wall Street. They've burst into the nonprofit sector, especially in the health care arena but also in a surprising array of other segments of this diverse community. Fundamentally, nonprofit mergers and other alliances are significantly different than corporate ones because they're not "stockholder" driven, and this underlying principle directly and indirectly affects many aspects of the merger. This clear, practical, step-by-step guide walks nonprofit managers through the merger process— from preliminary considerations to actual implementation. It focuses on the unique concerns of the nonprofit sector and contains easy-to-use checklists, analytical tables, real-world case studies, and insightful commentary. *Hardcover, 256 pages, $55.00*

Tax Reporting and Compliance

990 Deskbook

(PRACTITIONERS PUBLISHING COMPANY, 1999)

▶ *990 Deskbook* is a comprehensive reference manual (completely updated for changes made by the Revenue Reconciliation Act of 1993), designed to assist nonprofit accountants and accounting departments by providing line-by-line guidance for completing IRS Forms 990 (annual report), 990-PF (private funding return), and 1023 (application for 501(c)(3) status); along with dozens of time-saving, easy-to-use checklists and worksheets to help you simplify return preparation. It also includes information on Form 990 filing exceptions, disclosure requirements when soliciting nondeductible donations, identifying unrelated business income, determining when Form 990-T must be filed, and lobbying public charities. Also included are examples, sample completed forms, tables, and elections. Annual supplements are sent on approval. *906 pages, 2 volumes, $150 (includes shipping); 990 Print—$160, CD-ROM—$190, Both Versions—$240*

CCH Exempt Organizations Tax Library

(CCH)

▶ The Library is a comprehensive research tool, designed to assist not-for-profit and charitable organizations, as well as the tax, accounting, and legal professionals who advise them, in their handling of federal and state tax matters that confront exempt organizations. The Library addresses the tax needs of exempt organizations, and it provides the information needed to both qualify for and maintain tax-exempt status, and to meet compliance and reporting requirements to support an exemption. The CCH Tax Exempt Library consists of a collection of tax reference materials specific to exempt organizations, which cumulate to provide the information needed to structure effective strategies for tax-exempts. The Library includes: *The Tax-Exempt Advisor Newsletter* (designed to report monthly developments in the not-for-profit arena, as well as provide "how-to" insight by way of feature articles authored by recognized experts in the field); *The Practitioners Analysis* (provides practitioner-authored, experience-based explanations of the tax rules that affect exempt organizations); *Exempt Organizations Reporter* (includes exempt-related official text (Code, Regulations, cases, and rulings) as well as CCH-authored explanations and annotations); *State Exempt Laws and Explanations* (presents statutory text pertinent to exempt organizations for all 50 states as well as the District of Columbia, along with CCH explanations and digests to expedite research); *Internal Revenue Manual* (sets forth the IRS view of exempt-related matters with the *Exempt Organizations Handbook, Exempt Organizations Technical Guidelines Handbook,* and the *Private Foundations Handbook*); *IRS Technical Instruction Program Manual* (used by the IRS to help IRS Exempt Organization specialists keep abreast of the latest tax developments and learn examination techniques); *Forms and Publications* (supplies practitioners with interactive versions of the federal and state tax forms they need to meet the compliance requirements of not-for-profits and with pertinent IRS publications).

Subscriptions to *CCH Exempt Organizations Tax Library* are updated monthly. The text of the newsletter is seeded with hypertext links. When you click on a hypertext link, the full text of the document or explanation that pertains to the newsletter topic will appear. A "What's New" feature is also built into the menu of the "Welcome" segment of the Library, which lists those new developments of particular interest with hypertext links so that you can move directly to the new development that has been updated in the Library during the last update report cycle.

Completing Your IRS Form 990: A Guide for Tax-Exempt Organizations, Revised Edition
(Workbook/Manual)
ANDREW S. LANG AND MICHAEL SORRELLS (AMERICAN SOCIETY OF ASSOCIATION EXECUTIVES, 1999)

▶ This book is a line-by-line guide for preparing your organization's Form 990. It helps you understand the various items reported on the 990. The Form 990 you file may be much more widely circulated and available to the public at large in light of new federal public disclosure regulations. This increased exposure makes it even more important that your Form 990 be completed accurately, while reflecting your organization in the most favorable light possible. This exposure also may generate more questions. This guide will help you find many of the answers, helping you feel confident answering any questions that may arise. Authors Lang and Sorrells take you through Form 990 and IRS instructions section by section, examining areas of possible confusion and alerting readers to areas of particular scrutiny by the IRS. Throughout the guide, a hypothetical association is described to help you better understand each section of the form. The appendices to the guide include a sample completed Form 990 and the required schedules that were prepared for the hypothetical association. *Softcover, 136 pages, $38.40 (Nonmember), $32 (Member) (plus $6.25 shipping)*

Exempt Organizations Reports Library
(CCH)

▶ This resource provides the complete tax background that you need for structuring and advising organizations in the growing nonprofit sector. Monthly updates keep practitioners current on legislative and regulatory changes, rulings, cases, and other new developments. CCH explanations clarify complex federal rules. *Tax-Exempt Advisor* newsletter reports monthly developments with feature articles authored by experts in the area. CD-ROM/Internet also includes: *Internal Revenue Manual, IRS Technical Instruction Program Manual,* and *Select Forms and Publications. Volume 1— State Law* contains the full text of every state nonprofit corporation act, state registration and reporting requirements, and summaries of state charitable deductions and exemptions; *Volume 2—Federal Tax Law* contains provisions of the IRC pertaining to tax-exempt organizations, including regulations, explanations, and annotations; *Volume 3—New Developments* contains new developments and official materials affecting and regulating tax-exempt organizations. *Internet: Monthly updates; CD-ROM: One disc, Monthly updates; Print: Three loose-leaf volumes, Monthly updates*

Exempt Organizations Tax Digest
(WARREN, GORHAM & LAMONT, 1996)

▶ This comprehensive reference gives you instant access to important federal tax cases and rulings rendered since 1990 concerning tax-exempt organizations. All relevant reported decisions of federal courts and the IRS have been carefully reviewed, selected, and edited to present concise and easy-to-understand abstracts of complex cases affecting hospitals, private foundations, religious organizations, colleges and universities, charitable contributions, tax-exempt bonds, and compensation and benefits. Cumulative paperbound supplements are issued twice annually. *Casebound volume, $180.00*

Federal and State Taxation of Exempt Organizations
FRANCES R. BILL, BARBARA L. KIRSCHTEN, ROBERT E. ATKINSON JR., WENDELL R. BIRD, AND BONNIE S. BRIER (WARREN, GORHAM & LAMONT, 1994)

▶ This new treatise covers both state and federal taxation of fundraising and other activities of organizations that are tax-exempt under federal tax law. It focuses on current issues in the tax-exempt area (entrepreneurial initiatives, investment, and lobbying activities) that have resulted in closer governmental scrutiny. It helps your organization steer clear of trouble with in-depth analysis and practical guidance to help make certain your exempt organization is in full compliance with current rules and regulations. Provides guidance on such critical topics as unrelated business income tax (UBIT), health care organizations, lobbying rules (including newly enacted restrictions on deductibility of dues and disclosure requirements), comprehensive analysis of the private foundation rules, foreign organizations (especially activities conducted abroad by U.S. exempt organizations), in-depth analysis of tax issues relating to investments in derivative products, complex structures of affiliated tax-exempt organizations or exempt and taxable entities, and operations of exempt organizations. Also included is extensive coverage of trade associations, business leagues, and investment portfolios. Other features include a comprehensive topical index, tables of cases, IRS rulings and announcements, sections of the Internal Revenue Code and Treasury regulations, coverage of significant pending cases, and more. Cumulative loose-leaf supplements are issued twice annually. *Loose-leaf volume, $190.00 (plus $11.45 shipping)*

Getting Started With Not-for-Profit Organization Tax Issues (Continuing Professional Education)
ROB LYONS (AMERICAN SOCIETY OF ASSOCIATION EXECUTIVES)

▶ For public practitioners as well as financial managers, this program teaches how not-for-profits work, their fundamental tax problems, and how to achieve tax savings and address special needs to overcome their commonly faced obstacles. Course highlights include qualifying for not-for-profit status, unrelated business income taxes (UBIT), private foundations, joint ventures and alternative structures, Form 990, charitable organizations, and practical examples and case studies. *$149.00 (Nonmember), $119.00 (Member)*

Law & Taxation, Leadership Series, Volume I
JILL MUEHRCKE, ED. (THE SOCIETY OF NONPROFIT ORGANIZATIONS, 1993)

▶ In articles selected from the *Nonprofit World* journal, authors give practical advice on such topics as how to handle an IRS audit, how to avoid litigation, and how to safeguard your organization's tax-exempt status. *$20 (Nonmember), $17 (Member) (plus $4.50 shipping)*

Law & Taxation, Leadership Series, Volume II
JILL MUEHRCKE, ED. (THE SOCIETY OF NONPROFIT ORGANIZATIONS)

▶ This collection of articles from *Nonprofit World* (November 1989–September 1993) discusses such topics as the Americans with Disabilities Act, liability insurance for nonprofits, how to avoid litigation, and how to safeguard your tax-exempt status. *$20 (Nonmember), $17 (Member) (plus $4.50 shipping)*

The Law of Tax-Exempt Organizations *(See Legal Issues—Tax-Exemption for full description)*

Managing for Profit in the Nonprofit World *(See General Management—General for full description)*

Obtaining and Maintaining Exemption from Income Taxes
GERARD M. ZACK (NONPROFIT RESOURCE CENTER)

▶ This resource provides all the do's and don'ts of tax exemption, from the basic qualifying characteristics to thorough discussions of private inurement, excess benefit transactions, and political activities and lobbying; Also included is how to properly complete Form 990 and Schedule A and compliance with the contribution reporting and disclosure rules. *$49 (Nonmember), $36 (Member) (includes shipping and handling)*

Tackling Tough Tax Topics in Nonprofit Organizations (Continuing Professional Education)
ROBERT LYONS (AMERICAN SOCIETY OF ASSOCIATION EXECUTIVES)

▶ Refer here for specific, practical coverage of the hottest issues bedeviling CPAs who work for or advise nonprofits. You'll get the latest on UBIT, use of for-profit subsidiaries, compliance, and lobbying—along with savvy solutions to the problems "taxing" today's NPO. Course highlights include the latest tax law changes affecting nonprofits; dealing with tricky Form 990 issues; use of multiple structures within nonprofits; hot issues in unrelated business income; income ventures—current trends and techniques; effect of health care changes on nonprofits; and debt financed income. *$149.00 (Nonmember), $119.00 (Member)*

Tax Planning and Compliance for Tax-Exempt Organizations: Forms, Checklists, Procedures, 3rd Edition *(See also Legal Issues—Tax Exemption)*
JODY BLAZEK (JOHN WILEY & SONS, 1999)

▶ This book provides clear, concise instructions for filing 990s and other important IRS forms and documents; obtaining tax exemp-

tion; reporting to boards, auditors, and the IRS; testing ongoing tax compliance; and managing lobbying expenditures and unrelated business income. It also incorporates expanded discussions of definitions of different types of nonprofits, qualifying under various categories, unrelated business income, employment taxes, joint ventures and partnerships, loss of exemption, and bankruptcy. Includes easy-to-use checklists, line-by-line instructions for completing applications and forms, sample documents, practice aids, and tips and suggestions for handling special situations. It includes a section on the proposed regulation on the reporting and record-keeping requirements for voluntary donations, the most common form of income for a nonprofit organization and includes checklists and complete citations. Annual supplements keep subscribers apprised of relevant changes in IRS forms, requirements, and procedures. *Hardcover, 818 pages, $135*

Teitell's Portable Planned Giving Manual *(See Resource Development—Deferred and Planned Giving for full description)*

The Unrelated Business Income Tax
GERARD M. ZACK (NONPROFIT RESOURCE CENTER, 1999)

▶ A thorough exploration of all the rules and regulations associated with UBIT, including numerous letter rulings and court decisions as examples to aid in determining whether activities are taxable, as well as in planning to avoid UBIT. *$49 (Nonmember), $36 (Member) (includes shipping and handling)*

What a Difference Knowledge Makes: A Guide to Intermediate Sanctions for 501(c)(3) and 501(c)(4) Organizations (Accountants for the Public Interest)

▶ This publication will cover Intermediate Sanctions, a bill that was signed into law last year as part of the Taxpayer's Bill of Rights II. This law penalizes insiders who receive an excess benefit from their involvement with 501(c)(3) and 501(c)(4) organizations. Any person who is defined as having power or influence in an organization's decision making should learn about this bill. Intermediate Sanctions target two groups of individuals within 501(c)(3) and 501(c)(4) organizations: persons of influence and managers. This book provides the necessary information to navigate the regulatory pitfalls covered under the Intermediate Sanctions law. *$12.95*

PERIODICALS AND SUBSCRIPTION SERVICES

Accounting Technology (11 Monthly Issues)

Faulkner Gray Inc., 11 Penn Plaza, New York, NY 10001
Tel: 800-535-8403 (Subscription services), 212-967-7060
E-mail: bob_scott@faulknergray.com;
WWW: http://www.faulknergray.com/account/actt.htm

▶ *Accounting Technology* delivers practical answers and "how-to" guidance from accounting and tax professionals who know what you want from your systems, software, and telecommunications equipment. From boosting productivity to cutting technology acquisition costs, *Accounting Technology* brings you the issues that concern you and your colleagues most. It provides practical information you'll need to take full advantage of the time-saving, money-making potential of today's emerging technology that you will want to put to work. *$61/year (plus $4.95 postage and handling)*

Accounting Today—The Business Newspaper for the Tax and Accounting Community
(Biweekly Newspaper)

Faulkner Gray Inc., 11 Penn Plaza, New York, NY, 10001
Tel: 800-535-8403 (Subscription services), 212-967-7000
E-mail: rick_telberg@faulknergray.com (Rick Telberg, Editor);
WWW: http://www.faulknergray.com/account/acttoday.htm

▶ This is the only twice-monthly newspaper devoted to the business of accounting. *Accounting Today* delivers action-oriented news reports and hands-on guidance that will keep you up to date on the latest trends and developments in the accounting profession. Regular columns include Opinion, Tax Practice, Audit Accounting, Practice Management, Technology, New Products, People. Each issue also includes a few stories about news in the area of taxation or accounting. *36 pages, $84 (plus $4.95 shipping and handling)*

CFO: The Magazine for Senior Financial Executives
(Monthly Magazine)

253 Summer Street, Boston, MA 02210
Tel: 800-877-5416 (Subscriptions), 617-345-9700;
FAX: 617-951-4090
E-mail: JuliaHomer@cfopub.com (Editor);
WWW: http://www.cfonet.com

▶ Each month, *CFO* magazine provides 435,000 senior financial executives with the sophisticated analysis and innovative ideas they need to add value to their organizations. From refinancing to reengineering, from insurance to information systems, *CFO* magazine takes the latest financial thinking and shows how it is being implemented in the country's most innovative organizations. In the increasingly competitive arena of corporate finance, *CFO* keeps its readers on the inside track. It is distributed free to qualified senior financial executives in the United States.

CPA Government & Nonprofit Report (Monthly Newsletter)

Harcourt Brace Professional Publishing, 6277 Sea Harbor Drive, Orlando, FL 32821-9816
Tel: 800-831-7799; FAX: 800-874-6418/336-7377
WWW: http://www.hbpp.com/index.html

Editorial Offices:
Harcourt Professional Publishing, 525 B Street, Suite 1900, San Diego, CA 92101-4495
Tel: 619-699-6716; FAX: 619-699-6542
E-mail: propub@harcourtbrace.com (Rhett Harrell, Editor)

▶ This newsletter provides comprehensive and timely publication devoted exclusively to governmental and nonprofit accounting and auditing. It includes the latest updates and analyses of issues affecting your organization (guidance for audits of nonprofits, coverage of state and local government reporting issues, overviews of projects on which the FASB, GAO, AICPA, and the GASB are working); specific, detailed, and comprehensive coverage of all the issues affecting those who receive governmental financial assistance and those who perform audits of that assistance; and a "Question Corner" devoted exclusively to the financial issues and problems facing your organization. Each monthly issue is filled with strategies you can use immediately, including Late-Breaking News Affecting Recipients of Governmental Funds and Those Who Audit Them; Methods for Handling Endowments Under FASB 124; Guidance on Governmental and Nonprofit Accounting and Auditing; Coverage of the AICPA's New Single Audit Reports; Ongoing Analysis and Guidance Regarding OMB A-133; and overviews of FASB, GAO, AICPA, and GASB projects. *8 pages, $257/year (plus shipping)*

The CPA Journal

New York State Society of Certified Public Accountants, Attn: Circulation Dept., 530 Fifth Avenue, 5th Floor, New York, NY 10036-5101
Tel: 800-877-4522 (for credit card orders, or to request a subscription application), 212-719-8300
WWW: http://www.cpajournal.com,
http://www.nysscpa.org/cpaj.htm (Archives),
http://www.nysscpa.org/useful_links/accounting.html

▶ A technical-refereed publication aimed at public practitioners, management, educators, and other accounting professionals. It is edited by CPAs for CPAs. Its goal is to provide CPAs and other accounting professionals with the information and news to enable them to be successful accountants, managers, and executives in today's practice environments. Provides interpretative analysis of tax, accounting, and other professional developments. *The CPA Journal* is published monthly by the New York State Society of Certified Public Accountants. *$42/year*

The CPA Software News

110 North Bell Street, Suite 300, Shawnee, OK 74801
Tel: 800-456-0864, 405-275-3100; FAX: 405-275-3101
E-mail: editor@cpasoftwarenews.com,
tawn.rose@cygnuspub.com (Tawn Allen Rose, CPA,
Editor/Publisher); WWW: http://www.cpasoftwarenews.com/,
http://www.softwarenews.net/advertising/buyers_guide.htm

▶ As the independent voice for accountants' software, *The CPA Software News* is dedicated to making purchasing decisions easier for more accounting firms than any other publication. *The CPA Software News* helps accountants implement software productively by offering independent and in-depth software comparisons as well as detailed charts, tables, and graphs. It also assists accountants in advising business clients who are making software decisions. Over 500 reviews per year will keep you informed of the latest trends in accounting software. Regular features include The General Ledger, Marketing Your Firm, Practice Management, Tricks & Tips, The Bleeding Edge, and Networks. It provides the Buyer's Guide, available online at *http://www.cpasoftwarenews.com/advertising/buyers_guide.htm* and fee-based Software Search (*http://www.cpasoftwarenews.com/misc/software_search.htm*). $39.95/year

Charitable Gift Planning News

Moerschbaecher, McCoy & Simmons, P.O. Box 214373, Dallas, TX 75221
Tel: 214-978-3325, 214-328-4244; FAX: 214-349-2209
E-mail: carolcgpn@aol.com, stonec@tklaw.com

▶ $168/year

Charitable Giving and Solicitation (Monthly Service)

Warren, Gorham & Lamont, 117 E Stevens Avenue, Valhalla, NY 10595
Tel: 800-950-1216

▶ Written by three veteran tax attorneys, this monthly service provides the specialized tax-planning insight you need to help your donor clients realize the greatest possible tax benefits from charitable giving. *Charitable Giving and Solicitation* offers in-depth analysis of the tax ramifications of and filing requirements for current charitable contributions and deductions, as well as more sophisticated planned and deferred giving programs; examples, tips, and warnings that clarify and illustrate each discussion; monthly reports that alert you to the latest charitable giving laws, cases, rulings, and IRS requirements; practical worksheets that simplify the computation of charitable deductions; up-to-date IRS valuation tables that help you develop tax answers and sound recommendations for present and potential donors; and sample formats most approved by the IRS to help you quickly design tax-advantaged giving programs. Additionally, a special section on fund raising gives you case histories of effective campaigns and techniques, as well as practical guidance on how to make these successes your own. Annual subscription includes monthly updates and report bulletins. *One loose-leaf volume, $205/year*

Charitable Giving Tax Service

R&R Newkirk, 8695 South Archer, Suite 10, Willow Springs, IL 60480
Tel: 800-342-2375; FAX: 708-839-9207
E-mail: newkirk2@aol.com; WWW: http://www.rrnewkirk.com

▶ *Charitable Giving Tax Service* (CGTS) is a comprehensive, thoroughly indexed reference and resource library that is updated every other month to remain current with developments in the area of planned giving. It provides quick access to valuable tax and financial planning information and is presented in an easy-to-read style. The four-volume CGTS is divided into 12 sections covering the following topics: federal income tax, charitable contributions of individuals and corporations, gift annuities, the federal estate tax, the federal gift tax, charitable bequests, charitable remainder trusts, unrelated business income, pooled income funds, charitable lead trusts, state regulations, and life insurance gifts. *Four-Volume CGTS Library $250 (plus shipping and handling), Update Service 1-year subscription $186*

Community Risk Management and Insurance (Newsletter)

Nonprofit Risk Management Center, 1001 Connecticut Avenue NW, Suite 900, Washington, DC 20036
Tel: 202-785-3891; FAX: 202-296-0349
E-mail: info@nonprofitrisk.org; WWW: http://www.nonprofitrisk.org

▶ *Community Risk Management and Insurance* is the Nonprofit Risk Management Center's newsletter. The print edition is distributed three times each year to more than 15,000 nonprofits. Each issue of *Community Risk Management and Insurance* covers a wide spectrum of risk management issues, showcases the Center's training and workshop sessions, and highlights other crucial nonprofit risk management issues. It provides the latest updates on risk management and insurance as it relates to the nonprofit sector. It is a collection of practical articles about strategies for reducing risks, protecting against liability, obtaining all types of insurance, and managing employee benefits programs. *Nonprofit Organizations and Government Agencies—Free, For-Profit Businesses and Individuals—$25 per year*

Estate Planner (Bimonthly Newsletter)

Clark Nuber & Company, CPAs, Not-for-Profit Services Group, 10900 NE 4th St., Suite 1700, Bellevue, WA 98004
Tel: 425-454-4919; FAX: 425-454-4620
WWW: http://www.cnuber.com/default.asp,
http://www.cnuber.com/publications/default.asp#Books

▶ This bimonthly newsletter provides timely information to those interested in succession and wealth preservation strategies. Topics include tips for reducing estate and gift taxes, marital and retirement planning, creating wills, and protecting assets. *Estate Planner* deals with issues relating to minors, the elderly, and the disabled. Articles present strategies for leveraging gifts, using insurance, creating trusts, timing retirement plan distributions, transferring wealth between spouses, and making charitable gifts to take maximum advantage of tax breaks. *Estate Planner* also keeps you abreast of legislative and tax code changes that may affect your current succession plan. *Free*

Estate Planner's Alert (Monthly Newsletter)

RIA Tax, 117 East Stevens Avenue, Valhalla, NY 10595
Tel: 800-950-1216

▶ This newsletter provides a monthly spotlight on critical developments in estate planning with highlights of the latest issues, trends, and techniques. It offers practical guidance for minimizing your clients' taxes and enhancing your practice. Warnings of potential pitfalls help you avoid costly oversights. A binder is provided for easy storage. *$155/year*

Estate Planning Review (Monthly Newsletter)

CCH, 4025 West Peterson Avenue, Chicago, IL 60646
Tel: 800-248-3248
E-mail: info@cch.com; WWW: http://tax.cch.com

▶ Stay on top of the latest financial and estate planning trends with this monthly newsletter edited by CCH editors in consultation with renowned expert Sidney Kess. *Estate Planning Review* reports and interprets the meaning and planning implications of legislative, judicial, and administrative changes. Each monthly issue, covering a wide range of topics, keeps you in touch with current planning techniques and key financial and estate planning developments. Other helpful features, including a Table of Contents on the front page of every issue, along with annual indexing, make this newsletter perfect to retain for future reference. *$206.00/year*

The Exempt Organization Tax Review (Monthly Journal, with Quarterly Indexes and EOTR Weekly)

Tax Analysts, 6830 Fairfax Drive, Arlington, VA 22213
Tel: 800-955-2444 (Customer Service), 703-533-4400;
FAX: 7030533-4444
E-mail: webmaster@tax.org; WWW: http://www.tax.org/

▶ Each issue contains the latest news on significant developments from the IRS, Treasury, and Capitol Hill, along with insightful special reports written by leading EO practitioners. The EOTR is an excellent source for summaries of all letter rulings dealing with EO subjects, and many full-text documents. They also bring you interviews with EO newsmakers, the full text of pertinent IRS guidance, EO tax news from all 50 states and from around the world, and updates on current EO litigation. Each month *The Exempt Organization Tax Review* includes the latest developments from the IRS, Treasury, Capitol Hill, and the courts, along with insightful special reports written by leading EO practitioners. Each issue of the EOTR contains special features, such as the Letter Ruling Alert. Written by an EO tax practitioner, the letter ruling alert will keep subscribers informed on new and noteworthy technical advice memorandums (TAMs) and private letter rulings. Summaries of all TAMs and letter rulings dealing with EO subjects are also included, as are the full texts of significant rulings.

Special features include sections of the Internal Revenue Code pertaining to tax-exempt organizations, including private foundations, are reproduced, accompanied by pertinent regulations, explanations annotations similar to the coverage offered in *CCH Standard Federal Tax Reporter;* the federal tax and information returns forms required by exempt organizations and charitable trusts are reproduced in facsimile; descriptions of timely articles published in legal periodicals; Internal Revenue Service publications that relate to exempt organizations and charitable contributions, as well as the official texts of the Internal Revenue Service handbooks on exempt organizations and private foundations; a newsletter, *Tax Exempt Advisor,* accompanies each report, announcing and summarizing developments reported in full text in the loose-leaf pages.

In addition to news coverage and helpful, full-text documents, you will also find interviews with EO newsmakers and edited transcripts of the three ABA Exempt Organization Committee meetings held each year. Features include News and Analysis; Special Reports; ABA Transcripts; State Law Survey; Charitable Giving Update; Conference Notes; IRS Letter Rulings—Letter Ruling Alert; Focus on IRS; Focus on Treasury; Focus on Congress; Letters to the Editor; Court Opinions; Current Litigation Status Report—updates on current EO legislation; State Tax News—EO tax news from all 50 states; and Press Watch.

Included with your EOTR subscription is the *EOTR Weekly* newsletter containing the latest tax news and developments affecting exempt organizations. *EOTR Weekly* includes information on the latest IRS letter rulings, court opinions, and compliance initiatives. It will bring you up to speed on all the EO tax news you need each week at no additional cost. *EOTR Weekly* can also be subscribed to separately (see separate listing). *$749.95/year*

EOTR Weekly

Tax Analysts, 6830 North Fairfax Drive, Arlington, VA 22313
Tel: 800-955-2444 (Customer Service), 703-533-4400;
FAX: 703-533-4444
E-mail: webmaster@tax.org; WWW: http://www.tax.org/

▶ *EOTR Weekly* is designed to keep the tax professional in touch with all the important developments in exempt organizations tax law. This weekly newsletter contains timely reports from the IRS, Treasury, and the courts, as well as news of state level and international events that will affect exempt organizations. Features include articles on all EO tax news and developments from IRS, Treasury, and the courts; all state and local EO tax news and special reports; abstracts and citations; exemption rulings; and service releases. *EOTR Weekly* is also available for free with a subscription to *The Exempt Organization Tax Review* (see separate listing). *$129.95/year*

Exempt Organizations Reporter (Federal and State Coverage) (Monthly Service)

CCH Incorporated, 4025 West Peterson Avenue, Chicago, IL 60646
Tel: 800-449-8114 or 888-224-7377 (Sales); FAX: 800-221-4240
E-mail: Shellie_Mild@cch.com

2700 Lake Cook Road, Riverwoods, IL 60015
Tel: 847-267-7024
E-mail: larry_perlman@cch.com (Larry Perlman, Writer/Analyst); WWW: http://www.cch.com

▶ *Exempt Organizations Reporter* provides effective guidance on the fast-developing and changing federal rules that affect and regulate tax-exempt organizations, including private foundations. State laws are also covered. Monthly reports for use with three loose-leaf volumes keep subscribers posted on the sweep of new developments and changes in such pertinent federal tax areas as tax-exempt status, investment income, donor–foundation interactivity, trustees' dealings, unrelated business income, prohibited expenditures, information reporting rules, termination of private foundation status, and the like. New laws, amendments, regulations, administrative rulings, court decisions, and other official materials affecting and regulating tax-exempt organizations, including private foundations, are promptly reported and indexed by subject, case name, and number for quick reference. The monthly reports put the new rules in proper perspective and protect nonprofit organizations from loss of exempt status or excise taxation by pinpointing the complex federal requirements. Throughout, CCH Explanations help subscribers adapt their practices and activities to comply with the developing complex federal rules. Covered on the federal level are the rules and regulations for qualifying for tax-exempt status, income tax controls and sanctions, excise taxes on net investment income, donor–foundation transactions, mandatory income payout, speculative investments, unrelated business interests, voluntary and involuntary termination of private foundation status, charitable remainder trusts, and estate and gift tax consequences of charitable transfers.

Pertinent state not-for-profit statutes covering articles of incorporation, charter amendments, dissolution, and voting requirements are reproduced in a uniform manner to allow subscribers to check the rules in one state or in all the states. Also reproduced are the state provisions for registration and reporting by nonprofit corporations and charitable trusts. The state laws on charitable contribution deductions; exemption from income, property, and sales taxes; and nontax limitations on charitable giving are presented in summary form. *Annual Pricing: $956.00, Government: $823.00, School: $823.00*

Harvard Business Review *(See General Management— Periodicals for full description)*

Inc. (Magazine) *(See General Management—Periodicals for full description)*

Inside Nonprofit Accountability *(See Legal Issues— Periodicals for full description)*

Journal of Accountancy
American Institute of Certified Public Accountants (AICPA), 1211 Avenue of the Americas, New York, NY 10036-8775
Tel: 888-777-7077 (Subscriptions), 201-938-3100 (Membership Administration Division), 212-596-6003 (General Inquiries);
FAX: 212-596-6128
E-mail: joaed@aicpa.org;
WWW: http://www.aicpa.org/pubs/jofa/index.htm
▶ *Journal of Accountancy* is a monthly publication of the AICPA that focuses on the latest news and developments related to the field of accounting. The *Journal* is written for CPAs and other accounting professionals. *$59/year*

The Journal of Gift Planning (Quarterly)
National Committee on Planned Giving, 233 McCrea Street, Suite 400, Indianapolis, IN 46225
Tel: 317-269-6274; FAX: 317-269-6276
E-mail: ncpg@iupui.edu;
WWW: http://www.ncpg.org/journal.html
▶ *The Journal of Gift Planning* is intended to facilitate and encourage the education and training of the many different professionals in the planned giving community. It provides its readers with timely, advanced, and comprehensive information on all aspects of planned giving. Original articles and columns appear in each issue of the journal. Every issue includes an article in each of the following subject areas: technical, advanced gift planning, marketing/sales, and how-to/basics. Also included are legislative and tax updates, educational opportunities, panel discussions, letters to the editor, and more. A discounted subscription rate for *The Journal* is a benefit of membership in an NCPG-affiliated council. *$45.00 (Nonmember), $22.50 (NCPG Member)*

The Journal of Taxation of Exempt Organizations (Bimonthly Magazine)
Warren, Gorham & Lamont, 117 E Stevens Avenue, Valhalla, NY 10595
Tel: 800-950-1216
WWW: http://www.riatax.com/journals/eotj/eotjfred.html
▶ *The Journal of Taxation of Exempt Organizations* provides tax analysis and guidance to members of the exempt organization community. It is directed to the professional advisors of these organizations and their contributors, as well as to members of the

organizations' management. Its goal is to provide the tax information that these organizations need to negotiate the rapid changes of the new business and regulatory environment. Articles cover intermediate sanctions, combinations and joint ventures, health care organizations, exemption and compliance, private foundations, political and lobbying activity, the unrelated business income tax, charitable giving, compensation, and many other topics. It focuses on tax strategies, and tax-related business and financial strategies, that can help nonprofit organizations succeed financially while maintaining their exempt status. It offers analysis of the tax problems and concerns faced by nonprofit organizations and problem-solving approaches used by experts in exempt tax planning. *$195/year (includes shipping)*

Nonprofit Adviser
Reznick Fedder & Silverman, CPAs, Nonprofit Services Group, 4520 East West Highway, Suite 300, Bethesda, MD 20814-3319
Tel: 800-694-4376 (Baltimore), 301-652-9100;
FAX: 301-652-1848
E-mail: cpa@rfs.com, corines@rss.com (Corine Sheridan, Dir. of Marketing), gary@rfs.com (Gary Pokrant, Managing Editor);
WWW: http://www.rfs.com/non-profit_advisor.shtml
▶ *Nonprofit Adviser* is designed to enhance the role of the nonprofit association and its director and executive board by providing advice on critical issues such as fund raising, organizational strategies, working with the media, growth management, tax-advantaged donations, and assurance services. Also available online.

The Nonprofit Board Report *(See Governance— Periodicals for full description)*

Nonprofit Business Alert
Aspen Publishers, Inc., 7201 McKinney Circle, P.O. Box 990, Frederick, MD 21701-9782
Tel: 800-638-8437 (Subscriptions), 301-417-7500;
FAX: 301-417-7550
WWW: http://www.aspenpublishers.com
▶ Today's nonprofit must operate intelligently and efficiently to survive, prosper, and serve its public. *Nonprofit Business Alert* is a life vest for the modern organization, featuring up-to-the-minute business information and ideas. Included in each essential issue is fresh guidance on such hot button topics as taxation, donations, compensation, commercial ventures, retirement plans, and technology. For the chief executive, top financial officer, or savvy fund raiser, *Nonprofit Business Alert* offers intelligence, not fluff. Each issue is packed with insights on how to take advantage of exciting opportunities and how to avoid the pitfalls that are commonplace in today's rapidly changing landscape. *16 pages, $258/year*

The Nonprofit Counsel (Monthly Newsletter)
John Wiley & Sons, Inc., Subscription Department, 605 Third Avenue, New York, NY 10158-0012
Tel: 800-825-7750, 212-850-6347
E-mail: subinfo@wiley.com
▶ Edited by Bruce R. Hopkins, in eight fact-filled pages each month, *The Nonprofit Counsel* offers up-to-the-minute articles on subjects like federal, state, and local challenges to tax exemption; lobbying restrictions, court ruling related to unrelated business income, emerging opportunities for nonprofits, and more. *$179/year*

Nonprofit Issues *(See Legal Issues—Periodicals for full description)*

Nonprofit Legal and Tax Letter *(See Legal Issues— Periodicals for full description)*

Nonprofit Navigator (Quarterly Newsletter)
Harmon, Curran, Spielberg & Eisenberg, LLP, 1726 M Street NW, Suite 600, Washington, D.C. 20036
Tel: 202-328-3500; FAX: 202-328-6918
E-mail: navigator@harmoncurran.com,
dsmith@harmoncurran.com (Doug Smith, Assistant Editor),
HCSE@HarmonCurran.com (Gail Harmon);
WWW: http://www.harmoncurran.com

▶ *Nonprofit Navigator* is Harmon, Curran, Spielberg & Eisenberg, LLP's monthly newsletter on law and policy of interest to the nonprofit community. *Nonprofit Navigator* discusses and explains new developments in areas ranging from employment law to Federal Election Commission compliance to recent court cases and new regulations. *8 pages, $115 (includes shipping and handling)*

Nonprofit Report: Accounting, Taxation & Management (Newsletter)
Warren, Gorham & Lamont, Research Institute of America, Thomson Tax & Accounting, 395 Hudson Street, New York, NY 10014
Tel: 800-431-9025, 950-1216, 212-367-6300
E-mail: customer_services@riag.com;
WWW: http://www.riahome.com/default.asp

▶ This newsletter offers CPAs with nonprofit clients—and professionals working in the nonprofit sector—a practical, timely look at today's key nonprofit issues, including IRS rulings and pronouncements, AICPA changes, and legislation governing financial management of most nonprofit organizations. The *Report* delivers effective strategies for making these changes work to your advantage. *$190/year*

Nonprofit Tax & Financial Strategies (Biweekly Newsletter—24 Issues)
(Merger of Not-for-Profit Financial Strategies and Nonprofit Executive Tax Letter newsletters)
Harcourt Brace Professional Publishing, 6277 Sea Harbor Drive, Orlando, FL 32887-6777
Tel: 800-831-7799 (Subscriptions), 619-699-6848 (Article Inquiries); FAX: 201-592-0320

Harcourt Professional Publishing, 525 B Street, Suite 1900, San Diego, CA 92101-4495
Tel: 619-699-6716; FAX: 619-699-6542
E-mail: propub@harcourt.com;
WWW: http://www.hbpp.com/index.html

▶ Each issue of this biweekly publication includes tax law changes and rulings, plus practical ways for you to avoid crackdowns and take advantage of new opportunities. You'll also receive information about successful methods for increasing donations and building your organization's tax-free income. Written by a team of nonprofit experts, this resource will help to protect your organization's income from taxes and penalties. It will keep you up to date on charitable donations, compensation benefits, corporate giving, exempt status, IRS procedures, new legislation, payroll, foundations, and retirement plans, in addition to other issues that affect financing and your nonprofit organization. *$207.00/year*

Not-for-Profit Newsletter (Quarterly)
Clark Nuber & Company, CPAs, Not-for-Profit Services Group, 10900 NE 4th Street, Suite 1700, Bellevue, WA 98004
Tel: 425-454-4919; FAX: 425-454-4620
WWW: http://www.cnuber.com/default.asp

▶ *Not-for-Profit Newsletter* is published quarterly by Clark Nuber and contains current topics of interest to the not-for-profit community. The articles are written by Nuber's staff and are tailored to the relevant needs of nonprofit clients and friends. Recent articles include not-for-profit tax law changes such as corporate sponsorship payments, board development, directors' and officers' liability issues, and other similar topics. *Free*

The PPC Nonprofit Update (Monthly Newsletter)
Practitioners Publishing Company, P.O. Box 966, Fort Worth, TX 76101-0966
Tel: 800-323-8724; FAX: 817-877-1383/3694
E-mail: ppc@onramp.net, Customer.Service@ppctx.com;
WWW: http://www.ppcnet.com

▶ This newsletter keeps you current on new developments in accounting, auditing, taxation, and single audits of nonprofit organizations. Written specifically for nonprofit financial officers, accountant auditors, and tax advisors, it gives you news and highlighted tips that you can put to use immediately. It covers new developments in accounting, auditing, taxation, and single audits of nonprofit organizations. You will learn how to apply the newest accounting, auditing, and tax standards and regulations. It helps you determine exactly how the newest developments will affect your nonprofit organization. *6 pages, $132/year*

The Philanthropy Monthly (10 Issues) *(See also Legal Issues—Periodicals, Resource Development—Periodicals)*
Box 989, New Milford, CT 06776
Tel: 860-354-7132
E-mail: hsuhrke@AOL.COM

▶ *The Philanthropy Monthly* provides commentary on not-for-profit accounting. It concentrates on legal aspects of fund raising for grant makers and grant seekers, with particular focus on tax news, accounting, compensation and benefits, state and IRS regulations, congressional legislative developments, state and federal litigation on nonprofits, and academic research. Articles concentrate on general issues in philanthropy and tax and legal aspects of fund raising for grant makers and grant seekers. *$84/year, $65/year (501(c)(3) charities)*

The Planned Gifts Counselor (Monthly)
Practical Publishing, 1602 W. 1050 North, Provo, UT 84604-3062
Tel: 877-PGC-0499, 801-802-8930, 801-375-3155
E-mail: pschneit@inquo.net (Paul Schneiter, Editor);
WWW: http://www.premieradministration.com

▶ How do you identify the best planned giving prospects . . . how do you cultivate and solicit them? How do you recruit effective development board members . . . how do you train them, motivate them, honor them? How do you attract truly excellent individuals to your development staff (and how do you know they're truly excellent)? How do you organize and conduct effective estate-planning seminars? How do you prepare direct mail pieces that "pull"? How do you tactfully disengage from an ineffective board member? How do you market charitable bequests, life insurance policies, gift annuities, charitable trusts, and bargain sales? How do you use annual giving, special events, and other fund-raising methodologies to nurture your organization? Prepared by nonprofit professionals Paul H. Schneiter and Alden B. Tueller, JD, this newsletter focuses on news, analysis, announcements, and successful strategies. Regular features include Web Sites That Click, Seminars to Attend, and book reviews. *8 pages, $150.00/year*

Planned Giving Today (Monthly Newsletter)

100 Second Avenue South, Suite 180, Edmonds, WA 98020-3551
Tel: 800-525-5748 (KALL-PGT), 425-744-3837 (PG-4EVER);
FAX: 425-744-3838
E-mail: pgt@pgtoday.com, roger@pgtoday.com (G. Roger Schoenhals, Publisher and Editor);
WWW: http://www.pgtoday.com

► A publication dedicated to helping gift planners enable others to give generously, prudently, and joyfully, *Planned Giving Today* promotes thoughtful giving as a way of life for the universal benefit of society. Subscribers receive a resource supplement, *The PGT Marketplace*, containing news about services, products, and employment opportunities of interest to the charitable gift planner. *The PGT Marketplace* also includes a comprehensive listing of current training events for gift planners. In addition, subscribers receive a handy "Rate of the Month" card for easy access to the Applicable Federal Mid-Term Rate (AFR). Also available are PGT on CD and Index on Disk, as well as additional books and articles about planned giving. *12 pages, $179/year*

Practical Accountant (Monthly)

Faulkner Gray Inc., 11 Penn Plaza, New York, NY, 10001
Tel: 800-535-8403 (Subscriptions), 212-967-7060
WWW: http://www.faulknergray.com/account/prac.htm

► *Practical Accountant* is designed to keep accounting practitioners on the leading edge with monthly practical tax and accounting money-making advice and time-saving tips. From compliance to cost-effective management techniques, their regular features include: News Front, Practitioner's Update (news for CPAs), Tax Alert (new IRS regulations), Tax Briefs (judicial rulings), Inside the IRS (news about IRS practices), Financial Planning, Tech News (new software and hardware), Accounting & Audit Report, ERISA and Compensation Report, Products & Service Showcase, Web Directory, and Last Word. *Practical Accountant* is geared primarily to smaller practices, while its sister publication *Accounting Today* is geared toward large, "Big Six" accounting firms. *80 pages, $65/year (plus $4.95 postage and handling)*

The Tax-Exempt Organization Alert (Monthly Newsletter)

Nonprofit Resouce Center, 7731 Belle Point Drive, Greenbelt, MD 20770
Tel: 800-883-6247, 301-507-6247; FAX: 301-507-6250
E-mail: info@nonprofitresource.com, questions@nonprofitresource.com;
WWW: http://www.nonprofitresource.com

► This newsletter offers practical advice to keep you current on all important accounting, audit, tax, and financial developments in the nonprofit community for nonprofit CFOs and CPA firms serving nonprofit organizations. It includes feature articles and recurring columns such as Tax Update, MIS Corner, In The News, Lists & References, and Reminders. There is also an online version of the newsletter for members of the Nonprofit Resource Network on their Web site. *8–12 pages, $115/year*

Taxwise Giving (Monthly Newsletter) *(See also Resource Development—Periodicals)*

13 Arcadia Road, Old Greenwich, CT 06870
Tel: 800-243-9122; FAX: 203-637-4572
E-mail: info@taxwisegiving.com;
WWW: http://www.taxwisegiving.com/

► This newsletter is designed to provide accurate and authoritative information in regard to news of IRS private letter rulings, planned gift computation rates, charitable remainder trusts, and estate and gift taxes. Every month Conrad Teitel's *Taxwise Giving* delivers practical methods of demonstrating tax advantages to donors and clients what to do and how to do it; constant flow of information on the latest code changes, new revenue rulings, regulations, and court cases; and creative ideas for taking maximum advantage of the tax laws' encouragement to charitable giving. *12 pages, $195/year*

Trusts & Estates—The Journal of Wealth Management for Planning Professionals

Intertec Publishing, a PRIMEDIA Company, 6151 Powers Ferry Road NW, Atlanta, GA 30339
Tel: 877-296-3125, 770-955-2500; FAX: 770-618-0345
E-mail: jackie_kandell@intertec.com (Jackie Kandell, Associate Publisher); WWW: http://www.trustsandestates.com, http://www.trustsandestates.com/confer/calendar.html

► Providing technical information about estate planning, trust fund administration, and investing assets for financial planning and building wealth, *Trusts & Estates* is a source for financial advisors, trust administrators, wealthy individuals, and banks. Regular features include News Briefs, Viatical Info, Philanthropy, Finance, Editorial Index, Reprints, and Back to School. Each year *Trusts & Estates* prepares *The Directory of Trust Institutions,* a guide to the trust industry and its thousands of bank trust departments and independent trust companies. It is a good resource for information on the estate planning and trust administration arena. *$139/year*

INTERNET RESOURCES

General

Business Planning (For Nonprofits or For-Profits)

▶ This site contains a basic introduction for both for-profits and nonprofits about developing business plans. For nonprofits that are looking to become more professional and efficient, a clear business plan is a must have. This site helps to get the ball rolling. *www.mapnp.org/library/plan_dec/bus_plan/bus_plan.htm*

Nonprofit Financial Center

▶ The Nonprofit Financial Center offers nonprofits financing and management resources to enhance their financial management skills. *http://www.nonprofitfinancial.org*

Accounting, Reporting, and Auditing

Accounting—Charity USA

▶ CMA accounting firms specializing in charitable bookkeeping and auditing functions for nonprofits. Search engine for locating CMA firms in all states. *http://www.charityusa.org/pages/Service_Providers/Accounting/*

Accounting Professionals' Resource Center

▶ *http://www.kentis.com/*

Accounting Net—Online Resource for Accounting Professionals

▶ This site contains links to firms and societies, related accounting links, CPA associations, industrial news, national job database, products and services, and forums. *http://www.accountingnet.com*

AccountingNet

▶ *http://accounting.pro2net.com*

AccountingSource.com—Your Internet Source for Accounting Software

▶ *http://www.accountingsource.com/index.html*

AICPA Guidance Related to OMB Circular A-133

▶ "Audits of States, Local Governments, and Non-Profit Organizations" *http://www.aicpa.org/belt/a133main.htm*

Authoritative Government Accounting and Auditing Publications Site Seeker—Kent Information Services

▶ *http://www.kentis.com/siteseeker/govpub.html*

CPANet

▶ *http://www.cpanet.com*

Critical Issues in Financial Accounting Regulation for Nonprofit Organizations

▶ *http://www.muridae.com/nporegulation/accounting.html*

Cyber-Accountant

▶ This site contains tax research links arranged by state; also many state and federal tax forms available. *http://www.cyber-cpa.com/proserve.html*

Electronic Accountant

▶ Faulkner & Gray's site provides free access to news and critical accounting industry information. This site includes Newswire, weblinks and commentary, discussion groups, feature articles, and accounting/tax software exhibit halls. *www.electronicaccountant.com*

Financial and Accounting Resources—Thompson & Thompson

▶ *http://www.taxexemptlaw.com/thompson/rs-12.shtml*

Financial Accounting Standards Board

▶ This site provides summaries of the main policies of the board, which issues accounting rules followed by most nonprofit organizations. The site also includes information on the board's publications, projects, and forthcoming meetings. *http://www.rutgers.edu/Accounting/raw/fasb/index.html*

Governmental and Nonprofit Organization Resource Web Sites

▶ *http://web.missouri.edu/~accterw/a365f00/govsites.htm*

Information about Nonprofit Accounting

▶ *http://www.nonprofit.about.com/careers/nonprofit/cs/accountinghelp*

Kaplan's AuditNet Resource List (KARL)

▶ This site is a comprehensive list of electronic resources available for auditors, accountants, and financial professionals. *http://www.auditnet.org/karlpage.htm*

Non-Profit Accounting Resource Center

▶ Created by John Farino, a certified public accountant in New Jersey, this Web site explains key policies of the Financial Accounting Standards Board and several federal Office of Management and Budget circulars that set accounting and audit standards for nonprofit organizations that receive federal funds. It also provides links to other sites that provide information on government regulations that affect nonprofit accounting. *http://www.1800net.com/nprc*

Nonprofit Service Bureau

▶ *http://www.online.emich.edu/~acc_kattelus/bureau.htm*

Office of Management and Budget: OMB Circulars
(Educational and Nonprofit Institutions Documents)

▶ *http://www.whitehouse.gov/OMB/circulars/index-education.html*

Online Guide to Federal Program Compliance and Audits

▶ To receive a monthly e-mail alerting you to important changes to the Online Guide, including OMB's latest *Circular A-133 Compliance Supplement,* sign up here. *http://www.dc.thompson.com/audit/*

Rutgers Accounting Web

▶ *http://www.rutgers.edu/Accounting/raw*

Tax and Accounting Sites Directory

▶ *http://www.taxsites.com*

Unified Chart of Accounts (UCOA)

▶ A service of the Support Center of Washington, UCOA is an accounting method by which nonprofits can track financial activity so that their financial statements will be in direct compliance with IRS Form 990 requirements and other outside reporting. UCOA also seeks to promote uniform accounting practices throughout the nonprofit sector. *http://www.ucoa.org/*

Business and Finance

SBA Nonprofit

▶ *http://www.sbaonline.sba.gov/nonprofit/intro.html*

Estate Planning and Planned Giving

Charitable Gift Fund Resource Center

▶ *http://www301.charitablegift.org/resource/*

Charity Regulators in Other States—Maryland Secretary of State

▶ *http://www.sos.state.md.us/sos/charity/html/otstates.html*

Death & Taxes

▶ *http://www.deathandtaxes.com/nptoc.htm*

The Estate Planning Links Web Site

▶ This site is your link to wealth preservation resources on the Internet. For consumers and estate planning professionals, this site contains hundreds of well-organized, time-saving links to estate planning, elder law, tax, and related Web sites. *http://www.estateplanninglinks.com/*

GiftLaw

▶ GiftLaw is a free service to CPAs, attorneys, trust officers, gift planners, life underwriters, and other professionals. The Gift law free service is accessed through link files on the Web sites of participating charities. *http://www.giftlaw.com/*

The Importance of Charitable Trusts—The Monitor
(Investment Management Consultants Association)

▶ *http://www.imca.org/monitor/imca_jul_99.htm#ImportanceofCharitableTrusts*

Legal Information Institute Estate and Gift Tax Law Materials

▶ *www.law.cornell.edu/topics/estate_gift_tax.html*

PLANNED GIVING: Everyone (But the IRS) Benefits

▶ *http://www.raffa.com/interior/ArtPlangiv.html*

State Charitable Solicitation Requirements

▶ The most complete online collection of information on *state requirements for charitable solicitations.*

Financial Management

Answer Center: Financial Management—Delaware Association of Nonprofit Agenices

▶ *http://www.delawarenonprofit.org/FinMgmnt.htm*

Basic Guide to Non-Profit Financial Management—The Management Assistance Program for Nonprofits

▶ *http://www.mapnp.org/library/finance/np_fnce/np_fnce.htm*

Foundation & Endowment Money Management

▶ Institutional Investor, a company that publishes newsletters about investing, includes descriptions of selected articles from *Foundation & Endowment Money Management* on its Web site. *http://www.foundationendowment.com/femm/index.html*

GENIE: Financial Management

▶ *http://search.genie.org/genie/ans_result.lasso?cat=Financial+Management*

Nonprofit Financial Center

▶ The Nonprofit Financial Center is a nonprofit organization in Chicago that makes loans to charities in Illinois and offers advice and classes on nonprofit financial matters. The Center's Web site provides information on nonprofit financial management—including selected articles from its monthly newsletter. *http://www.nonprofitfinancial.org*

Insurance and Liability

GENIE: Insurance & Liability

▶ *http://search.genie.org/genie/ans_result.lasso?cat=Insurance*

Nonprofits' Essential Handbook on Insurance

▶ *http://www.independentagent.com/Consumer/Business/NonProf.htm*

Investing

Fidelity: Investment Basics

▶ *http://wps.fidelity.com/non-profits/basics/basics.htm*

Risk Management

Answer Center: Risk Management—Delaware Association of Nonprofit Agencies

▶ *http://www.delawarenonprofit.org/RiskFAQ.html*

Software

Nonprofit Financial Center: Fund Accounting Software Listing

▶ Developed by the Nonprofit Financial Center, a Chicago nonprofit organization that offers charities guidance on financial matters, this Web site lists contact information for companies that produce accounting software designed for non-profit groups. The site includes links to Web sites operated by the companies. *http://www.nonprofitfinancial.org/software.html*

Your Complete Guide to Nonprofit Accounting Software and Fund Accounting Software Technologies

▶ *http://www.nfpaccounting.com/accounting_software.htm*

Tax and Legal Issues

990 Online

▶ The 990online.com service was recently established to assist tax-exempt organizations that wish to fulfill the requirements of the new IRC Section 6104(d) regulations through online publication of their completed annual information returns and application for exempt status. *http://www.990online.com/*

Answer Center: Tax & Legal Issues—Delaware Association of Nonprofit Agencies

▶ http://www.delawarenonprofit.org/TaxFAQ.html

EOTEXT—Fast Updates on Tax-Exempt Issues

▶ To make your research on tax issues concerning exempt organizations easier, the EOTEXT file on Lexis is updated weekly and contains the news, documents, and commentary relating to tax-exempt issues published in the *Tax Notes Today, State Tax Today,* and *Worldwide Tax Daily* files. *http://205.177.50.92/catalog/products/specialty/eotext.htm*

Form 1023 Help

▶ *http://www.form1023help.com*

Free Management Library's On-Line Nonprofit Organization Development Program Module #8: Managing Your Nonprofit's Finances and Taxes

▶ *http://www.managementhelp.org/np_progs/fnc_mod/finance.htm*

Internal Revenue Service: Information for Tax-Exempt Organizations

▶ This site explains the different types of tax-exempt organizations and how to apply for tax-exempt status. The site also includes answers to frequently asked questions about tax-exempt organizations, IRS forms that can be downloaded, and articles on topics such as unrelated business income tax, lobbying by tax-exempt organizations, and charitable remainder trusts. The site also includes a database of nearly 500,000 nonprofit organizations, updated quarterly, that makes it possible to find all the groups in a certain city or state or to check whether a particular group has received tax-exempt status. *http://www.irs.ustreas.gov/prod/bus_info/eo*

Internet Nonprofit Center: The Nonprofit FAQ

▶ Sponsored by the Evergreen State Society, a Seattle charity that promotes civic involvement, this site provides information on legal and tax issues for nonprofit organizations. The information was compiled from the soc.org.nonprofit newsgroup, an on-line discussion about the nonprofit world. *http://www.nonprofits.org/npofaq*

Kent Information Services

▶ Tax Resources Site Seeker; an excellent collection of links to other tax sites. *http://www.kentis.com/siteseeker/taxlink.html*

Louisiana State University Libraries

▶ This is a first-rate site for downloading federal and state tax forms. *http://www.lib.lsu.edu/govdocs/taxes.html*

Nonprofit Forms

▶ *http://www.nfpaccounting.com/Form%20990.htm*

Online Compendium of Federal and State Regulations for U.S. Nonprofit Organizations

▶ Created by Eric Mercer, manager of services at DU Educational Technology Services, this Web site provides information on financial accounting regulations, rules for nonprofit postal rates, public disclosure requirements for charities, and the text of laws that regulate nonprofit organizations. The site plans to cover additional topics in the future, such as the steps that organizations must take to apply for tax-exempt status, registering as a charitable solicitor, and the laws that govern fund raising, as well as to provide information on nonprofit regulations in each state. *http://www.muridae.com/nporegulation*

Quality 990

▶ Operated by the National Center for Charitable Statistics at the Urban Institute's Center on Nonprofits and Philanthropy, this site features information about the Form 990—the informational tax return that charities with annual revenues of more than $25,000 are required to file with the IRS—and on projects that educate charities about the form's importance. Independent Sector and the National Council of Nonprofit Associations, both in Washington, and the National Society of Fund Raising Executives, in Alexandria, Virginia, are also sponsors of the site. *http://www.qual990.org*

Simplified Tax and Wage Reporting System

▶ *http://www.tax.gov/1stop.htm*

Tax Analysts

▶ Developed by Tax Analysts, a nonprofit organization that monitors tax policy, this site provides updates on congressional and Internal Revenue Service activities. The site also provides subscription information for 17 e-mail discussion lists that Tax Analysts staff members moderate, including lists that discuss exempt organizations, international philanthropy, tax-exempt bonds, and estates and trusts. *http://www.tax.org*

Tax and Accounting Sites Directory

▶ *http://www.taxsites.com*

Taxes and Tax Exemption Resources—Thompson & Thompson

▶ *http://www.taxexemptlaw.com/thompson/rs-11.shtml*

Tax-Exempt Organizations Tax Kit

▶ *http://www.irs.ustreas.gov/prod/bus_info/eo/eo-tkit.html*

Tax Law Resources

▶ *www.law.emory.edu/*

U.S. Tax Code Online

▶ This site provides access to complete text of the U.S. Internal Revenue Code. Based on U.S. Tax Code at some date in the past, consultation of an official copy is advised for confirmation. *http://www.fourmilab.ch/ustax/ustax.html*

U.S. Tax Code On-Line: Section 501

▶ This site includes the full text of Section 501 of the U.S. Internal Revenue Code, which deals with tax exemption for charities and other organizations. The tax code can be searched, and the site provides hypertext links to references to other parts of the tax code. *http://www.fourmilab.ch/ustax/www/t26-A-1-F-I-501.html*

E-MAIL DISCUSSION LISTS

AGVNFP-L *(For Discussion of Governmental and Not-for-Profit Accounting)*

▶ To subscribe, send the subject line SUBSCRIBE, with no text in the message body. *AGVNFP-L@listserv.csu.edu.au*

GIFT-PL

▶ GIFT-PL is an e-mail distribution center for gift planners that is administered by the National Center for Planned Giving. It was established as a forum for discussion on issues relating to gift planning. There is no charge for subscribing other than charges you ordinarily incur for access to the Internet. For instructions on using GIFT-PL, go to *http://www.ncpg.org/giftpl.html* or send a message to *listserv@iupui.edu.*

GIFTMANAGE

▶ This site covers all aspects of the management of endowment, charitable trust, and foundation funds. *http://www.charitychannel.com/archives/giftmanage.html*

TAX-NONPROFIT

▶ This site is an online forum to discuss the tax and legal matters that affect nonprofit organizations, maintained by the American Bar Association's Section of Taxation and its Exempt Organizations Committee. To subscribe send an e-mail message to *listserv@mail.abanet.org* that states in the body of the message "subscribe tax-nonprofit." Leave the subject blank, and do not include e-mail addresses in the body of the message.

Tax Analysts Discussion Archives

▶ You may subscribe to a group by sending e-mail to *majordomo@lists.tax.org* with the following in the message body: subscribe *groupname*

Example: subscribe accounting archives

You should receive a response back from Majordomo, requesting confirmation of your subscription.

Similarly, you may unsubscribe to a group by sending e-mail to *majordomo@lists.tax.org* with the following in the message body: unsubscribe *groupname*

Tax Analysts Discussion Archives of interest to nonprofits include: Accounting Archives; Employment Taxes Archives; Estate, Gift, Trusts Archives; Exempt Organizations Archives; Insurance Archives; Pensions, Benefits; ERISA Archives; Policy & Reform Archives; State and Local Taxation Archives; and Tax-Exempt Bonds Archives.

Online Newsletter

Nonprofit Agendas

▶ This is a newsletter for executives, board members, and others involved in managing nonprofit organizations. This bimonthly publication discusses such topics as fundraising, nonprofit management, governance, compliance, technology, UBIT, employee compensation, and regulations affecting nonprofits. You'll find it a helpful source of information about ways to operate more efficiently and better accomplish your mission. *http://kdvnonprofitupdate.listbot.com*

To subscribe, send a blank e-mail to *kdvnonprofitupdate-subscribe@listbot.com*

Nonprofit Issues

▶ Selected articles from the current and past issues of *Nonprofit Issues,* a monthly newsletter on nonprofit legal matters, are included on its Web site. *http://www.nonprofitissues.com*

Not-for-Profit Perspectives—Grant Thornton

▶ This is a quarterly newsletter for not-for-profit service organizations sponsored by Grant Thorton, an international accounting and management consulting firm. *http://www.grantthornton.com/content/10497.asp*

Taxing Issues—Grant Thornton

▶ *http://www.grantthornton.com/resources/not-for-profits/taxissues/taxissues_recent.html*

PART III

General Management

ORGANIZATIONS

(See also Assessment and Evaluation; Financial Management; Human Resource Management; Organizational Development; Strategic Planning)

NATIONAL AND REGIONAL MANAGEMENT SUPPORT ORGANIZATIONS

Alliance for Nonprofit Management

1899 L Street NW, 6th Floor, Washington, DC 20036
Tel: 202-955-8406; FAX: 202-955-8419
E-mail: alliance@allianceonline.org, Wendy Reed, Database
Coordinator: wendy@allianceonline.org;
WWW: http://www.allianceonline.org/

► Formed by the merger of the Support Centers of America and the Nonprofit Management Association, the purpose of the Alliance is to challenge and strengthen those who deliver management and governance support services to nonprofit organizations. Its efforts focus on board development, financial management, strategic planning, and fund raising, and its Web site contains answers to frequently asked questions regarding each of these subjects, along with its online newsletter *PULSE!,* and links to the sites of its members. Members include management support organizations (MSOs), individual professionals, and a range of national/regional, umbrella, research and academic, publishing, and philanthropic organizations that provide technical assistance (training and consulting) to nonprofits. The Alliance Resource Center includes a comprehensive compilation of Web sites, books, videos, and other valuable resources relating to nonprofit management. The Alliance CareerBank is designed to assist nonprofit management support professionals (capacity builders) in locating new jobs. It publishes the *Gold Book: Success Stories in Nonprofit Management* and the *MSO Salary & Benefits Survey* and holds an annual conference.

American Society of Association Executives

1575 I Street NW, Washington, DC 20005-1168
Tel: 202-626-2723; FAX: 202-371-8825
E-mail: asae@asaenet.org; WWW: http://www.asaenet.org,
http://www.asaenet.org/find/

► Described as the "association for association executives," ASAE is dedicated to enhancing the professionalism and competency of association executives, promoting excellence in association management, and increasing the effectiveness of associations to better serve members and society. Its ASAE Services, Inc., provides business products and services to the association marketplace. It offers educational programs and meetings. ASAE works in conjunction with allied societies in providing a full range of services and support to the association community. Sections include Association Management Company, Chapter Relations, Communication, Executive Management, Finance and Administration, Government Relations, International, Legal, Marketing, Meetings and Expositions, Membership, Professional Development, and Technology. ASAE publishes a monthly magazine, *Association Management;* 13 newsletters; and numerous books and survey reports. Its Web site offers a large number of resources designed to enhance the association professional's performance. The site also contains their online Allied Societies Directory, a by-state listing of each ASAE allied society, its president or chairman (chief volunteer leader), and a staff contact. It holds an annual conference.

Business Volunteers Unlimited *(See Financial Management—Support and Advocacy Organizations for full description)*

Center for What Works

680 North Lakeshore Drive, Suite 1230, Chicago, IL 60611
Tel: 800-34-WORKS; FAX: 312-640-5010
E-mail: breames@whatworks.org, cchamp@whatworks.org;
WWW: http://www.whatworks.org

► The mission of the Center for What Works is to improve the effectiveness of social policy by assisting public and nonprofit sector organizations to systematically identify and replicate best practices. The Center has pioneered the practice of benchmarking for best practices in the nonprofit sector. It is the Center's work to identify, evaluate, and disseminate successful solutions to social problems to policy makers, corporations, foundations, academics, nonprofits, and the public at large. The Center for What Works helps nonprofits and foundations to allocate their funds efficiently by providing up-to-date information on the practices most likely to ensure success. Consulting services include best practices, implementing performance measures, case studies of other programs, successful approaches to the same problem in other countries, and names of organizations that fund similar approaches. Their On-Line Benchmarking Center provides nonprofit organizations a clearinghouse to find the state-of-the-art knowledge of effective programs and strategies.

Christian Management Association

P.O. Box 4090, San Clemente, CA 92674-4090.
Tel: 800-727-4CMA (4262); FAX: 949-487-0927
E-mail: cma@cmaonline.org; WWW: http://www.cmaonline.org

► Christian Management Association was founded in 1976 and today serves more than 3,400 CEOs, managers, pastors, and church administrators representing more than 1,400 Christian organizations and larger churches. Services and programs include Leadership Training (CEO Dialogues, one-day roundtables limited to 25 CEOs); *CMA's Annual Leadership & Management Conference for Christian organizations and larger churches* offers more than 100 workshops and general sessions providing training in CEO and board leadership, financial management trends and updates, fund raising, human resources, information technology, tax/legal issues, church management, communications and marketing, personal development, management case studies, and much more; *CMA School of Management,* one- and two-day seminars on cutting-edge management, leadership, financial, and HR issues and trends; The Executive Leadership Program) Management Resources (Christian Management Report, CMA's's bimonthly; *CMA Management Monthly,* newsletter; *Christian Ministries Compensation Handbook; Christian Management Resources*—catalog of books and resources—with discounts for CMA members; CMA audiocassettes, a library of CMA's most popular workshops and general sessions on cassette; complete list of workshop tapes available at: *http://www.iwc.com/acts/conf.html*); Networking (*Who's Who in Christian Management,* CMA's Annual Membership Directory of Christian Organizations, plus the Directory of Business and Professional Services; CMA Chapter Meetings in which CMA members in key cities join together for additional training and networking opportunities; CMA Management Classifieds).

The Peter F. Drucker Foundation for Nonprofit Management

320 Park Avenue, 3rd Floor, New York, NY 10022-6839
Tel: 212-224-1174; FAX: 212-224-2508
E-mail: info@pfdf.org; WWW: http://www.pfdf.org/,
http://www.pfdf.org/innovation/index.html (The Drucker Innovation Discovery Site)

▶ The Peter F. Drucker Foundation for Nonprofit Management, founded in 1990, is named for and inspired by the acknowledged father of modern management. By providing educational opportunities and resources, the Foundation furthers its mission to lead social sector organizations toward excellence in performance. The Foundation pursues this mission through the presentation of conferences, video teleconferences, the annual Peter F. Drucker Award for Nonprofit Innovation, and the development of management resources, partnerships, and publications. Since its founding, the Drucker Foundation's special expertise and role has been to serve as a broker of intellectual capital, bringing together the finest leaders, consultants, authors, and social philosophers in the world with the leaders of social sector voluntary organizations. The Drucker Nonprofit Innovation Discovery Site (*http://www.pfdf.org/innovation/innovation/index.asp*) aims to share lessons and discoveries contained within the hundreds of annual nominations for the Peter F. Drucker Award for Nonprofit Innovation. The Discovery Site will be revised each year to include new discoveries of innovation in a variety of areas from fund development to management, from decision making to alliances and partnerships. The Foundation publishes *Leader to Leader,* a quarterly journal (see separate listing under Periodicals) and a quarterly newsletter, *Foundation News,* selections from which are available online at *http://www.pfdf.org/publications/news/index.html.* It holds an annual Leadership and Management Conference as well as other conferences.

Environmental Support Center

4420 Connecticut Avenue NW, Suite 2, Washington, DC 20008-2301
Tel: 202-966-9834; FAX: 202-966-4398
E-mail: lmclark@envsc.org; WWW: http://www.envsc.org/

▶ ESC was created to strengthen the grassroots environmental movement by supporting the organizational development needs of regional, state, and local groups. It subsidizes training and organizational assistance to help groups increase their fund-raising, strategic, communications, and organizational capacities; works to obtain and distribute free or low-cost equipment; promotes creation of environmental federations that use workplace solicitation to raise money. Since 1990, ESC has assisted almost 1,300 local, state, and regional organizations working on environmental issues. Its Training and Organizational Assistance Program, Technology Resources Program, Workplace Solicitation Program, and Environmental Loan Fund help these environmental groups become better managed, funded, and equipped.

Independent Sector *(See Study and Research of the Nonprofit Sector—Support and Advocacy Organizations for full description)*

Innovation Network *(See Strategic Planning for full description)*

Institute for Nonprofit Organization Management *(See Professional Development—Education for full description)*

Learning Institute for Nonprofit Organizations *(See also Professional Development—Education)*

Director of Education, Society for Nonprofit Organizations, 6314 Odana Road, Suite 1, Madison, WI 53719
Tel: 800-214-TEAM (8326), 800-257-2578 (PBS Customer Service); FAX: 608-274-9978
WWW: http://www.uwex.edu/li/,
http://www.uwex.edu/li/nonprofit/.learner/library.htm,
http://www.uwex.edu/li/nonprofit/.learner/sites.htm,
http://www.uwex.edu/li/nonprofit/.learner/courses.htm,
http://www.learningstream.net/pbs_nonprofit/

▶ Begun in 1996, the program is a collaboration involving The Society for Nonprofit Organizations, the University of Wisconsin–Extension, and the PBS Adult Learning Service. The Institute distributes, via satellite, educational programs for nonprofits, featuring leading experts in the field. It augments these satellite-delivered programs with local facilitation and a host of other educational tools and services: audiocassettes, videotapes, CD-ROMs, and various printed and online materials. The Learning Institute is the producer of the *Excellence in Nonprofit Leadership and Management* educational series. The instructional design of the LI programs include the following program elements: nationally recognized faculty members; video case studies illustrating profiles of excellence in the nonprofit sector; print materials including practical management tools, an organizational assessment tool, teaching outline, bibliography, glossary of terms, and other resources; complimentary Web-based resources including articles, an annotated and categorized list of nonprofit web links, FAQs, and course assignments; group/individual learning activities. Participants have the option of viewing the programs as live events via satellite with other nonprofit leaders in the community, or registering as an individual learner for the videotape or Web-based programs that are available on an anytime/anywhere basis. The curriculum incorporates the core principles of governance, leadership, and management.

Logistics Management Institute (LMI)

2000 Corporate Ridge, McLean, VA 22102-7805
Tel: 703-917-7217
E-mail: bmoeller@lmi.org (Bill Moeller, Director of Contracts);
WWW: http://www.lmi.org/lmi_abot.html

▶ LMI is a private, nonprofit corporation that provides management consulting, research, and analysis to government and nonprofit organizations. Although historically focused on logistics, LMI today provides its clients with expertise across the full spectrum of management functions. It seeks to improve the efficiency of public sector operations and the effectiveness with which public resources are used. LMI maintains a strong awareness of academic research and of private sector technologies and business practices. It maintains field offices in Bel Air, Maryland; Brussels, Belgium; St. Louis, Missouri; Montgomery, Alabama; and Petersburg, Virginia.

Management Assistance Group

1555 Connecticut Avenue NW, Suite 3F, Washington, DC 20036-1107
Tel: 202-659-1963; FAX: 202-659-3105
E-mail: magmail@msn.com; WWW:
http://www.managementassistance.org/

▶ Management Assistance Group is a nonprofit 501(c)(3) that builds the effectiveness of nonprofit groups by strengthening their internal structure, leadership, planning, and management; provides individualized, in-depth assistance to groups with organizational growth, change problems, or simply seeking greater effectiveness; helps to pinpoint the problems, reframe the issues, and develop a process for resolving them; concentrates on assisting organizations working in areas of broad social concern (peace, human rights, civil liberties, environmental protection, and social and economic justice). Assists in the areas of purposes, goals, and priorities; organizational and management structures; leadership and managerial styles; working relationships; board issues; planning; and financial development. The Group maintains an office in Santa Barbara, California, for West Coast clients.

National Council of Nonprofit Associations (NCNA)

1900 L Street NW, Suite 605, Washington, DC 20036-5024
Tel: 202-467-6262 (467-NCNA); FAX: 202-467-6261
E-mail: ncna@ncna.org; WWW: http://www.ncna.org

▶ Created in 1989, the National Council of Nonprofit Associations is an umbrella, state-based network of associations of nonprofits that collectively represents more than 20,000 community nonprofits. Advancing the vital role and capacity of the charitable sector, NCNA fosters the development of state and regional associations of nonprofit organizations to become more effective supporters of and advocates for community nonprofits; promotes the highest levels of accountability and ethics to broaden public support for and increase confidence in the nonprofit sector; and creates interchanges and alliances with other organizations that work to strengthen the charitable sector. Programs and services include information clearinghouse, publications, and networking; capacity-building and development, involving peer-to-peer mentorships, and individualized technical assistance; and advocacy and public policy education to connect community nonprofits with a shared vision based on their charitable tax-exempt status and public benefit missions.

National Executive Service Corps

120 Wall Street, 16th Floor, New York, NY 10005
Tel: 212-269-1234; FAX: 212-269-0959
E-mail: info@nexc-ny.org; WWW: http://www.help4nonprofits.org

▶ Since 1977, the National Executive Service Corps has effectively applied business planning and management skills to the nonprofit sector. There are 42 ESC organizations nationwide, all independently run, but all affiliated through the national office in New York. NESC's consulting specialties and programs include: board development, business planning, earned revenue generation, executive search, executive advisory and coaching (including mentoring for small arts groups), facilities, management, finance and control, fund-raising management, human resource management, leadership development, information systems, marketing, communications and public relations, operations/cost reduction, organizational analysis, peer advisory support, program development, and strategic planning.

Nonprofit Education Initiative (NEI)

Center for Women in Government, University at Albany, Draper Hall 302, 135 Western Avenue, Albany, NY 12222
Tel: 518-442-3875; FAX: 518-442-3877
E-mail: saidel@csc.albany.edu (Judith R. Saidel,, Executive Director), mcs@albany.edu (Margery C. Saunders, Director); WWW: http://www.cwig.albany.edu/NEI.htm

▶ The Nonprofit Education Initiative is a four-year collaborative enterprise that involves nonprofit organizations that work on issues related to women, children, and families; regional voluntary sector leaders; government policy makers and business representatives; and the Center for Women in Government and the Nelson A. Rockefeller College of Public Affairs and Policy at the University at Albany. The purposes of NEI are to advance collaborative learning and information exchange about critical nonprofit leadership and management needs, and to strengthen the leadership and competencies of a broadly diverse population of voluntary sector organization management and staff. The goals of the NEI are to strengthen collaboration among statewide associations; build stronger connections between nonprofit organizations, the communities they serve, and the university; increase the capacity and competence of statewide nonprofit organizations; and strengthen the technology capacity and competence of the core consortium.

Nonprofit Resources of Southern New England

160 Broad Street, Providence, RI 02903
Tel: 401-861-1920; FAX: 401-861-8198
E-mail: jbeauchemin@nonprofitresourcessne.org, jbeauchemin@altavista.com (Joan Beauchemin); WWW: http://www.nonprofitresourcessne.org/

▶ Nonprofit Resources is Southern New England's support network for nonprofit organizations. It was created to supply nonprofits with the knowledge and expertise needed for effective operation and future growth. Their mission is to support the advancement of nonprofit organizations and the nonprofit sector as a whole. Services include advocacy; information and referral; networking; grantsbook; subscription to *nonprofit quarterly;* group purchasing; technology assistance; and member profile on the NPR Web site. It sponsors the NonProfit Resources Annual Nonprofit Recognition Awards.

OMG Center for Collaborative Learning

1528 Walnut Street, Suite 805, Philadelphia, PA 19102
Tel: 215-732-2200; FAX: 215-732-8123
WWW: http://www.omgcenter.org/work/orgcap.htm

▶ OMG offers several types of consulting services specifically designed for not-for-profit and public sector organizations that wish to enhance their organizational capacity for financial and performance management. OMG uses a team approach in which indicators and systems are co-developed with the client organization, which means you understand the systems being developed at every step. Client services include program and operations analysis, management systems development, and tools and training.

Society for Nonprofit Organizations

6314 Odana Road, Suite 1, Madison, WI 53719-1141
Tel: 800-424-7367; FAX: 608-274-9978
E-mail: snpo@danenet.wicip.org;
WWW: http://www.danenet.wicip.org/snpo

▶ Society for Nonprofit Organizations is a 501(c)(3) nonprofit national membership organization that serves as a clearinghouse of information and facilitates a variety of educational, training, and support services. It offers substantial discounts on books, audiotapes, and videotapes geared specifically to nonprofits. It created The Learning Institute for Nonprofit Organizations, the provider of satellite-based education for the nonprofit sector, and publishes the monthly magazine, *Nonprofit World* (see separate listing under General Management—Periodicals), and the newsletter *Nonprofit World Funding Alert* (see separate listing under Resource Development—Periodicals).

State and Local Nonprofit Consulting Organizations

ALABAMA

Nonprofit Resource Center of Alabama

3324 Independence Drive, Suite 100, Birmingham, AL 35209
Tel: 205-879-4712; FAX: 205-879-4724
E-mail: resource@wwisp.com; WWW: http://nonprofit-al.org

▶ The Nonprofit Resource Center of Alabama is a membership organization open to any 501(c)(3) organization or any group applying for 501(c)(3) status in Alabama. Individual and Business memberships are also available. Members can access services from anywhere in the state by telephone, e-mail, visits, or participation in programs held in locations throughout Alabama. The Resource Center is Alabama's only centralized source of information, programs, and services specifically designed to meet the needs of Alabama's nonprofit community. Services include education (community, governance, fund development, agency management, the Nonprofit Summit, an intensive day-long training program focusing on leading trends and critical issues in the nonprofit sector); information and referral (resource library, Web site, affinity groups, advocacy, the bimonthly newsletter *Nonprofit Notes,* The Friday Letter weekly FAX to members highlighting upcoming events or important nonprofit sector. Its Jobline is searchable at *http://www.nonprofit-al.org/jobline.htm.*

ALASKA

Association of Nonprofit Corporations

Contact: Nancy Scheetz-Freymiller, 420 Kayak Drive,
Anchorage, AK 99515
Tel: 907-274-1880; FAX: 907-345-6714
E-mail: 102736@compuserve.com

ARIZONA

The Institute for Nonprofit Management at ASU

Arizona State University, 502 E Monroe Street, 2nd Floor,
Phoenix, AZ 85004
Tel: 480-727-5330; FAX: 480-965-3660
E-mail: ssheldon@asu.edu (Scott Sheldon);
WWW: http://www.asu.edu/xed/npmi

▶ Established in 1993, the Nonprofit Management Institute (NMI) has enhanced the management skills of over 2,800 professionals serving the nonprofit sector. Through a selection of courses, one-day seminars, and a certificate program, NMI presents key issues affecting the nonprofit industry.

Nonprofit Management Center

Arizona State University, P.O. Box 874905,
Tempe, AZ 85287-4905
Tel: 480-965-0607; FAX: 480-727-8878
E-mail: nonprofit@asu.edu, ashcraft@asu.edu (Dr. Robert Ashcraft); WWW: http://www.asu.edu/copp/nonprofit

▶ The Center for Nonprofit Leadership and Management will serve as a catalyst to promote the understanding and improved practice of nonprofit organizations in Maricopa County, in Arizona, the Southwest region, and the nation. The Center for Nonprofit Leadership and Management, developed from Arizona State University's respected American Humanics undergraduate program, will enhance the effectiveness of nonprofits, especially those involved in positive youth development and human services, through interdisciplinary strategies. These strategies include facilitating curriculum development, promoting relevant research, providing technical assistance, and convening people and ideas around pertinent issues of the nonprofit sector. Components include Curriculum & Education Development, Applied Interdisciplinary Research, Communications and Convenings, and Technical Assistance to Nonprofits.

ARKANSAS

Nonprofit Resources, Inc.

500 Broadway, Suite 403, Little Rock, AR 72201-3342
Tel: 501-374-8515; FAX: 501-374-6548
E-mail: nonprofit@aristotle.net, mmullins@nonprofitarkansas.org (Maria Mullins, Program Director);
WWW: http://www.nonprofitarkansas.org/

▶ Nonprofit Resources, Inc. was established in 1980 to improve the ability of nonprofit organizations to fulfill their missions. Services include library; group health insurance; *Grantseeker's Horizon* (includes information about private and public grant opportunities and other subjects of interest to nonprofits); *Corporate Connection* (book provides tips on approaching funders and writing grants); Grant Search (NRI conducts individualized computer grant searches based on key words to help groups identify appropriate potential funders for their projects); training (financial management, legal issues, basics of nonprofit management and development); information (NRI staff will help you find answers to your questions about nonprofit management and organizational development. They also have printed materials available on a wide variety of topics).

CALIFORNIA

California Management Assistance Organizations
WWW: http://search.genie.org/genie/cmap.lasso

▶ The California Management Assistance Partnership (C-MAP) is a consortium of 13 regional, nonprofit support organizations providing training and technical assistance to local nonprofit organizations throughout California. The regional partners established C-MAP in 1996 to encourage collaboration and sharing of efforts among the partners to enable them to serve their local communities more effectively. Each of these organizations provides workshops in nonprofit management and fund raising, assistance with information, and referrals to other community resources. C-MAP maintains the Nonprofit GENIE Web site (see Internet Resources for full description) as a free service to help nonprofit staff and board members manage more successfully.

California Association of Nonprofits
315 West Ninth Street, Suite 705, Los Angeles, CA 90015
Tel: 213-347-2070; FAX: 213-347-2080
E-mail: info@CAnonprofits.org;
WWW: http://www.canonprofits.org

▶ Founded in 1984, CAN is a private, nonprofit, tax-exempt membership organization of more than 2,000 California professional nonprofit managers, directors, and consultants. As a collective voice and leading advocate, it works to expand and strengthen the power and effectiveness of the nonprofit sector in order to improve the economic, social, and environmental well-being of all communities. Services include management consultation, research, lobbying, and training. A toll-free Managers' Helpline for members offers information on personnel law, accounting, insurance, legal issues, and other management matters; the Executive Search service assists nonprofit staff and boards with the finding and hiring of executive directors, development managers, financial officers, and other key personnel. Annual conferences and seminars throughout the state provide opportunities to discuss common problems, find workable solutions, offer a forum for sharing ideas and resources, meeting prospective funders, consultants, board members, and new employees or employers. CAN coordinates the Nonprofit Public Policy Agenda Project in assisting nonprofits more easily fulfill their missions by improving public understanding, the sector's image, the regulatory climate, and government regulation. It monitors legislative affairs, advising policy makers and promoting public awareness in areas such as government funding, regulation, tax, and postal rate benefits. CAN sponsors annual conferences and seminars; publishes *CAN Alert: The Newsletter for Nonprofit Managers, Employee Handbook, Nonprofits Yellow Pages Resource Directory,* and other publications.

Center for Excellence in Nonprofits
1515 The Alameda, Suite 302, San Jose, CA 95126
Tel: 408-294-2300; FAX: 408-294-8600
E-mail: mailcen@cen.org; WWW: http://www.cen.org/

▶ The Center for Excellence in Nonprofits (CEN) provides the nonprofit community with in-depth leadership development and continuous improvement programs through an innovative learning community model pioneered by CEN. It provides a range of educational programs, transition management, consulting services, and research activities; and maintains a resource center containing reference materials on nonprofit management, financial development, and boards of directors. Programs include Best Practice Exchange™, Organizational Development Planning Service, institutes, workshops, executive leadership initiatives, Pinnacle Volunteer Program (offers nonprofit members opportunities to engage in systemwide organizational improvements with the support of CEN's corporate volunteer consultants. Pro-bono consultants work solo or in teams to provide expertise to nonprofits in the areas of quality improvement, management information systems, team development, marketing, human resource management or finance); and Wired for Good (CEN and Smart Valley, Inc. are collaborating to improve the effectiveness of Silicon Valley nonprofits by helping them strategically apply appropriate technology and publish *Wired for Good: The Nonprofit Technology Planning Guide*). In addition to learning programs, CEN makes available the latest management and leadership information through its Web site CEN Online, its newsletter, *The Connection,* and its publications.

Center for Nonprofit Management in Southern California
606 South Olive Street, Suite 2450, Los Angeles, CA 90014-1604
Tel: 213-623-7080; FAX: 213-623-7460
E-mail: main@cnmsocal.org; WWW: http://www.cnmsocal.org

▶ The Center for Nonprofit Management is a nonprofit organization whose mission is to support nonprofit organizations in Southern California, and provide information, education, and consulting. The Center for Nonprofit Management assists the boards and staffs of nonprofit organizations in Los Angeles and surrounding counties to improve management effectiveness through these programs: Opportunity NOCs, a biweekly nonprofit job listing resource; Wage & Benefit Survey, an annual report of wages and benefits given by nonprofit organizations in southern California; Seminars (a seminar program of topics relevant to nonprofit management taught by experts in their fields on a volunteer basis); Nonprofit Manager's Helpline; Customized Training; Consulting; Nonprofit Resource Library (a Foundation Center cooperating collection, featuring the FC Search CD-ROM, microfiche copies of foundation IRS Form 990s, as well as Internet access, plus hundreds of titles on nonprofit management issues).

Center for Nonprofit Resources
43430 East Florida Avenue, Suite F-323, Hemet, CA 92544
Tel: 909-927-1873; FAX: 909-927-5871
Contact: Beverly Copeland, Director

▶ The Center for Nonprofit Resources specializes in fund raising and business management for the nonprofit sector. Services include an extensive philanthropic reference library, a series of workshops, and consulting services provided at a nominal fee. Service area: Riverside County, California. Clients: 501(c)(3) organizations. Services: Consulting, public workshops, and nonprofit management reference library.

Community Resource Connection

413 North State Street, Ukiah, CA 95482
Tel: 707-467-3204; FAX: 707-462-0191
E-mail: ncocsbg@pacific.net
Darla Gibson, Community Resource Connection,
306 East Redwood Avenue, Suite 7, Fort Bragg, CA 95437
Tel: 707-964-2586
E-mail: crc@mcn.org

▶ A program of North Coast Opportunities, Inc., Community Resource Connection is an information clearinghouse and support center designed to meet the needs of the not-for-profit community of Mendocino and Lake Counties. They have available for use a collection of computer databases, publications, periodicals, and other resources for organizations' staff, board members, and volunteers. The grant research library is designed to help fund raisers target those funders whose goals and objectives most closely match their own. For nonprofit professionals who need other forms of assistance, they also have a selection of materials on nonprofit management, human resources, organizational development, and board development. For those who prefer a more hands-on approach, they offer half-day and full-day seminars and workshops on a variety of related topics (human resource development, strategic planning, fund raising, grant writing, board development, and executive director training). They are also working with other nonprofit assistance programs in neighboring counties to deliver collaborative training programs.

CompassPoint Nonprofit Services (Formerly The Support Center for Nonprofit Management/Nonprofit Development Center)

706 Mission Street, 5th Floor, San Francisco, CA 94103-3113
Tel: 415-541-9000 (General information), 415-541-9197
(Workshop information); FAX: 415-541-7708

Suite 212, San Jose, CA 95126
Tel: 408-248-9505; FAX: 408-248-9504
E-mail: info@compasspoint.org;
WWW: http://www.compasspoint.org

▶ With offices in San Francisco and Silicon Valley, CompassPoint Nonprofit Services is a nonprofit consulting and training organization. They provide nonprofits with the management tools and concepts necessary to best serve their communities. Services include workshops; consulting; Executive Transitions Board Match Plus; electronic newsletters (co-published with the National Center for Nonprofit Boards, *Board Cafe* is the first electronic newsletter exclusively for members of nonprofit boards of directors; *Food for Thought*, the San Francisco Bay Area's online newsletter for nonprofit organizations); Silicon Valley Funders (a searchable database of funders serving Silicon Valley nonprofits); the Nonprofit Development Library; Nonprofit GENIE (online information and resources on fund raising, boards, grant makers, and more, updated weekly); Consultants ONTAP (a searchable database of consultants who work with the Bay Area nonprofit community); The Bay Area Nonprofit Techie Listserv (a focused forum in which people involved in technology administration can post resources, exchange ideas, and troubleshoot common problems); *Medianet* (a Web-based tutorial for media and public relations on the Internet); events (CompassPoint provides major conferences each year that promote skills enhancement and community building for the nonprofit sector: Technology Conference, Nonprofit Day, Beyond the Line, Media Day).

East Bay Management Assistance Partnership Project

National Economic Development & Law Center,
2201 Broadway, Suite 815, Oakland, CA 94612
Tel: 510-251-2600, ext. 147; FAX: 510-251-0600
E-mail: info@eastbaymapp.org, jean@nedlc.org (Jean Wiley,
Director); WWW: http://eastbaymapp.org,
http://eastbaymapp.org/mta_resource.html (Resource Library),
http://eastbaymapp.org/partners.html,
http://eastbaymapp.org/mta_links.html,
http://eastbaymapp.org/mtatools/best_practices_tools.html

▶ In 1996 and 1997, The East Bay Community Foundation (EBCF) and National Economic Development & Law Center (NEDLC) surveyed over 200 local nonprofit agencies, asking these organizations what would help them become more successful and effective. The East Bay Management Assistance Partnership Project (East Bay MAPP) is a result of this survey. East Bay MAPP supports the nonprofit communities of Contra Costa and Alameda Counties by offering a vast amount of accessible information, tools, and resources.

The East Bay Resource Center for Nonprofit Support

Preservation Park, 1203 Preservation Park Way, Suite 100,
Oakland, CA 94612
Tel: 510-834-1010; FAX: 510-834-2525
E-mail: r_center@pacbell.net;
WWW: http://www.eastbaymapp.org/ebrc.html

▶ The East Bay Resource Center is a 501(c)(3) nonprofit organization, founded in 1986, to serve the thousands of nonprofit community-based organizations working to serve the East Bay's diverse population. The East Bay Resource Center promotes the growth and stability of East Bay nonprofits by providing access to funding information, support services, and knowledge of effective resource development and management. The Center's Funding Research Library provides access to a wide collection of materials on fund raising and nonprofit management. Available to the public free of charge, these reference materials and electronic information services are supported by a trained library coordinator who is available to help researchers locate funding information and prospects.

Executive Service Corps of Southern California (ESCSC)

520 South Lafayette Park Place, Suite 210,
Los Angeles, CA 90057-1607
Tel: 213-381-2891; FAX: 213-381-2893
E-mail: exec@soca.com

PMB 522, 14252 Culver Drive, Suite A, Irvine, CA 92604-0326
Tel: 800-466-4114
WWW: http://www.escsc.org, http://www.escsc.org/hotlinks.htm

▶ Executive Service Corps of Southern California is a nonprofit organization devoted to enhancing management skills in the nonprofit sector through involvement of retired executives in volunteer consulting service. ESCSC links retired executives and professionals with nonprofit organizations to serve as management consultants and board members on a volunteer basis. The following six services are available to nonprofits for a nominal fee: Management Consulting Services; One-Time "Sounding-Board" Sessions, the Board Coaching Program, Executive Advisory Program, Retainer

Partnership, and the Board Bank Program. Their Web site includes information on volunteering, highlights current projects, and offers links to other sites relating to the nonprofit world in California.

Grant & Resource Center of Northern California (GRC)

2280 Benton Drive, Bldg. C, Suite A, Redding, CA 96003
Tel: 530-244-1219; FAX: 530-244-0905
E-mail: library@grcnc.org, dennis@shastarcf.org (Dennis Kessinger, Executive Director); WWW: http://www.grcnc.org

▶ GRC offers the north state communities the advantages of a professional staff, a resource library, and periodic seminars and workshops. Their services are geared toward supporting the not-for-profit community and other philanthropic endeavors in northern California. Services/programs include library, workshops, Outreach Project, grantwriter's listserve, GRC Research Services, and Consulting.

Humboldt Area Foundation/ Rooney Resource Center

373 Indianola Road (mailing address is P.O. Box 99),
Bayside, CA 95524
Tel: 707-442-2993; FAX: 707-442-3811
E-mail: hafound@hafoundation.org;
WWW: http://www.hafoundation.org

▶ The Rooney Resource Center is the North Coast's information clearinghouse and support center for nonprofits. It includes a nonprofit management and grant resource library, training workshops and special events, direct one-on-one technical assistance, technical assistance awards, and a free meeting room for nonprofits.

Institute for Nonprofit Organization Management, University of San Francisco *(See Professional Development—Education for full description)*

Long Beach Nonprofit Partnership

3515 Linden Avenue, Long Beach, CA 90807
Tel: 562-290-0018; FAX: 562-290-8018
E-mail: lbnp@ixnetcom.com; Web: http://www.lbnp.org

▶ To enhance the lives of the people of Long Beach, the Partnership's mission is to provide local access to educational, technical assistance, and networking opportunities to enable Long Beach Nonprofits to build relationships, share resources, and strengthen agency infrastructure so they may better serve their constituencies. Services include a resource library; information and referral services; board and staff training and consultation; workshops and conferences; networking and collaborative opportunities; and advocacy for nonprofit sector.

Management Assistance Group/Western Office

2685 Puesta Del Sol, Santa Barbara, CA 93105
Tel: 805-569-0364; FAX: 805-687-1805
E-mail: magmail@msn.com;
WWW: http://www.managementassistance.org
(See National Consulting and Management Assistance/Support Organizations for full description)

The Management Center

870 Market Street, Suite 360, San Francisco, CA 94102-30091
Tel: 800-344-NOCS (6627), 415-362-9735; FAX: 415-362-4603
E-mail: tmc@tmcenter.org; WWW: http://www.tmcenter.org,
http://www.opportunitynocs.org (Professional Development)

▶ Established in 1977, the Management Center is a leading resource for nonprofit management support in Northern California. Programs and services include board and organizational development; human resources management (Executive Search and TempExecs, Opportunity NOCs, Wage & Benefit Survey, Skillbuilders, Human Resources Consulting Services, Creating Your Own Employee Handbook, Compensation Guide, Best Practices Conference); support for Nonprofit Leadership (Executive Director 101, Executive Director Retreat, Executive Exchange, Nonprofit Study Section, The Management Center Quarterly, TMC E-Notes, OpportunityNOCs); Recognition of Nonprofit Excellence; consulting services (Information Services, Human Resources, Organizational Development); OpportunityNOCs.org (Internet source of nonprofit jobs and career opportunities); and board fairs.

Marin Council of Agencies (MCA)

650 Las Gallinas Avenue, San Rafael, CA 94903
Tel: 415-479-5710; FAX: 415-479-9878
E-mail: mca@marin.org; http://www.marinnonprofits.org/

▶ MCA is an association of 140 Marin nonprofits. It provides management assistance programs including seminars on fund raising, nonprofit management, board responsibilities, as well as supporting peer programs for CEOs, development directors, and financial managers. In addition, MCA provides information about and referral to technical assistance resources for nonprofits, publishes a monthly newsletter, and provides opportunities for its members to meet with decisionmakers important to nonprofits. MCA has organized an informal network of independent consultants who provide services to Marin's nonprofit organizations. This network allows participants to exchange resources and ideas and gain a better understanding of the needs of the nonprofit community. It publishes *The Information Bulletin,* a monthly newsletter designed to provide MCA members with news of the local nonprofit community, as well as to offer them technical assistance by way of print, online, and other resources.

Nonprofit Advancement Center–Fresno Regional Foundation

Fresno Regional Foundation, 3425 North First Street, Suite 101,
Fresno, CA 93726
Tel: 559-226-5600; FAX: 559-230-2078
E-mail: frfjesse@lightspeed.net (Jesse R. Arreguin, Director of Operations); Web: http://bizweb.lightspeed.net/~frf

▶ The Nonprofit Advancement Center serves as a resource library where nonprofit organizations can research available funding opportunities from private foundations and other potential funding sources. The Center offers the following services: a comprehensive library to help organizations with board development, strategic planning, grant writing, fund raising, management, marketing, and public relations; a computerized database listing over 43,000 private foundations, available for use at the facility, that represents the state-of-the-art technology; and numerous workshops and training seminars designed to benefit local organizations. Nominal fees will be charged for these services.

Nonprofit Management Solutions (Formerly Support Center/Executive Service Corps)

8265 Vickers Street, Suite #C, San Diego, CA 92111
Tel: 619-292-5702; FAX: 619-292-9943
E-mail: npsolutions@earthlink.net;
WWW: http://www.npsolutions.org/

▶ Nonprofit Management Solutions is the major provider of management training, consulting, and information resources to nonprofit organizations in San Diego County, with outreach to clients in Riverside, San Bernardino, and Imperial Counties. Their resource portfolio includes the following: board development and leadership training, public and on-site management training, retreat and meeting facilitation, strategic planning, program and service feasibility studies, organization assessment and consulting services, as well as information and referral resources. It publishes *Opportunity NOCs,* nonprofit job listings for Southern California.

The Nonprofit Partnership

P.O. Box 3472, Palm Desert, CA 92261
Tel: 760-770-7897 (Hilary Bendon) or 760-340-4560
(Chris Stone)
E-mail: Csmith@mccallum-theatre.org (Cameron Smith)

▶ The Nonprofit Partnership is a networking association that is improving the quality of nonprofit management and social programming in the Coachella Valley by increasing effective collaboration and providing cooperative support and resources. An ongoing project of the Partnership is the development of a community-wide information and referral resource for individuals and agencies.

Nonprofit Resource Center

828 I Street, 2nd Floor (2nd Floor Sacramento Public Library),
Sacramento, CA 95814
Tel: 916-481-4916; FAX: 916-481-7287
E-mail: NRC@nonprofitresourcectr.org,
jstohr@sacramento.lib.ca.us (Jan Stohr, Director),
chowland@sacramento.lib.ca.us;
WWW: http://www.sacramento.org/nprc/index.html,
http://www.boardlink.net/ (BOARDLINK)

▶ The Nonprofit Resource Center, a 501(c)(3), opened in 1989 aiming to increase funding and improve management of Sacramento region nonprofit organizations. Center services include workshops on proposal writing, fund raising, and nonprofit management; consulting services; books, periodicals, audio and video tapes, grant research databases and other materials covering fundraising and management; knowledgeable staff who provide help in using the resources; information and referral to resources specifically serving nonprofit needs; registry of consultants serving nonprofit organizations; calendar of major regional special events; nonprofit job information; BOARDLINK (program that matches interested people with the boards of nonprofit organizations in the Greater Sacramento area). The Nonprofit Resource Center is a cooperating collection of the Foundation Center and a National Society of Fund Raising Executives (NSFRE) Affiliate Library.

Nonprofit Resource Center

Volunteer Center Orange County, 1901 East 4th Street, Suite 100,
Santa Ana, CA 92705
Tel: 714-953-5757; FAX: 714-834-0585
E-mail: chirtler@volunteercenter.org,
admin@volunteercenter.org; WWW:
http://www.volunteercenter.org/nrc

▶ The Nonprofit Resource Center is Orange County's training, educational, and research center for nonprofit agencies, charitable organizations, and the community. The Nonprofit Resource Library is a complete source of up-to-date information that contains a collection of reference materials for funding research and nonprofit management. The Resource Library currently houses CD-ROM resources, newsletters, newspapers, videos, and a complete collection of 990s (tax returns) for the private foundations in California. Other services include online nonprofit job opportunities, customized research, and funding searches. In addition, NRC offers over 100 seminars annually that are taught by trainers and practitioners in areas such as fund raising, volunteer management, board development, marketing, and public relations. NRC also offers customized training and retreats to address specific needs of nonprofits and publishes the *Guide to Orange County and Los Angeles County Foundations,* an annually updated reference resource for local funding opportunities. NRC is a member of the Foundation Centers Cooperating Collection. As a member, NRC receives up-to-date foundation directories and funding guides from the Foundation Center. The Board Excellence Conference is a focused conference for executive directors and new and experienced board members to discover the latest trends affecting Orange County boards and organizations. NRC offers a five-step Core Competency Certificate Program that deals with the fundamentals of efficient nonprofit organizations, spanning such topics as volunteer management, board development, nonprofit operations, marketing and public relations, and fund raising. For individuals interested in intensive professional development, the Administration of Nonprofit Programs certificate course (offered in collaboration with California State University, Long Beach) provides a practical framework and overview for the study of nonprofit operations.

Nonprofit Support Center of Santa Barbara County

2950 State Street, Suite A, Santa Barbara, CA 93105
Tel: 805-687-8560; FAX: 805-687-8570
E-mail: resource@nscsb.org; WWW: http://www.nscsb.org

Satellite Office, Columbia Business Center, 910 East Stowell
Road, Suite 114, Santa Maria, CA 93454
Tel: 805-928-2503; FAX: 805-928-0894

▶ The Nonprofit Support Center (NSC) of Santa Barbara County is a regional training, consulting, and resource center for board members, staff, and volunteers of nonprofit organizations. Founded in 1995 under the auspices of the Santa Barbara Foundation and with the support of the James Irvine Foundation, the NSC became an independent nonprofit organization in 1998. UCSB Extension, in cooperation with the Nonprofit Support Center and the Hutton Foundation, offers a certificate program in Nonprofit Financial Management. This certificate program is designed to develop professional fiscal management capacity within local nonprofit organizations.

Peninsula Nonprofit Center

1700 South El Camino Real, San Mateo, CA 94402
Tel: 650-358-9392; FAX: 650-358-0141
E-mail: georgia@pcf.org (Georgia McDaniel, Manager);
WWW: http://www.pcfnonprofitcenter.org

▶ Services and programs include workshops (grant seeking, fund raising, board development, and general management topics in addition to periodic seminars); grant seeking support; career advancement resources (nonprofit job announcements, list of academic programs for nonprofit leaders, Wage & Benefit Survey of Northern California Nonprofit Organizations); networking opportunities; Peninsula Silicon Valley Funders Fairs; and information and referral. The Center is a Cooperating Collection of the Foundation Center in New York.

Resource Center for Nonprofit Management

Ventura County Community Foundation, 1317 Del Norte Road, Suite 150, Camarillo, CA 93010
Tel: 805-988-0196; FAX: 805-485-5537
E-mail: vccf@vccf.org; WWW: http://www.vccf.org/resource.html

▶ The Resource Center for Nonprofit Management was created in 1991 by the Ventura County Community Foundation to meet the needs of the county's nonprofit organizations and institutions. The Resource Center for Nonprofit Management provides the following services: Library for Nonprofit Research and Development; Seminars for Nonprofit Excellence; Community Needs Profiles; and Technology Resource Network.

Resource Center for Nonprofits

153 Stony Circle, Suite 100, Santa Rosa, CA 95401
Tel: 707-573-3399; FAX: 707-573-3380
E-mail: NPResource@volunteernow.org,
snelson@volunteernow.org, edraper@volunteernow.org;
Web: http://www.volunteernow.org/training

▶ The mission of the Resource Center for Nonprofits is to foster excellence in nonprofit management. Services include workshops on such topics as fund raising, grant writing and board development, board excellence training, board bank matching service, a nonprofit conference, information, and referral, and roundtables for professional development.

The San Diego Association of Nonprofits (SANDAN)

Leslie Hine-Rabichow, Executive Director, P.O. Box 300896, Escondido, CA 92030-0896
Tel: 619-518-5182; FAX: 760-745-3300
E-mail: sandan1@home.com

▶ The San Diego Association of Nonprofits (SANDAN) is an association of San Diego County nonprofit organizations established to represent the role of the nonprofit sector in advancing community well-being. Services/programs include: Communication (maintains a Web site posting important meeting schedules, upcoming events, issue analysis, etc.; produces and distributes a bimonthly Director Updates; convenes monthly general meetings open to any nonprofit organization for the purpose of information sharing and discussion; convenes forums focusing on specific issues for the purpose of education, analysis, and dialog); San Diego Nonprofit Sector Capacity Building (InfoTap, a collaborative effort to develop a nonprofit technology support center; training forums in collaboration with other nonprofit support organizations that increase provider readiness to provide services under managed care and other new service financing realities; written and oral presentations and analyses, which identify trends in nonprofit organization development and resources available for organizational transformation); State & Federal Nonprofit Policy Initiatives (SANDAN is a member of the California Association of Nonprofits' Nonprofit Policy Council); and Nonprofit Sector Value-Added Research.

Volunteer Center of the Inland Empire, Inc.

255 North D Street, Suite 311, San Bernardino, CA 92401
Tel: 909-884-2556; FAX: 909-381-8822
E-mail: kelley@yourvolunteercenter.org (Robin L. Kelley);
WWW: http://www.yourvolunteercenter.org

▶ The Volunteer Center of the Inland Empire is taking the lead in the development of the Nonprofit Executive Network (NEN). The mission of the NEN is to provide executive directors of nonprofit organizations an opportunity to gain mutual support, understanding, and assistance to effectively meet the needs of the communities their agencies and organizations serve. The primary purpose of the Network is to provide executive directors the opportunity to share ideas, learn the latest information affecting the nonprofit sector, meet other executive directors, further develop their leadership skills, and strive for excellence in the management and operations of nonprofit organizations serving San Bernardino County. Membership is open only to executive directors and/or senior management staff of public and/or private, charitable health, human services, arts, and cultural 501(c)(3) nonprofit organizations serving San Bernardino County that meet the membership criteria and pay annual dues.

Support Center for Nonprofit Management *(See Compasspoint)*

COLORADO

The Center for Nonprofit Excellence

715 Galapago Street, Denver, CO 80470
Tel: 303-446-2221; FAX: 303-727-5745
E-mail: CNEparsons@aol.com (Richard Parsons, Managing Consultant)

▶ To improve an organization's effectiveness and/or service delivery, CNE's consortium of experienced consultants offers practical, hands-on assistance in developing and implementing appropriate, achievable action plans. Based on the mission and objectives of the organization, CNE customized problem-solving services including board development, staff team building, strategic or business planning resource development, and interim executive services.

Colorado Association of Nonprofit Organizations (CANPO)

225 East 16th Avenue, Suite 1060, Denver, CO 80203
Tel: 800-333-6554 (Colorado only), 303-832-5710;
FAX: 303-894-0161
E-mail: canpo@canpo.org, pread@canpo.org (Patricia Read);
WWW: http://www.canpo.org,
http://www.canpo.org/fresources.htm

▶ The Colorado Association of Nonprofit Organizations (CANPO) is the largest network of nonprofit organizations in the state. This diverse community of over 1,000 charitable and philanthropic agencies includes human service providers, health care facilities, cultural organizations, educational institutions, and more. As the leader of this growing alliance, CANPO provides a voice for the sector that builds public confidence and support for Colorado's nonprofit organizations; develops and maintains an information network that connects nonprofit organizations to resources for the "best practices" of nonprofit management and governance; sponsors educational forums where nonprofit professionals can broaden their knowledge, network among peers, and strengthen CANPO's statewide alliance of nonprofits; offers quality insurance programs that help nonprofits responsibly manage their agencies; creates partnerships with other organizations who provide special benefits to nonprofits that participate in our network. Programs/services include Information Hotline; *Nonprofit Colorado,* CANPO's bimonthly newsletter (also available online); CANPO Bookstore (a selection of publications for the nonprofit Community); Nonprofit Startup Information; Resources for Job Seekers; the *Colorado Directory of Nonprofits;* the Nonprofit Library; Colorado Nonprofits Listserv (an electronic mailing list in partnership with Regis University's Master of Nonprofit Management program). CANPO sponsors Colorado Nonprofit Day an annual event organized by the Colorado Association of Nonprofit Organizations that recognizes and celebrates the vital contributions that nonprofit organizations make to their communities.

Colorado Nonprofit Development Center

4130 Tejon Street, Suite A, Denver, CO 80211
Tel: 720-855-0501; FAX: 720-855-8273
E-mail: condc@qadas.com, mhiggs@startnonprofit.org (Melinda Higgs); WWW: http://www.startnonprofit.org
▶ The Center was founded by a group of foundation leaders, lawyers, and civic leaders who came together to discuss a different approach to nonprofit start-up. The Center's founders saw a need for an approach that would encourage innovation and community leadership in new charitable ventures; bring increased efficiency and effectiveness to the nonprofit development process; and reduce the risk to funders, lawyers, and other professionals who are interested in investing time and resources in new nonprofits. After extensive research and much input from the nonprofit, legal, and funding communities, the Center was created as an incubator without walls to support new nonprofit activities in Colorado.

Colorado Springs Chamber Nonprofit Partnership
(Formerly the Chamber Nonprofit Center)
Colorado Springs Chamber of Commerce, 2 North Cascade Avenue, Suite 110, Colorado Springs, CO 80903
Tel: 719-575-4346, 719-575-4324 (Susan Saksa, Director);
FAX: 719-635-1571
E-mail: csnc@cscc.org, info@cscc.org, susan@cscc.org
(Susan Saksa, Director);
WWW: http://www.coloradospringschamber.org/cf/index.htm
▶ The Colorado Springs Nonprofit Partnership, run through the *Colorado Springs Chamber of Commerce,* was established in 1991 to promote, support, and strengthen the growing nonprofit sector. The Colorado Springs Nonprofit Center assists nonprofit organizations by offering networking, technical assistance, consulting, education and training, and group insurance programs geared toward

board members, staff, and volunteers. Additionally, the El Pomar Center (see separate listing) was established to provide a location to hold seminars and training for nonprofits.

Community Resource Center
655 Broadway, Suite 300, Denver, CO 80203-3426
Tel: 303-623-1540; FAX: 303-623-1567
E-mail: info@crcamerica.org; WWW: http://www.crcamerica.org
▶ Established in 1981, the Community Resource Center (CRC) is a 501(c)(3) nonprofit organization that provides leadership training, technical assistance, and consultation to community-based organizations in Colorado and across the country. The Community Resource Center also publishes the Colorado Grants Guide, and offers a year-long series of mini-workshops designed for nonprofit executive directors, board members, and staff. The 2½-hour workshops cover a variety of issues ranging from how to incorporate and obtain your 501(c)(3) tax-exempt status to nonprofit budgeting, board development, how to best use the Colorado Grants Guide, and resource development. CRC's Consulting and Technical Assistance services give organizations the tools to develop and implement activities that address their present needs and future goals, including Getting Started, Board Development, Staff Development, Strategic Planning, Resource Development, Financial Management, Constituency Building & Community Outreach, Marketing/Public Relations Strategy, and Personal Leadership. Other services include workshops, training, and conferences; Colorado Nonprofit Leadership and Management Program; and community organizing. For additional consulting techniques, innovations, pointers, and strategies, visit their (TIPS) Resource Page at *http://www.crcamerica.org/tips/index.htm.*

El Pomar Nonprofit Resource Center at Penrose Library (Pike's Peak Library District)
A Cooperating Collection of the Foundation Center,
20 North Cascade Avenue, Colorado Springs, CO 80903
Tel: 719-389-8968; FAX: 719-632-5744
WWW: http://library.ppld.org/El_Pomar/ResourceCenter.ASP,
http://library.ppld.org
▶ The El Pomar Nonprofit Resource Center (EPNRC) has relocated to the Penrose Public Library. It is a cooperating collection of the Foundation Center located in the reference area of the Penrose Public Library. It also offer workshops and classes on grant writing and fund raising, and researching corporations and foundations. For more information regarding the El Pomar Nonprofit Resource Center, contact Lynn Harrison at 531-6333, ext. 2335 or *lharrison@ppld.org.*

Metro Volunteers (Formerly Technical Assistance Center)
225 East 16th Avenue, Suite 200, Denver, CO 80203
Tel: 303-894-0103; FAX: 303-832-4483
E-mail: metrovol@metrovolunteers.org;
WWW: http://www.metrovolunteers.org
▶ Metro Volunteers offers a full range of consulting and training services, including consulting (in-depth assistance and coaching on a specific management problem), customized training services; grant writing coach (to get you started with a proposal, and/or review and critique your work when it is done); strategic planning (to facilitate a customized strategic planning retreat with your orga-

nization's board and/or staff), facilitation services (provides skilled facilitators for board meetings and board/staff retreats), board candidate training and development (to assist your board of directors with any issue along the governance continuum, from committee structure to board self-assessment), group training (a trainer will design and deliver workshops tailored to your organization's need), and volunteer management consulting and training (will assist your organization in maximizing its volunteer resources).

CONNECTICUT

Connecticut Association of Nonprofits

90 Brainard Road, Hartford, CT 06114
Tel: 860-525-5080; FAX: 860-525-5088
E-mail: info@ctnonprofits.org, Agiliberto@aol.com,
rcretaro@ctnonprofits.org (Ron Cretaro);
WWW: http://www.ctnonprofits.org

▶ The Connecticut Association of Nonprofits is a private, nonprofit trade association of over 515 nonprofit organizations in Connecticut. The Connecticut Association of Nonprofits provides services to its members, including advocacy, informative meetings and publications, professional training, insurance and group purchasing programs, an unemployment trust, a retirement program, and much more. The Connecticut Association of Nonprofits membership consists of human service, arts, health, educational, recreational and cultural organizations, as well as private philanthropic foundations. It publishes *Nonprofit Advantage,* a quarterly newsletter that features articles on topics that are important to the entire nonprofit sector. It also has updates on the latest in cost-saving products and services for association members, as well as tips on other helpful resources. It also publishes *Connecticut Nonprofits,* a magazine that focuses on the work and accomplishments of nonprofits in Connecticut, and what they give back to their communities. The Connecticut Association of Nonprofits organized the first annual Connecticut Nonprofit Day.

DELAWARE

Nonprofit Assistance Initiative

Waterbury Foundation, 81 West Main Street, Fourth Floor,
Waterbury, CT 06702
Tel: 203-753-1315; FAX: 203-756-3054
E-mail: jcowan@waterburyfoundation.org (Judy Cowan,
director), info@waterburyfoundation.org;
WWW: http://www.waterburyfoundation.org/

▶ The Nonprofit Assistance Initiative was established in 1998 as a joint project between the Waterbury Foundation and the United Way of the Central Naugatuck Valley to provide organizational development support to nonprofit agencies in northwest Connecticut. Services available to individual nonprofit organizations are: Technical Assistance Workshop Fund (provides minigrants to hire a trainer or attend training workshops; applications are accepted at anytime during the year); basic workshops (board development, strategic planning, fund raising, marketing, and grant writing, as well as seminars in new models of organizational development); organizational assessment (designed to help an agency identify its specific organizational development needs. Upon completion of the organizational assessment, the following are available: consulting services in board development and strategic planning; grants for hiring consultants). Services are available to

organizations with tax-exempt status under Sections 501(c)(3) or 501(c)(4) of the Internal Revenue Code and nonprofit organizations located in Beacon Falls, Bethlehem, Bridgewater, Cheshire, Goshen, Litchfield, Middlebury, Morris, Naugatuck, New Milford, Oxford, Prospect, Roxbury, Southbury, Thomaston, Warren, Washington, Waterbury, Watertown, Wolcott, and Woodbury.

Delaware Association of Nonprofit Agencies (DANA)

Contact: Drew Hastings, 100 West 10th Street, Suite 102,
Wilmington, DE 19801
Tel: 302-777-5000; FAX: 302-777-5386
E-mail: dana@delawarenonprofit.org;
WWW: www.delawarenonprofit.org,
http://www.delawarenonprofit.org/AnswerCtr.htm

▶ DANA is composed of more than 375 charitable and community-based institutions throughout the state of Delaware. Its members represent the entire spectrum of the nonprofit sector—the arts, education, health, human service, religious, and philanthropic institutions. Programs and services include advocacy; information and referral (DANA on Demand; Nonprofit Resource Library; *Delaware Nonprofit,* bimonthly magazine; *DANA Monthly; Opportunity NOCs,* monthly newsletter listing nonprofit job opportunities in the Delaware Valley jointly published with LaSalle University's Nonprofit Management Development Center; Nonprofit Career Center; Your Help Is Needed, a joint venture with *The News Journal,* which publishes volunteer opportunities every Saturday in the local section of the newspaper program); professional development (The Nonprofit Institute, Leadership Delaware, Service-Learning Connection); research (Delaware Nonprofit Research Center, Delaware Community Service Directory, Nonprofit Wage & Benefit Report); and government affairs. DANA sponsors Delaware Nonprofit Day as well as the Annual Conference and Nonprofit Expo.

DISTRICT OF COLUMBIA *(See Greater Washington, DC)*

FLORIDA

Florida Association of Nonprofit Organizations (FANO)

7480 Fairway Drive, #206, Miami Lakes, FL 33014
Tel: 800-362-3266, 305-557-1764; FAX: 305-821-5528
E-mail: FANO@ix.netcom.com (Marina Pavlov);
WWW: http://fano.communityisoft.com, http://www.fano.org

▶ FANO was founded by nonprofit leaders to enhance the well-being of all people and communities in the state of Florida by building the capacity of the private nonprofit sector. FANO assists Florida's 22,000 nonprofits, in strengthening their leadership, management, and financial and public policy capacity to reach their missions. FANO publishes a newsletter and offers a Certificate in Nonprofit Management Workshop Series.

Leadership Center of the Community Foundation of Collier County

2400 Tamiami Trail North, Suite 300, Naples, FL 34103
Tel: 941-649-5000; FAX: 941-649-5337
E-mail: leadcenter@naples.net, pdbecker@att.net (Pam Becker,
Director); WWW: http://gator.naples.net/~leadcenter

▶ The Center is the management assistance and technical assistance arm of the Community Foundation of Collier County. It coordinates a series of seminars, provides free short-term consulting and advice on governance and management issues, provides information and referral, maintains a library of nonprofit resources, and facilitates custom board retreats. As the only nonprofit resource center in the area, it draws from Lee County as well, which is the Ft. Myers area. The Leadership Center is open to any charitable, civic, or governmental organization in Collier County. Nonprofits outside of Collier County are welcome to use any of the fee-based services.

Non Profit Resource Center (NPRC)

335 Beard Street, Tallahassee, FL 32303
Tel: 888-442-8966, 850-222-6000; FAX: 850-681-2890
E-mail: bob@hmgnet.com; WWW: http://www.nonprofitcenter.org
▶ NPRC offers a wide range of consulting services to meet every association and nonprofit organization need in communications/public relations, education, fund raising, general administration, leadership training and development, meeting planning, membership management and marketing, and strategic planning services. NPRC also offers in-depth commentary and analysis on various nonprofit management topics through its available publications. Six members running MSOs or TA programs in Florida have recently begun holding quarterly meetings to share resources and support. Sherry Abbott, Executive Director of the Philanthropy and Nonprofit Leadership Center at Rollins College, is their informal coordinator. Her e-mail address is sabbott@rollins.edu.

GEORGIA

Georgia Center for Nonprofits (Formerly Nonprofit Resource Center)

50 Hurt Plaza SE, Suite 220, Atlanta, GA 30303-2914
Tel: 404-688-4845, 800-959-5015 (outside Atlanta);
FAX: 404-521-0487
E-mail: info@nonprofitgeorgia.org (Karen Beavor),
nonprofitga@mindspring.com;
WWW: http://www.nonprofitgeorgia.org
▶ Begun by The Community Foundation for Greater Atlanta in 1990 and known originally as the Nonprofit Resource Center, it is Georgia's association for nonprofit, charitable organizations. Services and programs include Managing for Excellence Workshops and Events (nonprofit management and governance training and workshops); board/staff helpline (connects nonprofit staff and board members with information, resources, and referrals); consultation, training, and board member matching; TeamTECH (provides information technology training and consulting); *Opportunity NOCs* newsletter listing employment opportunities in the nonprofit sector, published every other week; listing of résumés for nonprofit employers to review; cost-saving opportunities for member organizations; and advocacy efforts on behalf of Georgia nonprofit agencies. Alexander Haas Martin & Partners offers Center members a 20 percent discount on DoNET, an online fund-raising resource specially designed for Georgia nonprofits.

GREATER WASHINGTON, DC

Cultural Alliance of Greater Washington

1436 U Street NW, Suite 103, Washington, DC 20009
Tel: 202-638-2406; FAX: 202-638-3388
E-mail: rmills@cultural-alliance.org (Rebecca Mills);
WWW: http://www.cultural-alliance.org
▶ The Cultural Alliance of Greater Washington, the nation's largest regional arts service organization, works with its members to ensure that the arts survive and prosper. Founded in 1978, the CAGW provides a forum for addressing common challenges to arts organizations and individual artists. The CAGW provides a number of services to members and the community, including helping artists and arts organizations with the business side of their endeavors by providing management and marketing assistance, group-buying health care plans, and educational programs. The CAGW advocates for the arts, cultivates public participation in the arts, and creates partnerships between Washington's artistic and business communities.

Greater Washington Society of Association Executives (GWSAE)

1426 21st Street NW, Washington, DC 20036
Tel: 202-429-9370; FAX: 202-833-1129
E-mail: general@gwsae.org; WWW: http://www.gwsae.org/,
http://www.vcanet.org (The Virtual Community of Associations)
▶ The Greater Washington Society of Association Executives (GWSAE) serves thousands of association professionals who work in the Washington region's 3,500-plus trade, professional, and philanthropic associations. GWSAE accomplishes this by focusing on three principal areas—professional development for association professionals, knowledge development for the association profession, and relationship and partnership building among association executives and industry partners. The Society and the GWSAE Foundation for Association Leadership offer educational programs and information resources, including The Nation's Capital Distinguished Speakers Series; Springtime in the Park®, a trade show for association meeting professionals; Associations Innovate™, a conference designed to encourage greater innovation in associations; *Executive Update,* GWSAE's magazine; the GWSAE Career Services Center, which helps association professionals become more marketable and matches candidates with association positions; and nearly 100 other professional and career development programs for association CEOs, senior executives, and staff specialists. Check out JOBSmart on their Web site (*http://www.gwsae.org/JOBSmart*), the marketplace for association careers in the Greater Washington, DC area. The GWSAE Business Connection is a searchable database of GWSAE supplier members. It is in the process of creating a Center for Association Leadership. Their Virtual Community of Associations (VCA) Member Directory provides a resource for locating associations and their Web sites.

Social Action and Leadership School for Activists (SALSA)

The Institute for Policy Studies, 733 15th Street NW, Suite 1020,
Washington, DC 20005
Tel: 202-234-9382, ext. #229, FAX: 202-387-7915
E-mail: netfas@hotsalsa.org (Netfa Freeman, Executive
Director); WWW: http://www.hotsalsa.org

▶ This is an evening learning program providing classes in the Washington, DC area on scores of topics in nonprofit management, communications, fund raising, direct action, and career development.

Support Center of Washington

2001 O Street NW, Washington, DC 20036-5955
Tel: 202-833-0300; FAX: 202-857-0077
E-mail: supportcenter@scw.org; WWW: http://www.scw.org

▶ In addition to training and consulting programs, the Center coaches executives and board members, facilitates dialogue within and among nonprofits, and encourages networking that leads to collaborative efforts to improve service and make the best use of funding. Services include consulting (strategic planning, board, staff, and client diversity, organizational development, fund raising, leadership and management skills, information systems planning and acquisition, data management, application of information technology, desktop publishing, Internet resources and development, board development, volunteer management, conflict management, supervision, human resource development, team building, and financial management); training (Planning & Managing for Results, professional development, board development, effective supervision, effective communication, fund raising, Meet the Funders, financial management, marketing and public relations, and computer applications).

Washington Council of Agencies (WCA)

1001 Connecticut Avenue NW, Suite 925, Washington, DC 20036
Tel: 202-457-0540; FAX: 202-457-0549
E-mail: wca@wcanonprofits.org (Betsy Johnson);
WWW: http://www.wcanonprofits.org

▶ The Washington Council of Agencies is a membership organization of nonprofit organizations based in the Washington, DC metropolitan area. WCA provides advocacy/community building activities, educational and networking opportunities, and group-buying purchasing power. Membership is open to any 501(c) organization in the Washington, DC metropolitan area. Founded in 1979, WCA currently has over 700 members. Programs/services include educational opportunities (brown-bag lunch workshops, New Executive Director Support Group, Nonprofit Management Skill Development Series); publications (offers publications to assist area nonprofit organizations); *The WCA Nonprofit Agenda* (the newsletter for the Washington area nonprofit community); the Clearinghouse on Nonprofit Management Issues (offers assistance with a wide variety of nonprofit management issues); the *Washington Post* Award for Excellence in Nonprofit Management; and advocacy (WCA advocates on behalf of its membership and the entire nonprofit community; monitors and analyzes relevant local-level, sector-wide legislation and public policy issues that impact regional nonprofit organizations; read about current legislative and community building in the latest *WCA Advocacy Alert!*). Additionally, the WCA Nonprofit e-Genda (available at *http://www.wcanonprofits.org/newsletter1852/newsletter.htm*) serves as the online newsletter of the Washington Council of Agencies. Included in this section is late-breaking news, important information from the current newsletter, *The WCA Nonprofit Agenda,* as well as classic information from past newsletters.

ILLINOIS

Institute for Voluntary Organizations, Inc.

Center for Creative Management, 4800 Prince,
Downers Grove, IL 60515
Tel: 630-964-0432
E-mail: billconrad@mediaone.net (Bill Conrad, President);
WWW: http://www.ifvo.org/

▶ Their primary mission since 1975 has been to support and help preserve our voluntary traditions by assisting voluntary organizations strengthen their leadership/management systems. They provide reasonably priced, practice-proven, and conceptually consistent publications, training, and consultations. Their fully integrated management practices model for nonprofit organizations maximizes the collective effort and effectiveness for all the publics involved with successfully providing community services.

Center for Nonprofit Excellence (CNE)

Professional Development Institute at Illinois Central College,
Illinois Central College, Peoria Campus, Perley Bldg.,
115 SW Adams Street, Peoria, IL 61635-0001
Tel: 309-999-4550; FAX: 309-999-4549
E-mail: eswiontkowskidenardis@icc.cc.il.us (Eva M.
Swiontkowski-de Nardis, Coordinator), fthomas@icc.cc.il.us;
WWW: http://www.icc.cc.il.us/pdi/nonpft.htm

▶ CNE is committed to developing efficient and effective nonprofit management skills by offering quality educational programming while providing information and resources to area nonprofits. It offers small, individualized classes and instructors with practical nonprofit experience. CNE serves nonprofit organizations of central Illinois and their benefactors by providing assessment, tools, consultation, training, and administrative support services, all designed to enhance the efficiency, productivity, and effectiveness of the entire nonprofit process. Through membership in the CNE, local organizations with federal tax-exempt status receive an award certificate entitling them to free and/or discounted classes in nonprofit management and computer training. Individuals may earn a Certificate in Nonprofit Management.

Executive Service Corps of Chicago

30 West Monroe Street, Suite 600, Chicago, IL 60603
Tel: 312-850-1840; FAX: 312-580-0042
E-mail: info@esc-chicago.org, nancy.fuhrman@esc-chicago.org;
WWW: http://www.esc-chicago.org/

▶ The Executive Service Corps of Chicago is a consultant to nonprofit and government organizations on board and management issues. Executive Service Corps's consulting services cover the following areas: management issues (administration, human resources, communications/PR, information management, facilities, marketing, finance, organization analysis); board issues (board development, strategic planning, revenue generation); facilitation services (retreat, focus groups).

Illinois Association of Non-Profit Organizations (IANO)

8 South Michigan Avenue, Suite 3000, Chicago, IL 60603
Tel: 312-357-1707; Fax: 312-236-9679
E-mail: iano@iano-online.org;
WWW: http://www.iano-online.org/

▶ The Illinois Association of Non-Profit Organizations (IANO) was founded in 1989 as a statewide membership organization for nonprofit organizations, consultants, for-profit businesses serving the nonprofit community, and individuals interested in the nonprofit sector. The purpose is to provide educational and managerial programs, technical assistance, advocacy, and information/referral services to nonprofit organizations in the state of Illinois. Of special interest to IANO is the fostering and nurturing of newly formed nonprofit agencies to see that they receive skill building to help them survive. Services/programs include Information Network (IANO's central clearinghouse gives nonprofits the opportunity to share critical information through *Illinois Non-Profit Chronicle,* a quarterly newsletter to inform members about current laws, regulations, resources, grant deadlines, and information, free materials, and more; *Monthly Memo and Job Line,* a monthly newsletter about current jobs, current events, grants, gifts-in-kind, donations, programs, and more; Information Hotline, a telephone reference service to answer basic questions about nonprofit management, services, referrals, start-up information, insurance, etc.; Directory of Internships in Illinois Non-Profit Organizations); educational programs (Board Development Institute; Annual Non-Profit Convention; Special Events Extravaganza; Statewide Housing Conference; Nonprofit Certificate Program); and partnerships with other organizations (IANO is able to negotiate discounted services and products for its members). IANO also maintains an office in Oak Park, Illinois.

Nonprofit Leadership Initiative

The Center for Organizational Research and Development, Campus Box 1456, Southern Illinois University–Edwardsville, Edwardsville, IL 62026-1456
E-mail: rbush@siue.edu (Richard Bush, Director, Community and Nonprofit Leadership Initiative), aparisi@siue.edu (Ann Parisi); WWW: http://www.rrds.siue.edu/non-prof.htm

▶ Nonprofit Leadership Initiative provides comprehensive assessment services to evaluate existing community-oriented programs, determine their accomplishments, and provide measurement tools to track results. The team works closely with clients to improve management and processes within nonprofit organizations, voluntary associations, and the community as a whole. This is accomplished through the variety of services that they offer. Services include fund raising/development, grant writing training, board development, strategic planning, search conferencing, capacity building, collaboration/partnership building, recruitment of interns/volunteers, needs/capacity assessment, and human resources for nonprofits.

Support Center of Chicago

3811 North Lawndale Avenue, Suite 100, Chicago, IL 60618
Tel: 773-539-4741; FAX: 773-539-4751
E-mail: supportchi@aol.com (Valerie Zimmer); WWW: http://www.sc-chicago.org/

▶ SCC serves nonprofit organizations throughout the metropolitan Chicago area and is affiliated with the Alliance for Nonprofit Management. Programs/services include training: providing workshops on organizational and leadership development, human resource management, fund raising, marketing, financial management and computer applications; consulting: addressing critical organizational needs in board and staff leadership, marketing, resource development, program and systems design and evaluation, and computer systems development; board development: Training customized to meet specific needs, including roles and responsibilities, board/staff relations, fund raising planning and strategy, strategic planning, and business development; on-site training: tailoring any of the workshops listed in its catalogs and more, exclusively for an organization or conference—all the benefits of public training plus custom features for the specific group; management assistance: taking an objective and realistic look at an organization's current internal strengths and weaknesses as well as opportunities and threats that exist in the environment; strategic planning: creating a road map for any organization's future, whether starting from scratch or updating an existing plan; meeting and retreat facilitation: giving every participant the opportunity to enter fully and equally in planning problem solving and decision.

United Way (Chicago)

560 West Lake Street, Chicago, IL 60661
Tel: 312-575-2578 (Phyllis Bracey)
E-mail: info@uwonline.org, mleonard@uwonline.org (Michael Leonard, Management Consultant and Trainer); WWW: http://www.uwcmercy.org/resources/services.asp

▶ United Way's Agency Services unit develops and delivers management support services in these areas: Agency Workshops (United Way offers two kinds of agency training in a full array of nonprofit management topics. They offer customized training available at your site; Customized Training (They customize workshops to meet your needs and conduct them at your site. In addition to bringing their regular workshops to your site, they provide training in areas such as sexual harassment and progressive discipline policies and procedures that are better suited for on-site delivery. United Way's agency-based trainings reflect a core curriculum of management support topics. Course length can range from half days, several days, or over a period of several weeks based on your needs and schedule. They design the programs in consultation with you. Examples of trainings include: first-time supervisors; advanced supervisory skills; progressive discipline; sexual harassment; team building; conflict resolution; diversifying the funding mix; program planning and evaluation; the role of the board in successful fundraising; understanding financial statements); consulting services (they provide consultation to management and boards of directors in a variety of areas, such as: board development; planning [operational assessments, strategic planning]; organizational development; communication and conflict resolution; team building; human resources; personnel policy reviews; salary surveys; resource development; fundraising plans and assessments; membership campaign assessments); faciliation of meetings and retreats (they have skilled and impartial facilitators to keep your group focused and on schedule. They regularly facilitate board retreats, management planning sessions, meetings of community groups, and agency collaborations. They have worked with groups ranging in size from five to over 100); Staff development planning (they work with your management and HR staff to design and deliver training geared to the needs of your staff. They have developed training series for managers in supervision, staff evaluation, conflict resolution and time management); executive coaching (their consultants provide confidential one-on-one coaching and support for new executive directors and individuals with new development director/management responsibilities. It is a pro-bono service providing a safe place for individuals to explore their new role and responsibilities).

INDIANA

Indiana Nonprofit Resource Network

Indiana Association of United Ways, 3901 North Meridian Street, Suite 306, Indianapolis, IN 46208-4026
Tel: 800-457-1450; FAX: 317-921-1397
E-mail: lisa.hanger@iauw.org (Lisa Hanger);
WWW: http://www.iauw.org

▶ The Network is a partnership of four United Ways and the United Way of Central Indiana's Nonprofit Training Center. They work as a team with IAUW to meet Indiana United Ways/Funds and other nonprofit organizations' training and development needs. By partnering with organizations such as Ivy Tech, National Center for Nonprofit Boards, Indiana University Center on Philanthropy, and Indiana Grantmakers Alliance, the Network is able to increase access to valuable speakers, programs and events. Basic services include workshops, consultant referral, library resources for loan or reference, and nonprofit certificate programs.

KANSAS

Community Association of Nonprofit Business Executives (CANBE)

P.O. Box 3743, Olathe, KS 66063-3743
Tel: 913-393-0316
E-mail: canbinfo@canbe.org; WWW: http://www.canbe.org/

▶ Supports and strengthens Greater Kansas City nonprofit organizations in their administrative, financial, and human resource functions by bringing together professionals to share expertise and to gain new skills and knowledge. CANBE is a membership-based, professional development organization. Your membership entitles you to the following benefits: discounts to attend quarterly seminars featuring area experts in nonprofit administration, finance and human resources; discounts to attend its annual Fall Symposium featuring national speakers who discuss cutting-edge trends in the nonprofit field; free members-only brown bag lunches to discuss topics selected by members that impact your job and career; discounts through CANBE's Group Purchasing Agreement with Kansas City Council for Regional Education for office supplies, custodial supplies, office furniture, computer equipment, long distance, car and van rental, even natural gas for your agency's facility; discounts for health insurance through First Guard, offering 5 percent off its already affordable rates, rate caps for continued coverage, and a simplified enrollment process for medical and vision coverage; networking opportunities with colleagues in the nonprofit field; access to vendor representatives to help you save time and money; exclusive member updates, including *News You Can Use,* which highlight management trends, book reviews, and meeting summaries; members-only access to job postings of regional positions in administration, finance, and human resources; membership directory organized by name and area of expertise; and a display booth at its annual symposium for corporate associate members.

KENTUCKY

Center for Nonprofit Excellence

2001 Newburg Road, Louisville, KY 40205
Tel: 502-452-8272; FAX: 502-452-8376
E-mail: kconnelly@cnpe.org; WWW: http://www.cnpe.org/

▶ The Center for Nonprofit Excellence was created as the result of a 14-month planning process headed by the Donors Forum of Louisville, Metro United Way, the City of Louisville, the Community Foundation of Louisville, and other civic leadership groups. Bellarmine College has provided space for the Center. It plans to complement the mission of Bellarmine's five-course certification program in Nonprofit Leadership (*http://www.bellarmine.edu/conteduc/noncredit/nonprofit.asp*). Its newsletter, *The Schedule Plus,* provides information about upcoming training and educational opportunities. Also featured will be trends in nonprofit organizations, best practices, and ways to access funding sources. Services include training; consultation; research; forums on special topics to nonprofit staff and board leadership; training bulletins and publications about educational opportunities for nonprofit leaders, their staff, and volunteers; and networking with other nonprofits in the area.

LOUISIANA

Center for Nonprofit Resources

3801 Canal Street, Suite 309, New Orleans, LA 70119
Tel: 504-483-8080; FAX: 504-483-8087
E-mail: nonprof@iamerica.net (Monica Roers, President and CEO); WWW: http://www.geocities.com/center_nonprofit, http://www.nonprofitresources.org/GeneralInformationGSAI.htm

▶ Nonprofit management assistance organization serving the greater New Orleans area. The mission of the Center for Nonprofit Resources is to increase the effectiveness and efficiency of the private, not-for-profit community by providing a wide range of high-quality management support services to address the needs of staff and volunteer leadership of private, not-for-profit organizations. Services include training programs (the Center offers various workshops throughout the year designed to help nonprofit staff and volunteers acquire the latest tools and resources for effective management. The Center's most in-demand training program is BoardsWork!, the premiere board training and development program in the New Orleans area. BoardsWork! is for individuals who aspire to be nonprofit board members); consulting services (board development, strategic planning, fund development, organizational assessment, outcome evaluation). The Center annually hosts the Grantsmanship Center for a five-day, hands-on grantwriting workshop. It also offers the Managing for Excellence conference, a four-day, annual conference that offers high-quality management workshops to staff, boards, and volunteers of nonprofit organizations. Seminar topics include leadership development, fund raising, financial management, marketing, office management, and much more. The Center offers a three-hour workshop three times a year at which an attorney, a certified public accountant, an IRS representative, and a nonprofit executive director address the legal, financial, and organizational issues to be considered before starting a nonprofit organization. The Center houses a collection of nonprofit management resource materials that are available during business hours.

Louisiana Association of Nonprofit Organizations (LANO)

700 North 10th Street, Suite 250, Baton Rouge, LA 70821
Tel: 225-343-5266; FAX: 225-343-5363
E-mail: contactus@lano.org, melissa@lano.org (Melissa Flournoy); WWW: http://www.lano.org

▶ The Louisiana Association of Nonprofit Organizations (LANO) was convened by the Council for a Better Louisiana (CABL). LANO has received planning grants from the Foundation for the Mid-South, the Frost Foundation, and the National Council on Nonprofit Associations to support the development of a statewide network of nonprofit leaders. LANO helps nonprofits work together by providing a technical assistance network; information, education, and public policy assistance; cost-saving services and benefits such as health insurance and group purchasing options. Programs and services include Nonprofit Management Institute, state conference, legislative events, and advocacy training. LANO publications include: *The Nonprofit News of Louisiana* (quarterly newsletter); *$ and Sense: Profile of Louisiana Nonprofits; Capitol Views: State and National Public Policy Perspectives; LANO Notes* (periodic reports on topics of interest; *LANO Technical Assistance Guide* (a statewide listing of community-based technical assistance resources); *LANO Nonprofit Policy Makers Guide; The Louisiana Directory of Nonprofit Organizations; Monthly Member Mailings* of events, national activities, opportunities for funding and trainings; and *Public Policy Alerts.* LANO holds an annual conference.

MAINE

Maine Association of Nonprofits (MANP)

565 Congress Street, Suite 301, Portland, ME 04101
Tel: 207-871-1885; FAX: 207-780-0346
E-mail: manp@nonprofitmaine.org, jwalker@nonprofitmaine.org (John Walker); WWW: http://www.nonprofitmaine.org

▶ Formed in 1994 by a core of seven nonprofits, MANP is a statewide organization dedicated to strengthening the leadership and management effectiveness of Maine's nonprofits. The Association's current initiatives include Nonprofits First Employer Coalition (a program of MANP dedicated to supporting the nonprofit employer); Nonprofit Sector Future Search Initiative (find out what nonprofit stakeholders have been doing over the last two years as a result of this project); technical support (advocates for well-trained staff and effectively governed boards); group services (negotiated bulk-purchase discounts for nonprofits, and a full-range health plan offered through the Nonprofits First Employer Coalition); networking opportunities through regional forums and other collaborative efforts; and *Advocacy,* which promotes an understanding of nonprofit work.

Membership benefits include professional development (monthly workshops in areas that will assist nonprofits in building their organizations in such areas as human resources, fund raising, and many more; *Nonprofit Maine Newsletter,* the quarterly which provides the most current news in the nonprofit world in Maine and nationally and also includes a special technical section; annual conference (attracts nonprofit leaders from all over the state to address issues concerning all nonprofit organizations and offers technical training workshops); involvement; and support services (MANP OnLine, Wage & Benefit Survey, Nonprofit Employers Coalition, group purchasing, consultant databank, staff help line, resource clearinghouse).

MARYLAND

The Development Training Institute, Inc. (DTI)

2510 St. Paul Street, Baltimore, MD 21218-4510
Tel: 410-338-2512,129; FAX: 410-338-2751
E-mail: drothman@dtinational.org;
WWW: http://www.dtinational.org

▶ Founded in 1981, The Development Training Institute (DTI) is a trainer of leaders in community development. It offers comprehensive services to individuals and organizations working in community development. DTI provides a continuum of services and a range of levels of assistance. Services include training, consulting/technical assistance, information and the ability to build your skills without leaving your office through online skill-building tools and training, and DTI's Community Building Investment Program (CBI), which can help you cover the costs associated with organizational and/or project development, including computers and staff (these awards are currently only available to HUD-certified Community Housing Development Organizations).

Maryland Association of Nonprofit Organizations

Main office: 190 West Ostend Street, Suite 201,
Baltimore, MD 21230
Tel: 800-273-6367 (MD only), 410-727-6367; FAX: 410-727-1914
E-mail: pberns@mdnonprofit.org (Peter Berns)

Suburban Washington office: 8720 Georgia Avenue, Suite 303,
Silver Spring, MD 20910
Tel: 877-565-0707 (MD only), 301-565-0505; FAX: 301-565-0606
E-mail: mdnp@mdnonprofit.org;
WWW: http://www.mdnonprofit.org/

▶ The Maryland Association of Nonprofit Organizations (Maryland Nonprofits) is a statewide association of more than 790 member organizations dedicated to strengthening the individual nonprofits as well as the entire nonprofit sector. Membership benefits include training and technical assistance (classroom-style training programs, house calls training programs, technical assistance, consultant databank, lawyers clearinghouse); cooperative buying programs; information sharing and networking (monthly member mailing, roundtables, and monthly member meetings); public policy advocacy; researching and promoting the nonprofit sector (through projects and programs like the Ethics and Accountability Initiative and Private Action/Public Good, Maryland's Nonprofit Sector in a time of change).

MASSACHUSETTS

The Executive Service Corps of New England (ESCNE)

87 Summer Street, 3rd Floor, Boston, MA 02110
Tel: 617-357-5550; FAX: 617-423-2510
E-mail: arubin@escne.org (Annette Rubin), jschultz@escne.org (Jim Schultz, Director of Consulting);
WWW: http://www.escne.org

▶ The Executive Service Corps of New England is a 501(c)(3) nonprofit corporation with headquarters in Boston. The mission of the Executive Service Corps is to improve the quality of life in the community we serve by enabling nonprofit agencies, principally in the fields of human services, the arts, and education, to operate more efficiently and effectively to meet the needs of their constituents. ESCNE works with the nonprofit community in Boston, eastern Massachusetts, Cape Cod, Rhode Island, New Hampshire, and Maine. They offer a wide array of support for nonprofits that includes in-depth management consulting with organizations throughout eastern Massachusetts (including Cape Cod), Rhode Island, New Hampshire, and Maine on a variety of issues ranging from board development to strategic planning; supporting the work of public school administrators through the Leadership Program—

an intensive leadership development and skills-building program; publishing *Opportunity NOCs,* the biweekly job bulletin and Web site linking nonprofit practitioners with jobs in the nonprofit sector; sponsoring an acclaimed annual day-long nonprofit Management Conference, which brings together nonprofits throughout New England for a unique interactive learning experience. ESCNE offers consulting services in strategic planning, board development, fund raising, human resources management, information technology, communications, and public relations. It also works in a broad range of other areas, including mergers, marketing, market research, operations management, facilitation, real estate, risk management, feasibility studies, budgeting, accounting controls, startups, and turnaround management. ESCNE holds an annual nonprofit management conference.

Human Service Forum

P.O. Box 3040, Springfield, MA 01102-3040
Tel: 413-773-2691, ext. #115; FAX: 413-788-4130
E-mail: forum@unitedwaytogo.org

▶ Founded in 1986, the Human Service Forum is an association of over 160 nonprofit and public agencies and individuals providing human services in the Pioneer Valley. The Forum serves as a vehicle for members to network, address problems of mutual concern, and discuss major trends and changes impacting social services. Services and programs include information (training; workshops, conferences, and educational series are offered. Topics include: supervision and leadership, legal issues, fiscal management, public relations, professional skills for support staff, problem solving, and board development; networking: at informal gatherings, roundtable discussions, and dialogues, human service workers meet, work together, and learn from each other; breakfast meetings: speakers address cutting-edge issues of interest to human service professionals; newsletter: distributed five times a year with items of interest, including a human service event calendar, member news, public relations suggestions, and technology updates); advocacy; public relations; and marketing member agencies (ongoing efforts to increase positive media coverage of member agencies and the work they do).

Interaction Institute for Social Change

20 University Road, 4th Floor, Cambridge, MA 02138
Tel: 617-234-2750; FAX: 617-234-4410
E-mail: mparra@interactioninstitute.org

600 Townsend Street, Suite 550, San Francisco, CA 94103
Tel: 415-241-8000; FAX: 415-241-8010
E-mail: scourtney@interactioninstitute.org;
WWW: http://www.interactioninstitute.org/

▶ Its mission is to transfer the skills and tools of collaboration to nonprofit and community-based organizations that want to transform communities and to promote the spirit and practice of collaborative action by facilitating partnerships between corporations and low-income groups. Products and services include training, consulting, facilitation, partnerships, and education practice.

Management Assistance Program/Justice Resource Institute

100 Boylston Street, Suite 860, Boston, MA 02116
Tel: 617-988-2605; FAX: 617-988-2629
E-mail: MAP@JRIHealth.org, jcarey@jrihealth.org (Juliet Carey, Director); WWW: http://www.jrihealth.org/programs/map/www/

▶ The Management Assistance Program (MAP) is designed to provide an array of management support and development services to community-based, nonprofit organizations. MAP's services are based on a holistic systems approach in order to build learning, participative organizations. By strengthening the organizations from within, MAP helps ensure that they remain dynamic, viable, and responsive to the changing needs of their communities. MAP's activities fall into four categories: organizational assessments, management consultant services, staff and board trainings and topical conferences and forums.

Massachusetts Council of Human Service Providers

250 Summer Street, Suite 1, Boston, MA 02210
Tel: 617-428-3637; FAX: 617-428-1533
E-mail: mweekes@providers.org (Michael Weekes),
Naomi@providers.org; WWW: http://www.providers.org/

▶ The Providers' Council is a statewide association of private, community-based, care-giving organizations that provide educational, health, and social services. Founded in 1976, the Providers' Council is the state's largest human service trade association and is widely recognized as the official voice of the private provider industry. Benefits of membership include political representation, education and training, leadership opportunities, supplier partnerships, communications (through their Provider newspaper, the *Provider Insider,* fax alerts, letters, media strategy, and phone calls, they keep you abreast of the most important developments as they happen, and interpret their impact on the industry), and information. *The Provider* is the flagship publication of the Massachusetts Council of Human Service Providers, Inc. As a major publication of the human service trade association, it serves as a source of news and views, not only for Council members, but also other trade associations, nonmembers, and state managers. The Council holds an annual nonprofit convention and expo.

Nonprofit Center

Isenberg School of Management, University of Massachusetts, Amherst, MA 01003
Tel: 413-545-5685; FAX: 413-545-3858
E-mail: skulik@som.umass.edu (Suzanne Kulik),
diamond@mktg.umass.edu (William Diamond),
http://www.som.umass.edu/som/community/nonprofit/

▶ The Nonprofit Center at the Isenberg School of Management at the University of Massachusetts, Amherst offers a variety of services to strengthen the links between the school and the nonprofit community, including research on topics of value to nonprofit organizations, such as image development and the design of direct-mail fund raising appeals; graduate and undergraduate student consulting to provide assistance to local nonprofits in a variety of business areas under faculty supervision; graduate-level nonprofit management courses offered through the Isenberg School of Management; professional development courses, workshops, and in-service training offered to volunteers and staff of nonprofit organizations; and business student volunteers available for short-term or ongoing placement in local nonprofit agencies. SOM students have business skills to share in addition to an interest in community service, and liaison services with other resources at the University of Massachusetts that can serve nonprofit organizations. The Center helps agencies find the assistance they need among the many departments and programs available on campus.

The Nonprofit Support Center

Greater Worcester Community Foundation, 44 Front Street,
Worcester, MA 01608
Tel: 508-755-0980; FAX: 508-755-3406
E-mail: grandall@greaterworcester.org (Gail Randall);
WWW: http://www.greaterworcester.org/nonprofit.htm

▶ The Nonprofit Support Center was founded in 1991 as the Coalition for Not-for-Profit Management Assistance by the United Way of Central Massachusetts, the Colleges of Worcester Consortium, and the Greater Worcester Community Foundation. It works to help nonprofit leaders manage their limited resources more effectively and creatively. The Nonprofit Support Center exists to stimulate the development of a capable, forward-thinking, and collaborative nonprofit sector. Its programs and services help organizations think strategically, govern effectively, and work cooperatively with community partners. Services to senior managers and governing board members of Central Massachusetts nonprofit organizations include seminars, workshops, and conferences (programs on a wide range of strategic management and governance issues); organizational assessment (tools and guidance to help nonprofit groups assess their operations); short-term consultation (time-limited intervention on management and governance concerns); technical assistance grants (financial support for strategic redirection efforts that meet Nonprofit Support Center guidelines); and resources and referral (information on nonprofit trends, consultants, and best practices including manuals, books, and computer disks on a wide range of topics).

Third Sector New England (TSNE)

18 Tremont Street, Suite 700, Boston, MA 02108
Tel: 617-523-6565; FAX: 617-523-2070
E-mail: jspack@tsne.org (Jonathan Spack, Executive Director);
WWW: http://www.tsne.net/

▶ Third Sector New England (TSNE) is an evolving resource center for nonprofit organizations, foundations, and others involved in voluntary activity. Its mission is to help the sector improve its understanding of its role and potential impact within a rapidly shifting economy, and to provide materials and services that build knowledge, skills, and capacity. Programs and services include information and education programs (*New England Nonprofit Quarterly;* The New England Nonprofit Exposition; TSNE Web site, which serves as a forum for discussion about topics raised in the *New England Nonprofit Quarterly* and at the Exposition, which also acts as a bulletin board for events, training, and educational opportunities and other resources, while providing hyperlinks to literature on various topics of interest to the region's nonprofits; research and original writing); Collaborative Capacity Building Services (consulting and training to support the development of learning organizations, capacity building among multiple organizations, and large scale events); Management for the Purely Mission Based (to provide management support and capacity building that allows unincorporated groups to maintain an exclusive focus on mission and program until they choose to build their own institutional infrastructure).

MICHIGAN

Detroit Executive Service Corps (DESC)

23815 Northwestern Highway, Southfield, MI 48075
Tel: 248-213-1780
E-mail: descdm@worldnet.att.net, (Deanna McGraw, Executive Director); WWW: http://comnet.org/desc

▶ DESC's mission is to facilitate the development of more effective managerial and operational practices by nonprofit and governmental organizations in the greater Detroit area. It provides consultation and management advice to nonprofits and government agencies. Specializes in organizational analysis, strategic planning and board development. Its volunteer consultants are retired and active business executives.

Direction Center

118 Commerce Avenue SW, Suite 210,
Grand Rapids, MI 49503-4106
Tel: 888-790-NPOS (6767), 616-459-3773; FAX: 616-451-4390
E-mail: nelsonp@river.it.gvsu.edu (Paul Nelson, President);
WWW: http://www2.gvsu.edu/~directct

▶ Direction Center is a nonprofit organization that provides training, consulting, and research services to West Michigan nonprofits to strengthen and support their operations, board governance, and leadership capacities. It is part of the Alliance for Nonprofit Management. If offers consulting and other types of assistance to nonprofit organizations in western Michigan. Services/programs include consulting services (strategic planning, board training and development, needs assessment, evaluations, market research, management training and consultation, proposal/grant application critique, research on community issues and opportunities, leadership building, staff development, diversity training, human resource management, total quality service consultation); online computer research (grants database, electric library); diversity video program; and publications. Direction Center has teamed up with Michigan Nonprofit Association and Crain's Nonprofit News (*http://www.crainsdetroit.com/nonprof.html*) to place West Michigan nonprofit classified ads in *Crain's Nonprofit News*—a biweekly newsletter that covers Michigan's nonprofit sector. This service offers agencies an inexpensive and easy way to place classified ads to recruit personnel. Direction Center will also receive a small commission for each classified ad it places.

Jackson Nonprofit Support Center

325 W. Michigan Avenue, Jackson, MI 49201
Tel: 517-796-4750; FAX: 517-796-5981
E-mail: shelly@jacksonnonprofit.org (Shelly Schadewald,
Executive Director); WWW: http://www.jacksonnonprofit.org/

▶ The Jackson Nonprofit Support Center provides management and volunteer support to nonprofits through services including information clearinghouse functions, training, consulting, and an on-site resource library. Services include personalized technical assistance; profiles of Jackson County nonprofit organizations and their programs and services; volunteer job descriptions and vacancies; calendars of fund-raising events and campaigns; calendars of seminars and education workshops; organizational assessments; consulting services on how to become a community partner; consulting services on the promotion of volunteerism; and an extensive resource library

Michigan League for Human Services

300 North Washington Square, Suite 401, Lansing, MI 48933
Tel: 517-487-5436; FAX: 517-371-4546
WWW: http://www.milhs.org

▶ Michigan League for Human Services offers lobbying support and member services, including insurance plans; low-interest loans;

seminars on legal, human resource, liability, and financial management topics; and several publications. A subsidiary, the Michigan League Insurance Project for Nonprofits Inc., helps agencies save insurance premium dollars.

Michigan Nonprofit Association (MNA)

Contact: Sam Singh, 29 Kellogg Center,
East Lansing, MI 48824-1022
Tel: 888-242-7075 (Michigan only), 517-353-5038, 487-5436;
FAX: 517-355-3302
E-mail: singhsam@pilot.msu.edu (Sam Singh, President and
CEO), jharper@pilot.msu.edu (Jan Harper, Director of Nonprofit
Outreach); WWW: http://www.mna.msu.edu

▶ Statewide membership organization devoted to promoting awareness and effectiveness of Michigan's nonprofit sector and to advance the cause of volunteerism and philanthropy. It offers members public policy updates, conferences, training, and technical assistance. It co-sponsors an annual Grant-makers/Grant-seekers conference with the Council of Michigan Foundations as well as Nonprofit Day. It is affiliated with two volunteer promotion groups—Michigan Campus Compact and Volunteer Centers of Michigan. Publications include the *Michigan Association and Nonprofit Compensation and Benefit Survey.* Its print and online Nonprofit Management Training Catalog features the training resources of Michigan's universities and management support organizations in supporting effective management of the nonprofit organizations serving the citizens of Michigan. Services include board management, ethical and legal issues, financial planning/auditing, fund raising, governing documents, leadership development, personnel management, public policy, program management, strategic planning, technology/computer management; and volunteer management. Membership benefits include public policy alerts; regional training; discounts; member publications (the MNA *Member Update* features nonprofit classified ads, public policy news, funding opportunities, calendar of events, and feature articles of interest to Michigan's nonprofit organizations; MNA generates publications for the following: MNA public policy updates and alerts; mini-grant information, brochure and information packet, monthly member update, membership directory, nonprofit employment classified ads, MSAE/MNA Compensation & Benefit Survey, NCNB publications and *Michigan in Brief*).

NonProfit Alliance (NPA)

Willard Public Library, 7 West Van Buren Street,
Battle Creek, MI 49017
Tel: 616-968-8166, ext. 548
WWW: http://www.willard.lib.mi.us/npa/npahome.html

▶ A membership organization dedicated to serving, supporting, and strengthening the nonprofit community of Calhoun County, Michigan. NPA connects member agencies to appropriate consulting resource by conducting an initial assessment to identify strengths and opportunities, identifying the goals to be achieved, providing the member agency with several referrals for agency screening and selection, developing a service agreement, and providing services to ensure that the goals of the relationship have been met. A prime focus of NPA is to help agencies themselves and build their capacity to serve the community. Types of services include strategic planning, needs assessment, board development, marketing, fund raising, grant writing, staff development, leadership building, team building, initial grant planning, market research,

management consultation, evaluations, legal liability information, financial management, diversity training, agency assessment, and information and referral. NPA provides initial technical assistance and referrals to both paid and volunteer consultants based on the needs of the organization. Membership benefits include: quarterly newsletter regarding nonprofit topic; *NonProfit Alliance Membership Directory;* stipends to fund organizational development activities; *Journal Information Alert* (synopsis of nonprofit journal articles); *Funding Opportunities* (biannually); voting privileges: NPA board of directors; eligibility for nomination to NPA board of directors; Web page development and server space; training calendar information; Great Lakes Free Net *Members Only* site with nonprofit information; and a discount on Foundation Center materials (20%).

Nonprofit Enterprises at Work (NEW)

1100 North Main Street, Suite 101, Ann Arbor, MI 48104
Tel: 734-998-0160; FAX: 734-938-0163
E-mail: new@new.org; WWW:
http://comnet.org/local/orgs/newcenter/

▶ Nonprofit Enterprises at Work is a nonprofit organization located in Ann Arbor, Michigan, that provides a variety of services to the nonprofit sector and the larger community. NEW promotes the value of nonprofit services to society while helping to strengthen nonprofit organizations through improvements in resource utilization and management practices. NEW accomplishes this through the efforts of a professional management team, a network of experts, and a complement of volunteers and interns. NEW fosters collaboration between nonprofits and provides facilities, information and support services, educational programs, and leadership development. Services include: conference (the Working Together for a Better Community Conference brings together community leaders to facilitate the creation of alliances and the sharing of knowledge through a biannual working conference); consulting (NEW's Consulting Consortium provides accessible and affordable consulting services to nonprofit organizations); excellence awards (the Nonprofit Excellence Awards celebrate the central role and achievements of Washtenaw County's nonprofit community); library (NEW offers a one-of-a-kind resource center for nonprofit organizations at the NEW Center, as well as a collection of online resources from a wide variety of sources; recent additions is available on their online book store); Nonprofit Leadership Forum (brings prominent speakers from throughout the region to speak on sector trends and engage in dialogue with nonprofit leaders); office and meeting space (NEW Center is home to 21 nonprofit agencies to whom it provides shared facilities at below-market rent; it also has conference facilities available to other community nonprofits); Online management resources; on-site training; Web development; workshops (NEW's workshop series, "Managing for Nonprofit Excellence," provides opportunities to improve management skills in areas pertinent to the nonprofit sector). Additional training opportunities for nonprofits, offered by other agencies, are also available.

Nonprofit Leadership and Administration

School of Public Affairs and Administration,
Western Michigan University, Kalamazoo, MI 49008
Tel: 616-387-8930; FAX: 616-387-8935
E-mail: barbara.liggett@wmich.edu (Dr. Barbara Liggett);
WWW: http://www.wmich.edu/nonprofit/index.html

▶ Western Michigan University, with support from the W.K. Kellogg Foundation, is helping nonprofit organizations meet the challenges of a new millennium. Mutually beneficial partnerships with nonprofits are allowing the university to learn from nonprofit leaders in the community while providing the nonprofit community with university-based concepts and theories to improve and increase organizational capacity. Toward these goals, WMU proudly offers a graduate certificate in nonprofit leadership and administration.

MINNESOTA

Amherst H. Wilder Foundation
919 Lafond Avenue, St. Paul, MN 55104
Tel: 651-642-2083; FAX: 651-642-2088
E-mail: consultants@wilder.org; WWW: http://www.wilder.org/

▶ The Amherst H. Wilder Foundation provides training and consulting services to nonprofit, government, and community organizations in the Twin Cities area, with emphasis on the central urban communities of Saint Paul. Areas of expertise include collaboration planning and development, including cross-sector collaboration; community capacity building; community planning; conflict management, and mediation; convening large groups of people for a specific purpose; training; leadership development; meeting facilitation; organizational planning; strategic planning; board development; team building; and specialized subject-area technical assistance such as community organizing, economic development, housing, and urban planning. The Foundation also produces publications on planning, marketing, collaboration, and other issues, including *Strategic Planning Workbook for Nonprofit Organizations, The Nonprofit Mergers Workbook, Resolving Conflict in Nonprofit Organizations* and *Marketing Workbook for Nonprofit Organizations,* step-by-step guides with worksheets and examples (see separate listings under Publications in the Strategic Planning and Marketing and Communications sections). The Foundation's catalog of practical books for nonprofits and community groups is available online at *http://www.wilder.org/pubs/pubs.html.*

The Center for Nonprofit Management
University of St. Thomas Graduate School of Business
Mailing address: 25H 525, 1000 LaSalle Avenue,
Minneapolis, MN 55403-2001

Physical Address: 1125 Harmon Place, Suite 525,
Minneapolis, MN 55403-2001
Tel: 800-328-6819, ext. 2-4300, 651-962-4300;
FAX: 651-962-4810
E-mail: veschmeling@stthomas.edu (Vicki Schmeling, Program Coordinator), pswilder@stthomas.edu (Patricia Wilder, Director), askshamblin@stthomas.edu;
WWW: http://www.gsb.stthomas.edu/centers/nonpro.htm

▶ The Center is dedicated to helping the community's nonprofit practitioners improve their skills and knowledge. It provides a unique opportunity for practitioners, researchers, and educators to come together to better understand the nonprofit sector and to share information, knowledge, and experience. Provides educational services (over 50 educational and training programs offered, including the Mini MBA for Nonprofit Organizations); information services (publications, networking on community problem-solving, creating quality management process); research (database on new

research, identifying critical research needs); and Institute of Community Leadership. It publishes the newsletters *Nonprofit Management News, Legal-Ease,* and *Memorandum.*

Management Assistance Program for Nonprofits (MAP)
2233 University Avenue West, Suite 360,
St. Paul, MN 55114-1629
Tel: 651-647-1216; FAX: 651-647-1369
E-mail: mail@mapnp.org; WWW: http://www.mapnp.org/,
http://www.mapnp.org/library/index.html (Free Management Library), http://www.mapnp.org/library/topics.htm (Index of Topics in the Free Management Library)

▶ Although originally designed to serve the nonprofit organizations within and surrounding the Twin Cities area of Minnesota, thanks to the Internet this organization is now serving nonprofits all over the country. MAP's Web site includes information on classes and area services, conferences and news, a discussion group, volunteer postings, and online publications. Be sure to check out the Checklist of Nonprofit Indicators and the Nonprofit Managers Library.

MAP provides management support services and collaborating with other organizations to achieve their goals. MAP provides management consulting and board recruitment services to more than 600 organizations each year and engages over 700 volunteers in helping manage nonprofit organizations. Among its services/ programs are online resources for nonprofits (Free Management Library, MAP News Wire, other helpful Web sites); classes and workshops; services to organizations (accounting and financial management, governance and strategic leadership, information technology, legal counsel, marketing and communications, human resources, facilities and operations, Technology Partnership Fund); MAP publications; professional coaching service for nonprofit leaders; and a business development initiative.

Minnesota Council of Nonprofits
2700 University Avenue West, Suite 250, St. Paul, MN 55114
Tel: 800-289-1904 (Greater Minnesota), 651-642-1904;
FAX: 651-642-1517
E-mail: info@mncn.org, MCN@mncn.org (Jon Pratt,
Executive Director); WWW: http://www.mncn.org,
http://www.mncn.org/manage.htm

▶ MCN makes connections with experts from around the state and nation to gather the management, policy, and fund-raising information its members need. Services include The Nonprofit Library; publications (*Minnesota Grants Directory, Minnesota Grants Calendar, Nonprofits' Yellow Pages, Minnesota Nonprofit Salary and Benefits Survey,* and *Minnesota Nonprofit Directory*); MCN newsletters (*Nonprofit News,* MCN's bimonthly members-only newsletter, provides alerts about proposed legislation affecting the nonprofit sector, the latest developments in technology, and upcoming education and training programs; *Minnesota Grants Alert,* a monthly members-only electronic newsletter covering both national and Minnesota grant makers, including new grant programs, upcoming deadlines, personnel changes, and new fundraising resources); Education and training programs (offers over 40 low-cost workshops and briefings to cover proven methods and new trends in fund raising, technology, management, and public policy); annual conference (features national speakers and Minnesota's nonprofit leaders); *cost-saving programs; endorsed service providers; advocacy; research; events and workshops* (a complete schedule and descriptions can be found on the Web site at *http://www.mncn.org/events.htm*); public policy projects; management, legal, and fund-raising resources; links to Minnesota's nonprofit management allies; *online nonprofit job* board (job postings are from nonprofit organizations throughout Minnesota available online at: *http://www.mncn.org/jobs*); and Find a Nonprofit (*http://www.mncn.org/find.htm*).

University of St. Thomas Center for Nonprofit Management *(See The Center for Nonprofit Management)*

MISSISSIPPI

Mississippi Center for Nonprofits

612 North State Street, Suite B, Jackson, MS 39202
Tel: 601-968-0061; FAX: 601-352-8820
E-mail: mcn@msnonprofits.org, misscnp@netdoor.com (Nathan Woodliff-Stanley); WWW: http://www.msnonprofits.org
▶ The Mississippi Center for Nonprofits serves the needs of all 501(c)(3) organizations in Mississippi, from the smallest charity to the largest hospital or university. Whether your purpose is educational, artistic, religious, environmental, medical, human service, or social justice, the Mississippi Center for Nonprofits offers valuable assistance to help you accomplish your mission more effectively. Member benefits include networking and information (access to their library of reference materials; the quarterly newsletter, the *501 News,* monthly informational updates and alerts; a directory of member organizations; a one-year subscription to *Nonprofit World*); training and technical assistance (a place to call with management questions; workshops, discussions, seminars, and publications to help you improve your fund-raising strategy, comply with state and federal regulations, and manage your programs more effectively; trained facilitators for board retreats or custom workshops); cost-saving opportunities; and advocacy. The Center sponsors the Annual Mississippi Management Seminar for Nonprofits.

MISSOURI

Center for Management Assistance

170 Rivergate Business Center, 600 Broadway, Suite 170, Kansas City, MO 64105
Tel: 816-283-3000; FAX: 816-283-3005
E-mail: chanback@coop.crn.org (Cheryl Hanback); http://www.cmakc.org/
▶ The Center for Management Assistance is a network of community volunteers, staff associates, and organizational affiliates capable of responding effectively to any request for assistance, recognized as a national leader in consulting for the nonprofit sector. Services include board development; financial management; fund development; human resources management; information technology; marketing assistance; organizational planning; staff development; and a technology assistance program (TAP). Member benefits include leadership and management forums; free initial consultation; discounts on center products and services; consulting discounts; training discounts; products discounts; other services (discounts are also available for association management, technology, and personnel services); *Access to Essential Information* (monthly cyber newsletter e-mailed once a month and archived on

the Center's Web site; interactive information sharing; *Nonprofit World Magazine* subscription); and group purchasing arrangements. It hosts the annual conference, *Convergence.*

Midwest Center for Nonprofit Leadership (MCNL)

Mailing address: 5110 Cherry Street #310, University of Missouri–Kansas City, Kansas City, MO 64110-2499

Location address: 5100 Rockhill Road, Kansas City, MO 64110-2499
Tel: 800-474-1170, 816-235-2305; FAX: 816-235-1169
E-mail: mcnl@umkc.edu; WWW: http://mwcnl.bsbpa.umkc.edu/
▶ Its mission is to enhance the performance and effectiveness of individuals and organizations in the nonprofit sector, through high-quality community-focused education, applied research, problem solving, and service. The Midwest Center for Nonprofit Leadership was created in 1991 to serve the six-state region of Missouri, Kansas, Iowa, Nebraska, Arkansas, and Oklahoma. MCNL applies the resources and talents of the University and the sector to the problems and issues facing the nonprofit sector so that its members are better prepared to serve their communities. While creating opportunities for exchange among the members of this vital community, the Midwest Center actively works to support and enhance leadership in all areas of the nonprofit community. A calendar of events is available online at http://mwcnl.bsbpa.umkc.edu/calendar/calendar.htm. An online forum is also available at http://mwcnl.bsbpa.umkc.edu/mcnldiscussion.

Nonprofit Management and Leadership Program

University of Missouri–St. Louis, 318 Lucal Hall, St. Louis, MO 63121
Tel: 314-553-6701; FAX: 314-553-5910
WWW: http://www.umsl.edu/divisions/graduate/mppa/npmlmppa.htm
▶ The Nonprofit Management and Leadership Program is designed for current managers and volunteer leaders of nonprofit organizations, as well as students wishing to explore a future in the field. Managers, other professional staff, board members, and other leaders in a wide variety of nonprofit, voluntary organization areas, including human and social services, the arts and culture, education, public issues advocacy, religion, and voluntary and community associations, will benefit from this program. Typical course offerings include Leadership and Management of Nonprofit Organizations; Management Issues in the Nonprofit Organization (NPO): Financial, Legal, and Staff Management Issues; Effective Grant Making for Donors; Accessing Federal Grants; and Creating and Managing a Successful Planned Giving Program. Extensive custom-designed seminars and consulting services for specific organizations are also offered. The University offers graduate and undergraduate certificates in nonprofit management and leadership.

Nonprofit Services Consortium

319 North Fourth Street, Suite 501, St. Louis, MO 63102
Tel: 314-621-8678; FAX: 314-588-8088
E-mail: sue@stlcf.org (Susan Richards, Executive Director); WWW: http://www.nonprofitservices.org
▶ The Consortium provides a repository of hard copy informational holdings related to health and human issues and services as well as to the nonprofit sector in general; a social indicators database containing key indicators on the demographic, social, and economic conditions of the communities that comprise the St. Louis

metropolitan area; a regional health and human services and non-profit organizational database of agency information on more than 1,600 agencies; a clearinghouse and referral service to other regional holders and providers of data, information, and management and technical resources; a computer workstation to access the Internet and the electronic holding of the Electronic Nonprofit Special Collections Library; and technical assistance, including workshops, training, and nonprofit consultants. The Consortium publishes the *Directory of Nonprofit Training and Technical Assistance Providers* (lists nonprofit service providers by provider profiles and by service indices. Topic areas include accounting/financial management, board development, board/staff roles, budgeting, fund raising, grant writing, leadership development, legal issues, marketing, mergers, needs assessment, networks/collaboration, personnel administration, program development, program evaluation, public relations, strategic planning, technology/information systems, volunteer management).

United Way of Greater St. Louis Nonprofit Resource Center

1111 Olive Street, St. Louis, MO 63101
Tel: 314-539-4292; FAX: 314-539-4270
E-mail: nrc@stl.unitedway.org, harrisj@stl.unitedway.org;
WWW: http://www.stl.unitedway.org/non_profit.htm

▶ The United Way's Nonprofit Resource Center (NRC) is a library and information clearinghouse, linking organizations and individuals in the St. Louis region with the resources that are critical for effective health and human service delivery, nonprofit management, and volunteerism. The mission of the NRC is to build the capacity of the St. Louis Region's health and human service organizations and nonprofits to efficiently and effectively define, plan for, respond to, and meet the community's needs through the provision of data, information, management, and technical resources.

The United Way Nonprofit Resource Center Catalog of Publications and Products (http://www.stl.unitedway.org/publications.htm) is published quarterly. This catalog provides a comprehensive listing of all United Way publications and products available for distribution through the Nonprofit Resource Center. Materials listed in the catalog are divided into four broad topical areas: Health and Human Services Research, Health and Human Services Resources, Nonprofit Management, and Volunteerism.

NEW HAMPSHIRE

Granite State Association of Nonprofits

6 Loudon Road, Suite 404, Concord, NH 03301-5327
Tel: 603-225-1947; FAX: 603-228-5574
E-mail: lindaquinn@chi.tds.net (Linda Quinn);
WWW: http://www.nhnonprofits.org/

▶ The Granite State Association of Nonprofits (GSAN) is a statewide association of New Hampshire 501(c)(3) nonprofit organizations who are interested in working together to benefit themselves and their communities. GSAN membership includes nonprofits of all types and sizes serving every community in New Hampshire. Services to Nonprofits include: information and advocacy on the state budget; *advocacy for nonprofit sector issues and ethics and accountability; management training and materials* (offers an ongoing series of management roundtables covering a wide range of topics such as fund raising, strategic planning, mergers, planned giving, accounting software, health insurance, retire-

ment plans, buying insurance and risk management, workers' compensation, nonprofit ethics, property tax exemptions, controlling conflicts of interest, budgeting, volunteer recruitment and management, board development, meeting the requirements of labor and nonprofit law, personnel administration, and governance; group purchasing; *property, casualty, workers' compensation, and unemployment insurance* (GSAN is a licensed insurance broker serving nonprofits exclusively); property and casualty and directors' and officers' insurance (GSAN's in-house professional staff provide nonprofits with property and casualty insurance packages specially designed for nonprofits); health, life, dental, vision, and disability insurance (GSAN is a licensed broker for health and life insurance); benefits administration; regular member mailings (members receive the *CONNECTOR* newsletter and "Member Mailings" each year—a packet of topical resources such as legislative directories, official labor posters, meetings and seminars, new laws and rulings, resource lists, management checklists, and model policies).

NEW JERSEY

Center for Non-Profit Corporations

1501 Livingston Avenue, North Brunswick, NJ 08902
Tel: 732-227-0800; FAX: 732-227-0087
E-mail: center@njnonprofits.org (Contact: Linda Czipo);
WWW: http://www.njnonprofits.org

▶ Founded in 1982, the Center is a charitable umbrella organization serving New Jersey's nonprofit community. Over 600 charitable organizations statewide are Center members, supporting and participating in programs such as government relations (the Center works to promote sound policies to boost the ability and effectiveness of nonprofits throughout New Jersey); legal and management assistance (provides guidance to charitable organizations on a wide range of topics such as nonprofit incorporation and tax exemption, insurance issues, IRS regulations, lobbying laws, board/staff roles and responsibilities, fund-raising laws, and many others); public information (the Center is a hub of an extensive information network that connects nonprofits to valuable information and serves as a bridge to the government and business sectors); collaboration (fosters collaborations between and among nonprofits, government, and business); publications (resources for nonprofits include *Front & Center,* the Center's newsletter; *Hiring, Firing, Retiring: A Personnel Practices Guide for New Jersey Nonprofits,* a reference book on employment law; and the *New Jersey Grants Guide,* an up-to-date resource for and about New Jersey funding resources); cost-saving programs (provides access to directors' and officers' liability insurance, volunteer insurance, health insurance, and a nonprofit unemployment trust); job opening announcements (available online at *http://www.njnonprofits.org/Jobs.html*).

NEW YORK

Cause Effective: Nonprofit Resource Development Center

505 Eighth Avenue, Suite 1212, New York, NY 10018
Tel: 212-643-7093; FAX: 212-643-0137
E-mail: info@causeeffective.org, laureng@causeeffective.org (Lauren Goldstein);
WWW: http://www.causeeffective.org/glance.html

▶ Founded in 1981, Cause Effective is a New York-based nonprofit that helps nonprofit organizations build their capacities to develop human and financial resources through consulting, workshops, and publications. Cause Effective helps nonprofits plan and implement special events, train and develop their boards, manage individual donors, enlist and manage volunteers, and promote and market their organizations.

Community Resource Exchange (CRE)

39 Broadway, 10th Floor, New York, NY 10006
Tel: 212-894-3394; FAX: 212-616-4994
E-mail: fbarrett@crenyc.org (Fran Barrett, Executive Director),
wlam@crenyc.org (Wei Lam, Contract Manager);
WWW: http://www.crenyc.org

▶ CRE is a not-for-profit organization that provides management assistance to the diversity of not-for-profit groups serving the poor and disenfranchised. By ensuring the stability, growth, and effectiveness of these organizations, CRE strives to improve the lives of New Yorkers most in need. It works with not-for-profits of all sizes but is known for its ability to assist indigenous start-up organizations emerging from their neighborhoods. CRE uses management assistance to encourage, facilitate, and enable community-based organizations to improve their impact on the needs of the poor and disenfranchised. CRE offers one-to-one relationships, small grants, volunteer matches, internships, and publications. CRE also provides technical assistance in the areas of organizational development, fund raising, financial management, human resources, continuous quality improvement, boards of directors, and computer technology, including technology planning, database development, and the Internet. CRE has on staff (not via affiliated consultants) expertise in a full range of management areas, including strategic planning; financial management/bookkeeping; individual, foundation, and government fund development; human resource management; board of directors development; and organizational development including mergers, dissolution, restructuring, and replication. Services include board of directors (train new board members in their basic roles and responsibilities or to assume greater leadership in a particular area, for example, fund raising or finance; restructure the board to operate more effectively; develop and implement a board expansion plan; help the board develop and implement executive director evaluations); financial management (prepare groups for organizational and program audits, analyze accounting systems, computerize financial management systems, perform cost analysis to determine overhead rate and unit cost of service); fund raising: (develop a fund-raising plan that includes diverse income sources; identify likely funding sources and how to approach them; help increase board involvement in fund raising, including planning and organizing events and donor campaigns; help write winning proposals for both private and public funding sources or a case statement to guide an individual donor plan); human resources (develop or update job descriptions, employee evaluation systems and personnel policies; restructure staffing patterns, including the formation of management teams; organize and update benefits packages, including switching or acquiring health, life, or other benefits; develop executive-level compensation plans; implement executive-level staff searches); and organizational development (guide the development or revision of an agency's mission and goals and shape action plans to achieve goals as part of a strategic planning process; organizational self-assessment; analyze and improve internal management systems; help leadership evaluate the effectiveness of the agency's programs and services; restructure the organization, including replication of a program, mergers, and downsizing). Special Projects include The Search

Company (helps community organizations to identify and hire the best candidates to assume leadership positions); *Technical Assistance to AIDS Service Organizations* (offers technical assistance at no cost to AIDS service organizations); *NYNMAC* (Community Resource Exchange, Cause Effective, and Lawyers Alliance for New York formed the New York Nonprofit Management Assistance Collaborative, whose mission is to coordinate their collective skills and resources to help the city's nonprofit organizations facing downsizing, mergers, or bankruptcy); *Media Jumpstart Affiliation* (helps community-based organizations in the New York City metro area to use the tools of new technologies to accomplish their missions and goals). You can subscribe to its listserv to receive periodic announcements via e-mail.

Council of Community Services of New York State (CCSNYS)

200 Henry Johnson Boulevard, Box 17, Albany, NY 12210
Tel: 800-515-501C, 518-434-9194; FAX: 518-434-0392
E-mail: info@ccsnys.org, dsauer@ccsnys.org (Doug Sauer,
Executive Director); WWW: http://www.ccsnys.org/

▶ The Council of Community Services of New York State, Inc. (CCSNYS) is a 501(c)(3) membership-based nonprofit organization dedicated to improving the quality of community life in the state through the provision of nonprofit capacity-building services and community-based health and human services planning. The Council is a membership of over 650 nonprofit agencies. The Council is a member of the National Council of Nonprofit Associations, the Alliance for Nonprofit Management, and the National Association of Planning Councils. Services/programs include nonprofit services (develops, sponsors, and administers capacity-building services that benefit charitable nonprofit organizations); Leadership and Management Institute (provides nonprofits with organizational assistance and information to build governance and management efficiency and capacity); general organizational assistance (board training and development, agency merger planning, strategic planning, meeting and retreat facilitation, executive director/CEO search, employee compensation consultation, management analysis, marketing and fund development); legal assistance (bylaws, personnel policies, contracts and leases, tax exemption application, incorporation and amendments, general consultation, policy information on tax exemption, advocacy and lobbying regulations); Nonprofit Accounting Service Center (fiscal agent services, budget development and review, budget projections, fiscal procedures, accounting software, selection of an auditing firm); public policy and information; annual publications (*Greater Capital Region Human Services Directory, Nonprofits' Guide to New York State Policymakers, Compensation Study of New York State Nonprofits*); newsletters and journal (*Nonprofit FOCUS* quarterly newsletter for CCSNYS member organizations; *NEXUS,* highlights community planning, evaluation, and research activities in the Greater Capital Region community; *Capital-Eyes,* the newsletter about state government for nonprofit organizations; and *Journal for Nonprofit Management*); special initiatives (Donor Choice & Accountability Project—two working groups to develop nonprofit ethics and accountability standards, and to develop and distribute information on donor education and informed-choice charitable giving; and New York State EGrants Initiative—a collaborative project between New York State grant-making agencies to improve the distribution of grant information and the application process).

CCSNYS sponsors the annual Nonprofit Expo, three days of training for nonprofit staff and board members. Choose from over

45 workshops and "toolboxes" in seven tracks: administration, advocacy and lobbying, communications and marketing, governance, program development, resource development, and nonprofit technology.

Nonprofit Advisory Service

Rochester Area Community Foundation, 500 East Avenue, Rochester, NY 14607-1912
Tel: 716-271-4100; FAX: 716-271-4292
WWW: http://www.racf.org/community/nonprofit/

▶ This innovative community foundation initiative provides experienced management guidance to aid nonprofit organizations in maximizing their potential and fulfilling their mission. Services include individualized needs assessments as well as referrals to outside consultants and academic training opportunities. In addition, the advisory service offers workshops on long-range planning, marketing, evaluation, board and committee effectiveness, and financial management.

The Nonprofit Connection (Formerly Brooklyn In Touch Information Center)

1 Hanson Place, Suite 2504, Brooklyn, NY 11243
Tel: 718-230-3200; FAX: 718-399-3428
E-mail: tnc@nonprofitconnection.org;
WWW: http://www.nonprofitconnection.org

▶ The Nonprofit Connection provides management services to the community-based organizations of the nonprofit sector. The Nonprofit Connection provides consulting services and workshops in the following areas of organizational development: fund raising and resource development, planning and strategic management, accounting and financial management, board development, marketing, human resources management, organizational design and restructuring, coalition building, and the facilitation of retreats and meetings. Special initiatives that provide targeted information and resources to New York's nonprofit community include the Brooklyn Connection Library, the Community Development Institute, and the Strategies 2001 Institute. Access resources and publications that will provide useful information and opportunities for your organization at *http://www.nonprofit-connection.org/advscripts/frmresrc.asp.*

Nonprofit Coordinating Committee of New York (NPCC)

1350 Broadway, Suite 1801, New York, NY 10018-7802
Tel: 212-502-4191; FAX: 212-502-4189
E-mail: pswords@npccny.org (Peter Swords), jsmall@npccny.org (Jon Small); WWW: www.npccny.org,
http://www.npccny.org/databank.htm

▶ NPCC unites nonprofits from all subsectors—social services, the arts, religion, philanthropy, health, education, housing, and economic development. NPCC provides members with technical and managerial support, informs members of government activities that affect them, represents the nonprofit sector in legislative matters, and promotes a better understanding of the role of nonprofits in the economy and culture of New York. Membership services include information on governmental actions affecting nonprofits; identification of funding opportunities with Federal Grants Information Service; legal assistance on employment and labor relations issues; low-fee retirement plan; discounted directors' and officers' (D&O)

liability insurance policy; savings on office supplies; discounts on payroll processing; affordable computers; conference room rental; health insurance information and referrals; workshops and roundtables for nonprofit managers; bimonthly newsletter; active Web site and information databank; and online member directory listing. *New York Nonprofits* is NPCC's bimonthly newsletter, available online at *http://www.npccny.org/newslet.htm.* The Information Databank (*http://www.npccny.org/databank.htm*) contains articles and memos from previous issues of *New York Nonprofits* and from *NPCC Informational Memos.* NPCC's Workshop Calendar is also available on the Web site at *http://www.npccny.org/workshop.htm.*

NonProfit Management Center

6342 Pin Cherry Court, East Amherst, NY 14051-1557
Tel: 800-610-6564, 716-741-9735 (Home Office), 716-741-7403;
FAX: 716-741-9735
E-mail: FCP@aol.com (Frank Polkowski, Senior VP)

▶ NMC was founded in 1993 by Fern E. Koch, Frank C. Polkowski, and Gretchen E. Stringer. All three principals have a long history of involvement with United Ways, nonprofit agencies, boards of directors, associations, and corporations on local, regional, and national levels. NMC presents a neutral, cross-organizational, cross-agency, and cross-cultural perspective of the nonprofit world. Its mission is increasing the effectiveness of nonprofit organizations. It provides resources and support through training, consulting, partnering, and mentoring for all aspects of nonprofit endeavors including the management of staff, board, volunteers, and all other aspects involved in the operation of nonprofit organizations. Services include training, development, and consultations; over-the-counter, telephone, and mail-order book sales, videos, and materials; a lending library; training videos; and retreat facilitation and custom-designed conferences, workshops, and seminars.

Support Center of New York

305 Seventh Avenue, 11th Floor, New York, NY 10001-6008
Tel: 212-924-6744
E-mail: info@supportctr.org; WWW: http://www.supportctr.org/

▶ Support Center for Nonprofit Management strengthens the leadership and management capacity of nonprofit and public interest organizations to fulfill their missions and vitalize their communities. They provide management training and consulting, disseminate information to the sector, and build strategic alliances. They offer training workshops, consulting services, and meeting facilitation specifically designed to increase your organizational effectiveness. Services include workshops (offered in the areas of organizational development, human resources development, fund raising, financial management, and marketing); consulting (the Center has helped organizations with strategic plans and long-range fund-raising strategies, board development and board retreats, conflict management, financial management, organizational assessment and development, meeting facilitation, and search consultations); customized on-site training; publications; and Info Express Listserv (*http://www.supportctr.org/info.html*). The Center's Web site has the current workshop catalog; an opportunity to engage in online dialogue on management, leadership, and organizational issues; and links to other helpful sites, including FAQs on nonprofit financial management, fund raising, strategic planning, board development, and risk management.

Volunteer Consulting Group, Inc. *(See Governance—Support and Advocacy Organizations for full description)*

NORTH CAROLINA

North Carolina Center for Nonprofits

1110 Navaho Drive, Suite 200, Raleigh, NC 27609-7322
Tel: 919-790-1555; FAX: 919-790-5307
E-mail: nccenter@aol.com; WWW: http://www.ncnonprofits.org,
http://www.ncexchange.org/techsupports/database.html,
http://www.ncnonprofits.org/vltrctrs.html,
http://www.ncnonprofits.org/westnc.html

▶ The North Carolina Center for Nonprofits is a private, 501(c)(3) nonprofit organization that serves as a statewide network for nonprofit boards and staffs, an information center on effective practices, and an advocate for the nonprofit sector as a whole. It offers services directly to all sizes and types of 501(c)(3) nonprofits, and works closely with other local, state, and national groups that assist nonprofits. Services/programs include regional and statewide forums with nonprofit and philanthropic leaders to exchange ideas and to learn about emerging issues that affect your organization; *North Carolina Nonprofit Network Statewide Directory* (link your nonprofit's Web site and e-mail address to the Center's Web page); nonprofit workshops and seminars; *Common Ground: Linking North Carolina's Nonprofit Sector* (a bimonthly source of practical information and updates on critical issues for nonprofits in North Carolina, available only to Members, Associates, and supporters; regular columns include legislative and legal updates, a statewide calendar of professional development for nonprofit staff and volunteers, and "Good Stuff Free"); board and staff helpline; Nonprofit Resource Center (includes books, articles, and other resources on a wide variety of topics including nonprofit sector, boards of directors, communications, conservation of resources, evaluation, financial management, funding and philanthropy, human resources, legal issues, membership, partnerships and collaboration, planning, tax issues, technology, and volunteers); peer and consultant referral networks; One-Hour Pro Bono Program for Legal Assistance (for use by nonprofits with budgets under $750,000); publications and tapes (a complete listing is available online at *http://www.ncnonprofits.org/publications.html*); special projects (*Tech Supports for Nonprofits: A Resource Directory,* a directory of local, state, and national technology resources to help North Carolina's nonprofits strengthen their access to and use of technology; and a list of resources currently offered for nonprofit organizations in western North Carolina available at *http://www.ncnonprofits.org/westnc.html.*

NORTH DAKOTA

North Dakota Association of Nonprofit Organizations (NDANO)

1459 Interstate Loop, Suite F2, Bismarck, ND 58503-0567
Tel: 888-396-3266, 701-258-9101; FAX: 701-255-2411

Plaza Center Office Building, 1025 North Third Street,
Bismarck, ND 58501
Tel: 800-396-3266, 701-258-9101; FAX: 701-222-8257
E-mail: ndano@nisc.cc (Brenda Dissett, Executive Director);
WWW: http://www.ndano.org,
http://www.ndano.org/html/resources.html

▶ NDANO's goals include promoting awareness of the role of the sector, enhancing the integrity and capacity of the sector, becoming proactive in public policy processes, improving management practices among nonprofits, encouraging networking and collaboration across the sector, encouraging cooperative and effective leadership for the betterment of the entire state and its people. It provides leadership, services, and technical assistance to its membership of nonprofit organizations, making them efficient and effective within their communities. NDANO publishes *Nonprofit Network,* the bimonthly newsletter for distribution throughout North Dakota's nonprofit sector, a free service to members, and is available to nonmember subscribers. Links to articles from the most recent issue are available at *http://www.ndano.org/html/newsletter.html.* NDANO holds an annual conference.

The Resource Center

Box 1127, Fargo, ND 58107-1127
Tel: 877-233.8966, 218-233-8966; FAX: 218-236-7387
E-mail: hersrud@rrnet.com (Cher Hersrud, Director)

▶ The Resource Center operates as a semiautonomous division of the North Dakota Community Foundation to provide technical assistance to the many small nonprofit organizations operating primarily in North Dakota. Support from the Otto Bremer Foundation allows the Center to provide free, or low-cost assistance to the primarily volunteer organizations operating within this rural state. Resource Center services include assistance in planning, project development, fund raising, and other forms of capacity building. Additionally, the Resource Center can provide workshops and resource and reference material on a variety of nonprofit and community issues. A computer recycling effort has been developed to solicit computer and office equipment from businesses for placement in nonprofit organizations. An annual publication (self-published) is developed, addressing a specific issue within the context of North Dakota.

OHIO

Business Volunteers Unlimited *(See Financial Management—Support and Advocacy Organizations for full description)*

Center for Nonprofit Resources of Ohio, Inc. (CNR)

1133 Edwin C. Moses Boulevard, Suite 380, Dayton, OH 45406
Tel: 937-225-3057; FAX: 937-222-0995
E-mail: info@cnrohio.org, Tgardner@cnrohio.org (Tim Gardner, Consulting/Training Manager); WWW: http://www.cnrohio.org,
http://www.cnrohio.org/career_cnr.html

▶ CNR is the resource center for nonprofit organizations and volunteers in Ohio. It is a management and consulting organization that provides nonprofits with the tools and concepts necessary to best serve their communities. Services include workshops (Iams Nonprofit Management Series, Basic Volunteer Management Series, Board Development Series, Leadership Series, Fund-Raising Series, Human Resources Series, Train the Trainer Series, Information and Technology Workshops, Facilities Workshops, Marketing Tools and Topics Workshops, Charter Schools Workshops, Legal-Ease, Personal & Professional Development; its training calendar is available online), on-site training and consulting services (CNR's Consulting Group offers assistance in the areas of board governance, strategic planning, human resource development, organizational development, marketing, print media design, grant writing, volunteer program design, and conference presentations and keynotes), Board Match, and Regional Bulletin Board. CNR also maintains a consultancy database for organizations that desire one-to-one training and consultations. Hosts Nonprofit Neighbors, a weekly television show on DATV providing a question-and-answer session aimed at educating the public about issues of interest in the nonprofit sector.

Nonprofit Resource Center (Formerly the Nonprofit Management and Governance Clinic) *(See also Governance)*
The Mandel Center for Nonprofit Organizations,
Case Western Reserve University, 10900 Euclid Avenue,
Cleveland, OH 44106-7164
Tel: 800-863-6772, 216-368-5883, 216-368-5214 (Ann Lucas);
FAX: 216-368-5065
E-mail: def2@po.cwru.edu, jay@po.cwru.edu (John A.Yankey, Director of Community Service), ael@po.cwru.edu (Ann Lucas, Assistant Director of Community Service Projects & Center Operations); WWW: http://www.cwru.edu/mandelcenter, http://www.cwru.edu/msass/mandelcenter/mc_nmgc.html
▶ The Center offers workshops, lectures, and some publications as well as customized leadership education programs.

The Nonprofit Management and Governance Clinic (NMGC) was created to expand and formalize the assistance of the Mandel Center for Nonprofit Organizations and to provide to the local nonprofit community consultants. The NMGC enables many area nonprofit organizations to successfully complete a variety of tasks and projects and to operate more efficiently and effectively. Services include The Nonprofit Law Clinic (assisting organizations in the process of filing for 501(c)(3) status), The Trusteeship Initiative (facilitating and training board members in carrying out their volunteer responsibilities), The Management Information Systems program (assisting nonprofit organizations with their technology needs), student externships (individual and classroom projects that enable nonprofit organizations to complete grant writing, marketing campaigns, volunteer programs, program development, special events management, and other discrete projects), complex projects (strategic planning, management audits, demographic and marketing surveys, and program evaluations), referral sources (compensation and benefits information; assistance with creation of job descriptions), Grantwriting Workshop (held in collaboration with Grantmaker's Forum), community forums (held throughout the year with topics based on a profile of the requests received by the Clinic), and mentoring program (nonprofit executives work with master's degree students each year).

Ohio Association of Nonprofit Organizations (OANO)
42 East Gay Street, Suite 1000, Columbus, OH 43215
Tel: 888-480-6266, 614-280-0233; FAX: 614-280-0657
E-mail: info@oano.org, robertmatthews@oano.org (Robert D. Matthews, Assistant Director), rick@oano.org or rickmoyers@yahoo.com (Richard Moyers, Executive Director); WWW: http://www.oano.org, http://www.oano.org/LINKS/links.html
▶ Incorporated in 1994, the mission of the Ohio Association of Nonprofit Organizations (OANO) is to strengthen the effectiveness of the charitable nonprofit sector in Ohio. To carry out that mission, OANO offers programs and services to strengthen the leadership,

governance, and management capacity of nonprofit organizations; expand public awareness and understanding of the nonprofit sector; create opportunities for networking, information sharing, and professional development for the leaders of nonprofit organizations; and provide access to affordable products and services, including health insurance, pension plans, liability insurance, and other group purchasing opportunities. Programs and services include an annual leadership conference that provides opportunities for training, networking, and professional development; a quarterly newsletter, *Ohio Nonprofits,* that provides timely information on issues and trends facing nonprofit organizations, co-sponsoring the *Ohio Grants Guide,* a comprehensive listing of Ohio grantmakers, sponsoring and co-sponsoring workshops and training opportunities throughout the state, serving as a resource for identifying affordable products for nonprofit organizations, including health insurance, pension and retirement plans, directors' and officers' liability insurance, and other group purchasing discounts. Members are eligible to utilize OANO's online listing of consultants and pro-bono legal assistance through OANO's partnership with the Ohio Legal Assistance Foundation. OANO is a member of the National Council of Nonprofit Associations.

Strength in Partners, Inc.
17600 Hampton Place, Cleveland, OH 44136
Tel: 440-572-7510; FAX: 440-572-7519
E-mail: psadallah@strengthinpartners.org (Patty Sadallah); WWW: http://www.strengthinpartners.org, http://www.strengthinpartners.org/best.htm
▶ A nonprofit consultation network that supports and facilitates nonprofit-to-nonprofit partnerships in Northeast Ohio so that these organizations may be stronger and more able to further their own missions of service to the greater Cleveland community. Strength in Partners, Inc. offers consultation, training, and resource networking services to nonprofit organizations primarily in the state of Ohio. Consultation services (includes organizational assessment, strategic planning, strategic marketing, interorganizational projects/mergers, board development, expert consultation (help with legal, human resource, financial, public relations, or fund raising); training services (half-day, full-day, or two-day increments; training can be brought to your site on any of the following topics: the skills of leading change, effective team and interteam development, building strategic relationships, the nuts and bolts of strategic leadership), and resource networking (they help find you the help you need, either through their own network of consultant trainers or by researching other helping resources). Information regarding research networking is available at *http://www.strengthinpartners.org/Need%20Help/canhelp.htm* (go to the *Need Help/Can Help* page and submit your specific request).

OKLAHOMA

Center for Nonprofit Management (CNM)
525 NW 13th Street, Oklahoma City, OK 73103-2238
Tel: 405-236-8133; FAX: 405-272-0436

Physical address: 110 West 7th Street, Suite 2611
Mailing address: 1120 South Utica Avenue,
Tulsa, OK 74104-4090
Tel: 918-579-1900; FAX: 918-579-7899
E-mail: lbillen@cnm-ok.org; WWW: http://connections.oklahoman.net/nonprofit, http://www.cnm-ok.org

▶ Since 1981, the Center for Nonprofit Management (CNM) has been helping nonprofit organizations and public agencies across Oklahoma to improve their results. By offering top-quality management programs and services at affordable prices, CNM's help is accessible to all organizations that need it. Services include consulting, training and development, workshops and seminars, on-site contract training, conferences, computer training, strategic planning facilitation, diagnostic services, SUPPORT-NET (members receive discounts on most CNM services, including workshops, computer training, consulting and use of the Center's bulk mail permit; they also receive reduced rates on board and workers' compensation insurance and payroll services); Board Builders (offers a variety of services that train, motivate, and improve the effectiveness of nonprofit governing boards; these include board retreat facilitation, on-site workshops, public programs, and conferences and consulting), and *The Nonprofit Exchange,* CNM's quarterly newsletter.

OREGON

Pacific Non-Profit Network/Grantsmanship Library

(See also Resource Development)
Southern Oregon University, Education Resource Center
in the Rogue Valley Mall, 1600 North Riverside, Suite 1094,
Medford, OR 97501
Tel: 541-779-6044; FAX: 541-858-0715
E-mail: lori@theerc.org, arnold@sou.edu (Lori Arnold),
pam@theerc.org (Pam Hall, Coordinator, Medford Community
Education), orpnn@aol.com;
WWW: http://www.sou.edu/ecp/business/pnn.html

▶ Pacific Non-Profit Network (PNN) provides management support and resource development services to nonprofit organizations in southern Oregon. PNN is a program of Southern Oregon University's Extended Campus Programs. PNN hosts the Foundation Center's Grantsmanship Resource Library, which contains information about foundation and corporate funding sources in printed or CD-ROM format. Internet access for funding information is available. The library has many books and materials to assist nonprofit organizations with all aspects of management, boards of directors, and fund raising. Information can also be found about how to start a nonprofit agency. From time to time, PNN offers workshops for nonprofit organizations as well as an annual conference.

Technical Assistance for Community Services (TACS)

1903 SE Ankeny, Portland, OR 97214
Tel: 888-206-3076, 503-239-4001; FAX: 503-236-8313
E-mail: info@tacs.org, al@tacs.org (Al Llebrez, technology
assistance); WWW: http://www.tacs.org/

▶ TACS provides consultations, facilitations, and training programs designed for individual nonprofit organizations. TACS provides workshops, networks, and consultations on financial management, board development, strategic planning, building diversity, organizational development, and leadership issues. TACS charges fees for its services on a sliding scale. Services and resources include board development, conflict resolution, financial management, diversity issues, organizational development; strategic planning; executive directors network (monthly breakfast meetings for executive directors to meet their peers, share strategies, and discuss

planning, management, and funding issues with expert speakers), Nonprofit Fiscal Managers Association (monthly breakfast meetings featuring outstanding professional speakers for financial managers to discuss current issues and network with their peers); Diversity Leaders Network (bimonthly breakfast meetings for people leading the diversity efforts within their organizations to get support, share ideas, and network among peers); tech help (comprehensive assessment of hardware, software, and networking needs and opportunities; development of realistic technology plans; help with acquisition, installment, training, and implementation of new systems; training and professional networking opportunities for IT staff in nonprofits); Building Community Connections (statewide workshop series); Workshops (Portland-based series); Nonprofit Organization Information and Referral Helpline (888-206-3076 or 503-233-9240); technical assistance grants; publications (*Oregon Nonprofit Corporation Handbook,* guide to creating, governing, and managing nonprofit corporations in Oregon; *Oregon Foundation Databook; TACSNEWS,* TACS' quarterly newsletter, which highlights emerging issues in nonprofit management and planning, lists resources, and provides a calendar of TACS' training events); access to pro-bono professional services: TACS helps smaller Portland metro-area nonprofits connect with attorneys and other professionals seeking opportunities to provide volunteer assistance with legal and management issues. The TACS training calendar is available online at *http://columbia-pacific.interrain.org/tacs.*

PENNSYLVANIA

Center for Nonprofit Management at Robert Morris College

718 Fifth Avenue, Pittsburgh, PA 15219
Tel: 800-762-0097, 412-227-6814 (Peggy M. Outon, Executive
Director), 412-227-6784 (Yvonne H. Van Haitsma, Director,
Collaboration Project); FAX: 412227-4097
E-mail: vanhaits@robert-morris.edu (Yvonne H. Van Haitsma,
Director, Collaboration Project), outon@robert-morris.edu
(Peggy M. Outon, Executive Director, RMC Center for Non-Profit
Management); WWW: http://www.robert-
morris.edu/SentryHTML/LearnMoreAtRMC-2.htm

▶ The Center provides management and governance information, tools, education, and research to nonprofit organizations, to strengthen their ability to meet their mission and to make the best possible use of the investment made by the public. Services include information and referral (staff is aware of all management support programs and services available to the local nonprofit customer and, when appropriate, refers customers to the best provider); consulting services (offers consulting services through staff and contracted consultants in the areas of collaboration, technology, fund development, financial management, human resources, business planning, and organizational effectiveness; local consultants will receive training from national experts in the primary areas of the Center's work to improve consulting practices throughout the service area); educational programs (through its affiliation with the Robert Morris College, the Center offers a masters of science in management with a concentration in nonprofit management; students will also be offered a nonprofit management concentration in the MBA program; certificate programs will also be available each semester; public workshops with national trainers will be offered 8 to 12 times a year); research (conducts commissioned research on topics of interest to its nonprofit clients and the philanthropic community).

Community Technical Assistance Center Inc. (CTAC)

901 Western Avenue, Pittsburgh, PA 15233
Tel: 412-231-2822; FAX: 412-231-6150
E-mail: CTAC@city-net.com

▶ For organizational development and planning assistance, community organizations can turn to the Community Technical Assistance Center, a facility supported by PPND, in order to put expertise at the disposal of Pittsburgh's communities. CTAC provides help in running, financing, and managing organizations, through one-on-one sessions or through its series of workshops. Economic development advice, capacity building, and strategic planning are some areas of expertise offered.

The Elmer J. Tropman Nonprofit Management Institute

William J. Copeland Fund, The Pittsburgh Foundation,
One PPG Place, 30th Floor, Pittsburgh, PA 15222-5401
Tel: 412-391-5122; FAX: 412-391-7259
E-mail e-mail@pghfdn.org; WWW:
http://www.pittsburghfoundation.org/supportorg.html

▶ Named for the founder of the Copeland Fund, the Institute provides continuing education and professional development programs for staff, management, executive directors, and board members of human service/nonprofit organizations. This nationally recognized Institute consists of a consortium of five Pittsburgh colleges and universities (Duquesne University, University of Pittsburgh School of Social Work and Graduate School of Public and International Affairs, Carnegie Mellon University, H. John Heinz School of Public Policy and Management, Robert Morris College, and the Community College of Allegheny County), which coordinate their training efforts to reach a wide range of nonprofit leaders. In addition to providing scholarships to the programs, the Institute supports seminars and publications that either advance new techniques in nonprofit management or address current environmental trends that affect the organizational health of the nonprofit sector.

Executive Service Corps of the Delaware Valley (ESC)

119 Coulter Avenue, Suite 200, Ardmore, PA 19003-2427
Tel: 610-649-2284; FAX: 610-649-7224
E-mail: escdv@escdv.org; WWW:
http://www.executiveservicecorps.com

▶ A nonprofit organization, the Executive Service Corps of the Delaware Valley Executive Service Corps of the Delaware Valley is a 501(c)(3) nonprofit organization dedicated to a unique goal: helping area 501(c)(3) nonprofit institutions become more effective through ESC volunteer management consultants. ESC can provide guidance on strategic planning, systems and procedures, fund raising, governance, marketing, and other aspects of managing a nonprofit. The Executive Service Corps of the Delaware Valley was established in 1983. It is patterned after the National Executive Service Corps (NESC) in New York, founded by Frank Pace in 1977. ESC is one of 40 affiliates nationwide, but functions as a completely autonomous and independent organization with its own board of directors and professional staff. ESC publishes a quarterly newsletter, *Consultant.*

Executive Service Corps of Western Pennsylvania (ESC)

425 6th Avenue, Suite 1610, Pittsburgh, PA 15219-1819
Tel: 412-263-6718; FAX: 412-263-2106
E-mail: escwpa@trfn.clpgh.org (Laurie Anderson, Executive
Director); WWW: http://trfn.clpgh.org/escwpa

▶ The Executive Service Corps of Western Pennsylvania (ESC) is a 501(c)(3) nonprofit organization that provides professional management, planning, legal referral, and technical assistance to nonprofit organizations in the southwestern Pennsylvania area that could not otherwise afford these types of services. ESC makes these services affordable through volunteer professionals who donate their time and expertise to helping the nonprofit community. ESC seeks to enhance the effectiveness of the nonprofit community by providing management consulting assistance and coordinating legal assistance related to the challenges facing nonprofits. Services include accounting and finance, board development, facility planning and management, human resources, information systems, marketing and public relations, organizational development, outcomes measurement, risk management, strategic planning. Management volunteers can also serve in such capacities as meeting facilitators and mentors for administrative staff. ESC will consider requests for assistance from any nonprofit organization in southwestern Pennsylvania (primarily Allegheny and contiguous counties). We work closely with other technical assistance providers and independent consultants in our area to avoid competition and duplication of services. Arts and cultural organizations are usually referred to ProArts (Western Pennsylvania Professionals for the Arts). ESC also offers educational seminars.

Good Neighbors

United Way of Allegheny County, One Smithfield Street, P.O. Box
735, Pittsburgh, PA 15230-0735
Tel: 412-261-6010, 456-6779; FAX: 412-394-5376
WWW: http://www.uwac.org/goodneighbors/trantech.htm

▶ Good Neighbors is a volunteer resource center that provides an interactive management information system for volunteer recruitment and referral, training and technical assistance to nonprofit agencies and organizations, a resource library on volunteer management, and coordination of county-wide volunteer special events.

Nonprofit Assistance Center

SEDA–Council of Governments, RR 1 Box 372,
Lewisburg, PA 17837
Tel: 570-522-7216; FAX: 570-524-9190
E-mail: dmccormi@seda-cog.org (Danielle McCormick, Program
Director); WWW: http://nac.seda-cog.org/

▶ The Nonprofit Assistance Center, an initiative of SEDA–Council of Governments and Susquehanna Institute, provides technical assistance in addition to practical trainings and workshops to the nonprofit organizations of the SEDA–COG region. The Nonprofit Assistance Center provides limited technical assistance to nonprofit organizations in the areas of allocating grant sources, fund-raising development, grant proposal writing, support materials creation, Web site development, board development, 501(c)(3) applications, and the development of bylaws and articles of incorporation. The Center publishes a bimonthly newsletter and maintains a listserv for its members.

Non-Profit Council/Non-Profit Assistance Network

Greater Philadelphia Chamber of Commerce, 200 South Broad Street, Suite 700, Philadelphia, PA 19102
Tel: 215-790-3647; FAX: 215-790-3720
E-mail: bsaverino@gpcc.com (Barbara Saverino, Manager);
WWW: http://www.gpcc.com/nonprofit/index.htm

▶ Members of the Greater Philadelphia Chamber of Commerce's Non-Profit Council can call to receive free advice and assistance from knowledgeable volunteers. Expertise includes accounting and finance, advertising/public relations, board relations and training, computers/MIS, employee relations/benefits, fund raising/marketing, investment management, legal issues, operations management, strategic planning, and volunteer management. It also offers events and seminars, a *Nonprofit Membership Directory,* links to area nonprofits on its Web site, and an online newsletter.

Nonprofit Management Development Center (NMDC)

La Salle University, 1900 West Olney Avenue, Philadelphia, PA 19141-1199
Tel: 888-LSU-7480, 215-951-1701; FAX: 215-951-1488
E-mail: simmons@lasalle.edu (Karen Simmons, Executive Director), nmdc@lasalle.edu, slawinsk@lasalle.edu
(Lisa Slawinski, Information, Referral and Publications Director);
WWW: http://www.lasalle.edu/services/nmdc
http://alpha.lasalle.edu/services/nmdc/links.htm

▶ Since its programs began in 1981 and with the official founding of the Center in 1986, the mission of La Salle University's Nonprofit Management Development Center (NMDC) has been to increase the capacity of Delaware Valley nonprofit staff and board members to manage and govern their organizations in a responsible, humanistic manner so nonprofits can better carry out their nonprofit missions to serve the public good. NMDC builds nonprofit capacity by providing on-site, individualized problem-solving consultations for executive directors and board members as well as customized staff and board training sessions. NMDC works primarily with midsized arts, culture, environmental, human service, social justice, and social service organizations whose budgets range from $75,000 to $10 million. It draws its consultants and trainers primarily from the La Salle University academic and professional staff and alumni community. Services/programs include workshops, customized consulting services (board development, resource development/fund raising, strategic planning, collaboration and partnering, executive coaching, human resources management, marketing and market research, organizational development, program evaluation, social entrepreneurship and revenue generation, team building), Board of Directors Institute (a semicustomized, interactive, two- to three-hour training session, which clarifies board members' roles, responsibilities, and functioning in the areas of board, management, and volunteer roles; legal liability; financial management and control; policy making; fund raising and resource development; strategic planning; key organizational phases and their impact on board roles; board self-appraisal; identification of the board's development goals for the year); information, referral, and publications (advocacy, board of directors, evaluation/outcomes assessment, financial management, fund raising, human resources, marketing, proposal writing, starting a nonprofit, strategic planning; also available online); research (areas of research emphasis include strategic planning, board development, resource development, leadership, and evaluation); education (offers certificates in nonprofit management); e-mail list (mailing list to receive notices of board events, management seminars, and special events); *Opportunity NOCs* (listing nonprofit jobs in the Delaware Valley area in arts, conservation, education, environment, human service, religion, social justice, and social service).

Nonprofit Resource Directory

The Foundation Center, The Carnegie Library of Pittsburgh, 4400 Forbes Avenue, Pittsburgh, PA 15213-4080
Tel: 412-622-1917; FAX: 412-622-6561
E-mail foundati@alphaclp.clpgh.org;
WWW: http://www.clpgh.org/clp/Foundation/directory-resource/hp.htm

▶ The Directory lists services available to nonprofit organizations in southwestern Pennsylvania. Services include technical assistance in all aspects of running a nonprofit, including management, finance, law, marketing, communications, and computerization with a special emphasis on fund raising. Also included are organizations that provide training, educational programs, volunteers, or interns in these areas. Can search by name or type of service.

Pennsylvania Association of Nonprofit Organizations (PANO)

132 State Street, Harrisburg, PA 17101
Tel: 717-236-8584; FAX: 717-236-8767
E-mail: jgeiger528@aol.com (Joseph M. Geiger, Executive Director); WWW: http://www.pano.org/,
http://www.pano.org/conslt.htm

▶ PANO is a statewide organization serving and strengthening the charitable nonprofit sector through leadership, advocacy, and education. Services and programs include education (offers seminars on a variety of topics in various parts of the state; members receive discounts on these programs), affiliations and public policy (PANO is involved with a number of organizations which affect the nonprofit sector, including the National Council of Nonprofit Associations), technical assistance and networking (PANO provides free technical assistance to its members when possible. For long-term assistance, PANO provides a free referral service to consultants in fields such as accounting, fund raising, legal services, tax services, etc.) publications (their quarterly newsletter, *Keynotes,* provides updates on current legislation and issues, lists upcoming events, posts current member benefits, and keeps members educated about what PANO is doing statewide; *Pennsylvania Nonprofit Handbook: Everything You Need to Know to Start and Run Your Nonprofit Organization,* an A-to-Z guide for new and established nonprofits in Pennsylvania), communications and outreach (Executive Director Joe Geiger conducts monthly interviews with leaders in the nonprofit sector and public officials for the Lincoln Radio Journal; PANO participates in an annual charitable survey with the Lincoln Institute on Public Policy). Upcoming workshop and event schedule is located online at *http://www.pano.org/events.htm.* PANO also offers cost-saving discounts (members only).

ProArts

425 Sixth Avenue, Suite 360, Pittsburgh, PA 15219-1819
Tel: 412-391-2060; FAX: 412-394-4280
E-mail: proarts@artswire.org (Marilyn Coleman, Executive Director); WWW: http://www.proarts-pittsburgh.org,
http://www.proarts-pittsburgh.org/artscal.html (ProArts Library)

▶ ProArts is southwestern Pennsylvania's arts service organization serving not-for-profit arts organizations and independent artists. Established in Pittsburgh in 1994 as Western Pennsylvania Professionals for the Arts, ProArts provides programs to support and strengthen the greater Pittsburgh arts community, and opportunities for arts supporters in the business and legal communities to volunteer and become active in the cultural life of our region. Services include Business Volunteers for the Arts (a program that helps to strengthen business practices of arts organizations by recruiting and placing executives with not-for-profit arts organizations to provide free management consulting assistance; volunteers are needed with expertise in marketing and public relations, financial management and systems, planning, facilities studies, information systems, and more), *Volunteer Lawyers for the Arts* (provides pro-bono assistance to low-income artists and smaller arts organizations for arts-related legal needs), and a calendar of area workshops.

RHODE ISLAND

Nonprofit Resources of Southern New England (NRSNE)

160 Broad Street, Providence, RI 02903
Tel: 401-861-1920; FAX: 401-861-8198
E-mail: craigk@intap.net (Craig Kercheval),
jbeauchemin@altavista.com,
jbeauchemin@nonprofitresourcessne.org (Joan Beauchemin);
WWW: http://www.nonprofitresourcessne.org

▶ Nonprofit Resources was created to supply nonprofits with the knowledge and expertise needed for effective operation and future growth. Their mission is to support the advancement of nonprofit organizations and the nonprofit sector as a whole. NRSNE offers an array of services to support the advancement of nonprofit organizations to improve community life and foster a civil society and advocates for the interests of the nonprofit sector. It is Southern New England's support network for nonprofit organizations. It provides a place for nonprofit organizations to learn, share, and develop solutions to problems that typically confront agencies in the nonprofit sector. Services include advocacy, information and referral, networking, grantsbook, subscription to nonprofit quarterly, group purchasing, technology assistance, and member profile on the NPR Web site.

SOUTH CAROLINA

South Carolina Association of Nonprofit Organizations (SCANFO)

Mailing address: P.O. Box 11252, Columbia, SC 29211

Physical address: 625-C Taylor Street, Columbia, SC 29201
Tel: 800-438-8508, 803-929-0890; FAX: 803-929-0173
E-mail: info@scanpo.org (Contact: Erin Hardwick);
WWW: http://www.scanpo.org,
http://www.scanpo.org/Useful_Links/useful_links.html

▶ Founded in 1997, the South Carolina Association of Nonprofit Organizations is a private, 501(c)(3) nonprofit organization that serves as a statewide network for nonprofit boards and staffs, a growing information center on effective practices and an advocate for the nonprofit sector as a whole. They offer services directly to all sizes and types of 501(c)(3) nonprofits, and work closely with other local, state, and national groups that assist nonprofits. Programs/services include public policy (regular communications on federal and state public policy issues through *The Nonprofit Advocate,* SCANPO's quarterly newsletter; Action Alerts; representation at the statehouse on issues affecting the nonprofit sector as a whole and with regulatory agencies, such as the Secretary of State, state Department of Revenue, and the state Attorney General's office; educational information to assist organizations to understand and comply with state and federal regulations; leadership opportunities on an advocacy committee that guides SCANPO's legislative priorities; collaboration with other organizations and coalitions to strengthen the force of the nonprofit voice at the state level), communication and public education (*The Nonprofit Advocate* keeps you current on state and national issues, trends, and events of interest to the nonprofit sector; *Member Memo,* a mailing of timely and important information sent to members between newsletters; online resources on the SCANPO Web site, which include the opportunity to post job openings and share suggestions with the SCANPO; leadership opportunities with your colleagues on a communications committee that guides SCANPO's communications activities); education and training (educational seminars and workshops offered around the state; a calendar of events is available online at *http://www.scanpo.org/Education_and_Training/education_and_tr aining.html;* SCANPO's Annual Conference; members-only discounts on seminar, workshop, and annual meeting registration fees for member; leadership opportunities with your colleagues on an education committee that plans and evaluates SCANPO's training seminars), cost savings, resources (a statewide forum with nonprofit, corporate, and philanthropic leaders to exchange ideas and to learn about emerging issues that affect your organization; SCANPO's annual conference offers information along with an exposition showcasing the latest products and services; the Board & Staff Helpline for assistance on issues such as fund raising, boards, personnel, accounting, legal concerns, communications, advocacy, evaluation, volunteers, and collaboration; referrals to consultants, CPAs, attorneys, and nonprofit peers experienced in your topics of concern). SCANO publishes *The SCANPO Nonprofit Resource Directory,* a statewide directory of nonprofit members of SCANPO.

Nonprofit Management Institute

132 S. Dakota Avenue, Sioux Falls, SD 57104
Tel: 800-641-4309, 605-367-5380
E-mail: Jean.Layton@dsu.edu (Prof. Jean Layton, CFRE, Director); WWW: http://www.departments.dsu.edu/npmi/

▶ Nonprofit Management Institute provides public service assistance for both nonprofit and for-profit organizations in South Dakota. Established in 1990 through partial state funding, the Institute has grown from providing assistance with grants to offering comprehensive assistance with issues affecting nonprofit organizations. Through the Institute, organizations may receive assistance with a variety of steps in the grant-writing process, strategic planning, finding appropriate resources, and other areas. Non-Profit Management Institute is a division of the College of Business and Information Systems and is located in Sioux Falls. Assistance can be provided at the Sioux Falls office or on site. The Institute also is involved in delivery of academic program resulting in a minor or certificate in nonprofit management.

TENNESSEE

Center for Nonprofit Management (CNM)

44 Vantage Way, Suite 230, Nashville, TN 37228
Tel: 615-259-0100; FAX: 615-259-0400
E-mail: info@cnm.org or editor@cnm.org;
WWW: http://www.cnm.org

▶ Services include *Educational Services* (core courses, specialized and advanced courses, executive forums, briefings, "hot spot" briefings, in-agency training), consultation (consultation engagements, MentorMatches, and their InfoLine), Nonprofit Tool Kit (Assessment-for-Development Service, *A Grantseeker's Guide to Tennessee Funders, Human Resource Policy Manual*), Excellence Network (E-Net), a constituent group of nonprofit organizations affiliated with the Center committed to management excellence, administrative cost containment, and collective buying power. *Events* (the CNM Board of Directors hosts the annual Salute to Excellence event, which turns the spotlight on the nonprofit sector and celebrates achievement in the nonprofit community. CNM sends fax broadcast announcements providing information on CNM products and services by e-mail.

Tennessee Nonprofit Association (TNA)

2012 21st Avenue South, Nashville, TN 37212
Tel: 800-330-9871, 615-385-2221, ext. 34; FAX: 615-385-2157
E-mail: spoulton@ccs1.org (Sandra Poulton),
stewc98545@aol.com (Stewart Clifton);
WWW: http://www.expage.com/page/TNasc

▶ The Tennessee Nonprofit Association (TNA) was formed in 1994 to assist local nonprofit agencies across the state in meeting the increasing demands of organizational leadership. TNA works to help nonprofits enhance their efficiency, funding, and service coordination by providing information, advocacy, specially designed publications, and cost-saving programs and benefits.

TEXAS

Abilene Center for Nonprofit Management *(See The Nonprofit Resource Center)*

Amarillo Area Foundation Nonprofit Services Center

801 South Fillmore, Suite 700, Amarillo, TX 79101-3545
Tel: 806-376-4521; FAX: 806-373-3656
E-mail: ashley@aaf-hf.org (Ashley Allison, Director of Community Services); WWW: http://www.aaf-hf.org

▶ A program of the Amarillo Area Foundation, it provides nonprofit management assistance to the 26 counties of the Panhandle. Services include consulting (organization development; long-range planning; program development; nonprofit establishment; financial and legal issues; membership and fund-raising strategies; endowment programs; management strategies; volunteer programs); grant-writing assistance (project strategies, proposal development, funding source research, collaboration development); and workshops (board training; team building; management skills; volunteer training).

Business Volunteers for the Arts/Houston (BVA)

6406 Teal Run Drive, Houston, TX 77035
Tel: 713-658-2483
WWW: http://www.fine-art.com/org/bva.html

▶ BVA currently has consultants serving about 90 organizations. Its main consulting services include communications, graphic design, marketing, development strategy, strategic planning, general management, personnel policies, financial planning, data processing, and information systems. BVA's services are provided without a fee to nonprofit arts organizations. All BVA consultants receive orientation and training on working with nonprofit arts groups. The consultants are then matched in team or individual situations through an extensive interview process. This consultancy program is the core of Business Volunteers for the Arts. All other BVA activities and programs orbit around this core and all are intended to facilitate and support the partnership between the business and arts communities.

Center for Nonprofit Management/ Nonprofit Loan Center

2900 Live Oak Street, Dallas, TX 75204
Tel: 214-826-3470; FAX: 214-821-3845
E-mail: atwood@cnmdallas.org (Jennifer Atwood, Director of Communications); WWW: http://www.cnmdallas.org

▶ The mission of the Center for Nonprofit Management is to enhance the management effectiveness of the nonprofit sector as it seeks to enhance the quality of life of its community. Services include management seminars (continuing education seminars; listing online at *http://www.cnmdallas.org/pages/seminar.htm;* management consulting services (board training, fund development, strategic planning, organizational assessments); low-interest loans (loans and financial guidance); employment (*Opportunity NOCs,* a classified publication listing nonprofit employment opportunities); membership (resource information and referral service); meeting space: Center for Community Cooperation (access to free meeting space); programs and services (Collaboration Program—Building Effective Partnerships; facilitation teams; management sonsulting services in the areas of organizational assessment, board training, development audit, development consultation, development workshop, strategic planning, human resources consultation, legal consultation, financial management consultation, customized management consulting services). The Center sponsors the annual GET ON BOARD! Fair and publishes the members-only *NewsBriefs,* a bimonthly resource newsletter

Center for Community-Based and Nonprofit Organizations

Austin Community College, 5930 Middle Fiskville Road, Room 506.4, Austin, TX 78752
Tel: 512-223-7076; FAX: 512-223-7895
E-mail: bsilverb@austin.cc.tx.us (Barry Silverberg, Director)

▶ The Austin Community College Center for Community-Based and Nonprofit Organizations works collaboratively with public and private ventures to broaden the horizons and possibilities for nonprofits in Travis County and the greater Austin area. It identifies NPO and CBO needs and develops low-cost services to respond to them by supplementing and complementing existing community services. The Center's Nonprofit Training Initiative is a collaborative effort of businesses and nonprofits providing training at low or no cost to Austin area nonprofits. The Center also establishes partnerships with professional associations to better serve the CBO and NPO community. The Austin Chapter of American Society for Training and Development, the Center's first partner, helped create the Center's Anne Durrum Robinson & ASTD Resource Center. It serves CBO and NPO professionals, volunteers, and consultants and the college's students and faculty. It offers courses, seminars, forums, workshops, and mentoring. It publishes a monthly newsletter, *Update.*

Executive Service Corps of Tarrant County (ESC)

Sterling Lauer, Executive Director, Executive Service Corps of Tarrant County, 3209 South University Drive, Fort Worth, TX 76109
Tel: 817-924-5393, 817-923-0950
E-mail: esctc@flash.net

▶ ESC provides leadership and management resources to nonprofit organizations and government agencies in the Tarrant County area. Services include low-cost consultations, educational programs, information, and referral in these areas: strategic planning, board development, human resource management, financial management, fund-raising strategies, organizational management, marketing and communication, and computer technology. ESC also offers an Executive Advisory Program for executive directors, conducts executive searches and publishes a *Guidebook for Starting a Nonprofit Organization in Texas.*

Funding Information Center

329 South Henderson, Fort Worth, TX 76104
Tel: 817-334-0228
E-mail: klibassi@fic-ftw.org (Karen LiBassi, Executive Director); WWW: http://www.fic-ftw.org, http://www.fic-ftw.org/links.htm

▶ The Funding Information Center (FIC) is a free, self-service library of research materials on grants, fund raising, and nonprofit management. Services/programs include library, workshops, *Directory of Tarrant County Grantmakers,* newsletter (available online); Events Calendar, volunteer opportunities, and nonprofit job opportunities.

Laredo Nonprofit & Volunteer Center

Laredo Public Library, 1120 East Calton Road, Laredo, TX 78041
Tel: 956-795-2400, ext. #2255; FAX: 956-795-2403
E-mail: janice@laredolibrary.org (Janice Weber, Library Director); WWW: http://www.laredolibrary.org/nonprofit.htm

▶ The City of Laredo Nonprofit Management & Volunteer Center provides technical assistance to all not-for-profit organizations within a 150-mile radius. It is a member of the Texas Nonprofit Management Support Network. Services include management counseling, funding information, grants research assistance, critique of grant proposals, continuing education seminars, board training, volunteer services referral, selected dissemination of information, and calendar of events.

Management Assistance Program

Volunteer Center of Coastal Bend, 400 Mann Street, Suite 402, Corpus Christi, TX 78401
Tel: 361-887-8282, ext. 4; FAX: 361-887-8286
E-mail: gilnan@aol.com (Gilna Nance, Executive Director), vccb@caller.infi.net; WWW: http://www.callernetwork.com/volctr, http://3rdrock.coserve.org/nrc/cc.html

▶ The Management Assistance program is a member of the Texas Nonprofit Management Support Network; it collaborates with Texas A&M University–Corpus Christi and Del Mar College and other community organizations to deliver the best services possible to the nonprofit sector. Services offered include seminars and workshops on fund raising, outcome evaluation, and grant writing, in addition to management and development audits. Consultations are also provided in the areas of board training, grant writing, financial and strategic planning, team building, 501(c)(3) start-up, personnel training, and meeting management and committee goals; all services are tailored to the needs of individual agencies. Areas of expertise lie in volunteer management and total quality management (TQM), board training, and strategic planning.

Management Assistance Program

United Way of the Gulf Coast, 2200 North Loop West, Houston, TX 77018
Tel: 713-685-2787; FAX: 713-685-5575
E-mail: map@maphouston.org, rhagerty@uwtgc.org (Ronnie Hagerty, MAP Director), http://www.maphouston.org, http://www.uwtgc.org/servicesnonprofit.htm, http://www.uwtgc.org/MAPweb.htm

▶ The Management Assistance Program (MAP) is a program of the United Way of the Texas Gulf Coast. MAP provides management assistance and training for all 501(c)(3) nonprofit organizations. The Management Assistance Program offers management consulting, seminars and computer training designed to enhance the management of nonprofit organizations. Training addresses nonprofit concerns such as financial planning, budgeting, fund raising, board development, special events, legal issues, and other topics of interest to nonprofit managers. In addition to computer classes on the most used software packages, MAP addresses other technology issues such as planning, data modeling, database development, and software and hardware selection and maintenance. MAP is a member of the Texas Nonprofit Management Assistance Network.

The Nonprofit Center

3710 Cedar Street, Suite 130, Box 10, Austin, TX 78705
Tel: 512-451-5315; FAX: 512-451-0651
E-mail: ljebo@flash.net (Lois Jebo, Executive Director); WWW: http://www.main.org/nonprofit

▶ Established in 1988 as part of a statewide network funded by the Meadows Foundation, the Nonprofit Center serves over 250 organizations annually and continues to fulfill the original mission set forth by the Meadows Foundation: to maximize the effectiveness of community agencies thereby improving the lives of all citizens of Texas. Services include: consulting services (accounting and financial development; organizational development; strategic planning; development and fund raising; laws, rules, and regulations; computer programs/network setup; marketing and public relations; board and staff relations; management audits; organizational audits; volunteer management); technical assistance (starting a nonprofit organization; locating funding sources; specific regulations affecting your agency; obtaining grants; management or board issues; starting and running a volunteer program); training and seminars (workshop on such topics as fund raising and grantsmanship; board member development; organizational assessment; effective nonprofit management; strategic planning; collaboration); partnership (the Center invites nonprofits to join as partners in being informed and educated about nonprofit issues; partnerships will bring you

The Inside Link, Nonprofit News Bulletins, preferential notification of workshops, seminars, scholarships, intern opportunities, board service opportunities, and limited job announcements. In return, the Center will seek your input and voluntary participation in Center programming and also participation in activities that contribute to setting the agenda for the entire nonprofit sector).

Nonprofit Management Center of the Permian Basin

Physical address: 550 West Texas, Suite 1260, Midland, TX 79701

Mailing address: P.O. Box 10424, Midland, TX 79702
Tel: 915-682-4704; FAX: 915-498-8999
E-mail: info@pbaf.org, nmc@pbaf.org (LaNell Honeyman, Executive Director); WWW: http://www.pbaf.org/nmc/index.html

▶ The purpose of the new Nonprofit Management Center is to provide programs and services to help civic and charitable organizations better serve their communities. The Center's services include providing training for staff and volunteers of nonprofit agencies, as well as consulting and information resources. Among specific issues with which the Center will offer assistance are community needs assessment, starting a nonprofit organization, leadership training, strategic planning, fund raising and grant writing, budgeting and financial administration, and public relations.

The Nonprofit Resource Center (Formerly Abilene Center for Nonprofit Management)

P.O. Box 3322, Abilene, TX 79604
Tel: 915-677-8166; FAX: 915-676-4206
E-mail: nonprofit@abilene.com (Jody Grigsby, Director); WWW: http://coserve1.panam.edu/nrc/ab.html

▶ A program of the Community Foundation of Abilene, the Center has been in operation since 1987 and serves Abilene and the 19-county Texas Midwest. The Nonprofit Resource Center works with any nonprofit organization that has or is applying for IRS tax-exempt status. Services include: training and consulting (strategic and long-range planning, analysis, and planning; board and staff development consultations, customized board training, and a board bank; fund raising, marketing, and public relations assistance; management audits; organizational assessment; budgeting; information on nonprofit incorporation, legal liabilities, and tax issues; information on and assistance in starting a nonprofit organization; guidelines for writing effective grant proposals; funding information library; workshops/seminars on topics of general interest); customized board training retreats (roles and responsibilities of a board member; committee structure; legal liabilities of the board; strategic planning; board/staff relations; fund raising and the board; board composition and recruitment); The Funding Information Library (the FIL is one of 13 Foundation Center Cooperating Collections in Texas and maintains the most current editions of foundation directories, FC Search [CD-ROM], and the *Directory of Texas Foundations,* in addition to resource materials on the nonprofit management topics); the Center's publication, *The Inside Link,* published three times a year, concerns issues and trends affecting the nonprofit sector; *Board Bank* (free information and referral service matches individuals with community boards).

Nonprofit Resource Center of Texas

P.O. Box 15070, 111 Soledad Avenue, Suite 200, San Antonio, TX 78205
Tel: 210-227-4333; FAX: 210-227-0310
E-mail: nprc@nprc.org; WWW: http://www.nprc.org

▶ The Center offers technical assistance, consultation, and training opportunities for board members, staff, and volunteers of nonprofit and philanthropic organizations. Services/programs include: library services (the library of the Nonprofit Resource Center is a specialized collection of information on private funding sources and the nonprofit sector; a Cooperating Collection of The Foundation Center since 1976); publications (publishes the most current information available on Texas private and community foundations including *Texas GrantSeekers Link, Directory of Texas Foundations Online, Directory of Texas Foundations, Trustee Listings, Am I Liable? Responsibilities & Liabilities of Texas Nonprofit Organization Directors,* and Information *LINK*); center partnerships (as a partner, you help to build and make available a valuable collection of materials on nonprofit management, organizational leadership, fund raising, and private and corporate philanthropy; special privileges available); training and consulting services (workshops are designed to help nonprofit managers, staff and board members improve management skills, enhance efficiency and effectiveness, and diversify funding sources; consulting services are designed to provide confidential assistance to nonprofits with specific management and development issues that cannot be addressed in a public workshop setting; topics include fund raising, marketing, organizational assessments, human resources, financial management, strategic planning, board development, compensation studies, and customized training; course schedule available online); custom training (special workshops taken from the regular curriculum or tailored to the specific needs of the client organization including board training, fund raising, planning, marketing, and personnel management); online job board (listing of available positions in the areas of development, financial operations, management, programming and services, support services, position wanted).

North Texas Center for Nonprofit Management

1105 Holliday, Wichita Falls, TX 76301
Tel: 940-322-4961; FAX: 940-322-4962
E-mail: deedecker@cst.net (Dee Decker, Executive Director)

▶ The Center provides nonprofits in north Texas as well as those in southern Oklahoma with all areas of management assistance. Workshops and seminars provide valuable information in such areas as efficient and effective service delivery, grant writing, personnel management, and board development. The Center is one of 12 Foundation Center Cooperating Collections in Texas housing 2,500 books and periodicals in its library. The Center is a member of the Texas Nonprofit Management Assistance Network.

Southwest Border Nonprofit Resource Center (SENRC)

Mailing address: The University of Texas–Pan American, 1201 West University Drive, Edinburg, TX 78596
Tel: 956-384-5920; FAX: 956-384-5922
E-mail: nrc@panam.edu (Irene Sanchez-Casas, Director); WWW: http://3rdrock.coserve.org/nrc

▶ The Southwest Border Nonprofit Resource Center (SBNRC) is a component of the University of Texas–Pan American's Center for

Office Operations and Community Service (COSERVE). This component provides outreach to the nonprofit community in the Rio Grande Valley and South Texas by providing funding resource information, technical assistance, and a philanthropic organizations' network. The Southwest Border Nonprofit Resource Center (SBNRC) serves as a catalyst for sustainable, long-term development of nonprofit organizations in the Rio Grande Valley and South Texas. It provides a variety of resources, services, and technical assistance to build a viable, efficient network of nonprofit organizations. Service areas include: library of funding resources (maintains a database of nonprofit resources available on the Internet, which they make available to nonprofits interested in doing such searches; a quarterly newsletter keeps member nonprofit organizations apprised of new developments within the funding arena); technical assistance (continuing education coursework, seminars and workshops and consulting services in the areas of board, volunteer, and staff development; fund raising such as grant proposal writing, special events, planned giving campaigns; public relations; marketing; management audits; financial management; legal issues; CEO evaluations; computer training including onsite computer assessments along with brochure, Web page development, and marketing production); issue-driven network (SBNRC serves as a liaison for nonprofit organizations interested in creating collaborative efforts centered on a single issue); Funders Information Forum (in collaboration with participating nonprofits, SBNRC organizes an annual meeting of funding entities and nonprofit organizations); publications (*Directory of Rio Grande Valley 501(c)3 Organizations*, quarterly newsletter available online).

Texas Association of Nonprofit Organizations

P.O. Box 12963, Austin, TX 78711
Tel: 512-627-8266, FAX: 888-467-4238, 512-478-5014
E-mail: info@tano.org, kirchoff@rayassociates.com (Kim Kirchoff); WWW: http://www.tano.org,
http://www.tano.org/centers.html

▶ The Texas Association of Nonprofit Organizations (TANO) offers access to awareness and education about nonprofit policies and management issues, nonprofit insurance and group purchasing, and online information and publications

Texas Nonprofit Management Assistance Network, Inc. (Formerly Texas Nonprofit Management Support Network)

9901 IH 10 West, Suite 800, San Antonio, TX 78230
Tel: 210-558-2845; FAX: 210-558-4207
E-mail: texasnetwork@stic.net, rmfry@texasnetwork.org or rmfry@stic.net (Rose Mary Fry, Executive Director);
WWW: http://www.nprc.org/advanced/tips/,
http://3rdrock.coserve.org/nrc/tips.html,
http://www.texasnetwork.org/pages/members.html

▶ Incorporated in 1999, its mission is to develop a coordinated network of centers and organizations, strategically located throughout Texas, that delivers quality management support services and resources to the nonprofit sector. The Texas Nonprofit Network members work each day with nonprofit organizations of all types and budget sizes. The clients of the current providers range from small start-up organizations to large, established organizations. Members provide help in these areas: information and referral (Network members provide help to questions over the phone and in person by qualified staff); libraries (there are 16 Cooperating

Collections libraries in Texas affiliated with the Foundation Center in New York); workshops (Network members offer ongoing public workshops throughout the state and the calendar lists upcoming workshops); consulting services (call your local center to discuss available consulting services; each Network provider has a fee schedule often based on the budget size of the organization and the work to be completed); publications (several Network members publish useful tools for their nonprofit clients such as grant directories, a human resources manual, a board manual on legal responsibilities, and a directory of area nonprofit organizations); other services (Network members offer a variety of other services such as a classified newsletter for jobs, collaborative program, a loan fund, and community convener); partnership programs (some Network providers offer partnership programs for the benefit of their clients, which provide discounts on programs and services and checkout privileges from library collections).

United Way of the Texas Gulf Coast (*see also MAP*)

Management Assistance Program, 2200 North Loop West, Houston, TX 77018
Tel: 713-685-2787; FAX: 713-685-5575
E-mail: map@maphouston.org;
WWW: http://www.maphouston.org/tnpmanagement.htm

▶ The Management Assistance Program (MAP) is a program of the United Way of the Texas Gulf Coast. MAP provides management assistance and training for all 501(c)(3) nonprofit organizations. Housed in United Way of the Texas Gulf Coast headquarters, the Management Assistance Program offers management consulting, seminars and computer training designed to enhance the management of nonprofit organizations. Training addresses nonprofit concerns such as financial planning, budgeting, fund raising, board development, special events, legal issues, and other topics of interest to nonprofit managers. In addition to computer classes on the most used software packages, MAP addresses other technology issues such as planning, data modeling, database development, and software and hardware selection.

Volunteer Center of Lubbock

1706 23rd Street, Suite 101, Lubbock, TX 79411-1214
Tel: 806-747-0551; FAX: 806-747-8640
E-mail: vclubbock@aol.com (Louise Cummins, Executive Director); WWW: http://www.volunteerlubbock.org,
http://sql.ofthe.net/scripts/volunteer/links/output.idc

▶ The Volunteer Center of Lubbock is a community agency organized for the purpose of meeting community needs through the promotion and enhancement of volunteerism, and for the provision of management assistance services for nonprofit organizations. Services include management assistance consultation (technical assistance; consultations with nonprofits; criminal background checks; The Leadership Connection, a program that links people from minority populations who want to serve the community to nonprofit boards; Nonprofit Executives Association, a colleagues group that offers professional development and networking for agency directors); seminars and workshops; volunteer services (provides assistance with volunteer management, recruitment, recognition, and training to help people find volunteer positions). The Center is a member of the Texas Nonprofit Management Support Network.

UTAH

Utah Nonprofits Association (UNA)

1901 East South Campus Drive, Room 2120,
Salt Lake City, UT 84112
Tel: 801-581-4883
E-mail: jrandall@cppa.utah.edu (Jolaine Randall);
WWW: http://www.nonprofit.utah.org/una

▶ The UNA is the umbrella membership association of 501(c)(3) organizations in Utah. Incorporated in 1990, UNA was created by, and for, people who want a stronger, more professional not-for-profit community in Utah. The organization focuses on responding to the training needs of the sector as well as providing mutual support and sector-wide advocacy. UNA is Utah's official statewide affiliate of the National Council of Nonprofit Associations. UNA current membership includes over 100 nonprofit organizations as well as individual members. Its goals are to improve the practice of nonprofit organization management; foster a climate conducive to the growth of nonprofit organizations; promote greater understanding of the role of the nonprofit sector; and encourage networking and cooperative efforts among nonprofit organizations. Programs/services include executive roundtables (focus on key issues in the nonprofit sector and provide an opportunity for representatives of nonprofits to discuss these issues with experts as well as providing an opportunity to network with other nonprofit professionals); training programs (designed to provide representatives of nonprofit organizations with information and expertise to improve their management strategies); *annual meeting and biennial conference* (the annual meeting and biennial conference feature top speakers and panelists that are active in the sector; workshops on topical issues are also offered); *The UNA Newsletter* (the quarterly UNA newsletter, *The Nonprofit News,* includes a calendar of key professional development and networking events, updates on trends, and information about regulation and practice affecting the sector); Web site (includes online access to community nonprofit calendar, classified ads, training event announcements, and links to Utah nonprofit organizations and national resources; it also links to the Utah nonprofit organization database); *Utah Nonprofits Directory;* insurance discounts (provides access to the National Unemployed Insurance Fund and referrals to directors' and officers' liability, property, and health insurance programs).

VERMONT

Technical Assistance Programs (TAP)

Vermont Community Foundation, P.O. Box 30,
Three Court Street, Middlebury, Vermont 05753
Tel: 802-388-3355; FAX: 802-388-3398
E-mail: vcf@vermontcf.org, psharpe@vermontcf.org (Pat Sharpe); WWW: http://www.vermontcf.org

▶ Established in 1991, TAP-VT is sponsored by The Vermont Community Foundation. TAP provides technical training, support, and encouragement to charitable organizations to assist them in dealing effectively with change and to help them increase their efficiency. TAP offers a full schedule of workshops (available online) as well as an online Directory of Nonprofit Consulting Services (*http://www.vermontcf.org/consult.html*).

The Vermont Alliance for Nonprofit Organizations

P.O. Box 8345, Burlington, VT 05402
Tel: 802-862-0292; FAX: 802-862-0292
E-mail: VTNONPROF@aol.com (Jane VanBuren);
WWW: http://www.vermontcf.org/vanpo.html

▶ Benefits of membership include easier access to and less cost for health, life, disability, and directors' and officers' insurance; reduced costs on office supplies and office equipment; easier access to resources, and consultation on retirement, profit sharing, and pension services; pooled or shared computer technicians and other technical assistance; action on issues of accountability, reporting, deductions for charitable contributions, etc.; a unified examination of state contracts, and the relationship of nonprofits to state agencies; promotion of broad-based initiatives to increase charitable giving; and training and education for board members and staff.

WASHINGTON STATE

The Evergreen State Society

Physical address: 1122 East Pike Street, Suite 444,
Seattle, WA 98122-3934

Mailing address: P.O. Box 20682, Seattle, WA 98102-0682
Tel: 206-329-5640; FAX: 206-322-8348
E-mail: pbarber@eskimo.com (Putnam Barber);
WWW: http://www.tess.org

▶ The Evergree State Society is a nonprofit organization addressing policy issues and management questions in order to strengthen the nonprofit sector in Washington State and beyond. Programs and activities include: The Internet Nonprofit Center and the NONPROFIT FAQ (an extensive library and archive of information for leaders and observers of the nonprofit sector in the United States; to access this resource, visit *http://www.nonprofits.org;* the Evergreen State Society maintains the *NONPROFIT FAQ* and provides Web services through the Internet Nonprofit Center for related activities such as the Multi-State Filer project of the National Association of State Charities Officials).

Management Assistance Program

Volunteer Center—United Way of King County, 107 Cherry Street,
Seattle, WA 98104-2266
Tel: 206-461-3700
E-mail: give@uwkc.org

▶ The Volunteer Center provides a full array of services for community volunteers, nonprofit community organizations and workplace volunteer programs on a year-round basis. In addition to the benefits of volunteer recruitment assistance, your organization will automatically receive information about upcoming training opportunities and other services that strengthen nonprofit organizations. Services include: volunteer recruitment and referral, management and technical assistance, training opportunities, volunteer program management, leadership development opportunities, workplace services, networking and seminars, wage and benefit survey for nonprofits, downloadable resources, executive director survey, and agency update newsletter.

The Nonprofit Center

1121 Court C, Suite 208, Tacoma, WA 98402
Tel: 253-272-5844; FAX: 253-272-0916
E-mail: info@npcenter.org; WWW:
http://www.npcenter.org/about.html

▶ The Nonprofit Center is a 501(c)(3) organization formed in 1999, serving the South Puget Sound area, which includes Pierce, Kitsap, Mason, South King, and Thurston Counties. Service areas include education (a rigorous schedule of seminars and workshops is offered throughout the year on topics relating to nonprofit management. Custom designed training is provided to individual organizations with specific needs. Each fall a major conference is held focusing on nonprofit boards); volunteer leadership development: (Center staff and trainers work with nonprofits in providing board training and in expanding and improving recruitment and leadership development activities. Work also is done in the community to expand the pool of knowledgeable potential board members. BoardLink, a system for linking skilled leadership volunteers with nonprofit organizations seeking board members, is under development.); consultation and facilitation services (Center staff and other facilitators are available to lead or facilitate nonprofit planning meetings and board retreats. As the Consultant Program is developed, nonprofit organizations will be linked with skilled consultants on a pro bono or subsidized basis to provide assistance with a full range of nonprofit issues); building connections (Center staff work to increase and strengthen networks among nonprofit organizations for collaboration, program enhancement, and better utilization of resources. Included in these activities are the convening of the Executive Directors' Forum and the Development Directors' Forum, both of which meet regularly throughout the year. The Center also presents the annual Grantmakers' Roundtable, which brings funders and grant seekers together).

Northwest Nonprofit Resources (NNR)

525 East Mission Avenue, Spokane, WA 99202-1824
Tel: 509-484-6733; FAX: 509-483-0345
E-mail: sgill@iea.com (Sandy Gill);
WWW: http://www.indra.com/nnr

▶ Northwest Nonprofit Resources (NNR) is a resource center for nonprofit organizations and their leaders in Washington, Idaho, and Montana. NNR serves as a vehicle through which leaders of nonprofit organizations can strengthen their effectiveness, efficiency, and professionalism as they serve their communities. NNR was formed in 1993 to bring awareness among nonprofit leaders about the issues and trends facing their organizations and the knowledge, skills, and practices leaders need to address those issues. Member services include communication (publishes *Northwest Nonprofit,* a newsletter that provides thought-provoking articles on issues and trends facing nonprofit organizations, management and development tips and techniques, and access to resources important to nonprofit leaders; *Policy Alerts,* condensed updates about federal and state policy issues facing nonprofits focusing on issues such as charitable giving, lobbying and advocacy, accountability, taxes, impacts of federal programs and nonprofit image; electronic networking, a mechanism for nonprofit leaders to ask and answer questions facing their colleagues; *Member Update and Dialogue,* information compiled quarterly and distributed electronically or by mail; toll-free Helpline); cost-saving services; learning (resource center, events); bookstore; nonprofit policy dialogue and strategy.

Technical Assistance for Community Services *(See listing under Oregon)*

WISCONSIN

Greater Milwaukee Nonprofit Institute

3505 North 124th Street, Milwaukee, WI 53005
Tel: 262-790-6831; FAX: 262-790-6753
E-mail: learn@gmni.org (Executive Director Paul Sturm);
WWW: http://www.gmni.org/

▶ The Greater Milwaukee Nonprofit Institute strengthens nonprofit effectiveness and collaboration through learning, technology, and follow-up support. Since 1997, over 200 organizations from seven counties have benefited from the Institute's cutting-edge programs and resources.

The Nonprofit Center of Milwaukee, Inc.

2819 West Highland Boulevard, Milwaukee, WI 53208-3217
Tel: 414-344-3933; FAX: 414-344-7071
E-mail: npcm@execpc.com
WWW: http://www.execpc.com/~npcm

▶ The Nonprofit Center promotes the organizational effectiveness of nonprofit groups dealing with the broad scope of urban issues. The Nonprofit Center is committed to the empowerment of nonprofit organizations through community-based decision making, leadership development, effective management, resource sharing, and other collaborative efforts. The Nonprofit Center was founded in 1967 as an association of nonprofit organizations. The Nonprofit Center provides comprehensive services through three major programs: The Resource Center (the leading source of training and technical assistance in southeastern Wisconsin); The School for Leaders (a program to provide community organizing skills training to local organizations); The Data Center (a technical resource collecting and distributing maps and graphs of Milwaukee neighborhoods); Management Assistance Program (consists of a pool of consultants who provide services and consultation to Milwaukee-area nonprofit organizations through the Nonprofit Center of Milwaukee, are recruited by the Center and the Volunteer Center of Greater Milwaukee offering expertise in areas including organizational management, strategic planning, program review and evaluation, fund raising/resource development, conflict resolution, and a host of other areas pertaining to strengthening agency capacity). Major service/program areas include training and education (provides assistance in the core areas of board training and development, data and demographic analysis, financial management, fundraising and development, human resources, information technology, marketing and communications, program development and evaluation, strategic planning, consultation and administrative and management services (conference planning, conflict resolution, executive searches, nonprofit accounting, personnel policy review, retreat and meeting facilitation).

Consultants

Adams and Associates Consulting

444 West 22nd Avenue, Spokane, WA 99203
Tel: 509-747-3878, FAX: 509-624-6045
E-mail: adams.associates@ior.com

▶ Services include annual giving, major gifts, financial development planning, feasibility studies, capital campaigns, communications, planned giving, and board/staff training and development to clients in the Pacific Northwest.

The Addison Group

PMB 409, 6300-138 Creedmoor Road, Raleigh, NC 27612
Tel: 919-881-0836; FAX: 919-881-9655
E-mail: addgroup@bellsouth.net; WWW: http://addgroup.net

▶ Services include organizational assessment, issues research/advocacy, board development, strategic planning, feasibility studies, project management, leadership workshops, executive search, mediation, and marketing.

The Alford Group Inc.

7660 Gross Point Road, Skokie, IL 60077
Tel: 800-291-8913, 847-966-6670; FAX: (847) 966-6782
E-mail: info@alford.com;
WWW: http://www.alford.com/splash/index.html

▶ The Alford Group was founded in 1979 to provide leadership in improving the quality of life by serving not-for-profits. The firm has worked with over 430 organizations whose budgets and missions span the range of the not-for-profit sector. The firm tailors its services to the needs and budget of each client. Services include management counsel (strategic planning assistance; board development; staff skill analysis and job description review; plan implementation counsel, and staff or volunteer training); resource development (feasibility study, capital campaign design and counsel, annual fund assistance, TAG Planned Giving Services, development assessment, major and planned gift counsel, strategic resource development planning). Clients include organizations in the following areas: human services; arts, culture, and humanities; health; education; religion; environment/wildlife; association/parent; international affairs/public policy. It maintains regional offices in Seattle and Washington, DC; an area office in San Diego; and a nationwide network of local strategic partners. Recent issues of the Alford Group newsletter are available as portable document format (PDF) files, which can be read using the freely available Adobe Acrobat Reader.

Association Management Services, Inc. (AMS)

33 South Catalina Avenue, Suite 202, Pasadena, CA 91106
Tel: 626-449-4356; FAX: 626-564-8540
E-mail: pam@assnmgmt.net (Pamela Hemann, President);
WWW: http://www.assnmgmt.net

▶ Association Management Services, Inc. (AMS) is an association management company specializing in service to nonprofit organizations in both full-service headquarters management and management consulting. The organizations they serve are professional, trade, and philanthropic in nature and range from local to international in scope. Services include full service headquarters management (administrative services, membership recruitment and retention, member service programs, accounting, publications, meetings and professional development programs, board of directors and committee participation); management consulting services (organizational development, board leadership design, governance and structure process, strategic planning and direction, executive search, project outsourcing, meetings and events, convention and trade show management, fund raising and strategic alliances development, newsletters, and publications).

Association Works

P.O. Box 741325, Dallas, TX 75354
Tel: 800-986-8472; FAX: 214-553-5585
E-mail: jpaul@associationworks.com (John Paul, Partner);
WWW: http://www.associationworks.com

▶ Areas of specialization include board development, executive recruitment, management, marketing, organizational development, strategic planning, training and facilitation, executive searches, retreat and conference facilitation, feasibility studies, managing change, merger management, performance management, diagnostic consultation, relationship fund raising, using technology effectively, enhancing the volunteer staff partnership, and customer and donor delight training. John Paul and Sherry Paul co-authored *Achieving Customer Delight in Your Organization: Positioning Your Organization to Stand Out,* and *Field Book* targeted to nonprofit organizations.

Avatar Company

2907 Red Bug Lake Road, Casselberry, FL 32707
Tel: 407-695-6618; FAX: 407-695-4832
E-mail: avatarway@avatarcompany.com,
avatarway@aol.com (Bob Kovacevich);
WWW: http://avatarcompany.com

▶ Avatar is a full service consultancy serving an international clientele. Services range from market research and strategic planning to fund-raising programs and coaching. Its consulting philosophy is driven by the principle that substantive support will not occur until a charity understands and meaningfully serves the needs and interests of its diverse audiences. Avatar is committed to helping a charity understand its audiences by conducting market research and using the findings to influence institutional strategic decision making. The outcome is an audience-compatible experience in which earned and contributed income, volunteerism, foundation funding awards, and overall growth can flourish. Avatar's specialties are board development, computers and technology, direct mail services, evaluation of programs, fund raising, grant writing, graphic design, marketing, research, and strategic planning. Workshops are provided.

Bates & Associates, Inc.
13640 Spinning Wheel Drive, Germantown, MD 20874-2819
Tel: 301-515-1660; FAX: 301-515-1661
E-mail: BA2GEO@aol.com
▶ Bates and Associates provides strategic management counsel to nonprofit organizations whose missions relate to education, arts, culture, and religious and charitable work. Services are available in the following areas: strategic planning, governance, management, programs, and consumer and market research.

Berthoud/Greene *(See also Organizational Development)*
111 Lee Avenue, Suite 305, Takoma Park, MD 20912
Tel: 301-270-1512 (Robert Greene); FAX: 301-270-1519 (Robert Greene)
Tel: 301-891-3224 (Heather Berthoud); FAX: 301-891-3225 (Heather Berthoud)
E-mail: bgreene@erols.com, hberth@erols.com
▶ Organization development consultants, they assist executives, boards, and staff to achieve organizational excellence so they can better serve the community. All of their work is customized. Services include organizational assessment (conduct comprehensive review of organization including program development, program effectiveness, and internal dynamics; provide analysis, recommendations, implementation, and evaluation); strategic planning (design and facilitate processes to evaluate environment, stakeholders, vision, mission, strategic goals, operational plans, organizational structure, and policies and procedures; integrate ongoing assessment with implementation; constant focus on interplay between vision, guiding principles and daily operational realities including management systems, and project output requirements), program planning (guide the development of clear goals and implementation steps including responsibility assignments and timelines; attention to both concrete action steps and flexible implementation options); team development (facilitate development of high-performance teams through attention to joint goal setting, performance measures, role negotiation, division of labor, conflict resolution, decision making, and accountability; certified in the use of the Myers-Briggs Type Indicator™); leadership coaching (assess leadership and management skills, competencies and attitudes; provide tailored training, individual coaching, and consultation to build leadership and management skills including vision, problem-solving, staff development, and management of work-style differences); diversity development (design processes to ensure inclusion and productivity of all organizational members; options include creating opportunities for dialogue across differences, building competencies in cross-cultural work relationships, and developing problem-solving flexibility); group facilitation (design and facilitate groups toward their desired outcomes; jointly determine overall approach in keeping with group's culture. Groups can include boards, task forces, committees, and work units; size can range from 3 to 300); training design and delivery (design tailored workshops on topics such as leadership, facilitation skills, training of trainers, planning, and diversity; focus on both theory and practical experience).

Browning Associates
209 Cooper Avenue, Upper Montclair, NJ 07043
Tel: 973-746-5960; FAX: 973-746-0189
E-mail: info@browning-associates.com;
WWW: http://www.browning-associates.com
▶ Browning Associates is a full-service development consulting firm that also specializes in searches for heads of school. Services include annual fund, capital giving, institutional studies, development office audits, head searches, strategic planning, and board retreats.

CLB & Associates
2538 E. Pine Bluff Lane, Highlands Ranch, CO 80126
Tel: 303-791-9220; FAX: 303-791-9224
E-mail: clbassociates@aol.com (Carol L. Barbeito, President)
▶ CLB & Associates specialize in nonprofit management and leadership; applied research; planning, including long range, annual, and project; needs assessment; evaluation; governance and structure of organizations; resource development, including fund raising and earned income; aspects of human resource management such as stress management and leadership skill development; building communities and developing effective citizens through strengthening the nonprofit sector and its organizations. Their services include consultation, training, train the trainer, advanced education, presentations; and research.

The Center for Public Skills Training
2936 North Hackett Avenue, Milwaukee, WI 53211
Tel: 414-961-2536; FAX: 414-961-7749
E-mail: frankwill@aol.com (Frank Martinelli, President);
WWW: http://www.createthefuture.com
▶ The Center specializes in the recruitment, training, and development of voluntary leadership. Areas of expertise include strategic planning, board development, volunteer management, community partnerships and alliances, and community organizing. Services include training (programs offered include Increasing the Impact of Your Strategic Planning Efforts; Developing and Managing Volunteers: New Tools for Changing Times; Building the Nonprofit Board of the Future; Forging Effective Collaborations and Strategic Alliances; Building a Learning Organization; Systems Thinking Tools for Nonprofit Leaders. Other training can be custom designed to meet the special needs of your organization); consultation (can design specialized technical assistance programs to meet the unique needs of your organization. Areas of expertise include strategic planning facilitation, assisting leaders in planning and conducting high-priority meetings and conferences, board and staff retreats, developing community collaborations and alliances, annual reviews/updates of strategic plans, specialized consultation to address particular organizational problems).

Charitable and Philanthropic Management Counsel
257 Bolton Street, South Boston, MA 02127-1303
Tel: 617-268-4960; FAX: 617-268-4961
E-mail: rita1st@worldnet.att.net;
WWW: http://home.att.net/~rita1st
▶ Chartiable and Philanthropic Management Counsel provides management, organizational development, and fund-raising development counsel for not-for-profit organizations; volunteers; con-

tributors and foundations dedicated to education, arts, culture, historic preservation, health care, sports, and youth; and professional and civic associations.

Coalescence

100 NE 100th Street, Miami, FL 33138
Tel: 305-759-8235; FAX: 305-759-8236
E-mail: info@dowelldogood.com;
WWW: http://www.dowelldogood.com,
http://www.dowelldogood.com/tips2.html

▶ Coalescence is a nonprofit and corporate consulting firm that works with corporate partnerships, strategic planning, volunteer management, program development and evaluation, special event management, earned income ventures, and board and staff development.

Community Consulting Network (CCN)

1441 West Chase, Suite 201, Chicago, IL 60626
Tel: 773-761-6564; FAX: 773-761-6561
E-mail: info@changenet.org

▶ The Community Consulting Network assists nonprofits in managing change in order to build more effective organizations and programs. The Community Consulting Network works with organizations to increase their organizational capacity and resources so that they can negotiate the best possible opportunities for their constituents, both within and outside of their communities. CCN assists organizations to fulfill their missions through consultation, training, research, and evaluation.

The Conservation Company

One Penn Center, Suite 1550, Philadelphia, PA 19103
Tel: 888-222-2281, 215-568-0399; FAX: 215-568-2619

50 East 42nd Street, 19th Floor, New York, NY 10017
Tel: 212-949-0990; FAX: 212-949-1672
E-mail: info@consco.com

2300 N. Lincoln Park West, Chicago, IL 60614
Tel: 312-327-7148; FAX: 312-327-7483

▶ Formed in 1980, it is a multidisciplinary firm with a team approach to consulting with nonprofit organizations, philanthropies, corporate community affairs departments, and public agencies. Services include strategic planning; program feasibility, design, and evaluation; organizational assessment and development; board development; executive search; and forming a nonprofit organization. Its clients are in fields as diverse as education, arts and culture, community and economic development, human services, health care, children and family issues, and the environment.

Ralph Copleman

44 Titus Avenue, Lawrenceville, NJ 08648
Tel: 609-895-1629; FAX: 609-896-0423
E-mail: ralph@earthdreams.net

▶ Mr. Copleman's consulting practice focuses on closer connections between people's ideals and their work life. He helps apply the motivation behind dreams directly to responsibilities. Consulting activities: long-range planning (employs system-wide programs and large-scale activities to help organizations and communities reformulate visions, strategies, and ways of operating; leadership development (designs challenging programs for people

at any level of an organization; delivers concentrated explorations of vision, ethics, realism, and courage); team building (conducts powerful workshops for teams seeking to harness their collective ability to make an important difference to their organization and the world); executive coaching (works closely with individuals at all levels of responsibility to clarify life goals, align organizational priorities, and/or change interpersonal behavior). Copleman created and maintains a Web site devoted to free management support and fund-raising advice for environmental nonprofits (*www.EarthDreams.net*).

Corporate Alternatives, inc. (CAi)

301 West Cook Street, Springfield, IL 62704
Tel: 217-544-5687; FAX: 217-544-5738

1014 11th Street, Sacramento, CA 95814
Tel: 916-944-0535
E-mail: corpalt@fgi.net, brinck@delphi.com;
WWW: http://www.fgi.net/~corpalt/

▶ Established in 1982, CAi works only with nonprofits providing consultation and training in board development and recruitment strategies, strategic planning and organizational development, new business start-up, property acquisition, management audits, finding capital, board–staff retreat planning and facilitation, marketing, surveys and focus groups, and corporate restructuring. CAi provides staff training and curriculum development on all the above. It offers the Enterprise Forum, a seminar on business development, and training session "How to Achieve Financial Empowerment for Your Not-for-Profit."

Designs in Development, Inc. (DID)

P.O. Box 4460, Seminole, FL 33775
Tel: 800-411-1477; FAX: 727-397-6497
E-mail: designdev@aol.com (Nancy L. Brown, President);
WWW: http://ephilanthropy.com,
http://members.aol.com/designdev/index/nancy.html

▶ Designs in Development serves the Southeast through campaign consultation, strategic planning, training, and executive search, specializing in organizations with budgets of $100,000 to $10 million. The firm provides a full range of services from strategic planning and executive search to campaign consultation, development audits, and planned giving. DID has worked with all types of nonprofit institutions, and is especially experienced with human services, economic development, arts, and humane organizations. Nancy L. Brown, President and chief counsel for the firm, is a nationally noted trainer and speaker in philanthropy. In addition to having authored and published the audio workshop "Increasing Board Effectiveness," she has developed 10 day-long curricula for training boards, staff, and volunteers. Services include management consulting (strategic planning facilitation, tactical planning facilitation, board development, policies and procedures, executive search, leadership training, quality management consultation, marketing and communications planning, association management, 501(c)(3) applications); fund-raising consulting (capital campaigns and feasibility studies, major gift planning, fund-raising planning, grant writing, donor cultivation training, in-house training, workshops, development audits, and keynote speeches). Nancy Brown authored and published the audio workshop "Increasing Board Effectiveness."

The Dini Partners, Inc.

2727 Allen Parkway, Suite 700, Houston, TX 77019
Tel: 713-942-8110; FAX: 713-942-8708

3400 Carlisle Street, Suite 348, Dallas, TX 75204
Tel: 214-754-9393; FAX: 214-754-9363

The Dini Partners, Inc., 3724 Jefferson Avenue, Suite 348,
Austin, TX 78731
Tel: 512-302-1943; FAX: 512-302-5254
E-mail: dinipart@dinipartners.com;
WWW: http://www.dinipartners.com

▶ Services provided by the Dini Partners include management consulting (strategic planning, leadership development, executive search, and trustee planning retreats); fund raising (development staff and volunteer training, development program assessment, fund-raising feasibility studies, capital campaign consulting and management, major gift fund raising, and endowment development).

Draper Consulting Group (DCG)

10811 Washington Boulevard, Suite 380,
Culver City, CA 90232-3659
Tel: 310-559-3424; FAX: 310-559-4586
E-mail: office@drapergroup.com (Lee Draper, President);
WWW: http://www.drapergroup.com

▶ Founded in 1990, DCG is a full-service firm offering a broad range of management and technical assistance services. DCG provides essential consulting services that strengthen nonprofit organizations and position them for long-term success. Services include strategic planning, fund development, capital campaigns, board and staff development, planning retreats. DCG has worked with over 60 nonprofit service providers in health, human services, conservation, education, and the arts.

f3t Nonprofit Consulting

1524 Bayview Drive, Fort Lauderdale, FL 33304
Tel: 954-868-2897; FAX: 954-563-1759
E-mail: mail@f3t.com, joel@f3t.com (Joel Greenbaum,
Founder/President); WWW: http://www.f3t.com

▶ f3t consulting helps nonprofit organizations with marketing/communications, fund development, management evaluations, and technology improvements.

Full Circle Associates

4756 U Village PL NE #126, Seattle, WA 98105-5021
E-mail: nancyw@fullcirc.com (Nancy White, Founder);
WWW: http://www.fullcirc.com/about.htm#services,
http://www.fullcirc.com/resources.htm

▶ Full Circle is the consulting practice of Nancy White and a network of independent professionals who provide services individually and collectively for clients in the community, and nonprofit and business sectors. Using communications as its centerpoint, it provides strategic facilitation, online community development, marketing, and project management services for the community and nonprofit and business sectors. Full Circle has a deep interest in successful online interaction in online communities and virtual workgroups, and maintains a free collection of resources in this area. In collaboration with Knowise, Full Circle provides training in online facilitation. It does business in geographic and cyberspaces and provides an e-mail newsletter. Current services provided include Wise Circle Training; online community building services; online facilitation and moderation; strategic and program planning; public, media, and government relations; marketing; message development; focus group testing; writing, editing; group facilitation (online and offline); project management; Internet strategic planning; community organizing; and Internet research.

Glenwood Associates

24 Old Georgetown Road, Princeton, NJ 08540
Tel: 732-821-5522; FAX: 732-821-5955
E-mail: info@glenwoodassociates.com;
WWW: http://www.glenwoodassociates.com/services.htm

▶ Services include meetings and conferences; major gifts (develop the case for major gift support; identify donors and prospects; plan for cultivation and relationship building; develop a purposeful solicitation packet; and build partnerships with donors), special events, cultivating and soliciting donors or members, organizational studies and program audits, marketing and community outreach, leadership and volunteer development, corporate partnership programs, chapter and field development, staff recruitment, and Web site design and promotion.

Hayes Briscoe Associates

322 West Bellevue Avenue, San Mateo, CA 94402
Tel: 650-344-8883; FAX: 650-344-3387
E-mail: hbaconsult@aol.com; WWW: http://www.hbaconsult.com

85 Sterling Street, Beacon, NY 12508
Tel: 914-831-9741
6671 SW 70th Terrace, Miami, FL 33143
Tel: 305-667-2795; FAX: 305-667-3195

▶ Hayes Briscoe Associates offers full-service consulting to nonprofit organizations throughout the United States and abroad. They specialize in nonprofit management with an emphasis on governance (board recruitment, board/staff relations, board counsel, bylaws development, start-up coaching, public policy, self-assessment, program evaluation, board retreats, board/staff training, board organization, coalitions/alliances, mergers), planning (executive coaching, strategic planning, mission development, goals/objectives, internal audits, budgeting, data system audits, staffing needs, personnel policies, program expansion, government relations, interim management, organization capacity building, accreditation preparation) and fund development (capital campaigns, planning/feasibility studies, development audits, case development, program marketing/marketing audits, annual fund development/coaching, volunteer development, development planning, prospect identification, planned giving, foundation/corporate outreach, endowment building, software design/selection, software implementation, development writing, major gifts).

Ivan Price Associates (IPA)

P.O. Box 413, Indio, CA 92202-0413
Tel: 760-413-7320; FAX: 760-342-3907
E-mail: ipa@ezwebservices.com (Ivan Price, President/Owner);
WWW: http://www.ezwebservices.com/ipa

▶ Established in 1984, IPA is a full-service consulting firm that works with all types of not-for-profit organizations. Services include fund raising, special events, planned giving, feasibility studies, campaign management, foundation development, grant writing and management, foundation and corporate research, fund raising, special events, planned giving, feasibility studies, campaign management, foundation development, grant writing and management, foundation and corporate research, marketing, strategic planning, interim management, audits and evaluations, publication development, board/staff development, organizational development, and community and public relations.

J/C Consulting Group

236 Wahelani Road, Kula, Maui HI 96790-9409
Tel: 808-876-1205; FAX: 808-879-1305
E-mail: jeanconger@aol.com (Jean Conger CFRE, Principal)

▶ Services include planning and implementing annual and capital campaigns, grantsmanship nonprofit board training/development, retreat/meeting facilitation, executive coaching, strategic planning, and mergers. The group is experienced with diverse economic development, human services, education, health care, and arts and cultural organizations, including Native Hawaiian.

Jackson, Fields, Allen (JFA) & Associates

6983 Montana Avenue, Las Vegas, NV 89110-5221
Tel: 702-452-0333; FAX: 702-452-9505
E-mail: jfaassoc@aol.com, (Dr. Barbara P. Jackson)

▶ JFA & Associates is a management consulting firm devoted to providing consulting services specifically for small and medium-sized nonprofit organizations as well as governmental agencies. JFA specializes in providing management services such as meeting facilitation, annual meetings, retreats, consultation (management and organizational issues, administrative and operational policy development, governmental collaborations), customized training (board of directors, volunteers, staff, membership), seminars/workshops (strategic planning, board of director development, volunteer management, board/staff diversification).

James Dunlop & Co., Inc.

85 Clifton Avenue, Marblehead, MA 01945
Tel: 781-631-0821; FAX: 781-593-8940
E-mail: jdunlop272@aol.com

▶ Dunlop provides nonprofit organization management and organizational consulting, including strategic planning, governance, and staff organization.

Jean Block Consulting, Inc.

7624 Verona NW, Albuquerque, NM 87120
Tel: 505-899-1520; FAX: 505-890-5285
E-mail: jblockinc@aol.com (Jean Block, President);
WWW: http://www.jblockinc.com

▶ Jean Block Consulting provides nonprofit management and fund-raising services for staff and volunteers, strategic planning, and how to develop a stronger, more effective board of directors, and is the author of *Fast Fundraising Facts for Fame & Fortune* (1997). The Web site contains an electronic copy of all past newsletters offering tips on fund raising, board development, and volunteer management.

John R. Frank Consulting

14642 NE 174th Street, Woodinville, WA 98072
Tel/FAX: 425-488-1362
E-mail: JohnRFrank@aol.com (John R. Frank, President);
WWW: http://www.JohnRFrank.com

▶ John R. Frank Consulting counsel in development, management (strategic planning, marketing, management and development audits), and leadership (board/staff training and retreats, organizational development, executive coaching) to nonprofit organizations, specializing in capital campaigns, major donors, and boardsmanship.

Kumamoto Associates

4130 Seaview Lane, Los Angeles, CA 90065
Tel: 323-233-6473; FAX: 323-342-0817
E-mail: akumamoto@aol.com

▶ Kumamoto Associates is a consulting firm serving corporate, governmental, and nonprofit clients in management consulting, communications, and marketing. Alan Kumamoto is a founding partner with over 30 years of experience in management consulting, resource development/fund raising, and human relations training. Mr. Kumamoto works with public agencies, nonprofit organizations, and private businesses in strategic business planning, community needs assessment and evaluation, board development, volunteer recruitment, program planning, resource development, proposal writing, coalition building, and community outreach.

La Piana Associates

43 Estrella Avenue, Piedmont, CA 94611
Tel: 510-655-34355; FAX: 510-655-3408
E-mail: info@lapiana.org; WWW:
http://www.lapiana.org/lapiana/index.html

▶ La Piana Associates is a management consulting firm located in the San Francisco Bay Area, but serving nonprofits and their funders throughout the country. It works in the following areas: strategic restructuring (through its foundation-sponsored Strategic Solutions project, it assists with all aspects of mergers, joint ventures, consolidations, alliances, and other forms of nonprofit partnership); strategic planning (has developed a fast-track strategic planning methodology that addresses critical issues in the organization's future); organizational change management (helps the people of your nonprofit to adjust to and embrace change and use it to strengthen the organization in dealing with executive changes, contemplated mergers, or changing markets); board/management issues (provides experienced help to executives and board members experiencing conflicts, misunderstandings, or other cross-purposes that can hamper the organization's ability to advance its mission); funder consultation (works with funders to develop strategies that enhance their grantees' organizational effectiveness and can also help groups of funders to develop joint ventures or, in the case of small foundations, to consolidate administrative activities).

Logistics Management Institute (LMI)

2000 Corporate Ridge, McLean, VA 22102-7805
Tel: 703-917-7217
E-mail: bmoeller@lmi.org (Bill Moeller, Director of Contracts);
WWW: http://www.lmi.org/lmi_abot.html

▶ LMI is a private, nonprofit corporation that provides management consulting, research, and analysis to government and nonprofit organizations. Although historically focused on logistics, LMI today provides its clients with expertise across the full spectrum of management functions. It seeks to improve the efficiency of public-sector operations and the effectiveness with which public resources are used. It maintains a strong awareness of academic research and of private-sector technologies and business practices. It maintains field offices in Bel Air, Maryland; Brussels, Belgium; St. Louis, Missouri; Montgomery, Alabama; and Petersburg, Virginia.

Management Consulting Services (MCS)

95 Berkeley Street, Suite 412, Boston, MA 02116
Tel: 617-556-0099; FAX: 617-556-0275
E-mail: mcs@tmfnet.org; WWW: http://tmfnet.org/mcs

▶ Management Consulting Services (MCS), itself a nonprofit organization, is a partner to Boston's philanthropic community. It provides other nonprofits with flexible and constructive management assistance so that they can build viable organizations that are better equipped to serve their communities. Since its founding in 1987, it has assisted hundreds of nonprofits with strategic planning, board development and training, organizational development, fundraising, financial management, and human resource planning. MCS maintains an extensive database of management consultants who specialize in working with nonprofit organizations. In addition to consultant referrals, MCS also provides information on other technical assistance resources, including training opportunities, to the organizations it serves.

Margo Morris & Co.

910 North Lake Shore Drive, Suite 519, Chicago, IL 60611
Tel: 312-335-3686; FAX: 312-335-3687
E-mail: mmorrisco@aol.com, EErhart@aol.com (Erika Erhart);
WWW: http://www.nonprofitconsult.com

▶ A consulting firm that serves nonprofit organizations throughout Chicago, Margo Morris & Co., established in 1992, provides creative consulting services that include fund raising, marketing, publications, and board development. Skilled at creating, developing, implementing, and managing programs to increase revenues, Margo Morris & Co. provides counsel for a wide range of development needs. Services include fund raising (plans, develops, and implements capital campaigns and annual fund programs; researches prospects and writes grant proposals; conducts feasibility studies; and plans special events); marketing (designs innovative programs that expand audiences, increase revenues, and promote organizational identity); publications (creates publications including newsletters, solicitation brochures, and annual reports that drive revenue growth and support organizational goals); board and staff development (conducts board and staff retreats that help build organizational capacity; trains board and staff members to lead successful capital and annual fund campaigns).

McConkey/Johnston Associates

Corporate office: P.O. Box 370, Woodland Park, CO 80866-0370
Tel: 719-687-3455; FAX: 719-687-3772
E-mail: cienfuegos@aol.com, Becca1305@aol.com;
WWW: http://www.mj1.com

▶ McConkey/Johnston Associates is a consulting and marketing services firm that specializes in serving Christian organizations in the areas of marketing, fund development, management, and organizational development. Specific services include development/fund raising (development audits, current giving strategies, planned giving, capital fund programs, staff support development, events, annual development planning); marketing programs (marketing audits, market research, advertising, public relations, data-

base design and analysis); development services (creative services, development systems, production services, development reporting, staff training). They can also help with organization development, strategic and long-range planning, management and leadership seminars and training, Feasibility and planning studies, campaign planning and analysis, leadership enlistment/cultivation for campaigns, specialized audits, and development management reporting systems. McConkey/Johnston also maintains offices in Madison, Wisconsin, Colorado Springs, and St. Louis.

McGann Associates

1429 Walnut Street, Suite 1500, Philadelphia, PA 19102
Tel: 215-854-9393; FAX: 215-854-0097
E-mail: info@thinktankconsultants.com; WWW:
http://www.thinktankconsultants.com/index4.htm

▶ A private consulting firm with over 25 years of combined program and management experience in the public and private sectors in the United States and abroad, McGann Associates specializes in strategic planning, organizational design and development, and research and analysis for nonprofit organizations and private foundations. Specific services include program evaluations and program planning; program, resource, and management audits; program design and management; leadership development workshops, seminars, and briefings for boards and staff; strategic planning and organizational development; and recruitment and selection of senior staff.

The Metanoia Group

700 Terrace Heights, Suite 3, Winona, MN 55987-1399
Tel: 507-457-1750; FAX: 507-457-1722
E-mail: metanoia@smumn.edu (Tim Burchill, President and Co-Founder);
WWW: http://www.smumn.edu/academics/affiliation/metanoia.html

▶ The Metanoia Group provides development consulting to small nonprofit organizations; campaigns, planning, audits, searches, and a wide range of studies. They serve a wide variety of not-for-profit organizations, including religiously affiliated elementary and secondary schools and consolidated systems, parishes, dioceses, congregations of religious women and men, homeless shelters, elder care facilities, medical centers, agencies serving children at risk, and other organizations with religious affiliation and/or heritage. Services include organizational analysis, organizational effectiveness, external relations, and resource development.

Netzel Associates, Inc.

Corporate office: 9696 Culver Boulevard, Suite 204,
Culver City, CA 90232-2753
Tel: 310-836-7624; FAX: 310-836-9357
E-mail: fundraising@netzelinc.com;
WWW: http://www.netzelinc.com

▶ Netzel Associates offers a full range of services for nonprofit organizations delivered through organization management assistance; counseling in the planning, executing, and monitoring of programs or projects; and staff training. It provides counsel to management and volunteers in planning and building stronger boards and committees and strengthening the staff–volunteer participation, in addition to a full range of fund-raising services.

New Ventures Consulting

18 Frasco Road, Santa Fe, NM 87505
Tel: 505-466-0326; FAX: 505-466-2730
E-mail: AEgan@roadrunner.com (Ann Hays Egan, President);
WWW: http://www.npresources.com

▶ New Ventures works regionally and nationally with nonprofit agencies, networks, and national organizations as well as state associations, management assistance centers, government agencies, community planning groups, and grant makers. Key areas of focus include managing change, devolution, nonprofit system development, community planning and network development, and workforce development.

NFP Consulting Resources, Inc.

1690 Starling Drive, Sarasota, FL 34231
Tel: 941-922-1690
E-mail: nfpconsulting@aol.com (Norman Olshansky, President);
WWW: http://www.nfpconsulting.com

▶ NFP Consulting Resources, Inc., provides a wide range of consulting services to not-for-profit corporations. NFP Consulting has worked with small locally based organizations as well as with large national and international associations. Services include board development, communications, evaluation of programs, event planning, executive recruitment, fund raising, human resources, insurance, management, organizational development, planned giving, professional development, project management, public affairs and policy, public relations, research, retirement and pension plans, strategic planning, training and facilitation, and volunteer program development.

Nonprofit Management Inc. (NMI)

1555 Connecticut Avenue NW, Suite 200, Washington, DC 20036
Tel: 202-462-9600 X18
E-mail: keith@nonprofitmgt.com (Keith Krueger, President);
WWW: http://nonprofitmgt.com

▶ MNI's focus is managing national and international nonprofit organizations, particularly organizations in the fields of health, information technologies, education, and libraries. Services include organizational development (they manage the legal and support details of establishing new nonprofit organizations, e.g., incorporation, developing bylaws, securing tax-exempt status, selecting your initial Board of Directors, etc.); membership (they breathe new life into existing organizations, as well as build new membership organizations from scratch); financial services (they meet your financial needs from monthly financial reports to accounts payable to securing audits and filing 990 IRS forms); meetings/events management; grants management (they seek and administer major private and public grants and contracts for our nonprofit clients); strategic planning (they facilitate strategic planning efforts for their clients or even on a project basis for other nonprofits); Web design/Listserv management/technology (they specialize in using the Internet/WWW and other emerging information tools to manage nonprofits).

Nonprofit Management Services (NMS)

PMB361, 402A West Palm Valley Boulevard,
Round Rock, TX 78664-4200
Tel: 512-341-0197; FAX: 512-341-0197
E-mail: Marilyn@NonProfitMS.com, marilyn157@aol.com
(Marilyn L. Donnellan); WWW: http://www.nonprofitms.com/

▶ The firm can provide assistance in just about any nonprofit management issue, specializing in board/staff development, organizational assessments, new CEO mentoring, and strategic planning. NMS publishes and distributes the *Executive Director's Handbook* in addition to other publications. NMS offers workshops and on-site consulting services.

NonProfit Management Solutions, Inc.

P.O. Box 7536, Hollywood, FL 33081
Tel: 954-985-9489; FAX: 954-989-3442
E-mail: terriet@nonprofitmgtsolutions.com (Terrie Temkin, President);
WWW: http://www.nonprofitmgtsolutions.com/index.htm

▶ A national consulting firm that helps to facilitate the visioning, growth, and management of nonprofits through training, coaching support, and hands-on task management. Services include board development, defining roles and responsibilities, enhancing communication facilitating change, facilitating retreats, facilitating training, mission-based planning, needs assessments, organizational audits, policy development, staff development, team building, visioning, and volunteer program development. Additional services include annual reports, community impact projects, evaluations, focus groups, fund-raising training, interim executives, leadership development, meeting planning, motivational speakers, newsletters, publicity and public relations, speakers' training, special events fund raising, development, strategic planning, surveys, and volunteer and personnel manual. It offers a no obligation consultation with your leadership to discuss your organization's vision and objectives in order to determine how it can best meet your needs. It publishes the quarterly newsletter *Nonprofit Management Solutions* (video also available). A schedule of upcoming workshops is available online at *http://www.nonprofitmgtsolutions.com/upwork.htm*.

NonProfit Team, Inc.

10 West Market Street, Suite 480, Indianapolis, IN 46204
Tel: 317-464-5156; FAX: 317-464-5146
E-mail: sellisnpt@aol.com (Susan)

▶ Nonprofit Team is a nonprofit consulting, outsourcing, and association management firm providing services including a wide range of nonprofit management needs in such areas as fund development, technology, marketing, human resources, training, financial, board development, and general management issues.

Nonprofit Training Associates

Mailing address: P.O. Box 684664, Austin, TX 78768-4664

Physical address: 5515 New Haven, Austin, TX 78756-1801
Tel: 512-467-0420
E-mail: nonprofittraining@e-mail.com;
WWW: http://www.nonprofittraining.com

▶ Nonprofit Training Associates provides training seminars and consulting services. A list of upcoming seminars is available online at *http://www.angelfire.com/biz/nonprofittraining/courses.html*.

Nonprofit Works Inc. *(See also Information Technology, Resource Development, Marketing and Communications, Strategic Planning)*
10 Gibbs Street, Suite 250, Rochester, NY 14604
Tel: 716-546-2420; FAX: 546-2423
E-mail@nonprofitworks.com;
WWW: http://www.nonprofitworks.com/planning/default.asp
▶ Services include grantwriting, planning, Web development, Web hosting, and computer training.

Carol O'Brien Associates
120 West State Street, Ithaca, NY 14850
Tel: 607-272-9144; FAX: 607-272-9180
E-mail: info@carolobrienassociates.com

3904 Chippenham Road, Durham, NC 27707
Tel: 919-403-2500
▶ Services include organizational design and evaluation, constituency development, feasibility studies, campaign counsel, internal assessments, board development, volunteer and staff training, and workshop, retreat, and seminar presentations.

Olszak Management Consulting, Inc.
Administrative offices: 812 Robinson Street,
East Brady, PA 16028
Tel/FAX: 724-526-5747

Satellite office: Regional Enterprise Tower, 425 Sixth Avenue,
Suite 1320, Pittsburgh, PA 15219
Tel: 412-281-9262; FAX: 412-281-9261
E-mail: olszak@olszak.com, olszak@penn.com;
WWW: http://www.third-wave.com/olszak/
▶ They provide a wide range of nonprofit management services tailored specifically for those clients in the public sector, with particular emphasis on projects within the fields of education, community development, and health and human services. Primary services in this area include outcomes and evaluation research, social entrepreneurship and earned income ventures, strategic and business planning, and strategic alliances: partnerships and mergers.

The Osborne Group
70 West Red Oak Lane, White Plains, NY 10604
Tel: 914-697-4921; FAX: 914-697-4899
E-mail: HQ@theosbornegroup.com;
WWW: http://www.theosbornegroup.com
▶ Olszak is a full-service consulting company providing expertise across a broad spectrum of management issues. Services are in the areas of development (capital campaigns, fund raising, capital campaigns, major gifts, planned giving, board development, staff development, and institutional advancement); board and staff training; and operations (executive management, program assessment, strategic planning, government relations, and marketing).

Laurence A. Pagnoni & Associates
549 West 123rd Street, Suite 18H, New York, NY 10027
Tel: 212-932-8001; FAX: 212-932-8801
E-mail: lapagnoni@mindspring.com (Laurence A. Pagnoni);
WWW: http://www.lp-associates.com
▶ Pagnoni & Associates conducts feasibility surveys to test entrepreneurial ideas, write business plans or grant proposals, and will

help identify investors, philanthropists, and potential partners to implement plans. They work to establish well-researched, cultivated, and diverse revenue sources and often work to integrate private sector strategies with nonprofit values. Specialties include board development, fund raising, grant writing, management, marketing, organizational development, professional development, and strategic planning.

Pappas Consulting Group, Inc.
One Stamford Landing, 68 Southfield Avenue, Suite 116,
Stamford, CT 06902
Tel: 203-357-7058; FAX: 203-357-7092
E-mail: info@pappas-consulting.com,
WWW: http://www.pappas-consulting.com/
▶ Founded in 1992, Pappas Consulting Group is a corporation registered in the state of Connecticut, serving the needs of educational institutions and nonprofit organizations. It is an Equal Opportunity Employer that contracts work with small businesses, businesses owned by women, and businesses owned by minorities. It serves organizations in such areas as strategic planning and positioning; governance (board, faculty, student, staff, volunteer); policy and procedure analyses; operations/business process redesign; organizational analyses (individual institution, postsecondary system of education, national office, and chapter/affiliate relations); program assessment and redesign, including benchmarking and best practices; change management and continuous quality improvement; interim management; staff training and development; enrollment services; fund raising and development; marketing and communications; IT planning; facilitation; distance consulting services; and distance education.

Perille Consulting Group
26 Grovenor Road, Boston, MA 02130
Tel: 617-524-8171; FAX: 617-522-6690
E-mail: perilleconsult@aol.com
▶ Services include program (design, assessment, outcome measurement); planning (strategy and business plan development); research (policy, survey, and market analysis); writing (grant proposals, reports, and curricula).

Peterson Consulting
885 Sherburne Avenue, St. Paul, MN 55104
Tel: 877-915-0245, 651-221-0065; FAX: 877-915-0235,
651-291-3252
E-mail: contact@peterson-consult.com;
WWW: http://www.peterson-consult.com/
▶ Services include strategic planning; leadership and board development; management strategies/systems; cultural competence; community building; quality initiatives; organizational restructuring; collaboration, strategic alliances, and partnerships; and conflict resolution and mediation.

Philanthropic Alternatives
5 Barry Avenue, Annapolis, MD 21403
Tel/FAX: 410-626-0828
E-mail: at relpc@aol.com (Dr. Ronald E. Limoges);
WWW: http://www.shirenet.com/harmony/pa.htm
▶ Philanthropic Alternatives offers temporary, short-term professional services on an hourly or per diem basis, specializing in pro-

ductive planning, management, and operational activities with not-for-profit corporations and community agencies on a cost-effective, as-needed basis. It shares continuing organizational burdens, such as defining goals and tasks; strengthening internal and external communication; enhancing staff, board, and volunteer performance; improving operations; and expanding resources.

The Philanthropy Group

2600 72nd Street, Suite F, Des Moines, IA 50322-4724
Tel: 800-538-4483; FAX: 515-270-1437
E-mail: pkirpes@whatmattersmost.com (Paul J. Kirpes, CFRE, President and CEO)

▶ The Philanthropy Group is a full-service fund-raising, marketing, communications, and management firm, specializing in capital campaigns, endowment building, planned giving, development audits, feasibility studies, major gifts, grants, board/volunteer development, and project management.

Pioneer Consulting Services

2200 Rainier Avenue South, Seattle, WA 98144
Tel: 206-322-6645, ext. #211, FAX: 206-325-8009
E-mail: consulting@p-h-s.com;
WWW: http://www.pioneerhumanserv.com

▶ Pioneer Consulting Services specializes in consulting with other nonprofit organizations in two major areas: program outcomes measurement and entrepreneurial analysis and assistance.

RPA Inc.

951 Westminster Drive, Williamsport, PA 17701
Tel: 800-992-9277; FAX: 570-321-7160
E-mail: rpainc@suscom.net

▶ RPA Inc. provides the following consulting services to nonprofits: executive recruitment, campaign consultation/management, public relations support of fund raising, organizational management, and planned giving.

Raffa & Associates, PC

1899 L Street NW, Suite 600, Washington, DC 20036
Tel: 202-822-5000; FAX: 202-822-0669
E-mail: raffa@raffa.com; WWW: http://www.raffa.com,
http://www.iknow.org, http://www.raffa.com/interior/mcs.html

▶ Management consulting services include the following: financial projections and forecasts; budgeting and cash management; strategic planning; due diligence procedures; investment analysis; evaluation and structuring of business transactions and mergers; evaluation and structuring of dispositions and reorganizations; establishment of new organizations, charter organizations, and affiliates; establishment of profit and nonprofit subsidiaries; grant and contract applications and administration; applications for the Combined Federal and United Way Campaigns; assistance in audits by granting, contracting, and taxing authorities; establishing and reevaluating indirect cost rates; establishment and compliance reviews of employee benefit programs; temporary assistance as the acting CFO or other accounting positions; interviews of potential candidates for our clients' staff; litigation support; annual membership surveys; establishing or expanding banking relationships; developing policies and procedures manuals; assistance in establishment of endowments and capital campaigns; assistance with lease negotiations; implementing systems that deal effectively with

foreign banks and currency translations; enhancing membership dues billing process; establishing the membership dues allocation to comply with lobbying regulations; structuring the financial operations among subsidiaries and affiliates; and serving on the board of directors.

Rafferty Consulting Group

45-775 Indian Wells Lane, Indian Wells, CA 92210-8835
Tel: 760-776-9606; FAX: 760-776-9608
E-mail: raffcons@ix.netcom.com;
WWW: http://www.raffertyconsulting.com

▶ Rafferty Consulting Group provides comprehensive consulting and training services for nonprofit organizations, public agencies, and philanthropies operating in areas including education, the arts, health, and community and social services. Services include organizational assessment (diagnostic evaluation, program assessment); long-range and strategic planning; board development (structure and bylaws, training/evaluation, recruiting/reorganization, retreat facilitation); staff development (organizational structure, performance evaluation, executive search, team-building and in-service, mentor service, volunteer management); fund development (fund development program assessment, fund development master planning, capital campaign feasibility and counsel, corporate and foundation funding, endowment planning, major gift programs, annual campaign, support groups and auxiliaries, special events); marketing (competitive analysis and market research, marketing campaign, development, Multimedia and publications, public relations/community relations, sales programs); financial planning and controls (budget analysis, compensation and benefits). The Group is available to work with your organization on a one-time, limited-term, or continuing basis. They also offer workshops and seminars in these and other areas of interest to the nonprofit, philanthropic, and public sectors, which can be tailored for your organization's specific needs and audience.

Rebecca Leet & Associates

2501 North Quantico Street, Arlington, VA 22207-1053
Tel: 703)-533-8966; FAX: 703-533-8971
E-mail: info@leetassociates.com, rleet@leetassociates.com;
WWW: http://www.leetassociates.com

▶ Since its founding in 1985, Rebecca Leet & Associates has helped organizations develop clear strategic directions, solve management and marketing problems successfully, and create effective communications. Services include strategic planning; meeting and retreat facilitation; strategic marketing planning; message development; program and communication audits; communication planning; and corporate charitable involvement: assessment and planning.

Results Group International

230 West 41st Street, Suite 1602, New York, NY 10036
Tel: 212-869-3373, ext. 43; FAX: 212-869-5535
E-mail: Get@resultsg.com, ClaudiaC@ResultsG.com (Claudia Chouinard, President); WWW: http://www.ResultsG.com

▶ Results Group International is a full-service management consulting firm assisting cultural, educational, and advocacy nonprofits. Services include full-service planning capabilities (board and staff retreats, strategic planning, feasibility studies, staff and trustee training, deficit reduction planning, program audits, management counsel, results assessment, planning process management, and organization audits); full-service marketing capabilities (new program feasibilities, continuity and loyalty programs, membership and sales campaigns, earned income audits, corporate sponsorship, constituency research, print and media strategies, Web site strategies and designs, marketing plans, database and fulfillment system reviews, renewal and upgrade programs, marketing office setup/reviews, staff service training, and outsourced executive services); full-service fund-raising capabilities (retention programs, major donor programs, annual fund campaigns, feasibility studies, capital and endowment campaigns, pre-capital and pre-endowment campaign preparation, development program audits, strategic fundraising plans, prospect research, development office setup/reviews, volunteer and solicitor training, international issues, outsourced executive services); full-service search capabilities (executive search, search committee support, trustee recruitment, volunteer recruitment, temporary leased executives, outsourced executive services).

Sheppard and Brown Consulting Group Nonprofit Sector (SBC Group)

5625 Southampton Drive, Springfield, VA 22151
Tel: 703-764-1799; FAX: 703-764-0646
E-mail: info@sbcgroup.com;
WWW: http://www.sbcgroup.com/nonprofit.htm

▶ The SEC Group offers a broad range of services geared to the nonprofit sector. SBC Group business services for nonprofit organizations include business process and client service audits, technology assessment, workflow analysis, and process redesign. Services include business services (business process and client service audits, technology assessment, workflow analysis, and process redesign); program and budget planning (service utilization projections, cost–benefit and comparative analyses, grant preparation assistance, presentation graphics, and program funding strategies); Software Solutions (develops user-friendly and easily maintained software solutions for budget, planning, financial, and client service needs of nonprofit organizations. SBC Group specializes in meeting needs unaddressed by mass market packaged software through relational database solutions, data warehouses, and analysis tools designed for networked and desktop applications); performance metrics (nonprofit funding and policy strategies, including development of "dashboard" program and financial indicators for governing boards, life-cycle replacement funding for information technology, depreciation funding for plant maintenance, CPI-indexed tuition pricing and financial aid packaging strategies for higher education, and numerous others).

Social Research Associates, Inc. (SRA)

5638 Glen Avenue, Minnetonka, MN 55345
Tel: 952-974-0892; FAX: 952-974-1021
E-mail: jhiller@codenet.net

▶ SRA assists nonprofit agencies with strategic planning, program planning, needs analysis, evaluation design and implementation, data and forms management, development of internship and volunteer programs, fund-raising plans, grant writing, and board of directors basic training. In addition, SRA has also conducted independent evaluations of programs and projects as required by state or federal grant contracts.

Sadlon & Associates, Inc.

100 East Linton Boulevard, Suite 127B, Delray Beach, FL 33483
Tel: 561-266-2757; FAX: 561-266-8909
E-mail: sadlon@mindspring.com

▶ Sadlon & Williams helps nonprofits improve client services through better management. Services include outcome measurement; strategic planning (facilitate board planning meetings small to large; design, research, and coordinate board retreats; develop actionable plans and tracking systems); board development (provide training for boards at all stages of nonprofit life cycle; tailor a board manual to your agency's needs and approach; facilitate board orientation).

Schultz & Williams, Inc.

421 Chestnut Street, Suite 400, Philadelphia, PA 19106-2422
Tel: 215-625-9955; FAX: 215-625-2701
E-mail: mail@sw-inc.com (L. Scott Schultz, President);
WWW: http://www.sw-inc.com

▶ Schultz & Williams is a national full-service development, marketing, and management consulting firm specializing in capital campaigns, annual campaigns, direct mail, planned giving, major gifts, prospect research, board development/training, and strategic planning.

Scribner and Associates

49 Coronado Avenue, Long Beach, CA 90803
Tel: 562-433-6082; FAX: (562) 439-3025
E-mail: scribner@aol.com; WWW: http://www.scribner.qpg.com

▶ Scribner and Associates offers financial development, trainings, retreats and facilitations, and organizational development for nonprofit organizations.

Smith Beers Yunker & Company

2300 Lincoln Park West, Suite A-9, Chicago, IL 60614-4163

431 Ohio Pike, Suite 105 North, Cincinnati, OH 45255-3372
Tel: 800-698-6537
E-mail: info@smithbeers.com; WWW: http://www.smithbeers.com

▶ This is an international management and fund-raising consultancy to organizations in the United States and the United Kingdom, specializing in management reviews, board and leadership development, donor research, staff recruitment and training, volunteer coaching, annual and capital campaign planning and counsel, planned giving counsel, and graphic design and writing.

Social Entrepreneurs, Inc.

100 Washington Street, Suite 300, Reno, NV 89503
Tel: 775-324-4567; FAX: 775-324-4941
E-mail: msmith@socialent.com; WWW: http://www.socialent.com

▶ Social Entrepreneurs, Inc. (SEI) is dedicated to building strong management and operating infrastructures within human service organizations. They provide management support packages, consulting, training, and computer systems that merge the best management practices from the business world with those of the social service community. SEI can assist all types of human services through three categories of management support: strategic development, organizational development, and program management. SEI services all of Nevada and California.

Summit Consulting Collaborative (See also Information Technology)

61 Lincoln Avenue, Amherst, MA 01002
Tel: 413-549-0014; FAX: 520-447-3998
E-mail: info@summitcollaborative.com,
marcosten@mediaone.net;
WWW: http://www.summitcollaborative.com

▶ Its mission is to provide strategic technology and management expertise to the nonprofit sector. It works in close collaboration with foundations, management support organizations, nonprofit networks, technology support providers, and nonprofit organizations to develop programs that meet critical nonprofit sector needs. Services include Internet outreach campaigns and solutions, strategic technology planning, and nonprofit executive technology leadership. It offers presentations and workshops as well as individual consultations. Norwottuck Technology Resources, Summit's sister organization, specializes in Web site design, including HTML, CGI, database connectivity, and Javascript. Norwottuck has worked primarily with nonprofits on technology projects since its founding.

Technical Assistance & Support Consultants

1133 15th Street NW, Suite 1200, Washington, DC 20005
Tel: 202-822-8272
E-mail: mvassall@technicalassistance.com;
WWW: http://www.technicalassistance.com,
http://www.technicalassistance.com/links.htm,
http://www.technicalassistance.com/magazine.htm

▶ An African American, woman-owned firm that assists progressive organizations with institutional development. Established in 1991, TASC offers the following services: fund development, writing and publishing, World Wide Web marketing, accounting services, and grantsmanship and proposal writing workshops.

Waters, Pelton, Ostroff & Associates, Inc.

7108 Fairway Drive, Suite 235, Palm Beach Gardens, FL 33418
Tel: 561-626-0026; FAX: 561-626-9119
E-mail: wpojkw@aol.com (J. Keith Waters, Chairman and CEO);
WWW: http://www.wpoassociates.com

▶ A full-service professional planning and fund-raising firm offering a variety of specialized services to nonprofit organizations across the country. Services include management consulting; long-range strategic planning; development program assessments; fund-raising feasibility studies; capital campaign management; fund-raising counsel; grantwriting (corporate, foundation, government); public relations/media relations.

Clyde P. Watkins and Associates

1144 Lake Street, Suite 204, Chicago, IL 60301
Tel: 708-848-3340; FAX: 708-848-0637
E-mail: cwatkins@watkinsandassoc.com (Clyde P. Watkins, CFRE, President);
WWW: http://www.watkinsandassoc.com/index2.html

▶ Clyde P. Watkins and Associates assists colleges and universities, independent schools, health care organizations, cultural institutions, human services agencies, and other not-for-profit organizations with a wide range of institutional advancement services. Services include institutional planning, organizational and program assessment, board and volunteer leadership development, campaign planning and oversight, and ongoing fund-raising programs and operations.

The Whelan Group, Inc. (TWG)

155 West 19th Street, New York, NY 10011
Tel: 212-727-7332; FAX: 212-727-7578
E-mail: twg@whelangroup.com;
WWW: http://www.whelangroup.com/manage/manage.htm

▶ The Whelan Group, Inc. (TWG) is a private management consulting firm. Founded in 1980, the firm provides fund-raising management, strategic and financial planning, and management consulting services to nonprofit institutions and organizations. They complement these core services with an array of innovative prospect identification and gift targeting services. TWG provides assistance to organizations seeking to attract significant new financial resources for their work through expanded fund-raising and development programs. They help growth-oriented nonprofits to prepare for and conduct capital campaigns that address their facility and endowment needs. They offer technical assistance, with the goal of strengthening each client's financial management and long-term fund-raising capacity.

Zimmerman, Lehman & Associates

582 Market Street, Suite 1112, San Francisco, CA 94104
Tel: 800-886-8330 (outside the Bay Area), 415-986-8330;
FAX: 415-986-2048
E-mail: zi@zimmerman-lehman.com;
WWW: http://www.zimmerman-lehman.com

▶ Zimmerman, Lehman & Associates is a consulting firm that offers assistance to large and small nonprofits. Services include motivation and training for fund-raising and board development; fund raising (planning, individual campaigns, fund-raising events, corporate campaigns, grant-seeking); marketing and public relations; executive and board recruitment; and organizational planning and facilitation.

RESOURCES

General/Basics

The 21st Century Nonprofit
PAUL B. FIRSTENBERG (FOUNDATION CENTER, 1996)

▶ In this book the author encourages nonprofit organizations to apply business techniques to a broad range of activities, including fund raising, personnel management, and board operations. Drawing on his extensive experience in the for-profit and nonprofit sectors, Paul Firstenberg develops in this new book a systematic plan for organizational governance that draws on the latest management techniques. *The 21st Century Nonprofit* helps nonprofits become more vital social and cultural forces by encouraging managers to adopt the strategies developed by the for-profit sector in recent years; expand their revenue base by diversifying grant sources and exploiting the possibilities of for-profit enterprises; develop human resources by learning how to attract and retain talented people; and explore the nature of leadership through short profiles of three nonprofit CEOs. Firstenberg insists that nonprofits cannot simply rely on their altruistic intentions and past records of achievement. He suggests that nonprofits must establish specific aims and then account for how well they achieve them and that accountability is the key to credibility for nonprofits.

The 21st Century Nonprofit encourages executives to transform their organizations into more vital social and cultural forces by implementing the most successful managerial policies recently adopted by U.S. businesses. The book demonstrates that restructuring that focuses on organizational processes—the systems by which work is accomplished—can be applied to a nonprofit's advantage. Firstenberg encourages nonprofit organizations to develop a "marketing approach" to increase the effectiveness of their fund-raising programs and to diversify their income base by exploiting the possibilities for earned income. He discusses mergers and conversion to for-profit enterprises, options likely to receive more attention in the future. He focuses on human resources, illustrating how nonprofit organizations can create environments that encourage individuals to maximize their commitment and further their own career goals. Convinced that strong and innovative leaders provide the most effective impetus for instituting the management structures he advocates, Firstenberg closes with insightful profiles of leaders of the Ford Foundation, Princeton University, and Children's Television Workshop. *Softcover, 320 pages, $34.95*

Activity-Based Management for Service Industries, Government Entities, and Nonprofit Organizations
JAMES A. BRIMSON & JOHN ANTOS (JOHN WILEY & SONS, 1998)

▶ This book demonstrates how activity-based management (ABM), a form of managerial accounting, can be applied to service groups, government agencies, and nonprofit entities. It examines why traditional accounting methods have become obsolete and introduces a five-step approach to calculating activity cost. It outlines activity-based budgeting and illustrates its advantages in settings such as insurance, banking, government agencies, and hospitals. Now revised and expanded, this indispensable resource illustrates how ABM can be applied to all types of organizations—including service groups, government agencies, and nonprofit entities—and any department within them. Using a variety of examples, authors James A. Brimson and John Antos examine a company structure and break down its separate activities to measure each activity's cost/performance effectiveness. Supplemented annually (no supplement to date). *Softcover, 364 pages, $42.95*

Best Practices of Effective NonProfit Organizations: A Practitioner's Guide
PHILIP S. BERNSTEIN (FOUNDATION CENTER, 1997)

▶ Enhance your organization's impact by learning from Philip Bernstein, former member of the board of directors of Independent Sector, who has drawn on his extensive experience as a nonprofit executive, consultant, and volunteer to produce this review of the "best practices" adopted by successful nonprofit organizations. In Best Practices of Effective Nonprofit Organizations, the author identifies and explains the procedures that provide the foundation for social achievement in all nonprofit fields. Bernstein's coverage of crucial topics will help you to define purposes and goals and adhere to missions, obtain and retain high-quality volunteers and staff, create comprehensive financing plans, respond to change by adjusting services and operations, evaluate services to assess effectiveness, communicate goals both internally and externally. Best Practices illuminates the importance of these procedures and many others as well. *Softcover, 186 pages, $29.95*

Board of Directors & Management (*See Governance for full description*)

The Complete Guide to Nonprofit Management, 2nd Edition
SMITH, BUCKLIN & ASSOCIATES, ROBERT H. WILBUR, ED. (JOHN WILEY & SONS, 2000)

▶ This practical how-to book addresses such vital issues as the importance of mission statements, the boards of directors' role in daily operations, planning a publicity campaign, coordinating special conventions, basic office management and information services, and more. A practical, how-to-run-your-business book designed specifically for nonprofit managers and volunteers; it covers the general areas of nonprofit activities with an emphasis on real-world advice and examples. It addresses such vital nonprofit business management issues as the importance of mission statements, the board of director's role in day-to-day operations, basic office administration, information systems, human resources, public relations, planning a publicity campaign to enhance fund-raising activities, marketing, strategic planning, fund raising, special events, law, and financial management. This revised and expanded edition identifies and addresses the unique concerns of nonprofit organizations. It provides dozens of real-world examples and case studies and up-to-date, vital strategies and techniques for dealing with virtually every nonprofit business management issue. *Hardcover, 374 pages, $29.95*

The Effective Management of Volunteer Programs
(See Volunteerism—Leadership and Management for full description)

Effectively Managing Human Service Organizations
RALPH BRODY (SAGE PUBLICATIONS, 1993)

▶ *Effectively Managing Human Service Organizations* is a resource for middle managers, line supervisors, and those who aspire to work in these roles. The author addresses five major issues: leadership, getting things done, interacting with staff, assessing and rewarding performance, and enhancing employee productivity. Many other important issues not normally included in human service management books are covered, including firing unproductive staff, dealing with sexual harassment, managing cultural diversity, and handling stress. A final chapter concludes with ways to bolster the morale and spirit of staff by humanizing the organization. Includes information on leading an organization, the culture of a productive organization, strategic planning, action plans, problem solving, productive meetings, communication and conflict, staff supervision and evaluation, and other topics. *Softcover, 288 pages, $29.95 (includes shipping)*

The Entrepreneurial Nonprofit Executive: A Guide to Prudent Risk-Taking in the Service of a Larger Mission
(THOMAS A. MCLAUGHLIN (TAFT GROUP, 1991)

▶ This book exposes "the seven deadly myths of nonprofit management" and pitfalls of conventional thinking that have led the term *nonprofit* to be associated with the term *nonprofitable* and how to avoid them; challenges the restrictive and self-defeating assumptions and attitudes that have traditionally dominated nonprofit management; and shows how to successfully bring the entrepreneurial spirit to a nonprofit and take the risks necessary to fulfill the organization's mission. Lessons include: (1) how to bring money into the organization; (2) how to spend it wisely once it's there; (3) how to budget for success; (4) the secrets of accounting, financial reports, and liability insurance; (5) how to get and keep employees and volunteers; and (6) how to deal with the board, the executive director, lawyers, consultants, lobbyists, and the media. *Softcover, 264 pages, $24 (includes shipping)*

Essential Volunteer Management *(See Volunteerism—Leadership and Management for full description)*

The Executive Guide to Strategic Planning *(See Planning—Publications for full description)*

Financial and Strategic Management for Nonprofit Organizations: A Comprehensive Reference to Legal, Financial, Management, and Operations Rules and Guidelines for Nonprofits, 3rd Edition
HERRINGTON J. BRYCE (JOSSEY-BASS, 1999)

▶ Now in its third edition, *Financial and Strategic Management for Nonprofit Organizations* provides an encyclopedic account of all the key financial, legal, and managerial issues facing nonprofit

executives. Organized into 20 detailed chapters, this comprehensive reference provides a firm grounding in the five fundamental pillars of effective nonprofit management: Mission, Money, Marketing, Management, and Membership. It then shows managers and trustees how to strengthen operations in each of these vital areas ethically, legally, and efficiently. Bryce explores such diverse topics as nonprofit law, financial planning, fund raising, compensation and benefits, strategic planning, risk management, and more. He also adds several new features, including: an expanded section explaining all the technical and legal foundations of managing a nonprofit; timely advice on developing ethical procedures to protect the organization against fraud and incompetence; new and practical discussions on tax-exempt status, American and Canadian law for associations, corporate contributions, trust management, audits, antitrust issues, program evaluation, partnerships, business revenue; and more. *Hardcover, 816 pages, $49.95*

From the Top Down: The Executive Role in Volunteer Program Success *(See Volunteerism—Publications for full description)*

From Vision to Reality: A Guide for Forming and Sustaining Community-Based Efforts
(COMMUNITY RESOURCE EXCHANGE, 1996)

▶ This is the definitive reference for those forming a not-for-profit organization or strengthening a voluntary community effort. This kit contains a wealth of how-to guides on developing not-for-profit management systems, including: getting started, creating fiscal systems, program planning, personnel management, fund raising, and much more. The kit also contains reproducible worksheets and samples of basic organizational documents such as bylaws, personnel policies, and annual reports. Included free with every copy is a computer diskette containing the worksheets and sample documents for you to adapt for your own use. Softcover, $39.95

Gold Book, 2nd Edition
(THE ALLIANCE FOR NONPROFIT MANAGEMENT, 2001)

▶ Discover an array of successful strategies in nonprofit capacity-building; a collection of experiences, offered as the beginning of a sustained, long-term conversation about quality; success stories designed as a collection of vignettes to illustrate excellence in the nonprofit management arena; and contacts (story authors) eager to talk with you about their experiences.

The Alliance *Gold Book* is filled with terrific success stories about Alliance members who have made a real difference working with their nonprofit clients in their local communities. This dynamic tool will help us to better "see" and understand quality management assistance—and how it might be adapted in other locales. The first edition was published in November 2000 with 23 success stories in nonprofit technical assistance. *Spiral-bound, 180 pages, $20*

High Performance Nonprofit Organizations: Managing Upstream for Greater Impact
CHRISTINE W. LETTS, WILLIAM P. RYAN, AND ALLEN S. GROSSMAN (JOHN WILEY & SONS, 1998)

▶ This book clearly and concisely shows nonprofits how to make general business management guidance relevant and effective by providing a framework for analyzing management, and by translating business lingo into an accessible vocabulary for nonprofit managers. Drawing on management techniques used by successful managers in both businesses and nonprofits, *High Performance*

Nonprofit Organizations outlines approaches that nonprofits can use to build their capacity for learning, innovating, ensuring quality, and motivating staff. Illustrated with case studies and examples, the book outlines processes for achieving these goals. *High Performance Nonprofit Organizations* goes further, laying out an agenda for changing the nonprofit environment, making it more supportive of its managers and more aware of the potential of organizational capacity. *Hardcover, 224 pages, $29.95*

Harvard Business Review on Nonprofits (The Harvard Business Review Paperback Series)
(HARVARD BUSINESS PRESS, 1999)

▶ All aspects of the work of modern nonprofit organizations are explored in this volume. The eight essays examine such essential topics as the importance of earning the public trust and how nonprofit managers can learn from the success of venture capitalists. *The Harvard Business Review* Paperback Series is designed to bring today's managers and professionals the fundamental information they need to stay competitive in a fast-moving world. Here are the landmark ideas that have established the *Harvard Business Review* as required reading for ambitious businesspeople in organizations around the globe. Articles include "Can Public Trust in Nonprofits and Governments Be Restored?," by Regina E. Herzlinger; "Effective Oversight: A Guide for Nonprofit Directors," by Regina E. Herzlinger; "The New Work of the Nonprofit Board," by Barbara E. Taylor, Richard P. Chait, and Thomas P. Holland; "When a Business Leader Joins a Nonprofit Board," by William G. Bowen; "Virtuous Capital: What Foundations Can Learn from Venture Capitalists," by Christine W. Letts, William Ryan, and Allen Grossman; "Profits for Nonprofits: Find a Corporate Partner," by Alan R. Andreasen; "Enterprising Nonprofits," by J. Gregory Dees; and "Do Better at Doing Good," by V. Kasturi Rangan, Sohel Karim, and Sheryl K. Sandberg. *Softcover, 224 pages, $19.95*

How to Help Your Board Govern More and Manage Less *(See Governance—Roles and Responsibilities for full description)*

Improving Quality and Performance in Your Nonprofit Organization
GARY M. GROBMAN (NONPROFIT ISSUES, 2000)

▶ This is the latest book authored by Gary Grobman, *Pennsylvania Nonprofit Report*'s contributing editor. It introduces to the nonprofit sector quality management and improvement strategies that are prevalent in business circles. Among them are total quality management (TQM), business process reengineering (BPR), benchmarking/best practices, outcomes-based management (OBM), and large group interventions (LGI). The book also includes easy-to-read, up-to-date, and practical applications of chaos theory and organization theory. It is designed to help nonprofit organizations respond to uncertainty and organizational turbulence, reduce mistakes and infuse their staff with a quality ethic, rebuild their work processes from the ground up, and find and implement "best practices" of comparable organizations. *Softcover, 155 pages, $16.95 (plus $4.00 shipping and handling)*

The Jossey-Bass Handbook of Nonprofit Leadership and Management
ROBERT D. HERMAN AND ASSOCIATES, EDS. (JOSSEY-BASS, 1994)

▶ With a collection of 25 articles by scholars and practitioners, this book brings together the leading experts in the nonprofit field, to describe what is currently known about effective practice in all the distinctive and important functions, processes, and strategies of nonprofit organization and leadership. Based on the most up-to-date research, theory, and experience, this comprehensive volume provides a panoramic view of the nonprofit sector and offers practical advice on every aspect of managing nonprofit organizations, including board development, strategic planning, lobbying, marketing, government contracting, volunteer programs, fund raising, financial accounting, compensation and benefits programs, risk management, and more. It offers an insightful perspective on how nonprofit organizations have been shaped and how their leadership and management will continue to be affected by historical roots, law and regulations, political and economic forces, and the increasing internationalization of the world; the authors detail the key leadership issues facing nonprofit organizations and explain how boards of directors can provide necessary leadership in defining their organizations' missions and values. They offer guidance on the day-to-day challenges of managing nonprofit operations, including advice on evaluating performance and programs. *Hardcover, 682 pages, $64.95 (plus $5.50 shipping)*

Leadership and Management of Volunteer Programs: A Guide for Volunteer Administrators
(See Volunteerism—Management and Leadership for full description)

A Legal Guide to Starting & Managing a Nonprofit Organization *(See Legal Issues—Incorporation for full description)*

Management & Planning, Leadership Series, Volume I (Booklet) *(See also Strategic Planning)*
JILL MUEHRCKE, ED. (THE SOCIETY OF NONPROFIT ORGANIZATIONS, 1990)

▶ In articles selected from *Nonprofit World,* authors explore such diverse aspects of effective nonprofit management as developing a collaborative strategy, fostering creativity, and making the best possible decisions. *123 pages, $35 (Nonmember), $25 (Member) (plus $4.50 shipping)*

Management & Planning, Leadership Series, Volume II (Booklet)
JILL MUEHRCKE, ED. (THE SOCIETY OF NONPROFIT ORGANIZATIONS, 1993)

▶ In this second volume of articles from *Nonprofit World* (November 1989–September 1993), authors continue to explore diverse aspects of effective nonprofit management; topics include creating cosponsored programs, strategic planning, incorporation, financial review, total quality management principles, collaborative strategies, and optimum decision making. *130 pages, $35 (Nonmember), $25 (Member) (plus $4.50 shipping)*

Managing a Nonprofit Organization in the Twenty-First Century, 3rd Edition
THOMAS WOLF (FIRESIDE BOOKS/SIMON & SCHUSTER, 1999)

▶ Since this classic work was originally published in 1984, there have been major shifts in the nonprofit world—the growth of more profit-oriented ventures, the overhaul of accounting rules, new partnerships, and an emphasis on customer-oriented service and leadership. In easy-to-understand language, Thomas Wolf explains how to cope with these changes and deal with the traditional challenges of managing staff, trustees, and volunteers. Now updated and revised, this "bible" for nonprofit organizations focuses on recent changes and pinpoints their impact on staffing, governance, and fund raising. 30 charts. It contains theory and practical advice and covers everything you need to know about managing a nonprofit organization. It covers a vast range of issues and strikes a balance between theory and detail. Once you've incorporated, good workers need to be hired, money raised, an accounting system implemented, and volunteers recruited, motivated, and coordinated. How to get all this to happen with a minimum of fuss and a maximum of effectiveness is covered, as well as staffing, fund raising, choosing trustees, financing, marketing, computerizing, planning, succeeding, and more. *Softcover, 368 pages, $14*

Managing for Impact in Nonprofit Organizations: Corporate Planning Techniques and Applications

JAMES M. HARDY (ESSEX PRESS, 1995)

▶ *Managing for Impact in Nonprofit Organizations* is a comprehensive, clear, and practical book written especially for CEOs and board chairs. It is a book that will help organizational leaders (non-profit and for-profit) to clarify and implement the role of board and staff in strategic and operational planning and management; formulate a driving mission and long-term corporate goals that give direction and vitality to their organizations; obtain commitment to the organization's desired future and broaden the base of responsibility to achieve that future through meaningful and real involvement of people; apply marketing principles and techniques as an integral part of planning and management; create and implement long-term financial development strategies to make goal achievement possible; obtain measurable objectives, action steps and clear accountabilities that are integrated and that provide effective fiscal control; help people grow and develop and overcome performance problems; and review, update, and keep planning current and on target. The book is complete with examples, exhibits, forms, diagrams, and designs, which can either be reproduced directly from the large format or changed to meet particular organizational needs. *Hardcover, 238 pages, $36.45*

Managing Nonprofit Organizations in the 21st Century

JAMES P. GELATT (ORYX PRESS, 1992)

▶ Dr. James P. Gelatt discusses the five basic principles that should guide all nonprofit organizations: mission, leadership, management, professionalism, and financial stability. Each principle is thoroughly explored and is enhanced by instructive examples of notable managers and successful organizations. The contents also feature a strategic planning guide, tips on building an effective staff, and public relations and marketing advice, plus: Successful Fund Raising; Fiscal Management; Communication: Creating a Knowledge Industry in Your Organization; Board and Staff: Toward a Partnership; Volunteers; and Maintaining the Edge: What You Don't Learn in Management School. It offers quick access to a wide range of proven facts, effective procedures, successful ideas, and working solutions. The guiding principles for successful nonprofit organizations are identified, explored, and practically applied to the specific needs of management, board, staff, and volunteers. Beginning with the importance of defining an organization's mission and planning the strategies to achieve that mission, the book outlines the challenges all nonprofit executives face. Each chapter begins with an organizer in the form of an executive summary. *Softcover, 256 pages, $35.50 (plus $3 shipping)*

Managing the Non-Profit Organization: Principles and Practices

PETER FERDINAND DRUCKER (HARPER BUSINESS, 1992)

▶ The world's most renowned management guru teaches you how to become a mission-oriented leader in this revised edition. He offers guidelines and advice on how to manage nonprofit organizations effectively, convert good intentions into results, and overcome the two major challenges of (1) making "contributors" out of "donors" and (2) instilling a sense of community and common purpose. The book includes interviews with nine experts on key issues in the nonprofit sector. Drucker gives examples and explanations of mission, leadership, resources, marketing, goals, people development, decision making, and much more. Included are interviews with nine experts that address key issues in the nonprofit sector. *Softcover, 256 pages, $13.50*

Market-Driven Management: Lessons Learned from 20 Successful Associations (See Marketing and Communications for full description)

Mission-Based Management: Leading Your Not-for-Profit into the 21st Century

PETER C. BRINCKERHOFF (JOHN WILEY & SONS, 1998)

▶ This core volume in the Mission-Based Management Series provides a comprehensive plan for successfully meeting all challenges facing nonprofit organizations (meeting the changing needs of the community, securing the funding to make ends meet, and responding to the often conflicting demands of founders, clientele, staff, and trustees) while remaining true to the overall mission of the organization. It provides everything you need to know about current trends and how to use them to lead your organization to success as well as insights into the needs, functions, and output of not-for-profit agencies, offering practical recommendations based on institutional missions. Chapters include: (1) Introduction (core philosophies to make nonprofits successful), (2) The Environment (seven trends that will influence the future of nonprofits), (3) What Works (the nine things your nonprofit must do to be successful), (4) The Mission Is the Reason (four key uses of the mission statement), (5) A Businesslike Board (six characteristics of a successful board), (6) Building a Better Board (five keys to recruiting and retaining the board you want), (7) Managing Staff (the upside-down organization—six critical management factors), (8) Controls (nine control policies that let you sleep at night), (9) Marketing (discover who your markets really are, and how to meet their wants), (10) Vision (how to plan for the future—nine steps of a good planning process), (11) Financial Empowerment (how to put the five key characteristics of financial empowerment into your organization), (12) More on Financial Empowerment (how to keep what you earn and create an endowment), (13) Social Entrepreneurship (taking prudent risks on behalf of clients—the 10 biggest mistakes nonprofits make in planning for growth), (14) Change (how to facilitate positive change and be responsive to the future), and (15) A National Agenda (what nonprofits and their funders can do to be more effective in serving the needs of the community and their clientele). It includes a bibliography of resources and an index. *Hardcover, 258 pages, $51.95 (includes shipping)*

Nine-Part Nonprofit Management Series

BRIAN O'CONNELL (INDEPENDENT SECTOR, 1988)

▶ This series provides guidelines for fund raising, evaluation of effectiveness, board development, planning, budgeting, accountability, and more. It is a nine-part management series designed to help you now with: (1) *The Role of the Board and Board Members*, (2) *Finding, Developing, and Rewarding Good Board Members*, (3) *Operating Effective Committees*, (4) *Conducting Good Meetings*, (5) *The Roles and Relationships of the Chief Volunteer and Chief Staff Officers, Board and Staff: Who Does What?*, (6) *Recruiting, Encouraging and Evaluating the Chief Staff Officer*, (7) *Fundraising*, (8) *Budgeting and Financial Accountability*, and (9) *Evaluating*. The series brings you essential guidelines in the nine key areas; each publication is a valuable reference source in itself, and in combination, the series provides leadership for successful, effective, efficient funding and volunteer action. *Individual Booklets: $5 (Nonmember), $3.50 (Member) (plus $3.50 shipping); Entire nine-part set: $35 (Nonmember), $24.50 (Member) (plus $3.50 shipping)*

The Nonprofit Handbook: Everything You Need to Know to Start and Run Your Nonprofit Organization, 2nd Edition

GARY M. GROBMAN (WHITE HAT COMMUNICATIONS, 1999)

▶ This is a reference manual for starting up and running a nonprofit corporation in the United States. Information about how to incorporate, register to lobby, apply for tax exemptions, and comply with charitable solicitation laws is included for every state and the District of Columbia. Also included are the addresses and telephone numbers of the government contact offices in each state with jurisdiction over these issues. The book's 30 chapters provide all one needs to know to manage an effective nonprofit organization. The *Handbook* includes information about current federal laws, regulations, and court decisions that apply to nonprofits, as well as practical advice on important organizational concerns such as fund raising; grantsmanship; applying for tax-exempt status; setting up and dealing with boards of directors; obtaining liability insurance; hiring, firing, and other personnel issues; office management; advocacy; strategic planning; volunteer management; involvement in political activities and lobbying; bookkeeping; organizational communication; use of the Internet; running coalitions; dealing with challenges to tax exemptions; and much more. Preprinted postcards are included to assist readers in obtaining useful forms and instruction booklets. *Hardcover, 353 pages, $29.95 (plus $3.50 shipping)*

The Nonprofit Handbook: Management, 3rd Edition

TRACY D. CONNORS, ED. (JOHN WILEY & SONS, 2001)

▶ The revised and expanded format provides more coverage to both "sides" of the nonprofit equation; management and fund raising. In practice, these two aspects of a nonprofit's organizational structure each keep to themselves. *The Nonprofit Handbook: Management* offers information from experts in the field on every facet of a nonprofit's daily operations: management and leadership, human resources, benefits, compensation, financial management, marketing and communications, and law and regulations. *The Nonprofit Handbook: Fund-Raising* covers every aspect of the practice from preparatory, organizational, and managerial issues to both annual and major giving to specialized types of nonprofit organizations. Talk shop with more than 30 legal experts, management consultants, and nonprofit executives, and get the insights, answers, and solutions to improve your nonprofit organization. It includes numerous sample letters and forms, organizational flowcharts, checklists, and real-world examples demonstrating how to apply and use these critical tools for success. It is supplemented annually. *Hardcover, 960 pages, $105 (includes shipping if prepaid); Two-volume set (includes Management and Fund Raising), $200*

Nonprofit Management Case Collection

(INSTITUTE FOR NONPROFIT ORGANIZATION MANAGEMENT, UNIVERSITY OF SAN FRANCISCO, 1994)

▶ To augment and enhance existing educational materials, the Institute has created a collection of teaching cases covering the major functional areas of nonprofit management. The cases are written by academics and practitioners from around the world and cover such areas as planning, governance, finance, and public relations. These cases are available through the Institute's International Nonprofit Management Teaching Resource Center (INOM-TRC). *$120 (includes shipping)*

Nonprofit Organization Management: Forms, Checklists, and Guidelines, Revised Edition (Manual)

(ASPEN PUBLISHERS, 2001)

▶ A one-stop source of practical guidance for nonprofit executive directors, it will help you: (1) develop a better working relationship with your board by gaining a deeper understanding of the key aspects of managing a nonprofit organization, knowledge that will help you draw and maintain the line between board and administrator responsibilities, (2) become thoroughly knowledgeable about and gain a clear direction for implementing a wide variety of fundraising options, as well as advice on soliciting donors and getting board and staff member participation, (3) expand your understanding of an extensive array of key management concerns, and quickly and easily pinpoint the useful information you need to tackle day-to-day management issues; and more. It includes more than 200 ready-to-use documents, checklists, and guidelines applicable to policies and procedures for every area of your organization; materials can be adapted to meet your organization's unique needs. Content highlights include: Chapter 1, Strategic Planning and Marketing; Chapter 2, Fund-Raising; Chapter 3, Staff Management; Chapter 4, Compensation and Benefits; Chapter 5, Financial Management; Chapter 6, Program Management; Chapter 7, Board Relations; and Chapter 8, Community Public Relations. Each chapter is prefaced by a table of contents and separated by tabbed dividers; a complete index helps you locate or cross-reference any item. Annual supplements provide the latest management tools and techniques, along with updates on new social, legal, and regulatory issues, fully indexed and ready to insert in your loose-leaf binder. It includes new sections on Advocacy, Program Evaluation, Tax Tips and Guidelines, Board Service & Performance, and Internet & E-mail Guidelines. Loose-leaf binder, 800+ pages, *$175 (plus shipping)*

A Nonprofit Organization Operating Manual: Planning for Survival and Growth (Manual)

ARNOLD J. OLENICK & PHILIP R. OLENICK (THE FOUNDATION CENTER, 1991)

▶ The authors, a CPA/MBA attorney team, pool their nonprofit expertise in this all-inclusive desk guide for nonprofit executives. It covers all aspects of starting and managing a nonprofit: legal problems; the qualification process for obtaining tax-exempt status; organizational planning and development; board relations; legal structures; operational, proposal, cash, and capital budgeting; marketing; grant proposals, fund raising, and for-profit ventures; accounting; computerization; and tax planning and compliance. It is ideal for small- or medium-sized nonprofits. Softcover, 484 pages, *$29.95 (plus $4.50 shipping)*

Nonprofit Organizations' Business Forms, Disk Edition (Book & Disk)
(JOHN WILEY AND SONS, 1997)

▶ The checklists, forms, and samples on this disk provide the guidance and documentation for the management activities that nonprofit executives and their professional advisors (accountants, lawyers, and consultants) oversee on a daily basis. These self-explanatory documents include forms for establishing a nonprofit organization, checklists for maintaining tax-exempt status, real estate development forms, and much more. It contains 300 forms on diskette; includes sample articles of incorporation, unrelated business income tax checklists, fund-raising documents, accounting and budgeting worksheets, charitable gift agreements, internal management policies, maintaining tax-exempt status, and managing fund-raising programs. It includes a 96-page manual and is supplemented annually. *Softcover, w/three 3.5" IBM-compatible disks, 144 pages, $130.00; 3½" IBM-compatible disk, $105*

The Not-for-Profit CEO: A Survivor's Manual
GEORGE B. WRIGHT (C3 PUBLICATIONS, 1993)

▶ This "first aid" manual for the nonprofit CEO presents six key "checkpoints" for managers of nonprofit organizations to follow in order to lead their organizations effectively: building successful relationships between the CEO and the organization's board, staff, and volunteers; effective recruiting of board, staff, and volunteers; a well-run volunteer component; good budget management; successful relationships with other community organizations; and planning for the future. *Softcover, 138 pages, $11.95 (plus $2.25 shipping)*

Pathways to Leadership: How to Achieve and Sustain Success
JAMES LAWRENCE POWELL (JOSSEY-BASS, 1995)

▶ *Pathways to Leadership* is a practical, nuts-and-bolts guide written for nonprofit chief executives and those on the career path to becoming chief executives. In this book, author James Lawrence Powell provides realistic advice and offers illustrative examples for developing the skills necessary to become a successful nonprofit leader. The book is filled with numerous checklists, case examples, and a valuable resource section containing a list of questions interviewers ask, guidelines on negotiating the initial contract and holding the first senior staff meeting, scenarios on asking for gifts, and tips on learning to use the computer. For those who aspire to the position of CEO, the author details the search interview process from the perspective of the candidate, explains how to maximize the chances of getting a job offer, and offers sensible suggestions for salary negotiations. For those already in a leadership role, Powell surveys several crucial administrative skills—including time management, making meetings productive, the art of delegation, and control and use of technology. He illuminates the often difficult task of building a successful team and describes how to employ the best aspects of total quality management. Powell describes how to select qualified personnel and evaluate senior staff members in order to achieve maximum potential from staff. Also, he outlines the steps necessary for gaining and maintaining financial stability. In this age of increasing accountability, the author demonstrates how to evaluate the productiveness of an organization's administrative operations and projects. In addition, he offers the chief executive seasoned advice on how to deal most effectively with trustees. And he offers recommendations on how to assess when the time has come to seek a new position. *Hardcover, 253 pages, $25.95*

Principles of Association Management: A Professional's Handbook, 3rd Edition
HENRY ERNSTTHAL (AMERICAN SOCIETY OF ASSOCIATION EXECUTIVES, 1996)

▶ Ernstthal shares his 20+ years as an association executive, giving you a comprehensive insider's look at virtually every aspect of association management, including the unique nature of associations, governance structures, volunteer management, finance, marketing, membership, publishing, education and meetings, standards, research, government relations, foundations, strategic planning, and the association of the future. *Softcover, 131 pages, $43.95 (Nonmember), $34.95 (Member) (plus $6.25 shipping)*

Profiles of Excellence: Achieving Success in the Nonprofit Sector
(See Organizational Dynamics and Design—Publications for full description)

Starting and Managing a Nonprofit Organization: A Legal Guide
(See Legal Issues—Incorporation for full description)

Starting and Running a Nonprofit Organization
(See Legal Issues—Incorporation for full description)

Steering Nonprofits: Advice for Boards & Staffs
(See Governance—Roles and Responsibilities for full description)

Strategic Management for Nonprofit Organizations: Theory and Cases
SHARON M. OSTER (OXFORD UNIVERSITY PRESS, 1995)

▶ This book applies powerful concepts of strategic management developed originally in the for-profit sector to the management of nonprofits. It describes the preparation of a strategic plan consistent with the resources available; it analyzes the operational tasks in executing the plan; and describes the ways in which nonprofits need to change in order to remain competitive. The book draws clear distinctions between the different challenges encountered by nonprofits operating in different industries. *Hardcover, 360 pages, $39.95*

Strategic Management of Public and Third Sector Organizations: A Handbook for Leaders
PAUL C. NUTT AND ROBERT W. BACKOFF (JOSSEY-BASS, 1992)

▶ This handbook goes beyond strategic planning to show how an organization can be managed strategically. Comprehensive in scope, it provides a framework for understanding strategic issues in the public and nonprofit sectors. It also explains strategic management concepts and describes the process step by step, details support techniques, and includes useful forms and worksheets. *Hardcover, 558 pages, $43.95 (plus $4.50 shipping)*

Sustaining Innovation: Creating Nonprofit and Government Organizations That Innovate Naturally
PAUL C. LIGHT (JOSSEY-BASS, 1998)

▶ In this book, Paul Light reviews the work of the Surviving Innovation Project, a study of 26 public agencies and nonprofit organizations in Minnesota, between 1991 and 1995. The lessons learned from the study of these groups help to explore and explain the causes and consequences of innovation. He discovers that the organizations that are flexible and adaptable are the ones that innovate most successfully. In this volume, Light gives nonprofit managers the know-how and tools to overcome obstacles to innovation, and he also debunks the myths that create those obstacles. *Hardcover, 350 pages, $26.95*

What a Difference Understanding Makes: Guides to Nonprofit Management *(See Financial Management—General for full description)*

A Working Guide for Directors of Not-for-Profit Organizations *(See Governance—General for full description)*

Stress Control

Preventing Job Burnout: Transforming Work Pressures into Productivity (Fifty-Minute Series), Revised Edition
BEVERLY A. POTTER (CRISP PUBLICATIONS, 1995)
▶ Introducing eight proven strategies for beating job burnout, this newly revised edition also contains expanded information on networking, growing your social support system, and personal goal setting. *Softcover, 104 pages, $12.95*

You Don't Have to Go Home from Work
Exhausted! *(See Professional Development—Personal Growth for full description)*

Time Management

101 Ways to Make Every Second Count: Time Management Tips and Techniques for More Success with Less Stress
ROBERT W. BLY (CAREER PRESS, 1999)
▶ *101 Ways to Make Every Second Count* can help you become more effective in today's competitive, fast-paced world. This book goes beyond the usual time management books to bring you a broad range of strategies and tactics to gain the personal productivity boost you so desperately need. It shows how to maximize your time by setting priorities, creating useful schedules, and overcoming procrastination. Robert Bly describes how proper diet and exercise—or lack thereof—affect our energy levels and how using the latest technology allows us to manage information and to communicate more efficiently and effectively. Time management tips include the three types of to-do lists every person should keep; how to eliminate bad habits and unnecessary activities that slow you down; the Speed-Weeding Method for handling paperwork; mastering the art of saying no; how to deal with information overload; and why scanning should replace reading—and how to do it effectively. Readers benefit by meeting deadlines and commitments, increasing customer satisfaction, enhancing on-the-job performance, having more time for family, reducing pressure and stress, and feeling better about themselves and happier at work. *Softcover, 224 pages, $14.99*

201 Ways to Manage Your Time Better (Quick-Tip Survival Guides)
ALAN AXELROD, JIM HOLTJE, JAMES HOLTJE (MCGRAW-HILL, 1997)

▶ Focusing on the personal and interpersonal skills crucial to success, the Quick-Tip Survival Guides mine and refine the nuggets of essential business know-how: time-tested truths, as well as savvy from the cutting edge. *201 Ways to Manage Your Time Better* is no weighty tome on efficiency theory, but a compact quick-read collection of practical tips and easy steps that will start saving you time today. Here are real-world moves for people who need to make the very most out of every business day. *Softcover, 150 pages, $10.95*

ABC Time Tips
MERRILL E. DOUGLASS (MCGRAW-HILL, 1998)
▶ For all who've wondered why time isn't on their side, here's an essential, quick-access guide to everyday time management. Designed to eliminate the habits that keep people running behind while honing the skills that help them catch up, *ABC Time Tips* is organized into 80 alphabetically listed topics, such as "Attitudes," "Distractions," "Lists," "Perfectionism," and "Saying No." Each topic has pages of practical and proven tips and techniques to help time-strapped readers gain more control over their schedules. The book includes more than 1,000 proven tips and techniques that put you in charge of your day. Learn to distinguish "urgent" from "important"; overcome procrastination; conquer the clutter on your desk; create and use quiet time; and reserve time for play. This guide will tell you everything you need to know to be more on top of things at work and at home—and show you how to have more time for what's really important, like family, friends, and time for yourself. *Softcover, 224 pages, $12.95*

Commonsense Time Management (Worksmart Series)
RAY ALEXANDER (AMACOM BOOKS, 1992)
▶ Easy-to-follow tips, techniques, and guidelines for making better use of your time. This instructive guide to time management is full of tips, techniques, and commonsense advice that will make you more productive and free up your schedule. Topics include using a to-do list, setting priorities, and reducing stress through time management. You'll also learn how to handle distractions, stop procrastinating, delegate tasks, deal with meetings, use the telephone, and manage time effectively while traveling—all of which will help you make the most of your working time and your time off. *Softcover, 120 pages, $10.95*

How to Be Organized in Spite of Yourself: Time and Space Management That Works with Your Personal Style, Revised Edition
SUNNY SCHLENGER, ROBERTA ROESCH (SIGNET, 1999)
▶ Revised and updated, this is a fabulous resource for one of the hottest topics of the last decade—getting organized! Recognizing that just one organizational system is not for everyone, the authors have devised solutions that provide 10 different systems to match 10 basic personality types, such as Perfectionist Plus, Hopper, Fence Sitter, Pack Rat, and Total Slob. *Softcover, 256 pages, $6.50*

The Personal Efficiency Program: How to Get Organized to Do More Work in Less Time, 2nd Edition
KERRY GLEESON (JOHN WILEY & SONS, 1999)
▶ Get more done—faster and easier than you ever dreamed possible. Kerry Gleeson's Personal Efficiency Program is the famed system for multiplying productivity that has already revolutionized the work lives of over 300,000 people around the globe. Now, in *The Personal Efficiency Program*, Gleeson offers an updated and

expanded edition of his classic guide to working faster and smarter, giving you all the tools you need to get control of your workload—and your career. You'll learn how to save a month of work a year by following the simple *Do It Now!* rule; conquer an endless stream of interruptions and paperwork; create easy, effective methods of organizing paper and computer files; and manage meetings, schedules, and other horrific time wasters. This second edition also includes expanded information on conquering information overload, using the Internet to save time and energy, and managing today's faster-paced and multilocated work environments. *Softcover, 224 pages, $16.95*

Time Management for Dummies, 2nd Edition

JEFFREY J. MAYER, AND MARY GOODWIN (IDG BOOKS WORLDWIDE, 1999)

▶ Here, you find practical, how-to advice that you can implement right away to get your life back in balance and be more successful at home and at work. Jeffrey J. Mayer, one of the United States' foremost authorities on time management, shares his expert tips on such topics as organizing your desk and files, prioritizing your to-dos, setting goals, and scheduling time for yourself, your family, and your friends. It offers the latest in time-saving tips, including how to clear office clutter, use a daily planner, work within deadlines, and stay on track while away from the office or home. His commonsense approach to time management will get you organized, make you more productive, and get you home for dinner. Gain an hour a day and learn how to organize your desk and files in just a few hours; master your day by creating a master list for tasks; prioritize your business and personal life with a daily planner; put your calendar, Rolodex, and to-do list inside your computer with ACT!; optimize your time on the phone and with voice mail and e-mail systems; and improve your ability to communicate effectively. *Softcover, 372 pages, $21.99*

Time Trap, 3rd Edition

ALEC MACKENZIE (AMACOM, 1997)

▶ Since it was first published, *The Time Trap*, by internationally known authority Alec Mackenzie, has indeed become *The Classic Book on Time Management*, as proclaimed in its subtitle. Based on the theory that self-management is the key to handling the time crunch that we all face, it focuses primarily on Mackenzie's 20 biggest time wasters, such as telephone interruptions, the inability to say "no," and personal disorganization, and offers clear step-by-step ways to combat them. The updated third edition also includes information on time problems caused by technology, downsizing, and self-employment. *The Time Trap* shows readers how to squeeze the optimal efficiency—and satisfaction—out of their workday as they learn how to recognize how human nature is usually the root cause of dwindling time; pinpoint and combat the 20 most tenacious time wasters; avoid the technology trap and so-called "time-savers"; and use time management techniques for professional and personal success. *Softcover, 240 pages, $17.95*

Working with Consultants

Succeeding with Consultants: Self-Assessment for the Changing Nonprofit

BARBARA KIBBE AND FRED SETTERBERG (THE FOUNDATION CENTER, 1992)

▶ Providing practical advice for inexperienced nonprofit executives, the authors explain how the appropriate use of consultants can generate exciting methods of forwarding your organization's goals (in terms of advice, perspective, tools, inspiration, skills, and time not available to solve your own problems). This book guides nonprofits through the process of selecting and utilizing consultants to strengthen their organization's operations; emphasizes self-assessment tools, and covers six different areas in which a nonprofit organization might benefit from a consultant's advice: governance, planning, fund development, financial management, public relations and marketing, and quality assurance. *Softcover, 79 pages, $20 (plus $4.50 shipping)*

PERIODICALS

(See also Financial Management; Information Technology—Internet Resources; Marketing)

Association Management (Monthly Magazine)
American Society of Association Executives (See also Financial Management, Resource Development, Human Resource Management, Legal Issues, Volunteerism)
1575 I Street NW, Washington, DC 20005-1168
Tel: 202-626-2723; FAX: 202-371-8825
E-mail: feedback@asaenet.org; WWW: http://www.asaenet.org
Association Management is edited specifically for association executives. It provides timely, practical information to help association executives succeed in their dual role as manager and visionary. Articles address issues, programs, news, and trends important to nonprofit organizations of all sizes and scopes. Departments include: The Human Resource, Legal, Calendar, Board of Directors, Careers, Sources & Resources, Good Ideas; and many useful articles about managing nonprofit organizations. *$50 (Member and Nonmember)*

Board & Administrator: Nonprofit Edition (See *Governance—Periodicals for full description*)

The Chronicle of Philanthropy: The Newspaper of the Non-Profit World (See also *Information Technology, Philanthropy, Resource Development*)
1255 Twenty-Third Street NW, Washington, DC 20037
Tel: 202-466-1212; FAX: 202-659-2236
E-mail: editor@philanthropy.com (General inquiries),
subscriptions@philanthropy.com
WWW: http://www.philanthropy.com
▶ *The Chronicle of Philanthropy* is the newspaper of the nonprofit world. Published every other week, it is a major news source for charity leaders, fund raisers, grant makers, and other people involved in the philanthropic enterprise. In print, *The Chronicle* is published biweekly except the last two weeks in June and the last two weeks in December (a total of 24 issues a year). A subscription includes full access to its Web site and news updates by e-mail. Features include Guide to Grants, Facts & Figures, Conferences, Workshops and Seminars (organized by region), Deadlines, Products and Services, and Jobs as well as *The Directory of Services, The Consultants Guide, The Technology Guide*. The Web site offers the complete contents of the new issue, an archive of articles from the past two years, and more than four years' worth of grant listings, all fully searchable. You can browse by topic (Gifts & Grants, Fund Raising, Managing Non-Profit Groups, Technology, For Donors and Trustees). Some of this material (including the fully searchable version of the 2000 edition of *The Chronicle's Non-Profit Handbook*, containing more than 1,000 resources on fund raising and nonprofit management) is available only to *Chronicle* subscribers. The Guide to Grants is an electronic database of all foundation and corporate grants listed in *The Chronicle* since 1995. *Chronicle* subscribers can search grants from the two most recent issues. Complete access to the *Guide to Grants* requires a separate subscription. *$67.50/year*

Communication Briefings (Monthly Newsletter)
Briefings Publishing Group, 1101 King Street, Suite 110, Alexandria, VA 22314
Tel: 800-888-2084, 703-548-3800; FAX: 703-684-2136
E-mail: customerservice@briefings.com;
WWW: http://www.briefings.com/,
http://briefings.com/cb/Resources.html,
http://www.briefings.com/tr/index.html#videos,
http://www.briefings.com/tr/index.html#reports,
http://www.briefings.com/tr/index.html#tips
▶ Each month, you'll discover tips and techniques to help increase workplace communication and productivity. An ideal source for decision makers in thousands of nonprofit organizations, it provides concise, practical communication ideas and techniques you can put into action to sharpen your personal skills in writing, speaking, listening, organizing, problem solving, and decision making; spur employee productivity with better communication; increase your effectiveness with clients and customers; generate enthusiasm and imagination within your organization; gain public support for your organization's policies and activities; improve your reports, memos, presentations, letters, and publications; gain acceptance for the importance of effective communication; and give your staff and employees advice and suggestions on how to communicate more effectively. Regular features include Tips of the Month, Face-to-Face Communication, Customer Service, Time Management, Media Relations, As We See It, Publications, Test Yourself, Getting Ahead, Training, Productivity, Marketing, Employee Communication, Speaking, Books to Read, Computer Tips; Special Reports, Employee Tip Sheets, and videos on a variety of topics also available. Online area of interest include Team Management, Customer Service, Speaking & Presenting, PR & Publicity, Employee Communication, Writing, Dealing with Difficult People, and Teamwork. *8 pages, $79/year*

Contributions Magazine (See *Resource Development— Periodicals for complete description*)

Crain's Nonprofit News (Twice-Monthly Newsletter)
Crain Communications
Subscriber Services: 965 East Jefferson Avenue, Detroit, MI 48207-3187
Tel: 888-909-9111 (subscriptions)
Editorial Offices: 1400 Woodbridge Avenue, Detroit, MI 48207-3187
Tel: 313-4460-0399; FAX: 313-446-1687
E-mail: MKramer@crain.com (Mary Kramer),
dguilfor@crain.com;
WWW: http://www.crainsdetroit.com/nonprof.html
▶ *Crain's Nonprofit News* is a source of news and ideas for Michigan nonprofits that can help you and your organization with every decision you face with staff, volunteers, board members,

donors, grant makers, grant seekers, trustees, tax and legal advisors, committees, and more. Excerpts from the latest issue are available on the Web site. It includes a calendar of activities, job ads, and more. *$49/year*

501(c)(3) Monthly Letter: A Management Tool for Nonprofits *(See also Resource Development)*

Great Oaks Communication Services, 400 Chestnut Street,
P.O. Box 192, Atlantic, IA 50022
Tel: 712-243-4750; FAX: 712-243-2775
E-mail: jkenney@nisha.net, mmiller@nishna.net,
kmeickle@nishna.net, http://www.nishna.net/501c3/index.html

▶ The *501(c)(3) Monthly Letter* features articles by leaders in the nonprofit world on such varied topics as fund raising, grants, computerization, communication, special events, working with volunteers, selecting board members, attracting media attention, postal rate savings, and more. It covers the full range of issues with concise articles and other features, including Calendar of Events and Books of Interest. It also provides Internet access to nonprofits on the World Wide Web home page (see Information Technology—Products and Services for further details). *12 pages, $46/year*

Food for Thought *(See also Internet Resources—Online Publications)*

CompassPoint, 706 Mission Street, 5th Floor,
San Francisco, CA 94103-3113
Tel: 415-541-9000; FAX: 415-541-7708
E-mail: info@compasspoint.org;
WWW: http://www.compasspoint.org

▶ The San Francisco Bay Area's source of news for nonprofit organizations, *Food for Thought* provides timely information about funding opportunities, conferences, online resources, and more in every issue.

Harvard Business Review *(See also Financial Management)*

Mail: Harvard Business School Publishing, Corporate Customer Service Center, 60 Harvard Way, Box 230-5C, Boston, MA 02163

Delivery Address: Harvard Business School Publishing
Attn: Fulfillment Center, 300 North Beacon Street
Watertown, MA. 02472
Tel: 800-988-0886; FAX: 617-496-1029
E-mail: corpcustserv@hbsp.harvard.edu;
WWW: http://www.hbsp.harvard.edu/products/hbr/index.html

▶ Learn about original research and new business developments from top executives around the world, faculty members at the Harvard Business School, leading consultants, and distinguished teachers from other graduate schools of business. Every issue contains these regular features: Incisive Articles (thought-provoking ideas and insights on managerial excellence, from the best minds in business), First Person (personal accounts of experienced managers' trials and triumphs, and the lessons they learned), Interviews (question-and-answer sessions with men and women in various managerial fields), Case Studies (spotlights how managers reacted to specific business situations at the crucial moment of decision), World View (emerging trends with international implications or applications), In Question (a review of hot policy issues-in-progress that may affect your decision-making process). Also included are management tips and tactics, opinions, humor, and more. Topics covered include marketing, communications, computers, executive compensation, strategy, finance, and dealing with your board. *$75/year*

Inc. Magazine *(Monthly)*

100 First Avenue, 4th Floor, Building #36,
Charlestown, MA 02129
P.O. Box 54129, Boulder, CO 80322
Tel: 800-234-0999, 303-604-1465 (Subscriptions);
FAX: 617-248-8277 (Editorial)
E-mail: inc@neodata.com; WWW: http://www.inc.com

▶ Although designed for people who run businesses, most of the ideas and information in this vibrant publication are also applicable to nonprofit managers; reading it is a good way to become more "businesslike" in your management approach. Contents include case histories, user guides to resources, business Q&A, book reviews, and regular columns on marketing, banking and capital, financial strategies, managing technology, and managing people. *Inc.* is full of practical, hands-on information to help you succeed in business. Full contents of the 14 annual issues of *Inc.* and four annual issues of *Inc. Technology* are posted at inc.com, with the current issue available to subscribers only. Stories back to 1988 are available for free in the online archives. Also provided are a broad array of books, videos, software, conferences, seminars, consulting services, and awards programs. *$19/year*

Innovating *(Quarterly Journal)*

The Rensselaerville Institute, Rensselaerville, NY 12147
Tel: 518-797-3783; FAX: 518-797-5270
E-mail: info@tricampus.org; WWW: http://www.tricampus.org

▶ *Innovating* is the publication for people who practice innovation in public- and private-sector organizations and in their lives. Contributors to *Innovating* are distinguished by their proven ability to make change happen. Their articles connect theory and practice. In each issue you will find Assumptions, Essays, Viewpoints, Interviews, and Passages, all carefully selected to help those who believe that change starts with themselves. This quarterly publication instructs on how to trigger change through example by using small projects to test new thinking in immediate ways. Names and phone numbers are included for follow-up, as well as personal accounts of innovators and a timely digest of innovations in government, schools, and businesses. It presents experiences and viewpoints of innovative scholars and in public- and private-sector organizations. *$30/year*

Leader to Leader *(Quarterly Journal) (See also Leadership)*

Jossey-Bass Publishers, 350 Sansome Street,
San Francisco, CA 94104-1342
Tel: 888-378-2537, 415-433-1767 (mention priority code W98DF); FAX: 800-605-2665, 415-433-0499
E-mail: webperson@jbp.com (include your mailing address, daytime phone number, and mention priority code W98DF);
WWW: http://www.jbp.com/JBJournals/ltl.html,
http://www.josseybass.com/catalog/isbn/LTL/

▶ Sponsored by the Peter F. Drucker Foundation for Nonprofit Management, *Leader to Leader* is published jointly by the Drucker Foundation and Jossey-Bass. It offers current thinking on leadership, management, and strategy written by today's top thought leaders from the private, public, and social sectors. In each issue, the Drucker Foundation brings together a peerless selection of world-class executives, best-selling management authors, top consultants, and respected social thinkers. *Leader to Leader* gives you unique insight into what other top executives and thought leaders are planning for, what they see as the major challenges ahead, and how they are dealing with change. Tables of contents for recent and forthcoming issues are posted on the *Leader to Leader* homepage. *$149/year, $99 (501(c)(3) nonprofit organizations)*

Monthly Management Review (Monthly Magazine)
American Management Association
Editorial office: 1601 Broadway, New York, NY 10019
Tel: 212)-586-8100; FAX: 212-903-8168

P.O. Box 169, Saranac Lake, NY 12983-9986
Tel: 800-262-9699 (Customer Service), 518-891-5510;
FAX: 518-891-0368
WWW: http://www.amanet.org, http://www.amanet.org/start.htm

▶ Devoted to improving your management skills, this practical management tool takes you behind the scenes to reveal how key decisions are made, how strategies are put into action, and how problems are resolved. It keeps you in touch with the latest trends and ideas and gives you inventive, resourceful solutions to management problems. Bound into each issue, Monthly Forum Newsletters provide informative articles, news briefs, editorials, and an active exchange of information on problems, issues, and innovations in the areas of human resources, information systems and technology, finance, and marketing. Each feature article includes a special "Workbook" with specific suggestions to help you implement the ideas presented in that article. *$45/year*

Manager's Edge
Briefings Publishing Group, 1101 King Street, Suite 110,
Alexandria, VA 22314
Tel: 800-888-2084, 703-548-3800; FAX: 703-684-2136
E-mail: customerservice@briefings.com;
WWW: http://briefings.com/me

▶ This resource offers problem-solving ideas middle- and upper-level managers can use immediately. Each issue offers advice on building leadership skills, teamwork, delegating, motivating, juggling multiple priorities, and more. The Web site offers free advice from the ME archives on management problems, such as leadership, employee communication, coaching, employee motivation, problem solving, teamwork, employee development, and managing change. *$97/year*

New England Nonprofit Quarterly
18 Tremont Street, Suite 700, Boston, MA 02108
Tel: 800-281-7770 ext. 223, 617-523-6565; FAX: 617-523-2070

Contact Name: David Garvey, Executive Director
E-mail: editor@newenglandnonprofit.org;
WWW: www.newenglandnonprofit.org,
http://www.nonprofitquarterly.org/technology/index.htm

▶ Circulates the best in thinking, research, and practice in the nonprofit sector. Because of its critical rigor, it is broadly read by funders and researchers as well as by nonprofit leaders and managers who prize it for its on-the-ground practicality. Originally a regional journal for New England nonprofits, it has expanded to national distribution. Learn from the challenges others have faced, and meet the nation's nonprofit pioneers and leaders. Keep current on new trends in development, marketing, management, major gifts and planned giving, finance and accounting, governance, collaborations, technology, and volunteers. Subscribers have a resource and learning center open to them 24 hours a day. *$39/year*

Nonprofit Alert Newsletter (Monthly Newsletter)
The Law Firm of Gammon & Grange, PC,
8280 Greensboro Drive, 7th Floor, McLean, VA 22102
Tel: 703-761-5000 or 402-292-5653; FAX: 703-761-5023
E-mail: sjschmidt2@earthlink.net (Sarah J. Schmidt, Editor),
npa@gandglaw.com; WWW: http://gandglaw.com/

▶ This newsletter provides concise summaries highlighting legal, regulatory, and administrative developments that shape the nonprofit world, along with practice tips and resources for managing any associated risks. *$75/year*

Nonprofit and Voluntary Sector Quarterly
(Quarterly Journal) (Formerly Journal of Voluntary Action Research) *(See also Nonprofit Sector Overview—Study and Research; International Third Sector—Periodicals)*
Sage Publications, 2455 Teller Road, Newbury Park, CA 91320
Tel: 805-499-0721; FAX: 805-499-0871
E-mail: order@sagepub.com;
WWW: http://www.gspa.washington.edu/nvsq/index.html

▶ Sponsored by the Association for Research on Nonprofit Organizations and Voluntary Action (ARNOVA), this journal contains articles on national and international theoretically grounded research that applies to management of nonprofit organizations, voluntary action, and collaboration of organizations. It is the only scholarly journal dedicated exclusively to exploring the unique dynamics, needs, and concerns of today's nonprofit and voluntary organizations. It offers a forum for interdisciplinary exchange, incorporating the insights of scholars and practitioners in such key areas as sociology, public administration, management, organizational behavior, social work, health, and education. It includes up-to-date book reviews. *Nonprofit and Voluntary Sector Quarterly* welcomes queries or finished papers that report research on voluntarism, citizen participation, philanthropy, civil society, and nonprofit organizations. *$67/year (Individual), $163/year (Institution)*

Nonprofit Management and Leadership (Quarterly Journal)
Jossey-Bass Inc. Publishers, 350 Sansome Street,
San Francisco, CA 94104
Tel: 415-433-1767, ext. 424; FAX: 800-605-BOOK (2665)
WWW: http://www.jbp.com/JBJournals/nml.html
Mandel Center for Nonprofit Organizations, Case Western
Reserve University, 10900 Euclid Avenue,
Cleveland, OH 44106-7164
FAX: 216-368-8592

▶ This is a scholarly publication co-sponsored by the Mandel Center for Nonprofit Organizations at Case Western Reserve University and the Centre for Voluntary Organisation at the London School of Economics. It presents five articles by nationally and internationally known writers in the field. It brings together the best thinking and most advanced knowledge about the special needs, challenges, and opportunities of nonprofit organizations. It includes authoritative insights of top executives and scholars on the common concerns of nonprofit leaders in all settings (social services, the arts, education, foundations, community development, advocacy work, religion, professional associations). It includes interviews and case studies, research reports, book reviews, Letters to the Editor, and Calendar of Events. *$56/year (Individual), $115/year (Institution)*

Nonprofit Nuts & Bolts: Practical Tips for Building Better Non-Profits (Monthly Newsletter)

Nuts & Bolts Publishing, 4623 Tiffany Woods Circle, Oviedo, FL 32765
Tel: 407-677-6564; FAX: 407-677-5645
E-mail: info@nutsbolts.com, lbeach@nutsbolts.com (Lisa Beach, Editor); WWW: http://www.nutsbolts.com/

▶ *Non-Profit Nuts & Bolts* aims to provide nonprofit professionals with practical "how-to" management tips to build a better organization. It strives to be the number one information-packed resource for busy, budgetstretching, lean-staffed nonprofit professionals. The newsletter covers fund raising, volunteer management, public relations, special events, team building, board relations, committees, communications, leadership, time management, marketing, media relations, technology, meetings, staff management, budget-stretching ideas, and other key areas of nonprofit management. Each monthly issue contains approximately 30 to 35 articles on a variety of key nonprofit management topics. Regular features include Freebies (one or two items each issue that highlight an offer of free resources, such as booklets, idea kits, brochures, sample products, and checklists from other companies and organizations), Budget-Stretching Ideas (a few brief, money-saving ideas that readers can implement immediately), Off the Shelf (periodic reviews of nonprofit resources, such as books, reports, workbooks, videotapes, audiotapes, etc.), Success Stories (periodically share readers' success stories of how they effectively solved a management problem or how they took a creative approach to improve the way they currently manage their nonprofit). The Web site includes Freebies, Reports, Articles, and Resources. *8 pages, $89/year, $49 (electronic version)*

The Nonprofit Report: Accounting, Taxation & Management *(See Financial Management—Periodicals for full description)*

Nonprofit Times (Monthly)

Circulation Department, Suite 318, Cedar Knolls, NJ 07927
Tel: 973-734-1700; FAX: 973-734-1777
E-mail: ednchief@nptimes.com; WWW: http://www.nptimes.com, http://www.nptimes.com/main/directory.html

▶ This publication is for executives of nonprofit organizations, with articles on philanthropy, volunteering, and nonprofit issues and developments; includes general news, features, editorials, and display advertisements. Also, the online version offers the Employment Marketplace, Resource Directory, and access to previous issues. It publishes the Direct Marketing Edition (six issues per year), the Financial Management Edition (three issues per year), the NPT 100, and the NPT Salary Survey. Free subscriptions are offered only to full-time U.S. nonprofit executives whose organizations qualify for a free subscription. *$59/year*

Nonprofit World: The National Nonprofit Leadership and Management Journal (Bimonthly Magazine)

The Society for Nonprofit Organizations, 6314 Odana Road, Suite 1, Madison, WI 53719
Tel: 800-424-7367, 608-274-9777
E-mail: snpo@danenet.wicip.org;
WWW: http://danenet.wicip.org/snpo, http://danenet.wicip.org/snpo/NPWIndex/NPWindex.htm

▶ Comprehensive national leadership, management, and governance-focused journal; each issue addresses the key management areas all nonprofits deal with on a daily basis and includes feature articles, news on impending federal legislation, critical legal issues, successful fund-raising ideas, promotion and marketing tips, planning strategies, reviews of current literature in the field, and organizational success stories. It also contains The *Resource Center Catalog: The National Bookstore for the Nonprofit Sector* (a listing of outstanding educational materials available through the Society), and the *National Directory of Service/Product Providers* (a listing of highly regarded companies with services and products specifically designed for nonprofit organizations). *$79/year (Nonmember); Society members (included in membership)*

The Not-for-Profit CEO Monthly Letter (Monthly Newsletter)

C3 Publications, 3495 NW Thurman Street, Portland, OR 97210-1283
Tel: 503-223-0268; FAX: 503-223-3083
E-mail: gwryter@teleport.com (George B. Wright, Editor);
WWW: http://www.teleport.com/~gwryter/publications.html#ML

▶ This newsletter provides practical, nuts-and-bolts information and strategies for the nonprofit practitioner; each monthly issue features a Focus section, exploring a specific issue of interest and concern to nonprofit managers, in addition to Expert Witness (advice from a professional), From the Ranks Editorial, On My Mind, and periodic supplements and survey results. Features include discussion about boards; CEO Surveys (opinions of readers on current issues); From the Ranks (NFP CEOs speak out); Expert Witness (advice on the technical issues facing you every day); Focus (current issues); and Hands-On Tools (special supplements to help you do your job). *8 pages, $89/year*

Pennsylvania Nonprofit Report (Monthly Newsletter)

Patterbury Publications, P.O. Box 252, Wayne, PA 19087
Tel: 610-356-3160; FAX: 610-356-8153
E-mail: editor@panonprofitreport.com;
WWW: http://www.panonprofitreport.com/

▶ Pennsylvania Nonprofit Report (PNR) is the news and information resource for Pennsylvania nonprofits. This monthly publication is developed and published exclusively for the nonprofit sector in Pennsylvania—the only publication of its kind in the state. PNR delivers indispensable information that helps you get your job done, carry out your mission, develop leaders, recruit staff, plan programs, identify funding sources, and hone the budget. Features include Meet the Newest Funders—up to five profiles of newly formed foundations from the editor of the *Directory of Pennsylvania Foundations;* profiles/interviews with leaders and doers; spotlight on grantors and grantees, and programs making a difference; timely listings of funding sources and grant awards; expert management and technical assistance; surveys, stats, trends, and opinions; and *The Harrisburg Report*—monthly reports direct from the state capitol. *16 pages, $120 (Nonmember), $95 (Member)*

Team Management Briefings (Monthly Newsletter)

Briefings Publishing Group, 1101 King Street, Suite 110, Alexandria, VA 22314
Tel: 800-888-2084, 703-548-3800; FAX: 703-684-2136
E-mail: customerservice@briefings.com, dhackett@briefings.com; WWW: http://www.briefings.com/

▶ This newsletter offers practical ideas that team leaders and team members can use right away to build and maintain strong teams. It covers the following areas: conflict, performance, recognition/rewards, communication, morale/motivation, increasing participation, coaching, leadership. *$99/year*

INTERNET RESOURCES

(See also Information Technology, Internet Resources)

General

About.com–Nonprofit Charitable Organizations

▶ Extensive number of links and articles on various aspects of nonprofit organizations. *http://nonprofit.about.com/careers/nonprofit*

Alliance for Nonprofit Management

▶ The Alliance Web site is the home of *Pulse!,* an online newsletter serving the nonprofit management community. The Alliance Resource Center provides a compilation of Web sites, books, videos, other resources. *www.allianceonline.org, http://www.allianceonline.org/ providersearch.html*

American Society of Association Executives—ASAE on the Net

▶ *http://www.asaenet.org/main*

Association of Executive Search Consultants Online Management Library

▶ *http://www.aesc.org/management1.html*

Basic Skills in Management and Leadership—Free Management Library's On-Line Nonprofit Organization Development Program Module #4

▶ *http://www.managementhelp.org/np_progs/mng_mod/mng_ldr.htm*

California Management Assistance Organizations

▶ The California Management Assistance Partnership (C-MAP) is a consortium of 13 regional, nonprofit support organizations providing training and technical assistance to local nonprofit organizations throughout California. The regional partners established C-MAP in 1996 to encourage collaboration and sharing of efforts among the partners to enable them to serve their local communities more effectively. Each of these organizations provides workshops in nonprofit management and fund raising, assistance with information, and referrals to other community resources. C-MAP maintains the Nonprofit GENIE Web site (see Internet Resources for full description) as a free service to help nonprofit staff and board members manage more successfully. *http://search.genie.org/genie/cmap.lasso*

CompassPoint Nonprofit Services (Formerly the Support Center/Nonprofit Development Center)

▶ The site includes: *Board Café* (co-published by CompassPoint and the National Center for Nonprofit Boards, *Board Café* is the first electronic newsletter exclusively for members of nonprofit boards of directors. Sign up today for a free subscription); workshops (the latest courses and workshops offered by CompassPoint Nonprofit Services to Bay Area nonprofits. Classes are available in San Francisco, San Jose, San Mateo, and the East Bay); and *Food for Thought* (the San Francisco Bay Area's source of news for nonprofit organizations). *http://www.compasspoint.org*

Delaware Association of Nonprofit Agencies Answer Center

▶ *http://www.delawarenonprofit.org/AnswerCtr.htm*

Peter F. Drucker Foundation for Nonprofit Management

▶ For social sector organizations, the Peter F. Drucker Foundation provides educational opportunities and resources, such as conferences, video teleconferences, partnerships, publications, links to other foundation sites and resources, and internal and external searches. Included is a link to the Nonprofit Innovation Discovery site *(http://www.pfdf.org/innovation/index.html). http://www.pfdf.org*

East Bay MAPP Online: Management and Technical Assistance Tools and Resources for Nonprofit Organizations

▶ *http://www.eastbaymapp.org/*

Excellence in Nonprofit Leadership and Management Certificate Series

▶ *http://www.pbs.org/als/nonprofit/index.html*

Free Management Library—Management Assistance Program for Nonprofits (MAP)

▶ This is a well-organized, no-frills library of free, self-directed management courses in topics such as board roles and responsibilities, communications skills, finance and taxes, program development, program evaluation, and consultants. Users can browse through the management materials at this online library, using any of 69 categories to find information on any of their 675 topics. This site has good links to other resources on the Internet. *http://www.mapnp.org/library, http://www.mapnp.org/library/topics.htm*

IKNOW

▶ IKNOW is a product of Raffa & Associates, an accounting and business management firm that specializes in the nonprofit sector. IKNOW identifies and organizes information of concern to the nonprofit community into the following major categories: business services, education, fringe benefits, fund raising, governance, human resources, legal issues, legislation, strategic planning, and volunteerism. IKNOW also has an Internet resource directory for nonprofits. *http://www.iknow.org*

Internet Nonprofit Center & the Nonprofit FAQ

▶ *http://www.nonprofit-info.org*

InnoNet's Workstation for Innovative Nonprofits

▶ Created by Innovation Network, a nonprofit consulting organization in Washington that helps charities plan and evaluate programs, this Web site offers interactive worksheets that help nonprofit staff members develop program, fund-raising, and evaluation plans for their projects, and sample evaluation tools, such as surveys and questions for focus groups, that can be downloaded, as well as links to other Internet resources for nonprofit organizations. *http://www.innonet.org*

Kalamazoo County Virtual Nonprofit Resource Network

▶ *http://www.knrn.org/*

Kern, DeWenter, Viere, Ltd. Nonprofit Management Tips

▶ KDV maintains a library of nonprofit management tips. Topics include new regulations, tax legislation, UBIT, finance, nonprofit management, fund raising, technology compliance, and employee compensation. Membership is free. *http://www.kdv.com/articles.html*

La Piana Associates

▶ *http://www.lapiana.org/tips/index.html*

Management Center

▶ A searchable site with an organization library, extensive job listings, a nonprofit assessment tool, programs and services, and other resources. *http://www.tmcenter.org*

Management—General—Canadian Centre for Philanthropy Information Centre

▶ This area contains information on a variety of management concepts and practices, as well as a listing of awards available to the nonprofit sector. *http://www.ccp.ca/information/management/general/mgmtgen.html*

Management Toolkit—501Click

▶ *http://www.501click.com/mt_main.html*

Milano Nonprofit Management Knowledge Hub

▶ The Milano Nonprofit Management Knowledge Hub provides annotated links to Web sites of interest to the nonprofit world. The site includes links to research reports on nonprofit topics, Web sites that provide advice on fund raising and management, online calendars of nonprofit events, e-mail discussion lists, online publications, and more. The site is a project of the Nonprofit Management Program of the Robert J. Milano Graduate School of Management and Urban Policy of the New School University. *http://www.newschool.edu/milano/hub*

National Council of Nonprofit Associations

▶ The NCNA Web site includes: NCNA news, the chance to order NCNA publications, contact information for state associations. *http://www.ncna.org*

Nonprofit Coordinating Committee of New York (NPCC)

▶ The NPCC Web site has a newsletter for nonprofit organizations, a workshop calendar, and a list of useful articles and information. In collaboration with Philanthropic Research, Inc., users can search for New York nonprofit organizations. *http://www.npccny.org*

NonProfit Gateway

▶ Network of links to federal information and services for nonprofit organizations. *http://www.nonprofit.gov/*

Nonprofit Genie (Global Electronic Nonprofit Information Express)

▶ The Nonprofit Genie is provided by the California Management Assistance Partnership (C-MAP). The site includes a list of recommended publications; links to selected nonprofit resources; answers to frequently asked questions about management; interviews and articles by experts, grant makers, and other leaders; and tips for accounting, retirement, and other human resource issues for nonprofit managers. *http://www.genie.org*

Nonprofits Grassroots MBA Program

▶ This highly accessible, results-oriented program is geared to develop the complete range of basic systems needed by learners to start and run a nonprofit organization. The program is not accredited for granting a degree. *http://www.mapnp.org/library/mgmnt/mba_prog.htm*

Nonprofit Management Resources—Thompson & Thompson

▶ *http://www.t-tlaw.com/rs-13.shtml*

The Nonprofit Resource Center

▶ Fund-raising and grants information, legal links, research, management resources, books, and other areas. *http://www.not-for-profit.org/index.html*

The Nonprofit Zone

▶ *http://www.nonprofitzone.com/mgmnt.htm*

Organizational Literacy and Leadership *(See also Human Resource Management; Organizational Development; Strategic Planning)*

▶ This site provides information on organizational issues facing nonprofit organizations, in-service short courses in organization studies for those working in nonprofit organizations, and a clearing house for information on human resource development opportunities for those working in nonprofit organizations. *http://Web sites.quincy.edu/~chasemi/iopsych.htm*

PhilanthropySearch.com

▶ *http://www.philanthropysearch.com/managing.html*

Principals and Practices for Nonprofit Excellence

▶ A fine paper on this subject from the Minnesota Council of Nonprofits. *http://nonprofit.about.com/careers/nonprofit/gi/dynamic/offsite.htm?site=http://www.mncn.org/pnp%5Findex.htm*

Resources for Nonprofits—Helping.org

▶ *http://www.helping.org/nonprofit/general.adp#npmgt*

Starting a Nonprofit Organization: One-Stop Answer Page

▶ If you're thinking of starting a nonprofit organization, this is the place to begin. You'll find links to basic information such as planning, legal resources, and fund raising. *http://nonprofit.about.com/careers/nonprofit/library/weekly/blonestart.htm*

Online Newsletters

501(c)(3) Monthly Letter

▶ The *501(c)(3) Monthly Letter* features articles by leaders in the nonprofit world on such varied topics as fund raising, grants, computerization, communication, special events, working with volunteers, selecting board members, attracting media attention, postal rate savings, and more. Subscribers include the entire spectrum of the nonprofit world: arts; culture, human services, education; health, environment, and so on in all 50 states and a few foreign countries. First published in 1980 by Margaret Stewart Carr, it was purchased by Jim and Marilyn Kenney of Great Oaks Communication Services in December 1988. The *501(c)(3) Monthly Letter* is a practical, no-nonsense type of publication with lots of "how-to" ideas in an easy-to-read format. *http://www.nishna.net/501c3/index.html*

The Chronicle of Philanthropy

▶ *The Chronicle of Philanthropy's* Web site offers a summary of the contents of the current issue of their newspaper, which is published every other week. The site includes a list of forthcoming conferences and workshops, job opportunities in the nonprofit world, and other information. The news summary is updated on the Monday preceding the print edition's issue date. The job announcements are updated on the Monday following the issue date.

Like its biweekly print analog, *The Chronicle of Philanthropy's* Web site is full of useful information for fund raisers, grant makers, nonprofit managers, and others. The site is organized into broad topic areas—gifts and grants, fund raising, managing nonprofit groups, and technology—and offers, among other items, a summary of the contents of the Chronicle's current and previous issues, a listing of award and RFP deadlines, job opportunities in the nonprofit sector, a listing of forthcoming conferences and workshops, and annotated links to other nonprofit resources on the Internet. Visitors can also sign up for free e-mail updates about changes at the site as well as breaking news stories. *http://www.philanthropy.com/*

Contributions Magazine

▶ The "how-to" source for nonprofit professionals. Also available in print. *http://www.contributionsmagazine.com*

Crain's Nonprofit News

▶ Includes a copy of the latest newsletter. *http://www.crainsdetroit.com/nonprof.html*

Food for Thought—CompassPoint

▶ The San Francisco Bay Area's source of news for nonprofit organizations. If you would like to have *Food for Thought* delivered via electronic mail, send an e-mail message to majordomo@igc.org and in the body of the message type subscribe Food-for-Thought. *Food for Thought* will be delivered to you every three weeks via e-mail or fax. *http://www.compasspoint.org*

Leader to Leader

▶ Sponsored by the Peter F. Drucker Foundation for Nonprofit Management, *Leader to Leader* is published jointly by the Drucker Foundation and Jossey-Bass. It offers current thinking on leadership, management, and strategy written by today's top thought leaders from the private, public, and social sectors. This site provides select articles from current and past issues. *http://www.jbp.com/JBJournals/ltl.html*

Nonprofit Management and Leadership *(Select Articles)*

▶ This is the first journal to bring together the best thinking and most advanced knowledge about the special needs, challenges, and oportunities of nonprofit organizations. Each issue of NML offers readers the authoritative insights of top executives and scholars on the common concerns of nonprofit leaders in all settings, including social services, the arts, education, foundations, community development, advocacy work, religion, professional associations, and others. It is co-sponsored by the Mandel Center for Nonprofit Organizations at Case Western Reserve University and the Centre for Voluntary Organisation at the London School of Economics. *http://www.josseybass.com/JBJournals/nml.html*

Non-Profit Nuts and Bolts: Practical Tips for Building Better Non-Profits

▶ A companion site to the monthly newsletter *Non-Profit Nuts and Bolts,* it includes back issues and articles, links to nonprofit resources, and a directory of free publications on nonprofit management issues. *http://www.nutsbolts.com*

Nonprofit Online News

▶ This is a site by the Gilbert Center devoted to news and commentary relating to the nonprofit online community, with a particular emphasis on issues related to organizational renewal, outreach, and Internet strategies in use by nonprofits. News announcements or comments can be sent to *news@gilbert.org. http://www.gilbert.org/news/*

The NonProfit Times: The Leading Publication for Nonprofit Management

▶ A monthly trade journal by the Davis Information Group, Inc., focusing on current events and issues affecting the nonprofit industry. The online version offers selected articles from current and back issues, a directory of service providers and consultants in the nonprofit area, and links to other nonprofit sites on the Web. *http://www.nptimes.com/*

NonprofitXpress Nonprofit News

▶ This online daily newspaper publishes state, national, and international news on fund raising, giving, managing, volunteering, innovation, and technology in the philanthropic community. The Web newspaper, a publication of the A.J. Fletcher Foundation in Raleigh, North Carolina, also features editorials, opinion columns, letters, job opportunities and electronic links to nonprofit resources. Readers can submit and post announcements about people, organizations, grants, gifts, events, and fund-raising results. *Nonprofitxpress* also publishes a free weekly e-mail newsletter and will conduct and publish electronic surveys on critical issues facing nonprofits. The site offers a free headline service for organizations that want to publish nonprofit news on their Web sites. The online newspaper is edited by Todd Cohen, who founded and edited the Philanthropy News Network and the *Philanthropy Journal of North Carolina. Nonprofitxpress* aims to expand to other states the kind of local coverage it provides in its home state of North Carolina. For more information, visit the Web site or contact Krista Bremer, online reporter, at 919/890-6243 or by e-mail at kbremer@ajf.org. *http://www.npxpress.com/*

PULSE!

▶ *PULSE!* is a free newsletter from the Alliance for Nonprofit Management. Subscribe by sending e-mail to *alliance@allianceonline.org* and typing in the body of the message "subscribe pulse." *PULSE!* can be also found online at *http://www.allianceonline.org.*

TMC E-Notes: News and Information about Management Center Events and Programs

▶ To subscribe to E-Notes, send an empty e-mail to *tmcenter-subscribe@egroups.com*. You may unsubscribe to *E-Notes* at any time by sending an empty e-mail to *tmcenter-unsubscribe@egroups.com*. For additional questions about this list, e-mail *tmcenter-owner@egroups.com*. All the information included in *E-Notes* and more can be found on The Management Center's Web site at *http://www.tmcenter.org.*

PART IV

Governance Support and Advocacy

ORGANIZATIONS

(See also Accountability and Ethics; General Management; Leadership; Legal Issues; Strategic Planning; Resource Development)

Alliance for Nonprofit Governance (ANG)

c/o ANG Task Force, New York Junior League,
130 East 80th Street, New York, NY 10028
Tel: 212-831-0272; FAX: 520-447-2455
E-mail: carolynlp.ang@HotOffice.net (Carolyn L. Patterson, Chair)

▶ The Alliance for Nonprofit Governance (ANG) is a coalition of nonprofit technical assistance providers, nonprofit umbrella organizations, funders, public regulators, and academics that share an interest in promoting good governance for nonprofit organizations. They believe that volunteer boards, composed of concerned citizens, can and often do provide diligent and informed oversight to nonprofit organizations. They also realize that this model is an ideal that is not always reflected in common practice. They have formed this group because they believe that, collectively, they can address these barriers to successful governance in New York. With the goal of raising the standards of nonprofit governance in New York nonprofit organizations, members of the Alliance for Nonprofit Governance are committed to working collaboratively to clearly define what constitutes excellence in approaches to governance, raise awareness of the need for effective governance, educate people about governance, and advocate for effective governance with those who influence nonprofits.

American Institute for Managing Diversity, Inc.

(See Human Resource Management—Support and Advocacy Organizations for full description)

Association of Governing Boards of Universities and Colleges (AGB)

One Dupont Circle, Suite 400, Washington, DC 20036
Tel: 800-356-6317, 202-296-8400; FAX: 202-223-7053
WWW: http://www.agb.org/

▶ AGB is the only national organization providing university and college presidents, board chairs, and individual trustees of both public and private institutions with the resources they need to enhance their effectiveness. Its mission is to advance the practice of citizen trusteeship and help ensure the quality and success of our nation's colleges and universities. To accomplish its mission, AGB has developed programs and services that strengthen the partnership between president and governing board; define the responsibilities of governing board members; provide guidance to regents and trustees, inspiring a level of professionalism for a voluntary function; provide guidance to regents and trustees, inspiring a level of professionalism for a voluntary function; identify issues that affect tomorrow's decision making; and foster cooperation among all stakeholders in higher education. AGB serves as a continuing education resource to trustees, regents, presidents, chancellors, and senior-level academic administrators in addition to foundations affiliated with public colleges and universities, professional schools, seminaries and theological schools, other higher-education–related governing and state coordinating boards, and independent K–12 school boards. Services include publications (publishes many publications, all listed in the annual *Trustee Resource Guide;* the three-times yearly newsletter *Priorities* for AGB members; and the bimonthly magazine *Trusteeship* (see separate listing under Periodicals); programs and services (conducts programs in many cities on diverse topics, and provides consulting services to help institutions examine and improve their performance; offers on-campus workshops and presentations on issues of greatest interest to board members and chief executives, including board education services, board–mentor workshop, fund-raising workshops, presidential search workshop, board and presidential assessment service, academic restructuring roundtable; conferences and seminars include Institute for Trustee Leadership, annual National Conference on Trusteeship, held every spring, National Luncheon Series); The J.L. Zwingle Resource Center for Academic Trusteeship and Governance (a repository for the best research and scholarship on trusteeship, governance, and the academic presidency; to learn more about the Zwingle Research Center, visit *http://www.agb.org/zrc2.cfm).*

Board Bank/Metro Volunteers

225 East 16th Avenue, Suite 200, Denver, CO 80203
Tel: 303-894-0103, 303-832-4483
E-mail: joyc@metrovolunteers.org (Joy Criminger, Director of Corporate Programs); WWW: http://www.metrovolunteers.org/np_training/bmember/index.htm

▶ Their Board Bank Program connects individuals interested in serving as board members with Denver area boards that have completed agency registration forms. The steps are as follows: (1) Register with the Board Bank; (2) attend an "Introduction to Board Membership" training session; (3) meet with Board Bank Coordinator to discuss your skills and interests; and (4) meet with board members of agencies that match your interests. Metro Volunteers offers seminars on topics of interest to board members throughout the year.

Board/Committee Placement Program

Volunteer Center of Greater Milwaukee,
225 East Michigan Street, Suite 5, Milwaukee, WI 53209
Tel: 414-273-7887 (HELP); FAX: 414-273-0637
E-mail: info@volunteermilwaukee.com (Becky Turner, Executive Director), opportunities@volunteermilwaukee.org;
WWW: http://www.volunteermilwaukee.org

▶ The Board/Committee Placement Program maintains a file of agencies actively seeking board members. They also help board candidates review their individual interests. Introductions are made to boards according to candidate preference. When there is a direct match between an interest and a need, an introductory meeting is arranged. The Program sponsors the Community Board Institute, an annual event covering a broad range of board issues including nonprofit finance, board development, fund raising, and meeting management co-sponsors, which include Marquette University, Future Milwaukee, Jewish Family Services, Junior League of Milwaukee, the Nonprofit Center of Milwaukee, and the Wisconsin Institute of Certified Accountants.

Board Connection

Volunteer Center Orange County, 1901 East Fourth Street, Suite 100, Santa Ana, CA 92705
Tel: 714-953-5757, ext. 115; FAX: 714-834-0585
E-mail: volunteering@volunteercenter.org, ddalton@volunteercenter.org (Debbie Dalton); WWW: http://www.volunteercenter.org/board

▶ Board Connection matches local area leaders with nonprofit organizations. It also provides Board Connection coaches, volunteers that oversee and participate in connecting potential board candidates and participating nonprofit agencies.

Board Match Plus

1675 California Street, San Francisco, CA 94118
Tel: 415-982-8999, ext. 229; FAX: 415-982-0890
E-mail: bmp@vcsf.org, info@boardclassifieds.org, syuen@vcsf.org (Sandy Yuen, Director);
WWW: http://boardmatchplus.org, http://www.compasspoint.org/consulting/board_match_plus/board +.html

▶ A collaboration of the CompassPoint and the Volunteer Center of San Francisco, it is a program designed to help introduce qualified candidates to nonprofit boards of directors, as well as support those individuals already on boards. Board Match Plus Switchboard is a service that introduces qualified candidates to a selected group of San Francisco–based nonprofits seeking new board members. Board candidates bring a wide array of professional backgrounds (finance, law, marketing, human resources, etc.) and are trained in basic board roles and responsibilities. Over 40 percent of the individuals participating in Switchboard to date are people of color. Each year, Board Match Plus publishes two Switchboard registries containing the information on participating candidates and distributes each to a pool of about 20 nonprofits. Nonprofits are targeted based on their readiness to take part in this type of recruitment process.

The Board Network

P.O. Box 15200, Portland, ME 04112-5200, 400 Congress Street, 4th Floor, P.O. Box 15200, Portland, ME 04112-5200
Tel: 207-874-1000, ext. 329; FAX: 207-874-1007
E-mail: vrc2@unitedwaygp.org (J. Bart Morrison, Executive Director), tjhopps@mindspring.com (Tory Dietel Hopps, Director); WWW: http://www.unitedwaygp.org

▶ The Board Network is a community-wide initiative connecting talented, civic-minded citizens to nonprofit organizations in need of qualified board members. The Board Network also provides training and support to nonprofit boards to enhance efficiency and effective use of board talent and time, ultimately having a positive impact on each organization's ability to develop a competitive and forward vision, garner financial resources, lead the organization through change, and ensure sufficient staffing (paid and volunteer) to accomplish organizational goals.

Board Placement Initiative

Future Milwaukee , 759 North Milwaukee Street, Suite 622, Milwaukee, WI 53202
Tel: 414-276-1540; FAX: 414-276-4760
E-mail: ajohnson@futuremilwaukee.org (Anita Johnson, Program Coordinator), robm@futuremilwaukee.org (Robert A. Meiksins, Executive Director); WWW: http://futuremilwaukee.org/ Bridges.html, http://futuremilwaukee.org/leadership.html

▶ The Board Placement Initiative facilitates Future Milwaukee graduates into leadership-level positions where they can be effective in serving the community. Thus, a prerequisite for its assistance to board candidates is involvement in the core Leadership Development Program (an intensive, nine-month program developing the skills and community awareness of up to 60 participants per year as they prepare themselves for leadership positions. Components of the curriculum include building understanding of community issues; exposure to boardmanship roles, responsibilities, and skills; development of personal leadership skills; and involvement in a community project). The Mentorship Program offers support and access to an active network to recent leadership graduates. The Executive Orientation Program, called Get to Know Milwaukee, is offered in collaboration with the local chamber of commerce to management-level executives new to the community. The eight-session series introduces decision makers in the community as well as an in-depth understanding of some of the issues critical to the community, offering a window to opportunities to serve the community the participants have newly adopted.

BOARDLINK
FIRSTLINK

370 S. Fifth Street, Columbus, OH 43215
Tel: 614-221-6766; FAX: 614-224-6866
E-mail: info@firstlink.org;
WWW: http://www.firstlink.org/Volunteerism/BoardLink/

▶ BOARDLINK, a program of FIRSTLINK for information, resources, services, and training, links volunteers interested in serving on a nonprofit board to nonprofit organizations seeking board members. Through BOARDLINK, volunteers are able to communicate their areas of interest and expertise to over 600 nonprofit organizations in Franklin County.

BOARDLINK

Nonprofit Resource Center, 828 I Street, Sacramento, CA 95814
Tel: 916-264-2719; FAX: 916-264-2787
E-mail: angie@boardlink.net, chowland@sacramento.lib.ca.us, Kathryn C. Hannah (hannahkc@aol.com);
WWW: http://www.sacramento.org/nprc/index.html, http://www.boardlink.net/

▶ BOARDLINK is a program of the Nonprofit Resource Center that matches interested people with the boards of nonprofit organizations in the Greater Sacramento area. The project's ultimate aim is to raise the standard of leadership and service in the nonprofit community. Its purpose is to strengthen the effectiveness of Sacramento area nonprofit boards to lead and to govern. Board candidates and nonprofit organizations that have participated in BOARDLINK may borrow from the BOARDLINK library. The library includes books, videos, audiocassettes, and other materials that focus on issues of concern to board members. In addition, the Nonprofit Resource Center offers year-round workshops, technical assistance, and training on all aspects of nonprofit leadership and management (e.g., fund raising, marketing, fiscal management, volunteerism, board roles and responsibilities, etc).

BoardNet

Volunteer Center of San Mateo County, 800 South Claremont, Suite 108, San Mateo, CA 94402
Tel: 650-348-4314; FAX: 650-348-4313
E-mail: info@vcsmco.org, arobinson@vcsmco.org (Andrew Robinson), mlukin@vcsmco.org (Melissa Lukin); WWW: http://www.vcsmco.org/boardnet.shtml

▶ BoardNet brings to San Mateo County the best practices, latest techniques, and newest research on building and maintaining boards for our rapidly changing world. Services include facilitation, consulting, and training, along with matching individuals with boards.

BoardsWork!/On-Board Leadership Series

The Center for Nonprofit Resources, 3801 Canal Street, New Orleans, LA 70119
Tel: 504-483-8080, ext. 222 or 223 (Lisa Amos, Director of Consulting Services, or Pamela Frank, Director of Training Programs); FAX: 504-483-8087
E-mail: roers@usa.net (Monica Roers, President and CEO); WWW: http://www.geocities.com/center_nonprofit/board development.html

▶ BoardsWork! is a board training and development program for individuals who aspire to be board members of nonprofit organizations. Participants attend a series of six evening workshops on the following topics: board roles and responsibilities, committee structure, financial management, fund raising, strategic planning, and diversity. Upon completion of the training, participants are placed on the board of local nonprofit organizations for a one-year internship. The training takes place in the fall, and annually trains and places about 50 new board members. The Center for Nonprofit Resources offers consultation services in the area of board development to nonprofit organizations throughout the Metropolitan New Orleans area. The Center's consultants facilitate full- and half-day board retreats, conduct orientations for new board members and help strengthen the nominating process, committee structure, and functioning of a nonprofit board of directors. The Center for Nonprofit Resources maintains a collection of books, articles, pamphlets, and videotapes on board development (and on a variety of other nonprofit management topics).

Business Volunteers Unlimited (EVU)

Tower City Center, Suite 950, 50 Public Square, Cleveland, OH 44113-2204
Tel: 216-736-7711
E-mail: AKent@busvol.org (Ann C. Kent, Director, Services to Nonprofits); WWW: http://www.businessvolunteers.org

▶ Board development services include training and placement of business executives on boards, educating trustees, and consults to board. BVU was founded by corporate leaders in Cleveland who saw the need for a vehicle to help companies get involved in the community beyond contributing money. Initially, BVU focused on helping nonprofit boards find and train new members. Soon, nonprofits asked BVU to provide training for all of their board members, followed by requests for ongoing consulting. Nonprofits pay a $100 to $1,000 annual membership fee, based on their budget, to become BVU members and gain access to training and consulting. Access to trained board candidates and corporate professionals who want to volunteer their expertise is free.

BVU has been particularly successful in expanding the racial, ethnic, and gender diversity of Cleveland's nonprofit boards. BVU encourages corporations to nominate women and minorities as board candidates and actively seeks relationships with minority business leaders who help BVU identify and reach out to potential candidates in minority communities. BVU maintains an e-mail Nonprofit Forum for Chief Executives.

Center for Management Assistance *(See Management—Support and Advocacy Organizations for full description)*

The Center for Non-Profit Corporations *(See Legal Issues—Support and Advocacy Organizations for full description)*

Center for Nonprofit Excellence *(See Management—Support and Advocacy Organizations for full description)*

Center for Nonprofit Management

2900 Live Oak, Dallas, TX 75204
Tel: 214-826-3470; FAX: 214-821-3845
E-mail: trammell@cnmdallas.org (Adrienne Cox-Trammell); Website:http://www.cnmdallas.org/pages/gob_events.html, http://www.cnmdallas.org/pages/events.html

▶ Each year the Center sponsors a Board Fair for individuals interested in serving on a nonprofit board, as well as for boards wishing to add to their governing group. This event brings over 70 nonprofit organizations to one convenient location, where individuals wanting to serve on a nonprofit board of directors discover how their time and talent can benefit the community they call home. Organizations representing a variety of missions, from social services to health care and housing, find the Fair to be a great way to meet qualified individuals representing a diverse segment of the community. Additional programs include board training, board leader's breakfast series, *Executive Director Performance Review Handbook;* and human resources policies for nonprofit organizations (suggestions and sample policies).

Center for Nonprofit Management In Southern California *(See General Management—Support and Advocacy Organizations for full description)*

Community Resource Center *(See General Management—Support and Advocacy Organizations for full description)*

The Forbes Fund

One PPG Place, Pittsburgh, PA 15222-5401
Tel: 412-394-2634; FAX: 412-394-2641
E-mail: kubelickc@pghfdn.org (Cheryl Kubelick, Interim Advisor)

▶ The Forbes Fund gives technical assistance grants to improve the management capacity of the Pittsburgh area nonprofit community. Individuals wishing to serve on boards should complete *boardnetusa's* Board Profile (see Volunteer Consulting Group Web site) and send that to United Way's Volunteer Service Board Bank. Nonprofit Leadership Institute is a governance enhancement program, specifically for nonprofit board members, offered by Duquesne University's Division of Continuing Education. Call Constance Mokenhaupt at 412-396-6231.

Grant and Resource Center of Northern California

(See Resource Development—Support and Advocacy
Organizations for full description)

Leadership Albuquerque

Greater Albuquerque Chamber of Commerce, P.O. Box 25100,
Albuquerque, NM 87125
Tel: 505-764-3733; FAX: 505-764-3714
E-mail: jhoneycutt@gacc.org (Janice Honeycutt),
lhschlu@sandia.gov (Lynne Schluter), svarela@gacc.org;
WWW: http://www.gacc.org

▶ Leadership Albuquerque is active in connecting its alumni with local nonprofit boards of directors seeking new members. After an initial two-day retreat each September, Leadership participants spend one day together each month in the Albuquerque area to review issues and learn skills important for community leadership. For Albuquerque boards interested in the involvement of young leaders, this program selects high school juniors each year and prepares them for responsible participation in community affairs. Graduates of the program are available for board service following their junior year. It offers a Board Governance Training Program (a one-day program for current, new, and potential board members to explore best practices of board governance; national and local speakers present examples of model board member behavior).

Leadership Green Bay (LGB)

400 Washington Street, PO Box 1660, Green Bay, WI 54305-1660
Tel: 920-437-8704; FAX: 920-437-1024
E-mail: lgb@titletown.org (Jeanne Agneessens, Program
Manager); WWW: http://www.titletown.org/LGB/index.htm

▶ Leadership Green Bay is an initiative of the Green Bay Area Chamber of Commerce, whose mission is to develop, strengthen, and challenge the community's leadership. Each Leadership Green Bay class year begins with a two-day retreat in September. October through May, participants meet one day each month. The monthly sessions focus on the area's economy, education, local history and heritage, diversity and cultural awareness, human services, government, and environment. In addition to the scheduled sessions, LGB participants work in small groups on projects designed to help the community. The small groups meet during their own time. Upon completion of the year's activities, educational opportunities, including board training, bring members together regularly.

Leadership OnBoard

Leadership Pittsburgh, 425 Sixth Avenue,
Pittsburgh, PA 15219-1811
Tel: 412-392-4505; FAX: 412-392-4520
E-mail: info@lpinc.org, info@leadershippittsburgh.org
(Beth Wainwright, Executive Director);
WWW: http://www.lpinc.org/lobinfo.htm

▶ The OnBoard program places Leadership Development Initiative (LDI) graduates—ages 22 to 34—onto nonprofit governing boards. Thus, a prerequisite is attending LDI. The OnBoard program is a one-year internship—attending board meetings and joining one board committee. OnBoard members are not required to contribute financially nor do they carry voting privileges. Many OnBoard participants are invited to become full board members at the end of the year. Leadership Development Initiative (LDI): thirty young adults, ages 22 to 34, are selected through a competitive application process to participate in the 11-month program. Participants have a proven interest in future community leadership and represent a diverse cross-section of backgrounds and organizational affiliations. They meet two Thursday evenings a month to develop their leadership capacities and to gain knowledge of our region. Participants are matched with Leadership Pittsburgh graduates who serve as mentors and community resources during the year. Teams of participants also implement projects to meet various needs in the community.

MAP for Nonprofits *(See General Management—Support and Advocacy Organizations for full description)*

Management Assistance Group *(See General Management—Support and Advocacy Organizations for full description)*

The Management Center

870 Market Street, Suite 360, San Francisco, CA 94102-3009
Tel: 415-399-2651; FAX: 415-362-4603
E-mail: tmc@tmcenter.org; WWW:
http://www.tmcenter.org/programs/bf.html

▶ The Center offers the annual San Francisco and Contra Costa Board Fairs. With a focus on local communities, their recruitment efforts now also cover the entire Bay Area. They have made diversifying the cultural, ethnic, and economic backgrounds of candidates a top priority. They provide orientation sessions at the Board Fair to better prepare candidates to meet you. Check their advance calendar regularly for other upcoming dates.

Management Resources Center—United Way of Central Maryland *(See General Management—Support and Advocacy Organizations for full description)*

National Center for Nonprofit Boards

1828 L Street NW, Suite 900, Washington, DC 20036-5104
Tel: 800-883-6262, 202-452-6262; FAX: 202-452-6299
E-mail: ncnb@ncnb.org; WWW: http://www.ncnb.org

▶ NCNB was established in 1988 by the Association of Governing Boards of Universities and Colleges (AGB) and Independent Sector to improve the effectiveness of the more than one million nonprofit organizations throughout the United States by strengthening their boards of directors. Through its programs and services, NCNB provides solutions and tools to improve board performance, acts as convener and facilitator in the development of knowledge about boards, promotes change and innovation to strengthen governance, and serves as an advocate for the value of board service and the importance of effective governance.

Primary programs/services offered include consulting services (provides customized governance consulting for nonprofit boards and the staff that work with those boards; topics of the board programs vary greatly depending on the specific needs of your organization. Some of the most common topics are assessment of governing board's and chief executives' performance; functions, roles, and responsibilities of the board and of individual board members; criteria for attracting, selecting, and retaining qualified people to serve on the board; building a partnership between the board and the chief executive; learning to govern more and manage less; preparing for changes in board structure and in the organization's structure and operations; engaging the board in strategic planning, fund raising, and fiscal and program oversight; associates consist of facilitators, presenters, and consultants who have been trained through NCNB's Professional Development Program); retreats (NCNB can develop an agenda and provide a trained expert to facilitate a day-long or multiday session during which your board members reflect upon a particular topic, such as strategic planning or organizational mission. Retreats offer a chance for board members to discuss and work through leadership issues thoroughly and with candor); Board Self-Assessment Services (working from a special assessment tool that NCNB designed, tested, and revised based on work with hundreds of boards, your board members undertake a self-study that helps to reveal both strengths and weaknesses of the board as a whole); workshops and conference speakers (workshop agendas can be designed for the board and executive staff of a cross-section of organizations that are meeting for a regional gathering or at a national conference. These programs focus on specific governance issues and use an array of techniques, including presentations, case studies, and small- and full-group discussions); National Leadership Forum (each year the National Leadership Forum brings together more than 650 nonprofit leaders from around the world to learn, network, and share ideas on how boards can contribute to a nonprofit organization's success); The Governance Consulting Professional Development Program (designed specifically for experienced consultants, nonprofit practitioners, and management assistance providers; drawing on the resources and curricula that NCNB has developed through its board development programs, NCNB's Governance Consulting Professional Development Program provides an effective orientation to board development practices and resources for trainers and consultants); publications (as the world's largest publisher of materials on nonprofit governance, NCNB offers more than 100 publications covering key issues related to the work of nonprofit boards; offers special bundled selections of their publications including: *Building Better Boards* (*Six Keys to Recruiting, Orienting, and Involving Nonprofit Board Members*), *Meeting the Challenge: An Orientation to Nonprofit Board Service* (video), *The Nonprofit Board's Guide to Bylaws, Building Boards That Work* (video), *How to Build a More Effective Board, The Board Member's Fund-Raising Essentials* (*Speaking of Money*) (video), *Fearless Fund-Raising for Nonprofit Boards, Fund-Raising and the Nonprofit Board, Planned Giving: A Board Member's Perspective, The Development Committee*) and *Complete Financial Resources Kit* (*Creating and Using Investment Policies, The Audit Committee, The Finance Committee, Merging Mission and Money, Financial*

Responsibilities of the Nonprofit Board, Understanding Nonprofit Financial Statements). Also, subject packages including: *Governance Series, Board Development, Financial Oversight, Fund Raising, Board Basics, Board Effectiveness, Legal Issues, Strategic Planning, Organizational Development, Board Committees*. Descriptions of their publications and ordering information can be found on their Web site at: *http://www.ncnb.org/bookstore/index.htm*); information and referral (NCNB runs a Board Information Center, which provides guidance and referral services to persons and organizations who call with specific questions and concerns; the Board Information Center is a free information clearinghouse on board-related topics, providing information to hundreds of nonprofit leaders, educators, consultants, and journalists. Simply e-mail them with your question and the Board Information Center staff will respond promptly. To speak with the center directly, call 800-883-6262 or 202-452-6262. Also, check out AskNCNB online at: *http://www.ncnb.org/askncnb/index.htm*. There you will find links to Frequently Asked Questions at *http://www.ncnb.org/askncnb/faq.htm*, as well as Question of the Week Archive at *http://www.ncnb.org/askncnb/archive.htm*); *Board Café* (NCNB and CompassPoint Nonprofit Services serve as co-publishers of this free electronic newsletter for board members of nonprofit organizations).

National Center for Strategic Nonprofit Planning and Community Leadership

1133 20th Street NW, Suite 210, Washington, DC 20036
Tel: 888-528-NPCL or 6725; FAX: 202-822-5699
E-mail: info@npcl.org; WWW: http://www.npcl.org

▶ The National Center for Strategic Nonprofit Planning and Community Leadership (NPCL) is a nonprofit organization created for charitable and educational purposes. The mission of NPCL is to improve the governance and administration of nonprofit, tax-exempt organizations

New York Junior League Nonprofit Boards Clearinghouse

130 East 80th Street, New York, NY 10021-0306
Tel: 212-288-6220, ext. 276; FAX: 212-734-9364
E-mail: info@nyjl.org (Lois Kauffman, Administrative Director)

▶ The Clearinghouse seeks to increase the effectiveness of the New York City nonprofit sector by training qualified women and placing them on the governing bodies of nonprofit agencies. The only program of its kind available in New York City, the Clearinghouse has placed more than 100 qualified women on boards and committees of nonprofit agencies throughout New York City. The program is not limited to NYJL volunteers and is open to any woman who has demonstrated an interest in community volunteer service and the nonprofit sector.

Nonprofit Board Builders Program

Nonprofit Resource Center, 50 Hurt Plaza, Suite 220,
Atlanta, GA 30303
Tel: 404-688-4845; FAX: 404-521-0487
E-mail: psugarman@nonprofitgeorgia.org (Pam Sugarman, Director, Management & Government Services),
nonprofitga@mindspring.com;
WWW: http://www.nonprofitgeorgia.org,
http://www.nonprofitgeorgia.org/mangov.html

▶ The Nonprofit Board Builders Program is an initiative of the Nonprofit Resource Center. Board Builders offers consulting, matching, and training services to address the needs of three target audiences. Those audiences and related services include *Corporations and professional groups:* Consultation on strategies for community involvement, information on available board positions, training for key staff/members in the governance of nonprofits and introduction of key staff/members to nonprofit boards. *Individuals:* Consultation on how to choose the right board, identification of boards requiring one's expertise, training in principles of governance and trusteeship, opportunity to expand personal and professional networks. *Nonprofit organizations:* Consultation on board development, training in effective board governance, profiles of pre-qualified candidates, facilitated introduction to candidates and follow-up evaluation of the match after three and six months. Candidates and nonprofits pay a fee based on their affiliation and budget size, respectively. *Board/Staff Helpline:* The Center connects nonprofit staff and board members with information, resources, and referrals. Georgia nonprofits call 800-959-5015. In Atlanta, call 404-688-4845, ext. 3104.

Nonprofit Leadership Institute (NLI)

Duquesne University, Division of Continuing Education,
210 Rockwell Hall, 600 Forbes Avenue, Pittsburgh, PA 15282
Tel: 800-283-3853, 412-396-6231; FAX: 412-396-4712
E-mail: nli@duq.edu, kumer@duq.edu (Michael Kumer,
Executive Director)

▶ Duquesne University's Nonprofit Leadership Institute (NLI) is western Pennsylvania's resource center for nonprofit boards. Founded in 1996, the NLI provides training, information resources, and consulting for current and prospective trustees in order to enhance the quality of nonprofit governance. The NLI offers a wide variety of programs, including Leadership Academy (a comprehensive skill enrichment seminar) and Advanced Leadership Academy (The 21st Century Nonprofit; breakfast sessions; special collaborative projects; customized board training and consulting services; focus forums). Areas of NLI expertise include mission and vision, strategic planning, image and identity, marketing and public relations, fund raising, board structure and development, program evaluation, and legal issues. The NLI also disseminates information about best practices of peak-performing boards. To date, more than 1,000 persons have attended NLI academies, breakfast sessions, and other programs. Nonprofit organizations served by the NLI include agencies in education, social services, arts and culture, health, economic development, and foundation sectors.

Nonprofit Resource Institute (Formerly Board Connection)

Leadership Palm Beach County, 324 Datura Street, Suite 303,
West Palm Beach, FL 33401
Tel: 561-802-6280, 748-8182; FAX: 561-802-6282
E-mail: boardcon@bellsouth.net (Rosalind Murray),
leadershippbc@hotmail.com,
http://www.gopbi.com/community/groups/leadershippbc/,
http://www.nonprofitinstitute.org

▶ Board Connection, a project of Leadership PBC, has formally merged with The Center for Nonprofit Know-How. The new organization is now known as The Nonprofit Resource Institute (NRI). Its new mission statement is "NRI is the comprehensive resource for improving the management and governance of nonprofit organ-

izations in Palm Beach and Martin counties." NRI is the only organization in the state of Florida that provides both board connection services and individual one-on-one organizational technical assistance. Additional service areas include consultant referral and workshop training programs.

The mission of NRI is to achieve and sustain effective and diverse leadership for Palm Beach County nonprofit boards. Leadership is most effective when it is drawn from the broad and diverse cultures and communities that make up the greater whole it is seeking to serve. We recruit, train, and place people on nonprofit boards to expand diversity and leadership in our community. The program is open to all individuals who are committed to community service and community betterment and has as its goals: to introduce participants to nonprofit governing board service, to clarify governing board roles and responsibilities, and to provide tools and strategies for being an effective board member. At different times of the year, NRI offers an eight-hour course (in two sections) on board governance. Issues covered include officer and committee structures and roles and responsibilities of board members, including finance, strategic planning, legal, and fund raising.

Nonprofit Risk Management Center *(See Financial Management—Support and Advocacy Organizations for full description)*

Pacific Non-Profit Network *(See General Management—Support and Advocacy Organizations for full description)*

The Peter F. Drucker Foundation for Nonprofit Management *(See General Management—Support and Advocacy Organizations for full description)*

San Diego Board Connection

c/o Nonprofit Management Solutions (formerly Support
Center/Executive Service Corps), 8265 Vickers Street, Suite C,
San Diego, CA 92111
Tel: 858-292-5702; FAX: 858-292-9943
E-mail: audreytan@npsolutions.org, npsolutions@npsolutions.org;
WWW: http://www.npsolutions.org/onsite/board_connection.htm

▶ A collaboration between Nonprofit Management Solutions and The Volunteer Center of United Way of San Diego County, San Diego Board Connection is designed to recruit qualified individuals interested in nonprofit board service and link them with nonprofit organizations in need of new board members. The program offers aggressive recruitment and training of qualified and diverse individuals, follow-up to promote successful matches, ongoing board development opportunities for individuals and organizations.

Society for Nonprofit Organizations *(See General Management—Support and Advocacy Organizations for full description)*

Trustee Leadership Development

719 Indiana Avenue, Suite 370, Indianapolis, IN 46202
Tel: 877-564-6853, 317-636-5323; FAX: 317-636-0266
E-mail: info@tld.org; WWW: http://www.tld.org

▶ The mission of Trustee Leadership Development, Inc., is the education and development of transformational leaders with the capacity to hold individuals, organizations, and communities in trust. Programs and services provided include annual leadership education workshops, institutes, and forums; organizational consultation, assessment, and development; board leadership development; executive coaching and mentoring; customized, skill-based workshops; training of professional educators to work with the not-for-profit sector; consultation and training; change management; design and development of leadership programs; and development and dissemination of research-based, practitioner-oriented educational resources. A detailed listing of its resources is available online at *http://www.tld.org/resources.htm*, or request a copy of its print catalog. It publishes *Leading Ideas Newsletter* (see separate listing under Periodicals).

UJA-Jewish Federation of New York Philanthropies

Volunteer & Leadership Development Division, Agency Board Referral Service, 130 East 59th Street, New York, NY 10002
Tel: 212-836-1447; FAX: 212-836-1524
E-mail: fleishmanl@ujafedny.org (Laura Fleishman, Assistant Director, Recruitment & Placement)
▶ The boards of directors of UJA-Federation agencies need a "braintrust" of management talent—in finance, strategic planning, real estate, human resources, marketing and more—to face today's challenges. The Agency Board Referral Service helps (1) network agencies find needed board members and (2) individuals interested in board service to find placement on a board that needs their expertise. Placement of qualified candidates is by mutual agreement of all parties. Its Observership Program provides an opportunity to individuals between the ages of 28 and 35 to participate on an agency board of directors as a nonvoting observer. This program includes training components and is designed to prepare young Jewish professionals for future leadership positions. UJA-Jewish Federation of New York also offers board consulting and board training to its network agencies.

Volunteer Center of the Pike's Peak Region

Chamber Nonprofit Partnership, 2 North Cascade Avenue,
Suite 110, Colorado Springs, CO 80903
Tel: 719-575-4342; FAX: 719-635-1571
E-mail: brendac@cscc.org (Brenda Clifton, Director),
ppvc@cscc.org, csnc@cscc.org, susan@cscc.org (Susan Saksa);
WWW: http://www.coloradospringschamber.org/perl/chamber/build
▶ The Chamber Nonprofit Partnership has three main programs: The Colorado Springs Nonprofit Center (their membership and education program), The Volunteer Center of the Pike's Peak Region (volunteer opportunities, clearinghouse, etc.), Leadership Initiatives (runs Colorado Springs Leadership Institute in collaboration with the Center for Creative Leadership). The Volunteer Center serves as a clearinghouse to enhance corporate volunteer participation for community projects. The Center is currently planning to develop a program to help boards and potential board members find each other, with a special emphasis on placing graduates of the Colorado Springs Leadership Institute. The Nonprofit Leadership Conference, an annual spring conference, is one of the premier nonprofit management conferences in the United States, focusing on providing the latest knowledge board members need to lead their organizations into the next century. Its Nonprofit Resource Library includes publications on board governance. The

Center and the Colorado Springs Chamber of Commerce Government Affairs Division jointly sponsor educational offerings including board-level seminars.

Volunteer Consulting Group, Inc. (VCG)

6 East 39th Street, 6th Floor, New York, NY 10016
Tel: 212-447-1236; FAX: 212-447-0925
E-mail: boardinfo@vcg.org, bmahoney@vcg.org, http://www.vcg.org/,
http://www.vcg.org/boardnetusa/programs_individuals_corporatio
ns.htm, http://www.vcg.org/boardnetusa/net.asp,
http://www.vcg.org/boardnetusa/net_postings.asp#74
▶ The Volunteer Consulting Group (VCG) was founded in 1969 by the Harvard Business School Club of New York. It is a nonprofit organization that works nationally and regionally to strengthen the governing and management capability of nonprofit boards of directors. Fundamental to the organization's mission is bringing outstanding leadership into service as board members of health, human service, educational, cultural, advocacy, and community development nonprofit organizations. VCG assists nonprofit boards in defining recruiting objectives, and then conducts a targeted search for business, professional, and community leaders with the desired expertise, diversity of perspective, and resources and helps people who wish to serve as board members to explore their interests, review nonprofit board opportunities, and be introduced to chosen boards. VCG's Boardmember's FORUM is a membership organization for men and women who serve on nonprofit boards. The FORUM provides a way for trustees to learn from each other, share ideas, explore issues, and compare experiences. Primary services include board consulting (strengthening and clarifying the board/staff partnership, developing methods to assist the board to work as a team effectively and efficiently, planning and implementing leadership succession strategies for incorporating new board members into the working rhythm of the board, developing trustee job descriptions); board recruiting (VCG assists nonprofit organizations with headquarters in the Northeast Corridor in defining their board recruitment objectives, and then conducts a targeted search for business, professional, and community leaders with the desired expertise, diversity of perspective, and resources); serve on a board (VCG maintains a database of individuals who live and work in the Northeast Corridor interested in nonprofit board service); Boardmember's Forum (VCG's response to meet the needs of men and women who serve on nonprofit boards in the Northeast Corridor who are seeking common ground to learn from each other; benefits include *boardmember's KIOSK*, a compilation of events and seminars—drawn from over 100 organizations—that focuses on nonprofit board level issues and published twice a year; *boardmember's FYI*, providing insider interviews with board members about what really happens in boardrooms in our region; access to information online, including the BOARD DOCTOR, a unique on-line service to discuss your board issues; *Directory of Nonprofit Directors*, a publication divided into three sections—by name, by nonprofit board, and by company—that illuminates the men and women leading boards); corporate board placement (the Corporate Board Placement Program has worked to increase the pool of potential board candidates for the nonprofits of the community it serves); Boardnet USA (a national network of programs, individuals, and corporations involved in strategically matching nonprofit boards and potential board members); Web site (*wwwboardnetusa.com*) (will offer the following features: information resources about how to find a board to serve; a searchable national database of boards needing trustees; a Board Candidate Profile to

send directly to boards of interest; and an e-mail helpline); *The Board Market Place Program: A Community Action Plan to Bridge the Gap Between Board and Potential Board Members* (free manual to volunteer centers, leadership programs, management support organizations, and community foundations that have or are interested in developing a program that strategically connects nonprofit boards and potential board members); and Annual Board Connectors Meeting.

Volunteer Trustees

818 18th Street NW, Suite 410, Washington, DC 20006
Tel: 202-659-0338; FAX: 202-659-0116
E-mail: VT@sprintmail.com;
WWW: http://www.volunteertrustees.org

▶ Volunteer Trustees is a national organization of not-for-profit hospital and health system governing boards. The organization was founded in 1980 to give voice to the trustees of America's voluntary health care system and is dedicated to preserving and furthering the not-for-profit healthcare sector. Volunteer Trustees provides the only national forum run by trustees for trustee-to-trustee exchange, discussion, and education. Volunteer Trustees Foundation for Research and Education was created in 1986 to support the research and educational activities of the Association. It has conducted research on a variety of issues and has hosted numerous educational forums. Volunteer Trustees provides a platform from which not-for-profit health care trustees can influence policy at all levels of government. It holds an annual National Trustee Conference.

PRODUCT AND SERVICE PROVIDERS

Consultants

Bates & Associates, Inc.

13640 Spinning Wheel Drive, Germantown, MD 20874-2819
Tel: 301-515-1660; FAX: 301-515-1661
E-mail: BA2GEO@aol.com

▶ Bates & Associates provides strategic management counsel to nonprofit organizations whose missions relate to education, arts, culture, and religious and charitable work. Services are available in the following areas: strategic planning, governance, management, programs, and consumer and market research.

Board Builders

Carol Weisman, 48 Granada Way, St. Louis, MO 63124
Tel: 888-500-1777, 314-991-3018 (office); FAX: 314-991-0202
E-mail: info@CarolWeisman.com, cewfer@aol.com;
WWW: http://www.carolweisman.com,
http://www.carolweisman.com/pages/resources.html

▶ Board Builders is a company dedicated to helping nonprofits reach a higher levels of success, and to help board and staff achieve greater joy in their work. It offers seminars, training, and consultation services.

Carver Governance

Carver Governance Design, Inc., P.O. Box 13007,
Atlanta, GA 30324-0007
Tel: 404-728-9444; FAX: 404-728-0060
E-mail: polgov@aol.com, johncarver@carvergovernance.com;
WWW: http://www.carvergovernance.com

▶ Carver Governance provides seminars, workshops, consultations, and consultant training focusing on the board's governance responsibilities and the relationship of the board to its constituents, its chairperson and committees, and its chief executive officer. John Carver consults regularly in the United States and Canada and occasionally in other parts of the world, particularly in Europe. Beyond providing initial exposure to the principles of board excellence, Dr. Carver is available to assist individual boards to implement and maintain model operation. After the initial work, continued assistance is offered only to boards that have made an official group decision to proceed. Carver Governance originated the Policy Governance Model.

The Conservation Company

50 East 42nd Street, 19th Floor, New York, NY 10017
Tel: 212-949-0990; FAX: 212-949-1672
E-mail: info@consco.com; WWW: http://www.consco.com

▶ The Conservation Company offers strategic planning, board development, and program design and evaluation for nonprofit organizations.

Craig and Vartorella, Inc

P.O. Box 1376, Camden, SC 29020
Tel: 803-432-4353 or 803-432-9841
E-mail: globebiz@camden.net

▶ Craig and Vartorella, Inc., specializes in strategic planning, training, and development projects for nongovernmental organizations (NGOs) and nonprofits worldwide. Craig and Vartorella, Inc.'s work on global philanthropy is read regularly in publications distributed in more than 30 countries, as well as online. The firm maintains several proprietary donor databases for projects related to exploration, biodiversity, cardiovascular health care, ballet, and archaeology, and has trained more than 6,000 nonprofit executives worldwide in its fund-raising and board development seminars. Craig and Vartorella, Inc. works worldwide and is available for consultancies, fund raising, and training on a daily or project basis.

Doug Eadie Presents

1 Spyglass Court, Frisco, TX 75034
Tel: 800-209-7652; FAX: 469-384-1441
WWW: http://www.dougeadie.com/presentations.htm

▶ Doug Eadie Presents offers presentations and workshops, retreats, and books.

Gene Royer/Luztbooks

Gene Royer Consulting, 9210 Beringwood Drive,
Houston, TX 77083
Tel: 281-495-7009; FAX: 281-495-1323
Lutzbooks, 624 Roberts Avenue, Glenside, PA 19038
Tel: 215-858-7577
E-mail: sirgeno@mindspring.com, governance2000@juno.com;
WWW: http://www.lutzbooks.com/governance

▶ Gene Royer is an author, consultant, and speaker who offers training in John Carver's Policy Governance Model. Clients include national nonprofit organizations, schools, institutions of higher education, and city governments in the United States and Canada. He is the author of School Board Leadership 2000.

The Governance Group

200—1765 West 8th Avenue, Vancouver, B.C. V6J 1V8
Tel: 604-731-0307; FAX: 604-731-0509
E-Mail: vince@governance.bc.ca;
WWW: http://www.governance.bc.ca

▶ The Governance Group provides consulting on management and governance for nonprofit associations. It also conducts public and in-house workshops and seminars. It provides consulting, facilitation, and coaching services for conducting organizational (governance and operations) effectiveness reviews; organizational transformation and renewal; strategic planning and strategic plan annual reviews; outcomes-based goal setting and performance measurement; productive annual retreats and planning sessions; addressing issues/problems related to all aspects of governing practices, structures, and processes; building and maintaining effective stakeholder relationships; developing business plans; designing and conducting the CEO/executive director performance evaluation; conducting new board member orientation sessions; conducting difficult meetings or meetings in which achieving agreement or consensus is essential or important.

Hanna & Associates

4678 W. Hoffer Street, Banning, CA 92220
Tel: 888-922-0856, 909-922-0856; FAX: 909-922-0956
E-mail: barbhanna@bigfoot.com, BFHanna@aol.com (Barbara Hanna); WWW: http://www.hanna-policygovernance.com,
http://www.hanna-policygovernance.com/articles/index.html,
http://www.hanna-policygovernance.com/materials/index.html

▶ Hanna & Associates trains nonprofit boards of directors and staff in the Policy Governance Model (a registered service mark of Dr. John Carver).

Hayes Briscoe Associates

322 West Bellevue Avenue, San Mateo, CA 94402
Tel: 650-344-8883; FAX: 650-344-3387
E-mail: hbaconsult@aol.com; WWW: http://www.hbaconsult.com

85 Sterling Street, Beacon, NY 12508
Tel: 914-831-9741

6671 SW 70th Terrace, Miami, FL 33143
Tel: 305-667-2795; FAX: 305-667-3195

▶ Hayes Briscoe Associates offers full-service consulting to nonprofit organizations throughout the United States and abroad. They specialize in nonprofit management with an emphasis on governance (board recruitment, board/staff relations, board counsel, bylaws development, start-up coaching, public policy, self-assessment, program evaluation, board retreats, board/staff training, board organization, coalitions/alliances, mergers), planning (executive coaching, strategic planning, mission development, goals/objectives, internal audits, budgeting, data system audits, staffing needs, personnel policies, program expansion, government relations, interim management, organization capacity building, accreditation preparation), and fund development (capital campaigns, planning/feasibility studies, development audits, case development, program marketing/marketing audits, annual fund development/coaching, volunteer development, development planning, prospect identification, planned giving, foundation/corporate outreach, endowment building, software design/selection, software implementation, development writing, major gifts).

Hiller Associates Incorporated

6 Water Street/Long Wharf, Mattapoisett, MA 02739
Tel: 800-482-4498, 508-758-3436; FAX: 508-758-6975
E-mail: tom@hiller.com (Thomas P. Hiller, President)

Regional office: 406 Farmington Avenue, Farmington, CT 06032
Tel: 860-676-7711
WWW: http://www.hiller.com/part3.html

▶ With an understanding of the special needs and time constraints of board members, Hiller Associates, Inc., has designed several successful programs that help the not-for-profit board understand and accept the importance of philanthropic giving and the significance of its leadership role in promoting its growth for the institution. Hiller Associates, Inc., helps your organization identify the skill areas needed by the board (resource development, finance, legal, etc.) and works with you to recruit board members with those skills.

LORAC & Associates, Inc.

11915 Stonehollow Drive, Austin, TX 78758
E-mail: inquiry@boardconsulting.com,
Chief@boardconsulting.com (Carol J. Hinkley Thompson, Chair, President and CEO); WWW: http://www.boardconsulting.com

▶ Services include board trustees training and development; strategic planning and implementation seminars, with ongoing guidance; Internet advising, by prior arrangement, for trustees and CEOs; fund-raising consulting; program development to facilitate self-sufficiency; Web site design; special events; and volunteer training.

Miriam Carver Consulting

P.O. Box 13849, Atlanta, GA 30324
Tel: 404-728-0091; FAX: 404-728-0060
E-mail polgov@aol.com; WWW: http://www.miriamcarver.com

▶ Miriam Carver is available to make presentations on Policy Governance® to individual boards, community groups, conferences, and governmental policy makers. Miriam Carver works with individual boards to facilitate the process of policy development necessary for the adoption of the Policy Governance Model. She provides coaching for boards new to the model, assisting with the establishment of monitoring, board self-evaluation, and owner consultation. Miriam Carver will provide CEO coaching where the board is using Policy Governance.

Nonprofit Training Associates (NTA)

Mailing address: P.O. Box 684664, Austin, TX 78768-4664

Physical address: 5515 New Haven, Austin, TX 78756-1801
Tel: 512-467-0420
E-mail: nonprofittraining@e-mail.com (Ron Ayer, Lead Trainer);
WWW: http://www.angelfire.com/biz/nonprofittraining

▶ NTA offers the Board Development Course. The NTA Board Development Seminar is an intensive, one-day course that takes members of a nonprofit board through a variety of exercises designed to assess the present functioning of the board and explore options to enhance the board's effectiveness. Topics including board structure, member responsibilities, the relationship between the board and organization executives, group dynamics, conflicts of interest, liability coverage, recruiting new members, meeting management, ethics and the law, and organization communications are addressed. Board members will leave with practical, ready-to-use systems critical to the successful functioning of a nonprofit board of directors.

Strategic Nonprofit Resources

2939 Van Ness Street, NW, Suite 1248, Washington, DC 20008
Tel: 202-966-0859; FAX: 202-966-3301
E-mail: cpirtle@compuserve.com (Connie Pirtle);
WWW: www.volunteertoday.com/Connie.html

▶ Provides guidance and assistance to nonprofit organizations in the areas of board/staff development and volunteer program management. Services include Volunteer Program Management (assessments of volunteer programs—either one or more elements or the entire program; customized training workshops for small and large groups tailored to meet the needs of the group; executive coaching for volunteer officers, volunteer program managers, senior staff, and executive directors; management of volunteers for special events; public speaking on all elements of volunteer program management) and boards of directors (one- or two-day retreats customized to meet the needs of the board; self-assessment tools; executive coaching for board presidents and executive directors; resources to strengthen board committees; public speaking on the roles and responsibilities of boards).

Transitions in Leadership

2371 Baxton Way, Chesterfield, MO 63017-7808
Tel: 636-386-1193; FAX: 636-386-1293
E-mail: info@tilnonprof.com;
WWW: http://www.tilnonprof.com/seminars.htm

▶ Transitions in Leadership conducts training seminars in the areas of Board Roles & Responsibilities; "Shared Leadership": Board & Staff Relationships; Leading Change Successfully; Leadership & Supervisory Skill Enhancement; and Team Building Skills: Reducing Staff Turnover and Ensuring Quality Services. These hands-on seminars are designed to improve participants' understanding of the topic, while also providing very specific recommendations for applying what is learned.

GENERAL RESOURCES

(See also Assessment and Evaluation; Legal Issues [Employment Law, Incorporation, Risk Management and Liability]; Organizational Development; Resource Development)

GENERAL/BASICS

(See also Board Effectiveness; Board Recruitment and Development)

AGB Pocket Publication Series

(AGB PUBLICATIONS)

▶ Pocket-size booklets, 10 to 20 pages in length, including the following titles: (1) *Trustee Responsibilities* (John W. Nason), (2) *A Guide for New Trustees* (Nancy R. Axelrod), (3) *Trustee Orientation and Development Programs* (Richard T. Ingram), (4) *The Board Chair–President Relationship* (John W. Pocock), (5) *Distinguishing Between Policy and Administration* (Charles A. Nelson), (6) *The Fund-Raising Role* (Richard D. Legon), (7) *Resource Management Responsibilities* (Charles A. Nelson), (8) *Endowment Management* (J. Peter Williamson), (9) *The Board's Role in Planning* (Dabney Park), (10) *Trustees and Preventive Law* (Kent Weeks), (11) *The Board's Role in Accreditation* (Various Authors), (12) *The Tenure Issue* (Richard P. Chait and Andrew T. Ford), (13) *The Role of the Board Secretary* (Daniel H. Perlman), (14) *Making Advisory Committees and Boards Work* (Richard T. Ingram), (15) *Governing the Multicampus University* (C. Peter Magrath), (16) *The Role of the Foundation Board* (Curtis R. Simic), (17) *The Business of Presidential Search* (Charles B. Neff and Barry Munitz), and (18) *Introduction to Fund Accounting* (John W. Pocock); see separate listings under "Publications" for Nos. 1, 2, 3, 4, 5, 6, 9, 10, and 18. *$5.50 each ($4.95 bulk); series: $79.95*

The Board and Its Responsibilities: Guidelines for Effective Management of Citizen Boards

(UNITED WAY OF GREATER ST. LOUIS)

▶ This manual provides guidelines for the effective management of citizen boards. The manual addresses the critical aspects of board management, including board organization, board education, the responsibilities and functions of boards, and reviewing board performance. In addition, the causes of ineffective boards and the importance of good interaction of the board and the chief executive are noted. *Softcover, 34 pages, $10*

Board Link

(SEE RESOURCE DEVELOPMENT—PROSPECT RESEARCH FOR FULL DESCRIPTION)

Board Manual Workbook

G.E. STRINGER WITH K.B. ARSEM (VOLUNTEER CONSULTANTS—AVAILABLE FROM MBA PUBLISHING)

▶ To promote the effective functioning of the board of a nonprofit organization, each member needs to have appropriate information about the organization. This workbook is the tool to assure that the information is accurate and complete. It can be used as an elementary text in a classroom setting or individually by board members searching out their own answers. *(See also Instructor's Guide: Companion to the Board Manual Workbook). Softcover, $12.50*

The Board Member's Book: Making a Difference in Voluntary Organizations, 2nd Edition

BRIAN O'CONNELL (THE FOUNDATION CENTER, 1993)

▶ This is a basic handbook on the roles of board members, volunteers, and staff, including advice on finding, developing, and rewarding good board members; recruiting and evaluating the executive director; effective fund raising and financial planning; and maintaining the public trust. It offers solutions for the problems and challenges facing board members and how board members can help their organizations make a difference. This updated and revised version reflects the current issues facing nonprofit boards serving as a valuable resource on the issues, challenges, and possibilities that emerge from the interchange between a nonprofit organization and its board. Filled with inspiration and practical advice, it covers: (1) the impact of nonprofit organizations on the United States today; (2) the different responsibilities of board members, volunteers, and staff; (3) finding, developing, and rewarding good board members; (4) recruiting, encouraging, and evaluating the executive director; (5) effective strategies for fund raising and financial planning; (6) how to make the most out of meetings and evaluate results; and (7) budgeting and financial accountability. It addresses the ethical issues facing nonprofit organizations and provides advice on how to conduct both internal and external ethical evaluations to inspire essential public confidence. It is recommended for nonprofit management programs and universities. *Softcover, 198 pages, $25 (plus $2.50 shipping)*

The Board Member's Guide: A Beneficial Bestiary

JEANNE H. BRADNER (CONVERSATION PRESS, 1995)

▶ Bradner's handbook is for any member of any kind of board who wants to carry out his or her duties effectively while avoiding the many pitfalls that can sabotage that goal. It takes a lighthearted look at the animal characteristics displayed by human board members to make serious points about such perpetual challenges as goal setting, power struggles, and nonproductive behavior. The author, a nationally known consultant for not-for-profit and volunteer activity, offers practical guidelines for the role of the chair, the executive director, and the board member in making board meetings more satisfying for all participants. It is helpful for volunteers and paid staff alike, whether on social service, arts, church, education, professional, or governmental boards.A cartoon menagerie of 15 animals, representing personality traits of board members, decorates practical advice on nonprofit management. Denizens of Ms. Bradner's bestiary include the elephant, who is unwilling to try new ideas because she never forgets the old ones that failed, and the wolf, who marks his territory and believes himself to be the expert on everything. The author is a consultant on nonprofit management and leadership develoment. The illustrator, Carl R. Granath, is a newspaper cartoonist and animator. This book does not pretend to be either a comprehensive textbook on the legal obligations of board directors or a detailed manual on board management. Instead, it is a guide to effective board behavior for the board member, the board chair, and the organization's chief staff officer. *Softcover, 128 pages, $9.95*

Board of Directors & Management (Training materials)

(ZIMMERMAN LEHMAN & ASSOCIATES, 1994)

▶ Unlock the potential of your board; learn how to ensure your board's full participation in fund raising and planning, good management techniques, and what makes a good leader. Discover the techniques you will need to recruit new board members with "clout." It discusses the responsibilities of board members, recruitment, developing strategic and marketing plans, insurance, the board's role in fund raising, committees, structure, team building, and more. It includes articles, forms, a delegation checklist, 100 time management shortcuts, time management outline, and performance appraisal. *Softcover, 45 pages, $30 (plus $1.50 shipping)*

Board Overboard: Laughs and Lessons for All but the Perfect Nonprofit

BRIAN O'CONNELL (JOSSEY-BASS, 1995)

▶ If you think your board is in shambles, wait until you read about the board portrayed in this book. It is a spoof of nonprofit organizations written by Brian O'Connell, founding president of Independent Sector, who draws on 40 years of experience with nonprofit groups. Presented in the form of minutes from a fictitious nonprofit's board meetings, *Board Overboard* is a send-up of a world that is too seldom treated with humor. In this witty account, we eavesdrop on an outrageous group of inept but very funny board members. Every incriminating word has been captured in the recording secretary's riotous minutes. This book is a perfect gift for all board members and nonprofit executives for whom the laughs and lessons may produce more lighthearted and effective boards. *Hardcover, 240 pages, $25 (plus $5.50 shipping)*

Board Passages: Three Key Stages in a Nonprofit Board's Life Cycle

NONPROFIT GOVERNANCE SERIES (AVAILABLE FROM AMERICAN SOCIETY OF ASSOCIATION EXECUTIVES)

KARL MATHIASEN (NATIONAL CENTER FOR NONPROFIT BOARDS, 1990)

▶ The Nonprofit Governance Series addresses governance issues of immediate concern to executive staff and board members. The practical and concise booklets (12 to 28 pages each) answer questions relating to the board's fundamental responsibilities and involvement in specific key areas. *$12.00 (Nonmember and Member)*

Boardroom Verities: A Celebration of Trusteeship with Some Guides and Techniques to Govern By, Reissue Edition

JEROLD PANAS (PRECEPT PRESS, 1998)

▶ This book is a salute to trusteeship that looks at why men and women are willing to join boards and give their time, compassion, and commitment. In 80 brief chapters, time-tested truths are presented covering virtually every aspect of what it takes to have a healthy and effective board. It is based on interviews with over 100 trustees—some famous, others localized fund raisers in organizations just like yours. Filled with philosophy and commonsense advice, these stories and anecdotes will be the motivation for your board members to strive to be the best trustees they can be. What's the optimum size of boards? What's the necessary number and types of committees? On what basis do you select officers and new members? Who are your "roaring advocacy" board members? These and every possible question about your board will be answered in detail. Jerry Panas's exclusive board assessment rating system is also included. Newly revised and written by a specialist in trustee development for every trustee and nonprofit staff member, this book looks at why men and women are willing to join boards and give their time, compassion, and commitment. It presents 80 time-tested "trustee truths" that govern board membership in a series of brief chapters, based on interviews of over 100 men and women trustees. These truths include: "Be Guardian of the Vision," "Be Open to Change," and "Beware the Letterhead Trustee." Stories and anecdotes cover virtually every aspect of what constitutes a healthy board and effective trustees, including the optimum size of boards, the number of necessary committees, the amount of time required, and the need for "a roaring advocacy" from board members. The author's exclusive "board assessment" rating system provides essential guidelines to having an effective board and trustees and encourages board members to give even more. *Hardcover, 238 pages, $40 (plus $4 shipping)*

Boards That Make a Difference: A New Design for Leadership in Nonprofit and Public Organizations

JOHN CARVER (JOSSEY-BASS, 1997)

▶ John Carver's groundbreaking Policy Governance Model has influenced the way public and nonprofit boards operate around the world. Now, as widespread experience with the model continues to grow, Carver enriches his definitive exposition with updated policy samples, a new chapter on the process of policy development, and additional resources for various types of boards. He debunks the entrenched beliefs about board roles and functions that hamper dedicated board members. With creative insight and commonsense practicality, Carver presents a bold new approach to board job design, board–staff relationships, the chief executive role, performance monitoring, and virtually every aspect of the board–management relationship. In their stead, he offers a board model designed to produce policies that make a difference; missions that are clearly articulated; standards that are ethical and prudent; meetings, officers, and committees that work; and leadership that supports the fulfillment of long-term goals. *Hardcover, 256 pages, $29.95*

CarverGuides (Booklets)

(JOSSEY-BASS, 1996–1997)

▶ These booklets deal with one governance topic at a time. But unlike all other such "tips" booklets on the market, these are consistent with the Policy Governance Model. Titles currently out: #1, *Basic Principles of Policy Governance;* #2, *Your Roles and Responsibilities as a Board Member;* #3, *Three Steps to Fiduciary Responsibility;* #4, *The Chairperson's Role as Servant–Leader to the Board;* #5, *Planning Better Board Meetings;* #6, *Creating a Mission That Makes a Difference!;* #7, *Board Assessment of the CEO;* #8, *Board Self-Assessment;* #9, *Making Diversity Meaningful* in the Boardroom; #10, *Strategies for Board Leadership;* #11, *Board Members as Fundraisers, Advisors, and Lobbyists;* and #12, *The CEO Role Under Policy Governance.* Some booklets in the series are co-authored with Miriam Mayhew Carver.

The Corporate Employee's Guide to Nonprofit Board Service (Booklet)

CAROL E. WEISMAN (NATIONAL CENTER FOR NONPROFIT BOARDS, 1996)

▶ Employees of major corporations face a number of special considerations when they agree to serve on nonprofit boards. Employees with a business background may not understand the role of the board, the differences between for-profit and nonprofit organizations, or what will be expected from them as a board member. This guide was designed for employees who are about to join their first board. It includes sections on choosing a board that fits the employee's needs and interests and on clarifying expectations, including what the nonprofit will expect from the employee and the company, as well as what the company expects from the employee. It also includes a primer on board service that answers many of the most common questions related to board service. Whether you are a corporate employee joining a nonprofit board or a board member seeking to recruit and welcome corporate employees on the board, this booklet is required reading for a smooth transition to fruitful board service. *28 pages, $14 (Nonmember), $10.50 (Member) (plus $3.50 shipping) (DC residents add 5.75% sales tax)*

The Drucker Foundation Self-Assessment Tool for Nonprofit Organizations (See Assessment and Evaluation—Publications for full description)

Foundation Trusteeship: Service in the Public Interest

JOHN NASON (COUNCIL ON FOUNDATIONS/THE FOUNDATION CENTER, 1989)

▶ This book identifies the roles of foundation trustees. Topics include board compensation, board size, role of members, and length and frequency of meetings. It is applicable to all nonprofit organizations. *Softcover, 173 pages, $19.95 (plus $2 shipping if ordered from Council on Foundations) (plus $4.50 if ordered from Foundation Center)*

The Fundamentals of Trusteeship (Package)

(ASSOCIATION OF GOVERNING BOARDS OF UNIVERSITIES AND COLLEGES PUBLICATIONS)

▶ Become a better board member with AGB's one-of-a-kind audio–video training package, designed to help presidents and boards operate as a more cohesive, effective team; give trustees the knowledge and insight they need to help their institutions flourish; and help them carry out their often ambiguous roles. These materials will benefit new trustees and veterans alike. The package contains three components: a 40-minute videotape; *Trustee Responsibilities* audiotape (also available separately); and a 20-page *Leader's Guide.* Separate versions for public and independent institutions are available. *$99.95*

Fundamentals Set (Seven-Booklet Series)

(ASSOCIATION OF GOVERNING BOARDS OF UNIVERSITIES AND COLLEGES)

▶ The set includes the following Board Basics booklets: *AGB Statement on Institutional Governance; Policy Making and*

Administrative Oversight; Trustee Responsibilities: A Basic Guide for Governing Boards of Independent (or Public) Institutions; Financial Responsibilities; The Board's Role in Fund-Raising; A Guide to Conflict of Interest and Disclosure; and Institutional Ethics and Values. $59.95 ($54.95 for 10 or more)

Governance Is Governance, 2nd Edition

KENNETH N. DAYTON (INDEPENDENT SECTOR, 1998)

▶ This essay by philanthropist and former chairman and CEO of the Dayton Hudson Corporation spells out what governance means, how management and governance are different, how similar good governance is in business and the nonprofit sector, and how board members can measure up to their responsibilities. It includes sample job descriptions for a CEO, board chair, and board members. The booklet ends with a question-and-answer session that further clarifies Ken Dayton's wise advice. Bulk prices are available. *Softcover, 15 pages, $7.00 (Nonmember), $5.00 (Member)*

Governing Boards: Their Nature and Nurture

CYRIL O. HOULE (PROJECT OF NATIONAL CENTER FOR NONPROFIT BOARDS/JOSSEY-BASS PUBLISHERS, 1997)

▶ This book offers practical guidance to the common issues, problems, and challenges that all boards of nonprofit and public organizations face, including: (1) how a board can help the nonprofit organization carry out its mission; (2) current challenges and problems facing the nonprofit sector; (3) how a board, chief executive, and staff can work together effectively and harmoniously; (4) determining the proper size of the board; (5) choosing committees to establish within the board; (6) selecting, monitoring, and supporting the chief executive; and more. There is a 25 percent discount to NCNB members. *Softcover, 256 pages, $21.95*

Governing Independent Colleges and Universities: A Handbook for Trustees, Chief Executives, and Other Campus Leaders

RICHARD T. INGRAM AND ASSOCIATES (JOSSEY-BASS, 1993)

▶ Eighteen contributors offer expert guidance on all the major responsibilities of governing boards, including the importance of board–chief executive relationships, the elements of a sound board development program, better board meetings, good staffing and information systems, and board performance assessment. It helps volunteer trustees, chief executives, and other institutional officers think and act more strategically, assess performance and effectiveness, serve a more effective advocacy role, and cope with an increasingly litigious environment. This is a companion volume to *Governing Public Colleges and Universities* (see separate listing). *Hardcover, 516 pages, $55*

Governing, Leading, and Managing Nonprofit Organizations

DENNIS R. YOUNG, ROBERT M. HOLLISTER, AND VIRGINIA A. HODGKINSON AND ASSOCIATES (INDEPENDENT SECTOR, 1993)

▶ Drawing on management research and inquiries into the nature of voluntary organizations, this volume provides insights into how managers, board members, and other leaders in the nonprofit sector can meet the pressing challenges of governance and management, and lead their organizations with informed vision and renewed purpose. Often used as a textbook at nonprofit management programs across the country, this book serves as a guidebook for managers, researchers, and students. *Hardcover, 338 pages, $36.95 (Nonmember), $25.95 (Member)*

Governing Public Colleges and Universities: A Handbook for Trustees, Chief Executives, and Other Campus Leaders
RICHARD T. INGRAM AND ASSOCIATES (JOSSEY-BASS, 1993)

▶ This book helps volunteer trustees, chief executives, and other institutional officers think and act more strategically, assess performance and effectiveness, serve a more effective advocacy role, and cope with an increasingly litigious environment. It is a companion volume to *Governing Independent Colleges and Universities* (see separate listing). *Hardcover, 510 pages, $55*

Inside the Boardroom: Governance by Directors and Trustees
WILLIAM G. BOWEN (NATIONAL CENTER FOR NONPROFIT BOARDS/JOHN WILEY & SONS, 1994)

▶ At a time when both nonprofit and for-profit boards are under increasing pressure and scrutiny, this book offers recommendations on how both types of boards can better serve the interests of organizations and their stakeholders. It offers an overview of the role, functions, constitution, and structure of nonprofit boards, as well as covering issues of informing and recruiting directors of nonprofit corporations. The author, an experienced board member of nonprofit and for-profit organizations, uses well-known incidents in both sectors to illustrate his points. It examines the following questions: (1) Do boards really matter?, (2) Is it wise to allow chief executives to serve as board chairs?, (3) In what ways is a board's ability to act effectively influenced by the type of information reported to it and by the reporting mechanisms themselves?, and (4) Is there an optimal board size and optimum balance between inside and outside members? It is attentive to the differences between for-profit and nonprofit boards and includes profiles of each type. *Hardcover, 184 pages, $35 (plus $6.50 shipping)*

Inside the Nonprofit Boardroom
CHARLES WILLIAM GOLDING, TEDROWE WATKINS, AND CRAIG W. STEWART (DOCUMENTARY BOOK PUBLISHERS, 1999—AVAILABLE FOR UNITED WAY–SEATTLE)

▶ A no-nonsense primer for folks who serve on nonprofit boards. This handbook provides sound insight into navigating the nonprofit board world. This guidebook is a "must read" for those considering participation on a nonprofit board or those who have recently joined one. *Softcover, 79 pages, $15.95*

Instructor's Guide: Companion to the Board Manual Workbook
G.E. STRINGER WITH K.B. ARSEM (VOLUNTEER CONSULTANTS—AVAILABLE FROM THE POINTS OF LIGHT FOUNDATION AND MCDUFF/BUNT ASSOCIATES, 1986)

▶ This book is a companion to the *Board Manual Workbook* (see separate listing). Instruction for board members of nonprofit organizations is essential to the effective involvement of these administrative volunteers. This guide to the implementation of board training has been designed for use by the directors, designers, and/or teachers of sessions on boardsmanship. It includes detailed plans using *The Board Manual Workbook* as well as additional exercises to supplement those in the workbook. For the instructor or trainer, this companion guide to the best-selling *Board Manual Workbook* provides activities and exercises to help create effective board members. The "learn by experience" method will give your class valuable insights into board service. Session plans, quizzes, and instructional tools make this guide a valuable resource. *Softcover, 43 pages, $20.50*

NCNB Nonprofit Governance Series
(NATIONAL CENTER FOR NONPROFIT BOARDS)

▶ This series of 10 booklets addresses governance issues of immediate concern to executive staff and board members. The practical and concise booklets answer questions about the board's fundamental responsibilities and involvement in specific key areas. Titles include: (1) *Ten Basic Responsibilities of Nonprofit Boards;* (2) *The Chief Executive's Role in Developing the Nonprofit Board;* (3) *Fund Raising and the Nonprofit Board Member;* (4) *Creating Strong Board–Staff Partnerships;* (5) *The Chair's Role in Leading the Nonprofit Board;* (6) *How to Help Your Board Govern More and Manage Less;* (7) *The Board's Role in Strategic Planning;* (8) *Understanding Nonprofit Financial Statement: A Primer for Board Members;* (9) *Financial Responsibilities of the Nonprofit Board;* and (10) *Evaluation and the Nonprofit Board.* There is a 25 percent discount to NCNB members. *12–28 pages, $99 (Series) (plus $8.50 shipping), $12 (Individual booklets) (plus $3.50 shipping each)*

Nonprofit Board Answer Book: Practical Guidelines for Board Members and Chief Executives
ROBERT C. ANDRINGA, THEODORE WILHELM ENGSTROM, AND TED W. ENGSTROM (NATIONAL CENTER FOR NONPROFIT BOARDS, 1998)

▶ This book provides answers to virtually all of your board questions under one cover. Written for seasoned as well as new nonprofit leaders, this book covers virtually every issue you're likely to encounter in nonprofit board governance in an easy-to-follow question-and-answer format. The nuts-and-bolts information you'll read about includes recruiting committed and active board members; ensuring board diversity; how to involve your board in fund raising; defining responsibilities of the board chair, chief executive, and board members; assessing board performance; getting to the heart of strategic planning; involving board members in assessing board performance; showing a board member the door; and stepping down: a dozen soul-searching questions for the chief executive. It includes action steps, real-life examples, and worksheets. CEOs of nonprofits should take special note of the practical suggestions in Chapters 5, 14, 19, 21, and 26. Board members who are serious about making a contribution will benefit greatly from Chapters 1, 4, 5, 7, 16, 22, 28, and 34. This book is fully indexed. *Hardcover, 208 pages, $29.95 (Nonmember), $22.50 (Member)*

Nonprofit Boards and Leadership: Cases on Governance, Change, and Board–Staff Dynamics
MIRIAM M. WOOD, ED. (JOSSEY-BASS, 1995)

▶ This book offers detailed case studies that demonstrate the crucial strategic issues facing nonprofit governing boards and offers board members new methods for dealing with them. In this practical book, each chapter is actually a story that outlines the context of the case and is followed by questions for discussion. Readers are encouraged to study the case scenarios and develop their own solutions to the dilemmas they present. *Nonprofit Boards and Leadership* provides a hands-on understanding for the complex issues that challenge today's board members. Designed for graduate students, professors, nonprofit professionals, and board members, it provides a behind-the-scenes view of the inner workings of real-life boardrooms; based on actual examples from such nationally known organizations as the United Way of Massachusetts Bay, California Hospital Medical Center, the University of Bridgeport, and AIDS Project Los Angeles. Contents include: Introduction: Governance and Leadership in Theory and Practice; Part I: The Role of External Stakeholders in Governance; Part II: Complexities in the Board–Staff Relationship; and Part III: Interpreting Mission and Accountability. It is supplemented with annotated bibliographies. *Hardcover, 266 pages, $24.95 (plus $4.50 shipping)*

Nonprofit Boards of Directors: Analyses and Applications

ROBERT D. HERMAN AND JON VAN TIL (TRANSACTION PUBLISHERS, 1989)

▶ This book presents articles mixing analysis of what nonprofit boards actually do with suggestions for enhancing their contributions. It looks at what kinds of people join boards and why they continue to serve, describes subgroups that form within boards and how they affect organizational transitions and relations with the chief executive, and offers advice on meeting the board's information needs. *Hardcover, 256 pages, $35 (plus $3.50 shipping)*

Nonprofit Boards: What to Do and How to Do It

JOHN E. TROPMAN AND ELMER J. TROPMAN (CHILD WELFARE LEAGUE OF AMERICA, INC., 1999)

▶ What are nonprofit boards supposed to do? *Nonprofit Boards: What to Do and How to Do It* is an operator's manual for chairs and members of today's nonprofit boards of directors. This guide details the responsibilities of boards; explains how to articulate the nonprofit organization's vision, mission, and goals; describes processes for evaluating the performance of board chairs and directors; explains how to evaluate a board's decision-making processes; and outlines how to improve the dreaded board meeting. Chapter exercises allow readers to assess how well their own boards are doing, while popular cartoons from *The New Yorker* satirize common board afflictions. It is an essential resource for every nonprofit executive director and board leader. *Softcover, 247 pages, $22.95*

Nonprofit Governance: The Executive's Guide

VICTOR FUTTER AND GEORGE W. OVERTON, EDS. (AMERICAN BAR ASSOCIATION, 1997)

▶ *Nonprofit Governance: The Executive's Guide* discusses virtually every problem that nonprofit executive directors or their staff are likely to face. Based on the expertise of corporate and nonprofit executives, attorneys, and professionals who have hands-on experience facing board organization and management problems, this informative guide is filled with step-by-step guidelines, sample forms and letters, useful checklists, and bibliographies. Whether nonprofit entities are large or small, they face many similar management problems. *Nonprofit Governance* will help you identify potential risks and implement appropriate solutions. Topics include conflicts of interest—sample policies and procedures to follow; risk exposure to nonprofits—how to identify, analyze, and reduce risk; tax and insurance issues—what details the executive director needs to know; lobbying activities—restrictions and statutory requirements; fund raising—the problems and responsibilities of the board and the staff; strategic planning—how to better meet the needs of clients, employees, and the community; records retention—what records should be retained, and how; and total quality management—how to improve the effectiveness of your organization. *Nonprofit Governance* explains how effective boards are created,

how they are best organized and served, and how and why they need staff support to achieve optimum performance. Chapters cover important issues to consider in the composition and operation of the board—profiling a board; the purpose and function of board committees and their relationship to staff; the criteria for compensation of the executive director; how and why to develop a mission statement, plan a retreat, and train new directors—including sample bylaws and the critical questions they raise; what types of information to provide a board and when; and tax and accounting considerations. *Softcover, 400 pages, $79.95*

Nonprofit Leadership Seminars (Training Materials)

(VOLUNTEER CONSULTING GROUP)

▶ Touching every aspect of a nonprofit board's structure and function (from nominating new members to strategizing for the future), this series in three volumes contains the knowledge every nonprofit board needs in order to direct its resources in the most efficient possible manner and sharpen its competitive edge. Each volume offers step-by-step procedures for organizing a seminar; additionally, there are comprehensive teaching notes, sample flip charts, a case study, and a seminar workbook for participants. Titles include *Strategy Formulation: How to Compete in Today's Nonprofit World, Chairing the Board: The Challenge of Leadership,* and *Building a Board: There Is a Way* (see separate listings). *$175 (Individual Seminars), $475 (All three volumes), $10 (Additional Participants Workbooks)*

Nonprofit Organization: Essential Readings (See General Management—Publications for full description)

A Nonprofit Organization Operating Manual: Planning for Survival and Growth (See General Management—Publications for full description)

The Policy Governance Fieldbook: Practical Lessons, Tips, and Tools from the Experiences of Real-World Boards

CAROLINE OLIVER, MIKE CONDUFF, SUSAN EDSALL, CAROL GABANNA, RANDEE LOUCKS, DENISE PASZKIEWICZ, CATHERINE RASO, AND LINDA STIER (JOSSEY-BASS, 1999)

▶ Boards all around the world have adopted the revolutionary Policy Governance principles to improve their leadership and performance. This field book is the latest addition to growing literature on the landmark model. Endorsed with a foreword by John Carver, this practical resource closely examines 11 diverse organizations that have implemented Policy Governance in the United States and Canada. The authors analyze what works and what doesn't in real-world practice. *The Policy Governance Fieldbook* is for organizations considering, beginning to use, or already using Carver's principles. Readers will discover practical advice based on the real-life experiences of organizations that have tried and tested Policy Governance for themselves. *The Policy Governance Fieldbook* is not a theoretical treatise, but a practical study. Its authors are concerned with real people in real organizations with real challenges. Each chapter is built around a framework, first introducing a specific Policy Governance activity or challenge, exploring the experiences of boards that met this challenge, and then drawing key lessons from those experiences. It is a practical exploration of real organizations facing real challenges. *Softcover, 272 pages, $29.95*

The Role of the Board and Board Members
(Booklet)
BRIAN O'CONNELL (INDEPENDENT SECTOR, 1988)

▶ This booklet is part one of a nine-part series on nonprofit management (Nine-Part Nonprofit Management Series) (see separate listing under Publications in Management section), which looks at the moral and legal responsibilities, strategies and goals, performance and rewards, staffing, and ways to involve boards of director members. *20 pages, $5 (Nonmember), $3.50 (Member) (plus $2.50 shipping)*

Running Nonprofit Organizations: Fifteen Essential Steps and Concepts for Board Members and Managers
HERBERT HEATON (COGENT PUBLISHING, 2000)

▶ Today, there are over one and a half million nonprofit organizations. What are their missions? How can they rigorously assure their productivity and performance quality? What should board members and managers do? This book helps board members and managers of nonprofit organizations sketch their roles and fill them effectively. It puts practical ideas, drawn from experience and observation, into a conceptual framework. Fifteen essential steps and concepts are presented as priority projects to be taken in order—like steps in a stairway.

Mr. Heaton, an accountant and a consultant to nonprofit groups, begins his 15 steps by discussing how to acquire start-up funds for a nonprofit organization and to craft a mission statement. In the second section, he outlines management techniques, including how to exercise control over the organization and encourage responsibility among employees. Managers and trustees of charities should clearly define each employee's role, he writes, as that will make it easier to delegate work. The third section contains advice on how to recruit and retain workers and how to develop and approve programs. Finally, Mr. Heaton provides methods for measuring an organization's performance. He contends that successful organizations foster a sense of discovery daily. "Board members, managers, employees and volunteers must not be locked in windowless boxes by job descriptions, established routines or their own mindsets," he writes. *Softcover, 128 pages, $15.95*

Self-Study Guide for Family Foundation Boards
(Training Materials)
(COUNCIL ON FOUNDATIONS, 1994)

▶ Identify ways to help improve your board operations and measure your goals and progress with the *Self-Study Guide for Family Foundation Boards*. Sections explore seven key trustee responsibilities and assess overall board performance, as well as that of each trustee. The book offers step-by-step instructions for conducting a board self-assessment. *$20.00 (Member), $45.00 (Nonmember) (Set includes five self-study guides and a user's guide) (plus $2 shipping)*

Self-Study Guide for Independent Foundation Boards
(Training Materials)
(COUNCIL ON FOUNDATIONS, 1994)

This guide helps the board evaluate and increase its knowledge of the foundation it serves. Trustees complete a survey and use the results to evaluate their understanding of board membership, fiduciary responsibilities, board organization, management, and grant making. Through the survey, trustees also consider the foundation's recent successes and areas that need more attention in the future. It

is an excellent tool for board retreats or other meetings when the board considers the entire scope of its current operations. *$20.00 (Member), $45.00 (Nonmember) (Set includes five self-study guides and a user's guide) (plus $2 shipping)*

Serving on the Board of a Not-for-Profit Corporation: A Layperson's Guide (Booklet)
MARTHA J. OLSON (LAWYERS ALLIANCE FOR NEW YORK, 1993)

▶ This manual is designed to assist board members and executives of a nonprofit organization in addressing a financial crisis. Topics include assessing the financial health of the organization, negotiating with creditors, and an overview of federal bankruptcy laws and dissolution procedures under New York state law. *$5 (plus 75 cents shipping)*

A Snapshot of America's Nonprofit Boards: Results of a National Survey
LARRY SLESINGER AND RICHARD L. MOYERS, EDS. (NATIONAL CENTER FOR NONPROFIT BOARDS—AVAILABLE FROM THE AMERICAN SOCIETY FOR ASSOCIATION EXECUTIVES, 1995)

▶ Results of NCNB's first national survey of more than 1,100 chief executives of board practices and composition. The survey was conducted in 1994; the responses provide a first look at America's nonprofit boards, including valuable and surprising information on board size, frequency of meetings, voting status of the chief executive, and fund raising. It is intended to answer such questions as: (1) How often do most boards meet?, (2) How many members does the average board have?, (3) Do most boards have conflict-of-interest policies?, (4) How many boards reimburse their board members for expenses incurred in attending board meetings?, and others; based on responses from nearly 1,200 nonprofits from all major mission areas to a national survey conducted in 1994. It includes graphs and charts suitable for reproduction as overheads or handouts. *Softcover, 20 pages, $19.50*

Taking Trusteeship Seriously
RICHARD C. TURNER, ED. (INDIANA UNIVERSITY CENTER ON PHILANTHROPY, 1994)

▶ This book offers a diverse look at trusteeship, including insights by experts in fields such as history and the law, the anecdotes and wisdom of trustees, consultants, and executives of nonprofit organizations. Selected from papers presented at the 1993 annual symposium sponsored by the Center, the book offers definitive information about boards and how they work and raises questions that call for further research. In the introduction, Dr. Turner says the volume will give readers "a renewed sense of trusteeship and its place in our thinking about philanthropy and a new conviction about the value of pursuing the questions and issues which surround the work of trustees." *$9.95 (plus $2 shipping)*

Trusteeship for Individuals: Renewing the Legacy of Trusteeship (Video)
(TRUSTEE LEADERSHIP DEVELOPMENT)

▶ This video describes the process that helps individuals examine the history and meaning of their service to others, determine their personal mission, and plan effectively for future service. *$35.00*

Turning Vision into Reality: What the Founding Board Should Know About Starting a Nonprofit Organization
(NATIONAL CENTER FOR NONPROFIT BOARDS, 1999)

▶ Many nonprofits get their start from the vision of an individual or a small, committed group. Knowing how to create a viable nonprofit organization from that vision is the job of the founding board. In this latest booklet from NCNB, founding board members will learn the necessary steps for gaining nonprofit status, including where to request and file necessary forms, choosing and registering a name for the organization, and how to set up an accounting system. This booklet provides key questions and answers for boards embarking on this process, including: How big should the board be?, What should the role of the organization's founder be?, What committees should the board have?, Is it necessary to incorporate?, and Will we need a lawyer? Also included are sample job descriptions for board officers, case studies, and helpful resources. *Softcover, 38 pages, $16.00 (Nonmember), $12.00 (Member)*

Accountability/Ethics

(See also Liability; Roles and Responsibilities)

Developing an Ethics Program: A Case Study for Nonprofit Organizations

CHARLES E.M. KOLB (NATIONAL CENTER FOR NONPROFIT BOARDS, 1999)

▶ Today's nonprofits operate in an era of accountability. When a nonprofit's reputation is damaged, it's not easy to recover the public's trust. Set against the United Way of America scandal of the early 1990s, author Charles Kolb, former general counsel for the United Way of America, discusses the process the organization undertook in creating its ethics program and describes how to develop, implement, evaluate, and revise a code of ethics. Board members will learn how having an ethics program can help clarify and communicate the organization's values to staff, board, funders, and the general public and the importance of having organization-wide acceptance of the code in order for it to be effective. Included is full text of the United Way of America code of ethics and a discussion of various ethics code provisions. *Softcover, 24 pages, $16.00 (Nonmember), $12.00 (Member)*

Entrusted: The Moral Responsibilities of Trusteeship

DAVID H. SMITH (INDIANA UNIVERSITY PRESS, 1995)

▶ This book contains thoughtful essays on the morality, obligation, practice, and virtues of trusteeship. It seeks to answer questions such as: Is governance by a board of trustees the best way to oversee nonprofit institutions?, What are the major duties of a trustee and what are their common problems?, How should trustees be related to the rest of the organization?, and What are the prime virtues of a trustee? Smith proposes three principles that should guide the work of trustees and examines them in light of case studies of trusteeship and trusteeship gone wrong. He presents intriguing arguments for governance grounded in a broader sense of organizational and public stewardship. This book is part of the IU Press Philanthropic Series. *Hardcover, 148 pages, $19.95 (plus $3.75 shipping)*

Fulfilling the Public Trust: Ten Ways to Help Nonprofit Boards Maintain Accountability (Booklet)

PETER D. BELL (NATIONAL CENTER FOR NONPROFIT BOARDS, 1993)

▶ Unlike business leaders, who answer to stockholders, or political leaders, who are elected by voters, nonprofit board members act as stewards for the public. This booklet is intended to assist members of nonprofit boards understand and fulfill its crucial, yet often neglected, role in maintaining organizational accountability. It outlines 10 mechanisms for accountability and five common obstacles to avoid in helping boards fulfill this vital responsibility. The author's goal is for nonprofits to not just avert institutional calamities, but also to achieve higher levels of effectiveness in pursuit of their social purposes. There is a 25 percent discount to NCNB members. *16 pages, $15 (Nonmember), $11.25 (Member) (plus $3.50 shipping) (DC residents add 5.75% sales tax)*

How to Manage Conflicts of Interest: A Guide for Nonprofit Boards (Booklet)

DANIEL L. KURTZ (NATIONAL CENTER FOR NONPROFIT BOARDS/AMERICAN ASSOCIATION OF MUSEUMS, 1995)

▶ Even though conflicts of interest are at the heart of a growing number of controversies involving nonprofit governance, few board members and chief executives understand exactly what constitutes conflict of interest and how board members can avoid it. Attorney Daniel Kurtz, a former New York charity regulator, explains the legal context of conflict of interest, offers examples of potential conflicts, and suggests guidelines for avoiding them. The booklet includes samples of conflict-of-interest policies and a checklist of items to consider when establishing a policy. Despite the fact that conflicts of interest are at the heart of a growing number of controversies involving nonprofit governance, few board members and chief executives understand exactly what constitutes conflict of interest and how board members can avoid it. The author, an attorney, explains the legal context of conflict of interest, offers examples of potential conflicts, and suggests guidelines for avoiding them. It includes a sample conflict-of-interest policy, a sample conflict-of-interest statement and a questionnaire for board members to complete, and a checklist of points to consider when establishing a conflict-of-interest policy. There is a 25 percent discount to NCNB members. *16 pages, $12 (Nonmember), $9 (Member) (plus $3.50 shipping) (DC residents add 5.75% sales tax)*

Leaving Nothing to Chance: Achieving Board Accountability Through Risk Management

(NONPROFIT RISK MANAGEMENT CENTER, 1998)

▶ Risk management plays a fundamental role in the governance of a nonprofit, and every board is both responsible for the overall well-being of the organization and accountable to its constituencies. This new booklet outlines 10 steps for achieving board accountability through risk management, including formulating risk management policies, creating models for safe volunteer and staff activities, organizing a risk management committee, establishing sound financial management policies, ensuring proper management of the board's activities, and seeking expert help from trustworthy sources. *Softcover, 34 pages, $12.00*

Nonprofit Governance: The Executive's Guide

VICTOR FUTTER AND GEORGE W. OVERTON, EDS. (ABA SECTION OF BUSINESS LAW, 1997)

▶ This comprehensive guide discusses virtually every problem that nonprofit executive directors or their staff are likely to face. Based on the expertise of corporate and nonprofit executives, attorneys, and professionals who have hands-on experience face board organization and management problems, this informative guide is filled with step-by-step guidelines, sample forms and letters, useful checklists, and bibliographies. Chapters cover how to build and maintain a productive board of directors; potential problem areas for nonprofits, including conflicts of interest, lobbying activities, fund raising, records retention, and tax and accounting issues; and much more. *Softcover, 400 pages, $79.95*

Oversight or Interference? Striking a Balance in Nonprofit Governance
(NATIONAL CENTER FOR NONPROFIT BOARDS)

▶ This January 1995 special edition of *Board Member* examines the delicate balancing act board members must face in dealing with increasing pressures for accountability and admonishments not to interfere with the day-to-day management of the organization; using the comments of keynote speakers and participants of NCNB's second National Leadership Forum, this publication discusses the traditional distinction between governance and management, examines why boards tend to interfere in management, and offers advice on how boards can strike the right balance. It includes separate articles on governance on grant making, nonprofits and government, redesigning the board, and evaluating the chief executive, as well as a list of resources for further study. There is a 25 percent discount to NCNB members. *16 pages, $12 (plus $3.50 shipping)*

Better Board Meetings

Conducting Good Meetings (Booklet)
BRIAN O'CONNELL (INDEPENDENT SECTOR, 1988)

▶ Part four of a nine-part series on nonprofit management, *Nine-Part Management Series* (see Management) looks at do's and don'ts for effective, smoothly conducted meetings with full and fair participation for all. *20 pages, $5 (Nonmember), $3.50 (Member)*

Getting Involved (Booklet)
(AMERICAN SOCIETY OF ASSOCIATION EXECUTIVES, 1980)

▶ This booklet presents tips on chairing and participating in committee meetings. Also provided is information on committee meeting structure and how to set agendas. Bulk discounts are available. *$3.30 (Nonmember), $2.20 (Member) (plus $5.25 shipping)*

Meditations for Meetings: Thoughtful Meditations for Board Meetings and for Leaders
EDGAR STOESZ, ED. (GOOD BOOKS, 1999)

▶ Here are dozens of two-page-long meditations, written expressly for board meetings by seasoned board members. Each meditation begins with a scripture, moves on to a personal story, and ends with a brief prayer. Each is about leadership—the courage it requires, the clarity it demands, the celebrations it sometimes offers. *Softcover, 192 pages, $9.95*

Meetings That Work
KAREN E. SILVA (MCGRAW-HILL-BUSINESS SKILLS EXPRESS, 1994)

▶ This book gives readers the tools to organize meetings that are more productive and efficient. It includes strategies and techniques for setting meeting agendas, choosing the most effective meeting setting, developing meeting participation skills, and more. Strong meeting skills are in demand, especially with today's increasing use of teams for planning and decision making; here are the tools you need to organize meetings that are more productive and efficient. Topics include setting agenda, encouraging participation and motivation, choosing appropriate settings, and more. For meeting par-

ticipants, this book explains how to make a valuable contribution, how to communicate effectively, and how to turn meetings into more rewarding experiences. *Softcover, 100 pages, $10.95*

Modern Parliamentary Procedure
RAY E. KEESEY (AMERICAN PSYCHOLOGICAL ASSOCIATION, 1994—AVAILABLE FROM AMERICAN SOCIETY OF ASSOCIATION EXECUTIVES)

▶ Keesey's models for more efficient democratic action modernize parliamentary terminology, eliminate superfluous motions, and provide valuable ideas for preventing and handling disruptions. Using this book will make it easier for members of your organization to participate openly, effectively, and democratically. It simplifies the traditional complex, overly technical rules of procedure. Author Ray E. Keesey presents models for more efficient democratic action by modernizing parliamentary terminology; presenting a simpler, more logical classification of motions; eliminating superfluous motions; and providing valuable ideas for the prevention and handling of disruptions. It is ideal for associations, clubs, student groups, and other deliberative bodies seeking flexible, effective procedural rule. *Softcover, 160 pages, $14.95*

The Modern Rules of Order, Second Edition
DONALD A. TORTORICE (AMERICAN BAR ASSOCIATION, 1999)

▶ Learn how to run any business meeting with confidence and efficiency. An alternative to the cumbersome *Robert's Rules of Order, The Modern Rules of Order* is a simplified system for running any business meeting and can be mastered in less than an hour. For quick reference during meetings, this guide has a handy one-glance chart summarizing how to handle any motion. It includes the 15 Rules of Order, discussion/explanation of the rules, sample bylaw or resolution adopting the rules, general guidelines for the conduct of meetings, discussion of minutes, typical meeting agendas; typical minutes, one-glance motions chart, index for quick reference, wide margins, and extra pages for note taking. *Softcover, 80 pages, $24.95*

Planning Better Board Meetings: Carver Guide 5
JOHN CARVER (JOSSEY-BASS, 1996)

▶ This booklet examines how to restrict crowded agendas, scattered focuses of discussion, and all the familiar weaknesses of group discipline—and use board energy efficiently and effectively. It tells how to select subject matter for meetings, how to plan use of board time, and control the agenda, and discusses how long a board meeting should be in order to fulfill its task of governing. *Softcover, 24 pages, $10.95*

We Can't Keep Meeting Like This! A Guide to More Effective Meetings (See Organizational Dynamics and Design—Publications for full description)

Board Chair

The Chairperson's Role as Servant–Leader to the Board: Carver Guide 4
JOHN CARVER (JOSSEY-BASS, 1996)

▶ As the chairperson of the board, your role, on behalf of the board, is to protect and further the integrity of governance. This Carver Guide helps you and your board develop your role as leader in this process, yet as servant to the board as a body. It describes the fundamental responsibilities of the chairperson of the board: to ensure the functioning of the board and the integrity of the board process. It offers invaluable tips for helping the chair lead more effectively, such as leading the board to define its own job, design its discipline, and evaluate its performance. *Softcover, 24 pages, $10.95*

Dare to Chair: The Art of Chairing a Nonprofit Board of Directors
(COMMUNITY RESOURCE EXCHANGE, 1990)

▶ This elementary guide for board chairpersons addresses the role of the board chair and the strategic importance of the not-for-profit board of directors. It provides advice on such topics as increasing attendance at board meetings, planning meeting agendas, developing bylaws, fund raising, replacing a founder/director, and increasing board membership. Each section includes real-life examples and hands-on tools. It is particularly useful for those individuals new to board leadership. *Softcover, $10*

Getting Involved (Booklet)
(AMERICAN SOCIETY OF ASSOCIATION EXECUTIVES, 1980)

▶ This booklet presents tips on chairing and participating in committee meetings. Also provided is information on committee meeting structure and how to set agendas. Bulk discounts are available. *$3.30 (Nonmember), $2.20 (Member) (plus $5.25 shipping)*

The Chair's Role in Leading the Nonprofit Board
ELLEN HIRZY (NATIONAL CENTER FOR NONPROFIT BOARDS, 1998)

▶ The principles of effective leadership, the personal characteristics of a qualified board chair, and applying those principles are outlined to help the board chairperson, candidates for this important office, the executive director, and other board members understand this vital position. An excellent tool for use in the board development process, it includes a list of responsibilities critical to serving as chairperson of a nonprofit board and annotated resources for further study. It is part of the Nonprofit Governance Series (see separate listing under General/Basics for additional titles). There is a 25 percent discount to NCNB members. *Softcover, 16 pages, $12 (Nonmember), $9 (Member) (plus $3.50 shipping)*

The Role of the Board Chairperson
NONPROFIT GOVERNANCE SERIES (AVAILABLE FROM ASAE)

▶ The Nonprofit Governance Series addresses governance issues of immediate concern to executive staff and board members. The practical and concise booklets (12 to 28 pages each) answer questions relating to the board's fundamental responsibilities and involvement in specific key areas. *$12 (Nonmember and Member)*

Board Committees

(See also Better Board Meetings; Roles and Responsibilities)

Audit Committee
JOHN S. OSTROM (ASSOCIATION OF GOVERNING BOARDS OF UNIVERSITIES AND COLLEGES PUBLICATIONS, 1996)

▶ Part of the Effective Committees Set, this concise booklet describes the roles and responsibilities of well-managed audit committees, including their role in overseeing regular audits of financial activities, adhering to laws and regulations, and monitoring the institution's conflict of interest policies. The author, the controller emeritus of Cornell University, also describes a typical committee

structure and includes a suggested reading list. *12 pages, $9.95 ($7.95 for 10 or more) (plus $3 shipping)*

The Audit Committee: A Key to Financial Accountability for Nonprofit Organizations
(Booklet)
SANDRA JOHNSON (NATIONAL CENTER FOR NONPROFIT BOARDS, 1993)

▶ In the wake of financial scandals that have put board members in the media spotlight, boards should be increasingly wary of ignorance about their organizations' accounting procedures and financial standing. This booklet describes who should be on the audit committee and what the committee's responsibilities are, as well as offers guidelines on implementing internal accounting controls and understanding financial reporting requirements. It also suggests how the committee might be chartered, what type of members should serve on the committee, and how often it should meet. All board members are accountable for the finances of their organizations and should make sure they understand how the audit works and what the results mean. It is part of the Committee Series. *16 pages, $12 (plus $3.50 shipping)*

Building Effective Volunteer Committees, 2nd Edition
NANCY MACDUFF (MCDUFF/BUNT ASSOCIATES, 1998)

▶ The backbone of volunteer efforts is provided by functioning committees. This publication presents an excellent 10-step process to building committee strength and effectiveness. With short narrative sections describing each step, the book contains useful reproducible forms to assist staff and committees in beginning the process. Detailed explanations are given for recruiting the right people, writing guidelines, establishing annual work plans, holding members accountable for their responsibilities, and evaluating individuals and committee work. Each chapter is followed by forms suitable for copying that can be used at your next committee meeting. New and revised. *Softcover, 82 pages, $23.50*

Development Committee
GARY EVANS (ASSOCIATION OF GOVERNING BOARDS OF UNIVERSITIES AND COLLEGES PUBLICATIONS, 1996)

▶ Part of the Effective Committees Set, this booklet describes the committee's general roles and responsibilities, suggests ways in which committees might be composed and structured, and focuses on the essential tasks for developing sound policies that support successful fund raising and other exacting duties. The author is the vice president for development and college relations at Lafayette College. *12 pages, $9.95 ($7.95 for 10 or more) (plus $3 shipping)*

The Development Committee: Fund Raising Begins with the Board (Booklet)
EUGENE R. TEMPEL (NATIONAL CENTER FOR NONPROFIT BOARDS, 1996)

▶ The development committee plays a critical role in an organization's financial survival. In addition to discussing general issues of committee size and composition, the booklet stresses the committee's relationship with staff; emphasizes the importance of involving the committee in planning; suggests specific ways that committee members can be involved in identifying, cultivating, and soliciting prospects; and discusses the ethical issues related to the work of the development committee. This thorough booklet reviews general issues of committee size and composition, including the committee's relationship with staff; the importance of involving the committee in planning; specific ways committee members can be involved in identifying, cultivating, and soliciting prospects; and ethical issues related to the work of the development committee. Appendices include a sample job description for the development committee chairperson, a sample charge, and a worksheet that can be used to evaluate the committee composition. See separate listings for *Nonprofit Board Committees, The Finance Committee, The Nominating Committee, The Executive Committee, The Audit Committee,* and *The Nonprofit Board's Guide to Committees. 16 pages, $12 (plus $3.50 shipping)*

Effective Committees Set (9 Booklet Series)

(ASSOCIATION OF GOVERNING BOARDS OF UNIVERSITIES AND COLLEGES PUBLICATIONS)

▶ These booklets constitute one of the topic clusters in the Board Basics Series. They are intended to strengthen the role of key standing committees, in which much of the day-to-day work of boards occurs. These concise and practical publications will help you understand the roles and responsibilities standing committees play in developing effective policies. All members of every committee— committee chairs, newly named members, or seasoned members, plus the president and the board chair, should keep these important booklets handy. The set includes the following Board Basics booklets: *Academic Affairs Committee, Audit Committee, Buildings and Grounds Committee, Committee on Trustees, Development Committee, Executive Committee, Finance Committee, Investment Committee,* and *Student Affairs Committee. $49.95 ($44.95 for 10 or more)*

Enhancing Committee Effectiveness

JOHN F. SCHLEGEL (AMERICAN SOCIETY OF ASSOCIATION EXECUTIVES, 1994)

▶ One of the most practical reference tools you can give your committee members, this handbook offers a quick how-to reference for carrying out committee responsibilities. The booklet provides checklists and sample job descriptions for both staff liaisons and committee chairs. Learn helpful tips for developing agendas, conducting orientation, writing reports, and presiding over meetings. *Softcover, 30 pages, $10 (Nonmember), $8.50 (Member) (plus $6.25 shipping)*

Executive Committee

RICHARD T. INGRAM (ASSOCIATION OF BOARDS OF UNIVERSITIES AND COLLEGES, 1996)

▶ The executive committee has a mandate to strengthen the efficiency and effectiveness of the entire governing board. Written by the president of AGB, this booklet presents a fresh look at the standing committee that has greater potential for good or harm than any other. It discusses the committee's charge, reviews the committee's four critical responsibilities, and suggests language boards may want to follow or adapt for describing the committee in its bylaws. It is part of the *Effective Series Set. 12 pages, $9.95 ($7.95 for 10 or more) (plus $3 shipping)*

The Executive Committee: Making It Work for Your Organization (Booklet)

ROBERT C. ANDRINGA (NATIONAL CENTER FOR NONPROFIT BOARDS, 1994)

▶ An executive committee can be an asset to good governance, or it can detract from the board's effectiveness. The author presents a

thorough guide to one of the most important and often misused board committees. It will help you ensure that your executive committee complements the board and improves its effectiveness. This practical booklet includes: (1) a checklist for determining whether your board should have an executive committee, (2) guidelines for establishing the committee's level of authority, and (3) an overview of 10 key areas of responsibility. There is a 25 percent discount to NCNB members. *20 pages, $12 (plus $3.50 shipping)*

Finance Committee

JAMES E. MORLEY, JR. (ASSOCIATION OF GOVERNING BOARDS OF UNIVERSITIES AND COLLEGES, 1996)

▶ This valuable booklet explains how a board's finance committee should operate to oversee an institution's fiscal operations most effectively, develop a long-range financial plan, ensure adequate income, and communicate financial policies to the rest of the board and campus administration. The author is the executive director of the National Association of College and University Business Officers. *12 pages, $9.95 ($7.95 for 10 or more) (plus $3 shipping)*

The Finance Committee, The Fiscal Conscience of the Nonprofit Board (Booklet)

NORAH HOLMGREN (NATIONAL CENTER FOR NONPROFIT BOARDS, 1995)

▶ In a time of increased public scrutiny of the financial decisions and activities of nonprofit organizations, the role of the finance committee is more important than ever before. Sound financial decisions and appropriate financial planning are critical to the survival of any nonprofit organization, and essential to maintaining public trust. This booklet confronts the challenge of engaging the board in a meaningful way so that all board members can understand the financial picture. The fifth in the NCNB's Nonprofit Board Committees Series, this concise guide discusses the finance committee's key responsibilities, including ensuring that appropriate financial records are being kept, budgeting in anticipation of financial problems, safeguarding and managing the organization's assets, monitoring compliance with federal and state regulations, and encouraging sound financial planning and responsible growth. The relationship between the finance committee and the organization's staff and chief executive are also explored. This comprehensive overview of the finance committee's responsibilities will benefit treasurers, finance committee chairs, committee members, chief executives, and financial staff. There is a 25 percent discount to NCNB members. *20 pages, $12 (plus $3.50 shipping)*

Investment Committee

JOHN H. BIGGS (ASSOCIATION OF GOVERNING BOARDS OF UNIVERSITIES AND COLLEGES PUBLICATIONS, 1996)

▶ The investment committee must develop strategies and guidelines to support the board's larger investment initiatives. Discover how in this booklet written by the chairman and CEO of TIAA-CREF, who describes typical roles of investment committees, and how to establish an investment policy, and suggests guidelines for selecting an investment manager, among other committee responsibilities. It is part of the Effective Committees Set. *16 pages, $9.95 ($7.95 for 10 or more) (plus $3 shipping)*

The Nominating Committee: Laying a Foundation for Your Organization's Future (Booklet)

ELLEN COCHRAN HIRZY (NATIONAL CENTER FOR NONPROFIT BOARDS, 1994)

▶ The nominating committee is often called the most important nonprofit board committee, since the future of the board and the organization are deeply affected by its work. In this booklet, the fourth in NCNB's Nonprofit Board Committee Series, the author discusses the nominating committee's crucial role, including: (1) a thorough description of the committee's responsibilities, with emphasis on ongoing cultivation and board development activities that are often neglected; (2) points to consider when determining the committee's size and composition; (3) a discussion of the importance of having a year-round plan for board development and recruitment of new board members; and (4) strategies for evaluating the committee's performance and effectiveness; a valuable reference tool for board and nominating committee chairs, chief executives, and development officers; a 25 percent discount to NCNB members. *20 pages, $12 (plus $3.50 shipping)*

Nominating Committees as Change Agents: Making Decisions for the Future (Workbook/Manual)
ANNE HOOVER AND BARBARA BUGG (THE GREENLEAF CENTER, 1994)

▶ A curriculum for the nominating process, drawing upon Robert K. Greenleaf's ideas of trustees as servant–leaders, this manual offers a step-by-step process for achieving positive change within an organization. *$49 (plus $5 shipping)*

Nonprofit Board Committees: How to Make Them Work (Booklet)
ELLEN COCHRAN HIRZY (NATIONAL CENTER FOR NONPROFIT BOARDS, 1992)

▶ This concise guide explains the purpose, functions, and operation of important board committees. It helps you to understand: (1) when and why a board committee should have meetings; (2) how to select committee members; (3) the roles of committee members, including the role of the chair; (4) functions of various types of committees, including executive, development, nominating, finance, audit, personnel, and program committees; (5) the relationship between board committees and the staff; (6) the role of committees; (7) when to establish committees; (8) committee size; (9) committee composition; (10) committee leadership; and other topics. A helpful checklist of tips for successful committees is also included. There is a 25 percent discount to NCNB members. *16 pages, $12 (plus $3.50 shipping)*

The Nonprofit Board's Guide to Committees
(NATIONAL CENTER FOR NONPROFIT BOARDS)

▶ This comprehensive kit will prepare you for establishing and operating effective committees, often where the crucial work of the board is done. Contents include: Nonprofit Board Committees: How to Make Them Work; The Nominating Committee: Laying a Foundation for Your Organization's Future; The Executive Committee: Making It Work for Your Organization; The Audit Committee: A Key to Financial Accountability for Nonprofit Organizations; and The Finance Committee: The Fiscal Conscience of the Nonprofit Board. There is a 25 percent discount to NCNB members. *$45 (plus $6 shipping)*

Operating Effective Committees (Booklet)
BRIAN O'CONNELL (INDEPENDENT SECTOR, 1988)

▶ Part three of nine-part management series on nonprofit management, Nine-Part Nonprofit Management Series (see separate listing under Publications in Management section), which looks at why well-constructed committees are efficient and discusses the need for a written agenda and for keeping the committee focused. *20 pages, $5 (Nonmember), $3.50 (Member) (plus $2.50 shipping)*

Board Effectiveness
(See also Board/CEO Relations; Recruitment and Development)

Achieving Excellence in Association Governance
ANNE L. DECICCO (AMERICAN SOCIETY OF ASSOCIATION EXECUTIVES, 1996)

▶ This practical resource is a primer on governance evaluation for the chief staff executive. It presents a step-by-step approach to designing and managing a governance evaluation program. DeCicco guides you through a thinking and development process that will help you introduce governance evaluation to your association's chief elected officer and governing board, outline a program proposal, and create assessment tools. Sample forms provide a framework for developing your own governance evaluation, board member self-evaluation, board meeting evaluation, issue briefing papers, and definition of board of directors and executive committee roles. *Softcover, 76 pages, $27 (Nonmember), $22.95 (Member)*

Achieving Goals (Booklet)
(AMERICAN SOCIETY OF ASSOCIATION EXECUTIVES, 1980)

▶ This booklet can help you make your mark as a member of the board. Included is information on your legal and fiscal responsibilities, working with the chief elected officer, representing the membership, and working with the staff. *Softcover, $3.30 (Nonmember); $2.20 (Member) (plus $3.50 shipping)*

The Art of Trusteeship: The Nonprofit Board Member's Guide to Effective Governance
SUSAN HOUCHIN AND CANDACE WIDMER (JOSSEY-BASS, 2000)

▶ The well-being of any nonprofit organization rests first with its volunteer board of directors. This book offers board members the guidance they need to successfully govern their organizations, no matter what type or size of nonprofit they may lead. *The Art of Trusteeship* shows you how to fulfill ten key trustee responsibilities and includes much-needed detail on defining mission, strategic planning, executive selection and evaluation, fund raising, financial oversight, and board self-assessment. This hands-on guide is filled with illustrative case studies and real-life examples that clearly show how a variety of creative boards have tackled challenges and strengthened their organizations. *Hardcover, 192 pages, $25.95*

Association Management Magazine: The Leadership Issue 2000
(AMERICAN SOCIETY OF ASSOCIATION EXECUTIVES, 2000)

▶ The January issue of *Association Management* magazine is devoted entirely to the training of your board and volunteer leaders. Not a bind-in. Not a supplement. It's a full issue dedicated to making your board work better. Thousands of CEOs take advantage of the great quantity discounts on the Leadership issue of *Association Management* magazine to purchase one for every member of their board and every association volunteer leader. Sample article titles from the January 2000 Leadership issue: "Arriving at Authentic Leadership," "How Association Boards Add Value," and "Strategic Directions." Issue also includes the popular "Board Primer." For information on quantity discounts, call 202-371-0940 or e-mail *service@asaenet.org.*

Basic Principles of Policy Governance: Carver Guide 1

JOHN CARVER AND MIRIAM MAYHEW CARVER (JOSSEY-BASS, 1996)

▶ This Guide offers board members a clear understanding of the concepts and principles that are at the very heart of John Carver's innovative Policy Governance Model. It presents the guidelines needed to transform your board members into a unified group that consistently makes powerful contributions to its organization. *Softcover, 32 pages, $10.95*

Board Assessment of the Organization: How Are We Doing? (Booklet)

PETER L. SZANTON (NATIONAL CENTER FOR NONPROFIT BOARDS, 1992)

▶ This booklet illustrates the value of organizational assessment to both board members and executive directors; in addition to explaining the "why" behind evaluating the performance of the organization, the " who, what, when, and how" aspects of this responsibility are mapped out in a practical and useful approach that will assist all trustees, staff, and consultants involved in evaluation. It is part of the Nonprofit Governance Series (see listing under Publications for additional titles). There is a 25 percent discount to NCNB members. *Softcover, 13 pages, $9 (plus $3.50 shipping)*

Board Leadership & Governance, Leadership Series, Volume I (Booklet)

JILL MUEHRCKE, ED. (THE SOCIETY FOR NONPROFIT ORGANIZATIONS, 1993)

▶ In articles selected from *Nonprofit World*, writers clarify board responsibilities and advise readers on assuring the highest possible quality for their boards. *106 pages, $35 (Nonmember), $25 (Member)*

Board Leadership & Governance, Leadership Series, Volume I (Booklet)

JILL MUEHRCKE, ED. (THE SOCIETY FOR NONPROFIT ORGANIZATIONS, 1998)

▶ In articles selected from *Nonprofit World*, writers clarify board responsibilities and advise readers on assuring the highest possible quality for their boards. *115 pages, $35 (Nonmember), $25 (Member)*

Board Self-Assessment: Carver Guide 8

JOHN CARVER (JOSSEY-BASS, 1997)

▶ This Guide offers a novel, whole-systems approach to this primary task by outlining the guiding principles of successful self-assessment. Your board will learn how to craft a policy that will spell out its job description and plan its conduct. In addition, it will learn how it can best implement self-assessment to see if it is doing its job and acting as it had planned. *Softcover, 20 pages, $10.95*

Boards That Make a Difference: A New Design for Leadership in Nonprofit and Public Organizations

JOHN CARVER (JOSSEY-BASS, 1997)

▶ This book takes a candid look at how badly many boards fulfill their governance role and analyzes the failure of common prescriptions for boards. Readers will find the first part of the book exhilarating as Carver takes on the "anecdotal wisdom" that characterizes most board literature. Carver goes on to develop a highly structured approach where boards focus on "ends, not means," and where boards focus on results and staff have latitude in program selection, design, and budget. In this model, boards adopt policies about what staff can't do, not about what they should do. He debunks the entrenched beliefs about board roles and functions that hamper dedicated board members. Carver presents a bold new approach to board job design, board–staff relationships, the chief executive role, performance monitoring, and virtually every aspect of the board—management relationship. In their stead, he offers a board model designed to produce policies that make a difference; missions that are clearly articulated; standards that are ethical and prudent; meetings, officers, and committees that work; and leadership that supports the fulfillment of long-term goals. *Hardcover, 256 pages, $29.95*

Boards That Work: A Practical Guide to Building Effective Association Boards

DOUGLAS C. EADIE (AMERICAN SOCIETY OF ASSOCIATION EXECUTIVES, 1995)

▶ This constructive approach to board relations is based on flexibility, openness, and commitment to innovation. Eadie challenges the conventional wisdom surrounding board organization and training. This vision is applied to the board's mission, membership, leadership training, performance management, structure, strategic planning, public relations, retreats, implementation of change, and more. Take advantage of Eadie's practical experience—lessons learned as a consultant to more than 200 nonprofit boards—and help your leadership team work together more effectively. It also includes a resource list. *Softcover, 163 pages, $33 (Nonmember), $28 (Member)*

Building a Better Board, Book I: A Guide to Effective Leadership, 2nd Edition

ANDREW SWANSON (FUND RAISING INSTITUTE/THE TAFT GROUP, 1992)

▶ This guide has been hailed throughout the nonprofit sector as the leading primer on board governance. Fully revised, updated, and expanded, this second edition of *Building a Better Board, Book I* reveals ways to hold productive meetings, develop criteria for evaluating organizational performance, apply the principles of plan-based governance, establish the crucial role committees play, and more. *Softcover, 89 pages, $10 (includes shipping)*

Building Effective Boards for Religious Organizations: A Handbook for Trustees, Presidents, and Church Leaders

THOMAS P. HOLLAND AND DAVID C. HESTER (JOSSEY-BASS, 1999)

▶ Through their admirable energy, dedication, and leadership, religious board members sustain our world's most invaluable organizations. This handbook offers insights from veterans of religious and nonprofit work on governing an organization with a religious mission. Drawing on years of research, consulting, and hands-on religious nonprofit work, the authors show how board members can clearly define their roles and mission, transform hierarchical structures into models of collaborative leadership, and organize for greater impact. From congregations and seminaries to soup kitchens, hospital chains, and social service agencies, *Building Effective Boards for Religious Organizations* examines both the nature and nurture of religious boards. Filled with real-life examples, it demonstrates how a religious board can escape common problems, and how understanding the full depth of the organization's mission can help it best fulfill its intended purpose. *Hardcover, 240 pages, $25*

Called to Serve: Creating and Nurturing the Effective Volunteer Board

MAX DE PREE (WM. B. EERDMANS PUBLISHING, 2001)

▶ In *Called to Serve,* internationally respected CEO Max De Pree offers experienced advice on how to create a successful nonprofit board. Now retired as chairman of the board of Herman Miller Inc., Max De Pree has been lauded by *Forbes, Fortune,* and the *Wall Street Journal* as one of the most sensitive and successful leaders in the business world. This experience comes through clearly as De Pree lays out the nuts and bolts of nonprofit organizations and provides the direction necessary to establish and nurture a volunteer board. Based on De Pree's many years of service on nonprofit boards, his work as a consultant in the field, and his work as a teacher who has already used this material successfully in numerous seminar settings, Called to Serve will benefit readers involved with any of the wide range of volunteer-based organizations, from boards of churches, hospitals, and libraries to boards of public works, foundations, and schools. *Softcover, 72 pages, $10*

Creating a Mission That Makes a Difference: Carver Guide 6

JOHN CARVER (JOSSEY-BASS, 1996)

▶ This Guide looks at how to write a mission statement that delivers a powerful message. It shows how to make the statement one of concrete, practical utility, not just inspirational value. It provides a useful Mission Statement Checklist and advice on how to evaluate the completed statement. *Softcover, 24 pages, $10.95*

Developing Dynamic Boards: A Proactive Approach to Building Nonprofit Boards of Directors

JAMES M. HARDY (ESSEX PRESS, 1990)

▶ This is a helpful, hands-on book that is full of exhibits, worksheets, evaluation tools, and examples. This practical work looks at all elements of board development with a good understanding of the human considerations with which board chairs must always work. Information is well organized, accessible, and clear. There is a good balance between theory and advice that can be readily applied to any board of directors. The book begins with an overview of board roles, responsibilities, and functions. It then examines all the key components of board development: board assessment and evaluation; recruitment, orientation, training, and education of board members; organization and committees; operations and meetings; and decision making. Wherever action is recommended, a framework or a form is provided. Hardcover, *194 pages, $24.95 (plus shipping)*

Doing Good Better!: How to Be an Effective Board Member of a Nonprofit Organization, Updated Edition

EDGAR STOESZ AND CHESTER RABER (CONTRIBUTOR) (GOOD BOOKS, 1997)

▶ Well-meaning individuals become board members, but few are given adequate instructions about how to do their job well. In this manual, two veterans of many boards lucidly address the ideal relationship between a nonprofit organization and its board. They candidly cover the realities that often threaten that relationship, then suggest strategies for overcoming these common difficulties. They include many stories, guidelines, and suggestions. *Softcover, 150 pages, $9.95*

Drucker Foundation Self-Assessment Tool, 2nd Revised Edition

GARY J. STERN AND FRANCES HESSELBEIN (JOSSEY-BASS, 1998)

▶ This completely revised edition of the Self-Assessment Tool combines long-range planning and strategic marketing with a passion for dispersed leadership. It allows an organization to plan for results, to learn from its customers, and to release the energy of its people to further its mission. Peter F. Drucker helps nonprofit organizations uncover the truth about their performance, focus their direction, and improve their overall effectiveness. The fully enhanced edition not only provides expanded methods of evaluation and planning, but also places special emphasis on implementing the decisions made in the self-assessment process. *The Drucker Foundation Self-Assessment Tool* consists of a *Participant Workbook* by Peter F. Drucker and *Process Guide* by Gary J. Stern. The *Process Guide* features step-by-step guidelines as well as sample reports, customer surveys, agendas for discussions or retreats, and a completed plan. Nonprofit leaders and their teams will find detailed instructions on how to work through the three phases of self-assessment: Preparing for Self-Assessment, Conducting the Self-Assessment Process, and Completing the Plan. The revised and expanded *Process Guide* lays out the three phases of a full self-assessment process and gives step-by-step guidance. It also includes sample reports and customer surveys, retreat and meeting agendas, sample completed plan, practical facilitation techniques, and a method for developing the mission statement. *The Streamlined Participant Workbook* has introductions and worksheets that coach users through each stage of answering Peter F. Drucker's Five Most Important Questions, a stronger focus on direct customer input, and a new Afterword on Implementing the Plan. *Softcover, 176 pages, $29.95*

The Effective Board of Trustees, Revised

RICHARD P. CHAIT, THOMAS P. HOLLAND, AND BARBARA E. TAYLOR (ACE/ORYX, 1993)

▶ This book shares the practical and tested experiences of board members and college presidents. Various dimensions of board performance are covered, from the ability to discern the culture and norms of the organization to the importance of being well informed about the roles, responsibilities, and performance of board members. The book also examines the board as a group, its ability to foster a collective welfare and cohesiveness, as well as its capacity to dissect complex problems, draw upon multiple perspectives, and synthesize appropriate responses. The authors describe how a board can develop and maintain healthy relationships with key constituencies and how it shapes institutional direction. It is a companion book to *Improving the Performance of Governing Boards* (see separate listing). *Hardcover, 144 pages, $27.95*

Effective Committees Set (Nine-Booklet Series)

(ASSOCIATION OF GOVERNING BOARDS OF UNIVERSITIES AND COLLEGES PUBLICATIONS)

▶ These booklets constitute one of the topic clusters in the Board Basics Series. They are intended to strengthen the role of key standing committees, in which much of the day-to-day work of boards occurs. These concise and practical publications will help you understand the roles and responsibilities standing committees play in developing effective policies. All members of every committee—committee chairs, newly named members, or seasoned members—plus the president and the board chair should keep these important booklets handy. The set includes the following Board Basics booklets: *Academic Affairs Committee; Audit Committee;*

Buildings and Grounds Committee; Committee on Trustees; Development Committee; Executive Committee; Finance Committee; Investment Committee; and Student Affairs Committee. Softcover, $49.95 ($44.95 for 10 or more)

The Effective Nonprofit Board: Responsibilities & Recruitment
ANN W. LEHMAN AND ROBERT W. ZIMMERMAN (ZIMMERMAN LEHMAN PUBLICATIONS, 1998)

▶ This book is filled with hands-on information on recruiting and retaining top-quality board members, tips on developing a board-led strategic plan for the nonprofit, and specifics on the board's essential role in fund raising. This volume helps boards avoid the embarrassing conflicts of interest that occasionally occur and also teaches them how to evaluate the executive director. It includes a model job description and an ideal board member orientation package. An extremely instructive handbook for capable but busy people, it gives board members the information they need to serve with enthusiasm and imagination as directors of a successful nonprofit. It answers such questions as: How do you recruit effective new board members?, How do you guarantee that your board will be top-notch fundraisers?, What are the respective responsibilities of board and staff?, How does a nonprofit deal with conflicts of interest?, and What should a board member job description contain? Also published as an e-published book (you can print it off the Web for $10). Softcover, 28 pages, $20

Empowering Boards for Leadership: Redefining Excellence in Governance (Audiotape)
JOHN CARVER (JOSSEY-BASS, 1992)

▶ This audiotape draws on Carver's Boards That Make a Difference to reveal how boards can see past the clutter of day-to-day details to provide real governance for their organizations. 120 minutes, $34.95

Enhancing Committee Effectiveness
JOHN F. SCHLEGEL (AVAILABLE FROM AMERICAN SOCIETY OF ASSOCIATION EXECUTIVES, 1994)

▶ One of the most practical reference tools you can give your committee members, this handbook offers a quick how-to reference for carrying out committee responsibilities. The booklet provides checklists and sample job descriptions for both staff liaisons and committee chairs. Learn helpful tips for developing agendas, conducting orientation, writing reports, and presiding over meetings. Softcover, 30 pages, $10 (Nonmember), $8.50 (Member)

Excel!
JEROLD PANAS (BONUS BOOKS, 1999)

▶ This is a collection of essays intended to motivate and inspire board members. It is, at one and the same time, an inspirational book for board members, a reminder to staff of the leadership qualities needed in our volunteers, a personal treatise on excellence, a heartfelt invitation to be your humanly best. It explores leadership, courage, and integrity; will instill a pride of association within you; and, more importantly, convey in your trustees an empowering sense that anything and everything is possible. Miniature hardcover, 96 pages, $14.50

Extraordinary Board Leadership: The Seven Keys to High-Impact Governance
DOUG EADIE (ASPEN PUBLISHERS, 2000)

▶ Despite the best intentions, many nonprofits never take full advantage of board members' wisdom, talents, influence, and contacts. Nonprofit leadership expert Doug Eadie has a method for changing that! In his new book, Extraordinary Board Leadership, Eadie reveals the power of "high-impact governance." With Eadie's guidance, chief executives, board members, and the entire leadership team can join in forging a partnership that transforms ordinary boards into extraordinary leaders. Drawing on experience with more than 400 nonprofits, Eadie helps nonprofits reach beyond success with "nuts and bolts" issues (writing bylaws, running good meetings) to develop dynamic leadership that makes the board a true asset in leading change and achieving unprecedented results. Softcover, 243 pages, $39

For the Good of the Cause: Board-Building Lessons from Highly Effective Nonprofits
DON TEBBE (CENTER FOR EXCELLENCE IN NONPROFITS, 1998)

▶ Author Don Tebbe has prepared real-world examples of nonprofit CEOs and board members who work as a team, have high standards, and are of vital benefit to their clients and communities in his new book, For the Good of the Cause: Board Building Lessons from Highly Effective Nonprofits. This Governance Case Study project (from which the book is based) was sponsored by the Center for Excellence in Nonprofits, which is a laboratory on nonprofit effectiveness.

The book, which is based on interviews with the executive directors of 20 successful nonprofits from the Washington, DC, Silicon Valley, and northern Ohio areas, is divided into three parts, with the first part devoted to conclusions drawn from the interviews. In it, Tebbe acknowledges he is more interested in exploring the practical aspects of board governance than questions of theory and urges board members to be proactive. The roles of board members are then delineated in broad terms and successful board traits are highlighted. A set of questions at the end of each chapter challenge readers to expand their vision of what constitutes an effective board. The second section presents a series of case studies citing specific examples of effective board management. The last section highlights specific tools that nonprofits have found to be useful in their board operations and relations.

This book looks at board governance practices of nonprofits that funders identified as "highly effective." It reports the results of the Governance Case Study Project sponsored by CEN, which examined 20 excellent community-based nonprofit organizations in California, Ohio, and Washington, DC. For the Good of the Cause distills observations into lessons and examples you and your board can use. It includes five key roles (what these boards do and how they provide value to the organization), five success traits (how these boards function and approach their work), and lessons for getting the most out of your board (how to use the best practices ideas from these boards). Softcover, 134 pages, $20

How to Build an Effective Board
RANDALL R. RICHARDS (AMERICAN SOCIETY OF ASSOCIATION EXECUTIVES, 1997)

▶ This book is fundamentally about leadership and tools for excellence in governance. Richards's descriptive models and principles make the typically complex concepts of leadership understandable and employable. The appendices include a treasure trove of practical tools to help you get started, such as visions versus mission exercises, ends versus means exercises, board business exercises, a sample policy manual, and a sample board member survey. An important how-to resource for association leaders, staff executives and volunteers alike, this book can be used to benchmark your board's performance and plan for future challenges and opportunities. *Softcover, 200 pages, $42.95 (Nonmember), $35.95 (Member)*

Improving the Performance of Governing Boards

RICHARD P. CHAIT, THOMAS P. HOLLAND, AND BARBARA E. TAYLOR (AMERICAN COUNCIL ON EDUCATION/ORYX PRESS, 1996)

▶ In their 1991 book, *The Effective Board of Trustees,* authors Chait, Holland, and Taylor identified six skill sets or competencies that differentiate strong governing boards from weak ones. Now they have taken their research to the next level by conducting an in-depth study of how the boards of colleges, universities, and other nonprofit organizations can raise their level of competence. In *Improving the Performance of Governing Boards,* the authors detail the findings of this study and address the topics of effective trusteeship, board development, board cohesion, trustee education, and the improvement of board processes. They also discuss effective ways of responding to the resistance some trustees and institutional leaders exhibit toward board development efforts. All of the recommendations offered in the book have been field tested. The text is enhanced with charts and exhibits, and revealing quotes from board members who participated in the study appear throughout. Readers will find that this book directly addresses the questions most frequently raised by institutional leaders and trustees about improving the effectiveness of governing boards. This book is a companion to *The Effective Board of Trustees* (see separate listing). *Hardcover, 161 pages, $34.95 ($29.95 for 10 or more)*

Increasing Board Effectiveness (Audio Seminar and Workbook)

NANCY L. BROWN (DESIGNS IN DEVELOPMENT)

▶ Do your board members know what is expected of them? Is the board functioning as effectively as it could be? This audio seminar is designed to be a guide for board members of not-for-profit organizations. Because board members function to "protect the public trust" in all of their decision-making processes, they must be aware of their obligations to the organization, including legal, fiduciary, and managerial responsibilities; attendance requirements; committee participation; financial support; and advocacy. Based on the seminar, topics include staff versus board roles and responsibilities, guidelines for strategic planning, predictable stages of growth in organizations, the board's role in fund raising, board composition analysis and nominating, running meetings and utilizing committees, attracting community resources, and avoiding liability. *Spiralbound, 88 pages, six audiotapes (three hours), $89 (plus $9 shipping)*

John Carver on Board Governance (Videotape)

PRESENTED BY JOHN CARVER (JOSSEY-BASS, 1993)

▶ John Carver presents his revolutionary model of board governance in this information-packed, two-hour color video. His popular approach energizes board members to build a strong, vibrant organization that achieves its goals. He reveals a conceptual framework for individuals who work with or are members of boards of nonprofit or public institutions. Carver describes how board members can formulate practical, concise policy statements, establish self-governance systems, delegate authority to the executive officer, and more. A question-and-answer session addresses the issues and challenges of board. *Two hours, 1/2" VHS video cassette, $99*

Making Boards Effective: The Dynamics of Nonprofit Governing Boards

ALVIN ZANDER (JOSSEY-BASS, 1993)

▶ This book provides a basis for understanding the interpersonal dynamics of governing boards, why and how they function the way they do, and how these processes affect the quality of their performance. It demonstrates that clarifying the board's mission and setting realistic, yet challenging, goals will result in increased commitment and responsible decision making. It offers insights and practical guidance for improving the internal functions intrinsic to boards, including setting goals, making sound decisions, and resolving conflicts. It provides a basis for understanding a board's interpersonal dynamics that affect the quality of board performance. *Hardcover, 189 pages, $27 (plus $4.50 shipping)*

Nailing Down a Board: Serving Effectively on the Not-for-Profit Board

CHARLES CALDWELL RYRIE AND CHARLES CALDWELL (KREGEL PUBLICATIONS, 1999)

▶ This is a concise guide that all individuals currently serving, or considering serving, on a not-for-profit board of directors should be required to read. This text is a complete guide on how a board should function as a board. *Softcover, 96 pages, $5.99*

New Effective Voluntary Board of Directors: What It Is and How It Works

WILLIAM R. CONRAD, JR. (OHIO UNIVERSITY PRESS, 2001)

▶ This book provides clear answers, backed up with graphics, to heretofore ambiguous and bewildering questions, such as definitions of policy, the function of boards, the roll of board members, and many other issues. It deals with the delicate balance in nonprofit organizations, the legal implications of serving on a board, the nonprofit leadership and management model, and other matters of concern. Conrad applies his lifelong experience to providing a comprehensive, practical, and concise tool for those involved in the unique challenges associated with the leadership and management of nonprofit and voluntary groups. *Softcover, 288 pages, $16.95*

Nonprofit Boards That Work: The End of One-Size-Fits-All Governance

MAUREEN K. ROBINSON (JOHN WILEY & SONS, 2000)

▶ The number of nonprofit organizations is growing increasingly across the United States and abroad, yet many nonprofit boards find that their goodwill often outweighs their governance skills, one of the most undertaught and underdiscussed areas of a nonprofit manager's job. Nonprofit Boards That Work provides hands-on advice and real-world examples for nonprofit managers and boards to apply directly to their own organizations. Backed by the National Center for Nonprofit Boards, this easy-to-read guide contains case studies, checklists, sample questionnaires, forms, and explanations to guide boards and their executive directors toward the development of a more thoughtful, intentional, and mission-conscious approach to governance that their particular nonprofit requires.

Effective governance is a joint undertaking—it emphasizes the fundamentally positive relationship that a board must establish with its executive director if an organization is to succeed. *Nonprofit Boards That Work* addresses role definition, key responsibilities, working culture, structure, and leadership—critical issues that boards must tackle if they are to play a meaningful part in helping a nonprofit achieve success. It offers practical advice and encouragement to nonprofit boards ready to improve the quality of their work. *Hardcover, 224 pages, $29.95*

Perfect Nonprofit Boards: Myths, Paradoxes and Paradigms

STEPHEN R. BLOCK (PEARSON CUSTOM, 1998)

▶ This book will help nonprofit organization CEOs and boards of directors expand their understanding about the most common processes that lead to ineffective governing boards and discover new approaches for improvement. The author explains the effective approaches that are most often used and promoted in board training and board development. The reader is presented with alternative ways of thinking about these approaches and is offered powerful tools and methodologies to advance board and executive director effectiveness. The content and arguments laid out in this book rest heavily on three positions. The first advances the idea of giving up and letting go of any expectations that board members should know how to implement the concept of board effectiveness. The second position asserts a strong belief that an effective board of directors is an outgrowth of an executive director's leadership and ability to skillfully and sensitively facilitate each board member's involvement—helping board members use their strengths, skills, and community connections for the purpose of achieving mutually agreed upon organizational objectives. The third position of this book entails the development of a set of tools for improving board commitment and participation. *Softcover, 149 pages, $21.95*

The Policy Governance Fieldbook: Practical Lessons, Tips, and Tools from the Experiences of Real-World Boards

CAROLINE OLIVER, MIKE CONDUFF, SUSAN EDSALL, CAROL GABANNA, RANDEE LOUCKS, DENISE PASZKIEWICZ, CATHERINE RASO, LINDA STIER (JOSSEY-BASS, 1999)

▶ Endorsed with a foreword by John Carver, this practical resource closely examines 11 diverse organizations that have implemented Policy Governance in the United States and Canada. The authors analyze what works—and what doesn't—in real-world practice. *The Policy Governance Fieldbook* is for organizations considering, beginning to use, or already using Carver's principles. Readers will discover practical advice based on the real-life experiences of organizations that have tried and tested Policy Governance for themselves. Each chapter is built around a user-friendly, hands-on framework—first introducing a specific Policy Governance activity or challenge, exploring the experiences of boards that met this challenge, and then drawing key lessons from those experiences. Filled with tips and tools for implementation of key principles, the book is far from a theoretical treatise. It is a practical exploration of real organizations facing real challenges. *Softcover, 272 pages, $29.95*

Reinventing Your Board: A Step-by-Step Guide to Implementing Policy Governance

JOHN CARVER AND MIRIAM MAYHEW CARVER (JOSSEY-BASS, 1997)

▶ This book is John Carver and Miriam Mayhew Carver's recipe for putting Policy Governance into practice. It is a natural companion to the best-selling *Boards That Make a Difference*. With 25 figures, policy samples, forms, and other practical, put-the-model-in-motion materials, these are the nuts-and-bolts materials that the Carvers' followers have been requesting. The authors illustrate effective board decision making, show how to craft useful policies, and offer practical advice on such matters as setting the agenda, monitoring CEO performance, defining the board role, and more. Step-by-step instructions and sample policies make this a valuable resource for boards in the public and nonprofit sectors. *Hardcover, 342 pages, $29.95*

Revitalizing Your Board of Directors: A Q. & A. Guide to Getting the Most from Your Nonprofit Board

JAMES M. HARDY (EMERSON & CHURCH)

▶ When working with your board, have you ever encountered problems such as the need to recruit wealthy board members, what to do with do-little chairpersons, spotty attendance at meetings, the need to retire unproductive trustees, lack of follow-through after meetings, dealing with trustees who consider fund raising belittling, how to get your board to evaluate itself, personality conflicts on the board, what to do when the board splinters into factions, or the need to make wholesale board changes? It sets forth dozens of problems that invariably arise when working with boards and shows you, in a pragmatic way, how to solve each of them to your satisfaction and that of your board's. Grouped under six broad chapter headings, the problems deal with recruiting matters, how to maintain effectiveness, problem board members, board and staff relations, workings of the board, and fund raising. Almost every imaginable problem is presented. *Softcover, 128 pages, $24.95*

Secrets of Successful Boards: The Best from the Non-Profit Pros

CAROL E. WEISMAN AND SANDY SINEFF (F.E. ROBBINS & SONS PRESS, 1998)

▶ This is a fascinating collection of essays about board management, including chapters on building boards with passion, board fund raising, trustee roles, effective meeting strategies, liability issues, strategic planning, volunteer issues, board–staff relationships, and Internet strategies. *Softcover, 192 pages, $25.00*

Self-Assessment for Nonprofit Governing Boards: Questionnaire for Board Members, Revised (Self-Assessment Kit)

(NATIONAL CENTER FOR NONPROFIT BOARDS, 1999)

▶ NCNB's proven *Self-Assessment for Nonprofit Governing Boards* is designed to help nonprofit boards determine how well they're carrying out their responsibilities and identify areas that need improvement. This evaluation toolkit includes a user's guide and 15 board member questionnaires so you can easily distribute the printed resource to your board. Confidential questionnaires enable board members to evaluate the board's performance as well as their own contributions. The user's guide leads the board facilitator through the process. It includes sample forms and instructions for tabulating the results. New to the revised edition is an updated scoring system to better reflect the board. The *Self-Assessment* is an ideal preparation for a board retreat, provides a board "checkup," and is a valuable resource for consultants and others who promote good governance. *52-page user's guide, 20-page questionnaire. Self-Assessment Kit: Includes user's guide and 15 questionnaires; $169.00 (Nonmember), $126.75 (Member); Each additional Questionnaire: $40.00 (Nonmember); $30.00 (Member)*

Strategies for Board Leadership: Carver Guide 10

JOHN CARVER (JOSSEY-BASS, 1997)

▶ This Guide cuts across various aspects of the policy governance model and challenges board members to move from paradigm to performance. *Softcover, 24 pages, $10.95*

TLD Guide for Organizations
(TRUSTEE LEADERSHIP DEVELOPMENT)

▶ This Guide introduces an organization to TLD and the PLANT (Preparing Leaders and Nurturing Trustees) process and prepares it to participate by providing resources for assessing its effectiveness and critical issues. *$25.00*

TLD Guide for Participants
(TRUSTEE LEADERSHIP DEVELOPMENT)

▶ This is an essential resource for board members participating in the PLANT (Preparing Leaders and Nurturing Trustees) process. *$25.00*

Board/CEO Relations
(See also Board Performance and Appraisal; Roles and Responsibilities)

Artful Leadership: Managing Stakeholder Problems in Nonprofit Arts Organizations
MARY TSCHIRHART (INDIANA UNIVERSITY PRESS, 1996)

▶ Nonprofit organizations sometimes face problems with stakeholders, and the organization's manager must then decide how to respond. In this study, Mary Tschirhart addresses three questions: What types of problem do managers experience with their organizational stakeholders?, What are their responses to these problems?, and What governs the use of different responses? Examples are based on interviews with managers of 24 nonprofit arts organizations, which yielded information on three types of problems—involving organizational legitimacy, stakeholder legitimacy, and efficiency. Along with detailed discussions of these problems, the author gives practical advice on addressing complaints. *Hardcover, 144 pages, $24.95 (plus $3.75 shipping)*

Assessment of the Chief Executive: A Tool for Boards and Chief Executives of Nonprofit Organizations, Revised
JANE PIERSON AND JOSHUA MINTZ (NATIONAL CENTER FOR NONPROFIT BOARDS, 1999)

▶ By failing to adequately evaluate the chief executive, many nonprofit boards miss an opportunity to express support for the executive and strengthen his or her performance. Neglect can be costly, resulting in high turnover, mistrust, and ongoing poor performance. While there is no single "correct" process or instrument that will be effective for every nonprofit, this publication provides a valuable and comprehensive starting point for the assessment process. This resource provides a comprehensive tool boards can use to evaluate the chief executive in a humane and constructive way. After discussing the benefits of assessment, the booklet suggests a process and provides a questionnaire that addresses every major area of the executive's responsibility. It also includes a self-evaluation form for the executive to complete and share with the board; and a diskette for IBM-compatible computers that contains the assessment instrument in WordPerfect for DOS and Microsoft Word for Windows formats, as well as generic text files. See also separate listing for *The Nonprofit Board's Guide to Assessing the Chief Executive. 56 pages, $52 (Nonmember), $39 (Member) (plus $6.50 shipping) (DC residents add 5.75% sales tax)*

Board Assessment of the CEO: Carver Guide 7
JOHN CARVER (JOSSEY-BASS, 1997)

▶ Now the wisdom of John Carver is more accessible to busy board members with the Carver Guide Series on Effective Board Governance. In this new series, a specific topic is addressed and questions that concern both new and seasoned boards are answered. These new guides are concise and written in easy-to-digest language. This Carver Guide tackles the important task of assessing whether or not your CEO is getting the job done. It shows what is meant by CEO evaluation, how your board should approach the matter, and what technique will best carry it out. *Softcover, 10 pages, $10.95*

Board Assessment of the Chief Executive: A Responsibility Essential to Good Governance
(Booklet)
JOHN W. NASON (NATIONAL CENTER FOR NONPROFIT BOARDS, 1990)

▶ Features clear descriptions of various methods of assessment appropriate for nonprofit organizations, the value of assessment to the organization as a whole, and the importance of a self-assessment by the chief executive. Introducing principles and guidelines to help boards establish a constructive process to evaluate the chief executive, it features clear descriptions of various methods of assessment appropriate for nonprofit organizations, offers criteria to consider, the value of the assessment to the organization as a whole, and the importance of a self-assessment by the chief executive. It provides guidelines to help boards establish an effective process to evaluate the chief executive; part of the Nonprofit Governance Series (see separate listing for additional titles). There is a 25 percent discount to NCNB members. *Softcover, 16 pages, $11 (plus $3.50 shipping)*

Build a Better Board in 30 Days: A Practical Guide for Busy Trustees
CAROL E. WEISMAN (F. E. ROBBINS & SONS PRESS, 1998)

▶ This is a practical guide for busy trustees, with great reminders for experienced board members and an easy orientation for new board members. It provides effective strategies for improving the effectiveness of a board. The book is geared to volunteer service boards but is useful to anyone serving as a board member. *Softcover, 136 pages, $12.00*

CEOs and Their Boards (ASAE Background Kit)
(AMERICAN SOCIETY OF ASSOCIATION EXECUTIVES, 1996)

▶ This book presents a broad overview of this important relationship. Topics include the CEO's role, the politics of being a CEO, building partnerships with the board; and consensus building. It is supplemented with case studies. *Spiralbound, 185 pages, $46 (Nonmember), $38 (Member)*

The CEO Role Under Policy Governance: Carver Guide 12
JOHN CARVER AND MIRIAM MAYHEW CARVER (JOSSEY-BASS, 1997)

▶ Just as Carver's Policy Governance transforms the board's job, it also transforms the job of the CEO. This guide offers practical advice for nonprofit CEOs on working with board members under this powerful model. *Softcover, 24 pages, $10.95*

Chief Executive Compensation: A Guide for Nonprofit Boards
(NATIONAL CENTER FOR NONPROFIT BOARDS, 1999)

▶ Now more than ever, nonprofits must compete for talented executive leadership. And salaries of nonprofit executives have been under increasing public scrutiny. Nonprofit boards must be able to craft a competitive salary and benefits package that not only reflects the values of the organization but helps to attract and retain the right chief executive for the job. *Chief Executive Compensation: A Guide for Nonprofit Boards* discusses the factors that affect compensation, including the organization's budget and staff size, the candidate's experience and abilities, and the geographic location of the organization. Board members will learn about the aspects of an employment contract and components of a compensation package, including bonuses, qualified retirement plans, and other benefits. Included in this booklet is a discussion of the new standards set by the intermediate sanctions provisions for determining compensation, and Form 990 reporting. *Softcover, 20 pages, $16.00 (Nonmember), $12.00 (Member)*

The Chief Executive's Role in Developing the Nonprofit Board
NONPROFIT GOVERNANCE SERIES (AVAILABLE FROM AMERICAN SOCIETY OF ASSOCIATION EXECUTIVES)

▶ The Nonprofit Governance Series addresses governance issues of immediate concern to executive staff and board members. The practical and concise booklets (12 to 28 pages each) answer questions relating to the board's fundamental responsibilities and involvement in specific key areas. *Softcover, $12*

Essentials of Presidential Search
WILLIAM A. WEARY (AGB PUBLICATIONS, 1998)

▶ This Board Basics booklet features an overview of the essential roles and tasks associated with conducting a presidential search and as such, it is ideal for search and, executive committees and boards preparing for a presidential search. *Softcover, 12 pages, $9.95 ($7.95 for 10 or more)*

Evaluating the Nonprofit CEO: A Guide for Chief Executives and Board Members
JOHN GILLIS (ASPEN PUBLISHERS, 1996)

▶ *Evaluating the Nonprofit CEO* is designed to be read and used by board members and covers all the points administrators like their board members to know about the performance appraisal process. This resource provides information about how board members can conduct regular, consistent, and fair evaluations and salary reviews. It contains tips and strategies to actually conduct performance appraisals. It includes useful forms, checklists, and questionnaires to make sure board members are fully qualified to write job descriptions, evaluate performance, and formulate achievable and measurable goals. *Loose-leaf, 160 pages, $96.00*

Executive Leadership in Nonprofit Organizations: New Strategies for Shaping Executive–Board Dynamics
ROBERT D. HERMAN AND RICHARD D. HEIMOVICS (JOSSEY-BASS, 1991)

▶ This book presents strategies used by effective executives to position their organizations and offers guidance on how executives can work more productively with their boards. Two scholars of management and leadership of nonprofit organizations, based on extensive studies of chief executives in nonprofit organizations, reveal the skills and leadership strategies that distinguish the most successful nonprofit managers. The authors describe the strategic links effective CEOs forge with their boards and offer detailed, practical advice on how executives can work more productively with boards to achieve their common purpose: the fulfillment of the organization's mission. *Hardcover, 174 pages, $26 (plus $4.50 shipping)*

Hiring the Chief Executive: A Practical Guide to the Search and Selection Process (Handbook)
SHEILA ALBERT (NATIONAL CENTER FOR NONPROFIT BOARDS, 1993)

▶ The departure of a chief executive can cause turmoil for any organization. The key to maintaining a well-run organization is to have a new chief executive step in as soon as possible. This guide reviews the essential steps of the process of hiring a new CEO, including obtaining legal advice, identifying the most important characteristics of the next chief executive, and interviewing candidates. It also includes a sample job description and systems for rating candidates. It provides valuable insight into how a board should handle this monumental task and discusses all aspects of hiring a CEO, including: (1) obtaining legal advice; (2) revamping the job description; (3) identifying the most important characteristics of the next chief executive; (4) checklist for determining compensation, and adjusting salary and benefits; (5) creating a search committee; (6) advertising the position; and (7) screening, interviewing, and making the final selection. It also discusses responsibilities of board members and suggests resources for further study. Included are samples of appropriate questionnaires, job descriptions, and interview rating sheets. It provides a four-month timeline for hiring a chief executive, along with advice on which steps can be eliminated should less time be available. Use this handbook, along with its companion, *Finding and Retaining Your Next Chief Executive: Making the Transition Work* (see separate listing) to help guide you through the process of hiring a new chief executive. There is a 25 percent discount to NCNB members. *28 pages, $16 (Nonmember), $12 (Member) (plus $3.50 shipping) (DC residents add 5.75% sales tax)*

How to Help Your Board Govern More and Manage Less (Booklet)
RICHARD P. CHAIT (NATIONAL CENTER FOR NONPROFIT BOARDS, 1993)

▶ This booklet helps your board members distinguish between shaping policy and hands-on management; shows that boards work best when they focus on setting, direction, policy, and strategy, not on administration; suggests specific procedures and policies that chief executives, board members, and senior staff can follow to strengthen the board's capacity to govern; advises actions that will shift the focus of a board's attention from management to governance; and explores the executive's and the board's roles and contains a list of suggested resources for further exploration. There is a 25 percent discount to NCNB members. *16 pages, $12 (Nonmember), $9 (Member) (plus $3.50 shipping) (DC residents add 5.75% sales tax)*

Nonprofit Boards and Leadership: Cases on Governance, Change, and Board–Staff Dynamics
MIRIAM M. WOOD, ED. (JOSSEY-BASS PUBLISHERS, 1995)

▶ This book offers detailed case studies that demonstrate the crucial strategic issues facing nonprofit governing boards and offers board members new methods for dealing with them. It provides a behind-the-scenes view of the inner workings of real-life board-rooms. Based on actual examples from such nationally known organizations as the United Way of Massachusetts Bay, California Hospital Medical Center, the University of Bridgeport, and AIDS Project Los Angeles, this book offers detailed case studies that demonstrate the critical strategic issues facing nonprofit governing boards. These and other case studies have been contributed by leading scholars in the nonprofit field, and are based on real events and issues that actual board members have grappled with and solved. As a survey of key governance problems, this book can be used as the centerpiece of a syllabus or as a vehicle for board members and chief executives to use in reviewing thorny situations and reflecting on their boards' problems. Each chapter is an actual story that outlines the context of the case, followed by questions for discussion. Readers are encouraged to study the case scenarios and develop their own solutions to the dilemmas presented; contents include: Introduction: Governance and Leadership in Theory and Practice; Part I: The Role of External Stakeholders in Governance; Part II: Complexities in the Board–Staff Relationship; Part III: Interpreting Mission and Accountability. It is supplemented with annotated bibliographies. *Hardcover, 266 pages, $24.95 (plus $4.50 shipping)*

Oversight or Interference? Striking a Balance in Nonprofit Governance
(NATIONAL CENTER FOR NONPROFIT BOARDS, 1995)

▶ This January 1995 special edition of *Board Member* examines the delicate balancing act board members must face in dealing with increasing pressures for accountability and admonishments not to interfere with the day-to-day management of the organization. Using the comments keynote speakers and participants of NCNB's second National Leadership Forum, this publication discusses the traditional distinction between governance and management, examines why boards tend to interfere in management, and offers advice on how boards can strike the right balance. It includes separate articles on governance on grant making, nonprofits and government, redesigning the board, and evaluating the chief executive, as well as a list of resources for further study. There is a 25 percent discount to NCNB members. *Softcover, 16 pages, $10 (plus $3.50 shipping)*

Presidential Search Guidelines and Directory
WILLIAM A. WEARY (AGB PUBLICATIONS, 1998)

▶ This easy-to-use reference and guide will help boards carry out their most important task—finding and selecting a chief executive. It describes what a board needs to know and do to select an executive search firm that best matches its institution. The book also features 15 probing questions a search committee should ask search firms to ensure that the institution invests wisely in a consultant. It includes profiles of leading executive search firms so boards may conduct an initial assessment of firms' experiences, review their prior searches, evaluate their other qualifications, and determine if a search firm might be helpful in the complex academic presidential search process. *Softcover, 36 pages, $125.00*

The Roles and Relationships of the Chief Volunteer and Chief Staff Officers, Board and Staff: Who Does What? (Booklet)
(INDEPENDENT SECTOR, 1988)

▶ Part five of the Nine-Part Nonprofit Management Series (see separate listing under Publications in Management section), it looks at the staff and board and answers the question, Who does what? *Softcover, 20 pages, $5 (Nonmember), $3.50 (Member) (plus $2.50 shipping)*

Board Composition

Building Board Diversity (Booklet)
JENNIFER M. RUTLEDGE (NATIONAL CENTER FOR NONPROFIT BOARDS, 1994)

▶ First product of the NCNB Diversity Project, it is an important new resource to help boards examine the issues of diversity and inclusiveness. It offers guidance in defining diversity within an organization, outlines the benefits that diversity can bring, and proposes a "tour phase" process that boards can use to become more inclusive and effective. It includes: (1) step-by-step suggestions for launching a diversity initiative; (2) tools that boards can use throughout the process, including a diversity issues discussion guide, an organizational audit questionnaire, and an annotated list of additional resources; and (3) a summary of the results of NCNB's national survey on the diversity of nonprofit governing boards, including a first look at the composition of nonprofit boards, and an examination of attitudes about diversity in the nonprofit sector; 25 percent discount to NCNB members. *50 pages, $18 (Nonmember), $13.50 (Member) (plus $3.50 shipping) (DC residents add 5.75% sales tax)*

Making Diversity Meaningful in the Boardroom: Carver Guide 9
JOHN CARVER AND MIRIAM MAYHEW CARVER (JOSSEY-BASS PUBLISHERS, 1997)

▶ What are the governance implications of a commitment to diversity? What kind of diversity should a board pursue? In this CarverGuide, John Carver outlines both the need and the nature of diversity around the board table. *Softcover, 10 pages, $10.95*

Making the Most of Our Differences
(TRUSTEE DEVELOPMENT LEADERSHIP)

▶ This resource provides a usable conceptual framework for administrators and board leaders to build more effective nonprofit organizations through consensus building. *$15.00*

Perspectives on Nonprofit Board Diversity
JUDITH MILLER, KATHLEEN FLETCHER, AND RIKKI ABZUG (NATIONAL CENTER FOR NONPROFIT BOARDS, 1999)

▶ Board diversity encompasses much more than race and ethnicity. This new Research in Action booklet presents three different researchers' perspectives on board diversity: representativeness, racial diversity, and gender diversity. Judith Miller examines the concept of representativeness on boards by drawing upon studies of differences inside various cultural and ethnic groups. Kathleen Fletcher investigates racial diversity. Her research of board members of Planned Parenthood affiliates reveals their struggles in attaining true diversity. Rikki Abzug shares her findings about the evolving roles women have played on nonprofit boards this century. *Softcover, 60 pages, $19 (Nonmember), $16 (Member)*

The Value of Difference: Enhancing Philanthropy Through Inclusiveness in Governance, Staffing, and Grantmaking
(COUNCIL ON FOUNDATIONS, 1993)

▶ Discover what more than 200 people in the philanthropic and corporate world know about inclusion practices. From information about broadening the governance process to altering staff profiles and redefining grant-making practices, this reference gives you a complete philanthropic view from those who are in the know.

Illustrates a range of responses from more than 200 people in philanthropy and the nonprofit sector on challenges from broadening the governance process to altering staff profiles. *Softcover, 60 pages, $35 (Nonmember), $20 (Member) (plus $2 shipping)*

Board Liability

(See also Accountability & Ethics; Roles & Responsibilities)

Board Liability: Guide for Nonprofit Directors

DANIEL L. KURTZ (MOYER BELL, 1988)

▶ This is the authoritative guide to avoiding liability, geared for boards of directors of nonprofit institutions and their lawyers. It is an in-depth examination of board responsibilities, emphasizing care, loyalty, and obedience. *Softcover, 179 pages, $12.95*

Directors and Officers Liability Insurance and Indemnification, 2nd Edition

JOHN A. EADIE (COUNCIL ON FOUNDATIONS, 1993)

▶ This is the resource for the nonlawyer when it comes to answering questions about indemnification and directors' and officers' (D&O) insurance such as: What are the real risks and how can they be minimized? What should one look for in a good D&O policy? How much coverage is needed? It is a book for the nonlawyer board member looking for a primer or for the experienced board member who needs a refresher. This revised edition discusses risks, how they can be minimized, what to look for in a good directors' and officers' liability insurance policy, and the effect of new state immunity statutes. *Softcover, 38 pages, $25 (Nonmember), $15 (Member) (plus $2 shipping)*

Essentials of Risk Management

(ASSOCIATION OF GOVERNING BOARDS OF UNIVERSITIES AND COLLEGES, 1998)

▶ Institutions are vulnerable to events that can lead to serious loss: financial mismanagement, personnel actions, loss of accreditation, and natural disasters among them. Effective risk management can mitigate the loss. The key is to anticipate and respond to serious exposures. This booklet describes trustees' legal and fiduciary responsibilities to protect their institutions and their exposure to potential personal liability if they do not exercise sufficient oversight of institutional affairs. *Softcover, 16 pages, $9.95 ($7.95 for 10 or more)*

The Financial Responsibilities of Nonprofit Boards

(See Roles and Responsibilities for full description)

Fulfill the Public Trust: Ten Ways to Help Nonprofit Boards Maintain Accountability *(See Accountaibility/ Ethics for full description)*

A Guide to Conflict of Interest and Disclosure

(ASSOCIATION OF GOVERNING BOARDS OF UNIVERSITIES AND COLLEGES PUBLICATIONS, 1997)

▶ This booklet provides broad guidelines to help private and public institution boards develop and adhere to sound conflict of interest and disclosure policies. It defines conflict of interest and offers an illustrative policy and a sample disclosure form that boards can adapt for their own use. *Softcover, 16 pages, $9.95 ($7.95 for 10 or more)*

Guidebook for Directors of Nonprofit Corporations

GEORGE W. OVERTON, ED. (AMERICAN BAR ASSOCIATION, NONPROFIT CORPORATIONS COMMITTEE, ABA SECTION OF BUSINESS LAW/NONPROFIT RISK MANAGEMENT CENTER, 1993)

▶ Written for a general audience, this Guidebook is filled with practical advice and legal guidance to assist directors of all types of nonprofit corporations in their duties and obligations. It covers how nonprofit corporations are structured, how boards and committees function, and potential risks and conflicts of interest, and includes numerous checklists and appendices. You'll learn what issues and potential problems are important to all directors of corporations, including how boards work: what they do, how they do it, and for whom; what responsibilities can and should be delegated to committees; the procedures to follow if you believe a corporate activity may be illegal; potential conflicts of interest—how to identify and deal with them; the director's right to indemnification from the corporation; protecting the director through insurance, and the issues to consider when reviewing an insurance policy; and maintaining the nonprofit tax exemption. While directors are not required to have a detailed knowledge of the various tax statutes and regulations affecting nonprofit corporations, they should have a general understanding of the basic application of federal and local tax laws. In an extensive chapter, the Guidebook summarizes principal federal income tax issues, including qualifying for exemption from Federal Income Tax. It also explains the advantages and requirements of achieving 501(c)(3), 501(c)(4), and 501(c)(6) status; what types of activities can produce unrelated business taxable income and the risks to losing the corporation's tax exemption; and the special reporting requirements for noncharitable contributions and charitable contributions in return for items of value. It includes numerous checklists, appendices, and suggested questions. At the end of each chapter is a list of questions that highlight the issues that should be considered by the director, followed by a checklist of issues to be reviewed by the corporation's chair, board of directors, chief executive, executive committee, nominating committee, audit committee, and legal counsel. Appendices also include a Statement of Policy Governing Conflicts, an organization reference chart from the IRS publication *Tax-Exempt Status for Your Organization*, and a list of suggested reading. *Softcover, 118 pages, $19.95 (plus $3 shipping)*

How to Assess Board Liability (Pamphlet)

(NONPROFIT CONNECTION)

▶ This is a fact sheet for nonprofit managers and leaders on assessing board liability in nonprofit organizations. Risks and liability insurance policies are discussed. *$25 (25 copies), $90 (100 copies)*

How to Manage Conflicts of Interest: A Guide for Nonprofit Boards

DANIEL L. KURTZ (NATIONAL CENTER FOR NONPROFIT BOARDS, 1995)

▶ Even though conflicts of interest are at the heart of a growing number of controversies involving nonprofit governance, few board members and chief executives understand exactly what constitutes conflict of interest and how board members can avoid it. Attorney Daniel Kurtz, a former New York charity regulator, explains the legal context of conflict of interest, offers examples of potential conflicts, and suggests guidelines for avoiding them. The booklet includes samples of conflict-of-interest policies and a checklist of items to consider when establishing a policy. *Softcover, 16 pages, $12 (Nonmember), $9 (Member)*

Leaving Nothing to Chance: Achieving Board Accountability Through Risk Management
(NONPROFIT RISK MANAGEMENT CENTER, 1998)

▶ Risk management plays a fundamental role in the governance of a nonprofit, and every board is both responsible for the overall well being of the organization and accountable to its constituencies. This new booklet outlines 10 steps for achieving board accountability through risk management, including formulating risk management policies; creating models for safe volunteer and staff activities, organizing a risk management committee; establishing sound financial management policies, ensuring proper management of the board's activities; and seeking expert help from trustworthy sources. *Softcover, 34 pages, $12.00*

The Legal Guide for Association Board Members
JAMES G. SEELY (AMERICAN SOCIETY OF ASSOCIATION EXECUTIVES, 1995)

▶ This concise reference tool covers all legal aspects of board service, with sections on association legal structure, tax-exempt status, antitrust matters, association liability, and board members' personal liability. It also includes a glossary and an appendix on understanding bylaws. *Softcover, 96 pages, $24.95*

Legal Obligations of Nonprofit Board: A Guidebook for Board Members, Revised
JACQUELINE COVEY LEIFER AND MICHAEL B. GLOMB (NATIONAL CENTER FOR NONPROFIT BOARDS, 1997)

▶ This primer on the legal responsibilities of nonprofit boards has been revised and updated to reflect changes in law enacted since it was originally published in 1992. Written by two attorneys with extensive nonprofit experience for those without a legal background, this booklet translates technical law into everyday language to help board member better understand their legal and fiduciary responsibilities. It includes new sections on the Lobbying Disclosure Act, the Volunteer Protection Act, private inurement, intermediate sanctions, and changes to the Internal Revenue Code that increase the obligation of tax-exempt organizations to publicly disclose federal tax returns. In addition, the booklet outlines how to avoid personal liability, how to structure contracts with outside parties, standards of conduct for board members, and more. The guide is applicable to board members and executive directors working with every category of the IRS-defined 501(c) grouping. Find answers to many everyday questions and common scenarios. It covers: (1) requirements imposed by federal and state laws; (2) specific board member duties; (3) what should be included in internal board and organization documents, articles of incorporation, bylaws, contracts, policies, and procedures; (4) board member liability; (5) suggestions on how to comply with legal requirements; (6) D&O (directors' and officers') insurance tips; (7) how to avoid personal liability; (8) the limits on lobbying and political activities as an individual or on behalf of an organization; (9) standards of conduct for board members; and more. It includes case studies illustrating legal principles. There is a 25 percent discount to NCNB members. *Softcover, 32 pages, $28 (Nonmember), $21 (Member) (plus $6.50 shipping) (DC residents add 5.75% sales tax)*

The Nonprofit Board's Guide to Bylaws: Creating a Framework for Effective Governance (Booklet and Diskette)
KIM ARTHUR ZEITLIN AND SUSAN E. DORN (NATIONAL CENTER FOR NONPROFIT BOARDS, 1996)

▶ Bylaws, the set of rules governing a nonprofit organization's internal affairs, are often neglected as a tool for ensuring good governance and are sometimes a source of confusion and frustration to nonprofit leaders. Attorneys Kim Zeitlin and Susan Dorn demystify the subject in simple, nontechnical language. They offer advice on the pros and cons of common bylaws provisions, and emphasize the important role bylaws play in ensuring effective governance. The booklet also includes a checklist of the elements bylaws should contain and sample language for common bylaw provisions. This diskette provides 11 sample bylaws from a variety of local, state, and national nonprofit organizations, allowing organizations currently writing, updating, or revising their bylaws to see how other nonprofits handle specific bylaw provisions. It is available on one diskette in Microsoft Word for Windows, WordPerfect (for DOS), and generic text files. *Softcover, 36 pages, $16 (Nonmember), $12 (Member)*

The Role of the Board and Board Members
(Booklet)
BRIAN O'CONNELL (INDEPENDENT SECTOR, 1988)

▶ Part one of the Nine-Part Nonprofit Management Series (see separate listing under Publications in Management section), which looks at the moral and legal responsibilities, strategies and goals, performance and rewards, staffing, and ways to involve boards of director members. *Softcover, $5 (plus $2.50 shipping)*

Recruitment and Development

The Board Manual Workbook: For Effective Boardmanship and the Development of an Orientation Manual and Instructor's Guide: Companion to the Board Manual Workbook
G.E. STRINGER, WITH K.B. ARSEM (VOLUNTEER CONSULTANTS, 1989—AVAILABLE FROM POINTS OF LIGHT FOUNDATION AND McDUFF/BUNT ASSOCIATES)

▶ Designed to help a nonprofit develop a board orientation manual, this Workbook may be used in a classroom setting; helps the user assess board strengths and weaknesses, identify jobs and skills for effective action, strengthen organizational structure, and provide a framework in which your organizational materials can be used. The Instructor's Guide provides an instructor or trainer with activities and exercises that will give the class valuable insights into board service. *Softcover, 35 pages, $9*

Board Member Orientation: Strategies for Association Executives
JEFF STRATTON, ED. (ASPEN PUBLISHERS, 1995)

▶ With every new member, the face, personality, and skills of an association board change. The sooner that these newcomers are brought up to speed about the business of the association and the board, the sooner all will benefit from the abilities they possess. This guide is designed to help executives provide effective, in-house orientation to rookie board members. It will help them walk through the basic responsibilities of board members, and provide a structure through which specific issues and characteristics about each association and board can be discussed. This resource boasts a wide range of forms and worksheets to assist the busy executive in setting up a customized program in his or her organization. *Looseleaf binder, 160 pages, $102 (plus $4 shipping)*

Board Member Orientation: Strategies for Nonprofit Executives

HOLLY KLENSASSER, ED. (ASPEN PUBLISHERS, 1995)

► This manual is designed to help executives provide effective, in-house orientation to new or inexperienced board members. It helps them walk through the basic responsibilities of board members, and provides a structure through which specific issues and characteristics about each association and board can be discussed. Sections include: Why Orientation Is Important, What Does Orientation Entail?, What Should You Include in Your Orientation Kit?, and Ongoing Orientation Can Enhance Board Performance. It includes many forms, letters, checklists, agendas, and worksheets to assist the busy executive in setting up a customized program in their organization. Materials are also available on IBM and Macintosh diskette. An edition targeted at association executives is also available (see separate listing). *Loose-leaf binder, 160 pages, $102 (plus $4 shipping); Diskette, $102*

Boards from Hell, 3rd Edition

SUSAN M. SCRIBNER (SCRIBNER & ASSOCIATES, 1998)

► Do you have Phantom Board Members, Bored Board Members, Mutant Ninja Board Members? Boards are great when they work well, but when they don't it can be very frustrating as boards of directors can make or break nonprofit agencies. Now you can turn your motley crew into an effective board. This is a humorous, insightful look at nonprofit boards. This guidebook is designed to help you develop your board from strength, identifying and solving board problems, defining appropriate roles for board and staff, organizing effective committees, recruiting and managing volunteer board members, learning how to use (and lose) volunteers, and actual steps for terror-free strategic planning to improve the board's value to your agency. A disk edition is also available for DOS, Windows, or Macintosh. *Softcover, 62 pages, $15; Electronic version, $89*

Boards That Make a Difference: A New Design for Leadership in Nonprofit and Public Organizations

JOHN CARVER (JOSSEY-BASS, 1990)

► Taking the position that board difficulties "are not a problem of people, but of process," the author presents a radically new model of board governance that energizes board members to build a strong, vibrant organization that achieves their goals. It calls for a shift away from reactive roles and getting down to the real business of governance: policy making, articulating the mission of the organization, and sustaining its vision, and how they can work with managers to get them implemented. It explains a method for executives and boards to divide responsibilities most effectively, outlining procedures for delegating authority to staff, evaluating management's performance, and making decisions as a board, all of which will help your board stay on course toward its long-term goals. *Hardcover, 266 pages, $27 (plus $4.50 shipping)*

Boards That Work: A Practical Guide to Building Effective Association Boards

DOUGLAS C. EADIE (AMERICAN SOCIETY OF ASSOCIATION EXECUTIVES, 1995)

► Focusing on the principle of the leadership team (the board and its CEO), this groundbreaking title teaches you how to develop and maintain a positive, productive working partnership. This constructive, creative approach to board relations abandons the emphasis on discipline, control, and rules, and moves toward board relationships based on flexibility, openness, and commitment to innovation. The author's "Board Leadership Design" concept challenges the untested conventional wisdom surrounding board organization and training. This unique vision is applied to the board's mission, membership, leadership training, performance management, structure, strategic planning, public relations, retreats, implementation of change, and more. It includes a resource list. *Softcover, 163 pages, $33 (Nonmember), $28 (Member)*

Building a Better Board, Book I: A Guide to Effective Leadership, 2nd Edition

ANDREW SWANSON (FUND RAISING INSTITUTE/THE TAFT GROUP, 1992)

► A primer on board governance, this fully revised, updated, and expanded guide reveals ways to hold productive meetings, develop criteria for evaluating organizational performance, apply the principles of plan-based governance, establish the crucial role committees play, and more. *Softcover, 89 pages, $10 (includes shipping)*

Building a Better Board, Book II: The Role of the Nonprofit Board in Strategic Planning

ANDREW SWANSON (THE TAFT GROUP, 1992)

► This companion to Book I provides assistance in defining your board's role in strategic planning. Noted author Andrew Swanson takes you through the process of establishing your organization's mission and involving your board, where necessary, to meet your goals. Accessible to both experienced board directors and those just starting out, Book II will help you monitor the progress of your plan. *Softcover, 75 pages, $10 (includes shipping)*

Building Board Diversity (*See Composition for full description*)

The Chief Executive's Role in Developing the Nonprofit Board (Booklet)

NANCY R. AXELROD (NATIONAL CENTER FOR NONPROFIT BOARDS, 1990)

► This concise and helpful publication identifies eight ways the chief officer can strengthen the governing board so that both the board and chief executive can work effectively together to fulfill the organization's mission. It includes a practical grid to help identify and select new board members. It is part of the Nonprofit Governance Series (see listing under Publications for additional titles). There is a 25 percent discount to NCNB members. *Softcover, 16 pages, $12*

The Corporate Employee's Guide to Nonprofit Board Service (Booklet)

CAROL E. WEISMAN (NATIONAL CENTER FOR NONPROFIT BOARDS, 1996)

► Employees of major corporations face a number of special considerations when they agree to serve on nonprofit boards. Employees with a business background may not understand the role of the board, the differences between for-profit and nonprofit organizations, or what will be expected from them as board members. This Guide was designed for employees who are about to join their first board. It includes sections on choosing a board that fits the employee's needs and interests and on clarifying expectations, including what the nonprofit will expect from the employee and the company, as well as what the company expects from the employee.

It also includes a primer on board service that answers many of the most common questions related to board service. *28 pages, $14 (Nonmember), $10.50 (Member) (plus $3.50 shipping) (DC residents add 5.75% sales tax)*

Creating and Renewing Advisory Boards: Strategies for Success (Booklet)

NANCY R. AXELROD (NATIONAL CENTER FOR NONPROFIT BOARDS, 1990)

▶ This book analyzes the ingredients necessary to create and strengthen advisory boards or committees. Practical suggestions and case studies describe a range of advisory board situations that help executive directors, advisory committee members, and development directors understand how to build effective advisory groups. It is part of the Nonprofit Governance Series (see listing under Publications for additional titles). There is a 25 percent discount to NCNB members. *Softcover, $12*

Creating Caring and Capable Boards: Reclaiming the Passion for Active Trusteeship

KATHERINE TYLER SCOTT (JOSSEY-BASS, 2000)

▶ *Creating Caring and Capable Boards* is for the millions of people who serve on nonprofit boards and for the executive staff who work with those boards. It offers readers a new and proven model of board leadership. Based on more than 10 years of practical experience, this step-by-step process can help board members to refine their understanding of the organization, strengthen their commitment to mission and goals, and improve their ability to lead cohesively and effectively. Author Katherine Tyler Scott explores the historical context of board service, explains the duties of board trustees, and offers straightforward exercises to help trustees fulfill their unique roles. Much more than a guide, this book invites boards to renew their commitment to improving the social sector through caring and competent leadership. *Hardcover, 224 pages, $26.95*

Developing Dynamic Boards: A Proactive Approach to Building Nonprofit Boards of Directors

JAMES M. HARDY (ESSEX PRESS, 1990—AVAILABLE FROM THE POINTS OF LIGHT FOUNDATION)

▶ *Developing Dynamic Boards* is written especially for CEOs and board chairs of nonprofit organizations. It provides a practical, nononsense approach to building an organization's board of directors. This book will help leaders of nonprofit organizations understand comprehensive board development and its components; clarify the role, functions, responsibilities, and relationships of the board of directors and staff; assess board members in relationship to eight factors that should be present for effective board functioning and to take appropriate action; retire "tired" board members and recruit new ones; conduct board orientation and training; maximize board member participation; institute effective decision making processes; recognize productive board members; and evaluate boards. *Hardcover, 194 pages, $25*

The Effective Nonprofit Board: Responsibilities & Recruitment

ROBERT M. ZIMMERMAN AND ANN W. LEHMAN (ZIMMERMAN LEHMAN, 1998)

▶ The authors explain how board members should meet five responsibilities: planning and implementation policies, ensuring good management, fund raising, complying with the law, and governing. This book answers the questions: How do you recruit effective new board members?, How do you guarantee that your board will be top-notch fund raisers?, What are the respective responsibilities of board and staff?, How does a nonprofit deal with conflicts of interest?, and What should a board member job description contain? This book is filled with hands-on information on recruiting and retaining top-quality board members, tips on developing a board-led strategic plan for the nonprofit, and specifics on the board's essential role in fund raising. This volume helps boards avoid the embarrassing conflicts of interest that occasionally occur and also teaches them how to evaluate the executive director. It includes a model job description and an ideal board member orientation package. An extremely instructive handbook for capable but busy people, it gives board members the information they need to serve with enthusiasm and imagination as directors of a successful nonprofit. *Softcover, 28 pages, $16.95*

Empowering Boards for Leadership: Redefining Excellence in Governance (Audiotape)

JOHN CARVER (JOSSEY-BASS, 1992)

▶ This tape discusses how governing boards can develop leadership skills; using scenes from typical board meetings, illustrates what good governance is; through examples of common problems that boards face, demonstrates how boards can keep their focus on the goals of the organization, prescribing ends but leaving means to the staff; and describes the characteristics that make a mission statement a powerful instrument of board governance, helping to make its values explicit and tangible. *2 hours, 2-cassette audio program, $34.95*

Finding, Developing, and Rewarding Good Board Members (Booklet)

BRIAN O'CONNELL (INDEPENDENT SECTOR, 1988)

▶ Part two of Nine-Part Nonprofit Management Series (see Management), it looks at recruiting, training, and nurturing good board members. *20 pages, $5 (Nonmember), $3.50 (Member) (plus $2.50 shipping)*

Fundamentals of Trusteeship (Audiotape and Videotape with Training Materials)

(AGB PUBLICATIONS, 1991)

▶ Become a better board member with AGB's one-of-a-kind audio–video training package, designed to help presidents and boards operate as a more cohesive, effective team. It gives trustees the knowledge and insight they need to help their institutions flourish and help them carry out their often ambiguous roles. These materials will benefit new trustees and veterans alike. This package of materials helps guide trustee orientation and development programs; contains a videotape, an audiotape, and a leader's manual to help your board orient new members, as well as explain board functions to other constituent groups; separate versions of the tapes and leader's guides for public and private institutions capture the nuances of trusteeship, including the basic responsibilities of boards and the special problems they face. The leader's guide describes how to use the videotape in a comprehensive trustee orientation program you can tailor to the needs of your organization. The audiotape, which is also available separately, describes the responsibilities of individual trustees, an ideal educational resource to help new board members learn on their own. Fundamentals videotape, audiotape, and Leader's Guide: *$99.95 (Nonmember), $70 (Member) (plus $7 shipping); Fundamentals audiotape: $14.95 (Nonmember), $12 (Member) (plus $3 shipping)*

How to Recruit Great Board Members: A Guide for Nonprofit Agencies

DORIAN DODSON (ADOLFO STREET PUBLICATIONS, 1993)

▶ This is a user-friendly book on the process of board recruitment for the small nonprofit or an organization in its early stages of development. Dodson's book is a good guide through the process of identifying what a board needs and how to recruit to fill that need. It is a nuts-and-bolts manual on the importance of understanding a group's mission and conveying it honestly to any prospective board member. The book is quite specific about where to find new members and how to enlist them. It gives concrete recruitment strategies and details options for maintaining the commitment of the good board members and for removing deadbeats. How to Recruit Great Board Members captures all of the information board recruiters need to identify, find, and persuade excellent prospects to sit on their boards. It also gives ideas on how to best use the time and talents of people who may want to help an organization but who are not ready to join the board, at least not yet. The last section contains sample recruitment letters, brochures, press releases, and public service announcements geared toward recruitment of board members. They can be used as is or modified to fit an agency's unique situation. Finally, there is a companion book "Should I Become a Board Member," also by Dodson, that addresses the question of board membership from the viewpoint of the person being recruited. *Softcover, 132 pages, $14.95*

Meeting the Challenge: An Orientation to Nonprofit Board Service (Video)

HOSTED BY NATIONAL PUBLIC RADIO'S RAY SUAREZ (NATIONAL CENTER FOR NONPROFIT BOARDS, 1998)

▶ Nonprofit board service can be a rewarding experience, but it can also be a challenge. Equipped with the right information, board members can carry out their responsibility for making sure that organizations are being run effectively and that their missions are rightfully supported. *Meeting the Challenge,* hosted by Ray Suarez, voice of National Public Radio's Talk of the Nation, highlights four basic principles of board responsibility determining mission and program, ensuring effective oversight, providing resources, and participating in community outreach. The video features interviews with board members, executive directors, and experts in the field of board governance as they share their experiences and insights into nonprofit board service. *Meeting the Challenge* can be used as a board orientation tool and as a starting point for board development and strategic planning. Included is a helpful 16-page user's guide with suggestions for viewing the video and questions to facilitate board discussion. *35-minute video, plus user's guide, $62.00 (Nonmember), $46.50 (Member)*

Six Keys to Recruiting, Orienting, and Involving Nonprofit Board Members (Handbook)

JUDITH GRUMMON NELSON (NATIONAL CENTER FOR NONPROFIT BOARDS, 1995)

▶ Make your board more effective with the revised edition of this comprehensive handbook. It offers a step-by-step approach to help organizations and nominating committees maintain active boards by attracting qualified and committed new members. It guides board and nominating committees through the all-important process of assessing current board makeup, identifying and cultivating prospects, and recruiting and involving new board members. It provides detailed suggestions, and hands-on tools such as model forms, sample letters, and checklists of first-year goals can be used as is or modified to meet specific board needs. Included are sample board development plans for nominating committees, bylaw language for establishing nominating committees, agendas for orientation meetings, and a checklist of first-year goals for new board members. It is also available on diskette for Microsoft Word (DOS or Windows), WordPerfect (DOS), and generic text files. There is a 25 percent discount to NCNB members. *Softcover, 64 pages, $36 (Nonmember), $27 (Member); Diskette only: $15 (Nonmember), $11.25 (Member) (plus $6.50 shipping) (DC residents add 5.75% sales tax)*

Strategic Board Recruitment: The Not-for-Profit Model

J. MICHAEL LOSCAVIO AND ROBERT W. KILE (ASPEN PUBLISHERS, 1996)

▶ Board recruitment is one of the most important and least understood functions of nonprofit boards. The search for new members often involves well-intentioned volunteers with little or no recruiting experience contacting well-intentioned candidates with little or no board experience. Such an approach to board recruitment is too limited in today's competitive nonprofit environment where leadership, fund raising, diversity, and vision are needed more than ever. The eight-step Strategic Board Recruitment model is based on the systems and techniques used by executive search professionals. It has been tailored to guide nonprofits in their ongoing efforts to strengthen their boards. This model provides a framework for executing and institutionalizing a results-oriented recruitment process. *Spiral-bound, 160 pages, $64.00*

Trustee Orientation Resource

(COUNCIL ON FOUNDATIONS, 1993)

▶ Learn your responsibilities and legal duties as a new foundation board member through this compilation of insights from 12 grant-making experts. Contributors such as John Nason and John Edie expound on key issues including understanding board liability, empowering new board members, determining program areas, creating a board, and making the first grants. *Softcover, 112 pages, $30 (Nonmember), $15.00 (Member)*

Welcome to the Board: Your Guide to Effective Participation

FISHER HOWE (JOSSEY-BASS, 1995)

▶ This book provides you with expert guidance and basic nuts-and-bolts information about board membership. In easy-to-understand, jargon-free language, the author answers the most common questions and concerns of prospective board members, outlines the key areas of responsibilities, and details the rights, obligations, and liabilities of nonprofit board members. Howe details the seven key responsibilities of a nonprofit board member, including how to go about the process of approving the mission, long-range planning, fund raising, and selecting and evaluating a chief executive. Additionally, Howe explores the leadership role each board member must assume if their organization is to excel. He dispels the commonly held notion that running a nonprofit organization is the same as running a business. It describes how you can become active in the various aspects of board governance: evaluating the board's composition, recruiting new members, appointing officers, and participating in meetings, to help your board achieve maximum effectiveness. It outlines what you have the right to expect from the organizations you are serving and explores the leadership role all board members must assume if their organizations is to excel. It includes a useful resource section containing information all board members should know. *Hardcover, 138 pages, $19.95 (plus $4.50 shipping)*

Board Retreats

To Go Forward, Retreat!: The Board Retreat Handbook

SANDRA R. HUGHES (NATIONAL CENTER FOR NONPROFIT BOARDS, 1999)

▶ Whether your board is bringing on new members, starting a strategic planning process, or conducting a self-assessment, a board retreat is perhaps the best place to address head-on some of the challenging issues facing your board and organization. Find out the importance of gaining full commitment from the board's leadership, selecting an outside facilitator, and setting clear and realistic goals. This handbook provides the do's and don'ts of a successful retreat planning process, including tips on icebreakers, seating arrangements, and alternative meeting spaces; involving staff, guests, and spouses; getting input from participants in the preplanning process; using humor and joy as a force in "jelling" a group. Also included is a helpful board retreat checklist and preretreat planning questionnaires to help with the planning process. *Softcover, 40 pages, $30.00 (Nonmember), $22.50 (Member)*

Planning Successful Board Retreats: A Guide for Board Members and Chief Executives Nonprofit Governance Series (Booklet)

BARRY S. BADER (NATIONAL CENTER FOR NONPROFIT BOARDS, 1992—AVAILABLE FROM AMERICAN SOCIETY OF ASSOCIATION EXECUTIVES)

▶ This booklet offers a step-by-step process for organizing a board retreat. It covers choosing issues to discuss at the retreat, coordination of logistics, preretreat interviews, a follow-up plan, and other topics; sample checklists, conducting preretreat questionnaires, deciding whom to invite, managing the retreat, and other topics. Sample checklists, preretreat questionnaires, suggested agendas for one- and two-day board retreats, and action plans are included. *Softcover, 28 pages, $12 (plus $3.50 shipping)*

Board Roles and Responsibilities

(See also Accountability and Ethics; Board Liability; Recruitment and Development)

All Hands On Board! The Board of Directors in an All-Volunteer Organization

JAN MASAOKA (COMPASSPOINT/NATIONAL CENTER FOR NONPROFIT BOARDS, 1999)

▶ In organizations without paid staff, such as neighborhood associations, local youth soccer leagues, or flower clubs, the volunteers both govern the organization and do the hands-on work. In this booklet co-published in partnership with the Support Center for Nonprofit Management in San Francisco (recently renamed CompassPoint), author Jan Masaoka describes the 10 jobs common to boards of all-volunteer organizations. Written for a grassroots audience, this booklet discusses basic legal and fiduciary responsibilities, management and group leadership, and collective and individual responsibilities. It also includes a board checklist. *Softcover, 24 pages, $12.00 (Nonmember), $9.00 (Member)*

Assessment of the Chief Executive: A Tool for Boards and Chief Executives of Nonprofit Organizations, Revised

JANE PIERSON & JOSHUA MINTZ (NATIONAL CENTER FOR NONPROFIT BOARDS, 1999)

▶ By failing to adequately evaluate the chief executive, many nonprofit boards miss an opportunity to express support for the executive and strengthen his or her performance. Neglect can be costly, resulting in high turnover, mistrust, and ongoing poor performance. While there is no single "correct" process or instrument that will be effective for every nonprofit, this publication provides a valuable and comprehensive starting point for the assessment process. This resource provides a comprehensive tool boards can use to evaluate the chief executive in a humane and constructive way. After discussing the benefits of assessment, the booklet suggests a process and provides a questionnaire that addresses every major area of the executive's responsibility. It also includes a self-evaluation form for the executive to complete and share with the board and a diskette for IBM-compatible computers that contains the assessment instrument in WordPerfect for DOS and Microsoft Word for Windows formats, as well as generic text files. See also separate listing for *The Nonprofit Board's Guide to Assessing the Chief Executive. Softcover, 56 pages, $52 (Nonmember), $39 (Member) (plus $6.50 shipping) (DC residents add 5.75% sales tax)*

Beyond Strategic Planning: How to Involve Nonprofit Boards in Growth and Change

DOUGLAS C. EADIE (NATIONAL CENTER FOR NONPROFIT BOARDS, 1993)

▶ This booklet suggests a process called *strategic issue management* designed to close the gap between what an organization wants to do and be in the future and where it actually is now. Although strategic planning has gained wide acceptance among board members and executives, many nonprofit organizations have found their excursions into strategic planning to be unproductive and disillusioning. This publication focuses on the practical steps boards can take to play a meaningful role in the process, helping you identify key strategic issues, and implementing a plan to ensure that each issue is fully developed and addressed. There is a 25 percent discount to NCNB members. *Softcover, 24 pages, $12 (Nonmember), $9 (Member) (plus $3.50 shipping*

Blueprint for Success: A Guide to Strategic Planning for Nonprofit Board Members (Videotape)

HOSTED BY MARIA SHRIVER (NATIONAL CENTER FOR NONPROFIT BOARDS, 1997)

▶ Commitment and participation of the board is essential during a strategic planning process. NBC news broadcast journalist Maria Shriver guides an exploration of how two nonprofit organizations and their boards carry out strategic planning. Board and staff leaders from the Mid-America Chapter of the American Red Cross and the Levine School of Music explain why planning is important, why the board must be involved, and the benefits and challenges of the strategic planning process. The video is the perfect motivational tool for nonprofit boards considering a strategic plan or about to embark on the process. The user's guide includes guidelines and discussion questions that will make the video a starting point for in-depth discussion. *25-minute video, plus 20-page user's guide, $62.00 (Nonmember), $46.50 (Member)*

Board Assessment of the CEO, Vol. 7

JOHN CARVER (JOSSEY-BASS, 1999)

▶ This *Carver Guide* tackles the important task of assessing whether or not your CEO is getting the job done. It shows what is meant by CEO evaluation, how your board should approach the matter, and what technique will best carry it out. *Softcover, 22 pages, $10.95*

Board Fund Raising Manual (Workbook/Manual)

SHERI CAMPBELL AND DARLA STRUCK, EDS. (ASPEN PUBLISHERS, 1992)

► This guide will walk your board members through every aspect of the fund-raising process, from convincing them that it's part of their job to teaching them how to set up an endowment. Each chapter in the *Board Fund Raising Manual* covers one specific area of fund raising: how board members can use their personal contacts to raise money and support for their nonprofit, how they can make corporate solicitations really pay off, how to conduct an annual drive or capital campaign, how they can maximize the "take" at all their special events, and how to make the best use possible of planned giving techniques. Designed for both the veteran and the rookie board member, the *Board Fund Raising Manual* is full of forms, worksheets, and checklists that will help your board members take ownership of the fund-raising process. All the material has been compiled through interviews with successful administrators, development directors, and board members. *Spiral bound, 75 pages, $29*

Board Leadership and Governance, Leadership Series (Booklet)

JILL MUEHRCKE, ED. (THE SOCIETY FOR NONPROFIT ORGANIZATIONS, 1993)

► In articles selected from the *Nonprofit World* journal, writers clarify board responsibilities and advise readers on assuring the highest possible quality for their boards. *Softcover, 106 pages, $20 (Nonmember), $17 (Member) (plus $4.50 shipping)*

Board Leadership Orientation Guide

(MANAGEMENT ASSISTANCE PROGRAM FOR NONPROFITS)

► This guide provides a comprehensive, yet highly practical overview of the roles and responsibilities of a nonprofit board and its members. New board members or those considering joining a nonprofit board will find the guide highly useful in explaining the unique role of nonprofits and their boards. The guide is an excellent resource to train new members. Experienced board members will find the guide useful in grounding and integrating their board experience. Straightforward worksheets help the reader to collect and organize key information needed for board responsibilities and operations. *Softcover, 25 pages, $10*

Board Member Manual Video, Vols. 1 & 2

(ASPEN PUBLISHERS, 1998)

► Actively involve your board members in learning their proper roles and responsibilities with these outstanding training videos. This is the perfect way to illustrate why board training is so important, and helps initiate discussions about potential explosive board situations. Each video presents four brief scenarios in which professional actors portray board members dealing with situations that are sure to strike home with your board. *Vol. 1, $49.00; Vol. 2, $51.00*

Board Member Manual 2000

CHUCK ELLIOTT AND JOHN GILLIS, EDS. (ASPEN PUBLISHERS, 2000)

► The *Board Member Manual* gives board members of nonprofit organizations a thorough understanding of the essentials of effective service. The manual is full of practical advice, ideas, and strategies from successful board members to help your board members meet the challenge of serving effectively. It is a ready reference when a board member doesn't know the right thing to do. Filled with practical, ready-to-use worksheets, checklists, and proven strategies, it defines your board's six key areas of responsibility and emphasizes the importance of leaving day-to-day management to the executive. Board members learn proper procedures, how to keep meetings on track and on schedule, and how to resolve differences without disruptive confrontations. The board learns the critical importance of long-term planning, how to draft a strategic plan, techniques for improving public relations and fund raising, and how to recruit the best new board members. Revised training videos (see separate listings) present four brief scenarios followed by discussion questions and instructions directing board members to the appropriate section of the book (Volume I depicts these scenarios: Dealing with Board Conflict at the Board Meeting, Micro Managing Finances, Meddling with Staff, The Poorly Run Board Meeting; Volume II depicts these scenarios: Rehashing Committee Work, The Maverick Board Members, Ineffective Administrator Evaluations, Neglecting Long-Range Planning). *Spiral bound, 64 pages, $49 (plus $4 shipping); Board Member Manual Video Volume I: $49; Board Member Manual Video Volume II: $51*

The Board Member's Guide to Fund Raising: What Every Trustee Needs to Know About Raising Money

FISHER HOWE (NATIONAL CENTER FOR NONPROFIT BOARDS (JOSSEY-BASS, 1991)

► This book highlights effective techniques in seeking support from individuals, government agencies, and foundations and asking for a contribution. The book starts and ends with board leadership, describing fund raising responsibilities of the board and how members can be effective in fulfilling this aspect of their role. Author Fisher Howe views fund raising as a part of overall board responsibility, and ends with an informative discussion on board composition, organization, and motivation. He shows why board members must take the lead in fund-raising efforts and helps members discover how their role in raising money for an organization they believe in can be personally satisfying. He offers helpful do's and don'ts and answers to board members' most frequently asked questions. Key elements of a successful fund-raising program are featured, with discussion encouraging and motivating active board member participation, including: (1) various techniques in seeking support from individuals, government agencies, foundations, and other organizations; (2) raising capital funds via planned giving, capital campaigns, and insurance; (3) making the request; (4) support activities such as publicity, prospect cultivation, research, preparation, proposal writing, and more; and (5) special issues such as cause-related marketing, ethics, and the use of fund-raising consultants. It ends with an informative discussion on board composition, organization, and motivation. *Hardcover, 16 pages, $29.95*

The Board Member's Guide to Strategic Planning: Charting the Future for Your Nonprofit

FISHER HOWE (JOSSEY-BASS, 1997)

► Nonprofit board members know that strategic planning can lay the foundation for strong governance, sound management, effective fund raising, and the solid evaluation of mission fulfillment. Howe's practical, no-nonsense approach demystifies the often intimidating planning process, showing why it is essential and providing detailed instructions for successful execution. Presenting illustrative examples and straightforward action steps, Howe guides board members through each critical step, from preparing and conducting the planning to production of strategic and operational plans. This compact guide for busy nonprofit board members demonstrates how strategic planning need not be tedious, irrelevant, or expensive. It shows how strategic planning can generate interest, enthusiasm, and pride in the performance of an organization. *Hardcover, 114 pages, $22.95*

A Board's Guide to Comprehensive Campaigns

JAKE B. SCHRUM, ED. (ASSOCIATION OF GOVERNING BOARDS OF UNIVERSITIES AND COLLEGES)

▶ Learn from the experiences of fund-raising pros who have contributed chapters on such topics as assessing institutional readiness, achieving trustee ownership, and building the case for a comprehensive campaign. *Softcover, 122 pages, $44.95*

The Board's Role in Fund-Raising

(ASSOCIATION OF BOARDS OF UNIVERSITIES AND COLLEGES, 1997)

▶ The governing board sets the standards for institutional commitment and advocacy—most notably in fund raising. This is a detailed look at the responsibilities of trustees as active participants in fund raising, why trustees are important donors, how a board's structure can positively affect fund raising, the annual fund, the comprehensive campaign, and the case statement. *Softcover, 16 pages, $9.95*

The Board's Role in Fund-Raising: How Your Board Can Strengthen Its Fund-Raising Effectiveness (Videotape)

(ASSOCIATION OF GOVERNING BOARDS OF UNIVERSITIES AND COLLEGES PUBLICATIONS, 1989)

▶ This video features a frank discussion among higher education and corporate foundation leaders. Moderated by Hodding Carter, the panel discusses how trustees can prepare for their fund-raising responsibilities, identify and cultivate donors, budget for fund raising, and more. It is an effective tool for orientation sessions, development committee and foundation board meetings, campaign planning sessions, and board workshops. It is applicable to all nonprofit organizations and is available in VHS or Beta format. *40 minutes, $89.95 (Nonmember), $60 (Member) (plus $7.50 shipping)*

The Board's Role in Maximizing Volunteer Resources (Booklet)

SUSAN J. ELLIS (NATIONAL CENTER FOR NONPROFIT BOARDS, 1999)

▶ While the vast majority of nonprofit organizations involve volunteers in direct service or support roles, the subject of volunteers rarely—if ever—is raised in the boardroom. This newly revised booklet discusses the recent national trends in volunteerism, and issues affecting board members who also function as volunteer staff. This booklet will provide your board with some fundamental questions such as: Are volunteers incorporated into long-range plans for the organization?, Are we budgeting appropriately to support volunteers?, Is there adequate staffing for the volunteer program?, and Are volunteers providing the best possible service in support of our mission? *Softcover, 23 pages, $16 (Nonmember), $12 (Member)*

The Board's Role in Strategic Planning

KAY SPRINKEL GRACE (NATIONAL CENTER FOR NONPROFIT BOARDS, 1996)

▶ This best-selling booklet explains the importance of strategic planning and why board involvement is essential. It discusses types of planning, defines key planning terms, and outlines a sample process. It emphasizes the importance of ongoing monitoring eval-

uation and revision once the plan is in place. It is a companion to their video, *Blueprint for Success* and is also available on audiotape. *Softcover, 24 pages, $9.00 (Member), $12.00 (Nonmember)*

The Budget-Building Book for Nonprofits: A Step-by-Step Guide for Managers and Boards

MURRAY DROPKIN, BILL LaTOUCHE (JOSSEY-BASS NONPROFIT & PUBLIC MANAGEMENT SERIES, 1998)

▶ This nuts-and-bolts workbook guides nonprofit executives and boards through the budget cycle, offering practical instruction on completing each step of the process. This one-source budgeting toolkit is specifically designed to give nonprofits everything they need to prepare, approve, and implement their own budgets. It provides smaller nonprofit budgeters and nonfinancial nonprofit managers with a simple, systematic method to create, maintain, and track their budgets. Examples, to-do lists, worksheets, schedules, and other hands-on tools help readers get down to work. Murray Dropkin draws on years of experience in working with nonprofit financial management to make this workbook an essential tool for anyone involved in financial management within a nonprofit organization. *Softcover, 192 pages, $26.00*

Building a Better Board, Book II: The Role of the Nonprofit Board in Strategic Planning

ANDREW SWANSON (THE TAFT GROUP, 1992)

▶ A companion to Book I, this guide provides vital assistance in defining your board's role in strategic planning for results; discusses the process of defining the organization's mission and involving your board, whatever degree of involvement the board may have in completing its plan; and helps you monitor the progress of your plan. It is beneficial to both experienced board directors and those just starting out. *Softcover, 75 pages, $10 (includes shipping)*

Effective Fundraising: Challenging Your Board to Raise Real Money (Videotape)

LESLIE G. BRODY, PRESENTER (LES BRODY ASSOCIATES)

▶ This video was produced to take the mystery out of the fund-raising process and provide a clear and concise approach for realizing your fund-raising goals. Brody, author of the book *Effective Fund Raising: Tools and Techniques for Success* (see separate listing under Publications in the Resource Development section), is shown working with board members and volunteers from a local community organization. He reveals successful fund-raising strategies and alleviates board members' concerns by providing reliable solutions to common fund-raising obstacles. This presentation will guide you through the fund-raising process and help ensure that you and your organization meet your fund-raising goals. Specific questions answered on this video include: How do you approach individuals?, What is the effectiveness of fund raising at various times of the year?, What about approaching someone for the second time?, Is there a way to get "easy money"?, and Do you want to hire someone to do your fund raising on a contingency basis? *45 minutes, $43.95 (includes shipping)*

Essentials of Presidential Search

(ASSOCIATION OF GOVERNING BOARDS OF UNIVERSITIES AND COLLEGES PUBLICATIONS, 1998)

▶ This booklet features an overview of the roles and tasks associated with conducting a presidential search, including how to assemble a search committee and define its responsibilities; how to compile a position description that reflects institutional mission and priorities; how to find and retain a search consultant, when appropriate; and how to screen and interview candidates. Ideal for search committees, executive committees, and boards preparing for a presidential search. *12 pages, $9.95*

Evaluations of CEOs by Their Boards *(See Board/CEO Relations for full description)*

Executive Compensation: Establishing Appropriate Compensation for Chief Executives of Nonprofit *(See Board/CEO Relations for full description)*

Executive Compensation: A Primer for Board Members and Chief Executives *(Board/CEO Relations)*

Financial and Strategic Management for Nonprofit Organizations *(See Financial Management—General for full description)*

Evaluating the Nonprofit CEO: A Guide for Chief Executives and Board Members
JOHN GILLIS (ASPEN PUBLISHERS, 1996)

▶ *Evaluating the Nonprofit CEO* is designed to be read and used by board members, and covers all the points administrators tell us they'd like their board members to know about the performance appraisal process. This resource provides information about how board members can conduct regular, consistent, and fair evaluations and salary reviews. *Evaluating the Nonprofit CEO* contains tips and strategies to actually conduct performance appraisals. It's full of useful forms, checklists, and questionnaires to make sure board members are fully qualified to write job descriptions, evaluate performance, and formulate achievable and measurable goals. *Loose-leaf, 160 pages, $96.00*

Fearless Fund-Raising: The Video Workshop
(NATIONAL CENTER FOR NONPROFIT BOARDS, 2000)

▶ Few relish the thought of asking for money, however worthy the cause. But for most nonprofits, raising money is an important way to ensure the necessary resources for the programs and services. *Fearless Fund-Raising* features a team of fund-raising experts and nonprofit leaders who explore the board's role in the fund-raising process. The workshop format also provides answers to questions from real board members and nonprofit staff members. You'll learn how the board and staff differentiate their fund-raising roles, strategies for helping board members become effective fund-raisers, how to prepare the board to be successful in fund raising, and how the process of fund raising is managed on a day-to-day basis. The program also profiles the experience of the board and staff of a small nonprofit in its efforts to begin a capital campaign. The 20-page user's guide provides questions and exercises for additional discussion. Use it to orient new board members and stimulate discussion at board and staff retreats. A must for your fund-raising library. *60-minute video, plus 20-page user's guide, $52.00 (Nonmember), $39.00 (Member)*

Financial Responsibilities
(ASSOCIATION OF GOVERNING BOARDS OF UNIVERSITIES AND COLLEGES, 1998)

▶ Trustees have no greater responsibility than to ensure an institution's financial health in support of its mission. A Bowdoin College trustee and vice president for finance and administration discuss the board's role in meeting its financial responsibilities, four funda-

mental questions trustees must ask when overseeing finances, how to monitor performance, and how to use comparison groups and data sources. *16 pages, $9.95 ($7.95 for 10 or more)*

The Financial Responsibilities of the Nonprofit Board: An Overview of Financial Management for Board Members, Revised *(Booklet)*
ANDREW S. LANG (NATIONAL CENTER FOR NONPROFIT BOARDS, 1998)

▶ This comprehensive publication, written for both the experienced and the new trustee, helps your board members understand their critical responsibilities in the key area of financial oversight. It addresses financial questions board members should ask about systems that protect nonprofit organizations in financial matters and explains in nontechnical language: (1) the most important elements of sound financial practice for nonprofits, (2) key financial issues that are especially challenging to nonprofit boards, (3) common signs of organizational distress to watch out for, and (4) step-by-step guidelines for fulfilling this trustee responsibility. It includes checklists on tax and regulatory filings, specific questions you should ask to ensure that the organization is operating appropriately, and systems that can protect nonprofits from financial harm. There is a 25 percent discount to NCNB members. *24 pages, $12 (Nonmember), $9 (Member) (plus $6.50 shipping) (DC residents add 5.75% sales tax)*

Finding and Retaining Your Next Chief Executive: Making the Transition Work *(See Board/CEO Relations for full description)*

Fund Raising and the Nonprofit Board Member, Revised *(Booklet)*
FISHER HOWE (NATIONAL CENTER FOR NONPROFIT BOARDS, 1998)

▶ This publication describes five principles each board member should understand so the board can carry out its responsibility to raise funds for the organization. A useful checklist helps board members (including those reluctant to solicit potential donors) do as much as possible to help raise funds. It is part of the Nonprofit Governance Series (see separate listing for additional titles). A 25 percent discount is offered to NCNB members. The audiotape version is also available, based on the booklet by Fisher Howe, read and adapted by Kent Martin. Running time: 30 minutes. *Softcover, 14 pages, $12 (Nonmember), $9 (Member) (plus $3.50 shipping)*

Fund Raising for Nonprofit Board Members *(Training Package)*
DARLA STRUCK (ASPEN PUBLISHERS, 1995)

▶ Increasingly, nonprofits depend on volunteer board members to raise money and support for their organizations. But this can often be an intimidating prospect for trustees. This resource is designed as a tool for nonprofit executives, foundation directors, and development directors to help convince their boards to participate, and to provide them with the basic information they need to undertake a variety of fund-raising activities. An optional training video is also available to illustrate the need for board member involvement in this crucial area. It takes you step by step through the entire fund-raising process and is packed with specific ideas and techniques that will improve your nonprofit's bottom line. It serves as both a comprehensive training guide and a valuable long-term reference that you and your board members will turn to time and time again. It covers every area of fund raising, from selecting the best board members to locating alternative sources of funding. It includes more than 30 ready-to-use forms. An optional diskette available is Microsoft Word 4.0 and DOS WordPerfect 5.1. *Loose-leaf, 160 pages, $112 (Manual only); Complete training package (manual, diskette, video): $198; Training manual and video: $168; Training manual and diskette: $142; Video: $81*

Fund-Raising Realities Every Board Member Must Face: A 1-Hour Crash Course on Raising Major Gifts

DAVID LANSDOWNE (BONUS BOOKS/EMERSON & CHURCH, 1996)

▶ David Lansdowne has distilled the essence of major gifts fund raising, put it in the context of 47 "realities," and delivered it in clear prose. It is brief, concise, easy to read, and free of all jargon. Further, it is a work that motivates, showing as it does just how doable raising big money is. Lansdowne addresses every important principle and technique of fund raising, and explains them in a succinct way board members will grasp immediately. *Fund Raising Realities* puts everyone on a level playing field—board member with board member, and board member with staff. *Softcover, 112 pages, $24.95*

A Guide to Fund Raising for Nonprofit Board Members (Videotape and Guide)

HOSTED BY HUGH DOWNS (NATIONAL CENTER FOR NONPROFIT BOARDS, 1996)

▶ ABC News journalist Hugh Downs walks viewers through a series of candid interviews in which real board members explain why fund raising is an essential board responsibility, how board members work in partnership with staff, why each board member should make a personal contribution, and how to ask for a gift. It is equally suitable for use at board orientation sessions, development committee meetings, or board retreats. Written by Kay Sprinkel Grace, the user's guide reinforces the video's principal points with discussion material and dialogue-generating questions. *30-minute video, plus a 20-page user's guide, $62.00 (Nonmember), $46.50 (Member)*

Guidebook for Directors of Nonprofit Corporations

GEORGE W. OVERTON, ED. (AMERICAN BAR ASSOCIATION/NONPROFIT RISK MANAGEMENT CENTER, 1993)

▶ Reduce your board members' fear of lawsuits and help them govern effectively. This guide explains a board's legal responsibilities, and how it can govern effectively, and suggests how to conduct board business in conformity with the law. It is an indispensable guide that covers what every nonprofit corporation director, board member, and legal counsel should know about their activities and roles, duties and obligations, risks, and legal requirements. It covers legal principles as they apply to nonprofit corporations, legal requirements and special risks, and good corporate practice, and summarizes important tax considerations. Topics include mission statements, delegating responsibilities to committees, handling conflicts of interest, keeping adequate records, protecting your tax-exempt status, and dealing with other common situations that can cause legal problems. Each chapter is followed by related questions and issues checklists. Appendices included. *Softcover, 118 pages, $20 (plus $4 shipping)*

Hiring the Chief Executive: A Practical Guide to the Search and Selection Process *(See Board/CEO Relations for full description)*

How to Help Your Board Govern More and Manage Less *(See Board/CEO Relations for full description)*

Long-Range Planning Manual for Board Members (Workbook/Manual)

DARLA STRUCK, ED. (ASPEN PUBLISHERS, 1993)

▶ Long-range planning should be one of your board's top priorities. A quality plan gives direction, prevents problems, and makes decision making considerably easier. This manual provides your board with the skills and tools to do the job right. It is packed with practical hints, worksheets, and forms your board will use. Highlights include: Why Is Planning So Important—And Why Should Board Members Be Involved; The Four Components of a Well Written Plan; Good Information Is the Foundation for a Good Plan; How to Write a Plan; Models You Can Use to Help in Your Planning Efforts; and Set Aside Time in the Boardroom or on Retreat to Make Your Planning Efforts as Effective as Possible. *Spiral bound, 44 pages, $30 (plus $5 shipping)*

Making a Leadership Change: How Organizations and Leaders Can Handle Leadership Transitions Successfully *(See Board/CEO Relations for full description)*

Nonprofit Boards: Roles, Responsibilities, and Performance

DIANE J. DUCA (JOHN WILEY & SONS, 1996)

▶ Too often, a nonprofit organization's efforts to fulfill its mission or use its resources efficiently are frustrated by an ineffectual, poorly defined, or adversarial relationship between the board and staff. *Nonprofit Boards: Roles, Responsibilities, and Performance* will help executives and board members avoid these conflicts with invaluable guidance and strategies for effective board management. This hands-on guide, geared specifically to the nonprofit sector, explores that difference. On these pages, executive directors, as well as experienced and first-time board members, will find all the tools they need to effectively carry out their organization's mission and manage its financial resources. Clear, concise, and easy-to-implement strategies cover all the major areas: organization and structure, roles and responsibilities, and accountability and ethics. It presents a variety of board models, the pros and cons of each, and guidelines for determining which model to use. It provides case studies and other real-life examples. Diane Duca helps executives and board members avoid conflicts with invaluable guidance and strategies for effective board management in this book. Diane J. Duca offers different ways to approach organizing and utilizing a board by presenting different board models. Using case studies and illustrations from real-life situations, she explores every aspect of board management, clarifies the roles of board members and executives, and discusses the board's legal and ethical obligations. In her discussion of core responsibilities—strategic planning, policy setting, fiscal oversight, and fund raising—Ms. Duca focuses on creating a spirit of cooperation between board and staff. *Hardcover, 192 pages, $29.95*

The Nonprofit Board's Guide to Assessing the Chief Executive *(See Board/CEO Relations for full description)*

The Nonprofit Board's Guide to Chief Executive Compensation *(See Board/CEO for full description)*

The Nonprofit Board's Guide to Finding, Hiring, and Evaluating the Chief Executive (See Board/CEO Relations for full description)

Nonprofit Mergers: The Board's Responsibility to Think the Unthinkable (Booklet)

DAVID LAPIANA (NATIONAL CENTER FOR NONPROFIT BOARDS, 1994)

▶ If your nonprofit is struggling to survive or you are looking for ways to strengthen your organization, you may need to consider a merger. Although it may not be the first choice, a merger might be your best choice to ensure your ability to fulfill your mission. This concise booklet makes a strong case for mergers and discusses why a merger should be considered, common characteristics of successful mergers, how a merger should proceed, potential problems that can block the process, and the board's important role in a successful merger. It provides questions to determine if your organization is ready for a merger and steps to assure a successful transition. *Softcover, 28 pages, $12 (Nonmember), $9 (Member) (plus $3.50 shipping)*

Planned Giving: A Board Member's Perspective

GRANT THORNTON LLP (AVAILABLE FROM THE NATIONAL CENTER FOR NONPROFIT BOARDS, 1999)

▶ The responsibility of asking for major gifts belongs with the board—and planned giving campaigns are no exception. Understanding the complexities of deferred giving and cultivating relationships with donors is key to the campaign's success. Unlike most fund-raising efforts, which often raise immediate cash, results from planned giving campaigns are seen over the long term. Written by the accounting and management consulting firm of Grant Thornton, *Planned Giving: A Board Member's Perspective* explains the different planned giving options available to donors. Board members will learn about present and deferred gifts, bequests, charitable trusts, and annuities. A planned giving campaign requires the commitment of time, effort, and proper management on the part of both board and staff. Find out if planned giving is right for your organization and for your donor. *Softcover, 28 pages, $12 (Nonmember), $9 (Member)*

The Policy Sampler: A Resource for Nonprofit Boards

KATHLEEN FLETCHER (NATIONAL CENTER FOR NONPROFIT BOARDS, 2000)

▶ In addition to steering the nonprofit organization's activities, nonprofit boards are also responsible for setting policies that govern their own actions. This new resource from NCNB provides nonprofit leaders with more than 70 sample board policies and job descriptions collected from a wide variety of nonprofits. The user's guide, written by Kathleen Fletcher, provides a basic overview for each of the policies. The diskette contains the full selection of sample policies and job descriptions that can be easily customized to suit your organization. Some of the sample policies included are anti-discrimination, capital expenditures, check signing and cash disbursement, confidentiality, conflict of interest, expense reimbursement, grievance, indemnification, investments, nepotism, sexual harassment, and more. Also included are sample conflict-of-interest disclosure statements, a board member contributions form, and a board member contract for board members to fill out and sign. The section on board job descriptions includes a general board member job description; job descriptions for board officers, committee chairs, and the chief executive; and job descriptions for

board committees. The PC-formatted diskette comes with both Microsoft Word and generic text files. *Softcover, 52 pages, $52.00 (Nonmember), $39.00 (Member)*

Presidential Search Guidelines and Directory

(ASSOCIATION OF GOVERNING BOARDS OF UNIVERSITIES AND COLLEGES, 1998)

▶ This reference and guide will help boards carry out their most important task—finding and selecting a chief executive. It describes what a board needs to know and do to select an executive search firm that best matches its institution. The book also features 15 probing questions a search committee should ask search firms to ensure that the institution invests wisely in a consultant. It includes profiles of leading executive search firms so boards may conduct an initial assessment of firms' experiences, review their prior searches, evaluate their other qualifications, and determine if a search firm might be helpful in the complex academic presidential search process. Softcover, 36 pages, $125.00

The Role of the Board and Board Members (Booklet)

BRIAN O'CONNELL (INDEPENDENT SECTOR, 1988)

▶ Part one of the Nine-Part Nonprofit Management Series (see separate listing under Publications in Management section), which looks at the moral and legal responsibilities, strategies and goals, performance and rewards, staffing, and ways to involve boards of director members. *$5 (plus $2.50 shipping)*

The Roles and Relationships of the Chief Volunteer and Chief Staff Officers, Board and Staff: Who Does What? (Booklet)

(INDEPENDENT SECTOR, 1988)

▶ Part five of the Nine-Part Nonprofit Management Series (see separate listing under Publications in Management section), it looks at the staff and board and answers the question, Who does what? *20 pages, $5 (Nonmember), $3.50 (Member) (plus $2.50 shipping)*

Sample Board Governance Policies: ASAE Background Kit, Revised

(AMERICAN SOCIETY OF ASSOCIATION EXECUTIVES, 1998)

▶ This book provides practical information on board roles and responsibilities, governing structures, officer position descriptions, volunteer liability, conflict of interest, nomination and election procedures, parliamentary procedure, and more. It includes more than 100 sample policies and documents. *Spiral bound, 532 pages, $66 (Nonmember), $44 (Member) (plus $6.25 shipping)*

Ten Basic Responsibilities of Nonprofit Boards, Revised (Booklet)

RICHARD T. INGRAM (NATIONAL CENTER FOR NONPROFIT BOARDS, 1996)

▶ NCNB's most popular resource discusses 10 core areas of board responsibility that can be adapted to fit the differing needs and circumstances of most nonprofit organizations. Basic board responsibilities include determining the organization's mission and purpose, choosing and evaluating the chief executive, ensuring effective planning, and participating in fund raising. An appendix discusses individual responsibilities. It is an ideal reference for drafting board and board member job descriptions, and assessing board performance. An audiotape version is also available. *Softcover, 26 pages, $12 (Nonmember), $9 (Member) (plus $3.50 shipping)*

Three Steps to Fiduciary Responsibility: Carver Guide 3

JOHN CARVER (JOSSEY-BASS, 1996)

▶ This Guide offers a strategic approach to the issues of finances and board responsibility, revealing how a board can get down to the business of governing its organization's financial planning by controlling budget values rather than budget numbers. It shows how a board can address the issue of actual fiscal conditions by creating policies that safeguard an organization's real fiscal health. *Softcover, 24 pages, $10.95*

Understanding Financial Statements (Booklet)

JOHN H. MCCARTHY AND ROBERT M. TURNER, WITH SANDRA L. JOHNSON, ED. (ASSOCIATION OF GOVERNING BOARDS OF UNIVERSITIES AND COLLEGES, 1998)

▶ This clearly written booklet explains the three types of financial statements recently required by the Financial Accounting Standards Board: the statement of financial position, the statement of activities, and the statement of cash flow. The authors also suggest the fundamental strategic question each type of financial statement is intended to inform, and they describe various external market assessments. The booklet summarizes a new AGB book by the same authors (see separate listing). *Softcover, 16 pages, $9.95*

Understanding Financial Statements: A Strategic Guide for Independent College and University Boards

JOHN H. MCCARTHY AND ROBERT M. TURNER, WITH SANDRA L. JOHNSON, ED. (ASSOCIATION OF GOVERNING BOARDS OF UNIVERSITIES AND COLLEGES, 1998)

▶ This definitive Guide demystifies financial statements and—in plain language and easy-to-understand charts and sample statements—helps trustees read and understand three basic statements. This important publication, which updates AGB's 1994 guide, takes a look at the new standards from the Financial Accounting Standards Board (FASB), 116 and 117, which trustees and business officers need to understand to carry out their fiduciary responsibilities. *Hardcover, 100 pages, $39.95*

Understanding Nonprofit Financial Statements: A Primer for Board Members, Revised (Booklet)

JOHN PAUL DALSIMER (NATIONAL CENTER FOR NONPROFIT BOARDS, 1996)

▶ This booklet includes definitions of key accounting terms and concepts, sample nonprofit financial statements with notes and explanations, and a discussion of SFAS 116 and 117 (nonprofit accounting rules). Dalsimer's no-nonsense explanations are particularly helpful for board members new to financial responsibilities or nonprofit accounting. It is useful for treasurers, finance committee members, and staff who prepare financial information for the board. *Softcover, 24 pages, $10 (plus $3.50 shipping)*

Understanding the Planning Process

(ASSOCIATION OF GOVERNING BOARDS OF UNIVERSITIES AND COLLEGES, 1997)

▶ Governing boards should ensure that planning takes place and use it regularly for decision making. A professor of marketing who is a strategic planning expert discusses how trustees can recognize and promote the usefulness of planning, review and approve an institutional planning process, hold the chief executive accountable

for planning, participate in certain steps of the process, and use the institution's plan to set priorities and allocate resources. *Softcover, 12 pages, $9.95*

Your Roles and Responsibilities as a Board Member: Carver Guide 2

JOHN CARVER AND MIRIAM MAYHEW CARVER (JOSSEY-BASS, 1996)

▶ This Guide shows how board members must be successful strategic leaders, willing to cherish diversity, strive for accountability, and pinpoint board positions, for the good of the organization. Describes the essentials of the board member's job, and relates the job to Carver's Policy Governance Model. *Softcover, 24 pages, $10.95*

Mergers and Restructuring

Nonprofit Mergers: The Board's Responsibility to Think the Unthinkable (Booklet)

DAVID LAPIANA (NATIONAL CENTER FOR NONPROFIT BOARDS, 1994)

▶ If your organization is struggling to survive, has ever considered a merger, or is looking for ways to serve more people or strengthen it, you may need to consider the "unthinkable"—a merger. Although it might not be your first choice, a merger may be your best choice to ensure your organization's survival. In this concise booklet packed with practical advice, the author, who has helped several nonprofits merge, explains why a merger is not "the end of the world" but perhaps the start of something stronger and better. It discusses: (1) why a merger should be considered, (2) what characteristics successful mergers have in common, (3) how a merger should proceed, (4) potential problems that can block the process, and (5) the board's important role in a successful merger. It provides questions to determine if your organization is ready for a merger and steps to assure a successful transition. There is a 25 percent discount to NCNB members. *Softcover, 28 pages, $15 (plus $3.50 shipping)*

The Power of Mergers: Finding New Energy Through Mission-Based Restructuring

(NATIONAL CENTER FOR NONPROFIT BOARDS, 1997)

▶ In a time of tightening governmental purse strings and increasing competition for funds, nonprofits are finding new ways to meet the needs they were created to fill. Led by the nonprofit health care industry, organizations from all mission areas are exploring mergers and other restructuring options as ways to support their missions and streamline the nonprofit sector. This special edition of *Board Member* discusses the potential pitfalls and perils, as well as the advantages and improvements, that accompany strategic restructuring. The issue includes case studies of actual mergers, alliances, and consolidations that discuss what worked, what didn't, and why; information on how to assess whether a merger might be right for your organization; and Guidelines for selecting the right partner and moving forward. *Softcover, 16 pages, $10 (Nonmember), $7.50 (Member)*

Seven Steps to a Successful Nonprofit Merger (Booklet)

THOMAS MCLAUGHLIN (NATIONAL CENTER FOR NONPROFIT BOARDS, 1996)

▶ How do you make a merger happen? From choosing the right partner to structuring the new organization to conducting post-merger evaluation, this booklet offers straightforward suggestions and guidelines to help determine whether merger partners will be compatible, design a process that builds trust between the two parties and resolves key management and governance questions, make decisions about the structure and character of the merged organization, and work around issues that may threaten the process. *Seven Steps to a Successful Nonprofit Merger* helps leaders complete the process. *Softcover, 28 pages, $12 (Nonmember), $9 (Member)*

Board Transition
(See also Board Mergers and Restructuring)

Board Passages: Three Key Stages in a Nonprofit Board's Life Cycle (Booklet)
KARL MATHIASEN III (NATIONAL CENTER FOR NONPROFIT BOARDS, 1990)

▶ This booklet helps nonprofit leaders understand predictable transitions and stages in a board's evolution that result from a growing and changing organization. Board members and chief staff officers will be able to anticipate, recognize, and prepare for change in their own board structure and operations. It examines three distinct phases of board evolution, identifying issues that arise at each stage. Predictable changes in board roles, functions, and member-

ship during each phase are described. The three phases are defined as the organizing board, the governing board, and the institutional board. It provides sound advice you can use to help your governing board adapt to change. Although the process is not inevitable and boards develop in different ways, the issues addressed will help board leaders manage change through any transition. *Softcover, 20 pages $12 (Nonmember), $9 (Member) (plus $3.50 shipping)*

Executive Transitions (Booklet)
NEIGHBORHOOD REINVESTMENT CORPORATION
(AVAILABLE FROM THE NATIONAL CENTER FOR NONPROFIT BOARDS, 1999)

▶ Finding the right chief executive can be one of the most challenging and important jobs of the nonprofit board. Whether searching for the organization's first executive, finding a successor to an effective or founding director, or replacing an ineffective executive, the transition process is the same. This booklet highlights three major phases of the transition: determining the role of the board during the executive transition; the step-by-step process for identifying and hiring candidates; and managing the new executive's transition into the organization. Underwritten by a grant from the W.K. Kellogg Foundation, this practical, how-to booklet provides board members with sample forms, worksheets, tips for advertising, screening and interviewing prospective candidates, and suggestions for preparing the staff for the new arrival. *Softcover, 31 pages, $8.00 (Nonmember), $6.00 (Member)*

PERIODICALS

Board & Administrator: Nonprofit Edition (Monthly Newsletter)

Aspen Publishers, Inc., 7201 McKinney Circle, P.O. Box 990, Frederick, MD 21701-9782
Tel: 800-638-8437, 301-417-7500; FAX: 301-417-7550

150 Third Street (Editorial Office), P.O. Box 226, Akron, IA 51001
Tel: 712-568-2418, 712-568-2418 (Board Issues Hotline); FAX: 712-568-3427
E-mail: aspenia@acsnet.com; WWW: http://www.aspenpub.com

▶ *Board & Administrator* is a network of administrators who share their strategies for improving their relationships with board members—therefore making their jobs easier. The newsletter is broken into two sections: the eight-page For Administrators Only report offers inside information on techniques administrators use to get their board members more involved, conduct productive board meetings, and keep them from interfering in management and staff issues. The two-page report to your board members will help them understand their proper role and serve more effectively. *Board & Administrator* tells your board members everything you wish you could tell them, but can't! In addition to the regular newsletter, there are Special Reports six times a year to cover topics in-depth. Finally, as a member of the *Board & Administrator* network, readers can call the Board Issues Hotline to discuss their board problems, meeting ideas, or simply to talk boards. Hotline calls from administrators all across the U.S. and Canada keep *Board & Administrator* readers up to date with the latest trends. *10 pages, $156.00/year (Supplemental board reports, $6 each)*

Board Leadership: Policy Governance in Action (Bimonthly Newsletter)

Jossey-Bass Publishers, 350 Sansome Street, San Francisco, CA 94104-1310
Tel: 800-956-7739, 415-433-1767, ext. 600 (Customer Service), 415-433-1740 (Editorial); FAX: 800-605-BOOK (2665), 415-433-0499
WWW: http://www.jbp.com/JBJournals/bl.html; http://www.josseybass.com/catalog/isbn/BL/

▶ *Board Leadership* gives you the latest information on how to use the Policy Governance Model to improve every aspect of your board's performance. The concise articles allow you to stay on top of the best thinking on governance in a minimal amount of time. Discover new ways to confront and overcome the tough issues that have been holding your organization back from greater success. It offers the insights of one of America's most innovative and sought-after board consultants. John Carver's unique approach to governance has already radically improved the way hundreds of boards conduct business, and improving governance means improving the entire organization. It offers the insights of a well-known board consultant; rather than treating the symptoms of board shortcomings, it deals with the flaws built into most board designs that can frustrate the efforts of even the most dedicated and talented board. Tables of contents for recent and forthcoming issues are posted on the *Board Leadership* page. *8 pages, $105 (Individuals), $139.50 (Boards—per individual)*

Board Member (Bimonthly Newsletter) (Ten Issues)

National Center for Nonprofit Boards, 1828 L Street NW, Suite 900, Washington, DC 20036-5104
Tel: 800-883-6262, 202-452-6262; FAX: 202-452-6299
E-mail: ncnb@ncnb.org, rosenblatt@ncnb (Betsy Rosenblatt); WWW: http://www.ncnb.org/boardmember/current.htm

▶ *Board Member* brings you practical case studies, informative checklists, interviews with some of the country's best-known trustees, and vital statistics about the nonprofit sector and trusteeship, keeping you up to date about nonprofit leadership issues. It provides: (1) the latest issues and trends in trusteeship today, including summaries of the latest research on nonprofit governance; (2) thought-provoking interviews with board members, chief executives, and other nonprofit leaders nationwide dedicated to nonprofit success; (3) practical case studies that examine governance dilemmas and solutions, with hands-on advice; (4) checklists of information you can use immediately; (5) statistics on the impact of the nonprofit sector; (6) a digest of current news on board issues; (7) provocative opinion pieces by governance experts; and more. It will help you define key responsibilities of board members; motivate board members to raise money; fine-tune the relationship between the board and the chief executive; identify, recruit, and train the right people to join a nonprofit board; plan board retreats; and more. It includes at least two special editions and Nonprofit Governance Case Studies: Volume I (collection of 12 of case studies sections from the first two years). Included in your annual subscription are seven regular issues of *Board Member* and three special editions. Features include summaries of new research into the sector; reviews of nonprofit resources; the latest program and event news from NCNB; Member to Member, where members answer other members' questions; and more. Included are seven regular issues, two special editions about a particular topic, and a special edition focused on the theme of NCNB's annual National Leadership Forum. An abridged version is available online at *http://www.ncnb.org/boardmember/index.htm. $88/year (Includes NCNB membership)*

The Chronicle of Philanthropy: The Newspaper of the Non-Profit World (See The Nonprofit Sector— Periodicals full description)

Community Risk Management and Insurance (See Financial Management—Periodicals for full description)

Leadership *(See Volunteerism—Periodicals for full description)*

Leading Ideas Newsletter (Formerly Trustee Educator) (Quarterly Newsletter)
Trustee Leadership Development, 719 Indiana Avenue, Suite 370, Indianapolis, IN 46202
Tel: 877-564-6853, 317-636-5323; FAX: 317-636-0266
E-mail: info@tld.org; WWW: http://www.tld.org/
▶ This newsletter covers issues facing not-for-profit organizations and their boards of trustees, and those consultants and trainers who work with these organizations. It also provides information regarding trustee leadership development activities and programs. Each quarterly issue brings new perspectives on leadership and leadership development. Contributing writers are scholars in the field of leadership. A preview of the current issue is available online at *http://www.tld.org/leading_ideas.htm. $25.00/year*

Legal-Ease *(See Legal Issues—Periodicals for full information)*

Nonprofit Alert Newsletter (Monthly Newsletter)
The Law Firm of Gammon & Grange, PC, 8280 Greensboro Drive, 7th Floor, McLean, VA 22102
Tel: 703-761-5000 or 402-292-5653; FAX: 703-761-5023
E-mail: sjschmidt2@earthlink.net (Sarah J. Schmidt, Editor), npa@gandglaw.com; WWW: http://gandglaw.com/
▶ This newsletter provides concise summaries highlighting legal, regulatory, and administrative developments that shape the nonprofit world, along with practice tips and resources for managing any associated risks. *$75/year*

The Nonprofit Board Report (Monthly Newsletter)
Progressive Business Publications, 370 Technology Drive, Malvern, PA 19355
Tel: 800-220-8600/5000, 610-695-8600; FAX: 610-647-8089
E-mail: Customer_Service@pbp.com;
WWW: http://www.pbp.com/

▶ This newsletter serves both executive directors and board members by investigating the changing needs and responsibilities of nonprofits and providing information to help make the relationship between the executive director and board more effective. It regularly presents the latest examples of how various nonprofits have successfully resolved fund-raising, management, and financial planning problems. It answers vital questions regarding due diligence and provides concrete solutions to the challenging leadership problems nonprofit organizations face today. *8 pages, $249/year*

Nonprofit Issues *(See Legal Issues—Periodicals for full description)*

The NonProfit Times *(See The Nonprofit Sector—Periodicals for full description)*

Nonprofit World: The National Nonprofit Leadership and Management Journal
(See Management—Periodicals for full description)

Trusteeship (Bimonthly Magazine)
Association of Governing Boards of Universities and Colleges (AGB), One Dupont Circle, Suite 400, Washington, DC 20036
Tel: 800-356-6317, 202-296-8400; FAX: 202-223-7053
E-mail: danl@agb.org (editor);
WWW: http://www.agb.org/periodicals.cfm
▶ This magazine reports on issues, trends, and practices in higher education to help trustees and chief executive officers better understand their distinctive and complementary roles and to strengthen board performance. It includes feature articles on public policy matters, board procedures, and presidential concerns; also regular guest columns, and timely news about higher education. Regular features include: Perspectives on the News, Focus on the Presidency, Views from the Board Chair, State Lines, Sum & Substance, Board Briefing, One Dupont 400, On My Agenda, and Other Voices. *$65 (Nonmember), $40 (Member)*

INTERNET RESOURCES

General

Alliance for Nonprofit Management—Board Development
▶ *http://www.allianceonline.org/faqs.html*

Ask NCNB
▶ This site features Frequently Asked Questions and Question of the Week Archive. *http://www.ncnb.org/askncnb/index.htm*

Board Governance—501 Click
▶ *http://www.501click.com/mt_bg_main.html*

Carver Governance
▶ *http://www.carvergovernance.com/home.htm*

Check out links to:
Policy Governance (*http://www.carvergovernance.com/model.htm*), Training Events Calendar (*http://www.carvergovernance.com/train.htm*), Publications (*http://www.carvergovernance.com/pubs.htm*), Reprint File (reprints from *Board Leadership: A Bimonthly Workshop with John Carver,* published by Jossey-Bass [http://www.josseybass.com]; available at *http://www.carvergovernance.com/tr.htm,* Governance Forums (*http://www.carvergovernance.com/forum.htm*)

Delaware Association of Nonprofit Agencies Answer Center—Board Management
▶ *http://www.delawarenonprofit.org/BoardFAQ.htm*

Foundation Center FAQs
▶ *http://fdncenter.org/onlib/faqs/nonprofit_boards.html*

Free Management Library Resources for Nonprofit AND For-Profit Businesses—Boards of Directors
▶ *http://www.mapnp.org/library/boards/boards.htm*

Gilbert Accountancy Corporation
▶ Provides management tips for nonprofits and associations. These downloadable files contain valuable information for setting board policies. Includes lobbying do's and don'ts, establishing an internal control checklist, devising a sound investment strategy for your nonprofit, determining if a for-profit subsidiary can benefit your corporation, and more. *http://www.gilbertcpa.com/doc.asp?id=249*

Information about Boards of Directors—About.com
▶ *http://nonprofit.about.com/careers/nonprofit/cs/helpforboards/index.htm*

Internet Nonprofit Center: The Nonprofit FAQ
▶ Sponsored by the Evergreen State Society, a Seattle charity that promotes civic involvement, this site provides information on the responsibilities of board members and the relationship between board and staff members. The information was compiled from the newsgroup soc.org.nonprofit, an online discussion about the nonprofit world. *http://www.nonprofits.org/npofaq/keywords/1a.html*

Nonprofit Boards of Directors—How to Evaluate Their Performance
▶ *http://www.pnf.org/boards.html*

Nonprofit GENIE—Board Development
▶ *http://search.genie.org/genie/ans_result.lasso?cat=Board+Development*

Nonprofit Management Solutions
▶ *http://www.nonprofitmgtsolutions.com/resource.htm*

Robert's Rules of Order
▶ *http://dolphin.upenn.edu/~philo/roberts-rules/index.html*

Serving on the Board of a Not-for-Profit Organization: A Guide for New Directors (Grant Thornton)
▶ *http://develop.grantthornton.appliedweb.com/resources/not-for-profits/serving98/serving98_toc.html*

Serving on the Audit Committee of a Not-for-Profit Organization
▶ *http://develop.grantthornton.appliedweb.com/resources/not-for-profits/audit/audit_toc.html*

Strategic Solutions FAQ—La Piana Associates
▶ *http://www.lapiana.org/strategic/faq/index.html*

Volunteer Consulting Group
▶ Maintained by the Volunteer Consulting Group, an organization in New York that provides assistance to nonprofit boards, this Web site includes a list of more than 45 organizations across the country that help match professionals interested in board service with charities that are recruiting new board members. *http://www.vcg.org*

Zwingle Resource Center for Academic Trusteeship and Governance

▶ Association of Governing Boards of Universities and Colleges (AGB), *http://www.agb.org/zrc2.cfm*

This is a repository for the best research and scholarship on trusteeship, governance, and the academic presidency. Originally the Trustee Information Center—an information "brokering" service—the newly named and recently dedicated Zwingle Resource Center has been transformed into a more interactive, full-service resource center. In the coming years, new acquisitions and improved services will enable the center to better address member needs regarding the practical aspects of trusteeship as well as the strategic issues and challenges facing the nation's college and university board members.

Discussion Lists

Board-Sense

▶ Discussion of issues related to boards of directors of nonprofit organizations.

To subscribe, send e-mail to *majordomo@AZStarNet.com,* with SUBSCRIBE BOARD-SENSE as the message. Leave the subject line blank.

Boards

▶ From CharityChannel, focusing on all aspects of nonprofit/NGO governance, board issues such as board creation and function, board member responsibility in fund raising, board member liability, and other legal issues involving board members, policies, etc.). *http://charitychannel.com/Forums/, http://24.10.159.37/archives/BOARDS.html*

There are two methods to subscribe:

1. Send e-mail to *listserv@CharityChannel.com* with *SUBSCRIBE BOARDS YourFirstname YourLastname* as the message. Leave the subject line blank.
2. Visit the CharityChannel Web site at *CharityChannel.com/forums* and click on the subscription information for BOARDS.

Online Publications

Board Café—CompassPoint

▶ This is the electronic newsletter exclusively for members of nonprofit boards of directors. Each issue will bring you a cornucopia of "Little Ideas," as well as one "Big Idea" you can use in your board work. Board Café is a collaborative project of the National Center for Nonprofit Boards and CompassPoint Nonprofit Services (formerly the Support Center for Nonprofit Management), and is sponsored in part by the Charles Schwab Corporation

Foundation. Board Café will be delivered to you the second week of each month. The *Board Café Annual Report* is available from their bookstore. *http://www.ncnb.org/askncnb/boardcafe.htm, http://search.compasspoint.org/board_cafe/bc_subscribe.lasso*

National Center for Nonprofit Boards: Board Member

▶ *http://www.ncnb.org/boardmember/index.htm*

Board Member Online

▶ Selected articles from the current and past issues of *Board Member,* the members-only periodical of the National Center for Nonprofit Boards, are available on the Center's Web site. *Board Member,* published 10 times a year, is a magazine that discusses issues that face nonprofit boards and provides advice on how members can improve their board's performance. An abridged version of the print publication, Board Member Online is designed to give you highlights of each new regular issue of the publication, and to serve as a ready archive of past issues. *http://www.ncnb.org/boardmember/index.htm*

The Board's Role in Public Relations and Communications—National Center for Non-Profit Boards

▶ Written by Joyce L. Fitzpatrick, president of a public relations company in Raleigh, North Carolina, this book argues that nonprofit organizations should develop communications plans and explains the role of board members in communicating with the public. The guide, which was published by the National Center for Non-Profit Boards, in Washington, also discusses how to manage public relations crises. *http://www.ncnb.org/askncnb/free.htm*

Building Bridges—Transitions in Leadership

▶ *http://www.tilnonprof.com/news.htm*

The Effective Board Member's Orientation Manual—(67K PDF file)

▶ This is a straightforward manual covering the essential skills for effective board members. *http://www.ginsler.com/documents/bdman.pdf*

Right From the Start—A Handbook for Not-for-Profit Board Members

▶ *http://www.oag.state.ny.us/charities/duties.html*

Trusteeship—Association of Governing Boards of Universities & Colleges

▶ *http://www.agb.org/periodicals.cfm*

PART V

Human Resource Management

ORGANIZATIONS

(See also Financial Management [Risk Management, Insurance, and Liability]; General Management; Legal Issues [Employment Law]; Organizational Development; Professional Development [Career Advancement, Personal Growth]; Volunteerism [Volunteer Management, Risk Management, Insurance, and Liability])

Academy for Human Resources Development (AHRD)

Mailing address: P.O. Box 25113, Baton Rouge, LA 70894-5113
Physical address: Louisiana State University, Old Foresty
Building, Room 142, Baton Rouge, LA 70803
Tel: 225-334-1874; FAX: 225-334-1875
E-mail: office@ahrd.org; WWW: http://www.ahrd.org,
http://www.ahrd.org/publications/publications_main.html

▶ The Academy of Human Resource Development was formed to encourage systematic study of human resource development theories, processes, and practices; to disseminate information about HRD, to encourage the application of HRD research findings, and to provide opportunities for social interaction among individuals with scholarly and professional interests in HRD from multiple disciplines and from across the globe. It sponsors the *Human Resource Development Quarterly* along with the *American Society for Training and Development,* published by Jossey-Bass. It holds an annual conference.

American Institute for Managing Diversity, Inc. (AIMD)

50 Hurt Plaza, Suite 1150, Atlanta, GA 30303
Tel: 800-757-AIMD (2463), 404-302-9226; FAX: 404-302-9252
WWW: http://www.aimd.org; http://www.aimd.org/resource.html

▶ Founded in 1984, AIMD is a national nonprofit education and research institute in the field of managing diversity. Research helps the general public clarify their vision, strategies, and goals as it relates to managing diversity. Work contributes to an ever-increasing body of knowledge in the field at local, state, and national levels. The stakeholders or benefactors of its work fall into four groups: policy makers, academicians, diversity practitioners, and individuals. Work is primarily focused in three areas: research, advocacy, and education. AIMD produces diversity educational services and products that stem from its research efforts. It is a repository of current research and literature on management practices, cultural change, and other topics related to organizational renewal. An examination of an organization's values, assumptions, practices, and systems represents the central thrust of its managing diversity concepts and organizational change development strategies. AIMD offers public and in-house seminars, in addition to awareness sessions. It maintains a speaker's bureau and publishes the quarterly newsletter *Chronicles of the Institute.*

American Society for Training and Development (ASTD)

1640 King Street, P.O. Box 1443, Alexandria, VA 22313-2043
Tel: 800-628-2783, 703-683-8100; FAX: 703-683-1523;
Information Center: 703-683-8183
WWW: http://www.astd.org/, http://astd.expoventure.com/
ASTDBuyerGuidenoreg/Booths/Booths.html,
http://www.astd.org/virtual_community/library/links_main.html

▶ Founded in 1944, ASTD is a major resource on workplace learning and performance issues. ASTD provides information, research, analysis, and practical information derived from its own research, the knowledge and experience of its members, its conferences, expositions, seminars, publications, and the coalitions and partnerships it has built through research and policy work. Services/ programs include: research and information (ASTD's research projects are workplace based and are focused on several key themes: the ways in which individuals and organizations learn; the links between workplace learning and individual and organizational performance; the organizational interventions that best improve performance and enhance workplace learning; and the systems dimension of performance); *ASTD's publications* (cover all aspects of learning and performance in the workplace. Its books, magazines, periodicals, and reports address the leading performance issues facing business and the profession and provide practical workplace tools for managers, professionals and technical workers); benchmarking service (provides standard measures that organizations can use to measure their training investments, practices, and outcomes, and compare those with training of other organizations); *ASTD Buyer's Guide and Consultants Directory* (a directory of training suppliers in the field of workplace learning and performance. The online version is searchable); annual ASTD International Conference and Exposition (world forum for presentation and discussion of new issues and practices in learning and performance); the ASTD TechKnowledge Conference and Exposition (brings together the worlds of technical training and learning technologies into one venue); Human Performance Improvement Certificate Program (providing the skills and hands-on experience training and performance professionals desire to address the changing needs in the workplace); *Info-Lines* (created with training and performance professionals in mind, *Info-lines* are 16- to 20-page single-issue publications that provide practical, concise help for developing training curriculum); *ASTD Audio and Videotape Collection* (available online at *http://www.astd.org/ virtual_community/avcatalog*); *Human Resources Development Quarterly* (available online at: *http://www.astd.org/virtual_community/astd_press/hrdq_main.html*); and *Training & Development* magazine (*http://www.astd.org/virtual_community/td_magazine*).

Association of Executive Search Consultants (AESC)

500 Fifth Avenue, Suite 930, New York, NY 10110
Tel: 212-398-9556
E-mail: aesc@aesc.org; WWW: http://www.aesc.org,
http://www.aesc.org/ClientProducts.html

▶ The Association of Executive Search Consultants (AESC) is the professional association representing retained executive search consulting firms worldwide. The Association consists of executive search firms that are committed to the high standards of professional practice outlined in the *AESC Code of Ethics and Professional Practice Guidelines*. AESC activities include government and legal monitoring (The AESC Government Affairs Committee and legal advisors monitor and make representations on legislation and legal developments in North America and Europe that impact executive search); professional development (courses and workshops, featuring leading experts/speakers are provided by the AESC on subjects such as interviewing and assessment, research skills, presentations, marketing, Internet research, and executive compensation); publications (*Executive Talent Journal*, the quarterly professional journal of the AESC, published in partnership with Kennedy Information, offers articles and research on the recruiting and retention of executive talent, senior executive careers, the international executive search industry, etc.); *Membership Directory* (annual directory is a full listing of member firms and their offices around the world. It is available free to all consultants of member firms, and at a specially discounted price for members to provide a complimentary copy to clients and candidates. The directory is sold to members of the public via the AESC Web site or directly from the New York office. An online version of the directory is also available at the Web site); *Search Connection*, AESC's newsletter that provides coverage of regional activities, the annual conferences in the United States and Europe, news on legal and legislative developments, profiles of members, and guest articles on issues affecting executive search and the senior executive market); *public relations; research; events* (annual conferences and regional events); online Management Library (information on career management at the senior executive level, compiled from AESC publications, AESC members' research, Harvard Business School Publications, and various other news and print sources); special discounts for AESC members.

Center for Management Assistance *(See Management—Support and Advocacy Organizations for full description)*

Equal Employment Advisory Council

1015 Fifteenth Street NW, Suite 1200, Washington, DC 20005
Tel: 202-789-8650; FAX: 202-789-2291
E-mail: info@eeac.org; WWW: http://www.eeac.org,
http://www.eeac.org/links.htm

▶ The Equal Employment Advisory Council (EEAC) is a nonprofit association made up of more than 340 major companies that are committed to the principle of equal employment opportunity. Founded in 1976, EEAC provides a wide variety of services and benefits to its member companies, some of which also are available to nonmembers. Services/programs include training (among the services that EEAC makes available both to members and nonmembers is a full curriculum of highly acclaimed training programs and seminars. In addition, EEAC offers several off-the-shelf courses that any organization can use for its internal training); publications (EEAC also offers a variety of comprehensive publications that serve both as manuals for EEAC's training seminars and as handy desk references should an EEO-related question or problem arise); special services (in addition to its regular member services like weekly memoranda and telephone clearinghouse, EEAC also offers a variety of Special Services. Available for a modest charge, these services include EEO-related software packages, pamphlets, and agency opinion letters, to name a few).

The Human Resource Planning Society

317 Madison Avenue, Suite 1509, New York, NY 10017
Tel: 212-490-6387; FAX: 212-682-6851
E-mail: info@hrps.org; WWW: http://www.hrps.org/html/index.html,
http://www.hrps.org/html/index.html

▶ HRPS is an association of more than 3,000 human resource and business executives. HRPS is committed to improving organizational performance by creating a global network of individuals who function as business partners in the application of strategic human resource management practices to their organizations.The Society provides current perspectives on complex and challenging human resource and business issues. HRPS is a nonprofit organization representing a mix of leading-edge thinkers and practitioners in business, industry, consulting, and academia around the world. This network is enhanced by conferences, educational programs, publications, local affiliates, and two Web sites, which provide for global electronic interaction.

International Federation of Training & Development Organizations, Ltd. (IFTDO)

1800 Duke Street, Alexandria, VA 22314-3499
Tel: 703-535-6011; FAX: 703-836-0367
E-mail: iftdo@shrm.org; WWW: http://www.iftdo.org

▶ IFTDO is a worldwide network of human resource professionals committed to identify, develop, and transfer knowledge, skills, and technology to enhance personal and organizational growth, human performance, productivity, and sustainable development. IFTDO's diversified network of human resource management and development organizations links HR professionals in HR societies, corporations, universities, consultancies, government organizations, and nonprofit enterprises. Its 150 member organizations represent more than 500,000 professionals in over 50 countries. *World Human Resource Directory* (WHRD), a publication of the International Federation of Training & Development Organizations, is free to IFTDO member organizations. It will be published periodically in hard copy in alternate years and, in abbreviated version, perpetually, in electronic format on the IFTDO Web site. It sponsors the annual World Conference and Exposition.

International Society for Performance Improvement (ISPI)

1300 L Street NW, Suite 1250, Washington, DC 20005
Tel: 202-408-7969; FAX: 202-408-7922
E-mail: info@ispi.org; WWW: http://www.ispi.org/

▶ Founded in 1962, the International Society for Performance Improvement (ISPI) is the leading international association dedicated to improving productivity and performance in the workplace. ISPI represents more than 10,000 international and chapter members throughout the United States, Canada, and 40 other countries. ISPI's mission is to develop and recognize the proficiency of our members and advocate the use of Human Performance Technology.

Assembling an Annual Conference & Expo and other educational events like the Institutes, publishing books and periodicals, supporting research, and recognizing outstanding achievements through the Awards of Excellence program are some of the ways ISPI works toward achieving this mission.

Management Assistance Group *(See Management— Support and Advocacy Organizations for full description)*

The Management Center Executive Search and TempExecs

870 Market Street, Suite 360, San Francisco, CA 94102
Tel: 800-344-NOCS (6627), 415-399-2643 (Claire Taylor, Executive Search Director); FAX: 415-362-4603
E-mail: ctaylor@tmcenter.org (Claire Taylor, Executive Search Director); WWW: http://www.tmcenter.org/programs/ess.html
▶ Services offered include search committee formation, documented process and timeline, in-depth organizational assessment, new/refined position specification, salary range recommendations, advertising, networking and recruitment, candidate screening, interview facilitation, reference and background checks, and compensation negotiations.

The Management Center's Human Resources Institute

870 Market Street, Suite 360, San Francisco, CA 94102
Tel: 415-399-4645; FAX: 415-362-4603
E-mail: bserbin@tmcenter.org (Baillee Serbin);
WWW: http://www.tmcenter.org.
▶ An intensive training program for nonprofit consultants to learn professional human resources consulting skills. Preference will be given to candidates with human resources or organizational development experience, particularly within the nonprofit sector. The program will help expand the availability of expert human resources consulting assistance to nonprofits throughout northern California. In addition, TMC frequently contracts with affiliate consultants who are skilled in human resources to work with human resources consulting clients.

National Human Resources Association

c/o Judy Huschka, JH Association Management, 6767 West Greenfield Avenue, Milwaukee, WI 53214
WWW: http://www.humanresources.org/,
http://www.humanresources.org/hrlinks.html
▶ Established in 1951, the National Human Resources Association is a nonprofit organization numbering approximately 1,500 professionals, managers, and executives engaged in human resources management and related fields. The National Human Resources Association has a network of affiliates in major metropolitan areas across the country that offer programs and activities of their local organizations and those at the national level. Membership in the National Human Resources Association is also available for human resource professionals who do not live near a local affiliate. These Members-at-Large enjoy all the benefits of membership.

National Multicultural Institute (NMCI)

3000 Connecticut Avenue NW, Suite 438,
Washington, DC 20008-2556
Tel: 202-483-0700; FAX: 202-483-5233
E-mail: nmci@nmci.org; WWW: http://www.nmci.org,
http://www.nmci.org/links.htm
▶ A private, nonprofit organization founded in 1983 in recognition of our nation's growing diversity and the resulting need for new services, knowledge, and skills; NMCI's mission is to increase communication, understanding, and respect among people of different racial, ethnic, and cultural backgrounds, and to provide a forum for discussion of the critical issues of multiculturalism facing our society. Programs include: diversity training and consulting (works with corporations, government agencies, professional associations, nonprofit organizations, hospitals, schools, and universities to help meet the long-range challenges of diversity; programs focus on both individual and organizational change); resource materials (produces educational resource materials for educators, trainers, mental health, and social service professionals; these include a manual on training diversity trainers, and books and videos on issues of cross-cultural mental health; online catalog at: *http://www.nmci.org/catalog/index.htm*); national conferences (sponsors conferences and workshops on professional issues relating to diversity; intensive four-day training programs are offered three times a year, as well as shorter workshops and courses; its annual spring conference brings leaders in the diversity field together to consider and discuss the ramifications of our multicultural society; renowned speakers and presenters attract a national audience that includes managers, administrators, human resource specialists, educators, mental health and social service professionals, mediators, and law enforcement officials); counseling and referral (experienced mental health professionals associated with NMCI provide therapy in 25 languages to individuals and families; also maintains information on community resources for multilingual counseling in the Washington, DC area).

National Rehabilitation Information Center (NARIC)

1010 Wayne Avenue, Suite 800, Silver Spring, MD 20910-3319
Tel: 800-346-2742, 301-562-2400; FAX: 301-562-2401;
BBS: 301-589-3563
WWW: http://www.naric.com
▶ Founded in 1977 and funded by the U.S. Department of Education's National Institute on Disability and Rehabilitation Research (NIDRR), NARIC is a library and information center that houses more than 43,000 documents on all aspects of disability and rehabilitation. In addition to reference and referral services, it offers customized database searches of REHABDATA (a computerized, annotated bibliography of the NARIC collection) and ABLEDATA (listing information on more than 20,000 assistive devices), and a free service that answers just about any question pertaining to disabilities. With over 180 databases and a large file-system library, it provides information about adaptive equipment (listing of over 25,000 pieces of equipment to help those with disabilities; this equipment includes everything from very high-tech, such as adaptive computers, to low-tech, such as daily living aids); laws (legislation related to disability issues, including accessibility standards); education (resources, financial aid, vocational training, rehabilitation, etc.); employment (employment agencies, specialized training, disability awareness on the job, interview techniques, etc.); medical data (medical library databases that can retrieve informa-

tion covering every existing disability, syndrome, condition, and disease. Fact sheets, guides, directories, software, and periodicals are available.

Nonprofit Risk Management Center *(See Financial Management—Support and Advocacy Organizations for full description)*

Pacific Disability and Business Technical Assistance Center

440 Grand Avenue, Suite 500, Oakland, CA 94610-5085
Tel: 800-949-4232, 510-465-7884; FAX: 510-465-7885
WWW: http://www.pacdbtac.org/services.htm,
http://www.adata.org/index-dbtac.html

▶ The National Institute on Disability and Rehabilitation Research (NIDRR) has established 10 regional centers to provide information, training, and technical assistance to employers, people with disabilities, and other entities with responsibilities under the ADA. The centers act as a "one-stop" central, comprehensive resource on ADA issues in employment, public services, public accommodations, and communications. Each center works closely with local business, disability, governmental, rehabilitation, and other professional networks to provide ADA information and assistance, placing special emphasis on meeting the needs of small businesses. Programs vary in each region, but all centers provide the following: technical assistance; education and training; materials dissemination; information and referral; public awareness; and local capacity building.

Society for Human Resource Management

1800 Duke Street, Alexandria, VA 22314
Tel: 800-283-SHRM (7476), 703-548-3440; FAX: 703-535-6490
E-mail: shrm@shrm.org; WWW: http://www.shrm.org,
http://www.shrm.org/buyers/, http://www.shrm.org/hrlinks/,
http://www.shrm.org/consultants/directory/

1600 West 82nd Street (Distribution Center), Suite 200,
Minneapolis, MN 55431
Tel: 800-444-5006, 612-885-5500; FAX: 612-885-5569
E-mail: shrmstore@shrm.org

▶ The Society for Human Resource Management (SHRM) is the leading voice of the human resource profession. SHRM provides education and information services, conferences and seminars, government and media representation, online services and publica-

tions to more than 125,000 professional and student members throughout the world. The Society, the world's largest human resource management association, is a founding member of the North American Human Resource Management Association (NAHRMA) and a founding member of the World Federation of Personnel Management Associations (WFPMA). It provides access to HR information, products and services designed to meet the needs of human resource professionals. It publishes the monthly *HR Magazine®, HR News™* (monthly newspaper), Issues in HR (bimonthly newsletter), *Mosaics, Workplace Visions,* and *SHRM® Legal Report.* Membership entitles you to participate in such networking benefits as HR job openings, SHRM® White Papers and HR Talk. Also, members can access the SHRM® Information Center, the HR hotline for assistance. SHRM membership gives you a listing in the SHRM® Member Directory Online, a "Who's Who" of the human resource profession. More than 450 SHRM chapters are located throughout the country.

WorldatWork (Formerly American Compensation Association and Canadian Compensation Association)

14040 North Northsight Boulevard, Scottsdale, AZ 85260
Tel: 877-951-9191 (Customer Relations), 480-951-9191
(Main switchboard); FAX: 480-483-8352
E-mail: customerrelations@acaonline.org;
WWW: http://www.acaonline.org, http://www.acaonline.org/
buyersguide/generic/html/buyers-home.html

▶ WorldatWork, formerly American Compensation Association, is a not-for-profit association of more than 26,000 human resource practitioners who design and manage employee compensation and benefit programs in their respective organizations. It is dedicated to knowledge leadership in disciplines associated with attracting, retaining, and motivating employees. It serves the worldwide profession's information, training, networking, and research needs. More than 25,000 human resources professionals, consultants, educators, and others are members of the association, which emphasizes total rewards, specifically focusing on *compensation* and *benefits,* as well as other components of the work experience such as work/life balance, recognition, culture, professional development, and work environment issues. WorldatWork offers certification and education programs, online information resources, publications, conferences, research, and networking opportunities. It holds seminars on benefits management, compensation management, total compensation, and the public sector. Useful features on its Web site include the bookstore, Buyer's Guide, and *Newsline.*

PRODUCT AND SERVICE PROVIDERS

Background Checks

American Background Information Services

629 Cedar Creek Grade, Winchester, VA 22601
Tel: 800-669-2247 (Customer Service), 540-665-8056;
FAX: 540-722-4771
WWW: http://www.americanbackground.com

▶ Since 1988, American Background has assisted organizations in selecting quality employees by providing employment screening services. Trained consultants with the know-how to design employment screening programs to fit a wide range of positions and industries are available to walk you through every step of the screening process. Their detailed knowledge of the EEOC guidelines and federal laws such as the Fair Credit Reporting Act, the Consumer Reporting Clarification Act of 1988, and the Americans with Disabilities Act is a valuable resource in developing a screening program that is both legal and fair. A customer service representative (CSR) is assigned to each client contact in order to perform account monitoring, status inquiry, and finding clarifications; initiate progress reports, urgent communication, and supplemental requests; facilitate dispute arbitration, and provide Web assistance. Their experts can draft an employment screening policy that is specific to your organization. Issues covered can include company goals, necessary forms, procedure, legal issues, and applicant rejection criteria. Services include criminal history research, social security traces, driving records, credit reports, employment history verifications, education/professional license verifications, workers' compensation claims, drug screening, and training and education.

Management Consultants—General

Clear Management Solutions

7863 Virginia Oaks Drive, Gainesville, VA 20155
Tel: 703-753-8067; FAX: 703-753-8097
E-mail: info@clearmgmt.com, karenlehr@clearmgmt.com (Karen F. Lehr, President); WWW: http://www.clearmgmt.com/

▶ Clear Management Solutions provides human resources consulting for small to mid-size organizations, specializing in nonprofit and government clients. Services include human resources, compensation, salary surveys, salary administration, performance management, policy and procedures manuals, and employee handbooks. Most of their clients are located in Virginia, Maryland, and the District of Columbia, and include nonprofit organizations and associations, government and quasi-government agencies, and private sector companies in a variety of industries.

Compensation Connections, Inc.

P.O. Box 1256, Hightstown, NJ 08520
Tel: 609-490-0895; FAX: 609-490-1197
E-mail: jkaspin@juno.com (Joan A. Kaspin)

▶ Compensation Connections, Inc., provides consulting services to help nonprofit organizations to achieve improvements in service, performance, and job satisfaction through the integration of mission, teamwork, and human resource practices. Using a collaborative problem-solving approach, clients achieve the solution that best meets their needs. Services offered include job descriptions, hiring practices, performance appraisal processes, salary surveys and analyses, pay and incentive plans, employee handbooks, human resources audits, staff satisfaction surveys, and orientation programs. In addition, Dr. Kaspin is a trained facilitator in the Drucker Foundation Self-Assessment Tool for nonprofit strategic planning.

Employease

One Piedmont Center, Suite 500, Atlanta, GA 30305
Tel: 888-EASE NET, 877-450-5500 (Customer Support), 404-467-6481
E-mail: info@employease.com, support@employease;
WWW: http://www.employease.com

▶ The Employease Network is the leading HR and benefits administration application delivered as a service over the Web. The Employease Network simplifies the administration and communication of employee and benefits information by delivering Fortune 500 Web services to small and mid-sized employers, Administrative Service Providers, managed care organizations, insurance carriers, and other employer services providers. Employease provides Employee Information Commerce solutions that improve the management and communication of human resource, employee benefit, and payroll information. Employee Information Commerce brings together small and mid-size companies with their service providers via the Employease Network, the business-to-business network for employee information. By building the Employease Network from the ground up as an Internet business service, Employease helps employers and service providers avoid the cost and complexity associated with traditional software.

The Great Place to Work Institute

286 Divisadero Street, San Francisco, CA 94117
Tel: 415-503-1234; FAX: 415-503-0014
E-mail: info@greatplacetowork.com, 100best@greatplacetowork.com;
WWW: http://www.greatplacetowork.com/

▶ Dedicated to bettering society by helping companies transform their workplaces. They work both to improve corporate performance and to raise the quality of employee worklife. To further these goals, the Institute provides a variety of diagnostic and consulting services to organizations interested in becoming great places to work, studies progressive workplaces and maintains an extensive database of best practices, produces magazine articles and books; and offers speeches and workshops. The Great Place to Work Institute's work is based on workplace expert and Institute co-founder Robert Levering's pioneering research for best-selling books like *The 100 Best Companies to Work for in America*. The Institute has developed an employee opinion survey instrument to help companies accurately assess the level of trust in their organizations and take actions to improve the quality of workplace relationships. Called the Great Place to Work Trust Index, it measures the three main elements of workplace trust: management credibility, an attitude of respect toward employees, and fairness in the workplace. It also measures employees' pride in their job/company and camaraderie among employees.

HR Consultants, Inc.

Law & Finance Building, 133 West Main Street, Suite 200, Somerset, PA 15501-2005
Tel: 800-255-2912, 814-444-1380; FAX: 814-445-3295
E-mail: gem@hrconsults.com Glenn E. Miller, Jr., President), jonna@hrconsults.com (Jonna M. Contacos, Vice President); WWW: http://www.hrconsults.com

▶ HR Consultants specializes in training and development, human resource management, benefits consulting, and human resource audit and compliance.

Human Resources ANEW, Inc. (HRA)

P.O. Box 2634, Columbia, MD 21045
Tel: 410-740-8084; FAX: 410-740-4321
E-mail: Anew@home.com; WWW: http://www.hranew.com

▶ HRA is a human resources consulting and outsourcing firm. Its programs are flexible and range in scope from recruitment assignments to periodic consulting or auditing on distinct issues to completely "managing" a human resources department. They can customize their services to meet your requirements and resources. They offer the following services to your organization: recruitment and retention, employment advertising and marketing, executive and management coaching, employee handbook and policy development, compensation and benefit administration, Web page design, recruiting for diversity, employee/labor relations, training and development, cross-cultural communications, regulatory/legal compliance, and business and human resources strategic planning.

Laurdan Associates, Inc.

10220 River Road, Potomac, MD 20854
Tel: 301-299-4117; FAX: 301-299-7486
E-mail: radler@laurdan.com (Ronald Adler, President); WWW: http://laurdan.com

▶ Laurdan Associates, Inc., founded in 1983, is a human resource management consulting firm specializing in HR audits, employment practices risk management, employee attitude surveys, sexual harassment prevention, and general HR issues. Products and services include the auditing tool: the Employment–Labor Law Audit (ELLA), the ELLA Assistance Hotline, and ELLA training.

Laurdan's consulting activities help employers increase the value of their human resource asset and reduce their exposure to employment-related claims and lawsuits. Laurdan's consulting activities include human resource management and employment practice audits, employment issues (e.g., sexual harassment, training programs); employee handbooks, employer policies, and employee communications; and general human resource management assistance, including outsourced HR functions.

Linkage, Inc.

One Forbes Road, Lexington, MA 02421
Tel: 781-862-3157; FAX: 781-862-2355
E-mail: info@linkage-inc.com; WWW: http://www.linkageinc.com

▶ Linkage is a leading provider of corporate education and consulting for human resource, human resource development, organizational development, and training professionals worldwide. Services include conferences (hosts conferences and expositions worldwide on strategic human resource and training topics. Linkage conferences feature world-class speakers and best-practice case studies from leading organizations); consulting (its Consulting Group is composed of industry-specific practices, which focus on the design, development, and application of organizational development tools, techniques, and assessment instruments to enhance and sustain superior human performance); Best Practices Consortium (enables companies to benchmark the latest HRD and OD topics, network with others in the field, learn from new research and study results, and reap the benefits of Linkage's world-class educational programs); Linkage service and products (benchmarks organizational best practices to identify the critical success factors of twenty-first century organizations); educational resources (one-stop shopping for leading HR books, audiotapes, workbooks, tools, and conference proceedings); workshops (offers practical skill-building workshops and tools for HR practitioner development. Public workshops are offered in the United States, and on-site training can be customized for your organization); institutes (provides programs and services targeted at the long-term leadership development of individuals and teams from the best organizations); technology training programs (offered publicly with its University partners, or on-site for organizations, designed to give you or your employees the skills needed to succeed in today's high-tech environment); and satellite programs and distance learning.

The Management Center

870 Market Street, Suite 800, San Francisco, CA 94102-4010
Tel: 800-344-NOCS (6627), 415-362-9735; FAX: 415-362-4603
E-mail: tmc@tmcenter.org; WWW: http://www.tmcenter.org

▶ The Management Center provides human resource consulting expertise in the following areas: customized compensation and benefit studies, customized employee policy, and books; management training including team building, communication, and leadership; performance management systems; organizational reporting structure and reorganization; executive coaching; human resources needs assessments; diversity training; harassment prevention training; staff retreats; mediation; temp execs (interim management placement service); and executive search services. Its Human Resources Institute is an intensive training program for nonprofit consultants to learn professional human resources consulting skills. For additional information, visit its online TMC Human Resources Consulting (*http://www.tmcenter.org/tmc/consultants.html*) or send e-mail requests to Baillee Serbin at bserbin@tmcenter.org.

NFP Consulting Resources

1690 Starling Drive, Sarasota, FL 34231
Tel: 941-922-1690
E-mail: NOlshansky@AOL.COM (Norman Olshansky, President),
Info@nfpconsulting.com; WWW: http://www.nfpconsulting.com/
fundraising.html

▶ NFP Consulting can help you and your organization accomplish your goals and develop the skills and experience necessary for short- and long-term success. Norman Olshansky, President of NFP Consulting Resources, brings with him over 20 years of professional and executive level leadership and consulting within both the not-for-profit and for-profit sectors. His clients have included both large and small service, cultural, and faith-based organizations throughout the United States, Canada, and Israel. Services include board and staff development, executive mentoring, project management, interim staffing.

Performance Resource Center

Nonprofit Resource Center, 7731 Belle Point Drive,
Greenbelt, MD 20770
Tel: 301-507-6247; FAX: 301-507-6250
E-mail: nrc@clark.net (Gerard M. Zack, President);
WWW: http://www.nonprofitresource.com/index.html

▶ PRC is a highly specialized consulting and training firm focused on improving organizational performance. PRC identifies and measures the differences between actual and desired performance, identifies causes of performance gaps, and then identifies and delivers appropriate performance improvement recommendations and interventions. These interventions may involve staff training, modifications to processes or policies, or recommended environmental changes. PRC is also a licensed WORKPOINTS consulting firm. The WORKPOINTS model is an innovative new process for identifying workplace behavior issues and identifying and delivering a series of short training modules designed to improve workplace behavior and attitudes.

Personnel Computer Systems

7551 East Moonridge Lane, Anaheim Hills, CA 92808
Tel: 714-281-8337; FAX: 714-281-2949
E-mail: mding@SoCa.com; WWW: http://personnelsystems.com

▶ Personnel Computer Systems is a compensation, performance, and human resource management consultant. Areas of expertise include compensation (salary and benefit surveys, salary structure design, job evaluation, legal compliance assistance, *executive incentive plans, sales incentive plans, board of directors compensation,* employee bonus plans); personnel management (productivity improvement, policy development, policy surveys, attitude surveys, performance appraisal, compensation audits, employee communications, supervisory training); personnel computer systems (planning, selection, documentation, training, installation); expert witness testimony (lost wages and benefits, executive compensation, employment litigation, reasonable compensation); H-1B Wage Determination (research and compilation of published survey sources, custom prevailing wage surveys, directory of employee pay and benefits survey sources).

Richard Chang Associates

15265 Alton Parkway, Suite 300, Irvine, CA 92618
Tel: 800-756-8096; 949-727-7477; FAX: 949-727-7007
E-mail: info@rca4results.com;
WWW: http://www.richardchangassociates.com/

▶ Richard Chang Associates, Inc. (RCA) is an organizational performance improvement firm that offers a wide range of consulting services, training, curriculum and materials development, custom video and media production, and public seminars. They also provide a variety of off-the-shelf products and publications for building and maintaining a continuous learning environment. Their online catalog (*http://www.richardchangassociates.com/catalog.htm*) lists products and workshops in the areas of organizational performance, performance measurement, management development, high-performance teams, high-impact training, and personal growth and development

Benefits

Benefits Design Group, Inc. (BDG)

1133 Broadway, Room 1227, New York, NY 10010
Tel: 212-727-7990; FAX: 212-627-0477
E-Mail: bdg@webb.com;
WWW: http://www.benefitsdesigngroup.com

▶ Benefits Design Group is an independent insurance broker and employee benefits consulting firm since 1984 serving human resources and benefits managers. They serve the tri-state area of New York, New Jersey, and Connecticut. They offer health insurance, life insurance, dental insurance, and legal plans. The following is a list of plans available by BDG: medical plans; dental plans; custom-tailored salary continuation and life insurance plans; international travel insurance; international major medical insurance; international term life insurance; prepaid legal plan for yourself or your organization. They serve the nonprofit community, primarily in the New York metropolitan region, with employee benefit plans designed to your organization's budget.

Mutual of America

320 Park Avenue, New York, NY 10022
Tel: 800-468-3785
WWW: http://www.mutualofamerica.com

▶ Mutual of America has specialized in providing pensions and retirement-related products, programs, and services to nonprofit organizations and their employees since 1945. They also offer such products and services directly to the for-profit community and offer variable annuities to individuals as well. In addition, variable universal life insurance and group life insurance are also available. As specialists in employee benefit plans for not-for-profit organizations, they offer complete administrative services available, computerized hotline for easy plan administration, a 24-hour, toll-free telephone service for employees, 36 regional offices nationwide for local service, and quarterly statements mailed to employees. Plans offered include pension plans: defined benefit/contribution plans, 403(b) matching contribution plans, 457 deferred compensation for government agencies, simplified employee pension/IRA plans, tax-deferred annuities (TDA), payroll deduct individual retirement annuity (IRA), payroll deduct variable universal life insurance, and group life and disability plans.

Compensation

Compensation Connections, Inc.
P.O. Box 1256, Hightstown, NJ 08520
Tel: 609-490-0895; FAX: 609-490-1197
E-mail: jkaspin@juno.com (Joan A. Kaspin)

▶ Compensation Connections enables nonprofits to do extraordinary work by focusing the energy of their people. They work collaboratively with you in creating customized human resources solutions, which are designed to ensure that all staff are focused on their contribution to achieving the organization's mission, provide equitable and consistent policies and procedures, and improve communications. Specific services include human resources consulting, job descriptions, performance appraisal process, salary surveys and analysis, compensation advising and analysis, revising employee handbooks, coaching staff, and facilitating executive or other team problem-solving/conflict-resolution meetings.

Hay Management Consultants
World headquarters: Hay Group, 100 Penn Square East,
The Wanamaker Building, Philadelphia, PA 19107-3388
Tel: 215-861-2000; FAX: 215-861-2111
Report, Variable Compensation in Not-for-Profit Organizations
(Karen Flisek)
WWW: http://www.haygroup.com/default.asp

▶ Hay Management Consultants provides human resources consulting, particularly in the areas of compensation, work valuation, role design, and performance management. They are increasingly engaged to enhance the capabilities of entire organizations. These strategic, integrated engagements combine a variety of approaches that focus on people, their work, and how they are led, motivated, and developed. These engagements include clarification and communication of strategy; selection and development of leaders; enhancement of culture and values; assessment and development of emotional intelligence; creation of performance-enhancing reward strategies for executives and employees; creation of integrated human resource systems, including selection, development, and performance management; and design of new and more effective organizational structures, work processes, and roles.

Lawrence Associates
PMB 303, 200 Linden Street, Wellesley, MA 02482-7914
Tel: 781-237-9044; FAX: 781-237-9045
E-mail: lal@lawrenceassociates.com;
Web: http://www.lawrenceassociates.com

▶ Lawrence Associates provides compensation consulting services to health care organizations, colleges and universities, associations, foundations, and other tax-exempt and service industry organizations. Specific services include executive compensation (assistance to management and board members with competitive analysis, compensation strategy, compliance with Intermediate Sanctions, incentive plan design, capital accumulation, perquisites, benefits, and response to media and public disclosure); incentive, recognition and reward programs (incentive compensation, physician compensation, team-based compensation, management compensation, wage and salary administration, performance evaluation, competency-based pay, broadbanding, skill-based pay, and other reward programs); custom competitive analysis and surveys (custom-designed competitive market surveys ranging from one to 100 or more positions in selected national and local geographic areas, covering executive and management compensation issues, physician compensation issues, wage and salary, and related areas).

Diversity

Intercultural Development Inc.
755 San Mario Drive, Solana Beach, CA 92075
Tel: 858-755-3160; FAX: 858-755-8637
E-mail: selma@mailhost1.csusm.edu;
WWW: http://www.inetworld.net/smyers

▶ Intercultural Development is a consulting firm specializing in diversity that focuses on developing and implementing strategies to improve quality and productivity in the workplace. Intercultural Development/Myers Consulting specializes in programs and publications to help businesses take advantage of the opportunities that a culturally diverse workforce and customer base present. It conducts and analyzes needs assessments, facilitates focus groups, develops and delivers training programs, provides curriculum guidance, and helps organizations to explore diversity issues and create strategies to deal with them. Services offered include training programs (each program can be tailored to meet your specific needs or those of your organization. Any of these programs can be presented as a one-on-one consultation or through group seminars or workshops. Programs offered include Managing Cultural Diversity, Communication Skills for the Foreign-Born Professionals, Increasing Overseas Business Effectiveness, Pre-Departure Orientation, Designing and Implementing English as a Second Language Programs, Managing Cultural Diversity Train-the-Trainers Programs); publications (see list available online at *http://www.inetworld.net/smyers/smyerspb.htm*); and presentations (see the online list of presentations that can be given at your site and can be tailored to your specific needs at: *http://www.inet world.net/smyers/smyerspr.htm*).

Lambert & Associates
1945 Morningview Drive, Hoffman Estates, IL 60192
Tel: 847-429-9640; FAX: 847-429-9641
E-mail jonamaylam@aol.com; WWW: http://www.lambert-diversity.com/lambert.html

▶ Lambert & Associates is a consulting firm specializing in workplace diversity issues. Services include diversity communication support; cultural needs assessments to determine your diversity climate; focus groups; diversity strategy development; instructional design; current program updates and modifications; executive leadership development; diversity awareness and skill building to create better relationships; mentor programs for employee development; and train-the-trainer programs. Workshops offered include Customers, Co-workers and Culture; The Business Case for Diversity; Men and Women at Work; Stopping Sexual Harassment Before It Starts; Understanding Racism; Dialogue Sessions to Increase Understanding; Beyond Generation X; Conflict Resolution in a Multicultural Workforce; Multicultural Team Building for High Perfomance Teams; Coaching and Feedback; Communicating in a Diverse Workplace; Customer Service and the Diversity Challenge; Leadership: The Main Ingredient Needed for Diversity to Thrive; Resolving Disputes: Skills for Third-Party Intervention; Effective Meetings Across Cultures; Coaching for Career Management; and Action

Planning. Any of these can be customized and others developed for your specific needs. It also offers training and assessment guides.

George Simons International

236 Plateau Avenue, Santa Cruz, CA 95060
Toll-free voice & FAX: 888-215-3117
E-mail: info@diversophy.com; WWW: http://www.diversophy.com

▶ George Simons International is a consulting group that assists organizations and their people worldwide to meet the challenges of globalization through working, communicating, and negotiating effectively across cultural boundaries both virtually and face to face. It offers the following services: consulting (its professionals will partner with you to examine and address opportunities and challenges in the areas of diversity, intercultural management, working together across cultures and organizational development both online and face to face); coaching (GSI offers one on one or small group coaching on intercultural or diversity challenges for both proactive approaches to diversity issues and to address problem areas in an individual's behavior); training (design, training, and training of trainers); *CUSTOM DIVERSOPHY*® (intercultural training game that can be focused on your industry, core business, and the needs of your people in the form of a customized training instrument for seminars, conventions, workshops, and delivered in electronic form to your Intranet).

Executive Services

Coaching Vision

7604 Fairway Woods Drive, Sarasota, FL 34238
Tel: 941-922-1777; FAX: 941-921-5485
E-mail: Jbos@coachingvision.com;
WWW: http://www.coachingvision.com

▶ Coaching executives, leaders, and professionals to the next level of success. Services include assessments, coaching skills development, team development, executive coaching, marketing and sales coaching, management coaching, retreat facilitation, and keynote presentations.

Executive Search Firms

Arts Consulting Group

519 N. Windsor Boulevard, Dept. Web, Los Angeles, CA 90004
Tel: 888-234-4236; FAX: 323-463-1911
E-mail: artsconsult@artsconsulting.com;
WWW: http://www.artsconsulting.com/index2.htm

▶ Arts Consulting Group places executives in interim positions due to unforeseen circumstances or management changes in arts organizations of all sizes.

Ast/Bryant Consultants in Executive Search

1 Atlantic Street, Stamford, CT 06901
Tel: 203-975-7188; FAX: 203-975-7353
E-mail: info_east@astbryant.com

2716 Ocean Park Boulevard, Suite 3001,
Santa Monica, CA 90405
Tel: 310-314-2424; FAX: 310-399-5774
E-mail: info_west@astbryant.com (Chris Bryant);
WWW: http://www.astbryant.com

▶ Ast/Bryant Consultants specializes exclusively in the philanthropic sector. Its staff of five recruiters are search specialists in higher education, secondary schools, health care and human services, the environment, and the arts. It is a member firm of the Association of Executive Search Consultants (AESC), the professional association of retained search firms worldwide.

A.T. Kearney, Inc.

333 John Carlyle Street, Alexandria, VA 22314
Tel: 703-836-6210; FAX: 703-836-0547
E-mail: joan.Jackson@atkearney.com (Joan Jackson, Director)

153 East 53rd Street, New York, NY 10022
Tel: 212-751-7040; FAX: 212-350-3150
E-mail: james.abruzzo@atkearney.com (James Abruzzo, Vice President)

▶ A.T. Kearney Executive Search is able to meet the current needs of their nonprofit clients with an industry practice whose mission is "to improve the effectiveness of nonprofit organizations worldwide." Their nonprofit practice provides a full range of executive search and management consulting services to clients throughout North America and the world. The majority of their search engagements are for top-level positions such as CEOs, presidents, and other senior executives. Recent consulting projects have included feasibility studies, compensation surveys, strategic and long-range planning, development audits and fund-raising consulting, board retreats, business plans, earned income enhancement and cost reduction, organizational restructuring, and other strategic management issues facing nonprofit organizations. The practice also conducts industry surveys, and the consultants in the practice frequently speak at industry conferences.

Barnes & Roche, Inc.

919 Conestoga Road, Building 3, Suite 110,
Rosemont, PA 19010-1375
Tel: 610-527-3244; FAX: 610-527-0381
E-mail: consult@brnsrche.com (Mary D'Ignazio),
search@brnsrche.com

▶ The firm offers a full range of fund-raising consulting and executive search services.

Boulware & Associates, Inc.

175 West Jackson Boulevard, Suite 1841, Chicago, IL 60604
Tel: 312-322-0088; FAX: 312-322-0092
E-mail: boulware1@aol.com (Christine Boulware);
WWW: http://www.boulwareinc.com

▶ Boulware & Associates is an executive search firm working in the private, nonprofit, and government sectors.

Boyden Global Executive Search (Formerly Cal Douglas & Associates)

221 7th Street, Suite 302, Pittsburgh, PA 15238
Tel: 412-820-7559; FAX: 412-820-7572
E-mail: pittsburgh@boyden.com, Mary.Neville@boyden.com (Mary Neville); WWW: http://www.boyden.com/

▶ Since 1979, they have worked with clients nationwide to recruit CEOs, chief development officers, and planned giving/major gifts executives for the nonprofit sector.

Browning Associates

209 Cooper Avenue, Upper Montclair, NJ 07043
Tel: 973-746-5960; FAX: 973-746-0189
E-mail: info@browning-associates.com;
WWW: http://www.browning-associates.com

▶ Browing Associates is a full-service development consulting firm that also specializes in searches for heads of school.

Campbell & Company

One East Wacker Drive, Suite 2525, Chicago, IL 60601
Tel: 877-957-0000
E-mail: djb@campbellcompany.com (Daniel J. Burns, Director, Executive Search); WWW: http://www.campbellcompany.com/

▶ Campbell & Company has a 10-year track record of successful searches, helping clients find the best "match" for new senior-level professionals. With their broad knowledge of the nonprofit sector and our database of development professionals, Campbell & Company is able to identify candidates with the right qualifications and skills. Campbell & Company's work is focused solely on the nonprofit sector. Campbell & Company has developed an extensive database of qualified development professionals. This database is not only a key resource of potential candidates, but is also an important source for referrals.

CoachWise

The Helms International Group, 8000 Towers Crescent Drive, Suite 1350, Vienna, VA 22182
Tel: 703-760-7881 or 302-226-2389
E-mail: mhelms@coachwise.com;
WWW: http://www.coachwise.com/executivesearch.html

▶ CoachWise provides executive coaching and leadership development to nonprofit organizations. It is also a retainer-based executive search firm whose primary focus is on recruiting for key "people" positions within a nonprofit organization including chief executives and senior managers, senior communications, and human resource professionals.

Copley Harris Company, Inc.

106 High Street, Danvers, MA 01923
Tel: 978-750-1028; FAX: 978-750-6709
E-mail: chc@copleyharris.com; WWW: www.copleyharris.com

▶ Copley Harris Company recruits senior-level professionals for hospitals, colleges, museums, and social service agencies. In addition, they offer Interim Services, providing a full range of development program and management services for the short-term needs of organizations in transition. CHC keeps established development programs running smoothly while professional staff recruitment is underway. In addition, CHC is retained by clients for special project needs, including major gifts, annual fund and special events management, development program restructuring, and support services.

The Development Resource Group—DRG, Inc.

104 East 40th Street, Suite 304, New York, NY 10016-1600
Tel: 212-983-1600; FAX: 212-983-1687
E-mail: search@drgnyc.com, DRGDELL@AOL.COM (David E. Edell, President)

1629 K Street NW, Suite 802, Washington, DC 20006
Tel: 202-223-6528; FAX: 202-775-7465
WWW: http://www.drgnyc.com

▶ Since 1987, The Development Resource Group (DRG) has provided executive search services for nonprofit institutions. DRG conducts local, regional, and national searches for nonprofit executives including presidents, executive directors, chief financial and administrative officers, and public affairs officers. They also specialize in recruiting professionals for development positions. Recent and current searches in this field include executive directors, vice presidents and directors of development, regional directors, directors of major gifts, foundations and corporate relations, planned giving, annual giving, alumni affairs, and capital campaigns.

Arthur Diamond Associates, Inc.

4630 Montgomery Avenue, Suite 200, Bethesda, MD 20814
Tel: 301-657-8866; FAX: 301-657-8876
E-mail: info@arthurdiamond.com, towens@arthurdiamond.com (Thomas G. Owens, Executive Vice President);
WWW: http://www.arthurdiamond.com

▶ A retained executive search firm specializing in recruitment for corporations, nonprofit organizations, the real estate industry, and trade and professional associations. Since 1971, they have specialized in confidential searches for senior management and professional positions. In addition to their extensive recruitment network and personal contacts, their success and longevity as a company have relied upon the personalized attention they give to their clients.

Robert W. Dingman Company, Inc.

650 Hampshire Road, Suite 116, Westlake Village, CA 91361
Tel: 805-778-1777; FAX: 805-778-9288
E-mail: info@dingman.com; WWW: http://www.dingman.com

▶ They are retained search generalists with experience ranging broadly over a wide variety of industries and most functional fields. Their primary focus is doing searches at the CEO/president/general manager level, along with the functional vice presidents reporting to those positions.

The Diversified Search Companies

One Commerce Square, 2005 Market Street, Suite 3300, Philadelphia, PA 19104
Tel: 215-732-6666; FAX: 215-568-8399
E-mail: diversified@divsearch.com, nonprofit@divsearch.com;
WWW: http://www.divsearch.com/

▶ Founded in 1973 as a local Philadelphia firm specializing in financial services and the placement of women, Diversified has grown to a full-service national and international executive search firm. They specialize in not-for-profit and higher education, having placed chief executives, executive directors, development/fundraising executives, academic administrators, and other leaders in academic, cultural, public, and philanthropic organizations. As a result of their affiliation with Manchester Inc., Diversified has begun to provide services such as executive coaching, individual and organizational assessment and leadership assimilation to help ensure an investment in new talent pays off. Diversified also maintains offices in New York, Atlanta, Boston, San Francisco, and Charlotte, North Carolina.

Donovan Slone, Inc. (Formerly J. Donovan Associates, Inc.)

Corporate headquarters: One Derby Square,
Salem, MA 01970-3704
Tel: 800-370-0036, 978-744-8558; FAX: 978-741-1871
WWW: http://www.donovanslone.com,
http://www.jdonovan.com/services.htm

▶ Donovan Slone provides a search and placement service built on 17 years of networking with development professionals throughout North America.

Egmont Associates

521 Grove Street, Norwell, MA 02061
Tel: 781-659-2430; FAX: 781-659-9905
E-mail: emont@mediaone.net; WWW: http://www.consultantsnet
work.org/members/Egmont_Associates.htm

▶ Egmont Associates is an executive search firm providing services to nonprofit organizations and to corporations, foundations, and academic centers with interests in the nonprofit sector. The company helps its clients achieve their missions by assessing organizational readiness for new leadership, planning strategically for executive transitions, and matching talent and experience to achieve desired organizational outcomes. Services include search committee support and training, staff involvement in planning, development of written materials for recruitment, advertisement, candidate screening and interviewing, extensive reference interviews, preparation for committee meetings with candidates, offer negotiation, placement announcements, and coaching for positive adjustments for new executive directors. Among the firm's clients are organizations in human services, public policy, philanthropy, education, health, leadership, school-to-career, peace and justice, social change, and the arts.

Ford Webb Associates

Ted Ford Webb, P.O. Box 645, Carlisle, MA 01741
Tel: 508-371-2484; FAX: 508-371-4911

45 Walden Street, Concord, MA 01742
Tel: 978-371-4900; FAX: 978-371-4911
E-mail: jcodinha@fordwebb.com (Justin Codinha)

▶ Executive recruiting for the public sector and nonprofits.

Goodwin & Company

Tom Goodwin, 1150 Connecticut Avenue NW, Suite 200,
Washington, DC 20036
Tel: 202-785-9292; FAX: 202-785-9297
WWW: http://www.goodwinco.com

▶ They represent national, regional, and community foundations in recruiting senior-level management staff. The firm serves corporate, not-for-profit, and government clients including some of the largest and most influential organizations in Washington and around the country.

J.B. Groner Executive Search, Inc.

P.O. Box 101, 2805 B. Philadelphia Pike, Claymont, DE 19703
Tel: 302-792-9228, 610-494-7197 (Philadelphia area);
FAX: 302-798-8433.
E-mail: groner@execjobsearch.com (J.B. Groner);
WWW: http://www.execjobsearch.com

▶ J.B. Groner is a professional search firm primarily handling permanent placements, with some contract placement opportunities in the information technology fields. They have recruited many executive director, deputy director, controller, membership services, facilities manager, state bar association director, hospital administrator, health care administrator, medical director, university president, director of volunteer services, and development director positions.

The Hollins Group

Lawrence Hollins, 225 West Wacker Drive, Suite 2125,
Chicago, IL 60606-1229
Tel: 312-606-8000; FAX: 312-606-0213
E-mail: Lhollins@thehollinsgroup.com

▶ The Hollins Group are consultants who conduct executive searches for a variety of clients, including nonprofits.

Isaacson, Miller

334 Boylston Street, Boston, MA 02116
Tel: 617-262-6500; FAX: 617-262-6509
E-mail: info@imsearch.com;
WWW: http://www.isaacsonmiller.com

▶ Isaacson, Miller is a retained search firm serving mission-driven organizations. Since 1983, they have completed over 2,000 searches for hundreds of clients across the country, including leading universities, research institutes, academic medical centers, foundations, cultural institutions, economic development organizations, human service agencies, and national advocacy groups. Most of their clients are not-for-profit groups as well as socially responsible companies.

JDG Associates, Ltd.

1700 Research Boulevard, Suite 103, Rockville, MD 20850
Tel: 301-340-2210; FAX: 301-762-3117
E-mail: info@jdgsearch.com, degioia@jdgsearch.com;
WWW: http://jdgsearch.com/

▶ JDG Associates, Ltd., has been serving the executive and technical search needs of research and consulting organizations, and national trade and professional associations since 1973. Their searches are conducted on a retained or contingency basis depending on the level and nature of the position. Their team of professional consultants primarily serves clients within the mid-Atlantic area, but also supports clients located in other parts of the country.

Gary Kaplan & Associates

201 South Lake Avenue, Suite 600, Pasadena, CA 91101
Tel: 626-796-8100; FAX: 626-796-1003
E-mail: info@gkasearch.com, gkaplan@gkasearch.com;
WWW: http://www.gkasearch.com/

▶ Gary Kaplan & Associates is a retained executive search firm.

Kittleman & Associates

300 South Wacker Drive, Suite 1710, Chicago, IL 60606
Tel: 312-986-1166; FAX: 312-986-0895
E-mail: search@kittleman.net;
WWW: http://www.kittleman.net/index1.html

▶ Kittleman & Associates is an executive search firm serving exclusively nonprofit organizations nationwide. Kittleman & Associates offers full-service retained search capabilities backed by a team of experienced professional executive recruiters, research associates, and administrative support staff. Kittleman & Associates represents a roster of nonprofit clients across the country, including colleges and universities, hospitals and health care organizations, human service agencies, museums and historic sites, conservation organizations, performing arts organizations, professional associations, and foundations. It publishes *From Making a Profit to Making a Difference: How to Launch Your New Career in Nonprofits.*

Korn Ferry International

Presidential Plaza, 900 19th Street NW, Suite 800,
Washington, DC 20006
Tel: 202-822-9444; FAX: 202-822-8127
WWW: http://www.kornferry.com

▶ This international executive search firm with more than 70 offices in 40 countries specializes in senior-level searches for clients throughout North America, Europe, Asia/Pacific, and Latin America. Since its founding in 1969, it has conducted over 75,000 searches for clients in every industry and in all parts of the world. Formally established in 1988, the education/not-for-profit specialty practice comprises the education, association, not-for-profit (philanthropic and cultural arts) and government/public administration sectors—recruiting senior-level executives to colleges and universities, professional and industry associations, charitable and philanthropic organizations, cultural arts entities (symphonies, ballets, opera, and museums), and government and quasi-government agencies.

LaMalie Amrop International

Mary Wheeler, 200 Park Avenue, New York, NY 10166
Tel: 212-953-7900; FAX: 212-953-7907

225 West Wacker Drive, Suite 2100, Chicago, IL 60606
Tel: 312-782-3113

1601 Elm Street, Suite 4246, Dallas, TX 75201
Tel: 214-754-0019
WWW: http://www.amrop.com/

▶ LaMalie Amrop is an across-the-board executive search firm.

Leadership Recruiters

1315 Walnut Street, Suite 1315, Philadelphia, PA 19107
E-mail: prose@leadrecruit.com; WWW: http://www.leadrecruit.com/

▶ Leadership Recruiters is a consulting firm providing fundraising, programmatic, and organizational expertise to nonprofit organizations.

The Management Center

870 Market Street, Suite 800, San Francisco, CA 94102-4010
Tel: 800-344-NOCS (6627), 415-362-9735; FAX: 415-362-4603
E-mail: tmc@tmcenter.org, ctaylor@tmcenter.org (Claire Taylor, Executive Search Director); WWW: http://www.tmcenter.org

▶ The Management Center's Executive Search provides a full-time staff of experienced search professionals who exclusively help nonprofits recruit new leadership. Whether your organization needs a full-service search or just some recruiting assistance, the Center provides a comprehensive range of services suited to every situation and budget. Services provided include search committee formation; documented process and timeline; in-depth organizational assessment, new/refined position specification, salary range recom-

mendations, advertising, networking and recruitment, candidate screening, interview facilitation, reference and background checks, and compensation negotiations. In addition, TempExecs, The Management Center's interim professional placement service, will help you find an experienced nonprofit executive director to fill in for three months, six months, or as long as you need, ensuring an easy transition.

McCormack & Associates

5042 Wilshire Boulevard, Suite 505, Los Angeles, CA 90036
Tel: 323-549-9200
E-mail: jmsearch@earthlink.net;
WWW: http://www.mccormackassociates.com/

▶ McCormack & Associates' national team of retained search professionals specialize in diversity recruiting. Their mission includes working in partnership with professionals who are committed to recruiting top-quality candidates for senior-level executive and board positions with a breadth of experience and corporate leadership skills from a wide array of fields. Their expertise in diversity recruiting helps ensure a superior pool of candidates inclusive of race, ethnic origin, gender, age, sexual orientation, and physical ability. McCormack & Associates is a member of the Association of Executive Search Consultants (AESC).

Mersky, Jaffe & Associates

45 Rockefeller Plaza, Suite 2000, PMB 40, New York, NY 10111
Tel: 800-361-8689; FAX: 413-556-1074
E-mail: michael@merskyjaffe.com (Michael Jaffe),
david@merskyjaffe.com (David A. Mersky);
WWW: http://www.merskyjaffe.com

▶ This company offers executive search and placement for leadership, financial management, fund raising, and development for nonprofit organizations. It serves cultural, higher education, social service, and health-related enterprises.

Morris & Berger

201 South Lake Avenue, Suite 700, Pasadena, CA 91101
Tel: 626-795-0522; FAX: 626-795-6330
E-mail: jberger@morrisberger.com;
WWW: http://www.morrisberger.com/

▶ Founded in 1984, Morris & Berger is a generalist executive search firm that has developed a specialty practice serving the nonprofit sector, including the performing and visual arts, institutions of higher education, independent schools, foundations, and human and social service agencies. They have recruited presidents and other officers, board members, directors, and other professional staff.

Netzel Associates, Inc.

9696 Culver Boulevard, Suite 204, Culver City, CA 90232
Tel: 310-836-7624; FAX: 310-836-9357
E-mail: fundraising@netzelinc.com;
WWW: http://www.netzelinc.com/

▶ Netzel Associates manages the process to identify, recruit, and employ nonprofit CEOs and development staff. It maintains offices in California, Arizona, Colorado, Idaho, Montana, Nevada, New Mexico, Oregon, Oklahoma, Texas, Utah, Washington, and Wyoming.

The Oram Group, Inc.

275 Madison Avenue, New York, NY 10016
Tel: 212-889-2244; FAX: 212-986-2731
E-mail: hankus@juno.com

44 Page Street, Suite 604C, San Francisco, CA 94102
Tel: 415-864-7567; FAX: 415-621-2533
E-mail: mbancel@aol.com; WWW: http://www.oramgroup.com

▶ Oram Group executive search provides complete confidentiality for both client and candidate, a thorough knowledge of the nonprofit sector, and an objective, professional, knowledgeable look at the overall organization. They specialize in the recruitment of development and other external affairs executives. As management consultants to the nonprofit sector, they are able to look at an entire organization vis-à-vis the position to be filled. This helps in determining job responsibilities, specifications, title, compensation reporting, space requirements, support staff, and relationship to other positions within the organization.

Paschal•Murray

611 West G Street, Suite 500, San Diego, CA 92101
Tel: 619-702-8881; FAX: 619-702-8883
E-mail: info@paschalmurray.com;
WWW: http://www.paschalmurray.com

▶ A specialized executive search firm since 1978, they assist management in identifying and hiring outstanding professionals in fund raising, public relations, and management positions. Their clients are located throughout the United States and Canada and include universities, hospitals and health care systems, fine and applied arts organizations, museums, and social service agencies. Nearly 70 percent of their search contracts are for positions in philanthropy, public relations, and senior management. Most searches are for presidents, chief executive officers, chief operating officers, chief advancement officers, vice presidents, vice chancellors, and directors. They also place senior and midlevel planned giving officers, major and special gifts professionals, and executive directors of nonprofit organizations.

The Phillips Oppenheim Group

521 Fifth Avenue, Suite 1802, New York, NY 10175
Tel: 212-953-1770; FAX: 212-953-1775
E-mail: info@pogsearch.com (Jane Phillips Morrison or Debra Y. Oppenheim); WWW: http://www.pogsearch.com/

▶ Executive search consultants for the nonprofit community, the Phillips Oppenheim Group helps not-for-profit organizations identify and recruit talented people. They work with domestic and international organizations of all sizes in a diverse range of fields, and recruit for a full spectrum of positions including chief executives, financial and administrative officers, marketing and communications professionals, development officers, and program officers, as well as board members and trustees. The Phillips Oppenheim Group primarily serves not-for-profit organizations, domestic and international, in a diverse range of fields, including: advocacy/public policy, community and economic development, corporate and not-for-profit boards, education, environment, health care, human and social services, philanthropy/foundations, and visual and performing arts.

Professionals for NonProfits, Inc.

515 Madison Avenue, Suite 900, New York, NY 10022
Tel: 212-546-9091; FAX: 212-546-9094
E-mail: pnp@pipeline.com; WWW: http://www.nonprofit-staffing.com/intro.html

▶ It is the first personnel agency to recruit temporary, permanent, and special project consulting staff for museums, social services agencies, foundations, universities, and performing arts and other nonprofit organizations. PNP places staff in fund raising, finance, exhibitions, and programs—from executive, senior, and middle management staff to administrative and technical personnel. PNP has a pool of professionals (fund raisers, grant writers, special events and public relations personnel, educators, registrars, curators, bookkeepers) who are available to work on a permanent or temporary basis. In addition, the partners undertake executive search.

RPA Inc.

951 Westminster Drive, Williamsport, PA 17701
Tel: 800-992-9277; FAX: 570-321-7160
E-mail: rpainc@suscom.net, RPAInc@epix.net (Richard P. Allen); WWW: http://www.rpainc.org

▶ RPA Inc. has been providing executive recruitment services to nonprofits for more than two decades. It offers a network of development, public relations, not-for-profit, and educational professionals from 50 states and 11 countries.

Results Group International

230 West 41st Street, Suite 1602, New York, NY 10036
Tel: 212-869-3373; FAX: 202-869-5535
E-mail: get@resultsg.com; WWW: http://www.resultsg.com/

▶ Results Group International assists with retainer searches for staff at the director level and above and for talented candidates for board service. Trustee searches can include identifying minority candidates, diversifying board membership or seeking prospects with specific *pro bono* skills. They work not as head-hunters but rather as partners with your search committee, assisting with the process and the product of your search. Search committee chairs or executive directors are invited to call for further information. For nonprofits whose development needs are limited, they also offer an annual outsourced executive service that provides 30 to 50 percent time by a Results Group senior consultant. Full-service search capabilities include executive search, search committee support, trustee recruitment, volunteer recruitment, temporary leased executives, and outsourced executive services.

Bruce Robinson Associates

Bruce Robinson or Eric Robinson, Harmon Cove Towers, Suite 8, AL Level, Secaucus, NJ 07094
Tel: 201-617-9595; FAX: 201-617-1434

▶ Bruce Robinson Associates is an executive search firm for upper-level management jobs, including nonprofit positions.

Ruotolo Associates, Inc.

Horizon Square, 29 Broadway, Suite 210, Cresskill, NJ 07626
Tel: 201-568-3898; FAX: 201-568-8783
E-mail: info@ruotoloassoc.com;
WWW: http://www.ruotoloassoc.com

▶ Ruotolo Associates may be of valuable assistance to an institution in its search for effective development executives. To this end, Ruotolo Associates will interview current administration and board, evaluate and respond to the stated job and candidate requirements, prepare a job description, orchestrate a comprehensive search, screen candidates and references, present final candidates, and negotiate salary and benefits, if warranted. It maintains New England, Midwest, and Baltimore/Washington division offices.

Rusher, Loscavio & LoPresto

142 Sansome Street, 5th Floor, San Francisco, CA 94104
Tel: 415-765-6600; FAX: 415-397-2842
E-mail: rll@rll.com, rwkile@rll.com (Bob Kile);
WWW: http://www.rll.com

2479 East Bayshore Road, Suite 700, Palo Alto, CA 94303
Tel: 650-494-0883; FAX: 650-494-7231

▶ Since its inception in 1977, this firm has developed long-term relationships providing both board recruitment/executive search and consulting services with special emphasis in the nonprofit field. They have developed a reputation within the functional areas of general management, sales and marketing, management information systems, and human resources. Clients include arts organizations, associations, education, foundations, health care, and human services.

Robert Sellery Associates, Ltd

1155 Connecticut Avenue NW, Washington, DC 20036
Tel: 202-331-0090; FAX: 202-333-1167
E-mail: sellery@cais.com; WWW: http://www.sellery.com

▶ This is a medium-sized executive search firm with a strong practice finding senior people for a variety of nonprofit organizations. They work with large private and public universities, small private colleges, trade associations, professional membership organizations, national health groups, community hospitals, foundations, government agencies, human services organizations, arts and religious organizations, museums, "think tanks," and environmental and conservation organizations. They seek senior-level administrators for a wide range of management and professional positions, both line and staff. They have found executive directors, CEOs, presidents, chief development officers, chief financial officers, communications officers, chief academic officers, deans, scientists, NIS privatization officers, and program officers, along with people reporting to these positions.

Semple Bixel Associates, Inc.

653 Franklin Avenue, Nutley, NJ 07110
Tel: 973-284-0444; FAX: 973-284-0950

8 Deerfield Road, Mendham, NJ 07945
FAX: 973-543-6296
E-mail: RFSemple@aol.com, Marsemple@aol.com,
crawdeb@nac.net (Joan Crawford)

▶ A full-service fund-raising management consulting firm specializing in planning studies, campaign counseling, strategic planning, prospect research, and endowment building. They conduct executive searches for 501(c)(3) organizations in need of fund-raising personnel and executive directors. They have served nonprofit organizations for 25 years.

HC Smith Ltd.

Herb Smith, 20600 Chagrin Boulevard, Suite 200, Shaker Heights, OH 44122-5334
Tel: 800-442-7583, 216-752-9966; FAX: 216-752-9970
E-mail: info@hcsmith.com; WWW: http://www.hcsmith.com

▶ This is a generalist retained search firm with a national and international client base of corporations and nonprofit organizations. Its unique specialty is the recruitment of minority and women professionals. Their commitment is to provide clients with diverse slates of candidates.

Spencer Stuart Associates

401 North Michigan Avenue, Suite 3400, Chicago, IL 60611
Tel: 312-822-0080; FAX: 312-822-0116
E-mail: tsmith@spencerstuart.com (Toni Smith, Leader, Not-for-Profit Practice); WWW: http://www.spencerstuart.com/home/
content/en/us/sso-nolog.asp

▶ Spencer Stuart is a leading management consulting firm specializing in senior-level executive search and board director appointments. For 45 years, they have been at the forefront of their industry, creating a blend of management consulting and executive search that is best described as executive talent management and is focused on the long-term success of their clients. It is a global company whose core practice has reached 50 offices in 24 countries since its founding.

TAG Executive Services

The Alford Group, Inc., 7660 Gross Point Road, Skokie, IL 60077
Tel: 800-291-8913, 847-966-6670; FAX: 847-966-6782
E-mail: info@alford.com; WWW: http://www.tag-jobs.com

▶ This resource is an outgrowth of the Alford Group, Inc.'s 20-plus years of counsel for the not-for-profit community. TAG Executive Services' offerings fall into three integrated groups: executive search (use TAG Executive Services in any combination to help you find and hire experienced, highly qualified senior members of your staff); contingency staffing (rely on TAG Executive Services' contingency staffing services to keep temporary fluctuations in your professional staff and workload from affecting the fulfillment of your organization's mission); the Online Job Bank. (utilize their data bank to post résumés, search for open positions, post available jobs, and review resumes).

Transitions in Leadership (TIL)

1129 Lorien Court, St. Louis, MO 63131-4611
Tel: 314-822-4868; FAX: 314-966-6973
E-mail: info@tilnonprof.com; WWW: http://www.tilnonprof.com

▶ TIL provides a variety of management services during times of leadership change. Their niche is providing interim executive directors along with executive search services. They also facilitate the long-range visioning and strategic planning journey. TIL is available to evaluate and redesign management systems. Board and staff training is another component of their menu of services. Specific services include succession planning, executive search, interim executive directors, visioning and strategic planning, board and staff training seminars, and negotiating alliances and mergers.

Tuft & Associates, Inc.

1209 Astor Street, Chicago, IL 60610
Tel: 312-642-8889; FAX: 312-642-8883
E-mail: matuft@tuftassoc.com

▶ Tuft & Associates is a national executive recruitment firm that specializes in customizing searches for CEO or key staff in non-profits and foundations.

EMN/Witt/Kieffer Ford

2015 Spring Road, Suite 510, Oak Brook, IL 60523
Tel: 630-990-1370; FAX: 630-990-1382

2010 Main Street, Suite 320, Irvine, California 92614
Tel: 949-851-5070
E-mail: nicke@wittkieffer.com (Nick Fraunfelder);
WWW: http://www.wittkieffer.com/home.asp

▶ Through Educational Management Network, a division of Witt/Kieffer, the firm conducts executive search assignments for colleges, universities, community service, cultural, philanthropic, and other not-for-profit organizations. Educational Management Network/Witt/Kieffer has conducted more than 800 academic, administrative, and advancement searches on behalf of the nation's leading universities and colleges. EMN/Witt/Kieffer assignments on behalf of clients typically center on identifying and recruiting candidates for such prominent executive roles as presidents/chancellors; provosts; vice presidents for finance, student affairs, enrollment management, and technology; chief advancement officers; deans; and directors of major service/academic units. It maintains offices in Phoenix; Emeryville, California; Irvine, California; Atlanta; Burlington, Massachusetts; Nantucket, Massachusetts; Bethesda, Maryland; St. Louis; New York; Nashville; Dallas; and Houston.

Ward-Howell

William Tipping, 3350 Peachtree Road NE, Suite 1600,
Atlanta, GA 30326
Tel: 404-261-6532; FAX: 404-261-5339

▶ Ward-Howell is an executive recruiting firm with offices also in Phoenix, Arizona; Barrington, Illinois; Stamford, Connecticut; Los Angeles; Dallas; Houston; Chicago; New York City; and internationally.

Wilcox Miller & Nelson

Diane D. Miller, 100 Howe Avenue, Suite 155 North,
Sacramento, CA 95825
Tel: 916-977-3700; FAX: 916-977-3733
E-mail: wilcoxcareer@wilcoxcareer.com;
WWW: http://www.wilcoxcareer.com/

▶ This is a retained executive search and career transition firm providing executive search and outplacement services to nonprofit and for-profit employers at the mid- through executive management level.

Zimmerman Lehman & Associates

582 Market Street, Suite 1112, San Francisco, CA 94104
Tel: 800-886-8330 (outside the San Francisco Bay Area),
415-986-8330; FAX: 415-986-2048
E-mail: zl@zimmerman-lehman.com;
WWW: http://www.zimmerman-lehman.com

▶ This firm recruits executive and management staff. Zimmerman Lehman works with you and your board to hire top executive directors, development directors, and management staff. It helps your organization evaluate and develop job responsibilities, utilize Zimmerman Lehman's contacts in the field for candidates, draft and distribute job descriptions and advertisements, review résumés and references, assist with the interview process and/or perform preliminary interview screening, and check references.

Human Resource Information Systems

Advanced Personnel Systems

P.O. Box 1438, Roseville, CA 95678
Tel: 916-781-2900; FAX: 916-781-2901
E-mail: frantz@hrcensus.com (Richard B. Frantzreb, Editor &
Publisher); WWW: http://www.hrcensus.com

▶ Advanced Personnel Systems specializes in providing objective information on all types of HR software. They are currently monitoring 2,500 HR software products from 1,500 vendors—plus consultants and developers.

Ascentis Software

Mailing address: P.O. Box 53330, Bellevue, WA 98015

Physical address: 220 120th Ave NE, Building D,
Bellevue, WA 98005
Tel: 800-229-2713; FAX: 425-462-1313
E-mail: info@ascentis.com, sales@ascentis.com;
WWW: http://www.ascentis.com

▶ Ascentis was founded in 1994 with the vision of providing comprehensive, easy-to-use solutions for employee benefit and human resource information management. These solutions are designed to be connected throughout the enterprise, serving managers, employees, and external vendors of benefit and payroll services.

BMH, Inc. (Bonnecaze, McLeroy & Harrison, Inc.)

4004 Beltline Road, Suite 125, Dallas, TX 75001
Tel: 972-702-0892; FAX: 972-991-2983
WWW: http://www.open4.com

▶ BMH is the distributor of OPEN4 software, a fully integrated system that addresses the human resource department's diverse requirements, as well as complexities required by payroll. It includes 40+ predefined information categories, future and alert-date processing, organizational hierarchy, AAP, OSHA, VETS, EEO reporting, and seamless integration with Excel®/Word®.

Ceridian Employer Services

6800 LBJ Freeway, Suite 3100, Dallas, TX 75240
Tel: 972-385-5740; FAX: 972-385-5768
WWW: http://www.ceridian.com/

▶ Ceridian Employer Services is a leading provider of products and services that support the full employment life cycle. Ceridian solutions include innovative outsource and in-house HRMS, payroll and tax filing solutions as well as comprehensive benefits administration services. The Ceridian Source product suite provides integrated HRIS, employee self-service, payroll, tax filing, and time and attendance solutions.

Cyborg Systems, Inc.

2 North Riverdale Plaza, Chicago, IL 60606
WWW: http://www.cyborg.com

▶ Cyborg is a worldwide provider of quality, best-in-class Human Resource Management Systems (HRMS) solutions. Cyborg's best-in-class HRMS product line, The Solution Series/ST®, offers comprehensive integrated HR management, payroll processing, and benefits administration functionality. The company's e-business product line, eCyborg, brings e-business to HRM through The ESS Solution™, The MSS Solution™, and The XSS Solution™ products.

Employease, Inc.

One Piedmont Center, Suite 400, Atlanta, Georgia 30305
Tel: 888-EASE-NET, 404-467-6414, 877-450-5500 (Customer Support); FAX: 404-467-6466
WWW: http://www.employease.com/index2.php3

▶ Employease is a provider of Web-based human resource management systems. Employease brings together employers with their service providers via the Employease Network, the business-to-business network for employee information. Employers benefit from the Employease Network by reducing administrative costs, improving service to employees and increasing focus on strategic human resources. Service providers benefit from the Employease Network by improving customer service, reducing operating expenses, and delivering new services.

Genesys Systems and Services

5 Branch Street, Methuen, MA 01844
Tel: 978-685-5400; FAX: 801-761-2015
E-mail: info@genesys-soft.com; WWW: http://www.genesys-soft.com

▶ Genesys Systems is a full-service firm in the payroll, human resources, and benefits industry, providing a selection of services designed to meet all HRMS needs. Today's offerings include Web-enabled solutions, employee self-service kiosks, voice response systems, in-house licensed software, robust outsourcing services, and complete ASP capabilities. Genesys provides outsourcing services to handle your payroll, HR, ASP, BPO, and benefits administration needs. Genesys outsourcing provides integrated functionality; unlimited employer tax IDs; on-line, real-time access; compliance with all government regulations and legislation; online employee history; intranet- and Internet-based employee self-service functions; and much more. Choose from two outsourcing options: ONESource and FULLSource.

Human Resource Microsystems

160 Sansome Street, Suite 1050, San Francisco, CA 94104
Tel: 800-972-8470, 415-362-8400; FAX: 415-362-8595
E-mail: sales@hrms.com; WWW: http://www.hrms.com

▶ This firm provides software applications and services.

Meta4 USA

3391 Peachtree Road, Suite 300, Atlanta, GA 30326
Tel: 877-USMETA4; FAX: 404-760-4301
E-mail: usa@meta4.es; WWW: http://www.meta4.com/company/management.html

▶ Meta4 USA distributes Meta4Mind Set, Web-based products that combine an integrated people management system (PeopleNet)—comprising modules for payroll, benefits, training, recruitment, competency management, and performance appraisal—with a unique knowledge management system (KnowNet). It includes a Web-based application platform and set of design tools that enable customers to customize applications (Meta4Mind Works).

SAS Institute

SAS Campus Drive, Cary, NC 27513-2414
Tel: 919-677-8000; FAX: 919-677-4444
E-mail: software@sas.com; WWW: http://www.sas.com/

▶ HR Vision™ provides tools for accessing data from transactional systems, reorganizing and warehousing that data, and generating HR-specific report and analyses, while protecting the daily operations of those systems. This new product from SAS Institute will automate the delivery of HR information. HR Vision gives you a direct link into current and historical information on any HR subject, from headcount to turnover rates.

SPECTRUM Human Resource Systems Corporation

1625 Broadway, Suite 2600, Denver, CO 80202-4720
Tel: 800-334-5660, 477-3287; FAX: 303-595-9970
E-mail: info@spectrumhr.com; WWW: http://www.spectrumhr.com

▶ SPECTRUM is the exclusive provider of affordable software solutions for HR management, benefits administration, and training and development. They provide a full range of support services including system planning and implementation, training, customization, and data conversion and transfer. HR Vantage and iVantage complements our product line to meet the needs of companies of all sizes and HR budgets. SPECTRUM's HR products provide powerful HR functionality and system customization capabilities. iVantage, the first Web operational HRIS, fully exploits the powerful features and capabilities of Microsoft SQL 7.0, including English Query and OLAP. Both products allow you to create reports by using integrated reporting tools, or by using the standard queries and reports.

Technical Difference, Inc.

5256 South Mission Road, Suite 802, Bonsall, CA 92003
Tel: 800-809-5731; FAX: 760-941-6128
E-mail: marketing@people-trak.com;
WWW: http://www.people-trak.com

▶ Technical Difference distributes People-Trak, PC-based HR management products designed for organizations ranging in size from 25 to 10,000 employees. People-Trak automates all your HR functions, taking your information out of the filing cabinets and spreadsheets and making it accessible. With People-Trak, you will become proactive in letting management know pertinent information through reports.

Ultimate Software

2000 Ultimate Way, Weston, FL 33326
Tel: 800-432-1729, 954-331-7369; FAX: 954-331-7300
E-mail: E-mail: ir@ultimatesoftware.com, hotinfo@ultimatesoftware.com;
WWW: http://www.ultimatesoftware.com

▶ It provides employee-centric HRMS/payroll e-business solutions to organizations of all sizes. Offering Web-based self-service for managers and employees, UltiPro provides critical business value to everyone in the organization, minimizing the time spent on administrative duties and allowing managers to focus on strategic objectives. UltiPro is available as an in-house solution or hosted through Intersourcing, Ultimate Software's IBM-hosted model.

Publishers

Alexander Hamilton Institute

70 Hilltop Road, Ramsey, NJ 07446-1119
Tel: 800-879-2441, 201-825-3377; FAX: 201-825-8696
E-mail: custsvc@ahipubs.com; WWW: http://www.ahipubs.com

▶ The Alexander Hamilton Institute has been helping executives manage their companies and their careers since 1909. They currently publish newsletters, booklets, and loose-leaf manuals targeted to top management, human resource directors, personnel managers, front-line managers, and supervisors at small to medium-sized firms. Their publications deal with all aspects of employment law, and are specifically designed to keep managers and executives from making mistakes that could lead to fines and lawsuits. All their products are written in a practical and easy-to-read style that all levels of management can understand and apply immediately to solve or prevent workplace problems. Useful features on their Web site include publications, problem solvers, employment law talk, free reports, FAQs (frequently asked questions), E-mail newsletter (monthly updates containing what's hot in the world of legal personnel issues and also what's new on the AHI publications front; join online at *http://www.ahipubs.com/newsletter/index.html,* or by sending an e-mail message with a blank subject line to *join-ahi_newsletter@ice.lyris.net* with "join" [without the quotes] in the message body text).

Carlson Learning Company/Inscape Publishing

P.O. Box 59159, Minneapolis, MN 55459-8247
Tel: 800-777-9897
WWW: http://www.carlsonlearning.com/splash.htm

▶ Carlson is an international publisher of quality instruments and programs designed to increase self-awareness and improve personal effectiveness, thereby improving organizational performance. It uses a network of independent speakers, trainers, and consultants authorized to use and market its products.

Coastal Training Technologies

3083 Brickhouse Court, Virginia Beach, VA 23452
WWW: http://www.coastal.com/humanresources.html

▶ This company creates workplace training media that improves the quality of employees' lives around the world. It offers an extensive selection and convenient access to management training materials, whether you want to improve the effectiveness of your management team, upgrade customer service standards, or avoid legal pitfalls.

LRP Publications

1555 King Street, Suite 200, Alexandria, VA 22314
Tel: 800-727-1227, 703-684-0510
E-mail: lrpconf@lrp.com; WWW: http://www.lrp.com

▶ Founded in 1977 by Kenneth Kahn, a practicing employment law attorney, LRP (then known as Labor Relations Press) first published case report for the legal profession. In addition to its many professional resources, LRP Publications also provides top-quality training and educational development seminars, conferences, and symposiums through its Conference Division. The division's programs include the National Institute on Legal Issues of Educating Individuals with Disabilities—attended by thousands of education administrators, school psychologists, attorneys and others; the National Workers' Compensation and Disability Conference and Exhibit—the largest conference and trade show on workers' compensation in the nation; and the HR Technology Conference and Exposition—the world's leading conference on technology for human resources professionals.

West Group

P.O. Box 64833, St. Paul, MN 55164-0833
Tel: 800-328-4880, ext. 66470 (Customer Service), 800-328-9352 (Product Orders and Information), 800-295-9378, ext. 66302; FAX: 800-340-9378
E-mail: customer.service@westgroup.com, HRMarketing@westgroup.com, hreditorial@westgroup.com; WWW: http://westgroup.com/www.wg

▶ A member of the Thomson Corporation, West Group is the established leader in providing legal and regulatory information to legal, human resource, business, and other professionals. For the human resource professional, West Group provides in-depth coverage of general HR, compensation and benefits, EEO, and international HR. They offer the human resources professional a full range of comprehensive analytical and practical tool to meet their information needs. Known for easy-to-understand analysis of federal and state laws, helpful sample policies and best practices, West Group provides on-point solutions to the issues you confront everyday. To learn more about hr-esource.com, go to *http://hr-esource.com/contact/contacts.html.*

Workshops, Seminars, & On-Site training

(See also Support, Advocacy and Information Organizations)

American Management Association (AMA)

1601 Broadway, New York, NY 10019
Tel: 800-262-9299 (Customer Service), 212-586-8100; FAX: 212-903-8168
WWW: http://www.amanet.org/seminars/index.htm

▶ AMA offers more than 200 different seminars on today's key management topics for business professionals and organizations, held at their own conference centers in New York, Washington, DC, Atlanta, Chicago, and San Francisco, as well as dozens of other locations throughout the United States.

CareerTrack & Fred Pryor Seminars

Fred Pryor Seminars, P.O. Box 2951, Shawnee Mission, KS 66202
Tel: 800-255-6139, 800-488-0928 (Seminars and Products), 800-955-6147 (On-Site Training Consultants); FAX: 913-665-3434
E-mail: customerservice@careertrack.com; WWW: http://www.careertrack.com

▶ Fred Pryor and CareerTrack combine to offer an incredible selection of quality seminars on timely topics, all led by the most sought-after speakers and trainers. Services include online training, on-site seminars, career store (audiotapes, videotapes, and CD-ROMs).

Council on Education in Management

Oakhill Business Park, 1338 Hundred Oaks Drive, Suite DD, Charlotte, NC 28217
Tel: 800-942-4494 (Registration), 877-236-0265 (Office), 704-522-1236; FAX: 704-521-5380
E-mail: Customer Service and Registration: registration@ counciloned.com; In-House Training: inhouse@counciloned.com; Recruitment: recruit@counciloned.com; HR Helpline: hrhelpline@ counciloned.com; WWW: http://www.counciloned.com

▶ A subsidiary of Institute for International Research since 1972, the Council on Education in Management has been the nation's leading provider of HR, employment law, and management information and training. Their seminars, newsletters, and on-site training cover the most up-to-date personnel law developments in issues such as the ADA, Workers' compensation, FMLA, sexual harassment, the EEOC, internal investigations, and employer liability. They provide a hard-edged, no-nonsense approach to human resource training and labor law.

Creative Training Techniques International, Inc.

7620 West 78th Street, Minneapolis, MN 55439-2518
Tel: 800-383-9210, 612-829-1954; FAX: 612-829-0260
E-mail: custsvc@creativetrainingtech.com;
WWW: http://www.cttbobpike.com

▶ Services include public seminars (provider of professional development seminars for trainers with over 75,000 alumni. Over 150 seminars in 40 cities are held each year, modeling the best of participant-centered training); in-house training programs (over 18 customized programs using the participant-centered training process. Topics range from fundamental training instruction, advanced training techniques, training management courses, soft skills communication, and better business presentations); Train-the-Trainer conference (annual international conference designed to offer over 20 speakers demonstrating the Participant-Centered Training Process and giving you their best new, creative approaches to a wide variety of training topics); *Creative Solutions Catalog* (creative solutions and supporting information and tools for training leaders using the Participant-Centered Training Process). It publishes the *Creative Techniques Newsletter* and *TRAINING* magazine.

Langevin Learning Services

P.O. Box 279, 5510 Main Street, Manotick, ON K4M 1A3, Canada
Tel: 800-223-2209, 613-692-6382; FAX: 800-636-6869, 613-692-6373
E-mail: training@langevin.com, langevin@magi.com;
WWW: http://www.langevin.com

▶ Since 1984, Langevin Learning Services has provided workshops and professional trainer certification in many areas, including instructional design/development, training needs analysis/assessment, instructional techniques/facilitation, training management, training basics, marketing your training internally, advanced instructional techniques, the successful training manager, advanced instructional design, designing supervisory and management training, and training needs analysis.

Linkage, Inc.

One Forbes Road, Lexington, MA 02421
Tel: 781-862-3157; FAX: 781-862-2355
E-mail: info@linkage-inc.com; WWW: http://www.linkageinc.com

▶ Services include conferences (attracts over 13,000 professionals a year to business conferences in leadership, marketing, HR, and OD); consulting (help organizations around the world achieve and sustain superior performance by systematically connecting their vision and strategy to the work processes, development, learning, and competencies needed for success) and institutes (provide high-level programs and services targeted at the long-term leadership development of individuals and teams from the best organizations); workshops (offer practical skill-building learning and development programs in the areas of management and leadership development, organizational development, and HR practitioner skills. Public workshops are offered throughout the year in major U.S. cities. All programs can be brought on-site and customized to your organization); Best Practices Consortium (Consortium enables companies to benchmark the latest HRD and OD topics, network with others in the field, learn from new research and study results, and reap the benefits of Linkage's educational programs); Technology Training Programs (offered publicly with their University partners, or on-site for organizations, are designed to give you or your employees the skills needed to succeed in today's high-tech environment); distance education; research services and products (benchmark organizational best practices to identify the critical success factors of 21st century organizations and provide insight into the cutting-edge, practical skills that growth organizations will need); and resources (HR books, audiotapes, workbooks, tools, and conference proceedings). An e-newsletter is available.

National Seminars Group

A Division of Rockhurst College Continuing Education Center, Inc.
Mailing address: P.O. Box 419107, Kansas City, MO 64141-6107
Tel: 800-258-7246 (Registration), 913-432-7755;
FAX: 913-432-0824

Physical address: 6901 West 63rd Street, P.O. Box 2949, Shawnee Mission, KS 66201-1349
Tel: 800-344-4613 (Business Training & Development Service Department)
E-mail: info@natsem.com; Web Site: http://www.natsem.com

▶ National Seminars Group, a division of Rockhurst University Continuing Education Center, Inc., is a provider of continuing education. Each year, they provide more than 6,000 seminars and conferences in the United States and Canada. Besides offering a full range of training skills to all professional levels through their one- and two-day seminars and conferences, they also offer books and audiocassette, videocassette, and CD-ROM training products for individuals, teams, departments, or corporate reference libraries.

Padgett-Thompson

P.O. Box 8297, Overland Park, KS 66208
Tel: 800-255-4141, 800-356-5107 (In-House Seminar), 913-451-2900
E-mail: consumercare@amanet.org;
WWW: http://ptseminars.com/kcmain.htm

Padgett-Thompson Products, SourceCom Distribution, 14502 West 105th Street, Lenexa, KS 66215
Tel: 800-433-3635; FAX: 913-541-0010
E-mail: products@ptseminars.com

▶ Since 1977, Padgett-Thompson has been providing popular, skill-building training that improves the way people work. They provide business strategy, best practices, and skill-building information and training through our public seminars, online training, books, tapes, and software, and their Padgett-Thompson On-site division. It is an affiliate of the American Management Association.

Pinnacle Performance Group

7011 Martindale, Shawnee, KS 66218
Tel: 800-345-3098, 913-441-3001; FAX: 913-441-3011
E-mail: contact@pinnacleseminars.com;
WWW: http://www.pinnacleseminars.com/

▶ Pinnacle provides on-site training seminars. Topics include leadership, customer service, supervision, human resources, business strategy, secretaries/administration, compensation, facilities management, Internet, marketing, team building, management, communication, quality management, writing skills, purchasing, safety/OSHA, sales, security, accounting and finance, training skills.

Skillpath Seminars

A division of The Graceland College Center for Professional Development and Lifelong Learning, Inc., 6900 Squibb Road, P.O. Box 2768, Mission, KS 66201-2768
Tel: 800-873-7545, 913-677-3200; FAX: 913-362-4241
E-mail: custserv@skillpath.net; WWW: http://www.skillpath.com/, http://www.skillpath.com/ourbookstore/

▶ As a comprehensive training and skill improvement provider, Skillpath offers technology, self-improvement, and management seminars.

Training Media Review

TMR Publications, P.O. Box 381822, Cambridge, MA 02238-1822
Tel: 877-532-1838; FAX: 617-489-3437
E-mail: tmr1@tmreview.com, CustomerService@tmreview.com;
WWW: http://www.tmreview.com, http://www.tmreview.com/ Consulting.asp

▶ Training Media Review was founded in 1993 with a single mission: to facilitate decision making by providing the training community with authoritative, objective evaluations of media-based business training. Training Media Review is a service company offering content, online communities, and consulting to trainers, human resource professionals, and managers in corporations, government, and nonprofits. Their consulting network consists of experienced consultants and training professionals who contribute reviews to Training Media Review. They offer clients not only training content and design expertise but also product and media knowledge. Consultants in the network have a variety of subject matter specialties, from leadership and diversity to information technology.

GENERAL RESOURCES

General/Basics

The A-to-Z Book of Managing People
VICTORIA KAPLAN AND ROBERT KUNREUTHER (BERKLEY PUBLISHING GROUP, 1996)

▶ Managers who need answers to basic questions, from employee complaints of harassment or conflicts with co-workers to handling perfectionist behavior patterns, will find this a key tool in dealing with people. It surveys common managerial issues, providing tips on how to hire, fire, and manage people at all levels. Preventative measures as well as problem-solving approaches are outlined in this valuable collection of tips. Non-*Fortune* 1000 corporations without access to human resources professionals will find many common-sense answers in this alphabetical dictionary. More than 110 entries correspond to frequent workplace situations, from an HIV-positive worker to the use of time clocks. According to the authors, every issue must be analyzed in light of 10 tools, including taking the Golden Rule and other people's opinions into consideration. It is a quick-reference, practical guide for managers dealing with salaries, employee conflicts, job performance, ethical problems, and more. *Softcover, 133 pages, $14*

Best Practices for HR Managers
(RANSOM & BENJAMIN, 1998)

▶ Contents include lawsuit avoidance strategies (workplace privacy—the need not to know, whistle-blowing and retaliation, class action threats, how to ensure against employee lawsuits); how to comply with HR laws (AFA, FMLA, NLRB, OSHA, ERISA, FSLA, Title VII, affirmation action, CRA); how to manage employees (step-by-step recruiting plus specific tips, orientation, training, development, appraisal, discipline, and termination); how to find HR information (consultants, attorneys, publishers, government contacts, federal and state); special tasks of HR managers (giving depositions; conducting investigations and searches; facilitating problem solving, brainstorming); compensation and benefits laws; organizing the HR department; training and development; and more. Yearly updates are sent on approval (most recent 8/00). *3-ring binder, approx. 400 pages, $129.95*

Complete Do-It-Yourself Personnel Department, 2nd Edition
MARY COOK (PRENTICE HALL DIRECT, 1997)

▶ Build a great personnel department with this all-in-one resource. Here is everything a small to mid-size business needs to establish a professional, legal, efficient HR office. Included are 50 ways to cut your HR costs, performance evaluation forms you can copy, sample employee manuals, compensation and benefits surveys, checklists for correctly terminating employees, classified ad forms, and tips on how to recruit, hire, and fire. *Hardcover, 560 pages, $69.95*

Current and Emerging Non-Profit Management and Leadership Resource Needs *(See General Management—Publications for full description)*

Effective Human Resource Development: How to Build a Strong and Responsive HRD Function
NEAL F. CHALOFSKY AND CARLENE REINHART (JOSSEY-BASS, 1988)

▶ This book offers tested methods for assessing the effectiveness of HRD functions and identifying opportunities for improvement. It details three primary criteria and illustrates how each can be achieved. An in-depth case study shows how one HRD manager built a high-quality organization based on those criteria. *Hardcover, 164 pages, $39.95*

Effectively Managing Human Service Organizations *(See General Management—Publications for full description)*

Human Resource Accounting: Advances in Concepts, Methods, and Applications, 2nd Edition
ERIC G. FLAMHOLTZ (JOSSEY-BASS, 1985)

▶ This book is a must for any manager or professional concerned about human resource management and development. At a time when executives seek the bottom-line implications of HR efforts, these 13 chapters provide both a rationale and a system for translating training and personnel development endeavors into dollars that make sense to management. *Hardcover, 413 pages, $48.95*

Human Resources Management for Public and Nonprofit Organizations
JOAN E. PYNES (JOSSEY-BASS, 2000)

▶ This is a textbook in personnel management, devoted to the non-profit sector, which addresses the use of strategic human resources management—the integration of human resources management with the strategic mission of the organization—in both public and nonprofit agencies. Joan E. Pynes demonstrates how strategic human resources management is essential to proactively managing change in an environment of tighter budgets, competition from private organizations, the need to maintain and train a more diverse workforce, and job obsolescence brought about by shifts in technology. She offers students and practitioners the guidance and techniques necessary to implement effective human resources management strategies in public and nonprofit organizations, from job analysis to performance evaluation, from recruitment and selection to training and development, from compensation and benefits to collective bargaining. Pynes also covers topics such as recruiting and managing volunteers, working with a board of directors, and federal and state labor relations. *Human Resources Management for Public and Nonprofit Organizations* is a good resource for all involved in shaping, implementing, or studying human resources policies. *Hardcover, 304 pages, $38.95*

Human Resource Management in Associations

PHYLLIS RODERER & SANDRA SABO, EDS. (AMERICAN SOCIETY OF ASSOCIATION EXECUTIVES, 1994)

▶ With its provocative approach to managing employees, this practical guide is the most authoritative source available on human resource issues for associations. This up-to-date reference covers topics such as moving your workforce into the twenty-first century; position development and job descriptions; recruiting, interviewing, and hiring; compensation, salary administration, and rewards; benefits; performance appraisals; orientation, training, and development; disciplining and discharging employees; budgeting; employee handbooks; and personnel policies. Intended for CEOs as well as HR professionals, this volume is generously illustrated with samples and graphics. *Softcover, 221 pages, $35.95 (Nonmember), $29.95 (Member) (plus $6.25 shipping)*

Managing a Nonprofit Organization: Staffing, Fundraising, Choosing Trustees, Financing, Marketing, Computerizing, Planning, Succeeding

(See General Management—Publications for full description)

Managing Human Resource Development: A Practical Guide

LEONARD NADLER AND GARLAND D. WIGGS (JOSSEY-BASS, 1986)

▶ This provides specific managerial guidelines to help direct the day-to-day activities of the HRD unit. Its how-to approach would be of value to current or aspiring HRD managers, human resources specialists, and line managers asked to take on HRD activities. *Hardcover, 213 pages, $36.95*

Managing Human Resources Issues: Confronting Challenges and Choosing Options

WILLIAM J. HEISLER, W. DAVID JONES, AND PHILIP O. BENHAM, JR. (JOSSEY-BASS, 1988)

▶ This book identifies and analyzes the most pressing issues affecting the organization's productivity, morale, and legal posture, and provides HR professionals with advice on responding to them. *Softcover, 270 pages, $34.45*

Personnel & Human Resources Development, Leadership Series, Volume I (Booklet)

JILL MUEHRCKE, ED. (THE SOCIETY OF NONPROFIT ORGANIZATIONS, 1990)

▶ In articles selected from the *Nonprofit World* journal, authors discuss how to hire and retain the best employees and avoid conflicts, lawsuits, and emotional dysfunctioning in the workplace. *Softcover, 95 pages, $20 (Nonmember), $17 (Member) (plus $4.50 shipping)*

Personnel & Human Resource Development, Leadership Series, Volume II (Booklet)

JILL MUEHRCKE, ED. (THE SOCIETY OF NONPROFIT ORGANIZATIONS, 1993)

▶ In this second volume of articles from *Nonprofit World* journal (November 1989–September 1993), the authors discuss personnel handbooks, effective use of interns, and salary expectations. *Softcover, 72 pages, $20 (Nonmember), $17 (Member) (plus $4.50 shipping)*

Personnel Guide for NonProfits (Workbook/Manual)

KAREN McELROY (PHILADELPHIA VOLUNTEER LAWYERS FOR THE ARTS, 1995)

▶ This guide covers aspects of the employer–employee relationship from both employer and employee perspective, including hiring practices, compensation, personnel policies, and discrimination. *Softcover, $27.77 (includes shipping)*

Survival Skills for Managers *(See General Management for full description)*

Position Development/Job Descriptions

BLR's Job Descriptions Encyclopedia

STEPHEN D. BRUCE, ED. (BUSINESS & LEGAL REPORTS, INC., 1995—AVAILABLE FROM THE SOCIETY FOR HUMAN RESOURCE MANAGEMENT)

▶ The first section of the *Job Description Encyclopedia* explains how job descriptions are written and used and why they are important. The second offers hundreds of sample job descriptions arranged by functional job category. They may be used verbatim or as examples and resources. This title comes in two three-ring binders. An annual subscription from the publisher includes updates on this topic. *2 Binders, 1,040 pages, $159.95*

How to Write Job Descriptions (Handbook)

LOUISE SAMSON (ABBOTT, LANGER & ASSOCIATES, 1992)

▶ This succinct guide illuminates the entire process of writing job descriptions and making them quick and easy to prepare. You will learn: (1) the many vital uses of job descriptions, (2) the six components of setting up a job description program, (3) interviewing tips with sample questions to help you master information gathering, (4) the 11 pitfalls of writing job descriptions, (5) nine essential points to remember, (6) an overview of rating plans, (7) how to include the organization chart for clarity, (8) how to use job descriptions in management performance appraisal and career planning, and (9) the value of ongoing support and maintenance of your program; included are a handy glossary of 200 essential terms and a job description writing checklist. *Spiral bound, $27.95 (plus $4.75 shipping)*

How to Write Job Descriptions—The Easy Way

(BUSINESS & LEGAL REPORTS, INC., 1993)

▶ This resource is intended to help organize the HR function and simplify legal compliance. It includes ready-to-use samples and formats to save time in preparing clear and accurate job descriptions. *Softcover, 92 pages, $27.95 (plus $3.95 shipping and handling)*

More Results-Oriented Job Descriptions: 228 Models to Use or Adapt—With Guidelines for Creating Your Own

ROGER J. PLACHY AND SANDRA J. PLACHY (AMACOM BOOKS, 1997)

▶ Good job performance begins with defining the job properly. When employees don't fully understand their responsibilities and the results they are meant to achieve, the outcome is negative productivity. *More Results-Oriented Job Descriptions* is the ultimate resource for the organization wanting to create state-of-the-art job descriptions. It presents 228 model descriptions covering a wide range of job categories. Readers can use or adapt the models or learn to make their own. And all the descriptions are included on a free, easy-to-use computer disk. This book helps any organization prepare job descriptions tied to business goals, communicate expectations clearly, improve employee job performance, and save time and money. *Comb bound, 320 pages, $65*

Results-Oriented Job Descriptions

ROGER J. PLACHY AND SANDRA J. PLACHY (AMACOM BOOKS, 1993)

▶ This resource contains more than 225 models to use or adapt, plus guidelines for creating your own. Job descriptions that focus on results are essential now that businesses are demanding greater employee responsibility. In addition, the Americans with Disabilities Act requires that organizations redefine job essentials. This book provides a formula for preparing job descriptions that emphasize results. It gives users nearly 250 model job descriptions in 24 categories, from accounting and finance to warehousing and distribution; a firm grasp of the distinction between job duties and job results; and writing exercises, including explanations of do's and don'ts. *Comb bound, 300 pages, $65*

Sample Job Descriptions

(AMERICAN SOCIETY OF ASSOCIATION EXECUTIVES, 1996)

▶ This book offers more than 450 descriptions of key association jobs, covering 20 areas of concentration, with an extensive set of management information systems positions. The job descriptions included represent all functions of association management (large and small; national and state; professional, trade, and charitable organizations). It includes information on ADA regulations and formulating your own job descriptions. *Spiral bound, 405 pages, $78 (Nonmember), $65 (Member) (plus $6.25 shipping)*

Administration/Record Keeping/Forms

(See also Benefits; Compensation; Payroll; Policies and Procedures; Position Development/Job Descriptions; Reference Guides)

The Complete Collection of Legal Forms for Employers: All-Inclusive Sample Contracts, Forms and Checklists for Hiring, Firing, and Day-to-Day Employment

STEVEN MITCHELL SACK (LEGAL STRATEGIES, 1996)

▶ In today's litigious business climate, virtually any part of an organization's operations can come under legal scrutiny. Organizations must follow the letter of the law while avoiding the hassle and expense of hiring attorneys on every document used. *Softcover, 320 pages, $24.95*

The Complete Human Resources Writing Guide

DIANE ARTHUR (AMACOM BOOKS, 1997)

▶ Letters, forms, policies, evaluations, and handbooks—these are just a few of the documents that HR professionals produce every day. And it's not just the quantity that counts, it's the clarity and accuracy of the communications that are key. This is a writing manual designed especially for HR professionals. It combines complete, how-to-do-it guidelines on writing with more than 100 actual samples of HR documents. Readers discover how to master the seven stages of writing, from outline to revision; avoid employee and legal problems that can arise from poorly written communications; overcome "blank page syndrome"; save time and effort; and make every document achieve its purpose. *Hardcover, 400 pages, $55*

Creating Your Employee Handbook: A Do-It-Yourself Kit for Nonprofits (Book and Disk)

LEYNA BERNSTEIN (JOSSEY-BASS, 1999)

▶ The first comprehensive guide to writing, evaluating, and revising nonprofit employee handbooks—in a unique book/disk set. This book covers every type of personnel policy, including hiring and employee development, benefits, workplace health and safety, standards of conduct, work hours, and pay. Each sample policy is offered in three versions for large, medium, and small organizations. Readers can use the electronic versions on the disk to reproduce the policies verbatim, or mix and match the language, form, and style to suit the specific needs of their organization. *Softcover, 208 pages, $49.95*

Employer Forms Policies and Checklists, 3rd Edition (Book and Disk)

MAUREEN F. MOORE (MATTHEW BENDER, 1999)

▶ As an employer in an increasingly litigious society, you know the risks of failing to document each and every personnel action. Let Michie make your job easier with this time-saving collection of almost 200 sample forms, model policies, and checklists covering nearly every phase of the employment relationship from writing job descriptions to terminating employment. In addition to the sample forms, you get accompanying expert legal commentary and suggestions for developing your own system. Includes forms on diskette for simple customization and modification. *Loose-leaf and disk, $110*

Forms Used in Human Resources

LIFE OFFICE MANAGEMENT ASSOCIATION, INC. (CRC PRESS–ST. LUCIE PRESS, 1997)

▶ A lot has changed since 1985, when this collection of human resource forms was last published. It is fully revised with up-to-date forms for areas such as domestic partnership, the ethical use of computer software, and requests for translation services. It features contributions from over 55 U.S. and Canadian companies and includes 350 commonly used HR forms. It can be used as a source to create new forms or as a standard for evaluating your company's current forms with those used by others. It includes a wide variety of forms on employee termination, leave of absence, benefits enrollment, drug abuse policy, 401(k) plans, and more. It addresses current workplace issues such as sexual harassment, nontraditional dependents, medical leave, and employee profit-sharing plans. *Hardcover, 656 pages, $114.95*

HR Quick Forms: A Sourcebook for Association Professionals

(AMERICAN SOCIETY OF ASSOCIATION EXECUTIVES, 1996)

▶ ASAE has collected 115 forms on a range of human resource topics—and all may be reproduced from our forms book. You'll find basic forms including job applications, performance appraisals, leave slips, and time sheets. They have also included forms for more specialized needs, such as preparing job descriptions, intellectual property agreements, job sharing applications, employee recognition nomination forms, and more. *115 Forms and User Guide, $86 (Nonmember), $69 (Member)*

HR Quick Forms: A Sourcebook for Association Professionals (With Disk)

(AMERICAN SOCIETY OF ASSOCIATION EXECUTIVES, 1996)

▶ ASAE has collected 115 forms on a range of human resource topics—and all may be reproduced from their forms book or customized and printed from their Microsoft Word 6.0–compatible disk. You'll find basic forms including job applications, performance appraisals, leave slips, and time sheets. They have also included forms for more specialized needs, such as preparing job descriptions, intellectual property agreements, job sharing applications, employee recognition nomination forms, and more. *115 Forms, User Guide, and Microsoft 6.0–compatible diskette, $125 (Nonmember), $100 (Member)*

Managing a Small HRD Department: You Can Do More Than You Think

CAROL PRESCOTT MCCOY (JOSSEY-BASS, 1993)

▶ This hands-on tool kit is specifically designed to help small HRD departments maximize its resources. This operating manual will help you successfully adapt strategies used by large training departments to meet your organization's needs. You'll get numerous checklists, valuable case examples, and 15 reproducible worksheets to help you apply the techniques for budgeting, program development, evaluation, and more. The author gives you success stories from a huge variety of industries. Learn how to conduct a needs analysis study and make use of organizational data and feedback; employ internal and external resources to develop programs that meet strategic business needs; create and manage a budget; use meetings, newsletters, and electronic mail to effectively market programs and services; conduct program evaluations that accurately pinpoint the strengths as well as areas for improvement in their programs; and more. *Spiral bound, 302 pages, $43.95*

Nonprofit Personnel Forms & Guidelines

MATTHEW J. DELUCA, ED. (ASPEN PUBLISHERS, 1994)

▶ *Nonprofit Personnel Forms & Guidelines* provides an extensive inventory of essential personnel forms—close to 200 carefully designed documents—ranging from an ADA compliance form to a succession planning chart. These forms will enable you to collect, integrate, and access personnel data in an orderly, efficient way. You'll receive expert policy and practice guidelines for setting up a record-keeping system specifically for your nonprofit organization. You'll learn how to obtain information in each key area—recruitment, pay and benefits, staff planning, training, performance appraisals—and how to use the information to manage human resources for better results. Every form in *Nonprofit Personnel Forms & Guidelines* has been preapproved by the IRS, EEOC, OSHA, and DOL, so you can be absolutely certain that your organization is in full compliance with federal law. Annual updates inform you of the latest developments. All policies and forms are available on disk for Word Perfect, MS Word, and Macintosh (disk available only with purchase of manual). *Loose-leaf binder, 636 pages, $164 (plus shipping)*

Personnel ReadyWorks

JAMES JENKS (ROUND LAKE PUBLISHING COMPANY, 1994)

▶ Personnel ReadyWorks provides 160 easily customizable forms for every phase of personnel management, from hiring to firing—and everything in between. There are dozens of personnel policies, plus job applications, disciplinary forms, performance appraisals, benefit forms, interviewing guides, training documents, termination forms, and much more—plus guidance on how to use the forms most effectively. This book enables any organization to put together a comprehensive, forms-based program to deal with the complete

range of personnel matters easily and effectively. All the major areas of personnel management are explained in a way that anyone can understand, including those with no background in the field. Each chapter contains forms ready to customize for virtually any personnel management requirement plus guidance on how to use them most effectively. *Softcover, 368 pages, $119.95*

Reference Guides

The Blackwell Encyclopedic Dictionary of Human Resource Management (Blackwell Encyclopedia of Management)

LAWRENCE H. PETERS, CHARLES R. GREER, AND STUART A. YOUNGBLOOD, EDS. (BLACKWELL PUBLISHERS, 1998)

▶ *The Blackwell Encyclopedic Dictionary of Human Resource Management* provides concise, up-to-date definitions and explanations of the key concepts covering the whole of the fast-changing field of human resource management. Bringing together specially commissioned and carefully edited entries from an international team of the world's best-known and respected scholars and teachers, this will become the standard reference for students, researchers, academics, and practitioners. The *Dictionary* has been carefully designed to give both the expert and the newcomer overviews with succinct presentations of the most important traditional and contemporary issues in human resource management. With entries ranging from extended explorations of major topics to short definitions of key terms, this major reference work gives the user authoritative and comprehensive coverage of the whole field, from strategic to international HRM, with in-depth articles in technical areas such as personnel selection, compensation, and legal environment; a fully indexed and cross-referenced for detailed research with relevant citations for further study; definitive entries covering the very latest development in human resource management from downsizing and TQM to the effects of the World Wide Web; and a completely international perspective and author base. This dictionary is part of the *Blackwell Encyclopedia of Management,* which contains 10 further volumes of the key areas of management science. *Softcover, 400 pages, $31.95*

The Human Resources Glossary: A Complete Desk Reference for HR Professionals, 2nd Edition

WILLIAM R. TRACEY (CRC PRESS–ST. LUCIE PRESS, 1997)

▶ The fast-paced world of human resources (HR) management, development, and utilization requires HR professionals to fill many roles and speak many "languages." Finally, the demand for a single authoritative source that compiles and explains the vocabulary of HR practitioners is answered in *The Human Resources Glossary.* The *Glossary* defines HR terms and explains their context, use, and managerial implications in 56 of the most important HR areas. It features benefits, compensation, disability, discipline, employee services, health care, labor–management relations, organization development, productivity, hiring practices, employee testing, training, travel management, meeting management, work measurement, and more. *Hardcover, 640 pages, $69.95*

Human Resources Kit for Dummies, Book & CD-ROM Edition

MAX MESSMER (IDG/MACMILLAN, 1999)

▶ The authors give you all the tools you need to run a first-rate HR department. You'll find information about everything from fostering an employee-friendly workplace to developing legal and effective discipline procedures. Plus, the book features detailed information about current employment laws and regulations, benefits packages, compensation, and aspects of hiring and firing employees. Best of all, *Human Resources Kit for Dummies* comes with a CD-ROM that includes job application forms, sample employee policies, performance appraisals, benefits worksheets, and more. *Softcover, 384 pages, $24.99*

Human Resources Management & Development Handbook, 2nd Edition
WILLIAM R. TRACEY (AMACOM, 1993)

▶ A comprehensive, authoritative, and up-to-date reference and how-to guide available, this new edition is an absolute must-have for HR professionals at all levels. With 18 major topics and 102 chapters, this compendium of expert advice shows how to create an excellent department, as well as excellent programs. It covers the gamut of critical information HR managers need, including managing, staffing, and directing; facilities; program elements; employee and labor relations; employee services; organizational and management development; training system design and evaluation; and "hot" topics like workforce diversity, TQM, and training the disabled. *Hardcover, 1,444 pages, $99*

Stern's CyberSpace SourceFinder: HR and Business Management Internet Directory
GERRY STERN AND YVETTE BORCIA (MICHAEL DANIELS PUBLISHERS, 1998)

▶ *Stern's CyberSpace SourceFinder®: HR and Business Management Internet Directory* fully describes 1,717 primarily noncommercial Web sites, electronic mailing lists, and newsgroups, selected for their usefulness to human resource and general business management professionals. Indexes are provided by subject (cross-referenced, over 10,000 entries), title, and author. Entries provide (as applicable): name or title of the item; descriptive comments; frequency of publication; cost or fee; name of source; address; telephone number (many toll-free); fax number (many toll-free); e-mail address; and Internet address. *Softcover, 185 pages, $69.95*

Stern's SourceFinder: The Master Directory to Human Resources and Business Management Information and Resources (Single Volume)
GERRY STERN AND YVETTE BORCIA (MICHAEL DANIELS PUBLISHERS, 1998)

▶ *Stern's SourceFinder* is a comprehensive, annotated desk reference that offers access to thousands of information resources for human resources and general business management, including compensation and benefits, performance management, labor and employment law, recruitment, selection and staffing, human resource information systems, health and safety, training and development, leadership and management, organizational behavior and psychology, organizational development, organizational design, structure and processes, policy administration, strategic planning, labor and industrial relations, and much more. This compendium of resources contains 5,762 sources of business management information and resources, including associations, books, periodicals, surveys (1,000 pay and benefits surveys), research reports, databases, government agencies, training materials, information centers, training tools, self-study programs, electronic mailing lists, newsgroups, libraries, online news, forms, model policies software directories, and more. Stern's covers over 10,000 man-

agement topics, including compensation and benefits; consulting; culture, values, and ethics; diversity; future trends; health and safety; human resource information systems; human resource management; individual testing and development; innovation, technology and operations; job search; labor and employee relations; law; leadership and management; leading-edge, macro-, and meta-thinking; motivation and participation; organizational development and change; organizational psychology and behavior; organizational structure and processes; performance management and appraisal; personal development; policy, administration and employee services; productivity, quality, and service; recruitment, selection, and termination; references and research; staffing and labor markets; strategy and planning; training and development; training program design and evaluation; training resources; and training skills and techniques. It provides keyword, subject (fully cross-referenced), title, and author indexes. *Softcover, 631 pages, $199.95*

Stern's SourceFinder: The Master Directory to Human Resources and Business Management Information and Resources (Two-Volume Set)
GERRY STERN AND YVETTE BORCIA (MICHAEL DANIELS PUBLISHERS, 1998)

▶ *Stern's SourceFinder* is the only comprehensive, user-friendly desk reference to offer informed, fast access to thousands of information resources for human resources and general business management, including compensation and benefits; performance management; labor and employment law; recruitment, selection, and staffing; human resource information systems; health and safety; training and development; leadership and management; organizational behavior and psychology; organizational development; organizational design, structure, and processes; policy administration; strategic planning; labor and industrial relations; and much more. *Softcover, 815 pages, $239.95*

Information Systems

Human Resource Management Systems: A Practical Approach, 2nd Edition
GLENN M. RAMPTON, IAN J. TURNBULL, AND J. ALLEN DORAN (CARSWELL, THOMSON PROFESSIONAL PUBLISHING, 1999)

▶ This book is based on advancements in the professional literature, together with the authors' combined first-hand experience in developing, implementing, and using numerous human resources management systems in private- and public-sector organizations. The perspectives of payroll, human resources, operations, human resources information specialists, and management systems specialists are all addressed, as are the different issues facing small, medium, and large organizations. This book is designed to reach a diverse audience, including postsecondary school students taking a general HRMS course; human resources and/or payroll managers and functional specialists who want to know more about what an HRMS can do, or who are involved with, or contemplating the development of a new HRMS; information systems professionals who will be working on an HRMS project and want to learn more about the business and user perspective on such systems; and executives and general managers who understand that their human resources are their most important resource and are looking to the strategic and pragmatic value of an HRMS in terms of helping them manage their human resources. Though emphasis is on HRMS solutions in Canada, it is universally useful. *Softcover, 320 pages, $34.95*

Performance Appraisals and Evaluation

360-Degree Feedback: The Powerful New Model for Employee Assessment & Performance Improvement
MARK R. EDWARDS (AMACOM BOOKS, 1996)

▶ Once, the only opinion that counted in a performance evaluation was the supervisor's. Now, as teamwork and employee empowerment become more prevalent, organizations are turning to "360-degree feedback"—the multi-perspective approach perfected by the authors of this pioneering how-to guide. The 360-degree method assesses employee performance and development from several points of view: peers, customers, supervisors, and direct reports. It is a sensitive process that must be managed carefully. This practical book shows how to implement the process step by step—both what to do and what *not* to do. Based on 20 years of field research and rich with real-world examples, *360-Degree Feedback* will help organizations achieve a powerful positive impact on employee performance, more accurate and fair assessments, and better alignment of individual and organizational goals. *Hardcover, 256 pages, $27.95*

The Competency Assessment (Self-Assessment Tool and Software)
(SOCIETY FOR HUMAN RESOURCE MANAGEMENT)

▶ This tool is designed to help human resource executives enhance their strengths and recognize their weaknesses, guiding them toward developing the professional abilities necessary to succeed in human resource management. The assessment instrument allows individuals to solicit feedback from peers and supervisors on job performance in a format that is security-coded to protect the privacy of the anonymous evaluators. *$165 (Nonmember), $120 (Member) (plus $8 shipping)*

The Complete Guide to Performance Appraisal
DICK GROTE (AMACOM BOOKS, 1996)

▶ A good appraisal system can serve as an effective structure for culture change within an organization, and it can help ease one of every manager's most dreaded duties. Dick Grote gives readers everything they need to make the process work well, including what an ideal system looks like; the available options and approaches; how to evaluate performance, write a fair appraisal, and conduct the actual appraisal discussion; how to create a system from scratch or optimize the one already in place; critical issues that must be considered, including employee development, pay, and legal concerns; emerging trends that influence the process—such as 360-degree feedback, teams, the use of software; and actual appraisal forms from 12 companies, as well as scripts, diagrams, checklists, worksheets, flow charts, and sample policies. *Hardcover, 400 pages, $59.95*

Designing Performance Appraisal Systems: Aligning Appraisals and Organizational Realities
ALLAN M. MOHRMAN JR., SUSAN M. RESNICK-WEST, AND EDWARD E. LAWLER III (JOSSEY-BASS, 1989)

▶ This is a comprehensive guide to planning, designing, and implementing appraisal systems that are tailored to meet an organization's real needs. It shows human resource professionals and managers how to define performance, who should measure it, who

should give and receive feedback, and how often appraisals should be made. It examines and evaluates the common approaches to appraisals, those oriented to the performer, the behavior, the result, or the situation, and shows how they can be integrated into an effective system. *Hardcover, 256 pages, $39.95*

Employee Appraiser (SuccessFactors.com, formerly Austin Hayne) (Software)

▶ The product includes essential tools for documenting employee performance on an annual basis; writing employee reviews; and providing value-added coaching and feedback. Key features include: Writing Assistant, thousands of phrases taken from real assessments, enabling managers to write more effective reviews; Employee Action Folder, a convenient location for documenting important events annually and tracking performance against objectives; Coaching Advisor, advice and suggestions for developing employees and solving performance issues. It is available in the following versions: Standard; Deluxe; Lominger; and Employee Appraiser for Macintosh. Features include 600 professionally written phrases to get you started, Manager's Notebook (records important events throughout the evaluation period), and word-scanning glossary checks for inappropriate or illegal language. *$249 (plus shipping)*

Evaluating Employee Performance: The Management Skills Series #6
PAUL J. JEROME (JOSSEY-BASS, 1997)

▶ Evaluation should be an ongoing, interactive process. Learn how to objectively describe performance, business impacts, and on-the-job examples. Avoid disagreements on words or ratings while you effectively appraise performance, even if you have to use "less-than-desirable" forms. Develop your team members' potential with measurable plans. Support your decisions with substantive and legally sound documentation. This guidebook provides essential tools and techniques to everyone accountable for assessing, reinforcing, and redirecting the performance of individuals and teams—including themselves. *Softcover, $14.95*

The Human Touch Performance Appraisal #1
CHARLES M. CADWELL (JOSSEY-BASS, 1995)

▶ The Human Touch Performance Appraisal explains how to prepare and plan performance appraisals, conduct effective appraisal discussions, and set new objectives with employees. *Softcover, 100 pages, $14.95*

Performance Appraisal: State-of-the-Art in Practice
JAMES SMITHER (JOSSEY-BASS, 1998)

▶ Part of the successful SIOP (Society of Industrial and Organizational Psychology) series, this book fulfills the practitioner's long-standing need for a research-based guide to the best performance appraisal practices currently in use. Addressing an issue vital to all organizations, it introduces readers to thought and theories on the cutting edge of their profession. Plus, it provides nuts-and-bolts guidance to a broad spectrum of timely issues such as legality, fairness, team settings, and incentive programs. A seamless fusion of state-of-the-art research and practical application, it will prove of great interest to both academics and practitioners in the field looking for ways to elevate and refine their craft. *Hardcover, 608 pages, $46.95*

Performance Evaluation and Performance-Based Compensation (ASAE Background Kit)

(AMERICAN SOCIETY OF ASSOCIATION EXECUTIVES, 1996)

▶ Learn how to develop and manage effective performance evaluation and performance-based compensation systems. It includes information on the law of employee evaluations and managing for quality, plus sample performance evaluation forms and performance-based compensation plans. *Spiral bound, 132 pages, $45 (Nonmember), $35 (Member)*

Supervisor's Guide to Employee Performance Reviews, 3rd Edition

MIKE DEBLIEUX AND LEE T. PATERSON (MATTHEW BENDER, 1999)

▶ A step-by-step guide, this handy manual for effective employee performance reviews explains the necessity of a review policy and provides methods for writing and presenting reviews. New forms and examples of current trends help you identify the most effective methods for your company and avoid litigation by spotting problem areas in advance. Sample forms included are a checklist for preparing to write the review, employee performance questionnaire, performance review forms with instructions, performance review planner to identify major job functions, FOSA checklist, and employee evaluation of workgroup leader. *Softcover, $32.50*

Benefits

(See also Compensation)

The 401(k) Handbook

MARTHA PRIDDY PATTERSON (THOMPSON PUBLISHING GROUP)

▶ Written by 401(k) attorneys and specialists, this one-stop resource for employers, attorneys, and consultants guides you in plan design and administration of employer and employee contributions, nondiscrimination testing, reporting requirements, employee communications, valuation problems, hardship withdrawals, plan loans, rollovers, and investment vehicles. It contains detailed explanations of the complex 401(k) rules, plus proven trouble-shooting strategies and remedies. Time-saving sample plan documents and forms, checklists, and flowcharts are also provided. Your subscription includes a monthly bulletin on relevant congressional, IRS, and Department of Labor activities. You'll also receive monthly update pages to keep your *Handbook* current. *$348*

The 401(k) Plan Handbook

JULIE JASON (PRENTICE HALL DIRECT, 1997)

▶ This practical guide saves organizations the expense of hiring pension consultants, while giving human resources, benefits, and investment managers everything needed to implement and monitor 401(k) plans, including step-by-step guidance in plan design, communication of features to employees, asset management, participant loans, hardship withdrawals, and transfer or rollover of benefits. You also get sample forms, checklists, and compliance guidelines. *Hardcover, 448 pages, $79.95*

401(k) Plans: A Comprehensive Planning and Compliance Guide, 2nd Edition

MICHAEL E. LLOYD, BRUCE J. MCNEIL, AND WILLIAMS COULSON (JOHN WILEY & SONS, 1996)

▶ Consisting of a straightforward, easy-to-use, question-and-answer format, this edition provides the most current, practical information on all aspects of establishing, managing, and adminis-

tering the 401(k) plan. It addresses the benefits to employer and employee of a 401(k) plan, qualification and ERISA requirements, the tax consequences for all parties, and 401(k) variations. It discusses deferred compensation arrangements that are not qualified as cash or deferred arrangements described under Code Section 401(k). It includes helpful examples, sample language, and all the essential forms, documents, and other work papers. *Hardcover, 528 pages, $135*

The Complete Idiot's Guide to 401(K) Plans

WAYNE G. BOGOSIAN, DEE LEE (MACMILLAN DISTRIBUTION, 1998)

▶ Over one third of all American workers are covered by 401(k) plans. Yet confusion abounds for many who don't know what investments to select for their plan or how to manage them for maximum return. In idiot-proof language, this new guide explains all the ins and outs of these plans: how much to contribute, how to diversify investments, tax information, when and how to borrow, what to do at retirement or when changing jobs, and more. Featured are model portfolios for various stages of life. Larry Starr is president of an employee benefits consulting firm. This is the ultimate beginner's guide to profiting from America's hottest new employee benefits. It features model portfolios for various stages of life. *Softcover, 346 pages, $17.95*

403(b) Answer Book, 5th Edition

DONALD R. LEVY, BARBARA N. SEYMON-HIRSCH, AND JANET M. ANDERSON, EDS. (PANEL PUBLISHERS/ASPEN PUBLISHERS, 2000)

▶ This book provides detailed information about accounts that are widely used by nonprofit groups to help their employees save for retirement. The plans, known as 403(b) under the Internal Revenue Code, are tax-sheltered annuities that are purchased by charities and held in custody for their employees. Workers may contribute to the plans by having money withheld from their paychecks or by making after-tax donations. The earnings accrue tax free and are used to supplement a charity's pension plan or may even constitute the entire plan. In question-and-answer format, the book examines the different types of 403(b) contracts that are available to nonprofit groups. The book's contributors, mostly lawyers who advise nonprofit organizations on retirement plans, explain the rules that govern contribution limits, loans, and life insurance policies. They also delineate the tax aspects of church-run retirement plans and examine other subjects that fall under the audit guidelines issued by the Internal Revenue Service in 1995. This book offers a summary of the "Voluntary Correction" program adopted by the IRS to help charities monitor their retirement plans and correct potential problems.

Updates to this edition include chapters that note the latest guidelines for designating income to beneficiaries and that examine the effects of court decisions on benefits to domestic partners and spouses. The publishers offer a companion book that provides sample forms, documents, and worksheets related to 403(b) plans, such as the federal forms needed to maintain 403(b) tax status, and a worksheet that lists the pros and cons of switching from a 403(b) plan to a 401(k) plan—a cousin retirement account used by many businesses. *Hardcover, 1,128 pages, $136; 984 pages, $96 (Book of forms and worksheets)*

Coordination of Benefits Handbook

MARK C. HOLLOWAY, ROBERT J. TOTH JR., AND KRISTINA WOLFE, EDS. (THOMPSON PUBLISHING GROUP, 1999)

▶ The *Coordination of Benefits Handbook* provides step-by-step information on coordinating health coverage for employees, spouses, dependents, retirees, disabled employees, and former employees. The *Handbook* is an easy-to-use reference to help you determine when and how duplicate health benefits are coordinated. Written by specialists in the health benefits field, the *Handbook* provides you with information on making timely and accurate claim determinations for all types of health plans, including group insurance, self-insured and managed care plans, and federal programs such as Medicare. It also describes all pertinent state regulations for coordinating benefits and indicates when those laws are preempted by ERISA. Your subscription includes quarterly updates and news bulletins keep you abreast of changing requirements and new developments at the federal and state levels of government, as well as in the courts. *$318*

The Decision-Maker's Guide to 401 (k) Plans: How to Set Up Cost-Effective Plans in Companies of All Sizes *(See Financial Management—Employee Benefits for full description)*

Domestic Partner Benefits—An Employer's Guide
JOSEPH S. ADAMS AND TODD A. SOLOMON (THOMPSON PUBLISHING GROUP, 1999)

▶ *Domestic Partner Benefits—An Employer's Guide* helps plan sponsors investigate the advantages and pitfalls of offering pension and welfare benefits to employees' domestic partners. It examines the trends in providing domestic partner benefits and assists employers in considering whether and how to establish a program. It features an implementation strategy and model documents, and addresses such issues as how federal, state, and local laws and ordinances affect the provision of domestic partner benefits; how "domestic partner" should be defined; whether benefits should be offered only to same-sex domestic partners and what, if any, proof should be required to receive benefits; and what administrative issues, such as tax, payroll/withholding, FMLA, COBRA, and HIPAA, are involved when offering domestic partner benefits. *Softcover, 74 pages, $79*

Employee Benefits (ASAE Background Kit)
(AMERICAN SOCIETY OF ASSOCIATION EXECUTIVES, 1998)

▶ Which benefits are appropriate for your staff? Learn the most common policies and procedures associations use in administering employee benefit programs; in addition to an overview section that includes statistical analyses of association personnel policies, this kit covers insurance, retirement plans, the Family and Medical Leave Act, bonus and incentive plans, legal issues, and many other benefits. *Spiral bound, 228 pages, $58 (Nonmember), $48 (Member) (plus $6.25 shipping)*

Employee Benefits Basics: Developing the Benefits Component of Total Compensation (Booklet)
RICHARD A. HARVEY, ROBERT M. MCCAFFERY (AMERICAN COMPENSATION ASSOCIATION, 1993)

▶ This booklet provides an overview of the elements that comprise typical employee benefits programs and discusses how they relate to total compensation. It examines benefits as part of total compensation; mandated, core, and optional benefits; tax and regulatory issues; design and administrative considerations; flexible benefits; communications; and future strategies. *Softcover, 24 pages, $19.95*

Employee Benefits Guide
DAVID L. BACON, STEPHEN D. PRATER, AND DAVID W. TUCKER (MATTHEW BENDER, 1991)

▶ With detailed analysis of statutes, regulations, opinion letters, and case law, *Employee Benefits Guide* shows you the scope of ERISA and its relationship to state law; whether an ERISA welfare or pension plan exists, even if the employer had no intention of creating one; when group insurance programs may be excluded from ERISA coverage; whether severance pay becomes subject to ERISA requirements; ERISA's reporting and disclosure rules; IRS qualifications are rules for pension plans; contributions to qualified pension plans; distributions from qualified pension plans; nonqualified pension plans; health care plans; COBRA's health insurance continuation provisions; and how to determine "qualifying events" under COBRA. It is updated with supplements and revisions. It is also available on Authority Employment Law Library CD-ROM. It includes complete discussion of the Multi-employer Pension Plan Amendment Act (MEPPA), fiduciary liability, and ERISA's bar to lawsuits seeking damages for emotional distress and punitive damages. *$125*

Employer's Guide to Fringe Benefit Rules
MARY B. HEVENER AND MARIANNA G. DYSON, EDS. (THOMPSON PUBLISHING GROUP)

▶ *Employer's Guide to Fringe Benefit Rules* pulls together all the complicated IRS fringe benefit rules in one unique, easy-to-use reference. Its practical, step-by-step approach explains the dangers and the safe harbors of all the IRS rules on fringe benefits. Plus, it includes tables to value leased cars and forms to keep track of business travel expenses. It explains how to handle withholding and how to avoid an IRS audit and more. Each month, update pages explain the latest guidelines, rule changes, standard limitations and per diem figures issued by the IRS. Plus, a monthly news bulletin provides the latest developments in the field, including pending legislation, upcoming regulations, and insider reports on what other companies are doing. *$339*

Employer's Guide to Self-Insuring Health Benefits
TERRY HUMO AND KEITH KAKACEK (THOMPSON PUBLISHING GROUP, 1999)

▶ *Employer's Guide to Self-Insuring Health Benefits* shows you how to set up and administer a successful self-funded health plan. The *Guide* features comprehensive, easy-to-read explanations of all the laws, regulations, and legal precedents that apply to self-funded plans, including IRS nondiscrimination testing; ERISA requirements; the danger of discriminating against disabled employees under the Americans with Disabilities Act; COBRA continuation coverage; medical confidentiality and malpractice liability; annual Form 5500 filing requirements; and more. A subscription includes monthly updates to keep the *Guide* up-to-date. It also includes a monthly news bulletin with briefs on important developments in the courts, at the IRS and Labor Department, and on Capitol Hill, and provides commentary and analysis on issues that are interesting and useful for sponsors of self-funded plans. *$379*

Employer's Handbook: Complying with IRS Employee Benefit Rules
MARY B. HEVENER, MARIANNA G. DYSON, AND VALERI L. STEVENS, EDS. (THOMPSON PUBLISHING GROUP)

▶ Employee benefit plans are subject to many different testing requirements, definitions, deadlines, and other requirements enforced by the IRS. It provides clear explanations of how the various IRS requirements apply to different types of benefits, along with sample forms and documents. The *Handbook* answers tough compliance questions in plain English, untangling the complex web of IRS employee benefits rules. It covers self-insured plans, group term life insurance, dependent care plans, cafeteria plans, educational assistance plans, and fringe benefits. Your subscription includes a monthly supplement to keep the *Handbook* up to date. In addition, monthly bulletins report on current action inside Congress and the IRS. *$288*

The ERISA Health & Welfare Handbook: Questions and Answers on ERISA Compliance, 2nd Edition
TERRY HUMO (THOMPSON PUBLISHING GROUP, 1999)

▶ In this question-and-answer format, *The ERISA Health & Welfare Handbook* provides practical advice on the Employee Retirement Income Security Act (ERISA)—one of the most important federal laws affecting employee health and other welfare benefit plans. ERISA's scope and application is being continually amended and reinterpreted by Congress and federal agencies. *The ERISA Health & Welfare Handbook* offers guidance on more than 30 key issues involving ERISA and employee welfare plans, including benefits entitlement, HIPAA, plan document language, discrimination issues, and employer obligations under managed care plans. Humo shares his expertise in answers to the most frequently asked ERISA questions from employers and plan administrators, such as: An employer has established differences in insured health, vision and dental benefits based on employee groups. Under what circumstances would these differences be discriminatory under ERISA, tax code or civil rights laws?; An employer had an indemnity plan for 20 years. In a few weeks, a preferred provider organization will be offered instead. Is this a material change in health coverage that warrants providing an ERISA notice of the change to plan participants?; An employer collects certain information on medical and drug benefit use to control costs in a managed care environment. Is this a violation of a plan participant's privacy rights? It also provides indexes, a glossary, and lists of resources to help employers promptly find the advice they need. *Softcover, 350 pages, $97*

Family and Medical Leave: Policies & Procedures
RICHARD L. MARCUS, ESQ. (ASPEN PUBLISHERS, 1994)

▶ This manual explains the Family and Medical Leave Act in detail, from leave provisions to prohibited conduct to remedies. It provides a step-by-step guide to analyzing the applicability of the Act to all companies and also describes how the Act fits with other legislation and corporate policies. There are many sample policies and procedures, notices, and amendments to policies. Checklists are provided to ensure compliance with the Act. *Case bound, 200 pages, $110*

Family and Medical Leave Handbook
PETER SUSSER (THOMPSON PUBLISHING GROUP, 1999)

▶ *Family and Medical Leave Handbook* is an easy-to-use guide to the law featuring an extensive explanation of the complicated FMLA requirements, including eligibility, reporting, and employee leave and benefits rules. This comprehensive information service will help control costs and minimize the new law's potential disruption of your organization's operations. The manual also provides clear explanations of the relationship between the FMLA and state and other federal laws, including the Americans with Disabilities Act, the Fair Labor Standards Act, COBRA, and the Employee

Retirement Income Security Act (ERISA). Organized into tabbed sections, the *Handbook* offers quick access to every facet of the FMLA compliance process. Sample forms and documents are included to help you draft a family and medical leave policy, an application for family or medical leave, medical certification statements, and a notice of employee intention to return from leave. Your subscription includes monthly updates to the loose-leaf guide plus monthly news bulletins to keep you on top of new regulations and interpretations from federal agencies, court cases, and state actions. *Loose-leaf, $298*

Financial Statement Reporting and Disclosure Practices for Employee Benefit Plans
(AMERICAN INSTITUTE OF CERTIFIED PUBLIC ACCOUNTANTS, 1998)

▶ This comprehensive practice guide illustrates a wide range of employee benefit plan financial statement disclosures and auditor's reports for both full-scope and limited-scope audits. Such disclosures include plan mergers, plan terminations, investments, interest in master trusts, plan amendments, contracts with insurance companies, prohibited transactions, and information certified by trustees. Also included are illustrative Form 5500 schedules. *Softcover, $56 (Nonmember), $45 (Member)*

Flex Plan Handbook
LAWRENCE J. EISENBERG (THOMPSON PUBLISHING GROUP, 1998)

▶ The *Flex Plan Handbook* shows how to avoid costly pitfalls in introducing or refining your flex plan, how to simplify initial enrollment, how to conduct nondiscrimination tests, and how to gather, record, and report data easily and cost effectively. It features an extensive section on the administration of flexible spending accounts for dependent care and unreimbursed medical expenses. It shows what funding alternatives are best for your organization and what other employers are doing. Plus, it keeps you notified of flex-related measures pending in Congress and the IRS. Your subscription includes quarterly updates that keep you in step with changes in the law and new guidance from the IRS. You'll also receive a news bulletin that keeps you up to date with new developments. *$337*

Fringe Benefits and Working Conditions in Nonprofits, 4th Edition (Survey)
STEVEN LANGER (ABBOT, LANGER & ASSOCIATES, 1999)

▶ This is an extensive and intensive study, with an analysis of prevailing practices in over 1,400 nonprofit organizations. It answers questions of interest to employees in the nonprofit sector, such as working conditions, overtime practices, work hours, time-off practices (holidays, vacations, sick leave, special leaves), 14 insurance programs, retirement practices, special work expenses, tuition reimbursement, tax-advantaged programs, part-time employment, and employee services/assistance programs. Information for each fringe benefit/working condition is reported by type of organization, region, number of employees, annual budget, and geographic scope of organization. Separate volumes are available for chief executive officers, for other administrative/professional personnel, and for clerical/blue collar employees. *Softcover, 819 pages, $175 (plus shipping and handling and Illinois sales tax, if applicable)*

The Handbook of 401(k) Plan Management, Revised Edition
TOWERS PERRIN, ED. (MCGRAW-HILL BUSINESS, 1996)

▶ *The Handbook of 401(k) Plan Management* is a comprehensive guide to the fundamental issues and unique challenges of managing plans. It covers how to maximize yield on maturing and growing assets, complying with new and changing regulations, designing and administering a flexible plan. Written for anyone involved in the design, implementation, and day-to-day operation of 401(k) plans, this book is a guide to understanding the strategic and fundamental issues involved in successfully managing a plan. In addition to demystifying the complex tax and legal environment in which these plans must operate, this book guides the reader in designing an appropriate 401(k) plan and in managing operational issues such as plan investments and administration. *The Handbook of 401(k) Plan Management* includes communicating to plan participants to help them get the most from their 401(k) plan participation; dozens of examples, graphs, and tables that simplify complex legal, financial, and administrative issues; and strategies for increasing the value of 401(k) plans for both employee and employer. *Hardcover, 475 pages, $70*

The Handbook of Employee Benefits: Design, Funding and Administration, 4th Edition

JERRY S. ROSENBLOOM, ED. (MCGRAW-HILL PROFESSIONAL PUBLISHING, 1997)

▶ *The Handbook of Employee Benefits* contains chapters written by over 50 of the field's most prominent names, and has become the necessary reference for understanding and selecting the benefits plan that works best for both your employees and your organizations. Now divided into two volumes, this set includes expanded coverage of medical benefits issues; new chapters on managed care, HMOs, PPOs, and long-term care; flexible benefit plans; and employee benefit plan communication. The first volume of a two-volume set covers the regulatory environment of employee benefits plans—legislation, rules, and regulations; medical benefits and issues, including chapters on managed care HMOs, PPOs, and long-term care; disability income and other welfare benefit plans; and cafeteria and retirement and capital accumulation plans. It provides practical and authoritative information for managers. It includes practical examples, charts, and graphs that provide a handy reference for benefits professionals who need to make important on-the-job decisions. There are new chapters on mental health, substance abuse, employee assistance programs, and educational assistance plans, as well as major revisions in many other chapters. *Hardcover, 1,100 pages, $99.95*

The Leave & Disability Coordination Handbook

(THOMPSON PUBLISHING GROUP, 1999)

▶ *The Leave & Disability Coordination Handbook* offers employers a comprehensive resource to sort through the ADA, FMLA, and workers' compensation mandates, as well as comply with other laws (e.g., COBRA, Fair Labor Standards Act, Pregnancy Discrimination Act) that affect leave. In one tabbed, cross-referenced volume, the *Handbook* addresses thorny issues such as distinguishing between FMLA "serious health conditions" and ADA "disabilities"; establishing legitimate attendance policies; granting (or denying) extended leave as an ADA accommodation; and obtaining medical information. The *Handbook* also offers sample leave policies, flowcharts, scenarios, and tips for real-world solutions to compliance problems. To ensure that subscribers have the most current information, the *Handbook* is updated quarterly with new reference pages and a newsletter that covers developments from federal agencies, Congress, the courts, and employers. Between supplements, subscribers will be alerted to events through special updates. *One-year subscription (which includes the 450-page manual and quarterly updates), $286*

Mandated Benefits: 2000 Compliance Guide

RSM MCGLADREY, INC (ASPEN PUBLISHERS, 1999)

▶ This guide provides employers, HR managers, and benefits professionals with the most cost-effective strategies for dealing with the growing number of federal and state government benefit requirements. It employs dozens of easy-to-follow tables to illustrate compliance requirements for each state. It's important to remember that individual states may pass legislation that increases the federal compliance requirements, so it's vital that you know your state's particular provisions. This new reference contains analysis and charts covering all areas of employee benefits, including pay practices, work-required materials, time off from work, health care benefits, required training, layoffs and terminations, discretionary benefits, ADA, FMLA, protection from sexual harassment, and privacy in the workplace. Plus, there are checklists and sample forms, statements, and policies to help keep you in compliance. *Softcover, 1,176 pages, $165*

Mandated Health Benefits: The COBRA Guide

PAUL M. HAMBURGER (THOMPSON PUBLISHING GROUP)

▶ Thompson's *COBRA Guide* contains plain-English explanations of the law and regulations, model employee notices and election forms, record-keeping tools, and suggested compliance procedures. Topics include determining who is eligible to receive COBRA coverage; determining when premium payments are short by an insignificant amount; responding to provider inquiries during the election and premium grace periods; analyzing when COBRA coverage must be offered under a flex plan; dealing with HMO coverage when someone moves out of the service area; figuring out the COBRA liability during business sales and acquisitions; determining how COBRA's Medicare and disability extension rules apply; providing required notices; and conducting COBRA compliance rules. Your subscription includes monthly bulletins and updates providing up-to-the-minute information about court cases, new rules, any changes in regulatory or statutory requirements, actions by federal agencies and other current developments. *$295*

Nonprofit Compensation and Benefits Practices

CAROL L. BARBEITO, APPLIED RESEARCH AND DEVELOPMENT INSTITUTE (JOHN WILEY & SONS, 1998)

▶ Designed to show nonprofit organizations what their peers are doing, this book presents data and summaries of compensation packages in the private, government, and nonprofit sectors. In doing so, it examines the different elements of compensation and benefits packages, including salary, insurance, pension plans, tuition reimbursement, vacation, and more. It also presents some of the more innovative compensation and benefits packages nonprofits have designed to attract, retain, and motivate staff. With an ever-watchful eye on cost control and budget constraints, it examines such strategies as bonuses, raises, creative work schedules (from job-sharing to flex time), noncash compensation, and more. *Hardcover, 224 pages, $57*

Nonprofit Compensation, Benefits, and Employment Law

HOWARD PIANKO, ED. (JOHN WILEY & SONS/EPSTEIN BECKER & GREEN, 1998)

▶ As the importance of charitable and other nonprofit organizations continues to grow, nonprofits themselves face a growing number of challenges that often differ significantly from those faced by their for-profit brethren. Nowhere is this more true than in the areas of compensation and benefits, where federal and state laws impose complex and often confusing restrictions on executive compensation and employee benefits. Beyond benefits and compensation, broader issues of employment law—including discrimination, sexual harassment, disability law, and other areas—also have considerable applicability in a nonprofit setting. *Nonprofit Compensation, Benefits and Employment Law* will serve as an indispensable resource to nonprofit executives when struggling with these sometimes daunting issues. *Hardcover, 364 pages, $145*

Pension & Benefits Deskset

(RIA, 2000)

▶ This desk set puts complete pension and benefits laws and regulations and source material within easy reach. Includes full-text laws, committee reports, final and proposed regulations, and preambles, with helpful finding aids. Individual volumes are available. *Softcover, 6,000+ pages, $150.00*

Pension & Benefits Law

(RIA, 2000)

▶ Reduce your research time with the only reference featuring committee reports with tax, ERISA, and other statutes. Reduce your research time and get valuable insight into lawmakers' intent. Tax, ERISA, other important statutes, and a complete statutory history are part of the all-encompassing information you'll find right at your fingertips. It includes over 800 pages of Congressional Committee Reports. *Softcover, approx. 1,700 pages, $55.00*

Pension & Benefits Regulations

(RIA, 2000)

▶ This is the only pension professional's handbook that compiles all relevant final, temporary, and proposed regulations and proposed amendments to final regulations issued by the IRS, DOL, PBGC, SEC, FDIC, and EEOC. *Softcover, approx. 2,900 pages, $75.00*

Preambles to Pension & Benefits Regulations

(RIA, 2000)

▶ This is a concise research tool with fast explanations of tax, ERISA, and other relevant regulations. Here's the background information you need to quickly understand the intent of all final, temporary, and proposed pension and benefit regulations, tax and nontax. *Softcover, approx. 1,500 pages, $49.00*

Qualified Pension and Profit Sharing Plans

(WARREN, GORHAM & LAMONT, 1998)

▶ This reference examines the requirements governing defined benefit or defined contribution plans and gives you practical guidance on how to set and manage these plans to qualify for and maintain tax-favored treatment. It provides analysis of various types of plans and the requirements that must be met to maintain qualification; when employees are eligible to participate in a qualified pension or profit-sharing plan; employee eligibility and minimum participation requirements; how the qualification rules work when the employer leases employees or uses part-time personnel or independent contractors; annual dollar limits on the accrual of benefits; how to determine employer deductions under qualified plans and when deductions can be claimed; nondiscrimination rules; and more. *One softcover volume and one 3 1/2" disk*

Retirement Benefits Tax Guide, 2nd Edition

THOMAS RUTHERFORD (CCH INCORPORATED, 1996)

▶ *Retirement Benefits Tax Guide, 2nd Edition,* is designed as a comprehensive source of information on the federal taxation of retirement benefits. It approaches the subject from the perspectives of participants in retirement plans; beneficiaries of deceased participants in retirement plans; the professional advisors of participants and beneficiaries, and employers and plan administrators who advise employees of federal tax ramifications on these retirement plans. This book focuses heavily on distributions and how they are taxed in the hands of participants and beneficiaries. It explores how employer contributions are taxed to the employee. In addition to detailed coverage of distributions from "qualified" retirement plans (employer-sponsored plans meeting the requirements of Section 401(a) of the Internal Revenue Code), this book provides an in-depth analysis of distributions from individual retirement accounts (IRAs), savings incentive match plans for employees (SIMPLE plans), simplified employee pensions (SEPs), tax-sheltered annuity arrangements of tax-exempt organizations and public schools (TSAs), and nonqualified plans of both the funded and unfunded varieties. Update supplements for this are published periodically to reflect changes in the law and other new developments. Such supplements are sent on approval at additional cost to purchasers of the volume. Supplements published within three months of purchase of the volume are provided free of charge to such subscribers. *Looseleaf, 1,000 pages, $175*

Stern's Compensation and Benefits SourceFinder®: Directory to Compensation and Benefits Surveys, Books, Periodicals, Reports, Web sites, Associations and Other Resources

GERRY STERN AND YVETTE BORCIA (MICHAEL DANIELS PUBLISHERS, 1998)

▶ This directory is useful for those who design, implement, communicate, and administer compensation and benefits programs. You will find descriptions of over 1,700 sources of data, information, and knowledge about every aspect of compensation and benefits and numerous related subjects. This includes nearly 1,200 compensation and benefit surveys. In addition to a description of the content of each source, you are provided with the provider or source name; mailing address; local and toll-free telephone and FAX numbers; and e-mail and Web site addresses. All of the sources are organized into the following subject sections (the number of sources in each section are indicated in the parentheses): benefits: general (87); benefits: health and life (57); benefits: retirement and profit sharing (122); compensation and benefits: executive (44); compensation and benefits: general (61); compensation and benefits: surveys (1,179); compensation and payroll administration (94); compensation: incentives (50); and compensation: international (36). Within these subject sections, a few of the many topics covered are laws and regulations covering wage and salary administration, executive compensation and all areas of benefits; sales incentive compensation plans; short-term and long-term incentive plans; qualified and nonqualified stock option plans; job analysis and job descriptions; competency-based compensation programs; job evaluation; expatriate compensation; motivation of individuals and teams; executive perquisites; employment agreements and related contractual arrangements; and more. The subject index is complete and cross-referenced. *Three-ring binder, $99.95*

Taxation of 401(k) and Other Salary Reduction Plans (Book and Disk)
(WARREN, GORHAM & LAMONT, 1994)

▶ This new volume is an in-depth, authoritative guide to designing and operating tax-favored salary reduction plans, including cafeteria plans, 401(k) plans, tax-sheltered annuity plans, simplified employee pension plans, and noncorporate plans. You'll see how each type of plan works, what its advantages and disadvantages are, and how it is related to other types of employee benefit plans. You'll also gain a clear understanding of the complex system of laws and regulations that govern these plans, including ERISA, COBRA, the Budget Reconciliation Act of 1993, the Family and Medical Leave Act, and more. The book includes a free 3½" disk containing 11 model plans you can adapt for your own use, including a 401(k) plan, a summary plan description of the model 401(k) plan, a flexible benefits plan, and a dependent care assistance plan. *One loose-leaf compression-bound volume and one 3½" disk; cumulative paperbound supplements and supplement disk issued twice annually*

Compensation

(See also Benefits)

Association Executive Compensation & Benefits Study, 11th Edition (Report)
(AMERICAN SOCIETY OF ASSOCIATION EXECUTIVES, 1999)

▶ This report provides salary and benefits data on CEOs, deputy executives, and more than 30 other association staff positions. This human resource tool allows you to benchmark your association's salaries and benefits against associations of similar staff size, budget size, type, scope, and geographic location. This new edition of one of ASAE's most popular studies includes an updated benefits section with more offerings under nonqualified plans for the CEO; expanded defined benefit questions; the association's cost of its retirement plan; updated health coverage and life, accident, and disability insurance sections; and expanded questions on the administration of salary and benefits programs such as incentive compensation and severance provisions. It contains data from more than 1,500 associations on salary levels and fringe benefits for the chief paid executive, number two executive, and 27 other management positions. Data are broken down by association scope, type, budget, staff size, and geographic location. *Softcover, approx. 125 pages, $195 (Nonmember), $125 (Member) (plus $5.25 shipping)*

Compensation Basics for HR Generalists: Understanding the Role of Pay in Human Resources Strategy (Booklet)
ELAINE M. EVANS (AMERICAN COMPENSATION ASSOCIATION [NOW WORLD AT WORK], 1995)

▶ This booklet identifies the specific components of typical compensation programs for the benefit of HR generalists, who are not likely to be familiar with the sometimes highly technical language of compensation. Topics include compensation philosophy, base pay, job evaluation, marketing analysis, salary ranges, legal defensibility, incentive pay, pay for performance, salary surveys, and total compensation. A downloadable pdf version is also available on the online bookstore at *http://www.worldatwork.org/Content/Infocentral/info-bookstore-frame.html. Softcover, 20 pages, $19.95 (Nonmember), $14.95 (Member)*

Compensating Executives
ARTHUR KROLL (CCH, 1998)

▶ This book offers an insider's view of how successful companies create and implement executive compensation programs. This resource brings to life specific strategies and provides an experienced view of how things work at real companies in real situations. The author discusses motivating and rewarding executives through a number of tried approaches and walks through their own unique opportunities and pitfalls. It includes reproduced forms, plans, and checklists used in practice to help readers understand and implement their own programs. The reference is suitable for professionals charged with creating and implementing plans for companies, as well as for those who evaluate plans for individual executives. *Hardcover, 352 pages, $115.00*

The Compensation Handbook: A State-of-the-Art Guide to Compensation Strategy and Design, 4th Edition
LANCE A. BERGER AND DOROTHY R. BERGER, EDS. (MCGRAW-HILL PROFESSIONAL PUBLISHING, 1999)

▶ Completely revised and updated, this edition provides simple and direct answers to specific compensation problems. Written by the leading practitioners in the field, it covers such important topics as attracting and retaining outstanding employees in a tight market, executive compensation, computers and compensation, and how to use a mix of compensation devices. It is an authoritative reference in the field, providing simple, direct answers to every important problem in compensation. Edited by experts Lance and Dorothy Berger, it features 75 percent completely new material showing you how to attract, retain, and motivate the key employees and executives your business needs. *The Compensation Handbook* provides coherent strategies and well-orchestrated planning guidelines for all aspects of compensation; data and guidance from more than 50 top leaders in the field; up-to-date help with base compensation, variable compensation, executive compensation, performance and compensation, compensation and corporate culture, and international compensation; worksheets, checklists, evaluation forms, and other useful instruments; and more. *Hardcover, 646 pages, $62.97*

Compensation in Nonprofit Organizations, 12th Edition (Survey)
(ABBOTT, LANGER & ASSOCIATES, 1999)

▶ This unique report provides the most comprehensive, in-depth analysis of salaries, salary ranges, and total compensation ever attempted in the nonprofit sector. Based on information provided by over 1,489 nonprofit organizations for over 40,000 employees in 124 benchmark jobs, this wage and salary survey report analyzes employee compensation by level of supervisory/managerial responsibility and type of nonprofit organization (association/society [by field]), chamber of commerce, civic/social service, hospital/nursing home/clinic, social welfare, and many more)—the latter versus number of employees; total annual budget; geographic scope; and region, state, and metropolitan area. This report gives you information on many of these benchmark jobs and all of these demographic variables. Many of the benchmark jobs contained in this report were not identified in earlier reports. *Part 1: Professional Societies and Trade Associations; Part 2: Excluding Professional Societies and Trade Associations*—combined editions are available for mid-Atlantic states, southern states, Great Lake states, New York and New Jersey, California, Illinois, and Texas. A combined edition is available for just the CEO. *Softcover, 1,400+ pages, National Edition Parts 1 and 2 (together) (includes CEO)*

$265 (plus shipping & handling and Illinois sales tax, if applicable); National Edition Part 1: Professional Societies and Trade Associations (includes CEO), $165.00; National Edition Part 2: Other Types of Nonprofit Organizations (includes CEO), $185.00; Compensation of CEOs in Nonprofit Organizations, $40

Compensation Tax Course, 2nd Edition (CCH, 1999)

▶ CCH's *Compensation Tax Course, 2nd Edition,* unravels the complexity and explains in clear and concise language this critical area, providing current and comprehensive guidance. This updated edition reflects numerous and significant new developments, including the important changes enacted in the IRS Restructuring and Reform Act of 1998, the Tax and Trade Relief Extension Act of 1998, and significant Treasury regulations issued since publication of the last edition. This reference fills a void left by other works on executive and employee compensation, which primarily cover qualified plans and deferred compensation, by covering all of the common forms of compensation including salary, bonuses, fringe benefits (e.g., health and accident plans and cafeteria plans), qualified deferred compensation (e.g., pensions and profit-sharing plans), and nonqualified deferred compensation (e.g., rabbi trusts and restricted stock plans). *Compensation Tax Course* is presented in five major parts: Overview of Compensation Taxation, Current Compensation, Employee Fringe Benefits, Qualified Deferred Compensation, and Nonqualified Deferred Compensation. Among the special topics covered are new developments and changes resulting from recent legislation; employee fringe benefits; multi-employee qualified deferred compensation plans; requirements for qualified plans; special rules for Keogh, top-heavy, and 401(k) plans; employer deduction and funding rules; ESOPs; taxation of distributions; IRAs, SEPs, SIMPLE IRAs, and Roth IRAs; fiduciary responsibilities and prohibited transactions; reporting and disclosure rules; Code Section 83 restricted property and stock plans and Code Section 457 deferred comp plans; equity-oriented arrangements; and more. A comprehensive Study Guide/Quizzer (see separate listing) is provided as part of this course. *Hardcover, 664 pages, $125.00*

Compensation Tax Course Study Guide/Quizzer, 2nd Edition (Self-Study Course)
(CCH, 1999)

▶ *The Compensation Tax Guide—Study Guide/Quizzer, Second Edition,* is designed to reinforce and apply the concepts presented in CCH's *U.S. Master Compensation Tax Guide* book (see separate listing), which unravels the complexity of compensation taxation and explains it in clear and concise language. This special Study Guide/Quizzer emphasizes new developments and opportunities resulting from the numerous and significant new developments presented in the *U.S. Master Compensation Tax Guide* and is formulated to help readers enhance their understanding of the intricacies of compensation taxation and planning. The Study Guide/Quizzer includes valuable study questions with detailed answers to reinforce and test the user's comprehension of key concepts. *$85.00*

Employee Compensation Basics: Developing the Direct Pay Component of Total Compensation
WILLIAM H. CLAMPITT & JOHN POTEMPA (AMERICAN COMPENSATION ASSOCIATION, 1994)

▶ This booklet provides an overview of the characteristics of and design considerations for typical employee compensation programs, including business vision and strategy, ideal direct compensation program objectives, setting base salaries, salary increases,

evaluating pay programs, and looking ahead. *Softcover, 20 pages, $19.95 (Nonmember), $14.95 (Member)*

Executive Compensation: A Primer for Board Members and Chief Executives (*See Governance—Executive, Roles and Responsibilities for full description*)

Executive Compensation: Establishing Appropriate Compensation for Chief Executives of Nonprofit Organizations (*See Governance—Roles and Responsibilities for full description*)

Financial Compensation in Nonprofit Organizations (Booklet)
BRIAN O'CONNELL & E.B. KNAUFT (INDEPENDENT SECTOR, 1993)

▶ How should the chief executives of organizations dedicated to serving society and funded by voluntary contributions be compensated? This booklet offers a philosophy of financial compensation in nonprofits, addressing four very different problems and perceptions facing nonprofit executives. *Financial Compensation* also provides a model for determining salaries, factoring in responsibilities, costs, and market place realities. Use this booklet to develop a salary schedule for your organization that you can use to attract qualified employees, operate effectively, and maintain public trust. *Softcover, 26 pages, $5 (Nonmember), $3.50 (Member) (plus $2.50 shipping)*

Handbook of Compensation Management
MATT DELUCA (PRENTICE HALL DIRECT, 1993)

▶ This handbook provides guidelines for HR managers who need to establish or improve their wage and salary program. It tells how to analyze jobs and write job descriptions in order to determine appropriate pay levels, how to budget, how to audit and review the wage and salary program, and how to conduct performance appraisals and set merit pay levels. It addresses relevant legal issues, salary surveys, incentive issues, benefits, and prerequisites, and the interaction between the wage and salary program and payroll. it can create a compensation program that makes it easy to attract and retain outstanding employees, while keeping total compensation costs remarkably low. It covers everything from broadbanding and performance evaluation to salary auditing and legal compliance. It includes sample job descriptions, budgeting worksheets, and much more. *Hardcover, 400 pages, $89.95*

U.S. Master Compensation Tax Guide, 2nd Edition
(CCH, 1999)

▶ This updated edition reflects numerous and significant new developments, including the important changes enacted in the IRS Restructuring and Reform Act of 1998, the Tax and Trade Relief Extension Act of 1998, and significant Treasury regulations issued since publication of the last edition. It offers concise, practical coverage of the federal tax laws concerning executive and employee compensation. This title covers all of the common forms of compensation, including salary, bonuses, and other current compensation; employee fringe benefits; qualified deferred compensation; and nonqualified deferred compensation. This reference fills a void left by other works on executive and employee compensation, which primarily cover qualified plans and deferred compensation, by covering all of the common forms of compensation including salary, bonuses, fringe benefits (e.g., health and accident plans and cafeteria plans), qualified deferred compensation (e.g., pensions and profit-sharing plans), and nonqualified deferred compensation (e.g., rabbi trusts and restricted stock plans). A comprehensive Study Guide/Quizzer is available for use with this volume. *Hardcover, 650 pages, $54.95*

Workers' Compensation Guide for Employers (Manual)

CHARLES B. LEWIS (ASPEN PUBLISHERS, 2000)

▶ This title will bring you up to speed on the "hot" issues in workers' compensation, like ergonomics and managed care, as well as traditional concerns, like how to manage a doubtful claim. It includes over 20 charts showing the practices of each state on vital topics. Some vital topics are: getting Workers' Compensation insurance, injuries and illness covered, types of benefits, controlling medical claims, investigating and defending doubtful claims, disability discrimination and family and medical leave laws, conflicts with Workers' Compensation, safety programs and claim prevention, and ergonomics and repetitive injuries. *Three-ring binder, 546 pages, $119.50*

Diversity

(See also Interpersonal Relations; Risk Management, Insurance and Liability)

Addressing Sexual Harassment in the Workplace

(JOSSEY-BASS, 1992)

▶ This complete program gives you the tools to discuss sexual harassment and help every organizational member recognize it, respond appropriately, and prevent it from happening. The trainer's package includes a trainer's guide, three experiential activities, a self-scoring test, supplemental readings that can be used for lectures and take-home materials, and lists of resources. Participants learn about sexual harassment from three activities: The Woman and the Sailor helps participants identify factors that affect their judgments and demonstrates how values affect relationships and decisions; The Promotion promotes awareness of the complexity of human sexuality as an influential factor in organizational settings; Tina Carlan increases awareness of legal issues connected with sexual harassment complaints. It provides a systematic process for investigating and resolving sexual harassment within the organization; and provides a group learning forum for how to resolve sexual harassment in the workplace. Educate your employees about sexual harassment and lead the way to a more productive, safe working environment. Help your participants clarify personal values and how they view harassment; identify types of sexual harassment; and become familiar with issues, laws, and consequences relating to sexual harassment. It includes one each of Trainer's Materials, The Woman and the Sailor, The Promotion, Tina Carlan, The Sexual-Harassment Awareness Test, and Readings Section. *Loose-leaf, $99.95*

Beyond Awareness: Skills for Managing a Culturally Diverse Workforce

JONAMAY LAMBERT AND SELMA MYERS (LAMBERT & ASSOCIATES/INTERCULTURAL DEVELOPMENT)

▶ This trainer's guide provides additional skills beyond basic intercultural awareness training. It focuses on the next step: skills for managing a culturally diverse workforce. It offers a variety of exercises that will help participants understand the impact of change, learn skills for dispute resolution, and promote multicultural team building. It includes 12 proven exercises, sample agenda, 32 different charts, sample lecturettes, handouts, and hard copy for transparencies. *Softcover, 80 pages, $59.95 (plus $3.75 shipping)*

Beyond Race and Gender: Unleashing the Power of Your Total Work Force by Managing Diversity

THOMAS R. ROOSEVELT (AMACOM BOOKS, 1992)

▶ By the year 2000, only one in every seven new employees will be the standard-issue white male. The ability to manage this diversity successfully has become a basic strategy for corporate survival. *Beyond Race and Gender* supplies a sorely needed Action Plan, extensive case studies, and a series of tough questions and answers to get readers thinking deeply about what elements are blocking the full use of their employees. *Softcover, 208 pages, $15.95*

Building a House for Diversity: A Fable About a Giraffe & an Elephant Offers New Strategies for Today's Workforce

R. ROOSEVELT THOMAS, JR., WITH MARJORIE I. WOODRUFF (AMACOM BOOKS, 1999)

▶ What could an elephant and a giraffe teach people about working together? Some very important lessons, it seems, about the complex—and critically important—issues of dealing with diversity in the workforce. *Building a House for Diversity* begins with a short fable about how a friendship between the two animals is threatened when the house built for a tall, skinny giraffe cannot accommodate his invited guest, a broad, bulky elephant. Using this story as a vivid metaphor for the difficult issues inherent in diversity, the book goes on to demonstrate how managing diversity can be seen as a set of *skills* that anyone can learn—and use. In a way that makes diversity management "up close and personal," *Building a House for Diversity* offers compelling, real-life stories of individual experiences at work. It includes the perspective of both "insiders" (usually white males) and "outsiders" (usually minorities or women); commentary illuminating what these experiences tell us about the challenges and opportunities of diversity; a segment on Phil Jackson, former Chicago Bulls coach, and how he dealt with diversity issues in his relationships to Michael Jordan, Dennis Rodman, Scottie Pippin, and others; and hands-on guidance to help readers become "diversity mature" and take personal responsibility for their attitudes and actions. *Softcover, 228 pages, $27.95*

Communicating in a Diverse Workplace: A Practical Guide to Successful Workplace Communication Techniques (Workplace Diversity Series)

LILLIAN A. KUGA (RICHARD CHANG ASSOCIATES/JOSSEY-BASS, 1999)

▶ Many factors can hinder effective workplace communication—including authority levels, department structures, and unclear objectives. A diverse workplace can either add another complication, or, if managed well, can overcome other organizational obstacles. It features the need for a consistent approach to communicating, obstacles to communicating in a diverse workplace, understanding different communication styles related to diverse backgrounds, and clues and cues to effective communication. *Softcover, 110 pages, $16.95*

Cultural Diversity in the Workplace

SALLY J. WALTON (IRWIN PROFESSIONAL PUBLISHING, 1994— AVAILABLE FROM SOCIETY FOR HUMAN RESOURCE MANAGEMENT)

▶ Employees from different cultural backgrounds bring a wealth of creativity, insights, and skills to their jobs, and it is up to employers to recognize, cultivate, and value these contributions. This publication explores the issues surrounding workforce diversity, cultural differences, and management sensitivity. This essential guide brings you up to speed on the unwritten rules of communicating, writing, interviewing, mentoring, and coaching within a culturally diverse workplace. *Softcover, 75 pages, $10 (Nonmember), $9 (Member) (plus $6 shipping)*

Cultural Diversity in Organizations: Theory, Research, and Practice *(See Organizational Dynamics and Design—Publications for full description)*

Designing and Implementing Successful Diversity Programs

LAWRENCE M. BAYTOS (PRENTICE HALL DIRECT, 1995)

▶ This guide, with ideas, techniques, action items, plans, and a complete case study, gives managers an understanding of the new complexity of the workforce and enables them to create and implement programs that get the best from employees. Complete guidelines are given for a diversity process, including research strategies, converting those strategies into action plans, and organizing for sustained management commitment. Methods are included for enhancing affirmative action, integrating diversity and work/family initiatives, testing career mobility systems, and much more. *Hardcover, 400 pages, $69.95*

Diversity Activities and Training Designs

JULIE O'MARA (JOSSEY-BASS, 1994)

▶ *Diversity Activities and Training Designs* contains everything you need to facilitate a highly successful diversity training program. Use these diversity tools to change policies, systems, and practices; stimulate involvement for people who have been oppressed; encourage behavior changes that will create a harmonious work environment; and reveal the benefits of a diverse work force to management. Each of the 36 activities states its specific objective. *Loose-leaf, 400 pages, $159.95*

Diversity Bingo: An Experiential Learning Event

(JOSSEY-BASS, 1992)

▶ Based on the traditional game of bingo, the *Diversity Bingo* game is a great addition to any type of diversity training program. It's a fun, lighthearted way to help individuals recognize the complexities involved in determining cultural perceptions and assumptions. Participants also become aware of how they are *seen* or categorized by others. Perhaps most important, the awareness that results from playing the game will have a positive impact on an organization's culture. The game includes a package of bingo cards and a trainer's manual that gives an overview of the game, instructions on how to apply it to small or large groups, and an outline for debriefing each session. Master overheads and handouts are included, as well as other activities and uses for the bingo card. A fast-paced, interactive group learning experience, *Diversity Bingo* makes it easy for organizations to better understand and deal with their own cultural diversity. *Loose-leaf, $99.95*

Diversity Icebreakers: A Trainer's Guide

SELMA MYERS AND JONAMAY LAMBERT (INTERCULTURAL DEVELOPMENT/LAMBERT & ASSOCIATES, 1995)

▶ This guide is designed for all trainers, and especially diversity trainers, who need simple, effective, and ready-to-use icebreaker activities. It can be used to introduce the diversity topic, warm up a group, or lead into more in-depth discussions. It will help participants learn more about diversity issues through short and creative exercises, increase self-awareness and expand diversity "comfort zone," and relate diversity themes to everyday experiences. It consists of icebreaker activities that address informal cultural introductions, effective cross-cultural communication, personal awareness and perception, values, and assumptions. Includes 40 proven activities (most under 20 minutes) in a standard format, divided into six sections by overall topic. It offers interactive and suitable exercises, convenient and ready for immediate use. *Softcover, 60 pages, $59.95 (plus $3.75 shipping)*

Dynamics of Diversity: Strategic Programs for Your Organization

ODETTE POLLAR AND RAFAEL GONZALES (CRISP PUBLICATIONS, 1995)

▶ Diversity is an important element for any workplace. The benefits of being able to work with all sorts of people are many. This book will help you understand what is necessary for diversity training and how to supplement such a plan. Examples of successful companies are given to show the value of diversity training in our society. *Softcover, 79 pages, $12.95*

Gender at Work: Improving Relationships

SELMA MYERS AND JONAMAY LAMBERT (INTERCULTURAL DEVELOPMENT/LAMBERT & ASSOCIATES)

▶ This guide provides exercises that increase awareness about gender issues in the workplace. It will help participants understand how personal influences affect perceptions about the opposite sex, become more comfortable and reduce anxiety among men and women, and reduce stereotypes that both men and women often have about each other. It includes 11 proven exercises, sample agenda, and 20 different charts, sample lecturettes, handouts, and hard copy for transparencies. *Softcover, 56 pages, $59.95 (plus $3.75 shipping)*

Handling Diversity in the Workplace: Communication Is the Key

KAY duPONT (AMERICAN MEDIA, INC., 1997)

▶ Work culture, like society, is multicultural. To succeed, organizations must value the differences of a diverse population and the individuality of all people. Employees and customers alike should be treated with dignity. *Handling Diversity in the Workplace* helps readers understand how words and actions in today's diverse workplace affect people and productivity and ultimately an organization's bottom line. *Softcover, 104 pages, $12.95*

How Diversity Works

HARRIS SUSSMAN (1995)

▶ *How Diversity Works* is a handbook for anyone who works with people—in organizations, in education, in counseling. It contains the first years of Dr. Sussman's monthly Q & A column in the *Managing Diversity* newsletter plus 30 other articles, as well as checklists, handouts, diagrams, and worksheets. His chapters look at Workforce 2000, training, meetings, diversity as HR's opportunity of a lifetime, women, and work–family, and provides a consumer's guide to diversity. He offers a 20-item "white males pre-test" which could be used as a catalyst in an open training program. He emphasizes that diversity work is not linear and he provides a diversity process rating scales worksheet. *$12 (plus $3 shipping & handling)*

Implementing Diversity: Best Practices for Making Diversity Work in Your Organization

MARILYN LODEN (MCGRAW-HILL PROFESSIONAL PUBLISHING, 1995) (IRWIN PROFESSIONAL PUB; ISBN: 078630460X)

▶ This practical and provocative guide provides the strategies and tactics used by organizations committed to implementing diversity from the top down. Focusing on the necessity for a strategic change initiative, Loden discusses how to position diversity initiatives for maximum buy-in and support, proven strategies for managing resistance to this important change, and the 18 classic mistakes made when implementing diversity initiatives—and how to avoid them. *Hardcover, 192 pages, $24.95*

Making Diversity Happen: Controversies and Solutions

ANN M. MORRISON, MARIAN N. RUDERMAN, AND MARTHA HUGHES-JAMES (CENTER FOR CREATIVE LEADERSHIP, 1993)

▶ This book compares and constrasts views of researchers, corporate practitioners, and consultants on the meaning of diversity and the approaches to its implementation in organizations. *Softcover, 136 pages, $20 (plus 5 percent shipping—$3 minimum)*

Managing a Diverse Workforce: Regaining the Competitive Edge

JOHN P. FERNANDEZ (JOSSEY-BASS, 1991)

▶ Leverage the rich diversity of the American workforce. This eye-opening book candidly examines the ramifications of racism and sexism at work, and provides managers with practical advice on how to prepare their organizations for the next demographic revolution. *Hardcover, 322 pages, $25.95*

Managing Cultural Diversity: A Trainer's Guide

SELMA MYERS AND JONAMAY LAMBERT (INTERCULTURAL DEVELOPMENT, INC./LAMBERT & ASSOCIATES, 1993—ALSO AVAILABLE FROM SOCIETY FOR HUMAN RESOURCE MANAGEMENT)

▶ This guide offers practical approaches to increase awareness of the impact of culture in the workplace, identify cultural issues and underlying assumptions in managing a diverse workforce, and meet the needs of diversity trainers and improve their skills. It includes training exercises, sample agendas, charts, handouts, and hard copy for transparencies. *Softcover, 58 pages, $59.95 (plus $3.75 shipping)*

Managing Diversity: A Complete Desk Reference & Planning Guide, 2nd Edition

LEE GARDENSCHWARTZ AND ANITA ROWE (MCGRAW-HILL, 1998)

▶ *Managing Diversity* is a comprehensive reference on diversity with an excellent mixture of practical information, worksheets, and activities. It goes past diversity awareness to systemic, long-term, hands-on implementation of a diversity strategy. It is a guide to improving the level of efficiency in an organization through effective cross-cultural communication. It shows how to conduct a diversity audit in the organization to design an effective program; create a corporate culture that embraces diversity to maximize the potential of the workforce; build cohesive multicultural work teams; design interesting, effective meetings; and hire, train, and promote a diverse workforce. Included are approximately 100 charts, checklists, suggested activities, worksheets, systems audits, exercises, sample interview questions, and tip sheets. Each exercise, worksheet, and the like is accompanied by a full page of the author's suggestions on how it can be best utilized in the trenches

as well as how it fits in to the theory of what is being explained in the text. It covers everything from theory, implementation, evaluation, and measurement to what the future holds and why some programs have failed and what to do about it, as well as offering a comprehensive resource section. *Hardcover, 538 pages, $99.95*

The Managing Diversity Survival Guide: A Complete Collection of Checklists, Activities, and Tips (Book and Diskette)

LEE GARDENSWARTZ AND ANITA ROWE (IRWIN PROFESSIONAL PUBLISHING, 1993—AVAILABLE FROM SOCIETY FOR HUMAN RESOURCE MANAGEMENT)

▶ Packed with over 80 activities, worksheets, charts, surveys, checklists (all on diskette), and transparency masters that cover everything from interviewing to communicating to coaching employees in a diverse workplace, this book lends itself to all diversity training environments and provides ready-to-use, reproducible support materials for employees involved in any stage of diversity training. It helps you assess your organization's need and readiness for diversity training, prepares you for potential difficulties in training sessions, and improves communication and cooperation with the workforce. *Softcover (with diskette), 200 pages, $45 (Nonmember), $41 (Member) (plus $10 shipping)*

Managing Workforce 2000: Gaining the Diversity Advantage

DAVID JAMIESON AND JULIE O'MARA (JOSSEY-BASS, 1991)

▶ Using examples from over 80 organizations, this practical guide to human resource development strategies shows how to attract, make the best use of, and retain employees of different skills and perspectives. The authors reveal the strategies successful organizations are using to capitalize on today's increasingly diverse and nontraditional workforce and shows how organizations must change to mesh with the needs. *Hardcover, 272 pages, $34.95*

The New Leaders: Guidelines on Leadership Diversity in America

ANN M. MORRISON (JOSSEY-BASS, 1992)

▶ White males now represent less than one third of the American workforce. Who will the new leaders be, and how will their skills be developed? This book defines the practices that obstruct and those that encourage the advancement of women and people of color into the executive ranks. It presents specific recruitment, development, and accountability tools that foster diversity and help organizations compete effectively for the best management employees available. Learn how organizations can reach a broader market, improve employee satisfaction, and increase productivity when diversity becomes an integral part of the organization's strategy. *Hardcover, 343 pages, $27 (plus $4.50 shipping)*

A Peacock in the Land of Penguins: A Tale of Diversity and Discovery

BARBARA HATELY AND WARREN H. SCHMIDT (BERRETT-KOEHLER PUBLISHERS, 1995)

▶ This book follows the adventures of Perry the Peacock and other exotic birds as they try to make their way in the Land of Penguins. It is a tale of the perils and possibilities of being "different" in a world that values comfort, safety, and the predictability of conformity. Perry the Peacock is a bright, talented, colorful bird who is recruited to live in the Land of the Penguins. He soon runs into problems because the penguins have established an organizational climate that is formal, bureaucratic, and governed by a vast array of written and unwritten rules. Although his talent is recognized, his different and unusual style make the penguins feel threatened. As this book shows, being "different" is much more than a matter of race and gender. Diversity in its fullest sense involves a broad range of human uniqueness: personality, work style, perception and attitudes, values and lifestyle, work ethic, worldview, communication style, and much more. Valuing diversity means appreciating and encouraging people to be who they really are, helping them to develop their full potential, and utilizing their special talents, skills, ideas, and creativity. *Softcover, 120 pages, $10 (plus $4.50 shipping)*

Redefining Diversity

R. ROOSEVELT THOMAS JR. (AMACOM BOOKS, 1996)

▶ From the author of *Beyond Race and Gender* comes this work that proposes a completely new and wholly liberating definition of "diversity." In R. Roosevelt Thomas's words: "Diversity applies not merely to a collection of people who are alike in some ways and different in others, but also to intangibles: ideas, procedures, ways of looking at things." By applying the concept to broad business concerns, Thomas awakens us to the latent power of diversity. At the heart of Thomas's new model for diversity management is the Diversity Paradigm, with eight action options that can be applied. *Hardcover, 272 pages, $24.95*

Tools for Valuing Diversity

ANTHONY HARRIS AND SELMA MYERS (JOSSEY-BASS, 1999)

▶ Tools and exercises are important elements to increase staff awareness and provide the skills needed for a successful diverse workplace. With clear explanations and suggested applications provided in this guidebook, these tools can be integrated into regular group meetings, formal training, and impromptu small-group sessions. *Softcover, $14.95*

The Value of Difference: Enhancing Philanthropy Through Inclusiveness in Governance, Staffing, and Grantmaking *(See Governance—Composition for full description)*

Winning With Diversity: A Practical Handbook for Creating Inclusive Meetings, Events, and Organizations *(See Organizational Development— Publications for full description)*

Working Together: Succeeding in a Multicultural Organization, Revised Edition

GEORGE SIMONS (CRISP PUBLICATIONS, 1994)

▶ The workforce today is increasingly diverse. This easy-to-use reference guide helps managers create a positive, productive work environment in a diverse workforce. Realistic case studies and reader-involving worksheets sensitize you to gender and cultural differences to help you enhance communication throughout your organization. *Softcover, 85 pages, $12.95*

A Workshop for Managing Diversity in the Workplace

SANDRA KANU KOGOD (JOSSEY-BASS, 1991)

▶ This trainer's guide offers a workshop design with 18 activities and lecturettes for building awareness, knowledge, and understanding of the complex issue of diversity. The activities effectively help

participants learn from one another and apply their learnings in action planning and contracting. This complete guide includes background information on diversity, instructions on preparing for the workshop, more than a dozen participant handouts, and more. The workshop strives to improve participants' abilities in evaluating behavior, especially as it relates to work performance; identifying and working through their own stereotypes; responding effectively in encounters with individuals who are culturally different from themselves; building a repertoire of practical methods for overcoming cultural barriers in the organizational setting; capitalizing on people's differing talents; and more. *Loose-leaf, 109 pages, $99.95*

Interpersonal Relations/Employee Behavior/Conflict Resolution

(See also Diversity; Risk Management, Insurance, and Liability)

Building Staff/Volunteer Relations, Revised Edition

IVAN H. SCHEIER (ENERGIZE, 1993)

▶ This resource helps employees and volunteers work together successfully by exploring the reasons for conflict between volunteers and employees. Scheier eases the all-too-common stresses of this relationship with a step-by-step process for analyzing tasks and work preferences for both paid and unpaid staff. He offers a great number of creative and practical solutions. The book contains lots of useful planning guides. This practical book deals directly with one of the major challenges in volunteer management: helping employees and volunteers work together successfully. It advises a step-by-step process for analyzing tasks and work preferences for both paid and unpaid staff; demonstrates how concern for clear and desirable job descriptions avoids the pitfalls of blurry lines of responsibility; defuses the tension inherent in this subject, exploring the reasons for conflict between volunteers and employees and offering a great number of useful solutions; incorporates and updates three previous publications on staff relations; and includes many useful planning guides. *Softcover, 70 pages, $16.95*

The Healing Manager: How to Build Quality Relationships and Productive Cultures at Work

WILLIAM LUNDIN AND KATHLEEN LUNDIN (BERRETT-KOEHLER PUBLISHERS, 1993)

▶ This book squarely faces the tough emotional issues in the workplace (anger, fear, distrust, conflict, resentment) and to provide practical and proven methods for creating more productive work environments. Based on 15 years' experience using these methods inside workplaces, the authors show how to replace anger and suspicion at work with caring, trust, and cooperation, unlock the goodwill, learning, and creativity of everyone in an enterprise, and enable all employees to facilitate productive relationships at work. The "healing manager" the authors describe is any employee who helps others grow emotionally and intellectually, and who cultivates caring relationships on the job. They show that such well-being is the real secret to productivity, quality, and service. They draw on counseling techniques, improvisational theater, and common wisdom to offer practical tools to help all managers and employees change their workplace behaviors, attitudes, and relationships *Hardcover, 312 pages, $27.95*

Polishing the Potential of Volunteer/Paid Staff Teams" *(See Volunteerism—Interpersonal Relations for full description)*

Preventing Violence in the Workplace
CHARLES E. LABIG (AMACOM BOOKS, 1995)

▶ This book helps organizations address the causes of violence and take steps to assess and prevent a crisis. This sane and practical book translates psychological assessment theories into effective models for the corporate environment. Written in plain English, it can help companies protect their employees and avoid liability, by showing them how to assess the risks of violence in any situation; develop guidelines, policies, and procedures to prevent violence, including hiring and selection; organize a Violence Response Team; and handle potentially tense downsizings and terminations. It includes a chapter on legal and liability issues by Garry Mathiason, a leading expert on workplace violence. *Hardcover, 224 pages, $24.95*

Sexual Harassment in the Workplace: How to Prevent, Investigate, and Resolve Problems in Your Organization
ELLEN J. WAGNER (AMACOM BOOKS, 1992)

▶ A female employee walks into your office and claims she has been sexually harassed. What should you do? Just as important, what should you not do. In an area where it can be hard to get at the truth and where emotions run high, *Sexual Harassment in the Workplace* offers a legal expert's advice on how to investigate complaints in a way that is fair to all parties and protects your organization from legal liability. In addition, this book shows you how to establish policies and procedures to prevent harassment, to discipline harassers, and to save your company many dollars in legal fees, court judgments, and lost productivity. *Softcover, 148 pages, $17.95*

Why Didn't You Say That in the First Place?: How to Be Understood At Work
RICHARD HEYMAN (JOSSEY-BASS, 1994)

▶ Do you ever get the feeling that your co-workers don't understand you? Misunderstanding through poor communication is rampant in the workplace, yet most workers just shrug their shoulders and accept misunderstanding as a fact of life. In *Why Didn't You Say That in the First Place?*, the author offers a path to clear communication by demonstrating how we can always reach full mutual understanding with others by using the power of plain talk in a systematic way. You'll discover why nobody understands you, why misunderstanding is normal, the power of strategic talk, and communicating when understanding is critical. It is full of anecdotes, illustrations, sample conversations, and checklists to show readers how misunderstandings can be prevented in everyday settings. It explains why creating understanding is such a challenge (we can only understand each other by interpreting what we hear or read, and no two people interpret the same words in exactly the same way).

Payroll
(See also Administration/Record Keeping/Forms)

Bender's Payroll Tax Guide
DENNIS LASSILA AND BOB KILPATRICK (MATTHEW BENDER, 1982)

▶ This is a time- and money-saving guide to payroll tax planning. It has over 1,000 pages of procedures, forms, and examples to help you design and run a payroll system that is both economical and efficient, including: applicability of federal payroll taxes to you and your employees; alphabetical dictionary to help correctly determine what constitutes a wage payment; methods and systems for streamlining record keeping, tax deposits, personnel status changes, garnishments, wage assignments, terminating business operations, and more; all the facts on Social Security benefits; filled-in sample forms and reproducible blank forms; and annual Social Security and withholding tables. It is updated with a new volume annually. *Softbound, $117*

Payroll Practitioner's Compliance Handbook
(WARREN, GORHAM & LAMONT, 1997)

▶ This expert reference guides you step by step through increasingly complex year-end and quarterly payroll reporting requirements. You get guidance on filing Forms W-2, W-3, 940, 941, and 945, and on distributing W-2s, 1099s, and other year-end statements; help for complying with federal and state magnetic media reporting requirements; details on reconciling wage and tax data and on correcting federal returns; guidance in the taxation and reporting of employee relocation, nonqualified deferred compensation, educational assistance, third-party sick pay, group term life insurance, business expense reimbursements; discussion of statutory changes to expect in the upcoming year so you can begin your planning now; and more. *One loose-leaf volume, published annually in April with midyear updates, $185*

Principles of Payroll Administration
(WARREN, GORHAM & LAMONT, 1997)

▶ This guide is really three books in one: a complete collection of payroll essentials, with clear explanations of applicable laws, accounting procedures, and more—making it the ideal primer for members of your payroll staff; a quick-answer desktop reference, covering tricky items such as child support withholding, third-party sick pay, 401(k) plans, group term life insurance, and more; a step-by-step training manual with examples, charts, tables, and self-quizzes in a question-and-answer format to simplify learning. Use it to get strategies for coping with garnishments and levies, the federal tax deposit rules, avoiding penalty traps, the federal tax and reporting rules for benefits, as a guide through federal and state wage-hour law, and for guidance through ALL the federal employment tax forms. *One loose-leaf volume, published annually in April with midyear updates, $175*

Policies & Procedures
(See also Administration/Record Keeping; Risk Management, Insurance, and Liability)

Association Personnel Policies (ASAE Background Kit)
(AMERICAN SOCIETY OF ASSOCIATION EXECUTIVES, 1998)

▶ This background kit features sections on hiring, funded benefits, office procedures, employee handbooks, leave policies, health issues, and separation policies. It also includes samples of associations' policies and statements on affirmative action and equal opportunity employment, employee insurance, various types of leave, flextime, overtime and compensatory time, substance abuse, smoking and AIDS, resignation, disciplinary action, and termination. *Spiral bound, 292 pages, $66 (Nonmember), $55 (Member) (plus $6.25 shipping)*

Creating Your Employee Handbook: A Do-It Yourself Kit for Nonprofits, National Edition

LENYA BERNSTEIN (THE MANAGEMENT CENTER/JOSSEY-BASS, 1999)

► This book-and-disk set has everything you need to craft an employee handbook that is tailored to your organization's mission, culture, and goals. It is The Management Center's most comprehensive human resources toolkit for nonprofits across the country—filled with sample policies and examples of how to adapt each policy to your specific objectives. *Creating Your Employee Handbook* offers a three-level approach, capturing the complexity and diversity of your nonprofit. Many of the sample policies appear in versions that correspond to large, medium-sized, or small nonprofits. Sample policies also reflect different organizational cultures. For each policy, you can choose—mixing or matching as needed—the language, form, and style that best reflect your purpose and work culture. Topics include employment and employee development, benefits, workplace health and safety, standards of conduct, work hours and pay, and much more. You can create a new employee handbook from start to finish, update existing policies, or identify new ones. The do-it-yourself kit includes a computer disk complete with all of the sample policies in PC format. The policies are organized into folders that correspond to the size of your nonprofit. You can select or combine the policies according to your specific requirements. Also included are sample forms that can be copied or saved for future use. *Softcover and disk, 272 pages, $49.95*

Drafting and Revising Employment Policies and Handbooks

KURT H. DECKER (ASPEN PUBLISHERS, 1994)

► This practical guide contains all the information and forms needed to develop and maintain employment policies and handbooks that meet the needs of both the company and the employee. It details a method for conducting a human resource audit to determine the problems and needs of an organization. The text covers such issues as relevant laws, initial employment policies, introductory policies, drug testing policies, privacy policies, compensation and benefits policies, leaves of absence, discipline performance, layoff and dispute resolution policies, and human resource and employment litigation. *Case bound, 2 volumes, 916 pages, $255*

E-Mail and Internet Use Policies (Report)

LUIS HERNANDEZ (THOMPSON PUBLISHING GROUP, 1999)

► Access to online communications tools improves employee performance and workflow, but its abuse can result in reduced productivity and company liability. *E-Mail and Internet Use Policies* brings together the information employers need to craft and implement sound e-mail and Internet use policies. Such a policy can help maintain productivity and help protect the company from liability for sexual harassment, racial discrimination, defamation, and other employee misconduct. This special report addresses the many complex issues HR managers face when considering workplace e-mail and Internet policies, such as the reasons why employers need e-mail and Internet use policies, the liability and productivity issues employers face when employees improperly use online services at work, the implications of sending copyrighted and confidential business information via e-mail, the legal risks associated with not enforcing established e-mail and Internet policies, and the ethical and privacy considerations that lie behind the decision about who should monitor employee e-mail. It offers an analysis of online "misperceptions," discussions of confidentiality, copyright infringement and liability, a sample e-mail and Internet use policy, and lists of relevant court cases and Web sites. *Softcover, 24 pages, $39*

Encyclopedia of Prewritten Personnel Policies

SUE ELLEN THOMPSON, ROBERT L. BRADY, AND LEONARD PRESSON (BUSINESS & LEGAL REPORTS, INC., 1995—AVAILABLE FROM SOCIETY FOR HUMAN RESOURCE MANAGEMENT)

► With the *Encyclopedia of Prewritten Personnel Policies* you can write your own professionally developed, employer-proven policy manual by just selecting from or adapting more than 200 field-tested policy statements. This complete "how-to" guide includes a policy for every HR area, from absenteeism to workers' compensation, from conservative to progressive choices. An annual subscription includes updates on this topic. *3-volume binders, 1,500 pages, $159.95*

How to Develop an Employee Handbook, 2nd Edition

JOSEPH W.R. LAWSON II (AMACOM BOOKS, 1997)

► One of an organization's most important communication tools is the employee handbook. It must be legally sound, up to date, clearly written, and comprehensive. This ready-to-use guidebook, now in its second edition, practically writes the handbook by itself. Human resources professionals will appreciate its checklists that guide them every step of the way (and make sure all bases are covered); step-by-step instructions that make information easy to understand (and help avoid mistakes); more than 400 sample policy statements, all in use by actual companies and ready to go "as is" or to revise as needed; and plain-English explanations of federal and state regulations, with practical suggestions for implementation. *Spiral bound, 392 pages, $75*

How to Develop a Personnel Policy Manual, 6th Edition

JOSEPH W.R. LAWSON II (AMACOM BOOKS, 1998)

► This reference guides HR professionals through the entire process of planning, developing, and writing the manual. It includes hundreds of sample policies covering every important topic, from hiring to benefits to termination, along with planning checklists and synopses of relevant employment laws. This guide to writing a personnel policy manual begins with the basics and covers all areas of HR concern, including recent issues such as AIDS, computers, ethics, and drug and alcohol abuse. *Binder, 540 pages, $75*

Manual of Personnel Policies, Procedures, and Operations, 2nd Edition

JOSEPH D. LEVESQUE (PRENTICE HALL DIRECT, 1993)

► This comprehensive manual is really four books in one. Part 1 is a ready-to-use manual of model personnel policies covering such issues as equal employment opportunity hiring, orientation, probation, benefits, and termination. Part 2 provides sample records and forms—from job applications to time reports, and OSHA records, performance appraisal forms—and sample letters for use during employee hiring, promotion, and termination. Part 3 covers laws related to wages, fair employment, and discrimination. Part 4 provides guidelines for handling all other HR functions: preparing job descriptions, interviewing, conducting pay surveys, and handling employee evaluations. This second edition is updated in all areas, especially to include information on the Civil Rights Act of 1991 and the Americans with Disabilities Act and new benefits information in such areas as family leave. The author is a consultant specializing in personnel management and labor relations. He has 11 years of experience as a personnel director, has taught college courses and given corporate training programs on a variety of personnel subjects. *Textbook binding, 656 pages, $79.95*

The Nonprofit Management Handbook: Operating Policies and Procedures *(See General Management— Basics for full description)*

Nonprofit Personnel Policies Manual
JOHN GILLIS, ED. (ASPEN PUBLISHERS, 1993)

▶ This comprehensive manual offers sample policies, approved by legal and management experts, you can implement at your organization, covering a wide range of situations to make your nonprofit a more efficient, productive place to work. It includes actual legally approved, working policies, a detailed appendix with ready-to-use sample forms, and always current annual updates.

Topics covered include family leave, insurance, compensation, discrimination, overtime, and discipline. It explains why each policy may be beneficial to your nonprofit and what to watch out for. Contents include: Chapter 1: Organizational Structure & Expectations, Chapter 2: Nondiscrimination, Chapter 3: Employment Conditions and Provisions, Chapter 4: Benefits, Chapter 5: Performance & Discipline, and Chapter 6: Appendix. Use this manual to review your current policy handbook, and to update it where necessary. Policies and forms are available on disk for WordPerfect 5.1 (IBM DOS 5.0 or later) and Microsoft Word 4.0 (Macintosh 6.7 or later). Both disk and manual are supplemented annually. *Loose-leaf binder, 150 pages, $170 (plus $5 shipping); diskettes: $39 each*

Personnel Guide for Non-Profit Organizations
KAREN MCELROY, ED. (PHILADELPHIA VOLUNTEER LAWYERS FOR THE ARTS)

▶ Many nonprofits have difficulty coping with personnel problems due to limited amounts of time and resources. This comprehensive guide has been developed to enable nonprofits to answer often complex personnel questions and help maintain a well-managed organization. Content includes: Employee Compensation; Guide to Recruitment & Hiring; The Personnel File: Contents and Accessibility; The Personnel Manual vs. Employee Contracts; Constructing the Personnel Manual; State, Real Estate, and Business Taxes; Organization's Responsibility to Donors; Federal Laws Pertaining to Nonprofits including: the Civil Rights Act, Americans with Disabilities Act, Family and Medical Leave Act; plus much more useful information. *Softcover, $24.95*

Personnel Policy Handbook: How to Develop a Manual That Works
WILLIAM S. HUBBARTT (MCGRAW-HILL, 1993)

▶ This is a guide for managers, administrators, and others involved in defining personnel policies, to preparing an effective, workable, and up-to-date human resources manual. It not only covers all areas of employee relations that affect the company, but also tackles a range of critical contemporary issues including AIDS, substance abuse, chemical safety, family and medical leave, and sexual harassment. In addition to covering 100 employee handbook policy topics, the volume includes specific instructions on organizing and writing a manual, some 20 charts on competitive practices, checklists and worksheets, about 40 sample personnel forms, and current samples of policy manuals complete with forms and procedural

steps. It also shows you how to handle the full range of critical contemporary HR issues—from AIDS to chemical safety. *Hardcover, 583 pages, $74.95*

Writing Effective Policies and Procedures: A Step-By-Step Resource for Clear Communication
NANCY CAMPBELL (AMACOM BOOKS, 1998)

▶ A guide to writing clear policy and procedure documents for company administrators, this book includes discussions of the planning, analysis, and research necessary to writing effective policy; legal violations to avoid; proper wording and formatting; dealing with resistance; when and when not to revise documents; and developing an online system of policies and procedures. Each chapter includes sample memos and checklists to aid in writing. *Hardcover, 320 pages, $60*

Recruitment and Staffing
(See also Interviewing, Hiring & Retention; Risk Management, Insurance & Liability)

The AMA Handbook for Employee Recruitment and Retention
MARY F. COOK, ED. (AMACOM BOOKS, 1992)

▶ This comprehensive book combines the contributions of 14 experts to create a detailed guide to every aspect of recruiting highly qualified employees and keeping them (happily) on the job. It provides both classic and innovative approaches to the key areas involved: planning, recruitment and selection programs, performance management, training, compensation, benefits, and family issues. It shows readers how to recruit the most qualified prospects; establish flexible policies in compensation, benefits, and services that will attract a new breed of workers; and retain productive employees with ongoing training and a more honest, participative management style. It includes dozens of practical aids, such as sample policies and forms, worksheets, and guidelines. *Hardcover, 432 pages, $75.00*

Competency-Based Recruitment and Selection (The Wiley Series in Strategic Human Resource Management)
ROBERT WOOD, TIM WOOD, AND TIM PAYNE (JOHN WILEY & SONS, 1998)

▶ This book offers a step-by-step guide to the recruitment, selection, and assessment of candidates. It highlights the best-practice aspects of recruitment and selection based on professional research. It discusses the practical considerations important when implementing recruitment and selection processes, and utilizes leading-edge methods developed in the field not reported elsewhere. *Softcover, 160 pages, $60.50*

The Complete Reference Checking Handbook
EDWARD C. ANDLER (AMACOM BOOKS, 1998)

▶ This book is a comprehensive guide to the delicate art of reference checking. Managers and human resources professionals can stop troubles before they begin by using this book's dozens of proven techniques for getting at the truth. It shows readers how to detect lies or evasions on résumés and in interviews; avoid illegal questions during the interview and reference-checking process; get meaningful information from what references say—and don't say; and check public and official sources such as credit, criminal, and driving records—even workers' compensation claims. *Softcover, 240 pages, $29.95*

Employment Screening

LEX K. LARSON (MATTHEW BENDER, 1988)

▶ This important guide details each of the major employment screening devices currently in use, analyzing the legal and constitutional considerations, statutory restrictions and legal acceptance of each. Coverage includes employment applications, interview questionnaires, and background checks; personality, psychological, and other written tests; drug, alcohol, and AIDS testing; polygraph examinations (latest federal statute included). In addition to detailed federal law coverage, the volume provides a state-by-state analysis chapter: an employer's guide for avoiding potential liability, and an appendix with excerpts from various statutes, regulations, guidelines, technical reviews, and reports. It is updated with supplements and revisions. *Loose-leaf, $210*

High-Impact Hiring: A Comprehensive Guide to Performance-Based Hiring

JOSEPH ROSSE AND ROBERT LEVIN (JOSSEY-BASS, 1997)

▶ This book takes the mystery out of making good hires and serves as a comprehensive, systematic guide to understanding, planning, and perfecting the hiring process. Among the wealth of practical insights it offers, you will discover how to analyze a job in terms of overall organizational goals and hire accordingly; how to structure an interview that gets past superficial answers and uncovers critical information; how to develop a mix of selection procedures that efficiently and accurately assesses applicants' qualifications; how to make hiring decisions when information is limited; which hiring practices increase successful job performance, and what you should do before and after a hire to increase the opportunities for success. Complete with sample interview questions, a hiring decision guide, and a summary of legal obligations. *Hardcover, 315 pages, $37.95*

Keeping Your Valuable Employees: Retention Strategies for Your Organization's Most Important Resource

SUZANNE DIBBLE (JOHN WILEY & SONS, 1999)

▶ Retaining valuable employees is one of the most important problems facing today's human resource managers. Suzanne Dibble takes a systematic approach to help you figure out how to understand and respond to the new employment relationship. This how-to book gives you a framework to determine how the new employment relationship applies to your situation, techniques and tools for retaining employees, and methods to determine what works for your organization. *Keeping Your Valuable Employees* shows readers how to design, implement, and sustain actions that support the new employment relationship. *Hardcover, 280 pages, $34.95*

Recruit & Retain the Best

RAY SCHREYER AND JOHN MCCARTER (IMPACT PUBLICATIONS, 2000)

▶ This book addresses the *Real* issues behind labor shortage and retention concerns, advising employers of steps needed to successfully avoid the pitfalls of perilous planning. Two of America's leading recruitment specialists identify the key human resource strategies for creating a talent-powered company. Focusing on five competencies for predicting success, they dispel numerous myths and specify what HR professionals and hiring managers need to do in order to energize their human resources and productivity. They provide a critical examination of the latest in effective recruitment methods, from the use of Internet recruiting to developing em-

ployee referral programs. Talent-powered organizations not only recruit the best, they also retain the best through several employee-centered strategies. They focus on 10 building blocks: treat the workplace as a system; promote ethics, integrity, honesty, and trust; create organizational feedback loops; put people first; instill an ethic of fairness; accept diversity; encourage openness; make work and the workplace fun; develop employee connectivity; and view people management as a strategic business issue. *Softcover, 128 pages, $14.95*

Recruiting, Interviewing, Selecting, and Orienting New Employees, 3rd Edition

DIANE ARTHUR (AMACOM BOOKS, 1998)

▶ This updated and expanded edition of the how-to guide equips human resources professionals with the skills and tools to get the best people on board. Filled with sample forms, interview questions, and handy checklists, the book goes step by step through the entire hiring process, from effective use of recruitment sources to proper orientation of new hires. It also includes four completely new chapters on the hot issues of workplace diversity, electronic recruiting, competency-related interviewing, and other special interviewing techniques. *Hardcover, 400 pages, $59.95*

Interviewing, Hiring, and Retention

(See also Recruiting and Staffing; Risk Management, Insurance and Liability)

96 Great Interview Questions to Ask Before You Hire

PAUL FALCONE (AMACOM BOOKS, 1996)

▶ Falcone's title is invaluable in telling how to organize interviews to best identify high-performance candidates and how to spot evasions and untruths. It is a guide to turning general answers into specifics, and to using these candidates' specifics to assess strengths and weaknesses. *96 Great Interview Questions to Ask Before You Hire* focuses on getting past employers to "open up" on a reference check; making the employment offer and closing the deal; employing search firms, outplacement, and research firms in your candidate recruitment efforts; and salvaging offers when line managers have "given away the farm." It details how to elicit spontaneous, truthful responses; watch out for red flags that predict sub-par performance; solicit meaningful information from reference checking; and hire people that best fit the organization's needs. With questions covering 17 topics and all types of job openings, the book serves as both a ready reference for managers and a refresher course for seasoned human resources personnel. *Softcover, 240 pages, $17.95*

101 Hiring Mistakes Employers Make . . . and How to Avoid Them

RICHARD FEIN (IMPACT PUBLICATIONS, 2000)

▶ Based on interviews with key human resource professionals, this book identifies 101 hiring mistakes employers make—from asking the wrong questions to failing to verify credentials. This book shows its readers that the savvy HR professional needs to actively seek out and hire the "right" candidate for the job. Not only is it a mistake to hire the wrong person, but it is a mistake to fail to hire a successful candidate simply because the employer did not know where to look. Fein gives his readers tips on what to look for in a candidate, where to locate the specific characteristics that an employer desires, and how to draw out the potential in each job candidate in order to ensure a productive employee. *101 Hiring Mistakes Employers Make . . . and How to Avoid Them* catalogs the major hiring mistakes organizations make as well as outline key lessons to be learned from each mistake. Based on interviews with human resource professionals, the book reveals the top reasons for hiring mistakes: time pressures, lack of empathy for candidates, poor use of staff, flawed interviewing, inadequate reference checks, inappropriate offer letters, disparate staffing perceptions, overreliance on technology, and making HR solely responsible for hiring. *Softcover, 144 pages, $14.95*

267 Hire Tough Proven Interview Questions

MEL KLEIMAN (HTG PRESS, 1999)

▶ Until recently, it's been the norm for employers to invest a lot of time, money, and care in the selection of their management personnel and to view hourly employees as replaceable cogs in a wheel. This outdated, wrong-headed practice is exactly what will separate the losers from the winners in the new millennium. Today's exemplary organizations all have one thing in common—they place an unusually high significance on the selection of every employee: managers, supervisors, and hourlies. Over 70% of the U.S. workforce is composed of frontline workers and the firms that will fall by the wayside are those that continue to pay scant attention to how these hourly employees are interviewed and selected. *267 Hire Tough Proven Interview Questions* is a must-have for everyone who hires or manages hourly employees. *Softcover, 44 pages, $12.95*

Adams Streetwise Hiring Top Performers: 600 Ready-to-Ask Interview Questions and Everything Else You Need to Hire Right

BOB ADAMS (ADAMS MEDIA CORPORATION, 1997)

▶ This book furnishes authoritative tips on how to find, interview, and hire the best people for an organization, including 600 interview questions and tips on networking, writing ads, screening techniques, references, and hiring legalities. *Hiring Top Performers* includes 600 ready-to-go interview questions, plus information on all aspects of hiring, including writing help wanted ads, networking to find the right candidate, checking references, writing letters of rejection, legalities of hiring, and more. *Softcover, 464 pages, $17.95*

Build a Better Staff, Volume 1: Hiring, Evaluating and Firing Staff Members (Workbook/Manual)

DARLA STRUCK AND JEFF STRATTON, EDS. (ASPEN PUBLISHERS, 1992)

▶ This manual provides answers to the most perplexing problems administrators and supervisors face: how to hire staff, how to fire staff, and how to evaluate staff performance. It gives supervisors the essential information needed to perform their responsibilities properly and legally. It is full of pull-out forms and hands-on material to make the supervisors' job easier. Sections include: (1) How to Find, Interview, and Hire Top-Quality Staff Members walks you through all the important aspects of the hiring process (the importance of making good hiring decisions, legal issues associated with hiring, how to write clear job descriptions, interview skills, and ways to provide new staffers with a solid orientation to a nonprofit); (2) How to Provide Meaningful Feedback as You Evaluate Your Staffers emphasizes the importance of a sound evaluation procedure and how it benefits your nonprofit organization (shows you how to gather, organize, and provide valuable evaluation information and how to conduct an effective job performance meeting; in addition, sample evaluation forms used successfully by other non-

profits are provided); and (3) How to Approach the Unpleasant (and Legally Dangerous) Task of Firing Staffers demonstrates why caution is used when terminating staff members (includes material about the legal issues involved in firing staff, why it's important to know your nonprofit's policies and procedures and follow them in every firing decision, and how to handle a termination meeting. *Loose-leaf, 194 pages, $148 (plus $4 shipping)*

Build a Better Staff, Volume 2: Developing and Keeping Top Notch Staff

JAMIE WHALEY AND SHERI CAMPBELL, EDS. (ASPEN PUBLISHERS, 1998)

▶ Finding and keeping good staffers are problems every nonprofit faces. If you've ever wrestled with the question of where to find competent staff members or wondered how to provide useful and cost-effective training for staffers, this manual is the answer. It provides proven tips from your nonprofit colleagues for developing and keeping top notch staff. You will also find dozens of sample policies, forms, and guidelines. *Loose-leaf, $148 (plus $4 shipping)*

Competence-Based Employment Interviewing

JEFFREY A. BERMAN (QUORUM BOOKS–GREENWOOD PUBLISHING, 1997)

▶ Designed to assist practitioners in developing interview procedures for their organizations, this work shows how competence-based human resource management techniques can be applied to employment interviews. Leading the practitioner through the three-step interview process—preparation, interviewing techniques, and evaluation of applicants—this guide provides sample questions, a case study, and forms to help the reader conduct successful structured interviews. Also included is a chapter on issues related to equal opportunity employment and a comprehensive review of the literature on structured interviewing. *Hardcover, 184 pages, $59.95*

The Costs of Bad Hiring Decisions and How to Avoid Them, 2nd Edition

CAROL A. HACKER (CRC PRESS–ST. LUCIE PRESS, 1998)

▶ This hiring manager's guide gives you a comprehensive look at how to eliminate the pitfalls associated with bad hiring decisions. Includes information on preparing to search, screening, interviewing, checking references, and making the final selection. This book addresses the real costs of bad hiring decisions and their devastating effects, and offers 130 tips for avoiding them. This superb guide is easy to read and should be required reading for everyone who makes hiring decisions. Features include: conduct a search for candidates and eliminate accusations of prejudice, unfair treatment, and insensitivity; shorten the résumé/application screening process and still identify the best candidate; ask the right questions and interpret hidden meanings in candidate responses; use references to learn more about candidates and break down barriers to getting information even when references are reluctant to talk; and make final and defensible decisions based on the information you have gathered throughout the hiring process. *Softcover, 240 pages, $19.95*

Effective Hiring and ADA Compliance

ARLENE VERNON-OEHMKE (AMACOM BOOKS, 1994)

▶ This book clearly explains the full selection process under ADA: preparing job descriptions, advertising, interviewing candidates, and the final selection. It helps readers understand ADA employment requirements and simplify their company's compliance processes;

plan and conduct effective, legal interviews; avoid costly discrimination suits; be at ease interviewing candidates with disabilities; and hire qualified, productive employees. It is filled with pragmatic help, exercises, self-quizzes, scenarios of good and bad interviews, guidelines for "what you can and can't ask," and sample job descriptions, ads, and application forms. *Hardcover, 256 pages, $65*

The Essential Book of Interviewing: Everything You Need to Know from Both Sides of the Table

ARNOLD B. KANTER (TIMES BOOKS/RANDOM HOUSE REFERENCE, 1995)

▶ *The Essential Book of Interviewing* gives interviewers and interviewees the principles and techniques they need to master the process. Arnold B. Kanter explains how job seekers and interviewers can give and get the information they need, ask the right questions and avoid the wrong ones, prepare for the interview and make decisions, and achieve diversity and avoid illegal hiring practices. *Softcover, 221 pages, $15*

Finding and Retaining Your Next Chief Executive: Making the Transition Work (See Governance—Roles and Responsibilities for full description)

Finding & Keeping Great Employees

JIM HARRIS AND JOAN BRANNICK (AMACOM BOOKS, 1999)

▶ Based on extensive research into "best practices" at a wide variety of organizations, *Finding & Keeping Great Employees* is creating a workforce of people whose values and skills align closely with the organization's driving purpose—a match that ensures competitive advantage. This breakthrough book identifies four organizational cultures—operational excellence, customer service, innovation, and spirit. By focusing on one of these as their core purpose and using it to drive their selection and retention strategies, organizations become "aligned" (staffed by motivated employees who feel connected to their companies and their jobs). It offers dozens of illuminating case studies and examples and it provides action plans that enable you to adapt their cutting-edge recruiting and retention techniques to your own organization. Specifically, you'll learn how to end the cycle of "disconnection" between employees and their companies and build new, stronger, more stable employee/employer connections; simplify and streamline the recruiting process; hire and keep the best, most productive employees; decrease turnover—and all the associated costs—by making it tougher for great employees to leave; increase applicant "fit" and decrease potential "misfits"; become an employer of choice by creating an environment that has meaning beyond a paycheck and offers individuals a workplace that matches their values. *Hardcover, 240 pages, $24.95*

Hire the Best—and Avoid the Rest

MICHAEL W. MERCER (AMACOM, 1993)

▶ This pragmatic guide provides a three-pronged approach that helps employers choose the most promising candidates and eliminate hiring risks. The book shows readers how to interview effectively using such specific tools as a job analysis checklist, interview guide, and rating sheet; use pre-employment tests to evaluate behavior, mental abilities, character, and technical skills; and make the most of references to reveal useful information about a candidate. A multitude of tips and tools enables employers to ask the right questions, interpret answers, and coordinate the information they've gathered. The book's testing section contains numerous test samples. *Hardcover, 159 pages, $19.95*

The Hiring and Firing Book: A Complete Legal Guide for Employers

STEVEN MITCHELL SACK (LEGAL STRATEGIES, INC., 1998)

▶ This book contains the latest information about sexual harassment, discrimination, and family and medical leave. It includes dozens of contracts, forms, checklists, and hundreds of strategies, based on the author's legal experience to save thousands of dollars in lawyer's fees, settlements, and jury verdicts. *Hardcover, 368 pages, $150 (Nonmember), $128 (Member) (plus $12 shipping)*

Hiring: How to Find and Keep the Best People

RICHARD S. DEEMS (CAREER PRESS, 1998)

▶ This is a positive and practical guide that helps readers with every step of the hiring process: defining the position, searching most effectively, conducting an interview that really tells something, and more. *Softcover, 128 pages, $12.95*

Hiring the Best: A Manager's Guide to Effective Interviewing, 4th Edition

MARTIN YATE (ADAMS MEDIA CORPORATION, 1997)

▶ In *Hiring the Best,* over 400 questions give you the necessary material for the perfect choice. The updated fourth edition of this proven management tool also features an extensive review of the pros and cons of hiring temporary workers, part-time employees, consultants, and independent contractors. It has been updated to include the very latest information on the legal guidelines you must follow under the Americans with Disabilities Act. *Softcover, 230 pages, $10.95*

Hiring Top Performers: 350 Great Interview Questions for People Who Need People

CAROL A. HACKER (AMERICAN SOCIETY OF ASSOCIATION EXECUTIVES, 1995)

▶ Make sound, defensible hiring decisions with this valuable resource—and cut the costs of bad hiring decisions by quickly selecting questions that will help you get the information you need. Includes questions on education, work experience, initiative, leadership, interpersonal skills, sales, problem solving, and decision making. *Softcover, 36 pages, $15*

Hiring Winners

RICHARD J. PINSKER (AMACOM, 1991)

▶ Hiring a winner is simple, if you've got the right method. The P.I.E. Selection System set forth in *Hiring Winners* presents a clear-cut, easy-to-use approach to finding excellent people to fill managerial, executive, and professional positions. Defying conventional "wisdom," *Hiring Winners* says that many employers get trapped into looking at formal job descriptions. In fact, the book explains, you should first analyze the results for which the position is accountable, and then work backwards to decide on the qualifications. P.I.E. explains how to do just that—create a Profile of the desired results, then Interview and Evaluate candidates based on your original Profile. Using the example of a fictitious organization and a leading job candidate, *Hiring Winners* shows how to formulate an accurate profile; tap a multitude of candidate sources; conduct an interview that probes behind a candidate's protective façade, and avoid the 7 Deadly Sins of Hiring including falling for the "halo effect," ignoring intuition, or indulging in wishful thinking. *Hardcover, 160 pages, $19.95*

The Manager's Book of Questions: 751 Great Interview Questions for Hiring the Best Person

JOHN KADOR (MCGRAW-HILL PROFESSIONAL, 1997)

▶ In *The Manager's Book of Questions,* you will find hundreds of questions to make your interviews more productive and give you the ammunition you need to make a smart decision. Questions are guaranteed to identify leadership, initiative, people skills, stress management, organization, technical competence, and creativity. It contains a wide assortment of carefully worded queries that help make the process more effective. Logically organized by topics such as work history, motivation, teamwork, and skill assessment, it also includes favorite questions of top recruiters and personal questions that should never be asked. It includes pressure questions, icebreakers, exploratory questions, and much more. Arm interviews with powerful tools that help anyone who hires to find and keep top-notch talent. The questions cover the complete range of jobs, from entry level to senior management. Special "Top Ten" lists include the top ten best interview questions, the top ten toughest interview questions, and the top ten worst or illegal questions. *Softcover, 224 pages, $14.95*

The Older Worker: Effective Strategies for Management and Human Resource Development

NOREEN HALE (JOSSEY-BASS, 1990)

▶ This book presents model programs used to redesign jobs, create opportunities for part-time work, and keep workers age 50 and over productively on the job. It provides a career planning model for assessing the interests and skills of older employees and facilitating successful career changes. *Hardcover, 197 pages, $29 (plus $4.50 shipping)*

Reference Checking Handbook

(SOCIETY FOR HUMAN RESOURCE MANAGEMENT, 1993)

▶ This revised handy desk reference explains the importance of and need for reference checking, the different types of reference checks and how to conduct them, as well as the process and legal questions involved. It includes a sample telephone reference checklist and extensive bibliography. *Softcover, 37 pages, $20 (Nonmember), $16 (Member) (plus $6 shipping)*

Secrets of Motivation: How to Get and Keep Volunteers & Paid Staff! *(See Volunteerism—Recruitment, Motivation, and Retention for full description)*

Smart Hiring: The Complete Guide to Finding and Hiring the Best Employees, 2nd Edition

ROBERT W. WENDOVER (SOURCEBOOKS TRADE, 1998)

▶ In this competitive business environment, employee selection mistakes can cost you money, customers, your reputation—maybe even a lawsuit. *Smart Hiring* covers everything you need to know to hire the right candidates in a legal and practical fashion every time. *Softcover, 240 pages, $12.95*

Staff Screening Tool Kit: Building a Strong Foundation Through Careful Staffing Organization

JOHN PATTERSON (NONPROFIT RISK MANAGEMENT CENTER, 1994)

▶ Since the original Tool Kit (*Staff Screening Tool Kit: Keeping Bad Apples Out of Your Organization*) was first published, changes have taken place that influence the screening process and govern access to records. Besides these issues, the second edition addresses the increased focus on official agency records as tools for staff screening, and features a state-by-state directory of agencies that maintain records useful for screening. It is designed to effectively screen adults who work with children, based on a nationwide study of screening practices. It primarily focuses on screening out abusers but its scope extends to providing guidance for spotting individuals who are unsuitable for specific tasks, such as handling money, driving vans, and other individuals who are bad risks for particular positions. Topics include reference checks, criminal histories, interviewing, position descriptions, applications, consent forms, and confidentiality ("staff" refers to paid and volunteer staff equally; most of the examples pertain to volunteers). It covers the law and practice for reference checks, interviews, applications, psychological tests, and other techniques. *Softcover, 135 pages, $30 (plus $3 shipping)*

Executive Search

Aiming High on a Small Budget: Executive Searches & the Nonprofit Sector

EFFECTIVE SECTOR LEADERSHIP/MANAGEMENT PROGRAM (INDEPENDENT SECTOR, 1990)

▶ When faced with the important work of hiring a new executive, here's a wealth of information from some of the leading experts in the field. This collection of short writings includes advice on when and when not to use a search firm, how to select a firm, how to be a good client, and how to hire an executive without external help. This series of helpful articles that serves as a resource to aid both individuals and organizations involved in planning executive searches. *Softcover, 40 pages, $5 (Nonmember), $3.50 (Member) (plus $2.50 shipping)*

Directory of Executive Recruiters

(KENNEDY INFORMATION)

▶ Published since 1971, the famous "Red Book" lists 12,820 recruiters at 5,008 search firms in the United States, Canada, and Mexico. It indexes management functions, industries, geography, key principals, and 550 individual recruiter specialties. Listings include phone, fax, e-mail, and Web addresses. It is updated annually. *Softcover, 1,320 pages, $47.95*

Executive Recruiters of North America, Volume I— Retained Firms Edition

(HUNT-SCANLON)

▶ Both volumes are packed with information to help you evaluate more than 6,000 executive recruiters in over 1,000 executive search firms. The directory covers a wide array of search organizations, ranging from solo practitioners and midsized boutiques to the 25 largest firms in the industry. The guide displays vital statistics on each firm listed, as well as an indexing system that allows users to find recruiters according to industry specialization, functional specialization, or geography. *Hardcover, 1,800 pages, $235*

Hiring the Chief Executive: A Practical Guide to the Search and Selection Process *(See Governance— Roles and Responsibilities for full description)*

Managing Executive Transitions: A Handbook for Nonprofit Organizations

(NATIONAL ASSEMBLY OF HEALTH AND HUMAN SERVICE ORGANIZATIONS, 1999)

▶ Developed and made available by the Neighborhood Reinvestment Corporation and a network of community-based agencies, this handbook is for nonprofit organizations that face or are going through an executive transition. It covers the three major phases of getting ready, recruitment and hiring, and post-hiring. *Softcover, 30 pages, $4.00*

The Nonprofit Board's Guide to Finding, Hiring, and Evaluating the Chief Executive *(See Governance— Roles and Responsibilities for full description)*

Disciplining and Discharging Employees

(See also Interviewing, Hiring and Retention; Recruitment and Staffing; Risk Management, Insurance, and Liability)

Build a Better Staff, Volume 1: Hiring, Evaluating, and Firing Staff Members *(See Interviewing and Hiring, Recruiting)*

From Hiring to Firing: The Legal Survival Guide for Employers in the 90's
STEVEN MITCHELL SACK (LEGAL STRATEGIES PUBLICATIONS, 1995)

▶ It offers practical guidance to employers in all aspects of the employment process, including pre-employment considerations, negotiating and confirming the job, on-the-job benefits, protecting the company from dishonest employees, employee privacy rights, on-the-job policies, avoiding discrimination and defamation, and how to fire properly. The chapters are subdivided, making it easy to find the information you are looking for. It provides all the essential information you need to properly protect yourself and your organization. *Softcover, 352 pages, $35 (Nonmember), $32 (Member) (plus $8 shipping)*

The Hiring and Firing Book: A Complete Legal Guide for Employers
STEVEN MITCHELL SACK (LEGAL STRATEGIES, INC., 1993)

▶ This book contains the latest information about sexual harassment, discrimination, and family and medical leave. It includes dozens of contracts, forms, checklists, and hundreds of strategies, based on the author's legal experience to save thousands of dollars in lawyer's fees, settlements, and jury verdicts. *Hardcover, 368 pages, $150 (Nonmember), $128 (Member) (plus $12 shipping)*

Supervisor's Guide to Documenting Employee Discipline, 4th Edition
LEE T. PATERSON AND MIKE DEBLIEUX (MATTHEW BENDER, 1998)

▶ This book provides supervisors with proper procedures for documenting employee behavior and discipline. Text includes forms, flowcharts, explanations of regulations, and sample documentation. It shows you how to be objective in verbal and written documentation, counsel employees with disciplinary problems, and keep a Critical Incidents Diary. *Softcover, 70 pages, $25*

Risk Management, Insurance and Liability

(See also Compensation; Disciplining and Discharging Employees; Diversity)

The ADA Answer Book: Answers to the 146 Most Critical Questions about the Americans with Disabilities Act
(BUILDING OWNERS AND MANAGERS ASSOCIATION, 1992)

▶ This book offers advanced information about Title III: the fine points and gray areas that have been examined and defined in greater detail by regulatory authorities. In plain English, it explains obligations and options about alterations to buildings, lease language and legal agreements, exemptions, possible enforcement actions, and tax incentives. *Softcover, 78 pages, $60*

ADA Compliance Guide
BARBARA ANDERSON AND CHARLES D. GOLDMAN, EDS. (THOMPSON PUBLISHING GROUP, 1999)

▶ This "how-to" *ADA Compliance Guide* shows you how to cope with this complex law. It covers recruiting, hiring, promoting, providing benefits, accommodating disabilities, and evaluating performance. The Guide gives you step-by-step instructions for compliance and practical advice on what you can do, what you must do, and what you cannot do. Monthly updates feature the *ADA Compliance Guide Monthly Bulletin,* a time-saving source for accurate, timely news as the courts and federal agencies revise and refine your responsibilities under the law. Your subscription also includes regular updates to the loose-leaf guide. Separate "specialty" chapters are also available to provide hands-on, specific guidance for several industries and public agencies. *Loose-leaf binder, $287*

ADA Compliance Manual, 2nd Edition
MAUREEN F. MOORE (MATTHEW BENDER, 1997)

▶ This edition of *ADA Compliance Manual for Employers* provides the latest statutes, case authorities, and useful tips on this burgeoning area of law. This work is a complete guide to handling the impact of the Americans with Disabilities Act on your employment practices, now and in the future. *Loose-leaf, $95*

Accessible Computer Technology: Meeting the Needs of People With Disabilities (Special Report)
(THOMPSON PUBLISHING GROUP, 1999)

▶ Whether barriers are to Web sites or to computers themselves, individuals with disabilities are seeking to get access to the electronic information that is readily available to the nondisabled. Employers, schools, and service providers are trying to give all of their employees, students, and clients the tools they need to compete and to ensure compliance with the Americans with Disabilities Act and Section 504 of the Rehabilitation Act. This Special Report analyzes the progress being made toward full electronic access, including standards the federal Access Board is developing that will apply to the federal government in all of its purchases of electronic equipment. Included are tips on how to design accessible Web sites and provide access to computer input and output features; strategies used by organizations seeking to provide electronic access; an overview of two recently reauthorized laws that will affect access efforts; how to make a school's computer labs accessible to persons with all sorts of disabilities; and resource lists for employers, schools, and service providers. Also included is the text of the

Workforce Investment Act's amendments to the Rehabilitation Act and the Access Board's latest working draft of federal standards. *Softcover, 40 pages, $29*

Accommodating Employees with Psychiatric Disabilities: A Practical Guide to ADA Compliance
(THOMPSON PUBLISHING GROUP, 1999)

▶ One of the most challenging issues facing employers under the Americans with Disabilities Act is how to "reasonably accommodate" individuals with psychiatric disabilities. Second to those involving back impairments, more complaints are filed against employers alleging discrimination based on mental impairments than any other disability. *Accommodating Employees with Psychiatric Disabilities: A Practical Guide to ADA Compliance* explains the EEOC's guidelines for employers. The Guide gives employers the answers they need to effectively handle accommodation requests from individuals with psychiatric disabilities, answering such questions as: What is a "psychiatric disability"?, When is an employee with a psychiatric disability covered by the ADA?, What accommodations does the ADA require—or are appropriate—for an employee with a psychiatric disability?, What should an employer do before disciplining or discharging an employee with a psychiatric disability?, and How should human resource managers handle morale problems for co-workers of employees with psychiatric disabilities? This publication is packed with practical scenarios, analyses of case law, charts and checklists, and accommodation tips and examples. A copy of the EEOC's guidance is also included in the Guide. *Softcover, 128 pages, $79*

The American Bar Association Guide to Workplace Law: Everything You Need to Know About Your Rights as an Employee or Employer
BARBARA J. FICK (RANDOM HOUSE/TIMES BOOKS, 1997)

▶ *The ABA Guide to Workplace Law* is the complete and easy guide to the laws that affect the workplace. Organized in easy-to-follow chapters, with plenty of informative sidebars and checklists, *The ABA Guide to Workplace Law* covers all of the topics that are important to employees and employers, from the law that surrounds hiring and firing to specific questions about workplace safety. Like all of the books in the American Bar Association series, *The ABA Guide to Workplace Law* is written and reviewed by a group of America's top lawyers and provides expert recommendations. *Softcover, 224 pages, $13*

Americans with Disabilities Act: Employee Rights & Employer Obligations
JONATHAN R. MOOK, ESQ., DIMURO, GINSBERG & MOOK, P.C. (MATTHEW BENDER, 1992)

▶ This practice-oriented guide shows you, in directly applicable step-by-step form, how to meet all the ADA legal requirements that affect employment policies and procedures. With its help, you will be able to: establish fully compliant hiring policies, from advertising through screening to the offer of employment; write job descriptions compatible with the ADA/Essential functions clause; evaluate and restructure policies for discipline, evaluation, promotion, and termination of employees; provide auxiliary aids and services for employees with disabilities; keep records and file notices as required by the EEOC; renegotiate collective bargaining agreements to comply with the new law; avoid statements or activities that may give rise to liability for regarding an individual as a person with disabilities; includes essential checklists and forms; examples of fact situations in question-and-answer format; highlighted

notes and warnings; and the texts of the Americans with Disabilities Act and EEOC regulations. Revised annually. Includes one year of updating service after which publisher will send annual updates for a subscriber fee. *Loose-leaf binder, 1,000+ pages, $125*

Americans with Disabilities Act: Making the ADA Work for You, 2nd Edition
MICHAEL J. LOTITO, FRANCIS P. ALVAREZ, AND RICHARD PIMENTEL (SOCIETY FOR HUMAN RESOURCE MANAGEMENT, 1992—AVAILABLE FROM AMERICAN SOCIETY FOR ASSOCIATION EXECUTIVES)

▶ This resource provides basic information and answers to important questions on the ADA. A thorough overview of the ADA, it answers the questions: Who is protected?, Who are qualified individuals with disabilities?, What is discrimination?, What is reasonable accommodation?, and What is undue hardship? The authors offer 10 steps every organization should take to implement the ADA and an extensive list of resources. *Spiral binder, 163 pages, $47 (Nonmember), $40 (Member) (plus $6.25 shipping)*

Avoid Employee Lawsuits: Commonsense Tips for Responsible Management (Quick & Legal)
BARBARA KATE REPA (NOLO PRESS, 1999)

▶ *Avoid Employee Lawsuits: Commonsense Tips for Responsible Management* is the quick reference guide every employer needs. Practical, but still weighing in at less than a pound, it addresses hiring and firing, paper-trail control, discrimination, sexual harassment, disciplinary procedures, disputes, benefits, and privacy rights. *Softcover, 320 pages, $17.47*

Avoiding a Lawsuit: Legal Issues in Hiring and Evaluating Employees
(THE NATIONAL ASSEMBLY OF HEALTH AND HUMAN SERVICE ORGANIZATIONS, 1995)

▶ This report provides an overview of key issues employers and supervisors need to know in order to avoid litigation in the workplace. *Softcover, 64 pages, $11.95*

Building a Better Staff, Volume 3: Legal Issues and Your Nonprofit
JAMIE WHALEY, ED. (ASPEN PUBLISHERS, 1994)

▶ This manual provides complete coverage of discrimination issues, important information that will alert you to the pitfalls and danger zones that can put your nonprofit in legal trouble. Topics covered include the ADA, sexual harassment, and civil rights, as well as other issues affecting groups protected by additional state or federal laws. Many case studies are included to give you real-life examples to follow. It is a worthwhile investment that will keep your nonprofit out of the courtroom. *Loose-leaf, $148 (plus $5 shipping)*

The Complete Guide to Human Resources and the Law
DANA SHILLING (PRENTICE HALL DIRECT, 1998)

▶ This comprehensive, easy-to-read handbook guides HR professionals through the legal minefield of personnel management and staffing issues they face every day. Packed with practical, step-by-step solutions, sample forms, and nontechnical explanations of legal concepts, it helps HR pros deal proactively with personnel problems, while effectively managing situations related to plan design, implementation, and administration. It is supplemented annually to keep readers up to date with the many legal changes in this field. The paperback Supplement edition (January 2000) is available for *$39.95. Hardcover, 648 pages, $69.95*

The Complete Reference Checking Handbook: Smart, Fast, Legal Ways to Check Out Job Applicants
EDWARD C. ANDLER (AMACOM BOOKS, 1998)

▶ Noting that it would be unusual (and unwise) to purchase a major piece of equipment without first examining its background and evaluating its suitability, Edward Andler, a nationally recognized authority on improving hiring practices, marvels at how many businesspeople will take on new employees without a similarly thorough inquiry. His *Complete Reference Checking Handbook: Smart, Fast, Legal Ways to Check Out Job Applicants* begins by puncturing the popular perception that truly significant information about work applicants is strictly off limits. It then shows how to obtain the requisite data as efficiently as possible. This book is a comprehensive guide to the delicate art of reference checking. Managers and human resource professionals can stop troubles before they begin by using this book's dozens of proven techniques for getting at the truth. It shows readers how to detect lies or evasions on résumés and in interviews; avoid illegal questions during the interview and reference-checking process; get meaningful information from what references say—and don't say; and check public and official sources such as credit, criminal, and driving records—even workers' compensation claims. *Hardcover, 256 pages, $29.95*

Employer's Guide to the Fair Labor Standards Act
(THOMPSON PUBLISHING GROUP, 1999)

▶ The *Employer's Guide to the Fair Labor Standards Act* leads you through the maze of regulations and case law to proper compliance with the law. This guide shows how to classify employees, compute overtime compensation, understand what constitutes hours worked, and maintain your employee records in proper order. It is complete with statutes and regulations. The *Guide's* monthly updates and newsletters keep subscribers abreast of the latest FLSA action from Capitol Hill, the Department of Labor, and the courts, and provide analysis of the most current developments in this complex and ever-changing area of law. *Summary of contents:* Coverage of Employees and Employers; White-Collar Exemptions; Other FLSA Exemptions; Minimum Wage and Overtime Compensation; Working Time; Child Labor; Recordkeeping; Enforcement and Remedies; and Sample Forms and Documents. *Loose-leaf, $299*

The Employer's Legal Handbook, 3rd Edition
FRED S. STEINGOLD (NOLO PRESS, 1999)

▶ A complete guide to your legal rights and responsibilities, *The Employer's Legal Handbook* shows you how to comply with the most recent workplace laws and regulations, run a safe and fair workplace, and avoid lawsuits. Learn everything you need to know about: hiring—understand the legal guidelines for hiring employees, writing job descriptions, conducting interviews, investigating applicants; smart personnel practices—what to include in employee personnel files, employee handbooks, performance reviews, and references for former employees; employee benefits—learn the ins and outs of wage and hour laws, retirement plans, and health insurance; workplace health and safety—how to comply with OSHA requirements, implement policies on smoking, drug and alcohol abuse; discrimination—how to comply with laws prohibiting sexual harassment and discrimination based on age, race,

pregnancy, sexual orientation, and national origin; termination—how to avoid wrongful termination cases, conduct a final meeting, and protect your business information when employees leave; and laws affecting small business practices—what you need to know about the Americans with Disabilities Act, the Family and Medical Leave Act, health and safety issues, and employee testing. *Softcover, 456 pages, $27.97*

Employment and Personnel: A Legal Handbook, 2nd Edition (Workbook/Manual)
RICHARD S. HOBISH AND LORI YARVIS, EDS. (LAWYERS ALLIANCE FOR NEW YORK, 1997)

▶ This is a guide to the federal as well as New York State and New York City employment laws affecting nonprofit organizations. It includes discussion of development of personnel policies and manuals, hiring and firing, treatment of independent contractors, and employees and antidiscrimination laws. *Softcover, $18 (plus $2 shipping)*

Employment Discrimination, 2nd Edition
PAUL N. COX (MATTHEW BENDER, 1992)

▶ With the downsizing of the U.S. economy has come a rise in employment discrimination cases. Your clients want answers to their questions and resolutions to their disputes—immediately. Master the dynamic law of employment discrimination with Michie's comprehensive reference for legal and business professionals on both sides of the discrimination issue. Operate with confidence with the latest information on new legislation: the Civil Rights Act of 1991 and the Americans with Disabilities Act of 1990; disparate treatment and disparate impact theories; accommodation obligations; and affirmative action. Learn, for example, who is a covered employee, who may be sued, what constitutes a violation of the law, how to defend against a claim, how to prove your case, how to proceed, what remedies are available, and more. *Loose-leaf, 2 volumes, $185*

Employment Law Answer Book, 4th Edition
MARK R. FILIPP, THOMAS L. BOYER, AND JAMES O. CASTAGNERA (ASPEN PUBLISHERS, 1997)

▶ Fast, accurate answers to all your questions about personnel law. Noted employment and labor attorneys Mark R. Filipp, Thomas L. Boyer, and James O. Castagnera cover all the essentials in an accessible question-and-answer format. It is an authoritative, time-saving desk-reference for employers who need to keep track of and comply with the latest employment law requirements. The book makes it possible and easy to determine whether your company's policies and practices meet the latest legal rules and guidelines, so you can protect your company's rights, and those of your employees. This comprehensive guide answers more than 1,000 key questions, from the simple to the complex. Specific topics include the latest developments on affirmative action; job terminations; sexual harassment; Family and Medical Leave Act; the Americans with Disabilities Act; discrimination; compensation; health and fringe benefits; employer/employee relationship; employee privacy; and more. *Case bound, 776 pages, $125*

Employment Law Answer Book: Forms & Checklists
(ASPEN PUBLISHERS, 1994)

▶ Now you can implement all human resources laws and regulations with ease. This handy volume is packed with sample employment contracts; independent contractor agreements; employee evaluation and discipline forms; executive compensation plans; severance and collective bargaining agreements; and a model employee handbook. An easy-to-use format allows you to easily photocopy forms and insert them directly into your file. The forms and checklists will help ensure that all of your human resources practices are in compliance with EEOC, NLRB, OSHA, and DOL requirements. You'll have all the tools you need to keep your company up to date in compliance—and out of court. It is a useful companion volume to *Employment Law Answer Book* (see separate listing). *Softcover, 728 pages, $96*

Employment Law Deskbook
SHAWE & ROSENTHAL (MATTHEW BENDER, 1995)

▶ Written by employee relations specialists, this handy deskbook will make employment law accessible to the human resources professional. *Features:* covers every stage of the employer/employee relationship, from the initial employment application through termination; offers guidance for complying with the law and for recognizing those practices that may give rise to legal action; discusses the entire range of important issues confronting employers: drug and alcohol testing, sexual harassment claims, employee benefits; incorporates practical material throughout including checklists, charts, tables, and sample forms; and provides a state-by-state summary of key employment-related statutes. It is a day-to-day resource that will increase your understanding of complex employment law, telling you what's legal, what's not, and how to prevent problems from arising in the future. It is updated with annual revisions. *Loose-leaf binder, 1,000+ pages, $150*

Employment Law Update 1999
HENRY H. PERRITT JR. (ASPEN PUBLISHERS, 1999)

▶ This reference comprehensively covers recent developments in the rapidly changing employment and labor law field. Composed of nine chapters, each written by an expert in employment law, the 1999 update provides timely, incisive analysis of critical issues. Issues discussed include: independent contractor or employee? Navigating the maze of worker classification; workplace English-only rules; current FLSA issues; beyond 40-hours and time and a half; the after-acquired evidence doctrine after McKennon; evidence of prior employer acts in discrimination cases; actions against individual supervisors and fellow employees; insurance for employment discrimination and wrongful termination claims: coverage issues and new directions in insurance policies; guide to pre-employment practices and policies; and overview of immigration law principles. *Softcover, 544 pages, $150*

Employment Relationships: Law & Practice
MARK W. BENNETT, HOWARD J. RUBIN, AND DEAN DONALD J. POLDEN (ASPEN PUBLISHERS, 1998)

▶ This book analyzes the state and federal employment laws and recent trends in case law affecting the employment relationship. Topics covered include federal discrimination law, including ADEA, ADA, the Equal Pay Act, and the Family and Medical Leave Act; sexual harassment, with a discussion of same-sex harassment; severance pay, golden parachutes, and COBRA; employee's fiduciary duties to his employer; employee privacy, with discussions of privacy issues relating to employee e-mail and computer files; and Tort actions, such as defamation, breach of the covenant of good faith and fair dealing and infliction of emotional distress. Practice pointers throughout the chapter provide practical advice from the authors. The set also includes over 50 forms on

disk, including forms for employment contracts, personnel manual forms, litigation forms, sample severance plans and golden parachutes, and an online access policy. *Binder, 1,218 pages, $179*

Equal Employment Opportunity 2000 Compliance Guide
JOHN F. BUCKLEY IV (ASPEN PUBLISHERS, 2000)

▶ This sourcebook covers all the regulations and key EEOC publications and decisions, providing the only comprehensive, thoroughly annotated analysis of the EEOC regulations available. This reference examines all the major administrative and judicial decisions, interpretive memoranda, and other publications of the EEOC, providing compliance advice as well as reprinting the text of the most important of these publications and supplying vital information on the use of EEOC regulations by the states. It presents explanations of the EEOC regulations, together with annotations to the relevant judicial decisions, while giving you fast access to the regulations through quick-reference charts. Designed to meet the needs of both employment law attorneys and human resources professionals, the Guide presents thorough EEO coverage that mirrors the continuity that exists between EEO claims avoidance strategy and EEO litigation strategy. *Softcover, 1,137 pages, $145*

Fair, Square, and Legal: Safe Hiring, Managing, and Firing Practices to Keep You and Your Company Out of Court, 3rd Edition
DONALD H. WEISS (AMACOM, 1999)

▶ Employees today are more aware of their legal rights than ever before and they're more willing to sue if they think those rights have been violated. Completely updated and revised, it provides readers the current information on EEOC guidelines and the confusions they create; affirmative action issues (including the ramifications of Proposition 209); new legislation governing team formation; and a wealth of new court decisions regarding sexual harassment, negligent hiring practices, managing people with disabilities, the Family and Medical Leave Act, and other issues. This revised edition presents a "do's and don'ts" discussion of everyday issues, such as defamation, privacy and wrongful discharge, and unusual situations. *Hardcover, 368 pages, $29.95*

HR Manager's Legal Encyclopedia
(RANSOM & BENJAMIN)

▶ This is a comprehensive guide to all aspects of HR and employment law, with special emphasis on avoiding applicant and employee lawsuits. *Hardcover, $245*

The Hiring and Firing Book: A Complete Legal Guide for Employers
STEVEN MITCHELL SACK (LEGAL STRATEGIES, INC., 1993)

▶ This book contains the latest information about sexual harassment, discrimination, and family and medical leave. It includes dozens of contracts, forms, checklists, and hundreds of strategies, based on the author's legal experience to save thousands of dollars in lawyer's fees, settlements, and jury verdicts. *Hardcover, 368 pages, $150 (Nonmember), $128 (Member) (plus $12 shipping)*

How to Comply with Federal Employee Laws: A Complete Guide for Employers Written in Plain English
SHELDON I. LONDON (SOCIETY FOR HUMAN RESOURCE MANAGEMENT, 2000)

▶ Whether you have two employees or 200, protect your company from the devastating expense of employee lawsuits with this book. This up-to-date, authoritative book covers everything an employer needs to know about workplace laws including: FMLA, ADA, overtime pay rules, age discrimination, sexual harassment, drug and alcohol testing, pregnant workers' rights, and much more. *Softcover, 240 pages, $49.95*

Investigating Sexual Harassment: A Practical Guide to Resolving Complaints

Bernice R. Sandler (Thompson Publishing Group, 1999)

▶ *Investigating Sexual Harassment: A Practical Guide to Resolving Complaints* provides practical, tested advice on thoroughly investigating and resolving sexual harassment complaints to help employers understand their obligations under the evolving body of sexual harassment law. Written by the editors of the authoritative *Educator's Guide to Controlling Sexual Harassment*, it addresses such issues as how quickly employers should respond to sexual harassment complaints and how long investigations should take; how to choose an investigator; how to properly interview the complainant, alleged harasser, and witnesses; how employers should structure their sexual harassment policies and complaint procedures to limit their liability; when an employer is liable for sexual misconduct by a supervisor, co-worker, or nonemployee; and what impact the 1998 Supreme Court rulings on sexual harassment will have on employers. It offers workplace scenarios, analyses of case law, sample sexual harassment policies, and expert tips. *Softcover, 240 pages, $79*

Labor and Employment Law Desk Book, 2nd Edition

Gordon E. Jackson (Prentice Hall Direct, 1995)

▶ This revised second edition puts every employment law that affects you and your company right at your fingertips. It covers the full range of federal and state laws affecting mediation and arbitration, employment-at-will, wage/hour laws, and more. This comprehensive volume gives court-tested answers to questions that arise to such important areas as protected employee activities, discrimination and wrongful discharge, equal pay, mediation and arbitration, employee benefits, discrimination against the handicapped, and occupational health and safety. Includes annual cumulative supplement. *Hardcover, 1,179 pages, $79.95*

NARIC Guide to Resources for the Americans with Disabilities Act *(See Human Resource Management—Internet Sites for complete description)*

Personnel Compliance Guide

(Warren Gorham & Lamont)

▶ This guide takes a practical, action-oriented approach, delivering proven personnel management tips and techniques, legal requirements of the employer, and information on what personnel management areas contain hidden risks. This is the one source for successfully managing the diverse and difficult tasks of the small business personnel function. Features include over 50 sample handbook policies, numerous forms and checklists for identifying exempt employees and independent contractors, charts summarizing state requirements in various areas, survey data on the key provisions of benefit and retirement plans, resource lists, and state and federal addresses. Updated annually. *Three-ring binders, $195*

The Practical Guide to Employment Law

Bureau of Business Practice Legal Publications Staff, and Mary-Lou Devine (Aspen Publishers, 1999)

▶ This is a comprehensive desk manual for HR managers, risk managers, and employment lawyers. It covers federal employment laws in plain English, giving readers the practical information necessary to apply the laws. Essential court cases and tips for compliance appear in every chapter. This book includes a compliance checklist section—where readers can learn the various laws that apply to such topics as hiring, terminations, and benefits. It also includes a supervisory training section on several laws, including FMLA and ADA. An annual update is issued every January (whole chapters replaced with each update). *Loose-leaf, 816 pages, $225*

Pocket Guide to the ADA: Americans with Disabilities Act Accessibility Guidelines for Buildings and Facilities, Revised Edition

Evan Terry Associates (John Wiley & Sons, 1997)

▶ This book is intended to help users understand the facilities requirements of the Americans with Disabilities Act Accessibility Guidelines (ADAAG). Incorporating all of the latest guideline amendments within a compact and easy-to-use format that contains no confusing abbreviations, this revised edition presents the technical building requirements for accessible elements and spaces in new construction, alterations, and additions. The Guide is augmented with more than 60 illustrations from the Americans with Disabilities Act Accessibility Guidelines, and covers special requirements for businesses, restaurants, medical care facilities, libraries, and much more. It includes the scope and technical requirements for accessibility elements and spaces. *Softcover, 144 pages, $29.95*

Quick Guide to Employment Law

(Business and Legal Reports, 1997)

▶ This guide lets you look up the subject in the index, pick the subheading you are interested in, and go to the page that is referenced. If you need more information regarding a specific law, check the cross-reference index. Federal and state laws shown side by side with overlapping and sometimes contradictory federal and state employment laws, this guide ensures that your HR policies are in full compliance with all applicable regulations. Regulations are explained in plain English for use by all levels of HR professionals. *Softcover, 369 pages, $149.95*

Sexual Harassment in the Workplace

Ellen J. Wagner (AMACOM Books, 1992)

▶ *Sexual Harassment in the Workplace* offers a legal expert's advice on how to investigate complaints in a way that is fair to all parties and protects your organization from legal liability. In addition, this book shows you how to establish policies and procedures to prevent harassment, to discipline harassers, and to save your company many dollars in legal fees, court judgments, and lost productivity. Here is everything we need to know about handling sexual harassment claims, from prevention through investigation to corrective action. This guide enables you to take sexual harassment out of the closet in a manner that will protect our people and strengthen your organization. In addition to addressing the prevention of sexual harassment, it is an excellent road map through the minefield of investigating and resolving these serious and sensitive issues when they do arise, complete with checklists, how-tos, do-nots, and scripts of questions to ask. *Softcover, 148 pages, $17.95*

Sexual Orientation and Legal Rights

ALBA CONTE (ASPEN PUBLISHERS, 1998)

▶ This comprehensive guide covers gay rights issues and legal development in the areas of employment law, civil rights law, and family law. It covers topics such as constitutional issues, employment discrimination, same-sex harassment, same-sex couple benefits, tort and contract claims, same-sex marriage, dissolution of relationships, child custody and adoption issues, housing and property rights, federal and state statutory and case law, and a state-by-state survey of gay-related statutes and case law. *Case bound, 2 volumes, 1,500 pages, $265*

State-by-State Guide to Human Resources Law

JOHN F. BUCKLEY IV, SENIOR ATTORNEY, AND RONALD M. GREEN (ASPEN PUBLISHERS, 2000)

▶ Now you can find the employment laws of all 50 states. This guide has been revised and updated to cover every vital aspect of employment law and to reflect the changes enacted by state legislatures over the past year. Find out your state's position on frequently contested employment practices in minutes. Through the use of dozens of charts and tables as well as convenient referencing features, you'll find special attention given to state new-hire reporting requirements; employment at will; wage and hour laws (including penalty provisions); fair employment laws; group health insurance; continuation of benefits; drug, AIDS, and polygraph testing; parental leave; workers' compensation; unemployment benefits; smoking ordinances; Older Workers Benefit Protection Act; ADA; and FMLA. Plus, the guide provides complete citations to the original source for every law and regulation discussed, so you'll know precisely where to go for further research. *Softcover, 1,056 pages, $175*

Stay Out of Court: The Manager's Guide to Preventing Employee Lawsuits

RITA RISSER (PRENTICE HALL DIRECT, 1993)

▶ A comprehensive guide to employment law; its legal explanations are provided in plain, "user-friendly" language, with case examples and guidelines for implementing the law. Every potential trouble area is addressed, including discrimination, harassment, wrongful termination, drug testing, and references. *Stay Out of Court* serves as a clear, practical guide to help mangers avoid these danger zones, comply with government regulations, and keep their organizations out of court. Included in the book are detailed laypersons' explanations of today's complex hiring and firing laws; guidance for making personnel policies legally airtight; and scores of case histories of successful lawsuits, as well as the costly mistakes that a company can avoid. *Softcover, 352 pages, $19.95*

Taking the High Road: A Guide to Effective and Legal Employment Practices for Nonprofits

(NONPROFIT RISK MANAGEMENT CENTER, 1999)

▶ Are you taking the "high road" when it comes to your employment practices? If not, you could be vulnerable to lawsuits for wrongful discharge, sexual harassment, workplace discrimination, negligent referral, and more. *Taking the High Road: A Guide to Effective and Legal Employment Practices for Nonprofits* contains valuable information on developing sound, defensible employment practices that are practical as well as fair and compassionate. It provides up-to-date information and advice on complying with the ADA, FMLA, Title VII, and more. The book includes 27 sample policies and checklists, and 12 state-by-state comparisons of key employment laws. *Softcover, 217 pages, $45*

Wage and Hour Law: Compliance & Practice

LES A. SCHNEIDER AND J. LARRY STINE (CLARK BOARDMAN CALLAGHAN, 1995)

▶ This book provides the attorney with a complete analysis of wage and hour law organized in an easy-to-use format plus practical checklists, forms, and mathematical formulas to help prevent problems before they arise. *Wage and Hour Law* will help you quickly and effectively solve wage and hour compliance problems under the Fair Labor Standard Act (FLSA) and other contract acts the government enforces. This resource will help you avoid unnecessary errors that can result in expensive litigation, costly damage awards to employees, and steep civil penalties; give you compliance examples, coverage tests, summaries, and calculation methods to put the law into practice; and give you all the compliance information for compensable time, overtime, child labor exemptions, minimum wage, government contracts, and more. It will serve as a good reference when identifying compliance problems before they become litigation headaches. It will help you to determine workers' status of independent contractors or employees; define compensation and work policies for people engaged in various types of work; follow proper procedures for obtaining sub-minimum wage certificates; comply with the laws surrounding the minimum wage requirements; handle overtime under many different circumstances; and follow record-keeping requirements. It includes a Cumulative Supplement, updated annually. *Loose-leaf binder, 3 volumes, $365*

Wages and Hours: Law & Practice

LAURIE E. LEADER (MATTHEW BENDER, 1990)

▶ This source covers all aspects of federal and state laws governing minimum wage, overtime, and child labor standards. The publication focuses on the federal wage-hour statutory scheme, including laws regulating work under government procurement contracts and federally assisted projects. Coverage includes the Fair Labor Standards Act, including the Equal Pay Act; the Portal-to-Portal Act; the Walsh-Healy Public Contracts Act; the Davis-Bacon Act; the Copeland Anti-Kickback Act; the Contract Work Hours and Safety Standards Act; and evaluation and investigation of a wage-hour claim. It includes sample litigation forms. In addition, state wage-hour provisions and their relationship to federal legislation are discussed and analyzed in detail, featuring a state-by-state review of the laws of each jurisdiction on minimum wages, overtime provisions, and child labor. It includes analysis of federal and state regulation of minimum wage, overtime, equal pay, and child labor laws; evaluation of wage-hour disputes; and state-by-state review of wage-hour laws. It includes one year of updating service, after which the publisher will send annual updates for a subscriber fee. *Loose-leaf binder, 1,000+ pages, $140*

What Every Manager Needs to Know about Sexual Harassment

DARLENE ORLOV AND MICHAEL T. ROUMELL (AMACOM, 1999)

▶ This book provides managers with vital information to protect themselves and their companies from lawsuits, bad publicity, decreased employee morale, and other associated miseries. Topics covered include laws and court decisions (including the most recent Supreme Court rulings), what behavior is acceptable and what isn't; preventive policies and staff training; investigating complaints, and more. This is the complete "answer book"—with real-life scenarios, self-help quizzes, checklists, and analysis. *Softcover, 240 pages, $24.95*

What Managers & Supervisors Need to Know about the ADA

MICHAEL J. LOTITO, RICHARD PIMENTEL, AND DENISE BISSONNETTE (MILT WRIGHT & ASSOCIATES, 1992)

▶ This practical guide conveys clearly and concisely the basic information that HR managers and supervisors need to know and follow in implementing the ADA. *Softcover, 55 pages, $18.50 (plus $8 shipping)*

Whose Computer Is It Anyway? Office Policy for Internet and Other Computer Use

(THE NATIONAL ASSEMBLY OF HEALTH AND HUMAN SERVICE ORGANIZATIONS, 1999)

▶ This handbook collects computer policy examples from the MIS/Technology Group members of the National Assembly. The book features real-life examples of policies covering personal privacy issues, offensive use of technology, and other areas of legal risk. *Softcover, 18 pages, $4.00*

Workplace Accommodations Under the ADA

BARBARA ANDERSON AND CHARLES D. GOLDMAN, EDS. (THOMPSON PUBLISHING GROUP, 1999)

▶ *Workplace Accommodations Under the ADA* helps employers understand their obligations under the law and provides practical solutions to effectively handle accommodation requests from individuals with disabilities. It also discusses recent Supreme Court decisions on who is "disabled" and how those rulings will affect the duty to accommodate. Written by the editors of the authoritative ADA Compliance Guide (see separate listing), the book addresses such issues as when employers must provide unpaid leave, keep jobs open or reassign workers as accommodations for employees with disabilities. Also discussed is whether employers can use cost–benefit analysis when determining if a requested accommodation is an undue hardship. It also provides examples of low-cost accommodations and a directory of resources. *Softcover, 124 pages, $79 (plus shipping and handling)*

Workplace Sexual Harassment Law: Principles, Landmark Developments, and Framework for Effective Risk Management

FRANCIS ACHAMPONG (QUORUM BOOKS/GREENWOOD PUBLISHING GROUP, 1999)

▶ Workplace sexual harassment law can be a tangle for business. The chapters are a self-contained discussion of issues such as retaliation and constructive discharge, merged with substantive topics like quid pro quo and hostile environment sexual harassment. Achampong devotes significant attention to landmark developments shaping the law, and provides a holistic approach to managing the risk of liability for sexual harassment. This volume is an ideal reference and text for law and business professors and students, human resource managers, risk management consultants, and attorneys. Achampong devotes several chapters to landmark developments such as third-party and same-sex sexual harassment and the only one that goes beyond merely discussing workplace harassment prevention to discussing risk management of liability for sexual harassment. It also discusses esoteric rules that apply to federal sector sexual harassment complainants. The appendices provide guidelines on discrimination; excerpts from the Civil Rights Acts of 1964 and 1991; a discussion of landmark Supreme Court cases; excerpts from the EEOC Compliance Manual; and EEOC policy guidelines on current issues of sexual harassment. *Hardcover, 264 pages, $69.50*

Training and Development

The 1999 Training and Performance Sourcebook, 4th Edition

MEL SILBERMAN, ED. (MCGRAW-HILL PROFESSIONAL PUBLISHING, 1999)

▶ Tools that reflect the top trends and newest techniques in training and performance are what you get in this annual. It gives you 40 ready-to-copy laser-edged instruments for the tasks and issues that are taking up much of your training and consulting time. You get activities and exercises that teach specific skills, such as effective communicating. You also receive creative participant handouts, how-to guides, assessment instruments, and more, plus complete training design instructions, all developed and field-tested by the top names in performance and training. This toolset gives you ready-to-use tools for cyberlearning, career development, personal effectiveness, diversity, sales coaching, management skill building, change, training design, and much more. *Hardcover, 384 pages, $79.95 (also available in softcover)*

Achieving Results from Training: How to Evaluate Human Resource Development to Strengthen Programs and Increase Impact

ROBERT O. BRINKERHOFF (JOSSEY-BASS, 1987)

▶ Shows how to design and conduct evaluations of human resource development programs and demonstrate their worth and value to the organization: how to use evaluation methods to determine results, to develop, implement, and "debug" newly designed programs, or to refine existing ones. *Softcover, 268 pages, $33 (plus $4.50 shipping)*

CEO: Mentor and Protégé *(See Leadership for full description)*

Coaching and Teambuilding Skills for Managers and Supervisors *(See General Management—Teams and Teambuilding for full description)*

Coaching Skills: A Guide for Supervisors *(See General Management—Coaching/Mentoring for full description)*

Improving On-the-Job Training: How to Establish and Operate a Comprehensive OJT Program

WILLIAM J. ROTHWELL AND H.C. KAZANAS (JOSSEY-BASS, 1994)

▶ This complete, step-by-step action guide to establishing or improving a comprehensive on-the-job training program, in all job categories in any occupation or industry, can be used both to improve one-on-one OJT conducted by supervisors and as a reference guide for performance specialists and instructional designers. It draws on extensive research that includes a survey of 500 members of the American Society of Training and Development to go far beyond a simple description of what OJT is. It offers detailed guidance on managing the entire OJT effort, from identifying goals to evaluating OJT's impact on the organization. The authors of *Mastering the Instructional Design Process* offer a complete, step-by-step action guide to establishing or improving a comprehensive on-the-job training program for all job categories. This research-based guide helps you to identify needs and establish goals, prepare trainees to learn, determine when on-the-job training is appropriate, plan an on-the-job training program, evaluate the results, and much more. Includes checklists, hands-on tools, case studies, charts, and more. *Hardcover, 186 pages, $36.95*

On-the-Job Orientation and Training
LARRY R. SMALLEY (JOSSEY-BOSS, 1994)

▶ Get new employees up to speed quickly and efficiently with these proven orientation tools and techniques. You can use them for virtually any position or set of responsibilities. The book includes questions, checklists, and examples so you can create a custom orientation. *Softcover, $14.95*

Self-Directed Learning: A Practical Guide to Design, Development, and Implementation
GEORGE M. PISKURICH (JOSSEY-BASS, 1993)

▶ This book provides a cost-effective and time-saving alternative to traditional instructional designs. It offers practical guidance on each step of the process, including analyzing trainees' needs and abilities, designing SDL materials, choosing the right implementation strategy, and constructing the most useful evaluation tools. It shows how to identify training needs that match organizational needs, determine the specific tasks that must be learned to meet those needs, and then develop objectives and SDL materials based on those tasks. It provides practical learning aids, including checklists at the end of each chapter, and includes simulations that illustrate step-by-step how theory becomes reality. *Softcover, 379 pages, $36 (plus $4.50 shipping)*

Structured On-the-Job Training: Unleashing Employee Expertise in the Workplace
RONALD L. JACOBS AND MICHAEL J. JONES (BERRETT-KOEHLER, 1995)

▶ This is a step-by-step guide for developing effective on-the-job training, proven successful in a diverse range of organizations and fields, and for a wide variety of job tasks. The authors describe an approach to on-the-job training that combines the structure of most off-site training programs with the inherent efficiency of training conducted at the job site. They define a structured approach to OJT that encompasses a planned process of developing task-level expertise by having an experienced employee train a novice employee in the actual job setting. They show how structured OJT helps employees bridge the gap between learning job information and actually using that information on the job. The book provides step-by-step guidelines for designing, delivering, and evaluating on-the-job training programs. *Hardcover, 220 pages, $30 (plus $4.50 shipping)*

Training and Development in Organizations
IRWIN L. GOLDSTEIN (JOSSEY-BASS, 1989)

▶ Sponsored by the Society for Industrial and Organizational Psychology, a Division of the American Psychological Association, this book brings together research findings from I/O psychology and related disciplines to identify new approaches and strategies for making training more effective. They also provide models for measuring the benefits of training in terms of increased output, payroll savings, and more. You'll discover how better to evaluate training needs, how to design better training methods, and how to structure questionnaires to get the information you want. It includes instructional techniques based on cognitive and behavioral theory and covers such diverse factors as work-group settings, informal training by peers, and the socialization process of the newcomer. *Hardcover, 555 pages, $45.95*

Training and Development Organizations Directory, 6th Edition
JANICE MCLEAN, ED. (GALE RESEARCH, 1994)

▶ This reference is a guide to more than 2,500 companies that produce more than 12,000 workshops, seminars, videos, and other training programs that can enhance skills and personal development. *Softcover, $395*

Training Evaluation Handbook
A.C. NEWBY (JOSSEY-BASS, 1992)

▶ Based on the author's Training Evaluation Audit Method (TEAM), this book will help trainers in any kind of organization to develop more effective programs. The first part of the book examines the strategic role of training evaluation and discusses some of the political issues involved. Part II presents a range of techniques for improving training effectiveness and shows how to develop instruments that both assess and reinforce learning. In the final part, a series of case studies shows how the author's methods have been used in a wide variety of businesses and functions. If what you are looking for is a systematic way of reviewing and strengthening the training provision in your own organization, then Training Evaluation Handbook is for you. *Hardcover, $39.95*

Training for Impact: How to Link Training to Business Needs and Measure the Results
DANA GAINES ROBINSON AND JAMES C. ROBINSON (JOSSEY-BASS, 1989)

▶ In this hands-on guide, two top human resources consultants present a results-oriented, 12-step approach that directly links training to specific organizational goals. Here is all the information and guidance you need to create a work environment that reinforces new skills and maximizes training results. You'll also learn to document the effect your efforts have on the bottom line, track subtle but important changes in employee values and beliefs, and demonstrate increased sales and productivity. *Hardcover, 336 pages, $40.95*

Workplace Basics: The Essential Skills Employers Want
ANTHONY P. CARNEVALE, LEILA J. GAINER, AND ANN S. MELTZER (JOSSEY-BASS, 1990)

▶ This book presents the findings of a three-year ASTD/U.S. Department of Labor nationwide study on how to develop a skilled workforce capable of meeting today's business requirements. It explains how to implement training programs that develop the new basic skills workers will need. *Softcover, 508 pages, $40/$55.95 (plus $4.50 shipping)*

Workplace Structure—Teams and Team Building

(See also General Management—Coaching and Mentoring; Teams and Team Building)

Building Productive Teams: An Action Guide and Resource Book
GLENN H. VARNEY (JOSSEY-BASS, 1989)

▶ This book provides practical step-by-step guidance on how to improve teamwork and increase the productivity and efficiency of groups within an organization. It shows how to recognize symptoms of unproductive teams, improve team member relations, and clarify roles and goals. It gives strategies for solving problems that often plague work groups and demonstrates how to apply them. *Hardcover, 170 pages, $26 (plus $4.50 shipping)*

Change at Work: The Total Transformation Management Process *(See Organizational Development for full description)*

Designing Effective Work Groups
PAUL S. GOODMAN AND ASSOCIATES (JOSSEY-BASS, 1986)

▶ This book provides ways to design, manage, and maintain more useful work groups, including labor–management committees, staff meetings, advisory groups, and policy committees. It reviews current knowledge about groups and explores new directions for understanding them and improving their effectiveness. *Hardcover, 423 pages, $39 (plus $4.50 shipping)*

Designing Work Groups, Jobs, and Work Flow
TONI HUPP, CRAIG POLAK, AND ODIN WESTGAARD (JOSSEY-BASS, 1995)

▶ This source offers an integrated approach to using the most powerful tools of reengineering to design single work units that are productive, responsive, and build participant ownership and commitment. With numerous checklists, reusable worksheets, and flowcharts, the authors present practical techniques for analyzing and designing the daily work flow, group structure, and job responsibilities of intact work groups. They provide the step-by-step procedures for capturing such detailed information as who performs what function, why, when, how, and to what outcome, and offer guidelines for improving these processes. *Softcover, 272 pages, $40 (plus $4.50 shipping)*

Empowered Teams: Creating Self-Directed Work Groups That Improve Quality, Productivity, and Participation
RICHARD S. WELLINS, WILLIAM C. BYHAM & JEANNE M. WILSON (JOSSEY-BASS PUBLISHERS, 1993)

▶ A workplace revolution is taking place today—a movement toward empowered work teams. More and more organizations are demonstrating that work teams do improve quality, customer service, and productivity as well as reduce costs and boost morale. This book is a thorough examination of how teams work, how to prepare for teams, and how to build strong teams. Although based on corporate models, all the team-building principles apply equally well to nonprofit organizations. The book provides answers to questions about how self-directed teams work, what makes them effective, when they are useful, how to get them going, and how to maintain their vigor and productivity over time. *Softcover, 292 pages, $16.50 (plus $3.50 shipping)*

The Group Member's Handbook *(See General Management—Teams and Team building for full description)*

Groups That Work (and Those That Don't): Creating Conditions for Effective Teamwork
J. RICHARD HACKMAN, ED. (JOSSEY-BASS, 1989)

▶ This book explores the design and leadership of groups, providing detailed descriptions of 27 diverse work groups, including task

forces, top management groups, production teams, and customer service teams, to offer insights into what factors affect group productivity and what leaders and group members can do to improve work group effectiveness. *Hardcover, 548 pages, $37 (plus $4.50 shipping)*

Sculpting the Learning Organization: Lessons in the Art and Science of Systematic Change
KAREN E. WATKINS AND VICTORIA J. MARSICK (JOSSEY-BASS, 1993)

▶ This book offers a unique perspective from adult educators experienced in organizational change. It shows human resource professionals, front-line managers, and others how people learn in the workplace and how to support that learning in programs that foster high employee involvement, in self-directed teams, or by addressing core organizational concerns such as balancing work and home life. In 18 illustrative case vignettes, individuals describe in their own words the action imperatives that help create learning at four key levels: the individual, the team, the organization, and society. *Hardcover, 324 pages, $30 (plus $4.50 shipping)*

The Skilled Facilitator: Practical Wisdom for Developing Effective Groups
ROGER M. SCHWARZ (JOSSEY-BASS, 1994)

▶ Writing for consultants, peer facilitators, and managers alike, the author offers a comprehensive reference that pinpoints the skills needed to produce highly creative groups. This guidebook will show you how to be a facilitative leader, improve the overall effectiveness of an organization, increase employee commitment, sharpen cooperative and problem-solving skills, improve company flexibility, intervene effectively with groups, and more. *Hardcover, 336 pages, $30 (plus $4.50 shipping)*

Who's Got the Ball (and Other Nagging Questions About Team Life): A Player's Guide for Work Teams
MAUREEN O'BRIEN (JOSSEY-BASS, 1995)

▶ Friendly and conversational, the author offers experience-based, easy-to-implement guidelines that are practical and fun; her concise coaching notes, illustrated by real-life organizational situations, address every aspect of daily team life. *Softcover, 211 pages, $22 (plus $4.50 shipping)*

The Wisdom of Teams
JON R. KATZENBACH AND DOUGLAS K. SMITH (HARPERBUSINESS, 1993—AVAILABLE FROM ASAE)

▶ This book identifies and examines the characteristics of top-performing teams, helping today's managers take maximum advantage of this powerful concept. Learn how working dynamics function within a team, how to build your staff into a team, and how to overcome obstacles to this process. It also features the "Teams Question and Answer Guide," contrasting commonly held notions of teams with the authors' findings. *Softcover, 317 pages, $16 (Nonmember), $13 (Member) (plus $4.50 shipping)*

Independent Contractors

Independent Contractors: A Manager's Guide and Audit Reference *(See Financial Management—Accounting/Reporting for full description)*

Legal Guide to Independent Contractor Status, 3rd Edition

ROBERT W. WOOD (ASPEN PUBLISHERS, 1999)

▶ This comprehensive volume gives you contracts that satisfy current court review, along with checklists of critical issues to be resolved within each industry. You can learn the standards established for independent contractor status by the IRS, federal labor and employment laws, and state workers' compensation and unemployment compensation laws. Also addressed are the consequences of erroneous classification, including tax considerations, pension and benefit plans, and tort liability. *Case bound, 880 pages, $165*

PERIODICALS

(See also Financial Management [Employee Benefits/Compensation]; General Management; Legal Issues; Organizational Development; Volunteerism [Volunteer Management])

Accommodating Disabilities Newsletter (Monthly Newsletter)
CCH, 4025 West Peterson Avenue, Chicago, IL 60646
Tel: 800-248-3248
E-mail: info@cch.com; WWW: http://onlinestore.cch.com/
▶ Ensure Americans with Disabilities Act (ADA) and Rehabilitation Act compliance with this newsletter. You'll find current information and helpful tips on how to address most accessibility and accommodation requirements, interviews with leading experts, and up-to-the minute news on key issues. *$159/year*

At Work (Formerly Beyond the Bottom Line) (Six Issues)
Berrett-Koehler Publishers, 450 Sansome Street, Suite 1200,
San Francisco, CA 94111-3320
Tel: 800-929-2929, 415-288-0260; FAX: 415-362-2512,
802-864-7626 (orders)
E-mail: bkpub@bkpub.com;
WWW: http://www.bkpub.com/contactus/bkp.html
▶ *At Work* is a newsletter dedicated to supporting the work of those who are pioneering new approaches to management, leadership, organizational structure, success, and corporate accountability. Unlike most publications, which focus either on individual and organizational development or the larger business and financial issues, *At Work* presents the insights of people who are working in both areas. The result is a unique combination of reporting on new practices and insights into the realities of commerce and finance that sometimes determine whether these practices can truly take hold. *At Work* features reports on innovative practices (at the heart of each issue of *At Work* are reports on the innovative experiments in management and business that are transforming our workplaces. These reports help readers keep on top to the latest approaches to workplace reform, while offering valuable insights into what it takes to make these approaches work in real life); visions (every issue of *At Work* includes an interview with or essay by an innovative thinker in the areas of business, economics, organizational development, or social change); hearts and minds (essays in which individuals offer reflections and stories that shed light on our personal relation to work); reviews of new resources; news briefs; letters; and more. Past articles and excerpts from current issues available on the *At Work* Web site: www.atworknews.com. *24 pages, $75/year*

Benefits & Compliance Alert (Biweekly Newsletter)
395 Hudson Street, New York, NY 10014
Tel: 212-367-6300
117 East Stevens Avenue, Valhalla, NY 10595
Tel: 800-431-9025 (Customer Assistance), 800-950-1216 (Sales),
914-749-5000; FAX: 914-741-2412
E-mail: RIAhome@riag.com, Customer_Services@riag.com;
WWW: http://www.riahome.com/store/detail.asp?ID=BCA

▶ This newsletter focuses on nonpension and benefits compliance issues. It highlights activity within Congress and the federal agencies that affect the establishment and administration of benefit plans, particularly in the nonpension area. It includes in-depth analysis of benefits laws, regulations, other government releases, and court decisions. It also provides guidance on compliance issues, including the new EFAST program and the evolving Form 5500 submission program. *Benefits & Compliance Alert* highlights trends in the benefits community and notes recent forms, publications, or other releases by IRS, DOL, PBGC, and other agencies or groups of interest to benefits professionals. It also warns of upcoming benefits notice and filing deadlines. Most issues include a calendar of upcoming benefits events (for example, conferences and seminars). Occasional issues include practitioner articles discussing a particular benefits topic or concern. *8 pages, $215/year*

Community Risk Management & Insurance
(See Financial Management for full description)

Compensation & Benefits Management Law Journal (Quarterly Journal)
Aspen Publishers, 200 Orchard Ridge Drive, Gaithersburg, MD 20878
Tel: 301-417-7500; FAX: 301-695-7931
E-mail: customer.service@aspenpubl.com;
WWW: http://www.aspenpub.com/pgCBM.html
▶ The professional forum for the nation's experts in the compensation and benefits field, this journal is the leading source of timely analysis and valuable insights from the very people who create important new policies and practices nationwide. *Compensation & Benefits Management* helps you step back from the fray and refocus your energy on goal-oriented benefits planning. Every issue delivers thoughtful reflection, expert advice, and creative strategies from some of the top minds in the business, plus scores of practical ideas you can use. You'll discover ways to design a flexible deferred compensation plan; help employees allocate 401(k) assets for a better retirement; work with employees to control workers' compensation costs and increase productivity, reevaluate your salary management program, and remain competitive; and use the right information tools to reduce health benefits costs. Contributors may include government policy makers, as well as professionals like yourself who have to make difficult compensation and benefits decisions every day. *$164/year*

Compensation & Benefits Report (Monthly Newsletter)
Bureau of Business Practice, a division of Aspen Publishers, Inc.,
200 Orchard Ridge Drive, Gaithersburg, MD 20878
Tel: 800-638-8437 (Subscriptions), 301-417-7500;
FAX: 301-695-7931
E-mail: customer.service@aspenpubl.com;
WWW: http://www.aspenpub.com/pgBBP-CBM.html

▶ This newsletter keeps you in federal compliance by providing plain English explanations of the latest benefits laws, regulations, and cases. It also offers compensation survey results to keep your company competitive. The contents of each issue examine new tax laws and regulations, IRS announcements, news from the SSA and the Department of Labor, court cases, and proposals regarding benefits and compensation. Articles not only explain how the news affects compensation and benefits, but include a "what to do" angle to help the company cope with the change. *8 pages, $199/year*

Compensation & Benefits Review: The Journal of Total Compensation Strategies (Bimonthly Newsletter)

Sage Publications, Inc., 2455 Teller Road,
Thousand Oaks, CA 91320
Tel: 805-499-9774 (Customer Service); FAX: 805-499-0871
E-mail: order@sagepub.com; WWW: http://www.sagepub.com/

▶ Addresses the specific information needs of compensation specialists. *Compensation & Benefits Review* provides the most thorough and up-to-date information available on issues, trends, and what is working in the marketplace for senior executives who develop and update compensation and benefits policies. This journal supports human resources and compensation and benefits specialists who design cutting-edge programs that will not only attract and retain a superior workforce, but also motivate them to beat the competition. *Special features:* CBR provides Web site information on public/private sources of current news on compensation and benefits issues; Metrics Reports provides a compilation of statistics on numerous important topics in the field; Quick Response surveys keep you up-to-date on the best practices in new and emerging areas; Roundtable Discussions offers information from other professionals on current topics; Opinion and Response Dialogues present the pros and cons of new issues. CBR also keeps you on the cutting edge with sections on Global Strategy, News and Analysis, Best of the In-Box, Case Studies, and Legal Alert. An online version is also available. *$240/year*

Disability, Leave, and Absence Reporter (Monthly Newsletter)

Aspen Publishers, 200 Orchard Ridge Drive,
Gaithersburg, MD 20878
Tel: 800-638-8437 (Subscriptions), 301-417-7500;
FAX: 301-695-7931
E-mail: customerservice@aspenpubl.com;
WWW: http://www.aspenpub.com/pgDLM.html

▶ This newsletter provides HR professionals with expert advice and guidance on how to deal with the often overlapping and sometimes conflicting requirements of laws and regulations dealing with employee disability and leave—the Family & Medical Leave Act, the Americans with Disabilities Act, workers' compensation laws, state laws, and company policies. A solid panel of experts from across the country answers questions and provides practical guidance on dealing with employee disability, absences, and leave requests. Leading lawyers and other experts are interviewed on a wide range of disability and leave issues. Recent court cases are reported and analyzed in each issue. Special supplements (8- to 12-page white papers) are issued as needed to give greater in-depth coverage of new decisions in this complex area. *12 pages, $195/year*

Diversity Monitor (Newsletter) (Ten Issues)

Hunt-Scanlon Corporation, 445 Park Avenue,
New York, NY 10022
Tel: 212-752-3075, 212-679-0282 (Edith Updike, Editor-in-Chief); FAX: 212-752-3077
E-mail: Eupdia@aol.com (Edith Updike, Editor-in-Chief);
WWW: http://www.hunt-scanlon.com/us.htm

▶ *Diversity Monitor* covers employee diversity in mid- and large-sized organizations. *$190/year*

Employee Relations Law Journal (Quarterly Journal)

William J. Kilberg, Editor-in-Chief and Dianne C. Scent, Editor
Aspen Publishers, 200 Orchard Ridge Drive,
Gaithersburg, MD 20878
Tel: 800-638-8437 (Subscriptions), 301-417-7500;
FAX: 301-695-7931
E-mail: customerservice@aspenpubl.com;
WWW: http://www.aspenpub.com/pgERLJ.html#1284

▶ Senior human resource executives, in-house counsel, and attorneys specializing in employment law have turned to this prestigious quarterly to find out what the law says, how the courts are ruling, and what to do to comply. Practicing professionals provide you with clear and authoritative articles on key issues such as the Americans with Disabilities Act, family medical leave, sexual harassment, terminations and RIFs, age discrimination, alternative dispute resolution, key NLRB decisions, controlling benefits costs, and trends in employment law. Regular columnists explore the meaning of new laws, regulations, and cases in benefits, safety and health, and labor–management relations. *$256/year*

Executive Search Review (Ten Issues)

Hunt-Scanlon Corporation
Corporate offices: 20 Signal Road, Stamford, CT 06902
Tel: 203-352-2920; FAX: 203-352-2930

Editorial offices: 445 Park Avenue, New York, NY 10022
Tel: 212-752-3075; FAX: 212-752-3077
E-mail address: lashsp@aol.com (Lisa A. Sanders—Editor-in-Chief); WWW: http://www.hunt-scanlon.com/newsletters/search.htm

▶ Published since 1989, *Executive Search Review* is the leading source for information on executive recruiting worldwide. Each month, their editorial team explores key market trends in this important industry, giving readers the benefit of our expert opinion, insight, and perspective. They also profile key executive recruiters and important industry decision makers you need to know. Over 10,000 companies receive *Executive Search Review* each month. *$190/year*

Fair Employment Practices Guidelines (Newsletter)

Bureau of Business Practice, a division of Aspen Publishers, Inc.,
200 Orchard Ridge Drive, Gaithersburg, MD 20878
Tel: 800-638-8437 (Subscriptions), 301-417-7500;
FAX: 301-695-7931
E-mail: customerservice@aspenpubl.com,
http://www.bbpnews.com/hr/hr_portal.shtml,
http://www.aspenpub.com/pgFEP.html

▶ The focus of Fair Employment Practices Guidelines is primarily fair employment laws and regulations, such as Title VII of the Civil Rights Act of 1964 and the Civil Rights Act of 1991. It covers equal employment opportunity issues, changes in laws and regulations, recent cases of significance from federal and state courts, and emerging trends in fair employment law issues. It also provides commonsense advice to improve employer–employee relations and reduce employer liability. The publication helps HR managers strike a balance between the needs of the employer and the rights of the employees. Each issue begins with a two-page update on what's new in employment law, court decisions, or regulations. In-depth articles focus on issues such as discrimination and compliance with ADA, Title VII, FMLA, etc. *8 pages, $179/year*

HR Briefing (Newsletter)

Bureau of Business Practice, a division of Aspen Publishers, Inc., 200 Orchard Ridge Drive, Gaithersburg, MD 20878
Tel: 800-638-8437 (Subscriptions), 301-417-7500;
FAX: 301-695-7931
E-mail: customerservice@aspenpubl.com,
http://www.aspenpub.com/pgPML.html

▶ *HR Briefing* provides HR professionals and other business people with concise, up-to-date information on employment practices and trends, with an emphasis on compliance with federal employment laws. *HR Briefing* is a timely source of information on successful business practices, employment legislation and regulation, and workplace trends. The focus is on presenting proven solutions to common workplace problems and comprehensible guidelines for complying with employment laws and regulations. Specialists in employment practices and law, many of whom are recognized nationally for their expertise, offer practical guidance on and analyses of traditional HR functions. The quick-read format and concise writing style make legal, technical, and other complex information easy to comprehend. *8 pages, $199/year*

HR Fact Finder (Monthly Newsletter)

Jamestown area Labor–Management Committee, P.O. Box 819, Room 340, 1093 East Second Street, Jamestown, NY 14702-0819
Tel: 800-542-7869, 716-665-3654; FAX: 716-665-8060
E-mail: jalmc@netsync.net; WWW: http://www.jalmc.org/fct-fnd1.htm, http://www.cbs4u.com/jalmc/ (HR Computing product list)

▶ This newsletter brings its readers capsulizations of the most timely human resource information from over 100 publications. Subscribers receive "must have" information on a wide variety of HR topics in a condensed, quick-to-read format. Topics covered include absenteeism, the Americans with Disabilities Act, communications, compensation, downsizing, employee benefits, employment law, employment policies, interviewing, managing people, safety, termination, workers' compensation, workplace violence, plus much more. *$89/year*

HRFocus (Monthly Newsletter)

Institute of Management and Administration (IOMA), 29 West 35th Street, New York, NY 10001-2299
Tel: 212-244-0360 (press 1 for Subscriber Services);
FAX: 212-564-0465
E-mail: subserve@ioma.com;
WWW: http://www.ioma.com/nls/hr.shtml?hrf

▶ This newsletter keeps HR directors up to date on the latest developments in the rapidly changing field of human resources. It includes information about benefits, financial management, hiring/retention, technology, training, and more. It also offers case studies of what the best HR departments are doing now to stay up to date. *$179/year*

HR Information Systems

Institute of Management and Administration (IOMA), 29 West 35th Street, New York, NY 10001-2299
Tel: 212-244-0360; FAX: 212-564-0465
E-mail: subserve@ioma.com;
WWW: http://www.ioma.com/products/newsletters.shtml

▶ This newsletter covers issues critical to building and maintaining human resources software, hardware, and Internet activities, such as controlling costs, selecting new software, and using new technology better. It provides salary data for HR information systems employees. *$239/year*

HR Magazine (Monthly)

Society for Human Resource Management, 1800 Duke Street, Alexandria, VA 22314
Tel: 703-548-3440; FAX: 703-535-6490
E-mail: hrmag@shrm.org;
WWW: http://www.shrm.org/hrmagazine

▶ The official voice of the HR profession, it features timely, in-depth articles, practical case studies, analysis of legal issues, and book and product reviews. Each issue offers thorough analysis of a major HR issue, plus additional coverage trends and activities in areas such as benefits, hiring practices, training, and compensation. Special issues provide nationwide salary survey results, buyer's guides, detailed information on the SHRM® Annual Conference and Exposition, and more. *$70/year (Nonmember), Free (Member)*

HR Manager's Legal Reporter (Monthly Newsletter)

Ransom & Benjamin Publishers, P.O. Box 160, Mystic, CT 06355
Tel: 800-334-3352, 860-536-2000; FAX: 860-536-1545
E-mail rbpubs@aol.com, Keatins@aol.com;
WWW: http://www.rbpubs.com/pi/pi1.htm

▶ *HR Manager's Legal Reporter* is reports on developments in employment law and providing practical, how-to guidance on HR policies and lawsuit prevention. It provides practical policy and practice tips, particular advice for avoiding employee lawsuits, and insightful analysis of new regulation and legislation. Each issue includes feature articles, Washington Watch, Briefs and States, and the ever-popular You Be the Judge. *$129.95/year*

HR News (Monthly Newspaper)

Society for Human Resource Management, 1800 Duke Street, Alexandria, VA 22314
Tel: 703-548-3440; FAX: 703-535-6490
WWW: http://www.shrm.org/hrnews/

▶ This newsletter provides late-breaking coverage of hot topics and trends in the HR field. Each issue brings you people in the news, legislative updates, legal and regulatory analysis, and conference activity. It also has the largest national help wanted section in the HR field. It is also available online. *$49/year (Nonmember), Free (Member)*

Human Resource Development Quarterly (Quarterly Journal)

Jossey-Bass Publishers, 350 Sansome Street, San Francisco, CA 94104
Tel: 415-433-1767, ext. 424; FAX: 800)-605-BOOK (2665)
WWW: http://www.jbp.com/JBJournals/hrdq.html

▶ Sponsored by the American Society for Training and Development (ASTD) and the Academy of Human Resource Development (AHRD), *Human Resource Development Quarterly* is the first scholarly journal focused directly on the evolving field of human resource development. It assembles the work of scholars and practitioners in management, training, industrial psychology, vocational education, organizational behavior and development, economics, industrial relations, adult education, and instructional technology to present a comprehensive resource on the latest advances in HRD theory and practice. Tables of contents for recent and forthcoming issues are posted on the *HRDQ* page. *$58 for individuals, $130 for institutions*

Human Resource Executive (16 Issues)

747 Dresher Road, Suite 500, Horsham, PA 19044-0980, ext. 238
Tel: 215-784-0910; FAX: 215-784-0870
Customer service: P.O. Box 10804, Riverton, NJ 08076-0804
Tel: 800-386-4176
E-mail: heverson@lrp.com; WWW: http://www.hrexecutive.com,
http://www.hrexecutive.com/web_guide.htm

▶ *Human Resource Executive* was established in 1987 and continues today as the premier publication focused on *strategic* issues in HR. Written primarily for vice presidents and directors of human resources, the magazine provides these key decision makers with news, profiles of HR visionaries, and success stories of human resource innovators. Stories cover all areas of human resource management, including personnel, benefits, training and development, HR information systems, relocation, retirement planning, workplace security, and health care. In November, the magazine also produces an HR Executive's Purchasing Resource, which assists the reader in evaluating and selecting HR products and services. *$89.95/year*

Human Resource Management (Quarterly Journal)

John Wiley & Sons, Inc., Attn: Subscription Department,
605 Third Avenue, New York, NY 10158-0012
Tel: 800-825-7750, 212-850-6645; FAX: 212-850-6021
E-mail: subinfo@wiley.com; WWW: http://www.shrm.org/wiley/

▶ Published in cooperation with the School of Business Administration, The University of Michigan, and in alliance with the Society for Human Resource Management, this journal covers the broad spectrum of contemporary human resource management. It provides practicing managers and academics with the latest concepts, tools, and information for effective problem solving and decision making in this field. Broad in scope, it explores issues of societal, organizational, and individual relevance. Journal articles discuss new theories, new techniques, case studies, models, and research trends of particular significance to practicing managers. It brings you management ideas and insights from the world's top HR experts—from the academic thought leaders to the professional managers who provide cutting-edge leadership. You'll find out about the trends before they become mainstream. You'll discover organizational design ideas that will help you rework management initiatives. And you'll learn about cultural changes that will affect your workforce in years to come. *$195/year (SHRM Nonmember), $125/year (SHRM Member)*

Human Resources Department Management

Institute of Management and Administration (IOMA),
29 West 35th Street, New York, NY 10001-2299
Tel: 212-244-0360; FAX: 212-564-0465
E-mail: subserve@ioma.com; WWW: http://www.ioma.com/
products/newsletters.shtml

▶ This publication focuses on the manager's multifaceted role as leader, innovator, and motivator of the department. It offers practi-

cal ideas for reducing HR department costs, motivating staff, adopting new HR information management systems, and using Internet and intranet applications. *$219/year*

Info-Line (Monthly Newsletter)

American Society for Training and Development,
1640 King Street, P.O. Box 1443, Alexandria, VA 22313-2043
Tel: 800-628-2783, 703-683-8100; FAX: 703-683-8103/1523
WWW: http://www.astd.org

▶ Created with training and performance professionals in mind, *Info-Line* is a 16- to 20-page single-issue publication that provides practical, concise help for developing training curriculum and to get you up-to-speed on a variety of topics that address your profession. Each issue is packed with valuable, focused information on topics from basic training to the industry's current practices—all in an easy-to-read, quickly digestible format. You'll find detailed information that guides you step-by-step through the learning process, how-to tips and techniques on subjects important to you, diagrams and illustrations you can use in training, worksheets and job aids to guide you through essential processes, case studies that illustrate practical applications, and templates and forms that make your job easier. *Info-Line* is known throughout the industry as a major tool for training the training professional. And much of the information covered by *Info-Line* issues can reach to all areas of management. Each issue provides how-to information on one training topic, task, or issue, such as games and icebreakers, instructional technology, benchmarking, workplace diversity, and performance technology. It includes practical information, easy-to-follow guidelines, job aids, and comprehensive bibliographies to help reduce your research time and learn the latest on current training issues. *$119/year (Nonmember), $79/year (Member)*

Legal Ease (See Legal Issues for full description)

Managing Diversity (Monthly Newsletter)

Jamestown area Labor–Management Committee, P.O. Box 819,
Room 340, 1093 East Second Street, Jamestown, NY 14702-0819
Tel: 800-542-7869, 716-665-3654; FAX: 716-665-8060
E-mail: jalmc@netsync.net; WWW: http://www.jalmc.org/mg-
diver.htm

▶ To attract and retain good employees, employers have to hire and motivate minorities, women, and others different from the mainstream in age, appearance, physical ability, experience, and lifestyle. The old ways of managing a heterogeneous workforce simply won't work anymore. *Managing Diversity* will help you develop new ways to manage. Each month, some of the nation's top diversity experts will bring you ideas and practical suggestions about how to effectively manage the emerging new workforce. *$99.00/year*

Organizational Dynamics

Elsevier Science, 655 Avenue of the Americas,
New York, NY 10010-5107
Tel: 888-437-4636 (USA/Canada), 212-633-3730;
FAX: 212-633-3680
E-mail: usinfo-f@elsevier.com;
WWW: http://www.elsevier.nl/locate/issn/00902616

▶ *Organizational Dynamics'* domain is primarily organizational behavior and development, and secondarily HRM and strategic management. The objective is to link leading-edge thought and research with management practice. *Organizational Dynamics* publishes articles that embody both theoretical and practical content, showing how research findings can help deal more effectively with the dynamics of organizational life. *$74/year (Individual), $171 (Institution)*

Pension & Benefits Week (Weekly Newsletter)

Research Institute of America (RIA), A Thomson Tax and Accounting Company, 90 Fifth Avenue, New York, NY 10011
Tel: 800-950-1216 (Customer Service), 212-645-4800;
FAX: 212-337-4192
WWW: http://www.riahome.com

▶ A comprehensive look at the latest developments in pension and benefits each week, *Pension & Benefits Week* brings you in-depth analysis of recent developments at the agencies, in the courts and in Congress. A Practitioner to Practitioner column offers valuable, practical insights on vital current issues. And there's a summary of each week's relevant IRS Private Letter Rulings, ERISA Opinion Letters, and court cases. A checklist of highlights of that week's coverage speeds review of the latest developments. Updates on important surveys and conferences keep you abreast of emerging issues. It also includes a cumulative quarterly index. A binder is provided for easy storage. *$290/year*

The Personnel/HR Assistant (Monthly Newsletter)

Council on Education in Management, Oakhill Business Park, 1338 Hundred Oaks Drive, Suite DD, Charlotte, NC 28217
Tel: 877-236-0265, 800-942-4494, 704-522-1236
E-mail: registration@counciloned.com (Customer Service and Registration); WWW: http://www.counciloned.com/ie4000.html, http://www.counciloned.com/news2.html

▶ This monthly newsletter is specially designed to inform, train, and update personnel/HR administrative staff. It is written by experienced professionals in the field of HR. In each issue you'll find techniques to improve your skills; facts and data you can use on the job; information on trends that affect your job; news on legal developments; methods to reduce wasted time and effort; skills to enhance your professionalism; and tips on recruiting, record keeping, reference checking, and other essential HR functions. *$199/year*

Personnel Journal *(See Workforce Magazine)*

Personnel Law Update (Monthly Newsletter)

Oakhill Business Park, 1338 Hundred Oaks Drive, Suite DD, Charlotte, NC 28217
Tel: 877-236-0265
E-mail: registration@counciloned.com (Customer Service and Registration); WWW: http://www.counciloned.com/ie4000.html, http://www.counciloned.com/news2.html

▶ Each month, our legal editors bring you change in legislation, regulations, and court decisions. Recent topics include privacy issues in e-mail and computer files, wrongful termination, same-sex sexual harassment, FMLA, and psychiatric disabilities under the ADA. Twelve versions are available. Written in clear, simple language, every issue features condensed case decisions and legislative development of the current month. The Council produces *Personnel Law Update* newletters that are state specific: California, Florida, Illinois, Indiana, mid-Atlantic (MD, WV, VA, NC, SC), Michigan, Missouri/Kansas, mountain states (AZ, CO, MT, NM, UT, WY), New England (CT, MA, ME, NH, RI, VT), New Jersey, North Central (ND, SD, WI, NE, MN, IA) Ohio, Pacific Northwest (AK, ID, WA, OR), Pennsylvania, public sector, southern states (LA, MS, AL, GA, KY, TN), and Texas. *$199/year*

STAFF Leader (Monthly Newsletter)

Aspen Publishers, 200 Orchard Ridge Drive, Gaithersburg, MD 20878
Tel: 800-638-8437 (Subscriptions), 301-417-7500;
FAX: 301-695-7931
E-mail: customerservice@aspenpubl.com;
WWW: http://www.aspenpub.com

150 Third Street (Editorial offices), Box 226, Akron, IA 51001
Tel: 712-568-2418 (Staff Issues Hotline)

▶ This practical, informal, up-to-the-minute newsletter guides any nonprofit administrator through the toughest of personnel problems, and connects successful nonprofit administrators across the United States and Canada. Learn what legal experts say about how to safely terminate incompetent staffers, how to avoid discrimination hassles, and how the latest employment laws affect you. Receive personnel policies that have already been proven successful and strategies about how to include staff members in long-range planning, how to make staffers more cost-conscious, and how to add low-cost benefits and perks to your compensation package. If you have questions that you need answers to right away, call the special Hotline and get the answers from noted labor and management experts who offer their professional opinions on these questions. Each issue is also filled with successful team-building, motivating, and disciplinary strategies for you and your supervisors. Two pages are written specifically with supervisors in mind, to help them become better managers, and one page can be distributed to staffers to improve communications. It includes six Special Reports throughout the year. Subscription includes the *STAFF Management Guide* (staff management strategies and advice focusing on legal and regulatory pitfalls, tips to help you manage your staff, solutions to tough staff problems, how to increase morale and motivate staffers, staff rewards, teambuilding tips). *12 pages, $153/year*

Training & Development (Monthly Magazine)

American Society for Training and Development, 1640 King Street, P.O. Box 1443, Alexandria, VA 22313-2043
Tel: 800-628-2783, 703-683-8100; FAX: 703-683-8103
E-mail: Customercare@astd.org; WWW: http://www.astd.org/ virtual_community/td_magazine

▶ An official publication of ASTD, its mission is to help ASTD members and readers do their jobs better by providing useful, how-to information on best practices; sharing new theories and their applications; reporting emerging trends; and addressing relevant and pivotal issues to the training and workplace performance improvement field. It includes feature articles, interviews, and columns that keep you ahead of issues and trends and give you practical training techniques. Learn new techniques and strategies for the reorganization of work, women as global managers, performance technology, training for small business, and other current topics. *T&D* EXTRA is a free, weekly information service of *T&D* magazine. Seven years of *T&D* magazine (1992 through 1998) are now available on a searchable CD-ROM. For more information or to order, call APEX at 888-936-5527. The price is $199.95 (ASTD members pay $109.95). *$85/year (Nonmember), Free (Member)*

Training Media Review (Bimonthly Newsletter)

TMR Publications, P.O. Box 381822, Cambridge, MA 02238-1822
Tel: 877-532-1838; FAX: 617-489-3437
E-mail: tmr1@tmreview.com, CustomerService@tmreview.com;
WWW: http://www.tmreview.com/

▶ This newsletter helps trainers, HR professionals, and managers make better choices about media-based training. It's the only comprehensive source for objective evaluations of media products. All of the reviewers are working training professionals with a single agenda: Is the product quality training or not? *$229 (print and online membership), $189 (online), $99 (print—by request)*

Workers' Comp Update

Council on Education in Management, Oakhill Business Park, 1338 Hundred Oaks Drive, Suite DD, Charlotte, NC 28217

*350 North Wiget Lane, Suite 100, Walnut Creek, CA 94598-2406
Tel: 800-942-4494, 925-934-8333; FAX: 925-988-1888
E-mail: registration@counciloned.com (Customer Service and Registration); WWW: http://www.counciloned.com/ie4000.html, http://www.counciloned.com/news2.html*

▶ Statewide monthly publications geared to workers' compensation claims administrators, attorneys, medical providers, and insurance representatives to stay up to date on workers' compensation systems. Information covers claim management, avoiding litigation, calculating benefits, cutting costs, workers' comp fraud, defining eligibility, administering leave, returning employees to work issues, vocational rehabilitation issues, and much more. *(California edition) $199/year*

Workforce Magazine

*245 Fischer Avenue, Suite B2, Costa Mesa, CA 92626
Tel: 800-444-6485, 714-751-1883, ext. 223; FAX: 714-751-4106
E-mail: carroll@workforcemag.com (Carroll Lachnit, Managing Editor); WWW: http://www.workforce.com/section/04*

▶ *Workforce* (formerly *Personnel Journal*) is the business magazine for leaders in human resources. *Workforce* will answer your questions, give you solutions and help you make decisions that will move your organization and your career in the right direction. These articles and departments are exclusive to *Workforce* magazine and are not available on Workforce.com. A subscription includes copy of *Workforce*'s annual *HR Products & Services Directory. $59/year*

INTERNET RESOURCES

General

About.com—Human Resources

▶ *http://humanresources.about.com/careers/humanresources/?once=true&*

Briefings Publishing Group's Online Solutions Center

▶ *http://www.briefings.com*

ACCESS Article Archive—Information for Nonprofit Employers

▶ *http://www.accessjobs.org/articles/*

Council on Education in Management Links and Online Resources

▶ *http://www.counciloned.com/linx.html*

Delaware Association of Nonprofit Agencies Answer Center: Human Resources

▶ *http://www.delawarenonprofit.org/HRFaq.html*

HRNet

▶ This site provides all company-based human resource directors, personnel managers, and training and development staff a single point of reference for technical questions and queries. It also enables HR professionals to locate consultants and HR services quickly and easily. Only registered users can access this site, but registration is free. When you register you will be able to choose a user name and password that allows access to the site and to one of the specialist forums (there is currently a forum aimed specifically at HR professionals and an equivalent forum aimed at HR consultants). *http://www.the-hrnet.com/*

HR Links—National Human Resources Association

▶ *http://www.humanresources.org/hrlinks.HTML*

HR OnLine

▶ *http://www.hr2000.com/*

hr-resource.com—West Group

▶ *http://hr-esource.com/*

HRStore

▶ The Human Resource Store, a Chicago-based human resources firm, provides recruiting, training, and consulting services to employers and posts jobs for candidates seeking employment. *http://www.hrstore.com/*

HRIM Mall

▶ The HRIM Mall consolidates a wide variety of information from around the world on the subjects of human resources, information management, and technology. The objective is to provide "one-stop service" for practitioners, programmers, business analysts, and others interested in this field. *http://www.hrimmall.com/*

Human Resource Executive

▶ *http://www.hrexecutive.com/web_guide.htm*

Human Resources—The Michigan Electronic Library

▶ *http://mel.lib.mi.us/business/BU-hr.html#per.html*

Human Resources Channel—Institute of Management and Administration

▶ A collection of IOMA's sample materials on human resources. *http://www.ioma.com/nls/hr.shtml*

Human Resources "USA"

▶ *http://www.netegories.com/usa/h-links/human_resources_usa.htm*

Human Resources Learning Center

▶ *http://www.human-resources.org/*

Human Resources Mailing Lists

▶ *http://www.iplabs.com/hr_ml.htm*

Human Resource Management Resources on the Internet

▶ (aka Ray's List of HRM Connections) *http://www.nbs.ntu.ac.uk/depts/hrm/hrm_link.htm*

Human Resources—501 Click

▶ *http://www.501click.com/mt_hr_main.html*

Human Resources Channel—Institute of Management & Administration (IOMA)

▶ *http://www.ioma.com/nls/hr.shtml*

Human Resources Management—The Management Assistance Program for Nonprofits

▶ *http://www.managementhelp.org/hr_mgmnt/hr_mgmnt.htm*

Interviewing—The Management Assistance Program for Nonprofits

▶ *http://www.managementhelp.org/commskls/intrvews/intrvews.htm*

The Management Center Library—Human Resources

▶ *http://tmcenter.org/library/nparticles.html*

Prometheon Learning Resource Network—Human Resources

▶ Helps you find seminars, continuing education, and Web-based training courses matching your interests. *http://www.seminarfinder.com/topic/HumanResources/*

SHRM Buyer's Guide—Society for Human Resource Management

▶ *http://www.shrm.org/buyers/listing.asp?ADID=000*

SHRM Consultants Forum Directory Online— Society for Human Resource Management

▶ *http://www.shrm.org/consultants/directory*

SHRM HR Information Center—Society for Human Resource Management

▶ *http://www.shrm.org/whitepapers/*

Society for Human Resource Management HR Links

▶ This site is an excellent central resource for all sorts of online information about human resource issues such as compensation, benefits, labor laws, recruiting, and personnel management. *http://www.shrm.org/hrlinks/, http://www.shrm.org/hrlinks/allLinks.asp*

Workforce—Human Resources Trends and Tools for Business Results

▶ *http://www.infoxpress.com/workforcebg/workforce/buyers-guides/bg1/search.asp*

***Workforce Magazine* Product Information**

▶ *http://www.infoxpress.com/acc/workforceonline*

World at Work Buyers Guide

▶ *http://www.worldatwork.org/Content/Infocentral/info-buyers-frame.html*

Yahoo—Human Resources

▶ *http://dir.yahoo.com/Business_and_Economy/Companies/Corporate_Services/Human_Resources/*

Assessment and Evaluation

Employee Performance Management—The Management Assistance Program for Nonprofits

▶ *http://www.managementhelp.org/emp_perf/emp_perf.htm*

Group Performance Management—The Management Assistance Program for Nonprofits

▶ *http://www.managementhelp.org/grp_perf/grp_perf.htm*

Group Skills—The Management Assistance Program for Nonprofits

▶ *http://www.managementhelp.org/grp_skll/grp_skll.htm*

Guiding Skills—The Management Assistance Program for Nonprofits

▶ *http://www.managementhelp.org/guiding/guiding.htm*

Human Resources Indicators

▶ An excellent online self-evaluation for an agency's human resource systems and practices, including management of volunteers, Human Resources Indicator is part of a series of Nonprofit Indicators (internal evaluation tools) at *http://www.mapnp.org/library/org_eval/uw_list.htm* that can help identify strengths and weaknesses in an agency's governance (board), planning, financial activities, fund raising and legal protection. Developed by the Management Assistance Program for Nonprofits. *http://www.mapnp.org/library/org_eval/uw_hr.htm*

Performance Management—Basic Concepts (The Management Assistance Program for Nonprofits)

▶ *http://www.managementhelp.org/perf_mng/perf_mng.htm*

Background Checks/Employee Screening

Backgrounds Online

▶ A nationwide provider of online pre-employment screening solutions and employee background checks, Backgrounds Online provides the complete solution, offering SSN verification, criminal history checks, workers' compensation, DMV, reference checks (employment, education, personal, and credential), credit reports, and more. *http://www.backgroundsonline.com/*

Benefits and Compensation

BenefitsLink

▶ The purpose of this site is to provide compliance information and tools about U.S. employer-sponsored benefit plans. BenefitsLink is designed to be useful to employers of all sizes, as well as the employees who participate in benefit plans. This site is intended to be especially helpful to the many companies and persons who provide legal, administration, consulting, and other services to employee benefit plans. *http://www.benefitslink.com*

Employee Benefits and Compensation—The Management Assistance Program for Nonprofits

▶ *http://www.managementhelp.org/pay_ben/pay_ben.htm*

Employee Wellness Programs—The Management Assistance Program for Nonprofits

▶ *http://www.managementhelp.org/emp_well/emp_well.htm*

Guide to Compensation and HR-Related Sites

▶ *http://www.claytonwallis.com/otherhr.htm*

HRCompDepot™

▶ HRCompDepot™ is a warehouse of compensation tools, data, and information. HRCompDepot™ is the shopper's club for compensation and human resources professionals. Here you'll find the tools and information you need to do your job as an HR professional. The Depot is stocked with new tools and resources every day. *https://www.hrcompdepot.com*

Other Web Sites Concerning Pension and Benefits

▶ *http://www.thompson.com/tpg/pen_ben/p_blinks.html*
Panel Employee Benefits Library On-Line (Aspen Publishers)

▶ *http://www.aspenpub.com/pg720.html#1780*

This fee-based library puts six of Panel's most trusted benefits law references right on your desktop, combining ease of access with authoritative information and reliable advice. From the fundamentals of plan design and administration to the latest developments in regulations, everything you need is here in fast-access, searchable form. The online version includes the current editions of Panel's core benefits references, up to date and unabridged: *Employee Benefits Answer Book; Employment Law Answer Book; Flexible Benefits Answer Book; Health Insurance Answer Book; Managed Care Answer Book; COBRA Handbook.* Includes subscriptions to two benefits journals, indispensable tools for keeping up with trends in benefits law and practice: *Compensation & Benefits Management* and *Benefits Law Journal.*

Web Sites Concerning the Family and Medical Leave Act

▶ *http://www.thompson.com/tpg/person/time/timelinks.html*

Where can I find information on employee compensation in the nonprofit sector? *http://foundationcenter.org/onlib/faqs/faq46.html*

Conflict Resolution

Mediation Works

▶ This site contains resources for the prevention, management, and resolution of workplace conflicts and disputes in business, government, health care, and nonprofit organizations. *http://www.mediationworks.com/*

Diverstiy and Disability

Americans with Disabilities Act Document Center

▶ *http://janweb.icdi.wvu.edu/kinder*

ADA Information Center

▶ *http://www.ada-infonet.org/*

Americans with Disabilities Act Information on the Web

▶ *http://www.usdoj.gov/crt/ada/*

Diversity Issues—Lambert & Associates

▶ *http://www.lambert-diversity.com/lambert.html*

Diversity Online—Hunt-Scanlon Corporation

▶ DiversityOnline is the official Web site of The Institute for Corporate Diversity, a leading diversity database and research publisher in the U.S. acquired by market research firm Hunt-Scanlon in 1999. The Institute currently publishes the monthly newsletter *Diversity Monitor;* the weekly news update *Diversity Newswire;* as well as the award-winning directory *Diversity in Corporate America,* a 500-page reference packed with essential information for executives managing diversity programs in America's largest organizations. *http://www.diversityonline.com/*

Diversity Web

▶ *http://www.inform.umd.edu/diversityweb/*

Harris Sussman on the Internet (Diversity)

▶ *http://www.sussman.org/*

Harry Sussman Diversity Links

▶ *http://www.sussman.org/links.html*

Managing Diversity—Links and Updates

▶ *http://www.btinternet.com/~alan.price/hrm/chap9/ch9-links.html*

NARIC Knowledgebase: **Americans with Disabilities Act Resources**

▶ *http://www.naric.com/naric/search/kb/ada.html*

National Rehabilitation Information Center (NARIC)—National Institute on Disability and Rehabilitation Research

▶ *http://nhic-nt.health.org/Scripts/Entry.cfm?HRCode=HR0012*

Other Web Sites Concerning People With Disabilities

▶ *http://www.thompson.com/tpg/person/able/ablelink.html*

Resources for Diversity

▶ *http://alabanza.com/kabacoff/Inter-Links/diversity.html*

The University of Maryland's Diversity Database

▶ A comprehensive index of multicultural and diversity resources. *http://www.inform.umd.edu/Diversity/*

U.S. Department of Justice Americans with Disabilities Act

▶ *http://www.usdoj.gov/crt/ada/adahom1.htm*

Workplace Diversity Initiative—Society for Human Resource Management

▶ *http://www.shrm.org/diversity*

Employee Relations

Prometheon Learning Resource Network— Employee Relations

▶ Helps you find seminars, continuing education, and Web-based training courses matching your interests. *http://www.seminarfinder.com/topic/EmployeeRelations/*

Employment Law

AHI's Employment Law Resource Center— Alexander Hamilton Institute

▶ *http://www.ahipubs.net/products/index.html*

Americans with Disabilities Act Document Center

▶ This site contains ADA Statute, Regulations, ADAAG (Americans with Disabilities Act Accessibility Guidelines), Federally Reviewed Tech Sheets, and other assistance documents. *http://janweb.icdi.wvu.edu/kinder/*

Employment and Labor Law: Related Resources

▶ *http://www.ljx.com/practice/laboremployment/labrel.html*

HR Law Index

▶ A service that provides an index to specific HR-related articles published on the Web by law firms, legal publications, and government organizations. *http://www.hrlawindex.com/*

Human Resources and Employment Law—Bureau of Business Practice (Aspen Publishers)

▶ *http://www.bbpnews.com/hr/hr_portal.shtml*

Executive Search and Recruitment

DeepSweep

▶ DeepSweep is a web-facilitated, executive search service for nonprofit executives and employers. *http://www.deepsweep.com*

ExecSearches.com

▶ ExecSearches.com was originally created in 1997 to assist Isaacson, Miller, one of the nation's most prestigious executive search firms with recruiting top executive and senior management talent. In 1999, ExecSearches.com expanded its services to serve top nonprofit, public sector, and socially conscious organizations and other search firms and third-party recruiters in the United States and around the world. ExecSearches.com offers an easy-to-navigate interface for recruiters to post jobs and for job seekers and those just browsing to quickly find employment opportunities in their areas of interest. Job seekers may also sign up to receive personalized delivery of new job postings by e-mail. ExecSearches.com also offers résumé review and editing services for job seekers as well as additional services for recruiters and employers including reference checking, Internet recruiting training, and position profiling services. *http://www.execsearches.com/exec/*

Headhunter.net

▶ *http://www.headhunter.net/*

Nonprofit Career Network

▶ *http://www.nonprofitcareer.com*

Recruiter Link

▶ *http://www.recruiterlink.com/database/*

Recruiters Online

▶ A global community of recruiters, headhunters, and professional staffing firms. *http://www.recruitersonline.com/*

Legal

KnowledgePoint's Policy-Specific Web Links

▶ *http://www.knowledgepoint.com/kplinks.htm*

U.S. Equal Employment Opportunity Commission

▶ *http://www.eeoc.gov/index.html*

U.S. EEOC Quick Start—Employers

▶ *http://www.eeoc.gov/qs-employers.html*

Fair, Square, and Legal Web Resources

▶ *http://www.amanet.org/selfstudy/01120links.htm*

Prometheon Learning Resource Network—Legal

▶ This site helps you find seminars, continuing education, and Web-based training courses matching your interests. *http://www.seminarfinder.com/topic/Legal/*

Outsourcing

Outsourcing Center

▶ *http://www.outsourcing-suppliers.com/html/1aboutus.html*

Personnel Policies

Personnel Policies, Handbooks and Records—The Management Assistance Program for Nonprofits
▶ *http://www.managementhelp.org/policies/policies.htm*

Software

Guide to Human Resource Management Software Vendor Web Sites
▶ *http://www.claytonwallis.com/hrmsven.htm*

Human Resources Software Internet Guide—HR Software Online
▶ *http://www.hr-software.net/*

Taxes

Tax and Wage Reporting—STAWRS
▶ *http://www.tax.gov/*

Tax Exempt/Employee Plans Statistics
▶ *http://www.irs.ustreas.gov/prod/tax_stats/exempt.html*

Teams and Team Building

Self-Directed Work Teams
▶ An excellent site loaded with information on team building and the effective use of teams within organizations. *http://www.users.ids.net/~brim/sdwth.html*

Training and Development

Learning and Training FAQs
▶ *http://www.learnativity.com/training_FAQs/*

Overview of Training and Development—The Management Assistance Program for Nonprofits
▶ *http://www.mapnp.org/library/trng_dev.htm*

Seminar Information Service, Inc.
▶ *http://www.seminarinformation.com*

Training & Development Resource Center
▶ *http://www.tcm.com/trdev.*

TrainingNet
▶ *http://www.trainingnet.com*

The Training Registry
▶ *http://www.tregistry.com/*

TrainingSuperSite
▶ *http://www.trainingsupersite.com/*

Where Can I Find Information on Training Opportunities?
▶ *http://foundationcenter.org/onlib/faqs/faq15.html*

Web-Based Training Information Center
▶ *http://www.filename.com/wbt/*

Discussion Lists

SHRM HR Talk
▶ *http://www.shrm.org/hrtalk*

TeamNet
▶ This site is for discussions about teamwork and team-related topics. The goal of TeamNet is to build a network of researchers and business people who are interested in team topics and to facilitate discussion and collaboration within this network. To subscribe, visit the Web site. *http://www.workteams.unt.edu/teamnet.htm*

Training and Development
▶ Though not specifically aimed at the nonprofit sector, this high-volume list (up to 20 messages/day) includes discussion of human resource issues including training, development, and general management of employees. To subscribe, send e-mail to: *trdev-l @psuvm.psu.edu* with the subject line empty and the message: "subscribe tradev-1 (your full name)" without quotes.

Workcommunication
▶ This site is for discussion of all aspects of workplace communication—corporate, management–employee, staff. *workcomm-subscribe@egroups.com* To subscribe, send blank e-mail or visit the Web site at *http://www.egroups.com/group/workcomm/.*

Newsgroups

HRNET Discussion Archives
▶ Since April 1998, the posts to HRNET have been mirrored on eGroups (*http://www.egroups.com/group/hrnet*), a searchable archive. While this is focused on the management of paid staff, the discussions include things of interest to volunteer managers (conflict in the workplace, recognition, etc.). The discussion group is now defunct, but its archives provide excellent information.

Human Resources Newsgroups
▶ *http://www.magi.com/~broadb/hr-1st.html*

Online Newsletter

Compensation & Benefits Advisor (Grant Thornton)

▶ A quarterly newsletter focusing on Benefits and Human Resource Issues.

Diversity Issues—Lambert & Associates

▶ *http://www.lambert-diversity.com/lambert.html*

HR Magazine Online—SHRM

▶ *http://www.shrm.org/hrmagazine/*

HR-Today.com

▶ *http://www.hr-today.com/*

PART VI

Information Technology

ORGANIZATIONS

(See also General Management; Marketing & Communications; Resource Development)

Policy-Centered Organizations

Alliance for Community Media

666 11th Street NW, Suite 740, Washington, DC 20001-4542
Tel: 202-393-2650; FAX: 202-393-2653
E-mail: acm@alliancecm.org, briedel@alliancecm.org (Bunnie Riedel, Executive Director), bosnie@aol.com;
WWW: http://www.alliancecm.org/

▶ The Alliance for Community Media is committed to assuring everyone's access to electronic media. The Alliance accomplishes this by creating public education, advancing a positive legislative and regulatory environment, building coalitions, and supporting local organizing.

A nonprofit, national membership organization founded in 1976, the Alliance represents the interests of over 1,000 public, educational, and governmental ("PEG") access organizations (generally known as "public access") and public access Internet centers throughout the country. It also represents the interests of an estimated 1.5 million individuals, through their local religious, community, charitable, and other groups, who utilize PEG access television centers and Internet providers to speak to their memberships and their larger communities. The Alliance for Community Media provides critical support services for these community media centers and for the primarily volunteer staff that keep these electronic outposts of democracy in operation. The Alliance's activities in providing technical assistance, political advocacy, and opportunities to share expertise promote the broader goals of supporting our nation's communities and families, and promoting effective communication through community uses of media. Alliance for Community Media currently offers two mailing lists created for the purposes of sharing information and providing a forum for discussion of issues of interest.

Alliance for Community Technology (ACT)

Media Union, 2281 Bonisteel Boulevard,
Ann Arbor, MI 48109-2094
Tel: 734-647-8038; FAX: 734-936-3107
E-mail: atkins@umich.edu (Daniel E. Atkins, Executive Director),
wlodek@umich.edu (Vlad Wielbut, Technology Resources Manager), jmkerr@umich.edu (JoAnne M. Kerr, Project Associate); WWW: http://www.communitytechnology.org,
http://www.communitytechnology.org/demo_lib/index.html,
http://www.communitytechnology.org/lists.html

▶ The Alliance for Community Technology was launched in 1997 as a strategic partnership between the W.K. Kellogg Foundation and the University of Michigan through its new School of Information. The partnership was motivated by the perspective that information technology has emerged to the point that it could have an increasingly vital role in the Foundations's fundamental mission to help people help themselves through the practical application of knowledge and resources to improve their quality of life and that of future generations. The mission of the Alliance for Community Technology (ACT) is to lead in advancing the use of computing and communication technology globally to serve people (to help people help themselves) through community-serving organizations. It is committed to a human-centered focus on the creation, use, understanding, training, and dissemination of appropriate technologies to support communities whether these communities are defined by geography, organizational structure, or common interest (i.e., whether they are defined physically or conceptually). It will focus particularly on disadvantaged communities. ACT publishes a newsletter and holds an annual conference.

Alliance for Public Technology (ACT)

919 18th Street NW, 10th Floor, Washington, DC 20006
Tel: 202-263-2970; FAX: 202-263-2960
E-mail: apt@apt.org; WWW: http://www.apt.org/

▶ APT is a nonprofit membership organization open to all nonprofit organizations and individuals, not members of the affected industries, concerned with fostering access to affordable and useful information and communication services and technologies by all people. APT is composed of public interest groups and individuals, some of whom historically have been left out of the Information Age, including the elderly, minorities, low-income groups, and people with disabilities. Membership in the Alliance is open to individuals and nonprofit users of information services and communication technologies who support the goals of the Alliance. Members may be individuals, nonprofit organizations, government agencies and officials, and not-for-profit information providers. Services provided to its members are educating nonprofit groups and the general public about technology and telecommunications services; bringing nonprofit groups, government officials, regulators, and industry members together to network on issues and matters of common concern; researching barriers to access and developing programs and proposals to eliminate those barriers; bringing its program and goals to regulatory officials and legislators entrusted with ensuring the affordability and availability of telecommunications technology; and creating opportunities for industry, government, and nonprofit groups to form partnerships that foster greater access.

Americans Communicating Electronically (ACE)

ACE (ECS-CSREES), 4429 Water Front Centre,
800 9th Street SW, Washington, DC 20024
Tel: 202-720-2727 (Tom Tate)
E-mail: ttate@reeusda.gov (Tom Tate), ace2chair@hotmail.com
(Glynis Long); WWW: http://www.ace.org,
http://www.reeusda.gov/ecs/ace.htm

► The ACE network of more than 7,000 national, state, and local members assist their communities to explore, invest in, and adopt the appropriate information technology for strengthening their community. ACE volunteers are helping millions become comfortable with the Internet through "Internet Master" training initiatives. ACE volunteers are helping local educational leaders become aware of funding sources and announcements for sponsoring improvements in their community information infrastructure.

Association for Community Networking

840 University City Boulevard, Suite 5, P.O. Box 10155,
Blacksburg, VA 24060
Tel: 540-231-1619; FAX: 540-231-2139
E-mail: cohill@bev.net (Andrew Cohill, President),
shsnow@mindspring.com; WWW: http://www.afcn.net/afcn.html,
http://www.rtpnet.org/afcn/afcn_forum/wwwboard.html,
http://www.afcn.net/resources/resources.html

► The Association for Community Networking (AFCN) is an educational nonprofit corporation dedicated to fostering and supporting "Community Networking"—community-based creation and provision of appropriate technology services. AFCN's mission is to improve the visibility, viability, and vitality of Community Networking by assisting and connecting people and organizations, building public awareness, identifying best practices, encouraging research, influencing policy, and developing products and services.

Benton Foundation

950 18th Street NW, Washington, DC 20006
Tel: 877-2-BENTON (1-877-223-6866), 202-638-5770;
FAX: 202-638-5771
E-mail: benton@benton.org; WWW: http://www.benton.org/

► Since 1981, the Benton Foundation has worked to realize the social benefits made possible by the public interest use of communications. Through its projects, the foundation seeks to shape the emerging communications environment in the public interest. Bridging the worlds of philanthropy, public policy, and community action, Benton demonstrates and promotes the use of digital media to engage, equip, and connect people to solve social problems. The Benton Foundation promotes public interest values and noncommercial services for the National Information Infrastructure through research and policy analysis, outreach to nonprofits and foundations, and print, video, and online publishing. To advance these goals, Benton initiates projects in three interdependent areas: defining and promoting public policies that support the public interest services and capacities of new media; helping nonprofit organizations use communications tools and strategies to be information providers and social advocates; and creating knowledge centers in the new media that are trusted sources and guides to nonprofit information and action. Resources include its virtual library (online versions of most Benton publications); discussion lists (participate with public interest advocates in CPP's "Up for Grabs" discussion about current and future trends in communications policy and practice); and electronic news services (subscribe to one of their several

news and information services). The Benton's Best Practices Toolkit (*http://www.benton.org/Practice/Toolkit*) provides tools to help nonprofits make effective use of communications and information technologies.

Center for Civic Networking (CCN)

P.O. Box 600618, Newtonville, MA 02460-0006
Tel: 617-558-3698; FAX: 617-630-8946
E-mail: ccn-info@civicnet.org. mfidelman@civicnet.org (Miles R.
Fidelman, President and Director, Municipal Telecommunications
Strategies Program); WWW: http://civic.net/ccn.html
E-mail: ccn-info@civicnet.org; WWW: http://civic.net/ccn.html

► The Center for Civic Networking (CCN) is a 501(c)(3) nonprofit organization dedicated to applying information infrastructure to the broad public good, particularly by putting information infrastructure to work within local communities to improve delivery of local government services, improve access to information that people need in order to function as informed citizens, broaden citizen participation in governance, and stimulate economic and community development. CCN conducts internally initiated projects, conducts projects in partnership with other organizations, consults with government and nonprofit organizations, and conducts policy research and analysis. CCN staff members engage in ongoing educational, writing, and speaking activities. Major programs include CCN's Municipal Telecommunications Strategies Program (supports local governments as they deal with telecommunications issues; publishes the peer-reviewed Journal of Muncipal Telecommunications); The Public Webmarket (helps small businesses and community-based economic development organizations experiment with electronic commerce and Internet marketing); Civic Dialog and Citizen Participation; and additional projects from their West Coast office.

Center for Democracy and Technology (CDT)

1634 Eye Street NW, Suite 1100, Washington, DC 20006
Tel: 202-637-9800; FAX: 202-637-0968
WWW: http://www.cdt.org, http://www.cdt.org/links/,
http://www.cdt.org/publications/

► The Center for Democracy and Technology works to promote democratic values and constitutional liberties in the digital age. With expertise in law, technology, and policy, CDT seeks practical solutions to enhance free expression and privacy in global communications technologies. CDT is dedicated to building consensus among all parties interested in the future of the Internet and other new communications media.

Center for Media Education

2120 L Street NW, Suite 200, Washington, DC 20037
Tel: 202-331-7833; FAX: 202-331-7841
E-mail:cme@cme.org; WWW:http://www.cme.org/

► The Center for Media Education (CME) is a national nonprofit organization dedicated to improving the quality of the electronic media. CME fosters telecommunications policy making in the public interest through its research, advocacy, public education, and press activities. CME has played a leading role in organizing nonprofit organizations to address critical telecommunications issues. As a co-founder of the telecommunications Policy Roundtable, CME has helped over 200 groups become involved in the policy debate over the information superhighway.

Citizens Communications Center Project

The Institute for Public Representation, Georgetown University Law Center, 600 New Jersey Avenue NW, Washington, DC 20001
Tel: 202-662-9535; FAX: 202-662-9634
E-mail: gulcipr@law.georgetown.edu;
WWW: http://www.law.georgetown.edu/clinics/ipr

▶ The Citizens Communications Center Project represents advocacy, consumer, and civil rights organizations before the FCC, FTC, and courts on matters relating to mass media, common carrier, Internet, and new technologies. Their objective is to make the communications media accessible, diverse, and responsive to all segments of the community. The Institute for Public Representation is a public interest law firm and clinical education program established at Georgetown University Law Center in 1971. Currently, the Institute staff works in three project areas: civil rights, communications law, and environmental law.

Civil Rights Forum on Communications Policy

818 18th Street NW, Suite 505, Washington, DC 20006
Tel: 202-887-0301; FAX: 202-887-0305
E-mail: forum@civilrightsforum.org,
mlloyd@civilrightsforum.org (Mark Lloyd, Executive Director),
bforbes@civilrightsforum.org (Barry Forbes, Director of Community Programs); WWW: http://www.civilrightsforum.org/,
http://www.civilrightsforum.org/text/links.htm

▶ A project of the Tides Center, the Civil Rights Forum on Communications Policy works to bring civil rights organizations and community groups into the debate over the future of our media environment—that environment is the key to the future of the nation.

Community Technology Centers' Network (CTCNet)

372 Broadway Street, Cambridge, MA 02139
Tel: 617-354-0825; FAX: 617-354-8437
E-mail: info@ctcnet.org, kchandler@ctcnet.org (Karen Chandler, Acting Executive Director);
WWW: http://www.ctcnet.org/contact.html

▶ CTCNet is a national, nonprofit membership organization of more than 450 independent community technology centers where people get free or low-cost access to computers and computer-related technology, such as the Internet, together with learning opportunities that encourage exploration and discovery. CTCNet envisions a society in which all people are equitably empowered by technology skills and usage. CTCNet is committed to achieving this end.

Computer Professionals for Social Responsibility

P.O. Box 717, Palo Alto, CA 94302-0717
Tel: 650-322-3778; FAX: 650-322-4748
E-mail: cpsr@cpsr.org; WWW: http://www.cpsr.org,
http://www.cpsr.org/links/

▶ CPSR is a public-interest alliance of computer scientists and others concerned about the impact of computer technology on society. We work to influence decisions regarding the development and use of computers because those decisions have far-reaching consequences and reflect our basic values and priorities. As technical experts, CPSR members provide the public and policy makers with realistic assessments of the power, promise, and limitations of computer technology. As concerned citizens, we direct public attention to critical choices concerning the applications of computing and how those choices affect society. CPSR's flagship publication is the *CPSR Newsletter,* a quarterly magazine containing in-depth analysis of major issues involving technology along with updates on CPSR activities (now available online only). Back issues of the newsletter, along with the publications, reports, and books listed on this page, are currently available using their online form or from the national office.

The Electronic Frontier Foundation

1550 Bryant Street, Suite 725, San Francisco, CA 94103
Tel: 415-436-9333; FAX: 415-436-9993
E-mail: info@eff.org; WWW: http://www.eff.org,
http://www.eff.org/archive.html

▶ Uphold rights to digital free expression from political, legal, and technical threats. EFF is a nonprofit, nonpartisan organization working in the public interest to protect fundamental civil liberties, including privacy and freedom of expression in the arena of computers and the Internet. EFF was founded in 1990, and is based in San Francisco, California, with a satellite office in Washington, DC. EFF, in conjunction with many other organizations, has formed and participates in a number of coalitions and summits to bring together thinkers from the nonprofit/NGO world, communications and computing industry leaders, government policy makers (when appropriate), and grassroots advocates in a nonpartisan setting to discuss communications policy goals and strategies and to form balanced solutions to problems. Such efforts to date have included the Communications Policy Forum, the Digital Privacy and Security Working Group, and the Intellectual Property Working Group (EFF organized), as well as the Interactive Working Group and the Stop S.314 Coalition (with EFF as an active participant). More recently, EFF has been a charter member of the Digital Future Coalition, the Global Internet Liberty Campaign, and the Internet Free Expression Alliance. EFF publishes an electronic bulletin, *EFFector Online,* at *http://www.eff.org/effector.*

Electronic Privacy Information Center

1718 Connecticut Avenue NW, Suite 200, Washington, DC 20009
Tel: 202-483-1140; FAX: 202-483-1248
Washington, DC 20003
E-mail: info@epic.org; WWW: http://www.epic.org,
http://www.epic.org/alert/

▶ EPIC is a public interest research center in Washington, DC. It was established in 1994 to focus public attention on emerging civil liberties issues and to protect privacy, the First Amendment, and constitutional values. EPIC is a project of the Fund for Constitutional Government. EPIC works in association with Privacy International, an international human rights group based in London, and is also a member of the Global Internet Liberty Campaign, the Internet Free Expression Alliance, the Internet Privacy Coalition, and the Trans Atlantic Consumer Dialogue (TACD).

Internet Policy Institute (IPI)

601 Pennsylvania Avenue NW, North Building, Suite 250, Washington, DC 20004
Tel: 202-628-3900; FAX: 202-628-3922
E-mail: info@internetpolicy.org;
WWW: http://www.internetpolicy.org,
http://www.internetpolicy.org/resources/index.html

▶ The Internet Policy Institute (IPI) is the nation's first independent, nonprofit research and educational institute created to provide objective, high-quality analysis, research, education, and outreach on economic, social, and policy issues affecting and affected by the global development and use of the Internet. IPI maintains IPI News, a free e-mail discussion list.

Internet Public Policy Network (IPPN)

919 18th Street NW, 10th Floor, Washington, DC 20006
Tel: 202-263-2932; FAX: 202-263-2962
E-mail: hechtl@internetpublicpolicy.com (Lawrence Hecht, Founder and Administrator); WWW: http://www.internetpublicpolicy.com, http://internetpublicpolicy.com/links.cfm

▶ The Internet Public Policy Network (IPPN) is a network of Internet policy experts that provide content and services dealing with telecommunications, electronic commerce, and community technology issues. IPPN connects organizations to leading experts on telecommunications, electronic commerce, and community technology issues. IPPN both provides services directly to information technology companies and facilitates the relationship between the aforementioned experts and organizations that wish to retain their services. It provides facilitated networking services such as an expert referral service, speakers bureau, a directory, and custom research. IPPN has made its directory available to the public for free. It can be accessed at *http://www.internetpublicpolicy.com/directory.cfm.*

Internet Society

11150 Sunset Hills Road, Suite 100, Reston, VA 20190-5321
Tel: 800-468 9507, 703-326-9880; FAX: 703-326-9881
E-mail: isoc@isoc.org; WWW: http://www.isoc.org/

▶ The Internet Society is a nonprofit, nongovernmental, international, professional membership organization. It focuses on standards, education, and policy issues. Its more than 150 organization and 8,600 individual members in over 170 nations worldwide represent a veritable who's who of the Internet community. ISOC is the organizational home for the Internet Engineering Task Force, the Internet Engineering Steering Group, and the Internet Architecture Board, the groups responsible for developing the Internet's technical underpinnings. Through their efforts, broad-based consensus is achieved on bringing technical change to the Internet.

Its principal purpose is to maintain and extend the development and availability of the Internet and its associated technologies and applications, both as an end in itself, and as a means of enabling organizations, professions, and individuals worldwide to more effectively collaborate, cooperate, and innovate in their respective fields and interests. ISOC is involved in a variety of initiatives stemming from technological, educational, social, economic, standards, political, ethical, and legal sources that influence the direction of the Internet. Since 1992, the Internet Society has served as the international organization for global coordination and cooperation on the Internet, promoting and maintaining a broad spectrum of activities focused on the Internet's development, availability, and associated technologies.

Its *OnTheInternet Online,* the electronic resource for the Internet Society's magazine, is available online at *http://www.isoc.org/oti.* Published monthly and distributed by e-mail, ISOC Forum reports on activities of the Internet Society and the Internet Engineering Task Force, delivers news about Internet developments worldwide, and features a truly global list of Internet-related conferences, seminars, and workshops. The Forum is published for the benefit of ISOC individual and organizational members. INET is the annual ISOC conference that focuses on global issues of the Internet by bringing together the cyberspace leaders who are developing and implementing Internet networks, applications, and policies for the worldwide infrastructure.

Media Access Project (MAP)

950 18th Street NW, Suite 220, Washington, DC 20006
Tel: 202-232-4300; FAX: 202-466-7656
E-mail: webmaster@mediaaccess.org;
WWW: http://www.mediaaccess.org/programs/index.html, http://www.mediaaccess.org/web/index.html

▶ Founded in 1973, MAP is a nonprofit tax-exempt public interest telecommunications law firm that through its programs promotes the public's First Amendment right to hear and be heard on the electronic media of today and tomorrow. MAP is the only Washington-based organization devoted to representing listeners' and speakers' interests on electronic media and telecommunications issues before the Federal Communications Commission, other policy-making bodies, and in the courts. MAP's staff attorneys provide guidance and representation to scores of national and local nonprofit groups annually. Among MAP's goals are promoting policies for deployment of the Internet and other advanced telecommunications networks, cable, and direct broadcast satellites, which ensure affordable and nondiscriminatory access to speak and to be heard; ensuring open access on broadband Internet facilities; ensuring that broadcasters honor their commitment to promote civic discourse and democracy locally and nationally, as they convert to digital transmission; full implementation of the fairness doctrine and related policies ensuring access for divergent points of view and alternative artistic perspectives; encouraging competition and content diversity in video services; and enforcement of laws and FCC rules promoting minority and female ownership and employment in broadcasting, cable TV, and telecommunications.

National Telecommunications and Information Administration (NTIA)

Office of Telecommunications and Information Applications, National Telecommunications and Information Administration, U.S. Department of Commerce, Room 4096, 1401 Constitution Avenue NW, Washington, DC 20230
Tel: 202-482-5802; FAX: 202-501-8009
E-mail: otia_assoc_adm@ntia.doc.gov, sdowns@ntia.doc.gov (Steve Downs, Director), bmcguire-rivera@ntia.doc.gov (Dr. Bernadette McGuire-Rivera, Associate Administrator); WWW: http://www.ntia.doc.gov

▶ The National Telecommunications and Information Administration (NTIA), an agency of the U.S. Department of Commerce, is the Executive Branch's principal voice on domestic and international telecommunications and information technology issues. NTIA works to spur innovation, encourage competition, help create jobs, and provide consumers with more choices and better quality telecommunications products and services at lower prices. NTIA's Office of Telecommunications and Information Applications (OTIA) assists state and local governments, educational and health care entities, libraries, public service agencies, and other groups in effectively using telecommunications and information technologies to better provide public services and advance other national goals. This is accomplished through the administration of the Technology Opportunities Program (TOP) (formerly, Telecommunications and Information Infrastructure Assistance Program) and the Public Telecommunications Facilities Program (PTFP). TOP promotes the widespread use of advanced telecommunications and information technologies in the public and nonprofit sectors. The program provides matching demonstration grants to state and local governments, health care providers, school districts, libraries, social service organizations, public safety services, and other nonprofit entities to help them develop information infrastructures and services that are accessible to all citizens, in rural as well as urban areas.

NetPoint Center for Nonprofits and Technology

c/o CompassPoint Nonprofit Services, 1922 The Alameda, Suite 212, San Jose, CA 95126
Tel: 408-248-9505, ext. 375, 415-541-9000, ext. 313 (Nelson Layag); FAX: 408-248-9504
E-mail: scottw@netpointcenter.org (Scott W. Walton), nelsonl@compasspoint.org (Nelson Layag, Director of Technology, CompassPoint Nonprofit Services);
WWW: http://www.netpointcenter.org/

▶ This is a joint project of CompassPoint Nonprofit Services and HandsNet (see separate listings for both in Technology Assistance Organizations section). The NetPoint Center, based in Silicon Valley, addresses the *digital divide* faced by nonprofit organizations; helping them to access, integrate, and use computer and communication technologies within their work and to achieve their missions. The NetPoint Center will conduct research and develop responses to identified needs, design and operate Silicon Valley/Bay Area projects testing model solutions, and offer national resources and promotion of successful models. The NetPoint Center will serve as a collaborative interface for nonprofit organizations, technology companies, and funding institutions. Based in Silicon Valley with national networks, the NetPoint Center will bring together funders, technology corporations, consultants, and leaders in nonprofit management for research and development of effective technology services, testing and demonstrating programs, supporting collaborations to replicate successful responses, and producing information to support effective technology utilization. The NetPoint Center will provide programs and services in three main areas: research and development (will conduct research and data collection focused on and supporting nonprofit technology needs and practical applications); local services (will create, operate and assess strong services and programs in California that can serve as national models); and national programs (will develop information and provide referral regarding program assessment, resources, and solutions. Program models, including the collaborations that support them, will be promoted. The Center will provide mobile labs at events and conferences where nonprofit professionals can access workshops and direct technology consulting). The Center will sponsor the annual Silicon Valley Conference on Nonprofits and Technology, in partnership with CompassPoint, HandsNet, CompuMentor, and Wired for Good.

OMB Watch

1742 Connecticut Avenue NW, Washington, DC 20009-1171
Tel: 202-234-8494; FAX: 202-234-8584
E-mail: ombwatch@ombwatch.org;
WWW: http://www.ombwatch.org,
http://www.ombwatch.org/html/npi.html,
http://www.ombwatch.org/npadv/snapdes.html,
http://www.ombwatch.org/html/forum.html

▶ OMB Watch was formed in 1983 to lift the veil of secrecy shrouding the White House Office of Management and Budget (OMB), which oversees regulation, the budget, information collection and dissemination, proposed legislation, testimony by agencies, and much more. They now concentrate on five main areas: budget and government performance issues; regulatory and government accountability; information for democracy and community; nonprofit advocacy and other cross-cutting nonprofit issues; and nonprofit policy and technology. OMB Watch co-chairs the Let America Speak Coalition along with Independent Sector and Alliance for Nonprofit Management. In 1999, the Lincoln Filene Center for Citizenship and Public Affairs at Tufts University and OMB Watch in Washington, DC launched the Nonprofits' Policy and Technology Project to identify and better understand the factors that affect nonprofits' participation in the public policy process. OMB Watch is working with a number of organizations to increase the awareness of community technology centers. OMB Watch maintains several e-mail mailing lists (listservs). To subscribe to any of their lists, click on the name of the list (*http://www.ombwatch.org/forum.html*) and complete the form on the Web page that follows. If your browser does not support forms, please send an e-mail to *ombwatch@ombwatch.org* with your name, organization (if any), mailing address, phone, and FAX. They will respond via phone, FAX, or e-mail with more information. They also send out an online newsletter twice a month (*OMB Watcher Online*) updating OMB Watch's current activities and issues of interest. View past issues and subscribe to the OMB Watcher Online at *http://www.ombwatch.org/ombwatcher/index.html.*

Technical Assistance Organizations

Black Data Processing Associates (BDPA)

9315 Largo Drive West, Suite 275, Largo, MD 20774
Tel: 800-727-BDPA, 301-350-0001; FAX: 301-350-0052
E-mail: nbdpa@ix.netcom.com; WWW: http://www.bdpa.org

▶ Since 1975, BDPA has served as an invaluable conduit between the information technology and African American communities. Through more than 40 local chapters across the country, they offer career counseling, technological assistance, networking opportunities, workshops, computer competitions, and more to students eager to join the information age and IT professionals seeking advancement. They offer extensive educational and executive programs, an annual conference, and online resources. BDPA publishes the *BDPA Journal*. Its Web site provides job listings, *BDPA Journal Online*, Conference Central, and the BDPA Store.

CharityFocus, Inc.

P.O. Box 2711, Santa Clara, CA 95055
Tel: 888-FOCUS-45, 408-247-1830; FAX: 603-506-8384
E-mail: helpers@charityfocus.org;
WWW: http://www.charityfocus.org,
http://www.charityfocus.org/services/resources

▶ CharityFocus is a volunteer-run 501(c)(3) nonprofit organization, started in 1999, to empower nonprofits with Web-based technological solutions. For nonprofits, they provide a complete Web presence for free and there is no catch. Their FAQ lists some of the ways in which nonprofits can benefit. They charge for some of the custom features not to make money but to maintain their focus on helping smaller nonprofits with their basic needs. Main packages include Standard WebPack (this package is completely free. It includes a Web page designed by their technical team, Web hosting of your own virtual domain, e-mail setup, submission to search engines, and can include a host of other goodies like online donations and a shopping mall.); Custom WebPack (this package includes features like messages boards, customized graphics, chat rooms, etc. They charge an hourly fee for this service to maintain their focus on helping smaller nonprofits.); UpdateWeb (for a very nominal cost, they will manage and enhance your Web site, from updating regular schedules to adding new features like an online shop); TechHelp (while geared toward the Internet, they are not limited to it. They can guide you with any/all other technical requests and provide this service without charge.).

CommuniTech

E-mail: commtech@seas.upenn.edu, rossf@seas.upenn.edu;
WWW: http://wtg.wharton.upenn.edu/communitech

▶ Started in January 1999, CommuniTech is a not-for-profit University of Pennsylvania student organization that seeks to provide technical services and solutions to service-based nonprofit organizations at factor cost. Their goal is to help Philadelphian, and particularly West Philadelphian, nonprofits to be technically aware and to reap the rewards of our twenty-first-century technology age. Services include Internet (offer complete services including Web site development, Web site hosting, database-enhanced Web sites, security, and network design); Custom Database and Application Development (can help you determine your specific software application needs and develop a custom solution for your organization. They can develop new database systems or help you leverage existing legacy database systems with graphical user interfaces and Internet technology.); training (can train you and your staff in an array of applications and operating systems. They offer free biweekly group training sessions at the University of Pennsylvania and on-site one-on-one training upon request.); strategy (can help you formulate your organization's technology plan—your response to the rapidly evolving technology arena); and CommuniTech Listserv.

Community Resource Network (CRN)

106 East 31st Terrace, Suite 222, Kansas City, MO 64111
Tel: 816-960-0708; FAX: 816-960-3790
E-mail: services@crn.org; WWW: http://www.crn.org

▶ CRN is Kansas City's cybercenter for nonprofits. It is composed of community development and telecommunications professionals dedicated to helping nonprofits. They provide computer and telecommunication resources to help nonprofits advance their missions by doing business more effectively. Services include Internet access, electronic mail, Web site host, domain name administration, intranet, network administration, IP network address allocation, data file storage, computing application/device collocation, technical design assistance and coordination, affiliate network start-up support, network administration support, integrated connectivity options, and on-site technical support.

Community Technology Centers' Network (CTCNet)

372 Broadway Street, Cambridge, MA 02139
Tel: 781-684-0830, ext. 205
E-mail: ctcnet@edc.org, info@ctcnet.org;
WWW: http://www.ctcnet.org, http://www.ctcnet.org/members.html

▶ Started in 1990, CTCNet, now an independent, nonprofit corporation, was from 1990 through 2000 a project of the Education Development Center. It is a network of more than 400 community technology centers where people get access to computers and computer-related technology, such as the Internet. The 400+ sites are enormously diverse in program areas and participating populations. Some are stand-alone centers; others operate as one part of a larger organization, such as a multiservice agency or museum, job training center, shelter, cable public access center, and the like (see some centers' Web sites and related links). All support equitable access to computers. Its directory of affiliated community technology centers is available at *http://www2.ctcnet.org/ctc.asp*.

CompuMentor

487 Third Street, San Francisco, CA 94107
Tel: 800-659-3579, 415-512-7784; FAX: 415-512-9629
E-mail: realperson@compumentor.org;
WWW: http://www.compumentor.org/

▶ CompuMentor is the largest nonprofit computerization assistance organization in the country. Since 1987, CompuMentor has utilized its consulting staff and volunteer mentors to provide training and support services and low-cost software to more than 6,000 nonprofits and schools across the country. CompuMentor provides a wide range of technology assistance services to schools and nonprofits across the United States, including Mentor Matching Program (computer volunteers work with you to solve problems and move your organization forward); TEAM (TEchnology Assessment and Mentoring) Program (a member of CompuMentor's staff assists small and medium-sized nonprofit organizations with their technology planning); staff-based consulting (CompuMentor's staff provide in-depth consulting on a wide range of technology areas); *Software Redistribution Program* (schools and nonprofits can order some of today's most popular software titles at very reasonable prices). It is a co-sponsor with Handsnet, Wired for Good, and CompassPoint Nonprofit Services of the annual Nonprofits & Technology Conference.

Computers & Technology

22832 Hatchell Road, Tonganoxie, KS 66086
Tel: 913-369-2255; FAX: 913-369-2255
E-mail: chanback@grapevine.net (Cheryl Hanback)

▶ Computers & Technology helps assists nonprofits to develop a Web site or get connected to the Internet, empower their staff's decision making through timely delivery of information, improve staff productivity by automating routine tasks, provide staff and funders with timely performance data, and make decisions about your computer operating systems, hardware, and software.

Fund for the City of New York

121 Avenue of the Americas, New York, NY 10013
Tel: 212-925-6675; FAX: 212-925-5675
E-mail: info@fcny.org, aaltmueller@fcny.org (Alicia Altmueller,
Director of Technology Training and Community Outreach),
tking@fcny.org (Tamica King); WWW: http://www.fcny.org

▶ A private foundation and public charity, the Fund offers computer training and assistance for nonprofits through its Nonprofit Computer Exchange (NCE) and its Internet Academy programs. The Nonprofit Computer Exchange and Internet Academy of the Fund for the City of New York help organizations streamline operations, expand services, and make best use of the latest technology through computer classes, Internet classes, technology seminars and conferences, and technology consulting. The primary NCE programs are consulting services (provide research, planning, needs assessment, database design and development, and network design and configuration; fees are based on the scope of the work) and training (includes regularly scheduled classes that are offered at several levels for a selection of popular computer software and hardware, primarily Windows-based applications. The Internet Academy offers classes in Web-related programs including Beginning and Advanced HTML, Building Your Own Web Site, Java Script, CGI and Perl Scripting, and multimedia and graphics for the Web. Also offered is an introductory class to the World Wide Web for Windows). In 1995, the Fund established the Center for Internet Innovation to help government and nonprofits obtain the benefits of the Internet as well as shape its future.

Geekcorps

87 Marshall Street, Suite 6, North Adams, MA 01247
FAX: 413-664-0032
E-mail: volunteer@geekcorps.org;
WWW: http://www.geekcorps.org/,
http://www.geekcorps.org/dd.html (Digital Divide Resources)

▶ Geekcorps is a nonprofit 501(c)(3) organization committed to expanding the Internet revolution internationally by pairing skilled volunteers from the high-tech world with small businesses in emerging nations. Geekcorps and its partner businesses in emerging nations evaluate technical needs. Then Geekcorps selects volunteers with the expertise to meet those needs. Geekcorps trains its volunteers to teach their skills to people from different backgrounds. Volunteers spend three months on-site in developing nations, supported by Geekcorps' in-country staff. They spend their working hours helping the partner businesses and spend their free time exploring their host country and meeting its people. They also assist partner businesses in finding venture capital from partners throughout the world.

Handsnet

2 North Second Street, Suite 375, San Jose, CA 95113
Tel: 408-291-5111; FAX: 408-291-5119

HandsNet Training & Resource Center, 1990 M Street NW,
Suite 550, Washington, DC 20036
Tel: 202-872-1111; FAX: 202-872-1245
E-mail: hninfo@handsnet.org; WWW: http://www.handsnet.org

▶ HandsNet is a national nonprofit organization headquartered in Silicon Valley. It provides Internet training and interactive online information and communication services to help human service professionals strengthen programs and policy work on behalf of children, families, and people in need. HandsNet offers an innovative online information service, WebClipper, and operates a Training and Resource Center in Washington, DC, where it has developed highly acclaimed Internet curricula and pioneered the practice of customized and mobile training for nonprofits. The HandsNet Web site also offers alerts and calls to actions for and from members of the human service community. It promotes information sharing, cross-sector collaboration, and advocacy among individuals and organizations working on a broad range of public interest issues. For more than a decade, HandsNet has worked to make online collaboration and information sharing a reality for the human services community. It enables organizations to effectively

integrate new online strategies, strengthening their program and policy work on behalf of people in need. Services offered include training (hands-on training classes teach a range of skills, from the basics of using electronic mail to finding and managing Internet resources and publishing on the World Wide Web. Custom group training is provided to organizations wishing to train their staff, volunteers, board members, constituents, or strategic partners); management seminars (introduce senior-level staff to the potential of online technologies, with a focus on practical applications as well as the organizational implications of maintaining an online presence); Strategic Planning Workshops (help managers systematically analyze online solutions within the context of their organization's mission and overall communications plan); conference seminars (provide customized training in conjunction with human services conferences and events throughout the United States); WebClipper (online networking clipping service searches more than 500 Web sites that provide information for social services groups and sends members a daily e-mail message with new information in their fields of interest. It also allows members to conduct Internet searches on social services topics, publish reports online, and contact other members). Further information is available at *http://www.webclipper.org*.

Human Service Information Technology Applications (HUSITA)

E-mail: husita@husita.org; WWW: http://www.husita.org

▶ HUSITA is an international association of information technology (IT) innovators in human services dedicated to promoting the ethical and effective use of IT to better serve humanity. HUSITA's focus and expertise is situated at the intersection of three core domains: information technology, human services, and social development. With an emphasis on human centeredness and social justice, HUSITA strives to promote international knowledge development and dissemination and transfer of technology within human services. It achieves this through multidisciplinary leadership in international conferences, publications, collaboration, and consultation directed particularly at IT applications and innovations that promote social betterment. The interest domain of HUSITA is covered by two journals, each with its own Web site with information on how to subscribe and how to submit and an index to past articles: *New Technology in the Human Services* and *Journal of Technology in the Human Service* (previously Computers in Human Services). An extensive free indexing and abstracting service on information management in human services is available through SWBIB at *http://www.fz.hse.nl/causa/swbib*. It maintains *HUSITA*, a listserv. Discussion lists are available specifically dealing with the application of information technology or information management in human services. HUSTIA holds an annual conference.

iComm

Box 371, 253 College Street, Toronto, Ontario, Canada M5T 1R5
Tel: 416-410-4067
E-mail: icomm@icomm.ca; WWW: http://www.icomm.ca

▶ iComm is a nonprofit, Internet-based organization that exists to help other nonprofit, charitable, and community organizations all over the world by giving them Internet services and volunteer support. They are currently helping about 200 organizations in Canada, the United States, and around the world. iComm is supported by individual and corporate donations of hardware, Internet bandwidth, and money for their operating expenses. They offer Web hosting and e-mail services, including multiple e-mail addresses and mailing lists, and expert technical support. Some of their volunteers may be able to help you design your Web site. The iComm Account Services page offers a complete description of what they provide with each account on their system.

IT Resource Center (Formerly the Information Technology Resource Center)
29 East Madison Street, 16th Floor, Chicago, IL 60602
Tel: 312-372-4872; FAX: 312-372-7962
E-mail: itrc@npo.net, timmg@earthlink.net (Tim Mills-Groninger); WWW: http://itresourcecenter.org/
▶ The IT Resource Center enables nonprofit organizations to achieve their goals through effective use of technology. This mission is accomplished through providing the Center's constituents services in advocacy regarding the importance of technology to nonprofits; planning and implementing technology approaches to nonprofit activities; technology consulting, training, and problem solving for nonprofits; and providing objective information regarding technology as it pertains to nonprofits. Services include training (Web design and development, technology management, the Internet, desktop publishing/presentations, word processing, spreadsheets/accounting, databases, networking); consulting (IT Resource Center staff are experts in nonprofit management and technology. Their consultants provide critical support in areas ranging from Web design to database management to technology planning. Services are available on-site, off-site, or by phone); The CompuMentor/Chicago Project (matches skilled technology volunteers with the IT Resource Center's diverse roster of Chicago-area nonprofits); npo.net (a World Wide Web information service for the Chicago-area nonprofit community; experts located anywhere can collaborate on specific projects as part of their regular workday; available at: *http://npo.net*); and the Nonprofit Mailing List (includes 3,200+ Chicago metropolitan area nonprofit organizations. This joint product of six local technical assistance organizations is managed by the IT Resource Center. The IT Resource Center charges royalties for the use of the list. Executive Director or CEO contact names are available for most entries; the user may specify use of these names or request a slug such as "Director of Development" or "Finance Manager." The List is available on disk or by e-mail.).

Institute for Global Communications (IGC)
Presidio Building 1012, First Floor, Torney Avenue,
P.O. Box 29904, San Francisco, CA 94129-0904
Tel: 415-561-6100; FAX: 415-561-6101
E-mail: support@igc.apc.org (User Support);
WWW: http://www.igc.org
▶ A project of *Tides,* the mission of IGC is to advance the work of progressive organizations and individuals for peace, justice, economic opportunity, human rights, democracy, and environmental sustainability through strategic use of online technologies. IGC Internet is providing Internet access services through MindSpring Enterprises, the Internet service provider. In addition, IGC's e-mail list services are now being posted for free by Topica, Inc., but remain tightly integrated into the IGC Internet online community with e-mail discussions and newsletters. They also provide flexible online collaboration tools and act as a clearinghouse for technological advancements. IGC Internet partners with Idealist/Action Without Borders, Project Change, Entango, Independent Source,

MetaEvents, and Protest.net to bring software solutions for nonprofits' special needs.

InterConnection
P.O. Box 3496, Eugene, OR 97403
Tel: 425-0280-4577
E-mail: info@interconnection.org;
WWW: http://www.interconnection.org
▶ A nonprofit group that donates Web sites and Internet hosting to organizations dedicated to benefiting the local community or environment, InterConnection provides an online presence to community groups and projects in developing countries. Their mission is accomplished by providing the following services: Website Donation Program, Reduced Rate Website Program, World Wide Web Volunteer Program, and Computer Donations. InterConnection provides its services to primarily four groups (community-based tourism, artisans, community activism, and nonprofits). InterConnection encourages environmental stewardship and community development. They support nonprofit organizations and nongovernmental organizations with these common goals. By providing an online venue for these groups, InterConnection expands their visibility and their capacity for obtaining increased financial resources. They target these groups because they receive the most tangible benefits from Internet training and technology.

LINC (Low Income and Communications) Project
Welfare Law Center, 275 Seventh Avenue, Suite 1205,
New York, NY 10001
Tel: 212-633-6967
E-mail: dirk@welfarelaw.org; WWW: http://www.lincproject.org/
▶ The LINC Project is where technology and organizing meet to build power for low-income communities. It is a unique source of information for and about groups of low-income people organizing to confront the shredding of our social safety.

Media Jumpstart
39 Broadway, 10th Floor, New York, NY 10006
Tel: 212-894-3386; FAX: 212-616-4994
E-mail: info@mediajumpstart.org;
WWW: http://www.mediajumpstart.org
▶ Media Jumpstart is a nonprofit organization committed to working closely with New York City's nonprofit community to strengthen the impact of their work through effective use of technology. Their staff members are organizers and activists with a history of working on technology projects for nonprofits. They are dedicated to providing technology resources and information that is appropriate and relevant to organizations of all sizes, particularly those with limited resources. Media Jumpstart is affiliated with Community Resource Exchange, a nonprofit organization that provides management assistance to the diversity of nonprofit groups serving the poor and disenfranchised. Services include technology and communications planning, database design, and Web design.

The Morino Institute
11600 Sunrise Valley Drive, Suite 300, Reston, VA 20191
Tel: 703-620-8971; FAX: 703-620-4102
E-mail: info@morino.org, feedback@morino.org,
mmorino@morino.org (Mario Morino, Chairman);
WWW: http://www.morino.org

▶ The Morino Institute is a nonprofit organization dedicated to empowering people and communities to achieve positive social and economic change through the use of the Internet. The Institute focuses its energies on netpreneurs, who are creating new Internet-related business and are the drivers of the New Economy, and youth in low-income communities who at present lack the opportunity to fully participate in the New Economy. The Institute is both catalyst and facilitator to help individuals, institutions, and communities understand the opportunities and risks presented by the Internet. It supports and collaborates with other organizations to enhance their own effectiveness. It also incubates and launches new initiatives.

New Deal Foundation

20 Holland Street, 4th Floor, Somerville, MA 02144
Tel: 617-625-6180; FAX: 800-310-6180
E-mail: kavita@ndfound.org; WWW: http://www.newdeal.org/

▶ This foundation provides royalty-free donations of New Deal software to educational, nonprofit, community, and religious organizations. Its mission is to promote computer literacy and Internet access for all, through wise use of existing technology, co-sponsorship of pilot programs that lead the way; and research and advocacy of technology access issues. New Deal Foundation works closely with nonprofit and community-based organizations, as well as traditional and nontraditional educational organizations, to develop high-impact technology access programs. One pilot program of interest to nonprofits is Project @ccess, a nonprofit alliance to extend computer and Internet access through government and corporate PC donations.

Non-Profit Computing, Inc. (NPC)

125 East 63rd Street, New York, NY 10021-7302
Tel: 212-759-2368; FAX: 212-793-5723
E-mail: german63@hotmail.com (John German, Founder and Director); WWW: http://www.geocities.com/SiliconValley/Peaks/2126/

▶ Founded in 1985, NPC is a New York State–chartered nonprofit management assistance provider to nonprofit organizations, educational institutions, and government agencies. NPC's mission is to help such entities become more effective and self-sufficient through appropriate governance, direction, management, and use of technology. It works to coordinate nonprofit management and technology assistance providers locally, regionally, and nationally, identifying and disseminating best practices, and to foster, nurture, and support collaboration with potential institutional partners. It provides pro bono computer, telecommunications and new media volunteers, and arranges in-kind donations of computers across the United States and as far away as Mongolia. It arranges donations of goods and services to nonprofit organizations, educational institutions, and government agencies, including computers, software, printers, scanners, modems, other peripherals, cables, accessories, and supplies; network and Internet servers, software, cards, hubs, routers, and wiring; handheld electronic devices, PDAs (personal digital assistants), electronic organizers, and software; audiovisual equipment, TV/film/radio/recording studio, and broadcasting equipment; cell phones, answering machines, fax machines, and telephone systems; calculators, typewriters, photocopiers, other office equipment, cubicles, and furniture; medical equipment, warehouse equipment, and vehicles; and real estate, financial, and other assets. Items that cannot be placed for reuse, are refurbished, upgraded, mined for parts, or recycled. One of NPC's current major programs is the donation of computer labs (learning and access

facilities) primarily to community centers located in public schools, to support disadvantaged communities and community organizations as well as the schools themselves. NPC increasingly convenes, develops, and advises community development and support projects that implement computing and telecommunications technology in support of people, family, neighborhood, and community, with emphasis on providing access for the disadvantaged. The Career Development Group for computer and telecommunications professionals, a job networking group that operates as a division of NPC, helps employers and search firms find candidates, arranges internships and apprenticeships, and refers candidates to education, training, and support.

Nonprofit Tech Association

40 Benton Avenue, San Francisco, CA 94112-1104
Tel: 415-337-7412; FAX: 415-337-7927
E-mail: help@nonprofit-tech.org, alnisa@nonprofit-tech.org (Alnisa Allgood, Executive Director); WWW: http://www.nonprofit-tech.org

▶ One of the new breed of nonprofit social entrepreneurs, Nonprofit Tech was designed to work with the nonprofit sector to increase organizational effectiveness. Its mission is to inform, educate, and support and advocate for nonprofits in their efforts to implement and use technology. Its purpose is to make nonprofits more responsive and capable in providing life-critical services. Its goals are to enhance the adaptive capacity of nonprofits to create learning organizations, to harness organizational knowledge using technology, to revitalize missions, instruct providers, strengthen organizational infrastructure, and expand intra- and inter-agency collaboration and communication efforts. Services include user support and training, computer maintenance, technical support, user training, systems management, network administration, systems administration, information management, database development, data mining, presentations and publications, slides and presentation, print and web publishing, Internet and electronic, web planning and coding, electronic distribution. Features on their Web site include The Tech Library for Nonprofits (find research, articles, and reviews on technology for the nonprofit sector; browse their learning series that provides step-by-step how's and why's on a variety of topics at *http://www.tech-library.org*); The Tech Forum (a meeting place for individuals interested in nonprofits and technology. Individuals can schedule chats, participate in hosted chats, post resources, questions, and more at *http://forums.delphi.com/nonprofittech*); The Tech eGroup (allows you to sign up to receive regular notification of new articles, announcements, projects, and other information from Nonprofit Tech); *Nonprofit-TechWorld* (*http://www.nonprofit-techworld.org*); and Nonprofit Techworld's Tech TALKS (provides an array of new forums to the nonprofit sector located at *http://techtalk.infopop.net*).

Nonprofit Technology Enterprise Network (NTEN)

E-mail: mcg@halcyon.com (Michael Gilbert, President of the NTEN Founding Board of Directors); WWW: http://www.nten.org

▶ The NonProfit Technology Enterprise Network (NTEN) is a leadership network of nonprofit staff members, funders, and technology assistance providers working together to analyze and support the technology needs of the nonprofit sector. It is dedicated to connecting and supporting individuals and organizations that empower nonprofits to use technology to achieve their missions. NTEN was developed in response to the feedback and discussion generated by the National Strategy for Non Profit Technology

(NSNT). NSNT was an 18-month analysis of the nonprofit sector's technology needs, and from it came a blueprint of how the sector could use technology more effectively and efficiently. NSNT involved front-line technology assistance providers, interested funders, and nonprofit organizations.

NTEN will work for a world where all nonprofits, regardless of size, can skillfully and confidently use information technology to meet community needs. In pursuit of this vision, NTEN will make its mission to support and serve the diverse people and organizations that help nonprofits understand and employ technology effectively. NTEN will be an association made up of members from the following stakeholder groups: (1) individuals and organizations who provide nonprofits with technology assistance; (2) members of the philanthropic community with an interest in the effective use of technology; and (3) nonprofits whose approach to technology is self-help.

NTEN will serve its membership through five interrelated roles: Meetinghouse (where those delivering nonprofit technology assistance can find peers, share know-how, and form collaborative enterprises); Clearinghouse of knowledge and tools for nonprofit technology assistance; Incubator of new technology assistance organizations, programs, and projects; Rainmaker, who mobilizes new resources to advance nonprofit's technology capacity; Think Tank (scanning the horizon for new technology developments, analyzing their potential applications, and communicating these to members). Subscribe to the NTEN listserv at *http://www.egroups.com/group/nten.*

Nonprofit Technology Resources

1508 Brandywine Street, Philadelphia, PA 19130
Tel: 215-564-6686
E-mail: pokras@libertynet.org; WWW: http://www.libertynet.org/ntr
▶ NTR provides computer consulting, hands-on training, used computer hardware, and technical support to over 200 nonprofit organizations annually in the Greater Philadelphia region. They are the only computer consulting and training organization in the area devoted exclusively to nonprofit organizations and the people they serve. Services include consulting (can help with accounting systems, fund-raising systems, client service records, budget planning tools, mailing lists; merged mailings, and print and data communications); training (over 40 class titles are available for staff of your organization); computer donations (accepts the donation of used "486" (or better) computers, VGA monitors, small dot-matrix printers, ink-jet and laser printers, and other computer accessories); computer reuse (its Computer Adoption Program distributes donated computers to community organizations; the Learning Through Technology program serves low-income people through their community groups, churches, and schools); technical support (offers on-site technical support for your staff. They support most common software on DOS, Windows 3.1, 95, and 98, and Macintosh computers. They can help set up your office network, but do not provide electrical wiring services.).

NPInfotech.org

P.O. Box 582, Ambler, PA 19002-0582
Tel: 215-205-9254; FAX: 707-202-3344
E-mail: info@npinfotech.org, kleintop@npinfotech.org (Bill Kleintop, President/CEO); WWW: http://www.npinfotech.org/, http://www.npinfotech.org/TNOPSI/updates/news02.htm

▶ NPInfotech.org is an incorporated nonprofit organization with the mission of bringing together nonprofit organizations and providers of information technology services and products to better the ability of nonprofit organizations to achieve their goals and objectives. They meet their mission by matching information service providers with nonprofits, conducting educational seminars about information technology and related topics, operating *The Nonprofit Software Index,* and providing information about information technology, computer software, and the Internet to nonprofit organizations through a variety of media. NPInfotech.org provides an online newsletter.

NPower

The Nickerson Marina Building, 1080 West Ewing Place, Suite 300, Seattle, WA 98119
Tel: 206-286-8880; FAX: 206-286-8881
E-mail: People@NPower.org, Joan@NPower.org (Joan Fanning, Executive Director); WWW: http://www.npower.org
▶ NPower's mission is helping nonprofits use technology to better serve their communities. At present, NPower focuses on nonprofits around Seattle and Puget Sound. Through a new partnership, they will also be assisting other communities around the United States to develop their own independent NPower programs or organizations. The services of an NPower reflect a particular community's unmet needs. For nonprofits in the Puget Sound region, their services include assessment and planning (can help you assess your organization's technology status quo, and make plans for moving forward); hands-on assistance (can lend hands-on tech help, like wiring a computer network, designing a database, or launching a Web site); skills-building classes (offer technology training classes on everything from basic word processing, to graphing with spreadsheets, to constructing a database, to administering an intranet); technology libraries (print and online resources to build your technology know-how and confidence); technology volunteers (provide a matchmaking service that finds skilled community volunteers to pitch in on critical short-duration technology projects); and consulting (offer a wide variety of consulting services, including planning, budgeting, networks, databases, Web sites, pre-scheduled support (available to NPower members).

Organizers' Collaborative

Box 400897, Cambridge, MA 02140
Tel: 617-776-6176
E-mail: org-c@organizenow.net (Rich Cowan);
WWW: http://www.organizenow.net/,
http://www.organizenow.net/techtips/index.html
▶ Organizers' Collaborative is a nonprofit group harnessing the collaborative potential of the Internet and working to make computers accessible as a tool in support of community-based social change organizing. Organizers' Collaborative was established in 1999 to help nonprofit and activist groups all over the United States more effectively use computers and the Internet to achieve social change. They do this by collecting, classifying, and disseminating information about grassroots uses of technology; developing, testing, and distributing at no charge software that is easy to use and widely applicable to social change organizations; providing online methods of collaboration and resource sharing for organizers; and providing occasional technical assistance to selected groups. Its work is divided into three areas: creating Web sites to promote

social change networking and resource sharing; studying the impact of the Internet on social justice efforts; and developing software tools and printed "how-to" resources (through the TechTips section of their Web site [http://www.organizenow.net/techtips/index.html] and through their listserv, which you can join through their home page [http://www.organizenow.net/home.html]. They are available to do work for a modest fee for small to medium-sized nonprofits, particularly in the areas of membership databases, setting up computers for desktop publishing or financial accounting, and forming a new nonprofit group.

Progressive Technology Project (PTP)

1436 U Street NW, Suite 201, Washington, DC 20009
Tel: 202-387-9660; FAX: 202-387-1852
E-mail: info@progressivetech.org;
WWW: http://www.progressivetech.org,
http://www.progressivetech.org/Resources/index.htm

▶ Progressive Technology Project (PTP) is a collaboration that seeks to raise the scope and scale of technology resources available to grassroots organizing groups working for environmental, economic, and social justice. PTP provides technical assistance and makes grants to develop the capacity of grassroots organizing groups to use information technology to strengthen their social change efforts. PTP's goals include building the capacity of grassroots groups to sustain new technology skills that advance their ability to improve the quality of people's lives; exploring, creating and sharing models of technology use that increase the organization's power and effectiveness by adding value to grassroots organizing; developing a program of technical assistance to address the unique needs that grassroots organizations face in their use of technology; leveraging resources to support the use of information technologies by grassroots organizations; and creating a place for strategic discussions about the relationship between grassroots organizing and technology.

TEAMing for TECHnology

Mailing address: c/o Triangle United Way, P.O. Box 14428, Research Triangle Park, NC 27709

Street address: 1100 Perimeter Park West, Suite 112, Morrisville, NC 27560
Tel: 919-460-8687; FAX: 919-460-9019
E-mail: KJones@unitedwaytriangle.org (Kamira T. Jones, Webmaster); WWW: http://comnet.org/acconf/,
http://teamtech.home.mindspring.com/,
http://teamtech.home.mindspring.com/links.html

▶ TEAMing for TECHnology is a collaborative effort on the parts of Americorps*VISTA, IBM, and United Way of America to help nonprofits in 17 cities across the country bridge the digital divide. In each city, there are three to eight VISTA volunteers housed in a United Way facility with funding provided by IBM. The Teams are working diligently to implement a plan that will enhance technology for the interested nonprofits in their area. The TEAMing for TECHnology initiative is designed to encourage strong leadership and technological skills among nonprofit organizations in an effort to help them enhance delivery of services and improve office efficiency. TEAMing for TECHnology's focus includes volunteer matching, consulting services, and aquisition of hardware and software, while emphasizing the need for long-term technology planning and self-sufficiency. Their mission is to assist nonprofits in

developing and maintaining technological competency in the administration and delivery of services, create a permanent community-supported technical service to the nonprofit community, and increase the ability of the low-income community to access the Internet.

TeamTech San Francisco

50 California Street, Suite 200, San Francisco, CA 94111-4696
Tel: 415-772-4486; FAX: 415-391-8302
E-mail: t2sf@hotmail.com, larry.best@ncccsf.org (Larry Best, Project Supervisor; WWW: http://www.ncccsf.org/teamtech/ home.html, http://www.ncccsf.org/teamtech/resources.html

▶ Its mission is to assist nonprofits in effectively using technology to increase the impact of their work in the low-income communities they serve. Services include technology assessments, technology planning, IBM hardware donation, technical training, resource referrals, and volunteer matching. TeamTech is a collaborative effort on the parts of Americorps*VISTA, IBM, and United Way of America, as a response to America's Promise to bring nonprofits in 11 cities across the country up to date technologically. In each city, AmeriCorps*VISTA members work through the local United Way and its affiliates with technology funding from IBM, to implement a plan that will enhance technology for selected community-based organizations in their area. TeamTech San Francisco has joined with the Northern California Council for the Community, through the United Way, to strengthen the capacity of CBOs to provide services throughout the Bay Area. They collaborate with San Francisco State University's Office of Community Service Learning and SFSU College of Extended Learning's Multimedia Studies Program to create commercial-quality Web sites for Bay Area nonprofits. Its Techportal lets you look up technology resources for nonprofits and the community. Topics covered include volunteer recruitment, discounted hardware and software, computer recycling, computer technology centers, Web resources, and more. The bimonthly *TeamTech News* newsletter is available online in PDF format.

Tech Corps

Two Clock Tower Place, Suite 230, Maynard, MA 01754
Tel: 978-897-8282, 978-897-2241 (Karen Smith, Executive Director); FAX: 978-897-4204
E-mail: info@techcorps.org, ksmith@techcorps.org (Karen Smith, Executive Director); WWW: http://www.techcorps.org, http://www.techcorps.org/resources/index.html

▶ The mission of Tech Corps is threefold: recruit, place, and support volunteers from the technology community who assist schools with the introduction and use of new technologies; bring additional technology resources to schools and communities through local and national projects; and build partnerships in support of educational technology among educators, businesses, and community members at the local, state, and national levels. Tech Corps is a national nonprofit organization that is funded through corporate contributions and implemented through state chapters. A national staff oversees the Tech Corps mission and agenda, assists in the formation and maintenance of effective state chapters, provides a national media focus, and ensures quality at all levels. The broader organization is based on a bottom-up philosophy and draws on the expertise and enthusiasm of technology-literate members of the local community.

TechFoundation

20 University Road, Cambridge, MA 02138
Tel: 617-234-2141; FAX: 617-234-2121
E-mail: info@techfoundation.org, finn@techfoundation.org
(Deborah Finn, Nonprofit Liaison Officer),
altshuler@techfoundation.org (David Altshuler, Executive
Director); WWW: http://www.techfoundation.org

▶ TechFoundation was founded in 2000 to make the world a better place by bringing state-of-the-art technology and resources to the nonprofit sector. Their management and staff have decades of experience in the intersecting areas of technology, philanthropy, and nonprofit management. Their vision is to revolutionize the way nonprofits achieve their mission through the power of technology. They create opportunities to manifest this vision through partnerships with venture capitalists, corporations, foundations, and nonprofit technology providers—bringing social investment and vision to meet the needs of nonprofits across the sector. They are committed to effective use of technology with real impact and a demonstrated return on social investment. TechFoundation also maintains offices in New York, Seattle, and Washington, DC.

The Technology Resource Consortium (TRC)

c/o Information Technology Resource Center,
29 East Madison Street, 16th Floor, Chicago, IL 60602
Tel: 312-372-4872; FAX: 312-372-7962
E-mail: timmg@earthlink.net (Tim Mills-Groninger);
WWW: http://www.npo.net/itrc/

▶ The Technology Resource Consortium is an association of nonprofit technology assistance organizations that provide education about and access to information technology to private and public nonprofit organizations. The TRC is an affinity group of the National Alliance for Nonprofit Management. TRC's mission is to enhance the ability of its members to support the effective use of information technology by nonprofit organizations and government agencies; promote collaboration among its members, and encourage the formation of new technology assistance provider organizations and provision of services, particularly in unserved and underserved areas.

Technology Works for Good

1436 U Street NW, Suite 303, Washington, DC 20009
Tel: 202-234-9670; FAX: 800-848-5110, 202-234-9672
E-mail: info@technologyworks.org;
WWW: http://www.technologyworks.org

▶ Technology Works for Good is to form an infrastructure to help Washington-area community-based organizations become savvy users of modern technology in ways that strategically support their individual missions. Their approach is threefold: (1) public/private partnerships: partnering with for-profit technology providers to make solutions more affordable and more effective for nonprofits; (2) educating and informing nonprofit leaders: providing up-to-date information, training, executive education, and technical support to nonprofit leaders; (3) providing direct nonprofit technology consulting: "Circuit Riders," roving staff who are funded to work with specific organizations in specific issue areas, help organizations develop plans to increase their organizational effectiveness through the use of technology.

TechRocks (Formerly the Technology Project)

One Penn Center, 1617 John F. Kennedy Boulevard,
Philadelphia, PA 19103
E-mail: info@techrocks.org; WWW: http://www.techrocks.org

38 South Last Chance Gulch, Suite 2A, Helena, MT 59601
FAX: 208-361-0149
E-mail: marshall@techrocks.org (Marshall Mayer, Principal)

▶ TechRocks (formerly the Technology Project) is a result of the merger in 1999 of the Rockefeller Technology Project and Desktop Assistance. TechRocks is dedicated to accelerating social and political progress by building technological capacity for community collaboration and citizen engagement. TechRocks encourages and enables foundations, advocacy groups, and leading activists to use technology to achieve their goals, to increase participation from interested constituencies, and achieve change more quickly than by traditional organizing and advocacy methods alone. TechRocks programs are targeted at a growing national market of citizen-based nonprofits, especially nonprofits with budgets under $1 million. They serve a market underserved by industry, and provide accessible services translated specifically for a nonprofit context. Programs and products offered include ebase (gives nonprofits a sophisticated and cost-effective system to manage information about their supporters, including their transaction profiles. More than 10,000 organizations have downloaded ebase, and use it to strengthen their organization through increased revenues and volunteer involvement); eriders (TechRocks's field staff provide nonprofits the education, training, and on-site assistance they need to effectively use these tools. eRiders have helped hundreds of nonprofits and foundations learn about information technology and how it can be integrated to accelerate their mission); estrategies (provides leadership to the field of nonprofit technology assistance). TechRocks spearheaded the National Technology Enterprise Network (NTEN), sponsors the yearly Circuit Rider's Round-up, and incubated TechnologyWorks, a new technology assistance organization in Washington, DC. TechRocks promotes strategic networks of foundations, private-sector companies, technology providers, and nonprofit groups.

TechRocks is creating an Internet-based platform for effective citizen engagement through constituency outreach and profiling technologies. At the same time, TechRocks is developing a series of related and sustainable service infrastructures to support and scale advanced technology adoption within the nonprofit sector.

Telecommunications Cooperative Network (TCN)

20 University Road, 4th Floor, Cambridge, MA 02138
Tel: 877-400-5594, 800-669-4826 (Customer Service);
FAX: 800-214-0351
E-mail: info@tcn.org; WWW: http://www.tcn.org/

▶ Since 1980, TCN has specialized in helping the nonprofit community—providing thousands of charitable organizations with high-quality, affordable telecommunications services. TCN offers a wide variety of voice and data services, including long distance service (switched and dedicated), toll-free numbers, calling cards, conference calling, cellular, and DSL. TCN offers a comprehensive affinity program for organizations that would like to promote TCN services to their members /chapters/affiliates. TCN can customize an affinity program to meet the specific needs of your constituency. TCN's residential program allows individuals to take advantage of the same affordable services that organizations are using. TCN also has offices in Washington, DC, New York City, and Montgomery, Alabama.

Web Lab

155 Avenue of the Americas, 14th Floor, New York, NY 10013
Tel: 212-563-9251; FAX: 212-563-9271
E-mail: lkertz@weblab.org, ellen@weblab.org;
WWW: http://www.weblab.org/home.html,
http://www.weblab.org/about/resources.html

▶ Founded in 1997 by Marc Weiss, the creator of the public television series *P.O.V.*, a program of the New York Foundation for the Arts, it is a nonprofit that encourages and supports innovation on the Web, with a special emphasis on developing the potential of the medium to bring people together to explore both personal and public issues in powerful, transforming ways. It was created on the premise that the Web can be more than an efficient place to find and buy commercial products or to access information on any topic under the sun. It is also an extremely powerful communications medium that provides unprecedented opportunities for people with diverse backgrounds and experiences to connect with, and learn from, each other. One of Web Lab's first projects is the Web Development Fund (WDF), which provides funding and support services for innovative sites proposed by independent producers. It also created a Web Development Fund Partnership Program that will allow a range of organizations—from foundations to technology companies to nonprofits—to support innovative and unique special projects on the Web.

COMPUTER DONATIONS & RECYCLING/REUSE SOURCES

(See also Internet Resources for Online Databases)

Individual Donation and Recycling Programs

(For more comprehensive listings see Internet Resources–Computer Donations and Recycling/Reuse Online Databases)

American Computer Exchange

385 River Valley Road, Atlanta, GA 30328
Tel: 800-786-0717, 404-250-0050; FAX: 404-252-4265
E-mail: broker@amcoex.com; WWW: http://www.amcoex.com/

▶ Since 1988, the American Computer Exchange has brokered tens of thousands of used microcomputers worldwide. Sellers with quantities (five or more) list equipment for sale on their database. When buyers call, they locate what they need and charge the seller a 10 percent to 15 percent commission. To protect both the buyer and the seller, the buyer sends money for their purchase to them. They deposit the money in an escrow account. They hold the buyer's money for two business days after they receive the equipment. This two-day period constitutes an operational warranty: The buyer cannot change his or her mind, but if anything is missing or malfunctioning, the seller must rectify the situation. It is the seller's option to resolve the problem or take the equipment back and the buyer receives a refund.

AnotheR BytE, Inc.

c/o Gary Lagoy, 355 South Groseta Drive, Camp Verde, AZ 86322
E-mail: public@recycles.org; WWW: http://www.recycles.org, http://www.recycles.org/byte/others/index.htm

▶ AnotheR BytE has been recycling older computers from across America since 1994, providing low- and no-cost computers, computer instruction, and technical services to organizations and individuals in need. The groups have a regional focus within the Four Corner states and upon Indian reservations, but also arranges direct donations worldwide from donor to recipient. Requests for services can be made directly from their Web site, which is also host to a Non-Profit Computer Recycling eMail Discussion List.

Computer Bank Charity

15062-B 15th Avenue NE, Seattle, WA 98155
Tel: 206-365-4657, 206-631-0894
E-mail: compubank@seanet.com

▶ Computer Bank Charity's Computer Distribution Program accepts donations of computers and peripheral equipment that are in good working condition (will accept some broken machines). Donated computers are placed with individuals who have exceptional needs or with small nonprofit agencies.

Computer Reclamation

Monmouth Wire & Computer Recycling, Inc., 3230 Shafto Road, Tinton Falls, NJ 07724
Bill Lloyd, Technical Director
Tel and FAX: 732-922-3320; FAX: 973-597-0171
E-mail: amweintraub@computerreclamation.com, salmassaro@computerreclamation.com (Salvatore Massaro, President and CEO); WWW: www.ComputerReclamation.com

Computer Reclamation, Inc.

912 Thayer Avenue, Suite 210, Silver Spring, MD 20910
Tel: 301-495-0280
E-mail: 74463.3466@CompuServe.com (Contact: Michael Wiggins)

▶ A 501(c)(3) organization that obtains surplus computers from business and government sources. These computers are then fully refurbished and made available to schools and nonprofit organizations for a nominal cost. Computer Reclamation also builds new Pentium-class computers at greatly reduced prices. Multimedia-capable systems are available for well under $1,000, and many times in the $500 to $700 range, depending on the installed features. The computers are built and refurbished by certified repair technicians trained at their facilities. Computer Reclamation provides low-cost and reduced-cost training to individuals, preparing them to take the A+ PC Repair Technician certification exam, and then Computer Reclamation helps to place these individuals in jobs throughout the Washington, DC area.

The Computer Recycling Corporation/Computers & Education

1245 Terra Bella Avenue, Mountain View, CA
Tel: 415-428-3700; FAX: 415-428-3701

2971 Mead Avenue, Santa Clara, CA 95051
Tel: 408-327-1800; FAX: 408-327-180
E-mail: info@crc.org; WWW: http://www.crc.org

▶ Computers and Education has an effective computer reuse program. They loan newly built computers for free to public schools and nonprofit community programs. They partner with government and nonprofit programs working to bridge the "digital divide," and provide low-cost computer systems and parts to the public. Their volunteer program lets technical and non-technical individuals work in a friendly environment. They test computer equipment to recycle bad product and keep it out of the landfill, and to refurbish usable product giving it a second, third, even fourth life to benefit the community. Drop-off centers are in Santa Clara, Santa Rosa, San Francisco, and the Palm Springs/Indio area.

Computer Recycling Center

Carnegie Mellon University, Cyert Hall, Room B-25, Pittsburgh, PA 15213
Tel: 412-268-8609; FAX: 412-268-8192
E-mail: retread@andrew.cmu.edu

Computer Recycling Project

1041-A Regent Street, Alameda, CA 94501
Tel: 510-523-2858, 415-342-2244
E-mail: dale@wco.com (Dale Tersey, Director),
lstnspac@lodinet.com (Richard Blackston);
WWW: http://www.wco.com/~dale/crp.html,
http://www.wco.com/~dale/list.html

▶ Computer Recycling Project is a nonprofit clearinghouse for older computers to go to education and nonprofit programs to further computer literacy. It was established as a California nonprofit corporation to collect surplus computers and funnel them off to nonprofits and educational programs that wouldn't otherwise have computer resources available to them.

Computer Recycling Project

Center for Creative Activities, 635 North 5th Street,
Philadelphia, PA 19123
Tel: 215-923-7635; FAX: 215-829-8954
E-mail: cca@libertynet.org, charles.greens@juno.com (Charles Sherrouse, Coordinator);
WWW: http://www.libertynet.org/cca/about.html

▶ CCA is refurbishing donated computers and components to be donated to underfunded nonprofit and not-for-profit organizations in order to improve their efficiency and to establish electronic communications and networking.

Computers 4 Kids Foundation

Danielle J. Washington, President, P.O. Box 1562, Upland, CA 91784
Tel/FAX: 909-395-0202

150 Brookside Road, Waterbury, CT 06708
Tel: 203-754-5560; FAX: 203-756-6312
E-mail: info@computers4kidsinc.org;
WWW: http://www.computers4kidsinc.org/

▶ The foundation that makes a difference by enhancing the educational development of children at risk in Southern California, Computers 4 Kids Foundation is a nonprofit, tax-exempt agency registered under IRS Section Code 501(c)(3). Its mission is to advance the educational interest of economically disenfranchised children by granting them ownership of Internet-ready PC systems, delivered and installed at their home, free of charge. In addition, user training is given on a one instructor for one student ratio, during the first month after delivery of the equipment, and longer if required. Computers 4 Kids Foundation's unique programs bring connection and self-expression to children long too isolated from

the world of equal opportunity. Computers 4 Kids Foundation focuses on children attending grades K through 12, whose parents are unable to buy them a PC system for home study. Intellectual merit and scholastic achievement are the main criteria used in selecting the most deserving students to receive donated equipment. Computers 4 Kids Foundation serves the local geographic region better known as the Inland Empire in Southern California, including 11 cities contiguously located within Los Angeles and San Bernardino counties. Of greatest concern are residential areas where larger concentrations of low-income families are on social welfare programs, and qualify for other forms of government subsidies.

Computers for Schools Program

Detwiler Foundation, 3642 North Springfield Street,
Chicago, IL 60618
Tel: 800-939-6000; FAX: 773-583-7585
E-mail: pcsforschools@aol.com, comp4sch@aol.com;
WWW: http://www.detwiler.org/cfs.html,
http://www.detwiler.org/national.html

▶ The Computers for Schools Association is a nonprofit organization founded in September 1991 by John, Carolyn, and Diana Detwiler. The Computers for Schools Program has program activity nationwide and, in some states, is the largest source of computer equipment for K through 12 schools. The program is established to provide schools with computers needed to enhance instruction and to meet the needs of employers for qualified workers; facilitate the donation of equipment that could be better utilized in schools, and to help businesses establish ongoing donation programs; provide equipment to train students in vocational computer repair; and dramatically improve the quality of computers in schools.

Detwiler Foundation (*See Computers for Schools Program*)

East–West Development Foundation

504 Dudley Street, Roxbury, MA 02119
Tel: 617-442-7448; FAX: 617-442-7228
E-mail: ewf@eastwest.org, sales@eastwest.org;
WWW: http://www.eastwest.org/home.html

▶ Since 1990, East–West Foundation (EWF) has provided nearly 11,000 remanufactured computers to nonprofits and schools around the world. EWF bridges the gap between businesses seeking a convenient way to donate their surplus equipment and budget-strapped organizations seeking the technology that will make them successful into the twenty-first century. EWF provides low-cost, high-quality technology that enhances programs and management practices of nonprofit and educational organizations. With computers, nonprofits can improve operations such as fund raising, record keeping, financial management, client services, and communication. Schools can put more computers in classrooms, increasing student access to interactive learning and the Internet. EWF works with each recipient to select equipment appropriate to its needs *and* provides required follow-up. EWF guarantees every one of its remanufactured computers with a warranty. EWF accepts computer donations from companies and individual donors and provides a receipt for these tax-deductible contributions. At its warehouse, usable equipment is remanufactured into the technology that will ultimately reach a nonprofit or school. Unusable equipment is recycled in accordance with EPA guidelines. EWF's operations employ a core of 14 full-time staff and four part-time disabled individuals from Boston's Community Work Services. EWF also provides intensive training opportunities for area students interested in technology and recycling.

Educational Assistance Limited

P.O. Box 3021, Glen Ellyn, IL 60138
Tel: 630-690-0010; FAX: 630-690-0565
E-mail: scholar@eduassist.org (Claudia Mancini, Executive Director)

▶ Educational Assistance Limited accepts donations of new and used excess inventory, including computers, software, office equipment, maintenance equipment, cleaning supplies, furniture, and more from corporations and individuals worldwide. Their priority is to exchange these goods for scholarships within a national network of accredited colleges and universities.

Educational Technology & Conservation Exchange Program (ETCEP)

FundingFactory.com, 108 West Franklin Avenue, Suite I-8, Pennington, NJ 08534
Tel: 888-883-8237, 609-730-1300; FAX: 609-730-1772
E-mail: info@fundingfactory.com; WWW: http://www.etcep.com/

▶ Each and every day, individuals and businesses are recycling thousands of empty laser and inkjet cartridges. With the ETCEP Program, participating schools are collecting these empty cartridges from their communities. The collected cartridges earn points, which are then exchanged for free classroom technology products. Choose from over 5,000 technology products for your school, all available free of charge through the FundingFactory's extensive *Online Product Catalog.*

Free Bytes NP, Inc.

P.O. Box 550371, Atlanta, GA 30355-0371
Tel: 404-846-8414; FAX: 501-421-7903
E-mail: freebytes@mindspring.com (Charles F. Shufeldt, Executive Director); WWW: http://www.freebytes.org/

▶ Its mission is to make computer equipment available to educational and charitable organizations, through the acceptance of donated computer equipment that corporations and individuals have found no longer useful for their purposes. Using volunteer labor including high school students and youth groups, they will rehabilitate equipment, create usable systems, and place systems with organizations that could not otherwise obtain such equipment in the commercial marketplace.

Goodwill Computer Recycling Center

Tel: 412-481-9005, ext. 353
E-mail:crc@goodwillpitt.org;
WWW: http://www.goodwillpitt.org/crc/crc.htm

▶ Operating as a business unit of Goodwill Industries, the Computer Recycling Center solicits donations of PCs and related equipment from corporations, small businesses, educational institutions, health care facilities, government agencies, and individuals. Using these donations as "raw material," they utilize a combination of volunteers, Goodwill clients/consumers, and paid staff to test the donated equipment, refurbish what is usable, and disassemble the nonfunctioning computers for recycling. The final phase of the CRC operation is selling refurbished computers to the public and to nonprofit groups.

Goodwill's Computer Recycling Center

300 East Lea Boulevard, Wilmington, DE 19802
Tel: 302-761-4644, ext. 249; FAX: 302-761-9868
E-mail JZeiglergw@aol.com;
WWW: http://www.goodwill.org/localweb/delaware/dewilm15.htm

▶ This program helps the local community in the following ways: tests donated equipment, refurbishes usable equipment; trains people with disabilities and other barriers to employment for jobs as computer-repair technicians; prepares a computer-literate workforce for the marketplace; supports the accessibility of computers for individuals who have a disability or who are disadvantaged; helps corporations and individuals dispose of outdated computer equipment responsibly and with minimum impact on the environment; sells refurbished computers and parts at low cost; and supplies computer repair technicians and computer dealers with used parts and accessories through our wholesale business.

Interconnection's Computer Recycling Center

InterConnection, Charles Brennick, 2015 North Machias Road, Lake Stevens, WA
Tel: 425-280-4577

P.O. Box 3496, Eugene, OR 97401
E-mail: info@interconnection.org, brennick@interconnection.org (Charles Brennick) truett@interconnection.org (Jed Truett); WWW: http://www.interconnection.org/support/computers.htm

▶ They accept computer hardware, computer-related books, and software from individuals and companies and place computers at community centers around the globe.

Lazarus Foundation

10378 Eclipse Way, Columbia, MD 21044
Tel: 410-740-0735, 410-531-8485 (Don Bard), 410-997-5924 (Larry Medoff); FAX: 410-381-4762
E-mail: lazaruspc@aol.com (Don Bard), videogrape@home.com (Larry Medoff); WWW: http://www.lazarus.org/

▶ The Lazarus Foundation is a nonprofit, charitable organization, ruled tax-exempt by the Internal Revenue Service under IRC 501(c)(3). They accept tax-deductible donations of your surplus computer equipment. Volunteers test and restore them to working condition and install donated software. They distribute the recycled computers to other charitable organizations and educational institutions.

Learning and Information Networking for Community via Technology (LINCT Coalition) EPIE Institute

Tel: 516-728-9100; FAX: 516-728 9228
E-mail: info@linct.org, Komoski@EPIE.ORG (Kenneth Komoski, Executive Director); WWW: http://www.linct.org/

▶ This organization refurbishes/recycles donated legacy computers that are learned and earned as "green PCs" (kept out of landfills).

Lotus Development Corporation

The Philanthropy Software Donation Program, 55 Cambridge Parkway, Cambridge, MA 02142
Tel: 617-693-1667
WWW: http://www.lotus.com/home.nsf/rightframe/1philanthropy

▶ Lotus's Product Donations Program focuses on organizations working in K through 12 education reform, workforce development, and global workforce diversity, with donations also available for technology enhancements for the not-for-profit sector.

Mindscape (Formerly Software Toolworks)

88 Rowland Way, Novato, CA 94949
Tel: 415-895-2000; FAX: 415-895-2102
E-mail: cust_serv@learningco.com

One Athenaeum Street, Cambridge, MA 02142
WWW: http://www.toolworks.com/

▶ Mindscape donates computer software to nonprofits.

National Christina Foundation

181 Harbor Drive, Stamford, CT 06902
Tel: 203-967-8000; FAX: 203-406-9725
E-mail: ncf@cristina.org; WWW: http://www.cristina.org/

▶ The National Cristina Foundation is a not-for-profit foundation dedicated to the support of training through donated used technology. It provides computer technology and solutions to give people with disabilities, students at risk, and the economically disadvantaged the opportunity, through training, to lead more independent and productive lives.

Nonprofit Computer Exchange (NCE)

Fund for the City of New York, 121 Sixth Avenue,
New York, NY 10013-1509
Tel: 212-925-6675; FAX: 212-925-5675
E-mail: info@fcny.org, aaltmueller@fcny.org (Alicia Altmueller,
Director of Technology Training and Community Outreach);
WWW: http://www.fcny.org

▶ The Fund established the Nonprofit Computer Exchange (NCE) in 1986 to give New York City's nonprofits quality, low-cost assistance in acquiring and using information systems.

Purchasing Services Agency (PSA) (Formerly Nonprofit Services)

50 California Street, Suite 200, San Francisco, CA 94111
Tel: 888-488-0772
E-mail: info@psagency.org;
WWW: http://www.psagency.org/psa_info.html

▶ PSA is a nonprofit organization that negotiates with vendors for preferential pricing of goods and services on behalf of their member agencies and simplifies the ordering process for individual agencies. PSA negotiates with vendors for preferential pricing of goods and services on behalf of a large number of member agencies and simplifies the ordering process for individual agencies. Nonprofits, child care providers, and other social service agencies throughout the United States can combine their purchasing power to achieve savings that would be unavailable to them individually. Merchandise is primarily furniture, but some computers are free to recipient nonprofits.

RECA (Realizing Every Community Asset) Foundation

1326 West 7th Place, Suite #J1, Kennewick, WA 99336
Tel: 509-543-2910
E-mail: bmccomb@tcfn.org (Bruce McComb, Executive
Director); WWW: http://www.tcfn.org/cbpin/recycle.htm

▶ The RECA Foundation solicits donations of used computer equipment, refurbishes systems, and provides computers to those in need (low-income families, disabled, nonprofit organizations, and other "have-nots"). Recipients are expected to perform some form of community services such as volunteering for work in the recycling center, tutoring, or mentoring in a Community Technology Center. The Computer Recycling Center is located in the Arborwood Learning Center (take a look at some recent pictures). Volunteers are assisting a few hours a week—more are needed, as is cash for supplies and equipment. Recipients of refurbished computers are currently limited to Kennewick Family Self Sufficiency Program participants and other human services organizations.

Share the Technology Computer Recycling Project

P.O. Box 548, Rancocas, NJ 08073
Tel: 856-234-6156; FAX: 856-234-5809
E-mail: recycle@sharetechnology.org, share@libertynet.org
(Barry Cranmer, President); WWW: http://sharetechnology.org,
http://sharetechnology.org/rdb_start.html

▶ This is an all-volunteer 501(c)(3) nonprofit corporation registered in New Jersey. Their mission is to salvage used computers that they repair, upgrade, and donate to nonprofit organizations, schools, and people with disabilities.

Silicon Graphics

Community Relations Representative, 2011 North Shoreline
Boulevard, Mountain View, CA 94043-1389

University Donations Program, SGI Computer Systems,
2011 North Shoreline Boulevard M/S 40U-005,
Mountain View, CA 94043
Tel: 650-960-1980; FAX: 650-969-6289
E-mail: helpdesk@corp.sgi.com;
WWW: http://www.sgi.com/company_info/community/

▶ Silicon Graphics donates cash and used computer equipment to nonprofits providing job training and social services, as well as used equipment to schools. It gives new equipment to higher education institutions, especially those with computer science departments.

The Software Toolworks (See Mindscape)

Sun Micro Systems

Corporate Affairs, 901 San Antonio Road, Palo Alto, CA 94303
Tel: 650-336-5337; FAX: 650-336-1559
WWW: http://www.sun.com/aboutsun/comm_invest/foundation.html

▶ Sun Micro Systems donates cash grants to groups in the San Francisco Bay area and the Merrimack Valley in Massachusetts to support business development and job and leadership training for low-income people; also (in those areas) to schools that provide economics instruction and programs to motivate youth to attend college. It gives software and hardware to colleges, universities, and other nonprofits that support academic research. To apply for hardware aid, contact the Academic Equipment Grant Program.

Surplus Exchange

1107 Hickory, Kansas City, MO 64105
Tel: 816-472-0444
E-mail: rgoring@crn.org (Rick Goring, Executive Director),
danab@crn.org (Dana Byron, Nonprofit & Computer Sales);
WWW: http://www.surplusexchange.org

▶ Its mission is to benefit Not-for-Profit Organizations by providing them with refurbished and new electronics, furniture, materials and other equipment; to preserve the environment by keeping unwanted and obsolete business equipment out of the waste stream; and to utilize the resources and expertise from these operations to provide education and human service programs to the general community. Surplus Exchange collects discarded and surplus business equipment from area, regional, and national businesses. They bring this equipment into their 50,000-square-foot warehouse, refurbish, rebuild, or repair the items if necessary. This equipment is made available to their primary concern, the nonprofit community, and to general public secondary markets. Sales to secondary markets help fund our environmental, educational, and human service programs and help keep prices lower to their charities.

Tech Corps Georgia (TCGA)

1514 East Cleveland Avenue, Suite 110, East Point, GA 30344
Tel: 404-768-9990; FAX: 404-768-9993
E-mail: chris.miller@techcorpsga.org;
WWW: http://www.techcorpsga.org

▶ TCGA is the outgrowth of Computers for Classrooms, Inc., a nonprofit organization, whose Computer Refurbishing and Computers for Teachers programs have provided computers and training to over 500 teachers and low-income families with children in Georgia's K through 12 schools. Its mission is to bridge the technology gap that exists in many of Georgia's K through 12 minority and low-income schools, school districts, and surrounding educational communities. To accomplish this mission TCGA utilizes three main strategies: recruit, place, and support volunteers from the technology and business community to advise and assist these schools and communities in the introduction and integration of new technologies; bring additional technology resources to schools through local and national partnerships with large and small technology companies; and build partnerships in support of educational technology among educators, businesses, and community members at the local, state, and national levels. Tech Corps (TC) is a national nonprofit organization, funded through foundation, business, and corporate contributions, and implemented through state chapters. A national staff oversees Tech Corps' mission and agenda, assists with the formation and maintenance of effective state chapters, provides national media focus, and ensures quality at all levels. The broader organization is based on a bottom-up philosophy and draws on the expertise and enthusiasm of technology-literate members of the local community.

PRODUCT AND SERVICE PROVIDERS

Computer Services Consultants

Arisen Consulting

P.O. Box 50, Milton, WA 98354
Tel: 253-318-9714; FAX: 253-926-1732
E-mail: dale@arisenconsulting.org; WWW: http://askanmcse.com/

▶ Arisen serves nonprofit and religious organizations with their computing and networking needs.

Bentz Whaley Flessner

2150 Norwest Financial Center, 7900 Xerxes Avenue South,
Minneapolis, MN 55431-1104
Tel: 612-921-0111; FAX: 612-921-0109
E-mail: bwf@bwf; WWW: http://www.bwf.com,
http://www.bwf.com/service/techpresen.htm

▶ It is critical for organizations to stay current with today's latest software and hardware capabilities and the level of information management that is crucial to fund-raising effectiveness and efficiency. Bentz Whaley Flessner provides operations audits; systems selection; data management; systems conversion and implementation, and staff training and development.

Coyote Communications

P.O. Box 152473, Austin, TX 78715-2473
Tel: 512-440-0835, 512-440-0835
E-mail: jcravens@coyotecom.com (Jayne Cravens),
http://www.webcom.com/jac/consult.html

▶ Coyote specializes in both online and offline communications services for not-for-profit organizations and public-sector agencies. Current fee-based services, each available on a monthly or project basis, include Online Technologies (preparing long-term strategic planning and implementation for the development, upgrade and/or maintenance of a Web site; promoting your activities and services as appropriate; integrating online activities into your existing communications activities; training staff in how they can do the same with online technologies; and exploring online culture and how an agency can build online community among supporters, clients, and others); training and presentations (workshops and orientations for many national and major regional conferences in the areas of online culture, how to use the Internet to enhance offline community outreach and service delivery, database management, how volunteer managers and service leaders can use the Internet to find or involve volunteers and to connect with resources to help them in their professions, and introducing technology into an organization). Be sure to check out the *Coyote Communications Technology Tip Sheets* that Jayne Cravens provides as a public service and *The Best Free Internet Resources for Not-for-Profit Organizations*.

Hewitt and Johnston New Media

99 Atlantic Avenue, Suite 411, Toronto, ON, Canada M6K 3J8
Tel: 416-588-7780; FAX: 416-588-7156
E-mail: info@hjc.on.ca; WWW: http://www.hjc.on.ca

▶ Hewett and Johnston is a full-service consulting firm that assists nonprofits in developing, implementing, and improving their direct response fund-raising programs. In addition, HJC offers specialized communications services to nonprofit organizations so that their messages get out to constituents. HJC New Media helps nonprofit organizations effectively integrate new communications media, such as the Internet, into meeting their missions and mandates. They provide expertise in Web site design, online fund raising, and strategic planning in the use of new communications media. HJC also helps plan the client's workspace (through extranet Web pages for internal communications within nonprofit organizations). HJC helps nonprofits develop, implement, and improve their direct-response fund-raising programs as well as planned giving efforts. HJC also offers specialized communications services to nonprofit organizations as well as Internet Skills for Nonprofit Managers, a 12-week online course and the accompanying books *The Fund Raiser's Guide to the Internet* and *The Non Profit Guide to the Internet: How to Survive and Thrive*. Take a virtual tour of the course at *http://www.hjc.on.ca/learning/online_learning.htm*

Information Age Associates, Inc.

Martin B. Schneiderman, 47 Murray Place, Princeton, NJ 08540
Tel: 609-924-6936; FAX: 609-924-6993
E-mail: info@iaa.com

▶ Information Age Associates, Inc., is a management consulting firm that was founded in 1984. The company specializes in the design, development, and implementation of state-of-the-art integrated information and communications systems. Its mission is to assist our clients to achieve their goals through the effective and appropriate use of information systems. Clients include U.S. private and corporate foundations, family foundations, no-profit organizations, professional associations, educational institutions, and government agencies. Our services include strategic planning; project planning and management; needs analysis and workflow review; system benchmarking and evaluation; cost–benefit analysis; independent evaluation of products and services; system design and acceptance testing; design of Web-based applications; implementation of LAN, WAN, client/server, and thin client systems; optimizing and troubleshooting network systems; development of RFPs, proposal review, and contract negotiations; Web site design and usage tracking; client satisfaction surveys and focus groups; Web-based survey design, hosting and data analysis; product design and marketing; development of marketing materials; multimedia graphic presentations; development of policies and procedures; staff reviews and skills assessment; and professional development services.

InfoWeb Services

10040 NW Blum Road, Kansas City, MO 64152
Tel: 816-587-0944
E-mail: info@infowebservices.com, carmen@infowebservices.com
(Carmen Liimatta); WWW: http://www.infowebservices.com

▶ Their mission is to enable nonprofit organizations to more efficiently serve and accomplish their missions by providing consultation on the use of the technologies of the Internet. InfoWeb designs Internet strategies with long-term value to fit the unique goals of nonprofit organizations. These goals include public service, fund raising, membership recruitment, public relations, and professional certification. A consulting firm that specializes in assisting nonprofit organizations and associations to use the Internet for promotion and public relations. Services include Internet Web sites (develop attractive sites using professional layout and design, ensuring that the content is consistent with your nonprofit mission and has maximum appeal to your target audience); consulting and strategic planning (help you define goals and objectives for your new media project); site maintenance and updates (provide timely maintenance and updates to the Web site we create for you or to an existing site so your target audience has the latest information); project makeovers to increase impact and effectiveness; evaluation and tracking through measurable statistics (provide daily and monthly statistics that give you feedback on the nature and amount of activity on your site, helping you measure progress toward accomplishing your objectives); Web site audits (provide audits of existing Web sites that include branding and marketing strategy, setting performance objectives, as well as consideration of organizational infrastructure to meet future functionality; also assist organizations planning Web sites to save time and money writing an RFP and hiring a development firm through their Project Profiler system).

Interactive Applications Group (iapps)

2639 Connecticut Avenue NW, Suite 210, Washington, DC 20008
Tel: 202-265-3700; FAX: 202-478-5110

315 West 39th Street, Suite 1208, New York, NY 10018
Tel: 212-465-1800; FAX: 212-658-9323
E-mail: info@iapps.com; WWW: http://www.iapps.com,
http://www.iapps.com/newsletter1999/newsletter.htm

▶ Interactive Applications Group (iapps), a leading developer of Web sites for nonprofits and foundations, is a full-service Internet consulting, development, and design firm. It provides consulting on interface design, database integration, needs analysis, market research, and online community-building strategies. It provides consulting on interface design, needs analysis and market research, database integration and architecture, and online community-building strategies. iapps specializes in relational database design and systems integration, and has extensive experience building intranet, extranet, and public Web sites using Cold Fusion and enterprise relational database technology.

Jacobson Consulting Applications, Inc.

330 West 42nd Street, 30th Floor, New York, NY 10036
Tel: 212-465-2336; FAX: 212-465-2349
E-mail: solutions@jcainc.com, |steve@jcainc.com (Steven Jacobson, President), steveb@jcainc.com (Steven Birnbaum, Director of Database Services); WWW: http://www.jcainc.com, http://www.jcainc.com/links.html

▶ Jacobson Consulting Applications, Inc., is a full-service consulting firm dedicated to providing technical assistance to not-for-profit organizations. They specialize in helping organizations select and implement the fund-raising system that fits their needs. Services offered include fund-raising systems (data conversion, system implementation); consulting (needs assessment and planning, configuration, purchase advising); networking (Microsoft and Novell certified technicians, installation and support, support and troubleshooting, thin client solutions, network and operating system upgrades, hardware and software support); other services (custom applications, e-mail, and Internet connectivity, training); and reports exchange.

MRB Communications

4520 Wilde Street, Suite 2, Philadelphia, PA 19127
Tel: 215-508-4920; FAX: 215-508-4590
E-mail: info@mrbcomm.com; WWW: http://www.mrbcomm.com

▶ MRB is a full-service Internet communications firm with expertise in technology and marketing. It serves as an Internet presence provider for nonprofit organizations. They are specialists with backgrounds in technology, advertising, strategic planning, and research for nonprofits. Services include communications consulting (team building, integrated marketing strategies, site promotion, Web site and technical assessments); Web design and development (information architecture, graphic design, engineering, e-commerce); maintenance planning (custom template training, maintenance models, Web management); and products (e-mail marketing tools, affinity group communities, virtual tours, courseSeek solution, and customized plans and documentation).

Millwheel Systems

7807 Woodlawn Avenue, Philadelphia, PA 19027
Tel: 215-545-3424, 215-635-2526 (Paul Miller);
FAX: 215-545-3425
E-mail: pmiller@millwheel.com (Paul Miller);
WWW: http://www.millwheel.com

▶ Millwheel Systems specializes in consulting to nonprofit groups. Over the past 14 years, they have worked with more than 50 nonprofits and a few ethical for-profit organizations. In most cases, their focus is to help build or to improve our client's infrastructure. Millwheel has assisted clients with computer systems, FAX systems, accounting systems, fund-raising systems, client tracking systems, and contact management systems. The common thread of all Millwheel projects is getting "mission critical" jobs done more efficiently, more accurately, and more cost effectively. Millwheel works to reengineer the infrastructure (computers, programs, procedures, and training). With improved infrastructure their client organizations have put many of their problems behind them and are better able to focus on delivering service to the community. Services include database development; business process reengineering; and client and development systems.

NSL Associates

2411 A Delancey Place, Philadelphia, PA 19103
Tel: 215-732-6311; FAX: 215-732-0123
E-mail: sales@nslassociates.com; WWW:
http://www.nslassociates.com/nonprof.html,
http://www.nslassociates.com/comptips.html

▶ NSL is a computer consulting and value-added reseller company. NSL's Web Services for NonProfit Organizations include planning assistance; assistance in choosing your Internet service provider and acquiring your Internet account; creation of the actual site design plan; creation of the overall graphical design of your WWW pages; content authoring or editing as desired; creation of WWW logos, mappable graphics, color text and picture graphics, and photo conversion and retouching for your WWW site; creation of user inputable forms; creation of the WWW site itself, including debugging; creation of "Transfer" documents for inclusion in your WWW site; creation of database and database services to enable your database to be searched by users on the WWW; programming in HTML and CGI, Java, and Javascript where desirable, to carry out the needs of your WWW site; initial transfer of your pages, graphics, and other files to the server; creation of e-mail on your WWW site along with various e-mail services; and WWW site maintenance (Web mastering) and updating, or training your personnel to do the same. For those organizations with a desire to provide their own server, NSL Associates can plan and execute the entire server creation including all software and hardware.

Net-Resources.com
Tel: 800-641-7432, 281-419-9456
E-mail: brett@net-resources.com (Brett Thomas, Consulting);
WWW: http://www.net-resources.com/philanthropy/,
http://www.net-resources.com/links.html
▶ Services include Internet consulting, Web design and development, Web site hosting, promotion, electronic commerce/shopping carts, knowledge-base design, and advanced database features; virtual communities; and advanced interactive features.

NonprofitSolutions.Net
75 West End Avenue, Suite P23A, New York, NY 10023
Tel: 888-522-6676, 212-769-7942; FAX: 888-522-6676
E-mail: info@nonprofitsolutions.net (Jason Hutchins, Business Relations, Paul Pak, Operations);
WWW: http://www.nonprofitsolutions.net
▶ NonprofitSolutions.Net builds your online presence directly into your core business strategy by providing your consumers with the latest information and giving them the means to interact directly with your organization. They are with you every step of the way, from content organization and information management to sales implementation and e-commerce solutions. Services include: connecting people, Network Services (they handle all aspects of your communication infrastructure needs including hardware assessment, LAN configuration, Internet connectivity, and enterprise-wide communication tools); on-site training (group training and individual sessions); partners in resource development (following an assessment, they provide developers with the materials and background information needed to effectively communicate your technology vision and secure resources. They are also available for follow-up meetings and board presentations to assist in presenting your communications strategy); custom programming (modular-designed and database-driven solutions increase your capacity, enhance your Web offerings, and provide a custom front end for your staff to update and distribute information through multiple channels). Complimentary phone support is included with each product you purchase, and additional pay-as-you-go options and annual support contracts are available to meet your ongoing support needs.

Norwottuck Technology Resources
11 Norwottuck Circle, Amherst, MA 01002
Tel: 413-253-9600; FAX: 413-253-7638
E-mail: info@norwottuck.com, E-mail: mpm@norwottuck.com (Michelle Murrain, President); WWW: http://www.norwottuck.com/
▶ A multidimensional technology consulting firm, whose focus is working with small businesses and nonprofit organizations to help them implement technology to better accomplish their mission. They leverage database and Internet technologies to help organizations better handle data, communicate with constituencies, and accomplish goals.

Online Strategies
9919 Corsica Street, Vienna, VA 22181
Tel: 800-871-4033, 703-242-6078
E-mail: info@onstrat.com; WWW: http://www.onstrat.com
▶ Online Strategies trains researchers to use the Web more effectively. The content is based on an analysis of your needs. The instructor, Randolph E. Hock, PhD, has trained over 7,000 online researchers nationally and abroad over the last 20 years and is author of *The Extreme Searcher's Guide to Web Search Engines*. He has created courses on searching the Web for professional associations, government agencies, schools, libraries, and companies. Courses have included such topics as Effective Browser Usage, Understanding What Is (and Isn't) on the Web, Categories of Web Sites, Finding and Using Metasites, Using Search Engines Effectively, Finding Quick Facts, Library Catalogs, News Sources, Alternatives to Expensive Databases, Full-Text Books and Journals, Major Sites for Your Area of Interest.

Public Systems, Inc. *(See also Financial Management, Human Resource Management)*
114 East 32nd Street, Suite 1306, New York, NY 10016
Tel: 212-684-9667; FAX: 212-684-9672
E-mail: info@psnyc.com (Laird Cummings, President);
WWW: http://www.psnyc.com/pages/public_systems_inc.asp
▶ Public Systems has been providing services to the not-for-profit community since 1988. Our principal has worked in not-for-profits for over 25 years. They provide a full range of services, including network design, installation and support for offices, wide-area network integration, and Internet connectivity and access; Intranet and Web site development and hosting; database systems development and internet integration; selection, installation, and support of fund accounting systems; and payroll and human resource application software specifically designed to meet the needs of the not-for-profit agency, integrated with fund accounting applications.

R I Arlington
806 W. King Road, P.O. Box 1414, Malvern, PA 19355
Tel: 610-647-2648
E-mail: hunsaker@riarlington.com (Charlie Hunsaker, President); WWW: http://www.riarlington.com/
▶ This is a systems consulting firm that serves nonprofit organizations and development offices with a variety of services. The firm was established in 1988 with the recognition that nonprofits have many of the same systems requirements as their corporate counterparts, and they also need high-quality, objective assistance in undertaking important, nonrecurring systems tasks. Services include systems audit, needs assessment, system selection, systems implementation, and general systems consulting.

Sentient, Inc.

4950 Yonge Street, Suite 1500, North York, ON M2N 6K1
Tel: 416-590-0660, ext. 302 Canada
E-mail: asherwin@sentientinc.com (Andrew J. Sherwin,
Owner/Principal); WWW: http://www.sentientinc.com/

▶ Sentient is an information technology consulting firm specializing in the provision of turnkey information technology–based systems specifically developed to meet the unique needs of not-for-profit organizations. This encompasses the delivery and implementation of hardware, software, and consulting-related solutions. Sentient has been providing solutions to this market since 1987, and during the past decade has developed the widely acknowledged reputation as Canada's leading vendor of information technology solutions for not-for-profit organizations. Sentient, Inc., specializes in the implementation of information technology solutions that are designed specifically to meet the unique data processing needs of not-for-profit organizations such as associations, charities, boards of trade, and other member-driven organizations. Products provided include computer hardware and LAN software solutions, iMIS membership database applications, iMIS fund-raising software solutions, Express! Internet Web site solutions specifically for not-for-profits, and Great Plains Dynamics Accounting software solutions. Sentient also offers seminars and courses.

Sheppard and Brown Consulting Group Nonprofit Sector (SBC Group)

5625 Southampton Drive, Springfield, VA 2215
Tel: 703-764-1799; FAX: 703-764-0646
E-mail: info@sbcgroup.com;
WWW: http://www.sbcgroup.com/nonprofit.htm

▶ SBC Group offers a broad range of services geared to the nonprofit sector. Its technology consulting services include technology assessments (designed to meet your budget and objectives for enhanced technology utilization, networking, and Internet and intranet applications. Their focus is on the optimal deployment of desktop, networked, and client–server systems to meet your operating and management requirements. In addition, SBC Group designs and manages streamlined system selection and implementation processes for enterprise or specialized software applications. As software developers, they also will design systems to meet unique information technology needs that are not addressed by mass-marketed software.); software solutions (develops user-friendly and easily maintained software solutions for budget, planning, financial, and client service needs of nonprofit organizations. They specialize in meeting needs unaddressed by mass market packaged software through relational database solutions, data warehouses and analysis tools designed for networked and desktop applications. They use a variety of development platforms based on your organizational standards and specifications.); Web services (include domain registration, Web site hosting, Web page development, Web site administration, utilization tracking, search engine registration and updating, and Web page optimization to ensure top listings in Web search engines. They also develop corporate sponsorships for your Web site, and work with third-party vendors to provide for credit card contributions to your nonprofit organization.).

Summit Consulting Collaborative

61 Lincoln Avenue, Amherst, MA 01002
Tel: 413-549-0014; FAX: 520-447-3998
E-mail: info@summitcollaborative.com,
marcosten@mediaone.net, mosten@summitcollaborative.com
(Marc Osten, Founder and Principal);
WWW: http://www.summitcollaborative.com,
http://www.summitcollaborative.com/links.html,
http://www.summitcollaborative.com/resources.html

▶ Its mission is to provide strategic technology and management expertise to the nonprofit sector. It works in close collaboration with foundations, management support organizations, nonprofit networks, technology support providers, and nonprofit organizations to develop programs that meet critical nonprofit sector needs. Services include Internet outreach campaigns and solutions, strategic technology planning, and nonprofit executive technology leadership. It offers presentations and workshops as well as individual consultations. In close collaboration with foundations, management support organizations, and technology support providers, they develop programs that meet critical nonprofit sector needs. The outcome is the building of organizational capacity, power, and effectiveness. Working directly with nonprofit networks and specific organizations, they plan and implement Internet outreach and organizing campaigns to stimulate offline action. Services provided include presentations and workshops (nationwide on various technology and Internet-related issues to conferences, associations, boards. and organizations. For example, they can help you motivate an audience to support the use of technology, show your board how technology will improve your organization, and train/prepare a group to take advantage of particular technology initiatives.); individual consultations (help clients plan for, implement, and evaluate technology programs. Their consultations range from phone support to one-time site visits that are narrowly defined to more long-term assistance such as developing a strategic technology plan and grant proposal; launching an Internet outreach, marketing or advocacy campaign; improving the design, function, and success of your Web site; and preparing staff training and technical support programs.); peer-learning program (prepares nonprofit executives to take assertive leadership on technology issues within their organization. You leave the program with a highly specialized strategic technology plan to guide your use of technology.); and tools (develop easy to use and practical tools that help you understand, plan for, and evaluate technology use within your organizations). Norwottuck Technology Resources (see separate listing), Summit's sister organization, specializes in Web site design, including HTML, CGI, database connectivity, and Javascript. Norwottuck has worked primarily with nonprofits on technology projects since its founding.

Walker & Company, LLP

5100 Wisconsin Avenue NW, Suite 407, Washington, DC 20016
Tel: 202-363-9300; FAX: 202-363-0531
E-mail: cecountee@walkerllp.com;
WWW: http://www.walkerllp.com/

▶ Walker & Company, LLP, is a multiservice accounting and consulting firm serving clientele throughout the United States. The firm provides information technology services in the following areas: information technology planning and evaluation; rapid application development; information systems development support; database design and development; and Financial Management System, Internal Control, and Computer Security Reviews.

Hardware and Software Distributors

Consistent Computer Bargain, Inc.

Headquarters: 6220 Washington Avenue, Suite D, Racine, WI 53406
Tel: 800-342-4222; FAX: 800-440-5036
E-mail: office@ccbnpts.com; WWW:http://www.ccbnonprofits.com

▶ Consistent Computer Bargains, Inc. is in the business of reselling via marketing, quoting, securing special pricing, and selling and shipping computer software and hardware. CCB strives to provide the best value and customer service available to the nonprofit marketplace. Maintains offices in Chicago, Los Angeles, Philadelphia, Seattle, and Nashville. CCB's basic strategy is to assist nonprofit organizations in saving money so their budgets may be stretched to expand their focus. Based on quantity commitments, CCB has special offers each quarter, which publishers provide. CCB can offer you competitive price quotes on whatever your hardware or software requirements may be. They serve both small and large organizations. Specialties include computers and technology, information systems, office services and products, and supplies.

Third Sector Technologies, Inc.

751 Old Richardson Highway, Suite 235, Fairbanks, AK 99701
Tel: 907-452-2461; FAX: 907-452-3143
E-mail: info@infoinsights.com, doug@thethirdsector.com (Doug Toelle, CEO); WWW: www.infoinsights.com

▶ This company provides integrated Web-based tools to nonprofits and governmental agencies to help them effectively and economically deliver their services. The focus of Third Sector Technologies is software and online services designed specifically to improve the efficiency and quality of nonprofit management. Third Sector Technologies was spun off from Information Insights, a management consulting firm with years of experience working with nonprofit and government agencies that deliver human services. Third Sector Technologies is developing a browser-based software suite that will be available for nonprofits. The software will provide management information solutions for human service nonprofits and associations. These products, currently Third Sector Manager and Third Sector Universal, integrate client, volunteer, staff, fundraising, grant and proposal, inventory, and board management functions in a Web-based application.

Internet Application Services

APT, Inc.

P.O. Box 2264, 2900 East Broadway, Suite 5,
Bismarck, ND 58502-2264
Tel: 701-224-1815; FAX: 701-224-9824
E-mail: aptinc@aptnd.com; WWW: http://www.aptnd.com

▶ An association management and lobbying services company, offering state of the art Internet technology, APT, Inc., offers state and national associations, state regulatory boards, and nonprofit organizations, management, and Internet technology services. They provide complete Web site design, hosting, and maintenance services. Since 1988, APT, Inc., services have been used by state associations, state boards, special interest organizations, national affiliations, and Washington, DC–based firms. The APT, Inc., approach to association management allows your association or client to access the complete range of management, Internet technology, lobbying, and support services in order to remain a functional, well-organized, proactive association of members and maximize your influence of issues relating to your profession.

Dream Team Technologies

1425 Kalamath Street, Denver, CO 80204
Tel: 303-534-3334; FAX: 303-534-5442
E-mail: info@dreamteamtech.com, drewg@dreamteamtech.com (Drew Gerber), drew@dreamtech.com (Drew McDowell); WWW: http://home.dreamteamtech.com/start.html

▶ With Dream Team Technologies' Web site application, organizations can create, manage, control, and administer the content on their Web site. Your staff can log on to your Web site, point and click, and change the content. Dream Team offers Web packages that enable nonprofits to have a professional Web presence that can be managed internally without IT staff. Dream Team's packages can include such functionality as online calendaring, feedback forms, membership registration, intranet, extranet, and e-commerce, to name a few, creating an enterprise-level solution. All packages include setup, design, training, and support.

e-advocates

1800 K Street NW, Suite 301, Washington, DC 20006
Tel: 202-955-3001; FAX: 202-955-0664
E-mail: info@e-advocates.com;
WWW: http://www.e-advocates.com/

▶ E-advocates is the first full-service Internet advocacy consulting firm backed by the commitment and expertise of Capitol Advantage, the nation's top provider of cyber-lobbying technology. E-advocates helps organizations harness the power of the Internet to achieve legislative and political objectives. They offer public affairs clients a full-range of affordable cyber-advocacy consulting services, including e-mail activist recruitment and e-mail list management; federal and state legislative tracking; Internet campaign planning, design, and execution; issue advocacy; online advertising design and placement; on-site management of cyber-lobby events; public affairs Web site design and development; training and capacity building; and writing services.

EFax.com

1378 Willow Road, Menlo Park, CA 94025
Tel: 877-EFAXCOM, 650-324-0600; FAX: 650-326-6003
E-mail: info@efax.com

5385 Hollister Avenue, Santa Barbara, CA 93111
eFAX: 630-604-0023
WWW: http://www.efax.com

▶ Products offered include eFax Free (a service that lets you receive faxes by e-mail. Simply sign up for a personal eFax number. Then, when people send faxes to your eFax number, you receive them as e-mail attachments that you can view, edit with annotations, and forward easily. On the same eFax number you can also receive voice mail. Customers, clients, and friends can leave you voice messages that you can access by telephone or by e-mail. As an eFax Free user, your eFax number is assigned by eFax.com. Numbers assigned in the United States are based on where eFax.com has available numbers and not where you live. If you prefer a U.S. number in your local area code or a U.S. toll-free number, you will need to upgrade to eFax Plus.); and eFax Plus (all of the features and benefits of eFax Free plus a convenient way to send faxes. Compose a document or spreadsheet on your computer, add your signature, and fax it to a friend directly from your computer. With eFax Plus, you can receive and send faxes by e-mail. eFax Plus captures your document and uses your e-mail client to send the document. When you sign up as a Plus member, you can select your eFax number. Numbers are available in major metropolitan cities across the United States.).

FaxforFree.com (Now j2 Global Communications)
Attn: Help Desk, 2752 Loker Avenue West, Carlsbad, CA 92008
Tel: 888-718-2000, 800-241-0147, 323-860-9207, 860-9218
E-mail: help@mail.j2.com, support@fax4free.com;
WWW: http://www7.fax4free.com/home.asp,
http://jsource.j2.com/login.asp
▶ Fax4Free.com lets nonprofit groups send faxes from anywhere in the world to the United States, Canada, Australia, and the United Kingdom for free.

ForMyCause.com
11111 Santa Monica Boulevard, Suite 1200, Los Angeles, CA 90025
Tel: 800-246-6801, 310-479-1750; FAX: 310-479-9774
E-mail: customerservice@formycause.com;
WWW: http://www.formycause.com
▶ ForMyCause.com™ is dedicated to serving as the online link between worthwhile causes, individual supporters, and cause-friendly corporate sponsors. Their MyBar™ application is the best way that concerned people can help their cause, stay in touch, and never have to pay a cent.

GivingCapital, Inc.
Harry E. Cerino, Lewis Tower, 225 South 15th Street, 28th Floor,
Philadelphia, PA 19102
Tel: 877-MYGIVING (877-694-4846) (Donor Support),
877-MYGIVING (877-694-4846) (Nonprofit Support);
FAX: 215-735-8343
E-mail: sales@givingcapital.com (Partnering us),
help@givingcapital.com (Donor Support),
support@givingcapital.com (Nonprofit Support),
talent@givingcapital.com (Careers with us),
cmead@givingcapital.com (Public Relations);
WWW: www.givingcapital.com
▶ GivingCapital is dedicated to increasing charitable giving through online solutions to the philanthropic community. They provide a simple and secure way to donate online. They help nonprofit organizations harness the collaborative power of the Internet to acquire new donors and increase contributions. With their patent-pending technology, donors click a banner on your Web site to make their gift. From straight donations to membership drives, to creating a matching or challenge campaign, GivingCapital provides an array of tools to create and monitor your campaign. Use GivingCapital to lower your online fund-raising costs and reach new donors with this innovative Internet technology. In partnership with the National Philanthropic Trust, they also enable individuals to balance philanthropic interests with their estate planning and financial needs through donor-advised funds. Donors can open a donor-advised fund account on their Web site or on the Web sites of their financial service partners.

I Belong, Inc.
950 Winter Street, Waltham, MA 02451
Tel: 800-395-8122, 781-684-8280; FAX: 781-684-8252
E-mail: info@ibelong.com; WWW: http://www.ibelong.com
▶ I Belong, Inc., is a provider of custom Internet portals (start pages) to nonprofits/affinity groups for revenue generation and enhanced relationships.

LocalVoice.com
3265 17th Street, Suite 304, San Francisco, CA 94110
Tel: 415-522-1200; FAX: 415-522-1270
E-mail: info@localvoice.com;
WWW: http://www.localvoice.com/index.htm
▶ Founded in 1998, LocalVoice.com is an application service provider delivering a cost-efficient Internet platform that empowers schools, universities, and other member-supported organizations to engage members in an online dialogue. The LocalVoice.com Platform features integrated, self-service Web applications designed to engage alumni and members online. LocalVoice.com clients access these applications via the client console, a secure area designed for data collection, storage, management, and export. Services include e-mail marketing; fund raising; member activation/renewal; event management; member profiling; surveys; member directory; branded e-mail, chat room, and search functionality.

Non-Profit Technologies, Inc.
23 Arnold Street, Wakefield, RI 02879
Tel: 401-788-9415 (main), 401-933-5488 (beeper);
FAX: 617-249-0780
E-mail: info@nonprofittech.com; WWW: http://nonprofittech.com,
http://nonprofittech.com/Links/links.html
▶ Non-Profit Technologies was formed in 1998 to help nonprofits make the best use of technology to fulfill their missions and to do so at an affordable price. They specialize in building databases, networks, and Web sites.

Social Ecology
1818 Summit, Seattle, WA 98122
Tel: 206-726-0047, 800-485-8170 (Sales Line)
E-mail: info@socialecology.com, support@socialecology.com
(Technical Support); WWW: http://www.socialecology.com
▶ Social Ecology's mission is to get technology out of the way of the work of nonprofit organizations. To that end, using the Application Service Provider model, they offer systems that drive down the total cost of ownership and remove the barriers between people and their work. Founder and CEO is Michael Gilbert, editor of Nonprofit Online News. Based on their years of experience helping nonprofits keep up with changing information technologies, they exist to provide communication systems that fit the needs, as well as the budgets, of nonprofit organizations. Products include OrgMail IT, their group e-mail system, and InWeb IT, an intranet-style knowledge management tool.

TerraGold—Web Services for Nonprofit and Small Businesses
1852 West 11th Street, Suite 411, Tracy, CA 95376
Tel: 877-532-5875; FAX: 877-532-5875
E-mail: info@terragold.com; WWW: http://www.terragold.com

▶ TerraGold is a master agent and reseller of discount long distance, especially international long distance. They can assist your organization with fund-raising alternatives. They can provide you a turn-key long distance information and online sign-up site that will provide discount long distance service for your customers. Other competencies are in the field of graphic design, Web site development, and Internet marketing. TerraGold specializes in the creative look and feel aspect of Web sites, as well as doing the standard graphic design work of banners, buttons, and logos. TerraGold is also a full-service Internet advertising agency that can deliver traffic to any site, by means of selected Cost-Per-Click and Cost-Per-Impressions, advertising, press releases, as well as other less conventional means to get the word out about your e-business. TerraGold charges on the sliding scale, as they believe deeply in doing good things for good people, especially those who care about the Earth, and the innocents—children and animals.

WeCareToo

2719 West Lunt Avenue, Chicago, IL 60645
Tel: 773-764-2000
E-mail: richard@wecaretoo.com (Richard J. Schaefer);
WWW: http://www.wecaretoo.com

▶ WeCareToo offers free Web pages, no-cost optional fund-raising programs, and low-cost online shopping malls. Their Web site also includes links to other resources for the NPO community, an opt-in e-mail newsletter, and a free search engine registration page.

Internet Service Providers and Web Hosting Services

APT, Inc.

P.O. Box 2264, 2900 East Broadway, Suite 5,
Bismarck, ND 58502-2264
Tel: 701-224-1815; FAX: 701-224-9824
E-mail: aptince@aptnd.com; WWW: http://www.aptnd.com

▶ APT, Inc., offers state and national associations, state regulatory boards, and nonprofit organizations, management, and Internet technology services. They provide complete Web site design, hosting, and maintenance services. Since 1988, APT, Inc., services have been used by state associations, state boards, special interest organizations, national affiliations, and Washington, DC–based firms. The APT, Inc., approach to association management allows your association or client to access the complete range of management, Internet technology, and lobbying and support services in order to remain a functional, well-organized, proactive association of members and maximize your influence of issues relating to your profession.

Drizzle

P.O. Box 12829, Seattle, WA 98111
Tel: 800-378-7405, 206-447-2702; FAX: 206-447-2784
E-mail: info@drizzle.com; WWW: http://www.drizzle.com

▶ They offer all of their services (dial-up, DSL, Web hosting, secure server, mailing lists, e-mail, etc.) at deeply discounted annual rates. Because the rates are so low, they prefer not to publish them, but encourage eligible not-for-profits to call for a quote. Eligible not-for-profits include all 501(c)(3)s, most schools, and churches.

Flatiron WebWorks

Chelsea Networks, Inc., Flatiron WebWorks Division,
130 West 24th Street, Suite 4A, New York, NY 10011
Tel: 212-627-4806; FAX: 212-627-4919
E-mail: sales@chelsea.net; WWW: http://www.flatiron.org

▶ Flatiron WebWorks, an arm of Chelsea Networks, Inc., located in New York City, is an organization dedicated to creating and promoting affordable Internet presence and customized World Wide Web pages for nonprofit organizations and small businesses. Their technical specialists support an infrastructure designed specifically to host Web pages. They also maintain a broad base of consultant references including graphic designers, content developers, copywriters, and programmers to accommodate specific client needs. Through Chelsea Networks, Inc., Flatiron WebWorks provides Internet hosting services and connectivity so that Internet users worldwide can access your Web site. They also offer a range of consulting services.

Hubris Communications

Tel: 316-275-1900
E-mail: hubris@gcnet.com; WWW: http://www.hubris.net/,
http://www.nonprofit.net

▶ Hubris Communications is an Internet presence provider specializing in providing low-cost, high-quality services for the nonprofit and local communities. They offer the following services: HTML design (they will create professional, effective Web pages for your organization); WWW hosting (host your site on the World Wide Web); announcement (register your page with the major directories and search engines); FTP hosting (make files available for transfer via FTP); mailing lists (host your own distributed mailing lists); mailback service (auto-answer incoming mail); and mail forwarding (have a permanent e-mail address, even if yours changes).

ICobb

AWE, Inc., 1951 Canton Road NE, Suite 140, Marietta, GA 30066
Tel: 888-717-1832, 678-355-9016; FAX: 678-355-9017
E-mail: sales@icobb.com; WWW: http://me.icobb.com/,
http://icobb.com

▶ iCobb.com offers complete online solutions. Provides full online support and training and tools in their standard package. They are geared for the large organization (3,000 members and up) as well as the small organization (500 members and down). All receive personal service. For the small organization with high budget restrictions, there is *http://me.icobb.com,* which provides free online services and free access to their online development tools. 501(c)(3) Christian service organizations dealing with children, single-parent families, families, refugees, and the homeless (in that exact order) are most likely to receive the greatest benefit of their services. After that, they will consider community 501(c)(3) organizations that share the same interests. They also provide concessions for other Christian organizations. For any nonprofit organization, they will provide free Web hosting and free access to their standard set of online development tools. This allows the tightly budgeted organization to create and manage their online presence in a very professional manner without cost. Any entity that agrees to their standard terms (as outlined at the free site) is welcome to participate. You may visit that site at *http://me.icobb.com.* Any 501(c)(3) providing their mission statement and proof of their public charity status may be entitled to an upgrade on service at the free site that would allow more Web space and a few tools not included in the standard set.

Laughing Squid Web Hosting

Tel: 877-467-7843 (GO SQUID), 415-333-0995;
FAX: 415-333-0996
E-mail: info@laughingsquid.net;
WWW: http://www.laughingsquid.net

▶ Laughing Squid is an independently run Web hosting service that specializes in Web hosting for artists, individuals, nonprofits, and small organizations. For $15 a month, you get 100 MB of file space and 3,000 MB of monthly data transfer.

NonprofitSpace

14518 6th Avenue NE, Shoreline, WA 98155-6944
Tel: 206-418-9980
E-mail: hawthorne@cybervpm.com;
WWW: http://www.nonprofitspace.org/

▶ NonprofitSpace offers Internet services for nonprofit organizations and associations. Services offered to nonprofit organizations include Web site hosting; page updates; staff instruction on how to use the new Web site; technical assistance; retain copyright to content, choice of basic template designs; up to six prompt updates (within five business days); assistance finding Web server space or access to NonprofitSpace's hosting program; optional hosting on NonprofitSpace's Web server, for additional fee; additional features, such as mailing lists, forms, and so on, available for additional fee; custom image design for additional fee; e-mail–based instruction on use of the new site for your staff; submission of your site to eight top search engines; and additional pages for additional fee.

WeCareToo

2719 West Lunt Avenue, Chicago, IL 60645
Tel: 773-764-2000
E-mail: richard@wecaretoo.com (Richard J. Schaefer);
WWW: http://www.wecaretoo.com

▶ WeCareToo offers free Web pages, no-cost optional fund-raising programs, and low-cost online shopping malls. Their Web site also includes links to other resources for the NPO community, an opt-in e-mail newsletter, and a free search engine registration page.

Software Products and Distributors

Computer Training Services (CTS)

131 Rollins Avenue, Suite 1, Rockville, MD 20852
Tel: 800-433-8015, 301-468-4800; FAX: 301-468-2309
E-mail: support@ctsguides.com; WWW: http://www.ctsguides.com

▶ Publishers of software evaluation tools, CTS helps you select the right software with its *Guide to Selecting Software for Nonprofit Organizations and Trade Associations* (see separate listing under Publications).

ebase

TechRocks, One Penn Center, 1617 John F. Kennedy Boulevard, Philadelphia, PA 19103
E-mail: info@techrocks.org;
WWW: http://www.ebase.org/about.htm,
http://www.techrocks.org/about

▶ A free interactive database for nonprofit organizations, ebase™ is a series of Filemaker Pro templates developed for use by nonprofit organizations to manage communications with their members, donors, activists, and volunteers. Originally developed by Desktop Assistance in 1996, it is currently distributed and supported by TechRocks (formerly The Technology Project). Ebase™ was created to address a critical technology need in the nonprofit sector, where the cost of fund-raising management applications published by private companies averages $5,000. With ebase you can keep all your organization's data (memberships, donations, activist information) in one place, and provide secure, easy-to-learn access to everyone who needs to use it; send e-mail directly from your database, merging data in the text of an e-mail message to personalize communications; and customize your database to make it match the unique and changing needs of your organization. Technical support for ebase™ is provided through their Web site, the ebase listservers, and a small but growing group of independent consultants and trainers who have committed to supporting the needs of nonprofit organizations.

Web Design and Development

Home Page Service Bureau

501(c)(3) Monthly Letter: A Management Tool for Nonprofits, Great Oaks Communication Services, 400 Chestnut Street, P.O. Box 192, Atlantic, IA 50022
Tel: 712-243-5257, 712-243-4750; FAX: 712-243-2775
E-mail: kmeickle@nishna.net, jkenney@nisha.net, mmiller@nishna.net, http://www.nishna.net/501c3/index.html

▶ Home Page Service Bureau offers nonprofit organizations access to the Internet via the World Wide Web. Services provided include typesetting, editing and professional design, scanned logos and graphics, button graphics, separators, hyperlinks to other sites, mail/fax forms, free e-mail link to your home page, and your own World Wide Web address.

Kathy Canfield Web Design and Development

410 West 24th Street, 6L, New York, NY 10011
Tel/FAX: 212-243-5295
E-mail: kathy@kathycanfield.com;
WWW: http://www.kathycanfield.com

▶ This is a Web design and development practice specializing in Web sites for arts and nonprofit organizations. Owned and operated by Kathy Canfield, a Web designer and developer with an extensive performing arts background as a musician (and Web designer), Kathy Canfield Web Design and Development effectively serves the online needs of the arts and nonprofit communities. Services include planning and strategizing (education in all areas of Web design and development; creation of proposals and RFPs for new Internet projects); design (site architecture and planning, visual design of screens for use in Web site production); production (building of static Web sites using approved designs, integration of approved site design into template pages for use in dynamically generated sites); maintenance (monthly maintenance of existing Web sites); marketing (registration of completed sites with major search engines); management (supervision of production staff in new development and maintenance); and other services (sound clips: digitization of sound clips from music CD to RealAudio format; PDF files: preparation of PDF files from Quark documents).

New Media for Nonprofits

4401 North Ravenswood Avenue, Suite 303, Chicago, IL 60640
Tel: 773-334-2983; FAX: 773-784-3790
E-mail: info@fornonprofits.com;
WWW: http://www.fornonprofits.com/index.shtml

▶ This organization provides a full range of short- and long-term services to create effective online communications campaigns. Services include, but are not limited to, new site design and development, site redesigns, needs assessments, open-ended site maintenance, and online promotions services. Specific services offered include project management (specification, planning, scheduling, staffing); graphic and information design (information flow and navigation design, interface design, graphic design, and image optimization for display on the Internet, identity design, printed works conversions); site development (domain name registration, Web site/e-mail hosting account setup, content development, content organization and copy editing, programming/database integration [HTML, CGI, Perl, Java, Javascript, Cold Fusion]); supplementary formatting (Adobe Portable Document Format (PDF), audio formats (Real Audio, MPEG, WAV); site promotion (search engine registration, topic-specific directory listings, online publication announcements, like-minded site listings, newsgroups, chat sessions, and listservs); long-term support (site promotion, site usage statistical analysis, regular content updates, technology updates); and Beyond Web Sites (E-mail list setup and management, document distribution, application design, internal document solutions).

PUBLICATIONS

(See also Marketing & Communications; Resource Development)

Computers—General

Compact American Dictionary of Computer Words: An A to Z Guide to Hardware, Software, and Cyberspace
EDITORS OF THE AMERICAN HERITAGE DICTIONARIES (HOUGHTON-MIFFLIN TRADE & REFERENCE, 1998)

▶ The language of computing is changing and expanding daily. *The Dictionary of Computer Words* contains the most up-to-date vocabulary, information on how to operate a computer, and help with understanding manuals, documentation, and publications about the computer industry. Detailed entries are written in a clear, straightforward style and provide definitions and explanations in context, with many cross-references to other entries in the book. The subject index groups related entries at a common topic or category for easy reference. More than 60 charts, tables, and diagrams illustrate important concepts and make information easy to locate. *Hardcover, 448 pages, $12*

Complete Idiot's Guide to Computer Basics
JOE KRAYNAK (QUE, 2000)

▶ From the author of *The Complete Idiot's Guide to PCs* (see separate listing) comes this introduction covering the most popular aspects of computers online and offline. When you first get a PC, you want to do something with it. You didn't buy it to learn about it any more than you buy a car to learn about its engine. You want to write a letter, send an e-mail message, check out some Web sites, make a greeting card, or personalize the Windows desktop. Whatever it is you want to do, you don't want to have to read a book describing what a Pentium processor is or how your AGP adapter produces the pretty image on the screen. You want something more tangible; you want to do something practical. The only trouble is that the darn computer won't cooperate. It's just not as easy as it looks. That's the purpose of the *Complete Idiot's Guide to Computer Basics*. This book identifies the 20 to 30 tasks that you as a PC novice want to perform and then it draws a map showing you how to achieve your goal. You'll follow simple steps to print a greeting card, reconcile a checkbook balance, decorate the Windows desktop, make the PC run faster, and more. Learn how to perform basic PC operations in Windows. This book instructs you with hands-on, computer-related tasks. It includes a "speak like a geek" glossary. *Softcover, 408 pages, $16.99*

Complete Idiot's Guide to PCs, Seventh Edition
JOE KRAYNAK (QUE, 1999)

▶ This book takes the novice by the hand for a very ambitious tour of the world of possibilities available to the PC user. After a section of basic training for those who've flipped the "On" switch for the first time, the book surveys the world of software and hardware opportunities. Chapters cover everything from gaming software to file management to educational software, business uses for the computer, and a hefty introduction to modems, online services, and the Internet. Descriptions are task oriented, reasonably well detailed, and useful for the beginner. Also included is a lengthy computer terms glossary, as well as a large chunk of site listings from Lycos in an appendix. The book also includes a CD-ROM packed with Web software, editors, e-mail programs, and all kinds of utilities. For the new user of a PC, these will be useful additions. The book does a good job covering a very wide subject matter. It's an effective and useful guide for those who have a new computer and are looking to get more out of it. *Softcover, 380 pages, $16.99*

Computer Desktop Encyclopedia, 2nd Edition
(Book and CD)
ALAN FREEDMAN (AMACOM BOOKS, 1999)

▶ Alan Freedman has updated and expanded his magnum opus on computers and computing, the *Computer Desktop Encyclopedia*. With 2,000 new terms—and 3,000 revised terms, a grand total of over 10,000—this is truly an encyclopedic computer reference. The new edition contains completely updated Internet and World Wide Web terms, new telecommunications technologies and vendors, even a TCP/IP micro-lesson. Packed with graphics (over 750 illustrations altogether) and tutorials, it will appeal to anyone who wants a deeper understanding of all things computer. The book also includes a CD-ROM (complete with Windows help and "how to" entries) that provides heavy browsing capabilities in a multimedia format, while freeing up considerable desk space. *Softcover, 1082 pages, $45*

The Computer Glossary: The Complete Illustrated Dictionary, 8th Edition (Book and CD-ROM)
ALAN FREEDMAN (AMACOM BOOKS, 1998)

▶ This edition is substantially expanded, with over 6,000 computer terms. This dictionary covers basic computer vocabulary, graphics and multimedia terminology, and a sampling of cyberslang and Internet terms, plus programming, networking, UNIX, and PC jargon. Profiles on industry leaders and historic happenings make this glossary interesting as well as useful. Definitions are tailored to the type of word. Basic terms are defined in layman's language, while the specific technical jargon is defined with more technical terms. Comprehensive cross-referencing gives you quick access to what you're looking for. It covers trends such as client/server issues, multimedia, and object-oriented programming, and includes profiles of companies, industry leaders, and new technologies, as well as some 200 black-and-white illustrations. The accompanying disk contains the glossary for both DOS and Windows programs, plus a

DOS tutorial and enhanced Microsoft Windows help. *Softcover, 700 pages, $29.95*

Jargon: An Informal Dictionary of Computer Terms

ROBIN WILLIAMS AND STEVE CUMMINGS (PEACHPIT PRESS, 1993)

▶ This book explains over 1,200 computer terms in a way that readers can understand. It is an excellent resource for beginning and intermediate users. Although entries are alphabetically arranged, a nice feature is the thorough indexing, giving access to terms used in more than one context or having more than one meaning. An appendix thoroughly explains how to read a computer ad. This book is a straightforward guide that not only defines computer-related terms but also explains how and why they are used. It covers both the Macintosh and PC worlds. Now there is no need to ask embarrassing questions. *Softcover, 688 pages, $22 (plus $4 shipping)*

Microsoft Press Computer Dictionary, 4th Edition
(Book and CD)

(MICROSOFT PRESS, 1999)

▶ An authoritative source of definitions for computer terms, concepts, and acronyms, with over 8,000 entries, the fourth edition is fully updated to include the latest technology, including expanded coverage of e-commerce, cyberculture, networks, standards, enterprise and component terminology, Windows® 98, and UNIX. As an added bonus, the dictionary expands its coverage of jargon and slang, which are often the most confusing terms in the computer world. The dictionary also now includes stylish new line drawings to help· clarify concepts and illustrate key terms. The dictionary focuses on providing beginning and intermediate computer users with a solid grounding in terms, technologies, and concepts related to productivity software, databases, and networks. Communications technologies—such as those related to mobile phones—get attention too. The latest release of the reference includes extensive coverage of Internet, Web, and intranet-related terms and acronyms; software products from all manufacturers; terminology relating to PC, Macintosh, and UNIX; hardware; and words relating to mathematical, mainframe, networking, and programming concepts. Of particular help to newcomers are the pronunciation guides, especially identifying which acronyms to pronounce and which to spell out. It is well cross-referenced and illustrated. The accompanying CD-ROM contains the text, and is searchable by Microsoft Internet Explorer. Quarterly updates and revisions are available on the World Wide Web. *Softcover, 600 pages, $34.99*

Microsoft Press® Computer User's Dictionary

(MICROSOFT PRESS, 1999)

▶ This book gives you fast, easy explanations of terms covering the most recent trends in computing, including the Internet, the Web, multimedia, virtual reality, hardware, networks, and workgroup computing. In 400 pages, you get over 4,800 terms, along with concise versions of the in-depth definitions featured in the third edition of the Microsoft Press Computer Dictionary (Microsoft Press, 1997), described by Booklist as "The Webster's of computer dictionaries." In addition, you can view regular quarterly updates to the dictionary on the Microsoft Press Web site. Features include a traditional dictionary format—including parts of speech and numbered lists for separate definitions, succinct definitions of all the basic computing terms you need, and a handy size that makes it perfect to keep by your desktop or carry with a laptop. *Softcover, 400 pages, $19.99*

Webster's New World Dictionary of Computer Terms, Seventh Edition

BRYAN PFAFFENBERGER (IDG BOOKS, 1999)

▶ More than just a dictionary of computer and Internet terms, Bryan Pfaffenberger's book explains why a term is important and how it is related to other terms. Terms listed within this resource range from supergeeky, such as "symmetric key encryption algorithm," to superslang, such as "snaf." Within his definitions, Pfaffenberger italicizes any other words that you may not know, but that you can also access in the dictionary. One interesting feature is the list of common abbreviations used on Internet Relay Chat and Usenet (such as TTYL, for "talk to you later," and IMHO, for "in my humble opinion"). *Softcover, 580 pages, $12.95*

Computer and Information Systems

Smart Selection and Management of Association Computer Systems

THOMAS J. ORLOWSKI (AMERICAN SOCIETY OF ASSOCIATION EXECUTIVES, 1995)

▶ This book was written for CEOs and senior staff specialists who work with computer experts. Here's the information you need to make the right technology decisions for your association. This commonsense guide will help you wisely assess your organization's computer system needs, make sound purchasing decisions, and implement system changes. Topics include defining project scope and timetable, evaluating staff skills, working with consultants, selecting the system, and managing the project. Softcover, 85 pages, $20 (Nonmembers), $12.95 (Members)

Wired for Good: A Technology Guide Book for Nonprofits

(CENTER FOR EXCELLENCE IN NONPROFITS)

▶ The *Technology Guide* provides information to help nonprofit leaders determine the potential benefits of various technology applications in the organization; make good decisions about the organization's technology needs; ask informed questions when choosing vendors; and make an informed commitment of time, money, and people necessary to plan, implement, and sustain a viable technology environment that is appropriate to your needs. The *Technology Guide* is organized into two parts. Part One is an orientation to technology, how it can be used in an office environment, and what basic equipment and services are available. The final chapter in Part One helps you examine your current work systems to determine if any technology, or more technology, will be useful to you. Part Two assumes that you have decided to get serious about technology planning and that the plan will involve some level of networking, that is, connecting computers to each other to share information. The chapters help you translate technology requirements into a general network design and offer planning details about technical support needs, security matters, and budgeting. The final chapter contains lessons learned about technology planning, installation, and support. Throughout the book are "Stories from the Field," which feature real-life examples of how nonprofits are using technology to further their mission. *Softcover, 114 pages, $25 (plus $4 shipping)*

E-Commerce

The Nonprofit Organization's Guide to E-Commerce

GARY M. GROBMAN (NONPROFIT ISSUES)

▶ This book is the definitive guidebook for nonprofit executives who want to use the Internet for generating revenues. Read *The Nonprofit Organization's Guide to E-Commerce* and learn how to sell your products, handle Internet payments, fulfill orders, charge sales tax, and provide customer service; add an e-commerce component to your Web site, and where to find everything you need; write for the Web; set up an online shopping mall, charitable online auction, or online community; address security, privacy, copyright, and other legal issues; and effectively market your Web site. This book also includes capsule site reviews of more than 150 World Wide Web sites where you can obtain free e-commerce software, tools for your Web page, partner with online retailers, and much more. *Softcover, 182 pages, $19.95 (plus $4.00 for shipping)*

Information Technology—General

Association Technology Trends

(AMERICAN SOCIETY OF ASSOCIATION EXECUTIVES, 1997)

▶ Chronicling the current state of technology use in associations, this study thoroughly examines the development, use, and financing of Internet activities within associations. It also explores associations' use of computer systems, software, hardware, and member communication technologies such as broadcast faxing and voice mail. The study assesses the technology use of nearly 1,200 associations and is designed as a management tool that can be used by association executives to benchmark or compare the technology use in one's own organization with those in similar entities. *Softcover, 62 pages, $58 (Nonmembers), $48 (Members)*

Strategic Thinking for Information Technology

BERNARD H. BOAR (JOHN WILEY & SONS, 1996)

▶ In this jargon-free guide, IT strategist Bernard H. Boar surveys the terrain of the emerging information age and reveals how successful IT organizations have adapted their business strategies to this new environment and triumphed. He defines strategy in terms of its goals, its relationship to actions, and its impact on organizational structure, and points out specific ways in which IT affects the overall strategic plan, including 40 different strategic ideas and how they can be directly applied to information technology; four actions that the IT organization must take to enable the business to succeed in the information age; five ideas that encourage the breeding of new strategies in the marketplace—the cybermarketplace in which businesses will compete for share IT organizational design structures for the information age; and 50 flowcharts, templates, and tables that help explain and develop the techniques of strategic thinking. A special chapter reviews 40 strategic ideas and shows information technology managers how to directly apply them to their system. *Softcover, 288 pages, $54.99*

Internet—General

Associations Online: Making the Most of the Internet (Background Kit)

(AMERICAN SOCIETY OF ASSOCIATION EXECUTIVES, 1997)

▶ The Internet represents a new medium for association marketing, distribution, instruction, and interactive communication. This Background Kit is a collection of articles from ASAE publications and other sources, as well as samples, relevant to the subject of association Internet use. It includes an overview of the subject, several case studies of Web site development, discussions of Internet marketing applications, electronic mail applications, legal issues, and staff use issues. Statistics from ASAE surveys are provided as well as an extensive list of other resources including many Internet sites. *Spiral bound, 273 pages, $66 (Nonmember), $55 (Member)*

Atlas for the Information Superhighway, Book & CD-ROM Edition

PATRICK DOUGLAS CRISPEN (SOUTH-WESTERN EDUCATIONAL COMPUTER PUBLISHING, 1996)

▶ This book is adapted from Crispen's online *Roadmap Workshop* to direct students, newbies, and casual sightseers on a tour of the Internet and its many resources. Features include directions for use with Netscape Navigator, Mosaic, Microsoft's Internet Explorer, MacWeb, and IBM Web Explorer; on-line activities; 15 tabbed dividers for quick access to sections, including Usenet, the World Wide Web, Gopher, Telnet, and FTP; PC and Mac screen illustrations; a glossary of terms; and appendices that list addresses of Internet locations. An Internet training textbook, this guide for the general public also serves as an ancillary text for teachers who want to add Internet training to their curriculum; each chapter in the Atlas uses hands-on activities and end-of-chapter reviews to reinforce Internet knowledge and break down the material in the chapters so they are not so ominous to the reader, and 15 tabbed chapter dividers. There is also an Instructor's Manual available. An end-of-text glossary defines important Net language in understandable terms, and appendices provide an excellent highway atlas to great Internet locations and present a report citation style endorsed by the Alliance for Computers and Writing. *Spiral bound, 160 pages, $33.75*

Best Bet Internet: Reference and Research When You Don't Have Time to Mess Around

SHIRLEY DUGLIN KENNEDY (AMERICAN LIBRARY ASSOCIATION EDITIONS, 1998)

▶ As an Internet trainer in libraries, author Shirley Duglin Kennedy knows firsthand the frustration librarians feel when applying their professional research skills to the Internet. *Best Bet Internet* offers tips and tricks designed to help librarians satisfy their patrons on the spot. With the skeptical eye of a journalist and a librarian's sensibility, Kennedy has compiled a list and profiled more than 500 ready-for-reference sites. She also examines the best subject directories; offers tips on the various search engines; explains how e-mail discussion lists and news groups can aid in reference; evaluates and categorizes each site; and suggests when to use forgotten tools such as Gophers, Veronica, and Jughead. Kennedy's book on Web research sites is for anybody who's ever been frustrated by getting millions of useless hits out of a search engine. She shows you where to look when you need information, but don't have all day to slug through out-of-date, deserted, and plain inaccurate Web pages. Although Kennedy gives some guidelines for good search techniques—primarily when providing tips on using specific search sites—her emphasis is on reference sites that will lead you to dependable information.

The book mentions the big guns, such as Yahoo! and AltaVista, but the value of this collection lies in the more specialized sites. Kennedy devotes a chapter, for example, to sites that knowledgeable librarians and journalists depend on. Another chapter concentrates on sites particularly useful for tracking down people. The chapter on evaluating Internet resources is loaded with information everyone should know before attempting to do meaningful research online. In addition, Kennedy provides witty commentary on all the sites she reviews, on the state of the Internet, and on Internet culture as a whole. *Softcover, 208 pages, $35*

The Complete Idiot's Guide to the Internet, 6th Edition
PETER KENT (QUE, 1999)

▶ *The Complete Idiot's Guide to the Internet* is a great resource for the inexperienced cybertraveler. You'll learn how to get up and running on the Internet, to send and receive e-mail messages, to navigate around and find what you're looking for on the World Wide Web, to participate in Internet discussion groups, and to communicate with friends and family. The Guide also introduces you to Web multimedia, Gopher, Chat, and Telnet and teaches you how to create your own Web page. All topics are presented in the easy-to-understand language that is customary within the *Complete Idiot's Guide* series. The attached CD-ROM includes everything you need to get connected plus numerous Web tools and electronic copies of this and other books in the series. Featuring a disk packed with free software, this guide has everything reluctant users need to access the Internet. It introduces the must-know resources that make the Internet so popular, including electronic mail, government databases, news services, and much more. The humorous, nontechnical approach helps beginners learn their way around. Includes "Speak Like a Geek" definitions, E-Z Shortcuts, and Techno-Nerd tips for the curious. A full-color tear-out road map shows users how to get to the most popular Internet services. It covers the Internet for IBM and Compatibles. *Softcover, 496 pages, $15.99*

Dr. Bob's Painless Guide to the Internet . . . and Amazing Things You Can Do With E-Mail
BOB RANKIN (NO STARCH PRESS, 1996)

▶ No matter how you connect to the Internet (whether through e-mail alone or the latest Netscape beta), *Dr. Bob's Painless Guide to the Internet* will show you how to use *every* Internet tool—not just the World Wide Web. You will learn all about e-mail—what it is, what the rules are, and how to send and receive it; the World Wide Web—how to find the cool and useful sites; and how to connect to the Internet—what you need and what kind of account to get; search the Internet for the files you want (using Archie, Veronica, Gopher, and the World Wide Web) and then how to download them (using FTP) from computers around the world; access almost anything on the Internet using e-mail, saving time and money in the process; read newsgroups and subscribe to mailing lists that can help you to pursue your interests or advance your career; log onto and use computers around the world with Telnet; and chat online with Internet Relay Chat. Plus, you get a glossary of terms and the "Internet Mini-Yellow Pages," which lists lots of useful Internet resources that you'll be able to enjoy right now. Quantity discounts available for groups and classes. *Softcover, 145 pages, $12.95 (plus $2 shipping)*

Everybody's Guide to the Internet
ADAM GAFFIN (MIT PRESS, 1994)

▶ First "published" (made public) as *The Big Dummy's Guide to the Internet* electronically on the Net, Gaffin's work covers history, uses, and utilities. *Everybody's Guide* has moved to the top of the rapidly deepening stack of books on The Revolution. *Everybody's*

Guide is designed to make you comfortable in the virtual world of the Internet with its insider language and peculiar local culture. It offers a clear, bare-bones introduction to the Internet, with just enough technical information to get you online. Additional help is offered at the end of each chapter in the form of a section on what to do "when things go wrong," and another section, called "FYI," tells you where to look for further information. *Everybody's Guide* covers everything you need to know about the complex Internet environment: e-mail (including advanced e-mail); the "global watering hole" called Usenet and its essential newsgroups; mailing lists and bitnet; bulletin board systems; downloading files via FTP; information utilities such as Telnet, Gopher, Archie, Veronica, WAIS, and the World Wide Web; information services such as library catalogs, weather reports, and traveling advisories; news services; IRC and MUDs; and the network in the classroom. *Softcover, 211 pages, $14.95*

How the Internet Works: Millennium Edition, 5th Edition
PRESTON GRALLA (QUE, 1999)

▶ Have you ever wanted to know how data travels from computer to computer, around the world? Have you ever wondered how Web sites can track users or how newsgroups work? *How the Internet Works* shows you how with easy-to-follow, four-color visual spreads tracking the path data flows and the hardware involved. *How the Internet Works* helps you understand the latest in Internet and networking technology from cookies and data tracking to Web sound and video. Its visual approach demystifies the technology in a format that appeals to readers of all levels. Content includes explanations of digital certificates, extranets, Internet telephony, and metasearches and scripting languages such as XML and dynamic HTML. A basic introduction to the Internet and the World Wide Web explains how online information services and communications technologies work, answering questions about ISDN lines, modems, Java, offline browsers, push and pull, and other important topics. Topics cover Internet architecture, addressing, domain names, routers, connectivity, e-mail, newsgroups, Web browsers, push technologies, and Internet safety and security. *Softcover, 324 pages, $29.99*

How to Use the Internet, Fifth Edition
ROGERS CADENHEAD (SAMS, 1999)

▶ *How to Use the Internet, Fifth Edition,* visually steps you through everything you need to know in order to get connected to the Internet, browse and create Web pages, send and receive e-mail, read and post to newsgroups, and apply the Internet to your everyday office and home life. Over 100 two-page spreads illustrate and clearly explain each Internet task, from entry-level, beginning concepts to sophisticated techniques for more advanced users. Illustrations and figures lead you through each task with easy-to-follow directions and visual cues. *Softcover, 240 pages, $24.99*

The Instant Internet Guide
BRENT HELSOP AND DAVID ANGELL (ADDISON-WESLEY, 1994)

▶ This is a hands-on beginner's guide that provides a good quick introduction to Internet and quick reference sections on using e-mail, Usenet, Gopher, Telnet, file transfers, very basic UNIX, and so on; and a checklist of questions to ask when shopping for Internet access. It is oriented entirely toward a dial-up terminal user on a UNIX system. *Softcover, 209 pages, $14.95*

Internet 101: A Beginner's Guide to the Internet & the World Wide Web

WENDY G. LEHNERT (ADDISON-WESLEY LONGMAN, 1998)

▶ This is a textbook written by an experienced teacher as she designed a college-level course on the subject. *Internet 101* is written specifically with students in mind. It strives to nurture and enrich their interest and enthusiasm about the Internet. Written in a fun, relaxed style, this book teaches you everything that you need to know about the exciting world of the Internet and the World Wide Web. It contains the latest information on the Internet and includes discussions of social and ethical issues, in addition to exercises and special sidebars highlighting historical facts. Features include "FYI" warnings, "Real-Life Boxes," "Technical Definitions," "Help," and an abundance of screen shots to motivate and reinforce key concepts; a chapter on how to construct your own Web page; a frequently updated Web site that allows readers to find platform-specific information (PC, UNIX, MAC), read up-to-date information on links, and gain experience using the World Wide Web. *Softcover, 513 pages, $51.15*

Internet & Web Essentials: What You Need to Know

ERNEST ACKERMANN & KAREN HARTMAN (FRANKLIN, BEEDLE & ASSOCIATES, 2000)

▶ Like Ackermann's *Learning to Use the World Wide Web* and *Internet Today!*, co-authored by Karen Hartman, this latest effort covers the basic topics you need to know to master the ever-changing Internet. Furthermore, this book expands on vital topics such as searching and researching strategies and Web-page design issues that all students want to learn, with exercise examples shown for both Netscape Navigator and Internet Explorer browsers. *Hardcover, 608 pages, $27.95*

Internet Basics: The Non-Technical Guide to Cyberspace (Video and Manual)

BRETT THOMAS (NET-RESOURCES/THOMAS VIRTUAL GROUP)

▶ This state-of-the-art video course is designed for anyone who wants to learn to use the Internet to its full potential. This course, ideal for beginners, makes using the Internet easy . . . and fun. It covers navigating in cyberspace, the World Wide Web, browsers, e-mail, directories, search engines, downloading free software, online communities, 3D virtual worlds, and how to tap the global storehouse of knowledge that's available on the Net. *Video (purchased separately)—$59; Mastering the Internet Course (includes video, 85-page Learning Manual and HotLinks Software)—$99*

The Internet Companion: A Beginner's Guide to Global Networking, 2nd Edition

TRACY LAQUEY (ADDISON-WESLEY, 1994)

▶ This pocket-sized overview companion guide explains what the Internet is (including a detailed history), and the various tools available, as well as how to get connected. *The Internet Companion* explains in nontechnical language the structure, culture, and resources of the Internet. This book teaches you how to tap into university research databases, online archives, and vast social networks of up-to-date information; learn how to hook up to the Internet from your PC or Mac, use the Internet's e-mail, file transfer, and remote login; and understand the do's and don'ts of Internet etiquette. Covering the latest developments of this fast-changing world, it explores the growing commercialization of the Internet and examines the advantages of doing business on the Internet. With the second edition, LaQuey has updated the book to cover many of the new areas about the Internet, such as commercialization, and the increasingly sophisticated multimedia browser tools. The expanded Appendix includes many more Internet resources—with URLs (Uniform Resource Locators or Internet addresses for each). This updated edition is also available as *The Internet Companion Plus,* which comes bundled with Delphi's Internet access software enabling anyone with a PC and a modem to join the Internet. Primarily aimed at the general public, it is also being made available online (see separate listing in Information Technology—Internet Resources—Internet Tutorials, Guides, and Online Training). *The Internet Companion Plus* (includes DOS disk) is also available. *Softcover, 262 pages, $12.95 (The Internet Companion Plus, $19.95)*

The Internet for Busy People, Millenium Edition, 3rd Edition

CHRISTIAN CRUMLISH (OSBORNE MCGRAW-HILL, 2000)

▶ Get up and running on the Internet right away using this visually powerful learning tool. Packed with four-color art, annotated figures, and step-by-step directions, *The Internet for Busy People, Millennium Edition,* shows you the best, most efficient way to accomplish your tasks—while offering you insights into how you can be more productive while using the Internet. *Softcover, 264 pages, $19.99*

The Internet for Dummies®, 7th Edition Starter Kit

JOHN R. LEVINE, CAROL BAROUDI, MARGARET LEVINE YOUNG (IDG BOOKS, 2000)

▶ Covering the latest tools and techniques to get you up and running on the Internet in no time, *The Internet for Dummies, 7th Edition Starter Kit* delivers plain-English explanations describing how to go online. The seventh edition of this best-seller has been updated to focus on the parts of the Net that are most interesting to typical users—finding things on the Web with Netscape, Internet Explorer, and Opera; sending and receiving e-mail for person-to-person communications; chatting online; and downloading interesting things from the Web. Included with the book is a bonus CD-ROM, which offers the following tools to make every visit to the Web more productive. Web browsers: Netscape Communicator 4.7 and Microsoft Internet Explorer 5.0; E-Mail programs: Eudora Light and Outlook Express 5.0; Usenet newsgroups: Free Agent and InterNews; Compression and downloading tools: WS FTP LE, Anarchie, and StuffIt Expander; Web-page editors: HotDog Web Editor and BBEdit Lite; Graphics tools: Paint Shop Pro and GraphicConverter. *Softcover, 408 pages, $24.99*

The Internet Glossary and Quick Reference Guide

ALAN FREEDMAN, ALFRED GLOSSBRENNER, AND EMILY GLOSSBRENNER (AMACOM BOOKS, 1998)

▶ Computer lingo seems to be expanding about as fast as the Internet itself. The authors of this book provide an aid for those at risk of getting lost in the language. That includes everybody with a nontechnical background who suddenly has to do more than simply log on and check e-mail. Those who find they must deal with their company's Internet sites or in-house intranets will find this work invaluable in communicating with technical people, whether on their own staff or from vendors. This is quite helpful when it's important to know that the techie talking about ATM isn't discussing getting money from the automated teller machine but making data move across the network in Asynchronous Transfer Mode. More than providing definitions of the terms an Internet user or administrator is likely to fall across, the authors explain the backgrounds of terms and phrases, making the work almost like a mini-encyclopedia. For example, they not only define the term *bus* ("a common pathway, or channel, between multiple devices"), but they also provide an illustration of the concept, clearly describe types of buses, and even explain why it's called a *bus* in the first place. They also conveniently divide the entries into alphabetic and numeric, eliminating any confusion as to where to find, for example, 32-bit processing (which is not a reference to a processor worth $4) or 6 x 86 MX. *Softcover, 500 pages, $24.95*

Internet in a Nutshell
VALERIE QUERCIA (O'REILLY ASSOCIATES, 1997)

▶ *Internet in a Nutshell* is a guide to the Internet that goes beyond the "hype" and right to the heart of the matter: how to get the Internet to work for you. This is a second-generation Internet book for readers who have already taken a spin around the Internet and now want to learn the shortcuts. *Internet in a Nutshell* starts with a quick tour of the Internet, focusing on the technology that makes it work. It then dives into details on using the popular browsers, including their associated mail and news readers. Even the most seasoned Web surfer will find new tips on using their favorite browser. As with most tools, Internet software is useless if you don't know what to do with it. *Internet in a Nutshell* gives complete, concise coverage of how to find information on the Internet, with comparisons of the most popular search engines and how to use them to their best advantage. At the core, the Internet is about sharing information, which is often stored in discrete files. The book covers the various file types that are used across the Internet. It covers FTP, the file transfer protocol that is used today primarily for transferring downloadable programs and source code. It discusses how to deal with sending and receiving files over e-mail, both through attachments and more traditional means, and how to deal with compressed files. *Softcover, 450 pages, $24.95*

Internet Quick Reference
BILL EAGER (QUE, 1999)

▶ *Internet Quick Reference* delivers a valuable and convenient source of information on using common Internet and World Wide Web features. By focusing on a more referential approach, the same amount of feature coverage is provided in fewer pages. This highly visual approach also allows for much more coverage as one or two figures can often explain what would take several pages of text. The text is categorized by key Internet functions, then alphabetized within the group. *Softcover, 224 pages, $9.99*

Internet: The Complete Reference, Millenium Edition
MARGARET LEVINE YOUNG, ED. (OSBORNE MCGRAW-HILL, 1999)

▶ Make the most of all the Net has to offer with help from Internet author Margaret Levine Young. In *Internet: The Complete Reference, Millennium Edition,* you'll learn how get connected, choose an Internet service provider (ISP) and Web browser, send e-mail, chat, use plug-ins, purchase goods safely, find tons of helpful and fun information online—even create your own Web page. Inside, you'll find out how to connect to the Net via dial-up networking, TCP/IP, cable, or through a LAN; send and receive e-mail and attached files and handle security issues, including encryption and digital signatures; chat online using IRC, AOL, ICQ, and other methods; read Usenet newsgroups; use voice and videoconferencing technology; browse the Web with Netscape Navigator,

Netscape Communicator, and Internet Explorer; download and install software and other files using FTP; locate a wealth of useful information online—news, weather, books, investing tips, health issues, and more; find and install plug-ins and configure your browser to respond to ActiveX, Java, and other advanced controls; create basic to advanced Web pages with HTML, Frontpage, Javascript, and Active Server Pages; and register your domain name. Offering well beyond a simple description, readers will find advanced, detailed topics that cover connecting to the Internet and finer points of e-mail, chat sessions, conferences, and subscriptions. *Softcover, 956 pages, $39.99*

The Little Online Book
ALFRED GLOSSBRENNER (PEACHPIT PRESS, 1994)

▶ This beginner's guide gives you everything you need to begin exploring the electronic universe from your desktop. You can correspond with people all over the world, look up information, shop, join electronic clubs, download free software, and more with the help of this friendly, nontechnical book. It covers modems, communication software, the Internet, commercial online services, bulletin boards, and many other topics. It includes a step-by-step cookbook explaining common online tasks. In this book, Glossbrenner shows readers how to get connected and how to choose the online service best suited to their needs. He offers time- and money-saving tricks for using bulletin boards and tips for sending a message via modem to anyone, anywhere on the planet. Plus, he reveals the best reason for going online—the thousands of special interest groups (SIGs) and clubs that bring people together from all over the world. He shows how to find them and how to tap into them. Each chapter is short and to the point. *The Online Cookbook* at the end of the book takes readers by the hand, showing them exactly what steps they need to follow to get to where they want to go. Unlike other online books, this one assumes no prior knowledge on the part of the reader, and the focus is on accomplishing specific tasks as efficiently as possible. *Softcover, 426 pages, $17.95*

Pocket Guides to the Internet
(INFORMATION TODAY)

▶ This is a series of guides, published in 1994. The series includes the following titles: Vol. 1: Telnetting; Vol. 2: Transferring Files with FTP; Vol. 3: Using and Navigating Usenet; Vol. 4: The Internet E-mail System; Vol. 5: Basic Internet Utilities; and Vol. 6: Terminal Connections. *Softcover, 64–80 pages, $9.95/each*

The Whole Internet: The Next Generation
KIERSTEN CONNER-SAX AND ED KROL (O'REILLY & ASSOCIATES, 1999)

▶ *The Whole Internet: The Next Generation* is a book for a new generation of Internet users. There are more applications, more exciting information, and more problems to deal with, ranging from mere annoyances to outright theft. It is a book that illuminates how you can use the Internet effectively in today's environment. It explains how to deal with everyday problems like unsolicited e-mail and security alerts. It also tells you how to take advantage of new services on the Web. You will also find a next generation catalog of Internet resources, a wide-ranging selection of sites with special focus on "meta-sites" that provide extensive lists of related resources. *Softcover, 558 pages, $24.95*

Internet—Government and Politics

Electronic Democracy: Using the Internet to Influence American Politics
GRAEME BROWNING (CYBERAGE BOOKS, 1996)

▶ Here is everything you need to know to become a powerful player in the political process from your desktop. An experienced Washington reporter uses case studies to illustrate techniques for using the Internet to influence legislation inside the Beltway. Author Graeme Browning, formerly a congressional reporter with the respected *National Journal,* offers real-world strategies for using newsgroups, mailing lists, and the World Wide Web to impact decision makers in Washington. *Softcover, 186 pages, $19.95*

Internet—Nonprofits

200 Terrific Web Sites for NonProfit Organizations
BROWNIE S. HAMILTON (THE GRANTSMANSHIP SERVICE/GRANTS CONNECTION, 1998)

▶ Want to explore funding possibilities on the Internet? This must-have reference book will get you started. Consisting of 200 carefully chosen sites, the book identifies corporate, foundation, and government sites where grant seekers can match funding criteria to their organization's needs, download grant application forms, and read the funder's latest annual report. Included also are numerous sites of interest for the prospect researcher, sites that identify philanthropic publications, and sites of general interest to the fund-raiser. The book begins with a detailed introduction on how to use search engines for maximum effectiveness. *Softcover, 57 pages, $10*

Getting Started on the Internet
GARY M. GROBMAN AND GARY B. GRANT (AMHERST H. WILDER FOUNDATION, 1999)

▶ If all that's standing between you and the Internet is a little fear, lack of know-how, or both, this concise guide will help you quickly get connected to the world's largest library. *Getting Started on the Internet* shows you how to use e-mail, search engines, Web browsers, mailing lists, bulletin boards, and more. It also includes information on useful nonprofit Internet sites. *Softcover, 64 pages, $15*

The Nonprofit Guide to the Internet: How to Survive and Thrive, 2nd Edition
MICHAEL W. JOHNSTON (JOHN WILEY & SONS, 1999)

▶ This easy-to-use guide provides nonprofits with the information they need to not only survive on the Internet, but also thrive. Completely updated, it includes the latest technical advances, market trends, and cutting-edge tools that all nonprofits need if they want to maintain a cyber-advantage. It provides everything nonprofits need to boot up, log on, and benefit from the Net. Covering everything from computer basics to designing your own Web site, it shows you how to get connected, conduct research, raise funds, expand your outreach—with both adults and kids—electronically, and much more. With complete details on the latest technological advances, market trends, and cutting-edge tools, *The Nonprofit Guide to the Internet, Second Edition,* surveys the most up-to-date hardware and software you need to get online. *Softcover, 240 pages, $29.95*

The Non-Profit Internet Handbook *(See The Wilder Nonprofit Field Guide to Getting Started on the Internet)*

Top 300 Websites for Nonprofit Organizations (Disk)
MARILYN GROSS (EDUCATIONAL FUNDING STRATEGIES)

▶ Marilyn Gross has tamed the beast—the beast of proliferating Web sites, that is. In one convenient resource, one of the masters of the Internet has gathered together a definitive list of Web sites of importance and utility to nonprofit professionals, and painstakingly critiqued each and every one. A prodigious and time-consuming undertaking to be sure, but one that will prove enormously helpful for those who have grown weary of surfing for hour upon hour with precious little to show for it. The Web sites are organized into 15 categories. Among them are management and administrative, staffing, marketing and public relations, board issues and responsibilities, fund raising, specific interest sites (such as the arts, environment, education, health, etc.), volunteer recruitment and management, technology, educational resources, jobs and careers, and five additional groupings. With your Web browser open at the same time as your disk drive, you can click on any of the links and go directly to the sites. *$39*

The Wilder Nonprofit Field Guide to Getting Started on the Internet (Wilder Nonprofit Field Guide Series)
GARY M. GROBMAN, GARY B. GRANT (AMHERST H. WILDER FOUNDATION, 1999)

▶ This is your hands-on guide to getting connected quickly and easily. If all that is standing between you and the Internet is a little fear, lack of know-how, or both, this concise guide will help you quickly get connected to the world's largest library. Don't know what equipment you need? The authors make it simple, explaining what kind of computer, monitor, modem, telephone line, and software you'll need. A handy chart helps you compare the differences between local, national, and commercial Internet service providers. Don't know what an Internet service provider is? The Guide's five-page glossary demystifies terms that maybe you've heard but never quite understood. Once you know the lingo, it will be easier to do everything from buying a computer to surfing the Web. *Getting Started on the Internet* gives you all the basics so you can begin using this remarkable resource right away. You'll wonder why you didn't get connected sooner. *Getting Started on the Internet* shows you how to use e-mail, search engines, Web browsers, mailing lists, bulletin boards, and more. It also includes information on useful nonprofit Internet sites. *Getting Started on the Internet* also shows you how to use the Internet to uncover valuable information and help your nonprofit be more productive. E-mail is just one of many Internet benefits you'll learn to use. Through instruction, diagrams, and examples, the guide also shows you how to use search engines to track down information; how to use mailing lists and bulletin boards for everything from finding job candidates to finding solutions to management problems; what chat lines are and how to use them; how to use a Web browser (and what they look like); useful nonprofit Internet sites, such as Charity Village, the Internet Nonprofit Center, Nonprofit Genie, and more. *Softcover, 64 pages, $15*

Internet Subject Guides and Directories

Finding Government Information on the Internet: A How-to-Do-It Manual

JOHN MAXYMUK (NEAL-SCHUMAN, 1995)

▶ There's a wealth of government information available on the Internet, some of it available in no other format—much of it free! Depository and nondepository libraries can use this invaluable manual to locate and deliver the latest government information to patrons, and enhance their collections via the Net with highly current documents or resources it does not receive. *Softcover, 264 pages, $49.95*

Government Information on the Internet, 3rd Edition

GREG R. NOTESS (BERNAN ASSOCIATES, 2000)

▶ *Government Information on the Internet* helps researchers find answers to their research questions from one of the most reliable sections of the Internet—government information. In addition to comprehensive coverage of the U.S. government sites, entries for state, foreign, and international resources are included. Lists of finding aids and multiple indexes help users refine and focus their research. The new edition contains updated URLs and new content descriptions for over 2,000 government Web sites—more than 300 new. It provides comprehensive coverage of federal sites, plus state, international, and foreign sites. A particularly valuable feature of this work is its identification of online publications available from hundreds of Web sites. *Softcover, 800 pages, $39.50*

How to Access the Federal Government on the Internet

BRUCE MAXWELL (CONGRESSIONAL QUARTERLY BOOKS, 1999)

▶ With U.S. federal agencies and departments continuing to use the Internet to offer free information to the public, invaluable information and many hot tips are there for the taking. But many new sites have been added, many sites are still hard to find, and those that are found often provide only stale and misleading information. In this new edition of *How to Access the Federal Government on the Internet,* Bruce Maxwell helps turn the vast universe of information about the U.S. federal government into a world where readers can find the exact information they need. The detailed index points readers to specific information and the easy organization of topical chapters helps readers develop a general feel for "what's out there." The complete guide to locating government resources on the Internet, *How to Access the Federal Government on the Internet* should replace the "blue pages" of your local phone book as the best way to locate information from or about the United States federal government. This comprehensive reference to Web sites, bulletin boards, official e-mail addresses, mailing lists, and more is organized into 21 sections and covers all of the major areas of government, including defense, foreign affairs, education, energy, and transportation. The collection of sites and services is impressive and ranges from official government sites, such as THOMAS, to independent organizations, such as Project Vote Smart. Each source cited has an easy-to-navigate tabbed "Vital Stats" listing on the side of the page, which includes available access methods, guest login information, and e-mail addresses. A thorough review is given for each entry, citing the quality and quantity of information available. The detailed appendix contains a listing of e-mail addresses and Web sites for members of Congress, listed by state. The updated edition

includes nearly 200 new Internet government resources for a total of over 600 sites listed and reviewed. *Softcover, 328 pages, $29.95*

Internet Blue Pages: The Guide to Federal Government Web Sites

LAURIE ANDRIOT (CYBERAGE BOOKS, 1999)

▶ A portable search engine, this guide through the maze of official government Web sites is patterned after the *U.S. Government Manual*. The companion Web site at *http://www.fedweb.com* provides updates and links directly to every site that is listed. Readers will be able to quickly and easily access information on services and programs run by almost every department of the government. The alphabetically listed entries are numbered and fully indexed to make finding important governmental information easier than ever. With over 900 Web addresses, this guide is designed to help you find any agency easily. Arranged in accordance with the *U.S. Government Manual,* each entry includes the name of the agency, the Web address (URL), a brief description of the agency, and links to the agency or subagency's home page. For helpful cross-referencing, an alphabetical agency listing and a comprehensive index for subject searching are also included. Regularly updated information and links are provided on the author's Web site. *Softcover, 368 pages, $34.95*

Browsers

Sams Teach Yourself Internet Explorer 5 in 24 Hours

JILL FREEZE (SAMS, 1999)

▶ In just 24 sessions of one hour or less, you will be up and running with Internet Explorer 5. Using a straightforward, step-by-step approach, each lesson builds upon the previous one, allowing you to learn the essentials of Internet Explorer 5 from the ground up. *Softcover, 464 pages, $19.99*

Sams Teach Yourself Netscape Communicator 4.5 in 24 Hours

SHANNON TURLINGTON (SAMS, 1998)

▶ In just 24 sessions of one hour or less, you will be up and running with Netscape Communicator 4.5. Using a straightforward, step-by-step approach, each lesson builds upon the previous one, allowing you to learn the essentials of Communicator 4.5 from the ground up. Learn how to search the Web and find what you want quickly, go to your favorite Web pages quickly and find out automatically when they change, create your own personal and professional Web pages, keep in touch with friends and family by sending instant messages, make Web surfing safe for your family by filtering, get e-mail and news from the same window, and schedule group and personal activities with Calendar, a complete scheduling tool that comes with Communicator 4.5. *Softcover, 432 pages, $19.99*

Bulletin Board Systems

The Complete Cyberspace Reference and Directory: An Addressing and Utilization Guide to the Internet, Electronic Mail Systems, and Bulletin Board System

GILBERT HELD (JOHN WILEY & SONS, 1997)

▶ This comprehensive guide provides readers with everything they need to know to access and navigate the "Information

Superhighway," including how to transmit and receive information electronically, via a variety of electronic messaging services, bulletin boards, and the Internet; and what information is available electronically, and where to find it.

Beginning where most references end, *The Complete Cyberspace Reference and Directory* starts with a comprehensive glossary of terms, definitions, and abbreviations, which serves as an excellent introduction to the vast amount of information that the book provides. From there, the book discusses the procedures for electronic communications via a variety of channels, such as Internet FTP, Internet Telnet, CompuServe E-mail, and MCI Mail. Each chapter begins with a tutorial on using an electronic information system and then continues with a comprehensive listing of the information resources that users can access via the system. Over 10,000 electronic addresses—including more than 1,000 anonymous FTP sites and 300 libraries—are provided, making *The Complete Cyberspace Reference and Directory* the most complete resource currently available. Whether you are already an experienced traveler on the electronic highway, or just embarking on your first trip, *The Complete Cyberspace Reference and Directory* will give you all the information you need for a swift and prosperous journey. *Softcover, 765 pages, $30.95*

Creating Successful Bulletin Board Systems

ALAN D. BRYANT (ADDISON-WESLEY LONGMAN, 1994)

▶ Electronic bulletin board systems (BBS) offer limitless possibilities for advertising products and services, transacting business, and exchanging information. This guide shows how to put a BBS online for hobby, problem solving, or entrepreneurial purposes. It offers savvy advice on how to run a business using a BBS and how to use a BBS just for fun. *Softcover, 416 pages, $40*

The Essential Guide to Bulletin Board Systems

PATRICK R. DEWEY (INFORMATION TODAY, INC., 1998)

▶ As many as 12 million people may log on to the interactive computer databases known as bulletin board systems. BBS networks such as FidoNet now even rival the Internet for traffic. For new and prospective BBS operators, Illinois public library district director and microcomputer instructor Dewey consults on BBS types, hardware, software, business plans for success (with examples of successful BBSs), going global, operational troubleshooting, resources, and a glossary. This book details the setup and operation of bulletin board systems, which are interactive computer databases. There are chapters on hardware and software selection, software applications for personal computers, operational problems, and working with the World Wide Web, as well as examples of bulletin board system operations. These chapters are followed by invaluable resources such as a vendor list, Internet service providers, distributors, consultants, bulletin boards to call, and bulletin board system resources on the Internet. *Hardcover, 165 pages, $39.50*

Washington Online: How to Access the Government's Electronic Bulletin Boards, 4th Edition

BRUCE MAXWELL (CONGRESSIONAL QUARTERLY BOOKS, 1998)

▶ Access the federal government's vast bulletin board systems—free—and download the information to your own computer. Here are up-to-date descriptions of more than 200 federal bulletin boards arranged by 16 subjects, plus information on how to reach them and what they offer. *Softcover, 391 pages, $38.50*

Online and Internet Searching

Best Bet Internet: Reference and Research When You Don't Have Time to Mess Around

SHIRLEY DUGLIN KENNEDY (AMERICAN LIBRARY ASSOCIATION EDITIONS, 1998)

▶ *Best Bet Internet* offers tips and tricks designed to help librarians satisfy their patrons on the spot. With the skeptical eye of a journalist and a librarian's sensibility, Kennedy has compiled a list and profiled more than 500 ready-for-reference sites. She also examines the best subject directories; offers tips on the various search engines; explains how e-mail discussion lists and newsgroups can aid in reference; evaluates and categorizes each site; and suggests when to use forgotten tools such as Gophers, Veronica, and Jughead. Anyone can surf the Net, but Kennedy can show you how to use the Information Superhighway as a practical information-gathering tool. When there is no time to mess around, reach for *Best Bet Internet*. Kennedy's book on Web research sites is for anybody who's ever been frustrated by getting millions of useless hits out of a search engine. She shows you where to look when you need information, but don't have all day to slug through out-of-date, deserted, and plain inaccurate Web pages. Although Kennedy gives some guidelines for good search techniques—primarily when providing tips on using specific search sites—her emphasis is on reference sites that will lead you to dependable information. The book mentions the big guns, such as Yahoo! and AltaVista, but the value of this collection lies in the more specialized sites. Kennedy devotes a chapter, for example, to sites that knowledgeable librarians and journalists depend on. Another chapter concentrates on sites particularly useful for tracking down people. The chapter on evaluating Internet resources is loaded with information everyone should know before attempting to do meaningful research online. *Softcover, 208 pages, $35*

CyberSearch: Research Techniques in the Electronic Age

JOHN A. BUTLER (PENGUIN REFERENCE, 1998)

▶ This useful reference is appropriate for students, teachers, historians, writers, lawyers, librarians, doctors, and home browsers. Butler's text covers the basics of hardware, software, and getting Internet access; what CD-ROMs offer; and what research resources are available, and what they provide. From *Books in Print* to *Tapping the Government Grapevine* to *The Internet Directory*, Butler introduces a wonderful selection of resources that are worth adding to your list, if not to your personal library. Butler explores search strategies, introduces OPAC (online public access catalog) searches, and clarifies the use of e-mail, newsgroups, and Telnet, navigators, Gophers, and the World Wide Web. This handy reference includes material on Internet resources, CD-ROMs, public-access catalogs, news groups, library reference sources, and more. Written in jargon-free language, *CyberSearch* includes an index of useful Web sites, Uniform Resource Locators, telephone numbers, addresses, step-by-step instructions for conducting searches, and a glossary of terms and acronyms. *Softcover, $224 pages, $12.95*

Finding It on the Internet: The Internet Navigator's Guide to Search Tools and Techniques, Revised and Expanded, 2nd Edition

PAUL GILSTER (JOHN WILEY & SONS, 1996)

▶ Now extensively revised to reflect the dramatic growth of the Internet, this new edition explores the new generation of graphically based search tools designed for the World Wide Web and the Internet. It also features updated coverage of traditional UNIX search tools. Users find out how each tool works as well as research strategies. This guide gives you the tools and techniques you need to get the information you want. *Finding It on the Internet* shows you how to conceive, design, and execute focused and efficient searches to get the information you need as quickly as possible. Following the enormous success of its previous edition, this revised and expanded second edition clearly and concisely demonstrates the new generation of graphical Internet programs, including Netscape and Mosaic, WinWAIS, WSGopher, WSarchie; specialized Web search directories and engines, such as Yahoo!, Galaxy, Lycos, InfoSeek, and WebCrawler; the established successful tools, such as WAIS, Archie, Veronica, Jughead, and Gopher; and numerous other tools, tips, and techniques for getting what you want from the Internet. *Softcover, 379 pages, $24.95*

Great Scouts!: CyberGuides to Subject Searching on the Web

NORA PAUL AND MARGOT WILLIAMS (CYBERAGE BOOKS, 1999)

▶ *Great Scouts!* is a cure for information overload. Authors Nora Paul (The Poynter Institute) and Margot Williams (the *Washington Post*) direct readers to the very best subject-specific, Web-based information resources. Thirty chapters cover specialized "CyberGuides" selected as the premier Internet sources of information on business, education, arts and entertainment, science and technology, health and medicine, politics and government, law, sports, and much more. With its expert advice and evaluations of information and link content, value, currency, stability, and usability, *Great Scouts!* takes you "beyond search engines"—and directly to the top sources of information for your topic. As a reader bonus, the authors are maintaining a Web page featuring updated links to all the sites covered in the book. *Softcover, 320 pages, $24.95*

The Information Specialist's Guide to Searching and Researching on the Internet and the World Wide Web, 2nd Edition

ERNEST ACKERMANN AND KAREN HARTMAN (FRANKLIN, BEEDLE & ASSOCIATES, 2000)

▶ This book is for information specialists—researchers, librarians, and others whose work involves working with information. It's also very useful for almost anyone interested in tapping the Web and the Internet for information. Several different types of information resources—subject guides, search engines, and specialized databases—are discussed, along with research skills and strategies to help you find whatever interests you. Here are techniques and strategies for navigating the World Wide Web, with results in quick, efficient, and in-depth research results. The major databases are covered in detail, and the top search engines are described and contrasted. The enclosed CD-ROM contains Netscape Navigator 4. Ackermann and Hartman steer clear of the particulars of Internet technology in this straightforward treatise on searching and research. There is no mention of Java, CGI, or TCP/IP. Instead, the focus is on search engines, Boolean operators, Web site evaluation, and Internet resource identification. Roughly half of each chapter consists of step-by-step exercises in defining and resolving a research problem. The authors stress techniques and principles but also indicate some of the best sites for seeking various kinds of information. Includes useful appendices, a glossary, and a chapter on citation styles. *Softcover, 488 pages, $29.95*

Internet Power Searching: The Advanced Manual

PHIL BRADLEY (LIBRARY ASSOCIATION PUBLISHING/NEAL-SCHUMAN, 1998)

▶ Despite all the hype about how easy the Internet is to use, and how almost anything can be found, unless the user is a skilled searcher, this is far from the case. The book is designed to assist experienced users to get much more out of the Internet. It explains exactly how search engines work and how, when, and why to use particular engines. It also covers intelligent agents, virtual libraries, mailing lists, newsgroups, and hints and tips for better searching. It is written for anyone who wants to become a better and more effective searcher. The book contains visual devices such as screenshots, step-by-step examples, sidebars, icons, and search tips, as well as useful Web sites and valuable utilities. The main topics covered include main search engines; other available databases on the Internet; intelligent agents, virtual libraries and gateways; how to get the best use out of popular browsers, USENET newsgroups and mailing lists; and future developments of the Internet. The book is designed for both experienced and novice users of the Internet for information. Although it pays particular attention to the use information professionals can make of the Internet, it should be of use to anyone who wishes to find information quickly. *Softcover, 248 pages, $45*

The Internet Searcher's Handbook: Locating Information, People, & Software (Neal-Schuman Netguide Series), 2nd Edition

PETER MORVILLE, LOUIS B. ROSENFELD, JOSEPH JANES, AND GRACEANNE A. DECANDIDO (NEAL-SCHUMAN, 1999)

▶ Completely revised and expanded, this new edition of the highly acclaimed *Internet Searcher's Handbook* is ideal for reference librarians, students, and researchers of any kind. The authors provide a step-by-step tutorial for resource discovery on the Internet to help novice or advanced users conduct comprehensive research and find answers to quick reference queries. The *Handbook* offers in-depth coverage on all useful and usable resources, including virtual libraries, digital resources, bots and intelligent agents, metadata, search engines, Web guides, online communities, virtual libraries, Internet directories, and Internet search tools. Numerous quick reference charts for all the major search engines and directories will save hours of frustrating search time and help any reader streamline the searching process. *Softcover, 165 pages, $45*

Internet Searching for Dummies®

BRAD HILL (IDG BOOKS, 1998)

▶ No matter what you're looking for on the World Wide Web your chances for finding it quickly and painlessly get a welcome boost with the search tips, tricks, and techniques packed into online expert Brad Hill's *Internet Searching for Dummies*. Cut through the hype and the hyperbole about the Web and find the information you want fast with the friendly point-and-click advice you'll discover in *Internet Searching for Dummies*. From Web directories and portal sites to the top online search engines, you'll find out how to navigate the Web safely for topics and sites about news, entertainment, online shopping, people, health, education, finances, and software downloads. The book also features helpful advice on choosing the right browser, and the book's bonus CD-ROM contains personal search engine software, various Internet utilities, browser plug-ins (to help you enjoy the Web's multimedia effects), and more. *Softcover, 384 pages, $24.99*

Internet Today: E-mail, Searching & the World Wide Web

ERNEST C. ACKERMANN AND KAREN HARTMAN (FRANKLIN, BEEDLE & ASSOCIATES, 1999)

▶ In this illustrated introduction to the online world, the authors cover all the bases: key terms and concepts; using a Web browser; electronic mail basics; finding information; search engine strategies; writing your own Web pages; the non-Web Internet; and social, legal, and security issues. It includes exercises and a glossary ("acceptable use policy" to "WWW"). An instructor's guide and supporting Web site is also available. This is a thorough and well-documented description of e-mail, search techniques, and search tools. It is one of the few books designed specifically as a teaching text for beginners, but experienced searchers have much to learn as well from the comprehensive material. The format makes it easy to scan text, the index locates specific details, and chapters conclude with summaries, terms, and exercises. Web screens, bulleted lists, charts, and examples help illustrate the concepts. Published in 1999, it does not cover the most current changes, but it is an excellent resource for learners and teachers. *Softcover, 286 pages, $35.95*

NetResearch: Finding Information Online

DANIEL J. BARRETT (O'REILLY ASSOCIATES, 1997)

▶ Barrett's approach is to teach the techniques, strategies, and realities of finding information online. Topics covered include basics for beginners; starting points; search techniques and engines; finding places, people, and software; and putting new information online. It is an excellent teaching guide and a good work for individualized learning. In NetResearch, you'll learn successful search techniques that work with any Internet search programs, present or future, by using your instincts to track down what you need. NetResearch presents strategies of the Internet's expert searchers: how to choose effective starting points, follow hunches, narrow down possibilities, and even overcome failure by looking at search possibilities from different viewpoints. Whatever your profession or avocation, NetResearch teaches you how to locate the information you need in the constantly changing online world. It covers the Internet, America Online, CompuServe, Microsoft Network, and Prodigy, and includes quizzes for practicing your research skills or teaching others how to search effectively. *Softcover, 200 pages, $24.95*

The Online Deskbook: Online Magazine's Essential Desk Reference for Online and Internet Searchers

MARY ELLEN BATES (INFORMATION TODAY, 1996)

▶ A desk reference that covers all the major online services and the Internet, this book helps you identify important online information sources and put them to immediate use. Loaded with shortcuts, troubleshooting guides, tips, and techniques, this reference guide contains the nuts and bolts needed to get you up and running online. It provides information on every major professional and general online service and the Internet for experienced and novice users. It features command charts, troubleshooting guides, shortcuts, and answers to frequently asked questions, as well as nuts-and-bolts information on access codes, logging on, system requirements, e-mail availability, prices, and training. It includes lists of databases on each professional online service, plus top professional and consumer databases. *Softcover, 261 pages, $29.95*

Researching Online for Dummies®, 2nd Edition
(Book & CD-ROM)

REVA BASCH AND MARY ELLEN BATES, DUMMIES TECHNOLOGY PRESS (IDG BOOKS, 2000)

▶ *Researching Online for Dummies* shows you how to stay focused, find just what you need on the Net, and apply that information to the project you're working on. The authors cover the usual suspects (Yahoo! and its ilk) but go far beyond them, introducing specialized search engines, "ready reference" sources, industry-specific megasites, online libraries, and "gated information services" (some of which are fee-based; others are free). It includes a CD-ROM with demos of the best online research software, plus direct hyperlinks to all the sites mentioned in the book. Inside, find helpful advice on how to choose the best search engine for your research project; use search tools specialized for your area of interest; link up with a virtual guru for guidance on your quest; get just what you need from online libraries, archives, and gated information services; tackle governmental cyberbureaucracy like a special agent; make the most of the business and investing data on the Web; and verify your information, deal with copyright issues, and cite online resources properly. It also offers a 30-page directory dedicated to describing selected research sites, services, and other useful online resources. The book's bonus CD-ROM includes search engine help files from Northern Light and Lycos as well as demo versions of Copernic, BullsEye, and WebWhacker. The book concludes with the famous Dummies "Part of Tens," including Ten Timeless Truths about Search Engines and Ten Clarifying Questions for Better Research Results. The accompanying CD-ROM has three bonus chapters: "Life Choices," about using the Net to find information on finding a college, a car, a job, and other necessities; "Recreational Interests: Hobbies, Interests, and Leisure-Time Pursuits"; and "Ten Simple Tune-ups for Streamlined Searching." A bonus section on Boolean searches contains one of the better discussions of that misunderstood subject. *Softcover, 384 pages, $24.99*

Secrets of the Super Net Searchers

REVA BASCH (CYBERAGE BOOKS, 1996)

▶ Reva Basch, top online searcher and cyber-journalist, reveals the insights, anecdotes, tips, techniques, and case studies of 35 of the world's top Internet hunters and gatherers. These Super Net Searchers explain how to find valuable information on the Internet, including where the Internet shines as a research tool, distinguishing cyber-gems from cyber-junk, and how to avoid "Internet Overload." She asks the questions that reveal the secret strategies and planning techniques of the industry's top searchers in the fields of business, law, finance, communications, and the humanities. Learn how skilled searchers choose databases on professional online services, plan search strategies, cope with too many or too few hits, and know when the search is done. *Softcover, 335 pages, $39.95*

Search Engines

Complete Idiot's Guide to Yahoo!

MICHAEL MILLER (QUE, 2000)

▶ *Complete Idiot's Guide to Yahoo!* covers all content and services for the fastest-growing site on the Internet. Explore the capabilities of this global phenomenon by learning basic navigation and operation, searching for information, e-mail, chat, personal calendar/scheduling, and much more. See the hottest spots for news, sports, weather, finance, children's information, auctions, classified ads, personals, online shopping, and much more. You'll also see how easy it is to build a personal home page with GeoCities, create and send greeting cards, reconcile your checkbook balance, decorate your Windows desktop, and find ways to make your PC run faster. *Softcover, 339 pages, $19.99*

Neal-Schuman Authoritative Guide to Web Search Engines (Neal-Schuman Net-Guide Series)
SUSAN MAZE, DAVID MOXLEY, AND DONNA J. SMITH (NEAL-SCHUMAN, 1997)

▶ This guide describes, evaluates, and explains how to locate information with popular search tools that use automatic indexing software to efficiently and effectively discover, harvest, and index Web pages. Features of this manual include an introduction to search engines and chapters offering individual looks at the most widely known and used, such as WebCrawler, Lycos, Infoseek, OpenText, Altavista, Excite, and HotBot; a general explanation of how all Web search tools create and search their indexes and databases; a discussion of the interface (the medium that allows the user to enter a query, and then translates the query for the search engine); an explanation of how robots discover resources on the Web and their limitations, as well as depth-first versus breadth-first searching; and handy charts that help you compare search engine features, enabling you to choose the best one before you begin searching. Each description of a search engine contains information about who created it, the size of its database, the spiderbot or harvester it uses to retrieve information, how often it is updated, what is indexed, how this is determined, and the step-by-step methods to find information with each. Additional chapters offer a comparison of the various search engines, a look at the economics of search engines, an annotated listing of meta-engines, and a glossary. *Softcover, 179 pages, $55*

The Extreme Searcher's Guide to Web Search Engines: A Handbook for the Serious Searcher
RANDOLPH HOCK (CYBERAGE BOOKS, 1999)

▶ Whether you're a new Web user or an experienced online searcher, here's a practical guide that shows you how to make the most of the leading Internet search tools. Written by leading Internet trainer Randolph (Ran) Hock, this book gives an in-depth view of the major search engines, explaining their respective strengths and weaknesses, features, and providing detailed instructions on how to use each to its maximum potential. As a reader bonus, the author is maintaining a regularly updated directory online. *Softcover, 212 pages, $24.95*

Search Engines: For the World Wide Web, 2nd Edition (Visual Quickstart Guide Series)
ALFRED GLOSSBRENNER AND EMILY GLOSSBRENNER (PEACHPIT PRESS, 2000)

▶ Search engines are the keys that unlock the information treasure houses of the Internet. Unfortunately, most people have no idea how to tap their power. Like software applications, each search engine has its own unique features. People who know how to use these features are able to focus their searches more sharply and are more likely to find the information they want. Each search engine also has its strengths and weaknesses. It is important to select the right search engine for the job. It offers step-by-step, up-to-date chapters on each of the most popular Web search engines: AltaVista, Excite, HotBot, InfoSeek, Lycos, WebCrawler, and Yahoo!. The book also describes the more advanced features of

each engine, with step-by-step guides to access these features, and covers what each engine is best suited for. It also shows the reader how to quickly find particular people or companies via other search tools such as Four11, BigBook, and Big Yellow. From the basics of searching to the specifics of the major Web search sites, you'll find out what to look for, where to look for it, and how to get the best results the first time. Search Engines for the World Wide Web also gathers the quick reference charts into an appendix for even faster access. An introductory chapter discusses the basics of searching—unique keywords, Boolean operators, and the Seven Habits of Effective Web Searches—which will be valuable even if you consider yourself an expert at searching the Web. Other chapters cover specialized engines such as DejaNews for Usenet newsgroups, Liszt for mailing lists, Four11 for people-finding, Zip2 for yellow pages, and a whole host of sites for finding information on specific topics and subjects. *Softcover, 288 pages, $17.99*

Web Developer.com® Guide to Search Engines
WES SONNENREICH AND TIM MACINTA (JOHN WILEY & SONS, 1998)

▶ Written by a team of MIT Internet specialists, this comprehensive reference teaches Webmasters and Web developers how to choose, select, and implement the right search engine for their intranet or large Internet Web site. The book also describes and compares the most popular search engines and directories, explains their ranking systems, and teaches how users can get best results. The companion Web site contains freeware, shareware, and a demo version of a commercial search engine, as well as examples used throughout the book. *Softcover, 464 pages, $34.99*

Web Publishing

Beyond HTML
RICHARD KARPINSKI (OSBORNE MCGRAW-HILL, 1999)

▶ With its limited graphics and layout capabilities, HyperText Markup Language (HTML) is rapidly becoming a technology of the past. World Wide Web designers are now able to use more sophisticated electronic publishing formats that give them the flexibility and graphics capabilities associated with magazine and newspaper layouts. Organized into five sections, this book sorts out the contenders from the pretenders and provides you with an in-depth understanding of the key technologies you'll need to stay competitive. You'll discover everything from HTML alternatives—such as Adobe's Acrobat, to interactivity and multimedia products like Java, virtual reality, real-time audio, and multi-user environments. *Softcover, 512 pages, $27.05*

Dynamic HTML: The Definitive Reference
DANNY GOODMAN (O'REILLY & ASSOCIATES, 1998)

▶ After testing tags and techniques on multiple releases of the main browsers, Goodman came up with very practical information, some of which you may not find in any other resource. Goodman assumes a solid foundation, if not expertise, in basic HTML and an understanding of what DHTML is all about. From those assumptions, he presents a meaty, information-dense volume. The first of the book's four sections discusses industry standards and how to apply the basic principles of DHTML. He emphasizes the differences in Web browsers and discusses how to build pages so that they work well in both Netscape Navigator and Microsoft Internet Explorer. The second section is an extensive, quick reference of all the tags, objects, and properties of HTML, cascading style sheets,

Document Object Model, and core JavaScript. A particularly handy cross-reference guide to this information follows, helping you locate it in alternate ways. The final section contains appendices, with useful tables of values and commands. *Softcover, 1,073 pages, $44.95*

HTML 4 for the World Wide Web: Visual QuickStart Guide, 4th Edition

ELIZABETH CASTRO (PEACHPIT PRESS, 1999)

▶ HyperText Markup Language (HTML) is the lingua franca of the Web, and like any language, it's constantly evolving. That's why Elizabeth Castro has written *HTML 4 for the World Wide Web, Visual QuickStart Guide, 4th Edition,* an update to her guide to *HTML 4.* You'll find all the concise, practical advice—and fun examples—that made the first edition a worldwide bestseller, plus entirely new coverage of debugging, JavaScript, and using tables for page layout, and an expanded section on Cascading Style Sheets. This book breaks even the most complex tasks into easy-to-follow steps illustrated with hundreds of screenshots and the actual code. The book presumes no prior knowledge of HTML, making it the perfect introduction for beginners. It uses clear, concise instructions for creating each element of the Web page, from titles and headers to creating links and adding tables, frames, forms, and multimedia. It is a tutorial for novices and a reference for experienced users, featuring step-by-step instruction, tips, troubleshooting advice, and a visual approach with screenshots and code examples. This fourth edition contains a new debugging chapter, expanded coverage of cascading style sheets, a new section on attracting visitors to a Web page, and a set of CGI scripts for processing forms. Its tabbed format and info-packed appendices (on special HTML characters and Web-safe colors, for example) also make it a useful reference for those who build Web pages for a living. *Softcover, 384 pages, $19.99*

HTML Pocket Reference

JENNIFER NIEDERST (O'REILLY ASSOCIATES, 1999)

▶ The author of *Web Design in a Nutshell,* Jennifer Niederst delivers a concise guide to every HTML tag in this pocket reference. Targeted at Web designers and Web authors, it also contains detailed information on the tag's attributes as well as browser support information. Each tag entry includes detailed information on the tag's attributes; browser support information, including Netscape Navigator, Microsoft Internet Explorer, Opera, and WebTV; and HTML 4.0 support information, including whether the tag is deprecated in the current spec. In addition to tag-by-tag descriptions, the book also includes several useful charts, including character entities, decimal-to-hexadecimal conversions, color names. Niederst also provides context for the tags, indicating which tags are grouped together and bare-bones examples of how standard Web page elements are constructed. *Softcover, 96 pages, $9.95*

HTML: The Complete Reference (The Complete Reference), 2nd Edition

THOMAS A. POWELL (OSBORNE McGRAW-HILL, 1999)

▶ An industry expert gives detailed information about HTML through tutorials, important theory, and definitive references. The book contains 16 chapters and includes examples of why and when to use specific aspects of HTML. Tags new to HTML 4.0 are highlighted, and source code for the book will be posted on Osborne's Web site for easy access. Powell provides an introduction to the workings of the World Wide Web because it eventually makes it easier for readers to understand why their HTML Web sites behave as they do. Powell begins the book with introductory chapters that discuss HTML and Web background and set the limits of what HTML coding alone can accomplish. From there, he moves into lessons in basic HTML and progresses chapter by chapter to such high-end topics as advanced layout techniques, how to standardize Web-page presentation among browsers with style sheets, programmed Web pages, and client-side scripting and programming. He provides lessons, techniques, and examples based on his highly successful UCSD Extension Web Publishing Certificate Program. Discover how to use HTML in conjunction with the latest Web technologies, including CSS, JavaScript, DHTML, Cold Fusion, XML, and Active Server Pages, and learn how HTML works with Netscape Navigator and Microsoft Internet Explorer. The six appendices finish the book with a wealth of easy-to-use quick-reference information including HTML tags, color/HEX values, color names, fonts, and style sheets. *Softcover, 1130 pages, $39.99*

HTML: The Definitive Guide, 3rd Edition

CHUCK MUSCIANO AND BILL KENNEDY (O'REILLY & ASSOCIATES, 1998)

▶ HTML is changing so fast it's almost impossible to keep up with developments. *HTML: The Definitive Guide, 3rd Edition* covers Netscape Navigator 4.5, Internet Explorer 4.0, HTML, JavaScript, style sheets, layers, and all of the features supported by the popular Web browsers. The authors cover every element of HTML in detail, explaining how each element works and how it interacts with other elements. Many hints about HTML style help you write documents ranging from simple online documentation to complex marketing and sales presentations. With hundreds of examples, the book gives you models for writing your own effective Web pages and for mastering advanced features, like style sheets and frames. *HTML: The Definitive Guide, 3rd Edition* shows you how to use style sheets and layers to control a document's appearance; create tables, from simple to complex; use frames to coordinate sets of documents; design and build interactive forms and dynamic documents; insert images, sound files, video, Java applets, and JavaScript programs; create documents that look good on a variety of browsers; and use new features to support multiple languages. A handy quick reference card listing HTML tags is included. *Softcover, 576 pages, $34.95*

Practical HTML: A Self-Paced Tutorial

ROY TENNANT (LIBRARY SOLUTIONS PRESS, 1996)

▶ Rather than a comprehensive reference work on HTML, this book is a practical guide that teaches you in a very short time how to create a Web document complete with images, links, tables, and forms, and how to make it appealing according to principles of design and style. Following the author's step-by-step instructions for working through a series of practice exercises, you will create an increasingly attractive document using text and image files that are on disks (Macintosh and Windows) supplied with the book. You will also learn about HTML software for authoring, validating, and translating, as well as valuable tips and techniques. This book is almost a verbatim transcription of a live, hands-on workshop taught by this well-known Internet trainer who is recognized worldwide for his ability to boil down to essentials what you need to know to be a successful user of Internet tools. This workbook is divided into two main sections: the first module covers basic HTML such as tags for basic structure (head, title, body), general formatting (headers, paragraphs, line breaks, etc.), and linking; the second introduces some advanced HTML features (image mapping, tables, and forms). Each module introduces a set of concepts and tags followed by an exercise that requires readers to use what they have just learned. The value of this workbook is its simplicity and its practicality. With just a few tags, the reader who completes all of the exercises can create an elegant, professional-quality Web document that incorporates images, links, lists, forms, and tables. All that is required of the reader is a simple text editor and a Web browser; the image files necessary to complete the exercises are included in a diskette (both Windows and Mac versions) that comes with the workbook. Also useful in this volume is the quick reference guide at the end, which includes a glossary and lists of HTML tags ordered both in alphabetical order and by function. *Softcover, 106 pages, $54.00*

Teach Yourself Web Publishing With HTML 4 in a Week, Complete Starter Kit Edition

LAURA LEMAY (SAMS/MACMILLAN, 1998)

▶ The latest incarnation of this guide to learning HTML now comes as a complete starter kit. Along with the book, you get a CD-ROM featuring the author's recommended HTML editing tools, Web browsers, software, and information from related Sams books. Although the book's title refers to teaching yourself HTML 4 in a week, that idea assumes that Web-site development is your full-time job. Devoting just a few hours a day, however, you can work your way through all 14 regular chapters plus 4 more bonus chapters in about two weeks. Lemay begins her explanations with non-technical items. She explains the importance of planning a Web site's organization and provides the information to help you map out your pages. From there, Lemay shows how to build your skills, starting with simple page creation and advancing to more sophisticated skills, such as building image maps and frames. Each step along the way is clearly explained with illustrative samples. Lemay provides easy-to-follow exercises that allow you to learn by doing. The two quick reference sections—one a two-page "cheat sheet" and the other a more extensive appendix—are particularly handy when you need a rapid jog of the memory while putting your new skills to work on your dream site. The CD also includes full versions of Netscape Navigator and Microsoft Internet Explorer, in addition to a large collection of Web graphics, editing tools and utilities, JavaScript programs, CGI scripts, and Java applets, plus sample chapters from the Sams Teach Yourself family of books for Web publishing. *Softcover, 600 pages, $39.99*

Web Design in a Nutshell

JENNIFER NIEDERST (O'REILLY ASSOCIATES, 1998)

▶ *Web Design in a Nutshell* contains the nitty-gritty on everything you need to know to design Web pages. It's the good stuff, without the fluff, written and organized so that answers can be found quickly. Written by veteran Web designer Jennifer Niederst, this book provides access to the wide range of front-end technologies and techniques from which Web designers and authors must draw. It is a particularly good reference for HTML 4.0 tags (including tables, frames, and cascading style sheets), with special attention given to browser support and platform idiosyncrasies. The HTML section is more than a reference work, though. It details strange behavior in tables, for instance, and gives ideas and workarounds for using tables and frames on your site. *Web Design in a Nutshell* also covers multimedia and interactivity, audio and video, and emerging technologies like Dynamic HTML, XML, embedded fonts, and internationalization. The book includes discussions of the Web environment, monitors, and browsers; a complete reference to HTML and Server Side Includes, including browser support for every tag and attribute; chapters on creating GIF, JPEG, and PNG graphics, including designing with the Web palette; information on

multimedia and interactivity, including audio, video, Flash, Shockwave, and JavaScript; detailed tutorial and reference on cascading style sheets, including an appendix of browser compatibility information; and appendices detailing HTML tags, attributes, deprecated tags, proprietary tags, and CSS compatibility. *Softcover, 580 pages, $24.95*

Web Style Guide: Basic Design Principles for Creating Web Sites

PATRICK J. LYNCH AND SARAH HORTON (YALE UNIVERSITY PRESS, 1999)

▶ Lynch and Horton offer an informative book for Web designers who want to go beyond HTML to consider specific information architecture issues. It provides concise advice on creating well-designed and effective Web sites and pages. Focusing on the interface and graphic design principles that underlie the best Web site design, the book provides anyone involved with Web site design—in corporations, government, nonprofit organizations, and academic institutions—with expert guidance on issues ranging from planning and organizing goals to design strategies for a site to the elements of individual page design. Shifting away from the emphasis of many authors on HyperText Markup Language (HTML) and glitzy, gimmicky graphics, Patrick J. Lynch and Sarah Horton discuss classic principles of design, how these principles apply to Web design, and the issues and constraints of designing complex, multilayered sites. They address the practical concerns of bending and adapting HTML to the purposes of graphic page design. This book grew out of the widely used Web site on site design created by the Center for Advanced Instructional Media at Yale University (*info.med.yale.edu/caim/manual/*). At this site, readers will continue to find updated color illustrations and examples to complement and demonstrate points made in the book, as well as useful and current online references. *Hardcover/Softcover, 176 pages, $35/$14.95*

Webmaster in a Nutshell, 2nd Edition

STEPHEN SPAINHOUR AND ROBERT ECKSTEIN (O'REILLY ASSOCIATES, 1999)

▶ Webmasters make sure that the information on a site is accessible and usable; that the site is always available, that performance is good, that users can get the information they need, and that the site can collect the information it needs to serve those users. These disparate tasks require many different tools and skills. *Webmaster in a Nutshell* pulls together in a single volume all the essential reference information for Webmasters working on UNIX-based Web servers. In this second edition of *Webmaster in a Nutshell,* the authors have updated their material to include the latest versions of HTML and JavaScript, and also expanded the book to cover the newest technologies emerging on the Web. The book covers HTML 4.0, with special attention to forms, tables, and frames; CSS (cascading style sheets); XML, the next-generation markup language for the Web; CGI, with a chapter dedicated to the Perl module CGI.pm; JavaScript 1.2; PHP, the HTML-embedded programming language; HTTP 1.1, the underlying protocol that drives the Web; Apache server administration, including Apache modules; mod_perl, the Apache module for enhancing CGI performance and providing a Perl interface to the Apache API; and performance tips for the Web. *Softcover, 540 pages, $24.95*

World-Class Web Sites

DON DEA AND HUGH LEE (AMERICAN SOCIETY OF ASSOCIATION EXECUTIVES FOUNDATION, 1997)

▶ This easy-to-read guide can be used to evaluate your association's current Web site or help in the initial design stage of a new Web site. With the help of case studies of selected Web sites and explanations of the criteria used, you'll use this guide to perform a diagnostic checkup on where you are and how you might better capitalize on your site. *Softcover, 65 pages, $26.95 (Nonmember), $21.95 (Member)*

Web Searching

How to Search the Web: A Quick-Reference Guide to Finding Things on the World Wide Web, 3rd Edition
ROBERT S. WANT (WANT PUBLISHING, 2000)

▶ The third edition of this popular guide offers the latest information on search engines for those who use the Web to find things. The Web continues to expand (now consisting of 100 million sites and over 800 million Web pages and counting), and this very expansion threatens to overwhelm the user and make it difficult, if not impossible, to zero in on material of interest. Indeed, without search engines, the Web would be essentially useless for research and reference. *How to Search the Web, 3rd Edition*, explains, in simple, nontechnical terms, basic search techniques that will help turn the Web into a reference source that will challenge your imagination while it informs and entertains. It describes how the major search engines work, including Yahoo!, Infoseek, Excite, and AltaVista, among others, and the special requirements of each. Sample queries are included throughout. The third edition has added new search examples to speed you on your way and help make readily available the many wonders of the Web. *Spiral bound, 65 pages, $12.95*

Learning to Use the World Wide Web: Academic Edition Netscape 4 Update
ERNEST C. ACKERMANN (FRANKLIN, BEEDLE & ASSOCIATES, 1998)

▶ The book is written for people who want to learn how to use Netscape Navigator to access the World Wide Web and how to get the most from the resources available on the Internet. No prior experience with the World Wide Web or the Internet is assumed. It pays some attention to why things work the way they do, but the emphasis is on how to learn to effectively use the World Wide Web and associated services in a step-by-step, organized manner. The book can be used for self-study, or it can be used as a primary or supplemental text book in courses dealing with the Internet and the World Wide Web. *Softcover, 400 pages, $18*

Searching Smart on the World Wide Web: Tools and Techniques for Getting Quality Results
CHERYL GOULD (LIBRARY SOLUTIONS PRESS, 1998)

▶ *Searching Smart on the World Wide Web* shows how to find information efficiently and effectively. Using succinct explanations, pertinent examples, and helpful practice techniques, Ms. Gould teaches the reader to be a savvy searcher by weeding out all but the relevant and reliable information. She covers timeless Internet searching concepts that will hold true despite the inevitable changes in search tools and information resources. Since this book is an adaptation of the author's live workshop, the information is practical, and the reader comes away a smarter searcher. It does not intend to provide comprehensive coverage of the Internet but rather give exactly the amount and level of information you need to perform a successful search of the World Wide Web. In addition to clear explanations, useful examples, and well-spaced pages that make learning fun and easy, the book includes a disk containing bookmarks to use in practical exercises. You will have hands-on practice in using search engines and subject directories (and will know when to use which tool); you'll use advanced searching techniques that enable you to refine your search, avoiding an avalanche of retrievals and zeroing in on relevant information; you'll learn to manage your bookmarks or favorites for easy access to sites you want to return to; you'll receive guidelines for evaluating your retrievals (much of what is on the Internet is disguised as "truth" but in fact is advertising or unreliable); and much more. *Softcover, 102 pages, $40*

Web Search Strategies
BRYAN PFAFFENBERGER (MIS PRESS, 1996)

▶ Use this seven-step strategy for locating information on the Web, telling how to use the major Web search engines to locate initial subjects, and how to use more detailed search techniques offered in Boolean operators. This does more than outline Net sites: It tells how to conduct specialized searches to obtain specific information. Web browsers of all levels can follow seven steps to finding information on the World Wide Web and the Internet, thanks to *Web Search Strategies*. Learn to locate documents on the Web for virtually every topic of interest, how search engines and spiders work (including Infoseek, Lycos, WebCrawler, Yahoo!, Virtual Library), and how to locate Internet resources, including WAIS databases and Usenet postings. The disk includes valuable HTML files for all URLs in the book, as well as Bookware, a searching utility, and Web-O-Deck, a utility for organizing bookmarks. *Softcover, 448 pages, $29.95*

World Wide Web

Sorting Out the Web: Approaches to Subject Access (Contemporary Studies in Information Management, Policy, and Services)
CANDY SCHWARTZ (ABLEX PUB CORP., 2001)

▶ Search engines, subject gateways, descriptive metadata, Web cataloging—everyone is looking for ways to support information discovery and retrieval on the Internet. To become full partners in new digital access ventures, library and information professionals need to be familar with effective tools and stategies, and need to make decisions about what is appropriate for different resources, settings, and communities. This book takes a look at what has been done in providing subject access to networked resources, and what is around the corner. *Hardcover, 184 pages, $72.50*

The World Wide Web Complete Reference
RICK STOUT (OSBORNE MCGRAW-HILL, 1999)

▶ *The World Wide Web Complete Reference* offers an up-to-date comprehensive view of what's available to users. With thorough analysis of the most recent technologies, *The World Wide Web Complete Reference* offers an extensive comparison of browsers and connections and gives you the information you need to make the best choice. It describes creating Web pages from simple to complex—focusing on both the technical and artistic aspects of successful examples. It also covers creating interactive forms and securing your computers and data from intruders. For advanced connections, the book covers ISDN and frame relay technologies, registering domain names and addresses, and creating domain name aliases. If you're searching for business opportunities on the

Web, you'll find discussions about selling products over the Web, electronic cash and credit, selling access to the Internet, and even creating HTML documents for money. Filled with numerous examples of Web pages, the book also includes a catalog of the businesses and commercial services available on the Web. *Softcover, 656 pages, $29.95*

Software

Selecting Software for Non-Profit Organizations and Trade Associations

SHELDON NEEDLE (COMPUTER TRAINING SERVICES, 1998)

▶ This book identifies the probable computer software needs of assorted types of nonprofit groups and provides information on software packages offered by 64 companies. Mr. Needle, president of Computer Training Services, examines what features should be considered if one is seeking software to raise funds, keep up-to-date files on membership, plan conferences, or manage a university or religious organization. He then describes software packages that are tailored to the needs of nonprofit groups, and provides information on the companies that manufacture the software. Each entry contains a company address, telephone number, and a World Wide Web address, as well as a detailed description of the product offered and the features it provides. Most entries list how many installations the company has done, and note price ranges for single and multiple users, compatible operating systems, networks supported, types of technical support available, and hardware requirements. The book's final section consists of four spreadsheets that list all the companies under type of function provided, recommended budget size of the nonprofit group buying the software, type of nonprofit organization the software is intended to aid, and compatible operating systems. The CTS Guide offers tips and guidelines for what to look for when evaluating the following applications: Fund Accounting & Reporting; Membership Management; Fund Raising/Alumni Development; Meeting & Conference Management; Grant Management; Religious Organization Management; Publication Management; and School & University Accounting. Mr. Needle does not endorse any of the products contained in the book, but he does warn nonprofit groups against some common mistakes when selecting software. *Softcover, 269 pages, $99 (plus $5 postage and handling)*

PERIODICALS

(See also General Management; Information Technology [Internet Resources—E-zines, Online Newsletters, and News Services])

BiblioData's PriceWatcher (Semimonthly Newsletter)

BiblioData, P.O. Box 61, Needham Heights, MA 02194
Tel: 617-444-1154; FAX: 617-449-4584
E-mail: ina@bibliodata.com (Subscription),
lindacooper@erols.com (Editorial);
WWW: http://www.bibliodata.com/pw/pwdata.html

▶ A semi-monthly newsletter, it tracks current price announcements, price comparisons, low-cost searching tricks, and tips for negotiating good rates from the vendors of information products. It covers online vendors such as Dialog, Lexis-Nexis, and Dow Jones, as well as paid and free sources on the Internet and even print materials. Delivery format is your choice: print, FAX, e-mail text, or e-mailed PDF file. *$129/year (Nonprofits, AIIP members or individuals), $169/year (All others)*

CyberSkeptic's Guide to Internet Research (Ten Issues)

BiblioData, P.O. Box 61, Needham Heights, MA 02194
Tel: 617-444-1154; FAX: 617-449-4584
E-mail: ina@bibliodata.com (Subscriptions),
ruth@bibliodata.com (Editorial);
WWW: http://www.bibliodata.com/skeptic/skepdata.html

▶ A monthly newsletter in print, *CyberSkeptic's Guide to Internet Research* explores and evaluates important sites and strategies to help you use the Internet as a serious and cost-effective tool in your business and professional life. It provides concise, condensed information and expresses strong opinions. Geared toward business research, market research, and competitive intelligence, the newsletter is a "must" for every online searcher. *$104 (Nonprofits, AIIP members, or individuals); $159 (All others)*

Econtent (Formerly DATABASE) (Bimonthly Magazine)

Online, Inc., 462 Danbury Road, Wilton, CT 06897-2125
Tel: 800-248-8466, 203-761-1466; FAX: 203-761-1444
E-mail: info@onlineinc.com; WWW: http://www.ecmag.net/

▶ Written for the "hands on" searcher, managers of information facilities, and others who use information technology, it provides practical, how-to advice on effective use of databases and systems, plus innovative tips and techniques, reviews, and product comparison. It covers databases in online, CD-ROM, disk, and tape formats, and resources on the Internet. *$55/year*

Information Today (Monthly Newspaper)

Information Today, Inc. (Formerly Learned Information, Inc.),
143 Old Marlton Pike, Medford, NJ 08055-8750
Tel: 609-654-6266; FAX: 609-654-4309
E-mail: custserv@infotoday.com;
WWW: http://www.infotoday.com

▶ This is the only newspaper designed to meet the needs of the information professional. *Information Today* delivers total coverage of late-breaking news and long-term trends in the information industry. Accurate, timely news articles inform the reader of the people, products, services, and events that impact the industry, while hard-hitting, topical articles explain significant developments in the field. This news resource of the information industry gives you total coverage of online services; the Internet and intranets; CD-ROM, DVD, and other emerging optical technologies; new databases; electronic and Internet publishing; company activities; and library automation and technology. *$59.95/year*

Link-Up (Bimonthly Magazine)

Information Today, Inc. (Formerly Learned Information, Inc.),
Main Office, 143 Old Marlton Pike, Medford, NJ 08055-8750
Tel: 609-654-6266; FAX: 609-654-4309
E-mail: custserv@infotoday.com

Editorial Office, 2222 River Drive, King George, VA 22485
Tel: 540-663-0497

E-mail: 72105.1753@compuserve.com (Editor);
WWW: http://www.infotoday.com/lu/lunew.htm

▶ This is the only news magazine devoted exclusively to the users of online services, CD-ROM products, and the Internet. No other technology-related magazine matches its comprehensive news and editorial coverage. *Link-Up*'s late-breaking stories, regular columns, and special sections are designed to help you get the most out of your personal computer, modem, and CD-ROMs. In just one issue you'll find the latest information on online services, the Internet and World Wide Web, CD-ROM and multimedia, software and hardware, as well as details on bulletin board systems. *$32.95/year*

Linux Journal's WWWsmith section (Formerly WEBsmith™ Magazine)

Specialized Systems Consultants, Inc. (SSC), P.O. Box 55549,
Seattle, WA 98155-0549
Tel: 206-782-7733; FAX: 206-782-7191
E-mail: websmith@ssc.com (Subscriptions), wseditor@ssc.com
(Editorial); WWW: http://www.ssc.com/websmith/#wwwsmith

▶ *WEBsmith* was the how-to magazine for technicians of the World Wide Web. WEBsmith magazine offered articles that explain how to use the tools, techniques, and ideas that make up the Web. Now, *Linux Journal's* WWWsmith section continues this tradition. With its January 1997 issue, Linux Journal started its new WWWsmith section, bringing its readers the same useful technical information of the original *WEBsmith* magazine. *$22/year*

Online (Bimonthly Magazine)

Online, Inc., 462 Danbury Road, Wilton, CT 06897-2125
Tel: 800-248-8466, 203-761-1466; FAX: 203-761-1444
E-mail: info@onlineinc.com, ngarman@well.com (Nancy Garman,
Editor); WWW: http://www.onlineinc.com/onlinemag/index.html

▶ This magazine is written for information professionals and provides articles, product reviews, case studies, evaluation, and informed opinion about selecting, using, and managing electronic information products, plus industry and professional information about online database systems, CD-ROM, and the Internet. *$55/year*

Searcher: The Magazine for Database Professionals (Ten Issues)

Information Today, Inc. (formerly Learned Information, Inc.),
Main Office, 143 Old Marlton Pike, Medford, NJ 08055-8750
Tel: 609-654-6266; FAX: 609-654-4309
E-mail: custserv@infotoday.com

Editorial Office, 932 11th Street, Suite 9, Santa Monica, CA 90403
WWW: http://www.infotoday.com/searcher

▶ *Searcher* explores and deliberates on a comprehensive range of issues important to the professional database searcher. The magazine is targeted to experienced, knowledgeable searchers and combines evaluations of data content with discussions of delivery media. *Searcher* includes evaluated online news, searching tips and techniques, reviews of search aid software and database documentation, revealing interviews with leaders and entrepreneurs of the industry, and trenchant editorials. Whatever the experienced database searcher needs to know to get the job done is covered in *Searcher. $69.95/year*

Technology Grant News (Quarterly Newsletter)

561 Hudson Street #23, New York, NY 10014
Tel: 212-741-8101
E-mail: Service@technologygrantnews.com,
EditorsDesk@technologygrantnews.com (Editorial),
WWW: http://www.technologygrantnews.com

▶ *Technology Grant News* lists grant opportunities for technology programs from foundations, corporate giving programs, and government agencies. A sample issue of the newsletter is available on its Web site. *$125/year; $85 (Nonprofits)*

INTERNET RESOURCES

Application Service Providers

Abbycon.com's Directory of Application Service Providers
▶ *http://www.abbycon.com/internetservices/ASP.htm*

Application Service Providers—B2Business.net
▶ *http://www.b2business.net/infrastructure/Application_Service_ Providers/*

Application Service Providers—Computerworld
▶ *http://www.computerworldcareers.com/home/print.nsf/all/0001 17asp_links*

Application Service Providers Explained— workz.com
▶ *http://www.workz.com/content/1701.asp*

Community TechKnowledge
▶ *http://www.communitytech.net/aboutctk/index.html*

Evaluating On-Line ASP Options for Your Nonprofit
▶ In less than a year, a new Internet-based industry has quickly risen that may reinvent the way that your organization conducts much of its business. Known as application service providers, or ASPs, these new Web sites can host many traditional software applications, such as your external or intranet Web site, list management and database hosting, payroll service and HR support, bookkeeping and accounting, word processing and spreadsheets, and much more. Beyond software, many ASPs are beginning to offer a full range of customer services from strategy to support. *http://www.tmcenter.org/programs/techskill.html*

How ASPs (Application Service Providers) Work
▶ *http://www.howstuffworks.com/asp.htm*

The Nonprofit Matrix
▶ This is an online guide to Application Service Providers (ASPs) and portal providers in the nonprofit sector. ASPs offer outsourced services that can enhance your organization's Web presence with a minimum of programming and administrative effort. These include Web sites and Web "portals" that provide online databases of volunteering opportunities that the nonprofit agency controls, online donation accounts, and affinity shopping accounts. *http://www.nonprofitmatrix.com*

Tech Savvy: How Application Service Providers Will Change Your Life
▶ *http://www.wsaccess.com/theStreet/comment/techsavvy/759956.html*

Browsers

BrowserWatch
▶ *http://browserwatch.internet.com/*

Community Networks

Community Computer Networks
▶ *http://www.geocities.com/john_g_mcnutt/comm.htm*

Computer Equipment, Assistance, and Training

Camp Yahoo
▶ Gives away a basic Internet training curriculum intended for newcomers to the Web. These teaching materials are available free of charge to members of qualified nonprofit organizations, community centers, libraries, schools, and service groups. *http://camp.yahoo.com/*

Gifts in Kind International
▶ Directs donated products and services, including software and computer training, to nonprofit organizations. The organization's Technology Planning & Support (TPS) program links technology-savvy corporate volunteers with nonprofits needing technology assistance. *http://www.giftsinkind.org/*

National Cristina Foundation
▶ Provides computer technology and solutions to people with disabilities, students at risk, and the economically disadvantaged, helping them lead more independent and productive lives. *http://www.cristina.org/*

Computer Recycling Resource List

▶ A comprehensive list of organizations that recycle and/or donate computers. Compiled by Lauren Matthews for Philanthropy News Network. *http://www.pnnonline.org/technology/computerrecycle1.cfm*

Techsoup

▶ A Web-based resource center that offers technology assitance and solutions for small to midsize nonprofit organizations. The site offers information on where to find donated or discounted software and equipment; computer training; advice on technology funding; technology planning, and listings of available volunteers and consultants. *http://www.techsoup.org/*

Compumentor

▶ A provider of low-cost, volunteer-based computer assistance to schools and nonprofits. Also sells popular software packages at discounted prices. *http://www.compumentor.org/*

Technology Tip Sheets for Nonprofits

▶ Advice from Coyote Communications on how to reap money-saving, program-enhancing benefits from technology. Most of this material is geared to nonprofit and public-sector organizations. *http://www.coyotecom.com/tips.html*

Computer Donations and Recycling/Reuse Online Databases

AnotheR BytE's Non-Profit Computer Recycling Directory of Useful Links

▶ *http://www.recycles.org/byte/others/index.htm*

CPSR Links to Computers for Updated Equipment

▶ *Caution:* Last update was 1997. *http://www.cpsr.org/links/retool.html*

Comp-Recycle.com

▶ *http://www.comp-recycle.com/index.htm*

Computer Hardware Recycling—Index Page

▶ *http://www.compumentor.org/cm/resources/articles/108.html*

Computer Ownership for Neighbors

▶ *http://little.nhlink.net/nhlink/sada/conhome.htm*

Computer Recycling—Tech Corps

▶ *http://www.techcorps.org/resources/recycling.html*

Computer Recycling Organizations

▶ *http://www.wco.com/~dale/list.html*

Computer Recycling Programs—Center for Assistive Technology

▶ *http://wings.buffalo.edu/ot/cat/newsletters/comp_recycle.htm*

Computer Recycling Resource List—Philanthropy News Network

▶ *http://pnnonline.org/technology/computerrecycle4.cfm*

Computer Recycling Resources—The Super Start Project

▶ *http://www.superstart.org/computer_recycling_sites.htm*

Computers for Learning

▶ Schools and educational nonprofits can register online to request surplus federal computer equipment. *http://www.computers.fed.gov/School/user.asp*

Donated Computers: An Educator's Checklist

▶ *http://www.siia.net/program/education/check.htm*

Educational Technology & Conservation Exchange Program (ETCEP)

▶ *http://www.fundingfactory.com/etcep/visitorhome.asp*

EPR2 Project Electronic Equipment Recyclers Contact List

▶ *http://www.nsc.org/ehc/epr2/cntctlst.htm*

Electronics Reuse and Recycling Directory

▶ *http://www.epa.gov/epaoswer/non-hw/recycle/direlec.htm*

Gifts in Kind International—Recycle Technology Program

▶ *http://www.giftsinkind.org/rtopen.htm*

Hard Drives

▶ *http://www.l-and-k.com/page15.html*

Helping.org (AOL Foundation) Resources for Nonprofits

▶ *http://www.helping.org/nonprofit/index.adp*

How to Donate, Reuse, or Recycle Your Old Computer

▶ *http://www.nsc.org/ehc/epr2/donate.htm*

Institute for Local Self-Reliance

▶ *http://www.ilsr.org/*

Learning and Information Networking for Community via Technology (LINCT)

▶ *http://www.linct.org/*

The Mouse Hunter Page

▶ *http://www.geocities.com/SiliconValley/Park/7216/index.html*

National Computer Donation Database

▶ *http://www.nonprofit-services.com/reuse/index.html*

National Recycling Coalition

▶ *http://www.nrc-recycle.org/Programs/electronics/recycling.htm*

New Deal

▶ *http://www.new-deal.com*

Nonprofit Computer Recycling & Reuse Directory of Useful Links—AnotheR BytE

▶ *http://www.recycles.org/byte/others*

Parents, Educators, and Publishers (PEP) National Directory of Computer Recycling Programs

▶ A directory of national computer recycling programs that facilitate donations of used equipment for schools and community groups. *http://www.microweb.com/pepsite/Recycle/National.html, http://www.microweb.com/pepsite/Recycle/recycle_index.html*

Philadelphia Reuse Collaborative

▶ *http://www.reusers.org/cgi-bin/cgiwrap/reuse/index.cgi*

Philanthropy News Network—Philanthropy Journal

▶ *http://www.pj.org/technology/computerrecycle1.cfm*

Places to Donate and Recycle Old Computer Equipment

▶ *http://www.usedcomputer.com/nonprof.html*

reBoot

▶ *http://www.reboot.on.ca/*

Recycles.org Nonprofit Computer Recycling Directory

▶ *http://www.recycles.org/byte/others/board.htm*

Reuse Collaborative

▶ An association of organizations and individuals from private- and public-sector organizations who wish to develop the capacity of our community to efficiently recirculate computers that would otherwise be discarded or unused, assist businesses with equipment disposal, and create training opportunities for youth and others. *http://www.reusers.org/, http://www.reusers.org/cgi-bin/cgiwrap/ reuse/index.cgi, http://www.reusers.org/resources.html*

SAMI—Computer Recycle Projects

▶ A list of organizations that participate in local and national recycling by donating computers/supplies. *http://www.learner.org/sami/*

S.H.A.R.E. Network Computer Resources

▶ *http://members.aol.com/SHAREacrosstheUS/computer.htm*

Share the Technology

▶ *http://sharetechnology.org/*

Share the Technology Computer Donation Database

▶ *http://www.nonprofit-services.com/reuse/index.html*

Tech Portal

▶ *http://www.ncccsf.org/techportal/techportal.asp*

TechSoup Resources: Recycled and Refurbished Hardware

▶ *http://www.techsoup.org/resourcelist.cfm?resourcelistid=10&nav=tools*

Computing and Internet Technology (General)

AOL's Computing Webopedia

▶ *http://aol.webopedia.com/*

BABEL: A Glossary of Computer-Related Abbreviations and Acronyms

▶ *http://www.geocities.com/ikind_babel/babel/babel.html*

Acronym Finder

▶ *http://www.acronymfinder.com/*

Beginners Guide to Computing

▶ *http://computingcentral.msn.com/guide/beginner/default.asp*

CNET.com

▶ *http://cnet.com/*

CNET Glossary

▶ *http://coverage.cnet.com/Resources/Info/Glossary*

Deee's Computer and Internet Reference Guide

▶ *http://users.erols.com/foxdm/computer.htm*

Dictionary of PC Hardware and Data Communications Terms

▶ O'Reilly Publishing's online dictionary of PC Hardware and Data Communication terms. *http://www.ora.com/reference/dictionary/*

Explore the Internet (Library of Congress)

▶ *http://lcweb.loc.gov/global/explore.html*

FW: Free E-mail Providers Guide (FEPG)

▶ This is a searchable database of some 1,300 free e-mail services in over 85 countries, with comments and comparisons of the service features. It also provides listings on other free Internet communication services, including free ISPs, event planning tools, instant messaging, Internet answering machines and voice mail, Internet paging services, personal information managers, file storage, online FAX and phone-calling tools, and more. Listings are viewable by category and location, or by specific features, and there is a (free) weekly e-mail announcement distributed to interested users. *http://www.fepg.net/*

FreeWebspace.net

▶ *http://www.freewebspace.net/*

Glossary of Computer and Internet Terms

▶ *http://www.sharpened.net/glossary/index.html*

Glossary of Internet and PC Terminology

▶ *http://homepages.enterprise.net/jenko/Glossary/G.htm*

Glossary of Internet Terms

▶ *http://www0.delphi.com/navnet/glossary/*

Glossary of PC and Internet Terminology

▶ *http://homepages.enterprise.net/jenko/Glossary/G.htm, http://www.users. bigpond.com/jenkos/G.htm*

The Info Service—Internet/Computer Resources

▶ *http://info-s.com/comp.html*

Internet 101 Glossary of Internet Terms

▶ *http://library.thinkquest.org/11373/gloss.html*

Internet/Glossaries WebReference.com

▶ *http://www.webreference.com/internet/glossaries.html*

The Internet Help Desk

▶ *http://w3.one.net/~alward/*

Internet Hyper-Glossary

▶ *http://winfiles.cnet.com/howto/glossary.html*

Internet Magazines—Web Development

▶ *http://www.webreference.com/internet/magazines/webdev.html*

Internet Public Library Computers and Internet Resources

▶ *http://www.ipl.org/ref/RR/static/com0000.html*

Internet Tools Summary

▶ *http://www.december.com/net/tools/index.html*

Internet Web Text Index

▶ *http://www.december.com/web/text/index.html*

Internet.com Discussion Lists

▶ *http://e-newsletters.internet.com/discussionlists.html*

Internet.com Forums

▶ *http://forums.internet.com/*

Internet.com Internet Resources Channel

▶ *http://www.internet.com/sections/resources.html*

Jargon File Resources *(See also The New Hacker's Dictionary)*

▶ http://www.tuxedo.org/~esr/jargon, http://www.logophilia.com/jargon/jargon.html

Links to Resources on Computers and the Internet

▶ *http://www.nceo.org/resource/internet.html*

Looking for an Internet Glossary?

▶ *http://www.usd.edu/engl/internetglossary.html*

MSN Computing Central

▶ *http://computingcentral.msn.com/topics/internet/default.asp*

Matisse's Glossary of Internet Terms

▶ *http://www.matisse.net/files/glossary.html*

MyHelpDesk.com

▶ A unique source for technical support, MyHelpDesk.com serves as a Web portal for finding free assistance with myriad varieties of hardware and software. Typing in a model number or upgrade version yields a list of links to vendor support, training information, online forums, plug-ins, and other technical resources. Its specialized search engine also facilitates the process of retrieving highly customized information. *http://www.myhelpdesk.com/Membership/HomeVisitor.asp*

Netdictionary

▶ Netdictionary is a reference guide for terms related to the Internet. *http://www.netdictionary.com/html/index.html*

Netiquette

▶ *http://www.albion.com/netiquette/book/index.html*

Netiquette Guidelines

▶ *http://www.dtcc.edu/cs/rfc1855.html*

NetLingo: The Internet Language Dictionary

▶ *http://www.netlingo.com/*

The New Hacker's Dictionary *(See also Jargon File)*

▶ *http://www.tuxedo.org/~esr/jargon/jargon.html*

The Online World Resources Handbook

▶ *http://www.simtel.net/simtel.net/presno/bok/*

Open Directory

▶ *http://dmoz.org/Computers/*

Providing Information on the World Wide Web

▶ *http://lcweb.loc.gov/global/internet/dev.html*

RPInfo: Internet Information & Resources

▶ *http://www.rpi.edu/Internet/*

SoftSeek—Your Source for Shareware, Freeware, and Evaluation Software

▶ *http://www.softseek.com*

SquareOne Technology: Internet Glossary

▶ *http://www.squareonetech.com/glosaryf.html*

TechEncyclopedia

▶ *http://www.techweb.com/encyclopedia/*

Techni Help—Free Online Help

▶ *http://www.freepchelp.com/*

Virtual Dr.

▶ *http://www.virtualdr.com/*

Virtual University

▶ *http://www.vu.org/calendar.html*

The Web Reviewer

▶ This is the home of book and product reviews, articles, and other commentary written and published by Jim Moran. They have been collectively posted here for the benefit of the Internet community. They will assist readers to make more productive use of the Internet for profit, fun, and pleasure. *http://www.webreviewer.com/webreviewer.html*

Webopedia: Online Computer Dictionary for Internet Terms and Technical Support

▶ Webopedia is both an encyclopedia devoted to computer technology and a search engine. *http://www.webopedia.com/*

WhatIs.com Glossary of Internet Terms

▶ Whatis is a tool for understanding information technology. *http://whatis.com*

The World Wide Web Acronym and Abbreviation Server

▶ *http://www.ucc.ie/info/net/acronyms/acro.html*

Yahoo!: Computers and Internet

▶ *http://dir.yahoo.com/Computers_and_Internet/Internet/*

YIL: Surf Lingo

▶ *http://www.zdnet.com/yil/content/surfschool/lingo/lingotoc.html*

ZDNet: Help & How-To

▶ *http://www.zdnet.com/zdhelp/*

Computing and Internet Technology (Nonprofit)

All About Computers, Internet, Web—The Management Assistance Program for Nonprofits

▶ *http://www.managementhelp.org/infomgnt/infomgnt.htm*

ASAE Technology Solutions Directory

▶ A resource provided by the American Society of Association Executives. *http://www.asaenet.org/tech_dir/*

Automation & Computing for Nonprofits

▶ *http://www.nonprofit-info.org/npofaq/05/*

Benton's Best Practices Toolkit

▶ Benton Foundation's Best Practice Toolkit provides ideas on how nonprofits can make efficient use of communication and information technologies. This site includes articles on incentives for planning and implementing technology, effective examples of fund raising over the Internet, and tools for organizing and advocacy. *http://www.benton.org/Practice/Toolkit/*

CharityFocus Resources

▶ *http://www.charityfocus.org/services/resources*

The Chronicle of Philanthropy Internet Resources: General Technology Information

▶ *http://philanthropy.com/free/resources/technology/internet.htm*

Circuit Riders

▶ *http://www.rffund.org/techproj/circuit_riders/*

Community Action Technology Purchasing Guide

▶ Each CAT Guide edition provides expert recommendations for information technology products commonly used by community agencies, primary reference articles, and prices from national vendors. It is a great resource for quick hardware guidance. *http://www.catguide.org*

The Community Connector

▶ This is a Web site for community-service organizations, funders, academics, and students who are using technology to improve their local communities. Offerings include news updates, research reports, articles, handbooks, an original journal, a directory of community networks, and links to relevant resources. *http://databases.si.umich.edu/cfdocs/community/index.cfm*

Community Technology Centers' Network

▶ The Community Technology Centers' Network (CTCNet) works toward greater public access to computers. This network comprises more than 300 computer technology centers in 35 states, the District of Columbia, Ireland, and Scotland. Site resources include a complete listing of the centers in the network, some of the Centers' Web sites, a list of resources regarding "Equitable Access to Computer Technology." *http://www.ctcnet.org/*

CompuMentor Resource Center

▶ The site provides FAQs to help schools and nonprofits determine if the mentoring program will fit their needs; information on CompuMentor's software redistribution program and consulting services; and a Resource Center of "helpful information and advice on technology for nonprofits, schools, and volunteers." *http://www.compumentor.org/cm/resources/default.html*

Coyote Communications Database, Software & Technology Use Tip Sheets

▶ Coyote Communications is a consulting service for nonprofit and public sector organizations that specializes in online and offline communications services. The site provides a number of Technology Tip Sheets on Web development, database applications, other software, and the Internet. *http://www.coyotecom.com/tips.html, http://www.coyotecom.com/database/*

DOT ORG

▶ This e-newsletter, produced by Michael Stein and Marc Osten, is a practical how-to guide with tips, tools, techniques, and case studies about nonprofit use of the Internet. It is not intended as a source of news or a list of links. Each issue will have a central theme to focus the content. It covers such topics as e-mail newsletters, building Web site traffic, working with ASPs, collecting online donations, using HTML e-mail, evaluating Internet presence efforts, and more. For more information send e-mail to *mailto:mosten@summitcollaborative.com* or *mailto:michael@ michaelstein.net*. To subscribe, send an e-mail to *mailto:dotorg-subscribe@topica.com*. *http://www.summitcollaborative.com/ dot_org.html*

ERICA Ticker

▶ The official news bulletin of the Ericsson Internet Community Award. Every two weeks, they update interested parties on news and events related to the launch of the first-ever awards program aimed at bringing together three important communities: commercial Internet companies, Web developers, and nonprofit organizations. *http://www.npo.net/nponet/computer/erica.html*

Ericsson Internet Community Awards

▶ Any nonprofit organization in the world can compete for the annual Ericsson Internet Community Awards (ERICA). The five winning organizations share $500,000 worth of Web development services and technology. Winners are selected based on the innovation, feasibility, and community impact of their Web-based philanthropic ideas. Details are available at the ERICA Web site. The site also offers interactive community forums and information on the global philanthropic community. *http://www.ericsson.com/erica*

Getting Started on the Internet

▶ *http://www.idealist.org/getting-started.html*

Guidestar: Nonprofit Center: Links: Technology

▶ *http://www.guidestar.org/npo/nplinks/links_technology.html*

Helping.org (AOL Foundation) Resources for Nonprofits

▶ If your nonprofit organization or company needs technology (computer or Internet) assistance, you can search *Helping.org*'s "Find Computer Help Near You" database—located in the "Resources for Nonprofits" section of the Helping.org Web site. This new database, specifically designed to assist nonprofit agencies in finding computer assistance in their community, is searchable online by state. If your organization or company provides technology assistance, you can register its services using an online registration form. Managed by the Benton Foundation and sponsored by the AOL Foundation, the Resources for Nonprofits section of Helping.org is a starting point for nonprofits that are seeking learning tools. *http://www.helping.org/nonprofit/index.adp, http://www.helping.org/nonprofit/tools.adp, http://www.helping.org/nonprofit/findinghelp.adp*

Internet Introduction for Nonprofit Managers— Nonprofit Learning

▶ *http://www.nonprofitlearning.com*

LINC Project

▶ The LINC (Low Income Networking and Communications) Project is a site dedicated to fostering connections, cooperation, and information exchange between low-income organizations working in the human services area. Web site features include a directory of low-income organizations in the United States; "Organizers' Online Toolkit"; an events calendar; links to online newsletters; and a news section. *http://www.lincproject.org*

Managing Non-Profit Groups: Using the Internet for Advocacy Work Electronic Advocacy

▶ *http://www.geocities.com/john_g_mcnutt/electron.htm*

National Strategy for NonProfit Technology (N-TEN)

▶ The National Strategy for NonProfit Technology (N-TEN) has released a blueprint, based on 18 months of research and discussion, outlining the steps the nonprofit sector should take to use the Internet and information technology more effectively. *http://www.nten.org*

NcexChange Toolbox

▶ *http://www.ncexchange.org/toolbox/*

New Media for Nonprofits

▶ *http://www.fornonprofits.com/resources.html*

npo.net: Nonprofits and Technology

▶ *http://www.npo.net/nponet/computer/tools.htm*

Nonportal

▶ A commercial-free portal for nonprofits launched by the Gilbert Center. *http://www.nonportal.org/*

Nonprofit and the Net Resources—Full Circle Associates

▶ This site includes sections of links on communications and marketing resources, online community resources, volunteering, adding technology, and general Web sites for nonprofits. *http://www.fullcirc.com/nonprofit.htm*

Nonprofit Internet Standards Project

▶ Its purpose is to encourage a dialogue about data descriptions and interoperability standards that affect nonprofits in the era of universal networking. A central premise here is that standards should be open and nonprofits should play a central role in setting them. *http://standards.gilbert.org/*

Nonprofit Organizations and the Internet (First Monday Article)

▶ *http://firstmonday.org/issues/issue4_2/mjohnson/*

Nonprofit Quarterly Special Technology Issue

▶ *http://www.nonprofitquarterly.org/technology/index.htm*

Nonprofit Tech Library

▶ This technical library of resources for nonprofits provides easy-to-read, in-depth articles on relevant technology, tips and tricks for nonprofits to maximize their use of technology, as well as assistance in troubleshooting and maintaining both Macintosh and Windows-based computers. *http://www.tech-library.org*

Nonprofit TechWorld

▶ The online resource for nonprofits and technology. The source offers access to eight distinctive components of nonprofit technology: library, directory, software, links, talk, jobs, consultants, and news. *http://www.nonprofit-techworld.org*

Nonprofit Technology Infrastructure Support Organizations

▶ *http://www.nonprofits.org/npofaq/misc/000711npio.html*

Nonprofit Technology Resources—Foundation Center

▶ *http://fdncenter.org/onlib/npr_links/npr10.html*

Nonprofit Techworld's Tech TALKS

▶ If it has anything to do with nonprofits and technology, you'll find it in the forums listed here. *http://techtalk.infopop.net/1/OpenTopic/a/cfrm*

Nonprofits and Computer Technology—Nonprofit Charitable Organizations

▶ *http://nonprofit.about.com/careers/nonprofit/library/weekly/aa072298.htm*

Nonprofits and Technology—NPO.net

▶ *http://npo.net/nponet/computer/tools.htm*

NPower

▶ NPower's Web site is loaded with easy-to-access resources for online training, technology planning, and fund raising online. The site also offers well-organized links to general nonprofit resources and technology support organizations around the nation. One area not to miss on NPower's Web site is the Hands-On Technology How-To's section. Here you'll find great information on databases, networking, the Internet, virus protection, and much more. *http://www.npower.org/*

One Northwest: Online Networking for the Environment

▶ The One Northwest Web site is very easy to navigate and full of useful tools, especially for technology planning. They have online technical assessment forms that are worth a look. The online Activist Toolkit is a great resource for anyone interested in using online tools. Here you'll find information on hardware and software, e-mail, doing research online, and the basics of getting online. *http://www.onenw.org*

Open Studio: The Arts Online

▶ A national initiative of the Benton Foundation and the National Endowment for the Arts, this project provides Internet access and training to artists and nonprofit arts organizations to ensure that the communications environment of the twenty-first century thrives as a source of creative excellence and diversity. The site provides several features: a list of locations nationwide where artists can go for basic computer and Internet training or access the Internet for free; an online toolkit of resources and links; *Digital Canvas,* an online magazine; discussion forums that allow project participants, staff, advisors and the Internet public to share experiences, ask questions, and learn from one another. *http://www.openstudio.org*

Outcome Measurement

▶ Provides the following links: Learning Tech Evaluation cookbook, Article: Outcome-based Evaluation (6/97), Outcome Measurement and Program Evaluation—Online directory of web links and information resources of interest to nonprofits, Outcome Measurement Resource Network, Purposes of Evaluation, and Helping Your Nonprofit Track Outcomes with Technology. *http://www.libertynet.org/ntr/Bookmarks.html*

Philanthropy Journal Online

▶ This site has a wonderful technology section housing its many articles on how nonprofits are making use of the Internet. *http://www.nonprofitnews.org*

PNN Online: Technology

▶ *http://www.pj.org/technology/*

Philanthropy News Digest Special Issue: Nonprofits & the Internet

▶ *http://fdncenter.org/pnd/19991221/index.html*

Progressive Technology Project Resources

▶ *http://www.progressivetech.org/Resources/index.htm*

Resources for Nonprofits: Find computer help near you

▶ *http://www.helping.org/nonprofit/findinghelp.adp*

Share the Technology Resource Database

▶ The resource database provides links to information about the environment, recycling, volunteer issues, the digital divide, computer repair, computer salvage companies, nonprofit organizations, disability issues, and much more. *http://sharetechnology.org/rdb_start.html*

Strategic Technology.net—Summit Consulting Collaborative

▶ Summit's new Web site for dynamic strategic technology planning. *http://www.strategictechnology.net/*

Summit Consulting Collaborative—Summit Resources

▶ *http://www.summitcollaborative.com/resources.html*

SupportNET

▶ Offers online technical support resources and free online training courses, including communicating over the Internet, Internet networking, and Internet security and legal issues—all from a nonprofit or educational perspective. *http://supportnet.merit.edu*

TCN Library—Links of Interest (Telecommunications Cooperative Network)

▶ *http://www.tcn.org/library/links4.html*

Team Tech

▶ *http://comnet.org/acconf/, http://teamtech.home.mindspring.com/*

TeamTech Training/Resource Guide

▶ *http://www.ncccsf.org/teamtech/training/training.html*

TeamTech San Francisco Toolkit

▶ *http://www.ncccsf.org/teamtech/toolkit.html*

Tech Library for Nonprofits—The Computer Information Resource Center for Nonprofits and Public Agencies

▶ *http://www.tech-library.org*

Tech News: Enhancing Human Services Through Technology

▶ *http://www.uwnyc.org/tech.htm*

Tech Supports for Nonprofits—A Resource Directory

▶ This is a database compiled by NCExchange, a project of the Fund for the City of New York. *http://www.ncexchange.org/tech-supports/, http://www.ncexchange.org/techsupports/database.html*

Technical Tips for Small Nonprofits and Social Change Groups—Organizers' Collaborative

▶ *http://www.organizenow.net/techtips/index.html*

Technology Affinity Group—Council on Foundations

▶ Seeks to advance technology "best practices" in philanthropy through the formation of a network of technical and nontechnical foundation staff. *http://www.tagtech.org/*

Technology Guide—The Chronicle of Philanthropy

▶ *http://philanthropy.com/adv.dir/compute.dir/compmain.shtml*

Technology—The Nonprofit Zone

▶ *http://www.nonprofitzone.com/tech.htm*

Technology Libraries: Resources and Links— NPower

▶ *http://www.npower.org/resourcesandlinks/index.html*

Technology Planning

▶ This site provides the following links: Tech Planning for the Arts—Joe Matuzak, NSNT: Nonprofit Technology Assessment Tool, NSNT: Nonprofit Technology BenchMarks, National Center for Technology Planning—THE technology planning source, projects.scrt...techtips.html, Welcome to Techsoup.org, Concepts/ Processes/Methods/Tools: A Technology Planning Framework, Do's and Don'ts of Technology Planning, and Technology Planning. *http://www.libertynet.org/ntr/Bookmarks.html*

The Technology Project

▶ The Technology Project works to help nonprofits build their technological capacity, thereby furthering their work and bettering society. Site features include a free, downloadable program called ebase (a tool specifically suited to nonprofits' database and information management needs); information on current initiatives; and links to relevant publications and Web sites. *www.techproject.org*

Technology Project Resources

▶ The Technology Project eriders Resource section offers visitors a wide array of resources from the Technology Project and other organizations. The site offers you information on issues such as protecting your data, using your Web site effectively, and how to pick the right Internet service. The Technology Project's standards for using technology are important to check out. *http://www.techrocks.org/* (formerly Technology Project). *http://www.eriders.org/resources.html*

Technology Resources on the Internet (Technology Project)

▶ *http://www.techproject.org/resourceguide.html*

Techportal—TeachTech San Francisco

▶ This is a simple-to-use search tool that specializes on technology issues and the nonprofit sector. You can easily search on topics such as training, recycled computers, support and consultants, and discounted hardware. *http://www.techportal.org/*

TechSoup

▶ This is the one-stop information resource for all nonprofit technology issues. At TechSoup, you can find information covering topics such as hardware, finding the right software application, guidelines for selecting an appropriate database, planning your organization's network, how to get funding, and more. A free comprehensive resource, TechSoup aggregates the best in nonprofit technology across the Web, adds its own original content, and serves it all up in an easy-to-use interface that leads nonprofits to exactly the technology support and solutions they need. The site has a search engine built in so you can type a keyword, such as hardware, and all the records that match that word will come up in an easy-to-use table of contents. The site also features a useful tool called mytechsoup, which allows you to customize the site based on your personal interests. Sign up to receive their free e-newsletter, *By the Cup,* featuring nonprofit technology news, resources, and support. *http://www.techsoup.org*

TechVol

▶ TechVol is a completely nonprofit site that functions as a clearinghouse to link charitable organizations with technically skilled mentors, especially those who can help develop functional Web sites. Includes a page that lists resources for setting up a page on your own. *http://www.techvol.com/*

Towards a Linkages Guide for the National Strategy for Nonprofit Technoloy

▶ *http://www.ctcnet.org/nsntlnk.htm*

Web-Based Applications for Nonprofits

▶ *http://nonprofit.about.com/careers/nonprofit/library/weekly/aa061400a.htm*

Digital Divide

Bridging the Digital Divide: First You Need the Bridge

▶ The digital divide has many different definitions, and each week, somewhere in the world, representatives of different sectors meet to discuss ways of partnering to resolve it. Unfortunately, says Jonathan Peizer of the Open Society Institute, most are talk-fests with few results save the all-too-occasional cross-sector collaboration. Successful partnerships are the product of trust, mutually desired objectives, and mutual understanding. Sometimes, players are so focused on trying to resolve problems, they forget they still do not understand each other very well. This three-part series of essays seeks to provide some insight on how corporations, foundations, and nongovernmental organizations can improve their relations. *http://www.tagtech.org/topics2265/topics_show.htm?doc_id=30999*

Bridging the Digital Divide—*New York Times* Special Section

▶ *http://www.isoc.org/digitaldivide/*

Closing the Digital Divide

▶ Maintained by the National Telecommunications Information Administration (NTIA), this site is a central clearinghouse of data about the digital divide. The site offers useful audio/video excerpts from the December 1999 Digital Divide Summit as well as detailed government reports on the subject. *http://www.digitaldivide.gov/*

Digital Divide—John McNutt

▶ *http://www.geocities.com/john_g_mcnutt/digital.htm*

The Digital Divide Network

▶ This is a new site from the Benton Foundation, in association with the National Urban League. Users can search for news about efforts going on across the country, and research organizations and corporations involved in those efforts to bridge the gap. *http://www.digitaldividenetwork.org/*

Digital Divide PBS Series

▶ *http://www.pbs.org/digitaldivide/*

Digital Divide Resources—Geekcorps

▶ *http://www.geekcorps.org/dd.html*

LINC (Low Income and Communications) Project

▶ *http://www.lincproject.org/*

Making the Net Work—Bridging the Digital Divide

▶ *http://www.makingthenetwork.org/*

National Telecommunications Information Administration

▶ This Department of Commerce site provides detailed reports and guidelines on the government's efforts to address the digital divide. It includes a survey by the Census Bureau and specified charts and U.S. telecommunications data. *http://www.ntia.doc.gov/ntiahome/fttn99/contents.html*

PowerUP

▶ PowerUP: Bridging the Digital Divide is a major initiative to help ensure that America's underserved young people acquire the skills, experiences, and resources they need to succeed in the digital age. *http://www.powerup.org/index.shtml*

Seeking Solutions to the Digital Divide

▶ This growing site is designed to create solutions for bridging the digital divide and features links to various discussion forums, corporations, nonprofit organizations, and Web sites devoted to the issue. *http://www.digitaldivide.org/*

Electronic Advocacy

(See also Political)

Electronic Advocacy—John McNutt

▶ *http://www.geocities.com/john_g_mcnutt/electron.htm*

E-Mail Discussion List Search Sites

CataList—L-Soft Listserv Lists

▶ From this page, you can browse any of the 17,781 public listserv lists on the Internet, search for mailing lists of interest, and get information about listserv host sites. *http://www.lsoft.com/lists/listref.html*

Dejanews

▶ *http://www.dejanews.com*

DiscussionLists.com

▶ *http://discussionlists.com/*

List Tool

▶ A service for finding and subscribing to discussion lists, it also provides a good list of resources. *http://www.listtool.com/*

Liszt Directory of Listservs and Usenet Groups

▶ You can also browse topic-specific lists of discussion lists. *http://www.liszt.com/*

Meta-List.net

▶ *http://www.meta-list.net*

Net-Happenings

▶ A place to find Internet resources of all sorts, including announcements of new discussion groups. *http://listserv.classroom.com/archives/net-happenings.html*, *http://listserv.classroom.com/archives/net-happenings.html*

New-List

▶ An announcement list for new e-mail discussion groups. Also provides a searchable archive of past list announcements. This is a good way to find the list you are looking for or to get your new list publicized. *http://listserv.nodak.edu/archives/new-list.html*, *http://listserv.classroom.com/archives/new-list.html*

PAML—The Directory of Publicly Accessible Mailing Lists

▶ *http://paml.net/*

Search the List of Lists

▶ Search one of the largest directories of special interest group e-mail lists (also known as listservs) available on the Internet. *http://catalog.com/vivian/interest-group-search.html*

Tile.net

▶ A reference to Internet discussion lists listed by: name, subject, description, host country, and sponsoring organization. *http://www.tile.net/*

Tropica E-mail List Directory

▶ *http://igc.topica.com/lists/*, *http://igc.topica.com/resources/index.html*

Yahoo Mailing List Discussion Groups Listed by Subject Category

▶ *http://search.yahoo.com/bin/search?p=mailing+lists*

E-Mail Discussion Lists (Nonprofit)

(See also other sections of this directory for subject-specific lists)

Charity Channel

▶ Charity Channel, from American Philanthropy Review, offers more than 20 listservs for nonprofit professionals. In addition to CharityTalk, their all-inclusive "Big Tent" discussion list, topics covered include law, ethics, start-ups, consultants, and grants. It provides descriptions of and instructions for subscribing, as well as offering archive search access to their ever-increasing list of mailing lists. *www.charitychannel.com/forums*

CharityVillage Online Resources: Online Discussions

▶ *http://www.charityvillage.com/charityvillage/stand.html*

Grants and Related Resources—Mailing Lists and Discussion Forums

▶ *http://www.lib.msu.edu/harris23/grants/maillist.htm*

Online Discussion Groups, Portals, Mailing Lists, and Newsletters for Nonprofits

▶ *http://www.mapnp.org/library/gen_rsrc/newsgrps/np_grps.htm*

Accountability@charitychannel.com

▶ This site focuses on all aspects of ethics and accountability for nonprofits. There are two methods to subscribe:

1. Send e-mail to *listserv@CharityChannel.com* with *SUBSCRIBE Accountability YourFirstname YourLastname* as the message. Leave the subject line blank.
2. Visit the CharityChannel Web site at *CharityChannel.com/forums* and click on the subscription information for Accountability.

ALUMNI-L

▶ This is a listserv for alumni relations professionals at colleges, universities, and independent schools. It addresses issues related to alumni relations. To subscribe to ALUMNI-L: Send an e-mail message to *LISTSERV@BROWNVM.BROWN.EDU*. In your e-mail message type SUBSCRIBE ALUMNI-L followed by your name.

AnotheR BytE's Nonprofit Recycling & Reuse Network e-Mail Discussion List

▶ Objectives of this discussion list are to develop a worldwide network of nonprofit recyclers, donors, volunteers, and other interested parties in order to facilitate the exchange of information and equipment; discuss new, innovative, and practical methods for recycling, refurbishing, and redistributing things, especially older computer technology; discuss nonprofit recycling organizational development, and to assist others who may wish to get involved or who are just starting out; and discuss social and environmental issues involved with nonprofit recycling, refurbishing, and redistribution; share timely news stories, useful URLs, successes, pitfalls, discoveries, and other items of interest related to these objectives. To subscribe or unsubscribe, send blank e-mail to, *NRRN-subscribe@yahoogroups.com, NRRN-unsubscribe@yahoogroups.com, http://www.recycles.org/list/*

ARNOVA-L (Nonprofit Organizations and Voluntary Action)

▶ Aimed at researchers and research-oriented practitioners interested in nonprofit organizations, volunteerism, and philanthropy, this list was started by several members of ARNOVA (the Association for Research on Non-Profit Organizations and Voluntary Action) and continues to maintain informal ties to this organization. Past messages are archived at the listserv site. E-mail: *rlohman@wvnvm.wvnet.edu*. To subscribe: *listserv@wvnvm.wvnet.edu;* message: subscribe arnova-l [your first and last name]. To post: *arnova-l@wvnvm.wvnet.edu. http://www.arnova.org/list_srv.html*

ARNOVA-TEACH

▶ Sponsored by the ARNOVA Affinity Group on Nonprofit Curriculum and Teaching, its objectives are to promote the free exchange of ideas, mutual assistance, and collaboration toward the improvement of academic and professional education and training in the field of nonprofit organizations and management. Subscriptions to ARNOVA-Teach are offered as a free service to members of the Association for Research on Nonprofit Organizations and Voluntary Action (ARNOVA) and the International Society for Third Sector Research (ISTR). Others who would like to participate are asked to join either of those organizations. E-mail: *mcortes@castle.cudenver.edu* (Mike Cortes, list administrator). To subscribe, send the message "subscribe ARNOVA-Teach [your complete name]" to *listproc@carbon, cudenver.edu.* To post messages: *ARNOVA-Teach@carbon.cudenver.edu*

Bay Area Nonprofit Techie Listserv

▶ This is a lively and focused forum where people involved in technology administration can post resources, exchange ideas, and troubleshoot common problems. Recent discussions have included the pros and cons of purchasing home versus office machines and how to assess the best type of connection to the Internet (ISDN, DSL, or other options). CompassPoint Nonprofit Services also offers periodic evening forums for this community on topics such as hiring a technology consultant. To subscribe to the listserv, send e-mail to *<majordomo@npdc.org>*. For the body of your message, use the command "subscribe npo-mis" (without the quotes). The subject line doesn't matter and can be left blank. Once subscribed, you will receive a confirmation message. Once you have subscribed to the group, you can send e-mail to *<npo-mis@npdc.org>* and it will be forwarded to all of the members of the list. If you have any questions about the list, or if you need help subscribing or unsubscribing, contact the list owner at *<owner-npo-mis@npdc.org>*.

BOARD-SENSE

▶ This site covers boards of directors for nonprofits. To subscribe, send this e-mail message: subscribe to: *majordomo@AZStarNet.com.*

CFRNET

▶ This is a listserv intended for corporate and foundation fund raisers. It can generate a moderate to heavy amount of mail traffic. To subscribe to CFRNET, send an e-mail message to *LISTSERV@UNC.EDU*. In your e-mail message, type SUBSCRIBE CFRNET followed by your name.

Chardon Press Online: Nonprofit Forum

▶ Developed by Chardon Press, the Oakland, California, publisher of the *Grassroots Fundraising Journal*, the Nonprofit Forum is a Web-based discussion board designed to give employees at small, progressive nonprofit organizations the opportunity to discuss fund raising, management, and advocacy. *http://www.chardonpress.com/npforum/forums.shtml*

CharityBooks

▶ This site covers all aspects of writing, publishing, marketing, and review of nonprofit-sector books. There are two methods to subscribe:

1. Send e-mail to *listserv@CharityChannel.com* with *SUB-SCRIBE CharityBooks YourFirstname YourLastname* as the message. Leave the subject line blank.

2. Visit the CharityChannel Web site at *CharityChannel.com/forums* and click on the subscription information for CharityBooks.

Charitytalk@charitychannel.com

▶ CharityTalk is a "Big Tent" list, with folks from just about every discipline in the nonprofit sector actively participating. Unlike other lists, which are defined by a single subject area, this is the opposite: It's defined by the diversity of its subcribers across the several disciplines of the nonprofit sector. There are two methods to subscribe:

1. Send e-mail to *listserv@CharityChannel.com* with *SUB-SCRIBE CharityTalk YourFirstname YourLastname* as the message. Leave the subject line blank.

2. Visit the CharityChannel web site at *CharityChannel.com/forums* and click on the subscription information for CharityTalk.

The Chronicle Guide to Grants

▶ This is an electronic database of all corporate and foundation grants listed in *The Chronicle of Philanthropy* since 1995. Subscriptions are available for periods of one week to one year. There is a significant discount if you are also a subscriber to *The Chronicle of Philanthropy*. To learn more about the *Guide to Grants* and how to subscribe, see subscription information. *http://www.philanthropy.com/grants*

CNM@LISTSERV.UIC.EDU

▶ Nonprofit management list.

Cyber Accountability

▶ This site is the home of the Cyber Accountability listserv, which discusses, debates, and disseminates information on issues relating to nonprofits' use of technology to enhance nonprofit accountability. It is maintained by Harriet Bograd, a lawyer and consultant. Besides enabling users to sign up for the listserv, the site provides tutorials, relevant links, and news briefs. To subscribe, send an e-mail message to tlegg@fcny.org that includes your full name, e-mail address, organization, and location (city, state, and country). Information about the list is available at *http://www.bway.net/~bograd/cyb-acc.html#cybacc, http://www.bway.net/~bograd/cyb-acc.html.*

CYBERVPM

▶ This site covers volunteer recruitment and management. To subscribe, send this e-mail message: *SUBSCRIBE CYBERVPM* to: *listserv@listserv.aol.com.*

DigitalDivide

▶ The Benton Foundation's Communications Policy Program has developed the DIGITALDIVIDE listserv. DIGITALDIVIDE is a moderated discussion in which citizens can discuss the wide range of issues related to bridging the digital divide. The listserv, which currently includes over 800 members from around the world, cuts across disciplinary boundaries: community activists, educators, researchers, representatives of commercial and nonprofit enterprises, volunteers, students, and concerned citizens are all encouraged to take part in this online discussion. The listserv tackles the digital divide from a variety of angles, which include (but are not limited to) the following subjects: technology access issues; content creation for underserved populations and communities; combating illiteracy in its many forms; online diversity; economic development and workforce issues; community building; the Internet and cultural diversity; digital divide news and events; education and training; best practices from local, national, and international digital divide efforts; obstacles to bridging the digital divide; new tools for measuring the divide; public/private and commercial/nonprofit partnerships; and public policy issues. DIGITALDIVIDE is moderated by veteran listserv facilitator Andy Carvin, senior associate at the Benton Foundation. In order to subscribe to DIGITALDIVIDE, please visit their Web site: *http://www.DigitalDivideNetwork.org.* You can also join by sending an e-mail message to: *digitaldivide-request@list.benton.org.* In the first line of the body of the message, include the following line: *subscribe digitaldivide your-e-mail* with nothing else contained in the message. Once your e-mail address is confirmed, you'll be able to post messages to the list by sending e-mails to *digitaldivide@list.benton.org.* For more information, feel free to contact Andy Carvin at *andy@benton.org.*

DOVIA

▶ This site covers topics relevant to officers, board members, and committee members of DOVIAs (Directors of Volunteers in Agencies) or similar groups that support professional volunteer managers. To subscribe, send this e-mail message: *subscribe dovia-boards* [*YOUR E-MAIL ADDRESS*] to: *majordomo@angus.mystery.com.*

ESTPLAN-L

▶ This site covers estate and planned giving. To subscribe, send this e-mail message: *subscribe* to: *listserv@netcom.com.*

FOUNDATION-L

▶ This is an "announcement only" listserv, providing information about foundations. To subscribe, send this e-mail message: *Subscribe Foundation-L* [*YOUR FIRST AND LAST NAME*] to: *majordomo@fallingrock.com.*

FUNDCAN

▶ This site covers topics in the education fund-raising community in Canada. To subscribe, send this e-mail message: *subscribe fundcan* [*YOUR FIRST AND LAST NAME*] to: *listserv@qucdn.queensu.ca.*

FundClass

▶ This is an experimental online fund-raising "school" in which veteran fund-raisers share their experience with those new to the field. Participants discuss one topic at a time, with each "class" typically lasting two to three weeks. To subscribe, send this e-mail message: *subscribe* to: *fundclass-request@fundraiser-software.com.*

Fundlist

▶ This is a listserv for fund-raising professionals. It covers a variety of fund-raising topics, from major gifts to annual giving. Fundlist discusses just about everything at one time or another, and is a good way to acquaint yourself with some experienced people. Thirty to 50 messages a day is common. To subscribe, send this e-mail message: *subscribe fundlist [YOUR FIRST AND LAST NAME]* to: *listproc@listproc.hcf.jhu.edu.*

FUNDSVCS

▶ This is a listserv primarily for systems and computer professionals working in a fund-raising environment. Message traffic is oriented to discussion of database, administrative, and related issues. FUNDSVCS generates a light amount of traffic. To subscribe to FUNDSVCS, send an e-mail message to *MAJOR-DOM@ACPUB.DUKE.EDU.* In your message type *SUBSCRIBE FUNDSVCS.*

GIFT-MGT

▶ This is a forum for discussing planned giving alternatives after a gift is closed (investment issues, administration, reporting, etc.). To subscribe to GIFT-MGT, send an e-mail message to: *LIST-SERV@NETCOM.COM.* In the body of your e-mail message, type *SUBSCRIBE GIFT-MGT* followed by your name.

Gift-Pl

▶ This site covers fund-raising and planned giving topics. To subscribe, send this e-mail message: *subscribe gift-pl [YOUR FIRST AND LAST NAME]* to: *listserv@indycms.iupui.edu.*

Giving

▶ This site covers fund raising and giving, aimed at donors and volunteers. To subscribe, send this e-mail message: *subscribe giving [YOUR FIRST AND LAST NAME]* to: *listproc@envirolink.org.*

HTML-NONPROFIT

▶ This is an Internet mailing list provided by the Institute for Global Communications for people who enjoy the creative process of HTML coding, graphic design, and CGI-Perl programming, and want to donate some of their services and time to worthy nonprofit or community service Web site development. For information about this list and the new features, visit: *http://igc.topica.com/ lists/html-nonprofit.* To subscribe, send a blank message to: *html-nonprofit-subscribe@igc.topica.com.* To post a message to the list, send your message to: *html-nonprofit@igc.topica.com.*

HILAROS

▶ This site covers issues related to Christians in fund raising, a Christian perspective on work, sharing ideas, and information, and so on. To subscribe, send this e-mail message: *subscribe hilaros* to: *majordomo@mark.geneva.edu.*

INTFUND

▶ This site covers international fund-raising issues. To subscribe, send this e-mail message: *subscribe INTFUND [YOUR FIRST AND LAST NAME]* to: *listserv@vm1.mcgill.ca.*

Let America Speak

▶ This site is for organizations and individuals working to ensure the advocacy rights of nonprofits. To subscribe, go to *http://lyris.ombwatch.org/scripts/lyris.pl?enter=las&text_mode=0* and scroll down the registration page to add your name. For more information, visit *http://www.ombwatch.org/html/forum.html.*

NPTALK

▶ The discussion list for OMB Watch's Nonprofits' Policy and Technology (NPT) Project (*www.ombwatch.org/ombw/npt*) is an electronic forum for professionals, experts, researchers, and advocates interested in the issues related to how nonprofit organizations utilize information technologies in their public policy activities. This is a moderated discussion list and is distributed in digest form at most once a day to subscribers. To subscribe, send an e-mail message to *lyris@ombwatch.org* that states in the body of the message "subscribe nptalk Your Name." Leave the subject blank, and do not include e-mail addresses in the body of the message.The discussion list is also archived (*lyris.rtknet.org/scripts/lyris.pl?enter-nptalk&text_mode-0*).

NetAction Notes

▶ NetAction staff post suggestions and advice for advocacy organizations on how to use the Internet for effective organizing and coalition building. To subscribe, send e-mail to *majordomo@netaction.org* with the following message: *subscribe netaction.* *http://www.netaction.org/notes/.*

NONPROFIT (Formerly USNONPROFIT-L)

▶ Discussions include any subject of importance to people who care about nonprofit organizations such as leaders, funders, staff, volunteers, beneficiaries, or policy makers. NONPROFIT/soc.org. nonprofit is an online group for the discussion of nonprofit issues, such as program management, board recruitment and relations, volunteering/community service, staff issues, fund raising, accounting, taxation, evaluation, accountability, marketing/public relations, collaborating with other organizations, technology uses (computer hardware, software, and Internet), and various other issues of interest to nonprofit professionals, volunteers, and supporters. The group has been around since 1994. Its members are primarily in the United States, but a growing number of international organizations/NGOs post to the group as well. There are anywhere from 1 to 10 posts a day. NONPROFIT/soc.org.nonprofit is a great place to get the word out about everything from a local workshop to an international conference, as well as publications and other resources that would be of interest to nonprofit professionals. It's also a great place to ask questions.

There are two ways to access this group:

1. Via the e-mail list, NONPROFIT (formerly USNONPROF-IT-L). To receive each post as an e-mail, send the message "Subscribe" without quotes to: *nonprofit-request@rain.org,* or join the DIGEST version of the list, which will allow you to receive all of the day's postings in one e-mail. To do this, send the message "Subscribe" without quotes to: *nonprofit-d-request@rain.org.*

2. Via the newsgroup soc.org.nonprofit, which you can access via your newsgroup reader (for instance, most versions of Netscape come with a newsgroup reader) or via *http://www.dejanews.com.*

nonprofit-request@rain.org

▶ This discussion group, founded in 1994, has a gateway with the soc.org.nonprofit newsgroup, which means that a post sent to either group will appear on both. There are on average 5 to 10 posts a day to this group. Topics on NONPROFIT include management, board recruitment and relations, staff issues, volunteer management issues, fund raising, accounting, taxation, evaluation, accountability, marketing/public relations, collaborating with other organizations, technology uses (computer hardware, software. and Internet), and various other issues of interest to not-for-profit professionals, volunteers, and supporters. This group is managed by a group of volunteers, all professionals in the not-for-profit sector in various parts of the United States. NONPROFIT is an unmoderated discussion group; no one screens incoming messages. A core group of regulars try to answer questions and set a tone for the group, but the responsibility for the group ultimately falls on everyone who participates in it. NONPROFIT is hosted and technically maintained by RAIN (Regional Alliance for Information Networking), a not-for-profit organization (*http://www.rain.org*). You can read more about NONPROFIT/soc.org.nonprofit and its history at *http://www.nonprofit-info.org.* To subscribe, send e-mail with SUB-SCRIBE on the subject line. Leave the message area blank.

Nonprofit Computer Recycling E-mail Discussion List

▶ *http://www.recycles.org/list/.*

Nonprofit Intranets

▶ Discussion of issues relating to Intranets (private networks) for nonprofits. To subscribe, send e-mail with "subscribe intranet" (without quotes) in the body of the message. *autoshare@gilbert.org.*

NONPROFIT-NET

▶ This site covers nonprofit- and Internet-related topics. To subscribe, send this e-mail message: *SUB NONPROFIT-NET* to: *listproc@lists.nonprofit.net.*

NonProfit Tech

▶ This computer support and educational online resource center for nonprofit organizations, has organized a series of conversations

regarding nonprofits and technology. Topics range from current state of nonprofits using technology to future goals for the use of technology in nonprofits. *http://www.egroups.com/group/nonprofit-tech/.*

ORG-C

▶ ORG-C covers the use of the Internet in social change organizing and networking, the creation of open source software or technical assistance resources for nonprofit and activist users, social critiques of the Internet, and occasional events. To subscribe, send a blank e-mail message to: *org-c-subscribe@topica.com.*

OrgWeb

▶ This nonprofit online discussion group is focused on the Internet and how it can be used for the benefit of organizations and their membership. It is currently not very active, but don't let that stop you from subscribing and asking questions or sharing your experience. *www.orgitecture.com/discuss.*

Orgwebmasters Discussion Group

▶ List owner: Steve McGarry (*smcgarry@lexmundi.org*), *orgwebmasters-switch@mail-list.com,* *http://www.orgwebmasters.org/.*

PG-USA

▶ This list focuses on all aspects of planned giving in the United States. To subscribe, send this e-mail message: *subscribe pg_usa [YOUR FIRST AND LAST NAME]* to: *listserve@Philanthropy-Review.com.*

Practac@charitychannel.com

▶ This site brings together nonprofit-sector practitioners and academic researchers. There are two methods to subscribe:

1. Send e-mail to *listserv@CharityChannel.com* with *SUBSCRIBE PractAc YourFirstname YourLastname* as the message. Leave the subject line blank.

2. Visit the CharityChannel Web site at *CharityChannel.com/forums* and click on the subscription information for PractAc.

PRFORUM

▶ This site covers public relations topics. To subscribe, send this e-mail message: *subscribe PRFORUM [YOUR FIRST AND LAST NAME]* to: *listserv@indycms.iupui.edu.*

PROFNET

▶ This site is available for those doing public relations for nonprofit organizations. To subscribe, send this e-mail message: *INFORMATION* to: *dforbush@ccmail.sunysb.edu.*

PRSPCT-L

▶ This site covers prospect research and is, to some degree, for people who deal with the technology of alumni/fund-raising records. To subscribe, send this e-mail message: *subscribe PRSPCT-L [YOUR FIRST AND LAST NAME]* to: *listserv@bucknell.edu.*

RESADM-L

▶ This site is for staff in charge of research or sponsored programs at universities and other nonprofit organizations. To subscribe, send e-mail, leaving the subject line blank, with the message *subscribe resadm-l your name. listserv@uacsc2.albany.edu.*

STEWARDSHIPLIST

▶ This site covers donor cultivation and stewardship. To subscribe, send this e-mail message: *subscribe* to: *majordomo@ocaxpl.cc. oberlin.edu.*

TMC E-Notes

▶ To subscribe to TMC E-Notes, send an e-mail message: *tmcenter-subscribe@egroups.com.* To post a message: *tmcenter@ egroups.com. http://www.egroups.com/group/tmcenter.*

Tech Forum

▶ This site hosts dialogues on tech issues and questions. *http://www.tech-library.org/, http://login.prospero.com/dir-login/ index.asp?getDPref=0&webtag=NONPROFITTECH&lgnDST=ht tp%3A%2F%2Fforums%2Edelphi%2Ecom%2Fnonprofittech%2F start%2F*

TECHNOLOGY

▶ This list is focused on the broader voluntary-sector social, management, strategic, legal, policy, privacy, and other issues brought about by the ever-increasing pace of technology—especially Internet technology. Despite its name, it is not a "techno-geek" forum and welcomes individuals with little or no technical background, those who have a sweeping and in-depth knowledge of the Internet and other technologies, and everyone in between. You can subscribe to TECHNOLOGY either via e-mail or from the CharityChannel Web site. Send a message to: *listserv@charitychannel.com;* leave the subject blank. In the body of the e-mail message, type *SUBSCRIBE [FORUMNAME] FIRSTNAME LASTNAME.* From the CharityChannel.com Web site (*http://CharityChannel.com/ Forums*). Click on the link for forums, then on the link for TECHNOLOGY. Follow the instructions from there.

VIRTUAL VERVE

▶ A monthly e-mail update highlighting the latest news and resources about online volunteering, e-mentoring, and the like. It is produced by the Virtual Volunteering Project (*http://www.service-leader.org/vv/*). To subscribe (it's free) and receive this and future issues, send an e-mail to *listproc@lists.cc.utexas.edu* and in the body of the e-mail, type: *subscribe vverve YOURFIRSTNAME YOURLASTNAME.* The VIRTUAL VERVE e-mail list is managed by the Virtual Volunteering Project and is used exclusively for the distribution of this newsletter. E-mail addresses of subscribers are not sold or traded to any other organization.

What's New for Nonprofits@Helping.org

▶ Would you like to be notified by e-mail when we add new resources to the site? Send e-mail to *npupdates-request@list.benton.org,* and type *subscribe npupdates* in the body of the message. *http://www.helping.org/nonprofit/whatsnew.adp, http://www.helping.org/nonprofit/forums*

E-Mail Discussion List Guides and Tutorials

E-Mail Discussion Lists: A One-Stop Guide to Subscribing, Unsubscribing, and Searching

▶ *http://www0.delphi.com/navnet/faq/listsub.html*

E-Mail Discussion Groups/Lists and Resources

▶ *http://www.webcom.com/impulse/list.html*

Internet Resources: LISTSERV Lists

▶ *http://www.lib.utexas.edu/Pubs/guides/internetpubs/listservin.html*

Liszt: Intro to Mailing Lists

▶ *http://www.liszt.com/intro.html*

Establishing a Web Presence

CharityUSA

▶ Any nonprofit wanting a free Web page or discounted Web hosting can visit *www.charityusa.org/advanced.htm.*

Icomm.org

▶ This is a nonprofit, Web-based organization that supports other nonprofit, charitable, and community organizations by providing them with Internet services and volunteer support. Nonprofit organizations may apply to receive a free Internet account on Icomm's community server. Every community account includes at least one e-mail address, a Web home page, and 10 megabytes of space. *http://www.icomm.org*

Idealist

▶ Idealist provides a searchable database of volunteer organizations and opportunities worldwide, a career center with job and internship listings, links to nonprofit resources, and a directory of companies and consultants that provide products and services to nonprofit organizations. Nonprofit organizations can post information about their organization's mission, events, and volunteer opportunities free of charge. *http://www.idealist.org/*

Network for Change

▶ This is a nonprofit organization that unites hundreds of organizations and volunteers around the world with millions of people in more than 150 countries. Free Internet services, including Web hosting, automated e-mail lists, e-mail accounts, real-time chats, and bulletin board systems, are offered to nonprofit organizations within the environmental and animal rights communities. *http://www.networkforchange.com/*

The Web Author's Bootstrapping Toolkit

▶ This site offers graphics, authoring tools, and design advice from the Online Fundraiser's Resource Center. *http://www.fundonline.com/alabook/links/resource.htm*

WeCareToo

▶ The charitable division of TWT Marketing, Inc. The site works to assist charities and nonprofit organizations by giving them free publicity and help in raising funds. *http://www.wecaretoo.com*

Wego.com

▶ This site is the preview site for a company dedicated to helping the 1.5 million trade associations, churches, charities, unions, museums, sports leagues, alumni groups, and other organizations extend their communities online. *http://www.wego.com*

Impact Online

▶ Impact Online offers a listing of resources for organizations shopping around for low-cost Internet access. *http://www.impactonline.org/ services/resources/free.shtml*

E-Zines, Online Newsletters, and News Services

The American News Service

▶ *http://www.americannews.com/*

Association Trends Online

▶ *http://www.assntrends.com*

Brown & Company's *BCO Nonprofit Update* (See *KDV Nonprofit Update*)

▶ While Brown & Company gears its accounting, tax, and management consulting services to nonprofits in Minnesota primarily, its e-mail newsletter, *BCO Nonprofit Update,* serves the nonprofit community on a national level as well, offering nonprofit reports, guest articles, news briefs, announcements, and links of interest to the nonprofit community. *http://www.kdv.com/agendas.html*

Board Cafe

▶ Co-published by CompassPoint and the National Center for Nonprofit Boards, Board Cafe is a free electronic newsletter exclusively for members of nonprofit boards of directors. *http://www.boardcafe.org/*

By the Cup

▶ A free, monthly publication of CompuMentor's nonprofit technology portal TechSoup, *By the Cup* offers links and stories related to nonprofit technology, feature articles written by specialists, answers to frequently asked questions, and links to recommended resources. *http://www.techsoup.org/subscribe.cfm*

CPSR Newsletter

▶ CPSR's flagship publication is a highly regarded quarterly magazine containing in-depth analysis of major issues involving technology along with updates on CPSR, activities. If you are interested in getting timely newsletters from CPSR join CPSR. Online publication of the newsletter is delayed for several months after the print version release. Most newsletters are now online (older ones mainly in plain text, newer ones in HTML). There is a subject index listing all articles going back to the first issue in 1983. *Note:* Starting with winter 1999, the CPSR newsletter is being published online only. Back issues of the newsletter, along with the publications, reports, and books listed on this page, are currently available using our online form or from the national office: *Chicago Philanthropy, http://www.chicagophilanthropy.com/. http://www.cpsr.org/publications/newsletters/.*

CharityNews Daily

▶ Visit *http://charitychannel.com/forums/charitynews-a.htm# e-mail* to subscribe. An opt-in subscription e-newsletter is published Monday through Friday by CharityChannel and updated hourly.

The Chronicle of Philanthropy

▶ Like its biweekly print analog, *The Chronicle of Philanthropy*'s Web site is full of useful information for fund raisers, grant makers, nonprofit managers, and others. The site is organized into broad topic areas—Gifts and Grants, Fund Raising, Managing Non-Profit Groups, and Technology—and offers, among other items, a summary of the contents of the *Chronicle*'s current and previous issues, a listing of award and RFP deadlines, job opportunities in the nonprofit sector, a listing of forthcoming conferences and workshops, consultant and technology databases, and annotated links to other nonprofit resources on the Internet. Visitors can also sign up for free e-mail updates about changes at the site as well as breaking news stories. *http://philanthropy.com/.*

Community Technology Center Review

▶ *http://www.civicnet.org/comtechreview/*

Contributions Magazine

▶ *http://www.contributionsmagazine.com/*

Crain's Online: Technology Monday

▶ Lending tech smarts to local nonprofits. *http://www.chicagobusiness.com/cgi-bin/mag/article.pl?article_id=15159*

Craver Online—Craver, Mathews, Smith & Company

▶ *http://www.craveronline.com/*

Digital Voices

▶ This is a free, online editorial service of the Benton Foundation's Communications Policy & Practice program. *http://www.benton.org/DigitalVoices/*

DOT ORG

▶ This e-newsletter, produced by Michael Stein and Marc Osten, is a practical how-to guide with tips, tools, techniques, and case studies about nonprofit use of the Internet. It is not intended as a source of news or a list of links. Each issue will have a central theme to focus the content. It covers such topics as E-mail newsletters, building Web site traffic, working with ASPs, collecting online donations, using HTML E-mail, evaluating Internet presence efforts, and more. For more information, send e-mail to *mailto:mosten@summitcollaborative.com* or *mailto:michael@ michaelstein.net*. To subscribe, send an e-mail to *mailto:dotorg-subscribe@topica.com*. *http://www.summitcollaborative.com/dot_ org.html*

EFFectgor Newsletter—Electronic Frontier Foundation

▶ *http://www.eff.org/effector/*

ERICA Ticker

▶ This is the official news bulletin of the Ericsson Internet Community Award. Every two weeks, they update interested parties on news and events related to the launch of the first-ever awards program aimed at bringing together three important communities: commercial Internet companies, Web developers, and nonprofit organizations. *http://www.npo.net/nponet/computer/ erica.html*

Executive Update Online—Greater Washington Society of Association Executives

▶ This site provides content you won't find in the printed version. Look for interesting articles on career development, personal finance, travel, technology, self-help, health and fitness, lifestyle, time management, community service, recommended reading, and other interesting topics. *http://www.gwsae.org/ExecutiveUpdate/*

Food for Thought—Compasspoint

▶ Targeted at the San Francisco Bay Area, but with more general articles and information as well, this publication includes news about funding opportunities, conferences and online resources. The San Francisco Bay Area's source of news for nonprofit organizations, it provides timely information about funding opportunities, conferences, online resources and more in every issue. *Food for Thought* will be delivered to you every three weeks via e-mail or fax. If you would like to have *Food for Thought* delivered via electronic mail, send an e-mail message to majordomo@igc.org and in the body of the message type *SUBSCRIBE FOOD-FOR-THOUGHT*. To unsubscribe to *Food for Thought*, send e-mail to majordomo@igc.org and type *UNSUBSCRIBE FOOD-FOR-THOUGHT* in the body of the message. *http://www.compasspoint.org*

Foundation News and Commentary

▶ This site displays highlights from the current edition of *Foundation News and Commentary*, a bimonthly magazine published by the Council on Foundations, Inc. Users can also access back issues. *http://www.cof.org/foundationnews*

The Grantsmanship Center Magazine

▶ *TGCI Magazine* is packed with information on how to plan, manage, staff, and fund the programs of nonprofit organizations and government agencies. *http://www.tgci.com/publications/maga- zine.htm*

Ideas in Action

▶ This twice-monthly e-mail newsletter from the folks at Idealist offers a selection of news, tips, and useful resources for people working in the nonprofit sector. *http://www.idealist.org/newslet- ter.html*

The Internet Insider

▶ An e-letter published by Marilyn Gross and featuring Web sites and discussion lists of interests to charities and nonprofits. To subscribe, send an e-mail message to *mlgross@aol.com* with *subscribe insider* in the body of the message.

KDV Nonprofit Update *(See Brown & Company's BCO Nonprofit Update)*

▶ This newsletter is published monthly and features nonprofit reports, guest articles, news briefs, announcements, and links of interest to the nonprofit community. *http://kdvnonprofitupdate.list- bot.com/*

Leader to Leader

▶ This quarterly online journal of the Drucker Foundation contains articles by experts on leadership, management, and strategy. *http://www.pfdf.org/leaderbooks/l2l/index.html*

NetAction Notes

▶ This free electronic newsletter is published by NetAction to promote effective grassroots organizing on the Internet. To subscribe to *NetAction Notes*, send a message to *majordomo@netaction.org*. The body of the message should state: *subscribe netaction*. *http://www.netaction.org/notes/*

Netpulse

▶ This newsletter from PoliticsOnline covers political uses of the Internet. You can read the newsletter online or receive it via e-mail. *http://www.politicsonline.com/netpulsearchives/netpulse.asp*

Net Results—Lipman Hearne

▶ This is a monthly newsletter about new media published by Lipman Hearne to help clients and friends in the not-for-profit community think strategically about new media and net results for their institutions. Subscriptions are free. *http://www.lipman- hearne.com/net_results.htm*

Netsurfer Digest

▶ *http://www.netsurf.com/nsd/index.html*

New England Nonprofit Quarterly

▶ *http://www.newenglandnonprofit.org*

Nonprofit Agendas

▶ This newsletter is for executives, board members, and others involved in managing nonprofit organizations. This bimonthly publication discusses such topics as fund raising, nonprofit management, governance, compliance, technology, UBIT, employee compensation and regulations affecting nonprofits. You'll find it a helpful source of information about ways to operate more efficiently and better accomplish your mission. Subscribe: kdvnonprofitup- date-subscribe@listbot.com. *http://kdvnonprofitupdate.listbot.com*

Non-Profit and Voluntary Sector Quarterly

▶ This is an online publication covering nonprofit news and information. *http://www.evans.washington.edu/nvsq/*

Nonprofit Issues

▶ Don Kramer's *Nonprofit Issues* is a newsletter that addresses legal developments and events that affect nonprofit organizations and employees. Visitors to the Web site can read selected highlights from past issues and access Ready Reference Pages, which summarize the rules and regulations governing various aspects of nonprofit organization. Trial and regular subscription orders can be placed online. *http://www.nonprofitissues.com/*

Nonprofit News

▶ A service of OMB Watch, *Nonprofit News* contains news and analysis on technology, advocacy, and other topics relevant to nonprofits. *http://ombwatch.org/www/ombw/html/npi.html*

Non-profit News

▶ Monthly newsletter of the Virtual Community of Associations. *http://www.vcanet.org/vca/news.htm*

Non-Profit Nuts & Bolts Online

▶ *Nonprofit Nuts & Bolts Online* is a supplement to the print edition of *Nuts & Bolts,* available monthly by subscription. The online version gives users access to the current issue. The Web site also has a Nonprofit Resource Center. Users can find information about nonprofits and nonprofit management listservs, inquire about products, and research employment opportunities. It provides practical management tips for nonprofit executives, covering fund raising, board relations, volunteer management, special events, public relations, and the like. The Web site also features free resources, online articles and indexes, editorial guidelines, and links to other nonprofit Web sites. *http://www.nutsbolts.com/*

NonProfit Online News

▶ Michael Gilbert's news service is devoted to news and commentary relating to the nonprofit online community, with a particular emphasis on issues related to organizational renewal, outreach, and Internet strategies in use by nonprofits. *http://www.gilbert.org/news/*

The Nonprofit Quarterly: Technology

▶ *http://www.nonprofitquarterly.org/technology/index.htm*

NonProfit Times Online

▶ This is a monthly online news service of *The Nonprofit Times,* a U.S. print publication devoted to fund raising and management issues in the nonprofit sector. *http://www.nptimes.com*

Nonprofit Toolkit

▶ This new monthly online magazine from ArtsWire is designed to serve the technology needs of the nonprofit community. Along with relevant articles, the site provides links, reviews, and a bulletin board. *http://www.nptoolkit.org/*

Nonprofit World

▶ This online publication features excerpts from the bimonthly journal of the Society for Nonprofit Organizations. *http://danenet. wicip.org/snpo/newpage2.htm*

Nonprofitxpress: The Online Source for Nonprofit and Philanthropy News

▶ This online newspaper reports on philanthropy and the nonprofit world, publishing news every weekday. *Nonprofitxpress* is an online news source that focuses on news about fund raising, management, technology, and giving and volunteering in the nonprofit sector. The site contains in-depth reports on North Carolina issues but also has news about the entire country. Registered users can receive a weekly e-mail update on news stories; registration is free. Users can also submit grants and gifts announcements. *http://www.npxpress.com/*

NpoTech—Nonprofit Technology News

▶ *http://www.npotech.org/*

OMB Watch Nonprofit News

▶ This newsletter contains select articles and news and analysis on issues affecting nonprofits. OMB Watch was created when the Reagan Office of Management and Budget proposed a rule, first hatched by the Heritage Foundation, that would have "defunded the left," and in the process, a substantial segment of the nonprofit community generally. Since then, OMB Watch has been a leader in the fight against proposals that would limit nonprofit advocacy rights. OMB Watch now co-chairs the Let America Speak Coalition along with Independent Sector and Alliance for Justice to fight such proposals. OMB Watch's involvement in nonprofit issues, however, is no longer limited to nonprofit advocacy. OMB Watch also works to increase nonprofit access to the latest communications technology, including the Internet. *http://www.ombwatch.org/npadv/*

The OMB Watcher Online

▶ *The OMB Watcher* is a twice-monthly online newsletter that contains information on the federal budget and the activities of OMB Watch. *http://ombwatch.org/ombwatcher/index.html*

OnTheInternet Online

▶ This is the electronic resource for the Internet Society's magazine. Here you will find select articles that have appeared in the magazine as well as a comprehensive table of contents, editorial guidelines, and advertising information. Published bimonthly, *OnTheInternet* is distributed exclusively to Internet Society individual and corporate members. An *OnTheInternet* tradition, each issue focuses on Internet opportunities, challenges, and triumphs. For information about *OnTheInternet* magazine or *OnTheInternet Online,* send e-mail to *editor@isoc.org.* For information about *OnTheInternet* magazine or *OnTheInternet Online,* send e-mail to *editor@isoc.org. http://www.isoc.org/oti/*

Philanthropy Journal Online

▶ News about philanthropy, nonprofits, fund raising, volunteers, charity, and jobs. *http://www.nonprofitnews.org/*

Philanthropy News Digest

▶ This weekly online news service of the Foundation Center summarizes philanthropy-related articles and feature stories in the U.S. media. The Foundation Center's electronic publication can also be delivered weekly via e-mail. Includes Connections, a service of *Philanthropy News Digest* wherein every week they round up fresh links to the best the Web has to offer on issues related to the changing world of philanthropy (*http://fdncenter.org/pnd/connections. html*), *http://fdncenter.org/pnd/current/index.html*

Philanthropy News Network

▶ PNN is composed of PNN Online, PNN Alert (see separate listing), and *Nonprofits & Technology* newspaper. Users can find a discussion area in which experts respond to readers' questions and comments; announcements for conferences, jobs, books, and online classes; links to private, corporate, and community foundations; and meta-index of nonprofit sites. *http://pnnonline.org/*

Philanthropy News Network (PNN) Alert

▶ This is a free, twice-a-week newsletter for the nonprofit sector. Features include: News, Updates, Programs, and Tools. *http://www.pj.org/corporate/alert.cfm*

Philanthropy News Network/Nonprofits & Technology

▶ This free online journal offers new articles daily and includes a technology section detailing updates on technology in the nonprofit sector. *http://www.pj.org/technology*

Pulse!—The Online Newsletter of the Nonprofit Management Support Community

▶ This bimonthly newsletter, published by the Alliance for Nonprofit Management and delivered via e-mail, features articles on fund raising, management, and technology issues facing nonprofit organizations. *Pulse!* provides readers with a brief digest of what's happening in the management support community and the nonprofit sector as well as interesting ideas and relevant resources. To subscribe, send an e-mail message to *alliance@allianceonline.org* that states in the body of the message subscribe pulse! Leave the subject blank, and do not include e-mail addresses in the body of the message. More information is available at *http://www.allianceonline.org/pulse.html, http://www.allianceonline.org/pulse.html*

Tech News

▶ This newsletter, published bimonthly by the United Way of New York City and funded by IBM, concentrates on technology news related to human service organizations. It contains many articles on the topic of how nonprofit organizations can use computer technologies. It is also available in print format. Selected articles from the print edition are available online. *http://www.uwnyc.org/640/webres.html#*

TechSoup's By the Cup

▶ *By the Cup* is a free, monthly publication of TechSoup.org, CompuMentor's nonprofit technology portal. It is distributed by subscription to friends of CompuMentor and TechSoup. It is designed for nonprofits who want to learn more about using the World Wide Web to forward their missions. *http://www.techsoup.org/sub_btc.cfm*

Technology InSights

▶ Published quarterly in print and online by Third Sector Technologies to bring practical information about technology solutions to nonprofit organizations. *http://www.thethirdsector.com*

TMC E-Notes

▶ Published twice a month by The Management Center. *http://www.tmcenter.org*

WebActive

▶ WebActive sends you e-mail updates that highlight nonprofits on the Internet. Send e-mail to webactive@prognet.com, with *sign me up!* in the "Subject" header. *http://www.webactive.com/*

ZimNotes

▶ This is an electronic newsletter with information, articles, and news on fund raising, marketing, boards, and planning published by Zimmerman Lehman, a fund-raising consulting firm based in San Francisco. *http://www.mediate.com/zl/zimnotes.htm*

Funding for Nonprofit Technology

Benton Foundation's Nonprofits & Communities

▶ This site provides information to nonprofits and charities about useful technology updates and programs. The site offers a nonprofit toolkit and useful links to related services, articles, and other organizations. *http://www.benton.org/Nonprofits*

Community Connector

▶ This Web site for community-service organizations, funders, academics, and students who are using technology to improve their local communities offers news updates, research reports, articles, handbooks, an original journal, a directory of community networks, and links to relevant resources. *http://databases.si.umich.edu/cfdocs/community/index.cfm*

Digital Canvas

▶ The online magazine of Open Studio: The Arts Online, a project of the Benton Foundation, provides "Casting the Net—Creative Fundraising for Communications Technology," an overview of the funding landscape and fund-raising advice and resources. The current issue also includes "Fundraising Strategies for Technology," a tipsheet for finding long-term support for technology programs. *http://www.openstudio.org/homepage2450/index.htm*

"Enabling Technology Funding"

▶ This position paper is an overview of funding technology for nonprofits. The paper contains six parts: Calling the Question; Making the Case for Technology; Models for Guidelines and Proposals, Evaluating Technology and Effectiveness, Assessing Information, Management in an Organization, Advice to Grantseekers and Grantmakers; and Conclusion. *http://www.npo.net/nponet/computer/ETF_overview.htm*

ERICA

▶ This awards program created by Swedish telecommunications giant Ericsson is designed to recognize the community-building power of the Internet. The program seeks ideas from nonprofit organizations for technology applications that help nonprofits better manage their projects, deliver services, raise money, and communicate their messages. *http://www.ericsson.com/erica/*

Find Technology Funding

▶ *http://www.helping.org/nonprofit/grants.adp*

Markle Foundation's Interactive Communications Tech

▶ The Markle Foundation offers grants to organizations doing research in the area of information technology and emerging communications media. The Markle Web site provides application details as well as information about the organization's current projects. *http://www.markle.org*

Nonprofits' Questions about Tech Funding Have Answers

▶ *http://pnnonline.org/technology/techfunding0910.cfm*

Program Overview of the Telecommunications and Information Infrastructure Assistance Program (TIIAP)

▶ The Telecommunications and Information Infrastructure Assistance Program (TIIAP) promotes the widespread availability and use of advanced telecommunications technologies in the public and nonprofit sectors. As part of the Department's National Telecommunications and Information Administration (NTIA), TIIAP gives grants for model projects demonstrating innovative uses of network technology. *http://www.ntia.doc.gov/otiahome/top/index.html*

RealNetworks Foundation

▶ The Foundation funds programs that make innovative use of the Internet to promote free speech, enable technology access for underserved communities, or enhance the quality of life in specific geographic areas. *http://www.realnetworks.com/company/giving/rnfoundation.html?src=noref,ssph*

"Technology: Tech Funding: Elements of a Technology Plan"

▶ A two-part series on technology funding by Shane Tucker. *http://www.pnnonline.org/technology/techfunding1124.cfm*

Internet Access

Accessing the Internet by E-mail FAQ

▶ *http://www.faqs.org/faqs/internet-services/access-via-e-mail/*

ISPcheck—Internet Services Search Engine

▶ ISPcheck is a free service that lets one find, sort, and compare thousands of Web hosting and Internet access options offered by thousands of ISPs. *http://www.ispcheck.com/*

Internet News and Updates

First Monday

▶ *http://firstmonday.org*

Netsurfer Digest

▶ *http://www.netsurf.com/nsd/index.html*

The Network Observer

▶ Though discontinued, some of the back issues may be of interest and assistance to nonprofits and others. *http://dlis.gseis.ucla.edu/people/pagre/tno.html*

Red Rock Eater News Service

▶ *http://dlis.gseis.ucla.edu/people/pagre/rre.html*

Scout Report

▶ This is a very useful weekly gleaning from the wonders of the Web. To receive the electronic mail version of the *Scout Report* each week, join the scout-report mailing list. This is the only mail you will receive from this list. Send e-mail to listserv@lists.internic.net with the following message in the body of the message: *subscribe scout-report yourfirstname yourlastname. http://www.cs.wisc.edu/scout/report*

Weekly Bookmarkz

▶ A site and newsletter designed to inform and entertain the Internet community. What's new and cool on the Web? Find out every week in the *Weekly Bookmarkz* newsletter. You'll find cool site reviews of new and informative Web sites in over 15 categories. *http://www.bookmarkz.com/, http://www.mybookmarks.com*

Internet Search Tools and Strategies

(See also Internet Tutorials, Guides, and Online Training: Search Engine Guides and Tutorials; Searching the World Wide Web)

Complete Planet—Search Tutorial: Guide to Effective Searching of the Internet

▶ The tutorial provides a one-stop resource for the beginning to intermediate Web searcher. *http://www.completeplanet.com/tutorials/index.asp*

Dave Butler's Search the Net Page

▶ *http://www.voicenet.com/~dbut/netguide.htm*

Find It!

▶ *http://www.itools.com/find-it*

Find It on the Web—PC Magazine Online

▶ Offers advice on the best search engine to use in specific situations. *http://www.zdnet.com/pcmag/features/websearch98*

Finding Information on the Internet: A TUTORIAL

▶ Offers information for the beginner as well as the experienced Internet researcher—finding information on the Web, Internet tutorial, Web searching, choosing the best search tools or engines to refine searches and get the documents you want. *http://www.lib.berkeley.edu/TeachingLib/Guides/Internet/FindInfo.html*

Finding It Online: Web Search Strategies

▶ A free, interactive tutorial on how to search the Internet using basic and advanced search techniques. *http://home.sprintmail.com/~debflanagan/main.html*

Freeality Internet Search

▶ *http://www.freeality.com*

The Front Page Collection of Search Engines & Web-Site Links

▶ *http://www.thefrontpage.com/search*

Go Gettem WebSearch

▶ *http://www.gogettem.com*

How to Do Field Searching in Web Search Engines—Online Inc.

▶ *http://www.onlineinc.com/onlinemag/OL1998/hock5.html*

How to Search the World Wide Web: A Tutorial for Beginners and Non-Experts

▶ *http://204.17.98.73/midlib/tutor.htm*

Infomine Internet Enabling Tools

▶ *http://infomine.ucr.edu/search/enablesearch.phtml*

Inter-Links

▶ *http://alabanza.com/kabacoff/Inter-Links*

Internet Resources Meta-Index

▶ *http://www.ncsa.uiuc.edu/SDG/Software/Mosaic/MetaIndex.html*

Internet Scout Project

▶ *http://scout.cs.wisc.edu/index.html*

Internet Search Tools and Directories

▶ *http://ksgwww.harvard.edu/library/www_intdir.htm*

Internet Searching (Michigan COMNET)

▶ *http://comnet.org/net/search/index.html*

Internet Surfboard

▶ *http://www.geocities.com/Paris/1092*

Internet Tutorial: Search Engines and Search Strategies

▶ *http://www.geocities.com/SiliconValley/Mouse/5288/Search.htm*

Internet Tutorials, Guides, and FAQs

▶ *http://www.amdahl.com/internet/tutorials.html*

The Official Netscape Guide to Internet Research

▶ *http://www.researchbuzz.com/*

Phil Bradley: Searching the Internet

▶ *http://www.philb.com/search.htm*

Power Searching 101Tutorial: Guide to Effective Searching of the Internet

▶ Divided into 48 topics, it makes it easy to find the specific search information you need. *http://www.thewebtools.com/tutorial/tutorial.htm*

Scout Toolkit

▶ *http://www.scout.cs.wisc.edu/toolkit/*

Search IQ

▶ *http://www.searchiq.com*

Search Like the Pros

▶ *http://florin.syr.edu/webarch/searchpro/search_like_the_pros.html*

Search the Internet

▶ *http://alabanza.com/kabacoff/Inter-Links/search/search.html*

Searching and Researching on the Internet and the WWW

▶ *http://www.webliminal.com/search-web.html*

Searching and Researching Open Directory

▶ *http://www.webliminal.com/cgi-bin/dclinks/dclinks.cgi*

Searching the Internet

▶ *http://www.bartlesville.lib.ok.us/search.htm*

Searching the Internet: Recommended Sites and Search Techniques

▶ A comprehensive tutorial from the University at Albany. *http://www.albany.edu/library/internet/search.html*

Searching the Internet

▶ *http://home.worldstar.com/search/*

Sink or Swim: Internet Search Tools & Techniques

▶ Provides a detailed discussion of the different types of search tools available. *http://www.ouc.bc.ca/libr/connect96/search.htm*

WWW, USENET, and Mailing List Search Tools

▶ *http://amseed.com/asearch1.html*

WWW Virtual Library: Starter Tips for Internet Research

▶ *http://www.etown.edu/vl/starter.html*

Web Searching Tutorial

▶ How to use those Web search engines properly, and find what you are looking for. *http://www.askscott.com/tindex.html*

Yahoo! Computers and Internet: Internet: World Wide Web: Searching the Web

▶ *http://dir.yahoo.com/Computers_and_Internet/Internet/World_Wide_Web/Searching_the_Web/How_to_Search_the_Web/*

Yahoo! Internet Life

▶ *http://www.zdnet.com/yil/filters/channels/netezuser.html*

Internet Service Providers

Directory of Internet Service Providers

▶ *http://boardwatch.internet.com/isp/*

Internet Tutorials, Guides, and Online Training

An Incomplete Guide to the Internet (Especially for K–12 Teachers & Students)

▶ *http://www.ncsa.uiuc.edu/Edu/ICG/pt1.toc.html*

Arts Wire Spider School

▶ Arts Wire Spider School offers a guide and additional resources for using and understanding the Internet. *http://artswire.org/spider-school/workshops/internetprimer2.html*

Basic Guide to the Internet

▶ *http://www.albany.edu/library/internet/internet.html*

Beginners Central—A Users Guide to the Internet

▶ *http://www.northernwebs.com/bc/*

Beginners Guide to Life and the Internet

▶ *http://members.aol.com/JB44/index.html*

The Beginner's Guide to the Internet—A Novice's Guide to the World Wide Web

▶ *http://members.aol.com/bikerchris/main.htm*

Boston Phoenix Guide to the Net

▶ *http://www.bostonphoenix.com/supplements/TheNet/index.shtml*

Camp Yahoo!

▶ This site gives away a basic Internet training curriculum intended for newcomers to the Web. These teaching materials are available free of charge to members of qualified nonprofit organizations, community centers, libraries, schools, and service groups. *http://camp.yahoo.com*

The Complete Internet Guide and Web Tutorial

▶ *http://www.microsoft.com/insider/internet/default.htm*

Patrick Crispen's Internet Roadmap

▶ Easy to follow and fun Internet tutorial series. *Caution:* This site was established in 1996 and some of the information may need updating. *http://www.webreference.com/roadmap/, http://www.mcs.brandonu.ca/~ennsnr/Resources/Roadmap/Welcome.html, http://www.mobiusweb.com/~mobius/Roadmap/*

Explore the Internet (Library of Congress)

▶ *http://lcweb.loc.gov/global/explore.html*

Get It Joe's Internet Tour

▶ Provides three Internet tours (10-minute, one-hour, and complete)—foreign language versions (French, German, Italian, and Spanish) are under construction. *http://www.california.com/~getitjoe/joemain.html*

Help for Newbies: A Good Place to Start Learning about the Internet

▶ Everything you need to know about the Internet, but didn't know who to ask! Free Internet information for newbies. *http://www.fingertek.com/newbies.htm*

The Help Web—A Guide to Getting Started on the Internet

▶ *http://www.imaginarylandscape.com/helpweb/welcome.html*

ICYouSee—A Guide to the World Wide Web

▶ *http://www.ithaca.edu/library/Training/ICYouSee.html*

The Info Service—Internet Beginners Guides

▶ *http://info-s.com/internet.html*

Information about the Internet

▶ *http://www.usg.edu/galileo/internet/netinfo/netinfo.html*

Inter-Links

▶ *http://alabanza.com/kabacoff/Inter-Links*

Internet 101—Impact Online

▶ *http://www.glikbarg.com/internet/welcome.html*

Internet 101: A Beginner's Guide to the Internet and the World Wide Web

▶ *http://www2.awl.com/cseng/titles/0-201-32553-5/Website/index.html*

Internet 101: Introduction to the Internet—Impact Online

▶ *http://www.impactonline.org/services/internet/*

The Internet Companion—A Beginner's Guide to Global Networking
▶ *http://www.obs-us.com/obs/english/books/archives/editinc/top.htm*

Internet Detective
▶ *http://sosig.ac.uk/desire/internet-detective.html*

Internet for Beginners
▶ *http://netforbeginners.about.com/internet/netforbeginners/, http://netforbeginners.about.com/internet/netforbeginners/mbody.htm*

The Internet Guide
▶ *http://conted.fis.utoronto.ca/tig/demo/*

Internet Guides
▶ *http://members.tripod.com/~smanage/netguide.html*

Internet Guides and Information
▶ Includes: The Hitchhiker's Guide to the Internet, Zen and the Art of the Internet Bibliography, and Internet Timeline. *http://access.tucson.org/internet_info.html*

Internet Guides, Tutorials and Training Information
▶ *http://lcweb.loc.gov/global/internet/training.html*

Internet in a Nutshell (Infinite Ink)
▶ *http://www.best.com/~ii/internet/*

Internet Research
▶ *http://www.nuigalway.ie/soc/netsearch.html*

Internet Resources on the Web
▶ *http://austin.brandonu.ca/~ennsnr/Resources/Welcome.html*

Internet Tutorial: Search Engines and Search Strategies
▶ *http://www.geocities.com/SiliconValley/Mouse/5288/Search.htm*

Internet Tutorials
▶ *http://www.albany.edu/library/internet/*

Internet Tutorials—Surfing Sites and Guides to the Internet
▶ Would you like to learn more about the Internet? These guides give you simple explanations and answer your questions. Would you like to find some great surfing sites, then click on "Surfing." *http://www.useekufind.com/intutrl.htm*

Internet Tutorials, Guides, and FAQs
▶ *http://www.amdahl.com/internet/tutorials.html*

Internet Web Text Index
▶ *http://www.december.com/web/text/index.html*

Introduction to the Internet
▶ *http://myrin.ursinus.edu/cs100h/index.htm*

Learn Internet Basics—Fingertek Information Services
▶ *http://www.fingertek.com/*

Learn the Net: An Internet Guide and Tutorial
▶ This is a good primer to help you find your way around online. Learn the Net provides information and tips to help people discover how to use the Internet. It can be read in five different languages. *http://www.learnthenet.com*

Life on the Internet Beginner's Guide
▶ *http://www.screen.com/start/guide/default.html*

Netstrider Tutorials—Introduction to the Internet
▶ *http://www.netstrider.com/tutorials/internet/*

Newbie dot Org
▶ The newbie-friendly home of help for the newbie of all stages and ages, offers tutorials, trainers, online lessons, reference, and more. *http://www.newbie.org/*

Newbie U: New User University
▶ *http://160.79.240.59/*

NewbieNet
▶ *http://www.newbie.net/*

Newbies Anonymous
▶ *http://www.geocities.com/TheTropics/1945/index1.htm*

ONLearning.net Learning Resource Network—Prometheon
▶ *http://www.seminarfinder.com/topic/InternetWorldWideWeb/*

Online College (One/Northwest: Online Networking for the Environment)
▶ *http://www.onenw.org/college/default.htm*

Search Tutorial: Guide to Effective Searching of the Internet—The WebTools Company
▶ The tutorial provides a one-stop resource for the beginning to intermediate Web searcher. *http://www.completeplanet.com/tutorials/index.asp*

Searching and Researching on the Internet and the WWW

▶ *http://www.webliminal.com/search-web.html*

Self-Paced Tutorial on the Internet for Volunteer Program Staff

▶ *http://www.cybervpm.com/internet/tutorial/index.htm*

Tips and Suggestions for Internet Research—Net Gain

▶ *http://strategis.ic.gc.ca/SSG/ng00061e.html*

Tutorial: Guide to Effective Searching of the Internet

▶ *http://www.thewebtools.com/tutorial/tutorial.htm*

US Internet—Tutorial

▶ *http://www.usinternet.com/usi/tutorial.html*

Using and Understanding the Internet: Beginner's Guide (PBS)

▶ *http://www.pbs.org/uti/begin.html*

Virtual Internet Guide

▶ *http://www.virtualfreesites.com/internet.html*

WWW Internet Tutorials—Ferris State University

▶ *http://www.ferris.edu/weblinks/worldwideweb/webandinternet-tutorials.htm*

Web Searching Tutorial

▶ How to use those web search engines properly, and find what you are looking for. *http://www.askscott.com/tindex.html*

Webmonkey Guides

▶ *http://hotwired.lycos.com/webmonkey/guides/*

Yahoo! Beginner's Guides

▶ *http://dir.yahoo.com/Computers_and_Internet/Internet/Information_and_Documentation/Beginners_Guides/*

Yahoo! How-To: A Tutorial for Web Surfers

▶ *http://howto.yahoo.com/*

You Can Get There from Here: A Beginner's Guide to the Internet

▶ *http://www.angelfire.com/pa4/newbieweb*

Mailing List Directories and Search Engines

CataList—The Official Catalog of Listserv Lists

▶ *http://www.lsoft.com/catalist.html*

DiscussionLists.com

▶ *http://discussionlists.com/*

Liszt—The Mailing List Directory

▶ *http://www.liszt.com*

NEW-LIST

▶ NEW-LIST is a moderated distribution list that may be used to announce the establishment of new electronic mailing lists. Many of the people who maintain "lists of lists" subscribe to the NEW-LIST list as do direct users of the information. The NEW-LIST list exists primarily for initial announcements of new e-mail lists. Subscribers to NEW-LIST at *listserv@cs.wisc.edu* have some additional ways they can tailor the information they receive. *http://new-list.com/, http://scout18.cs.wisc.edu/cgi-bin/lwgate/NEW-LIST/*

Publicly Accessible Mailing Lists

▶ *http://paml.alastra.com*

Search the List of Lists

▶ *http://catalog.com/vivian/interest-group-search.html*

Tile.net

▶ *http://www.tile.net/*

Newsgroup Guides and Tools

AOL NetHelp—Newsgroups

▶ *http://aol.com/nethelp/news/news.html*

How to Use Newsgroups

▶ *http://startext.net/interact/forums/helpint.htm*

NewsGroups Guide

▶ *http://www.netspace.net.au/~quokka/NewsGroups.htm*

Usenet Info Center Launch Pad

▶ *http://metalab.unc.edu/usenet-i/*

Usenet News

▶ *http://alabanza.com/kabacoff/Inter-Links/usenet.html*

UseNet News (Information and Public Access)

▶ *http://psyche.uthct.edu/ous/UseNet.html*

Usenet References

▶ *http://www.faqs.org/usenet/*

Newsgroup Search Tools

Altavista.com

▶ *http://www.altavista.com/*

AOL NetFind's Newsgroup Finder

▶ Most newsreader programs give you the ability to search for keywords in newsgroup names. However, a more reliable way to find newsgroups that you're interested in, as well as specific newsgroup articles, is using a search engine that deals exclusively with newsgroups that will allow you to do both. Just specify whether you are looking for newsgroups or newsgroup articles, then type in words describing what you're looking for, and you're well on your way. *http://www.aol.com/netfind/newsgroups.html*

CyberFiber@ Newsgroups

▶ *http://www.cyberfiber.com/index.html*

Deja.com's Usenet Discussion Service

▶ This site presents a listing of "Top Forums" based on your keyword search of *article content*. The Usenet articles can be accessed directly via their Web interface. *http://www.deja.com/usenet*

Find Newsgroups

▶ *http://www.cen.uiuc.edu/cgi-bin/find-news-uiuc*

How to Search Mailing lists and Newsgroups—USUS

▶ *http://www.usus.org/techniques/discussionsearch.htm*

Infinite Ink's Finding News Groups

▶ *http://www.ii.com/internet/messaging/newsgroups/*

Internet Finder: Search the Usenet

▶ *http://www.access.ch/oblum/search/usenet.htm*

Internet Search Station

▶ *http://www.zetnet.co.uk/sigs/search/s_newsgr.html*

LEARN THE NET: Searching Newsgroups

▶ *http://www.learnthenet.com/english/html/27srchn.htm*

Liszt's Usenet Newsgroup Directory

▶ This is a searchable listing of some 30,000 newsgroups. You can browse by Usenet categories or search by keyword. Articles can be accessed either through your "local" news server or via Deja.Com's web interface. *http://www.liszt.com/news/*

Master List of Newsgroup Hierarchies

▶ A comprehensive list of local and regional newsgroup hierarchies. *http://www.magmacom.com/~leisen/mlnh/*

Newsgroup Index

▶ Listed in alphabetical order. *http://ben-schumin.simplenet.com/newsindex/*

Newsgroup Search Tools

▶ *http://rampages.onramp.net/~joenord/ng_list.htm*

Robot Wisdom Newsgroup Finder

▶ *http://www.robotwisdom.com/finder/index.html*

Search Usenet Newsgroups

▶ *http://www.lbl.gov/Glimpse/Usenet-search.html*

tile.net/news

▶ This is a complete index to Internet Usenet newsgroups. You can browse by subject, hierarchy, or search. There are links to newsgroup FAQs and use statistics. *http://tile.net/news/*

Usenet

▶ *http://www.personal.u-net.com/~yandy/search/Usenet.html*

Usenet FAQ Archives

▶ *http://www.faqs.org/faqs/*

Usenet Newsgroups Search Engines

▶ *http://home.worldstar.com/search/search.cfm?secid=news*

Newsgroups (Nonprofit)

soc.org.nonprofit

▶ This is a Usenet discussion newsgroup that covers all topics related to nonprofits. Most contributors are employees or volunteers. The site generates 5 to 10 messages a day. A Nonprofit FAQ for the group is occasionally updated. The frequently asked questions file, divided into 21 topics, include start-up and management issues, fund raising, marketing, nonprofit organizations and the Internet, education and training, and general theoretical discussions.

Online Applications

Designing Effective Action Alerts

▶ An action alert is a message that someone sends out to the Net asking for a specific action to be taken on a current political issue. Well-designed action alerts are a powerful way to invite people to participate in the processes of a democracy. Having seen many action alerts in my years on the Internet, I have tried to abstract some guidelines for people who wish to use them. *http://dlis.gseis.ucla.edu/people/pagre/alerts.html*

Online Lobbying and Political Action

Center for Responsive Politics

▶ This is a DC–based research group that tracks money in politics and its effect on elections and public policy. The Center's site offers a searchable database of political donors and "soft money" donations; the site can also be searched by state and politician. *http://dlis.gseis.ucla.edu/people/pagre/alerts.html*

e-advocates

▶ *http://www.e-advocates.com*

Netaction

▶ Dedicated to promoting the use of the Internet for effective grassroots citizen action campaigns and to educating the public, policy makers, and the media about technology policy issues, the Netaction site provides an online training program (*http://www.netaction.org/training*) on virtual activism, information about the organization's current projects, and links to helpful activism sites. *http://www.netaction.org/*

OMB Watch's Nonprofits' Policy & Technology Project

▶ The Nonprofits' Policy & Technology Project (NPT) is OMB Watch's three-year initiative to improve communications linkages within the nonprofit sector in order to strengthen public policy participation. The NPT site provides information about activities, resources, and project updates. *http://www.ombwatch.org/nptand-ctc.html*

Project Vote Smart

▶ This site researches, tracks, and provides independent factual information on over 13,000 candidates and elected officials. The site offers a searchable database of voting records, campaign issue positions, performance evaluations by special interests, campaign contributions, previous experience, and contact information. *http://www.vote-smart.org/*

Product and Service Directories

Association of Fundraising Professionals Marketplace

▶ *http://www.nsfre.org/afp_marketplace*

The Chronicle of Philanthropy: Products & Services

▶ *http://philanthropy.com/adv.dir/advmain.htm*

Contributions Magazine Wise Buyers Guide

▶ *http://www.contributionsmagazine.com/marketplace.html*

The Nonprofit Times Resource Directory

▶ *http://www.nptimes.com/main/directory.html*

Sources for Volunteer Recognition Materials

▶ *http://www.avaintl.org/resources/recog.html*

Search Engines and Directories

The following are menu-driven and/or keyword search engines and database indexes of sites available on the ever-expanding World Wide Web; these invaluable directories provide the fastest method of locating and accessing the literally millions of Web pages. *Caution:* All are not equal in speed or number of listings; trial and error will determine which ones work best for your particular needs.

Meta Search Engines

37.com

▶ This site has 37 major search engines. *http://www.37.com*

800go (12 Search Engines in One)

▶ *http://www.800go.com/800go.html*

AccuFind

▶ *http://www.nln.com/*

All4One

▶ *http://www.all4one.com/index.php3*

All-In-One Search Page

▶ *http://www.allonesearch.com/*

All in One Internet Searches

▶ *http://www.reverse-lookup.com/basict.htm*

AllSearchEngines.Com

▶ *http://www.allsearchengines.com/*

All the Best Search Engines

▶ *http://kresch.com/search/search.htm*

CNET Search

▶ *http://www.search.com/search*

Cyber411

▶ *http://www4.c4.com/*

Dr. Webster's Big Page of Search Engines

▶ Select the category you'd like to search—Business, Entertainment, Games, General, Government, Multi-searchers, Miscellaneous, News, Non-Web, People. *http://www.drwebster.com/search/search.htm*

Digisearch
▶ *http://www.digiway.com/digisearch*

Dogpile.com
▶ *http://www.dogpile.com/*

The Front Page Collection of Search Engines & Sites
▶ *Caution:* Somewhat outdated. *http://www.thefrontpage.com/search/*

Highway61
▶ *http://www.highway61.com/*

MegaSpider
▶ *http://www.megaspider.com*

Metacrawler
▶ *http://www.metacrawler.com/*

MetaGopher
▶ *http://www.metagopher.com/*

MetaIQ
▶ *http://www.metaiq.com/education/gov.html*

Meta Search/Index List
▶ *http://www.mindspring.com/~webgroup/angie/list.html*

Metor Search
▶ *http://www.metor.com/*

Netscape
▶ *http://home.netscape.com*

Prime Search
▶ *www.primecomputing.com/search.htm*

Search Engine Colossus—International Directory of Search Engines
▶ *http://www.searchenginecolossus.com/*

Search Engines and Servers
▶ *http://www.flex.com/~calvin/search.htm*

Search Engines Galore
▶ *http://searchitall.hypermart.net/subject3.html*

Speedy Q Meta Search: Find Internet Meta Search Engines
▶ *http://www.spdq.com/metasear.html*

The Ultimate Internet Search Index
▶ *http://www.geocities.com/SiliconValley/Heights/5296/index.html*

Use It Unified Search Engine
▶ *http://www.he.net/~kamus/useen.htm*

WWW3
▶ *http://cuiwww.unige.ch/meta-index.html*

Web Search Simple
▶ *http://www.web-search.com/simple3.html#70*

Individual Search Engines

@BRINT: Business & Technology Research Libary—A Business Researcher's Interests
▶ *http://www.brint.com/Sites.htm*

AltaVista
▶ *http://www.altavista.com/*

AOL NetFind
▶ *http://www.aol.com/netfind*

Ask Jeeves
▶ *http://www.aj.com/*

DirectHit
▶ *http://www.directhit.com*

Electric Library Personal Edition
▶ *http://www.elibrary.com*

Excite
▶ *http://www.excite.com* (Includes USENET)

Galaxy
▶ *http://www.galaxy.com/*

Go (Formerly Infoseek)
▶ *http://www.go.com/*

Google
▶ *http://www.google.com*

Goto

▶ *http://www.goto.com/*

HotBot

▶ *http://hotbot.lycos.com/*

Inference Find

▶ *http://www.infind.com/*

Inktomi Search Software

▶ *http://software.infoseek.com/*

Internet Search Station—Usenet Newsgroups Search

▶ *http://www.zetnet.co.uk/sigs/search/s_newsgr.html*

Jump City

▶ *http://www.jumpcity.com/start.shtml*

LookSmart

▶ *http://www.looksmart.com*

Lycos

▶ *http://www.lycos.com*

Magellan Internet Guide

▶ *http://magellan.excite.com/*

My Starting Point

▶ *http://www.stpt.com/*

Netscape Search

▶ *http://home.mcom.com/home/internet-index.html*

Northern Light

▶ *http://www.northernlight.com/*

Northern Light Research

▶ *http://nlresearch.northernlight.com/research.html*

Open Directory Project

▶ *http://www.dmoz.org/*

PhilanthropySearch.com

▶ This Web search engine is designed specifically for the non-profit sector. The site contains "speed searches" for fund raising, jobs, publications, tools and services, and more. Users can search for nonprofits by type (arts and culture, religious, health, etc.) and can do custom searches for organizations. The goal of

PhilanthropySearch.com is to help users find information about charitable giving, volunteering, and other nonprofit issues on the Web. Organizations that have an Internet presence may also submit their site for inclusion. *http://www.philanthropysearch.com/*

Search Engines, Indexes, Directories & Libraries—NetStrider

▶ *http://www.netstrider.com/search/*

Webcrawler

▶ *http://www.webcrawler.com*

WebDirect

▶ *http://www.wdirect.com/cgi-win/wdirect.exe*

WhoWhere?

▶ *http://www.whowhere.lycos.com/*

Yahoo! (Yet Another Hierarchical Officious Oracle)

▶ One of the original, best maintained, and most rapidly expanding catalogs on the Web, each site is classified by subject and tagged with a brief description, and the number of listings doubles each month; users can search by keyword or browse entries by subject heading. *http://www.yahoo.com*

Yellow Pages

▶ *http://yellow.com*

Yureka!—The Internet's First "Find" Engine

▶ *http://www.yureka.com/*

Search Engine Reviews

Choosing & Using Internet Search Engines, Part Three

▶ *http://www.indiana.edu/~librcsd/search/*

Find It on the Web—*PC Magazine Online*

▶ Offers advice on the best search engine to use in specific situations. *http://www.zdnet.com/pcmag/features/websearch98*

A Guide to Web Directories

▶ *http://www.crosswinds.net/~directories/home.htm*

Guides to Specialized Search Engines

▶ *http://www.searchability.com/*

Internet Research News

▶ Register for the free newsletter to stay informed on weekly search engine happenings. *http://www.researchbuzz.com/news/*

Internet Search Engines

▶ *http://www.fundsnetservices.com/engines1.htm*

Internet Search Engines

▶ *http://www.usg.edu/galileo/internet/netinfo/sengines.html*

Search Engine Guide

▶ This complete guide for search engine users offers functions (direct search, free submission), information and statistics, tutorial, and detailed description. *http://www.searchengineguide.org/*

The Search Is Over: The Search Engine Secrets of the Pros—PC Computing

▶ *http://www.zdnet.com/pccomp/features/fea1096/sub2.html*

Search Engine Showdown: The Users' Guide to Web Searching

▶ *http://www.searchengineshowdown.com/*

Search Engine Watch

▶ *http://www.searchenginewatch.com/*

Search Engines and Servers

▶ *http://www.flex.com/~calvin/search.htm*

Search IQ

▶ Also includes Directory of Specialty Engines and Search Tutorials. *http://www.searchiq.com*

Search Engine Guides and Tutorials

Rene Belson's Search Engine Index

▶ *http://www.rene.belso.dk/engines.html*

Choosing & Using Internet Search Engines, Part Three

▶ *http://www.indiana.edu/~librcsd/search/*

Emerson J. Dillon—Tutorial Search Engines

▶ *http://www.phoenix.k12.ny.us/ejd/info/computer/tutorial/search.htm*

Guide to Meta-Search Engines

▶ *http://www.indiana.edu/~librcsd/search/meta.html*

Guides to Specialized Search Engines (with Descriptions)

▶ *http://www.searchability.com/*

Internet Directories

▶ *http://www.usg.edu/galileo/internet/netinfo/director.html*

Internet Search Engines

▶ *http://www.fundsnetservices.com/engines1.htm*

Internet Search Engines

▶ *http://www.usg.edu/galileo/internet/netinfo/sengines.html*

Learning More about Search Engines and Subject Directories: FAQs

▶ *http://www.cln.org/searching_faqs.html*

Search Engine Glossary—Search Engine Watch

▶ *http://www.searchenginewatch.com/facts/glossary.html*

Search Engine Guide

▶ This complete guide for search engine users offers functions (direct search, free submission), information and statistics, tutorial, and detailed description. *http://www.searchengineguide.org/*

Search Engine Tutorials

▶ Links to tutorials, guides, articles, and resources to help you use search engines better. *http://www.searchenginewatch.com/tutorials.htm*

Search Engines, Indexes, Directories & Libraries— NetStrider

▶ *http://www.netstrider.com/search/*

Search Engine Watch: Tips about Internet Search Engines and Search Engine Submission

▶ *http://www.searchenginewatch.com/*

The Spider's Apprentice—A Helpful Guide to Web Search Engines (Monash Information Services)

▶ *http://www.monash.com/spidap.html*

Virtual Search Secrets

▶ *http://www.virtualfreesites.com/search.secrets.html*

Web Searching Tutorial

▶ How to use those Web search engines properly and find what you are looking for. *http://www.askscott.com/tindex.html*

Windweaver's Search Guide: Using the Best Directories and Search Engines

▶ *http://www.windweaver.com/searchguide.htm*

Searching the World Wide Web

(See also Internet Guides and Tutorials; Internet Search Tools and Strategies; Search Engines Guides and Tutorials)

Finding Information on the Internet: A TUTORIAL

▶ Finding information on the Web, Internet tutorial, Web searching, choosing the best search tools or engines to refine searches and get the documents you want. *http://www.lib.berkeley.edu/Teaching Lib/Guides/Internet/FindInfo.html*

Finding It Online: Web Search Strategies

▶ A free, interactive tutorial on how to search the Internet using basic and advanced search techniques. *http://home.sprintmail.com/~debflanagan/main.html*

How to Search the World Wide Web: A Tutorial for Beginners and Non-Experts

▶ *http://204.17.98.73/midlib/tutor.htm*

ICYouSee—A Guide to the World Wide Web

▶ *http://www.ithaca.edu/library/Training/ICYouSee.html*

Search Tools Chart

▶ *http://www.infopeople.org/src/chart.html*

Seven Habits of Effective Searchers

▶ *http://websearch.about.com/internet/websearch/library/weekly/aa010199.htm*

Seven Stupid Searching Mistakes

▶ *http://websearch.about.com/internet/websearch/library/weekly/aa051299.htm*

Super Searchers' Search Secrets

▶ *http://websearch.about.com/internet/websearch/library/weekly/aa010899.htm*

Tips for Searching the Web

▶ *http://www.neci.nec.com/%7Elawrence/searchtips.html*

The World Wide Web for the Clueless

▶ *http://www.mit.edu:8001/people/rei/wwwintro.html*

Yahoo! Computers and Internet: Internet: World Wide Web: Searching the Web

▶ *http://dir.yahoo.com/Computers_and_Internet/Internet/World_Wide_Web/Searching_the_Web/How_to_Search_the_Web/*

Software and Hardware

Charity USA Nonprofit Resources Search Engine & Directory: Products for Nonprofits: Software

▶ Charity USA's Directory of Software suited for nonprofit organizations. *http://www.charityusa.org/pages/Products_for_Nonprofits/Software/*

Community Action Technology Purchasing Guide

▶ A growing series of easy-reference guides to help you buy information technology products for your organization. *http://www.catguide.org/*

Indices of Software and Software Advice for Not-for-Profit and Public Sector Organizations

▶ *http://www.coyotecom.com/database/sites.html*

Inktomi Search Software

▶ *http://software.infoseek.com/*

Nonprofit Open Source Initiative (NOSI)

▶ The Nonprofit Open Source Initiative (NOSI) has been created to help facilitate a continuing discussion regarding the role of Open Source software in the nonprofit sector. Their goals are to educate technical assistance providers on the benefits of Open Source development by linking to relevant articles, sponsoring an online dialogue, and connecting people; and develop a technology think tank to assess the changing technical needs of the nonprofit sector. NOSI maintains an online discussion board and mailing lists (NOSI Announcments, General Discussions). Website: *http://nosi.net/*; E-mail: *nosi@nosi.net*

The Nonprofit Software Index

▶ Hosted by Seton Hall University's Center for Nonprofit Service, this low-graphics, frames-based site lists software packages in a variety of categories, including fund raising, financial, personnel, and volunteer management. Each entry includes a detailed description of the software, system requirements, and company contact information. *http://www.npinfotech.org/TNOPSI/*

NPWare.org

▶ NPWare.org is a software resource site that caters to nonprofit organizations. Here you will find only freeware or trial/demo versions of software offering discounts to schools, churches, charities and other nonprofit organizations. Submit your freeware or discounted software at *http://www.npware.org/submit.html*. *http://www.npware.org/links.html*

One/Northwest

▶ Site for finding major software donors and technology assessment tools. *http://www.onenw.org*

Selecting Software for Your Nonprofit

▶ A resource by Blackbaud, a software company that develops products for nonprofit organizations, this guide covers needs analysis, budgeting, conversion considerations, and getting buy-in from your board to approve the purchase of software. *http://www.blackbaud.com/products/select_registration.asp*

Softseek

▶ Online source for shareware, freeware, and evaluation software. *http://www.softseek.com*

Software & Hardware Resources

▶ Free software and hardware resources and links. *http://www.lincproject.org/toolkit/software_resources.htm*

TurboGuide: The CD-ROMs and Software Guide

▶ *http://turboguide.com/*

Useful Software—Michigan COMNET Virtual Library

▶ Links to popular software available online, as well as directories of software on the Web. *http://comnet.org/net/software.html*

Technology Assessment

One/Northwest's Technology Assessment Forms

▶ *http://www.onenw.org/assess/*

Technology News

CNN Technology News

▶ *http://www.cnn.com/TECH/index.html*

Crain's Online: Technology Monday

▶ Lending tech smarts to local nonprofits. *http://www.chicagobusiness.com/cgi-bin/mag/article.pl?article_id=15159*

DOT ORG

▶ This e-newsletter, produced by Michael Stein and Marc Osten, is a practical how-to guide with tips, tools, techniques, and case studies about nonprofit use of the Internet. It is not intended as a source of news or a list of links. Each issue will have a central theme to focus the content. It covers such topics as e-mail newsletters, building Web site traffic, working with ASPs, collecting online donations, using HTML e-mail, evaluating Internet presence efforts, and more. For more information, send e-mail to *mailto:mosten@summitcollaborative.com* or *mailto:michael@michaelstein.net*. To subscribe, send an e-mail to *mailto:dotorg-subscribe@topica.com*. *http://www.summitcollaborative.com/dot_org.html*

New York Times Computer News Daily

▶ *http://computernewsdaily.com/*

Tech Web

▶ *http://www.techweb.com/*

Virtual Volunteering

"Feeling Good About Doing Good"—CP Archives

▶ *http://www.cpuniverse.com/archives/2000/jun/probono.shtml*

Geekcorps

▶ *http://www.geekcorps.org/getinvolved.html*

Impact Online's Virtual Volunteering

▶ This site offers volunteer opportunities for individuals, including those with disabilities, who wish to contribute time via e-mail. The site's VolunteerMatch (*http://www.volunteermatch.org/*) service helps individuals nationwide find on-site volunteer opportunities posted by local nonprofit and public-sector organizations. *http://www.volunteermatch.org/virtual*

Interconnection

▶ *http://www.interconnection.org/volunteer/index.htm*

Service Leader's Virtual Volunteering Project

▶ Launched in 1996, the Virtual Volunteering Project works to encourage and assist in the development of volunteer activities that can be completed off-site via the Internet. It publishes *Virtual Verve*, a monthly electronic newsletter on virtual volunteering. *http://www.serviceleader.org/vv/*

Web Publishing

(Web Authoring, Design Tools, Utilities, Promotion)

123webmaster.com: Web Developing Tools, Scripts, Links, and Resources

▶ *http://www.123webmaster.com/*

Aaron's Fire Web Production

▶ *http://aaafire.hypermart.net*

BNB: HTML, Free CGI Scripts, Graphics, Tutorials, and More

▶ An all-free Webmaster's site featuring free CGI scripts, graphics, and over 300 original tutorials on all subjects important to a Webmaster. *http://bignosebird.com/*

Beginner's Guide to HTML—NCSA

▶ *http://www.ncsa.uiuc.edu/General/Internet/WWW/HTMLPrimer.html*

Building an Effective WWW: A Guide for Nonprofit Organizations

▶ *http://www.oxygenate.com/web101/*

CERN Web Services

▶ *http://webservices.web.cern.ch/WebServices/*

The CharityVillage Webmaster's Club

▶ Along with information about the CharityVillage Award, the club includes links to useful Web site building resources and online marketing links. *http://www.charityvillage.com/charityvillage/club.html*

CNET.com Web-Building

▶ One of the best sites for building a Web. *http://home.cnet.com/webbuilding/0-3880.html*

Dr. Watson

▶ Checks the HTML, load time, spelling, and other features of your Web site. *http://watson.addy.com/*

Elsop's Webmaster Resource Center

▶ *http://www.elsop.com/wrc/*

Essentials of Web Development

▶ *http://www.simpcoms.org/ewd/*

Free Site Tools—The Webmaster's Directory

▶ *http://www.freesitetools.com/*

Free Web Page Design Tools for Programmers

▶ *http://www.geocities.com/SiliconValley/Lakes/7362/index.html*

The Genius of Documentation

▶ Explains the power of writing things down to define a complex project: It becomes a tool for clarifying a collaborative vision. *http://www.shorewalker.com/pages/documentation-1.html*

Guide to Web Publishing

▶ *http://members.tripod.com/~jpsp1/freeweb.html*

HTML Editor Add-Ons for Windows

▶ *http://www.users.csbsju.edu/~eknuth/obcomp/addons.html*

HTML and Other Code Resources

Best Practices Toolkit: Web Stuff

Site-Building Tools for Webmasters

Webmonkey—Good tutorials for HTML

MediaBuilder—Free fonts, free code, free almost everything

Web Site Garage—Checks your Web site for browser compatability, load time, dead links, spelling, HTML design, with feedback

JoeExpert.com—Helpful answers on Web design questions and links to lots of resources

Dynamic Drive—no need to know code, just cut and paste. The site includes code for countdown clocks (how long until your fund drive ends?), games, and image and text effects.

JumpList—keep your offsite links current.

HTML Goodies

▶ *http://htmlgoodies.earthweb.com/*

HTML Quick Reference Guide—Academic Computing Services, University of Kansas

▶ *http://www.cc.ukans.edu/~acs/docs/other/HTML_quick.shtml*

The HTML Writers Guild

▶ *http://www.hwg.org/*

Hints from Hieran—Promoting Your Web Presence

▶ Once your site is up and running, whether you built it yourself or hired a firm to help you, you'll need to promote it aggressively. If you're using an outside firm, they may help you with the promotional aspect, but in either case, below are some ways to get the word out. *Hint from Hieran:* Most of these ideas are either free or relatively inexpensive, but there are a few paid promotional opportunities included as well. On the Internet, a small investment often goes a long way. *http://www.hieran.com/association/promote.html*

HitBox.com (Webmaster)

▶ *http://www.hitbox.com*

How to Set Up a Home Web Page

▶ *http://www.nonprofits.org/lib/start.html*

A How-To Guide for Do-It-Yourselfers in the Non-Profit Sector

▶ *http://www.netcastles.com/article.html*

Infomine Internet Enabling Tools

▶ *http://infomine.ucr.edu/search/enablesearch.phtml*

Internet Magazines—Web Development

▶ *http://www.webreference.com/internet/magazines/webdev.html*

Internet Survival Guide

▶ *http://www.prufrock.org/guide/*

InterNic

▶ Provides the public information regarding Internet domain name registration. *http://www.internic.net/*

Microsoft Site Builder Network: Authoring

▶ *http://msdn.microsoft.com/workshop/author/default.asp*

Mike's Clocks Clinic's Everything You Need to Know for Your Web Site Links

▶ *http://www.webcom.com/z4murray/Web site.shtml*

Net Tips for Writers and Designers

▶ *http://www.dsiegel.com/tips/index.html*

Phil Bradley's Web Design Page

▶ *http://www.philb.com/design.htm*

Promotion World

▶ *http://www.promotionworld.com/*

!Register-It!

▶ Allows you to register your site on multiple search engines. *http://register-it.netscape.com/*

Resources for Webmasters—FreeLinks

▶ *http://www.freelinks.com/*

Search Engine Tutorial for Web Designers

▶ *http://northernwebs.com/set/*

SiteOwner.com

▶ Provides several Web publicity services for your site. *http://www.siteowner.com/*

Spotster.net—Free Web Site Tools and Webmaster Resources

▶ *http://www.wsresource.com/*

Tips and Resources for Web Page Developers—Haas School of Business, University of California (Berkeley)

▶ *http://www.haas.berkeley.edu/groups/Webteam/tips.html*

Toolreviews—Overviews and Ratings of Free Programs and Online Tools for Webmasters

▶ *http://www.toolreviews.com/*

The Virtual Library of Web Development

▶ *http://www.stars.com/Vlib/*

W3C—World Wide Web Consortium

▶ Under the direction of Tim Berners-Lee, the creator of the World Wide Web, the WC3 has played a leading role since 1994 in developing and articulating the specifications and protocols at the heart of the Web. It is a touchstone in the evolution of the Web and a vitally important resource for Web developers. *http://www.w3.org/*

Web by Design

▶ *http://www.iupui.edu/~webtrain/*

The Web Developers Virtual Library

▶ The Web Developers Virtual Library is the original encyclopedia of Web design. *http://www.stars.com/, http://www.wdvl.com/*

Web Developer's Style Guides

▶ *http://www.stars.com/Authoring/Style/Guides/*

The Web Marketing Checklist: 27 Ways to Promote Your Site

▶ *http://www.wilsonweb.com/articles/checklist.htm*

Web Site Garage

▶ Check your Web site to get a five-point diagnosis of your page, covering load time, dead links, popularity, spelling, and design. *http://Websitegarage.netscape.com/*

Web Style Resources

▶ *http://www.devry-phx.edu/webresrc/webmstry/stylmanl.htm*

WebDeveloper.com

▶ *http://www.webdeveloper.com/*

Web Specialists Directory—Virtualis

▶ To find a Web specialist that fits your needs and budget, select the services that you require and press the *search* button. Each specialist is required to have one to three examples of their work. Categories include The Basics (HTML, Forms, Graphics, Logos, Webmastering, Marketing); Not So Basics (ImageMaps, Animation, RealAudio, Multimedia, FrontPage); and Programming (Database, mSQL, CGI/Perl, C programming, Java, JavaScript, VBscript, ActiveX). *http://www.virtualis.com/vr/kcann/specialists.html*

Webmonkey

▶ Webmonkey, an online forum provided by *Hotwired Magazine,* is an excellent source of information and tutorials for the Web developer and designer. Topics include JavaScript, Java, Dynamic HTML, Perl, Web interfaces for databases, and more. *http://hotwired.lycos.com/webmonkey/webmonkey/*

Weave Your Web—Getting Started on the World Wide Web

▶ *http://www.msg.net/tutorial*

Web Developer's Journal

▶ *http://www.webdevelopersjournal.com/*

The Web Developer's Toolkit (Online Resources)

▶ Graphics, authoring tools, and design advice from the Online Fundraiser's Resource Center. *http://www.fund-online.com/ala-book/links/resource.htm*

Web Development Tips for Nonprofits

▶ *http://www.ncexchange.org/toolbox/ncacdc.html*

Webcom—HTML Resources Guide

▶ *http://www.webcom.com/html/*

Webmaster T's World of Design

▶ *http://www.globalserve.net/~iwb/world/*

WebReference.com—The Webmaster's Reference Library: Web Site Design, Tips and Tutorials

▶ *http://www.webreference.com/*

Website Design & Technology—DANA Answer Center (Delaware Association of Nonprofit Agencies)

▶ *http://www.delawarenonprofit.org/WebFaq.htm*

WEBsmith

▶ Archive of articles from the discontinued *WEBsmith* magazine. *http://www.ssc.com/websmith/smith.html*

Webweavers Page—Tools for Aspiring Web Authors

▶ *http://www.nas.nasa.gov/NAS/WebWeavers/*

Yale Style Manual

▶ *http://www.info.med.yale.edu/caim/manual/*

Web Sites (Nonprofit) Megasites and Portals

About.com Guide to Nonprofit Charitable Organizations

▶ This is a mini-Web site within the comprehensive About.com site (formerly the Mining Company) that serves as a useful guide to resources and information about nonprofit organizations, foundations, jobs, educational opportunities, and the latest developments in the field. Visitors can search feature archives as well as the entire About.com site, participate in chats, and receive newsletters via e-mail. *http://nonprofit.about.com/index.htm*

altrue.com

▶ Easy-to-search databases of vendor products and services, plus content built around promoting their product categories, will allow you to get the latest information from this single Web site. Check through their product listings. *http://www.altrue.com/*

American Philanthropy Review

▶ Features include: *Discussion Forums*™—topics include grants and foundations, the law of tax-exempt organizations, college and university advancement, health care philanthropy, arts and social organization fund raising, international fund raising, and mentoring; *Career Search Online*™—career search and launch pad available to the U.S. nonprofit community; open positions are listed on the site; *We Review*—a series of reviews on nonprofit books, periodicals and software. *http://www.charitychannel.com/*

Ask Dr. Nonprofit (*Nonprofit Times*)

▶ *http://www.nptimes.com/main/askdrp.html*

Benton Foundation's Nonprofit Links

▶ *http://www.benton.org/Cyber/links.html*

Best of the Net: General Nonprofit Information & Advocacy Links

▶ *http://www.delawarenonprofit.org/resourceGenAdv.html*

CSC Non-Profit Resource Center (Formerly Campaign Service Consultants)

▶ *http://people.ne.mediaone.net/cscunningham/Foundation.htm*

Center for Excellence in Nonprofits

▶ The Center for Excellence in Nonprofits offers programs in leadership development, systemic change, continuous improvement, and best practices. The Web site offers a list of articles and information; a list of publications; links of interest to nonprofit managers; a best books page, which lists books CEN staff and board members have recommended to nonprofit executives and managers; and information on upcoming CEN programs. Site features: Technology Guide Book; Wired for Good Survey; Governance Best Practices Book; The Connection Newsletter; Best Books for Nonprofits; Excellence Articles; and links. *http://www.cen.org/*

Chardon Press Online: Nonprofit Forum

▶ Developed by Chardon Press, the Oakland, California, publisher of the *Grassroots Fundraising Journal,* the Nonprofit Forum is a Web-based discussion board designed to give employees at small, progressive nonprofit organizations the opportunity to discuss fund raising, management, and advocacy. *http://www.chardonpress.com/npforum/forums.shtml*

Charity USA's Search Engine Dedicated to Nonprofits and Their Supporters & Providers

▶ *http://www.charityusa.org/pages/*

Charity USA Nonprofit Portal Community

▶ Information for nonprofits. *http://www.charityusa.org/*

Charity Village

▶ CharityVillage is Canada's super-site for the nonprofit sector. This online service center is dedicated to encouraging, supporting, and servicing 175,000 Canadian charities and nonprofit organizations and the millions of staffers, volunteers, donors, and supporters who make them an important part of our national fabric. It is Canadian based, with a wealth of information for nonprofit management issues in general. It provides 3,000 pages of news, jobs, information, and resources for executives, staffers, donors, and volunteers. Visit their Welcome Centre for first-time visitors and the media. *http://www.charityvillage.com/*

CharityNews Daily

▶ Visit *http://charitychannel.com/forums/charitynews-a.htm#e-mail* to subscribe. An opt-in subscription e-newsletter published Monday through Friday by CharityChannel and updated hourly.

The Chronicle of Philanthropy Directory of Services

▶ *http://philanthropy.com/adv.dir/dos.dir/dosmain.shtml*

The Chronicle of Philanthropy: The Non-Profit Handbook

▶ This is a searchable database of more than 1,000 items—including books, periodicals, World Wide Web sites, e-mail discussion groups, videotapes, and audiotapes—that is available exclusively to *Chronicle* subscribers (*how to subscribe*). *http://philanthropy. com/handbook/*

Community Connector

▶ This Web site is for community service organizations, funders, academics, and students who are using technology to improve their local communities. Offerings include news updates, research reports, articles, handbooks, an original journal, a directory of community networks, and links to relevant resources. *http://databases.si.umich.edu/cfdocs/community/index.cfm*

Community Wealth Online

▶ A centralized resource and dialogue about community wealth, this site presents information on nonprofit/for-profit partnerships, social entrepreneurship, venture philanthropy, nonprofit businesses, and cause-related marketing guidelines from the Council of Better Business Bureaus. It also offers the following resources: a directory of organizations, a database of publications, job postings, a practitioner's toolkit, periodic updates of entrepreneurial efforts to generate resources to promote social change, models of community wealth through case studies and profiles, current research. *http://www.communitywealth.org*

Council on Foundations Glossary

▶ *http://www.cof.org/glossary/index.htm*

Delaware Association of Nonprofit Agencies

▶ *http://www.delawarenonprofit.org/*

Development Resource Center

▶ This site offers assistance and resources to nonprofit organizations. Sign up for *Development Resource Center News,* a free e-mail newsletter filled with practical fund-raising and marketing ideas, resources, and information. *http://www.drcharity.com*

Eagles.net

▶ This one-stop resource for nonprofit leaders, staff, and volunteers to find the tools they need to tackle the many challenges their organizations face emphasizes fund raising, operational efficiency, staff turnover, and time management. *http://www.eagles.net/*

East Bay MAPP Online

▶ Management and technical assistance tools and resources for nonprofit organizations. *http://www.eastbaymapp.org*

Echoing Green Foundation: Resource Center

▶ The Echoing Green Foundation, in New York, offers full-time fellowships to individuals who are starting innovative social change organizations. The "Resource Center" section of the foundation's Web site features articles, written by the foundation's fellows, on starting a charity, nonprofit management, fund raising, financial management, communications, and human resources, as well as links to other Web sites that provide additional information. *http://www.echoinggreen.org/resource/index.html, http://www.echoinggreen.org/resource/link/index.html*

eCommerce Info Center

▶ Links to nonprofit Web sites and institutes. *http://www.ecominfocenter.com/index.html?page=/nonprofit/resources.html*

E-mail Newsletters by Not-for-Profit and Public Sector Organizations

▶ Tips for content, design, sending schedules and techniques, marketing and evaluation; also includes sample e-mail newsletters and links to other resources. *http://www.coyotecom.com/enews.html*

eOrganizers Progressive Online Advocacy Network

▶ *http://www.nsnt.org/*

4npo.org

▶ *http://www.4npo.org/*

501Click.com

▶ This site offers solutions to management challenges that can arise in areas ranging from human resources to volunteer management, in the Management Toolkit; quick and easy ways to order the products and services that nonprofits need most at discounted prices in the marketplace; and opportunities to share ideas with your nonprofit peers in the 501(c)ommunity. *http://www.501click.com/*

FindIt.org

▶ *http://www.findit.org*

The Foundation Center Online

▶ *http://fdncenter.org*

Foundation Center's Online Librarian

▶ *http://fdncenter.org/onlib/librarian.html*

Free Management Library for For-Profit and Nonprofit Organizations

▶ *http://www.mapnp.org/library, http://www.mapnp.org/library/topics.htm, www.managementhelp.org*

Free Nonprofit Micro-eMBA

▶ The program is foundational and of a "nuts-and-bolts" nature. The program includes 12 online learning modules organized to lead the learner through a typical process to start and manage a nonprofit organization. Modules include specific online study materials, specific questions and assignments to learn concepts and build systems, and various assessments. The program does not grant a degree or certificate (unless a local provider adopts the program and includes certification when providing this program in their area). The program includes the following learning modules: Module 1: Program Orientation—Getting the Most from This Program; Module 2: Starting and Understanding Your Nonprofit; Module 3: Role of Chief Executive Officer (Executive Director); Module 4: Developing Basic Skills in Management and Leadership; Module 5: Building and Maintaining Your Board of Directors; Module 6: Developing Your Strategic Plan; Module 7: Designing and Marketing Your Programs; Module 8: Managing Finances and Taxes in Your Nonprofit; Module 9: Developing Your Fundraising Plan; Module 10: Staffing and Supervising Your Employees and Volunteers; Module 11: Evaluating Your Programs; Module 12: Complete Fitness Test of Your Nonprofit; OPTIONAL: Module 13: Managing Ethics in the Workplace: Practical Guide for Managers. *http://www.managementhelp.org/np_progs/org_dev.htm*

Frequently Asked Questions Files for soc.org.nonprofit

▶ *http://www.nonprofits.org/npofaq/*

General Nonprofit Resources and Information— United Cerebral Palsy Association, Greater Utica (New York) Area

▶ Maintained by the United Way of Greater Utica (New York), this Web site provides annotated links to Web sites divided into nearly 20 subcategories that provide information for nonprofit organizations. The site features links to topics of interest to all charities, such as grant seeking, fund raising, management, evaluation, and volunteerism, as well as more specialized categories such as children and families, education, and public policy. Each month, the site publishes an article about a featured Web site. In addition, there is also a site-of-the-month archive, along with a "News and Views" section that features topical articles selected by the site editors. *http://www.ucp-utica.org/uwlinks/directory.html, http://www.ucp-utica.org/uwlinks/generalinfo.html*

The Gilbert Center

▶ *http://www.gilbert.org/gilbert*

Grants and Related Resources—Nonprofit Virtual Library

▶ *http://www.lib.msu.edu/harris23/grants/znonprof.htm, http://www.lib.msu.edu/harris23/grants/znprofrg.htm*

GuideStar

▶ Users can find information on more than 700,000 nonprofits and the latest news on philanthropy, as well as resources for donors and nonprofits. Any 501(c)(3) organization can participate for free by registering and posting its information on GuideStar with easy-to-use templates. As part of GuideStar's mission to provide a comprehensive information source for both the nonprofit and donor communities, the Web site posts current images of organizations' IRS Forms 990. *http://www.guidestar.org/*

Guidestar's Nonprofit Center

▶ *http://www.guidestar.org/npo/*

HandsNet

▶ HandsNet empowers organizations to integrate effective online communications strategies that strengthen their programs and policies for children, families, and people in need. This site features its information about its WebClipper: Online Networking service (see separate listing), headlines, alerts, and training and capacity-building information (classes, strategic planning workshops, and management seminars). *www.handsnet.org*

HandsNet: WebClipper

▶ The WebClipper service searches more than 500 Web sites that provide information for social services groups and sends members a daily e-mail message with new information in their fields of interest. It also allows members to conduct Internet searches on social services topics, publish reports online, and contact other members. WebClipper is run by HandsNet, a San Jose, California, organization that provides technology help to other nonprofit groups. *http://www.webclipper.org*

Helping.org (AOL Foundation) Resources for Nonprofits

▶ If your nonprofit organization or company needs technology (computer or Internet) assistance, you can search Helping.org's "Find Computer Help Near You" database, located in the "Resources for Nonprofits" section of the Helping.org Web site. This database, specifically designed to assist nonprofit agencies in finding computer assistance in their community, is searchable online by state. If your organization or company provides technology assistance, you can register its services using an online registration form. Managed by the Benton Foundation and sponsored by the AOL Foundation, the Resources for Nonprofits section of Helping.org is a starting point for nonprofits that are seeking learning tools. The "Resources for Nonprofits" section is a gateway to an incredible bank of materials on everything from Web site design to online advocacy and finding computer help in your area. *http://www.helping.org/nonprofit/index.adp*

How Web Sites Benefit Nonprofit Organizations
▶ *http://www.kinesisinc.com/resource_article_Web sites.html*

IGC's Activism/Internet Resource Center
▶ This is a comprehensive directory of links to nonprofit resources on the Internet. The "activist toolkit" includes links to a number of e-zines, Web-based publications, and helpful legislative directories. *http://www.igc.org/igc/gateway/*

Idealist and Action Without Borders
▶ This is a huge index of international nonprofit organizations, organized by country and by issue of concern. Idealist is both a directory of nonprofits and a resource center for nonprofits. Idealist is a project of Action Without Borders, a nonprofit organization in New York. Site features include Take Action; Tools for Nonprofits; Find a Job; Where to Access the Web; Worldwide News; and Frequently Asked Questions. It provides links to "the most informative and frequently updated nonprofit news sites" pertaining to the United States and abroad; a database of over 20,000 nonprofit and community organizations in 150 countries; a list of links to "Organizations Promoting Global Volunteering" for users seeking assistance in volunteering worldwide; and the Nonprofit Career Center, which allows professionals, job seekers, and consultants to search for employment, internships, and public service fellowships worldwide; network with other professionals; seek professional advice; review salary surveys; learn about advanced degree programs for nonprofit managers and nonprofit awards; study strategies for writing effective résumés and cover letters; discover sector opportunities for high school students and educators. *http://www.idealist.org/*

IKNOW—Raffa & Associates
▶ IKNOW, Interactive Knowledge for Nonprofits Worldwide, is a free source of information on the web, expressly designed to give the nonprofit community information it can use. Unlike using a major search engine, the careful selection and organization of content on IKNOW is designed to save time usually spent weeding through tens and hundreds of pages that are not exactly what you were looking for. The editors of IKNOW seek out, identify, and organize only the best available information of concern to the nonprofit community into a dozen major categories: business services, education, fringe benefits, fund raising, governance, human resources, legal issues, legislation, marketing and media, strategic planning, and volunteerism. The site has recently added a new category of information on state requirements for charitable solicitations. *http://www.iknow.org/*

Impact Online
▶ This site offers a searchable database of opportunities for volunteers in 10 cities, as well as an online newsletter, a directory of nonprofits, volunteering tips, and a "Virtual Volunteering" program for those who wish to contribute time via e-mail/computer. *http://www.impactonline.org*

Independent Sector
▶ Committed to promoting philanthropy, volunteering, and citizen action, this coalition group brings together nonprofit organizations, foundations, and corporate giving programs. The site gives an overview of IS programs and includes a section on the basics of lobbying by charitable organizations. A media section includes facts and figures on the size and scope of the nonprofit sector and a statistical overview of the IS 1996 survey on giving and volunteering. "Giving Voice to Your Heart" is a starter kit to help guide visitors in their public relations efforts. The IS publications catalog can be searched electronically for material of interest. *http://www.independentsector.org/*

Information Centre—Canadian Centre for Philanthropy
▶ *http://www.ccp.ca/information/*

Institute of Nonprofit Management (INM)
▶ INM, the online Nonprofit Management University, has developed a series of self-study management courses to be offered on a continuing education basis. The program is designed for individuals who are involved with nonprofit organizations; students who plan to work in nonprofit organizations; and students who may simply desire a basic understanding of the nonprofit sector. *http://www.npmu.org/*

The Internet Nonprofit Center and the Nonprofit FAQ
▶ This site offers information for and about nonprofit organizations in the United States, including: The Locator assists with clarifying the legal name and exact location of any nonprofit registered with the Internal Revenue Service; the Nonprofit FAQ ("Frequently Asked Questions") presents information on a wide range of topics of interest to leaders and managers of nonprofit organizations; the Library offers longer essays and analysis of the nonprofit sector from a variety of points of view; and the Form 990 Project offers demonstrations of practical steps toward the day when it will be reasonable to expect nonprofits to use the Internet to file the required information with the Internal Revenue Service and also make the same information available to the public through the World Wide Web. Also included are INC news bulletins, a listing on nonprofit books, and a free weekly e-mail subscription. *http://www.nonprofits.org*

The Internet Public Policy Network Database
▶ A list of nearly 700 organizations that work with telecommunications, electronic commerce, and community technology issues, the Directory is an on-line database that can be downloaded to create mailing lists. It includes complete contact listings and brief descriptions for over 675 nonprofit groups, trade associations, government, academic institutions that work with telecommunications, electronic commerce, and community technology issues. To ensure the timeliness of the information, the Directory is updated bimonthly to include new organizations and different contact information. *http://www.internetpublicpolicy.com/directory.cfm*

Internet Resources for Nonprofit Public Service Organizations
▶ Somewhat outdated but may be of some use. *http://www-personal.si.umich.edu/~nesbeitt/nonprofits/nonprofits.html*

The Learning Institute (LI)

▶ LI offers an excellent list of resources including supplementary readings and online course assignments that are very useful. *http://www.uwex.edu/li/, http://www.uwex.edu/li/learner/*

Literature of the Nonprofit Sector, Internet Edition

▶ A bibliography with abstracts. *http://fdncenter.org/onlib/lnps/index.html*

Maine Philanthropy Center Index of Web Resources

▶ *http://www.megrants.org/bookmk98.html#Elec*

The Management Center Nonprofit Library

▶ *http://tmcenter.org/library/links.html*

Media Rights

▶ This site is designed to connect activists, nonprofit organizations, and media makers. It focuses on keeping communication open between media professionals across the country and on informing activists of other activities in the country. The site's goal is to stimulate more innovative media coverage of social issues. *http://www.mediarights.org*

Meta-Index of Nonprofit Sites—PNN Online

▶ *http://www.pj.org/links_metaindex.cfm*

Mickey's Nonprofit Resources

▶ *http://people.delphi.com/mickjyoung/resources.html*

National Center for Charitable Statistics

▶ Visitors to this site can download microdata on nonprofit organizations, view or download database documentation and data dictionaries, and download blank IRS forms from which most of the data is collected. *http://nccs.urban.org/*

National Strategy for Nonprofit Technology— Philanthropy News Network

▶ Series of 13 articles. *http://pnnonline.org/technology/about change0423.cfm*

NetAction

▶ A project of the Tides Center, this site has information on a variety of resources for "Virtual Activists" and organizations that want to use such activists via the Internet in grassroots campaigns. *http://www.netaction.org*

Nonline Nonprofit Network

▶ *http://www.nonline.com/*

Nonportal

▶ The Gilbert Center is beta testing a portal for the nonprofit sector that is free of advertisements. This site offers links to recent news sites and information by date; a search engine of news on philanthropy; and links to their current partners, which include: Action Without Borders, Benton Foundation, Internet Nonprofit Center, Nonprofit Manager's Library, Nonprofit Online News, OMB Watch, and Virtual Volunteering. *http://www.nonportal.org*

Nonprofit Center (Fundsnet Services)

▶ *http://www.fundsnetservices.com/nonproct.htm*

Nonprofit Connections

▶ *http://www.nonprofits.org/npofaq/06/02.html*

The Nonprofit Directory—The Plebius Press

▶ The Nonprofit Directory was created in August 1999 to help people locate nonprofit organizations with a presence on the Internet, as well as to help nonprofit organizations find the tools they need to be successful on the Internet. The Directory also indexes select activist and government Web sites. *http://www.plebius.org/directory*

Nonprofit Expert

▶ *http://www.nonprofitexpert.com/*

Nonprofit FAQ *(See also Internet Nonprofit Center and FAQ)*

▶ This frequently asked questions file is divided into 21 topics for the newsgroup soc.org.nonprofit. Categories include start-up and management issues, fund raising, marketing, nonprofit organizations and the Internet, education and training, and general theoretical discussions. *http://www.nonprofits.org/npofaq/*

Nonprofit Gateway

▶ A network of links to federal government information and services of interest to nonprofit organizations. *http://www.nonprofit.gov/*

Nonprofit Genie

▶ This Web site offers information on nonprofit management topics, such as board development, financial management, fund raising, and strategic planning. It also provides reviews of books on nonprofit subjects, interviews with grant makers and nonprofit leaders, and links to Web sites of interest to nonprofit professionals. The site is a project of the CompassPoint (formerly the Support Center for Nonprofit Management in San Francisco) and the California Management Assistance Partnership. *http://www.nonprofit.gov/*

Nonprofit Infogallery

▶ *http://www.infogallery.com/Nonprofit.htm*

NonprofitLearning.com

▶ *http://www.nonprofitlearning.com*

NonProfit Pathfinder

▶ Developed by Independent Sector and the University of Maryland's Civil Society Initiative, this site features annotated links to Web sites run by academic research centers and associations that study philanthropy, nonprofit organizations and commissions that promote civil society, think tanks, foundations, and periodicals that report on nonprofit activities. The site also describes and provides links to Web sites that offer information on evaluating nonprofit programs. A section of the site, entitled "Innovations," profiles creative local programs in areas such as arts and culture, economic development, housing, and technology. *http://www.independentsector.org/pathfinder*

The Non-Profit Presence on the World Wide Web

▶ Nonprofit organizations exist to serve and support a group or area of concern in society that is not represented by other interests. This is usually a result of the lack of financial returns for the endeavor. *http://webpages.shepherd.edu/ASULLI01/Global/start.htm*

The Nonprofit Resource Center

▶ The Nonprofit Resource Center, the one-stop Directory for Internet Resources of interest and value to nonprofit organizations, is provided as a service of Nonprofit Incorporators, a law firm whose sole business is low-cost incorporations of nonprofits. This site is designed for managers, board members, and volunteers of nonprofit and tax-exempt organizations, as well as people who are considering forming a nonprofit organization. It provides resources in the following categories: legal, grants and grantsmanship, support organizations and information for boards, financial and accounting services, staffing and volunteer management, fund raising, advocacy and public relations, management resources and consultants, publications and mailing lists, research and policy studies, and books for nonprofits. *http://www.not-for-profit.org/*

Nonprofit Resource Network—The Nonprofit Resource Center

▶ This is a Web site on which you'll find a searchable database of businesses that provide important products and services to nonprofit organizations, along with a special membership section for accountants and financial managers of nonprofit organizations and their external CPA firms. The database of vendors is open to the public as a free service to nonprofit organizations. Click on Business Directory to conduct a search for providers of specific products or services. *http://www.nonprofitresource.com/about.htm*

Non-Profit Resources (Non-Profit Nuts & Bolts)

▶ *http://www.nutsbolts.com/Non-Profit%20Resources.htm*

Nonprofit Solutions Fair—Technology Works for Good

▶ The Fair's goal is to promote the strategic use of technology to increase the effectiveness of organizations in meeting their missions. The focus is on reasonable, cost-effective strategies for using technology to improve nonprofit fund raising, client management, accounting, outreach, and marketing. *http://www.ltnsolutions.net/npohelp2/registration1.htm*

Nonprofit Virtual Library

▶ Part of an extensive set of link pages maintained by Jon Harrison, Main Library Reference Funding Center Supervisor at the Michigan State University Libraries. *http://www.ltnsolutions.net/npohelp2/registration1.htm*

Nonprofit Technology Enterprise Network

▶ *http://216.122.116.58/nten/index.html, http://www.nten.org/*

The Nonprofit Zone

▶ *http://www.nonprofitzone.com/*

The NonProfit Yellow Pages—The Internet Directory of Human Services

▶ *http://www.npyp.net/mainmenu.htm*

Nonprofitxpress

▶ *http://www.npxpress.com/*

The Not-for-Profit Advisor—Good Advice and Useful Information for Not-for-Profit Organizations, Schools, and Libraries

▶ *http://www.nfpadvisor.org/*

NPO-NET

▶ Created by the Internet Technology Resource Center (ITRC), NPO-NET provides a wide variety of resources for Chicago-area nonprofits, including links to a planners' calendar, the Donors Forum Philanthropic Database, nonprofit Internet resources, and information on jobs and volunteer opportunities in Greater Chicagoland. *http://www.npo.net*

Office.Com

▶ A business-oriented site that focuses on using the Internet in the business world. This link is to the site's section on nonprofits. *http://www.office.com/global/0%2C2724%2C62%2CFF.html*

Online Discussions: Benton's Lessons Learned

▶ *http://www.benton.org/Practice/Lessons/forumlessons.html*

The Online Nonprofit Information Center (TONIC)

▶ Whether you are a new or seasoned nonprofit professional or volunteer, this site has all the information you need to successfully start and run a nonprofit organization of any size. *http://www.socialworker.com/nonprofit/nphome.htm*

Open Directory—Society: Organizations: Nonprofit Resources

▶ *http://www.dmoz.org/Society/Organizations/Nonprofit_Resources*

Open Philanthropy Exchange

▶ Open Philanthropy Exchange (OPX) is a specification for data transfer between institutions in the philanthropy industry. The purpose of the OPX standard is to help philanthropic institutions communicate in a common language. *http://www.opxinfo.net/*

Organizers' Collaborative Comprehensive Links

▶ *http://www.organizenow.net/*

Philanthropy News Network Online

▶ *http://pnnonline.org/*

PhilanthropySearch.com

▶ A search engine serving the nonprofit and philanthropic sector that offers a general search; a search by category; free resources, including driving traffic to your nonprofit Web site, marketing tips, and the *NonProfit Times*™. The site contains "speed searches" for fund raising, jobs, publications, tools and services, and more. Users can search for nonprofits by type (arts and culture, religious, health, etc.) and can do custom searches for organizations. The goal of PhilanthropySearch.com is to help users find information about charitable giving, volunteering, and other nonprofit issues on the Web. Organizations that have an Internet presence may also submit their site for inclusion. *http://www.philanthropysearch.com*

Resource Central—Nonprofit Organizations

▶ *http://www.resourcehelp.com/qsernonprofit.htm*

Resources for Nonprofit Organizations

▶ The Grants Information Center at the University of Wisconsin offers information and links on using the Internet, as well as foundations and nonprofits. *http://www.library.wisc.edu/libraries/Memorial/ grants/nonprof.htm*

SERVEnet

▶ SERVEnet is a Web site dedicated to service and volunteering. Through SERVEnet, users can enter their zip code, city, state, skills, interests, and availability and be matched with organizations needing help. *http://www.servenet.org/*

TCAnet: Library—References for Nonprofits (Texas Commission on the Arts)

▶ Links to resources such as: Accounting Standards & Government Regulations for Non-Profits, Advertising on the World Wide Web, Americans for the Arts Publications, Copyright Laws, Disclosure of Charitable Contributions, Exempt Statistics: Exempt Organizations, Filing Requirements for Tax-Exempt Organizations, *Foundation News & Commentary,* Frequently Asked Questions About Nonprofit Governance, Frequently Asked Questions About Tax-Exempt Organizations, Independent Sector Online Bookstore,

Information for Tax-Exempt Organizations, Institute of Art and Law, Nonprofit Gateway, Tax Topic 506: Contributions, Tax Topic 705: Depreciation, The Nonprofit Genie, Tips on Marketing Your Non-Profit on the Internet, What Charity Can and Cannot Do. *http://www.arts.state.tx.us/templates/linkpage.asp?bid=lib&pid=096*

TONIC *(See The Online Nonprofit Information Center)*

Three Rivers Free-Net Nonprofit Resources

▶ *http://trfn.clpgh.org/nonprofits/*

Volunteer Centers

▶ The Points of Light Foundation's volunteer site map matches individuals with volunteer opportunities in their home state. *http://www.1800volunteer.org/1800VolunteerCenterMap.cfm*

VolunteerMatch

▶ A division of ImpactOnline, VolunteerMatch is a free online matching service for volunteers and nonprofits. *http://www.volunteermatch.org*

W.K. Kellogg Foundation: "E-Philanthropy, Volunteerism, and Social Changemaking: A New Landscape of Resources, Issues, and Opportunities"

▶ This report, published by the W.K. Kellogg Foundation, provides summaries of and links to more than 140 Web sites of interest to nonprofit organizations. The sites are organized into eight categories. Four of the categories involve online fund raising: shopping sites that allow consumers to donate a portion of their purchases to charity, sites that allow visitors to make charitable contributions online, sites that offer information for donors, and online fund-raising events. The other four types of sites included are those that focus on nonprofit news, volunteerism, and advocacy, as well as sites that provide multiple services. *http://www.wkkf.org/Publications/e-phil.pdf*

Web Sprouts—Web Resources for Nonprofits

▶ *http://members.tripod.com/~awchu/index.html*

Who Offers What Links—A Descriptive Forum for Products and Services for the Nonprofit Sector

▶ This database of products and services is of value to the nonprofit sector in the following areas: accounting; associations; awards, incentives, and recognition; board development; continuing education and training; database management; direct response; executive search; fund raising and campaign counsel; grant writing and foundation research; insurance; major gift/planned giving training and counsel; online fund raising; planned giving; prospect research; software; special events; strategic planning; telemarketing; and more. *http://www.contributionsmagazine.com/wow.html*

PART VII

Legal Issues

ORGANIZATIONS

(See also Accountability and Ethics; Financial Management [Insurance, Liability, and Risk Assessment; Tax Exemption]; Governance; Human Resource Management; Resource Development [Donor Solicitation])

Alliance for Justice Foundation

11 Dupont Circle NW, 2nd Floor, Washington, DC 20036
Tel: 202-822-6070; FAX: 202-822-6068
E-mail: alliance@afj.org, FAIcoordinator@afj.org;
WWW: http://www.afj.org

▶ A national association of environmental, civil rights, mental health, women's, children's, and consumer advocacy organizations, the Alliance for Justice Foundation seeks to increase foundation support to organizations that seek to influence policy and public opinion. Through its Foundation Advocacy Initiative, the Alliance for Justice seeks to increase foundation support to organizations that seek to influence policy and public opinion. The Foundation Advocacy Initiative was launched in 1995 with the release of the legal guide *Myth v. Fact: Foundation Support of Advocacy.* The book identifies and counters misperceptions about supporting activities that influence public policy. It also includes a sample agreement letter, requirements for expenditure responsibility, a glossary of relevant terms, and a short history of the rules and distinctions regarding types of advocacy. Since the release of *Myth v. Fact,* the Alliance has worked with regional associations of grantmakers and affinity groups to organize meetings and workshops to address pressing legal concerns, such as: May foundation proposals mention lobbying activities or intentions? May grantees discuss lobbying activities in their reports to foundations? May a foundation itself ever lobby on legislation? How do you handle grantee budgets that contain a line item for lobbying? The Alliance publishes the quarterly newsletter, *Pipeline, E-Advocacy for Nonprofits: The Law of Lobbying and Election Related Activity on the Net.* It makes available Nonprofit Advocacy Alerts (details can be found at *http://www.afj.org/napalert.html* or by sending a request to *advocacy@afj.org*).

Alliance of Nonprofit Mailers

1211 Connecticut Avenue NW, Suite 620, Washington, DC 20036
Tel: 202-462-5132; FAX: 202-462-0423
E-mail: alliance@nonprofitmailers.org;
WWW: http://www.nonprofitmailers.org,
http://www.nonprofitmailers.org/vendors/page6old.htm#N

▶ The Alliance of Nonprofit Mailers was established in 1980 as a national coalition of nonprofit organizations sharing a vested interest in nonprofit postal policy. The Alliance is the primary representative of nonprofit mailers before the Postal Rate Commission, at the United States Postal Service's (USPS) Headquarters, and on Capitol Hill. The organization's Web site provides information on nonprofit postal issues, from the latest rate charts to commonly asked questions about eligibility restrictions. To see a complete listing of Alliance sponsors along with a description of their products and services, go to their Preferred Commercial Vendors Directory (*http://www.nonprofitmailers.org/vendors/page6old.htm*). It publishes the newsletter *Alliance Report* and occasional special reports.

American Charities for Reasonable Fundraising Regulation, The Nonprofit Litigation Coalition (formerly Charities U.S.A., Inc.)

3124 North Tenth Street, Arlington, VA 22201
Tel: 703-243-7402; FAX: 703-243-7403
E-mail: gpeters@CDR-CDMI.COM (Geoffrey Peters)

▶ A 501(c)(3) public foundation, it is a coalition of nonprofit organizations, their national associations, and their supporters, formed for the purpose of combating excessive regulation by means of litigation. Legitimate, reputable charities have found it increasingly difficult in the past few years to express their concerns about excessive and fruitless regulation and to have those concerns seriously considered by those responsible for charitable and fundraising regulation. Thus, a number of nonprofits decided that, in order to have the charitable communities' views taken seriously, some of the most excessive and costly regulation should be challenged in court.

American Law Institute–American Bar Association Committee on Continuing Professional Education (ALI-ABA)

4025 Chestnut Street, Philadelphia, PA 19104-3099
Tel: 800-253-6397, ext. 1630, 800-243-CLE-NEWS, ext. 1650
(Customer Service), 215-243-1600; FAX: 215-243-1664
E-mail: jmendicino@ali.org, hkyriakodis@ali.org (Harry Kyriakodis, ALI-ABA Library); WWW: http://www.ali.org

▶ ALI-ABA was established in 1947 as a collaboration of the American Bar Association and the American Law Institute. Services provided include a wide range of educational materials and services, including book publishing, periodicals, courses of study, satellite programming, audiovisual materials, and a variety of projects and special studies to enhance professional education, competence, and responsibility. *The CLE Journal and Register* features articles on continuing legal education and lists courses, publications, and audiovisual aids of all continuing legal education providers. Upcoming courses of study are also listed in the monthly newspaper, *ALI-ABA CLE Review.* Separate course listings and a publications catalog are also available.

California Lawyers for the Arts

Fort Mason Center, C-255, San Francisco, CA 94123
Tel: 415-775-7200; FAX: 415-775-1143
E-mail: cla@calawyersforthearts.org;
WWW: http://www.calawyersforthearts.org/

▶ This is a nonprofit, tax-exempt service organization founded in 1974, which provides lawyer referrals, dispute resolution services, educational programs, publications, and a resource library to artists of all disciplines and arts organizations. It also has offices in Santa Monica, Sacramento, and Oakland.

Center for Non-Profit Corporations

1501 Livingston Avenue, North Brunswick, NJ 08902
Tel: 732-227-0800; FAX: 732-227-0087
E-mail: center@njnonprofits.org;
WWW: http://www.njnonprofits.org/Legal.html

▶ Founded in 1982, the Center provides individualized telephone consultation on nonprofit legal and management issues guidance to charitable organizations on a wide range of topics such as nonprofit incorporation and tax exemption, insurance issues, IRS regulations, lobbying laws, board/staff roles and responsibilities, fund-raising laws, and many others.

Charity Lobbying in the Public Interest

2040 "S" Street NW, Washington, DC 20009
Tel: 202-387-5048; FAX: 202-387-5149
E-mail: bob@independentsector.org (Bob Smucker, Project Director); WWW: http://www.indepsec.org/clpi/

▶ A project of Independent Sector, Charity Lobbying in the Public Interest is working to dispel the myths that lobbying by charities is unimportant, inappropriate, or illegal by providing information on the important role of lobbying in achieving an organization's mission. Their Web site includes detailed information on why lobbying is important, lobby laws for 501(c)(3) and (4) organizations, how to lobby, and motivating others to lobby.

Connecticut Volunteer Lawyers for the Arts (CTVLA)

Connecticut Commission on the Arts, 755 Main Street,
One Financial Plaza , 755 Main Street, Hartford, CT 06103
Tel: 860-566-4770; FAX: 860-566-6462
E-mail: tprioli@ctarts.org (Angela Capri);
WWW: http://www.ctarts.org/vla.htm

▶ This is a cooperative project of the Connecticut Commission on the Arts and the law firm of Sorokin, Gross & Hyde, PC. Typical matters that CTVLA attorneys handle include nonprofit incorporation, copyright information and infringements, tax information, and contract review. A law student intern is available at the Commission on the Arts five hours a week to handle CTVLA inquiries. In order to qualify for the CTVLA service, the client must be an individual or organization involved in arts-related activities within Connecticut only; the client's problem must be directly related to the client's arts activities; organizations must engage in not-for-profit activities; the client's financial status, as indicated by the amount of the organization's budget or the individual's annual income, must be such that the organization or individual could not afford a private attorney.

DMA Nonprofit Federation (formerly National Federal of Nonprofits)

815 15th Street NW, Suite 822, Washington, DC 20005-2201
Tel: 202-628-4380, 202-628-4383
E-mail: nfndc@aol.com;
WWW: http://www.federationofnonprofits.org/

▶ Created in 1982, the Nonprofit Federation gives voice to non-profits that want to be active on issues involving state and federal regulators, charity watchdogs, the postal service, and standards-setting groups such as the American Institute of certified public accountants (AICPA). The DMA Nonprofit Federation also serves as a knowledgeable advocate before Congress and a link to other organizations dealing with related issues. Its more than 400 members include charities, colleges and alumni associations, museums, voluntary health organizations, veterans groups, religious organizations, and other nonprofits. Originally organized to protect non-profit postage rates, it has expanded its programs to include working on any legislative, regulatory, and accountability issues, at both the state and federal levels, that affect nonprofits. It works to ensure that nonprofits and their suppliers are well represented and thoroughly informed about postal matters and other legislation and regulations that affect their ability to communicate with donors, members, and prospects. It also monitors and reports on the AICPA, Better Business Bureau, National Charities Information Bureau, and other organizations whose programs affect nonprofits. It holds two annual conferences, both in Washington, DC, and schedules additional conferences, presented in several cities around the country, when new developments create the need to explain in detail how the issue(s) will affect the nonprofit community. It publishes the monthly newsletter *NewsUpdate,* which provides timely and critical information about postal issues, current legislative activity, state regulations, accounting standards, court cases important to nonprofits, and items of interest suggested by members.

Financial Accounting Standards Board *(See Financial Management for full description)*

Georgetown University Law Center

Continuing Legal Education Division Office, 50 F Street NW,
Suite 8200, Washington, DC 20001-1564
Tel: 202-662-9890; FAX: 202-662-9891
E-mail: cle@law.georgetown.edu, center@law.georgetown.edu
(Lawrence J. Center, Executive Director);
WWW: http://www.law.georgetown.edu/cle

▶ GULC/CLE provides continuing legal education programs to meet the ever-changing needs of the legal profession both locally and nationally. Programs address the specific interests of practicing attorneys and help to develop their critical competencies while at the same time meeting the mandatory CLE requirements of various state bars. It offers the annual program *Representing & Managing Tax-Exempt Organizations* for attorneys, accountants, trust officers, nonprofit organization managers and consultants, and fund-raising and development personnel. Highlights include current IRS exempt organization priorities, exempt organization policy issues, anticipated legislation and how structural tax reform proposals affect your organization or clients, an up-to-the-minute analysis of current developments affecting exempt organizations, an examination of the latest developments in the unrelated business area, the latest trends and developments in international philanthropy, ways in which exempt organizations are participating in limited liability companies, issues affecting users of 501(c)(3) bonds and 403(b) plans, federal regulation of lobbying activities, and the future of tax-exempt organizations.

Georgia Volunteer Lawyers for the Arts (GVLA)

The Bureau of Cultural Affairs, 675 Ponce De Leon Avenue NE,
Suite 550, Atlanta, GA 30308
Tel: 404-873-3911
E-mail: georgiavla@hotmail.com; WWW: http://www.gvla.org/

▶ Founded in 1975, Georgia Volunteer Lawyers for the Arts (GVLA) exists to serve the legal needs of the artists and arts organizations of Georgia, to promote closer contact and understanding among the members of the legal profession and the arts community, and to educate artists about their legal rights and responsibilities. GVLA is organized to answer legal questions from visual artists, writers, performers, and musicians and make referrals to pro bono lawyers; give free legal advice to nonprofit arts organizations with budgets under $500,000; and conduct workshops on topical issues relating to the arts and the law including contracts and copyrights, taxes and record keeping, and nonprofit incorporation.

International Center for Not-for-Profit Law *(See*
International Third Sector for complete description)

Lawyers Alliance of New York

330 Seventh Avenue, 19th Floor, New York, NY 10001
Tel: 212-219-1800; FAX: 212-941-7458
E-mail: info@lany.org; WWW: http://www.lany.org

▶ Founded in 1969, Lawyers Alliance for New York is the leading provider of free and low-cost business and transactional legal services to nonprofit and community development organizations that are working to improve the quality of life in New York City. Their in-house attorneys, together with more than 650 volunteer lawyers from leading firms and corporations, provide pro bono legal services to their nonprofit clients, while leading firms and businesses also support their work in many other ways. They provide these services to nonprofits in all five boroughs of New York City. Clients employ thousands of New Yorkers as they promote economic development, create jobs and housing, and provide essential services such as child care and special programs for the elderly, young people, and those with special needs. Lawyers Alliance for New York offers workshops on topics of concern to nonprofits and legal professionals who advise them. All workshops are led by experts in the areas of nonprofit law addressed.

Lawyers for the Creative Arts (LCA)

213 West Institute Place, Chicago, IL 60610
Tel: 312-649-4111; FAX: 312-944-2195
E-mail: culture@ci.chi.il.us, babs@mcs.net (Barbara Koenen,
Project Manager); WWW: http://www.cityofchicago.org/Cultural
Affairs/CulturalProgramming/Lawyers.html (Chicago Department
of Cultural Affairs)

▶ LCA provides legal assistance to artists and arts organizations. Those requesting legal assistance are asked to fill out an application and supply pertinent financial data. Financial eligibility is determined on the basis of tax records for individual applicants and operating budgets for organizations. Artists and not-for-profit organizations qualify for pro bono legal counsel if their legal problems are related to artistic pursuits, and if they qualify as financially unable to retain counsel. Applicants who are ineligible for free legal assistance may still take advantage of other LCA services. In addition to direct legal assistance, LCA also offers conferences, workshops, a speaker's bureau, publications and expanded referral services.

The Legal Center for Connecticut Nonprofit Organizations

P.O. Box 693, New Haven, CT 06503-0693
Tel: 203-624-5415
E-mail: ldavis@connix.com; WWW: http://www.ctlegalcenter.org/,
http://www.ctlegalcenter.org/links.html

▶ Since its creation in 1991, the Legal Center for Connecticut Nonprofit Organizations, Inc., has been helping nonprofits across the state with legal problems. The Legal Center assists nonprofit organizations that cannot afford legal council to obtain pro bono legal services, through a matching system that pairs volunteer attorneys with nonprofits in their geographic area or area of expertise. To qualify for assistance from the Legal Center in finding pro bono legal counsel, the nonprofit organization must pass through the Legal Center's screening process by submitting an application. Screening assures the Legal Center and its volunteers that the organization qualifies or would qualify for tax-exempt status and is unable to pay for legal services. (Both criteria are discussed in the section entitled Eligibility Requirements.) The initial screening process generally takes one to four weeks, but it may take an additional four to six weeks for the Legal Center to find a volunteer willing to be "matched" to the organization.

Maryland Lawyers for the Arts (MLA)

218 West Saratoga Street, Baltimore, MD 21201
Tel: 410-752-1633
E-mail: lawgal@usa.net;
WWW: http://www.mlaonline.org/ mla/welcome.htm

▶ MLA is a 501(c)(3) nonprofit organization that offers pro bono legal assistance to income-eligible artists and arts organizations in the State of Maryland through its referral attorney panel. MLA offers many other services to the arts and entertainment community, including entertainment law library, educational seminars, speaker's bureau, fee-based lawyer referral, quarterly newsletter, and promoting the arts and entertainment community.

National Association for Public Interest Law (NAPIL)

2120 L Street NW, Suite 450, Washington, DC 20037
Tel: 202-466-3686; FAX: 202-429-9766
E-mail: napil@napil.org;
WWW: http://www.napil.org/HOME.html

▶ NAPIL was founded in 1986 by law students dedicated to surmounting barriers to equal justice that affect millions of low-income individuals and families. Today, NAPIL is the country's leading organization engaged in organizing, training, and supporting public service–minded law students, and is the national leader in creating summer and postgraduate public interest jobs. It publishes *Connection,* NAPIL's quarterly newsletter.

National Center for Nonprofit Law (NCNL)

2001 S Street NW, Suite 430, Washington, DC 20009-1125
Tel: 202-462-1000; FAX: 202-462-1001
E-mail: nonprftlaw@aol.com

▶ NCNL is a 501(c)(3) membership organization designed to help nonprofit organizations of all sizes and missions understand and satisfy the legal requirements and opportunities that apply to them and avoid unnecessary problems. It operates the National Clearinghouse of Nonprofit Legal Documents, a collection of hundreds of sample contracts, forms, memoranda, personnel policies, sexual harassment policies, leases, training materials, grievance procedures, and other documents (NCNL members contribute documents to the Clearinghouse), and conducts educational seminars for nonprofit staff, managers, lawyers, and volunteers on the practical aspects of understanding and handling nonprofit legal and operational issues (discount to NCNL members). Seminars focus on such issues as employment laws, financial operation restrictions, lobbying rules, corporate and tax filing requirements, and personnel matters. Each seminar explains the applicable law, illustrates how it can affect your organization, and wherever possible provides sample documents, operational checklists, and other written guidance. It publishes briefing papers in plain "how-to" language, which explain the law and discuss the practical aspects and implications of legal issues (legal self-audits, hiring independent contractors, hotel and fund-raising contracts, employee matters) affecting nonprofits in order that staff and legal counsel can better understand and effectively address the legal issues. Resource committees cover such issues as federal tax matters, nonprofit commercial activities, fund-raising registration, reporting and compliance, and state and local tax issues.

National Center on Philanthropy and the Law

New York University School of Law, D'Agostino Hall,
110 West Third Street, Room 205, New York, NY 10012-1074
Tel: 212-998-6168; FAX: 212-995-3149
E-mail: ncpl.info@nyu.edu; WWW: http://www.law.nyu.edu/ncpl/

▶ Launched in 1988, The National Center on Philanthropy and the Law was established at New York University School of Law to explore a broad range of legal issues affecting the nation's nonprofit sector and to provide an integrated examination of the legal doctrines related to the activities of charitable organizations. The Center is developing a unified field of study that provides central focus and leadership to scholarly research, conferences, teaching, and curriculum development. This approach is intended to add to and improve the overall quality of education and scholarship among law students, legal scholars, nonprofit organizations, practicing attorneys, judges, executives, administrators, and other professionals in the field. The Center sponsors periodic conferences providing a forum for scholars and practitioners, in law and related disciplines. Since the Center's inception, the NYU School of Law Library has made available, free of charge, a room for the use of scholars and students worldwide who wish to conduct scholarly research in the area of philanthropy and the law. NYU's entire collection is the most comprehensive ever assembled on the subject of philanthropy and the law. Scholars can arrange for access to the law and philanthropy room by calling the program coordinator, Niamh O'Brien, at 212-998-6168, or contacting her via e-mail at *ncpl.info@nyu.edu.*

Nonprofit Risk Management Center

1001 Connecticut Avenue NW, Washington, DC 20036
Tel: 202-785-3891; FAX: 202-296-0349
E-mail: info@nonprofitrisk.org;
WWW: http://www.nonprofitrisk.org

▶ The Center helps charities identify and reduce the legal and financial risks facing their organizations.

North Carolina Volunteer Lawyers for the Arts (NCVLA)

P.O. Box 26513, Raleigh, NC 27611-6513
Tel: 919-990-2575
E-mail: info@ncvla.org; WWW: http://www.ncvla.org/

▶ NCVLA's referral service received inquiries this past year from visual artists, writers, photographers, screenwriters, commercial artists, and arts organizations regarding contracts, copyrights, nonprofit incorporation, landlord/tenant, and infringement. In addition to their referral services, NCVLA sponsors educational programs in the form of seminars catering directly to the arts community and their needs as well as presenting continuing legal education programs for attorneys. NCVLA sponsors an annual seminar and publishes a newsletter.

Ocean State Lawyers for the Arts

P.O. Box 19, Saunderstown, RI 02874
Tel: 401-789-5686
E-mail: dspatt@artslaw.org; WWW: http://www.artslaw.org/

▶ This organization was founded in 1984 as the Rhode Island affiliate of a nationwide network of nonprofit public service organizations dedicated to providing legal assistance to visual artists, actors, performers, theater companies, museums, dance troupes, artists' groups, and any other artists or arts organizations in need of help regarding contracts, copyrights, trademarks, tax-exempt status, collection of accounts, and any other arts-related problems.

Philadelphia Volunteer Lawyers for the Arts (PVLA)

251 South 18th Street, Philadelphia, PA 19103
Tel: 215-545-3385; FAX: 215-545-4839
E-mail: pvla@libertynet.org;
WWW: http://www.libertynet.org/pvla,
http://www.libertynet.org/pvla/resources.htm

▶ PVLA is a nonprofit legal services organization, founded in 1978 to provide pro bono legal assistance and basic business counseling to area artists and cultural organizations. Over the years, PVLA has recruited hundreds of attorneys from large and small firms in Philadelphia and surrounding counties to their program. Volunteer attorneys work on projects such as negotiating performing contracts for actors, dancers, and musicians; preparing bylaws for newly formed nonprofits; negotiating short- and long-term workspace leases and exhibition agreements; securing protection of artwork; and setting up new community-wide arts initiatives. PVLA offers a wide selection of books on arts-related legal and business topics—including copyright, trademark, contracts, and nonprofit issues. Throughout the year, PVLA is involved with a variety of educational programs for professional artists, art students, and cultural nonprofits. PVLA is also an accredited *CLE* provider and offers programs designed to educate attorneys about arts law and nonprofit issues. Information on arts law and business development is available from PVLA's Small Business Development Center for the Arts and PVLA's Center for Arts Law Information.

Philanthropy Tax Institute *(See Financial Management—Products and Services for full description)*

Practising Law Institute (PLI)
810 Seventh Avenue, New York, NY 10019-5818
Tel: 800-260-4PLI, 212-824-5710; FAX: 800-321-0093
E-mail info@pli.edu; WWW: http://www.pli.edu/,
http://www.pli.edu/public/static/links.html,
http://www.pli.edu/public/publications.htm

▶ A nonprofit continuing legal education organization chartered by the Regents of the University of the State of New York, founded in 1933, PLI is dedicated to providing the legal community and allied professionals with the most up-to-date, relevant information and techniques that are critical to the development of a professional, competitive edge. Thy achieve these goals through the highest-quality seminars held annually in locations across the United States, annually supplemented reference books, audio and video programs, interactive multimedia CD-ROMs, course handbooks, Web programs, and customized training and specialized services, all with the guidance of practice-specific advisory committees. PLI is headquartered in New York City, with offices in California.

PLI's approximately 275 annual programs are known for their superior quality, expert faculty, and cutting-edge information for the legal community in just about every major discipline. They are approved for CLE credits in the 39 states that require MCLE in order to practice law. They also offer most programs for purchase as audio- or videocassettes.

PLI's Select Training Services Department offers customized training solutions for law firms, corporations, government agencies, legal services organizations, and nonprofit organizations. We work on a one-to-one basis with (1) lawyers and professional staff responsible for training to help you train your lawyers, legal support staff, and related professionals; (2) CLE coordinators to establish firmwide solutions to meeting mandatory CLE requirements; and (3) librarians, training directors, and others responsible for account management to resolve payment and billing issues. Additionally, this department works closely with law librarians and the law school community, and is responsible for PLI's Patent Bar Review Course.

ProArts
Volunteer Lawyers for the Arts, 425 Sixth Avenue, Suite 1220, Pittsburgh, PA 15219-1819
Tel: 412-391-2060; FAX: 412-394-4280
E-mail: proarts@artswire.org;
WWW: http://www.artsnet.org/proarts/

▶ A not-for-profit, tax-exempt organization, it is Southwestern Pennsylvania's arts service organization serving not-for-profit arts organizations and independent artists. Established in Pittsburgh in 1994 as Western Pennsylvania Professionals for the Arts, ProArts provides programs to support and strengthen the greater Pittsburgh arts community, and opportunities for arts supporters in the business and legal communities to volunteer and become active in the cultural life of the region. Volunteer Lawyers for the Arts provides pro bono assistance to low-income artists and smaller arts organizations for arts-related legal needs. VLA attorneys have provided

expertise in areas including (but not limited to) copyright and other intellectual property matters, contracts, nonprofit compliance and nonprofit, 501(c)(3) filings, facilities leases, insurance and tax matters, artist contracts, and responsibilities and liabilities of nonprofit boards of directors.

The Pro Bono Partnership
237 Mamaroneck Avenue, White Plains, NY 10605
Tel: 914-328-0674; FAX: 914-328-0538
E-mail: MelindaSherwood@princetoninfo.com,
information@probonopartner.org;
WWW: http://www.probonopartnership.org

Jennifer Chandler Hauge, Deputy Director, Pro Bono Partnership—New Jersey office, P.O. Box 225, Convent Station, NJ 07960
Tel: 973-984-1612; FAX: 973) 984-1527
E-mail: lawnonprof@aol.com

▶ Founded in 1997 by members of the Corporate Bar Association as a tax-exempt public charity, the Pro Bono Partnership has over 300 volunteer attorneys, primarily inside counsel of corporations in Westchester County (New York) and Fairfield County (Connecticut), consulting to nonprofits in the area. It has recently expanded its coverage to include New Jersey. Its primary purpose is to provide free business legal assistance to community-based nonprofit organizations serving the poor and disadvantaged populations in Westchester County, New York; Fairfield County, Connecticut; and northern New Jersey. It provides eligible community-based organizations with a variety of free services including advice and counsel on matters related to corporate structure and governance; contracts and leases; real estate; employment law; environmental law; tax law and tax exempt status; regulatory compliance (e.g., registration, annual reporting, charitable solicitation); and merger, bankruptcy, and dissolution. They also run workshops and training sessions on the laws pertaining to nonprofit and tax-exempt organizations and will publish easy-to-understand materials on legal issues that can be used for problem solving or practical guidance.

Program on Law & Global Philanthropy
(See Professional Development, Education [Pennsylvania] for full description)

St. Louis Volunteer Lawyers and Accountants for the Arts (VLAA)
3540 Washington, St. Louis, MO 63103
Tel: 314-652-2410; FAX: 314-652-0011
E-mail: vlaa@stlrac.org; WWW: http://www.vlaa.org,
http://www.vlaa.org/resources.asp

▶ More than 225 professionals offer their expertise in a wide range of arts-related matters. Cases are referred to attorneys and accountants based on their interests, experience, and availability. VLAA volunteers help painters, poets, musicians, playwrights, photographers, graphic artists, dancers, crafts groups, filmmakers, theater companies, orchestras, neighborhood arts councils, and others. Services include obtaining nonprofit, tax-exempt status; negotiating and drafting contracts; protecting intellectual property; and developing bookkeeping systems. To get help through VLAA, you must be a St. Louis, southwestern Illinois, or out-of-state Missouri artist or represent an arts organization and must submit an application. VLAA determines financial eligibility on the basis of an individual's income or an organization's operating budget, then refers the qualifying applicant to a volunteer. VLAA sponsors workshops for individual artists and arts organizations featuring "how-to" information on a variety of legal and business topics. It publishes a free monthly newsletter for Missouri and southwestern Illinois arts organizations entitled *Arts Law Memo.*

Texas Accountants & Lawyers (TALA)

1540 Sul Ross, Houston, TX 77006
Tel: 800-526-8252, 713-526-4876; FAX: 713-526-1299
E-mail: info@talarts.org; WWW: http://www.talarts.org/

▶ TALA is a nonprofit, tax-exempt 501(c)(3) statewide organization that has been providing legal and accounting services to the arts community of Texas since 1979. Over 700 attorneys and accountants donate their time to artists and arts organizations that are unable to afford professional services. Services include pro bono assistance, dispute resolution services, educational programs for the artistic and business community, publications, and a resource library. Programs are designed to help artists apply legal and accounting concepts for their benefit. TALA has provided counseling and representation across the spectrum of arts-related accounting and legal matters, including nonprofit organization formation; contract negotiation and review; copyright, trademark, and patent; arts-related landlord–tenant issues; dispute resolution/arts mediation; tax-exempt status; estate planning for artists; individual tax preparation; and basic accounting systems.

Volunteer Lawyers for the Arts

1 East 53rd Street, 6th Floor, New York, NY 10022
Tel: 212-319-ARTS (2787); FAX: 212-752-6575
E-mail: vlany@bway.net; WWW: http://www.vlany.org/

▶ This organization provides free arts-related legal advice and representation to low-income artists and arts organizations from all creative disciplines. It also offers low-cost legal publications, arts-related legal workshops and seminars, and special initiatives to help artists avoid legal entanglements.

Volunteer Lawyers for the Arts of Massachusetts (VLA)

P.O. Box 8784, Boston, MA 02114
Tel: 617-523-1764
E-mail: vla@world.std.com (James R. Grace, Executive Director); WWW: http://www.alliancefund.org/id104.htm

▶ VLA is a nonprofit organization established to meet the legal needs of the state's artistic community. VLA is the only organization in Massachusetts designed specifically to address the legal concerns of the arts community. VLA provides a Legal Referral Program, seminars, and workshops to artists and arts organizations from all creative disciplines, including visual arts, music, literary arts, performing arts, and film and video. A panel of more than 200 attorneys is available to provide free or reduced-fee legal assistance for arts-related problems. The Legal Referral Program can assist with issues such as specialized contracts, copyright and trademark, First Amendment, tax and nonprofit, estate planning, landlord–tenant, nonprofit incorporation, and employment. VLA also provides a

variety of seminars and workshops for artists and arts organizations and the attorneys who represent them. These sessions address specific aspects of art and entertainment law, such as nonprofit incorporation and tax-exempt status, public art contracts, trusts and estates, and copyright issues.

Volunteer Lawyers for the Arts/Western Florida
(A division of Business Volunteers for the Arts)

Pinellas County Arts Council, 14700 Terminal Boulevard, Suite 229, Clearwater, FL 33762
Tel: 727-507-4114; FAX: 727-507-4125
E-mail: bkotchey@co.pinellas.fl.us (Bruce Kotchey, Director), pcac@co.pinellas.fl.us;
WWW: http://www.co.pinellas.fl.us/ bcc/artscoun.htm

▶ Pairs attorneys with cultural organizations and artists for workshops and for individualized services regarding legal assistance.

Volunteer Lawyers Project

29 Temple Place, Suite 300, Boston 02111
Tel: 617-423-0648; FAX: 617-423-0061
WWW: http://www.neighborhoodlaw.org/volunteer_lawyers_ project.htm, http://www.neighborhoodlaw.org/otherlaw.htm

▶ Housing, including homeowner issues, consumer/bankruptcy, probate/wills, tax issues, disabilities/SSI, family law, unemployment, and assistance to nonprofit organizations.

Washington Area Lawyers for the Arts (WALA)

815 15th Street NW, Suite 900, Washington, DC 20005
Tel: 202-393-2826
E-mail: wala@juno.com; WWW: http://thewala.org/

▶ Since 1983, WALA has been meeting the legal needs of the arts community in the greater Washington metropolitan area, Maryland, and Virginia. WALA is a 501(c)(3) nonprofit organization that provides legal services to area artists and arts organizations through the WALA Legal Clinic and a corps of over 350 volunteer attorneys. WALA is also a public resource center for information about legal issues affecting artists and arts organizations. WALA offers educational programs, including legal seminars for artists and CLE programs for attorneys. WALA's services include legal advice and representation, professional business counseling, and education. It has a reference library, which is open to the public. It publishes *Portfolio,* a legal update newsletter, and numerous publications on specific arts-related legal issues written by volunteer attorneys.

Washington Lawyers for the Arts (WLA)

The Richard Hugo House, 1634 11th Avenue, Seattle, WA 98122
Tel: 206-328-7053; FAX: 206-568-3306
E-mail: info@wa-artlaw, director@wa-artlaw.org;
WWW: http://www.wa-artlaw.org/

▶ Founded in 1976, WLA is a 501(c)(3) nonprofit service organization with the mission to support the arts in Washington State by creating alliances and making legal resources accessible to artists and arts organizations of all disciplines. Since January 1996, WLA has sponsored and organized the Arts Legal Clinic in collaboration with Artist Trust. Attorneys specializing in intellectual property, tax, corporate, and arts and entertainment law donate pro bono services to the Clinic. It offers a lecture and workshop series.

PRODUCT AND SERVICE PROVIDERS

Law Offices of Barnaby Zall

7018 Tilden Lane, Rockville, MD 20852-4549
Tel: 301-231-6943
E-mail: bzall@aol.com;
WWW: http://www.lawyers.com/ taxexemptorganizationlaw

▶ Barnaby Zall is a nationally recognized expert in tax-exempt organizations, especially those that want to make a difference in public policy. He has helped start and run dozens of nonprofit organizations, from large professional and trade associations to specialized advocacy groups. He provides counseling on management, tax advice, and legal advice to the organizations, their managers, and their officers and directors. Clients include large universities and private foundations to tiny interest groups.

Bird & Associates, Attorneys at Law

1150 Monarch Plaza, 3414 Peachtree Road NE,
Atlanta, GA 30326
Tel: 404-264-9400; FAX: 404-365-9731
WWW: http://www.birdlawfirm.com/

▶ This firm's concentration in the nonprofit organization field includes the tax and corporate law needs of public charities, private foundations, and charitable trusts. They represent a number of large and small nonprofit organizations, and have never had an application for exemption or request for letter ruling turned down by the Internal Revenue Service. Their attorneys in this field include Wendell R. Bird, David J. Markese, and Thomas O. Kotouc. The firm represents charities nationwide.

Black Helterline, LLP

707 SW Washington Street, Suite 1200, Portland, OR 97205
Tel: 503-224-5560; FAX: 503-224-6148
E-mail: Stark Ackerman; WWW: http://www.bhlaw.com/

▶ This firm provides quality legal services to emerging growth and established Pacific Northwest businesses, individuals, governmental entities, and nonprofit institutions. Practice areas include bankruptcy and reorganizations; business law; employee benefits; employment law; litigation; mergers and acquisitions; services to professionals; taxation; and trusts, estates, and probate.

Caplin & Drysdale

One Thomas Circle NW, Suite 1100, Washington, DC 20005
Tel: 202-862-5000; FAX: 202-429-3301

399 Park Avenue, New York, NY 10022-4614
Tel: 212-319-7125; FAX: 212-644-6755
E-mail: tb@capdale.com (Terri L. Ballard, Firm Administrator);
WWW: http://www.caplindrysdale.com/

▶ Caplin & Drysdale represents a wide variety of tax-exempt organizations. Clients include major foundations, national associations of exempt organizations, public charities, and trade associations. They serve as advisors to the Department of Treasury internationally in its Tax Advisors program and assist the American Bar Association in law reform projects. The firm's attorneys provide ongoing advice to clients on all aspects of exempt organization creation, operation, and dissolution. The advice ranges from answering single questions to conducting comprehensive reviews of an organization's activities. In addition to tax matters, the firm provides general legal advice and representation to nonprofit entities. They also advise private individuals and for-profit organizations that support or engage in transactions with exempt organizations. Their lawyers have particularly strong experience and expertise in the following areas: establishing or restructuring an exempt organization, complying with restrictions on your ability to lobby, managing business activities and UBIT liability, facing an IRS audit, complying with private foundation rules, raising revenue and diversifying services through joint ventures with businesses and other nonprofits, monitoring legislative and regulatory developments, and advancing a legislative or regulatory strategy.

Coblentz, Patch, Duffy & Bass, LLP

222 Kearny Street, 7th Floor, San Francisco, CA 94108-4510
Tel: 415-391-4800; FAX: 415-989-1663
E-mail: nonprofit@cpdp.com

▶ This is a full-service law firm offering assistance and services in all aspects of tax and nonprofit corporate law fundamental to the operation of a nonprofit organization, including organization and tax exemption, operational issues, foundation issues, welfare exemption from property tax, directors' and officers' liability, political and lobbying activities, and charitable planning.

Copilevitz & Canter

423 West 8th Street, Suite 400, Kansas City, MO 64105-1408
Tel: 816-472-9000; FAX: 816-472-5000
E-mail: copcankc@copilevitz-canter.com

1815 H Street NW, Washington, DC 20006
Tel: 202-861-0740; Fax: 202-331-9841
E-mail copcandc@us.net;
WWW: http://www.copilevitz-canter.com

▶ This firm provides specialized legal services to nonprofit organizations, professional fund raisers, and commercial telemarketers, and legal counsel in all areas of First Amendment law relevant to this practice. Clients include hundreds of nonprofit organizations, which they advise in areas of federal tax, state regulatory compliance, royalty licenses, and copyrights and trademarks, as well as general corporate law. Services to nonprofits include federal and state tax laws (securing recognition of federal and state status, and maintaining tax-exempt status unrelated to business income issues; "private inurement" issues, advice as to preparation of Form 990, and local real estate tax exemptions); tax-exempt bond financing and development (assist organizations in taking advantage of special, tax-exempt bond financing techniques available only to 501(c)(3) organizations. Services include advising in connection with selecting an underwriter of all aspects of the offering); tax-advantaged, inter vivos fund raising (charitable remainder trust, pooled income funds, charitable gifts annuities, bargain sales, inter vivos and planned giving); estate planning for donor (will assist your donor in integrating a charitable request into his or her estate plan, in such a way as both to maximize the donor's tax advantage and the gift); United States Postal Service law (help your organization obtain and retain the special bulk, third-class charitable mail permit available only to tax-exempt organizations. They also will advise you to steer clear of types of solicitations that may trigger litigation with the USPS); state regulatory compliance (they have an automated, computer-based system designated to keep your organization registered in compliance with state law. They also defend organizations charged with violations of state consumer protection statutes); trademark and copyright services (will register and protect your organization's membership marks, service marks, trademarks, logos, and intellectual property); general corporate services (provide resolutions, minutes, bylaws, amendments, and the full panoply of corporate law services); contracts and lease review (review all forms of agreements); compensation and benefit planning (assist your organization with compensation, benefits, and retirement planning. They can prepare Section 403(b) tax-deferred annuity plans to fit all qualified, exempt organizations.).

Crosby, Heafey, Roach, and May

1999 Harrison Street, Suite 2600, Oakland, CA 94612-3572
Tel: 510-763-2000; FAX: 510-273-8832, 510-273-8898
E-mail: info@chrm.com, jkemp@chrm.com (John M. Kemp);
WWW: http://www.crosbyheafey.com/,
http://www.crosbyheafey.com/ expertise/non_profit.asp

▶ Crosby, Heafey lawyers have extensive experience in the organization and operation of tax-exempt and taxable nonprofit entities, including foundations, trusts, and other grant-making entities as well as operating nonprofits in education, health care, housing, and other areas. Lawyers counseling nonprofits often consult with their lawyers focusing on tax, health law, employment issues, education law, or other applicable areas of the law. They have offices in Century City, Los Angeles, San Francisco, Santa Rosa, and Sonoma.

Exemption Advisory Services

P.O. Box 75012, Seattle, WA 98125
Tel: 206-364-0758; FAX: 206-364-0064
E-mail: exempts@aol.com; WWW: http://members.aol.com/exempts

▶ This firm provides full-service preparation of an application for tax-exempt status under Section 501(c). As a public service, they maintain a Web site designed to help, with a do-it-yourself application, *http://members.aol.com/irsform1023* (see Internet Sites for detailed description).

Freeman, Freeman & Smiley, LLP

Los Angeles office: 3415 Sepulveda Boulevard, Penthouse,
Suite 1200, Los Angeles, CA 90034-6060
Tel: 310-255-6100

Orange County office: 2010 Main Street, Suite 220, Irvine, CA 92614
Tel: 949-833-7966
E-mail: sic@ffslaw.com; WWW: http://www.ffslaw.com/public_htm/

▶ Since its inception in 1976, Freeman, Freeman & Smiley, LLP, has developed a nationally recognized law practice specializing in the areas of estate planning and charitable and nonprofit organization planning. They provide counsel to nonprofit institutions in developing and operating their fund-raising programs.

Gammon & Grange, Attorneys at Law

8280 Greensboro Drive, 7th Floor, McLean, VA 22102
Tel: 703-761-5000
E-mail: sjs@gandglaw.com; WWW: http://www.gandglaw.com

▶ Gammon & Grange has a reputation for expertise in many areas of law, particularly those that affect nonprofits and tax-exempt organizations. The firm represents nonprofit and tax-exempt organizations of all types and sizes, from small local churches to large international foundations. Clients include schools and universities, religious organizations, social service and community action groups, trade associations, and professional organizations. Since 1979, Gammon & Grange has been one of the country's leading law firms in the practice of preventative law for nonprofit and tax-exempt organizations. Their work in the preventative law field has enabled hundreds of nonprofits to reduce their legal liability risks by improving their overall management and organizational skills. They also serve nonprofits on a wide range of issues, including incorporation and tax-exempt status (federal and state); charitable gifts and fund-raising laws (federal, state, and international); UBIT issues (unrelated business income tax); for-profit subsidiaries; executive compensation; employee and volunteer liability; director/officer liabilities and indemnification; board governance; lobbying and political activity; contract review. The firm publishes *Nonprofit Alert*, a monthly legal newsletter for nonprofit leaders.

Gilbert, Segall, and Young, LLP

430 Park Avenue, New York, NY 10022
Tel: 212-644-4025; FAX: 212-644-4051
E-mail: spaul@gsy.com (Sarah E. Paul), dkurtz@gsy.com (Daniel L. Kurtz); WWW: http://www.gsy.com/Pracarea.html

▶ This firm represents nonprofit organizations in all areas, including general corporate representation, exempt organization tax matters, real estate, estate administration and planned giving, and litigation. The firm assists clients in creating new nonprofit entities, and advises on all tax and corporate matters, including corporate governance issues. The firm also advises nonprofits on employment matters, charitable solicitation, the use and investment of endowment funds and restricted gifts, and intellectual property issues, as well as all types of transactions, including mergers, joint ventures, conversions and asset sales, and real property transactions. The firm represents nonprofits before regulatory agencies such as the Internal Revenue Service and state attorneys general. The firm's nonprofit clients include national and international charities, independent schools and universities, family and corporate foundations, cultural institutions, social service agencies, health care providers and research organizations, trade and professional associations, social clubs, religious organizations, and advocacy groups.

Hammar & Sommerville

1400 Summit Tower, Eleven Greenway Plaza, Houston, TX 77046
Tel: 877-537-4360; FAX: 972-354-7746
E-mail: fsommerville@abanet.org (Frank Sommerville, Attorney)

▶ Hammar & Sommerville is a law firm dedicated to performing tax compliance reviews for nonprofit organizations nationwide.

Heckscher, Teillon, Terrill, & Sager

Suite 300, 100 Four Falls Corp. Center,
West Conshohocken, PA 19428-2983
Tel: 610-940-2600; FAX: 610-940-6042
E-mail: info@htts.com, jaterrill@htts.com (John A. Terrill II);
WWW: http://www.htts.com

▶ This firm provides sophisticated legal services for charitable gift planning and documentation and estate and tax planning to tax-exempt and charitable organizations. The services provided by HTT&S attorneys include sophisticated estate and tax planning; trust, estate, and guardianship administration; fiduciary representation; fiduciary and tax litigation; and representing tax-exempt and charitable organizations. L. Pierre Teillon Jr., Esq., is counsel with advocacy and philanthropy.

Law Offices of Marshall A. Glick

10866 Wilshire Boulevard, Suite 1200,
Los Angeles, CA 90024-4336
Tel: 800-273-4849; FAX: 818-345-2263
E-mail: mglick@prodigy.net; WWW: http://www.glicklaw.com/

▶ This firm forms nonprofit, tax-exempt corporations, in every state of the United States, which function on a statewide, national, and worldwide basis. They provide their legal services quickly and affordably, and have never failed to obtain favorable tax-exempt status with the IRS for a nonprofit organization they have formed.

Gnossos Software, Inc.

1625 K Street NW, Suite 1250, Washington, DC 20006-1604
Tel: 202-463-1200; FAX: 202-785-9562
E-mail: info@gnossos.com;
WWW: http://www.gnossos.com/company/profile.htm

▶ This is a vertical market software company and the premier provider of government relations and corporate affairs software for *Fortune* 500 companies, associations, and public affairs consulting firms in the United States. It distributes the Keep In Touch® government relations management product line, which includes five products for grassroots, political action committee (PAC), lobby tax and disclosure, issues, and media relations management. Keep In Touch enables clients to comprehensively manage an entire public affairs or government relations effort of any size with efficiency, flexibility, speed, and accuracy. Keep In Touch comes with a complete database of federal and state legislators, including up-to-date contact information and committee assignments, and enables users to easily track contacts, activities, relationships, and financial transactions. Keep In Touch is Microsoft Office compatible and merges seamlessly with Microsoft Word, WordPerfect, Lotus, Delrina WinFax Pro, and association management software, such as iMIS. Keep In Touch also links easily with a myriad of other spreadsheet, broadcast faxing, and e-mail software.

Harmon, Curran, Spielberg & Eisenberg, LLP

1726 M Street NW, Suite 600, Washington, DC 20036
Tel: 202-328-3500; FAX: 202-328-6918
E-mail: HCSE@HarmonCurran.com (Gail Harmon),
rrooth@aol.com, bkingsley@harmoncurran.com (Beth Kingsley);
WWW: http://www.harmoncurran.com

▶ Since its beginning as Berlin, Roisman & Kessler in 1969, the firm has devoted its practice to the provision of affordable, high-quality representation to individuals and citizens' groups and nonprofit organizations that traditionally have lacked effective advocacy. Harmon, Curran, Spielberg & Eisenberg, LLP, provides strategic legal advice and planning services to help their nonprofit clients adopt structures and operating mechanisms that simultaneously comply with legal regulations and maximize organizational effectiveness. Clients range from large national and international organizations to small volunteer community groups. They include private foundations, public charities, advocacy and action organizations, associations, and PACs, as well as consultants, accountants, and businesses serving nonprofits. Services to nonprofits include federal election law (provide advice on federal election law compliance and represent organizations before the Federal Election Commission); general counsel services (address the full range of issues that arise in the course of running a nonprofit organization, including Lobbying Disclosure Act compliance, trademark and copyright questions, government grant conditions, fund-raising contracts and compliance with state and federal laws, insurance issues, contract and lease review, and drafting); employment law (counsel nonprofit clients on personnel matters, drawing on lessons learned from their representation of individuals and emphasizing the prevention and resolution of employment disputes before they reach litigation. Areas of expertise include federal and state employment law compliance, including Title VII of the Civil Rights Act, the Americans with Disabilities Act, the Family and Medical Leave Act; personnel practices audits; employee handbook preparation and review; employee benefit plan advice; contract preparation for employees and consultants; severance agreement preparation and negotiation; and sexual harassment investigations); Internet issues (advise clients about the emerging law of the Internet as it relates to nonprofits, including the application of established legal concepts such as IRS lobbying regulations and intellectual property law; drafting and negotiating contracts for creating Web pages and conducting business on and via the Internet and other electronic media). To alert nonprofits to legal rulings and legislative proposals that could affect their operation, the firm publishes the *Nonprofit Navigator,* a monthly newsletter also available online.

Labyrinth Inc.—Charitable Registration Requirements

932 Hungerford Drive, Suite 16B, Rockville, MD 20850-1713
Tel: 301-340-2030; FAX: 301-424-4495
E-mail: info@LabyrinthInc.com, register@LabyrinthInc.com,
software@LabyrinthInc.com; WWW: http://www.labyrinthinc.com

▶ Labyrinth assists with registration prior to the solicitation of contributions, registration of organizations that help prepare a solicitation campaign in any state, or organizations that solicit contributions in any state. They prepare all of the forms necessary to renew your registration in the states where you are currently registered or to register you in any new state in which your organization is not registered. They prepare the new and renewal forms for each state you request. In addition, they prepare extensions for those states that allow them when you haven't received your audited financial statement or Form 990 from your accountants. They also offer a state registration program that prints out all the forms and attachments needed to keep your registration current as well as detailed descriptions of how to file each form. The program is compatible with Windows 3.1, 95, 98, and NT, as well as Macintosh OS. Labyrinth, Inc., produces an e-mail publication to keep you abreast of the latest changes in the world of state registrations. In order to join our mailing list, send a message to *update@labyrinthInc.com.* Somewhere in the body of the message, type the word "subscribe" and the e-mail address you want information sent to. E-mail updates do not follow a set timetable, but are sent as changes or events occur.

Law Office of Paul E. Lee

35 South Raymond Avenue, Suite 405, Pasadena, CA 91105-1931
Tel: 626-440-5971; FAX: 626-449-4417
E-mail: inquiry@pellawoffice.com;
WWW: http://www.pellawoffice.com/

▶ This is a general practice and civil litigation law office with a special emphasis on cost-effective legal services for nonprofit organizations. It provides services in these and other areas and more: civil litigation, nonprofit and religious organizations, administrative and government law, real property transactions and litigation, arbitration and mediation, personnel and employer–employee relations, business transactions and litigation, consumer protection and rights, and incorporation and business entity creation.

Richard Alan Lehrman

777 Arthur Godfrey Road, Fourth Floor, Miami Beach, FL 33140
Tel: 305-534-1323; FAX: 305-531-0314
E-mail: Lehrman@Trustlaw.net, TrustLaw@ABAnet.org,
RickLehrman@ATT.net; WWW: http://www.lawyers.com/trustlaw

▶ This practice is devoted to planning, design, implementation, and administration of trusts and estates, business succession planning, and charitable gift planning.

Law Offices of Pamela A. Mann

225 Broadway, Suite 2501, New York, NY 10007
Tel: 212-566-3200
E-mail: pmann@pamelamann.com;
WWW: http://www.pamelamann.com

▶ The practice of the Law Offices of Pamela A. Mann is concentrated in the representation of tax-exempt organizations. Drawing on its comprehensive expertise in issues facing such organizations, the office is counsel to numerous public charities and private foundations, from newly formed family foundations to large charities specializing in education and scientific research, from trade associations to grassroots organizations providing services to impoverished communities. The office advises its clients in a wide range of governance, regulatory, tax, and general corporate matters. The office represents exempt organizations and their directors in a variety of litigated matters, including claims of breach of fiduciary duty, misuse of restricted assets, and disputes over election and dismissal of officers.

The Law Office of Harvey Mechanic

3755 Watseka Avenue #201, Los Angeles, CA 90034
Voice/FAX: 310-815-8936; FAX: 413-473-4376
E-mail: harvey108@mediaone.net;
WWW: http://www.com.org/law

▶ A large part of this practice consists of representation of tax-exempt organizations, including 501(c)(3) charities and religious organizations. They advise and secure appropriate federal and state tax exemption determinations. Additionally, they establish private foundations especially those to enable donors here in the United States to send funds overseas. They help establish nonprofit organizations in all 50 states.

Montgomery, McCracken, Walker & Rhoads

123 South Broad Street, Philadelphia, PA 19109
Tel: 215-772-1500; FAX: 215-772-7620

New Jersey office: Liberty View, 457 Haddonfield Road, Suite 600,
Cherry Hill, NJ 08002
Tel: 856-488-7700; FAX: 856-488-7720, 413-473-4376
E-mail: info@mmwr.com; WWW: http://www.mmwr.com/index2.html

▶ Montgomery, McCracken has earned a reputation for special interest and experience in representing nonprofit, health care, and educational organizations. In response to the growing needs of such organizations for legal services, the firm has established a unique Health, Education and Nonprofit Law Department to provide comprehensive counsel and assistance. To ensure that their nonprofit clients reap all the benefits of being served by a full-service law firm, they maintain an "Exempt Organizations Group" composed of more than a dozen experienced attorneys from each of their other practice groups: tax, estates, employment law, employee benefits, environmental law, real estate, antitrust, bankruptcy, and, of course, general corporate and litigation practice. The firm calls on them regularly for assistance in areas such as tax-exempt bonds, charitable giving, employee retirement and "cafeteria" flexible benefit plans, labor negotiations and personnel policies, partnership agreements, environmental counseling and litigation, antitrust counseling and litigation, trademark registration and protection, insurance coverage and litigation, computer software contracts, and bankruptcy counseling. They help structure their organizations and activities for maximum efficiency within the applicable tax and corporate law, particularly with new income-generating projects. They counsel on the requirements for tax-exempt status, qualification as a public charity, lobbying and electioneering, unrelated business income, charitable giving, and charitable registration issues. They obtain IRS private letter rulings, including "unusual grant" rulings. They advise those seeking funds on the requirements for foundation grants, and advise foundations on their responsibilities and opportunities in grant making. They have also worked extensively with economic and housing development projects, including the federal Low-Income Housing Tax Credit.

The Department has created a number of special services for nonprofits, including: legal audit (a comprehensive "legal audit" procedure to assess the needs of present and prospective clients. It covers more than 40 items including articles of incorporation, bylaws, tax status, personnel policies, operating licenses, real estate agreements, investment policies, insurance, trademark or patent rights, and charitable giving forms); Gift-Aide® (a charitable giving consultation service to assist charities in planning the most advantageous gifts for the institutions and their donors. The service provides telephone and personal consultation, occasional seminars, written materials, and other assistance); Quick Questions® (a telephone legal consultation service to smaller nonprofits, with budgets of less than $2 million, to give managers quick answers to quick questions of general applicability. The resources of the entire firm are available to help nonprofit managers determine whether they are moving in the right direction. Includes assistance with bylaws, federal taxes [unrelated business income tax, Form 990, payroll taxes], charitable giving, charitable solicitation registration, fundraising issues, lobbying, electioneering, employment law [personnel policies, hiring and firing, employee benefits, compensation], volunteer services, real estate taxes, sales and use taxes, copyright and trademark, antitrust issues, leasing or buying property or equipment, government and other contracts, private foundation rules, insurance, bonding, nonprofit mergers, bankruptcy, and more); *Nonprofit Issues*® (a highly regarded monthly newsletter, providing a comprehensive early warning system for important legal matters that affect nonprofit organizations. It covers the most significant cases, statutes, regulations, and other developments— see separate listing under Periodicals); seminar programs (conducts estate planning seminars; firm lawyers participate regularly in seminars and other presentations on nonprofit law, and the firm sponsors its own annual "This Year in Nonprofit Law" seminar each spring). It also maintains an office in Newark, Delaware.

Law Offices of Michael P. Mosher

Legal Service for Tax-Exempt Organizations, 19 South LaSalle Street, Suite 1202, Chicago, IL 60603
Tel: 312-220-0019; FAX: 312-220-0700
E-mail: info@mosherlaw.com, mmosher@mosherlaw.com;
WWW: http://www.mosherlaw.com/

▶ As its major focus, Mosher & Associates concentrates on the full range of issues that face tax-exempt organizations and for-profit businesses: tax law at the federal and state levels, corporate governance and organization, mergers and start-ups, regulation and reporting, real estate purchase and use, employment, financial management, multistate and international registrations, and trademark and other intellectual property. The firm works on a wide range of legal matters, with a primary client base of religious, charitable, and educational organizations in the Chicago metropolitan area. The firm concentrates on legal services for nonprofit organizations, including incorporation, tax exemptions and charitable solicitation, directors and officers, unrelated business income, charitable gifts, and religious and church issues. The firm represents more than 150 nonprofit organizations. Most are Illinois not-for-profit corporations, but many are incorporated in other states and several foreign countries. Clients range from newly organized entities with limited financial resources, to multimillion dollar organizations with lengthy histories of service. The firm makes frequent presentations at conferences and seminars.

National Charitable Solicitations Registry

12408 Preserve Way, Reisterstown, MD 21136
Tel: 410-526-7301; FAX: 410-526-7302
E-mail: CharitableRegistry@Home.com (Terri Ackerman);
WWW: http://www.charitableregistry.com/

▶ The Charitable Registry provides the following services: alleviates the administrative burden, simplifies, and promotes compliance with state charitable solicitations filing requirements; provides initial and renewal registration services for charitable organizations on a state-by-state basis; and help you keep up with constantly changing state registration requirements (it is likely that a charitable organization must register in any state where it conducts solicitations).

Nill & Johnston

30021 Tomas Street, Suite 300, Rancho Santa Margarita, CA 93453
Tel: 800-971-4438, 949-589-4318; FAX: 949-589-4399
E-mail: snill@nill-johnston.com (Stephen C. Nill, Esq.),
Stephen_Nill@CharityChannel.com

▶ Nill & Johnston is a southern California law firm that practices in the following fields: the law of tax-exempt organizations, planned giving, and estate planning. They offer expertise in nonprofit law, including corporate formation and dissolution, organization structure, compliance with federal and state exemption laws, taxation issues, risk management, personnel issues, and foundation issues. They have advised more than 100 nonprofit organizations.

Nonprofit Incorporators

14596 Round Valley Drive, Sherman Oaks, CA 91403-4631
Tel: 818-380-0222; FAX: 818-380-0234
E-mail: nonprofitinc@pobox.com; WWW: http://www.not-for-profit.org/npi/npi.html, http://www.not-for-profit.org/index.html

▶ This law firm exclusively serves small and start-up nonprofit organizations. Nonprofit Incorporators' primary service is their flat-fee incorporation and tax-exemption service for new nonprofits. For a flat fee of $1,400, they prepare, process, and follow up on every document a new 501(c)(3), 501(c)(4), 501(c)(6), or 501(c)(7) organization (i.e., a charitable, educational, religious, scientific, labor, lobbying, foundation, trade group, social club, or similar public service entity) must file with the Internal Revenue Service and state agencies in order to be recognized as a legal entity and to collect tax-deductible contributions. The only other charges to you are the filing fees required by the various government agencies. They serve a variety of other legal needs of nonprofits, all at a low cost commensurate with the financial resources of nonprofits. These services include board reorganization and other organizational changes; serving as general counsel to nonprofits; conflict resolution; structuring collaborative ventures between nonprofits and for-profits that satisfy IRS and California Attorney General's office requirements for nonprofits; general guidance on compliance with Internal Revenue Service rules applicable to nonprofits (i.e., maintaining tax-exempt status); counseling private foundations on the special rules applicable to them, including avoidance of excise taxes and penalties; revisions (amendments) and restatements of articles of incorporation and bylaws; conversions of for-profit corporations to nonprofits, and vice versa; dissolutions of nonprofits; guidance handling "unrelated business income"; corporate maintenance; and bringing corporate records up to date.

Nonprofit Works

10 Gibbs Street, Suite 250, Rochester, NY 14604
Tel: 716-546-2420; FAX: 716-546-2423
E-mail: mail@nonprofitworks.com;
WWW: http://www.form990online.com/contact.asp

▶ This organization provides nonprofits with affordable expertise in management, grant writing, communications, and computer training. One of its services is the Form 990 online Web site, which is designed to allow nonprofits to comply with the new IRS public disclosure regulations for federal Forms 990 and 1023.

Perlman & Perlman, Esqs.

220 Fifth Avenue, 7th Floor, New York, NY 10001
Tel: 212-889-0575; FAX: 212-889-5228
E-mail: FRISCOdANC@aol.com (Ed Mazlish);
WWW: www.perlmanandperlman.com

▶ The law firm of Perlman & Perlman specializes in counseling nonprofit organizations, professional fund-raising counsel, and professional solicitors and vendors who service these organizations. The firm specializes in advising charities and their agents in all aspects of fund raising, from incorporating and setting up bylaws, to applying to the IRS for tax exemption, to complying with state registration requirements on soliciting and on issuing charitable gift annuities, to defending state enforcement actions brought by attorneys general throughout the United States (including investigations and full-blown litigation), to bringing preemptive lawsuits against state regulations of charitable entities that they believe are unconstitutional. Clients have included a diverse group of religious organizations, health and welfare charities, educational organizations, private foundations, community foundations, professional fund-raising counselors, professional solicitors, commercial co-venturers, and numerous vendors who provide services to the philanthropic sector. They also perform contract work for charities, including employment agreements and setting up commercial co-venture and affinity card deals. Additionally, they advise charities with regard to intellectual property issues, particularly trademark issues. The contract and intellectual property work merges in the Internet context, where they also have done many deals for their clients, and they keep very abreast of all developments in e-commerce and the Internet, particularly (though not exclusively) as it pertains to charities.

Pfau Englund Nonprofit Law, PC

1451 Juliana Place, Alexandria, VA 22304-1516
Tel: 703-751-8203; FAX: 703-823-8692
E-mail: spfau@nonprofitlaw.com;
WWW: http://www.nonprofitlaw.com/pfaufirm.htm

▶ This firm provides legal services to a wide variety of nonprofit organizations—professional societies, charities, advocacy groups, and trade associations. The firm handles all necessary legal matters: incorporation and tax-exemption applications; tax-exempt status changes; antitrust issues; executive compensation contracts; lobbying rules and analysis; fund-raising regulations and negotiations; UBIT (unrelated business income tax); board governance matters; hotel, convention, technology, publishing, and other contract review, drafting, and negotiation; for-profit subsidiaries; and personnel and internal management issues.

Powers, Pyles, Sutter & Verville

1875 Eye Street NW, 12th Floor, Washington, DC 20006
Tel: 202-466-6550; FAX: 202-785-1756
E-mail: btesdahl@ppsv.com (Ben Tesdahl);
WWW: http://www.ppsv.com/

▶ The firm's nonprofit clients include schools, colleges, and universities; various health care organizations and institutions; medical research organizations; professional societies and business associations; public charities; private foundations; veterans' organizations; and advocacy organizations. The firm provides a full range of legal services for these tax-exempt organizations. Services include tax exemption and counseling (assist in establishing and qualifying tax-exempt organizations, under both federal and state law. Thereafter,

they provide ongoing counseling on tax, corporate, and other matters, including qualifications for public charity status, unrelated business income, reporting obligations, eligibility to conduct legislative and political campaign activities, and private inurement and private benefit. They are also experienced in preparing and monitoring private letter ruling requests to the IRS to ensure that desired transactions do not produce any adverse tax consequences. Additionally, they provide advice and counsel concerning many areas of the law as they relate to tax-exempt organizations, including leases, employment contracts, intellectual property matters, antitrust issues, labor law questions, nonprofit postal rate issues, and matters pertaining to employee benefits and executive compensation planning.); charitable giving and fund-raising programs (advise and assist in the development, maintenance, and expansion of charitable giving programs and other fund-raising activities. They work closely with charitable organizations in providing advice relating to contributions, record keeping, and reporting in the context of capital campaigns, special events, direct mail and annual fund programs, and planned giving. They work with clients and their prospective donors in designing appropriate vehicles for planned giving. They provide advice with respect to charitable remainder trusts, pooled income funds, charitable gift annuities, charitable lead trusts, charitable gifts of life insurance, and other major gifts [including bargain sales] of money and property. As part of their practice, they advise clients with respect to federal and state fund-raising regulation requirements, including the constitutionality of these laws. They also assist clients in registering and reporting under these laws.); tax controversy (represent clients in controversy matters at all levels within the IRS. During the audit phase, they assist clients in analyzing and evaluating factual and legal issues and in making persuasive presentations to local IRS officials and to the IRS national office in referrals for technical advice. In Coordinated Examination and Industry Specialization audits, they deal with IRS attorneys to narrow the issues and to minimize the need for litigation. Should litigation be necessary, they can handle cases in the various federal courts on any substantive or procedural issues affecting tax-exempt organizations.).

Pranschke & Holderle, LC, Attorneys at Law

1610 Des Peres Road, Suite 300, St. Louis, MO 63131-1813
Tel: 314-965-6455; FAX: 314-966-2144
E-mail: LPranschke@phlclaw.com (Leonard J. Pranschke),
EHolderle@phlclaw.com (Karl E. Holderle III);
WWW: http://www.phlclaw.com/

▶ Founded in 1982, the firm was established with an emphasis on the legal needs of nonprofit corporations, including charitable, religious, and educational organizations. Their attorneys have provided legal counsel to a wide variety of tax-exempt nonprofit organizations, including churches, church denominations and their related entities, mission and humanitarian organizations, primary and secondary schools, colleges, universities and seminaries, public and private foundations, hospitals, nursing homes, and continuing care retirement facilities. The spectrum of services provided by the firm for its clients includes the following: taxation (every effort is made to keep their attorneys current in those areas of tax law, such as unrelated business taxable income, tax-exempt status, and deductibility of charitable contributions. The firm assists its clients in obtaining and maintaining their tax-exempt status, and also provides guidance and direction to assist clients in identifying and capitalizing on opportunities for growth and expansion of their charitable activities, while avoiding pitfalls such as unrelated business taxable income. In addition, the firm has strong expertise in the areas of direct and deferred giving, including the establishment and ongoing maintenance of charitable remainder unitrusts, annuity trusts, pooled income funds, gift annuity programs, endowments, and donor advised funds.); corporate law (the firm regularly advises its clients on the formation of corporations and the ongoing operation of those corporations, and also provides continuing guidance and legal counsel to members, directors, and officers of corporations. To assist its clients in taking advantage of opportunities while avoiding the associated pitfalls, the firm has consulted with its clients to identify benefits to be gained from corporate restructuring and, where significant benefits are identified, has undertaken to create and implement new corporate structures for clients, including the creation of for-profit subsidiaries to enable clients to take full advantage of available opportunities.); securities law (the firm regularly advises its nonprofit clients concerning the unique application of federal and state securities laws to their operations. Another area of expertise is in the compliance of nonprofit organizations with federal and state regulation of deferred giving contracts, such as gift annuities, charitable remainder trusts, and pooled income funds.); employment law (the firm regularly advises its clients on many aspects of employment law, including preparation of employment agreements and policy manuals, employee benefits, including group health and cafeteria plans, and defense against employment-related claims, including those based on sexual misconduct or sexual harassment. The attorneys in the firm carefully monitor those areas of employment law, such as discrimination on the basis of religion, which are unique to religious nonprofit organizations, in order to be able to provide guidance to the firm's religious nonprofit clients in this unique area of employment law.); international nonprofit law (the firm represents mission and humanitarian organizations operating in foreign countries, advising them on how to obtain the legal right to engage in work in those nations; employment, visa, and tax issues; and how to comply with the wide range of local laws and regulations that affect their activities. The attorneys in the firm specialize in obtaining the legal right to operate in countries emerging from totalitarian rule and carefully monitor legal and religious freedom developments worldwide.).

Quarles & Brady

411 East Wisconsin Avenue, Suite 2550, Milwaukee, WI 53202
Tel: 414-277-5000; FAX: 414-271-3552
E-mail: jwd@quarles.com (John W. Daniels Jr.);
WWW: http://www.quarles.com/

▶ This firm provides services to tax-exempt organizations in the following areas: corporate (incorporation of nonprofit organizations; creation of charitable trusts; conversion of for-profit to nonprofit entities; mergers and acquisitions of nonprofit organizations; tax-exempt, taxable, and HUD financing; advising nonprofit boards of directors; conflict of interest policies); taxation (applications for recognition of exemption; revenue ruling requests; preparation of information returns and income tax returns; charitable gift planning, including charitable remainder trusts, charitable lead trusts, pooled income funds, and charitable gift annuities; property tax exemption appeals and litigation; charitable lotteries and auctions); employee benefits (tax-deferred annuities; qualified and nonqualified retirement plans; deferred compensation arrangements); labor and employment (employment issues, hiring, and terminations; wage-hour matters; employee handbooks); and intellectual property (trademark, service mark, trade name, and corporate name selection, adoption, registration, and protection; copyright registration and protection; obtaining and protecting utility, plant, and design patents; licensing intellectual property; protecting trade secrets).

The firm also maintains offices in Chicago; Phoenix; Madison, Wisconsin; Naples, Florida; and Tucson.

Rodriguez, Horii & Choi

777 South Figueroa Street, Suite 4207, Los Angeles, CA 90017
Tel: 213-892-7700; FAX: 213-892-7777
E-mail: al@rhclaw.com (Albert R. Rodriguez),
dwayne@rhclaw.com (Dwayne M. Horii), bill@rhclaw.com
(William C. Choi); WWW: http://www.rhclaw.com/

▶ The firm engages in the general practice of tax law. One of the areas of emphasis is exempt organizations. The firm has expertise in all aspects of nonprofit corporation law and the taxation of exempt organizations, including the unrelated business income tax, laws related to private foundations, intermediate sanctions, charitable remainder trusts, deferred giving, lobbying activities and state law corporate governance, charitable trust issues, and attorney general audits. The firm advises associations, charities, churches, museums, private foundations, cemeteries, social clubs, hospitals and health care organizations, scientific research organizations, educational organizations, and amateur sports organizations in connection with the foregoing matters.

Ropes & Gray

One International Place, Boston, MA 02110-2624
Tel: 617-951-7000, 617-951-7301 (Tax Practice);
FAX: 617-951-7050
E-mail: sjohnston@ropesgray.com (Susan A. Johnston);
WWW: http://www.ropesgray.com

▶ The Ropes & Gray tax practice group has experience in virtually every area of taxation. The tax department consists of both a general tax group and an employee benefits group (described separately under Employee Benefits). Within the general tax group, subgroups address a full complement of tax matters, including domestic and international tax planning and tax controversies, corporate mergers and acquisitions, partnerships and joint ventures, mutual funds and financial products, executive compensation and benefits, tax-exempt organizations, and tax-exempt financing. The firm maintains offices in Boston, Providence, and Washington, DC, and conference centers in New York and London.

Runquist & Zybach, LLP, Attorneys at Law

10618 Woodbridge Street, Toluca Lake, CA 91602
Tel: 818-760-8986, 714-990-5529
E-mail: lisa@runquist.com (Lisa A. Runquist);
WWW: http://www.runquist.com/

▶ This is a law firm specializing in nonprofit organizations, also as it relates to health care law, corporate law, and securities. They represent a diverse clientele, ranging from individuals, small nonprofits, and start-up business ventures to major public benefit and religious corporations.

Silk, Adler, & Colvin

Russ Building, 235 Montgomery Street, Suite 1220,
San Francisco, CA 94104
Tel: 415-421-7555; FAX: 415-421-0712
E-mail: SAC@silklaw.com, tm@silklaw.com (Terry Miller);
WWW: http://www.silklaw.com/

▶ This firm specializes in the law of nonprofit organizations. They represent domestic and international grant-making organizations, including family, independent, corporate, and community foundations; schools; trade and professional associations; churches and other religious organizations; social clubs; political committees; service clubs; and organizations devoted to social services, education, health care, environmental protection, peace and international understanding, human rights, arts and culture, animal welfare, and crime prevention. Services include formation of new charitable and other nonprofit organizations; determining whether a business or nonprofit form is most suitable to achieve their goals; form private and other grant-making foundations and prepare grant administration forms and procedures for them; alert clients to relevant legal developments, particularly those that may be useful to them in expanding or improving their programs; offer preventive advice so that clients may avoid troublesome legal issues in the future; counsel clients about distinctive matters that arise in the nonprofit sector, such as affiliation agreements; revisions to bylaws or other governing documents; endowment funds; fiscal sponsorship arrangements; nonprofit mergers, acquisitions, conversions and dissolutions; and compliance with applicable public support tests; advise clients regarding compliance with federal and state rules regulating the charitable sector, including limitations on charitable solicitations, lobbying, political activities, and commercial ventures; represent clients before regulatory agencies such as the Internal Revenue Service and state attorneys general; counsel directors and management of charitable and other nonprofit organizations with regard to the proper exercise of their fiduciary duties, and also counsel members of such organizations with regard to their rights and obligations; conduct periodic reviews of such organizations to assist directors and officers in satisfying their due diligence obligations; advise charitable grant makers, including private foundations and public charities, counseling them about general legal matters and also about specialized subjects such as program-related investments, self-dealing, donor-advised funds, expenditure responsibility requirements, and foreign public charity equivalence procedures; provide a full range of charitable giving services to both nonprofit organizations and individual philanthropists; assist nonprofit organizations to create and promote planned giving programs (donor presentations, specific gift proposals, gift structuring, and advice on gift program administration. They advise donors on the design and implementation of specific charitable gift opportunities to meet their charitable, financial, tax, and family goals. They assist individual philanthropists in evaluating their rights and obligations regarding family trusts and foundations. They also provide estate planning services—determining an individual's family and financial circumstances, designing a plan that meets his or her needs, and educating the client as to the estate planning process.).

Each lawyer in the firm is actively involved in law reform efforts in the nonprofit sector. They participate in committees of local, state, and national bar associations and act as advocates for the nonprofit sector by testifying at hearings held by the Internal Revenue Service, and by drafting recommendations for improvements in state and federal nonprofit laws and regulations. Each attorney also teaches nonprofit law and ethics.

Taxwise Giving (See Financial Management for full description)

Thompson & Thompson, PC, Attorneys at Law
39555 Orchard Hill Place, Suite 600, Novi, MI 48375
Tel: 248-348-5772; FAX: 248-449-2963
E-mail: thompson@exlaw.com; WWW: http://www.t-tlaw.com/
nonprof.shtml, http://www.npdomain.org/about.shtml,
http://www.taxexemptlaw.com

▶ This is a full-service law firm in representing charities, nonprofit organizations, and their related entities. They specialize in organization and restructuring of nonprofit organizations and their affiliated entities, obtaining qualification of tax-exempt status, rendering legal and tax opinions, and other transactional matters. They assist clients in obtaining and defending tax-exempt status (at both state and federal levels), forming and restructuring organizations, and providing a variety of legal and organizational consultation services. They represent nonprofit organizations of all kinds, not just charities. Their noncharitable nonprofit clients include: 501(c)(2) title holding companies; 501(c)(4) social welfare and action organizations; 501(c)(5) labor and agricultural organizations; 501(c)(6) business leagues and chambers of commerce; 501(c)(7) social and recreation clubs; 501(c)(10) fraternal orders and lodges; 501(c)(19) veterans posts and organizations; and other exempt and nonexempt organizations.

Since its founding, the firm has developed expertise in all areas of law necessary for the effective representation of nonprofit, tax-exempt organizations, and represents assorted and varied charities, including athletic associations, camps, churches, educational institutions, foundations (private and public), service clubs, historic societies, veterans groups, group homes, and the like. The firm's expertise extends to virtually all areas of civil transaction law applicable to nonprofit, tax-exempt organizations, including incorporation and organization of nonprofit, tax-exempt organizations, acquisitions and mergers, formation of subsidiaries and affiliates, and so on.

Tyler, Cooper & Alcorn, LLP
205 Church, P.O. Box 1936, New Haven, CT 06509-1910
Tel: 203-784-8481; FAX: 203-777-1181
E-mail: davislaw@connix.com (Lisa Nachmias Davis),
ldavi@cl-law.com, ldavis@connix.com;
WWW: http://www.tylercooper.com,
http://www.connix.com/~ldavis/,
http://www.connix.com/~ldavis/ faqtax.htm

▶ This firm provides legal services to nonprofit organizations including incorporation and tax exemption, issues regarding unrelated business income taxation, state tax exemptions, advice on deferred giving and deductibility issues, issues relating to corporate relationships such as subsidiaries, "supporting organizations," and the like; lobbying issues; excess benefit transactions and conflicts of interest to issues common to any organization: employment law problems, negotiating leases, and so on. Clients include public charities, private foundations, supporting organizations of various kinds, and non–501(c)(3) entities such as professional associations.

Webster, Chamberlain & Bean
Charles M. (Chip) Watkins, 1747 Pennsylvania Avenue NW,
Suite 1000, Washington, DC 20006-4693
Tel: 202-785-9500, ext. 34; FAX: 202-835-0243
E-mail: cwatkins@wc-b.com

▶ This law firm provides comprehensive legal services to trade associations, charities, churches and other religious organizations, and advocacy groups. Corporate law, charitable solicitation registration, tax law, election law, employment law and employee benefits, copyright and trademark matters, and trade regulation are among the specialties of attorneys in the firm.

Weinberg & Jacobs, LLP

Tax Exempt Organizations Practice Group, One Central Plaza, Suite 1200, 11300 Rockville Pike, Rockville, MD 20852
Tel: 301-468-5500; FAX: 301-468-5504
E-mail: paladin@wjlaw.com (Mark Weinberg, co-manager, Tax Exempt Organizations Practice Group and the Estate Planning and Administration Practice Group);
WWW: http://wjlaw.com/TaxExem.html

▶ They bring extensive experience to the representation of tax-exempt organizations, including 501(c)(3) charities and professional associations, 501(c)(4) social welfare organizations, 501(c)(6) trade associations, and other exempt groups. They provide advice to domestic and overseas nonprofits (public charities, private foundations, social action groups, and trade/professional associations, large and small) on initial organization, obtaining tax-exempt status, compliance with federal tax rules (including IRS audits), and governance. The firm organizes and secures appropriate federal, state, and local tax exemptions for a wide variety of exempt groups. They also create taxable subsidiaries, restructure contracts so as to minimize unrelated business income tax, and revise nonprofit governance systems for existing organizations. They provide tax planning for both the organizations and their prospective donors, configure nonqualified executive compensation, guide private foundations through the specific constraints applicable to them, and advise charities, social welfare groups, and trade and professional associations on related issues such as tax limits on lobbying and campaign activity by tax-exempt entities. Their attorneys have handled such specific matters as creation and operation of family private foundations, planned giving, mergers and acquisitions of nonprofits, creation of for-profit subsidiaries, and reorganizations. Clients include many public charities (such as public broadcasters, a national academy, and universities and museums here and abroad), private foundations, social welfare groups, trade and professional associations, and religious institutions. U.S. fund raising for overseas charities is a specialty.

Welty & Blair, PC

2111 Wilson Boulevard, Suite 550, Arlington, VA 22201-3051
Tel: 703-276-0114 (voice mail after business hours);
FAX: 703-522-9107
E-mail: info@weltyblair.com;
WWW: http://www.weltyblair.com/ attorneys.htm

▶ Primary practice areas include nonprofit corporations and tax-exempt organizations.

Weycer, Kaplan, Pulaski & Zuber, PC

1400 Summit Tower, Eleven Greenway Plaza, Houston, TX 77046
Tel: 713-961-9045; FAX: 713-961-5341
E-mail: fsommerville@wkpz.com (Frank Sommerville, Shareholder for Nonprofit Organizations); WWW: http://www.wkpz.com/

▶ Weycer, Kaplan, a 12-lawyer firm, provides full legal services to nonprofit organizations, including tax, human resources, corporate, and real estate.

GENERAL RESOURCES

General Exempt Organization Law *(See also Incorporation)*

Advising Nonprofits, 4th Edition
ALLEN R. BROMBERGER AND CATHERINE L. WOODMAN (LAWYERS ALLIANCE FOR NEW YORK, 1995)

▶ A comprehensive guide to legal issues that arise in the operation of nonprofit organizations, including fund raising, employee matters, political activity, and profit-making subsidiaries. *Softcover, $75 (plus $5 shipping)*

The Guide for Nonprofit Organizations: Legal, Organizational, Financial, and Accounting Information for Nonprofit Organizations (Handbook)
DON KRAMER AND VIRGINIA SIKES ET AL. (NONPROFIT ISSUES)

▶ This handbook outlines the basic legal, organizational, financial, and accounting issues regarding the start-up and ongoing operation of a nonprofit organization. Such critical issues as obtaining federal recognition of nonprofit status, charitable solicitation registration, basic financial statements, statement of activity, and balance sheets are outlined. A complete overview of nonprofit board responsibilities and financing requirements are discussed. Additionally, taxation and payroll requirements for nonprofit organizations with or without employees are included. The handbook also contains an information directory of the various agencies. *Softcover, 44 pages, $4 (plus shipping and handling)*

Law & Taxation, Leadership Series, Volume I
JILL MUEHRCKE, ED. (THE SOCIETY OF NONPROFIT ORGANIZATIONS, 1993)

▶ In articles selected from the *Nonprofit World* journal, authors give practical advice on such topics as how to handle an IRS audit, how to avoid litigation, and how to safeguard your organization's tax-exempt status. *$20 (Nonmember), $17 (Member) (plus $4.50 shipping)*

Law & Taxation, Leadership Series, Volume II
JILL MUEHRCKE, ED. (THE SOCIETY OF NONPROFIT ORGANIZATIONS, 1993)

▶ This collection of articles from *Nonprofit World* (November 1989–September 1993) discusses such topics as the Americans with Disabilities Act, liability insurance for nonprofits, how to avoid litigation, and how to safeguard your tax-exempt status. *$20 (Nonmember), $17 (Member) (plus $4.50 shipping)*

The Law of Tax-Exempt Organizations, 7th Edition
BRUCE R. HOPKINS (JOHN WILEY & SONS, 1998)

▶ Nonprofit organizations are subject to a complex set of regulations and laws that reflect the diverse organizations that are covered under these rules: charitable organizations, social welfare organizations, memberships organizations, advocacy groups, and many more. These organizations face a special set of rules governing everything from how they charter their organization, to their methods of measuring unrelated business income, and how they lobby (and if, in fact, they should continue to be allowed to lobby). Nonprofit lawyers, accountants, and directors need an easy-to-use reference work in understandable language to help them comprehend the issues and make informed decisions. This comprehensive, authoritative examination on the law of taxation of exempt organizations is widely recognized as the classic book on this subject. It provides detailed documentation and citations, including references to regulations, rulings, cases, and tax literature (including current articles and tax law review notes); an exhaustive index; Internal Revenue Code citations; tables of cases; and IRS rulings. It is supplemented annually. *Hardcover, 1,000 pages, $155.00*

The Legal Answer Book for Nonprofit Managers
BRUCE R. HOPKINS (JOHN WILEY & SONS, 1996)

▶ This is a business law strategies book that looks at different legal and legitimate strategies that nonprofit managers can use in running their organizations. Experienced professionals, actively involved in the nonprofit sector, present a variety of creative strategies to maintaining and enhancing an organization's activities and effectiveness. It provides workable solutions to nonprofit managers' most pressing concerns and problems including private inurement, lobbying limitations, board governance, establishing spin-off subsidiary organizations, liability, and directors' insurance. It is revised annually to keep subscribers up to date on the latest trends and developments. Designed to help nonprofit managers and their professional consultants, this comprehensive reference presents—in plain English—practical answers to the most frequently asked questions about nonprofit organizations. Nonprofit managers will find a wealth of workable, real-world solutions to their most pressing problems and concerns, including private inurement, lobbying limitations, subsidiary organizations, strategic alliances with for-profit and nonprofit organizations, board governance and responsibilities, liability insurance, planned giving vehicles, and much more. Written and edited by a leading legal authority on tax-exempt organizations, it also offers creative strategies for enhancing and expanding a nonprofit organization's activities. Periodic updates will keep readers informed of the latest trends and developments in the nonprofit sector. *Softcover, 285 pages, $79.95*

Nonprofit Enterprises: Law and Taxation
MARY E. PHELAN (CLARK BOARDMAN CALLAGHAN/WEST GROUP, 1991)

▶ This treatise explains in precise detail the effect of the many recent tax acts on nonprofit entities; accounting methods for reporting financial activities; use of tax-exempt bonds for financing; consequences of private foundations status; tax consequences of donors; and the concept of the unrelated business taxable income for hospitals, colleges, museums, and other nonprofit organizations. You'll also find the necessary forms for obtaining tax-exempt status and tax return forms for annual reporting purposes for several different types of exempt organizations. *Softcover, 3,500 pages, $325*

The Nonprofit Handbook, National Edition

GARY M. GROBMAN (WHITE HAT COMMUNICATIONS, 1998)

▶ The definitive handbook on starting and running a nonprofit corporation in the United States, this is a valuable resource for nonprofit executive staff, nonprofit board members, attorneys who practice nonprofit law, accountants who advise nonprofit organizations, and persons who plan to form a new nonprofit organization. *The Nonprofit Handbook* includes information about current laws, court decisions, and regulations that apply to nonprofits; practical advice on running a nonprofit corporation; sample corporate bylaws; and sources of information on how to start up a new nonprofit. This handbook is based on *The Pennsylvania Non-Profit Handbook,* a book originally published in 1992 with the help of more than two dozen nonprofit executives and attorneys and now in its fourth edition. Each easy-to-read chapter includes a synopsis, useful tips, and resources to obtain more information. Preaddressed postcards are included to obtain important government forms, instruction booklets, and informational publications. This reference tool includes information about current laws, court decisions, and regulations that apply to nonprofits—two full pages devoted to each state and the District of Columbia; practical advice on running a nonprofit, including chapters on communications, fund raising, lobbying, personnel, fiscal management, nonprofit ethics, and 19 other chapters; information on applying successfully for federal and state tax-exempt status; how to write effective grant applications; how to hire and fire; Internet resources for nonprofits; how to develop a strategic plan; and recent developments affecting nonprofits. *Softcover, 302 pages, $32.95*

Nonprofit Law Dictionary

BRUCE R. HOPKINS (JOHN WILEY & SONS, 1996)

▶ The vocabulary of nonprofit organizations is difficult for nonprofit managers to understand because so much of the activities of nonprofits are defined by laws and regulations; technical terms such as UBIT (unrelated business income taxation), pooled income fund, and the Commerciality Doctrine may mean something to lawyers and accountants practicing in this area, but they bewilder and intimidate laypeople running nonprofit organizations. It is intended for nonprofit executives, directors, and managers; fund-raising professionals; trustees and officers of nonprofit organizations; consultants; volunteers; accountants; and lawyers. Written by one of the country's leading authorities on tax-exempt organizations, this book is the first A-to-Z desktop reference on law and tax terminology for nonprofit managers, defining over 1,400 legal and tax terms in plain, straightforward English. *Softcover, 376 pages, $37.95*

Nonprofit Leadership and the Law (Handbook)

DON KRAMER, JEFFREY GARSON, AND ROBERTA SNOW (PHILADELPHIA VOLUNTEER LAWYERS FOR THE ARTS/NONPROFIT ISSUES)

▶ Written in a style that is accessible to both attorneys and laypersons, this handbook provides readers with the vital information needed to develop legally sound governance and operational practices. It includes discussion on topics such as state and federal laws that govern tax-exempt organizations, ethical and legal obligations

of board members and executive directors, business contacts and key financial management challenges, programmatic collaborations and joint ventures between nonprofits and for-profits, fund-raising realities, and organizational change including corporate restructuring. Chapters cover: Basic Legal Structures; Directors Rights and Responsibilities; Oversight of Finances; Liability Issues; Oversight of Operations; Organizational Change; Special Tax Issues; Rules Regulating Fundraising; and Deciding to Become a Board Member. *Softcover, 64 pages, $24.95*

The Nonprofit Management Handbook: Operating Policies and Procedures *(See General Management section for full description)*

A Nonprofit Organization Operating Manual *(See General Management section for full description)*

Nonprofit Organizations' Business Forms, Disk Edition

EDITORIAL STAFF (JOHN WILEY & SONS, 1997) (BOOK AND SOFTWARE)

▶ Save time and money preparing essential documents. On one easy-to-use disk, you'll find over 300 proven forms at your fingertips, prepared by nonprofit experts for nonprofit managers and their advisers. Included are sample forms such as articles of incorporation, bylaws, and agreements; checklists for tracking unrelated business income, maintaining tax-exempt status, and managing fund-raising programs; worksheets for accounting, budgeting, and completing IRS forms; and sample documents for charitable giving and internal management policies. It includes a 96-page manual and is revised periodically. *Softcover (with 3½" IBM-compatible disk), $130*

Representing Nonprofit Organizations (formerly Representing the Nonprofit Organization) (Workbook/Manual)

MARY E. PHELAN (CLARK BOARDMAN CALLAGHAN/WEST GROUP, 1999)

▶ This workbook covers organizing and operating a nonprofit organization; how charitable organizations can obtain and maintain public charity status; the consequences of private foundation status—and how to avoid prohibited activities and their associated penalty taxes; the extent to which nonprofit organizations may engage in lobbying activities or political campaigns without jeopardizing their status; potential liability of directors of nonprofit organizations and how to avoid it; accounting principles applicable to nonprofit organizations; practical approaches to handling unrelated business taxable income; and much more. It discusses establishing a nonprofit organization, including incorporation, obtaining and maintaining tax-exempt status, and obtaining and maintaining public-charity status. It also includes an explanation and consequences of private-foundation status, tax consequences to donors, concept and reporting of unrelated business taxable income, lobbying, liability, generally accepted accounting principles, and procedures to dissolve and liquidate a nonprofit organization. Cumulative supplement; updated annually. *Loose-leaf binder, 500 pages, $120*

The Second Legal Answer Book for Nonprofit Organizations (Nonprofit Law, Finance, and Management Series)

BRUCE R. HOPKINS (JOHN WILEY & SONS, 1998)

► In an increasingly competitive environment, nonprofit managers and their advisors need to know not only the law as it is written, but more importantly how to work with it and within its boundaries to maintain and enhance their organizations' activities. This book explores the many legal strategies that nonprofit managers can use in running their organizations effectively. Tailored exclusively to aid nonprofit managers and their professional advisors, this comprehensive reference presents—in plain English—guidance on the latest trends and developments in nonprofit law today. Nonprofit executives will appreciate the question-and-answer format and real-world, workable solutions to some of the key challenges facing nonprofit organizations, including intermediate sanctions, the competition and commerciality doctrines, partnerships and joint ventures, private foundation rules, disclosure and distribution rules, annual report requirements, and much more. Written by one of today's leading legal authorities on tax-exempt organizations, this book is a useful guide to understanding areas of statutes, regulations, and other laws governing tax-exempt organizations. Periodic updates will keep readers informed of the current statutes and regulations in the nonprofit sector, and citations will guide readers to more detailed references. *Softcover, 422 pages, $79.95*

Accountability and Ethics

Intermediate Sanctions: Curbing Nonprofit Abuse
BRUCE R. HOPKINS AND D. BENSON TESDAHL (JOHN WILEY & SONS, 1997)

► In the wake of recent nonprofit scandals, the United Way being the most notorious, Congress has raised the stakes for nonprofit organizations who stray too far from the law by enacting intermediate sanctions. The most important legislation to impact the nonprofit sector since 1969, intermediate sanctions legislation doesn't simply revoke an organization's priviledged tax-exempt status. It also imposes financial penalties. *Intermediate Sanctions* highlights major IRS legislation for dealing with a nonprofit organization's tax-exempt status. Easy-to-read accounts are given on the operations of all public charities and their boards, which outline excess benefit transactions, revenue sharing arrangements, loans, partnerships, and other areas that might invite government scrutiny. Bruce R. Hopkins and D. Benson Tesdahl examine the impact of these sanctions on the nonprofit sector. Tackling crucial issues resulting from the new legislation, Hopkins and Tesdahl equip readers with the vital information needed to understand the new rules and work with them effectively. What are the requirements of the new intermediate sanctions law? What is the definition of an excess benefit transaction? How will financial penalties be determined? How will sanctions be applied? What are the law's expanded reporting and disclosure requirements? What can nonprofits do to plan for compliance? These are just some of the questions you may be asking about intermediate sanctions, the most important legislation to affect the nonprofit sector in a generation. This unique guide tackles these crucial issues and more, equipping you with the vital information you need to understand these new rules and work with them effectively. Written by two of the country's leading authorities on tax-exempt organizations, *Intermediate Sanctions* reviews the history and background of the act, and systematically examines how this body of law promises to affect the operations of public charities and other tax-exempt organizations. Clear and direct in approach, the book features down-to-earth examples throughout,

making it an essential practical resource for lawyers, accountants, managers, and others working in the nonprofit arena. *Softcover, 194 pages, $69.95*

Advocacy, Lobbying, Political Activity, and Government Relations

Association Political Involvement (Including PACs)
(Background Kit)
(AMERICAN SOCIETY OF ASSOCIATION EXECUTIVES, 1995)

► This background kit includes information on forming and managing a PAC, alternatives to PACs, fund raising, criteria for endorsing candidates, legal and tax issues, and case studies of associations' experiences in the political arena. *Spiral bound, 173 pages, $66 (Nonmember), $47 (Member) (plus $6.25 shipping)*

Being a Player; A Guide to the IRS Lobbying Regulations for Advocacy Charities
GAIL HARMON, JESSICA LADD, AND ELEANOR A. EVANS (ALLIANCE FOR JUSTICE, 1995)

► This book explains how IRS rules apply to all types of lobbying, including grassroots lobbying, calls to action, referenda and ballot initiatives, mass-media communications, and foundation grants. *Softcover, 57 pages, $15*

Charity, Advocacy and the Law
BRUCE R. HOPKINS (JOHN WILEY & SONS, 1992)

► This book examines what nonprofit organizations can and cannot do to affect public policy. It defines various forms of advocacy as well as prohibited activities and explains how exempt functions are carried out. It includes sample forms from real-world examples and tables of cases, IRS rulings, and Federal Election Commission rulings. It includes appendices, tables, glossary, and index. It is supplemented annually. *Hardcover, 704 pages, $145*

E-Advocacy for Nonprofits: The Law of Lobbying and Election Related Activity on the Net
ELIZABETH KINGSLEY, GAIL HARMON, JOHN POMERANZ, AND KAY GUINANE (ALLIANCE FOR JUSTICE, 2000)

► A fundamental change is happening in the way nonprofit organizations engage in grassroots activism, driven by the growth of the Internet. However, while many organizations have recognized the Internet's power and have already begun to use it for organizing and advocacy, the law governing these activities has been slow in expanding to encompass these new techniques for advocacy. This guide tries to fill the gap, offering guidance, in plain language, about how nonprofits can use the Internet to participate in the policy-making process while staying within the law. *Softcover, 69 pages, $25*

Foundations and Lobbying: Safe Ways to Affect Public Policy
JOHN A. EDIE (COUNCIL ON FOUNDATIONS, 1991)

► Can foundations undertake lobbying without being penalized? What are the special rules for different foundation types? Learn the definitions of lobbying and exceptions to the definition, special rules for private foundations, regulatory schemes governing electing and nonelecting charities, and rules affecting expenditures by membership organizations. Also included is a list of references and appendices on private foundation and public charity regulations, background and summary leading to the 1990 regulations, tax on lobbying expenditures, and key definitions. *Softcover, $30 (Nonmember), $20 (Member)*

Guide to the Lobbying Disclosure Act

MICHAEL TRISTER (ALLIANCE FOR JUSTICE, 1995)

▶ With the passage of the 1995 Lobbying Disclosure Act, nonprofits have many questions about how to comply. This memorandum describes the two tests used to determine whether an organization is required to register and report, summarizes the types of activities that are covered, and outlines the enforcement of the act. *Softcover, 6 pages, Free*

Lobby? You? Yes, Your Nonprofit Organization Can! It Should! Elect to Come Under the 1976 Lobby Law (Pamphlet)

BOB SMUCKER (INDEPENDENT SECTOR, 1988)

▶ This bestseller booklet is a basic primer on why legislative work is important and how you can get started in using this tool to advance your organization's cause. *Lobby? You?* is written in easy-to-understand language designed to be useful for staff, trustees, and volunteers of 501(c)(3) public charities. The booklet also includes basic information on lobbying laws governing nonprofits. Take advantage of the bulk discount and distribute to each of your volunteers. It offers "how-to" guidelines for advancing causes by letting legislators know what grassroots organizations want and why. It also discusses federal lobbying rules for nonprofits and encourages groups to elect to come under the generous provisions of the 1976 Lobby Law. *12 pages, $1.25 (Nonmember), $.88 (Member) (plus $2.50 shipping)*

Lobbying by Associations

(AMERICAN SOCIETY OF ASSOCIATION EXECUTIVES, 1998)

▶ This background kit presents a wide range of information related to organizational lobbying; grassroots lobbying, forming and managing coalitions, state lobbying, working with congressional staffs, and evaluating legal and tax issues are among the featured topics. *Spiral bound, 195 pages, $66 (Nonmember), $44 (Member)*

Myth v. Fact

THOMAS ASHER (ALLIANCE FOR JUSTICE, 1995)

▶ From immunization to school reform, from clean air to fair housing, America's nonprofit organizations have played a powerful role in making change happen; as advocates, they've uncovered the problems, publicized the stories, helped frame the issues, created programs, and expanded public understanding. As their partners in the process of change, nonprofits have looked to the country's grant-making foundations; the myth persists, however, that foundations cannot support nonprofits doing advocacy and that nonprofits should not even discuss this aspect of their work with potential funders. This publication reiterates and emphasizes the fact that foundations have played a vital role in almost every important social movement and that their right to award grants to charities addressing critical issues is plainly protected by the IRS. It corrects these myths with clear and concise information about the laws governing grant making. *Softcover, 26 pages, $20*

Nonprofit Lobbying Guide: Advocating Your Cause and Getting Results, 2nd Edition

BOB SMUCKER (INDEPENDENT SECTOR 1998)

▶ *Nonprofit Lobbying Guide* demonstrates the many ways nonprofits can use lobbying to advance their causes in federal, state, and local legislatures. Author Bob Smucker draws upon his more than 25 years of experience as a lobbyist for charitable organizations to give jargon-free explanations of the laws governing lobbying limits, lobbying with private foundation and corporate grants, reporting to the IRS, and education efforts during a politcal campaign. Smucker also offers insightful tips on how to mobilize citizen support—and get results—at all stages of the legislative process, from the first contact with legislators to the final vote. You'll learn techniques for recruiting and organizing others into highly effective coalitions that achieve successful legislative outcomes. This second edition includes advice on using e-mail and the Internet to recruit volunteers, as well as updated information on the most current IRS regulations. This definitive guide to nonprofit lobbying is a must-have for nonprofits already engaged in public policy work—and an invaluable resource for nonprofits that want to get started. *Softcover, 144 pages, $12.00 (Member), $16.00 (Nonmember)*

The Rules of the Game: An Election Year Legal Guide for Nonprofit Organizations

GREGORY L. COLVIN AND LOWELL FINLEY (ALLIANCE FOR JUSTICE, 1996)

▶ This user-friendly report reviews the basic tax and election laws that govern nonprofits in an election year and explains the right (and wrong) ways to organize specific voter education activities. It explores topics such as voter registration, candidate questionnaires, voter guides, and candidate debates and forums. *Softcover, 52 pages, $20.00*

Seize the Initiative

GREGORY L. COLVIN AND LOWELL FINLEY (ALLIANCE FOR JUSTICE, 1996)

▶ The initiative/referendum has regained popularity as more and more citizen groups use the process to advance their issues. *Seize the Initiative* answers frequently asked questions by 501(c)(3) nonprofit organizations on the legal do's and don'ts of participating in ballot initiative campaigns. *Softcover, 60 pages, $20.00*

Worry-Free Lobbying for Nonprofits: How to Use the 501(h) Election to Maximize Effectiveness (Brochure)

(ALLIANCE FOR JUSTICE, 1999)

▶ This brochure describes how nonprofits and the foundations that support them can take advantage of the clear and generous provisions in federal law encouraging their lobbying activities via the 501(h) election. If you ever had questions about the appropriateness of lobbying by 501(c)(3) organizations—or if you have them now—this plain-language action guide has your answers. This publication was prepared so public charities and the foundations that support them will take full advantage of the clear and generous provisions in federal law that encourage their investment in the development of informed social policy through lobbying. *Worry-Free Lobbying for Nonprofits* demonstrates that lobbying is legitimate, encouraged, and protected; effective and essential, but often discouraged because of misconceptions; supported by the IRS under 501(h) at more generous levels than those to which most public charities now limit themselves; and legally fundable, within defined limits, by private and community foundations. The guide defines and describes lobbying, including principal exceptions. It gives answers to the nine most frequently asked questions about 501(h) election. It provides authoritative sources and opinions on 501(h) election, and it even has a copy of the simple one-page form you need to file to elect or revoke election. *12 pages, Free*

Charitable Giving

How Much Really Is Tax Deductible?—Deductibility of Payments Made to Charities (Booklet)
(INDEPENDENT SECTOR, 1997)

▶ This handbook helps nonprofit organizations and donors understand exactly how much is tax deductible for gifts, incentive programs, fund-raising events, athletic events, and other challenging situations. This version is updated with the latest IRS requirements. It is handy, concise guide for nonprofit organizations and donors alike. *28 pages, $7 (Nonmember), $5 (Member)*

Model Major Gift Policy Manual, 7th Edition
(Manual and Software)
STEPHEN C. NILL (AMERICAN PHILANTHROPY REVIEW, 1997)

▶ This edition has been extensively revised to reflect sweeping charitable giving changes imposed on U.S. nonprofit organizations by the Taxpayer Relief Act of 1997. It also contains a newly revised section on compliance with the often misunderstood provisions of the Philanthropy Protection Act. With the recent changes in the tax, securities, and other laws, it is more important than ever for U.S. nonprofit organizations to protect themselves—and their board members, officers, staff members, and benefactors—by ensuring that gift policies and procedures comply with IRS guidelines and other laws, industry practices, and ethical standards. Even if a nonprofit organization has a gift policy manual, it would take hours for its legal counsel to research and draft the necessary revisions to bring it into conformity with recent changes in the law that the *Model Major Gift Policy Manual* already tracks. The software consists of an extensively researched manual available in nearly every popular word processing file format. It is updated periodically. *Softcover, 59 pages, $189*

Outright Charitable Gifts: Explanation, Substantiating, Forms
CONRAD TEITELL (TAXWISE GIVING)

▶ This volume tells you everything you need to know about outright charitable gifts: (1) explains the general tax rules for deducting all types of outright charitable gifts, (2) translates the valuation and new substantiation rules into plain English, (3) tells about the various penalties for noncompliance and how to avoid them, (4) gives forms for reporting to the IRS, (5) explains the appraisal and appraisal summary requirements, and gives specimen forms, (6) tells how and when charitable institutions must sign a donor's appraisal summary, (7) details the valuation rules for all types of property, (8) explains the substantiation requirements for charitable gifts, and (9) gives the rules for gifts by individuals, partnerships, and corporations. Sections include Explanation, Forms and Miscellaneous Aids, Valuation, and Substantiation. It is supplemented and revised annually. *Loose-leaf binder, $175/year (plus $7 shipping)*

Planned Giving: Management, Marketing, and Law
(See Deferred and Planned Giving, Resource Development section, for full description)

Pledges to Nonprofit Organizations: Are They Enforceable and Must They Be Enforced? (Booklet)
(PROGRAM ON PHILANTHROPY & THE LAW, NEW YORK UNIVERSITY SCHOOL OF LAW)

▶ This booklet examines the legal theories by which the courts enforce charitable pledges and the impact of other areas of contract law. It also explores the duty of trustees, directors, or officers of nonprofit organizations to enforce such charitable pledges in the context of the duties imposed on nonprofit managers. The duty analysis is applied to practical situations with which charitable trustees, directors, and officers are frequently confronted. *$9.50 (includes shipping)*

Taxwise Giving Booklets
CONRAD TEITELL (TAXWISE GIVING)

▶ This is a series of booklets for donors on tax-encouraged giving with up-to-the-minute information on the latest tax laws. All booklets can be imprinted with your institution's name and address. The series includes these titles: *Planning Your Estate, Making Your Will, God's Will Is Not Subject to Probate, Personal and Financial Records, Taxwise Charitable Giving, You Can Be a Philanthropist, The Joys of Giving, The Charitable Remainder Trust, The Charitable Remainder Annuity Trust, The Charitable Gift Annuity, The Deferred Payment Gift Annuity, Pooled Income Fund Gifts, Counselor's Tax Guide to Charitable Contributions, Women's Financial Planner, The Charitable Lead Trust,* and *A Guide to Living Wills.* Bulk discounts are available. *$.93 each (12-page booklets), $1.01 each (24-page booklets), $1.05 each (32-page booklets), $4.95 (The Charitable Lead Trust) (plus $4.50 shipping)*

Teitell's Substantiating Charitable Gifts: The Complete Compliance Manual
CONRAD TEITELL (TAXWISE GIVING)

▶ This book has everything you need to know and do about the complicated and overlapping rules on substantiating, reporting, and disclosing charitable gifts, for income, gift, and estate tax returns. Recent changes in the law impose additional rules, but long-existing regulations must also be followed. Teitell figures it all out, puts it all together, and shows you how to comply with all the rules. *Softcover, 635 pages, $195 (plus $7 shipping)*

Charitable Solicitation and Fund Raising

The First Legal Answer Book for Fund-Raisers
BRUCE R. HOPKINS (JOHN WILEY & SONS, 2000)

▶ As the competition for dollars grows increasingly intense, managers and fund raisers need to know how to work with business law. This book looks at different legal strategies that fund raisers can use to optimize their return without jeopardizing their exempt status or donors' goodwill. It provides an accessible approach to understanding the various laws and offers solutions to enhance an organization's wealth and effectiveness. *Softcover, 320 pages, $49.95*

Fund-Raising Regulation: A State-by-State Handbook of Registration Forms, Requirements, and Procedures (Book and Forms Package)
BETSY H. BUSH AND SETH PERLMAN, EDS. (JOHN WILEY & SONS, 1996)

▶ Almost every state has a Charitable Solicitation Act that spells out fund-raising rules and regulations; nonprofits, fund raisers, and professional solicitors are required to register with each state, yet many do not because registration is such a time-consuming, expensive burden. As state governments enact more regulation and enforce it with greater frequency, nonprofits and fund raisers alike need to perform a "compliance check" to determine if their papers are in order. This guide presents all necessary fund-raising registration information for nonprofit organizations, fund-raising counsels, and professional solicitors in each state (with whom to file, when to file, what to file; includes attachments, registration costs, validity and expiration dates, and tips on filling out the forms). It contains a complete set of forms for every state, designed to be easily photocopied for quick filing (also includes an "exceptions" packet for nonstandard forms on colored or odd-sized paper), information about annual reporting requirements, exemptions for specific categories of exempt organizations (e.g., religious organizations), essential definitions for cause-related marketing (commercial co-ventures), and more. It helps avoid fines, penalties, and adverse publicity resulting from improperly completed forms, late filings, and failure to comply with ever-changing state laws. It is intended for lawyers, nonprofit executives and directors, fund-raising consultants, professional fund raisers and solicitors (tele-marketing and direct-mail companies), development directors, accountants, and boards of directors. It is supplemented twice annually. *Loose-leaf binder, 2 volumes, 1,024 pages, $370; supplements are $125 each*

Fundraising into the 1990s: State Regulation of Charitable Solicitation After Riley (Booklet)

(PROGRAM ON PHILANTHROPY & THE LAW, NEW YORK UNIVERSITY SCHOOL OF LAW, 1989)

▶ This booklet discusses the state of the law on charitable fund raising. After an examination of the often-competing interests of charities and state governments, it analyzes Supreme Court decisions. The final section focuses on the regulatory strategies and legislative options that are available, with particular emphasis on the tension points that remain unresolved. *$9.50 (includes shipping)*

Gifts and Favors: Privileges and Exemptions Enjoyed by Nonprofit Organizations—A Catalogue and Administrative Policy Analysis (Booklet)

(PROGRAM ON PHILANTHROPY & THE LAW, NEW YORK UNIVERSITY SCHOOL OF LAW, 1993)

▶ This book describes exemptions and benefits granted to charitable entities by federal and state governments: benefits accruing by virtue of tax-exempt status under Section 501(c)(3) of the IRS Code and benefits inferred because of nonprofit operations. It also discusses government approaches to policy making regarding charitable entities and the effect on the nonprofit community of having eligibility for benefits decided by a number of agencies. *$9.50 (includes shipping)*

The Law of Fund-Raising, 2nd Edition

BRUCE R. HOPKINS (JOHN WILEY & SONS, 1996)

▶ This book offers comprehensive summaries of each state's Charitable Solicitation Act. It discusses federal regulations and various state legal issues such as due process rights, equal protection rights, restraint on regulators, states' police power, and other issues. This book tackles the increasingly complex maze of fund-raising regulations. It details federal and state laws, with an emphasis on administrative, tax, and constitutional law. It also explains state and federal rules affecting the responsibilities of fund-raising professionals, as well as explores compliance issues, prospective laws, and regulatory trends. Annual supplements. *Hardcover, 704 pages, $145; $65 for each annual supplement*

Survey of State Laws Regulating Charitable Solicitation

HENRY C. SUHRKE (PHILANTHROPY MONTHLY)

▶ This resource digests the laws regulating charitable solicitation in each of the states providing updates as legislatures pass new or revised statutes or repeal existing statutes. *Loose-leaf binder, $148 (initial purchase including one year's updating service); $124 (annual updating service renewal)*

The Tax Law of Charitable Giving, 2nd Edition

BRUCE R. HOPKINS (JOHN WILEY & SONS, 2000)

▶ This book examines the highly complex set of rules and regulations that govern charitable giving, helping to optimize the tax benefits of tax-smart gift vehicles. It examines effective ways to make gifts to nonprofits, and discusses all the structure and timing considerations for one-time gifts and planned giving programs. Beginning with an introductory overview, it provides comprehensive information on the laws, definitions, and forms of various charitable gifts, ranging from art to real estate and beyond. It includes information on the most current tax laws and explains the fundamentals of establishing and maintaining a giving program. Additional topics include limitations on charitable giving, estate and tax considerations, special gift situations, gifts to charitable remainder and lead trusts, using life insurance, administration of charitable giving, disclosure rules, special events, and fund-raising regulations. Subscribers receive annual supplements. *Hardcover, 816 pages, $150*

Employment Law

2000 Employment Law Update

HENRY H. PERRITT JR. (ASPEN PUBLISHERS, 2000)

▶ This reference comprehensively covers recent developments in the rapidly changing employment and labor law field. Composed of nine chapters, each written by an expert in employment law, the *2000 Update* provides timely, incisive analysis of critical issues. Issues discussed include: independent contractor or employee? Navigating the maze of worker classification; workplace English-only rules; current FLSA issues; beyond 40-hours and time and a half; the after-acquired evidence doctrine after McKennon; evidence of prior employer acts in discrimination cases; actions against individual supervisors and fellow employees; insurance for employment discrimination and wrongful termination claims: coverage issues and new directions in insurance policies; guide to preemployment practices and policies; and an overview of immigration law principles for employers. *Softcover, 408 pages, $150*

2000 State by State Guide to Human Resources Law

JOHN F. BUCKLEY IV AND RONALD M. GREEN (ASPEN PUBLISHERS, 2000)

▶ Now you can find the employment laws of all 50 states literally at the turn of a page. This invaluable guide has been revised and updated to cover every vital aspect of employment law and to reflect the changes enacted by state legislatures over the past year. Find out your state's position on frequently contested employment practices in minutes. Through the use of dozens of charts and tables, as well as convenient referencing features, it gives you immediate access to vital information on state employment laws for all 50 states. You'll find special attention given to state new-hire reporting requirements; employment at will; wage and hour laws (including penalty provisions); fair employment laws; group health insurance; continuation of benefits; drug, AIDS, and polygraph testing; parental leave; workers' compensation; unemployment benefits; smoking ordinances; Older Workers Benefit Protection Act; ADA; and FMLA. Plus, the guide provides complete citations to the original source for every law and regulation discussed, so you'll know precisely where to go for further research. *Softcover, 1,056 pages, $175*

ADA Compliance Guide *(See Human Resource Management—Administration for full description)*

Employment and Personnel: A Legal Handbook, 2nd Edition
(Lawyers Alliance of New York, 1997)

▶ This manual focuses on how federal, state, and local employment laws affect nonprofit corporations. The treatment of independent contractors and employees, development of personnel policies and manuals, firing and hiring, record keeping, and antidiscrimination laws are also covered. *Softcover, $18.00 (plus $2.00 postage and handling)*

Employment and Personnel: A Legal Handbook *(See Human Resource Management—Administration for full description)*

Employment-Labor Law Audit *(See Human Resource Management—Administration for full description)*

Employment Law: A Checklist *(See Human Resource Management—Administration for full description)*

Employment Law Answer Book, 4th Edition
Mark R. Filipp, Thomas L. Boyer, and James O. Castagnera (Aspen Publishers, 1997)

▶ You'll reach for this up-to-date reference whenever you need accurate, in-depth information on human resources law. Noted employment and labor attorneys Mark R. Filipp, Thomas L. Boyer, and James O. Castagnera cover all the essentials in an accessible question-and-answer format. *Employment Law Answer Book* is the authoritative, time-saving desk reference for employers who need to keep track of and comply with the latest employment law requirements. The book makes it possible and easy to determine whether your company's policies and practices meet the latest legal rules and guidelines—so you can protect your company's rights, and those of your employees. This comprehensive guide answers more than 1,000 key questions, from the simple to the complex. Specific topics include the latest developments on affirmative action, job terminations, sexual harassment, Family and Medical Leave Act, Americans with Disabilities Act, discrimination, compensation, health and fringe benefits, employer– employee relationship, employee privacy, and more. *Hardcover, 776 pages, $125*

Employment Law Answer Book: Forms & Checklists
(Aspen Publishers, 1994)

▶ With this companion volume to *Employment Law Answer Book*, you can implement all human resource laws and regulations with ease. This handy volume is packed with sample employment contracts, independent contractor agreements, employee evaluation and discipline forms, executive compensation plans, severance and collective bargaining agreements, and a model employee handbook. An easy-to-use format allows you to easily photocopy forms and insert them directly into your file. The forms and checklists will help ensure that all of your human resources practices are in compliance with EEOC, NLRB, OSHA, and DOL requirements. You'll have all the tools you need to keep your company up to date in compliance—and out of court. *Softcover, 728 pages, $96*

Employment Law Manual *(See Human Resource Management—Administration for full description)*

Employment Relationships: Law & Practice
Mark W. Bennett, Howard J. Rubin, and Dean Donald J. Polden (Aspen Publishers, 1998)

▶ *Employment Relationships* analyzes the state and federal employment laws and recent trends in case law affecting the employment relationship. Topics covered include federal discrimination law, including ADEA, ADA, the Equal Pay Act, and the Family and Medical Leave Act; sexual harassment, with a discussion of same-sex harassment; severance pay, golden parachutes, and COBRA; employee's fiduciary duties to his employer; employee privacy, with discussions of privacy issues relating to employee e-mail and computer files; and tort actions, such as defamation, breach of the covenant of good faith and fair dealing, and infliction of emotional distress. Practice pointers throughout the chapter provide practical advice from the authors. The set also includes over 50 forms on disk, including forms for employment contracts, personnel manual forms, litigation forms, sample severance plans and golden parachutes, and an online access policy. *Binder, 1,218 pages, $179*

Hiring, Firing & Risk Management: Employment Law for New Jersey Nonprofits
Jennifer Chandler Hauge (Center for Non-Profit Corporations, 2000)

▶ When it comes to employment issues, the rules are constantly changing. The procedures your organization implemented ten, five, even two years ago may no longer be adequate, opening you up to serious legal challenges. Stay on top of the latest changes in employment law with the latest edition of *Hiring, Firing & Risk Management*. Completely updated and revised, it covers everything from wages and family leave to workplace harassment and discrimination issues. Written in plain language by an attorney experienced in employment law and nonprofit law, this comprehensive guide to personnel practices can help you navigate today's most common challenges as well as assist you with the more unusual situations that may arise. Without carefully crafted and executed policies and procedures, administrators and boards increase the potential for liability, financial penalties, or damage to their nonprofit's reputation. Learn how you can help your organization develop personnel policies and procedures that comply with the latest laws and regulations. Discover how you can protect your board, staff, and volunteers. Find out how to encourage your employees to perform their best. Take steps to reduce your employment-related liability risks. This book will show you how to do all this and much more. You will learn about the biggest liability risks, avoiding discrimination, anti-harassment policies, wage and hour traps, family leave, counseling the poor performer, legal interviewing and hiring procedures, and terminations. Though geared for New Jersey nonprofits, this book is valuable for any size nonprofit no matter where they are located. *Softcover, $183 pages, $29.95*

Hiring, Firing and Supervising Within the Law
(See Human Resource Management—Recruitment, Retention, and Termination for full description)

How to Avoid Employee Lawsuits *(See Human Resource Management—Risk Management for full description)*

How to Comply with the Americans with Disabilities Act *(See Human Resource Management—Policies for full description)*

Nonprofit Compensation, Benefits, and Employment Law
DAVID G. SAMUELS AND HOWARD PIANKO (JOHN WILEY & SONS, 1998)

► Issues surrounding executive compensation, employee benefits, and employment law are becoming increasingly important to non-profits. With the recent passage of intermediate sanctions, the government has signaled that they will be watching compensation and benefits of nonprofits very closely. This timely book fills the growing need by nonprofit executives for an accessible guide to legislation, case law, and IRS regulations. It not only covers those laws unique to the nonprofit sector, but, thankfully, addresses workplace-related statutes of broader applicability such as workplace discrimination, sexual harassment, the Family and Medical Leave Act, and so on. It even covers 401(k) plans, which until recently were unavailable to nonprofit organizations. *Hardcover, 364 pages, $125*

Personnel Matters in the Nonprofit Organization
(See Human Resource Management—General for full description)

Personnel Policies and Procedures for Nonprofit Organizations *(See Human Resource Management—Policies for full description)*

The Practical Guide to Employment Law
BUREAU OF BUSINESS PRACTICE LEGAL PUBLICATIONS STAFF, AND MARY-LOU DEVINE (ASPEN PUBLISHERS, 1999)

► This comprehensive desk manual for HR managers, risk managers, and employment lawyers covers federal employment laws in plain English, giving readers the practical information necessary to apply the laws. Essential court cases and tips for compliance appear in every chapter. The book includes a Compliance Checklist section where readers can learn the various laws that apply to such topics as hiring, terminations, and benefits. It also includes a supervisory training section on several laws, including FMLA and ADA. An annual update is issued every January—whole chapters are replaced with each update. Covered topics include the Age Discrimination in Employment Act (ADEA); the Americans with Disabilities Act (ADA); COBRA/HIPAA Healthcare Continuation Coverage; the Drug-Free Workplace Act and Drug Testing; Employee Polygraph Protection Act of 1988 (EPPA); Employee Retirement Income Security Act (ERISA); the Equal Pay Act (EPA); the Fair Labor Standards Act (FLSA); the Family and Medical Leave Act (FMLA); the Immigration Reform and Control Act of 1986 (IRCA); Pregnancy Discrimination Act of 1978 (PDA); Title VII and the Civil Rights Act of 1991 (CRA '91); the Worker Adjustment and Retraining Act (WARN); and the National Labor Relations Act (NLRA). Defamation, negligent hiring, employee privacy, whistle-blowing and retaliation, wrongful discharge, and affirmative action are also covered. *Loose-leaf, 816 pages, $225*

Sexual Orientation and Legal Rights
ALBA CONTE (ASPEN PUBLISHERS, 1998)

► This comprehensive guide covers gay rights issues and legal development in the areas of employment law, civil rights law, and family law. It covers topics such as constitutional issues, employment discrimination, same-sex harassment, same-sex couple benefits, tort and contract claims, same-sex marriage, dissolution of relationships, child custody and adoption issues, and housing and property rights. Federal and state statutory and case law is discussed, and a state-by-state survey of gay-related statutes and case law is included. *Hardcover, 2 volumes, 1,500 pages, $265*

Staff Screening Toolkit: Keeping the Bad Apples Out of Your Organization *(See Human Resource Management—Recruitment, Retention, and Termination for full description)*

Taking the High Road: A Guide to Employment Law for Charities
JENNIFER CHANDLER HAUGE AND MELANIE L. HERMAN (NONPROFIT RISK MANAGEMENT CENTER, 1999)

► The authors of this book urge employers at nonprofit organizations to strive for the moral high ground as they climb the executive ladder. They offer suggestions geared to creating a work environment that is efficient, equitable, and honest. Hauge and Herman begin with a state-by-state summary of laws that govern antidiscrimination policies and background checks. They explain regulations on severance pay, jury duty, and vacations, and recommend that organizations put their office policies and procedures in a handbook and distribute it to all employees. Should a nonprofit group have no other choice than to fire an employee, the authors outline steps that they say will promote fairness and decrease the likelihood of a lawsuit. Other topics include sexual harassment, drug abuse, and office safety. Hauge and Herman provide summaries of state employment laws that govern such areas, as well as sample forms and checklists relating to employment contracts, performance appraisals, and insurance. The book provides up-to-date information and advice on complying with the ADA, FMLA, Title VII, and more. It includes 27 sample policies and checklists and 12 state-by-state comparisons of key employment laws. *Softcover, 217 pages, $45*

For-Profit Ventures

For-Profit Subsidiary Corporations (Background Kit)
(AMERICAN SOCIETY OF ASSOCIATION EXECUTIVES, 1999)

► This resource contains a breadth of information on establishing and managing a for-profit subsidiary corporation, with an emphasis on tax and legal issues. It includes case studies and sample documentation such as articles of incorporation, a code of bylaws, licenses, and permits. *Spiral bound, 172 pages, $58 (Nonmember), $48 (Member) (plus $6.25 shipping)*

Joint Ventures Involving Tax-Exempt Organizations (Wiley Nonprofit Law, Finance and Management Series), 2nd Edition
MICHAEL I. SANDERS (JOHN WILEY & SONS, 2000)

► In this helpful resource, partnerships and joint ventures are clearly defined, and the tests used by the IRS to evaluate these relationships are explained. The book also surveys methods that nonprofits can use to raise capital and reviews the guidelines governing nonprofit eligibility for federal housing assistance. It includes a detailed examination of the laws, rules, and regulations governing partnerships and joint ventures involving nonprofit organizations, with an emphasis on maintaining exempt status. It contains a survey of other methods nonprofits can use to raise capital, a comprehensive review of the tax-exempt entity leasing rules, and a review of the guidelines governing nonprofit eligibility for federal housing assistance programs. *Hardcover, 672 pages, $150*

Partnerships and Joint Ventures Involving Tax-Exempt Organizations

Michael I. Sanders (John Wiley & Sons, 1998)

▶ This legal guide shows how to analyze partnerships and joint ventures involving tax-exempt organizations, whether two nonprofits are working together or a nonprofit is participating in a for-profit venture. It comprehensively examines the laws, IRS rulings, and court cases, with an emphasis on maintaining exempt status. It also gives you a discussion of nonprofits as investors and the implications of unrelated business income tax (UBIT) on these investments. It includes an analysis of the Revenue Reconciliation Act of 1993 and its effect on nonprofits, application of bargain sale techniques to "burned-out" shelters, and more. It contains a survey of other methods nonprofits can use to raise capital, a comprehensive review of the tax-exempt entity leasing rules, and a review of the guidelines governing nonprofit eligibility for federal housing assistance programs. It is supplemented annually (includes free 1996 supplement). *Softcover, 512 pages, $145*

Governance

Guidebook for Directors of Nonprofit Corporations

George W. Overton, ed. (American Bar Association/Nonprofit Risk Management Center, 1993)

▶ As nonprofit corporations continue to play a larger role in American life, they will face new risks and increasingly complex problems. *Guidebook for Directors of Nonprofit Corporations* will help you understand your obligations, protect your interests, and prepare you for the challenges ahead, whether you are currently serving on a board, or are considering joining one in the future. While directors are not required to have a detailed knowledge of the various tax statutes and regulations affecting nonprofit corporations, they should have a general understanding of the basic application of federal and local tax laws. Reduce your board members' fear of lawsuits and help them govern effectively. This guide clearly explains a board's legal responsibilities and how it can govern effectively and suggests how to conduct board business in conformity with the law. This indispensable guide covers what every nonprofit corporation director, board member, and legal counsel should know about their activities and roles, duties and obligations, risks, and legal requirements. It covers legal principles as they apply to nonprofit corporations, legal requirements and special risks, and good corporate practice and summarizes important tax considerations. Topics include mission statements, delegating responsibilities to committees, handling conflicts of interest, keeping adequate records, protecting your tax-exempt status, and dealing with other common situations that can cause legal problems. It covers the legal principles as they apply to nonprofit corporations and explains what is required by law, and equally important, what is good corporate practice. You'll learn what issues and potential

problems are important to all directors of corporations, including: how boards work: what they do, how they do it, and for whom; what responsibilities can and should be delegated to committees; the procedures to follow if you believe a corporate activity may be illegal; potential conflicts of interest—how to identify and deal with them; the director's right to indemnification from the corporation; protecting the director through insurance, and the issues to consider when reviewing an insurance policy; maintaining the nonprofit tax exemption; and regulations affecting nonprofit corporations. In an extensive chapter, the *Guidebook* summarizes principal federal income tax issues, including qualifying for exemption from federal income tax. It also explains the advantages and requirements of achieving 501(c)(3), 501(c)(4), and 501(c)(6) status, what types of activities can produce unrelated business taxable income and the risks to losing the corporation's tax exemption, and the special reporting requirements for noncharitable contributions and charitable contributions in return for items of value.

There are numerous checklists, appendices, and suggested questions. At the end of each chapter is a list of questions that highlight the issues that should be considered by the director, followed by a checklist of issues to be reviewed by the corporation's chair, board of directors, chief executive, executive committee, nominating committee, audit committee, and legal counsel. Appendices also include a Statement of Policy Governing Conflicts, an organization reference chart from the IRS publication *Tax-Exempt Status for Your Organization,* and a list of suggested reading. *Softcover, 118 pages, $19.95*

Nonprofit Governance: The Executive's Guide

Victor Futter and George W. Overton, eds. (ABA Publications, 1997)

▶ This book is intended to assist the executive director and other individuals in the nonprofit world who handle the various aspects of what, in the corporate for-profit arena, is called the corporate secretary's office. Because of the wide variation in size, structure, nature, and mission in the huge nonprofit world, the material and suggestions set forth in the chapters are not applicable in their entirety to all organizations. Rather, each organization should select the items applicable to it and helpful in its operations. Whether nonprofit entities are large or small, however, they face many similar problems. A number of these problems bear remarkable similarity to those faced in commercial, for-profit enterprises. Depending on the size, structure, nature, and mission of the organization, the nonprofit's secretary's office may be concerned with preparation for and organization of board meetings; recording, reviewing, and editing of minutes; corporate governance; accountability and responsibility; the fiduciary duties of directors; board and committee structure and effectiveness; what ethical and other policies (e.g., conflicts of interest) to adopt and what procedures to adopt to ensure the highest level of ethical leadership and to prohibit self-dealing by board and staff; bylaws; selection and retention of board members; records retention; the functions and operations of audit, compensation, executive, nominating, and other committees; tax exemption questions and filings; appropriate insurance coverage and risk management techniques to mitigate institutional risk; liability to third parties; what lobbying activities, if any, may be engaged in; compliance with federal and state laws and regulations; protection of directors through indemnification, insurance, and exoneration; and protection of the organization's intangible assets. Based on the expertise of corporate and nonprofit executives, attorneys, and professionals who have hands-on experience facing board organization and management problems, this informative guide is filled with step-by-step guidelines; sample forms and letters; useful checklists; and bibliographies. *Softcover, 400 pages, $79.95*

Grant Administration

Essential Grant Law Practice

PAUL G. DEMBLING AND MALCOLM S. MASON (AMERICAN LAW INSTITUTE–AMERICAN BAR ASSOCIATION, 1991)

▶ Each year, the federal government distributes billions of dollars through hundreds of grant programs. Created by statute, organized and run through administrative regulations, and subject to periodic litigation, these programs necessarily involve the professional skills of attorneys. Filling a conspicuous gap in materials available to the practitioner, this comprehensive text is a guide to the essentials of practice in the evolving grant law field. It provides authoritative instruction on the theory and practice of the grant system and includes discussion of the nature of grants, the principle types of grants, the basic legal rules of grants, the basic fiscal rules of grants, conditions attached to grants that affect their operation and the enforcement of those conditions, administrative appeals and court review processes, and advice on where to look for further guidance. *Hardcover, 254 pages, $33 (plus $3.25 shipping)*

Federal Grants Management Handbook (*See Taxes—Financial Management for full description*)

Incorporation and Bylaws

The Alpha Non-Profit Corporation Kit, 5th Edition

KERMIT BURTON (ALPHA PUBLICATIONS OF AMERICA, 1998)

▶ The complete do-it-yourself nonprofit corporation kit includes Articles, Bylaws, Minutes, Notices, Blank Resolutions, and Membership Certificates for either a Membership or Nonmembership Corporation. This *Alpha Non-Profit Corporation Kit* provides all of the forms necessary and required to organize either: (1) a membership public benefit nonprofit corporation; (2) a nonmembership public benefit nonprofit corporation; (3) a private foundation nonprofit public benefit corporation; or (4) a religious nonprofit corporation. Keep in mind that a nonprofit corporation is an entity created under state laws, and as such, some states may have statutory laws or rules that place additional requirements on the establishment of a nonprofit corporation.

Examples of the types of varying requirements that some states may impose are as follows: (1) that only the Articles of Incorporation supplied by the department of that state be used to incorporate, (2) that an attorney sign the Articles of Incorporation, and (3) the number of incorporators required to sign the Articles of Incorporation. All of this information can, of course, be obtained from the department of the state government that registers corporations. This nonprofit corporation kit includes a basic set of articles of incorporation (Forms ANP-1001 through ANP-1005), and additionally separate articles of incorporation for the states of California, Colorado, and New York. The basic set of articles of incorporation can be utilized in most states, with the exception of California, Colorado, and New York. This basic set also includes two page 1's; that is, one designated with the title "Articles of Incorporation" (ANP-1001a), and the other designated with the title "Certificate of Incorporation" (ANP-1001b), which are commonly

used in Delaware and Nevada. In addition to the Articles of Incorporation, this kit also includes: (a) notices, waivers of notices, and minutes of each of the first meeting of both members and directors, monthly meeting of directors, special meetings of both members and directors, and the annual meeting of both members and directors; (b) corporate resolution forms; (c) medical care reimbursement plan and resolution; (d) membership certificates, membership proxy, and a membership register. While this text provides an in-depth, but sometimes abbreviated, discussion of the Internal Revenue Code, as it pertains to nonprofit corporations, the information provided is more than adequate to permit a good understanding as to whether or not the proposed nonprofit venture can meet those tests required to gain a tax-exempt status. *Softcover, 163 pages, $24.95*

Bylaws: A Guide for Nonprofit Organizations and Their Lawyers (Booklet)

BARBARA A. SCHATZ AND WENDY P. SELIGSON (LAWYERS ALLIANCE FOR NEW YORK, 1983)

▶ Designed for use by community groups and their lawyers, this guide consists of two checklists to be used in bylaw preparation, one for community groups and another for their lawyers, with statutory requirements and citations. *$6 (plus $2 shipping)*

How to Form Your Own Profit or Non-Profit Corporation without a Lawyer

BENJI O. ANOSIKE (DO-IT-YOURSELF LEGAL PUBLISHERS, 1999)

▶ Probably the biggest roadblock to anyone's starting a business is a fear of doing something wrong and having to pay a lawyer exorbitant fees to fix it. This fear of giving one's major cash outlay to attorneys has stopped many a small business dead in its tracks, and Anosike's step-by-step how-to comes at the perfect time. With 14 other such do-it-yourself books to his credit, Anosike digs right in: What kind of business do you want to start? The forms for incorporating in every U.S. state are here, with how-to's on filling them out. Would you like to offer stock in your company? What kind of dental plan should you offer your employees? It is amazing that in our law-based society one can form a corporation without consulting a lawyer, but Anosike never once in the book advises asking for legal advice. But what if all fails, and the company needs to be dissolved? There's a chapter on that, too. *Softcover, $25.95*

How to Form a Nonprofit Corporation Book with Disk (DOS), 4th Edition

ANTHONY MANCUSO (NOLO PRESS, 1998)

▶ Incorporate your nonprofit without a lawyer and save the money for your worthy cause. Here is the definitive guide for arts groups, educators, social service agencies, environmentalists, and anyone who wants to start a nonprofit organization. It shows step-by-step how to form and operate a tax-exempt nonprofit corporation in all 50 states, and includes complete instructions for obtaining federal (501)(c)(3) tax exemption and for qualifying for public charity status with the IRS. Most organizations trying to gain legal nonprofit status don't have the money to pay a lawyer thousands of dollars for help. Fortunately, they don't have to. In this definitive guide for anyone who wants to start a nonprofit organization, corporation expert attorney Anthony Mancuso shows you step by step how to form and operate a tax-exempt corporation in all 50 states. *How to Form a Nonprofit Corporation* includes complete instructions for obtaining federal 501(c)(3) tax exemption and for qualifying for public charity status with the IRS. It also provides line-by-line instructions for completing your IRS tax-exemption application;

instructions and completed sample clauses for preparing articles of incorporation; ready-to-use bylaws for membership and nonmembership nonprofits; ready-to-use minutes for the organizational meeting; and state sheets with your state's specific nonprofit legal and tax requirements. The fourth edition includes the most up-to-date tax and legal information, along with all the forms for articles, bylaws, and minutes, both as tear-outs and on disk. *Softcover, 368 pages, $44.95*

How to Form a Nonprofit Corporation (National Edition), 4th Edition
Anthony Mancuso (Nolo Books, 2000)

► In this definitive guide for anyone who wants to start a nonprofit organization, corporation expert attorney Anthony Mancuso shows you step by step how to form and operate a tax-exempt corporation in all 50 states. If you're looking to start a nonprofit organization, it has everything you need to know to start a 501(c)(3) without hiring a lawyer for hundreds or thousands of dollars. The book walks you through the state incorporation process and the federal/IRS application process. It includes copies and a computer disk with preformatted samples of letters, articles of incorporation, organization bylaws, meeting minutes formats, and more. It also takes you step by step through the IRS Form 1023, which you must complete for 501(c)(3) determination. *How to Form a Nonprofit Corporation* includes complete instructions for obtaining federal 501(c)(3) tax exemption and for qualifying for public charity status with the IRS. It also provides line-by-line instructions for completing your IRS tax-exemption application; instructions and completed sample clauses for preparing articles of incorporation; ready-to-use bylaws for membership and nonmembership nonprofits; ready-to-use minutes for the organizational meeting; and state sheets with your state's specific nonprofit legal and tax requirements. The fourth edition includes the most up-to-date tax and legal information, along with all the forms for articles, bylaws, and minutes, both as tear-outs and on disk. *Softcover, 368 pages, $31.47*

How to Form a Nonprofit Corporation: With Forms
(Legal Survival Guides)
Mark Warda (Sphinx Press/Sourcebooks, 2000)

► Forming a nonprofit corporation is not difficult, and whether you want to start a local school or a national cause group, you can use this book to get the organization started. This book includes all of the forms and instructions needed to form a nonprofit corporation, including bylaws, minutes, notice, and much more. This book explains in simple language advantages and disadvantages, applying for tax exemptions of a nonprofit corporation, protecting your nonprofit status, types of nonprofits, charitable solicitation rules, step-by-step procedures for forming your nonprofit, and running your nonprofit. It includes state-by-state laws and addresses, useful Internet addresses, many resources for nonprofits, and 18 ready-to-use forms. *Softcover, 192 pages, $24.95*

Nonprofit Corporations, Organizations, and Associations, 6th Edition
Howard L. Oleck and Martha E. Stewart (Prentice Hall—Business & Financial Management, 1994)

► This is a standard reference to organizing, operating, merging, or dissolving any kind of nonprofit enterprise. It covers the drawing up of articles of incorporation, drafting bylaws, calling and conducting meetings, election procedures, committees, duties of officers, improper acts, special powers granted by the states, lawsuits, and maintaining tax exemption. This is the ultimate in resource

books for nonprofits; a one-volume library for successful day-to-day nonprofit management that covers every conceivable aspect of managing nonprofits, focusing on legal issues; updated by annual supplement. *Hardcover, 1,664 pages, 2 volumes, $110 (includes shipping)*

Nonprofit Corporations, Organizations, & Associations: 1998/1999 Cumulative Supplement
Stewart Oleck, Howard L. Oleck, and Martha E. Stewart (Prentice Hall Direct, 1998)

► This is the new edition of a standard reference to organizing, operating, merging, or dissolving any kind of nonprofit enterprise. It covers the drawing up of articles of incorporation, drafting bylaws, calling and conducting meetings, election procedures, committees, duties of officers, improper acts, special powers granted by the states, lawsuits, and maintaining tax exemption. *Softcover, 504 pages, $76.50*

Nonprofit Corporations: Qualify for Federal Income Tax Exemption (PDF Publications)
Anthony Mancuso (Nolo Press, 1999)

► Forming a nonprofit corporation doesn't make much sense unless you obtain a federal income tax exemption for your organization, a process that usually occurs under Internal Revenue Code Section 501(c)(3). This easy-to-read resource explains the basic requirements of this important tax exemption. Written by corporations expert attorney Anthony Mancuso, the eGuide carefully lays out what kinds of organizations are eligible for exemption, the limitations to be aware of when trying to qualify for the exemption, and the differences between public charities and private foundations. *$15.95*

Starting & Managing a Nonprofit Organization: A Legal Guide, 3rd Edition (Workbook/Manual)
Bruce R. Hopkins (John Wiley & Sons, 2000)

► Completely revised and updated, the second edition of this acclaimed work offers comprehensive, nontechnical guidance on the laws affecting nonprofit organizations. Written by renowned lawyer Bruce R. Hopkins, this invaluable resource not only offers a complete summary of the relevant laws and regulations affecting nonprofit organizations, it also offers full guidelines on how to successfully employ many powerful management strategies. It gives you practical information and advice about the laws governing nonprofit organizations so that you can successfully manage every stage of your group's development, and provides information on corporate, tax, and fund-raising laws and virtually every legal aspect of operating a nonprofit organization, including reporting revenue, nonprofits and private benefits, tax exemption, the rules pertaining to charitable giving, compensating the nonprofit employee, lobbying, using for-profit subsidiaries, and much more. Numerous easy-to-use checklists, charts, tables, and an expanded glossary of legal terms lead you step by step through the complex maze of rules and regulations. It has been revised and updated to include information on changes in laws, rules, and regulations governing the nonprofit sector. *Softcover, 320 pages, $26.95*

Starting and Running a Nonprofit Organization, 2nd Edition
Joan M. Hummel (University of Minnesota Press, 1996)

► *Starting and Running a Nonprofit Organization* is a book for people who are forming new nonprofits; thinking about converting an informal, grassroots group to tax-exempt status; reorganizing an existing agency; or currently managing a nonprofit. It provides practical and basic how-to information about legal, tax, organizational, and other issues particular to nonprofits. This one-of-a-kind resource has been an invaluable guide to nonprofit management for more than 15 years. Its unique, compact format provides all of the necessary information in an easy-to-understand style. The long-awaited revised edition retains all of the useful features of the original, adding important new insights and strategies for the challenges of today's nonprofit operating climate. The book describes, step by step, all of the phases of creating and operating a new nonprofit, including incorporation, establishing a board of directors, writing bylaws, obtaining tax-exempt status, creating a strategic plan, budgeting and grant seeking, understanding accounting principles, managing human resources, and creating a community relations plan. The information provided is specific enough to be immediately useful, yet can be generalized to any nonprofit practitioner in any state. It includes handy checklists and worksheets, as well as a list of sources for assistance and management development and a bibliography on nonprofit management. *Softcover, 152 pages, $13.45*

International Nonprofit Law

The International Guide to Nonprofit Law
LESTER M. SALAMON AND STEFAN TOEPLER (JOHN WILEY & SONS, 1997)

▶ With increased activity in the nonprofit world and a growing global business community, keeping up to date on the laws governing international philanthropy has become very complicated. This book is an easy-to-use reference on how nonprofits are governed around the world. Over 20 countries are covered, and the material for each country, provided by local experts, is comprehensive and consistent. Issues covered for each country include basic nonprofit law, types of organizations, internal management controls, taxation, business income, lobbying, reporting requirements, employee/board compensation and benefits, international activity, and general trends. Annual supplements will contain updates to rules and regulations and will feature additional countries. *Hardcover, 450 pages, $125*

International Legal Issues for Nonprofit Organizations
JEFFERSON C. GLASSIE (AMERICAN SOCIETY OF ASSOCIATION EXECUTIVES, 1999)

▶ This is the only international legal reference of its kind for nonprofit membership organizations. Based on more than 15 years of law practice, the book covers a wide variety of international legal issues including nonprofit incorporation, taxes, employment, membership, intellectual property, antitrust, trade, lobbying and political activities, litigation and dispute resolution, and more. The book also includes appendices of sample agreements for international affiliates, licenses and royalties, conference management services, office management, and antitrust policy. *Hardcover, 240 pages, $50 (Nonmember), $42 (Member)*

Investments

Program-Related Investments: A Primer (See Resource Development for full description)

Risk Management, Insurance, and Liability

Association Liability (Background Kit)
(AMERICAN SOCIETY OF ASSOCIATION EXECUTIVES, 1998)

▶ This background kit covers a full range of legal issues on liability, including hotel contract liability, hold-harmless agreements, copyright law, discrimination law, legal issues for the board, volunteer indemnification policies, sexual harassment, employee references, liability for pension plans, and numerous recently published articles on liability insurance. *Spiral bound, 138 pages, $66 (Nonmember), $44 (Member)*

The Best Defense: 10 Steps to Surviving a Lawsuit
(NONPROFIT RISK MANAGEMENT CENTER, 1998)

▶ This invaluable resource on lawsuits is a must-have text for nonprofit CEOs, executives, and board members. The text describes 10 steps to help a nonprofit survive litigation with minimal damage to morale, reputation, and the ability to focus on mission-critical activities. Chapters focus on working with your insurer, communicating with constituencies, understanding the process, minding the time clock, and much more. *Softcover, 52 pages, $12*

Board Liability: Guide for Nonprofit Directors
(See Governance—Roles and Responsibilities for full description)

The Board Member's Guide to Legal, Liability, and Insurance Issues *(See Governance—Roles and Responsibilities for full description)*

Child Abuse Prevention Primer for Your Organization
JOHN PATTERSON WITH CHARLES TREMPER AND PAM RYPKEMA (NONPROFIT RISK MANAGEMENT CENTER, 1995)

▶ As too many tragic incidents have shown, children and youth can become victims in programs designed to serve them. To help you protect the young people in your program, this book offers suggestions based on the best practices in the field. It begins by presenting the facts about abuse and abusers, building on that basis with suggestions for the four P's of child abuse prevention for any organization: Personnel, Program, Premises, and Participants. Liability implications of abuse in youth-serving organizations receive special attention. Reference sections list dozens of abuse-prevention books, videos, and other tools. *Softcover, 88 pages, $7.50*

Legal Barriers to Volunteer Service *(See Volunteerism—Risk Management, Insurance, and Liability for full description)*

Legal Issues for Service-Learning Programs *(See Volunteerism—Risk Management, Insurance, and Liability for full description)*

Legal Issues, Insurance, and Risk Management: An Invaluable Two-Part Satellite Series for Volunteer Program Leaders *(See Volunteerism—Risk Management, Insurance, and Liability for full description)*

Legal Obligations of Nonprofit Boards: A Guidebook for Board Members (See Governance—Roles and Responsibilities for full description)

Managing Legal Liability and Insurance for Corporate Volunteer Programs (See Volunteerism—Risk Management, Insurance, and Liability for full description)

Managing Volunteers Within the Law (See Volunteerism—Risk Management, Insurance, and Liability for full description)

No Surprises: Controlling Risks in Volunteer Programs (See Volunteerism—Risk Management, Insurance, and Liability for full description)

Nonprofit Litigation: A Practical Guide with Forms and Checklists
STEVE BACHMANN (JOHN WILEY & SONS, 1992)

▶ This book is an introduction to nonprofit litigation for nonprofit executives and a reference tool for lawyers. It highlights the unique aspects of litigating for nonprofit clients and contains checklists and forms as well as relevant case citations and examples. Annual updates will provide information on new cases and legislative developments. This easy-to-read reference is the first and only guide to nonprofit litigation, whether you are the plaintiff or the defendant. Learn how to take advantage of the unique opportunities and avoid the pitfalls inherent in the litigation process as it applies to nonprofit organizations. It covers all major areas of nonprofit litigation and provides an introduction to litigation for nonprofit executives and a reference tool for lawyers of nonprofit organizations: nonprofit executives (beginning with the basics of structuring your nonprofit organization to best withstand the rigors of litigation, and continuing into activities such as initiating and filing a complaint, injunctions, discovery, interrogatories, depositions, trial, and appeals, it gives you the nuts-and-bolts information needed for understanding all sides of nonprofit litigation. A clear description of the entire litigation process includes samples of all necessary legal forms to help you build a solid understanding of the subject. It covers ways you can control the costs of litigation while continuing to litigate effectively, litigation strategies that will help build your membership and constituencies, ways to litigate in order to advance your organization's objectives, and how nonprofit organization litigation differs from that involving for-profit companies), attorneys (provides a summary of legal procedures that apply to nonprofit organizations; organized for fast and easy access to specific information, including forms and case citations, it is divided into three sections: Organizational Structure, Litigation, and Other Government Encounters; includes litigation checklists, complaint, discovery, appeals checklists, tax status checklist, attorneys' fees checklist, and many more). It is supplemented annually (no supplement to date). *Hardcover, 400 pages, $165*

On-Board: Guiding Principles for Trustees of Not-for-Profit Organizations (See Governance—General for full description)

Planning It Safe: How to Control Liability and Risk in Volunteer Programs (See Volunteerism—Risk Management, Insurance, and Liability for full description)

Preventing Sexual Harassment in the Workplace (See Policies—Human Resource Management for full description)

Risk Management for Volunteer Programs (See Volunteerism—Risk Management, Insurance, and Liability for full description)

Standing to Sue in the Charitable Sector (Booklet) (PROGRAM ON PHILANTHROPY & THE LAW, NEW YORK UNIVERSITY SCHOOL OF LAW, 1993)

▶ This book traces the development of the laws regarding who may sue the management of charitable organizations for mismanagement, nonfeasance, failure to adhere to the purposes of the charity, and the like. Particular emphasis is placed on the growing tendency to allow minority board members and private parties with "special interests" to sue. *Softcover, $9.50 (includes shipping)*

Trustees and Preventive Law (See Governance—Roles and Responsibilities for full description)

Volunteers and the Law (See Volunteerism—Risk Management, Insurance, and Liability for full description)

What Nonprofit Managers Need To Know About Lawsuits (Booklet) (NONPROFITS' INSURANCE ALLIANCE OF CALIFORNIA)

▶ The publication is designed to help nonprofit managers, board members, and staff be better informed about the litigation process, so that they can work more effectively to manage lawsuits lodged against them. The 25-page booklet includes all of the basics in addition to a glossary and sample forms. To receive a free copy ($1 for each additional copy) call 800-359-6422, or go to *www.niac.org* and click on Loss Control to download a test version.

A Working Guide for Directors of Not-for-Profit Organizations (See Governance—General for full description)

Youth Law for Youth Workers (See Human Resource Management—Risk Management for full description)

Tax Exemption
(See also Financial Management, Tax Reporting and Compliance)

Federal and State Taxation of Exempt Organizations
FRANCES R. BILL, BARBARA L. KIRSCHTEN, ROBERT E. ATKINSON JR., WENDELL R. BIRD, AND BONNIE S. BRIER (WARREN, GORHAM & LAMONT, 1994)

▶ This resource focuses on current issues in the tax-exempt area (entrepreneurial initiatives, investment, and lobbying activities) that have resulted in closer governmental scrutiny; helps your organization steer clear of trouble with in-depth analysis and practical guidance to help make certain your exempt organization is in full compliance with current rules and regulations; and provides guidance on such critical topics as unrelated business income tax (UBIT), lobbying rules (including newly enacted restrictions on deductibility of dues and disclosure requirements), comprehensive analysis of the private foundation rules, foreign charitable organizations (especially activities conducted abroad by U.S. exempt organizations), in-depth analysis of tax issues relating to investments in derivative products, complex structures of affiliated tax-exempt organizations or exempt and taxable entities, and operations of exempt organizations. There is also extensive coverage of trade associations, health care organizations, religious organizations, schools, colleges and universities, business leagues, and investment portfolios. Other features include a comprehensive topical index, tables of cases, IRS rulings and announcements, sections of the Internal Revenue Code and Treasury regulations, coverage of significant pending cases, and more. *Hardcover, $175 (includes shipping)*

Financial and Accounting Guide for Not-for-Profit Organizations *(See Financial Management—Accounting for full description)*

Financial & Strategic Management for Nonprofit Organizations *(See General Management for full description)*

Gifts and Favors: Privileges & Exemptions Enjoyed by Nonprofit Organizations—A Catalogue and Administrative Policy Analysis (Booklet)
(PROGRAM ON PHILANTHROPY & THE LAW, NEW YORK UNIVERSITY SCHOOL OF LAW, 1993)

▶ This book describes exemptions and benefits granted to charitable entities by federal and state governments: benefits accruing by virtue of tax-exempt status under Section 501(c)(3) of the IRS Code and benefits inferred because of nonprofit operations. It also discusses government approaches to policy making regarding charitable entities and the effect on the nonprofit community of having eligibility for benefits decided by a number of agencies. *$9.50 (includes shipping)*

Guide to Unrelated Business Income Tax *(See Taxes—Financial Management for full description)*

The Law of Tax-Exempt Healthcare Organizations
THOMAS K. HYATT AND BRUCE R. HOPKINS (JOHN WILEY & SONS, 1995)

▶ This comprehensive source of detailed information on federal, state, and local laws combines Hyatt's industry-specific knowledge with the expertise of Hopkins, the country's leading legal authority on tax-exempt organizations. It explains complex legal issues in plain English and provides specific legal citations for further research. It covers the tax status of diverse types of health care providers, organizational topics, and operational matters. It is supplemented annually to keep subscribers up to date on legislative activity, IRS decisions, court opinions, and other developments in this rapidly changing industry. *Hardcover, 704 pages, $150*

Practitioners 990 Deskbook *(See Taxes—Financial Management for full description)*

Private Foundations: Tax Law and Compliance
BRUCE R. HOPKINS AND JODY BLAZEK (JOHN WILEY & SONS, 1997)

▶ Private foundations are subject to a unique and complex set of (mostly tax) regulations that govern everything from how much money they give away to their investment policies and procedures. This is the only single-volume reference that covers all aspects of tax compliance for private foundations. With approximately 50,000

private foundations in the United States and the increasing scrutiny of the IRS, this much-needed, annually updated manual provides a wide range of tax rules and regulations for these foundations. Co-authored by a lawyer and tax accountant, it includes practical tax compliance suggestions and in-depth legal explanations, line-by-line instructions, sample-filled IRS forms, and complete citations. *Hardcover, 520 pages, $135*

Protecting Your Organization's Tax-Exempt Status: A Guide for Nonprofit Managers
MARK BOOKMAN (JOSSEY-BASS, 1992)

▶ Bookman provides nonprofit leaders with a comprehensive examination of federal, state, and local laws affecting nonprofit organizations and recommends actions nonprofits can take to protect their organizations tax-exempt status. *Protecting Your Organization's Tax-Exempt Status* demonstrates how federal tax law applies to specific segments of the nonprofit sector. It provides comprehensive coverage in nontechnical language of federal, state, and local laws affecting nonprofit organizations, and recommends actions nonprofit leaders can take to protect nonprofit status for their own organizations. Using case studies, the author explains such crucial matters as preparing for an IRS audit, reporting unrelated business income, responding to claims of unfair competition, and fighting challenges to nonprofits' property tax exemptions. It discusses actual IRS audits and shows how nonprofits have made their case for tax exemption. *Hardcover, 296 pages, $51.95*

Tax and Financial Planning for Tax-Exempt Organizations: Forms, Checklists, Procedures
(See Financial Management—Taxes for full description)

Tax-Exempt Charitable Organizations—No. B511, 3rd Edition
PAUL E. TREUSCH (AMERICAN LAW INSTITUTE–AMERICAN BAR ASSOCIATION, 1988)

▶ This indispensable reference source focuses on the four major revenue acts affecting tax-exempt entities: the critical IRS regulations and revised procedures of monumental import to nonprofit organizations, the landmark decisions of the U.S. Supreme Court and trial and appellate courts that affect tax-exempt charitable organizations, and the extensive Congressional Committee hearings proposing further legislative changes; additional restraints considered by Congress and the IRS are also fully covered. It discusses expanded record-keeping, reporting, and disclosure requirements; the relative advantages and disadvantages of operating in tax-exempt form and the steps for securing and retaining exempt qualification; and the price imposed upon termination of private foundations status and available avenues for avoiding this penalty. *Hardcover, 706 pages, $42 (plus $7.50 shipping)*

Tax Planning and Compliance for Tax-Exempt Organizations: Forms, Checklists, Procedures, 3rd Edition
JODY BLAZEK (JOHN WILEY & SONS, 1999)

▶ Nonprofit organizations contend daily with the possibility of losing their tax-exempt status. From qualifying and applying for that status to maintaining and managing it, every nonprofit must plan and monitor ongoing procedures, activities, and forms to comply with federal, state, and local regulations. This book will keep you apprised of the latest developments affecting this area, including new 990, 990EZ, and 990PF, 990-T forms; the latest information on unrelated business income, including coverage of a ruling that allowed a child welfare organization to obtain "about half" of its revenues from a travel agency that it operated; a section on the techniques for reducing the excise tax private foundations pay on their investment income; and a section on the proposed regulation on the reporting and record-keeping requirements for voluntary donations, the most common form of income for nonprofit organizations. It provides concise instructions for filing 990s and other important IRS forms and documents; obtaining tax exemption; reporting to boards, auditors, and the IRS; testing ongoing tax compliance; and managing lobbying expenditures and unrelated business income. This guide focuses on changing UBI rules (joint ventures, sponsorships, deductions against UBI, preparation of IRS Forms 1023, 1024, and 99), evolving hospital and health care rules, and private foundations and public charities (fund-raising disclosures, communicating with the IRS, etc.). It also incorporates expanded discussions of definitions of different types of nonprofits, qualifying under various categories, unrelated business income, employment taxes, joint ventures and partnerships, loss of exemption, and bankruptcy. It includes easy-to-use checklists, line-by-line instructions for completing applications and forms, sample documents, practice aids and tips, complete citations on all tax aspects of the exempt organization, and suggestions for handling special situations. Annual supplements keep subscribers apprised of relevant changes in IRS forms, requirements, and procedures. It is supplemented annually. *Hardcover, 818 pages, $135*

Why Tax Exemption? The Public Service Role of America's Independent Sector (Special Kit)
(INDEPENDENT SECTOR, 1993)

► Today, as never before, voluntary and philanthropic organizations must be prepared to define their institutions and describe the public service roles they play. This kit is designed to help in that effort. It includes a booklet of definitions and descriptions for the sector as a whole and for nine major areas. The same material is included on loose sheets for your copying and use in whatever way you wish; three examples are included, showing how an organization might use the material in a brochure, testimony, and as general orientation in a grant proposal. *$12 (Nonmember), $8 (Member) (plus $2.50 shipping)*

Other

Certification and Accreditation Law Handbook
JEROLD A. JACOBS (AMERICAN SOCIETY OF ASSOCIATION EXECUTIVES, 1992)

► This book is a comprehensive and user-friendly review of legal principles and rules that apply to private, nonprofit voluntary organizations that issue credentials and operate certification or accreditation programs, or are considering doing so. Contents include liability to third parties, confidentiality of records, use of credentialing marks, tax exemption, and the Americans with Disabilities Act. Appendices include sample documents and excerpts from the *Federal Register. Hardcover, 194 pages, $150 (Nonmember), $100 (Member) (plus $6.25 shipping)*

Fiscal Sponsorship Arrangements, 3rd Edition (Booklet)
LORI YARVIS (LAWYERS ALLIANCE FOR NEW YORK, 1995)

► This manual, for nonprofit groups that have not yet obtained tax-exempt status but that are considering or involved in an arrangement with a fiscal sponsor, describes the relationship between the sponsor and the sponsored organizations. It includes negotiating tips and forms. *$5 (plus 75 cents shipping)*

Parliamentary Law and Practice for Nonprofit Organizations, 2nd Edition
HOWARD L. OLECK AND CAMI GREEN (AMERICAN LAW INSTITUTE–AMERICAN BAR ASSOCIATION, 1991)

► This book provides an authoritative, simple set of parliamentary rules of order, detailing meeting and convention procedures based on relevant statutory and case law and not merely an arbitrary preferences—a guide long needed by nonprofit organizations despite the availability of a number of proposed sets of such rules written by various individuals, commencing with General Robert's "Rules of Order in the 19th Century." This practice handbook contains a chart of parliamentary procedures that answers ordinary and special motions questions at a glance, concise rules, thorough analysis of each rule, and up-to-date citations to existing case law. It presents the parliamentary rules of order in a format that permits ready access to specific questions, lay or legal. Some of the discussion goes beyond strict matters of parliamentary procedure and touches on such thorny issues as conflicts of interest and indemnification, liabilities of members, and derivative actions. It includes a bibliography, table of cases, tables of statutes, and an index of subjects. *Softcover, 180 pages, $50 (plus $2.50 shipping)*

PERIODICALS

(See also Financial Management; General Management; Governance; Human Resource Management; Resource Development)

501(c)(3) Monthly Letter (Monthly Newsletter)
Great Oaks Communications Services, 400 Chestnut Street,
P.O. Box 192, Atlantic, IA 50022
Tel: 712-243-5257 or 4750; FAX: 712-243-2775
E-mail: kmeickle@nishna.net (Editor);
WWW: http://www.nishna.net/501c3/

▶ This newsletter features articles by leaders in the nonprofit world on such varied topics as fund raising, grants, computerization, communication, special events, working with volunteers, selecting board members, attracting media attention, postal rate savings, and more. It also offers financial advice for nonprofits, reports on nonprofit activities and legislation in different states, and recommendations on helpful products and service. *12 pages, $46/year*

The API Account *(See Financial Management—Periodicals for full description)*

Community Risk Management and Insurance (Newsletter)
Nonprofit Risk Management Center, 1001 Connecticut Avenue NW, Suite 900, Washington, DC 20036
Tel: 202-785-3891; FAX: 202-296-0349
E-mail: info@nonprofitrisk.org; WWW: http://www.nonprofitrisk.org

▶ The print edition is distributed three times each year to more than 15,000 nonprofits. Each issue of *Community Risk Management and Insurance* covers a wide spectrum of risk management issues, showcases the Center's training and workshop sessions, and highlights other crucial nonprofit risk management issues. It provides the latest updates on risk management and insurance as it relates to the nonprofit sector and a collection of practical articles about strategies for reducing risks, protecting against liability, obtaining all types of insurance, and managing employee benefits programs. *Free (Nonprofit organizations and government agencies), $25/year (For-profit businesses and individuals)*

EOTR Weekly (Weekly Newsletter)
Tax Analysts, 6830 North Fairfax Drive, Alexandria, VA 22213
Tel: 800-955-3444, 703-533-4400; FAX: 703-533-4444
E-mail: cwright@tax.org; WWW: http://205.177.50.92/catalog/products/specialty/eoweekly.htm

▶ Designed to keep the tax professional in touch with all the important developments in exempt organizations tax law, this weekly newsletter contains timely reports from the IRS, Treasury, and the courts, as well as news of state-level and international events that will affect exempt organizations. Features include articles on all EO tax news and developments from the IRS, the Treasury, and the courts; all state and local EO tax news and special reports; abstracts and citations; exemption rulings; and service releases. *$129.95/year*

Exempt Organizations Reporter (Biweekly Journal)
CCH Incorporated, 2700 Lake Cook Road, Riverwoods, IL 60015
Tel: 800-853-5224, 847-267-7024; FAX: 800-224-8299
E-mail: Cust_Serv@cch.com, larry_perlman@cch.com (Larry Perlman, Writer/Analyst); WWW: http://www.cch.com/, http://tax.cch.com

▶ This journal sets out and explains federal tax and state organizational and operational rules governing tax-exempt organizations, contributors, and managers. It emphasizes rules for tax-exempt status, investment income, state charitable trust laws, and the like, and details and describes current developments, IRS activity, and areas of special interest. It includes exempt-related official text (Code, Regulations, cases, and rulings) as well as CCH-authored explanations and annotations. The database also contains CCH new developments, including important new federal decisions and rulings on exempt law. Included are full texts of all IRS communications such as revenue rulings, revenue procedures, notices, announcements, news releases, letter rulings, and technical advice memoranda, as well as Tax Court decisions and other federal court decisions relating to tax-exempt organizations. *$865/year*

The Exempt Organizations Tax Review (Monthly Journal)
Tax Analysts, 6830 North Fairfax Drive, Alexandria, VA 22213
Tel: 800-955-3444, 703-533-4400 or 703-533-4419 (Carolyn D. Wright, Editor); FAX: 703-533-4444
E-mail: cservice@tax.org, cwright@tax.org (Carolyn D. Wright, Editor); WWW: http://www.tax.org/, http://205.177.50.92/ catalog/products/specialty/eotr.htm

▶ This journal provides monthly news coverage and analysis. Each monthly issue includes the latest developments from the IRS, Treasury, Capitol Hill, and the courts, along with insightful special reports written by leading EO practitioners. Each issue of the EOTR contains special features, such as the Letter Ruling Alert. Written by an EO tax practitioner, the Letter Ruling Alert will keep subscribers informed on new and noteworthy technical advice memoranda and private letter rulings. Summaries of all TAMs and letter rulings dealing with EO subjects are also included, as are the full texts of significant rulings. In addition to news coverage and helpful, full-text documents, you will also find interviews with EO newsmakers and edited transcripts of the three ABA Exempt Organization Committee meetings held each year. Features include News and Analysis; Special Reports; ABA Transcripts; State Law Survey; Charitable Giving Update; Conference Notes; IRS Letter

Rulings—Letter Ruling Alert; Focus on IRS; Focus on Treasury; Focus on Congress; Letters to the Editor; Court Opinions; Current Litigation Status Report—updates on current EO legislation; State Tax News—EO tax news from all 50 states; and Press Watch. Included with your EOTR subscription is the *EOTR Weekly* newsletter containing the latest tax news and developments affecting exempt organizations. *EOTR Weekly* includes information on the latest IRS letter rulings, court opinions, and compliance initiatives. It will bring you up to speed on all the EO tax news you need each week at no additional cost. *$749.95/year*

GIVING USA and Giving USA Updates (Quarterly Report)

American Association of Fundraising Counsel,
10293 N. Meridian Street, Suite 175, Indianapolis, IN 46290
Tel: 800-46-AAFRC (22372), 317-816-1613; FAX: 317-816-1633
E-mail: info@aafrc.org;
WWW: http://www.aafrc.org/giving/ catalog.asp

▶ This is a reference for timely legal, economic, and social developments affecting philanthropy. Recent reports have included Trends in Corporate Philanthropy, What Drives Charitable Giving, and the Annual Summary of State Laws Regulating Charitable Solicitations. *$125/year*

International Journal of Not-for-Profit Law (Quarterly Journal)

International Center for Not-for-Profit Law,
733 15th Street NW, Suite 420, Washington, DC 20005
Tel: 202-624-0766; FAX: 202-624-0767
E-mail: daitken@icnl.org, info@icnl.org;
WWW: http://www.icnl.org/journal/journal.html

▶ This journal provides up-to-date information on legal and regulatory developments affecting the not-for-profit sector in countries around the world; self-regulation, including information and resources about NGO codes of ethics and other sector-developed accountability mechanisms; the role of law in creating an enabling environment for private philanthropy; legal mechanisms for fostering development partnerships; tax law development affecting cross-border giving; summaries of topical articles, the full-text version of which will be accessible through hyperlinks to ICNL's Web site; book reviews; and discussions of important case law developments from national and international tribunals. An online version is also available. *$50/year*

Journal of Taxation of Exempt Organizations (Bimonthly Journal)

Research Institute of America, The Thomson Corporation,
395 Hudson Street, New York, NY 10014
Tel: 800-431-9025 (Customer Service) or 800-742-3348 (Editorial), 212-367-6300
E-mail: Customer_Services@riag.com, Editorial.Questions@ riag.com; WWW: http://www.riahome.com/store/detail.asp? ID=EOTJ

▶ This journal provides tax analysis and guidance to members of the exempt organization community. It is directed to the professional advisors of these organizations and their contributors, as well as to members of the organizations' management. Its goal is to provide the tax information that these organizations need to negotiate the rapid changes of the new business and regulatory environment. The journal offers in-depth analyses and updates by leading practitioners in an accessible and easy-to-read style. Articles cover intermediate sanctions, combinations and joint ventures, health care

organizations, exemption and compliance, private foundations, political and lobbying activity, the unrelated business income tax, charitable giving, compensation, and many other topics. An online version is also available. *$205/year*

Legal Ease (Quarterly Newsletter)

University of St. Thomas Graduate School of Business,
Mailing address: 25H 525, 1000 LaSalle Avenue,
Minneapolis, MN 55403-2001

Physical address: 1125 Harmon Place, Suite 525,
Minneapolis, MN 55403-2001
Tel: 800-328-6819, ext. 2-4300, 651-962-4300;
FAX: 651-962-4810
E-mail: pswilder@stthomas.edu, askshamblin@stthomas.edu;
WWW: http://www.gsb.stthomas.edu/centers/nonpro.htm

▶ This newsletter covers new federal and Minnesota state laws and regulations and related legal matters of prime interest to nonprofit managers and their boards. Each issue contains one or two feature articles and an update on new developments. Issues covered include tax deductibility of contributions, employment law, charitable gambling, nonprofit tax law, and nonprofit corporate structure. It is free to Minnesota-based nonprofits and foundations; $5 annually requested from others to cover printing and postage.

Nonprofit Alert Newsletter (Monthly Newsletter)

The Law Firm of Gammon & Grange, PC,
8280 Greensboro Drive, 7th Floor, McLean, VA 22102
Tel: 703-761-5000 or 402-292-5653; FAX: 703-761-5023
E-mail: sjschmidt2@earthlink.net (Sarah J. Schmidt, Editor),
npa@gandglaw.com; WWW: http://gandglaw.com/

▶ This newsletter provides concise summaries highlighting legal, regulatory, and administrative developments that shape the nonprofit world, along with practice tips and resources for managing any associated risks. *$75/year*

The Nonprofit Counsel (Monthly Newsletter)

John Wiley & Sons, 650 Third Avenue, New York, NY 10158
Tel: 800-225-5954 (Customer Service) or 800-359-3352,
800-753-0655, ext. 4457 (Account Representative), 212-850-6000
E-mail: brhop@pwvs.com (Bruce R. Hopkins, Editor);
WWW: http://www.wiley.com/products, http://www.wiley.com/
products/subject/business/nonprofit/catalog/hopkins5.html

▶ To keep pace with evolving laws and tax regulations, nonprofit executives and their legal counsel need an inside track on the laws affecting nonprofits. This newsletter gives you up-to-the-minute information on the issues that mean the most to your nonprofit organization—from emerging business opportunities to potential compliance pitfalls. *8 pages, $179.00/year*

Nonprofit Issues, Inc. (Newsletter, 11 Issues)

P.O. Box 482, Dresher, PA 19025
Tel: 888-NP-ISSUE, 215-542-7547 or 215-772-7277;
FAX: 215-542-7548
E-mail: info@nonprofitissues.com, dkramer@mmwr.com (Don Kramer, Editor); WWW: www.nonprofitissues.com,
http://www.nonprofitissues.com/ready.html

▶ This is a national newsletter of "Nonprofit Law You Need to Know." Written for nonprofit executives and their advisors, *Nonprofit Issues* provides clear, concise, and comprehensive coverage of real issues that affect nonprofits every day. They select from current federal and state cases the issues of critical importance to nonprofit executives and their advisors, such as federal tax law, employment law, board liability, volunteer law, corporate governance, foundation rules, charitable giving, insurance, copyright, and trademark. Each issue of the print newsletter includes a Ready Reference Page summarizing some aspect of the rules and regulations that control nonprofit activity and are sold individually online. (Each Ready Reference Page is two pages and in PDF format.) It offers e-mail updates, also available in PDF format. *$129/year (Nonprofit rate), $149 (Standard rate)*

Non-Profit Legal & Tax Letter (Newsletter, 18 Issues)

Organization Management, Inc., 42989 Ellzey Drive,
Ashburn, VA 20148-5026
Tel: 703-729-7052; FAX: 703-729-7053
E-mail: Taxletter@aol.com;
WWW: http://www.taxexemptresources.com/Tax%20Letter.htm

▶ The *Letter* provides regular (triweekly) updates on all significant developments affecting nonprofits. Written for nonprofit executives and their advisors, the style of the *Letter* is concise and factual, with just enough analysis to convey the significance of what is being reported. Subscribers include executives from all types of nonprofit and exempt organizations, including charitable institutions, educational organizations, private foundations, trade and professional associations, fraternal organizations, community and social welfare organizations, technical and scientific societies, advocacy groups, arts organizations, and more. Legislation and other actions by Congress; regulations, Revenue Rulings, private letter rulings, and other actions by the Internal Revenue Service; and court decisions from throughout the United States are all reported in the *Letter*. While developments related to tax exemption are emphasized, all issues relevant to nonprofits are covered, including, but not limited to, postal, governance, antitrust, tort liability, volunteer and charitable immunity, standards and certification, charitable solicitation, fiduciary duties of nonprofit officers and directors, raffles and lotteries, nonprofit executive compensation, executive employment agreements, and employment issues. In addition to the 18 issues of vital information, subscribers also receive special reports, published three times per year, that offer in-depth analysis of a particular topic. *8 pages, $235/year*

Nonprofit Navigator (Monthly Newsletter)

Harmon, Curran, Spielberg & Eisenberg, LLP, 1726 M Street NW,
Suite 600, Washington, DC 20036
Tel: 202-328-3500; FAX: 202-328-6918
E-mail navigator@harmoncurran.com;
WWW: http://www.harmoncurran.com/newsletters.html

▶ To alert nonprofits to legal rulings and legislative proposals that could affect their operation, the *Nonprofit Navigator* covers law and policy of interest to the nonprofit community. *Nonprofit Navigator* discusses and explains new developments in areas ranging from employment law to FEC compliance to recent court cases and new regulations. It includes recent court decision analysis, IRS guidance on the activities of nonprofits, "Tax Tips" to help organizations make financially sound decisions, Federal Election Commission actions and rulings, and significant developments in employment law. *$115/year*

Not-for-Profit Newsletter *(See Financial Management— Periodicals for full description)*

The PPC Nonprofit Update *(See Financial Management— Periodicals for complete details)*

Philanthropy Monthly (10 Issues)

2 Bennitt Street, P.O. Box 989, New Milford, CT 06776
Tel: 860-354-7132
E-mail: hsuhrke@AOL.COM (Henry Suhrke)

▶ Published since 1969, it has been a platform for informed and insightful reportage and commentary on philanthropy, voluntarism, nonprofits, particularly as they are affected by legal, regulatory, and policy trends. It provides commentary on not-for-profit accounting and concentrates on legal aspects of fund raising for grant makers and grant seekers, with particular focus on tax news, accounting, compensation and benefits, state and IRS regulations, congressional legislative developments, state and federal litigation on nonprofits, and academic research. It includes the Booknotes feature that once appeared in the ARNOVA newsletter. In addition to somewhat lengthier reviews and references, the new version features a brief commentary on matters of interest in nonprofits-related publishing. *$84/year (Charities eligible for discounted rate of $65)*

Planned Gifts Counselor (Monthly Newsletter)

Premier Administration/Practical Publishing,
1602 West 1050 North, Provo, UT 84604-3062
Tel: 888-58-TRUST (588-7878), 801-802-8930;
FAX: 801-802-8931
E-mail: alden@premieradministration.com (Alden B. Tueller);
WWW: http://www.premieradministration.com/pgc.htm

▶ Prepared by nonprofit professionals Paul H. Schneiter and Alden B. Tueller, JD, it focuses on news, analysis, announcements, and successful strategies. Easily scanned and quickly read, it nevertheless offers wide-ranging and pertinent information targeted toward your success. *8 pages, $150/year*

State Tax Trends for Nonprofits *(See Financial Management—Periodicals for full description)*

The Tax-Exempt Organization Alert *(See Financial Management—Periodicals for full description)*

Tax Monthly for Exempt Organizations *(See Financial Management—Periodicals for full description)*

Taxwise Giving *(See Financial Management—Periodicals for full description)*

INTERNET SITES

General Legal Resources Issues

411LegalInfo

▶ *http://www.411legalinfo.com*

Legal Services Corporation

▶ You can find a legal service program near you in the United States by clicking on Get Legal Assistance. *http://www.lsc.gov/index2.htm*

Nonprofit Legal and Tax Resources

AllExperts Nonprofit Law Q & A

▶ This site features Harvey Mechanic. Expertise in: nonprofit organizations, establishing and maintaining legal requirements for nonprofit organizations in all states, including state and Internal Revenue Service filings and requirements and other exempt organization tax issues. *http://www.allexperts.com/getExpert.asp?Category=2266*

Charitable Solicitation Over the Internet and State-Law Restrictions

▶ *http://www.bway.net/~hbograd/monaghan.html, http://members. aol.com/irsform1023*

Comparison of 501(c)(3) and 501(c)(4), (6), and (7) Status

▶ *http://members.aol.com/irsform1023/misc/comp501s.html*

Exempt Law—Copilevitz & Canter

▶ This Web site provides general information on topics of interest to people involved with nonprofit organizations. The site is also a marketing tool for the book *The Charity's Guide to Charitable Contributions*. *http://www.exempttaxlaw.com/*

Exempt Organizations Publications—Quarles & Brady

▶ *http://www.quarles.com/pub_eo.asp*

Fiscal Sponsorship

▶ *http://search.genie.org/genie/ans_result.lasso?cat=Fiscal+Sponsorship*

Internal Revenue Service: Information for Tax-Exempt Organizations

▶ This site explains the different types of tax-exempt organizations and how to apply for tax-exempt status. The site includes answers to frequently asked questions about tax-exempt organizations, IRS forms that can be downloaded, and articles on topics such as unrelated business income tax, lobbying by tax-exempt organizations, and charitable remainder trusts. The site also includes a database of nearly 500,000 nonprofit organizations, updated quarterly, that makes it possible to find all the groups in a certain city or state or to check whether a particular group has received tax-exempt status. *http://www.irs.ustreas.gov/prod/bus_info/eo*

Internet Nonprofit Center: The Nonprofit FAQ

▶ Sponsored by the Evergreen State Society, a Seattle charity that promotes civic involvement, this site provides information on legal and tax issues for nonprofit organizations. The information was compiled from the soc.org.nonprofit newsgroup, an online discussion about the nonprofit world. See various topics listed under subheadings "Organization," "Management," and "Regulation." *http://www.nonprofits.org/npofaq*

Legal Information Institute: Law about...Nonprofit Organizations

▶ *http://www.law.cornell.edu/topics/nonprofits.html*

Legal Issues—501 Click

▶ *http://www.501click.com/mt_li_main.html*

Legal Links for Nonprofit Corporations

▶ *http://www.not-for-profit.org/legal.htm*

Martindale-Hubbell

▶ For a list of lawyers who specialize in nonprofits and practice in your local area, refer to the Martindale-Hubbell lawyer locator. *http://lawyers.martindale.com/marhub/form?_form=by.html*

National Association for Public Interest Law

▶ This site provides an extensive listing of links to online public interest law resources. *http://www.napil.org/LINKS-FM.html*

Nonprofit Legal & Tax

▶ *http://www.taxexemptresources.com/*

Nonprofit-Specific Legal Information
▶ *http://www.managementhelp.org/legal/np_genrl/np_genrl.htm*

Other NPO Regulations Resources
▶ *http://www.paperglyphs.com/nporegulation/more_resources.html*

PNN Online: Law, Taxes, Money
▶ *http://pnnonline.org/law/*

Silk, Adler & Colvin—FAQs
▶ *http://www.silklaw.com/faqs/home.cfm*

Strategic Solutions FAQs—LaPiana
▶ *http://www.lapiana.org/strategic/faq/index.html*

Tax & Legal Issues—DANA Answer Center (Delaware Association of Nonprofit Agencies)
▶ *http://www.delawarenonprofit.org/TaxFAQ.html*

Tax Exempt Organizations—IRS
▶ *http://www.irs.ustreas.gov/prod/bus_info/eo/*

Thompson & Thompson FAQs
▶ *http://www.t-tlaw.com/nonprof.shtml, http://www.t-tlaw.com/ resource.shtml*

What Is a Nonprofit Corporation?
▶ *http://www.not-for-profit.org/page2.htm*

Charitable Contributions

GiftLaw
▶ *http://www.giftlaw.com/*

Planned Giving Resources—State Regulations for Charitable Gift Annuities
▶ *http://www.pgresources.com/regs.html*

Charitable Solicitation

The Copilevitz Telemarketing Fund Raising Resource
▶ Summarizes each state's current charitable fund-raising statutes to guide nonprofit organizations and those providing services to charitable organizations. *http://www.copilevitz-canter.com/fundresource.htm*

The National Association of State Charity Officials
▶ The NASCO board of directors has posted the Charleston Principles on using the Internet for charitable solicitation for comment by nonprofit leaders. *http://www.nasconet.org/stories/story Reader$10*

National Charitable Solicitations Registry FAQ
▶ *http://www.charitableregistry.com/FAQ.htm*

Online Compendium of Federal and State Regulations for U.S. Nonprofit Organizations
▶ Created by Eric Mercer, manager of services at DU Educational Technology Services, this Web site provides information on financial-accounting regulations, rules for nonprofit postal rates, public disclosure requirements for charities, and the text of laws that regulate nonprofit organizations. The site plans to cover additional topics in the future, such as the steps that organizations must take to apply for tax-exempt status, registering as a charitable solicitor, and the laws that govern fund raising, as well as to provide information on nonprofit regulations in each state. *http://www.muridae.com/nporegulation*

State Charitable Solicitations Requirements—Raffa & Associates
▶ This site contains a compilation of the registration requirements, state by state, required for charitable solicitation. Users can select the state they are interested in and find out the registration requirements, fees, dates, and statutory authorities. The site also includes a chart that shows which states you must file with before soliciting and which states allow soliciting before filing, and a chart that details each state's annual filing date and any extensions allowed. *www.raffa.com/interior/charsolic.html.*

Unified Registration Statement
▶ Many states require nonprofit organizations to register before asking their residents for charitable contributions. The Multi-State Filer Project has created the Unified Registration Statement (URS) to streamline the process of completing registrations for organizations that must file in several states. Organized by the National Association of State Charities Officials (NASCO) and the National Association of Attorneys General (NAAG), this site attempts to "consolidate the information and data requirements of all states that require registration of nonprofit organizations performing charitable solicitations within their jurisdictions." It also lists which states require registration and provides specific details for each state. More information about the URS, registration requirements, and the registration process are published at *http://www.nonprofits.org/library/gov/urs.*

Incorporation
(See also Starting a Nonprofit; Tax Reporting and Compliance)

123 EZ Corp
▶ *http://www.123ezcorp.com/*

Form 1023 Help
▶ *http://www.form1023help.com/*

Nonprofit Corporations—Nolo.com Legal Encyclopedia Articles
▶ *http://www.nolo.com/encyclopedia/nonprofit_corporations_ency.html*

Lobbying, Public Advocacy, and Political Action

(See also Marketing and Communications, Media)

Advocacy—Internet Nonprofit Center

▶ *http://www.nonprofits.org/npofaq/keywords/3a.html*

Alliance for Justice: Nonprofit Advocacy Resources

▶ Run by the Alliance for Justice, a national association of advocacy organizations, this Web site explains the Lobbying Disclosure Act of 1995, regulations that govern advocacy by charities that receive federal grants, and the "intermediate sanctions" law that authorizes penalties for excessive compensation at charities and new disclosure requirements for charities. The site also provides links to the Federal Election Commission, the Internal Revenue Service, and state agencies that oversee campaign finance and incorporation by nonprofit organizations. The Alliance for Justice will answer questions about nonprofit advocacy posed by users through its Web site. *http://www.afj.org/fai/napresource.html*

Answer Center: Advocacy & Lobbying—Delaware Association of Nonprofit Agencies

▶ *http://www.delawarenonprofit.org/AdvocacyFAQ.html*

Charity Lobbying in the Public Interest

▶ This site provides information on nonprofit lobbying regulations, permissible activities, and several tools and resources, including the recently updated *Nonprofit Lobbying Guide,* which can be downloaded from this site. *http://www.independentsector.org/clpi/index.html*

Independent Sector: Charity Lobbying in the Public Interest

▶ A project of Independent Sector, in Washington, Charity Lobbying in the Public Interest seeks to encourage nonprofit organizations to participate in the public policy process. The project's Web site explains the federal laws that govern lobbying and voter education activities by charities and provides examples of lobbying efforts by nonprofit organizations. Visitors can also download the 1999 edition of *The Nonprofit Lobbying Guide* by Bob Smucker, former vice-president for government relations at Independent Sector and project director of Charity Lobbying in the Public Interest. *http://www.indepsec.org/clpi*

Let America Speak

▶ Run by Let America Speak, a coalition of more than 3,000 organizations that seeks to protect charities' First Amendment rights, this Web site provides legislative updates, including the text of proposed anti-advocacy legislation, on issues that affect advocacy by nonprofit organizations. It also includes information on the regulations that govern advocacy by charities that receive federal grants, the Lobbying Disclosure Act of 1995, and what activities charities may conduct during political campaigns. *http://ombwatch.org/www/las/index.html*

Lobbying—The Nonprofit Zone

▶ *http://www.nonprofitzone.com/lobby.htm*

Netaction

▶ Dedicated to promoting the use of the Internet for effective grassroots citizen action campaigns and to educating the public, policy makers, and the media about technology policy issues, the Netaction site provides an online training program (*http://www.netaction.org/training/*) on virtual activism, information about the organization's current projects, and links to helpful activism sites. *http://www.netaction.org*

Nonprofit Advocacy—Western States Center

▶ *http://www.westernstatescenter.org/directory/advocacy.html*

Nonprofit Advocacy Tools

▶ *http://www.givevoicenetwork.org/advocacy.htm*

The Nonprofit Quarterly

▶ This is an advocacy issue of *The Nonprofit Quarterly,* Third Sector New England's national magazine. Nonprofits of all types need to know their rights regarding the use of advocacy. This edition of the *Quarterly* reviews legal issues, highlights sectorwide policy initiatives, and provides inspirational first-person accounts of nonprofit advocacy in action. *http://www.nonprofitquarterly.org/index intout.php3?from=intout*

Nonprofit Sector Research Fund—Projects and Findings: Advocacy

▶ *http://www.nonprofitresearch.org/newsletter1531/newsletter_list.htm?section=Advocacy*

OMB Watch's Nonprofits' Policy & Technology Project

▶ The Nonprofits' Policy & Technology Project (NPT) is OMB Watch's three-year initiative to improve communications linkages within the nonprofit sector in order to strengthen public policy participation. The NPT site provides information about activities, resources, and project updates. *http://ombwatch.org/npadv/, http://ombwatch.org/npt/*

Organizers' Collaborative

▶ The Organizers' Collaborative is a nonprofit organization in Cambridge, Massachusetts, that promotes the use of computers and the Internet as a tool for grassroots activism. The organization's site provides links to Web sites on computers, online advocacy, social justice, and the nonprofit world. The group plans to offer free software and sample documents that activists can download from the site. *http://www.organizenow.net*

Politics, Policy & Advocacy—Nonprofit Resource Center

▶ *http://www.not-for-profit.org/policy.htm*

Research Initiative on Nonprofit Advocacy— Center on Nonprofits & Philanthropy at the Urban Institute

▶ *http://www.urban.org/advocacyresearch/*

Service Leader

▶ This virtual volunteering project is a good source of information regarding advocacy and lobbying for nonprofits. It also has a comprehensive listing of other nonprofit advocacy Web sites. This organization feels that "your organization needs to know what activities staff and volunteers can engage in legally regarding lobbying, advocacy, and other public policy activities." This site contains useful information for any nonprofit that is interested in the ins and outs of advocacy work. *http://www.serviceleader.org/*

Update on Permissible Activities of 501(c)(3) Organizations During a Political Campaign

▶ *http://www.ombwatch.org/las/lobperm.html*

Parliamentary Procedure

Parliamentary Procedure

▶ Do you have questions about making motions in your board meetings? Visit parliamentarian Jim Slaughter's Web site for the answers. *http://www.jimslaughter.com/*

Public Disclosure

(See also Tax Compliance and Reporting)

Form990Online

▶ This site is designed to allow nonprofits to comply with the new IRS public disclosure regulations for federal forms 990 and 1023. *http://www.form990online.com/*

Information By State—National Federation of Nonprofits

▶ The NFN compilation of links to state information and regulation Web sites. *http://www.federationofnonprofits.org/statlink.htm*

Nonprofit Cyber-Accountability

▶ *http://www.bway.net/~hbograd/cyb-acc.html*

The U.S. Nonprofit Organization's Public Disclosure Regulations Site

▶ A surprising number of nonprofit organization administrators don't realize that federal law requires most tax-exempt nonprofit organizations to allow public inspection of their recent federal annual information returns (e.g., IRS Form 990 and Form 990 Schedule A) and their application for tax-exempt status (e.g., IRS Form 1023 or 1024), along with nearly all associated material. This site provides exhaustive and up-to-date coverage of NPO regulations. *http://www.muridae.com/publicaccess/access.html*

Risk Management

Answer Center: Risk Management—Delaware Association of Nonprofit Agencies

▶ *http://www.delawarenonprofit.org/RiskFAQ.html*

Volunteer's Legal Handbook

▶ Written by James D. DeWitt, a lawyer in Alaska, for the Volunteer Action Center of the United Way of the Tanana Valley in Fairbanks, Alaska, this Web site discusses how nonprofit organizations and their volunteers can protect themselves from potential lawsuits. *http://iciclesoftware.com/vlh/*

Starting a Nonprofit

(See also Incorporation; Tax Reporting and Compliance)

Answer Center: Nonprofit Start-Up

▶ *http://www.delawarenonprofit.org/StartUp.htm*

Five Steps to Starting a Nonprofit—Pfau Englund Nonprofit Law

▶ *http://www.nonprofitlaw.com/5steps.htm*

How to Establish a Nonprofit Organization— Foundation Center FAQs

▶ *http://fdncenter.org/onlib/faqs/starting_nonprofit.html*

Nonprofit Start Up—DANA Answer Center

▶ *http://www.delawarenonprofit.org/StartUp.htm*

Starting a Nonprofit Organization—Free Management Library

▶ *http://www.mapnp.org/library/strt_org/strt_np/strt_np.htm*

Starting a Nonprofit Organization: One-Stop Answer Page

▶ If you're thinking of starting a nonprofit organization, this is the place to begin. You'll find links to basic information such as planning, legal resources, and fund raising. *http://nonprofit.about.com/careers/nonprofit/library/weekly/blonestart.htm*

Starting a Nonprofit—Charity USA

▶ How to start a nonprofit organization in the United States. *http://www.charityusa.org/pages/Education_Information_and_Resources/Starting_a_Nonprofit/*

Starting a Non-Profit Organization: A Resource List

▶ *http://www.lib.msu.edu/harris23/grants/znpbib.htm*

Starting a Nonprofit Organization and Nonprofit Law

▶ *http://www.library.wisc.edu/libraries/Memorial/grants/npweb.htm*

Starting and Understanding Your Nonprofit—Free Management Library

▶ *http://www.managementhelp.org/np_progs/np_mod/orgs_crs.htm*

Tax Compliance and Reporting

(See also Public Disclosure)

Fast Links to IRS Tax Exempt Rules, Regulations— Joy Light Center

▶ *http://www.joylight.com/resource.html*

Federal Form 990—Nonprofit GENIE

▶ *http://search.genie.org/genie/ans_result.lasso?cat=Federal+Form +990*

The Form 990 Project

▶ The Form 990 Project developed a demonstration version of the annual information return nonprofits file with the Internal Revenue Service that could be completed online. The IRS and others are currently working on integrating such a form into the processing of returns for future use. Meanwhile, an editable version of Form 990 (and many other IRS forms) can be downloaded from the "Forms and Publications" section of the IRS Web site at *http://www.irs. ustreas.gov/forms_pubs/fillin.html*

Form 1023 Help

▶ *http://www.form1023help.com/*

GrantMasters, LLC

▶ *http://www.grantmasters.com/faqs.htm*

IRS Forms—Pfau Englund Nonprofit Law

▶ *http://www.nonprofitlaw.com/irsforms.htm*

990 Online

▶ This site was recently established to assist tax-exempt organizations that wish to fulfill the requirements of the new IRC Section 6104(d) regulations through online publication of their completed annual information returns and application for exempt status. *http://www.990online.com/*

Publication 557—Tax-Exempt Status for Your Organization

▶ *http://www.irs.gov/plain/forms_pubs/pubs/p557toc.htm*

Quality 990

▶ Operated by the National Center for Charitable Statistics at the Urban Institute's Center on Nonprofits and Philanthropy, this site features information about the Form 990—the informational tax return that charities with annual revenues of more than $25,000 are required to file with the IRS—and on projects that educate charities about the form's importance. Independent Sector and the National Council of Nonprofit Associations, both in Washington, and the National Society of Fund Raising Executives, in Alexandria, Virginia, are also sponsors of the site. *http://www.qual990.org*

Tax Analysts

▶ Developed by Tax Analysts, a nonprofit organization that monitors tax policy, this site provides updates on congressional and Internal Revenue Service activities. The site also provides subscription information for 17 e-mail discussion lists that Tax Analysts staff members moderate, including lists that discuss exempt organizations, international philanthropy, tax-exempt bonds, and estates and trusts. *http://www.tax.org*

Tax Exempt Organizations—IRS

▶ *http://www.irs.ustreas.gov/prod/bus_info/eo/*

Top Selected Tax Forms and Publications

▶ *http://www.irs.ustreas.gov/prod/bus_info/eo/eo-tkit.html*

U.S. Tax Code On-Line: Section 501

▶ This site includes the full text of Section 501 of the U.S. Internal Revenue Code, which deals with tax exemption for charities and other organizations. The tax code can be searched, and the site provides hypertext links to references to other parts of the tax code. *http://www.fourmilab.ch/ustax/www/t26-A-1-F-I-501.html*

E-Mail Discussion Lists

ABA-NONPROFIT

▶ This e-mail–based discussion group focuses on nonprofit and exempt organizations law. It serves as a forum for discussing the tax and legal issues affecting nonprofit organizations and philanthropy. The NonProfitGroup section of the 8000 Web site will complement the discussion group, providing a forum in which to post information and materials relating to the discussions. If you would like to be a charter subscriber or if you have any questions about ABA-NONPROFIT, please contact: Todd D. Mayo (*mailto:tmayo@may olawfirm.com*) Moderator, ABA-NONPROFIT. *http://www.c2. com:8000/NonProfitGroup*

Advocacy

▶ This site focuses on the business of nonprofits advocating for change. Social-change organizations face special challenges and opportunities not always faced by other organizations. ADVOCACY subscribers will discuss a range of topics, from the tightrope of lobbying disclosure requirements to the concerns of media exposure and coverage, from the benefits and perils of political struggles to the passion and, yes, even danger, of sometimes being affiliated with organizations and causes that arouse the passions of supporters and foes alike. ADVOCACY provides a place to discuss, advise, support, and question other professionals in the field. You can subscribe to ADVOCACY either via e-mail or from the CharityChannel.com Web site.

Via e-mail: Send an e-mail message to *Listserv@charitychannel.com*. The "subject" or "re" is ignored. In the body of your message, type: *SUBSCRIBE ADVOCACY YourFirstname YourLastname*

From the Web site: Point your Web browser to <*http://www.CharityChannel.com/Forums*> and click on "Subscribe . . ." for ADVOCACY. Follow the instructions.

CharityLaw

▶ This site focuses on all aspects of the law of tax-exempt organizations in the United States sponsored by American Philanthropy Review, it is open to any person interested in the topic. There are two methods to subscribe:

1. Send e-mail to *listserv@CharityChannel.com* with *SUBSCRIBE CharityLaw YourFirstname YourLastname* as the message. Leave the subject line blank.
2. Visit the CharityChannel Web site at *CharityChannel.com/forums* and click on the subscription information for CharityLaw.

CharityStart (discussion of the nuts and bolts of launching nonprofit organizations in the United States or Canada) *http://charity-channel.com/forumsnew/CharityStart.htm*

There are two methods to subscribe:

1. Send e-mail to *listserv@CharityChannel.com* with *SUBSCRIBE CharityStart YourFirstname YourLastname* as the message. Leave the subject line blank.
2. Visit the CharityChannel Web site at *CharityChannel.com/forums* and click on the subscription information for CharityStart.

http://www.charitychannel.com/cgi-bin/wa/exe?SUBED1=charity law&A=1, http://www.charitychannel.com/archives/charitylaw.html

Nonprofit Cyber-Accountability Listserv

▶ *http://www.bway.net/~hbograd/cyb-acc.html#cybacc [searchable archive]*

NonprofitOrganizations (Non-Profit Organizations/ Corporations Law List)

▶ Send the following message to *listproc@lists.washlaw.edu*: *subscribe nonprofitorganizations Your Name*

Starting a Nonprofit

▶ For people who are interested in starting a nonprofit and those who have started one and can offer expertise. To subscribe, send e-mail with message empty. *starting-nonprofit-subscribe@ egroups.com*

Tax Analysts' Exempt

▶ Subscribe: Automatic—send e-mail to *majordomo@lists. tax.org* with the body text: *subscribe exempt*. Tax Analysts offers a periodic exempt organization–related mail newsletter. This extremely low-traffic list is headed by Carolyn Wright, editor of *The Exempt Organizations Tax Reporter,* and Jon Almeras. Web site and archives: *http://www.tax.org/Discuss/discussion.htm*

Tax-Nonprofit

▶ This is an online forum to discuss the tax and legal matters that affect nonprofit organizations, maintained by the American Bar Association's Section of Taxation and its Exempt Organizations Committee. To subscribe to the Tax-Nonprofit discussion group, please send an e-mail message to *listserv@abanet.org* with a line *Subscribe tax-nonprofit your first and last name* in the body of the message. Leave the subject blank, and do not include e-mail addresses in the body of the message. If you are an ABA Tax Section member, you can access the Section Directory at *http://www.abanet.org/tax/*. Updated information about members will be contained in this directory. *http://www.abanet.org/tax/ groups/discuss.html*

Online Publications

Exotax on the Web

▶ Publications of KPMG's Exempt Organizations Tax Practice, including this newsletter, are now available on the World Wide Web. To reach the Exotax site, go to the KPMG-US homepage (*http://www.us.kpmg.com*). Once there, navigate to either the Tax page or the Products and Services page, where you will find a listing for Exempt Organizations Tax Practice.

Nonprofit Issues

▶ Includes past issues, current highlights, and links mentioned in the print version of this American newsletter about nonprofit law. *http://www.nonprofitissues.com/*

Nonprofit Navigator

▶ *http://www.harmoncurran.com/newsletters.html*

OMB Watch Nonprofit News

▶ *http://www.ombwatch.org/npadv/*

PART VIII

Resource Development

ORGANIZATIONS

(See also Financial Management [Charitable Giving, Grants Management, Tax-Exemption]; Legal Issues [Charitable Solicitation]; Marketing & Communications; Philanthropy [Corporate Philanthropy, Individual & Family Giving, Estate Planning & Planned Giving]; Social Entrepreneurship)

Advocacy

Alliance of Nonprofit Mailers *(See Legal Issues for full description)*

American Charities for Reasonable Fundraising Regulation (Formerly Charities U.S.A., Inc.)
3124 North Tenth Street, Arlington, VA 22201
Tel: 703-243-7402; FAX: 703-243-7403
WWW: http://www.muridae.com/nporegulation/documents/ acfrfr_flyer.html
▶ This coalition of nonprofit organizations, their national associations, and their supporters was formed for the purpose of combating excessive regulation by means of litigation.

Fund-Raising Information and Assistance Centers

CASE Matching Gifts Clearinghouse
1307 New York Avenue NW, Suite 1000,
Washington, DC 20005-4701
Tel: 202-478-5656; FAX: 202-387-4973
E-mail: matchinggifts@case.org;
WWW: http://www.case.org/matchinggifts/
▶ For more than 40 years, the CASE Matching Gifts Clearinghouse has been serving the nonprofit and corporate communities in all areas of matching gifts. Their primary goal is to encourage companies to match their employees' donations to nonprofits. They also maintain and update a comprehensive database of more than 7,500 parent companies, divisions, and subsidiaries with matching gift programs. With this data, the Clearinghouse provides a variety of products and free services to support matching gift programs. They help fund raisers raise more money for higher education and elementary and secondary schools, cultural organizations, and charities. They work with companies to improve their matching gift programs or start one, and they help matching gift administrators tackle ethical and program issues. They hold conferences of special interest to advancement services professionals. Conferences cover alumni relations, communications, fund raising, and advancement management, and are held in the United States, Canada, mainland Europe, the United Kingdom, and online.

Education Grants Resource Center
Alameda County Office of Education, 313 West Winton Avenue, Room 181, Hayward, CA 94544-1198
Tel: 510-670-4520
E-mail: egoldberg@acoe.k12.ca.us (Evan Goldberg, Grantwriting Specialist); WWW: http://www.alameda-coe.k12.ca.us/acoe/ grantcenter/gcinfo.html
▶ Established in 1992, the Grants Resource Center helps people in the community increase their capacity to generate new revenues for their endeavors. The Center provides resource materials, grant-writing workshops, and technical assistance to educators, parents, nonprofit and government administrators, community members, and businesses, especially in Alameda County, but also throughout the Bay Area. The Center has an extensive collection of information on funding opportunities from local, state, and national governments; private, corporate, and community foundations; and local and national corporations. They maintain the following information about funding sources: annual reports and funding guidelines; resource books, CD-ROMs and Internet access; weekly and monthly newsletters on current grant opportunities; and reference books on grant preparation and fund-raising strategies. Training sessions on all aspects of the grant-writing and fund-raising process are held throughout the year. *Funding Alert!* and *Technology Funding Alert!* are published monthly, September through June, and announce many local, state, and national funding opportunities that have specific deadlines. *Funding Alert!* identifies funding sources and training opportunities in a variety of areas for schools and community-based organizations. *Technology Funding Alert!* focuses on funding opportunities in technology for schools.

Environmental Support Center (ESC)
1500 Massachusetts Avenue NW, Suite 25, Washington, DC 20005
Tel: 202-331-9700; FAX: 202-331-8592
WWW: http://www.envsc.org/
▶ Since 1990, the Environmental Support Center (ESC) has repeatedly helped more than 1,500 local, state, and regional organizations working on environmental issues. ESC's goal is to improve the environment in the United States by enhancing the health and well-being of these organizations. Their Training and Organizational Assistance Program, Leadership and Enhanced Assistance Program, Technology Resources Program, Workplace Solicitation Program, Environmental Loan Fund, and State Environmental Leadership Program help these vital environmental groups become better managed, funded, and equipped.

The Foundation Center

79 Fifth Avenue, New York, NY 10003-3076
Tel: 800-424-9836; FAX: 212-807-3677
E-mail: library@fdncenter.org; WWW: http://fdncenter.org

▶ The mission of the Foundation Center is to foster public understanding of the foundation field by collecting, organizing, analyzing, and disseminating information on foundations, corporate giving, and related subjects. It maintains a comprehensive and up-to-date database on foundations and corporate giving programs by publishing directories and by analyzing trends in foundation support of the nonprofit sector. The Center publishes *The Foundation Directory,* the classic reference work for grant seekers, and some 60 other directories, guides, and research reports. It also makes information available electronically through FC Search: The Foundation Center's Database on CD-ROM and custom searching and online services. As a vital component of its outreach efforts, the Center offers information free of charge to the public at five Foundation Center libraries and more than 200 Cooperating Collections across the country and through its Web site.

Their audiences include grant seekers, grant makers, researchers, policy makers, the media, and the general public. The Center offers resources in book and electronic forms about fund raising and nonprofit development resources. Programs and services include: FC Libraries (located in Cleveland; San Francisco; Washington, DC; and Atlanta); Cooperating Collections (free funding information centers in libraries, community foundations, and other nonprofit resource centers that provide a core collection of Foundation Center publications and a variety of supplementary materials and services in areas useful to grant seekers. A complete list is available at *http://fdncenter.org/collections/index.html*); Associates Program (*http://fdncenter.org/about/associates/assoc1.html*); and Grantmaker Services (For Grantmakers, Foundation Folders, Electronic Grant Reporting, Grants Classification); Training and Seminars (free and fee-based). Additional help is available through the Online Library (*http://fdncenter.org/onlib/index.html*), including the Electronic Reference Desk and Online Training and Resources. (The Center produces the *Philanthropy News Digest* (available on their Web site at *http://fdncenter.org/pnd/current/index.html*).

The Fund Raising School *(See Professional Development—Education for full description)*

Grant and Resource Center of Northern California (GRC)

2280 Benton Drive, Building C, Suite A, Redding, CA 96003
Tel: 916-244-1219; FAX: 916-244-0905
E-mail: dennis@shastarcf.org (Dennis Kessinger, Executive Director), library@grnc.org, grc@c-zone.net;
WWW: http://www.grcnc.org

▶ Incorporated as a public service, nonprofit organization in the state of California, GRC offers the north state communities the advantages of a professional staff, a resource library, and periodic seminars and workshops. Their services are geared toward supporting the not-for-profit community and other philanthropic endeavors in northern California. They keep abreast of the latest trends, computer information retrieval systems and resources available to the not-for-profit sector and other charitable enterprises. They offer workshops on grant writing, strategic planning, fund raising, special events, and more. Services include library (contains more than

1,000 books and 40 periodicals covering corporate and independent foundations, federal funding, nonprofit management, fund raising, boardsmanship and volunteers; information on almost 53,000 different private, corporate, community, and operating foundations can be researched via the periodicals, directories, and computerized databases); workshops; outreach project; grant-writer's listserv; research services; and consulting.

Grantsmanship Center *(See Resource Development—Products and Services)*

National Planned Giving Institute *(See Products and Services—Workshops, Training, and Seminars)*

Philip E. Heckerling Institute on Estate Planning

University of Miami School of Law, P.O. Box 248087,
Coral Gables, FL 33124-8087
Tel: 305-284-2339 or 305-284-6752; FAX: 305-284-4762
E-mail: amiller@law.miami.edu (Amy Miller),
jghodges@IEX.NET (Joseph G. Hodges Jr.),
JuliaFisher@ewgf.com (Julia Fisher);
WWW: http://www.law.miami.edu/heckerling

▶ It is designed for sophisticated attorneys, trust officers, accountants, and insurance and financial planners who, through years of experience and practice, are familiar with the principles of estate planning. The Institute offers something of interest to every member of the estate planning team.

The Funding Information Center

The San Diego Foundation, 1420 Kettner Boulevard, Suite 500,
San Diego, CA 92101
Tel: 619-235-2300; FAX: 619-239-1710

North County: The San Diego Foundation, 6050 El Tordo Road,
Rancho Santa Fe, CA 92067
Tel: 858-756-8263, 619-235-2300; FAX: 858-756-7489
E-mail: maggie@sdfoundation.org (Maggie Maag, Funding Information Center Director), info@sdfoundation.org;
WWW: http://www.sdfoundation.org/grant/fundinginfocenter.shtml

▶ The San Diego Foundation Funding Information Center is a library for nonprofits that contains comprehensive information on government, corporate, and foundation funding sources as well as on fund raising, proposal writing, organizational management, and other issues relevant to nonprofit agencies. The use of the center is free and is open to the public during normal business hours, Monday through Friday from 8:00 A.M. to 5:00 P.M. and on Wednesday evenings until 7:30 P.M. Orientation sessions on basic grant seeking and how to use the library are provided each month.

In-Kind Products and Services/Excess Inventory

Gifts in Kind International

333 North Fairfax Street, Alexandria, VA 22314
Tel: 703-836-2121; FAX: 703-549-1481
E-mail: feedback@GiftsInKind.org,
ProductDonations@GiftsInKind.org;
WWW: http://www.giftsinkind.org

▶ Gifts in Kind International partners with businesses and non-profit organizations to provide quality products and services that improve lives in communities around the world. Gifts in Kind International directs donated quality products and services to the needy. They create partnerships that link companies and their valuable in-kind resources with a network of more than 50,000 non-profit organizations around the world. Annually, more than $350 million in computer technology, office products and supplies, personal care products, clothing, educational materials, emergency supplies, construction and building materials, furniture, appliances, and other critically needed materials are donated by thousands of generous corporations, including 30 percent of the *Fortune* 500 companies.

Purchasing Services Agency

50 California Street, Suite 200, San Francisco, CA 94111
Tel: 888-488-0772
E-mail: info@psagency.org;
WWW: http://www.psagency.org/index.cfm
▶ This is a nonprofit organization that negotiates with vendors for preferential pricing of goods and services on behalf of their member agencies and simplifies the ordering process for individual agencies.

Professional Associations

American Association of Fund-Raising Counsel (AAFRC)

10293 North Meridian Street, Suite 175, Indianapolis, IN 46290
Tel: 800-462-2372, 317-816-1613; FAX: 317-816-1633
E-mail: aafrc@compuserve.com; WWW: http://www.aafrc.org,
http://www.smithbeers.com/aafrc.htm
▶ Formed in 1935 to advance the philanthropic cause and the ethical approach to fund raising, AAFRC works to ensure that fund-raising counseling firms contribute positively to the cause that has been important to the nation's churches and community funds, cultural and arts institutions, colleges and universities, hospitals, character-building agencies, and health organizations. Member firms follow the concept that careful investigation and analysis of pertinent facts provide the foundation upon which successful fund-raising programs can be based. Each member firm exclusively or primarily provides fund raising counseling services, including feasibility studies, campaign management, and related public relations to nonprofit institutions and agencies seeking philanthropic support. Its Standards of Membership and Professional Conduct is accepted widely as the standard for professional conduct in fund-raising counsel. The Association cooperates with collegial groups and state and federal officials in formulating appropriate regulations and is a leading source of information on legislative developments affecting fund raising and philanthropy. In 1985, it founded the AAFRC Trust whose mission is to advance research, education, and public awareness of philanthropy.

Publishes annual compilation of statistics and trends, annual reports *Giving USA* and *Survey of State Charitable Solicitations* and the quarterly newsletter, *Giving USA Update*. The Web site of the AAFRC, whose membership is composed of consulting firms that advise nonprofits on fund-raising matters, leads visitors to useful data regarding trends in philanthropy and the distribution of the types of sources and recipients of giving. A particularly helpful feature on the site is its "8 Steps to Choosing Fund-Raising Counsel"

area, which elucidates various factors to consider in selecting the right firm.

American Association of Grant Professionals (AAGP)

c/o Iris Coffin, Treasurer, 1012½ 2nd Street, Perry, IA 50220
23410 Beech Road, Southfield, MI 48034
E-mail: MikeBrock@mediaone.net (Mike Brock, AAGP Association Administrator)
Home/Office: 248-356-8195; FAX: 248-356-8189
E-mail: prenninger@aol.com (Phyl Renninger, Secretary);
WWW: http://www.grantprofessionals.org/
▶ The AAGP serves grant developers who work for public or private organizations. The association offers professional certifications, maintains a code of ethics, promotes the public image of professional grant developers, enhances grant developers' relationships with funders and employers, and advances educational opportunities.

The American College of Trust and Estate Counsel

3415 South Sepulveda Boulevard, Suite 330, Los Angeles, CA 90034
Tel: 310-398-1888; FAX: 310-572-7280
E-mail: info@actec.org; WWW: http://www.actec.org/
▶ The purposes of The American College of Trust and Estate Counsel are to maintain an association, international in scope, of lawyers skilled and experienced in the preparation of wills and trusts; estate planning; probate procedure and administration of trusts and estates of decedents, minors, and incompetents; to improve and reform probate, trust, and tax laws, procedures, and professional responsibility; to bring together qualified lawyers, whose character and ability will contribute to the achievement of the purposes of the college; and to cooperate with bar associations and other organizations with similar purposes.

American Council on Gift Annuities

233 McCrea Street, Suite 400, Indianapolis, IN 46225
Tel: 317-269-6271; FAX: 317-269-6276
E-mail: acga@iupui.edu (Gloria Kermeen, ACGA Administrator);
WWW: http://www.ncpg.org/acga.html
▶ This qualified nonprofit organization was formed in 1927 as the Committee on Gift Annuities for the purpose of providing educational and other services to American charities regarding gift annuities and other forms of planned gifts. One of the primary activities of the Council is the publication of suggested charitable gift annuity rates for use by charities and their donors.

The Association for Healthcare Philanthropy

313 Park Avenue, Suite 400, Falls Church, VA 22046
Tel: 703-532-6243; FAX: 703-532-7170
E-mail: maryann@go-ahp.org; WWW: http://www.go-ahp.org/,
http://www.go-ahp.org/ric.htm (Resource Information Center)
▶ Founded in 1967, AHP is the only organization dedicated exclusively to advancing health care philanthropy and resource development. Members include 2,500 fund-raising executives working in health care, representing more than 1,500 hospitals and health care organizations throughout North America. AHP provides educational and networking opportunities to health care resource development professionals in the United States and Canada. Programs

include: Education Advancement (regional/national conferences, institutes, workshops, and courses, including AHP Core Curriculum accreditation; AHP's Certification Program, established in 1975, allows members to achieve professional recognition by documenting experience and testing knowledge in health care resource development. Currently, there are two levels of achievement in the program: the Certified Fund Raising Executive and the Fellow), publications; AHP Roundtables (regularly scheduled meetings that feature guest speakers, in-depth discussions, and networking opportunities); professional partners (pairs newcomers with experienced professionals in their region), government affairs; (keeps you abreast of legislation and proposals affecting health care delivery and philanthropy and provides advocacy); Resource Information Center (houses books, periodicals, pamphlets, articles, case statements, and other pertinent materials); publications (publishes monthly newsletter, *AHP Connect,* biannual *AHP Journal,* and annual *Membership Directory and Buyers Guide,* in addition to books, self-study guides, pamphlets, and reading packets, as well as videos).

Association of Direct Response Fundraising Counsel (ADRFCO)

1612 K St NW, Suite 510, Washington, DC 20006-2802
Tel: 202-293-9640; FAX: 202-887-9699
E-mail: ADRFCO@aol.com (Robert Tiger, General Counsel)

▶ Founded in 1986, it is the national trade association of companies or divisions of companies and individuals that specialize in consulting with nonprofit organizations about their direct response fund-raising campaigns. Member firms pledge compliance with ADRFCO's Rules of Business Ethics and Practice and promote the importance of maintaining the highest ethical standards in dealings with nonprofits, regulators, and the public. Its primary goals are to enforce the industry's set of comprehensive ethical standards, represent its members' interests before state and federal government, and educate nonprofit organizations and the general public about the use of direct response fund raising. Services provided by members include offering advice and counsel, conducting feasibility studies and tests, designing and managing campaigns, developing and producing solicitation materials, and providing mailing lists; providing timely reports on key changes in fund-raising law and legal advice on direct mail regulations. Members pledge compliance with the Rules of Business Ethics and Practice. ADRFCO sponsors local and national meetings and other events. A membership directory is available.

Association of Fundraising Professionals (Formerly the National Society of Fund Raising Executives)

1101 King Street, Suite 700, Alexandria, VA 22314
Tel: 800-666-3863 (FUND), 703-684-0410; FAX: 703-684-0540
E-mail: nsfre@nsfre.org, resctr@nsfre.org (Fund Raising Resource Center); WWW: http://www.nsfre.org/

▶ A not-for-profit corporation, it is the professional association for individuals responsible for generating philanthropic support for a wide variety of not-for-profit, charitable organizations. Founded in 1960 as NSFRE, it advances philanthropy through its more than 20,000 members in 154 chapters throughout North America. It advances philanthropy through education, training, and advocacy based on research and a Code of Ethical Principles and Standards of Professional Practice. It offers consulting, training, and career development services. It also produces various publications and

videos dealing with the subjects of general fund raising; not-for-profit planning, marketing, and management; not-for-profit boards; major gifts; planned giving; proposals and grants; direct mail; special events; prospect search and demographics; education; religion; philanthropy; fund raising as a profession; not-for-profit law, tax, and accounting; and general interest. Call the national number for a catalog. Programs and services include *Directory of Consultants* (Web version at: *http://www.nsfre.org/welcome/index.html*); Fund-Raising Resource Center; professional certification; educational opportunities; book publishing program; and *advancing philanthropy,* the member magazine.

Association of Lutheran Development Executives

P.O. Box 930303, Verona, WI 53593
Tel: 800-458-2363; FAX: 309-664-2931
E-mail: staff@alde.org; WWW: http://www.alde.org

▶ Organized in 1979 as a pan-Lutheran professional membership organization for Lutherans involved in resource development, ALDE promotes and provides professional growth opportunities for its members and advances the understanding and practice of Christian stewardship. ALDE members include professionals with Lutheran organizations and Lutherans working as development and communications staff in other not-for-profit organizations. *ALDE News,* published three times per year, serves as a valuable link between members and reports on news, plans, and ongoing activities of the organization. Other publications include *Legislative Alert,* published periodically and covering legislative, regulatory, and legal issues affecting ALDE members; The "Best of the Conference" series; and *Compensation Survey Report,* results from the latest of ALDE's biannual compensation survey. Additional services include executive searches, position announcements from member organizations, published on demand and distributed by a combination of first-class mail and e-mail to ALDE members. Copies of recent searches (within two months) are posted on this site in the Members Only area (password required); and education and professional growth. Their Web site provides information about legislative, regulatory, and legal issues that affect charities; the most recent issue of the association's newsletter; and links to Web sites of interest to fund raisers.

Association of Philanthropic Counsel

414 Plaza Drive, Suite 209, Westmont, IL 60559
Tel: 800-957-5666; FAX: 630-6555-0391
E-mail: APCInfo@InfoSyte.com; WWW: http://www.philanthropic counsel.org/, http://www.philanthropiccounsel.org/apc.htm (Membership Directory)

▶ This organization endeavors to support both the independent philanthropic consulting firm owner and consulting practitioners in developing and enhancing their consulting practices. It holds an annual conference.

Association of Professional Researchers for Advancement (APRA)

414 Plaza Drive, Suite 209, Westmont, IL 60559
Tel: 630-655-0177; FAX: 630-655-0391
E-mail: info@aprahome.org; WWW: http://www.aprahome.org/, http://www.aprahome.org/links.htm

▶ This international professional association addresses the changing needs and wide scope of skills required of advancement researchers and advancement service professionals working within the nonprofit community. It publishes *Connections,* a quarterly newsletter. Its Web site provides information about APRA's mission, membership, and events; "prospecting resources" links; and several FAQs on topics ranging from prospect research to netiquette.

Catholic Organization of Development

16647 Farnam Street, Omaha, NE 68118
Tel: 800-426-8198, 402-333-4279; FAX: 402-333-4284
E-mail: info@codesweb.com; WWW: http://www.codesweb.com/

▶ This is the original professional organization dedicated *exclusively* to serving and encouraging the development programs of America's Catholic schools. Programs/services include seminars and training, consulting, and publications.

Council for Advancement and Support of Education (CASE)

11 Dupont Circle, Suite 400, Washington, DC 20036-1261
Tel: 202-328-5948; FAX: 202-387-4973
E-mail: membership@case.org, library@ns.case.org;
WWW: http://www.case.org, http://www.case.org/links/fundrais.htm

▶ CASE is an international association of education advancement officers, who include alumni administrators, fund raisers, public relations managers, publications editors, and government relations officers. It is the product of a 1974 merger between the American Alumni Council (founded in 1913) and the American College Public Relations Association (founded in 1917). The ultimate goal of advancement professionals is to enhance their institutions by bringing in support, be it in the form of money, alumni loyalty, public esteem, or new students. In turn, CASE's purpose is to help these people advance the cause of education. It does this by offering information resources and training opportunities to aid members. CASE publishes an annual edition of *Matching Gift Details,* which itemizes which institutions match the gifts of their employees. Their membership includes more than 2,900 colleges, universities, and independent elementary and secondary schools in the United States, Canada, Mexico, and 27 other countries. CASE exists for educational advancement professionals whose responsibilities include budget, fund raising, alumni administration, and public relations. Other nonprofit organizations may affiliate with CASE as educational associates. Among these affiliates are hospitals, museums, arts organizations, and public broadcasting stations. CASE provides an educational training program. Its Web site contains job postings, discussion groups, information about CASE's awards and fellowships, training courses, member services, and related merchandise, an index of articles from its magazine *CURRENTS* since 1975, and links to other sites of interest.

Council for Resource Development (CRD) (Formerly the National Council for Resource Development)

One Dupont Circle NW, Suite 410, Washington, DC 20036-1176
Tel: 202-822-0750; FAX: 202-822-5014
E-mail: crd@aacc.nche.edu; WWW: http://www.ppcc.cccoes.edu/crd

▶ An affiliate and major council of the American Association of Community Colleges, CRD's mission is to educate and advocate for community college leaders dedicated to securing resources to increase the effectiveness of the institutions and students they serve. Current membership totals more than 1,000 contact people,

representing over 800 two-year colleges in the United States and Canada. Membership is open to anyone interested in the welfare of two-year colleges, and includes development officers, grant writers, foundation directors, college presidents, administrators, and staff. Programs/services include: Resource Development Network; Corporate Funding Initiative; Legislation/Grants Alerts; Resource Development Specialist Training Program; College Foundation Academy; Federal Funding Task Force; Summer Symposium on Emerging Issues; Executive Institute; and publications (Annual Membership Directory and Resource Guide, *DISPATCH Newsletter,* and annual *Federal Funding to Two-Year Colleges Report,* among others). CRD hosts a three-day annual conference in Washington, DC.

DMA Nonprofit Federation *(See Legal Issues, Organizations)*

Direct Marketing Association (DMA)

1120 Avenue of the Americas, New York, NY 10036-6700
Tel: 212-768-7277; FAX: 212-302-6714
WWW: http://www.the-dma.org/

▶ For over 75 years, DMA's mission has been to serve people and companies who are involved in direct marketing at any level. DMA is a professional community of direct marketers that has been a central force in the arena of government affairs, influencing legislation that directly and indirectly affects all direct marketers. DMA also plays a vital part in representing members' concerns over major governmental issues that directly affect the profitability of companies, including use tax, privacy, postal rate increases, alternate delivery, and many others.

Direct Marketing Fundraisers Association

224 Seventh Street, Garden City, NY 11530-5771
Tel: 516-746-6700; FAX: 516-294-8141
E-mail: info@dmfa.org; WWW: http://www.dmfa.org/

▶ This is the only professional association exclusively for direct-response fund raisers. Since 1972, DMFA has educated and connected individuals united by a common commitment to excellence and ethics in direct-response fund raising for nonprofit organizations. Its purpose/mission is to enhance the professionalism of all those engaged in the business of direct-marketing fund raising. They offer a selection of luncheons, workshops, and special events throughout the year.

International Alliance of Grantwriters and Nonprofit Consultants (IAOGWANC) (Formerly known as the National Association of Grantwriters and Nonprofit Consultants)

c/o Dr. Jorea Blount, 509 Marshall Street, Suite 729,
Shreveport, LA 71101
Tel: 318-459-1100; FAX: 318-459-1100

Dallas office: c/o Catherine Delaney
Tel: 972-378-3024
WWW: http://www.naogwanc.org

▶ IAOGWANC is a professional organization for grant writers and nonprofit consultants. Its mission is to represent all grant writers and nonprofit consultants, large and small; those well established and those just starting up; as well as those in all fields of the nonprofit effort: social service, education, health, and the like. IAOG-WANC furthers its mission to lead grant writers, nonprofit consultants, nonprofit organizations, its board, employees, and volunteers toward excellence in performance by providing a variety of resources, services, and technical assistance to build a viable, efficient network of nonprofit organizations. The group's Web site includes a directory of grant writers and consultants, organized by state, and links to Web sites of interest to nonprofit organizations.

National Association of Estate Planners and Councils (NAEPC)
270 South Bryn Mawr Avenue, P.O. Box 46,
Bryn Mawr, PA 19010-2196
Tel: 610-526-1389; FAX: 610-526-1310
WWW: http://216.149.57.170/

▶ This organization's primary goal and emphasis focus on a program of community awareness in the area of estate planning. The NAEPC is unique in that it spans the disciplines that contribute to the estate planning process and fosters a team concept of working together to accomplish the client's goals. A primary goal of the NAEPC is to encourage specialization programs to increase recognition and acceptance of estate planning as a specialty. Particular focus is on accounting, insurance, law, and trust services. NAEPC has two separate and distinct specialization programs: Accredited Estate Planner available to individuals in all four disciplines; Estate Planning Law Specialist is a board-certification program available only to attorneys.

National Association of Philanthropic Planners
24881 Alicia Parkway, Suite E-330, Laguna Hills, CA 92653
Tel: 800-342-6215; FAX: 714-692-7668
E-mail: info@napp.net, napp@napp.net, nappexec@flash.net
(Karen Mulder, Executive Administrator);
WWW: http://www.napp.net/

▶ This is a nationally organized group of financial professionals, estate planners, and philanthropic wizards whose unified purpose is to better the understanding of what exactly philanthropic planning is, what it involves, and how to educate potential consumers as to the rewards of organizing their fiscal benefaction in the best manner possible. It is committed to supporting the philanthropic planning practices of its members through a variety of association programs and benefits. It is the first formally organized group of its kind serving the philanthropic planning practitioner. It holds an annual conference.

National Catholic Development Conference (NCDC)
86 Front Street, Hempstead, NY 11550-3667
Tel: 888-TRY-NCDC (879-6232), 516-481-6000;
FAX: 516-489-9287
E-mail: hfernandez@ncdcusa.org or hafernandez@aol.com
(Henry A. Fernandez, President and CEO);
WWW: http://www.amm.org/ncdc.htm

▶ Since 1968, NCDC has grown to become the nation's largest association of religious fund-raising organizations. Active membership in NCDC is available to Catholic organizations and institutes that are listed in the Official Catholic Directory. Associate membership is available to nonCatholic entities. Corporate membership is available to suppliers of goods and services to the philanthropic

community. With a membership of 14,000 fund-raising organizations, the network extends across the United States into Canada and around the globe. It helps reach development professionals in religious congregations, social service agencies, mission groups, health care organizations, schools, dioceses, shrines, parishes, and many other charitable organizations whose fund-raising activities include direct mail, planned giving, major gifts, special events, foundation appeals, grant proposals, and endowment campaigns. It provides education, extensive networking opportunities and timely information. Member services and benefits include education and training, seminars and workshops, networking and peer support, annual NCDC Conference and Exposition, resource and audiotape libraries, advice and referrals, publications and postal/legislative bulletins, representation and affiliations. Its *Membership Resource Directory* lists products and/or services, their address, phone/FAX numbers, contacts, and a description. NCDC publishes a monthly newsletter, *Dimensions*. Fund raisers can also take advantage of NCDC's extensive tape library.

National Committee on Planned Giving (NCPG)
233 McCrea Street, Suite 400, Indianapolis, IN 46225
Tel: 317-269-6274; FAX: 317-269-6276
E-mail: ncpg@iupui.edu; WWW: http://www.ncpg.org,
http://www.ncpg.org/sites.html

▶ Established in 1988, it is the professional association for people whose work includes developing, marketing, and administering charitable planned gifts. Those people include fund raisers for nonprofit institutions and consultants and donor advisors working in a variety of for-profit settings. The National Committee on Planned Giving was formed in 1988 as a federation of planned giving councils to facilitate, coordinate, and encourage the education and training of the planned giving community, and to facilitate effective communication among the many different professionals in the community. It hosts the National Conference on Planned Giving. Programs and services include education (NCPG encourages the education and training of the planned giving community through the continuation and expansion of high-quality educational opportunities available to planned giving practitioners. Most of NCPG's educational programs and publications are keyed to the *Syllabus for Gift Planners,* a detailed outline of professional knowledge and skills); announcement listing service (offers a members-only Web-based job posting service); research (the majority of these projects are funded through grants and carried out in cooperation with other research organizations); government relations (through its Government Relations Committee, it recommends and coordinates efforts to promote a legislative environment favorable to charitable gift planning; news bulletin); GIFT-PL (an e-mail distribution center for gift planners that is administered by NCPG. It was established as a forum for discussion on issues relating to gift planning); publications (*Gift Planner Update,* a monthly newsletter covering professional issues, NCPG activities and policies, council activities, and planned giving resource reviews; *The Journal of Gift Planning*™—a quarterly publication intended to encourage professional education; *Syllabus for Gift Planners,* a detailed outline of professional knowledge and skills designed to be used as a training guide; and more); and *LEAVE A LEGACY*™, a community-based effort that encourages people from all walks of life to make gifts from their estates to the nonprofit organizations of their choice.

National Grant Writers Association (NGWA)

P.O. Box 1755, Irmo, SC 29063-1755
E-mail: contact@grantexperts.com;
WWW: http://www.researchassociatesco.com/ngwa.htm,
http://www.researchassociatesco.com/national_directory.htm

▶ The National Grant Writers Association (NGWA) began in 1997 by a group of grant writers who were seeking a national certification and recognition of their work in the grants field. The NGWA consists of approximately 1,000 Certified Grants Specialists who have completed 40+ hours of grants development training through Research Associates. The private, nonprofit organization's mission is to provide high level grants development education and to establish networks through which grant writers can communicate, exchange information, and provide professional support for each other. The National Grant Reviewers Association was formed in 1998 as a result of NGRA members desiring an advanced level of certification. They also wanted to receive training on how to not only review grant proposals, but also how to train others to be grant reviewers. In order to be a member, participants must attend their five-day grant development seminars scheduled in Columbia, SC, Hilton Head, SC, New York City, NY or Los Angeles, CA, and complete the two-day reviewer course. Upon completion of the training, members then become a Certified Grants Reviewer.

Planned Giving Design Centers (PGDC)

10800-D Independence Pointe Parkway, Matthews, NC, 28105
Tel: 704-849-0731; FAX: 704-849-2279
E-mail: info@pgdc.net; WWW: http://www.pgdc.net/pub/

▶ The Planned Giving Design Center helps charitable organizations create strategic alliances with legal, tax, and financial services professionals in their communities who have the capacity to influence philanthropy. The PGDC does this by offering the largest body of technical content and planning resources on the topic of charitable gift planning and taxation found anywhere on the Internet to professional advisors free of charge.

Women in Development of Greater Boston (WID)

93 Concord Avenue, Suite 8, Belmont, MA 02478
Tel: 617-489-6777; FAX: 617-489-7799
E-mail: widgb@widgb.org; WWW: http://www.widgb.org/

▶ Founded in 1980, WID is a nonprofit professional association of women in the field of institutional advancement. WID offers its members a variety of programs, services, and opportunities for volunteer involvement; membership is open to women working in the advancement profession as well as those considering careers in the field. It offers scholarship assistance toward membership dues and/or program fees to enable women from a broad spectrum of organizations and backgrounds to become actively involved. Services include regular programs (a broad range of topics of interest, including plenary meetings with speakers on a variety of professional development issues, smaller, skill-building workshops, and special seminars on such topics as public speaking and negotiation); mentoring program (matches senior members with those who have recently entered the field; provides small-group networking sessions around topics of common interest); membership directory (all WID members, listed alphabetically by institution, and by area of expertise; published annually), job listings (available development positions at a variety of experience levels and with a broad range of organizations); and WID Job Line (up-to-the-minute information on job openings). It also publishes the *Reference Guide to Compensation and Salary Negotiation* and the quarterly newsletter, *WID News.*

Special Events

Cause Effective

505 Eighth Avenue, Suite 1212, New York, NY 10018-6512
Tel: 212-643-7093; FAX: 212-643-0137
E-mail: info@causeeffective.org, judy@causeeffective.org (Judy Levine); WWW: http://www.causeeffective.org/

▶ Cause Effective is the nation's leading provider of special events management assistance for nonprofits. Founded in 1981, Cause Effective is a New York–based nonprofit that helps nonprofit organizations build their capacities to develop human and financial resources through consulting, workshops, and publications. Cause Effective helps nonprofits plan and implement special events, train and develop their boards, manage individual donors, enlist and manage volunteers, and promote and market their organizations. More than 2,000 nonprofit organizations serving tens of millions of people have been assisted by Cause Effective. Cause Effective extends its reach to thousands of additional organizations by training other management assistance providers nationwide to use its approach.

PRODUCTS and SERVICES
(Consulting Firms)

Annual Campaigns

Special Campaign Consultants, Inc. (SCC)
425 East 79th Street, Suite 6D, New York, NY 10021
Tel: 212-517-2557; FAX: 212-535-5983
E-mail: SCC-LS@att.net (Lucille Strauss CFRE, President)
▶ Established in 1985, SCC provides hands-on individual development support for annual and capital campaigns, board training, strategic planning, and feasibility studies. It conducts high-level annual capital and endowment fund campaigns and conferences for major nonprofit institutions in the United States and abroad. It works closely with specialists in public relations, communications, construction management, marketing, graphic arts, and planned giving. This enables SCC to offer its clients in-depth expertise and service, as well as providing customized attention and supervision to every project need.

Capital Campaigns

Affinity Resources
361 Woodlawn, Lawrence, KS 66049
Tel: 877-320-2299; FAX: 785-832-0682
E-mail: service@affinityresources.com (Marc Lee CFRE, Principal); WWW: http://www.affinityresources.com
▶ Services include capital campaigns, Virtual Community Internet solutions, development department audits, strategic planning, technology planning and assessments, and annual fund support for small and medium-sized organizations. They serve private schools, small colleges, churches, health and human services organizations, and other not-for-profits. They provide both development counsel and hands-on Web site support and offer a free e-mail newsletter.

Boris Frank Associates
7094 Paoli Road, Verona, WI 53593
Tel: 608-845-3100
E-mail: borisfrank@inxpress.com (Boris Frank, President)
▶ Specializing in capital campaign development, feasibility studies, and strategic planning, this organization is creator of the ACCELERATED PLANNING MODEL. It focuses on libraries, humane societies, and arts organizations. It conducts workshops, seminars, training on fund raising, marketing, planning, board development, and volunteer management. Its clients are primarily in Wisconsin, Illinois, Michigan, Iowa, and Minnesota.

Capital Quest, Inc.
6501 E. Grant Road, Suite B, Tucson, AZ 85715
Tel: 800-263-1976, 520-733-7229; FAX: 888-427-2230, 520-751-3918

300 Queen Anne Avenue North, Suite 377, Seattle, WA 98109
Tel: 206-364-1227; FAX: 206-364-1218

4226 Gravelly Hills Road, Louisville, TN 37777
Tel: 423-379-1234; FAX: 423-379-2034
E-mail: CQIWK@aol.com (William C. Krueger, President);
WWW: http://www.capitalcampaigns.com,
http://www.capitalcampaigns.com/tour.html,
http://www.capitalcampaigns.com/faq.html
▶ Founded in 1992 by William C. Krueger, it is a national capital campaign consulting firm. Provides two basic services to clients: design and marketing phase (personal interviews, direct mail surveys, focus groups, corporate and foundation research, identification of potential funding sources, a review of the organization's image, case, and leadership); and campaign management (develop a comprehensive campaign plan; instruct volunteers on methods of recruitment and solicitation; write a thorough campaign case statement; plan and coordinate the selection of top campaign leadership; identify and segment prospective donors; write appropriate Foundation proposals; organize all committees and direct their activities; prepare speaking notes and detailed agendas for speakers; devise appropriate gift plans; where desirable, solicit or assist in the solicitation of gift prospects; prepare all publicity and public relations activities; prepare campaign materials such as brochures, pledge cards, and newsletters; conduct orientation seminars for all important audiences; report regularly to campaign officials on activities and progress; prepare all records pertinent to the receipt of gifts; establish and monitor pledge redemption; prepare an official report embracing the campaign history; prepare recommendations for post-campaign development; provide pledge redemption service without fee.

Clover Development Strategies, Inc.
2677 South Ocean Boulevard, Suite 4C, Boca Raton, FL 33432
Tel: 800-741-4147, 954-429-8900; FAX: 954-429-8920
E-mail: CApelian@aol.com (Clover B. Apelian);
WWW: http://www.cloverfund.com
▶ This consulting firm manages nonprofit capital campaigns throughout the United States. In addition, they offer a broad array of fund-raising–related services including feasibility studies, board and/or organization development, plan facilitating, major gifts strategies, and more for not-for-profit organizations, and their staffs and volunteer leaders. Clover conducts workshops and seminars throughout the United States.

Cornerstone Consulting, Inc. *(See Full Service)*

Custom Development Solutions (CDS)
4 Allie Court, Isle of Palms, SC 29451
Tel: 800-761-3833; FAX: 843-886-9529
E-mail: dgp@cdsfunds.com (David G. Phillips),
kas@cdsfunds.com (Kim A. Stryker, Marketing/Administrative
Director); WWW: http://www.cdsfunds.com
▶ CDS specializes in the planning and resident direction of capital fund-raising campaigns. The firm raises money for colleges, schools, hospitals, cultural organizations, civic and social service agencies, and churches and church-related organizations. Services include capital campaign direction (specializes in the planning and resident direction of capital campaigns; provides a full-time campaign director on-site who will organize and monitor all aspects of the campaign process and ensure that all details of the program are run successfully); capital campaign consulting (offers campaign consulting services for organizations that already have established development operations; consultants provide fund-raising expertise and help to ensure that your organization reaches its fund-raising goals).

The David Mallison Company
145 West 85th Street, Suite Three B, New York, NY 10024
Tel: 212-721-1304; FAX: 212-721-1401
E-mail: dmc@rcn.com (David W. Mallison, President)
▶ This company concentrates on performing arts organizations, history and art museums, national libraries and archives, educational and recreational programs for schoolchildren, scholarly programs, biomedical research, and public health organizations. Mallison is a specialist in feasibility studies, capital campaigns, restoration projects, organizational strategic planning at New York and national levels, educational initiatives, annual fund drives, and marketing efforts.

Davidson Consulting Group
452 South Main Street, Suite C, Davidson, NC 28036
Tel: 704-892-9335; FAX: 704-892-9398
E-mail: blandess@dcg-nc.com (C. Barton Landess, Managing
Partner); WWW: http://www.dcg-nc.com
▶ This company offers capital campaign counsel and planned giving advice. Services include capital campaigns (strategic planning, planning/feasibility studies, development audit, government relations, prospect research, corporate/foundation support); and planned giving/fund-raising services (annual campaigns, board development). They offer other management consulting to complement and improve fund raising, to increase efficiency and productivity, to avoid potential problems, and to manage growth and success. Their consultants specialize in evaluating your organization's liability exposure and overall efficiency in the areas of risk management, human resources, financial management, financial controls, and student life facilities management. Clients include civic and cultural organizations, educational institutions, churches, human services organizations, and trade associations.

Durkin Associates *(See Full Service)*
Fund Consultants, Inc., 1525 Old Louisquisset Pike, Suite B-104,
Lincoln, RI 02865
Tel: 401-729-0100; FAX: 401-729-0122
E-mail: fciri@aol.com (Franklyn T. Cook CFRE, President)
▶ Fund Consultants, Inc., provides all types of institutional and organizational fund-raising and development services with an emphasis on capital campaigns.

Gloss and Company *(See Full Service)*

James A. Ravanelli and Associates
401 Cypress, Suite 414, Abilene, TX 79601
Tel: 800-353-0612; FAX: 915-675-0612
E-mail: jravanelli@jarsolutions.com;
WWW: http://www.JARSolutions.com
▶ Services include guerrilla capital campaigns with goals of $350,000 to $1.5 million, traditional capital campaign service, CEO coaching, direct-mail fund-raising service, annual fund campaign, newsletter for nonprofit organizations, student recruitment strategies for private schools PK through 12, coaching fund raisers with no experience, conducting board of trustees seminars, producing ads and brochures, stewardship literature and programs for churches, coaching CEOs in fund raising. Clients include private schools PK through 12, nursing homes and retirement centers, children's homes, homes for unwed mothers and adoption agencies, social service agencies, universities, churches, and para church organizations.

Kalish & Associates, Inc.
145 East 84th Street, Suite 5A, New York, NY 10028
Tel: 866-717-8935, 212-717-8935; FAX: 212-472-3057
E-mail: kalishinc@aol.com (Mark I. Kalish, President)
▶ Specialists in campaigns, strategic planning and assessments, and executive search, a full-service New York State–registered fund-raising and nonprofit management consulting firm founded in 1998. They specialize in capital campaigns, major gifts, board governance, leadership development, strategic planning, and interim management executive search for New York area organizations.

Special Campaign Consultants, Inc. (SCC)
425 East 79th Street, Suite 6D, New York, NY 10021
Tel: 212-517-2557; FAX: 212-535-5983
E-mail: SCC-LS@att.net (Lucille Strauss CFRE, President)
▶ Established in 1985, SCC provides hands-on individual development support for annual and capital campaigns, board training, strategic planning and feasibility studies. It conducts high-level annual capital and endowment fund campaigns and conferences for major nonprofit institutions in the United States and abroad. It works closely with specialists in public relations, communications, construction management, marketing, graphic arts, and planned giving. This enables SCC to offer its clients in-depth expertise and service, as well as providing customized attention and supervision to every project need.

Cause-Related Marketing
(See also Online Fundraising)

Diane Gingold & Associates (DG&A)
4812 Ellcott Street NW, Washington, DC 20016
Tel: 202-966-7121; FAX: 202-966-2341
E-mail: info@dga1.com, jennifer@DGA1.com (Jennifer Bricken);
WWW: www.strategic-philanthropy.com

▶ DG&A is a national consulting firm that assists corporations, nonprofit organizations, and individuals with strategic planning and programming designed to encourage good corporate citizenship as well as advance solutions for national social issues. DG&A designs and implements programs and negotiates partnerships by forming specialized teams that deliver strategies for effective philanthropy. Specializations include strategic planning and cause-related marketing, public awareness, special advertising sections and custom publishing projects, and museum consulting and fund-raising strategies.

Netcentives Cause-Related Marketing

475 Brannan Street, San Francisco, CA 94107
Tel: 415-538-1888, 415-615-2334 (Amon Rappaport),
415-307-9803 (Amon Rappaport); FAX: 415-538-1889
E-mail: nonprofits@netcentives.com, amon@netcentives.com
(Amon Rappaport); WWW: http://www.netcentives.com/solutions/
causerelated/index.html, http://www.emailmarketing.com/

▶ Netcentives offers an extensive array of technical integration, marketing, and loyalty promotion expertise and capabilities. It is a provider of relationship marketing technologies and services. Through a suite of technology products and services, Netcentives provides nonprofits with e-mail marketing and incentive solutions that generate significant online donations and Web traffic. For non-profits that want to enhance their direct marketing capabilities, Netcentives can design and deliver customized e-mail marketing programs to provide relevant and timely communication for fund-raising campaigns, newsletters, and advocacy alerts. Netcentives has additional offices in New York and Fort Lauderdale.

Communications

R. Gordon Talley Communication for Institutional Advancement

25 Magazine Street, Cambridge, MA 02139-3960
Tel: 617-497-7490; FAX: 617-497-2545
E-mail: info@rgtalley.com (R. Gordon Talley, Principal);
WWW: http://www.rgtalley.com

▶ This organization provides communication plans and strategic counsel to build board and donor awareness of needs, define campaign goals, and create compelling case statements. Services include campaign strategic planning, communications planning, staff motivation and training, key communications vehicles, and initiatives.

Computer Services

The Arlington Group

Tel: 703-893-9353; FAX: 703-893-9363
E-mail: info@arlgroup.com, lbair@arlgroup.com;
WWW: www.arlingtongroup.com

▶ Created in 1995, The Arlington Group has implemented data management solutions, addressing a diverse range of needs. It is experienced in the development of grants management systems and on-line application systems. Additional AG services include foundation management, contact management, membership management, data warehousing, custom software development, Web application development, and custom intranets/internets.

Bentz Whaley Flessner

2150 Norwest Financial Center, 7900 Xerxes Avenue South,
Minneapolis, MN 55431-1104
Tel: 612-921-0111; FAX: 612-921-0109
E-mail: bwf@bwf; WWW: http://www.bwf.com,
http://www.bwf.com/service/techpresen.htm

▶ It is critical for organizations to stay current with today's latest software and hardware capabilities and the level of information management that is crucial to fund-raising effectiveness and efficiency. Bentz Whaley Flessner provides operations audits, systems selection, data management, systems conversion and implementation, and staff training and development.

Jacobson Consulting Applications, Inc.

330 West 42nd Street, 30th Floor, New York, NY 10036
Tel: 212-465-2336; FAX: 212-465-2349
E-mail: solutions@jcainc.com; WWW: http://www.jcainc.com,
http://www.jcainc.com/links.html

▶ Jacobson Consulting Applications, Inc., is a full-service consulting firm dedicated to providing technical assistance to not-for-profit organizations. They specialize in helping organizations select and implement the fund-raising system that fits their needs.

S. Hellman Company, Inc. (SHC)

386 Park Avenue South, Suite 1914, New York, NY 10016
Tel: 212-689-5010; FAX: 212-684-5428
E-mail: info@shcco.com; WWW: http://www.shcco.com,
http://www.shcco.com/links.htm

▶ Established in 1983, S. Hellman Co. (SHC) delivers fund-raising and fund accounting software systems and solutions exclusively to nonprofits. Their client base includes organizations with the following missions: social services, religious, research, education, environmental, cultural arts; quasi-governmental, and foundations. SHC distributes iMIS Fund Raising software for nonprofits. iMIS Fund Raising provides your staff with the capability to plan, manage, and analyze simultaneous campaigns, appeals, and funds. They also provide consulting services.

Williamson Consulting Inc.

25 Farrar Road, Lincoln, MA 01773
Tel: 800-716-2681 (direct to voice mail and pager),
781-259-0091; FAX: 781-259-3447
E-mail: info@williamsonconsulting.com,
jim@williamsonconsulting.com (Jim Williamson);
WWW: http://www.williamsonconsulting.com

▶ Williamson Consulting works exclusively with nonprofit organizations on fund-raising systems design, selection, and strategic planning. It assists institutions, and their development offices in particular, in facing the complex issues related to information systems and their effective management. Among the range of services Williamson offers are information technology reviews, which can include assessments of current systems and the review of business processes, staffing plans, and organizational structure. Williamson also can provide assistance with the acquisition of a new fund-raising information system, including requirements analysis, the development of the RFP, the assessment of vendor proposals, and implementation planning. Clients include cultural, medical, international, educational, and general nonprofit organizations.

Corporate Contributions

Cain & Company Fundraising, Inc.
100 North Stone, Suite 1102, Tucson, AZ 85701
Tel: 800-687-3166, 520-918-1919; FAX: 520-918-1922
E-mail: info@cainandcompany.com (Shannon Cain);
WWW: http://www.cainandcompany.com

▶ The mission of Cain & Company is to support the work of progressive social service and advocacy organizations nationwide by helping them achieve the broadest possible base of financial support from foundations and corporations. They achieve their mission within a work environment in which employee input in company management is encouraged, information is shared, and openness, mutual respect, and health for all employees is acknowledged as a crucial component to their success. They specialize in fund raising and grant writing.

Contributions Academy
1150 Hungryneck Boulevard, Suite C-344,
Mount Pleasant, SC 29464
Tel: 843-216-3442; FAX: 843-216-3396
E-mail: Director@ContributionsAcademy.com,
Director@BNSInc.com (Curt Weeden, President);
WWW: www.ContributionsAcademy.com

▶ This is a management education organization dedicated to helping corporations and nonprofits establish powerful, creative, and mutually productive alliances. The Academy conducts Management Forums in Orlando, Florida, that are open to corporate contributions managers and other business executives looking to get maximum value from support provided to nonprofit organizations. The Academy also holds occasional programs for nonprofit leaders to acquaint them with the latest trends and developments in corporate philanthropy and related concepts. The Academy offers fund-raising guidance and assistance to nonprofit organizations through two initiatives: New Strategies conference that is held annually, and on-site workshops and speeches offered by Academy President Curt Weeden.

Direct-Mail and Direct-Response Marketing
(See also List Brokers; Membership; Telefundraising/Telemarketing)

Ahern Comunications, Ink.
10 Johnson Road, Foster, RI 02825
Tel: 401-397-8104; FAX: 401-397-6793
E-mail: A2Bmail@aol.com; WWW: http://www.aherncomm.com/nonprofit/index.htm

▶ This company offers best practices in marketing, employee, and nonprofit communications. They are a pool of writers, designers, and organizational development and fund-raising experts; a full-service research office; photographers; and several public relations veterans. Primary services are fund raising (appeal letters, special promotions, alumni materials, annual reports, case statements, endowment marketing materials, and campaign plans); and nonprofit communications (research and plans, public relations, ads, brochures, annual reports, newsletters, magazines, "Love Thy Reader," a seminar on how to create appealing nonprofit communications; more than 35 free expert tips for improving appeal letters, brochures, newsletters, press pitches, your Web site, etc.).

Amergent
9 Centennial Drive, Peabody, MA 01960
Tel: 978-531-1800; FAX: 978-531-0400
E-mail: jtrebbe@amergent.com (James Trebbe, Chairman and CEO); WWW: http://www.amergent.com

▶ This is a full-service direct-response fund-raising agency. They specialize in creative and strategic development, program analysis, database management, and integrated direct-mail production. Services include strategic planning, database services, creative services, analytic services, lifecycle analysis, vital signs analysis, direct-response fund raising, and major gift prospect identification. Their clients are serviced by account teams with specialized expertise in health care, social services, international and domestic relief agencies, membership organizations, and religious charities.

The Association of Direct Response Fundraising Counsel (ADRFCO)
1612 K Street NW, Suite 510, Washington, DC 20006-2802
Tel: 202-293-9640; FAX: 202-887-9699
E-mail: ADRFCO@aol.com

▶ The Association of Direct Response Fundraising Counsel represents firms that specialize in direct-response fund raising for nonprofit organizations. Member firms pledge compliance with ADRFCO's Rules of Business Ethics and Practice, and promote the importance of maintaining the highest ethical standards in dealings with nonprofits, regulators, and the public.

Black Mountain Communications, Inc.
34522 North Scottsdale Road #428, Scottsdale, AZ 85377
Tel: 480-595-9292; FAX: 480-595-9393
E-mail jgenette@aol.com (John Genette, President)

▶ Black Mountain specializes in direct-mail fund raising for nonprofit organizations. Clients include KUSC-FM public radio in Los Angeles and Scottsdale Healthcare Foundation. John Genette, President, has 24 years' experience in the nonprofit sector and serves as consultant to the Fundraising Group at Mal Warwick & Associates of Berkeley, California.

Craver, Mathews, Smith & Company (CMS)
4121 Wilson Boulevard, 11th Floor, Arlington, VA 22203
Tel: 703-258-0000; FAX: 703-258-0001
E-mail: markr@cms1.com (Mark Rover);
WWW: http://www.craveronline.com/

▶ CMS specializes in member and donor development and strategic fund raising. CMS also offers complementary services in planned giving, media strategy, and, through its CMSi division, Internet communications.

Epsilon
50 Cambridge Street, Burlington, MA 01803
Tel: 800-225-3333, 781-273-0250; FAX: 781-685-0800
E-mail: mrosen@epsilon.com (Matt Rosen);
WWW: http://www.epsilon.com/home.nsf/welcome

▶ Epsilon provides innovative, leading-edge, and cost-effective solutions in the fields of database management, fund raising, membership development, and direct-response marketing services. They specialize in serving nonprofit organizations and have maintained a leadership position by providing the following services: strategic consulting; direct-mail fund raising; creative design and development; database management and file processing; analytic research and modeling; list planning, management, and analysis; fulfillment services; production services.

European American Communications, Inc.

80 Eighth Avenue, Suite 1108, New York, NY 10011
Tel: 212-727-3876; FAX: 212-727-7954
E-mail: CorEuro@aol.com; WWW: http://www.eurodirectmail.com/

▶ This company focuses exclusively on marketing and direct-mail fund-raising campaigns for nonprofits. Services include analysis of your current direct-mail program, recommendations for expanding and/or improving your existing direct-mail program, media and list selection, copywriting of mailings, assistance in design (selection of graphic images, photos, color, paper stock selection, etc.), market research, comprehensive reports on findings, and application recommendations.

GB3 Group Nonprofit Marketing

430 North 1st Street, Suite 304, San Jose, CA 95112
Tel: 408-294-0035
E-mail: info@gb3group.com;
WWW: http://www.nonprofitmarketing.org/

▶ GB3 Group is a marketing, communications, and fund-raising consulting and training firm that services clients across the United States. The company provides training, consulting, coaching, and resources in marketing, communications, and fund raising to nonprofit and education managers, staff, and volunteers. Its nonprofit marketing site offers a variety of topical reference material and information about workshops, books, and related job openings in the field.

Gartner & Associates Inc.

728 West Jackson Boulevard, Suite 805, Chicago, IL 60661-5308
Tel: 312-454-0282; FAX: 312-454-0256
E-mail: GartnerAnd@aol.com

▶ Its development/fund-raising services include creative design, copy writing, final art preparation, printing production, lettershop management, mailing list research, computer applications, database management, acquisition campaigns, annual renewal campaigns, capital campaigns, planned giving programs, and special event planning and implementation. Clients include advocacy, arts and cultural, child welfare, colleges and universities, disabilities, educational training, elderly, environmental concerns, foundations (corporate and community), healthcare, low-income programs, professional associations, religious institutions, small agencies, social services, and welfare. Professional memberships include Association of Direct Response Fund Raising Counsel, Association of Consultants to Nonprofits, Chicago Association of Direct Marketing, and National and Chicago Councils on Planned Giving and National Society of Fund Raising Executives.

Hewitt and Johnson Consultants

99 Atlantic Avenue, Suite 411, Toronto, ON, Canada M6K 3J8
Tel: 416-588-7780; FAX: 416-588-7156
WWW: http://www.hjc.on.ca/

▶ This is a full-service consulting firm that provides expert guidance to nonprofits in developing, implementing and improving their direct-response fund-raising programs. HJC New Media helps nonprofit organizations effectively integrate new communications media, such as the Internet, into meeting their missions and mandates. They provide industry-leading expertise in Web site design, online fund raising, and strategic planning in the use of new communications media.

Huntsinger & Jeffer

809 Brook Hill Circle, Richmond, VA 23227-2503
Tel: 804-266-2499; FAX: 804-266-8563
E-mail: paulb@huntsinger-jeffer.com (Paul Braeckmans, President); WWW: http://www.huntsinger-jeffer.com

▶ Huntsinger & Jeffer is a full-service direct-response advertising agency founded in 1964, offering expertise in fund raising, business-to-business marketing, financial services, club and continuity marketing, travel/tourism, and consumer products.

KMA Direct

12001 North Central Expressway, Suite 900,
Dallas, TX 75243-3788
Tel: 800-KMA-4161, 972-560-1900; FAX: 972-980-1145
E-mail: tmccabe@kma.com (Tom McCabe), Smeyer@kma.com (Stan Meyer, General Manager); WWW: http://www.kma.com

▶ KMA partners with nonprofit organizations and ministries to develop personal, cost-effective strategies designed to build lasting relationships with donors. KMA direct services available include complete mailing services, CASS/PAVE certification, data processing, custom handwriting fonts, personalized cut-sheet lasering, personalized envelope addressing, hand match inserting, and machine inserting.

Kirk-Whitney Data Communications

7402-H Lockport Place, Lorton, VA 22079
Tel: 800-946-7674 (outside DC area), 703-339-8813;
FAX: 703-339-6802
E-mail: tiszard@Kirk-Whitney-Data.com (Tom Iszard, President);
WWW: http://www.Kirk-Whitney-Data.com

▶ Kirk-Whitney Data Communications exists to provide innovative mail communications solutions of the highest quality for nonprofit organizations. They emphasize new technology as a means of achieving breakthrough solutions for our customers. Their primary goal is to facilitate your communications with your customers or constituents by helping you understand the options, by clearing the obstacles to success, and by being responsive to your needs. They offer a complete range of services from data management, to laser personalization, bulk mail preparation, quick copy services, diskette duplication, and fulfillment.

L.W. Robbins Associates

201 Summer Street, P.O. Box 5838, Holliston, MA 01746-5838
Tel: 800-229-5972; FAX: 508-893-0212
E-mail: info@lwra.com, ledmonds@lwra.com (Lynn Edmonds, Executive Vice President); WWW: http://www.lwra.com,
http://www.lwra.com/Newsletters/news.htm,
http://www.lwra.com/Links/links.htm

▶ L.W. Robbins Associates, a direct-response fund-raising consulting firm, uses Donor (and Member) Relationship Management (DRM) for clients nationwide. With DRM, client teams incorporate database analysis, integrated media (including new and old technologies), customized creative and strategic programs, and competitive pricing to enhance value for the client. Founded in 1970, it has assisted over 300 nonprofit organizations serving local, regional, national, and international constituencies and represents virtually all sectors of the nonprofit world. L.W. Robbins Associates is a founding member of the Association of Direct Response Fund Raising Counsel (ADRFCO), and is also an active member of the National Society of Fund Raising Executives (NSFRE), the Direct Mail Association—Non-Profit Council, the New England Direct Marketing Association, the Direct Marketing Fundraisers Association, the National Catholic Development Conference, and the International Catholic Stewardship Council. Services include strategic direction, account management, creative/copy services, database solutions, production management, and internet fund raising.

Mal Warwick & Associates, Inc.

2550 Ninth Street, Suite 103, Berkeley, CA 94710
Tel: 510-843-8888; FAX: 510-843-0142
E-mail: info@malwarwick.com (Mal Warwick, Founder and Chair); WWW: http://www.malwarwick.com/,
http://www.malwarwick.com/publications.html

▶ Established in 1979, Mal Warwick & Associates can help you increase your membership base with a more effective direct-mail program; promote charitable bequests and other planned giving methods; find new members and cultivate the ones you have using e-mail and the Web; tune up your fund-raising programs with a development audit and consulting; and improve the creative impact of your direct-mail packages, newsletters, and other materials. Every January, Mal Warwick & Associates sponsors an intensive two-day Major Donor Fundraising Clinic in Berkeley, primarily for their clients. In addition, Mal Warwick, Nick Allen, Steve Hitchcock, Bill Rehm, and other staff members speak frequently at workshops and conferences, including conferences of the National Society of Fund Raising Executives (NSFRE), the Direct Marketing Association, and others. See their workshop page for information about upcoming events. They offer *Successful Fundraising Online*, a free e-mail newsletter on direct mail, telephone, and online fundraising. Mal is author of 10 books, including *Raising Money by Mail, How to Write Successful Fundraising Letters*, and *The Five Strategies for Fundraising Success.*

Mathis, Earnest & Vandeventer (ME&V)

6711 Chancellor Drive, Cedar Falls, IA 50613
Tel: 877-932-3279, 319-268-9151; FAX: 319-268-0124
E-mail: info@meandv.com, dee@MEandV.com (Dee Vandeventer, President); WWW: http://www.MEandV.com

▶ Specializing in annual/capital campaigns, development audits, direct mail, video production, Internet, training and public relations, ME&V puts power behind your fund-raising efforts. Services include feasibility studies, annual drives, capital campaigns, specialized constituent fund raising, strategic planning, marketing and communication audits, direct mail, fund raising by phone, new media development, fund-raising video, Web site development, architectural fly-through animation, volunteer/board training and development, and focus groups.

May Development Services (A Division of Axciom/Direct Media, Inc.)

200 Pemberwick Road, Greenwich, CT 06830
Tel: 203-532-2546; FAX: 203-532-1654
E-mail: lmay@ix.directmedia.com (Larry May, CFRE, President)

▶ May Development Services assists nonprofit organizations in the design and implementation of direct-response fund-raising campaigns. Services include strategic planning, list brokerage, list management, lettershop, copywriting and design, print production, computer services, and response analysis.

McGrath and Company

113 North Cass Avenue, Westmont, IL 60559-1603
Tel: 630-852-9900; FAX: 630-852-4567
E-mail: mcgrathco@msn.com (Kevin M. McGrath CFRE, President, Teresa A. Harkenrider, Director of Client Services); WWW: http://www.mcgrathco.com

▶ This fund-raising consulting firm specializes in the planning, budgeting, all creative (design and copy), materials (envelopes, letterheads), production (printing, lasering), list (rental), and mailing services of annual direct-mail fund-raising campaigns for nonprofit institutions across the country. The acquisition of new donors and the upgrading of current donors are areas of special expertise.

Membership Consultants

3868 Russell Boulevard, St. Louis, MO 63110
Tel: 314-771-4664; FAX: 314-771-2759
E-mail: email MemConsul@aol.com;
WWW: http://www.membership-consultants.com,
http://www.membership-consultants.com/memcomm&tsem.html

▶ This is a full-service membership marketing resource for membership organizations including zoos, museums, botanical gardens, arboretums, and nonprofit organizations. Services include direct-mail acquisition, membership audits and strategic marketing plans, on-site sales, annual appeals, telemarketing, member renewals, lapsed members, list services, membership surveys, membership management, and dues/benefits analysis. It conducts ongoing series membership seminars as well as customized seminars and individualized training seminars.

Meyer Partners

501 Pebble Court, Schaumburg, IL 60193
Tel: 800-676-4176, 847-524-1273; FAX: 847-524-8081
E-mail: info@meyerpartners.com;
WWW: http://www.meyerpartners.com/

9237 Ward Parkway, Suite 310, Kansas City, MO 64114
Tel: 816-363-858

▶ This is a full-service, direct-response advertising agency serving the not-for-profit community with fund-raising counsel and a wide range of donor development services. Services include fund-raising services (donor/member development programs, development program audits, file analysis, general fund-raising counsel, strategic counsel and implementation services, annual giving programs, major gift campaigns, planned giving promotion); direct mail (creative direction, copy, design, production services, results analysis); institutional planning and management (counsel on strategic and long-range planning for fund raising, board and leadership seminars); and marketing and communications (market research, identity and program materials, print advertising). It is a member of the following professional organizations: National Society of Fund Raising Executives, Direct Marketing Association Nonprofit Council, Association of Direct Response Fundraising Counsel, Association of Lutheran Development Executives, National Catholic Development Conference, Christian Management

Association, Chicago Association of Direct Marketing, Kansas City Direct Marketing Association, and the Greater Kansas City Council on Philanthropy.

Moore Response Marketing Services

1200 Lakeside Drive, Bannockburn, IL 60015-1243
Tel: 847-607-6000; FAX: 847-607-7205
WWW: http://www.rms.moore.com; http://www.moore.com/

▶ Serving the nonprofit industry as one of our core focuses over the past 25 years, Moore Response Marketing Services creates, manages, and produces world-class direct-marketing programs for the leading direct marketers in America. They deliver financial results using direct-marketing strategies, powerful technologies, and a wealth of experience. From strategic consulting, creative services, database and list services, and sophisticated production technologies, Moore Response Marketing is your single source for your direct marketing needs.

New Income Sources (NIS)

2070 Crabtree Drive, Greenwood Village, CO 80121
Tel: 303-794-9556; FAX: 303-794-9611
E-mail: pk@nisdm.com (Paula Kaye, CEO)

425 29th St., Manhattan Beach, CA 90266
Tel: 310-545-7793; FAX: 310-545-5429

▶ New Income Sources assists with all aspects of direct-mail programs for a variety of clients. They offer a range of database services to nonprofits, generally in the form of direct-mail services and consulting. NIS assists nonprofits in maximizing income from direct response and integrating efforts with telemarketers, Internet, and other newly emerging technologies and techniques. Services offered include strategic planning; database creation and maintenance; copy and concept through production and mail house; database enhancements; donor modeling; baseline data reporting; CHAID analysis on up to 13 mailing variables; auditing current direct-mail programs and making recommendation for improvements in data selections and analysis; evaluating whether direct mail is the right way for your organization to raise funds; planning and execution of direct-mail programs, including annual campaigns (renewal and membership), acquisition campaigns, capital campaigns, cultivation campaigns, high-dollar cultivation and solicitation; database development and maintenance; and segmentation (tracing and tracking) so that you know what is working and with what part of the universe mailed. Focus is on acquisition, annual renewal, special appeal, cultivation, cash collection, and alternative media.

Newport Creative Communications

33 Railroad Avenue, Duxbury, MA 02332
Tel: 800-934-0586, ext. #24, 781-934-0586, ext. #24;
FAX: 781-934-7514
E-mail: info@newportcreative.com,
jurquhart@newportcreative.com (Judi Urquhart, Senior Vice President); WWW: http://www.newportcreative.com

8 Hollis Street, Groton, MA 01450-1357

▶ Providing comprehensive direct-mail fund-raising programs that include strategic planning, creative services, list planning and management, production services and detailed analysis, Newport Creative Communications is a direct-mail marketing agency specializing in work with nonprofit organizations. They will develop winning direct-mail programs to meet your fund-raising objectives. Their clients are located from Maine to Hawaii in the following markets: animal welfare, children's causes, food banks, health care, hospices, social and environmental issues, religious causes, and human services.

Pinnacle Advertising

4700 De la Savane, Suite 102, Montreal, Quebec, H4P 1T7, Canada
Tel: 514-344-3382; FAX: 514-344-5394
E-mail: pinnacle@total.net (Israel Monzon, Art Director);
WWW: http://www.pinnacle-direct.com/html/welcome.html

▶ This is a full-service agency that specializes in direct mail campaigns. Services include production services, program planning and management, strategic planning, list brokerage, and database management services.

The Rubin Communications Group

5096-4 Heatherhill Lane, Boca Raton, FL 33486-8304
Tel: 561-395-4956; FAX: 561-395-3103
E-mail: leon@rubincomm.com, LMRubes@aol.com (Leon M. Rubin, President); WWW: http://www.rubincomm.com

▶ This organization creates campaign case statements, annual reports, fund-raising brochures, newsletters and magazines, solicitation letters, video scripts, advertising copy, public relations campaigns, fund-raising communications plans, speeches and special event scripts, and grant proposals. They have national clientele.

Sanky Perlowin Associates (SPA)

1501 Broadway, Suite 610, New York, NY 10036
Tel: 212-921-0680; FAX: 212-921-1821
E-mail: www.sankyperlowin.com, info@sankyperlowin.com;
WWW: http://sankyperlowin.com/

▶ Since 1977, Sanky Perlowin Associates (SPA) has launched or expanded direct marketing programs for more than 80 not-for-profit organizations, including social service agencies, environmental groups, museums, and hospitals. It also provides online marketing assistance with its SankyNet Internet Services.

SouthWest Direct

2129 Andrea Lane, Ft. Myers, FL 33912
Tel: 800-968-5798; FAX: 941-768-0408
E-mail: klehtoma@southwestdirect.net (Kirk Lehtomaa, Vice President for Nonprofit Fundraising);
WWW: http://www.southwestdirect.net

▶ SouthWest Direct is a family-owned business providing printing, mailing, and fulfillment services. Meeting the unique mailing needs of nonprofits is their specialty.

Steege/Thomson Communications

4606 Spruce Street, Philadelphia, PA 19139
Tel: 215-747-7700; FAX: 215-474-0279
E-mail: st@steegethomson.com, cthomson@steegethomson.com (Carol Thomson, Partner), msteege@steegethomson.com (Michele M. Steege, Partner); WWW: http://www.steegethomson.com

▶ This company provides marketing and fundraising communications strategies. Their fund-raising communications programs reflect each organization's character and speak to each organization's donors. Their services to more than 100 institutions have ranged from case statements to comprehensive campaign materials and campaign communications plans. Fund-raising services include campaign communications plans, case statements, campaign publications, and appeal letters. Steege/Thomson devises customized strategies in marketing, consulting, fund-raising campaign communications, print and multimedia, media relations and advertising, communications plans and audits, case statements, creative publications, and media and advertising strategies. Clients include higher education; secondary and elementary education; health care institutions; cultural and civic organizations; human services, philanthropic, and environmental organizations; professional firms; research organizations, and other clients.

The Stelter Company

10435 New York Avenue, Des Moines, IA 50322
Tel: 800-331-6881; FAX: 515-278-5851
E-mail: larry@stelter.com (Larry Stelter, President/CEO);
WWW: http://www.stelter.com

▶ Founded in 1962, its mission is to assist organizations nationwide in accomplishing their missions by writing, designing, producing, and distributing high-quality planned giving direct-mail marketing and other communication products. Stelter publishes print and web content for donors of all categories, bequest solicitations, a home-study charitable estate planning course, and custom-designed programs. The marketing staff provides on-site review, and planned giving consultants answer questions and can provide on-site consulting, seminars, and training. Stelter also offers donor-focused development training through its relationship-building workshop.

Stephen Thomas Associates

2383 Queen Street East, Toronto, Ontario, M4E 1H5, Canada
Tel: 416-690-8801; FAX: 416-690-7256
E-mail: mail@stephenthomas.ca, stevet@stephenthomas.ca (Steve Thomas CFRE, President); WWW: http://www.stephenthomas.ca

▶ This company offers direct-response fund-raising and communication expertise to a wide array of not-for-profit organizations.

Vital Data Management, Inc.

7 Alfred Street, Woburn, MA 01801
Tel: 888-624-5836, 781-935-9990; FAX: 781-935-9993
E-mail: Info@vitaldatamanagement.com,
jbetz@vitaldatamanagement.com (John R. Betz, Principal);
WWW: http://www.vitaldatamanagement.com

▶ Founded in 1985, Vital Data Management, Inc. provides mail marketing and fund-raising counsel. Services include program planning; creative services, printing services, database management, computer services, list services, mail processing, and program analysis. Clients include health care services, educational services, environmental services, and human/social service organizations.

Watson Mail Communications, Inc.

2401 Revere Beach Parkway, Everett, MA 02149
Tel: 617-389-5350; FAX: 617-387-7752
E-mail: MCIDP3@watsonmci.com (Les Gordon, Vice President);
WWW: http://www.watsonmci.com

▶ Watson Mail Communications, Inc., is a full-service direct-mail fund raising/marketing company offering program planning and

analysis creative services (copywriting and design), computer processing, personalized laser letters, prospect list rentals, donor database management systems, data processing, and mail processing, all in a single location. It services over 200 nonprofit organizations nationwide.

Zairmail

2800 NW 29th Avenue, Portland, OR 97210-1704
Tel: 877-921-MAIL, 503-525-2555; FAX: 503-525-2444
E-mail: sales@zairmail.com (Don Skloss, Vice President of Sales); WWW: http://www.zairmail.com

▶ Zairmail is a Web-based service that currently has two unique offerings: Zairmail Express Direct™ mail and Zairmail™ letters. Both provide convenient and fast ways to reach targeted audiences. Zairmail Express Direct allows nonprofit organizations, political organizations, associations, and businesses to easily launch effective direct-mail campaigns quickly and reliably, from the Internet. Currently, the average direct-mail program takes more than three weeks to expedite, according to the Direct Marketing Association. With Zairmail Express Direct, the automated process can take as little as one to two days from design to delivery to your target audience. Zairmail, the consumer offering, extends this further by allowing consumers to send overnight postal mail, via the Internet, for free.

Donation Processing

Capital Dynamics Corporation

P.O. Box 702095, Dallas, TX 75370-2095
Tel: 800-DYNAPAY (396-2729); FAX: 972-381-7303
E-mail: capdyn@aol.com; WWW: http://www.capitaldynamics.com

▶ Capital Dynamics Corporation was founded in 1992 for the purpose of assisting companies and organizations to increase their cash flow and enhance their profits by offering the most advanced technology of the banking industry, the electronic funds transfer.

EFT Corporation

2911 Dixwell Avenue, Hamden, CT 06518
Tel: 800-338-2435; FAX: 203-248-3512
E-mail: whs@etransfer.com (Will Sawyer CFRE, Chairman);
WWW: http://www.etransfer.com

▶ EFT is a full-service provider of electronic funds transfer from checking, savings, and credit card accounts for direct giving programs; offering professional expertise in EFT marketing, enrollment form design, and Web site fund raising. EFT Corporation processes monthly, quarterly, and yearly donations; dues and payments for associations; PBS stations; advocacy; and foundations and charitable organizations using electronic funds transfer (EFT). Twenty years of EFT fund development experience gives EFT Corporation a broad perspective on starting and marketing EFT programs. Along with EFT processing, they assist with EFT start-up and marketing, EFT materials design, related computer support, and EFT Web site and Internet donation services.

UniTEQ/PipeVine

50 California Street, Suite 200, San Francisco, CA 94111-4696
Tel: 415-772-4321; FAX: 415-291-8392
E-mail: info@uniteq.net; WWW: https://www.uniteq.org,
https://www.uniteq.org/faq.jsp

▶ A nonprofit organization that serves as a national fund-raising resource for corporations, organizations, individual contributors, and other nonprofit agencies, UniTEQ/PipeVine works in collaboration with several organizations to process donations made to nonprofit organizations. UniTEQ/PipeVine takes electronic transfer information from the donor and distributes the information and the donation electronically or by check to the recipient organization(s). They offer a wide range of donation processing services that ensures your organization's philanthropic efforts are more productive and easier.

Donor Recognition

Creative Hands Brick + Tile Engraving
8879 SW 131st Street, Miami, FL 33176
Tel: 800-463-9497, 305-253-8573; FAX: 305-253-4418
WWW: http://www.exhibit-art.com

▶ Art/photo on tile engraving/tile/brass/etc.

Gift Brick
9512 Washington Avenue, Racine, WI 53406
Tel: 800-537-5579; FAX: 262-886-1130
E-mail: giftbrix@wi.net; WWW: http://www.gift-bricks.com

▶ An international engraving company specializing in engraved brick and tile and other media as donor recognition items.

Recognition Resources
6121B Clark Center Avenue, Sarasota, FL 34238-2722
Tel: 800-446-8585; FAX: 941-921-8388
E-mail: rr@donorart.com;
WWW: http://www.recognitionresources.com,
http://www.donorart.com

▶ Successful recognition fund-raising programs, artistic donor acknowledgment displays, design, data, confirmation, and marketing support.

Donor Research and Prospect Identification
(See also Prospect Research)

Alexander Haas Martin & Partners Inc. *(See MaGIC Inc.)*

Bentz Whaley Flessner *(See Full Service)*
Campbell Research, 218 West Carmen Lane, Suite 110,
Santa Maria, CA 93458
Tel: 805-922-0880; FAX: 805-922-3909
E-mail: info@campbell-research.com;
WWW: http://www.campbell-research.com/

▶ They help organizations obtain quality research feedback in order to maximize nonprofit and for-profit marketing and fund-raising potential. Since 1991, Campbell Research has served the nonprofit and for-profit world. They specialize in focus groups, phone and mail surveys, in-depth interviews, and conducting major analysis such as conjoint, multivariate, regression analysis, and perceptual maps.

Community Counselling Service Company Inc.
(See Full Service)

Grenzebach Glier & Associates Inc. *(See Full Service)*

MaGIC Inc.
133 Carnegie Way, Suite 1200, Atlanta, GA 30303
Tel: 877-54MAGIC (546-2442); FAX: 404-524-2992
E-mail: magic@ahmp.com; WWW: http://magic.ahmp.com

▶ A division of Alexander Haas Martin & Partners (see separate listing under Full Service), MaGIC (Major Gifts Identification/Consulting) provides data on individual wealth and philanthropy and will identify major gift prospects. The MaGIC database is updated daily with the most current, individual-specific data available. Your constituency is matched with the MaGIC database, immediately identifying those potential major donors hidden inside your list. With MaGIC, you'll learn about your prospects' stock ownerships, corporate and foundation board positions, and philanthropic histories. A MaGIC representative will deliver your results in person and conduct a half-day consulting session to develop an implementation plan for using your MaGIC data now. Topics covered during the session include explaining the MaGIC identification process; identifying your top prospects; identifying your best prospects for a capital campaign, major gifts program, phonathon, etc.; planning for additional verification research; sorting the data; demonstrating the MaGIC Query computer program; outlining the next steps; and setting goals for the next few weeks to the next few months.

Marts & Lundy Inc. ES Solutions
1200 Wall Street West, Lyndhurst, NJ 07071
Tel: 800-526-9005; FAX: 201-460-0680
E-mail: information@martsandlundy.com;
WWW: http://www.selectnet.net,
http://www.martsandlundy.com/es_solutions.html

▶ ES Solutions gives you a constant stream of information to monitor both influential corporate insiders and elusive private company owners. Learn your top prospects' newfound abilities to make a major gift. You will also get a comprehensive analysis of the wealth and giving propensity of your entire database. You will learn how best to segment and organize your prospects for planned giving, major gifts, and annual giving appeals.

Prospect Information Network *(See Software)*

Target America/WealthKnowledge.com
10560 Main Street, Suite LL 17-19, Fairfax, VA 22030
Tel: 703-383-6905; FAX: 703-383-6907
E-mail: tamerica@erols.com, wealthknowledge@aol.com;
WWW: http://www.tgtam.com, http://www.wealthknowledge.com'

▶ This online service provides unmatched information about why and how affluent Americans choose to invest and make charitable donations. Founded by specialists in identifying the wealthy and studying their behaviors and attitudes, the company continuously conducts thousands of interviews with affluent Americans. The resulting information is made available to individual investors and donors, who may use it as a benchmark to improve their own financial decisions.

Thomson Financial Wealth Identification (Formerly CDA/Investnet)

1455 Research Boulevard, Rockville, MD 20850
Tel: 800-933-4446; FAX: 301-545-4493
E-mail: WEALTH_ID@cda.com; WWW: http://www.wealthid.com

▶ Wealth ID is a provider of wealth identification data and innovative prospecting solutions. Since 1983, Wealth ID has been tracking wealthy individuals for many of America's nonprofit organizations, banks, insurance companies, and brokerage firms. Wealth ID's products assist in identifying high-net-worth prospects, donors, and clients. Their Philanthropic Services Division continues to focus on offering more effective and efficient products that assist nonprofit organizations with their fund-raising efforts. Their trained staff specializes in providing solutions for identifying donors/prospects for major gift solicitation and cultivation.

Excess Inventory

Excess Access, LLC

5813 Geary Boulevard, Box 111, San Francisco, CA 94121
Tel: 800-846-9068; FAX: 800-846-9069
WWW: http://www.ExcessAccess.com

▶ This Internet and toll-free number database matches business and individual donations with nonprofit wish lists. The incentives for signing up include: donors get free removal of accepted donations and get tax-deductible receipts; nonprofits get access to donations and pay only for the delivery if they can't pick up the items themselves; delivery services get suggested for pick-ups in their area; volunteer organizations get referrals; recyclers get access to materials and parts; everyone gets publicity and PR opportunities; and Mother Nature is happy to see reusables being kept out of landfills. The processing fee is only $10.

Foundations

Cain & Company Fundraising, Inc.

100 North Stone, Suite 1102, Tucson, AZ 85701
Tel: 800-687-3166, 520-918-1919; FAX: 520-918-1922
E-mail: info@cainandcompany.com (Shannon Cain);
WWW: http://www.cainandcompany.com

▶ The mission of Cain & Company is to support the work of progressive social service and advocacy organizations nationwide by helping them achieve the broadest possible base of financial support from foundations and corporations. They achieve their mission within a work environment in which employee input in company management is encouraged, information is shared, and openness, mutual respect, and health for all employees is acknowledged as a crucial component to their success. They specialize in fund raising and grant writing.

Robert J. Miller & Associates, Inc. (RJMA)

124 Delaware Street, Tonawanda, NY 14150
Tel: 800-898-RJMA, ext. 29, 716-694-8181, ext. 29;
FAX: 716-694-8206
E-mail: rjma@rjma.com; WWW: http://www.rjma.com

▶ RJMA is one of the nation's oldest and largest consulting firms specializing in securing grants for nonprofit organizations, school districts, and counties, cities, towns, and villages. It developed and administers the nation's largest database of public and private grant-making organizations. RJMA seeks and secures grants from private and corporate foundations and all federal and state grant-making agencies. Services include conducting on-site grants development feasibility studies, complete project design and proposal development, comprehensive funding searches of available grant funds, and submission and tracking proposals through grant-maker review cycles.

Full-Service Fund Raising

A.L. Brourman Associates, Inc.

555 Grant Street, Suite 337, Pittsburgh, PA 15219
Tel: 412-261-6344; FAX: 412-261-6346
E-mail: fund@brourman.com; WWW: http://www.brourman.com

▶ This full-service firm offers a wide variety of professional services and expertise in marketing, fund raising, and institutional advancement to nonprofit organizations. They work with colleges and universities, cultural organizations, hospitals, artistic organizations, social service agencies, libraries, and others to meet their financial and planning goals. Services include strategic planning, development capability assessment, campaign planning study, marketing study, campaign brochure case statement, annual giving audit, resident campaign direction, and general campaign consulting. Additional client services include management of capital campaigns, management of annual campaigns, executive search, prospect research, specialized development and project support, events planning and management, board fund-raising training, board development, feasibility/planning studies, and planned giving programs. They are a member of the American Association of Fund-Raising Counsel.

Academic Research Associates

Dr. Holly C. VanScoy, Academic Research Associates, Inc.,
10102 Wild Dunes Drive, Austin, TX
Tel: 800-518-3538, 512-291-1593, 512-689-5677 (cell);
FAX: 512-291-0066,
E-mail: academres@aol.com; WWW: http://www.grants2go.com

▶ Academic Research Associates offers a full range of fund-raising and grant-writing services for nonprofit organizations and governmental entities in the United States. ARA consultants include individuals with training and expertise in research and evaluation, grant writing, human development, social justice, woman's studies, organizational effectiveness, environmental science, public and private education, community leadership development, cultural competence and diversity, economic development, instructional and graphic design, technical writing, and editorial services. The company operates on a project-by-project basis, selecting for each effort one or more ARA staff whose training and skills match a client's needs.

Accelerated Income Methods (AIM)

32 Madera Boulevard, Corte Madera, CA 94925-1227
Tel: 415-924-3202; FAX: 415-927-1635
E-mail: Listerg@usfca.edu (Gwyneth J. Lister)

▶ AIM offers full service fund-raising counsel, campaign management, development analysis, strategic planning, board development, feasibility studies, marketing, communications, and all related fund development strategies.

Adams and Associates Consulting

444 West 22nd Avenue, Spokane, WA 99203
Tel: 509-747-3878; FAX: 509-624-6045
E-mail: adams.associates@ior.com, kent@adams-associates.com
▶ This company provides development and management consulting to nonprofits. Services include annual giving, major gifts, financial development planning, feasibility studies, capital campaigns, communications, and planned giving and board/staff training and development to clients in the Pacific Northwest.

Advancement Partners, Inc.

5970 Blunden Road, Dublin, OH 43016
Tel: 888-717-9980, 614-761-2363; FAX: 614-798-0548
WWW: http://www.advancement-partners.com
▶ Services include development operations audit, capital campaign, interactive development assessment, development counsel, strategic planning, starting or upgrading a development operation, board of trustee development, planned giving, donor retention, stewardship, advancement, and client support services.

Advocacy and Philanthropy

180 Mansion Drive, Newtown Square, PA 19073-3407
Tel: 610-356-5507; FAX: 610-353-8860
E-mail: jwilwol@advanthropy.org (John P. Wilwol Sr., Principal);
WWW: http://www.advanthropy.org, http://www.advanthropy.org/ assessing_your_advancement_program.htm
▶ Founded in 1992, it consults with nonprofit leadership in strategic planning, fund raising, and professional search. It is a full-service consulting firm with particular strengths in the following areas: alumni relations; annual giving; board effectiveness; capital campaigns; charitable gift planning and documentation; direct-mail experiments, including copy testing and tracking studies; enrollment management; feasibility studies; major gifts programs; market research; membership development; professional search; program assessments; strategic planning; and writing and editorial services. They work exclusively with nonprofits located or headquartered in Pennsylvania, New Jersey, or Delaware.

Affinity Resources

361 Woodlawn, Lawrence, KS 66049
Tel: 877-320-2299; FAX: 785-832-0682
E-mail: service@affinityresources.com (Marc Lee CFRE, Principal); WWW: http://www.affinityresources.com
▶ Services include capital campaigns, Virtual Community Internet solutions, development department audits, strategic planning, technology planning and assessments, and annual fund support for small and medium-sized organizations. They serve private schools, small colleges, churches, health and human services organizations, and other not-for-profits. They provide both development counsel and hands-on Web site support and offer a free e-mail newsletter.

Alexander Haas Martin & Partners (AHM&P)

133 Carnegie Way, Suite 1200, Atlanta, GA 30303
Tel: 800-490-8039, 404-525-7575; FAX: 404-524-2992
E-mail: ahmp@ahmp.com; WWW: http://ahmp.com, http://ahmp.com/links/publication/publicat.html
▶ The professional staff of over 20, including associates, are specialists in campaign direction and management, communications, marketing, research, and all aspects of ongoing advancement consultation. AHM&P is a national firm serving clients throughout the United States and Latin America. Services include campaign direction and management; campaign strategy studies; annual fund counsel; development assessment studies; planned giving counsel; creative services; prospect research; campaign and general consultation; interim development staffing; Search Incorporated; board, staff, and volunteer training; and strategic visioning. Innovations in prospect research include the DoNet, an on-line service providing information on corporate, foundation, and individual donors; and MaGIC, the only prospect research service that will identify your best major gift prospects and give you a plan of action on how to reach them. Innovations in marketing include AHM&P's development of the computerized campaign case statement. The computer case statement is an interactive, multimedia presentation of your case for support. Innovation in giving includes the Gifts in Kind Program. Working with Chadwicks, Inc., AHM&P can help you to identify corporate donors with valuable items for in-kind donation. Chadwicks will then liquidate the assets for you and return the proceeds to your organization.

Alexander Macnab & Company

900 North Franklin Street, Suite 810, Chicago, IL 60610
Tel: 800-708-2060, 312-642-1239; FAX: 312-640-1994
E-mail: growfunds@aol.com
▶ This company offers personalized, practical solutions; major gift programs, feasibility studies, and campaigns; board and volunteer solicitation training; annual giving/direct-mail consultation; gift illustrations; and start-up planned giving. Services include capital and endowment campaigns; feasibility studies; major gift programs; new planned giving programs; program audits; board development; direct-mail annual giving programs; gift illustrations and record-keeping systems; executive searches; seminars (How to Solicit Major Gifts: Making Successful Solicitations; Gaining Through Giving: Doing Good While Doing Well; Developing Your Resources: The Process of Philanthropy; Starting a Planned Giving Program: Developing a Timeline and Budget; and Successful Annual Giving Programs: Fundamentals of Direct Mail).

The Alford Group Inc.

7660 Gross Point Road, Skokie, IL 60077
Tel: 800-291-8913, 847-966-6670; FAX: 847-966-6782
E-mail: info@alford.com; WWW: http://www.alford.com/splash/ index.html
▶ The firm tailors its services to the needs and budget of each client. Samples in this area include feasibility study, capital campaign design and counsel, annual fund assistance, TAG planned giving services, development assessment, strategic resource development planning, strategic planning implementation counsel, major and planned gift counsel, development assessment, executive search, and staff or volunteer training. It maintains regional offices in Seattle and Washington DC, an area office in San Diego, and a nationwide network of local strategic partners. Recent issues of the Alford Group newsletter are available as portable document format (PDF) files, which can be read using the freely available Adobe Acrobat Reader. It is a member of the American Association of Fund-Raising Counsel.

American City Bureau

Corporate headquarters: 1721 Moon Lake Boulevard,
Hoffman Estates, IL 60194
Tel: 800-786-GOAL (4625); FAX: 847-490-5860
E-mail: success@acb-inc.com; WWW: http://acb-inc.com

West Coast office: 595 Park Avenue, Suite 310,
San Jose, CA 95110
Tel: 888-786-GOAL (4625); FAX: 408-292-9823
E-mail: ACBWest@AOL.com

▶ Founded in 1913, American City Bureau is the oldest continually operating fund-raising consulting firm in the country. Services include developmental/feasibility studies, capital campaign direction, major/planned gift development, endowment development, board recruitment and training, development office audits, and marketing/communications services. In addition, they also offer consulting in endowment development, leadership development and training, and pre and post-campaign direction. It is a member of the American Association of Fund-Raising Counsel.

American Consulting Trust (ACT) for Philanthropy

1321 Harding Place, Charlotte, NC 28204-2921
Tel: 877-4-THE ACT, 704-334-1558
E-mail: mail@theact.com; WWW: http://www.THEACT.com,
http://www.theact.com/comp_info.htm

▶ A full-service fund-raising consulting firm dedicated to service, education, and advocacy to the not-for-profit sector and the field of philanthropy, they provide time, funding, expertise, and materials to educate individuals about philanthropy and fund raising, including, but not limited to, the sharing of information, sponsorship of seminars, and the development of educational materials and guidelines for campaign planning and readiness. Services include planning studies, position analyses and audits, campaign management, periodic counseling, resident direction, constituent relations, corporate giving programs, strategic planning, public relations, and custom services. ACT for Philanthropy publishes a quarterly newsletter you may subscribe to free of charge or from their Web site.

Anne Bergeron Consulting

18 Sherwyn Lane, St. Louis, MO 63141-7821
Phone and FAX: 314-569-5842
E-mail: abergeron@primary.net

▶ Anne Bergeron is an independent consultant who specializes in fund raising, strategic planning, and organizational development for the fields of nonprofit arts and education. She has expertise in annual giving and capital campaign fund raising that employs a wide range of strategies, including feasibility studies, grantmanship, direct mail, special events, and planned giving. She has further expertise in focus group facilitation, survey work, program development, and grants making.

Arnoult & Associates

2670 Union Avenue, Extended Suite 810, Memphis, TN 38112
Tel: 901-452-8145
E-mail: info@arnoultassoc.com;
WWW: http://www.arnoultassoc.com

▶ A marketing, management, and fund-raising consulting firm that works exclusively with nonprofit organizations, Arnoult & Associates provides development consulting for nonprofit organizations, especially strategic planning, market research, organizational development, public/private partnerships, strategic corporate giving, and philanthropic fund raising for capital and annual fund campaigns, including Internet strategies. They serve a variety of organizations, including educational, cultural, religious, social service, environmental, and public amenities. They are a member of the American Association of Fund-Raising Counsel.

Avatar Company

2907 Red Bug Lake Road, Casselberry, FL 32707
Tel: 407-695-6618; FAX: 407-695-4832
E-mail: avatarway@avatarcompany.com, avatarway@aol.com
(Bob Kovacevich); WWW: http://avatarcompany.com

▶ Avatar is a full-service consultancy serving an international clientele. Services range from market research and strategic planning to fund-raising programs and coaching. Their consulting philosophy is driven by the principle that substantive support will not occur until a charity understands and meaningfully serves the needs and interests of its diverse audiences. They are committed to helping a charity understand its audiences by conducting market research and using the findings to influence institutional strategic decision making. The outcome is an audience-compatible experience in which earned and contributed income, volunteerism, foundation funding awards, and overall growth can flourish. Their specialties are board development, computers and technology, direct-mail services, evaluation of programs, fund raising, grant writing, graphic design, marketing, research, and strategic planning. They also provide workshops.

Barnes & Roche, Inc.

Rosemont Business Campus, Building Three, Suite 110,
919 Conestoga Road, Rosemont, PA 19010-1375
Tel: 610-527-3244; FAX: 610-527-0381
E-mail: consult@brnsrche.com, consult@brnsrche.com
(Consulting), search@brnsrche.com (executive Search)

▶ Barnes & Roche, Inc., provides a comprehensive approach to Institutional Advancement and Resource Management. The firm offers a full range of fund-raising consulting and executive search services. In addition, related services include communications, public relations, market research, prospect research, and information systems consulting.

Baxter Farr Thomas & Weinstein, Ltd. (BFT&W)

1111 Kentucky NE, Albuquerque, NM 87110-6923
Tel: 800-325-2117, 505-256-3231; FAX: 505-265-0248
E-mail: bftwsw@bftw.com; WWW: http://www.bftw.com/bftw.
http://kumo.swcp.com/bftw/services.html#seminars

▶ BFT&W, a full-service fund-raising consulting firm, specializes in fulfilling the fund raising, marketing, and management needs of nonprofit organizations. Founded in 1988, the firm serves a broad spectrum of religious, environmental, health care, cultural, social service, educational institutions, and professional associations. They offer a full range of consulting services, including capital and endowment campaign planning studies, capital and endowment campaigns, strategic planning, planned giving programs, annual appeals, grant writing, comprehensive resource development planning, public relations and marketing, membership drives, development audits, fund-raising software, board development and retreats, executive search and training, and major gift initiatives, as well as seminars, workshops, and lectures. They have additional offices in Pennsylvania and Massachusetts.

Benefactors Counsel, LLC

1269 Grandview Avenue, Columbus, OH 43212
Tel: 877-437-3711, 614-437-3000; FAX: 614-437-3001
E-mail: info@bene-factor.com, laura@bene-factor.com (Laura MacDonald, Founder); WWW: http://www.bene-factor.com

▶ Benefactors Counsel provides innovative consulting services and management products to support fund raising, philanthropy, and voluntary leadership. Clients include nonprofit organizations, corporate community affairs departments, and individual donors. Services include leadership partners (governance/board assessments, long-range planning and implementation, leadership training and board placements, board retreat planning and facilitation); campaign partners (offers a variety of products and services to support the planning and management of major fund-raising campaigns, including campaign planning assessments and feasibility studies, campaign plans, campaign marketing materials, cases for support, grants templates, campaign management consulting, and leadership training); development partners (works to build the capacity of annual stewardship and fund-raising operations, working with volunteers and staff, providing products and services such as annual stewardship campaign planning and training, development evaluations, fund-raising marketing materials, special event planning and implementation, grant writing, evaluation, and compliance); corporate partners (provides services to build the capacity of these growing companies with products and services such as charitable giving audits, strategic planning for philanthropy and community affairs, development, implementation, and management of charitable giving procedures).

Bentz Whaley Flessner

7251 Ohms Lane, Minneapolis, MN 55439
Tel: 952-921-0111; FAX: 952-921-0109
E-mail: bwf@bwf.com, prospecting@bwf.com;
WWW: http://www.bwf.com

▶ Services offered include annual giving, development audits, campaign counsel, feasibility studies, prospecting services (including prospecting seminars), and technology and systems counsel.

Brakeley, John Price Jones Inc.

86 Prospect Street, Stamford, CT 06901
Tel: 800-486-5171, 203-348-8100; FAX: 203-978-0114
E-mail: brakeleyct@aol.com, bgallobrakeley@aol.com (Barbara A. Gallo, Consultant & Program Director);
WWW: http://www.brakeley.com,
http://www.brakeley.com/library.html

▶ Services include alumni relations, annual giving, communications, writing and editorial services, alumni and constituency relations, development office and management (operations audits), planned giving, development program and capital campaign consulting, prospect profiling and donor research, resident campaign management, strategic planning, fund-raising assessments (planning, marketing, and feasibility studies), executive search, and volunteer leadership training.

Browning Associates Inc.

209 Cooper Avenue, Upper Montclair, NJ 07043
Tel: 973-746-5960; FAX: 973-746-0189
E-mail: info@browning-associates.com;
WWW: http://www.browning-associates.com

▶ This full-service consulting firm provides counsel on all aspects of fund raising: annual funds, capital gift programs, enrollment management, institutional studies—assessment of fund-raising potential, development office audit, and planned giving as well as on board governance and strategic planning. Other services include assessments of fund-raising potential and board retreats. The firm also conducts school head searches.

CTE Associates

420 Lexington Avenue, Suite 2458, New York, NY 10170
Tel: 212-499-0866; FAX: 212-499-9075
E-mail: cte@changingourworld.com,
cwatson@changingourworld.com (Christopher Watson, President and CEO); WWW: http://www.changingourworld.com/CTE/cte6.htm

1776 I Street NW, 9th Floor, Washington, DC 20006
Tel: 202-756-4787; FAX: 202-756-1509

▶ CTE Associates specializes in helping to generate fund-raising and philanthropic revenue for trade associations, professional societies, and membership organizations. They work as a team of professionals, with senior executives supported by experts in research, grants management, planned giving, public relations, and communications. They specialize in capital campaigning, major gift fund raising, and in projecting realistic capital fund-raising potential.

Campbell & Company

Corporate office: One East Wacker Drive, Suite 2525, Chicago, IL 60601
Tel: 877-957-0000, 312-644-7100; FAX: 312-644-3559
E-mail: info@campbellcompany.com;
WWW: http://www.campbellcompany.com

▶ Founded in the mid-1970s, Campbell & Company is a full-service consulting firm. They offer extensive, hands-on experience in fund raising, management, marketing, and communications and serve not-for-profit organizations across the country. Their work with clients incorporates any combination of services in the following areas: philanthropic market studies, campaign counsel, planned and major gifts program, counsel, development program audits, annual giving program counsel, case development, volunteer training; strategic planning counsel, leadership development and training, staff development and training, executive search, online solutions. Their network of strategic partners address the following niche service areas for their clients: marketing and communications services, electronic screening, prospect research, telemarketing, systems consulting, online solutions, and estate planning services. They also maintain East Coast, Ohio, and West Coast offices. They are a member of the American Association of Fund-Raising Counsel.

Capital Development Services

111 Hampton Woods Lane, Raleigh, NC 27607
Tel: 800-729-4553, 919-854-9775; FAX: 919-854-9740
E-mail: jbennett@capdev.com (John Bennett, Founder and President); WWW: http://www.capdev.com/services.htm,
http://www.capdev.com/services.htm,
http://www.capdev.com/online/index.htm

▶ This is a fully licensed fund-raising counsel, research, and publications firm. Their Campaign Group specializes in capital campaign planning and implementation, feasibility studies, board and volunteer training, major gift solicitations, donor development, planned giving, grant writing, development office assessments, prospect identification and research, and development officer searches. They have worked throughout the Southeast providing fund-raising services for hundreds of nonprofit organizations, including cultural, environmental, educational, social, religious, health and human services, and economic development agencies and institutions. Capital Development Services' Research and Publications Group produces comprehensive directories on corporate and foundation giving for grant seekers in North Carolina, Virginia, and Georgia. In addition, their Resource Center provides a variety of services to all of their clients, including customized donor and leader prospect research, online access, and extensive databank information on philanthropic giving, material examples, and résumé files.

Carol O'Brien Associates

120 West State Street, Ithaca, NY 14850-5428
Tel: 607-272-9144; FAX: 607-272-9180
E-mail: cobaithaca@aol.com

3904 Chippenham Road, Durham, NC 27707
Tel: 919-403-2500

▶ Services include organizational design and evaluation; constituency development; feasibility studies; campaign counsel; internal assessments; board development; volunteer and staff training; and workshop, retreat, and seminar presentations.

Carlton & Company

National headquarters: 101 Federal Street, Suite 1900,
Boston, MA 02110
Tel: 800-622-0194; FAX: 800-622-5032
E-mail: Carlton@Seacoast.com;
WWW: http://www.fundraising.org

▶ This medium-sized consulting firm specializes in major gifts development, often in context of a client's first or nearly first capital campaign. Services include capital campaigns, annual giving programs, fund-raising planning studies, public relations programs, prospect research and development, planned giving, constituent development programs, case planning and development, solicitation of major gifts prospects, board development, special events management, volunteer training, market research and image studies, and print and video communication. It offers full-time resident direction of capital campaigns. It is a member of the American Association of Fund-Raising Counsel.

Charles H. Bentz Associates, Inc.

303 Washington Street NW, Warren, OH 44483
Tel: 800-582-3493, 330-399-9095; FAX: 800-677-1707,
330-399-9007
E-mail: fundcounsel@chbentz.com, CHBentz@worldnet.att.net;
WWW: http://www.chbentz.com/

▶ Services include fund-raising feasibility studies, leadership planning studies, campaign management, internal development audits, and board development. They also offer the following services: campaign planning, membership development, grant writing case statement development, prospect research, volunteer training,

annual giving consulting, mission statement development, not-for-profit marketing and public relations, annual giving consulting, long-range and strategic planning, and business plan development. They also maintain offices in the Midwest, metropolitan New York, and the South.

The Clements Group, LC

136 East South Temple, Suite 900, Salt Lake City, UT 84111
Tel: 801-355-0450; FAX: 801-355-0449
E-mail: clmgroup@mail.vii.com; WWW: http://www.clmgroup.com,
http://www.clmgroup.com/events.htm

▶ The Clements Group specializes in assisting organizations that change lives and communities. Since being organized in 1986, they have expanded to serve over 250 organizations in 43 states plus the District of Columbia, Canada, and Puerto Rico. Nearly 90 percent of their clients are community colleges and technical institutes. Consultation services include strategic visioning and planning, environmental scanning, institutional advancement assessment, foundation board organization and training, imaging and marketing campaigns, feasibility studies, major gifts campaigns, phone/mail communications and campaigns, workforce skills assessments, building alumni organizations, market surveys, and annual giving programs. In addition to these personalized consulting services, the Clements Group regularly offers other types of workshops and seminars, including a two-day Major Gifts Campaign Seminar, designed to serve as a guide to the conduct of successful major gifts campaigns at community colleges and technical institutes for presidents, institutional advancement officers, foundation executive directors, and other resource development professionals. This seminar is offered several times each year at various locations. They are a member of the American Association of Fund-Raising Counsel.

Clemow Consulting Group, LLP

120 Mountain Avenue, Suite 202, Bloomfield, CT 06002
Tel: 860-286-9396; FAX: 860-286-2787
E-mail: clemowcg@aol.com; WWW: http://www.fundraisingccg.com

▶ Clemow offers a broad range of development, strategic planning, financial, management, and marketing services to nonprofit organizations.

The Collins Group, Inc.

101 Stewart Street, Suite 840, Seattle, WA 98101
Tel: 800-275-6006
E-mail: info@collinsgroup.com; WWW: www.collinsgroup.com,
http://www.collinsgroup.com/free_tools.html,
http://www.collinsgroup.com/links.html

28 SW First Avenue, Suite 300, Portland, OR 97204
Tel: 503-274-9363; FAX: 503-274-1710
E-mail: TCGPDX@aol.com

▶ This fund-raising consulting firm specializes in capital campaign management, from feasibility studies and organizational assessments to project development and campaign management, institutional and development audits, and board and volunteer training. They are renowned for guiding arts, cultural, health care, educational, and human service institutions.

Community Counselling Service (CCS)

350 Fifth Avenue, Suite 7210, New York, NY 10118
Tel: 800-223-6733, 212-695-1175; FAX: 212-967-6451
E-mail: ccsnewyork@ccsfundraising.com;
WWW: www.ccsfundraising.com

▶ Since 1947, CCS has provided fund-raising and campaign management services to more than 7,000 nonprofit institutions. Services include campaign management and direction, campaign planning, prospect research, trustee development and orientation, case statement development, major gift strategies, recruitment of key leadership, public relations and communications, planned giving, and feasibility studies/development audits. CCS maintains research capabilities, including comprehensive profiles on individuals, corporate and foundation, utilizing on-line data services, demographic research, a comprehensive research library, CD-ROM databases, donor prospect profiles, prospect screening, online news services, and staff research. In partnership with PRIMARK, Inc., a data services corporation, CCS has developed Prospect Insight™, which provides geodemographics, wealth indicators, securities holdings, private company data, and real estate holdings on prospect donors in a robust search application format. CCS also maintains offices in Chicago; San Francisco; Washington, DC; Toronto; London; Dublin.

Copley Harris Company Inc.

106 High Street, Danvers, MA 01923
Tel: 978-750-1028; FAX: 978-750-6709
E-mail: chc@copleyharris.com;
WWW: http://www.copleyharris.com

▶ Copley Harris provides counsel to nonprofit health care, educational, cultural, and social service organizations seeking to advance philanthropy. Services include capital endowment campaigns, annual giving, feasibility studies, campaign management, development program start-ups, formation of new foundations, development audits, board retreats, planned giving counsel, general fund-raising counsel, interim services, and executive searches for nonprofits.

Cornerstone Consulting

320 North Kenhorst Boulevard, Reading, PA 19607
Tel: 610-796-9120, 610-796-9150
E-mail: CCILINDA@aol.com (Linda Lysakowski, President);
WWW: http://www.cornerstoneconsult.com

▶ Services include annual campaigns, board development, capital campaigns, donor management, special events, marketing and communications, planning, and training (see listing for Capital Venture under Training).

Cosgriff Company

One Continental Building, 209 South 19th Street, Omaha, NE 68102
Tel: 800-456-9902; FAX: 402-341-8590
E-mail: cosgriff@alltel.net (Michael J. Fitzpatrick,
CEO–President); WWW: http://www.cosgriffco.com

▶ Cosgriff provides fund-raising counsel and feasibility studies for churches, schools, museums, and libraries. Full-time resident campaign management means they work only on your project.

Cunneen Parish Fundraising Services

24 Rossotto Drive, Hamden, CT 06514
Tel: 800-842-4488; FAX: 203-407-5853
E-mail: info@cunneenfundraising.com;
WWW: http://www.cunneenfundraising.com

▶ A Catholic fund-raising organization, Cunneen Parish Fundraising began serving Catholic parishes in 1981. Cunneen has assisted over 5,000 Catholic parishes in all 50 states and Canada. Cunneen is a full-service firm and can develop and manage any type of fund-raising project (either individually or in combination) that a Catholic parish may wish to consider, including Introduction to Stewardship; large-project capital campaigns, small-project capital campaigns, campaign follow-up; feasibility and strategic planning analysis; direct-mail campaigns; donor recognition; memorial and tree of life programs; and capital, offertory, and annual appeal campaigns. The home office serves as a production facility and generates letters, campaign brochures, training guides, and campaign support material for their directors in the field. Its home office is supported by regional offices located in New York, New Jersey, Pennsylvania, Ohio, Michigan, and Iowa.

Custom Development Solutions (CDS)

4 Allie Court, Isle of Palms, SC 29451
Tel: 800-761-3833, 843-886-9969; FAX: 843-886-9529
E-mail: info@cdsfunds.com; WWW: http://www.cdsfunds.com,
http://www.cdsfunds.com/resources.htm

▶ Custom Development Solutions is a full-service fund-raising consulting firm dedicated to helping your organization meet or exceed its fund-raising goals. CDS provides advice and counsel to nonprofit organizations seeking money for operating expenses, new facilities, and capital improvements. CDS offers services to clients throughout the United States and Canada. Services include feasibility and planning studies, capital campaign direction, capital campaign consulting, development audits, and general fund-raising advice. CDS also offers many auxiliary services such as creating brochures, prospective donor research, executive search and training, and more. CDS offers free e-mail newsletter.

Davidson Consulting Group

452 South Main Street, Suite C, Davidson, NC 28036
Tel: 704-892-9388 or 704-892-9335; FAX: 704-892-9398
E-mail: info@dcg-nc.com; WWW: http://www.dcg-nc.com

▶ This is a cooperative effort of professionals with significant experience in all facets of nonprofit fund raising and management. Their principals and consultants include lawyers, MBAs, CPAs, CFREs, and other highly regarded specialists. Davidson Consulting Group offers capital campaign counsel and nonprofit risk management services as well as annual fund, corporate, foundation, and planned giving advice. Services include capital campaigns, planned giving, and annual campaigns. Clients include civic and cultural organizations, educational institutions, churches, human services organizations, and trade associations.

Demont & Associates Inc.

477 Congress Street, 5th floor, Portland, ME 04101
Tel: 207-773-3030; FAX: 207-773-5213
E-mail: demontassociates@compuserve.com;
WWW: http://www.demontassociates.com

33 Boston Post Road West, Suite 270, Marlborough, MA 01752
Tel: 800-291-9010; FAX: 508-481-7522

1233 Shelburne Road, Suite 400, South Burlington, VT 05403
Tel: 800-721-7171; FAX: 802-860-1625

▶ Established in 1994, it provides fund-raising counsel and related services to nonprofit organizations throughout the Northeast. It offers the following services: board and volunteer training workshops; precampaign feasibility studies to determine levels of interest and support for organizational needs and to determine the feasibility of a campaign for the optimum goal; major donor awareness programs designed to spread the word about organizational needs and to cultivate supporters; periodic advancement counsel; resident and periodic capital campaign counsel; campaign office management and training; computerized management of campaigns, including cost-effective and manageable software support and training; post-campaign and collections counsel; organizational financial planning counsel with staff and board members; internal audits to determine an organization's preparedness for a planned fund-raising campaign; strategic institutional planning workshops; and phonothon direction and counsel.

Designs in Development, Inc. (DID)

P.O. Box 4460, Seminole, FL 33775
Tel: 800-411-1477; FAX: 727-397-6497
E-mail: designdev@aol.com (Nancy L. Brown, President);
WWW: http://ephilanthropy.com, http://members.aol.com/design
dev/index/nancy.html

▶ DID serves the Southeast through campaign consultation, strategic planning, training, and executive search, specializing in organizations with budgets of $100,000 to $10 million. The firm provides a full range of service from strategic planning and executive search to campaign consultation, development audits, and planned giving. DID has worked with all types of nonprofit institutions, and is especially experienced with human services, economic development, arts, and humane organizations. Nancy L. Brown, President and chief counsel for the firm, is a nationally noted trainer and speaker in philanthropy. In addition to having authored and published the audio workshop "Increasing Board Effectiveness," she has developed 10 day-long curricula for training boards, staff, and volunteers. Services include management consulting (strategic planning facilitation, tactical planning facilitation, board development, policies and procedures, executive search, leadership training, quality management consultation, marketing and communications planning, association management, and 501(c)(3) applications); and fund-raising consulting (capital campaigns and feasibility studies, major gift planning, fund-raising planning, grant writing, donor cultivation training, in-house training, workshops, development audits, and keynote speeches).

The Dini Partners, Inc.

2727 Allen Parkway, Suite 700, Houston, TX 77019
Tel: 713-942-8110; FAX: 713-942-8708
E-mail: dinipart@dinipartners.com

3400 Carlisle Street, Suite 348, Dallas, TX 75204
Tel: 214-754-9393; FAX: 214-754-9363
E-mail: lstocklin@dinipartners.com;
WWW: http://www.dinipartners.com,
http://www.dinipartners.com/philanthropy.html

▶ Some of the services they provide include management consulting (strategic planning, leadership development, executive search,

and trustee planning retreats); and fund raising (development staff and volunteer training, development program assessment, fund-raising feasibility studies, capital campaign consulting and management, major gift fund raising, and endowment development).

Donovan Management, Inc. (DMI)

P.O. Box 195068, Winter Springs, FL 32719
Tel: 407-366-8340; FAX: 407-977-9668
E-mail: consultants@donovanmanagement.com,
DMIMGT@aol.com (James A. Donovan);
WWW: http://www.donovanmanagement.com,
http://www.donovanmanagement.com/Tips%20Free.htm

▶ Founded in 1986, DMI is a small consulting firm that assists clients in advancing philanthropy in communities, primarily in Florida and the Caribbean. It provides fund-raising, management, and training services for organizations engaged in philanthropy. DMI raises funds for annual, major/capital gift programs. They also solve fundamental organizational challenges (strategic direction, management efficiency, enhancement of board and staff performance or continued motivation throughout your organization). DMI provides three basic functions that clients cannot perform themselves: independent and objective assessment, study, and analysis of an organization's status, plans, and the performance of its staff and board; outside influence for making organizational change; and outside motivation of staff and board to exceed their goals. Services include strategic planning/major gifts counsel/solicitor training. DMI is publisher of major gift and board development books for staff and volunteers. They offer a free e-newsletter.

Donovan Slone, Inc. (Formerly J. Donovan Associates, Inc.)

Corporate headquarters: One Derby Square,
Salem, MA 01970-3704
Tel: 800-370-0036, 978-744-8558; FAX: 978-741-1871
WWW: http://www.donovanslone.com,
http://www.jdonovan.com/services.htm

▶ This full-service consulting firm offers clients a full complement of development and campaign service since 1983. Services include strategic planning; staff, board, and volunteer training; marketing, planning, and feasibility studies; executive search; development program assessments; capital campaign management; grant writing; prospect research; annual program development and support; comprehensive communication support; membership development; and periodic and resident counsel. They also maintain an office in East Greenwich, Rhode Island.

Douglas M. Lawson & Associates, Inc.

545 Madison Avenue, New York, NY 10022
Tel: 800-238-0004, 212-759-5660; FAX: 212-759-1893
E-mail: doug@douglawson.com;
WWW: http://www.douglawson.com

▶ They offer a full range of philanthropic services: campaign counsel and management (capital campaigns, endowment campaigns, annual campaigns, planned giving campaigns); fund-raising studies (campaign feasibility studies, development planning studies); motivation training events (board retreat seminars, staff training seminars, donor inspirational speeches); fund-raising audits; and fund-raising consultation (general fund-raising counsel to nonprofit organizations whether on-site, via telephone, FAX, correspondence, or directly through their offices in New York; Washington; Jacksonville, Florida; and Dallas, Texas).

Dragul Group

1500 Chiquita Center, 250 East Fifth Street, Cincinnati, OH 45202
Tel: 513-762-7828; FAX: 513-721-4628
E-mail: dragulgrp@aol.com (Marc Dragul);
WWW: http://members.aol.com/dragulgrp/dragul.html

▶ Dragul Group offers nonprofit entities and donors total fundraising consulting emphasizing support from planning and implementation to management and evaluation. Services include planning and performance studies, situational analyses, confidential survey interview, case statements and packages, annual giving development, planned giving programs, capital campaigns, donor relations, grantsmanship and proposals, major gifts, public relations, leadership development, solicitor training, seminars, volunteer programming, corporate giving programs, staff recruitment, corporate sponsorships, cause-related marketing, membership programming, testimonial banquets, golf tournaments, special events, databasing, and direct mail. They maintain offices in the United States and Brazil.

Draper Consulting Group

10811 Washington Boulevard, Suite 380,
Culver City, CA 90232-3659
Tel: 310-559-3424; FAX: 310-559-4586
E-mail: office@drapergroup.com (Lee Draper, President);
WWW: http://www.drapergroup.com

▶ Founded in 1990, it is a full-service firm offering a broad range of management and technical assistance services. A provider of high-quality consulting services to grantmakers and nonprofit agencies, it has expertise in the full range of strategic philanthropy: grant making and fund raising, organizational planning, and staff and board development. It serves grant makers, nonprofit arts and culture, social services, conservation, health and education organizations, and individuals and families of high net worth who have or are considering establishing philanthropic programs or foundations. Services include long-range/strategic planning; board/staff development, retreat planning and facilitation, fund development services, major donor solicitation, and capital campaigns.

Durkin Associates

1110 North Old World Third Street, Suite 650, Milwaukee, WI 53203
Tel: 414-967-7000; FAX: 414-967-7070
E-mail: info@wdurkin.com (William A. Durkin Jr., President)

▶ Founded in 1993, Durkin Associates has served 46 clients in five states. Engagements typically are for organizational and capital campaign planning activities, including feasibility studies, strategic and business planning processes, executive searches and staff development, donor file appraisals, major prospective donor profiles, interim management services, and professional support for volunteer solicitors. The firm has well-established relationships with vendors capable of supporting comprehensive campaign requirements. They are a member of the American Association of Fund-Raising Counsel.

The EHL Consulting Group, Inc.

2300 Computer Avenue, Building D-18, Willow Grove, PA 19090
Tel: 215-830-0304; FAX: 215-830-0351
E-mail: info@ehlconsulting.com, info@jewishare.com;
WWW: http://www.ehlconsulting.com

▶ Specialists in all aspects of financial resource development for nonprofit entities. Emphasis is on structuring and coordinating every type of fund-raising campaign: capital, endowment, special project, charitable gift planning, and annual giving. Clients include local, regional, and national groups, with annual budgets of at least $750,000, engaged in the full spectrum of nonprofit endeavors: education (universities, private schools, and academic institutions), social (youth programs, social service agencies), health (hospitals and medical centers, programs for children and adults with disabilities), arts and culture (community art centers, local and national theater programs, religious (houses of worship, schools and summer camps with religious affiliation), civic (veterans groups, honor societies, community centers). EHL also offers Jewishare.com (see *http://www.jewishare.com*). They are a member of the American Association of Fund-Raising Counsel.

Ferguson Development Group

110 DaCosta Avenue, Oceanside, NY 11572
Tel: 516-764-0930; FAX: 516-678-7436
E-mail: ferdevgp@chelsea.ios.com;
WWW: http://chelsea.ios.com/~ferdevgp

▶ This organization specializes in development and fund raising (capital and endowment campaigns, planning and strategy formulation, campaign planning and feasibility studies, development audits, capital campaigns, major gifts programs, board and leadership development, case and materials, planning retreats). Capabilities offered include managerial expertise in strategic planning and campaign implementation; areas of service (planning, management, leadership recruitment and training, prospect research and identification, case and materials development, and marketing); extensive computer hardware, software, and telecommunications capabilities used to support your campaign effort; online computer research systems including Dialog Information Systems and Dow Jones News Retrieval; information management systems used for prospect screening, rating, and review. They are a member of the American Association of Fund-Raising Counsel.

First Counsel, Inc.

428 East Fourth Street, Suite 100, Charlotte, NC 28202
Tel: 800-313-1645, 704-342-1100; FAX: 704-342-1700
E-mail: info@firstcounsel.com; WWW: http://www.firstcounsel.com

▶ First Counsel is a full-service fund-raising consulting firm. Services include development audit, planning study, resident campaign direction, executive counsel, leased executive program, board retreats, client support services (fund-raising management software, prospect research, statement of need/case for support writing, printed materials, cooperative banking, and marketing support).

Fund Consultants, Inc.

525 Old Louisquisset Pike, Suite B-104, Lincoln, RI 02865
Tel: 401-729-0100; FAX: 401-729-0122
E-mail: fciri@aol.com

▶ This firm provides fund-raising management services in the design, development, and execution of capital campaigns (for new construction, renovations, endowment, debt retirement); annual campaigns (for operating funds, membership, direct mail, phonathons); public relations programs (publications, graphics and design, media promotion, audiovisual materials); marketing services (surveys, audits, long-range plans); planned giving services (including seminars); and board training (including evaluations and retreats). They offer two basic options: counseling (their staff provides guidance and direction weekly or other periodic visits and meetings) and resident direction (a Fund Consultants, Inc. consultant is on the scene to provide staffing and on-site supervision of activities and events). They are a member of the American Association of Fund-Raising Counsel.

Fund Inc.

249 Market Square, Lake Forest, IL 60045
Tel: 847-295-0696; FAX: 847-234-8635
E-mail: fundinconline@hotmail.com, fundinc@yahoo.com (Rita Galowich); WWW: http://www.fundinconline.com

▶ Founded in 1987, Fund Inc. provides resource development management and consultation services to the not-for-profit community. Their team of associates offers consultation services for capital campaigns and feasibility studies, strategy development for major gift programs, coaching and consultation for board development and education, and hands-on assistance with both resource development start-ups and ongoing programs. Services include strategic planning, feasibility studies, capital campaign strategy development and management, major donor identification and strategy development, board and volunteer education, evaluation of resource development programs and staff, annual fund planning and implementation, proposal writing and case statements, prospect and donor database systems evaluation, facilitation of meetings, and special event assessment. They are a member of the American Association of Fund-Raising Counsel.

Fund Raising Innovations

36 Queensbrook Place, St. Louis, MO 63132
Tel: 314-991-0143; FAX: 314-991-1145
E-mail: jeanevogel@earthlink.net (Jeane Vogel, Owner);
WWW: http://www.nonprofit-innovations.com

▶ Established in 1994, it is a small consulting firm that specializes in helping small nonprofits in the United States and Canada find funding for programs, operating costs, and capital expenditures. It provides a full menu of fund-raising services. It offers fund-raising workshops in St. Louis. Author, "Let's Get a Grant to Do That" in *Secrets of Successful Fundraising, the Best of the Non-Profit Pros, http://www.nonprofit-innovations.com/Secrets.html.*

Ghiorsi & Sorrenti, Inc. (GSI)

Mack-Cali Corporate Center, 50 Tice Boulevard,
Woodcliff Lake, NJ 07675
Tel: 201-307-1970; FAX: 201-307-5632
E-mail: info@gsifundraising.com;
WWW: http://www.gsifundraising.com

▶ This full-service fund-raising and public relations firm for non-profit organizations specializes in planning and directing capital campaigns and major gift programs. Their staff includes senior campaign directors and experts in research, grants management, planned giving, public relations, and communications. GSI's full-service fund-raising and resource development services include planning, organizing, and directing capital campaigns for new and renovated facilities; special programs and services; equipment; endowment and other capital needs; campaign feasibility and planning studies; on-site campaign direction (full-time or part-time);

on-site development program management; general fund-raising consultation; development audits and assessments of financial potential; development strategic planning studies; foundation/grants management services; establishing fund development foundation operations; case statement research and writing; prospect identification; research and cultivation; trustee and leadership recruitment; board development; and *public relations.*

Glenwood Associates

24 Old Georgetown Road, Princeton, NJ 08540
Tel: 732-821-5522; FAX: 732-821-5955
E-mail: info@glenwoodassociates.com;
WWW: http://www.glenwoodassociates.com/services.htm

▶ Services include meetings and conferences; major gifts (develop the case for major gift support; identify donors and prospects; plan for cultivation and relationship building; develop a purposeful solicitation packet, and build partnerships with donors); special events; cultivating and soliciting donors or members; organizational studies and program audits; marketing and community outreach; leadership and volunteer development; corporate partnership programs; chapter and field development; staff recruitment; and Web site design and promotion.

Gloss and Company

2755 South Locust Street, Suite 113, Denver, CO 80222
Tel: 303-753-9079; FAX: 303-753-0099
E-mail: glossco@mountainpeak.com (Lawrence R. Gloss, AAHP, President); WWW: http://www.glossco.com

▶ Gloss and Company provides not-for-profit institutions with a full spectrum of resource development, marketing, and counseling services, capital and endowment campaigns; prospect research; and major gifts. They serve a wide range of not-for-profit institutions in cultural arts, health care, education, youth development, environmental, cultural, civic, legal rights, governmental, and human welfare areas. Services include capital campaign management; endowment campaign management; feasibility studies for capital and endowment campaigns; capital campaign development analysis; needs assessments and marketing analysis; campaign planning studies; major gift solicitation; foundation and corporate solicitation; development of case statements; prospect research and cultivation; formation of estate planning programs; annual giving programs; direct-mail solicitations; resource development audits; special event planning; computer and donor management systems; public relations; philanthropic marketing; multimedia presentations; board and volunteer training; organizational retreats; donor recognition programs; philanthropic marketing analysis; short- and long-range planning; recruitment of staff and volunteers; formation of resource development offices; solicitation training of staff and volunteers; and creation of publications, brochures, and newsletters.

Goettler Associates, Inc.

580 South High Street, Columbus, OH 43215
Tel: 800-521-4827, 614-228-3269; FAX: 614-228-7583
E-mail: info@goettler.com; WWW: http://www.goettler.com

▶ This full-service, client-oriented firm provides state-of-the-art analysis, consulting, and management in all areas of fund raising, marketing, and institutional advancement to nonprofit institutions large and small. They help their clients conduct successful capital campaigns, increase annual operating support, establish planned and deferred giving programs, and strengthen their endowments through their full range of services, including studies and assessments (campaign planning and feasibility studies, development assessments, and strategic planning); donor cultivation and campaign positioning (case for support development, leadership awareness programs, campaign identity and marketing, writing, print design, and video production); specialized development support (prospect research, endowment policy and management, executive search, planned and deferred gift services); campaign management (resident campaign direction, periodic campaign consultation, annual and deferred giving programs: consultation services). Goettler Associates has long supported efforts to educate nonprofit staff and volunteers about fund-raising issues. The ongoing *Goettler Series,* and quarterly newsletter *Fund-Raising Matters* have been used by countless individuals who seek reliable, basic information on key aspects of fund raising. Its Web site offers all 12 volumes of *The Goettler Series.* You may also browse the most current and previous issues of *Fund-Raising Matters.*

Gonser Gerber Tinker Stuhr, LLP

Naperville Financial Center, 400 East Diehl Road, Suite 380, Naperville, IL 60563
Tel: 630-505-1433; FAX: 630-505-7710
E-mail: info@ggts.com

▶ Founded in 1950, this firm has provided development and public relations counsel to more than 450 institutions. They provide a comprehensive approach to development consultative services to not-for-profit institutions nationally. Services include major gifts, planned gifts, annual fund, board development, volunteer development, capital campaigns, precampaign studies, program audits, strategic planning, endowment planning, marketing, communications, staffing, and student recruitment.

Goodale Associates

509 Madison Avenue, Suite 1112, New York, NY 10021
Tel: 212-759-2999; FAX: 212-759-7490
E-mail: TKGASSOC@aol.com; WWW: http://www.tkgoodale.com, http://www.tkgoodale.com/gast.htm

▶ This firm specializes in fund-raising and management counseling for nonprofit organizations. They offer a wide range of services, including feasibility and planning studies, capital campaigns, annual giving programs, major gifts programs, management counsel, planned giving programs, strategic planning, and solicitor training workshops.

Graham-Pelton Consulting, Inc.

16 Maple Street, Suite 5, Summit, NJ 07901
Tel: 800-562-3695, 908-608-1388; FAX: 908-608-1520
E-mail: info@grahampelton.com;
WWW: http://www.grahampelton.com

▶ Graham-Pelton Consulting, Inc., is a full-service fund-raising and nonprofit management firm specializing in capital campaigns for educational institutions, health care organizations, religious organizations, and cultural and community groups. They structure each project, capital, endowment, or annual campaign to maximize a client's opportunity to create positive relationships among staff and volunteers; cultivate and educate volunteer leadership; develop its donor prospect base; enhance its public image; plan for

strategic, long-term fund-raising initiatives; train its fund-raising staff; widen its donor base; and increase donor loyalty and satisfaction. Services include capital campaign management, annual fund management, feasibility/planning studies, development assessments, board training and development, development communications, planned giving.

The Greenwood Company

2351 Powell Street, Suite 505, San Francisco, CA 94133
Tel: 415-837-5858; FAX: 415-837-5850
E-mail: Greenwdco@aol.com, Littlejohn@thegreenwood company.com (William S. Littlejohn, Executive Vice President), WWW: http://www.thegreenwoodcompany.com/

▶ The Greenwood Company specializes in the design and management of comprehensive development programs and campaigns that support the capital and endowment needs of not-for-profit organizations. The company was founded in 1979 and now operates throughout the United States. The Greenwood Company's primary services are capital and endowment campaign management, campaign planning and feasibility studies, development audits, comprehensive long-range development plans, constituent education programs, solicitation training programs, case development, board development, board retreats, and executive recruitment.

Griesgraber & Associates (G&A)

125 Club Road, Pasadena, CA 91105-14211
Tel: 651-592-9215; Voice mail: 626-449-6446;
FAX: 626-795-0695
E-mail: jgriesg@aol.com; WWW: http://www.griesgraber.com/

▶ This consulting firm assists private schools, churches, and nonprofit institutions with organizational and financial development. G&A's approach is to learn as much as possible about your organization's vision, programs, staff, revenue, budgets, facilities, equipment, and its perspective on how effective its systems and staff are in fulfilling the organization's mission. Services include fund raising, feasibility studies, grant consulting, strategic planning, board retreats, leadership seminars, executive searches, and direct mail.

Grenzebach Glier & Associates, Inc. (GG&A)

55 West Wacker Drive, Suite 1500, Chicago, IL 60601
Tel: 312-372-4040; FAX: 312-372-7911
E-mail: gga@grenzglier.com;
WWW: http://www.grenzebachglier.com

▶ GG&A provides counsel to educational, medical, cultural, and other not-for-profit organizations throughout North America and western Europe. Their staff of professionals are available to review and refine specific advancement program areas, including annual giving, alumni programs, telemarketing, prospect research, proposals and publications, corporate and foundation relations, major gifts, and special events. Counsel services can assist with program design and management, program planning, and methods of evaluation and improvement. GG&A's client services include strategic planning and program consultation; development/advancement program reviews; feasibility, market, and planning studies; needs assessment; initiating and building advancement programs; precampaign and campaign consultation services; case development/gift opportunities documentation; writing, publications, and communications services; ongoing program consultation (annual fund, corporate/foundation relations, major gifts, etc.); training seminars and retreats for professional staff, academic leaders, and volunteers; prospect Profile℠ services (wealth demographics screening); information technology consulting (systems, databases); annual fund consultation and telephone solicitation programs; and executive search. They are a member firm of the American Association of Fund-Raising Counsel (AAFRC).

Gwen Mathews

8810-4 Furlong Drive, Louisville, KY 40242
Office/FAX: 502-420-2860; Home Tel: 502-420-9895
E-mail: gwenwm@earthlink.net (Gwen W. Mathews, Principal);
http://fundraiseronline.com

▶ Gwen Mathews provides a variety of development services to clients, including special events, grant writing, major gift solicitation, fund-raising plans, telemarketing, annual appeals, Internet research, capital and endowment campaigns, implementation and evaluation, direct-mail services, membership recruitment, alumni relations, volunteer management and training, public relations, organizational development, power point presentations, and strategic planning in a broad range of areas from working with nonprofit boards to program planning and development.

Hartsook and Associates Inc.

1501 Castle Rock, Witchita, KS 67230
Tel: 316-733-7100; FAX: 316-733-7103
E-mail: info@hartsookgroup.com, rhartsook@aol.com;
WWW: http://www.hartsookgroup.com,
http://www.hartsookgroup.com/hsook/seminars.shtml,
http://www.hartsookgroup.com/hsook/publications.shtml

▶ Founded in 1987, Hartsook and Associates specializes in quality fund raising and philanthropic management consulting and support to not-for-profit institutions. Hartsook and Associates is a full service fund-raising and philanthropic management consulting firm. The firm has consultants based in over 20 cities throughout the country. Services include capital or endowment campaigns, campaign feasibility, assessment and planning studies, campaign communications plan, and campaign consultant or resident program director services. Essential Philanthropic Services, a sister company with Hartsook and Associates, addresses the noncampaign needs of clients, such as annual funds, planned giving, board development, special events, and organizational development audits. The following services are available from *Essential Philanthropic Services:* annual giving programs, foundation and corporate campaigns, planned giving programs, long-range/strategic planning, publications and development of campaign materials, planned giving management, management counsel, establishment and evaluation of foundation status, board development, research and proposals, seminars and workshops, and candidate search and screening. The firm publishes *Hartsook on Philanthropy,* a special newsletter focusing on the issues that Hartsook and Associates have identified as critical to the philanthropic future. Founded in 1992, the newsletter is published periodically and available free of charge.

Harvest Development

200 Executive Way, Suite 213, Ponte Vedra Beach, FL 32082
Tel: 888-828-9250, 904-543-0117; FAX: 904-543-0364
WWW: http://www.harvestdevelopment.com/

▶ Harvest Development was formed to educate nonprofits on fund-raising methodologies and to empower them to grow and act independently. Their experience includes both professional gift solicitation and volunteer training and guidance. They handle a diverse client base around the world. Their services include strategic planning; campaign readiness assessment, campaign planning and management, financing, case statement preparation, prospect research services, communication services, board enhancement, major gift solicitation, donor cultivation, planned giving, and master planning.

Hayes Briscoe Associates

322 West Bellevue Avenue, San Mateo, CA 94402
Tel: 650-344-8883; FAX: 650-344-3387
E-mail: hbaconsult@aol.com; WWW: http://www.hbaconsult.com
85 Sterling Street, Beacon, NY 12508
Tel: 914-831-9741
6671 SW 70th Terrace, Miami, FL 33143
Tel: 305-667-2795; FAX: 305-667-3195

▶ Hayes Briscoe Associates offers full-service consulting to non-profit organizations throughout the United States and abroad. Their clients include national and international organizations and their state and local affiliates, universities, colleges and schools, churches and religious organization, arts organizations, museums, membership and advocacy organizations, civic organizations, professional associations, government agencies, foundations, corporate giving programs, health and human service agencies, and hospitals. Fund development services include capital campaigns, planning/feasibility studies, development audits, case development, program marketing/marketing audits, annual fund development/coaching, volunteer development, development planning, prospect identification, planned giving, foundation/corporate outreach, endowment building, software design/selection, software implementation, development writing, and major gifts.

Hiller Associates, Inc.

Corporate office: 6 Water Street/Long Wharf,
Mattapoisett, MA 02739
Tel: 800-482-4498, 508-758-3436; FAX: 508-758-6975
WWW: http://www.hiller.com
Regional office: 406 Farmington Avenue, Farmington, CT 06032
Tel: 860-676-7711

▶ Hiller Associates, Inc., works with a wide variety of not-for-profit organizations in implementing institutional analysis. Hiller Associates specializes in identifying and cultivating the not-for-profit organization's donors and market sectors. Services include capital campaign management, development program assessment, organization and start-up development, board and organizational development, marketing, and full computer and Internet services.

Hodge, Cramer & Associates Inc.

5060 Parkcenter Avenue, Suite E, Dublin, OH 43017
Tel: 800-978-9212; FAX: 614-761-9920
E-mail: russ@hodgecramer.com (Russ Hodge, President);
WWW: http://www.hodgecramer.com

▶ The largest minority-owned fund-raising agency in the Midwest, its services include comprehensive philanthropic planning, endowment campaigns, media relations, training and organizing of volunteers, feasibility studies, cause-related marketing, direct-mail development, deferred giving, capital campaigns, philanthropic marketplace positioning, board training and recruitment, development department, annual fund drives, foundation research, special event management, and organization and management. They are a member of the American Association of Fund-Raising Counsel.

Hope Primas Associates

3644 Worthington Road, Collegeville, PA 19426
Tel: 610-831-0390
E-mail: hopeconsulting@aol.com (Hope Primas, Principal)

▶ This firm provides fund-raising consulting and outsourcing alternatives to membership associations, clubs, and other nonprofit organizations. Their mission is to enhance the success of their clients by providing them with top consulting, outsourcing, and supplementary campaign services at affordable rates. Their services include interim development director services (provide professional fund development services on a contract basis, allowing clients access to management support for priority projects or fill gaps caused by staff vacancies); project outsourcing (carry out defined projects or assignments for clients, including fund-raising assessment and feasibility studies, market research, volunteer and board training, proposal writing, and fund-raising consulting services on a project basis); and functional outsourcing (manage ongoing fund-raising programs for their clients' fund-raising department; for example, they can manage a client's direct-mail program, special event, or phonathon campaign on an ongoing basis). They can also help assist your board in all types of campaigns, design a customized campaign plan, support leadership with training and materials, increase annual appeals giving, utilize prospect review to improve the bottom line, cultivate donors to become major gift prospects, train board members and volunteers in the ABCs of fund raising, and overcome the board's reluctance to solicit funds. In order to provide customers with tailored, innovative solutions, they provide a range of feasible options, including specialized consulting for long- and short-term needs; management services for high-priority projects or gaps caused by staff turnover; interim maintenance for specific projects; and technical expertise on site, by phone, or via the Internet. Their competencies include start-up/project management, nonprofit marketing, board development, membership development, strategic planning, volunteer training, annual giving. program planning, special events, grant writing, corporate and major giving, telemarketing, and direct mail. They closely partner with clients to set the direction for future service delivery.

Institutional Advancement Programs, Inc.

65 Main Street, Suite 208, Tuckahoe, NY 10707
Tel: 914-779-4092; FAX: 914-961-3114
E-mail: BrecherServices@aol.com (Bernd Brecher, President)
160 Gentian Hollow Road, Chester, MA 01011
Tel/FAX: 413-623-0024

▶ This firm provides strategic planning; governance; feasibility studies: IAP's Survey, Analysis, and Plan; retreats and board self-assessment; development audits; capital campaign consulting; leadership motivation; case and mission development; major gift cultivation; executive search; and training.

Irwin-Wells Associates

61 Catalpa Avenue, Mill Valley, CA 94941-2828
Tel: 415-383-9657; FAX: 415-383-9080
E-mail: SIWfund@aol.com (Suzanne Irwin-Wells, Principal);
WWW: http://www.irwin-wells.com

▶ Suzanne Irwin-Wells is the founder and principal of Irwin-Wells Associates, a firm providing a full range of fund-raising and management services to nonprofit organizations. The firm's clients include organizations devoted to the arts, community enhancement, education, the environment, health care, human services, and religion. Ms. Irwin-Wells works extensively with boards of directors, conducts planning studies, plans/directs capital campaigns, conducts development assessments (audits), provides coaching and training for boards and staff, and creates development plans. Irwin-Wells Associates offers comprehensive development services for nonprofit organizations, both large and small. Services include the following: planning (feasibility) studies; campaign counsel and management; board recruitment, development, and training; strategic plans; development assessments (audits); establishment of new development programs; and case (prospectus) development.

J.C. Geever, Inc.

417 Canal Street, 8th Floor, New York, NY 10013
Tel: 212-925-5800; FAX: 212-966-3074
E-mail: info@jcgeever.com (Jane Geever, Founder and Chairman); WWW: http://www.jcgeever.com/

▶ Founded in 1975, this firm provides guidance and support designed to help not-for-profit institutions overcome fund-raising challenges. The firm's services include consulting, management and training in support of organizations of every size across the United States. It offers a full range of consulting, training, and management services to help your not-for-profit organization meet its fund-raising challenges, including operating campaign, capital campaign, feasibility study, development planning, consulting, training. Clients are in health; museums, cultural, and science education; youth and social service; religion; education; libraries; YMCAs/YWCAs; and community service. Ms. Geever is co-author, with Patricia McNeill, of *The Foundation Center's Guide to Proposal Writing* (see listing under Publications).

J. Donovan Associates, Inc. (JDA) *(See Donovan Slone)*

Corporate headquarters: One Derby Square,
Salem, MA 01970-3704
Tel: 800-370-0036, 978-744-8558; FAX: 978-741-1871
E-mail: philanthropy@compuserve.com (Roy H. Temper, President); WWW: http://www.jdonovan.com/

▶ JDA is a full-service consulting firm, offering a broad range of services to clients in health care, education, human services, museums, the arts, research, and conservation. Services include strategic planning; staff, board, and volunteer training; marketing, planning, and feasibility studies; development program assessments; capital campaign management; annual program development and support; grant writing; prospect research; membership development; comprehensive communication support; periodic and resident counsel; and executive search.

The JM Advancement Organization

4370 S. Tamiami Trail, Suite 150, Sarasota, FL 34231
Tel: 888-921-5726; FAX: 941-927-0479
E-mail: jrmercier@aol.com (John R. Mercier)

▶ This firm serves Florida nonprofits, offering planning/feasibility studies, process-oriented endowment development/planned giving, direct mail—membership organizations or build new base, and capital campaign direction (in-residence or non) for national and local organizations. Programs offered are creatively integrated with ongoing fund raising. Also included are audits, strategic planning, and training for staff and volunteers. The firm primarily serves youth and health agencies and religious and affinity groups. Services include capital campaigns, planned giving/endowment, direct mail, and Internet resourcing.

JSM Consulting Group, Inc.
6777 Palmer Drive NW, Canton, OH 44718-1092
Tel: 877-305-9137, 330-305-9137; FAX: 330-305-9497
E-mail: judith@JSMConsulting.com (Judith Snyder, Principal);
WWW: http://www.jsmconsulting.com
▶ This consulting firm provides nonprofit fund-raising services. Their associates work with nonprofit organizations to develop and execute highly successful fund-raising plans, which include annual fund, board development, capital campaigns, endowment, feasibility studies, grant writing, special events, workshops, and more. Clients range from social service agencies to universities and hospitals. They will deliver services that are tailored to your organization's specific fund-raising needs. The firm has associates in Ohio, Pennsylvania, Colorado, and New York.

Jackson & Associates Inc.
P.O. Box 2827, 29713 Troutdale Scenic Drive,
Evergreen, CO 80437-2827
Tel: 800-824-8447; FAX: 303-670-1127
E-mail: jackson301@aol.com (Bryan Jackson, CFRE, President and CEO)
▶ Jackson & Associates have been fund-raising professionals since 1973, helping nonprofit organizations and foundations with powerful community awareness and resource development programs, successful capital campaigns, and profitable grant-writing programs.

JEADCO Enterprises, Inc.
P.O. Box 360973, Birmingham, AL 35236-0973
Tel: 800-745-2517, 205-424-1746; FAX: 205-424-6268
E-mail: JEADCO@aol.com (James Dobbin, President and CEO),
info@jeadco.com; WWW: http://www.JEADCO.com
▶ JEADCO (Just Everything About Development Enterprises) is a full-service fund-raising company. Services are designed individually and include resource developmental planning studies (to evaluate your fund-raising potential in terms of dollars and leadership); capital campaign management; annual and endowment giving programs; leadership training for boards of directors and staff; special event management; and collaborative efforts/partnership programs (for two or more not-for-profit organizations).

Jeff Conway and Associates, LLC
535 Rosario Drive, Thousand Oaks, CA 91362
Tel: 805-373-6891, 805-370-1131
E-mail: jconway@earthlink.net (Jeff A. Conway, Principal)
▶ Serving Los Angeles, Santa Barbara, and Ventura Counties, Jeff Conway and Associates offers a wide array of financial development services to nonprofit organizations and institutions. The firm specializes in fund-raising planning, capital campaigns, goal feasibility studies, and major gifts programs. Conway's experiences as a consultant include directing and working on eight successful multimillion dollar capital development campaigns for a wide variety of nonprofits—churches, health institutions, schools, and human service organizations. In addition, he has expertise in goal feasibility studies and has developed and directed many successful annual giving, major gifts, and special project campaigns. Since 1978, Conway has managed numerous board development programs, financial development plans, and long-range plans.

Jerold Panas, Linzy & Partners
500 North Michigan Avenue, Suite 2008, Chicago, IL 60611
Tel: 800-234-7777; FAX: 312-222-9411
E-mail: jpanas@jeroldpanas.com (Jerold Panas, Executive
Partner and CEO); WWW: http://www.panaslinzy.com,
http://www.panaslinzy.com/pages/material.html
▶ This full-service firm provides campaign services and financial resource development. Since its founding in 1968, the firm has served over 1,400 client institutions. They assist clients in the community, cultural education, health care, and religious fields, including YMCAs and YWCAs. Services include precampaign feasibility studies, development office audits, public relations and design communications, foundation research and grants, resident campaign services, and consultation for strategic, governance, and leadership attainment.

John Brown Limited, Inc. (JBL)
P.O. Box 296, 46 Grove Street, Peterborough, NH 03458
Tel: 603-924-3834; FAX: 603-924-7998
E-mail: johnbrownlimited@aol.com (John Brown);
WWW: http://www.johnbrownlimited.com
▶ This fund-raising firm specializes in providing consulting and training services to nonprofit institutions. Brown founded the company in 1978 to assist charitable organizations in developing, implementing, and marketing their major gifts and planned giving programs. The firm creates and services individualized major gift and planned giving programs, as well as implementing capital and endowment campaigns. Consulting services include major gifts and planned giving consulting, capital and endowment campaign consulting, development review (audit), and external market (feasibility) studies. JBL also provides donor seminars, board/trustee and staff training, and coaching services (see separate listing under Seminars). Clients include museums and symphonies, health/human service organizations, and educational and financial institutions.

John R. Frank Consulting
14642 NW 174th Street, Woodinville, WA 98072
Tel/FAX: 425-488-1362
E-mail: JohnRFrank@aol.com; WWW: http://www.JohnRFrank.com
▶ Development counsel services include current giving programs (direct mail, major gifts, special events, core/key Donor Groups, Corporations, Foundations); planned giving (establishing a planned giving program, marketing, developing heritage/membership clubs); capital campaigns (needs assessment, case statements, feasibility/planning studies, campaign plans, leadership training, campaign administration); and community relations (PR strategies, church relations, communications strategies).

Johnson, Grossnickle and Associates (JGA)

P.O. Box 576, Franklin, IN 46131
Tel: 317-736-1985; FAX: 317-736-1983
E-mail: jga@jgacounsel.com, ted@jgacounsel.com (Ted R. Grossnickle); WWW: http://www.jgacounsel.com

▶ JGA offers a comprehensive set of integrated services, designed to maximize your organization's ability to cultivate and secure philanthropic support. Clients include colleges and universities; independent schools; civic, religious, and fraternal organizations; cultural and educational organizations; social service organizations; and health care and research institutions. Services include an initial study, development audit, annual fund analysis, strategic capacity building, precampaign planning, feasibility study, and campaign counsel.

Joyaux Associates

10 Johnson Road, Foster, RI 02825
Tel: 401-397-2534; FAX: 401-397-6793
E-mail: SPJoyaux@aol.com (Simone P. Joyaux, Principal); WWW: http://www.aherncomm.com/nonprofit/joyaux_associates.htm, http://www.AhernComm.com/nonprofit/index.htm

▶ Joyaux Associates offers not-for-profits, from grassroots to major institutions, counseling on strategic planning and board and fund development. Services include board development, strategic planning, annual funds, capital campaigns, proposal development, marketing, and training. They offer free *Fund Raiser's Newsletter,* a quarterly containing more than a dozen brief articles covering trends, expert opinion, good advice, tips, statistics, checklists, Internet leads, and book reviews of use to the fund-raising professional. Call for case studies and resource materials. Author of *Strategic Fund Development* (see separate listing under Publications).

Kelleher & Associates

15240 Lotusgarden Drive, Canyon Country, CA 91351-1834
Tel: 661-251-7753; FAX: 661-251-7900
E-mail: JKelleher@KelleherandAssociates.com (John Kelleher); WWW: http://www.KelleherandAssociates.com

▶ This firm specializes in fund raising, marketing, and governmental affairs for organizations, from concept creation to expansion of existing programs and services. Their primary services are development audits, board and staff development, board and staff retreats, solicitation training programs, capital and annual campaign management, membership campaigns, major gifts, marketing and public awareness programs, special events, governmental affairs, government funding, grants (domestic, international, governmental), and customer relations.

The Kellogg Organization, Inc.

825 East Speer Boulevard, Suite 100-D, Denver, CO 80218
Tel: 800-621-7110, 303-871-0988; FAX: 303-871-0979
E-mail: info@kelloggorganization.com; WWW: www.kelloggorganization.com

Eastern office: 230 Tazewell Street, Suite 303, Norfolk, VA 23510
Tel: 757-627-1724

Western office: 1199 Bush Street, Suite 650, San Francisco, CA 94109
Tel: 415-567-8292

▶ Established in 1981, The Kellogg Organization, Inc., is a full-service, fund-raising counsel and management consulting firm specializing in planning and implementing capital, endowment, and annual operating campaigns. Clientele throughout the United States include performing arts institutions, historical and visual art museums, historic preservation societies, private and public colleges and universities, independent secondary schools, libraries, social service organizations, religious institutions, hospitals and medical centers, public broadcasting stations, and environment/wildlife organizations. Services include all phases of capital, operating, and endowment campaigns: preliminary development audit and analysis, philanthropic marketing studies, campaign master plans, campaign implementation, strategic development planning, graphics, planned giving, public relations, marketing and special events, marketing, campaign support materials and publications, as well as board and staff development and board and volunteer solicitor training. They are a member of the American Association of Fund-Raising Counsel.

Ketchum Inc.

Three Gateway Center, Suite 1726, Pittsburgh, PA 15222
Tel: 800-242-2161; FAX: 972-450-4477
E-mail: info@rsi-ketchum.com; WWW: http://www.rsi-ketchum.com, http://www.ketchumconnection.com/

12770 Merit Drive, Suite 900, Dallas, TX 75251
Tel: 972-404-7584; FAX: 972-450-4477

▶ Services include development audits, planning studies (to facilitate campaign planning and to determine fund-raising potential), campaign management, major gift and planned gift development, board and volunteer leadership development, communications counsel, staff development, access to research, strategic and long-range development planning, annual giving programs, funding proposals and presentations to foundations and corporations, donor relations and stewardship development, and postcampaign counsel. They are a member of the American Association of Fund-Raising Counsel.

Laudick/Brown & Associates

934 North Park Avenue, Indianapolis, IN 46202
Tel: 317-634-5319; FAX: 317-238-5444
E-mail: info@laudick.com, mlaudick@laudick.com (Michael Laudick, Principal), mlaudick@telocity.com (Michael Laudick, Principal)

14071 Mango Drive, Suite H, Del Mar, CA 92014
Tel: 858-509-0090; FAX: 858-509-4139

▶ This national, full-service firm specializes in feasibility studies; capital campaigns; strategic planning; annual giving programs; and board workshops and training programs.

Leigh & Associates

8916 69th Avenue NW, Gig Harbor, WA 98332
Tel: 253-219-0613; FAX: 253-858-6790
E-mail: jleigh@centurytel.net (James F. Leigh, President); WWW: http://home.centurytel.net/jleigh

▶ This Northwest firm specializes in capital campaigns, feasibility studies, annual giving, major gift programs, board/staff training and development, organizational management and executive searches. Services include annual giving and major gifts programs; capital fund-raising campaigns; development (goal feasibility) studies; financial and capital development planning: long-range (strategic) planning; board development; development office setup and organization; planned giving/endowment development; volunteer and staff training; communications and marketing; organizational management; grants development; project development; and executive search.

MGI Fund-Raising Consulting, Inc. (MGI)

600 South Highway 169, Suite 100, Minneapolis, MN 55426
Tel: 800-387-9840; FAX: 800-587-5579
WWW: http://www.mgifundraising.com; WWW: http://www.mgi
fundraising.com/About_Us/Preparing/preparing.html

▶ MGI is a full-service fund-raising and communications consulting firm operating across North America serving a wide range of not-for-profit clients, including hospitals and health care organizations; private schools; colleges, universities, and postgraduate schools; cultural and arts organizations; social service organizations; churches, ministries and religious organizations. MGI offers comprehensive services to nonprofit institutions and those who support them. Fund-raising services include philanthropic market/feasibility studies; planning studies and analysis; development program audits; strategic planning and case development; counsel and/or management services: capital and endowment campaigns, annual giving programs, corporate/foundation solicitation programs, planned and deferred giving programs and counsel, special events, and sponsorship and donor recognition programs; foundation and development office audits; consulting services: prospect identification and research, proposal writing; public relations and donor cultivation; volunteer identification and training and board seminars, telemarketing and capital-by-phone programs, and data management and computer support. MGI maintains offices in Toronto, Minneapolis, and Savannah.

Margo Morris & Co.

910 North Lake Shore Drive, Suite 519, Chicago, IL. 60611
Tel: 312-335-3686; FAX: 312-335-3687
E-mail: mmorrisco@aol.com, EErhart@aol.com (Erika Erhart);
WWW: http://www.nonprofitconsult.com

▶ Margo Morris & Co., established in 1992, provide creative consulting services that include fund raising, marketing, publications, and board development. Skilled at creating, developing, implementing, and managing programs to increase revenues, Margo Morris & Co. provides counsel for a wide range of development needs. Services include fund raising (plans, develops, and implements capital campaigns and annual fund programs; researches prospects and writes grant proposals; conducts feasibility studies; and plans special events); marketing (designs innovative programs that expand audiences, increase revenues, and promote organizational identity); publications (creates publications including newsletters, solicitation brochures, and annual reports that drive revenue growth and support organizational goals); board and staff development (conducts board and staff retreats that help build organizational capacity; trains board and staff members to lead successful capital and annual fund campaigns).

Maria Gitin & Associates

Box 216, Capitola, CA 95010-0126
Tel/FAX: 831-688-3373
E-mail: msgitin@got.net (Maria Gitin, Principal);
WWW: http://members.aol.com/GitinAssoc

▶ This independent consulting network has been providing development and training services to nonprofit organizations since 1983. They counsel, train, and empower nonprofit leaders to fund and fulfill their missions. Specialties are planning and directing capital, annual and endowment campaigns, board and staff development training, diversity and team-building training, conducting organizational assessments, and facilitating strategic plans for fund raising. They are frequent presenters at seminars and conferences. They conduct the Diversity in Fund Raising seminars co-presented nationally with Charles R. Stephens.

Marts & Lundy, Inc.

Meadowlands Corporate Center, 1200 Wall Street West,
Lyndhurst, NJ 07071
Tel: 800-526-9005, 201-460-1660
E-mail: information@martsandlundy.com,
jolly@martsandlundy.com (Richard T. Jolly, Vice President);
WWW: http://www.martsandlundy.com,
http://www.martsandlundy.com/nl9.html

▶ Marts & Lundy is a full-service consulting firm serving not-for-profit organizations since 1926. They offer counsel on total development programs or any specific area of such a program, including capital campaigns; annual funds; planned giving; audits; studies; major gift strategies; and prospect research, screening, and rating. In 1984, Marts & Lundy brought the concept of computerized screening for the identification of top donor prospects to the world of philanthropy with the introduction of ELECTRONIC SCREENING®. In 2000, Marts & Lundy established ES Solutions™—an integrated set of prospect segmentation and research tools. ES Solutions contains three different types of computerized prospect segmentation services: Potential Plus®, Prospect Data, and Prospect Select. It also contains two Internet-based research tools: ES Securities and ES Executives. Its counseling services support capital efforts at any phase of the campaign cycle—from precampaign feasibility studies to postcampaign development assessments. They also provide counsel in other development strategies that may or may not be immediately linked to a capital campaign. They can help you build and sustain a successful major gifts program, assess the effectiveness of your computer systems and database, suggest tactics for involving your trustee board in active fund raising, survey segments of your constituency, and/or assist you in planning an effective direct-mail campaign. They publish a Web newsletter, *Online Counsel*, several times a year.

McConkey/Johnston

P.O. Box 370, Woodland Park, CO 80866-0370
Tel: 719-687-3455; FAX: 719-687-3772
E-mail: cienfuegos@aol.com; WWW: http://www.mj1.com/

▶ This firm provides a wide variety of services aimed at helping you achieve comprehensive and integrated marketing and development programming. They also provide counsel in areas of organizational development; strategic and long-range planning; management and leadership seminars and training; feasibility and planning studies, campaign planning and analysis, leadership enlistment/cultivation for campaigns, specialized audits, and development management reporting systems. Development/fund-raising services include development audits, current giving strategies, planned giving, capital fund programs, staff support development, events, and annual development planning.

The Metanoia Group

700 Terrace Heights, Suite 3, Winona, MN 55987-1399
Tel: 507-457-1750; FAX: 507-457-1722
E-mail: metanoia@smumn.edu (Tim Burchill, President and Co-Founder); WWW: www.smumn.edu/metanoia

▶ The Metanoia Group provides development consulting to small nonprofit organizations: campaigns, planning, audits, searches, and a wide range of studies. They serve a wide variety of not-for-profit organizations, including religiously affiliated elementary and secondary schools and consolidated systems, parishes, dioceses, congregations of religious women and men, homeless shelters, elder care facilities, medical centers, agencies serving children at risk, and other organizations with religious affiliation and/or heritage. Services include annual funds, special projects, capital campaigns, constituent cultivation, campaign feasibility studies, planned giving, grant writing, direct mail, campaign design and planning, and volunteer training.

Meyer Partners

501 Pebble Court, Schaumburg, IL 60193-3149
Tel: 847-524-1273; FAX: 847-524-8081
E-mail: 71361.2463@compuserve.com

9237 Ward Parkway, Suite 310, Kansas City, MO 6114-3362
Tel: 816-363-8585; FAX: 816-363-6895
E-mail: bioneill@compuserve.com

▶ This firm was founded in 1989 to provide strategic consulting and related services in fund raising and marketing to selected nonprofit organizations. Services include direct mail, print advertising, major gifts campaigns, broadcast media, planned giving, file analysis, market research, marketing materials, creative development, and production services.

Mike Hoffman Associates, Inc. (MHA)

420 Lexington Avenue, Suite 2458, New York, NY 10170
Tel: 212-499-0866; FAX: 212-499-9075
E-mail: info@changingourworld.com;
WWW: http://www.changingourworld.com/mha.htm

▶ Formed in 1988, MHA is an independent full-service fundraising and development consulting firm. They provide on-site fundraising counsel for organizations as a more cost-effective alternative to a full-time executive director or director of development. They offer the following full range of consulting services on-site directors of development and executive directors of development, capital campaigns, corporate giving campaigns, planned giving campaigns, fund-raising audits and strategic planning, board recruitment and training, and communications/public relations.

Milano, Ruff & Associates, Inc.

609 Avery Place, Long Beach, CA 90807
Tel: 562-424-0058; FAX: 562-424-4438
E-mail: MilanoRuff@aol.com (Albert Milano/Michael Ruff, Managing Partners)

▶ A national management and fund-raising consulting firm.

Mirenda & Associates

360 South Monroe Street, Suite 270, Denver, CO 80209
Tel: 303-377-3389; FAX: 303-322-1445
E-mail: info@mirenda.com, ronm@mirenda.com (Ronald F. Mirenda, Founding Principal); WWW: http://www.mirenda.com, http://www.mirenda.com/messenger.htm

▶ They offer capital campaign experience, from limited consulting to total campaign management, from the smallest to the largest campaigns. They provide knowledge of issues such as budgeting, material production, major gift strategy development, and campaign timing. Services include feasibility studies, capital campaign management, strategic planning, annual programs, board development, communications programs, development programs, assessments, and strategies for corporate philanthropy.

NFP Consulting Resources

1690 Starling Drive, Sarasota, FL 34231
Tel: 941-922-1690
E-mail: infor@nfpconsulting.com, NOlshansky@AOL.COM (Norman Olshansky, President);
WWW: http://www.nfpconsulting.com/fundraising.html

▶ NFP Consulting can help you and your organization accomplish your goals and develop the skills and experience necessary for short- and long-term success. Norman Olshansky, President of NFP Consulting Resources, brings with him over 20 years of professional and executive-level leadership and consulting within both the not-for-profit and for-profit sectors. His clients have included both large and small service, cultural and faith-based organizations throughout the United States, Canada, and Israel. Services include major gifts, planned giving, feasibility studies, and capital campaign management.

Netzel Associates, Inc.

Corporate office: 9696 Culver Boulevard, Suite 204, Culver City, CA 90232-2753
Tel: 310-836-7624; FAX: 310-836-9357
E-mail: fundraising@netzelinc.com;
WWW: http://www.netzelinc.com/

▶ Established in 1985, Netzel Associates is a management and consulting firm specializing in fund raising and organizational development with not-for-profit organizations and institutions. It provides services including development/feasibility studies, capital and endowment fund-raising campaigns, planned giving/endowment development, executive search, major gift programs, annual giving and donor gift clubs, board development, foundation research and grant writing, planning, financial and capital development, volunteer and staff training, donor profile, and prospect identification. Netzel also maintains offices in Phoenix, San Jose, Phoenix, Las Vegas, and Seattle.

The New Castle Group LLC

1812 North Patrick Henry Drive, Arlington, VA 22205-3240
Tel: 703-237-9272; FAX: 703-237-8271
E-mail: ncastlegrp@aol.com, Ellen@esa.org (Ellen R. Cardwell, CFRE, Principal)

▶ Diane M. Carlson, Chairman, offers personalized attention from a small, creative, energetic team. The New Castle Group principals include highly experienced grant writers and CFREs with 24 years' experience in distinctive fund-raising events, customized leadership training for volunteers and staff (not-for-profits/government), events, conference, exhibits, annual fund and major gift campaigns, and corporate solicitations. Firm capabilities also include tactical/strategic planning: career and outplacement coaching. The Group specializes in meeting and event planning; awards events; general fund-raising activities; including feasibility studies in preparation for annual and capital campaigns; writing grant proposals; volunteer and staff training and coordination for fund-raising and strategic and long-range planning; and project management

NFP Consulting Resources, Inc.

1690 Starling Drive, Sarasota, FL 34231
Tel: 941-922-1690
E-mail: nfpconsulting@aol.com (Norman Olshansky, President);
WWW: http://www.nfpconsulting.com

▶ NFP Consulting Resources, Inc., provides a wide range of consulting services to not-for-profit corporations. NFP Consulting has worked with small locally based organizations as well as with large national and international associations. Fund-raising services include major gifts, planned giving, feasibility studies, and capital campaign management.

Nike B. Whitcomb Associates Inc.

205 West Wacker Drive, Suite 2022, Chicago, IL 60606
Tel: 800-822-9017, 312-346-9018; FAX: 312-346-9098
E-mail: wassoci159@aol.com;
WWW: http://members.aol.com/nbwhitcomb

▶ Serving not-for-profit organizations since 1981, its clients include nonprofits in the areas of social service, education, religion, arts and culture, health, and civic. Services include capital campaigns, assessment and planning, internal assessments, feasibility/planning studies, development programs, management support, marketing and communications (including marketing studies), prospect research, volunteer identification and recruitment, volunteer orientation and training, proposal writing (foundations, corporations, government), editorial production and coordination, and staff and board development (including board retreats).

Olwell Associates, LLC

1300 Old Bayshore Highway, Suite 100, Burlingame, CA 94010
Tel: 650-579-7925; FAX: 650-579-7928
E-mail: olwell@olwellassociates.com (Quentin M. Olwell, President); WWW: http://www.olwellassociates.com

▶ This is a full-service firm providing assistance with preappeal planning, audits, studies, leadership development, and capital and major gifts appeals.

The Oram Group, Inc.

Corporate offices: 275 Madison Avenue, Suite 1181,
New York, NY 10016-1184
Tel: 212-889-2244; FAX: 212-986-2731
E-mail: hankus@juno.com (Henry Goldstein, President and CEO)

44 Page Street, Suite 604C, San Francisco, CA 94102
Tel: 415-864-7567; FAX: 415-621-2533
E-mail: mbancel@aol.com; WWW: http://www.oramgroup.com

▶ The Oram Group helps clients in the fields of education, religion, health, welfare, social action, civil rights, the environment, and the visual and performing arts. Services comprise management counsel, fund-raising counsel, board development and empowerment, planning studies and development audits, organizational assessments, and executive search. The Oram Group has formed an alliance with Raybin Associates, Inc. The two firms offer over 80 years' experience, expertise, dedication, and creativity in serving philanthropic institutions. They are a member of the American Association of Fund-Raising Counsel.

The Osborne Group Inc.

70 West Red Oak Lane, White Plains, NY 10604
Tel: 914-697-4921; FAX: 914-697-4899
E-mail: HQ@theosbornegroup.com;
WWW: http://www.theosbornegroup.com

▶ A full-service consulting company with proven expertise across a broad spectrum of management issues, they focus primarily in the areas of health care management and consulting, fund raising for nonprofit organizations, and capital financing for commercial enterprises. Services include development (fund raising, campaigns, major gifts, planned giving, board development, staff development, institutional advancement); financial (debt and equity financing); operations (executive management consulting, program assessment, strategic planning, government relations, marketing).

Partners in Philanthropy, Inc.

1240 SW Oakley, Topeka, KS 66604
Tel: 785-354-4327; FAX: 785-354-9597
E-mail: pip@develop-net.com (Michael R. Maude, President);
WWW: www.develop-net.com

▶ This nonprofit management and fund-raising consulting firm has special expertise in leadership development, strategic planning, capital campaigns, and executive recruitment. Founded in 1994, the firm's clients include a broad array of nonprofits, including education, health care, and human service organizations. Additionally, it has developed a wide reputation among Catholic campus ministries throughout the country.

Paul Blanshard Associates, Inc.

645 East Butler Avenue, Doylestown, PA 18901
Tel: 215-345-4616; FAX: 215-345-4632
E-mail: sdhirt@prodigy.net (Stephen D. Hirt, President)

▶ Paul Blanshard Associates is a full-service development consulting firm serving small and mid-size nonprofit organizations within a 100-mile radius of Philadelphia. PBA has built a reputation for very personalized services to a broad spectrum of nonprofit organizations, including hospitals, independent schools, churches, human service and youth organizations, and civic and cultural organizations. They are a member of the American Association of Fund-Raising Counsel.

Paul J. Strawhecker, Inc.

4913 Dodge Street, Omaha, NE 68132
Tel: 402-556-5785; FAX: 402-556-7274
E-mail: pjsinc@uswest.net (Paul Strawhecker), jeanne@paul jstrawheckerinc.com; WWW: http://www.pauljstrawheckerinc.com

▶ This consulting firm specializes in providing fund-raising assistance to nonprofit organizations. They provide experience in connecting nonprofit organizations with individuals, corporations, and foundations to strategically raise funds and help achieve their goals. They support nonprofits through organizational development consulting, fund-raising software, annual giving, proposal research/writing, capital campaigns, any major and planned giving assistance. They provide services to a wide variety of community organizations, including church groups, educational organizations, medical institutions and social service agencies. They specialize in development assessment, organizational development, grant writing, feasibility studies, capital campaigns, major gift/planned giving, and training.

Payne, Forrester & Olsson, LLP/Payne, Forrester & Associates, LLC

790 Farmington Avenue, Suite 4B, Farmington, CT 06032
Tel: 860-409-2560; FAX: 860-409-2565
E-mail: pfo790@aol.com

▶ This firm provides counsel and support to nonprofit institutions on such matters as fund raising, communications, governance, long-range planning, finance, and management. Through its consulting services, the firm assists organizations and institutions in developing their own capacity for fund raising and effective leadership. The firm works with a variety of nonprofits and nongovernmental organizations on a worldwide basis and is particularly experienced in assisting organizations that are addressing change and/or planning new ventures. Over 350 clients have been served. Services can be engaged as retained counsel, campaign counsel, special project advisement, and, for special situations, bridge staff support, and cover fund-raising program assessment and development, campaign feasibility and planning, planned giving, annual giving, major gift development, strategic planning, grant writing; board governance issues, and staff recruitment and training.

The Philanthropy Group

2600 72nd Street, Suite F, Des Moines, IA 50322-4724
Tel: 800-538-4483; FAX: 515-270-1437
E-mail: pkirpes@whatmattersmost.com (Paul J. Kirpes CFRE, President and CEO)

▶ This is a full-service fund-raising, marketing, communications, and management firm, with specialized expertise in capital campaigns, endowment building, planned giving, development audits, feasibility studies, major gifts, grants, board/volunteer development, and project management.

Phillips & Associates

10877 Wilshire Boulevard, Suite 708, Los Angeles, CA 90024
Tel: 310-208-7772; FAX: 310-208-7066
E-mail: contact@phillipsontheweb.com;
WWW: http://phillipsontheweb.com/pa

▶ Phillips & Associates, established in 1971, is a professional management consulting firm specializing in organizational planning, financial planning, and fund-raising counsel for not-for-profit institutions and organizations, primarily within California, Arizona, Hawaii, Oregon, and Washington. Clients include community service organizations, cultural organizations, health and medical organizations, higher education, the performing arts, and private secondary education. Services include strategic planning, board and staff retreats, development program consulting and assessments, campaign readiness assessment and funding feasibility studies, campaign consulting and management, and volunteer and staff training. The firm also maintains San Francisco, Central Coast, and Orange County offices.

Phoenix Resources, Inc.

1830 Sherman Avenue, Evanston, IL 60201
Tel: 800-358-9386, ext. 24; FAX: 847-475-5111
E-mail: VerSchave@aol.com (Sally VerSchave, President)

▶ Services include fund-raising campaigns, feasibility studies, leadership development, strategic planning, communication, organizational development, and change management.

Pierpont & Wilkerson

P.O. Box 179, 1111 Route 9, The Stone House,
Garrison, NY 10524-0179
Tel: 914-737-4435; FAX: 914-737-7352
E-mail: bobp@pierpont-wilkerson.net (Robert Pierpont, Chairman and CEO); WWW: http://www.pierpont-wilkerson.net

Southeastern office: 1133 Bal Harbour Boulevard, Suite 1139, Box 300, Punta Gorda, FL 33950
Tel/FAX: 941-575-1609

▶ Pierpont & Wilkerson are senior professionals experienced in comprehensive development programs, capital and endowment campaigns, fund-raising management, board development, training, planning, and pre-campaign studies. Specialties include feasibility studies, major gift programs, program reviews, campaign counsel, constituency development, training and mentoring, campaign plans; case statements, campaign management, corporate and foundation grants; board development, and special projects.

Pride Philanthropy, Inc.

6508 Arbor Point, Flowery Branch, GA 30542
Tel: 888-417-0707, 770-967-0707; FAX: 770-965-8926
E-mail: pridephil@aol.com;
WWW: http://www.pridephilanthropy.com

▶ This firm is a national leader in helping health care organizations realize the full potential of their philanthropy programs. Services include education seminars, board retreats—design and facilitation, solicitation training, development audits/assessments, feasibility studies, strategic planning service, and ongoing program consultation.

Puffer & Associates

P.O. Box 16411, Saint Paul, MN 55116
Tel: 651-695-5558; FAX: 888-805-1070
E-mail: timpuffer@developmentresources.com (Timothy Puffer); WWW: http://www.developmentresources.com/Puffer& Associates.htm, http://www.developmentresources.com/index.htm

▶ This firm specializes in a full range of fund-raising services from audits and planning through grant writing, direct mail, telemarketing, and donor information management. Development-related coaching and technical assistance is also available. They offer the following services on a project-by-project or long-term contractual basis: development audits and planning, grant writing, case development, mail and phone appeals, donor information management, Internet presence, staff recruitment services, and coaching and technical assistance. They can offer flexible options and tailor arrangements to the individual needs of each client. Services can range from writing one appeal letter or grant to planning, implementing, and managing an organization's entire annual giving or grants program.

RPA Inc.

951 Westminster Drive, Williamsport, PA 17701
Tel: 800-992-9277; FAX: 570-321-7160
E-mail: RPAInc@epix.net (Richard P. Allen, President and Principal); WWW: http://www.rpainc.org/

▶ RPA Inc. provides organizational management, executive recruitment, and fund-raising consulting for national and international clients meeting education, health, cultural, and elder care management needs. Services include campaign consultation/management (assistance in planning, implementing and evaluating capital; annual and deferred giving campaigns); public relations support of fund raising (can develop programs to support capital campaigns, publish case statements and use the media to advance your cause); and planned giving (seminars for the public, strategies for specific prospects, individual solicitations as well as overall program management).

Raybin Associates, Inc.

275 Madison Avenue, Suite 1811, New York, NY 10016-1184
Tel: 212-490-0590; FAX: 212-986-2731
E-mail: Information@raybinassociates.com, nraybin@aol.com
(Nancy L. Raybin, Managing Partner), elowell236@aol.com
(Elizabeth M. Lowell, Partner), MDevlin@raybinassociates.com
(Mary Devlin), khawkins@raybinassociates.com (Kimberly
Hawkins); WWW: http:// http://www.raybinassociates.com

▶ This fund-raising, strategic planning, and management consulting group serves gift-supported and grant-making organizations. Founded in 1973 by the late Arthur D. Raybin, the firm has served as counsel to over 400 schools, colleges, human service agencies, hospitals, cultural organizations, religious institutions, and other gift-supported groups, as well as to a number of foundations. While the core of their practice is solving fund-raising problems, they view fund raising as part of an integrated system of sound management and governance. As a result, they work with many of their clients on board development, strategic planning, financial management, or organizational structure before launching major fund-raising initiatives. Their practice is focused on three inter-related areas: fund raising (capital campaign, planning, design and implementation; annual fund strategies; planned giving strategies); strategic planning (situation assessment; strategy retreats/workshops; ongoing counsel); and organization and management (organizational design; governance; leadership development and training for boards of trustees). They are a member of the American Association of Fund-Raising Counsel.

Resource Development Counsel

37 Round Hill Road, Dobbs Ferry, NY 10522-3310
Tel: 914-762-7187; FAX: 914-762-5642
E-mail: rmiss@email.msn.com (Robert E. Miss, Partner),
ghsavino@email.msn.com (Gae Hoffman Savino, Partner);
WWW: http://www.rdcfunds.org

▶ This full-service firm provides assistance in all areas of the development process, including board development, leadership training and technical assistance, prospect research, fund-raising campaigns; the case for support, feasibility studies, corporate and foundation relations, and project funding.

Resource Development, Inc.

Corporate headquarters: 1411 East Primrose, Suite A,
Springfield, MO 64804
Tel: 800-728-8805, 417-883-0202; FAX: 417-883-9140

Dallas office: 555 Republic Drive, Suite 200, Plano, TX 75074
Tel: 972-509-0010; FAX: 972-633-9107
E-mail: rdisgf@cland.net (Bill Jester);
WWW: http://www.resourcedevinc.com

▶ This financial consulting firm focuses on providing comprehensive fund raising. Since 1978, they have helped a wide variety of organizations, including missions, hospitals, universities, cultural, and social service groups to expand and improve their work. The scope of their fund-raising expertise includes feasibility studies, marketing analysis, direct mail, planned giving literature, proposal preparation, strategic planning, fund-raising program audits, planned giving and strategy, estate planning and tax counsel, and major gift solicitation. They also maintain a Los Angeles office.

Results Group International

230 West 41st Street, Suite 1602, New York, NY 10036
Tel: 212-869-3373, ext. 43; FAX: 212-869-5535
E-mail: Get@resultsg.com, ClaudiaC@ResultsG.com (Claudia
Chouinard, President); WWW: http://www.ResultsG.com

▶ This full-service management consulting firm assists cultural, educational, and advocacy nonprofits. It provides marketing, planning, and fund-raising capabilities. Fund-raising services include retention programs, major donor programs, annual fund campaigns, feasibility studies, capital and endowment campaigns, precapital and preendowment campaign preparation, development program audits, strategic fund-raising plans, prospect research, development office setup/reviews, volunteer and solicitor training, international issues, and outsourced executive services.

Ross, Johnston, & Kersting Inc. (RJ&K)

3326 Chapel Hill Boulevard, Suite C-220, Durham, NC 27707
Tel: 919-286-0721; FAX: 919-402-9199
E-mail: rjkinc@mindspring.com; WWW: www.rjkinc.com

▶ Established in 1981, RJ&K provides development counseling for nonprofit organizations and has worked on more than 145 campaigns. Typical clients include colleges and universities, health care institutions, independent and secondary schools, and cultural organizations. It offers assistance in the broad areas of feasibility studies, campaign plans, and counseling. Specific services available to clients include long-range planning, institutional promotion, support system development, special event planning, corporate and foundation guidance, annual support programming, deferred giving counseling, alumni affairs counseling, professional and volunteer staff training, and trustee workshops. RJ&K also performs executive searches to help you recruit and hire the best possible candidates for development and alumni affairs positions.

Ruotolo Associates, Inc.

Corporate headquarters/mid-Atlantic division: Horizon Square,
29 Broadway, Suite 210, Cresskill, NJ 07626
Tel: 201-568-3898; FAX: 201-568-8783
E-mail: info@ruotoloassoc.com, Rassoc1@aol.com;
WWW: http://www.ruotoloassoc.com ˘ Baltimore/Washington, DC

▶ This is a full-service fund-raising and public relations firm. Since 1979, they have specialized in service to schools, colleges, churches, and dioceses; libraries, social service, and health organizations; and cultural and community causes, throughout the United States. Specific services include feasibility/planning study; development program (capital campaigns, annual campaigns, planned giving); strategic planning; public relations; graphics; marketing; and executive search. They have divisions in Massachusetts, Missouri, and the Baltimore/Washington, DC area. They are a member of the American Association of Fund-Raising Counsel.

SFR Consulting

611 West Sixth Street, Suite 3250, Los Angeles, CA 90017
Tel: 213-239-9866; FAX: 213-629-3461
E-mail: sfrice@sfrconsulting.com (Susan F. Rice, Principal);
WWW: http://www.sfrconsulting.com

▶ SFR Consulting focuses on development requirements of non-profit organizations that provide essential educational and social services to the community. Services include increasing donor support for the mission and needs of the organization; training boards to lead the development program; mounting a major fund-raising campaign; and conducting special needs campaigns. They provide training for volunteers and/or staff, annual giving, board organizations, mentoring, corporate and foundation relations and marketing.

Schofield Associates

304 South Franklin Street, Suite 200, Syracuse, NY 13202
Tel: 800-724-6170, 315-472-9306; FAX: 315-472-4486
E-mail: billschofield@wcschofield.com;
WWW: http://www.wcschofield.com/about-us.htm

▶ Services include feasibility studies, campaign plan, marketing, and special events. Clients are in the following areas: cultural/civic, health, educational, cultural/educational, and human services/religious/youth. They also have offices in Clearwater and Ponte Vedra, Florida.

The Schrader Group

11715 26th Avenue NE, Seattle, WA 98125-5309
Tel: 206-368-8710; FAX: 206-368-2448
E-mail: Lynn@SchraderGroup.com (Lynn G. Schrader, President and Principal Consultant); WWW: http://www.SchraderGroup.com, http://www.schradergroup.com/philanthropy.htm, http://www.schradergroup.com/fundraising.htm

▶ Using a customized approach, The Schrader Group works collaboratively with boards and staff to develop the client's fund-raising capacity. They focus on building long-term donor relationships in the spirit of philanthropy while helping to generate support for immediate needs. As a team of consultants with complementary skills, they also use the latest in information technology to maximize fund-raising results while minimizing client expense. Services include capital and endowment campaigns, major gifts, planned giving, feasibility studies, prospect research, annual fund advancement, development audits, marketing communications, strategic planning, grant writing, board development and training, fund-raising through technology, and philanthropic education.

Schultz & Williams, Inc.

421 Chestnut Street, Suite 400, Philadelphia, PA 19106-2422
Tel: 215-625-9955; FAX: 215-625-2701
E-mail: mail@sw-inc.com (L. Scott Schultz, President);
WWW: http://www.sw-inc.com

▶ Schultz & Williams is a national consulting firm offering development, marketing, and management experience and skills. Schultz & Williams serves clients located throughout the country, including education, conservation, cultural and performing arts, public broadcasting, health, and community service organizations.

They meet clients' needs in traditional areas of development, including feasibility and campaign planning studies, annual funds, major gift programs, and board development/training. Clients also benefit from marketing, communications, and production services. Professional staff are located in Boston, Chicago, New York, San Francisco, and Los Angeles. Development services include strategic planning; development resource audits; campaign feasibility studies; campaign planning; fund-raising program planning (major gifts, annual giving, capital giving, planned giving, corporate and foundation relations); prospect research and identification; grant proposal preparation; communications; and board and volunteer training.

Semple-Bixel Associates, Inc.

653 Franklin Avenue, Nutley, NJ 07110
Tel: 973-284-0444; FAX: 973-284-0950
E-mail: rfsemple@aol.com (Maria Semple)

▶ This independent fund-raising management consulting firm specializes in planning studies, campaign counseling, staff/volunteer training, executive recruitment, prospect research, and endowment-building programs. They have designed and directed hundreds of fund-raising training programs and workshops in the United States and abroad. They are a member of the American Association of Fund-Raising Counsel.

Sinclair, Townes & Company

230 Peachtree Street NW, Suite 1601, Atlanta, GA 30303
Tel: 404-688-4047; FAX: 404-688-6543
E-mail: ask@sinclairtownes.com;
WWW: http://www.sinclairtownes.com,
http://www.sinclairtownes.com/shop.asp

▶ Since 1980, they have provided comprehensive fund-raising counseling services and products for nonprofit institutions and organizations. They consult with arts and cultural organizations, churches, colleges and universities, hospitals and medical centers, human service organizations, independent schools, membership organizations, and others on a local, regional, national, and international basis. The firm's fund-raising consulting services include capital campaign counsel, feasibility studies, planned giving consulting, annual giving consulting, membership programs, board development, executive search, development audits, board retreats, prospect research, multimedia case development; and internal readiness assessments. The firm offers extensive online prospect research on individuals, foundations, and corporations. The firm's electronic screening service, donor$earch, can identify which of a client's donors and prospective donors are the most affluent.

In addition to consulting services, the firm has developed a menu of publications, including fund-raising desk books and planned giving publications. They publish *The Digest of Southern Giving*, a bimonthly, eight-page newsletter featuring the latest fund-raising tips and trends, and the *Georgia Foundation Directory & Service*, providing information on more than 900 Georgia-based foundations. They also conduct seminars on such topics as charting capital campaigns, Planned Giving 101, and their annual Southern Giving Conference. Specific seminars and retreats for nonprofits and their board members, donors, and other friends are also conducted.

Smith Beers Yunker & Company, Inc.

Headquarters: 431 Ohio Pike, Suite 105 North,
Cincinnati, OH 45255-3372
Tel: 800-698-6537; FAX: 513-688-1151
E-mail: info@smithbeers.com; WWW: http://www.smithbeers.com

2300 Lincoln Park West, Suite A-9, Chicago, IL 60614-4163
Tel: 773-880-1680; FAX: 773-880-1681
E-mail: friedman@smithbeers.com (Carolyn Stolper Friedman
CFRE, Managing Director)

▶ This firm provides international management and fund-raising consultancy to organizations in the United States and the United Kingdom. Services include annual giving counsel, capital campaign planning and counsel, CoffeeCounsel^{sm}, donor research, leadership development, management reviews, planned giving counsel, volunteer coaching, staff recruitment and training, and writing and graphic design. They are a member of the American Association of Fund-Raising Counsel.

Social Research Associates, Inc.

5638 Glen Avenue, Minnetonka, MN 55345
Tel: 952-974-0892; FAX: 952-974-1021
E-mail: jhiller@codenet.net (J. Hiller)

▶ Nonprofit resource consultants in the areas of planning, evaluation, and fund-raising training.

Staley/Robeson®

733 Summer Street, Suite 204, Stamford, CT 06901
Tel: 800-659-7247, 914-694-2766; FAX: 914-694-2768
E-mail: uwin@staleyrobeson.com;
WWW: http://www.staleyrobeson.com,
http://www.staleyrobeson.com/new/WHONOT.HTM

▶ This organization serves independent schools, universities, medical centers, libraries, youth and human service agencies, hospitals, arts, cultural and other organizations, and health/service organizations. Primary services include capital campaigns, annual fund campaigns, and development studies. They are a member of the American Association of Fund-Raising Counsel.

Staley/Robeson/Ryan/St. Lawrence, Inc.

635 West Seventh Street, Suite 308, Cincinnati, OH 45203
Tel: 800-883-0809, 513-241-6778; FAX: 513-241-0551
E-mail: mail@staley-robeson.com, tconway@staley-robeson.com
(Thomas J. Conway, Managing Partner); WWW: http://www.staley-robeson.com

▶ This organization serves nonprofit organizations across America and throughout the world. Clients served include the following areas: colleges, cultural, health care, social service, religion, associations, schools, civic, and others. Services include fund-raising studies; fund-raising campaigns; planning and feasibility studies; capital campaign direction and management; annual fund development; institutional planning; major gifts development; planned giving programs and consulting; prospect research, including POW&R, Inc.; telephone fund raising; special events; staff recruitment and training; interim management; public relations; and editorial and graphic design services. They are a member of Downes Ryan International, the largest fund-raising consultancy in the world. They maintain Staley/Robeson Regional Offices in Atlanta, Chicago, St. Louis, Dallas, Phoenix, Cincinnati, and Washington, as well as an International Division office in Cincinnati.

Take Charge

2186 South Holly Street, Denver, CO 80222-5619
Tel: 888-426-9522, 303-504-9524; FAX: 303-504-9527
E-mail: carcan@ix.netcom.com (Carole Cantor, CFRE, Principal)

▶ The Take Charge team provides cost-effective consulting services for start-up to midsized nonprofit organizations to assist them in achieving their goals and increase productivity. Take Charge creates, develops, and implements programs that include annual and capital campaigns, development and organizational audits and renewal, board and membership development, and strategic planning and counsel for major gifts, as well as one-on-one solicitations. Planning and training seminars designed to address the needs of each individual organization are also available through Take Charge. Fund-raising counsel are available to assist NPOs in meeting their goals through annual and capital campaigns, as well as organizational and board development and training.

Talisman Associates, Inc.

711 North Elizabeth, Suite 2F, Chicago, IL 60622
Tel: 888-3-TALISMAN (outside Illinois), 312-733-7520;
FAX: 312-733-7530
E-mail: info@3talisman.com; WWW: http://www.3talisman.com,
http://www.3talisman.com/bestprac.html,
http://www.3talisman.com/bookrevu.html,
http://www.3talisman.com/mailing.html

2020 Pennsylvania Avenue NW, Suite 557, Washington, DC 20006
Tel: 888-3-TALISMAN; FAX: 877-5-TALISMAN
E-mail: info@3talisman.com

▶ Since 1983, Talisman Associates, Inc., has assisted not-for-profit organizations by providing developmental skills. Talisman Associates specializes in small/medium nonprofit agencies and serves clients nationwide from offices in Chicago and Washington, DC. Services include development audits, corporate giving, grant research/writing, annual campaigns, one-on-one/major gift campaigns, special events, and special campaigns. The firm also regularly sponsors "Best Practices" fund-raising training workshops and luncheons.

Ter Molen Brandt & Associates, Inc.

500 North Dearborn Street, Chicago, IL 60610
Tel: 312-222-0560
E-mail: info@termolenbrandt.com, gsbrandt@atlanta.com (Gene
S. Brandt), larryrichard@msn.com (Larry Richard);
WWW: http://www.termolenbrandt.com

▶ This full-service national consulting firm specializes in senior-level campaign consulting, feasibility studies development audits, and executive search. The firm serves nonprofit organizations by providing a wide range of senior-level consulting services designed to assist clients to achieve success in philanthropy and institutional advancement. These services include directing the development of strategic plans; conducting audits of the fund-raising function; assessing an institution's fund-raising readiness; conducting campaign feasibility studies; providing ongoing campaign counsel; assisting in strengthening key components of the fund-raising program; providing counsel on annual campaigns, planned giving programs, and special project funding; designing and implementing membership programs; and providing executive search services. Clients include educational institutions, museums and zoos, and performing arts organizations.

Thomas D. Wilson & Associates, Inc.

4495 NW Malhuer, Portland, OR 97229
Tel: 503-789-4366; FAX: 503-645-0175
E-mail: twilson789@aol.com; WWW: http://tdwa.webjump.com/

▶ Thomas D. Wilson & Associates, Inc., provides fund-raising consulting for capital campaigns (hospitals, museums, libraries, arts organizations, private secondary schools, institutions of higher education, public broadcasting facilities, churches, and social services). Wilson Fundraising Communications provides education and training seminars/retreats for volunteers and staff of not-for-profit organizations. Wilson Executive Search focuses on executive search for development officers. They are a member of the American Association of Fund-Raising Counsel.

Virtual Development Group

P.O. Box 2676, 724 Boston Street, Covington, LA 70434-2676
Tel: 504-809-1724; FAX: 504-892-9916
E-mail: meg3253@aol.com (Michael E. Guillot);
WWW: http://www.virtualdevelopment.net

▶ This full-service consulting firm specializes in campaigns, planning, major gifts, board retreats, and leadership development. They are the creators of the Million Dollar System, a systematic, 40-week fund-raising program, taught in their intensive one-day workshop. Services include leadership training, motivational speaking, capital campaigns, strategic planning, and the Million Dollar System. Clients include schools and school systems, higher education, religious organizations, and nonprofit organizations.

Vision Development Services, Inc.

1508 Starbeck Circle, Cedar Falls, IA 50613
Tel: 888-718-4746, 319-277-8562; FAX: 319-266-0638
E-mail: vision@cfu.net (Carolyn S. Hamrock, President);
WWW: http://www.visiondev.com

380 North Leoma Lane, Chandler, AZ 85225
Tel: 877-238-4746, 480-855-6659; FAX: 877-857-3736,
480-857-3736

8350 Hickman Road, West Des Moines, IA 50325
Tel: 888-718-4746; FAX: 888-768-4746
E-mail: visionaz@dancris.com (Jason Hamrock, Development Consultant)

▶ This full-service firm specializes in capital and endowment campaigns, feasibility studies, development assessments and major gifts. They serve a broad base of organizations: religious, educational, cultural, and health. They offer full-service marketing, public relations, graphic design, media services, and Web site development.

Waters, Pelton, Ostroff & Associates, Inc.

7108 Fairway Drive, Suite 235, Palm Beach Gardens, FL 33418
Tel: 561-626-0026; FAX: 561-626-9119
E-mail: wpojkw@aol.com (J. Keith Waters, Chairman and CEO);
WWW: http://www.wpoassociates.com

▶ This full-service professional planning and fund-raising firm offers a variety of specialized services to nonprofit organizations across the country. Services include management consulting, long-range strategic planning, development program assessments, fund-raising feasibility studies, capital campaign management, fund-raising counsel, grant writing (corporate, foundation, government), and public relations/media relations.

The Weber Group

26C Carillon Drive, Rocky Hill, CT 06067-2516
Tel: 860-257-3223; FAX: 860-563-5396
E-mail: thewebgroup@aol.com (Susan M. Weber, Principal);
WWW: http://www.thewebgrp.com,
http://www.thewebgrp.com/tips.htm

▶ Founded in 1995, services include executive search, feasibility studies, capital campaigns, retreat facilitation, strategic planning, annual support, major gifts, and leadership coaching in solicitation.

Whaley LeVay

790 East Colorado Boulevard, 9th Floor, Pasadena, CA 91101
Tel: 626-568-0267; FAX: 626-568-0367
E-mail: info@whaleylevay.com; WWW: www.whaleylevay.com

▶ Whaley LeVay are consultants in institutional advancement and philanthropy. Services include capital and endowment campaign counsel, strategic development planning, general fund-raising counsel, planned giving, and development services and systems (prospect research and management, gift processing and database management, system design, acquisition, and implementation).

The Whelan Group, Inc.

155 West 19th Street, New York, NY 10011
Tel: 212-727-7332; FAX: 212-727-7578
E-mail: twg@whelangroup.com;
WWW: http://www.whelangroup.com

▶ Services include capital campaigns, planned giving programs, annual giving programs, strategic fund raising and development planning, prospect identification and gift targeting, and management consulting.

Whitney Jones, Inc.

One Salem Tower, Suite 302, 119 Brookstown Avenue,
Winston-Salem, NC 27101-5245
Tel: 336-722-2371; FAX: 336-724-7381
E-mail: info@whitneyjonesinc.com;
WWW: http://www.whitneyjonesinc.com

▶ This firm has assisted nonprofit organizations and the communities they serve to accomplish their development goals service since 1981. Its clients include museums and cultural organizations, schools, health and human service agencies, conservation and public service organizations, and educational and religious organizations. Services include long-range and strategic planning; campaign surveys; capital campaigns; technology planning; support services (internal development audits, precampaign research and analysis, grantsmanship, membership and volunteer programs, prospect research, public relations/ marketing, campaign-related mailings, special events); and relationship management services (identifying potential major donors, creating event plans [talks, cultivation events, gocus groups], developing and maintaining donor contact, planning and implementing tiered annual giving program, "Board Development" workshops, planned giving programs). They are a member of the American Association of Fund-Raising Counsel.

William Jaques & Company, Inc.

Liberty Square, Danvers, MA 01923
Tel: 978-777-2289; FAX: 978-777-4758
E-mail: info@wljco.com; WWW: http://www.wljco.com/

▶ William L. Jaques & Company provides fund-raising counsel and related services to a broad array of nonprofit institutions. Services include general development program counsel, feasibility study, capital campaign counsel, annual giving improvement, planned giving program initiation/development, development program audit/planning study, and postCampaign program planning/definition. They are a member of the American Association of Fund-Raising Counsel.

Witzleben & Associates

1516 East Franklin Street, Suite 103, Chapel Hill, NC 27514
Tel: 919-942-0260; FAX: 919-942-1640
E-mail: wcw@witzleben.com (W. Charles Witzleben, Principal);
WWW: http://www.witzleben.com/

▶ Founded in 1986, it is a full-service development consulting firm providing counsel in institutional advancement to colleges and universities, health care institutions, independent schools, arts and cultural organizations, social services agencies, and religious organizations. Services include internal assessment of advancement programs (organizational design and evaluation; creation or strengthening of ongoing programs—annual giving, individual major gifts, planned giving, corporate and foundation support; establishment of infrastructure and systems—prospect research/management, major gift management and prospect tracking, donor relations and stewardship, gift processing and reporting); feasibility and strategic planning studies (needs assessment and documentation, personal leadership interviews, focus groups, telephone interviews, and mail surveys, prospect screening programs); campaign counsel and management (campaign plans, timetables, and budgets; campaign materials for donors and volunteers; cultivation and solicitation strategy plans; campaign volunteer planning); and general development counsel (annual and strategic operating plans, start-up development programs, grant and proposal writing). Additional services include board and volunteer leadership recruitment and training, training for professional and support staff, seminars and retreats, and staff selection assistance.

Woodburn, Kyle & Company

400 East First Street, Madison, IN 47250
Tel: 812-265-6551; FAX: 812-265-5840
E-mail: Woodburnfr@aol.com;
WWW: http://www.Woodburnkyle.com

▶ This midsize firm serves clients representing nearly every part of the not-for-profit sector, with services ranging from short-term, periodic consultation to complete on-site campaign management services. Services include campaign planning studies, preCampaign preparations, capital and/or endowment campaigns, development audits, and development counsel. They are a member of the American Association of Fund-Raising Counsel.

Worthington Associates Worldwide

Chelsea Hotel, 345 West 21st Street, Suite 3D,
New York, NY 10011-3059
Tel/FAX: 212-243-5883
E-mail: Worthworldtx@Sprintmail.com

1343 Bullock Lane, Bunker Hill Forest, Houston, TX 77055-4103
Tel: 888-262-4235; FAX: 713-827-0254

▶ Services include strategic planning/adaptive marketing; philanthropic marketing, including annual and capital campaigns; marketing new services, venture creation, and social entrepreneurship; corporate sponsorship and marketing of ideas and causes; event marketing; and managing and marketing through the use of incentives.

Zielinski Companies

2150 Hampton Avenue, St. Louis, MO 63139
Tel: 800-489-2150, 314-644-2150; FAX: 314-644-7132
E-mail: rnagel@zielinskico.com (Rick A. Nagel, Director of Development Services); WWW: http://www.zielinskico.com/

▶ Fund development services include grants (foundations, governments, corporations); planned giving and major gifts; (charitable gift annuities, wills and estate plans, plans to approach major givers); fund-raising consulting (annual appeals, capital campaigns, international programs, fund-raising software, market research, strategic planning, feasibility studies, direct mail, development staff training).

Zimmerman Lehman & Associates

582 Market Street, Suite 1112, San Francisco, CA 94104
Tel: 800-886-8330 (outside the San Francisco Bay Area),
415-986-8330; FAX: 415-986-2048
E-mail: zl@zimmerman-lehman.com;
WWW: http://www.zimmerman-lehman.com

▶ Services include fund-raising motivation and training (to enable boards of directors, staff, and volunteers to solicit funds enthusiastically, effectively, and without fear; public trainings also available); and fund-raising campaigns (to plan and implement annual and capital campaigns, major donor solicitations, direct-mail campaigns, planned giving efforts, special events, fund-raising plans, and solicitation of grants from public and private grantors).

Grant Administration

Grantmasters, LLC

33 Little Creek Lane, Fredericksburg, VA 22405
Tel: 540-371-9521; FAX: 540-371-9551
E-mail: rheiman@grantmasters.com;
WWW: http://www.grantmasters.com,
http://www.grantmasters.com/faqs.htm

▶ Grantmasters provides alternative solutions for grants administration, project planning and financial services to public broadcasters and other not-for-profits. Services include project development, project financial monitoring, and postproject administration.

Management Concepts Incorporated

8230 Leesburg Pike, Suite 800, Vienna, VA 22182
Tel: 703-790-9595; FAX: 703-790-1371
WWW: http://www.mgmtconcepts.com

▶ Management Concepts offers a comprehensive federal grants and assistance training curriculum. Courses focus on government-wide grants requirements and best practices to help federal awarding agencies, pass-through entities, and recipients effectively use scarce federal grant dollars. Offerings range from introductory courses on the grants process and application basics to advanced topics like assistance law and performance-based grants. We also offer the Grants Management Certificate Program.

Grant Proposals

(See also Grantwriting; Proposal Writing)

Grant Proposal & Research Services

806 Glensprings, Suite A, Knoxville, TN 37922
Tel: 865-694-3900
E-mail: travis_belcher@grantproposalservices.com;
WWW: http://www.grantproposalservices.com/home.html

▶ Since 1988 they have been writing grant proposals and searching for grant money. They have direct access to over 150 different government agencies who can tell them when, where, why, and how to apply for their grants. They also offer a proposal review, technical analysis or abstract preparation.

Grantmaster.com

8721 Oak Avenue, Orangevale, CA 95662
E-mail: Support@GrantMaster.com;
WWW: http://www.grantmaster.com/

▶ Grantmaster.com provides the tools you need to help yourself write quality proposals. They offer free grant/proposal resources, *GrantMaster Guidebook* with 3.5″ companion disk, subscriptions to the GrantWizard for Windows, online GrantMaster Wizard, a Web-based proposal writer that teaches you as you enter data about your proposal, and complete 4-hour reviews to ensure that you get the most out of your proposal.

Grants and Grant Seeking

Academic Research Information System (ARIS) Funding Reports

2940 16th Street, Suite 314, San Francisco, CA 94103
Tel: 415-558-8133; FAX: 415-558-8135
E-mail: info@grantsinfo.com; WWW: http://www.GrantsInfo.com

▶ For over 20 years, ARIS has been providing up-to-date information on federal and private sources of grants, fellowships, scholarships, contracts, and awards in the areas of Biomedical Sciences, Social and Natural Sciences, Creative Arts and Humanities, and Student Funding Sources. They now are offering to the public their complete database of funding information on a subscription basis.

Cain & Company Fundraising, Inc.

100 North Stone, Suite 1102, Tucson, AZ 85701
Tel: 800-687-3166, 520-918-1919; FAX: 520-918-1922
E-mail: info@cainandcompany.com (Shannon Cain);
WWW: http://www.cainandcompany.com

▶ The mission of Cain & Company is to support the work of progressive social service and advocacy organizations nationwide by helping them achieve the broadest possible base of financial support from foundations and corporations. They achieve their mission within a work environment in which employee input in company management is encouraged, information is shared, and openness, mutual respect, and health for all employees is acknowledged as a crucial component to our success. They specialize in fund raising and grant writing.

David G. Bauer Associates

3171 Green Valley Road, Suite 322, Birmingham, AL 35243-5239
Tel: 800-836-0732, 205-879-1457

P.O. Box 6592, Stateline, NV 89449-6592
FAX: 702-588-1255
WWW: http://www.dgbauer.com/consulti.htm

▶ David G. Bauer Associates provides educationally based grant-seeking and fund-raising consulting services to nonprofit organizations. From small nonprofits to large national organizations, they will evaluate your current grant-seeking and fund-raising efforts and help you develop dynamic and accountable strategies. They also offer training seminars (see separate listing under Training).

Grant Advisor

P.O. Box 650518, Potomac Falls, VA 20165.
E-mail: info@grantadvisor.com;
WWW: http://www.grantadvisor.com/about.htm

▶ Grant Advisor offers a subscription-based online information service for grantspersons and faculty in higher education.

Grant Results Alaska

1001 Boston Street, Anchorage, AK 99504
Tel: 888-755-4226, 907-333-8004; FAX: 907-868-7619
E-mail: inquiry@grantresults.com, cbarber@grantresults.com
(Chuck Barber); WWW: http://www.grantresults.com

▶ This firm provides funding source research, program planning, proposal writing and editing, and fund development consulting in Alaska and the Pacific Northwest. It assists nonprofit organizations to obtain annual operating and special project funds from foundations, corporations, and individual donors for a variety of social purposes.

GrantSearch

39 Ames Avenue, Marshfield, MA 02050
Tel: 781-834-8545
E-mail: projects@GrantSearch.org (William D. Taylor);
WWW: http://www.GrantSearch.org

▶ They are a research service assisting nonprofits and individuals develop contacts with government and foundation grantmakers. GrantSearch provides research services to identify grant-making sources whose objectives are to improve communities through prudent, philanthropic investments. They provide prospect research and grant-writing services to smaller organizations. GrantSearch works to redirect grant money to smaller charities that use volunteers to help people in need. This service may be of interest to over 500,000 nonprofits without dedicated researchers, or without volunteers with the time and knowledge for successfully pursuing grants. Organizations that they support, include social service, housing and shelter, health and mental health, education, community and civic issues, culture, environment, and religious groups of all denominations. They are a supporter of *The Fundraising Bank*, a directory of fund-raising products and services.

GrantStation

619 East Ship Creek Avenue, Suite 323, Anchorage, AK 99501
Tel: 877-78-GRANT; FAX: 907-297-6610
E-mail: info@grantstation.com, cadams@grantstation.com
(Cynthia Adams, President and CEO);
WWW: http://www.grantstation.com

▶ Its team is composed of individuals whose lives and careers have been dedicated to the creation and success of nonprofit organizations through creative strategies, exacting research, and innovative use of technology. Services include finding grants, funding strategies, and grant proposals. See their Web site for additional resources and services.

John L. Adams & Company, Inc.

P.O. Box 561565, Miami, FL 33256
Tel: 305-251-2203; FAX: 305-251-2773
E-mail: Info@FloridaFunding.com;
WWW: http://www.floridafunding.com/contactinfo.html

▶ This company was founded in 1976 as one of the first grants consulting firms in the country to provide grants acquisition expertise and services to local governments and nonprofit entities throughout Florida and the United States. Their services include the following: formulating development plans and project designs; identifying funding resources and acquisition strategies; preparing proposals and budgets; implementing funding awards; administering, evaluating, and closing out funded projects. Has helped clients from Puerto Rico to Massachusetts. The company has secured over $450 million in grant funds from federal, state, local, and private sources for a variety of needs and activities. Typical projects encompass economic and community development, historic preservation, recovery from natural disasters, environmental conservation, capital improvements, parks and recreation, planning, cultural affairs, education, law enforcement, social services, and youth programs.

Polaris

Three Bishop Street, Inman, SC 29349-6319
Tel: 800-368-3775, 864-472-5776; FAX: 864-472-5788
E-mail PolarisCo@aol.com, Polaris@ais-gwd.com (Kathryn Flick); WWW: http://www.polarisgrantscentral.net/

▶ Since 1984, the Polaris Grants Division has provided services for educational institutions (K–12, colleges, universities), government agencies (city, county, regional), hospitals, medical centers, health care organizations, nonprofit organizations, associations, United Ways, and other community-based organizations. Polaris assists organizations by providing step-by-step, how-to instruction and training in grants acquisition; in print, through how-to books and other publications; with technical assistance and support services to help acquire grant funding; through online advice in a "Dear Polaris," question-and-answer format on America On-Line (AOL); and through the Polaris Web site, which provides free basic information in the form of directories, lists, hints and tips, resources, and articles for grant seekers.

The Write Source

4671 Burnley, Bloomfield Hills, MI 48304-3720
Tel: 248-642-3808; FAX: 248-642-8956
E-mail: info@write-source.com, thewritesc@aol.com (Diane M. Gedeon-Martin); WWW: http://www.write-source.com

▶ Established in 1993, they offer total grant-seeking management, persuasive promotional materials, and expert hands-on training in the grant-seeking process. Services include grant proposal planning and preparation; proposal review and critique; funding and prospect research; direct mail and corporate solicitation packages; capital campaign materials, including case statements and brochures; and

interim and final grant reports. They also provide full and half-day workshops in the areas of proposal writing and funding research for board members, staff, and other groups.

Grant Writing

(See also Corporations; Donor Research and Prospect Identification; Foundations; Grants and Grantseeking; Proposal Writing; Prospect Research)

Academic Research Associates (ARA)

Tel: 800-518-3538, 512-291-0066
E-mail: academres@aol.com; WWW: http://www.grants2go.com

▶ Academic Research Associates offers a full range of fund-raising and grant-writing services for nonprofit organizations and governmental entities in the United States. ARA consultants include individuals with training and expertise in research and evaluation, grant writing, human development, social justice, women's studies, organizational effectiveness, environmental science, public and private education, community leadership development, cultural competence and diversity, economic development, instructional and graphic design, and technical writing and editorial services. The company operates on a project-by-project basis, selecting for each effort one or more ARA staff whose training and skills match a client's needs.

Bev Browing & Associates

1990 North Alma School Road, Suite 504, Chandler, AZ 85224
Tel: 480-786-9465; FAX: 480-899-0233
E-mail: grantsline@home.com;
WWW: http://www.grantsconsulting.com/

▶ This is a grants consulting firm. Services include grant writing, funding searches, customized grant writing workshops, grant review and critique, general grants consulting, and internships.

William Dingfelder, PhD, Grantwriting Services

431 Mary Watersford Road, Bala Cynwyd, PA, 9004
Tel: 610-667-5071; FAX: 610-667-7932
E-mail: Narberth@aol.com; WWW: http://libertynet.org/~grants/#2

▶ William Dingfelder is an independent development (fundraising) consultant with over 17 years of experience in the field. As a consultant, he has served a broad variety of nonprofit clients across the country. Experienced in almost every area of development, he specializes in grant proposals to corporations, foundations, and government agencies. He also "ghost writes" requests to major individual prospects for his clients. He creates written materials, including capital campaign literature, grant proposals, direct-mail letters, endowment brochures, and press releases. He also helps organizations build their prospect and donor base.

Erin E. Woods Grantwriting Services

1724 Jefferson Street, Stevens Point, WI 54481
Tel: 800-341-9757, 715-341-9757
E-mail: ewoods@coredcs.com (Erin Woods);
WWW: http://www.jcn.com/videos/woods/home.html

▶ Services offered are the following: an interactive video workshop that teaches the "step-by-step" process of prospect research and proposal writing. This workshop is a hands-on experience that includes outlines of research and writing tasks, elements of successful proposals, delegation of proposal writing tasks, checklist for key elements of proposals, current tips on following funding trends, a strategic plan example for large projects, delegation log for proposal writing tasks, an authorized application form from a grantmaking foundation, and more. Traditional services of prospect research and grant writing are performed by the Grantwriting Services staff as well as teaching at your on-site location. Development planning is also performed and taught, and columns for your newsletter are offered.

Especially NonProfits Consulting

P.O. Box 201, Tolleson, AZ 85353
Tel: 623-877-7811
E-mail: info@especiallynonprofits.com;
WWW: http://especiallynonprofits.com
▶ This firm offers technical support and classes in setting up a nonprofit (off and online) and writing grants. Services they provide are setting up nonprofits, grant writing and program development, marketing strategies, Web design and Web hosting, and workshops.

The Grant Doctors

P.O. Box 417212, Sacramento, CA 95841
E-mail: dave@thegrantdoctors.com (Dave Farley, Founder and Chairman); WWW: http://www.thegrantdoctors.com/
▶ This firm provides consulting, proposal writing and training services for local municipalities (governments) and not-for-profit organizations. Services include general consulting (provide a wide range of consulting services to meet all your grant-seeking needs. Examples of general consulting may include: fund and/or grant development strategy, program analysis/review, grant searches, proposal review and critique); proposal/application development (will partner with you and your staff to create a sound program plan, write your proposal, and complete all required application materials. As necessary, they will search for available grants and perform literature reviews/research for information to strengthen the proposal. They will attend all proposal strategy meetings to provide you with updates and advice on the proposal's development); and The Grants Clinic (a one-day workshop that shows participants how to improve their grant-seeking efforts from program conception to proposal submission).

Grants Link

P.O. Box 10140, 601 West Nifong Boulevard, Suite 4B,
5650A South Sinclair Road, Columbia, MO 65203
Tel: 800-396-8829; FAX: 573-443-3748
E-mail: info@grantslink.com; WWW: http://www.grantslink.com/
▶ Services include writing, training, research, consulting. Grants Link offers the fee-based Funders Online service (compiled for Arkansas, California, Illinois, Indiana, Iowa, Kansas, Michigan, Missouri, Ohio, Oklahoma, Texas, and Wisconsin; this series features corporations and foundations with funding programs in each state) and Help Link, a consulting service that encompasses grant critiques and reviews, research, question-answering, and training. Grants Link publishes the newsletter *Right on the Money* (see separate listing under Periodicals).

Grants Northwest

600 SW 10th Avenue, Suite 546, Portland, OR 97205
Tel: 503-294-2147; FAX: 503-294-0292
E-mail: mkwells@uswest.net (Michael Wells), leviner@uswest (Rick Levine); WWW: http://www.grantsnorthwest.com/

▶ This company brings together this region's two most experienced grantwriters, Michael Wells and Rick Levine, to assist organizations in obtaining grants to support their work. As principal partners, Levine and Wells head a team of seasoned grant writers and researchers who provide the most effective grantwriting and grants consultation available to public and private nonprofit organizations. Services of Grants Northwest include grant writing (foundation, corporate, local, state, and federal grant requests); grants consultation (assessing organizations' current and potential grants effort, review of grant requests, developing grants plans, and designing the most effective approaches to funders of interest); grants training (identifying key prospects, cultivation techniques, project development, strategy, and effective grant writing); grant prospect research (customized searches of local and national private funding sources, as well as federal and local government prospect research); grant organizing (engaging and energizing volunteers in support of grants activities); and grants information (informational Web site and publications).

Grantwriters Guild

18032-C Lemon Drive, PMB #117, Yorba Linda, CA 92886
Tel: 714-572-1975; FAX: 714-572-1976
E-mail: info@grantwritersguild.org, cgeisbauer@aol.com (Carol J. Geisbauer); WWW: http://www.grantwritersguild.org
▶ Services include grant writing; grantsmanship training; funding source research; and proposals to foundations, corporations, and government. They focus on community-based human service agencies. They offer three-day grant writing workshops in California.

The Medfield Group, Inc.

14 A North Meadows Road, Suite 301, Medfield, MA 02052
Tel: 508-359-8170; FAX: 508-359-8409
E-mail: tmginfo@aol.com
▶ The Medfield Group specializes in government relations, grant writing, and project management.

Nonprofit Works, Inc.

10 Gibbs Street, Suite 250, Rochester, NY 14604
Tel: 716-546-2420; FAX: 716-546-2423
E-mail: mail@nonprofitworks.com;
WWW: http://www.nonprofitworks.com,
http://www.nonprofitworks.com/links.asp
▶ Nonprofit Works provides the following grant-writing services: research and selection, writing of applications and proposals, budget development, and grant-writing training and coaching. They also offer courses.

Patricia Rife & Associates

725 Darymple Road 1-F, Atlanta, GA 30328
Tel: 678-596-6503
E-mail: prife@att.net (Patricia Rife, President),
prife@worldnet.att.net; WWW: http://www.patriciarifeassociates.com
▶ Services include grant writing and editing, training, and program evaluation.

Robert J. Miller & Associates, Inc. (RJMA)

124 Delaware Street, Tonawanda, NY 14150
Tel: 716-694-8181; FAX: 716-694-8206
E-mail: rjma@rjma.com; WWW: http://www.rjma.com

▶ One of the nation's oldest and largest firms specializing in grants development, RJMA seeks and secures grants from private and corporate foundations and all federal and state grant-making agencies. Services include conducting on-site grants development feasibility studies, complete project design and proposal development, comprehensive funding searches of available grant funds, and submission and tracking proposals through grant-maker review cycles.

The Write Source (*See Grants and Grant Seeking*)

Lists Brokers

(*See also Direct Mail and Direct Response Marketing; Telemarketing*)

21st Century Marketing

1750 New Highway, Farmingdale, NY 11735-1512
Tel: 631-293-8550; FAX: 631-293-8974
E-mail: Claire@21stcm.com (Claire Carpenter—List Brokerage); WWW: http://www.21stcm.com

▶ 21st Century Marketing seeks to identify and acquire the best possible direct marketing media for your needs. They assist you to earn the maximum income from your customer or prospect database and encourage you to take advantage of the power of e-commerce and the Internet by providing the necessary tools. In addition, they present new possibilities with value-added services such as an advanced database and analytical services, as well as strategic thinking and planning.

AccuData America

1625 Cape Coral Parkway East, Cape Coral, FL 33904
Tel: 800-732-3440; FAX: 941-540-5200
E-mail: info@accudata-america.com;
WWW: http://www.accudata-america.com/

▶ A national provider of mailing and telemarketing lists, they provide you with access to every compiled list available in America, and to deliver the data in the format you need. Their trained representatives have real-time access to all the major marketing databases in the country. They are continuously trained on the strengths and weaknesses of each to help you achieve your marketing objectives. They offer *AccuTips* newsletters.

All American List Corporation

A division of DM Group, 8903 Presidential Parkway, Suite 201, Upper Marlboro, MD 20772
Tel: 301-420-5760; FAX: 301-420-5765
E-mail: aalc@dmgroup.com; WWW: http://www.allamericanlist.com

▶ This is a registered list broker with over 25 years of expertise providing mailing lists for all types of mailers, including top telecommunications companies, health, utility, automotive, political groups, and more. They are available to assist you in any of the following ways: research and recommendation, list ordering, merge/purge, results analysis, national change of address (NOA) and nixie processing, and list management.

American List Counsel

88 Orchard Road, CN-5219, Princeton, NJ 08543
Tel: 800-ALC-LIST; FAX: 908-874-4433
E-mail: sgirt@amlist.com (Stacey Girt, Vice President—Direct Sales); WWW: http://www.amlist.com,
http://www.amlist.com/ALCWEB/alcweb.nsf/wproductshome/hom,
http://www.amlist.com/ALCWEB/alcweb.nsf/wknowledgehome/home

▶ ALC is a full-service mailing list and database broker, manager, and compiler. In addition, they provide their clients with a broad range of package insert and other alternative media brokerage and management services, data processing, and interactive marketing. Services include Buy a List, database management, interactive marketing, data management, and data acquisition. ALC also has regional offices in New York City, New England, and California. Under consideration are additional sales offices in Connecticut, Miami, Chicago, Denver, Dallas, and Los Angeles.

Dunhill International List Co., Inc.

1951 NW 19th Street, Boca Raton, FL 33431-7344
Tel: 800-DUNHILL (386-4455), 561-347-0200;
FAX: 561-347-0400
E-mail: info@dunhills.com, reaching@dunhills.com;
WWW: http://www.dunhills.com

▶ Dunhill International List Co. is the nation's largest compiler of specialty mailing and telemarketing lists. The company supplies local and national mailing lists of over 110 million U.S. households by age, income, gender, type of dwelling, home value, presence/age of children, marital status, and many other demographic selections. Consumer lists include wealthy individuals, investors, vacationers, contributors, yacht owners, executives and professionals at home, and hundreds more. Telephone numbers are available for most lists. There are now about 300 different categories of e-mail addresses totaling 15 million names.

The Listworks Corporation

One Campus Drive, Pleasantville, NY 10570
Tel: 914-769-7100; FAX: 914-769-8070
E-mail: wjm@listworks.com (Walter J. Monzi, Executive Vice President); WWW: http://www.listworks.com

▶ Established in 1982, The Listworks Corporation is a full-service list brokerage and list management company. In addition to brokerage and management services, Listworks offers list maintenance, list fulfillment, merge/purge operations, fund-raising marketing, creative services, and marketing consulting. Their state-of-the-art data processing capability gives their clients sophisticated data access and customized reports with support systems.

Major Gifts

CTE Associates (*See Full Service*)

Carlton & Company (*See Full Service*)

Glenwood Associates

24 Old Georgetown Road, Princeton, NJ 08540
Tel: 732-821-5522; FAX: 732-821-5955
E-mail: info@glenwoodassociates.com;
WWW: http://www.glenwoodassociates.com/services.htm

▶ Services include meetings and conferences; major gifts (develop the case for major gift support, identify donors and prospects, plan for cultivation and relationship building, develop a purposeful solicitation packet, and build partnerships with donors); special events; cultivating and soliciting donors or members; organizational studies and program audits; marketing and community outreach; leadership and volunteer development; corporate partnership programs; chapter and field development; staff recruitment; and Web site design and promotion.

Gloss and Company (See Full Service)

Institutional Advancement Programs Inc. (See Full Service)

John Brown Limited
Box 296, 46 Grove Street, Peterborough, NH 03458
Tel: 603-924-3834; FAX: 603-924-7998
E-mail: jblnh@aol.com; WWW: http://www.jblnh.com/
▶ This company assists charitable organizations in creating, implementing, and servicing individualized major gift and/or planned giving programs. It addresses the following areas in its major gift and planned giving consultation work: major gifts and planned giving consulting, capital and endowment campaign consulting, and development review (audit). It also offers seminar and training services.

McCord and Associates
5322 North 40th Street, Tacoma, WA 98407-3655
Tel: 253-759-2862; FAX: 253-759-4770
E-mail: jean@mccordassociates.com (Jean McCord, CFRE, President)
▶ McCord and Associates works in three main areas: planned giving (provide full services: audit present fund-raising efforts, plan and implement a planned giving program, train staff and volunteers, provide ongoing consulting and technical expertise); major gifts (evaluate gift potential, map strategies, train and coach staff and volunteers, integrate major and planned giving into the full development operation); and direct donor contact (phone calls and visits to your top individual major and planned giving prospects, either as part of an ongoing fund-raising effort or in a campaign context). Other services include board workshops, training for staff and volunteers, seminars for professionals, charitable seminars for donors, and written marketing materials.

Pentera, Inc.
8650 Commerce Park Place, Suite G, Indianapolis, IN 46268
Tel: 317-875-0910
E-mail: info@pentera.com; WWW: http://www.pentera.com/
▶ Pentera works together with hundreds of nonprofit organizations in promoting planned giving through personalized newsletters, booklets, seminars, consulting, and on the Web. They also offer customized staff training, target presentations to boards and/or trustees, key prospects, donors, and document preparation. Pentera offers educational and marketing seminars (advanced and intermediate) for development professionals with various degrees of skill and experience. They are designed both for the newcomer and the seasoned professional who wish to learn or refresh knowledge of major gifts and planned giving and their tax consequences.

Retriever Development Counsel
4125 Southeast 34th Avenue, Portland, OR 97202
Tel: 503-736-1102; FAX: 503-236-3183
E-mail: plannedgifts@email.msn.com (Kevin Johnson, CFRE, CSPG)
▶ Services include creation or expansion of planned giving programs, endowment campaign strategies, strategic planning, development and planned giving audits or assessments, board development and training, workshops for donors and professional advisors, gift planning for individuals, and charitable estate planning for individuals. It also offers a 12-session, year-long Planned Giving Action Program designed for nonprofits. Retriever also specializes in assisting individuals by helping identify charities to support that match their unique interests, how to make gifts in tax-smart ways, and charitable estate planning.

Thomson Financial Wealth Identification, Formerly CDA/Investnet (See Donor Research & Prospect Identification)

Matching Gifts

HEP Development Services
43212 Lindsay Marie Court, Ashburn, VA 20147
Tel: 800-681-4438, 703-858-5700; FAX: 703-858-5741
E-mail: info@hepdevelopment.com;
WWW: http://www.hepdevelopment.com.
▶ HEP development services works with nonprofit fund raisers who recognize the value of accurate data. They specialize in data enhancement—focusing in the areas of prospect research, matching gift identification, and address/phone updates. Products include GiftPlus, an authoritative electronic file of matching gift companies, which is available in several electronic and hard copy formats; and The Executive ID, their comprehensive database of more than 12 million private and public companies, which allows them to identify your constituents who are senior-level executives and owners at these businesses. In addition to a full summary of the company, HEP now provides a personal biographical history on your constituent executives. The entire output file is delivered in "easy to use" proprietary Web-based search engine. Also, Hep's InTouch program can electronically locate your lost constituents and verify and update their phone numbers.

Membership
(See also Direct Mail and Direct Response Marketing; Telemarketing/Telefundraising)

Craver Creative Services (See Direct Mail/Direct Response)

DirectLine Technologies Inc. (See Telemarketing/Telefundraising)

Membership Consultants
3868 Russell Boulevard, Saint Louis, MO 63110
Tel: 314-771-4664; FAX: 314-771-2759
E-mail: MemConsul@aol.com;
WWW: http://www.membership-consultants.com
▶ This is a full-service membership marketing resource for membership organizations. Services include direct-mail acquisition,

membership audits and strategic marketing plans, onsite sales, annual appeals, telemarketing, member renewals, lapsed members, list services, membership surveys, membership management, and dues/benefits analysis. They offer seminars.

Richard Hyland International

4515 Tyler Street, Hollywood, FL 33021
FAX: 954-985-1248
E-mail: info@richardhyland.net;
WWW: http://www.richardhyland.net/mcs.html

▶ They provide a computerized membership record-keeping and contribution database service for all nonprofit organizations.

Saturn Corporation

4701 Lydell Road, Cheverly, MD 20781-1116
Tel: 301-772-7000; FAX: 301-386-4538
WWW: http://www.Saturncorp.com

▶ This international database management and information services company specializes in online database maintenance services for nonprofit fund-raising and membership organizations. They currently provide online services to clients in the United States, Europe, and Canada. Other services include: predictive modeling, data entry, merge/purge, postal presort, NCOA, laser printing, and list rental fulfillment.

Online Fund Raising

(See also Philanthropy—Internet Resources; Resource Development—Internet Resources)

BenefitEvents.com—Online Fundraising Services

230 West 79th Street, Suite 94N, New York, NY 10024
Tel: 212-724-3443; FAX: 212-724-7690
E-mail: admin@benefitevents.com, jhw@benefitevents.com (James Wintner, President); WWW: http://benefitevents.com/home.html

▶ BenefitEvents.com provides online auction event and fund-raising services to the nonprofit community that are integrated with live events and cause-related activities. BenefitEvents supplies the tools that enable nonprofits to pursue their fund-raising goals via the World Wide Web, offering online applications combined with a range of personalized and custom services.

Charity Phone

2201 Broadway, 2nd Floor, Oakland, CA 94612
Tel: 888-426-6694, ext. 1003, 510-444-8744;
FAX: 603-698-0512
E-mail: Steve.Organek@charityphone.com (Steve Organek);
WWW: http://charityphone.com/11003/nonprofits.htm

▶ A socially responsible business committed to the creation of new wealth for nonprofits, its mission is accomplished by selling competitively priced services, such as long distance, Internet connectivity, and utilities, while donating a significant portion of its revenue to the nonprofit organizations that strengthen our communities. It provides a variety of services such as long distance and utilities. A portion of each monthly bill will be donated to a nonprofit specified by the customer. This enables customers to participate in philanthropic causes without incurring additional expense or effort while achieving the beneficial purpose of increasing donations to these organizations.

CharityWeb

1714 Fordham Way, Mountain View, CA 94040
Tel: 866-4eTools (866-438-6657), 650-938-8985
E-mail: khansen@charityweb.net (Kurt Hansen, CEO and Founder), AmyReid@CharityWeb.net; WWW: http://www.charityweb.net

▶ Founded in 1997, CharityWeb is an e-commerce application service provider (ASP) that provides custom e-commerce solutions for nonprofit organizations. Their credit card processing service includes custom designing donation/membership, shopping cart, and event registration pages that have the look and feel of your Web site; hosting the forms on their secure server; processing all financial transactions in real time; sending a custom thank you e-mail and receipt; and organizing donor data in an online database that is compatible with your organization's existing database. CharityWeb also offers a custom shopping mall builder service.

Contribute.Com

One Southwest Columbia Street, Suite 100, Portland, OR 97258
Tel: 503-973-5243; FAX: 503-973-5252
E-mail: info@contribute.com; WWW: http://www.contribute.com

▶ Contribute.com works quietly and invisibly behind the scenes to enable your donors to make contributions from your Web site. They custom build an online payment form to match the look and feel of your existing Web site.

Convio, Inc.

4801 Plaza on the Lake, Suite 1500, Austin, TX 78746
Tel: 888-528-9501, 512-652-2600; FAX: 512-652-2699
E-mail: info@convio.com (Vinay Bhagat, CEO and Founder);
WWW: http://www.convio.com/site/HomePage

▶ Convio is an online service provider of comprehensive solutions that allow nonprofits to market, fund raise, and manage relationships with their constituents using the Internet.

iDon8.com

426 Danbury Road, Wilton, CT 06897
Tel: 203-563-9363; FAX: 203-762-9826
E-mail: support@iDon8.com, sales@iDon8.com;
WWW: http://www.idon8.com/auction/Auctioneer

▶ This service-oriented online auction fund-raising site caters exclusively to the nonprofit industry. They offer branded "auction portals" customized with your message and identity. To maximize results, their auctions are designed to run simultaneously with multiple nonprofit participants in two-week events. This also allows you to enhance corporate sponsorship revenue.

Donate.net

Conscious Change, 931 Monroe Drive, Suite 102-281,
Atlanta, GA 30308
Tel: 404-874-7421; FAX: 404-352-0859
E-mail: info@donate.net, eric@donate.net (Eric Miller, President);
WWW: http://www.donate.net, http://www.donate.net/CCPage2.htm

▶ Donate.net helps you access donors on the Web in a simple, safe, and secure environment. Their goal is to provide you with the system that solves your fund-raising needs at a low cost and no risk.

DonorDigital.com

2819 Tenth Street, Berkeley, CA 94710
Tel: 510-647-2700; FAX: 510-647-3555
E-mail: info@donordigital.com, nick@donordigital.com (Nick Allen); WWW: http://www.donordigital.com/about.htm

▶ Founded in 1999 by Nick Allen and Mal Warwick, it is an Internet consulting and Web development company specializing in helping nonprofit organizations use the Internet for fund raising, marketing, and advocacy. It works with large and medium-size nonprofits to help them use e-mail and the Web to build online membership programs; acquire new donors; cultivate existing donors, members, and prospects; market their organizations; and educate and activate their target audiences. It offers online fund-raising workshops.

DonorLink IT

Social Ecology, 1818 Summit, Seattle, WA 98122
Tel: 800-485-8170 (Sales Line), 206-726-0047
E-mail: info@socialecology.com;
WWW: http://www.socialecology.com/dl/index.html

▶ DonorLink IT is a Web-based tool designed specifically for nonprofit organizations. It brings together and manages contacts, database, e-mail, and Web forms, giving you a powerful, complete communication system.

DonorNet

655 Broadway, Suite 725, Denver, CO 80203
Tel: 303-573-6226; FAX: 303-573-6228
E-mail: info@donornet.com, sales@donornet.com, help@donornet.com (Client Assistance);
WWW: http://www.donornet.com

▶ Donornet provides information technology and e-commerce solutions to fulfill the philanthropic needs of individuals, and not-for-profit and for-profit corporations. DonorNet was founded in 1999 as a joint venture between GS2.Net, an e-commerce software and solutions provider, and three national nonprofit consulting firms: Mirenda and Associates, Portnoy and Associates, and The Alford Group. Products include Give@Work™ (workplace giving), orgSolutions™ (nonprofit e-commerce), and DonorSpace™ (a public resource for private giving).

EContributor

655 15th Street NW, G Street Lobby, Suite 810,
Washington, DC, 20005
Tel: 877-406-1110, 202-628-0222; FAX: 877-406-1119, 202-628-9290

414 East Windsor Avenue, Alexandria, VA 22301
Tel: 703-837-8643; FAX: 703-968-5764
E-mail: info@eContributor.com, Email: cbclllvent@aol.com (Cliff Carnes, Sales and Marketing Manager);
WWW: http://www.econtributor.com

▶ eContributor was founded in January 1999 to meet the need for a fast, secure e-commerce solution for fund raising, grassroots development, and communications. eContributor brings proven strategies and techniques for nonprofit and political fund raising into the Internet environment. They help their clients acquire, retain, and build long-term relationships with their donors through powerful new online tools. These tools integrate directly into an organization's Web site. Their system is legally compliant in both the nonprofit and political fund-raising environments. eContributor services clients ranging from large nonprofits, educational institutions, presidential campaigns, and national political parties to local charities and congressional campaigns. eContributor also provides back-end fund-raising services to several nonprofit and political portals.

ForMyCause.com

11111 Santa Monica Boulevard, Suite 1200, Los Angeles, CA 90025
Tel: 800-246-6801, 310-479-1750; FAX: 310-479-9774
E-mail: customerservice@formycause.com;
WWW: http://www.formycause.com,
http://www.formycause.com/newsletter.html

▶ ForMyCause.com™ is dedicated to serving as the online link between worthwhile causes, individual supporters, and cause-friendly corporate sponsors. Their MyBar™ application is the best way that concerned people can help their cause, stay in touch, and never have to pay a cent.

FundRover.com

10333 Harwin Drive, Suite 195, Houston, TX 77036
Tel: 713-278-9341; FAX: 713-278-9338
E-mail: daniel@fundrover.com (Daniel Monks, Customer Relations); WWW: http://www.fundrover.com

▶ They help your organization accept secure, online credit card donations. FundRover.Com provides a self-service, self-administered collection Web site, which can lower your donation acquisition costs. You can promote your organization via their e-mail marketing tools, as well as track donation history. FundRover.Com does not require a merchant account, set-up costs, or monthly fees. Your organization pays nothing until you successfully raise funds with their service. FundRover.Com is a service of Compass Internet Solutions, Inc., a member of the Better Business Bureau.

Give to Charity

Storm Internet Services, Inc., P.O. Box 25332,
Tampa, FL 33622-5332
Tel: 813-886-3010; FAX: 813-290-0690
E-mail: admin@givetocharity.com (Michael Storm, President);
WWW: http://www.givetocharity.com

▶ They are dedicated to providing the most safe and secure way for nonprofit organizations to accept donations via the Internet, in the most cost-effective manner.

GivingCapital, Inc.

Harry E. Cerino, Lewis Tower, 225 South 15th Street, 28th Floor, Philadelphia, PA 19102
Tel: 877-MYGIVING (877-694-4846) (Nonprofit and Donor Support); FAX: 215-735-8343
E-mail: help@givingcapital.com (Donor Support), support@givingcapital.com (Nonprofit Support);
WWW: http://www.givingcapital.com

▶ GivingCapital is dedicated to increasing charitable giving through online solutions to the philanthropic community. They provide a simple and secure way to donate online. They help nonprofit organizations harness the collaborative power of the Internet to acquire new donors and increase contributions. With their patent-pending technology, donors click a banner on your Web site to make their gift. From straight donations to membership drives, to creating a matching or challenge campaign, GivingCapital provides an array of tools to create and monitor your campaign. Use GivingCapital to lower your online fund-raising costs and reach new donors with this innovative Internet technology. In partnership with the National Philanthropic Trust they also enable individuals to balance philanthropic interests with their estate planning and financial needs through donor-advised funds. Donors can open a donor-advised fund account on their Web site or on the Web sites of their financial service partners.

Givenation.Com

30 Cobble Hill Road, Somerville, MA 02143
Tel: 800-285-2989; FAX: 617-623-5439
WWW: http://www.givenation.com

▶ Givenation.com provides nonprofit groups with a risk-free revenue stream, while keeping donors informed and interested in philanthropy and in the accomplishments of the member nonprofits.

Hewitt and Johnson Consultants (HJC)

99 Atlantic Avenue, Suite 411, Toronto, ON, Canada M6K 3J8
Tel: 416-588-7780; FAX: 416-588-7156
WWW: http://www.hjc.on.ca/

▶ HJC is a full-service consulting firm that provides expert guidance to nonprofits in developing, implementing, and improving their direct-response fund-raising programs. HJC New Media helps nonprofit organizations effectively integrate new communications media, such as the Internet, into meeting their missions and mandates. They provide industry-leading expertise in Web site design, online fund raising, and strategic planning in the use of new communications media.

IBelong, Inc.

950 Winter Street, Waltham, MA 02451
Tel: 800-395-8122, 781-684-8280; FAX: 781-684-8252
E-mail: info@ibelong.com; WWW: http://www.ibelong.com

▶ IBelong is a provider of custom Internet portals (start pages) to nonprofits/affinity groups for revenue generation and enhanced relationships.

Jewishare.com *(See EHL Consulting—Full Service)*

LocalVoice.com

3265 17th Street, Suite 304, San Francisco, CA 94110
Tel: 415-522-1200; FAX: 415-522-1270
E-mail: info@localvoice.com;
WWW: http://localvoice.com/index.htm

▶ This firm provides online fund-raising systems customized to fit your institutions' needs.

Mal Warwick & Associates, Inc.

2550 Ninth Street, Suite 103, Berkeley, CA 94710
Tel: 510-843-8888; FAX: 510-843-0142
E-mail: info@malwarwick.com (Mal Warwick, Founder and Chair); WWW: http://www.malwarwick.com/,
http://www.malwarwick.com/publications.html

▶ Established in 1979, Mal Warwick & Associates can help you increase your membership base with a more effective direct mail program; promote charitable bequests and other planned giving methods; find new members and cultivate the ones you have using e-mail and the Web; tune up your fund-raising programs with a development audit and consulting; and improve the creative impact of your direct-mail packages, newsletters, and other materials. Every January, Mal Warwick & Associates sponsors an intensive two-day Major Donor Fundraising Clinic in Berkeley, primarily for their clients. In addition, Mal Warwick, Nick Allen, Steve Hitchcock, Bill Rehm, and other staff members speak frequently at workshops and conferences, including conferences of the National Society of Fund Raising Executives (NSFRE), the Direct Marketing Association, and others. See their workshop page for information about upcoming events. They offer *Successful Fundraising Online*, a free e-mail newsletter on direct mail, telephone, and online fund raising. Mal is the author of 10 books, including *Raising Money by Mail, How to Write Successful Fundraising Letters*, and *The Five Strategies for Fundraising Success*.

McPherson Associates, Inc.

312 East King Street, Malvern, PA 19355
Tel: 610-640-1555; FAX: 610-640-1456
E-mail: ideas@mcphersonassociates.com;
WWW: http://www.mcphersonassociates.com/mf.htm

▶ Services include internet planning and strategy; Web site enhancement and development; and secure online donation and e-services.

MyAssociation.com

50 W. Broadway #400, Salt Lake City, UT 84101
Tel: 801-363-0193; FAX: 801-363-0645
E-mail: info@myassociation.com (Brian Kelley, Director of Marketing); WWW: http://www.myassociation.com

▶ MyAssociation.com advances your cause by using its unique member benefits technologies to add value to your alumni, raise funds, and help you operate more efficiently.

MyWay.com

100 Brickstone Square, Andover, MA 01810
Tel: 888-717-7500, 978-684-3888; FAX: 978-684-3899
WWW: http://about.myway.com/

▶ MyWay.com provides custom portal solutions to nonprofits, empowering you to build community, secure funds, and communicate online with your constituents.

OnlineGiving.Com

16 Technology Drive West, Suite 206, Irvine, CA 92618
Tel: 949-789-7939; FAX: 949-789-7938
E-mail: Info@OnlineGiving.com;
WWW: http://www.onlinegiving.com

▶ OnlineGiving.com is an Internet fund-raising integrator. Its mission is to establish strategic partnerships with nonprofits that will facilitate both an increase in donations and more effective donor communications using the Internet. It enables nonprofits to receive charitable donations through their own Web site. They offer a safe, well-designed, and customized service that accepts donor contributions 24 hours a day, 365 days a year. Individual donors may opt-in for their own personalized giving portfolio. Additionally, their turnkey service will keep donors informed about campaigns with their e-mail communications tool.

WebCharity.com

36 Park Drive East, Branford, CT 06405
Tel: 888-432-4274 ext. #4002, 203-481-7600; FAX: 203-488-3251
E-mail: linda@webcharity.com (Linda Forgione);
WWW: http://www.webcharity.com

▶ WebCharity.com provides free Internet fund raising for non-profit organizations. WebCharity.com helps nonprofits raise money and awareness by providing free Internet and simulcast charity auction events, virtual thrift and gift shops, credit card donations, and member site featuring your organization.

WeCareToo

2719 West Lunt Avenue, Chicago, IL 60645
Tel: 773-764-2000
E-mail: info@wecaretoo.com, richard@wecaretoo.com (Richard J. Schaefer); WWW: http://www.wecaretoo.com

▶ WeCareToo offers free Web pages, no-cost optional fund-raising programs, and low-cost online shopping malls. Their Web site also includes links to other resources for the NPO community, an opt-in e-mail newsletter, and a free search engine registration page.

Online Grant Making and Grant Seeking

CyberGrants.com

790 Turnpike Street, Suite 300, North Andover, MA 01845
Tel: 978-794-0900; FAX: 978-794-9111
E-mail: info@cybergrants.com; WWW: http://www.cybergrants.com

▶ CyberGrants.com uses the World Wide Web to bring grant makers and grant seekers together. Proposals may be created online and submitted directly into the database of multiple foundations.

Easygrants.com *(See Software Vendors—Grants Management; Resource Development—Internet Resources)*

Planned Giving and Deferred Gifts

Ashton Associates

24 Robertson Street, Quincy, MA 02169
Tel: 617-472-9316
E-mail: debraashton@mediaone.net (Debra Ashton);
WWW: http://www.debraashton.com/,
http://www.debraashton.com/links.html

▶ Debra Ashton is best known as author of Planned Giving's "Blue Bible," *The Complete Guide to Planned Giving,* © 1988, © 1991. Her revised third edition will be published in 2001. Over the span of 25 years, Debra ran the planned giving programs for four charities: WGBH/TV; Wheaton College, Norton, Massachusetts; Boston University; and Boston College. Prior to that, she was Deferred Giving Administrator for Boston Safe Deposit and Trust Company. Debra's services include donor and board presentations, program evaluations, and general fund-raising or planned giving consulting for nonprofit organizations.

Barrett Planned Giving, Inc.

2000 L Street NW, Suite 200, Washington, DC 20036
Tel: 202-416-1667; FAX: 202-416-1668
E-mail: info@barrettplannedgiving.com, BarrettPln@cs.com;
WWW: http://www.barrettplannedgiving.com

▶ Services include marketing plan development, workshops, and telephone donor consulting.

Caswell, Zachry, Grizzard

8226 Douglas Avenue, Suite 655, Dallas, TX 75225
Tel: 800-972-3187 or 214-528-8084; FAX: 214-528-8456
E-Mail: czglin1@airmail.net; WWW: http://www.czg.net/index.html

▶ This firm offers planned giving products and seminars designed by fund raisers for fund raisers.

Charitable Gift Planning Associates (CGP Associates)

221 Elderberry Circle, Athens, GA 30605-4955
Tel: 706-543-4917
E-mail vsikes@negia.net (Scott Henderson Sikes, CFRE, President)

▶ Planned giving, gift planning, major current or deferred gifts, development research: create programs; assess existing programs; train staff, board, and volunteers.

The Charitas Group, Inc.

6250 Cape Haterras Way NE, Suite 4, St. Petersburg, FL 33702
Tel: 727-528-7755
E-mail: charitasinfo@charitasgroup.com, charitas@fdt.net (Doug Weatherby); WWW: http://www.charitasgroup.com

▶ This firm specializes in contacting preapproved prospects through phone and mail. The company's trained, licensed investment advisors promote your organization's planned giving opportunities, and their fees are tied directly to successful results. The company recognizes that there is much to learn even when someone says no. It will analyze the reasons why prequalified prospects with great potential turn you down. You'll benefit from honest information about how your institution is perceived, and you can find out how to improve the way you communicate with your best audience—current donors who are capable of making far more substantial gifts to your organization.

James E. Connell and Associates

Charitable Estate and Gift Planning Specialists,
4111 Darius Drive, Enola, PA 17025
Tel: 800-543-3809, 717-728-1900; FAX: 717-728-1993
E-mail: jec42644@supernet.com (James E. Connell, Principal),
connell@dickinson.edu (James E. Connell, FAHP),
jec42644@aol.com

▶ This consulting service is dedicated to building endowments for America's nonprofit organizations through charitable estate and gift planning. Demographic changes in America are creating an unparalleled opportunity for organizations to gain significant gifts by using charitable gift and estate planning techniques. James E. Connell and Associates maintains an active National Board of Advisors composed of attorneys, financial advisors, insurance agents, trust officers, and fund-raising professionals skilled in charitable gift development. The advisor network is available to clients to facilitate the cultivation, solicitation, and development of charitable estate planning gifts. James E. Connell, the author of more than 60 articles and book chapters on planned giving, is an experienced speaker. He has been Chair and the Dean of Planned Giving for the AHP's Institute of Hospital Philanthropy.

Davidson Consulting Group (See Capital Campaigns)

Deferred Giving Services

614 South Hale Street, Wheaton, IL 60187
Tel/FAX: 630-682-4301
E-mail: Schmeling@aol.com (David G. Schmeling, CFRE, Planned Giving Consultant); WWW: http://www.deferredgivingservices.com

▶ This fund development consulting firm specializes in helping charitable organizations, especially the smaller to midsize development office, build endowment through planned giving programs. The services and resource materials offered to clients are: planned giving audit for the integration of planned giving into the overall development program. Based on feedback from the charity's decision makers and answers to an extensive questionnaire, a personalized and written Action Plan is prepared to provide guidance in starting and managing the planned giving program; financial and estate planning newsletters for any size program and budget, even for the charity that can afford to send only 250 quarterly newsletters to its major donors; and customized and/or personalized planned giving brochures for building awareness of charitable giving in estate planning among all donor constituencies. Different styles are suitable for different purposes. They also offer tax-update newsletters for allied professionals, such as estate planning attorneys, trust officers, financial planners, and accounts (allow the development director to cultivate relationships with those to whom the donors will be going for advice and counsel); written illustration of benefits for prospective donors considering a particular gifting arrangement; training sessions/seminars for development staff members and volunteers; on-site/off-site consultant retainer agreements to assist in a comprehensive, wholly integrated planned giving program (allows the director of development to move forward confidently with the program, knowing that he/she has a reliable and experienced back-up); and creative estate planning seminars for donors, featuring the benefits and options of charitable gift planning.

Future Focus

101 Gregory Lane, Suite #52, Pleasant Hill, CA 94523
Tel: 800-737-3437, 925-686-3212; FAX: 925-686-3217
WWW: http://www.futurefocus.net

▶ Instant Web Pages for Planned Giving, the first combination of professional content and personalized design, provides nonprofit organizations a unique turn-key approach to an effective, engaging, and inexpensive method of tapping into this transfer (the fastest growing segment of Internet users today is the over 55 age group). The Future Focus Instant Web Pages will quickly, economically, and seamlessly add a planned giving presence to your Web site. Their planned giving content touches the heart with examples of the emotional rewards that donors experienced as a result of their gifts.

Gift Planning Associates (GPA)

223 Clipper Street, San Francisco, CA 94114
Tel: 415-970-2380; FAX: 415-970-2383
E-mail: Giftplanner1@cs.com (Richard Lamport, Principal, or Dick Rabin, Office Manager); WWW: http://www.giftplanner1.com/, http://www.giftplanner1.com/faq.html

▶ GPA specializes in the field of planned giving consulting to nonprofits, providing feasibility studies, lead generation mailings and seminars, board and staff training, evaluating gifting options with prospective donors, and working with prospects' advisors to answer questions and close the gifts. Their full range of services goes beyond highly effective lead generation to include extensive, one-on-one follow-up with donors and their advisors. During this critical phase, GPA continually maintains contact with prospects. They answer questions, address donors' concerns, provide unique alternatives, and facilitate the process that progresses from consideration to closing. Their in-house gift planning knowledge is supplemented by the expertise of carefully screened legal, accounting, and other planning professionals.

Henry & Associates Gift and Estate Planning Services

22 Hyde Park Place, Springfield, IL 62703-5314
Tel: 800-879-2098, 217-529-1958; FAX: 217-529-1959
E-mail: VWHenry@aol.com (Vaughn W Henry);
WWW: http://www.gift-estate.com

▶ Services include charitable trust and estate planning consulting services; professional development for NPO gift planners and for-profit advisers; workshops and private seminars for nonprofits and family groups; and they distribute a gift/estate tax calculator. Subscription information for the mailing list addressing CRT planning issues can be found at *http://gift-estate.com/crt.html*, or send an email to *VWHenry@aol.com* and you will be automatically subscribed.

John Brown Limited

Box 296, 46 Grove Street, Peterborough, NH 03458
Tel: 603-924-3834; FAX: 603-924-7998
E-mail: jblnh@aol.com; WWW: http://www.jblnh.com/

▶ This firm assists charitable organizations in creating, implementing, and servicing individualized major gift and/or planned giving programs. It addresses the following areas in its major gift and planned giving consultation work: major gifts and planned giving consulting, capital and endowment campaign consulting, and development review (audit). It also offers seminar and training services.

Kaspick & Company

Palo Alto office: 555 University Avenue, Palo Alto, CA 94301
Tel: 650-322-5477; FAX: 650-854-9023

Boston office: Four Liberty Square, 6th Floor, Boston, MA 02109
Tel: 617-357-0575; FAX: 617-357-0576
E-mail: info@kaspick.com; WWW: http://www.kaspick.com/

▶ Founded in 1989, they specialize in planned gift management. They manage approximately $2 billion for 46 charities nationwide. Clients include some of the preeminent educational, medical, and religious organizations in the nation. Services include asset management, gift administration, consulting on policies and practices, comprehensive reporting.

McCord and Associates

5322 North 40th Street, Tacoma, WA 98407-3655
Tel: 253-759-2862; FAX: 253-759-4770
E-mail: jean@mccordassociates.com (Jean McCord, CFRE, President)

▶ McCord and Associates works in three main areas: planned giving (provide full services: audit present fund-raising efforts, plan and implement a planned giving program, train staff and volunteers, provide ongoing consulting and technical expertise); major gifts (evaluate gift potential, map strategies, train and coach staff and volunteers, integrate major and planned giving into the full development operation); direct donor contact (phone calls and visits to your top individual major and planned giving prospects, either as part of an ongoing fund raising effort or in a campaign context). Other services include board workshops, training for staff and volunteers, seminars for professionals, charitable seminars for donors, and written marketing materials.

Pentera, Inc.

8650 Commerce Park Place, Suite G, Indianapolis, IN 46268
Tel: 317-875-0910
E-mail: info@pentera.com; WWW: http://www.pentera.com/

▶ Pentera works together with hundreds of nonprofit organizations in promoting planned giving through personalized newsletters, booklets, seminars, consulting, and on the Web. They also offer customized staff training, target presentations to boards and/or trustees, key prospects, donors, and document preparation. Pentera offers educational and marketing seminars (advanced and intermediate) for development professionals with various degrees of skill and experience. They are designed both for the newcomer and the seasoned professional who wish to learn or refresh knowledge of major gifts and planned giving and their tax consequences.

PhilanthroCorp

Mailing address: P.O. Box 6190, Woodland Park, CO 80866

Business address: 700 Valley View Drive, Suite B,
Woodland Park, CO 80863
Tel: 719-687-8777; FAX: 719-687-8780
E-mail: gring@plannedgift.com (Greg Ring, President and CEO),
dkeesling@plannedgift.com (Dave Keesling, Vice President and
COO); WWW: http://www.plannedgift.com

▶ PhilanthroCorp's process begins by looking at the donor's current situation to make sure there are viable planning strategies that can aid the donor. Information is then gathered to assist the donor in establishing or clarifying his or her goals. The next step is a proposal, which is an initial attempt to blend the goals of the donor with available trust and tax strategies. Strategies are fine-tuned as the donor begins to understand the ramifications of more or less inheritance to the children, more or less to charity, and so on. Finally, the implementation process begins, working with the donor's advisor or, if necessary, recommending advisors in the donor's geographic area. PhilanthroCorp is a fee-only, planned giving outsource company serving dozens of Christian ministries from coast to coast. Their goal is to expand the capacity of Christian nonprofits who have an existing planned giving program, or to establish the planned giving program of organizations who have not yet begun to work in this arena.

Planned Giving Resources, Inc.

P.O. Box 8300, Alexandria, VA 22306-8300
Tel: 703-799-8300; FAX: 703-799-8318
E-mail: jimbpotter@aol.com (James B. Potter);
WWW: http://www.pgresources.com/

▶ This firm provides assistance to nonprofits in starting or expanding a planned giving program, in the areas of bequest solicitation and wills emphasis, charitable remainder and lead trusts, and pooled income funds and endowment funds, including developing, accepting, processing, and managing charitable gift annuities, as well as assisting the charity with state compliance issues of state insurance/securities laws that regulate charitable gift annuity funds, where both the charity and annuitants are located. Help is available for charity's filing for state permits and state notifications of annuity gift activity to the various state regulators now required by at least 22 states, together with calculating the state-mandated required reserve obligations and the FASB liabilities for a charity's existing annuity agreements (and other life income plans).

Planned Giving Services

3147 Fairview Avenue East, Suite 200, Seattle, WA 98102-3019
Tel: 206-329-8144; FAX: 206-329-8230
E-mail: PlanGiv@aol.com (Frank Minton, Bill Zook);
WWW: http://www.plannedgivingservices.com/

▶ Services include consulting (assistance in starting a new planned giving program, ongoing support to a planned giving program, audit of an existing planned giving program, guidance in the completion of particular gifts); seminars; gift annuities (help charities to obtain certification to issue gift annuities in all 50 states as well as programmatic assistance in establishing and operating gift annuity programs); and cross-border gifts.

R.R. Newkirk

8695 South Archer, Suite #10, Willow Springs, IL 60480
Tel: 800-342-2375; FAX: 708-839-9207
E-mail: newkirk2@aol.com; WWW: http://www.rrnewkirk.com/

▶ This company has been providing planned gift promotional programs and training since 1967, serving more than 1,400 clients annually in all 50 states and Canada. Their talented team of writers, editors, tax attorneys, marketing consultants, artists, and design specialists provide planned gift officers the widest range of assistance. What's more, their newsletter clients are entitled to toll-free access to the editors of *The Charitable Giving Tax Service.* They offer donor/advisor seminars as well as week-long, comprehensive planned giving seminars.

Retriever Development Counsel

4125 Southeast 34th Avenue, Portland, OR 97202
Tel: 503-736-1102; FAX: 503-236-3183
E-mail: plannedgifts@email.msn.com (Kevin Johnson, CFRE,
CSPG)

▶ This firm works with nonprofit organizations, helping them to start or expand planned and major gift programs. Services include creation or expansion of planned giving programs, endowment campaign strategies, strategic planning, development and planned giving audits or assessments, board development and training, workshops for donors and professional advisors, gift planning for individuals, and charitable estate planning for individuals. It offers a 12-session, year-long Planned Giving Action Program designed for nonprofits. Retriever also specializes in assisting individuals by helping identify charities to support that match their unique interests, how to make gifts in tax-smart ways, and charitable estate planning.

Richard Alan Lehrman

777 Arthur Godfrey Road, Fourth Floor, Miami Beach, FL 33140
Tel: 305-534-1323; FAX: 305-531-0314
E-mail: Lehrman@Trustlaw.net, TrustLaw@ABAnet.org,
RickLehrman@ATT.net, 73670.435@compuserve.com,
RickLehrman@worldnet.att.net;
WWW: http://www.lawyers.com/trustlaw

▶ This practice is devoted to planning, design, implementation, and administration of trusts and estates, business succession planning, and charitable gift planning. Services that might be of interest to NPOs include charitable estate planning, applications for 501(c)(3) status, presentations to boards and donors on planned giving, setting up a planned giving program, marketing planned giving programs, setting up professional advisory committees, and establishing gift acceptance policies.

Robert F. Sharpe and Company

5050 Poplar Avenue, Suite 700, Memphis, TN 38157
Tel: 800-238-3253, ext. 360, 901-680-5303; FAX: 901-761-4268
E-mail: info@rfsco.com

DC area office: 17126 Briardale Road, Rockville, MD 20855
Tel: 301-977-4637; FAX: 301-977-0804
E-mail: dc@rfsco.com; WWW: http://www.rfsco.com/

▶ The Sharpe Company was founded in 1963 and is composed of three divisions: donor publications, training, and marketing support. The donor publications division offers a wide variety of newsletters, brochures, and booklets covering a range of gift planning topics. The training unit produces basic, intermediate, and advanced seminars for development, management, and support staff of nonprofit organizations as well as for trustees. The marketing support division offers one-on-one training and support to a limited number of client organizations across the country. The Sharpe Company serves nearly 2,000 organizations and institutions each year, representing at least 25 distinct areas of charitable endeavor.

Stelter Company *(See Direct-Mail/Direct-Response Marketing)*

Strategic Alliance of Planned Giving Consultants

WWW: http://www.giftplanners.com

▶ This organization serves the nonprofit sector with philanthropic consulting services, including readiness assessment, planned giving program design and implementation, charitable gift planning, board and staffing training, motivational seminars for donors, endowment building, and executive search. The Alliance is composed of the following consultants: Pamela Jones Davidson, JD, (Laura Hansen Dean & Associates); Laura Hansen Dean, JD (Laura Hansen Dean & Associates); Cynthia Wilson Krause, JD (Wilson & Krause); Betsy A. Mangone (Mangone & Co.); Kathryn W. Miree, JD (Kathryn W. Miree & Associates, Inc.).

Strategies for Planned Giving

15300 Pearl Road, Suite 203, Cleveland, OH 44136
Tel: 440-572-4790
WWW: http://www.s4pg.com

▶ Strategies for Planned Giving offers a wide variety of services within the planned giving arena. Some areas of their professional assistance include program audits, program development, training,

marketing, customized presentations, gift planning, ongoing counsel, and maintenance.

Tony Poderis

FundAmerica Press, 2901 Istra Lane, Willoughby Hills, OH 44092
E-mail: Tony@raise-funds.com (Tony Poderis);
WWW: http://www.raise-funds.com/workshop.html

▶ Tony Poderis can present a tailored program for half-day, full-day, or longer duration. The presentation can be integrated with your other programs and sessions for any local or national conference. It can stand alone or be part of a trustee or staff retreat for any nonprofit organization.

Young-Preston Associates

P.O. Box 280, Cloverdale, VA 24077
Tel: 800-344-5701
WWW: http://www.youngpreston.com/

▶ Young-Preston Associates are publishers of planned giving newsletters, booklets, brochures, and books for your own reading and for you to give to your donors.

Proposal Writing *(See also Grants and Grantwriting)*

Deborah Kluge—Independent Consultant

Columbia, MD
Tel: 301-596-7287
E-mail: dkluge@home.com; WWW: http://www.proposalwriter.com/

▶ Deborah offers proposal writing and management services for firms, organizations, and universities bidding on government contracts.

The Grant Doctors

P.O. Box 417212, Sacramento, CA 95841
Tel: 916-348-8460; FAX: 800-783 0238
E-mail: dave@thegrantdoctors.com;
WWW: http://www.thegrantdoctors.com

▶ The Grant Doctors is a full-service economic development consulting firm for local municipalities (governments), businesses, and not-for-profit organizations. Their services include program/project development, fund development planning, prepare responses to RFPs/RFAs, strategic planning, workshops, feasibility studies, needs assessments, proposal/application development, collaboration development, program evaluation, public/private partnership building, grant administration, funder relations, proposal review/examination (proofreading), grant searches, and one-on-one staff training.

Grantworks Proposal Writing Services

P.O. Box 365, Santa Monica, CA 90406
Tel: 310-312-5010; FAX: 310-826-7066
E-mail: info@grantworks.com (Katherine Kubarski, Principal);
WWW: http://grantworks.com

▶ This private consulting firm provides technical assistance and training to public and nonprofit organizations in the areas of grant proposal writing, program planning, and fund development. Serving both national and international agencies, it specializes in the development of programs and proposals for medical and social science research, health care and social services, child/family welfare, education, the arts, and community economic development. It regularly conducts comprehensive seminars for independent researchers, university faculty, and nonprofit managers in the preparation of grant proposals for foundation, corporate, and government funding. While the focus is on grant funding, planning and program development issues are always given in-depth attention. Customized training programs can be designed to meet agencies' special needs and interests.

Prospect Research

(See also Donor Research and Prospect Identification; List Brokers)

Bentz Whaley Flessner

7251 Ohms Lane, Minneapolis, MN 55439
Tel: 952-921-0111; FAX: 952-921-0109
E-mail: bwf@bwf.com; WWW: http://www.bwf.com,
prospecting@bwf.com

▶ Prospecting services include program assessment and planning, staff training, methodologies for the best in data acquisition and prospect management, and prospecting seminars.

Dick Luxner, MLS, Research Consultant

P.O. Box 277, Stow, MA 01775
Tel: 978-562-1288
E-mail: dluxner@ma.ultranet.com

▶ Services include research program evaluation; assistance in the selection of research personnel, software, and electronic screening services; training and workshops in establishing and managing a new state-of-the-art research office; selecting research tools and resources, print and electronic; searching libraries, CD-ROMs, online databases, and the Internet; writing profiles stressing giving capacity and major interests; compiling and analyzing foundation and corporate information; tracking the cultivation and solicitation of major prospects; conducting tracking and strategy meetings for fund-raising staff; and motivating board members, volunteers, cultivators, and solicitors.

HEP Development Services

43212 Lindsay Marie Court, Ashburn, VA 20147
Tel: 800-681-4438, 703-858-5700; FAX: 703-858-5741
E-mail: info@hepdevelopment.com;
WWW: http://www.hepdevelopment.com.

▶ HEP Development Services works with nonprofit fund raisers who recognize the value of accurate data. They specialize in data enhancement, focusing in the areas of prospect research, matching gift identification, and address/phone updates. Products include *GiftPlus,* an authoritative electronic file of matching gift companies, which is available in several electronic and hard copy formats; and *The Executive ID,* their comprehensive database of more than 12 million private and public companies, which allows them to identify your constituents who are senior-level executives and owners at these businesses. In addition to a full summary of the company, HEP now provides a personal biographical history on your constituent executives. The entire output file is delivered in an "easy to use" proprietary Web-based search engine. Also, Hep's InTouch program can electronically locate your lost constituents and verify and update their phone numbers.

Institutional Advancement Programs, Inc. *(See Full Service)*

Prasad Communications & Research

20 Sutton Place South, New York, NY 10022
Tel: 212-755-1309; FAX: 212-752-6672
E-mail: Prasadc@aol.com (Poonam Prasad, Principal)

▶ Prasad Communications & Research helps organizations craft major donor strategies that target groups with differing cultural values and sensitivities. Their work has included campaigns targeted specifically to Chinese, African-American, Hispanic, Scandinavian, Indian, gay and lesbian, elderly, and female populations. Services include prospect research (particularly major gift research for capital or other large campaigns through analysis of current givers, research on major donors and by identifying new sources of corporate, foundation and private support); publications (newsletters, brochures, case statements, annual reports, presentation materials, promotional materials); public relations; board development; donor event planning. Prasad Communications & Research assists development officers with analysis of current givers, research on major donors, and identifying new sources of corporate, foundation, and private support. Creating thorough and accurate reports, crafting major donor strategies, developing boards, producing campaign publications, and training development staff in research are PCR's strengths.

Prospect Information Network, LLC

501 North Grandview Avenue, Suite 203, Daytona Beach, FL 32118
Tel: 888-557-1326; FAX: 904-226-1154
E-mail: info@prospectinfo.com;
WWW: http://www.prospectinfo.com/home.htm

▶ Prospect Information Network was founded by David Lawson (*dlawson@prospectinfo.com*) in 1997 to create a service that would enable fund raisers to more efficiently identify and profile their share of today's new wealth. Services include Prospect I.D., Profile Builder 2.5 (see separate listing under Software), and training.

Target America

10560 Main Street, Suite LL17-19, Fairfax, VA 22030
Tel: 703-383-6905; FAX: 703-383-6907
E-mail: info@tgtam.com; WWW: http://www.tgtam.com/

▶ This prospect research company marries data and technology to bring you fund-raising programs that work. The Target America database contains more than 4 million records of the wealthiest and most generous people in the nation—the top 5 percent in terms of income, assets, and philanthropic history. 94 percent of the individuals on the database give more than $5,000 a year to charities. This database includes philanthropists, foundation trustees, private investors, individuals with income-producing assets of $250,000 to over $5 million, professionals with large private pension plans, executives of private companies with company financials, SEC insiders of publicly traded companies, luxury and estate property owners, and many more.

Veritas Information Services

9 Alton Street, Arlington, MA 02474
Tel: 781-643-7811; FAX: 781-643-1136
E-mail: Inquiries@Veritasinfo.com, ruderman@post.harvard.edu
(Susan Cronin Ruderman, Vice President);
WWW: http://www.veritasinfo.com/

▶ Veritas provides the following services to nonprofit organizations: development information systems audit; prospect identification (individuals, corporations, foundations, government); proposal writing; researcher recruitment and training; and staff training in prospect research techniques, including the Internet.

WealthEngine.com

4915 St. Elmo Avenue, Suite 300, Bethesda, MD 20814
Tel: 301-215-5980
E-mail: info@wealthEngine.com;
WWW: http://www.wealthengine.com/

▶ WealthEngine.com, formerly Prospects of Wealth & Resources, Inc. (POW&R), is a developer of wealth identification screening services and innovative prospecting solutions based on individual assets. It offers custom matching services to help you append information on your wealthiest prospects to your existing donor lists. Since 1989, WealthEngine.com has been tracking wealthy individuals for many of America's nonprofit organizations. WealthEngine.com's products assist in identifying high-net-worth prospects, donors, and clients. Services include subscriptions, batch matching, profiles, and list rental. Their products allow you to organize and segment your prospects for planned giving, major gift solicitation, and annual fund appeals.

Telemarketing/Telefundraising

Advantage Fund Raising Consulting

208 Passaic Avenue, Second Floor, Fairfield, NJ 07004
Tel: 888-599-3737; FAX: 973-575-5614
E-mail: advantage@advantageconsulting.com,
sales@advantageconsulting.com;
WWW: http://www.advantageconsulting.com

▶ This company provides off-site and on-site personalized telefundraising programs. Services include The Edge Tele-Mail Telecommunications Program (design and consultation on case and all mailing materials; pre- and postcall letters; individualized ask amounts; face-to-face simulated calling program using experienced fund raisers; three-, five-, and ten-time differentiated calling attempts; personalized thank you letters; fulfillment services); fulfillment services (entry of pledges, thank you letters; reminder statements; late payment letters; reminder calling reporting); on-site consulting services (design and consultation on case and all mailing materials, on-site monthly consulting meetings with your phone program staff, quarterly audits of the program, extensive reports with recommendations, full-service consulting for all your phone program requirements); automated calling stations (design, setup, and installation of network; customized automated systems to meet your need; software for call tracking and data entry; preview calling; customized statistical reporting; training of staff and calling team); Internet Web pages (consultation on benefits of using the Internet as a solicitation methodology, setup and design of Web site, reporting on Web-site traffic, address updates and pledges, Web site hosting; e-mail addresses for your team); and alumni surveys (design and consultation on preparation of the survey, face-to-face simulated calling program using experienced fund raisers; statistical reporting daily; evaluation report at the conclusion of calling program).

Aria Communications

717 West St. Germain Street, St. Cloud, MN 56301
Tel: 612-259-5206; FAX: 612-259-4314
E-mail: michele@ariaready.com, kimberly@ariaready.com;
WWW: http://www.careertimes.com/Profiles/AAA/Aria/

▶ Aria Communications is a telefundraising/sales and handwritten direct-mail service company. Since its founding in 1985, it has served over 200 clients in the following markets: education, public radio and television, health care, environmental groups, relief organizations, telecommunications, and others. It maintains operations in Sauk Centre and Duluth and a sales/administrative office in Minneapolis.

Artsmarketing Services, Inc.

260 King Street East, Suite 500, Toronto, Ontario M5A 4L5, Canada
Tel: 888-941-9333, 416-941-9000; FAX: 888-941-3381; 416-941-8989
E-mail: bspeyer@artsmarketing.com;
WWW: www.artsmarketing.com

▶ Provides telemarketing and telefundraising services exclusively to the nonprofit sector. Over the course of a year, Artsmarketing employs over 3,500 full- and part-time staff in offices across North America and has managed campaigns for hundreds of organizations. Its sister company, Legacy Leaders Inc., provides assistance with planned giving campaigns. Artsmarketing conducts telefunding component of Legacy Leaders Inc.'s planned giving by phone campaigns. They serve clients in performing arts, public broadcasting, conservation, museums, zoos, and health care.

DirectLine Technologies, Inc.

1600 N. Carpenter Road, Building D, Modesto, CA 95351-1145
1200 East Orangeburg Avenue, Suite 103, Modesto, CA 95350-4625
Tel: 800-448-1200; FAX: 209-491-2091
E-mail: martha_connor@directline-tech.com (Martha Connor);
WWW: http://www.directline-tech.com/DTI, http://www.directline-tech.com

▶ DirectLine specializes in annual fund and alumni membership telemarketing fund-raising campaigns to colleges and universities worldwide. They also provide full membership acquisition, renewal, and surveying services.

IDC

IDC Centre, 2920 North Green Valley Parkway, Suite 5-521, Henderson, NV 89014
Tel: 800-229-41DC (4432), 702-450-1000; FAX: 702-450-1020
E-mail: dmc@goidc.com; WWW: http://www.goidc.com

▶ IDC provides the following services to clients throughout the United States, Canada, the United Kingdom, and Australia: PHONE/MAIL®Centre Program, consultation and training, direct mail, survey program, letter generation, on-site PHONE/MAIL® program, comprehensive computerized reports, major gift prospect identification, and pledge fulfillment. They offer a series of ongoing workshops and seminars. Its Technology Group offers these services: database segmentation and management, letter generation, production, reporting. IDC is a member of the American Association of Fund-Raising Counsel.

Infocision Management Corporation
325 Springside Drive, Akron, OH 44333
Tel: 330-668-1400; FAX: 330-668-1401
WWW: http://www.infocision.com/

▶ Infocision is a teleservices company that specializes in nonprofit fund raising. It offers both inbound and outbound services and has developed a propriety inbound/outbound call-blending solution. It serves some of the largest nonprofit clients in the country, including health, humanitarian, religious, and membership associations.

Lester Telemarketing, Inc.
19 Business Park Drive, Brandford, CT 06405
Tel: 800-999-5265; FAX: 203-483-0408
WWW: http://www.lester-telemarketing.com

▶ Lester Telemarketing offers outbound telemarketing services for annual funds, capital campaigns, special challenges, and mop-up campaigns. It is a member of the Association for Healthcare Philanthropy, Council for Advancement and Support of Education, and National Society of Fund Raising Executives.

MSGi Direct (Formerly Steven Dunn & Associates)
1728 Abbot Kinney Boulevard, Venice, CA 90291
Tel: 310-301-1999; FAX: 310-301-9779
E-mail: Bschwan@sdatel.com, erudolph@msgidirect.com;
WWW: http://www.sdanda.com/

▶ MSGi Direct, previously known as Steven Dunn & Associates (SD&A), serves the nonprofit sector with state-of-the-art telemarketing and telefundraising campaigns. MSGi Direct specializes in annual fund, membership, capital, special gift, and subscription campaigns that are customized to the individual needs of each organization. Telefundraising for nonprofit organizations since 1983, MSGi offers individually designed fund-raising campaigns managed on-site, from a location provided by the client, or off-site, from their Calling Center in Berkeley, California. Clients include universities, public broadcasting stations, advocacy groups, environmental and performing arts organizations, museums, libraries, and zoos. The primary services provided for a campaign are: telefundraising (membership campaign, annual fund campaign, CapiTEL^{SM} campaign, Special Gift Campaign); telemarketing (Subscription Campaign); and Consulting.

RuffaloCODY
Corporate office: 221 Third Avenue, Suite 10, P.O. Box 3018,
Cedar Rapids, IA 52406-3018
Tel: 800-756-7483; FAX: 319-362-7457
E-mail: djasper@ruffalocody.com (Duane Jasper, President);
WWW: http://www.ruffalocody.com

▶ RuffaloCODY provides fund-raising, membership, and enrollment management solutions for nonprofit organizations. They serve the nonprofit community with three primary product and service offerings: off-site telemarketing, on-site telemarketing, and software. They maintain many locations all over the United States as well as many regional calling centers.

Telecomp, Inc.
3136 Winton Road South, Suite 301, Rochester, NY 14623
Tel: 888-272-1160, 716-272-1160; FAX: 716-272-1991
E-mail: telecomp@frontiernet.net (Kathleen E. Pavelka, CFRE,
Founder and President); WWW: http://www.telecomp.org

▶ Founded in 1986, it provides customized annual and capital telephone outreach programs for educational, health care, and cultural organizations since 1986.

Video Services

First Light Media Group
4 Oak Street, Needham, MA 02492
Tel: 781-449-7232; FAX: 781-449-7925
WWW: http://www.firstlightonline.com

▶ This independent production company creates custom films, video, and other media for use in marketing, training, and sales. It also offers consulting services in areas including instructional design, communication strategy, and concept development.

Lois Rice, LXR, Inc.
200 West 90th Street, New York, NY 10024
Tel: 212-873-1032; FAX: 212-873-0630
E-mail: ricenyc@aol.com

▶ Creative, effective, fund-raising videos and PSAs.

Workshops, Seminars, Training
(See also Professional Development—Education)

Alexander Macnab & Company
900 North Franklin Street, Suite 810, Chicago, IL 60610
Tel: 800-708-2060, 312-642-1239; FAX: 312-640-1994
E-mail: growfunds@aol.com; WWW: http://philanthropy.com/
adv.dir/consult.dir/ads.dir/asm.shtml

▶ Seminars offered include: How to Solicit Major Gifts: Making Successful Solicitations; Gaining Through Giving: Doing Good While Doing Well; Developing Your Resources: The Process of Philanthropy; Starting a Planned Giving Program: Developing a Timeline and Budget; and Successful Annual Giving Programs: Fundamentals of Direct Mail.

Avatar Company
2907 Red Bug Lake Road, Casselberry, FL 32707
Tel: 407-695-6618; FAX: 407-695-4832
E-mail: avatarway@avatarcompany.com, avatarway@aol.com
(Bob Kovacevich); WWW: http://avatarcompany.com

▶ Avatar provides the following workshops: Market/Audience Research; Fund-Raising Plan Development or Assessment; Marketing Plan Development or Assessment; Capital and/or Endowment Campaign Planning and Management; Case Statement Development; Solicitation Training; Prospect Identification; Cultivation and Solicitation Procedures; Grant Search and Assessment; Research and Application Development; Membership Program Development or Assessment; Annual/Major Gift Program Development; Deferred Giving Program Development or Assessment; Special Event Development or Assessment; Donor Acquisition Mail and Telemarketing; and Emergency Funding Appeals.

Axelrod Consulting Services

1301 Spring Street, #7E, Seattle, WA 98104
Tel: 206-325-1905; FAX: 206-325-5427
E-mail: info@raisingmoremoney.com, taxelrod@well.com (Terry B. Axelrod, Principal); WWW: http://www.raisingmoremoney.com/misc/misc12.shtml

▶ Axelrod provides training and coaching in building a self-sustaining individual giving program. They offer the Raising More Money® Basic Workshop and Raising More Money® Intensive Major Gifts Coaching Workshop.

Barrett Planned Giving, Inc.

2000 L Street NW, Suite 200, Washington, DC 20036
Tel: 202-416-1667; FAX: 202-416-1668
E-mail: info@barrettplannedgiving.com, BarrettPln@cs.com; WWW: http://www.barrettplannedgiving.com

▶ This firm presents interactive workshops for your board members, staff, and volunteers to help them become comfortable with planned giving concepts. Topics covered include: What Is Planned Giving?; How Your Organization Can Benefit from Planned Giving; How Planned Giving Works; How to Get Your Planned Giving Program Started Right; and How You Can Help Make the Planned Giving Program a Success.

Baxter Farr Thomas & Weinstein, Ltd.

1111 Kentucky NE, Albuquerque, NM 87110-6923
Tel: 505-256-3231, 800-325-2117; FAX: 505-265-0248
E-mail: bftwsw@bftw.com; WWW: http://www.bftw.com/bftw

▶ They can help your organization with board retreats and other similar gatherings. Among the subjects treated are fund-raising principals and practices; major gift solicitations: before, during, and after; building better boards; the board's role in fund raising; planned giving; developing your case for support; time management; and preparing for a capital campaign.

Bev Browning & Associates *(See Grant Writing)*

Boris Frank Associates

7094 Paoli Road, Verona, WI 53593
Tel: 608-845-3100
E-mail: borisfrank@inxpress.com (Boris Frank, President)

▶ This firm specializes in capital campaign development, feasibility studies, and strategic planning. It is the creator of the ACCELERATED PLANNING MODEL. It focuses on libraries, humane societies, and arts organizations. It conducts workshops, seminars, and training on fund raising, marketing, planning, board development, and volunteer management, with clients primarily in Wisconsin, Illinois, Michigan, Iowa, and Minnesota.

Capital Venture

320 North Kenhorst Boulevard, Reading, PA 19607
Tel: 610-796-9120; FAX: 610-796-9150
E-mail: CCILINDA@aol.com (Linda Lysakowski, President)

Ohio office:
Tel: 877-305-9137; FAX: 330-305-9497

Pennsylvania office:
Tel: 877-540-2896; FAX: 610-796-9150
WWW: http://www.cornerstoneconsult.com/page4.html

▶ This is a general partnership composed of JSM Consulting Group, Inc., and Cornerstone Consulting, offering expertise in the area of capital and endowment campaigns. They also work jointly with clients in the following areas: annual fund, board and volunteer development and training, development audits and plans, grant writing, and campaign planning and implementation.

Carol J. Geisbauer *(See Grantwriters Guild)*

Caswell, Zachry, Grizzard

8226 Douglas Avenue, Suite 655, Dallas, TX 75225
Tel: 800-972-3187, 214-528-8084; FAX: 214-528-8456
E-mail: czglin1@airmail.net; WWW: http://www.czg.net/index.html

▶ Planned giving products and seminars designed by fund raisers for fund raisers.

The Clements Group, LC

136 East South Temple, Suite 900, Salt Lake City, UT 84111
Tel: 801-355-0450; FAX: 801-355-0449
E-mail: clmgroup@mail.vii.com; WWW: http://www.clmgroup.com, http://www.clmgroup.com/events.htm

▶ The Clements Group regularly offers workshops and seminars, including a two-day Major Gifts Campaign Seminar, designed to serve as a guide to the conduct of successful major gifts campaigns at community colleges and technical institutes for presidents, institutional advancement officers, foundation executive directors, and other resource development professionals. This seminar is offered several times each year at various locations.

Clover Development Strategies, Inc.

2677 S. Ocean Boulevard, Suite 4C, Boca Raton, FL 33432
Tel: 800-741-4147, 954-429-8900; FAX: 954-429-8920
E-mail: CApelian@aol.com (Clover Apelian, President); WWW: http://www.cloverfund.com/about_us.html

▶ They can provide workshops on a variety of topics related to nonprofit management and fund raising. They usually charge only expenses when speaking to associations and charge expenses and a fee when retained by a specific not-for-profit client. Some of the workshops offered include: Taking the Mystery Out of the Capital Campaign; The Feasibility Study: The Most Important First Step; The Case for Support: Writing for Maximum Return; The Role of Planned Gifts: In Your Program; In Your Campaign; Major Gifts Fundraising: Cultivate to Win; Moves Management for Major Gift Fundraising Success; How to Make the Ask; Donor Recognition; Board Strengthening Through Better Organizing; Volunteer Management.

David G. Bauer Associates

3171 Green Valley Road, Suite 322, Birmingham, AL 35243-5239
Tel: 800-836-0732, 205-879-1457

P.O. Box 6592, Stateline, NV 89449-6592
FAX: 702-588-1255
WWW: http://www.dgbauer.com

▶ Established in 1981, David G. Bauer Associates is an educational-based consulting firm dedicated to assisting grant seekers and fund raisers develop the skills they need to succeed. The corporation's primary focus is to provide educational institutions and other nonprofit organizations with in-house seminars in grant seeking and fund raising. Mr. Bauer has trained over 15,000 individuals in grant seeking and fund raising. He has presented seminars at hundreds of colleges and universities, many school districts, and for major leaders in the education, health, and nonprofit arenas, including the American Council on Education, American Hospital Association, National 4-H Council, and the National Society of Fund Raising Executives. Clients can choose from one of four in-house seminars: How to Find—and—Win Government Grants; How to Find—and—Win Foundation and Corporate Grants; How to Develop and Operate a Successful Grants Office, and Strategic Fund Raising.

Deferred Giving Services

614 South Hale Street, Wheaton, IL 60187
Tel/FAX: 630-682-4301
E-mail: Schmeling@aol.com (David G. Schmeling, CFRE, Planned Giving Consultant); WWW: http://www.deferredgivingservices.com

▶ This firm offers the planned giving workshops/seminars. Their goals in the seminars for fund raisers are to answer their questions, raise their comfort level in starting a new program, and motivate them to act. Goals in the seminars for donors are to introduce them to the magic of charitable gift planning and help them understand that charitable giving through their estates is definitely a win-win-win situation—for them, their families, and the charities whose missions represent their lifetime values. Workshops/seminars include: Planned Giving for the One Person Development Office: Taking the First Steps; Introduction to Planned Giving: Learning the Basics and Getting Started on the Right Track; Endowment Building: What It Is, How to Make It Donor-Friendly, and How to Grow It; Creative Stewardship for the Local Congregation: Introducing Planned Giving into Our Members' Stewardship Awareness; Presentation to Boards and Committees: Establishing the solid foundation for a long-term program of helping donors perpetuate their lifetime values through estate planning; Creative Estate Planning for Donors: What Everyone Who Has Anything Should Know about Wills and Estate Planning; Creative Stewardship for Today's Christians: Helping God's People Today Endow Their Church's Ministries Tomorrow; and An In-depth Introduction to the Plans of Planned Giving: What They Are, How They Can Be Used, and The Benefits Which Accrue to Donors Who Use Them.

Development Resource Center

Administrative office: 4744 10th Avenue South,
Minneapolis, MN 55407
E-mail: yohen@aol.com

Marketing office: Box 15515, Seattle, WA 98115
E-mail: dhodiak@aol.com (Diane Hodiak);
WWW: http://www.drcharity.com/training.html

▶ Development Resource Center provides training services, workshops, and seminars for not-for-profit organizations in fund raising, management, and marketing. It offers a free e-mail newsletter filled with practical fund raising and marketing ideas, resources, and information.

Educational Funding Strategies, Ltd. (EFS)

79 Somerset Drive, Suffern, NY 10901
Tel: 845-368-2950, 845-357-8645
E-mail: mlgross@aol.com (Marilyn L. Gross, President);
WWW: http://www.efsinternet.com

▶ Since 1996, EFS has been a pioneer in designing and delivering low-tech, self-paced, e-mail- and Internet-based online courses for nonprofits, educational organizations, local governments, and public agencies. Their emphasis is on training, writing, and production of several computer-based products. They provide several low-tech (e-mail- and Internet-based) distance learning courses for grant seekers, fund raisers, and other nonprofit and educational professionals; in-person workshops and longer trainings related to using the Internet, grant seeking, proposal writing, and other aspects of nonprofit management and fund raising; *The Internet Insider for Grantseekers & Fundraisers,* a free, twice-monthly e-mail newsletter of great Web sites and other information related to fund-raising issues; and several computer disks (and book versions) with hot links to valuable, hard-to-find Web sites. Currently: "300 Top Web Sites for Fundraisers"; "300 Top Web Sites for Nonprofits"; "300 Top Web Sites for Grantseekers"; "Top Web Sites for Grantmakers and Donors."

The Foundation Center

79 Fifth Avenue, New York, NY 10003-3076
Tel: 800-424-9836, 212-620-4230; FAX: 212-807-3677
WWW: http://fdncenter.org/marketplace/training/index.html

▶ The Foundation Center accomplishes its mission of fostering public understanding of the foundation field by offering educational programs on the funding research process, proposal writing, grant makers and their giving, and related topics at all five of its offices. These include: FC Search Training Programs; Grantseeking on the Web: Hands-on Introductory Training Courses; Meet the Grantmakers; and Proposal Writing Seminars.

The Fund-Raising School

The Center on Philanthropy at Indiana University,
550 W. North Street, Suite 301, Indianapolis, IN 46202-3272
Tel: 800-962-6692 (The Fund-Raising School), 317-274-4200;
FAX: 317-684-8900
WWW: http://www.philanthropy.iupui.edu/fundschool.htm

▶ The Fund-Raising School is the only national fund-raising education program housed within a university. We are a part of the Indiana University Center on Philanthropy, which seeks to increase the understanding of philanthropy and improve its practice through research, teaching, and public service. It is intended for nonprofit managers who must raise funds as well as oversee operations, board members and volunteers who want to help their organization continue to grow, new development professionals who want a thorough foundation for success, and seasoned development professionals who want to hone their skills and learn new strategies. They offer a Certificate in Fund-Raising Management with the endorsement of the Indiana University Center on Philanthropy. You can partner with The Fund-Raising School to create a workshop or series of workshops that fit the fund-raising needs of your nonprofit. The Fund-Raising School faculty also conduct customized courses. You can save money by teaming up with other organizations in your area.

Gift Planning Associates

223 Clipper Street, San Francisco, CA 94113
Tel: 415-970-2380; FAX: 415-970-2383
E-mail: Giftplanner1@cs.com (Dick Rabin, Office Manager);
WWW: http://www.giftplanner1.com/

▶ Gift Planning Associates (GPA) specializes in the field of planned giving consulting to nonprofits, providing feasibility studies, lead generation mailings and seminars, board and staff training, evaluating gifting options with prospective donors, and working with prospects' advisors to answer questions and close the gifts. They offer a background in finance and planning, utilizing the research, reporting, and marketing techniques employed by the for-profit sector. One essential component of this approach is their feasibility study, which details specific planned giving strategies tailored to meet the needs of your organization and your donors. With the feasibility study as a foundation, they work with you to develop an individualized, executable marketing plan that will maximize results. GPA has served a variety of organizations in the fields of health care, social services, education, religion and religious education, and animal welfare.

Goodale Associates

509 Madison Avenue, Suite 1112, New York, NY 10021
Tel: 212-759-2999; FAX: 212-759-7490
E-mail: TKGASSOC@aol.com; WWW: http://www.tkgoodale.com,
http://www.tkgoodale.com/gast.htm

▶ Goodale Associates provides Solicitor Training Workshops to train board members, staff, and volunteers in fund-raising techniques. Solicitor Training Workshops are designed specifically for Development Professionals and Volunteer Leadership. Consisting of a presentation by Toni Goodale and a study of various hypothetical situations, the Solicitor Training Workshop is an indispensable tool for training solicitors in the "art of asking" and developing solicitation strategies.

The Grant Doctors

P.O. Box 417212, Sacramento, CA 95841
E-mail: dave@thegrantdoctors.com (Dave Farley, Founder and Chairman); WWW: http://www.thegrantdoctors.com/

▶ Presents The Grants Clinic (a one-day workshop that shows participants how to improve their grant-seeking efforts from program conception to proposal submission. It is intended for audiences of 10 to 50 individuals working on grant-related projects for their organizations. Participants will be able to develop new programs attractive to funders, identify private funding sources, locate state and federal grants, strengthen proposals, foster collaborations with other organizations, evaluate program effectiveness, and develop sustainable programs. It is designed for in-house proposal writers, program managers, executive directors (CEOs), board members, and volunteers.

Grant Proposal & Research Services

9805 Luna Vista, Suite A, Knoxville, TN 37922
Tel: 423-675-5411
E-mail: grantpro@bellsouth.net; WWW: http://members.tripod.com/~GrantPro/Workshop.html

▶ This firm offers the following workshops: Introduction to Grant Funding, Introduction to Grant Writing and Grant Funding, Introduction to Grant Writing and Grant Funding (Plus Internet Web Page Design).

The Grantsmanship Center

1125 W. Sixth Street, 5th Floor, P.O. Box 17220,
Los Angeles, CA 90017
Tel: 213-482-9860; FAX: 213-482-9863
E-mail: norton@tgci.com (Norton Kiritz);
WWW: http://www.tgci.com/training/training.htm

▶ TGCI conducts some 200 workshops annually in grantsmanship and proposal writing and has offered the continuously updated Grantsmanship Training Program since 1972. Designed for both novice and experienced grantseekers, this five-day workshop covers all aspects of searching for grants, writing grant proposals, and negotiating with funding sources. The program will teach you to use TGCI's widely used proposal writing format. During the workshop, you will search out funding sources and, as part of a team, you will develop a proposal for your own agency or help a classmate develop one. TGCI can provide customized (sponsored) training programs tailored to the specific needs of an agency or group of agencies. These are developed around the Grantsmanship Training Program and Grant Proposal Writing formats. TGCI publishes *The Grantsmanship Center Magazine, TGCI's Library of Winning Grant Proposals* (the best of funded federal grant proposals annually on CD-ROM), and the TGCI proposal writing guide, *Program Planning and Proposal Writing* (PP&PW).

Grantworks Proposal Writing Services

P.O. Box 365, Santa Monica, CA 90406
Tel: 310-312-5010; FAX: 310-826-7066
E-mail: kk@grantworks.com (Katherine Kubarski, Principal);
WWW: http://grantworks.com

▶ This private consulting firm provides technical assistance and training to public and nonprofit organizations in the areas of grant proposal development and program planning. One- to three-day seminars are regularly conducted, upon request, in the following areas: Introduction to Proposal Writing; Foundation and Corporate Proposal Writing; Government Proposal Writing; Collaborative Proposal Writing; Advanced Proposal Writing Clinics. Instruction is available in English, Spanish, and Portuguese. All instructors are practitioners with established track records in securing grants for organizations dedicated to the arts, child/family/youth services, community development, education, health care, and medical research.

Grantwriters Guild

18032-C Lemon Drive, PMB #117, Yorba Linda, CA 92886
Tel: 714-572-1975; FAX: 714-572-1976
E-mail: info@grantwritersguild.org, cgeisbauer@aol.com (Carol J. Geisbauer); WWW: http://www.grantwritersguild.org

▶ Grantwriters Guild offers three-day grant-writing workshops all over California.

Hartsook and Associates, Inc.

1501 Castle Rock, Witchita, KS 67230
Tel: 316-733-7100; FAX: 316-733-7103
E-mail: info@hartsookgroup.com, rhartsook@aol.com,
bob@hartsookcompanies; WWW: http://www.hartsookgroup.com,
http://www.hartsookgroup.com/hsook/seminars.shtml

▶ Hartsook and Associates specializes in training and workshop activities that equip the participant with fund-raising techniques necessary for today's professional fund raiser and leadership. Topics range from general development and giving essentials to specific time management tips for fund raisers. They offer a national seminar series on the Integrated Fund-Raising Campaign.

IDC

IDC Centre, 2920 North Green Valley Parkway, Suite 5-521, Henderson, NV 89014
Tel: 800-229-41DC (4432), 702-450-1000; FAX: 702-450-1020
E-mail: dmc@goidc.com; WWW: http://www.goidc.com

▶ IDC offers a series of ongoing workshops and seminars. Its Technology Group offers database segmentation and management, letter generation, production, and reporting.

Institute for Charitable Giving

500 North Michigan Avenue, Suite 2008, Chicago, IL 60611
Tel: 800-234-7777; FAX: 312-222-9411
E-mail: charity@pop.wwa.com;
WWW: http://www.philanthropymatters.com/,
http://www.philanthropymatters.com/Pages/store.html

▶ The Institute offers seminars to individuals within nonprofit organizations to teach successful major gift and planned gifts fundraising techniques. Seminars and training are conducted for professional fund-raisers, chief executives officers, volunteers, and board members to help implement specific motivation and cultivation techniques, which are necessary to successfully raise major gifts for nonprofit organizations. Benefits of attending these seminars are a resource notebook filled with presentation outlines, checklists, relevant reprints, and a host of fund-raising ideas; regular mailings in the future from the Institute regarding new ideas in fund raising, pertinent new techniques, and innovative approaches to getting the gift; regular mailings about vacancies and new job opportunities that involve major gifts, planned giving, and senior officer positions; and networking opportunities.

The Institute of Charitable Giving has developed a methodology called Moves Management (MM). This was designed to increase prospects and donors for nonprofit organizations. MM helps nonprofit organizations follow detailed steps and activities to move an individual from small donor to major gift giver. The Institute of Charitable Giving and eTapestry.com have developed an integrated software program that helps organizations track each step and activity of a donor. eTapestry.com is offering MM as an option to its customers. The selected option will allow the user to immediately access MM and fully integrate to eTapestry.com so that all functions are managed from within the donor database.

John Brown Limited, Inc.

P.O. Box 296, 46 Grove Street, Peterborough, NH 03458
Tel: 603-924-3834; FAX: 603-924-7998
E-mail: johnbrownlimited@aol.com (John Brown);
WWW: http://www.johnbrownlimited.com/Pages/
JBLseminars.html, http://www.johnbrownlimited.com/Pages/
seminarschedule.html

▶ This firm provides many interactive major gift and planned giving training services to nonprofit organizations. For the individual, they present the John Brown "Knowing the Essentials" three-day and the "Extending Your Experience" two-day seminars: Knowing the Essentials Seminars (the concepts of major gifts and planned giving in layman's terms with a focus on developing a program that can produce significant gifts) and Extending Your Experiences Seminar (communicating planned giving concepts to donors, trustees, staff, and volunteers; other strategies will be introduced that are designed for success in helping you meet your organization's goals). For institutions, they provide department-wide staff training or multi-institution staff training, where they present on-

site for one-, two-, or three-day sessions. They tailor each session to the institution's needs, goals, and objectives.

Membership Consultants

3868 Russell Boulevard, St. Louis, MO 63110
Tel: 314-771-4664; FAX: 314-771-2759
E-mail: email MemConsul@aol.com;
WWW: http://www.membership-consultants.com,
http://www.membership-consultants.com/memcomm&tsem.html

▶ This firm conducts ongoing series membership seminars as well as customized seminars and individualized training seminars.

The National Planned Giving Institute

The College of William and Mary

Gabrial Galt Building, 2nd Floor, P.O. Box 8795,
Williamsburg, VA 23187-8795
Tel: 800-249-0179, 757-221-1478; FAX: 757-221-1479
E-mail: npgi@wm.edu, npgi@facstaff.wm.edu;
WWW: www.wm.edu/NPGI

▶ The National Planned Giving Institute at the College of William and Mary offers a series of eight seminars covering all aspects of gift development through major current and deferred planned giving. Seminars are open to full-time employees of nonprofit institutions and accompanying trustees.

Nonprofit Training Associates

5515 New Haven, Austin, TX 78756-1801
Tel: 512-467-0420
E-mail: nonprofittraining@email.com (Taylor Maddux or Ron Ayer); WWW: http://www.nonprofittraining.com

▶ Nonprofit Training Associates offers the Proposal Writing Training Initiative course.

Philanthropic Quest International

28050 South Woodland Road, Cleveland, OH 44124
Tel: 216-831-3727; FAX: 216-831-8511
E-mail: Quest@Lord.org (James Gregory Lord);
WWW: http://www.boardworkshop.com/index.htm

▶ This organization offers 4 Steps to Generating the Largest Contribution in Your Organization's History. Includes special "lab" Mining the Lessons of Your Success, and preview of the new edition of the all-time best-selling book on philanthropy, *The Raising of Money: 35 Essentials Every Trustee Should Know.*

Planned Giving Seminars and Software

E-mail: PGSS1997@aol.com;
WWW: http://members.aol.com/pgss1997/Welcome.htm

▶ This company provides training in the form of two-day seminars entitled "Planned Giving: A Brisk Walk through the Basics," which covers the following topics: policies and guidelines, key estate and gift tax regulations, claiming the charitable deduction, valuing noncash gift assets, bargain sales/life insurance, gifts by will/dealing with probate, charitable gift annuities, charitable remainder annuity trusts, charitable remainder unitrusts, pooled income fund trusts, case studies and calculations, marketing. All material is covered in the 250-page seminar manual. Included is an introduction to planned giving calculation software. They developed and sell The Planned Giving Companion for Windows software.

Polaris

Three Bishop Street, Inman, SC 29349-6319
Tel: 800-368-3775, 864-472-5776; FAX: 864-472-5788
E-mail PolarisCo@aol.com;
WWW: http://www.polarisgrantscentral.net/ninetynine.htm

▶ Polaris provides one- and two-day high-content grants workshops in 48 states. Its workshops are known for their step-by-step, how-to nature and their well-organized content. Workshops are based on the Polaris project and proposal development processes. Polaris workshops are sponsored by K–12 education, postsecondary education, health care, government, and nonprofit organizations to train their staffs and, in many cases, as fund raisers. Workshops include: Grant Seeking Fundamentals; Grant Seeking Fundamentals for Technology Projects; Polaris Advanced Grant Seeking; How to Develop and Justify Your Project Budget; How to Effectively Evaluate Project Performance; Grant Seeking Fundamentals for Religious and Nonprofit Organizations; and How to Manage Your Grant Project. New workshops are in development.

Prospect Information Network

501 North Grandview Avenue, Suite 203, Daytona Beach, FL 32118
Tel: 888-557-1326; FAX: 904-226-1154
E-mail: info@prospectinfo.com, dlawson@prospectinfo.com
(David Lawson); WWW: http://www.prospectinfo.com

▶ This company founded by David Lawson in 1997 to create a service that would enable fund raisers to more efficiently identify and profile their share of today's new wealth. Products include Prospect ID and ProfileBuilder 2.5. They also offer training. Check their schedule at *http://www.prospectinfo.com/training/index.html.*

R&R Newkirk

8695 South Archer, Suite #10, Willow Springs, IL 60480
Tel: 800-342-2375; FAX: 708-839-9207
E-mail: newkirk2@aol.com; WWW: http://www.rrnewkirk.com/

▶ R&R Newkirk stages a week-long, comprehensive planned giving seminar. This week-long seminar features programs designed to increase your gift development skills. You will acquire technical knowledge, develop and practice solicitation techniques, and gain the confidence you need to solicit, close, and manage planned gifts. Don't miss out on this opportunity to increase your value to the charitable organization and prospects you represent. They also offer two-day Charitable Estate Planning workshops and an unusual one-day program on working with donors face to face and on the phone.

Research Associates

P.O. Box 1755, Irmo, SC 29063-1755
Tel: 803-750-9759
E-mail: contact@grantexperts.com;
WWW: http://www.researchassociatesco.com/grant_seminars.htm

▶ Established in 1986, it is a national firm providing grants development and training in collaboration with the National Grant Writers Association. Ten different courses and three national certifications are offered on how to locate, write, review, administer, and evaluate grants. On-site and conference grant seminars are delivered at your location nationwide. Grant training is national in its focus, and workshop presenters include very successful grant writers and foun-

dation representatives. Their goals are to illustrate innovative grant-writing techniques and strategies, help you to discover valuable secrets, and make the learning process fun and exciting. Over 400 grants will be available to examine and copy during the seminars. Each high-quality course includes a 100+-page notebook.

Resource Development, Inc. (RDI)

Corporate headquarters: 1411 East Primrose, Suite A, Springfield, MO 64804
Tel: 800-728-8805, 417-883-0202; FAX: 417-883-9140

Dallas office: 555 Republic Drive, Suite 200, Plano, TX 75074
Tel: 972-509-0010; FAX: 972-633-9107
E-mail: rdisgf@cland.net (Bill Jester);
WWW: http://www.resourcedevinc.com

▶ RDI seminars are taught by seasoned professionals—experts in strategic planning and direct contact with nonprofits and their donors across the country. Training dates are available by calling 1-800-728-8805 for more information.

Richard J. Condon & Associates

14673 SW 132nd Avenue, Miami, FL 33186
Tel: 305-252-8083; FAX: 305-252-8092
E-mail: LEGRANTS@aol.com;
WWW: http://members.aol.com/legrants/index.htm,
http://members.aol.com/legrants/seminaragenda.htm,
http://members.aol.com/legrants/fundingtip.htm

▶ This firm educates and equips persons serving public agencies and nonprofits with the knowledge and skills necessary to develop public and private funding and other resources for critical program, equipment, training, facility, and other needs. Two workshops have been developed to train and equip resource developers with the skills necessary to obtain public and private grant funding and other resources for critical program, equipment, and other needs.

1. **Developing Winning Grant Programs and Proposals**—a two-day workshop that provides participants with detailed training in how to develop a winning grant program and a winning letter of inquiry and grant proposal. This workshop will benefit beginners and those with more advanced program development and grant-writing skills. Instruction and workgroup exercises. Registration fee: $275.00

2. **Resource Development Workshop**—a three-day workshop that combines how to develop winning grant programs and proposals with training in developing public and private funding and other resources for critical program, equipment, facility, training, and other needs. Instruction and workgroup exercises. Registration fee: $325.00

3. **Resource Development Seminar**—a one-day seminar on public and private funding and other resources for programs, equipment, facility, training, and other needs. Registration fee: $200

Robert F. Sharpe and Company

5050 Poplar Avenue, Suite 700, Memphis, TN 38157
Tel: 800-238-3253, ext. 360, 901-680-5303; FAX: 901-761-4268
E-mail: info@rfsco.com

DC area office: 17126 Briardale Road, Rockville, MD 20855
Tel: 301-977-4637; FAX: 301-977-0804
E-mail: dc@rfsco.com;
WWW: http://www.rfsco.com/seminars/index.html

▶ The Sharpe company offers a variety of educational experiences to help all members of the development and management team learn more about major gift planning. There are three seminar levels to choose from: introductory, intermediate, and advanced. Their Web site provides details on each seminar offering, including a brief description, complete agenda, locations, dates, tuition, and a registration form.

Patricia Rife & Associates

725 Darymple Road 1-F, Atlanta, GA 30328
Tel: 678-596-6503
E-mail: prife@att.net (Patricia Rife, President),
prife@worldnet.att.net; WWW: http://www.patriciarifeassociates.com

▶ Services include grant writing and editing, training, and program evaluation.

Semple-Bixel Associates, Inc.

653 Franklin Avenue, Nutley, NJ 07110
Tel: 973-284-0444; FAX: 973-284-0950
E-mail: rfsemple@aol.com (Maria Semple)

▶ The firm has designed and directed hundreds of fund-raising training programs and workshops in the United States and abroad, including The Fund-Raising Fundamentals course. Topics include: Demographics & Direct Mail, Donor Identification and Research, Proposal Preparation, Public Relations, Designing an Annual Giving Program, Special Events, Capital Campaigns, Major Gift Solicitation, and Planned Giving.

Sinclair, Townes & Company

230 Peachtree Street NW, Suite 1601, Atlanta, GA 30303
Tel: 404-688-4047; FAX: 404-688-6543
E-mail: ask@sinclairtownes.com; WWW: http://www.sinclair townes.com, http://www.sinclairtownes.com/displayproduct.asp? Product_category=1561

▶ They conduct seminars and retreats for nonprofits and their board members, donors, and other friends on such topics as Charting Capital Campaigns, and Planned Giving 101.

Special Events Forum

1973 Schrader Drive, San Jose, CA 95124
Tel: 408-879-9392; FAX: 408-371-4752
E-mail: dnelson@specialeventsforum.com (David L. Nelson, President); WWW: http://www.specialeventsforum.com/

▶ Special Events Forum conducts nationwide seminars on special event fund raising. Topics include: Part One: Principles of Event Fundraising, or Why You Haven't Made $1,000,000 Yet (the symptoms of mission conflict; a confusion of standards; activities versus systems; management focus: volume versus profitability; market-oriented planning; how special events support the "Pyramid of Giving"; what creates a "unique" event; measuring the true cost and potential; recruitment and deployment of volunteers; what information is important; the mystery of ticket pricing; misuse of the media; sponsorship versus philanthropy; the importance of event follow-up); Part Two: Building the Million-Dollar System, or Making More Money With Fewer Hassles (integrating the elements of an event fundraising system; investment issues such as personnel, time, capital, etc.). The workshop will provide attendees with an action plan for accelerating the financial performance of special events; a diagnostic method for assessing the true worth of your current event fund-raising program; a comprehensive understanding of the nature of event fund raising and its unique investment requirements.

Talisman Associates Inc.

711 North Elizabeth, Suite 2F, Chicago, IL 60622
Tel: 888-3-TALISMAN (outside Illinois), 312-733-7520;
FAX: 312-733-7530
E-mail: info@3talisman.com; WWW: http://www.3talisman.com

2020 Pennsylvania Avenue NW, Suite 557, Washington, DC 20006
Tel: 888-3-TALISMAN; FAX: 877-5-TALISMAN
E-mail: info@3talisman.com

▶ Since 1983, Talisman Associates, Inc., has assisted not-for-profit organizations by providing professional, hands-on developmental skills that are client-focused and goal-oriented. They regularly sponsor "Best Practices" fund-raising training workshops and luncheons.

Target Funding Group, Inc. (TFG)

PMB 156, 4262 Northlake Boulevard,
Palm Beach Gardens, FL 33410
Tel: 800-345-0782; FAX: 561-626-4291
E-mail: mwinter@benefitauction.com;
WWW: http://www.benefitauction.com/index.html

▶ TFG developed and marketed AuctionOut, a simple to use software for the "Check-out" of an auction. This software has been sold throughout the country. In addition, TFG is a leading reseller for Auction Maestro, a comprehensive management software that coordinates every aspect of the auction process from catalogs, bid sheets, display cards, thank you letters, and invoices.

Third Sector Innovations, Inc.

480 31¼ Road, Grand Junction, CO 81504
Tel: 800-406-7274, 970-434-7621; FAX: 970-434-0955
E-mail: thirdsec@gj.net; WWW: http://www.gj.net/~thirdsec/

▶ They are available to provide one-to-one and group training on grant writing and grantsmanship, as well as fund-raising planning, special event fund raising, marketing, public and media relations, and other areas of interest to nonprofit managers. Trainings are interactive and hands-on. The material is not just theory-based, but proven successful and applicable to your distinct nonprofit organization.

Virtual Development Group

P.O. Box 2676, 724 Boston Street, Covington, LA 70434-2676
Tel: 504-809-1724; FAX: 504-892-9916
E-mail: meg3253@aol.com (Michael E. Guillot);
WWW: http://www.virtualdevelopment.net

▶ Virtual Development Group is the creator of the Million Dollar System, a systematic, 40-week fund-raising program, taught in their intensive one-day workshop. You will learn how to raise $1,000,000 for your nonprofit organization in as little as 40 weeks. They also schedule strategic retreats as well as board workshops and presentations.

The Write Source

4671 Burnley, Bloomfield Hills, MI 48304-3720
Tel: 248-642-3808; FAX: 248-642-8956
E-mail: info@write-source.com, thewritesc@aol.com (Diane M.
Gedeon-Martin); WWW: http://www.write-source.com
▶ They provide full and half-day workshops in the areas of pro-
posal writing and funding research for board members, staff, and
other groups.

Zimmerman Lehman & Associates

582 Market Street, Suite 1112, San Francisco, CA 94104
Tel: 800-886-8330 (outside the San Francisco Bay Area),
415-986-8330; FAX: 415-986-2048
E-mail: zl@zimmerman-lehman.com;
WWW: http://www.zimmerman-lehman.com/wkshps.htm
▶ This firm provides training for the board of directors and staff
and volunteers to help them solicit funds enthusiastically, effectively, and without fear. Professional materials, tailored to your organization's specific needs, are included in each training. Zimmerman
Lehman has trained thousands of individuals in the art and science
of fund raising and board development. A sampling of their most
popular workshops includes: Zimmerman's Twelve Rules of
Fundraising (an enthusiastic overview of fund-raising theory and
techniques); Individual Solicitation for Major Donor or Capital
Campaigns; Overcoming the Fear of Fundraising and How to Ask
for Money; Zimmerman's Eleven Ways Nonprofits Raise Money
(fund-raising planning for your organization); Effective Board
Recruitment and Orientation (includes developing a board profile
grid and job description that requires fund raising); Board of
Directors' Five Responsibilities; and Grantseeking: A Step-By Step
Approach. For a description of the above trainings, comments on
recent sessions, and a list of current trainings open to the public, see
their training page.

Software Vendors

Auction/Banquet/Event Management

Auction Systems

P.O. Box 8265, Colorado Springs, CO 80933-8265
Tel: 719-520-3245; FAX: 719-520-3246
E-mail: Info@auctionsystems.com;
WWW: http://www.auctionsystems.com

▶ Auction Systems is the developer and distributor of *Auction!*, a windows-compatible software package that automates bid sheets, invoices, catalog brochures, mailing labels, gift certificates, donor receipts, seating assignments, and more for silent and live auctions. They provide no-charge technical support, suggestions and guidance on event organization and management, creative ideas for operating within a tight budget, and more.

Campagne Associates, Ltd.

491 Amherst Street, Nashua, NH 03063
Tel: 800-582-3489; FAX: 603-595-8776
E-mail: info@campagne.com; WWW: http://www.campagne.com

▶ This company is distributor of EventMaker Pro software for both Windows and Macintosh computers. Campagne Associates also offers EventMaker Pro, which helps you plan, organize, and manage any fund-raising event with task management features, registration, event-day reports, and more. Combine these software options, with a variety of training options, data conversion options, and an annual support program, and you will have your complete fund-raising solution. EventMaker Pro streamlines registration and allows you to enter tickets purchased, food and seating preferences, guest information, and any other details all in one location. It helps you plan, organize, and manage all of your special events. With EventMaker Pro, you can easily handle the invitations, registration, and attendance of events as diverse as golf tournaments, black-tie galas, annual reunions, and conferences. EventMaker Pro can be used as a stand-alone system or as a module of GiftMaker Pro. Revenue and expense reporting gives you an instant snapshot of the status of your event, including paid/unpaid and complimentary ticket sales, actual versus estimated expenses, and event gains or losses. All event-day reports, such as seat listings, payment status, host and guests, and ticket revenue are standard. EventMaker Pro features a cloning function that lets users copy entire events including all of the specific tasks, to-do lists, and valuable notes, which helps you hit the ground running for next year's event. All the event information is stored in the software, so if there should be a turnover in your development office, all your important event data stays in-house and your organization doesn't suffer because of it.

MaestroSoft.com, Inc.

1200 112th Avenue NE, Suite C250, Bellevue, WA 98004
Tel: 800-438-6498, 425-688-0809; FAX: 425-688-0999
E-mail: Info@maestrosoft.com; WWW: http://crusader.paladin
data.com:7779/maestrodev/home.htm

▶ They design and produce user-friendly tools for organizations to orchestrate various events. Among their products of interest to non-profit organizations are Auction 2000 (as part of the Event Hub concept, the Web-enabled Auction 2000 product provides a new dimension for auction management); Meeting 2000 (combines the accessibility and power of the Internet with MaestroSoft.com Meeting software to effectively manage meeting events of virtually any scale); and Banquet 2000 (gives host planners a powerful set of tools to conduct dinners, banquets, award ceremonies, and other hospitality events for 5 guests or 5,000).

Northwest Software Technologies, Inc.

2418 California Avenue, Suite A, Everett, WA 98201
Tel: 425-252-7287
E-mail: sales@nwsoftware.com, nsti@sprynet.com (Jack D.
Wilson, Jr., President/CEO); WWW: http://www.nwsoftware.com

▶ Northwest is developer of special-event management software to the nonprofit and educational vertical market sectors. In business since 1985, their applications are sold in the United States, Canada, Australia, and England. Products include A'Thon-Tracker, Auction-Tracker, Banquet-Tracker, and Tournament-Tracker.

Sterling Sound Data

1121 Harvard Lane, Buffalo Grove, IL 60089
Tel: 847-459 7841
E-mail: sales@charityauctionsoftware.com;
WWW: http://www.charityauctionsoftware.com

▶ Distributor of Auction Express 2000 auction software for non-profits.

Sungard BSR, Inc.

1000 Winter Street, Suite 1200, Waltham, MA 02451
Tel: 781-890-2105; FAX: 781-890-4099
E-mail: info@bsr.com (Fred B. Weiss, Vice President)

▶ BSR provides software and services that support the friendraising and fundraising goals of our clients. Our systems and services are developed in response to specific user and industry requirements and in partnership with our user community, which includes colleges and universities, health care institutions, religious organizations, and other not-for-profit organizations. BSR offers a variety of software products for advancement: Advance, their premier product, is the core of what they do: the management of data to help organizations build relationships with their constituents; *The*

Special Events System helps organizations manage and track a diverse range of events, including reunions, seminars, luncheons, travel programs, and sporting events; *SmartCall* provides sophisticated telefundraising as well as calling capabilities for invitations, admissions, and stewardship. Both the Special Events and SmartCall systems can be used as "stand-alone" applications as well as optional add-ons to Advance, which has three other optional subsystems: Membership/Dues for managing dues-paying organizations; Web Access for remote and traveling staff and volunteers; and Web Community for online giving and directory information.

Target Funding Group, Inc. (TFG)

PMB 156, 4262 Northlake Boulevard,
Palm Beach Gardens, FL 33410
Tel: 800-345-0782; FAX: 561-626-4291
E-mail: mwinter@benefitauction.com;
WWW: http://www.benefitauction.com/index.html

▶ TFG's products provide tools for conducting all aspects of the auction event. TFG developed and marketed AuctionOut, a simple-to-use software for the "Check-out" of an auction. This software has been sold throughout the country. In addition, TFG is a leading reseller for Auction Maestro, a comprehensive management software that coordinates every aspect of the auction process from catalogs. The Target Funding Group, Inc., team has broadened their expertise to include seminars and media consulting and are able to develop a program to meet the needs and budget of any organization. Their clients range from small local nonprofits to chapters of national organizations, service clubs, and private schools throughout the United States.

Fund Raising/Donor Management

3rdSector.Net

Tel: 610-390-0965
E-mail: vic@3rdsector.net; WWW: http://www.3rdsector.net/index.htm

▶ An application software and service provider for the nonprofit sector, they offer small to midsize nonprofit organizations application software and over the Internet Web-enabled services that leverage the advantages of technology and the Internet. They are the developer of FUND-A-MENTAL Donor Management System, a software that allows you to track donors, prospects, campaigns, solicitations, gifts, and pledges. It also tracks volunteers, board members, special interests, and relationships. Using FUND-A-MENTAL, you can communicate with supporters through simple, automated mailings for solicitations, gift acknowledgment, pledge acknowledgment, and pledge reminders. Features include user-defined tables to facilitate data entry, access, and analysis; pledges and gifts tracked to campaign, find, solicitation, and memorials; tracks any changes in giving level of donor or prospect and provides detailed gift and pledge data; keeps track of volunteers so you can know when help has been provided and when; keeps a database of services offered by volunteers; allows you to set membership categories, bill dues, track renewal dates, and print membership cards; and it is fully integrated with Microsoft® Office.

Access International

432 Columbia Street, Suite 23, Cambridge, MA 02141
Tel: 617-494-0066; FAX: 617-494-8404
E-mail: sales@accessint.com (Courtney DeVries, Manager, Sales and Marketing); WWW: http://www.accessint.com

▶ This company distributes Enterprise/CS™ fund-raising software, which is client server software for larger, more complex not-for-profits. It unlocks the potential of your data, allowing you to approach fund raising from a strategic planning and individualized marketing perspective. It allows you to identify trends, monitor costs, and maximize results. From a centralized database, you can better manage direct marketing, prospect tracking, major donor research, planned gifts, and special events. Enterprise™ offers integration with list/data companies, NCOA providers, and fulfillment houses; advanced OCR, lockbox, barcoding, credit card authorization, and the Internet; integration of an organization's national database with its chapters and outlying offices; and seamless links to patient, ticketing, endowment, and accounting systems. They will even develop completely new modules if you need them.

Advanced Solutions International, Inc. (ASI)

901 North Pitt Street, Suite 200, Alexandria, VA 22314
Tel: 800-727-8682, 703-739-3100 ext. 330; FAX: 703-739-3218
E-mail: info@advsol.com, mdoyle@advsol.com (Michelle Doyle, Marketing Programs Lead); WWW: http://www.advsol.com/public/fund_raising

▶ An international provider of e-business software solutions for not-for-profit organizations. iMIS, ASI's flagship software, is a total not-for-profit solution with the addition of a fund-raising component that allows an organization to manage all types and sizes of donations and automate not only its fund-raising processes, but also its business functions such as order processing, inventory management, donor activity history, and special event planning. iMIS also seamlessly integrates back-end management systems (customer data, purchasing transactions, meeting records) with a front-end Web presence, creating a total e-business solution. iMIS Fund Raising, developed by Advanced Solutions International, is the scalable client server software to help any organization manage its fund-raising efforts efficiently and effectively, from capital campaigns and event management to matching gift management to personalized donor recognition. iMIS Fund Raising is sold, installed, trained, and supported locally. iMIS is available in three versions. The entry level product is iMIS LAN and is geared toward meeting the needs of small organizations with limited financial resources. iMIS Millennium is targeted for midsize organizations, and iMIS Enterprise is designed specifically for large and/or more technically demanding organizations. All versions of the iMIS software run on Windows 3.1, Windows 95, Windows NT, and/or Apple Macintosh workstations, and are available in single- and multiuser licenses. ASI has main offices in Alexandria, Virginia; Austin, Texas; Melbourne, Australia; and several regional offices throughout the United States.

Araize

1157 Executive Circle, Suite D, Cary, NC 27511
Tel: 800-745-4037, 919-319-1770; FAX: 919-460-5983
E-mail: sales@araize.com; WWW: http://www.araize.com/,
http://www.araize.com/ffR.htm

▶ They have database management software for fund raising as well as financial management components. They are the developer and distributor of FastFund Raising, fund-raising software for Windows 95/98/2000NT. FastFund Raising includes everything you need for fund raising: prospects and donor lists, campaign and appeal management, alumni and membership tracking, acknowledgments and receipts, solicitor results, and donor tributes. Wizards and on-screen help guide you through setup, data-entry, and donation processing. Sophisticated search, sort, and export capabilities allow you to generate letters and reports. All FastFund Raising users receive one year of free, unlimited 800 telephone support. A trial version of FastFund Raising is available for downloading from their Web site.

Ascend Technologies, Inc.
2658 Crosspark Road, Suite 200, Coralville, IA 52241
Tel: 800-624-4692; FAX: 319-626-5491
E-mail: info@ascend-tech.com; WWW: http://www.ascend-tech.com,
http://www.ascend-tech.com/html/fund-raising.htm

▶ An integrated fund-raising, fund accounting, and investment management system for educational and nonprofit organizations. Ascend helps organizations exceed their goals by managing all aspects of the development process, including prospect management, gift processing, profile information, special activity codes, matching gifts, pledges, alumni membership, fund accounting, and investment management. Ascend 2000 links together all of the information in an organization's database so users can quickly access the data they need. Data updates reflect instantly across the entire system so everyone is working with the most current information. Ascend is a suite of three major components that work seamlessly together. The Executive component allows you to quickly view, enter, and modify biographical and gift information. The second component, SelectPlus, allows you to zero in on prospects and generate reports, donor profiles, mailing labels, and other output. FastTrack speeds and simplifies administration and maintenance and produces comprehensive reports on all aspects of your efforts.

Batsch Group, Inc.
201 10435 178 Street NW, Edmonton AB Canada T5S 1R5
Tel: 780-489-9911; FAX: 780-487-3401
E-mail: ease@connect.ab.ca; WWW: http://www.batschgroup.com/

▶ Batsch Group is distributor of @ease Fundraising Asset Management System. They also offer seminars.

Blackbaud
2000 Daniel Island Drive, Charleston, SC 29405-8530
Tel: 800-468-8996, 443-9441; FAX: 843-216-6100, 216-6111
E-mail: sales@blackbaud.com; WWW: http://www.blackbaud.com

▶ Established in 1981, they are leading providers of fund-raising, accounting, academic, administration, grant-making, and planned giving software to philanthropic and nonprofit organizations. They are the distributor of fund-raising software including The Raiser's Edge; RE: Optional Modules; RE: NetDonors; MatchFinder; and Planned Giving Software. Clients include private schools, colleges, universities, hospitals, and other health care agencies, environmental organizations, museums, social service agencies, performing arts groups, and other charitable and cultural organizations. They also offer training and consulting services, data services, and customer support.

Bromelkamp Company
106 East 24th Street, Minneapolis, MN 55404
Tel: 612-870-9087; FAX: 612-870-9616
E-mail: info@bromelkamp.com;
WWW: http://www.bromelkamp.com/index.html

▶ This company distributes the Pearl fund-raising software package. Their Grants Management and Fundraising components can be developed "from scratch" to track your unique process. The Grants Management system can track matching gifts, scholarships, corporate contributions, multiple payees, multiple applicants for the same grant, grant modification history, panelist participation, application scoring, detailed project budget reporting, and more. The Fundraising system can keep track of stocks or in-kind gifts, special events or fund raisers, auctions, memberships, matching gifts, and the like. You can add Fund Accounting and/or Loan Tracking to your custom database, and can use their E-grant program as well.

Business Systems Resources (BSR) (A Sunguard Company)
1000 Winter Street, Suite 1200, Waltham, MA 02451
Tel: 781-890-2105; FAX: 781-890-4099
E-mail: info@bsr.com; WWW: http://www.bsr.com,
http://www.sungardbsr.com

▶ BSR provides software and services that support the friend-raising and fund-raising goals of their clients. Their systems and services are developed in response to specific user and industry requirements and in partnership with their user community, which includes colleges and universities, health care institutions, religious organizations, and other not-for-profit organizations. BSR offers a variety of software products for advancement including: Advance (their premier product, assists with the management of data to help organizations build relationships with their constituents); Special Events System (helps organizations manage and track a diverse range of events, including reunions, seminars, luncheons, travel programs, and sporting events); and SmartCall (provides sophisticated telefundraising as well as calling capabilities for invitations, admissions, and stewardship). Both the Special Events and SmartCall systems can be used as "stand-alone" applications as well as optional add-ons to Advance, which has three other optional subsystems: Membership/Dues for managing dues-paying organizations; Web Access for remote and traveling staff and volunteers; and Web Community for online giving and directory information.

Campagne Associates, Ltd.
491 Amherst Street, Nashua, NH 03063
Tel: 800-582-3489; FAX: 603-595-8776
E-mail: info@campagne.com; WWW: http://www.campagne.com

▶ Formed in 1987, they provide a suite of nonprofit software solutions, including Donor Management (GiftMaker Pro) and Special Event Management (EventMaker Pro) software for both Windows and Macintosh computers. GiftMaker Pro is a comprehensive donor and prospect management software that offers list management, gift processing, contact management, and detailed reporting and analysis features. The membership module manages all aspects of your membership, including daily processing of new members, renewals, membership cards, reporting, and trend analysis. The volunteer module enables you to maintain and create reports of the interests, skills, availability, and work history of your volunteers. GiftMaker Pro's Graphic User Interface allows you to access and maintain all constituent information from one central location through an icon-based toolbar at the top of the screen. GiftMaker Pro comes with a choice of low-cost and convenient training programs for your personnel, along with fast and easy data conversion options.

Ciconte & Associates

WWW: http://www.ciconte.com/

▶ This is a professional and technical services firm specializing in information systems, fund raising, and board development for the nonprofit sector. The firm combines technology expertise with fund raising and development experience to provide essential computer-related products, services, and consultations to nonprofit organizations of all sizes. Developer of the Resource Development System (RDS), a flexible, easy-to-use and easy-to-learn donor and member management system for nonprofits and associations, for use by any size organization. Highlights include: access and compile complete demographic, biographical, and giving history information; prepare personalized targeted mailings, including merge files, labels, and envelopes (RDS automatically suppresses duplicates); record contacts (letter, telephone, meetings, staff contacts) with donors, members, and major gift prospects; produce numerous statistical, financial, and analytical reports; manage events, including registration, cost analysis, attendance and seating reports, table assignments, nametags, and so on.

Datatel

4375 Fair Lakes Court, Fairfax, VA 22033
Tel: 800-328-2835, 703-968-4562; FAX: 703-968-4573
E-mail: mktg@datatel.com;
WWW: http://www.datatel.com/datatel.html

▶ Benefactor, Datatel's strategic planning and management tool designed specifically for fund-raising professionals, provides your organization with a competitive edge in its quest to identify and solicit the funds needed for success. Benefactor not only keeps complete and accurate records of your organization's fund-raising activities and efforts, but it also collects, calculates, and manipulates data to provide forecasts, progress reports, and prospect identification. Benefactor's features and functions provide the information access and tools necessary to effectively and efficiently manage a development staff while increasing the level of contribution and participation from donors. Benefactor tracks and stores detailed records on individuals and organizations, and then ties that information together to identify the personal and business relationships so crucial to successful fund raising. Benefactor also automates gift and pledge processing, tracking of matching contributions, identification and tracking of major prospects, campaign management, and scheduling and coordination of activities and events, so that all aspects of fund raising are integrated in one system. By consolidating financial and demographic data, Benefactor provides you with the ability to generate reports and perform analyses that help make informed decisions and develop future fund-raising strategies.

Diakonia

P.O. Box 5647, Diamond Bar, CA 91765
Tel: 800-DAKONIA (325-6642), 909-861-8787;
FAX: 909-861-0335
E-mail: info@faithfulsteward.com

▶ Diakonia is the developer of Faithful Steward, a solution that allows churches and nonprofit organizations to manage their membership and donation records. Faithful Steward™ streamlines your office paperwork. It quickly places members and donors into an unlimited number of "group" lists for future campaigns. You can send a personalized mailing to any "group" of donors. The software also prepares bulk mailings. View contribution results for each person, date, or fund-raising campaign. The software prints your donor's receipts efficiently using your organization's unique style. Faithful Steward™ is very flexible. It includes 50+ built-in reports, ranging from letters with your logo, to personalized announcement flyers with gray scale or color pictures, window envelope reports, mailing labels, directories, and much more! Faithful Steward™ integrates your information with the software you already own. You can export your membership, attendance, and donations to Microsoft Word, Wordperfect, Microsoft Excel, Lotus 1-2-3, and most other programs.

DonorAccess

P.O. Box 160801, Austin, TX 78716
Tel: 512-402-0632
E-mail: info@donoraccess.com; WWW: http://www.donoraccess.com

▶ This comprehensive fund-raising, event-planning, and volunteer tracking database uses Microsoft™ Access. Features include mailing lists (unlimited addresses, phone, e-mails, Web pages, automatic mail merges, lists, and labels); prospect research and tracking (employer, education, and membership information; solicitation schedule; tracking and history; quick information reports); donation and campaign tracking (pledge tracking, matching gifts, memorials, subcampaigns, anonymous gifts, daily batch, campaign and year-end reports); volunteer tracking (skill and availability matching queries, volunteer schedules, yearly reports); grant tracking (grant information and status, results and status reports); and event planning and tracking (reservation, payment, attendee lists, volunteer schedules and lists, event schedule, and budget reports).

Donor Automation, Inc.

912 New York Street, Suite B, Redlands, CA 92374
Tel: 909-793-1230
E-mail: dasales@donor.com, hayne@donor.com (Hayne Baucom, President); WWW: http://www.donor.com

▶ Incorporated in 1975, it produces software (DASCO II and CornerStone 2000) for nonprofit organizations involved in fund raising. Their primary clients are Christian and charitable organizations, rescue missions, and relief organizations. DASCO II is their flagship product for ministries with 100,000 to 2,000,000 names. CornerStone 2000 is a scaled-down version of DASCO II for ministries with 5,000 to 100,000 names.

Electro Acoustics

1504A Hickox Street, Santa Fe, NM 87501-3506
Tel: 505-986-0578
E-mail: info@fundimensions.com, frank@fundimensions.com (Frank Martin, President); WWW: http://www.fundimensions.com/

▶ Electro Acoustics is a computer software, networking, and support company. They publish FUNDimensions fund-raising software (Macintosh and Windows NT) for nonprofit organizations, and offer expert onsite troubleshooting, training, network design and installation, and consulting. A free demo is available.

eTapestry

5845 Lawton Loop East Drive, Suite 100,
Indianapolis, IN 46216-1064
Tel: 888-739-3827, ext. 252 (Phil Richmond or Steve Rusche),
317-545-4170; FAX: 317-545-4180
E-mail: info@etapestry.com, steve.rusche@etapestry.com (Steve Rusche); WWW: http://www.etapestry.com/

► This is fund-raising software you use over the Internet. To use eTapestry you don't need to buy software and install it on your computer. You log onto the Internet and use eTapestry anytime, anywhere, on any computer with Internet access. Donors, prospects, board members, volunteers, and staff can access the information you define from any Internet connection when they want it. There is no capital outlay required with eTapestry. Organizations use the system for a monthly fee based on number of users and amount of data. The monthly fee includes all eTapestry updates, online support, and automatic data backups and system administration. For organizations with fewer than 1,000 donor records, the base eTapestry applications—one user, all e-mail support, and donor records—are available at no charge. Additional users, data conversion, and training carry the usual charges. Information contained in eTapestry includes basic record information for donors, giving summaries, contact management, complete gift and pledge processing, mass e-mail, management reports, user queries, and online gift giving in a secure environment. eTapestry will also let volunteers keep personal information up to date including hours they are available, access a message center and see summary reports of their activities. Files can be exported to your computer for use with other third-party programs for creating thank-you letters or custom reports. eTapestry incorporates a variety of online links to outside services for easily finding address updates, phone numbers, creating maps, or running planned gift calculations. User support and training is provided online.

Executive Data Systems, Inc.

1640 Powers Ferry Road, Building 27, Marietta, GA 30067
Tel: 800-272-3374; FAX: 770-955-3374
E-mail: sales@execdata.com (Contact: G. William Spann, Vice President); WWW: http://www.execdata.com/

► Supplying nonprofits with software since 1983, their products include fully integrated fund raising and fund accounting software. They are the developer of Donor Records, a comprehensive donor tracking resource that has helped nonprofits of all types communicate their unique message to raise community awareness and to raise more money to support their programs. Donor Records lets you track individuals (prospects, donors, major contributors, etc.); foundations (current or potential grantors, grants pending, etc.); organizations (direct contributions and/or matching gifts); and memorials/tributes (with appropriate acknowledgments). More than 500 variables are captured, but you may use as many or as few as you need. More than 50 fields are user-definable. Donor Records records all gifts, pledges, dues/subscription payments and matching gifts for each individual. Membership records are automatically updated by dues/subscription payments. One of the largest suppliers of microcomputer software for nonprofit organizations in the United States, their products are currently in use by almost all types of nonprofit organizations, including voluntary health and welfare (social service); community action/economic development; private schools and universities; professional and trade associations; churches and other religious organizations; United Ways; college and university foundations; libraries and museums; zoological and historical societies; research/scientific organizations; performing arts organizations; and state and local government units.

FEOM Holdings, Inc.

1220 Hammonds Plains Road, Bedford, NS B4B 1B4, Canada
Tel: 902-835-9966; FAX: 902-835-9795
E-mail: info@feom.com;
WWW: http://www.feom.com/ezfund_win/main.htm

► FEOM is the developer of EZ-Fund, a financial management software system designed to help Canadian fund raisers to manage their donor databases and effectively track pledges and donations. The software tracks donations and pledges, and prepares mailings, reminder letters, and receipts. EZ-Fund™ is a multiuser, network-ready software system that has built-in security, user defined and searchable fields, import and export capabilities, and complete reporting capabilities. It captures credit card authorization numbers, correlates donations and deposit numbers, tracks gift-in-kind donations, and has built-in backup and restore capabilities. EZ-Fund™ is designed for Canadian fund raisers. EZ-Fund™ does conform to U.S. specifications and can be easily adapted to suit fund raisers from the United States and other countries. Telephone support is included in the purchase price of EZ-Fund™. Annual fees or maintenance fees are not assessed. Maintenance upgrades are free at their Web site.

Fund E-Z Development Corporation

106 Corporate Park Drive, White Plains, NY 10604
Tel: 914-696-0900; FAX: 914-696-0948
E-mail: sales@fundez.com;
WWW: http://www.fundez.com/products/pr-main1.htm

► Fund E-Z Fund Raising is a complete donor, gift, and pledge tracking software program designed for use by not-for-profit organizations. It organizes lists of prospects, donors, donations, and pledges. It categorizes lists by event, campaign, demographic, biographic, lifestyle, or giving history through the use of a comprehensive coding system. Query features extract only the data you want for reporting, exporting, statistics, tagging records, or screen inquiries. Create Mail Merge files for printing letters, labels, envelopes, or custom reports. Sort and report on donors, donations, events and pledges, with subtotal breaks to help you to analyze results.

FundTrack Software

PMB 489, 1500 West El Camino Avenue #13,
Sacramento, CA 95833-1945
Tel: 866-487-8444, 530-662-5799; FAX: 530-662-1923
E-mail: general@fundtracksoftware.com;
WWW: http://www.fundtracksoftware.com

► Their donor tracking software is written in today's most popular database product, Microsoft's Access®. They are the developer of the PhilanthrAppeal 2000+® Fund Raising and Donor Management software package. Features include comprehensive constituent tracking; volunteer tracking; grantsmanship; gift handling (gifts can be divided into unlimited fund accounts and campaigns); System Report Wizard (over 100 built-in reports); system report data can be exported as delimited or HTML (Internet) formats; build ad hoc searches and reports with their add-on report writer; Mailing Wizard (over 80 built-in mail queries to simplify your job); campaign tracking; fund budget tracking; unlimited group segmentation; and multiple address selection. Report Maker 2000+ (custom report generator designed to work with Microsoft Access 97® and Microsoft Access 2000® enables you to build custom searches and automatically build reports based on the searches) and more. A demonstration version of PhilanthrAppeal 2000+ can be downloaded from their Web site. A free fully functioning evaluation CD of PhilanthrAppeal 2000+® is available as well. Pricing for PhilanthrAppeal 2000+® Donor Management Software Package varies for Access 2000 and Access 97 versions and the number of concurrent users accessing the software. These prices plus prices for other software and services related to PhilanthrAppeal 2000+ are available on their Web site.

Granite Bear Development (GBD)

P.O. Box 1489, Columbia Falls, MT 59912-1489
Tel: 800-364-7953, 406-892-0087, 417-885-0990;
FAX: 303-265-9235
E-mail: info@granitebear.com; WWW: http://www.granitebear.com/

▶ Founded in 1992 from a part-time consulting firm started in 1985, it distributes DonorBase, a Windows-based fund-raising management database system for nonprofit organizations development professionals. It keeps track of donors, prospects, pledges, gifts, and funds. Queries, reports, and mail merges are customizable by the user. It is an open-architecture application that maintains an extensive demographic profile, pledge recording and tracking, gift entry, complete giving history, unlimited list management, and integrated mail/contact files. Key benefits include: manages donors, prospects, pledges, gifts, multiple funds; customizable queries, reports, mail merges, label printing, and more; open architecture solution based on Microsoft Access; currently available for Microsoft Access 2.0 (comes with a "runtime version" so you don't have to have a copy of Access), runs on Windows 3.x, Windows 95, Windows 98, Windows NT, with free upgrades and support for one year after purchase. Annual subscriptions are available to extend these benefits after the first year.

Harvey & Associates, Inc.

1160 Lakeview Court, Lake Geneva, WI 53147

10222 West College Avenue, Hales Corners, WI 53130
Tel: 265-245-2680; FAX: 265-245-2688
E-mail: sjhavey@aol.com;
WWW: http://members.aol.com/_ht_a/cms4ts/cms4ts/

▶ This firm distributes Campaign Management Systems software for multiyear and annual pledge campaigns. Campaign Management Systems provides you with the data needed to organize and track prospects and volunteers, project cash flow, and record pledges and payments, and provides numerous reports for keeping the decision makers up-to-date on the campaign. Features include quick entry batch processing; detailed prospect screens; numerous sort possibilities utilizing categories and groups; customized fields; unlimited fund account setup (both annual and multiyear pledge); volunteer tracking; pledge and payment data entry; payment collection utilizing reminder notices; auto alerts for reports and payment collection; named/memorial gifts program; restricted gifts program; matching gifts program; create relationships between prospects; donor giving history tracking (annual and multiyear); export data capability to word processing and spread sheets; and flexible report generator.

Heritage Designs, LLC

Mailing address: P.O. Box 10779, Phoenix, AZ 85064-0779

Office address: 5125 North 16th Street, Suite C-134,
Phoenix, AZ 85016
Tel: 602-996-7005, 800-752-3100; FAX: 602-265-6688
E-mail: info@matchmaker2000.com;
WWW: http://www.matchmaker2000.com/

▶ Heritage Designs is the developer of MatchMaker 2000, results-oriented fund-raising/donor management software package. It provides flexibility to manage all gifts including contributions, multiyear pledges, tributes, in-kind contributions, memberships and special events, and corporate matching gifts. Matchmaker 2000 provides unlimited capacity to maintain donor attributes and to track and analyze donors' contribution patterns and interests. A note system allows for the preservation of appropriate personal information about each donor that is accessible from all screens of MatchMaker 2000. Features include five security levels to protect sensitive information; multilevel query capability; accommodates individuals, corporations, foundations, and government entities; extensive set of reports, many of which can be modified by selection of variable codes and dates; gift and pledge management for multiple funds and campaigns; tracks in-kind contributions, matching gifts, and gifts in tribute; event management; membership and volunteer program management; and more.

Institute for Charitable Giving

500 North Michigan Avenue, Chicago, IL 60611
Tel: 800-234-7777; FAX: 312-222-9411
E-mail: charity@pop.wwa.com;
WWW: http://www.philanthropymatters.com/

▶ The Institute is the developer and distributor of Moves Management software, a tool for implementing both a prospect and a donor program. The Moves Management™ template is designed to help fund raisers manage and improve the relationship-building activities that are the basis of successful major and planned gift programs. In addition to the comprehensive "contact management" screen, there are eight screens designed precisely to apply Moves Management principles to any fund-raising program. It is designed to improve the effectiveness and efficiency of generalists, as well as those who specialize in major and planned gifts, all in an easy to use Windows 95/98/NT version. The system includes a comprehensive planning module for both cultivation initiatives and solicitation visits. There are planned giving donor recognition and corporate/foundation information elements. It includes software, manual, and support for one year.

Features include contact and action planning; strategic tracking for your donors and prospects (individuals, corporations, and foundations); coordination of individual, corporate, and foundation prospects and donors; call reports; tickler alerts and warning signals; prospect ratings; a design for donor upgrading; prospect and donor classifications; activity and results review; and fund raiser–friendly reports by prospect, worker classification, capability, or any combination. It works with all popular word processing systems to produce letters, notes, and other donor-winning communications. It lets you ask for the right gift, at the right time, by the right person.

Intrepid Systems, Inc.

701 Galer Street, Suite 504, Seattle, WA 98109
Tel: 800-952-8228, 206-270-1050; FAX: 800-533-9218
E-mail: Info@IntrepidSystems.com;
WWW: http://www.intrepidsystems.com/

▶ Intrepid Systems has been providing fund-raising management software since 1991. It develops, markets, and distributes DonorQuest Fundraising Management Software for Windows. DonorQuest for Windows is fund-raising software used for tracking donors, donations, pledges, linkages between donors, and so on. It supports in-kind gifts such as volunteer hours. Soft credits and matching gifts are supported. A demonstration program can be downloaded. Pricing information is available online.

JSI FundRaising Systems, Inc.

44 Farnsworth Street, 7th Floor, Boston, MA 02210
Tel: 800-521-0132, 617-482-9485; FAX: 617-482-0617
E-mail: frs@jsi.com; WWW: http://frs.jsi.com/

4732 Longhill Road, Suite 2201, Williamsburg, VA 23188
Tel: 800-574-5772
E-mail: millen@jsifrs.com; WWW: http://www.jsifrs.com/millennium

▶ JSI FundRaising has been providing software and services to a diverse range of nonprofit organizations since 1978. They offer two products (Paradigm, Millennium, and Donor$) to provide the nonprofit community a range of choices that vary in terms of technology, sophistication, and price. They maintain an operation for Paradigm in Boston and for Millennium in Williamsburg, Virginia. Together, these groups support a client base of 2,500. Millennium, released in 1991, has become the product of choice in some of the nation's most sophisticated development operations. The typical Millennium client has a staff of 25 to 300 and needs software to manage $100M campaigns. Recognizing that thousands of organizations did not have the need or means to support a product such as Millennium, they developed Paradigm. Released in 1995, Paradigm provides a cost-effective, easy-to-use solution.

KMA Interactive

12001 Central Expressway, Suite 790, Dallas, TX 75243-3788
Tel: 800-562-5150 (Sales Group), 972-560-7070;
FAX: 972-560-7071
E-mail: dthielker@kmainteractive.com (David Thielker, Sales);
WWW: http://www.kmssoftware.com/

▶ KMA distributes Donor ResponseAbility, a software product for capturing, organizing, managing, and analyzing valuable donor information quickly and easily. It will track and record unlimited details about the giving patterns of each individual donor, then produce comprehensive reports by segment to focus on specific donor groups. As part of their service, you receive full technical support with any purchase of a KMS software system. This service includes your initial training with the choice of instruction on-site at your location or in regularly scheduled classes at KMS. They also provide installation support to ensure the system is up and running smoothly. Once you are operational, you have unlimited telephone access to ongoing support.

KTS Systems Group

Concorde Gate, Suite 501, North York, Ontario, M3C 3N6
Canada
Tel: 416-449-4495; FAX: 416-449-4496
E-mail: info@kts.com WWW: http://www.kts.com/

▶ The Not-for-Profit Division develops and markets fund-raising systems for charities, foundations, hospitals, and academic institutions, as well as for the management of community centers. KTS is the distributor of giftTRAQ, a fully integrated management tool based on Windows and client/server technology that links all aspects of managing a modern fund-raising organization, including donation management, pledge maintenance, in memoriam processing, event management, canvasser control, project costing, demographics, endowment and planned giving and membership maintenance. giftTRAQ does more than just keep track of donors. Ultimately, it provides the ability to manage the donor pyramid and cultivate prospects through sophisticated relationship management software. Not-for-profit solutions from KTS are installed across North America in a broad range of client sites, from single organizations to large national and multidivisional operations maintaining large databases. KTS also distributes Top Giver (acquired from Hewitt-Anderson Corporation), the campaign and management software designed especially for United Way organizations. Top Giver Professional runs under Windows 95/98 and Windows NT/2000. Features include: Campaign Account Management; Accounts Receivable; Agency Designations and Allocations; Volunteer Management; and Built-in Report Writer. In addition, they are the creators of Rainbow Software, a leading software technology available for United Ways. Top Giver Professional is a comprehensive flexible tool designed to manage donor accounts, receivable, billing leadership givers, and donor choice. Top Giver Professional includes most everything needed to run a United Way campaign, including campaign account management, accounts receivable, agency designations and allocations, volunteer management, and a built-in report writer. The software supports multiple campaigns, unlimited numbers of donor designations per campaign, hundreds of built-in reports, as well as other capabilities. Top Giver Professional is fully supported with technical support and program updates.

LEV Software

Tel: 800-776-6538
E-mail: info@levsoftware.com, lev@bellsouth.net;
WWW: http://www.levsoftware.com/synlev.htm

▶ Synagogues, schools, and organizations are invited to fundraise with LEV Software's Hebrew packages.

Linked Software

78 Lake Frankston, Frankston, TX 75763
Tel: 800-546-5966 (Sales), 903-876-2224 (Support)
E-mail: linksoft@flash.net; WWW: http://www.linkedsoftware.com/

▶ The Membership Management System (MMS) from Linked Software is a universal membership and fund-raising software program for all nonprofits, clubs, churches, professional and trade associations, museums, country clubs, yacht clubs, health clubs, chambers of commerce, political organizations, fraternities and sororities, zoos, and many more.

LocalVoice.com

3265 17th Street, Suite 304, San Francisco, CA 94110
Tel: 415-522-1200; FAX: 415-522-1270
E-mail: info@localvoice.com;
WWW: http://www.localvoice.com/index.htm

▶ The LocalVoice.com suite of Web-based solutions uses the power of the Internet to help your organization build critical ties to your groups and communities. Not just a single solution, the LocalVoice.com product suite features five easy-to-use applications that give your organization the ability to engage communities via the web: Campaign Headquarters (create and manage online fund-raising campaigns; scalable to accommodate one or hundreds of campaigns simultaneously; users make secure credit card donations through your existing online presence; donation forms easily customized to match the look and feel of your Web site; provide an automatic return email/receipt for member tax records); E-mail Room (develop personalized e-mail campaigns that address individual interests of your community members; import existing lists of members from a variety of database programs; built-in filters to easily forward certain information to specific groups; field-based system allows for inclusion of individually oriented information; easily tracked to determine campaign effectiveness); Registrar (efficiently sign up members and register them for events and activities; easily managed forms permit capture of a wide variety of member information; customizable to include additional content such as maps, directions, and more; combined with e-mail, allows members to click through directly to registration sites); Polling Station (develop e-surveys that allow you to instantly learn the opinions of your community; capture data from members through your existing Web site; easily modify or add survey inquiries; variety of reporting functions provide instantaneous results); and Central Office (manage all your programs and community-provided information in one place; single location for administering all online fund-raising activity; password protected to manage access among several users; reporting available in several formats (Excel, HTML, flat file); intuitive interface for ease of use). An online demonstration of LocalVoice.com is available on their Web site.

MeadowBase

E-mail: francis@meadowbase.com (Francis Potter);
WWW: http://www.meadowbase.com/

▶ A free software, it is a customized database framework in Filemaker Pro (4.0 version 2 or higher) for single-site community organizations to manage their mailing list, contacts, donations, and other data. The Filemaker Pro files and a runtime application are both available for free for you to use, modify, and redistribute, following the terms of the GNU General Public License. Features include: keep the names and addresses of everyone connected to your organization in one centralized place: donors, volunteers, prospects, friends, and staff; generate mailing labels, merged letters, and reports quickly and easily from any computer in your office; track the history of your interactions with individuals and other organizations: donations, program participation, events, memberships, proposals and reports, and more; and quickly navigate through the information to find what you need, including name/address/phone data, current activities, historical information, and analysis. Technical support is provided online. Users of MeadowBase provide support to each other on an e-mail list. You can download MeadowBase online from their Web site.

Metafile

2900 43rd Street NW, Rochester, MN 55901-5895
Tel: 800-638-2445, 507-286-9232; FAX: 507-286-9065
E-mail Info@metafile.com; WWW: http://www.metafile.com

▶ Metafile has provided nonprofit software since 1985. They are the developer of Results/PLUS for Windows, a complete fundraising system designed to track prospects, donors, pledges, members, grants, gifts and solicitations. Results/PLUS returns in-depth analyses of giving trends, donors' lifetime values, solicitor performance, campaign and appeal performance, and much more. The product contains over 100 standard reports. For those organizations that have heavy event activity throughout the year, Events/PLUS for Windows, an add-on module to the Results/PLUS for Windows 5.0 software package, extends the capabilities of Results/PLUS by allowing you to set up and manage special events. They offer three levels of training.

PeopleSoft

6903 Rockledge Drive, Suite 1100, Bethesda, MD 20817
Tel: 301-571-5922; FAX: 301-581-2133

4460 Hacienda Drive, Pleasanton, CA 94588-8618
Tel: 925-694-4010
E-mail: rachel_cayelli@peoplesoft.com;
WWW: http://www.peoplesoft.com/

▶ PeopleSoft Advancement is an integrated and comprehensive software solution for philanthropic and nonprofit management. PeopleSoft Advancement supports all your fund-raising needs with eight functionally rich modules: Constituent Information, Gift and Pledge, Prospect Manager, Event Manager, Campaign Manager, Volunteer Manager, Membership Manager, and Planned Giving.

PowerNET Computer Systems Inc.

205 9th Avenue SE, Suite 199, Calgary, Alberta T2G 0R3,
Canada
Tel: 888-262-5130, 403-262-5100; FAX: 403-266-5829
E-mail: powernet@bowvalley.com;
WWW: http://www.powernetcalgary.com

▶ PowerNet is the developer of PowerOFFICE for fund raisers, an office automation system for nonprofit organizations. It records donations, donation status, tracks organizations, people, contacts, and provides reminders. It generates correspondence and electronically files documents. PowerOFFICE for fund raisers provides cash flows and online statistical reporting while allowing team access to information in the office, at home, or when traveling.

Professional Support Software

215 Humphries Drive, P.O. Box 901, West Plains, MO 65775-0901
Tel: 800-880-3454 (Sales), 417-256-4280; FAX: 417-256-6370
E-mail: mail@fundraiser-software.com (Gene Weinbeck,
Founder); WWW: http://www.fundraiser-software.com

▶ Founded in 1983, they are developers of the FundRaiser Family of Donor Management Software. The FundRaiser Family is a collection of three donor management programs for very small to medium-sized nonprofits. The products include: FundRaiser Basic (Windows and DOS), ideal for those new to computers or new to fund raising (or both); FundRaiser Jr for more sophisticated fundraising work (you can gather more information about your donors, then use that information to further personalize your letters and to better target your mailings); and FundRaiser Professional, an advanced level of fund raising. It includes modules for pledges, memberships, memorials, premiums, and the U.S. Postal Services's NCOA program. It can print USPS barcodes, has a tickler reminder system, and much more. Clients can also use an e-mail list to discuss the software.

Resource Management Software

1200 E. Woodhurst Drive, T200, Springfield, MO 65804
Tel: 417-887-9995; FAX: 417-887-9997
E-mail: lrfreund@aol.com (Larry Freund), wpgaut@aol.com (Bill Gaut); WWW: http://www.rmsoftware.com

▶ This firm distributes FundRaiser+™ software. FundRaiser+™, is a "vertically integrated" software package created because of a concern expressed by nonprofit organizations for an easy-to-use, powerful, yet reasonably priced program to manage fund raising records and automate many of the word processing and reporting chores associated with them. FundRaiser+™, handles an unlimited number of different giving levels or donor categories. It will handle an unlimited number of giving units, has flexible field definitions, calculates any type pledge (including varied frequency of giving), has a quick transaction entry screen for recording checks and gifts, powerful automatic, personalized letter writing system, integrates easily with Office, SmartSuite, or other applications, produces various "canned" standard reports for contributions, has an Open Custom Report Writer Engine for producing your own reports, produces pledge/giving report showing status of each giving unit, and produces receipt letter reminder complying with the IRS $250 rule. FundRaiser+™, is based on Foundation Open Database Technology.

Select Technologies

P.O. Box 959, Syracuse, NY 13201
Tel: 800-944-7277, 315-479-6663 (Marketing Specialist);
FAX: 315-471-2715
E-mail: sales@tickets.com;
WWW: http://www.select-info.com/product.html

▶ Fund Developer's Toolkit™ (FDT) was developed with tax laws and customer needs in mind, to incorporate the latest developments in fund-raising techniques and marketing practice. FDT provides membership management, links to other popular software, high data capacity, comprehensive reporting, automatic renewals, batch entry, and more. The system supports two to 2,000 users and accommodates two million or more members and donor files. Fund Developer's Toolkit is the fund-raising and membership module that is fully integrated with the ticketing and marketing functions of PASS. Features include: manage donors, members, and visitors from one database; generate membership reminders, renewals, confirmations and invoices; includes contact management, multiple pledge reminders, donor level analysis, corporate matching gifts, automatic renewals and more; and interface with Raiser's Edge.

Sherwood Systems Group

326 Heritage Drive, Sherwood Park, Alberta, Canada T8A 5R3
Tel: 780-467-0127; FAX: 780-467-2657
E-mail: rjohns@edmc.net; WWW: http://edmc.net/sherwood

▶ This group is the developer of Frequent-Funder software. Frequent-Funder maintains records about your donors, their donations and their pledges, as well as your volunteers and the work they have done. From these records, it can produce a great variety of reports, providing accurate and timely information about your donors, your finances, and your volunteers! Extensive mail-merge files are produced, and the software also prints all your tax and non-tax receipts. Split donations are supported, as well as designated donations. Donors and prospects can be easily classified into various demographic groups. It imports data in a number of formats, and exports it as well. The data you accumulate with this system

can be used in numerous other applications. Data is exported from the system so that donor data can be provided on diskette to bulk mailing houses in their preferred format. The software can be used with Windows 3.1x, Windows 95, or Windows 98, single-user or on a network. The system provides online help as well as an online manual. They also have other fund-raising programs, including their Door-to-Door system, used for the administration of door-to-door campaigns during which donations are solicited.

The Silent Partner

P.O. Box 1733, 617 Cherry Street, Sumas, WA 98295-1733
P.O. Box 633, Abbotsford, BC V2S 6R7 Canada
Tel: 604-852-3761
E-mail: info@silentpartner.ca;
WWW: http://www.silentpartner.ca/

▶ This firm distributes The Silent Partner, a fund-raising software package (free demo available) to help nonprofit organizations, charities, schools, colleges, foundations, churches, and radio stations with donor tracking, donation tracking, and pledge tracking. Features include donor tracking and reporting; convenient and fast donor entry; flexible donor coding and linking; printing receipts your way on demand; reprinting lost or misplaced receipts; preauthorized payment (PAP) plans; customized bank notification for PAP plans; appointment scheduler, notepad, and calculator; management and tracking of capital campaigns; and powerful and versatile list segmenting tools. It includes a 120-page manual.

Social Ecology, Inc.

1818 Summit, Seattle, WA 98122
Tel: 800-485-8170, 206-726-0047
E-mail: info@socialecology.com;
WWW: http://www.socialecology.com/products/dl/

▶ This firm is the developer of DonorLink IT, a web-based fundraising tool. DonorLink IT brings together and manages contacts, database, e-mail, and Web forms into one communication system. DonorLink IT combines elements of database and e-mail programs with web-based forms. A DonorLink IT administrator can create groups, send individual and mass personalized electronic mailings, accept donation data from major online giving sites, and create Web forms for gathering data through the Web, all without any specialized technical knowledge or training. Features include: Form Letter feature for writing, storing. and retrieving e-mail message forms for donor mailings; Web form that allows donors to fill out and submit forms to you via the Web (donors can update their own profile in your database); automatic notification of the receipt of contributions allowing you to reply with a personalized form letter; multiple criteria searches; contact groups can be created based on shared interests; and more.

SofterWare Inc.

540 Pennsylvania Avenue, Suite 200, Fort Washington, PA 19034
Tel: 800-220-4111, 215-628-0400; FAX: 215-628-0585
E-mail: info@softerware.com, info@donorperfect.com;
WWW: http://www.softerware.com

▶ This company is the distributor of DonorPerfect (see also listing for Starkland Systems). They have also established a partnership with Conscious Change, provider of the Donate.net Web-based fund-raising solution. The partnership will allow DonorPerfect clients to add online giving to their existing Web site with virtually no effort or expense. In addition, users of DonorPerfect will be able to quickly and easily download online gift transactions into their existing donor records. SofterWare and ECHO Management Group have formed a partnership under which SofterWare has assumed responsibility for supporting and marketing the TargetOne Fundraising System (TargetOne offers exceptional donor tracking and campaign management capabilities, a streamlined data-entry system, powerful reporting tools, and extensive mail merge functions. It handles donations, memberships, special events, foundation activities, and capital campaigns). Their agreement with ECHO provides programs for users of TargetOne to migrate to DonorPerfect. United Way clients are being offered special plans for migrating to Top Giver Software, a leader in specialized solutions for United Way Organizations.

SofTrek
2350 North Forest Road, Suite 10A, Getzville, NY 14068
Tel: 800-442-9211; FAX: 716-636-5401
E-mail: info@pledgemaker.com, jschultz@pledgemaker.com (John Schultz); WWW: http://www.pledgemaker.com
▶ Founded in 1987, they are providers of Oracle-based fundraising software for Windows and the World Wide Web. They are creators of PledgeMaker® Fund Raising Software, a comprehensive fund-raising system. PledgeMaker for Windows and the World Wide Web is designed to serve organizations with unlimited workstations, large databases, and sophisticated processing needs. Features include automated receipt/thank yous, billings, and premiums; customized giving clubs and recognition; pledge schedules; high-speed batch entry; relationship tree with hyperlink; shared addresses; corporate and foundation data; global updating; advanced security; contact history and tickler reports; E-mail, word processing interfaces, and paperclips; and matching gifts and soft credits. PledgeMaker is available in two versions: a Windows-based installed version and as PledgeMaker On-line™, a Web-based version accessible with a Web browser through the Internet. Optional modules provide increased functionality to meet individual organizational needs. A demonstration of PledgeMaker® can be viewed on the Web by first downloading a plug-in to run the demonstration in your browser. Clients include all types of nonprofits—hospital foundations and religious, human service, cultural, and political organizations.

Starkland Systems
3327 Freeman Street, San Diego, CA 92016
Tel: 800-748-6639, 619-696-7864; FAX: 619-696-1487
WWW: http://www.donorperfect.com/
▶ Creator and owner of DonorPerfect, they provide sales, support and programming services for DonorPerfect users in California and Oregon. In 1987, Starkland designed DonorPerfect based on the input of hundreds of fundraising professionals. DonorPerfect is a comprehensive development software system that has helped thousands of diverse organizations communicate their message and raise more money. DonorPerfect will streamline operations, expand resources, and strengthen fund-raising effectiveness. A working evaluation version of DonorPerfect is available on the vendor's Web site. Features include unlimited biographical information; gift and pledge management; receipts and acknowledgments; e-mail–enabled and other Web features; targeted mailings; comprehensive reports and analysis; membership management; volunteer coordination; relationships and affiliations; employer match pro-

grams; memorials and honorariums; special-event management; prospect research; major donor cultivation; capital campaigns; alumni tracking; grant requests; mailing house interfaces; import and export of data; and more. They offer training at your site or theirs. Other training options are seminars, phone instruction, and custom programming services.

StarSoft Technologies, Inc.
P.O. Box 10010, Spokane, WA 99209
Tel: 800-414-7990, 509-924-0814; FAX: 509-328-9835
E-mail: jackgordon@starsoft.com (Jack Gordon),
starsoft@starsoft.com (Technical Support);
WWW: http://www.starsoft.com/
▶ StarSoft is the producer of DonorWorks 5.0, a donor and prospect tracking, gift management program for Macintosh and Windows. Features include donor profiling; gift and pledge management, all the way through capital campaign tracking and major donor cultivation; and more. It tracks your donors' demographic information, relationships, contacts, volunteer abilities, giving histories, unlimited groups, classifications and 100+ user-defined fields. There are multiple ways to subset data for intelligent reporting and analysis. It includes a special events module, volunteer tracking, 300+ reports, a planned giving module, store scanned photographs in records for directories, custom report generator and a built-in word processor, spreadsheet, mapping program, CASS, and more. StarSoft Technologies offers support and training services plus data conversion services and custom programming to add specific additional functions to DonorWorks. A demonstration version of DonorWorks can be downloaded from the vendor's site. They also produce ChurchWorks 5.0, a church management and gift tracking program for Macintosh and Windows. It tracks demographics, relationships, contacts, volunteers, abilities, interests, renewals, alumni, and so on, and automates gift entry, receipting, reports, pledges, and more.

Straight Forward Software
P.O. Box 65317, Burlington, VT 05406-5317
Tel: 802-865-0480; FAX: 802-865-0480
E-mail: 102024.2545 @compuserve.com, TimnaGenz@aol.com
▶ LifeLine Non Profit Management System, Version 5, lets you manage up to a million constituents. For each constituent, record thousands of donations, pledges, memberships volunteer hours/ activities, print reports and custom list, print mailing labels in many formats, do merges for personalized mailing, and export in six formats to most other software. It includes a 180-page manual.

Summit Software Corporation
232 Goldfinch Turn, Newark, DE 19711-4112
Tel: 302-454-0839; FAX: 302-454-1976
E-mail: sales@summit-ware.com;
WWW: http://www.summit-ware.com/
▶ Summit is the distributor of Easy Gift, a comprehensive fundraising package for small to medium-sized nonprofit organizations. Easy Gift allows users to track dozens of facts about each donor or prospect, as well as their complete donation, contact, and mailing history. This stored information enables the creation of targeted mailings, solicitor assignments using common interests, relationships with donors and prospects, and customized presentations for individual donors. Features include multiple addresses and phone

numbers; pledge and donation history; e-mail and Web site addresses; family information; mailing and contact history; extensive notes; profiles for individuals and organizations; contact management; giving potential; annual and capital campaigns; statistical analysis; thank-you letters, and pledge reminders; memorials and honorariums; general ledger account assignments; multiple reports and graphs; and more. Easy Gift incorporates extensive help facilities named *The Helping Hand* that guides users through the use of the software.

SunGard BSR, Inc.

1000 Winter Street, Suite 1200, Waltham, MA 02451
Tel: 781-890-2105; FAX: 781-890-4099
E-mail: info@sungardbsr.com, sales@sungardbsr.com;
WWW: http://www.sungardbsr.com/

▶ SunGard BSR, Inc. supports the advancement efforts of not-for-profit organizations in higher education, health care, religion, social services, and the arts. They develop software and services for optimal constituent management, telefundraising, and event management. They also offer superior consulting, training, and outsourcing services. Their client list numbers more than 140 major institutions worldwide and their user group, the largest of its kind in the advancement field, provides a rich source of knowledge for members. BSR offers a variety of software products for advancement, including Advance (their premier product—it is the core of what they do: the management of data to help organizations build relationships with their constituents); The Special Events System (helps organizations manage and track a diverse range of events, including reunions, seminars, luncheons, travel programs, and sporting events); SmartCall (provides sophisticated telefundraising as well as calling capabilities for invitations, admissions, and stewardship). Both the Special Events and SmartCall systems can be used as "stand-alone" applications as well as optional add-ons to Advance, which has three other optional subsystems: Membership/Dues for managing dues-paying organizations; Web Access for remote and traveling staff and volunteers; and Web Community for online giving and directory information

Synergy Development Systems

11440 Okeechobee Boulevard, Suite 206,
Royal Palm Beach, FL 33411
Tel: 800-352-0312; FAX: 800-320-3256
E-mail: sales@denarisoft.com; WWW: http://www.denarisoft.com/

▶ Begun in 1994, Synergy is one of the premier vendors serving the nonprofit sector, with 100% of all products and services developed for the nonprofit community. Synergy serves over 450 nonprofits with the Denari product line of fund-raising software. They have developed three Fundraising Software products to meet your needs: DenariOnline, Denari2000, and Denari Client Server. Each is filled with innovative features that will reduce your data entry time, organize your donors to assist in targeted mailings, provide timely and accurate management and analysis reports, as well as receipts and reports that will keep your donors well informed. Denari 2000 for Windows (the ultimate in fundraising software for Windows. Robust features and expandability make this the perfect application for Windows 95/98/ME/NT/2000; Denari Online for the Web (access your data from anywhere. This feature-rich ASP runs in your Web Browser and is the perfect solution for small to large fund-raising organizations. Compatible with Windows 95/98/ME/NT/2000); Denari Client/Server (for large organizations,

their thin client application server will make short work out of even the largest networks. Centralize your data, and lessen administrative headaches with this intranet and Internet-compatible solution powered by MS SQL7).

Systems Support Services

8848-B Red Oak Boulevard, Charlotte, NC 28217
Tel: 800-548-6708; FAX: 704-522-8842
E-mail: sales@donor2.com (Steve Eshleman);
WWW: http://www.donor2.com/

▶ Since 1984, Systems Support Services has been providing software and support to nonprofit organizations nationwide. They are producers of Donor2 and Donor2 Enterprise, a comprehensive fund-raising software solution that manages all aspects of your development program, and features additional modules for prospect research, special events, volunteer tracking, planned giving, membership, alumni, and others. Features include donor management, gift management, fund-raising management, reporting/evaluation, and mail management. Donor2 also offers a fund accounting package that integrates with Donor2 and Donor2 Enterprise, and includes modules such as System Manager, General Ledger, Payroll, Accounts Payable, Bank Reconciliation, and others.

TMA Resources

World headquarters: 8201 Greensboro Drive, Suite 900,
McLean, VA 22102
Tel: 888-878-TMAR, 703-847-2800; FAX: 703-847-2899

1419 Lake Cook Road, Suite 300, Deerfield, IL 60015
Tel: 847-317-0900; FAX: 8470317-0955
E-mail: lingner_karen@tmaresources.com (Karen Lingner, National Marketing Coordinator); WWW: http://www.tmaresources.com

▶ Formed in 1996, they are a single-source provider of Association Management Software products and services. They distribute TIMSS RevUP fund-raising software to target markets more precisely. TIMSS RevUP tracks both hard and soft gifts, contributions of all types, and pledges by campaign, company, or individual, plus builds the donor history you need to keep improving your campaigns (Win 95/98 & NT/Unix or NT). For use by organizations involved in fund raising for: Capital Campaigns, Grants, Political Action, Research, and more. TIMSS RevUP was created in compliance with the FASB rules for nonprofit organizations, and has been tested and performance optimized for all types of organizations, including nonprofit organizations, trade associations, professional societies, labor unions, colleges, universities, hospitals, theaters, political groups, civic centers, and others. End-user benefits include the ability to track campaign activity; build donor profiles and history; create campaign teams and track solicitor activity; track contributions, gifts, and giving trends; and link events to campaigns.

TRAC (Technology Resource Assistance Center), Inc.

610 Cowper Avenue, Suite 1807, Palo Alto, CA 94301
Tel: 800-676-5831; FAX: 650-853-1677
E-mail: info@tracworld.com (Pam Hild);
WWW: http://www.tracworld.com,
http://www.tracworld.com/resources/links.html

▶ TRAC, Inc., has been developing fund-raising software since 1986. TRAC's software programs are available for Windows (Exceed!), Macintosh (MacTRAC), and for the Web with features such as donor tracking, gift management, electronic funds transfer, online gifts, volunteer scheduling, grant tracking, grant giving, mailing list management, contact management, intuitive reporting, automated mail merge, import/export, detailed giving history, easy reporting, contact management for major donors, grant tracking and special events, excellent technical support, and a variety of training options.

Target Software, Inc.

1030 Massachusetts Avenue, Cambridge, MA 02138
Tel: 617-583-8500; FAX: 617-354-0895
E-mail: info@targetsite.com (Elayna R. Bittner, Marketing Associate); WWW: http://www.targetsite.com

▶ Target Software was conceived in 1992 to create a sophisticated, integrated, state-of-the-art fund-raising application for large not-for-profit organizations. It is developer of Team Approach, client/server, a graphical user interface (GUI), Oracle-based fund-raising application. It is designed specifically to manage databases above 100,000 donors. Some of its primary features are: Constituent Management; Marketing and Benefit Programs; Gift and Pledge Management; Membership; Planned Giving; Corporate and Foundation Giving; Contact Management; Customer Service; Event Management; Volunteer Management; Queries and Outputs; Reports; and Production Scheduler.

TechRocks!

One Penn Center, 1617 John F. Kennedy Boulevard,
Philadelphia, PA 19103
Tel: 215-561-3608
E-mail: info@techrocks.org; WWW: http://www.ebase.org,
http://www.techrocks.org/ebase/index.lasso

▶ This company distributes ebase, an integrated database template for nonprofits that want to effectively manage interactive communications with their members, donors, and citizen activists. Using ebase, an organization can increase its capacity to conduct effective fundraising and constituency outreach campaigns. Based on FileMaker Pro® for Windows or Macintosh, ebase is easy to learn, use, and customize, making it a good choice for organizations that have no staff trained in database design or management. Originally developed by Desktop Assistance, a nonprofit group in Helena, Montana, it is a free database program that allows charities to keep track of such information as how much money donors have contributed to the group, the topics on which activists want information, and how people prefer to be contacted. Nonprofit groups can also e-mail members and donors directly from the program. It lets you keep all your organization's data, such as memberships, donations, and activist information, in one place, and provide secure, easy-to-learn access to everyone who needs to use it. You can use it to send e-mail directly from your database, merging data in the text of an e-mail message to personalize communications; and you can customize your database to make it match the unique and changing needs of your organization. It can be downloaded free, but to make modifications to the database, charities must own FileMaker Pro.

Viking Systems Inc.

236 Huntington Avenue, Boston, MA 02115
Tel: 800-23-VIKING; FAX: 617-425-0009
E-mail: info@vikingsys.com, rfrench@vikingsys.com;
WWW: http://www.vikingsys.com/

▶ A pioneer in the development of client-server and relational database technology for fund raising, it is the producer of the Viking Development System, a full-featured development system for fund raising and membership. It will help you to automate all of your fund-raising activities, including tracking and managing of constituents, organizations, prospects, proposals, campaigns and funds, financial accounts, gifts and pledges, planned gift tracking, stewardship activities, events, and membership payments. It also has a built-in Query Processor and Report Writer. Clients include schools, colleges, and universities of all sizes in the United States and Canada; nonprofits of all types, including large urban medical centers and radio stations; and membership organizations with chapters throughout the world.

Zoller Data Systems

7732 Goodwood Boulevard, Suite E, Baton Rouge, LA 70806
Tel: 504-928-7169

▶ The Zoller Donor/Member System combines donor records, database management, and office automation. The software includes gift and pledge processing, dues, database analysis and segmentation, mass mailing, correspondence control, direct mail, campaign, event and motivation reporting, matching gifts, grants, credit card and EFT processing, major donor prospecting with biographic/demographic data and solicitor tickler files, volunteer and underwriting management, premium inventory, telemarketing, planned giving, soft dollar accounting and payroll deductions with integrated word processing, spreadsheet, graphics, time scheduling, e-mail, and FAX-mail. Integrated fund accounting, budgeting, auction, program scheduling traffic control, and ticket sales support are also available.

Grant Research

The Canadian Directory to Foundations and Grants

Canadian Centre for Philanthropy, 425 University Avenue,
Suite 700, Toronto, ON M5G 1T6, Canada
Tel: 800-263-1178, ext. 221, 416-597-2293
WWW: http://www.ccp.ca/directory/index.html

▶ This is a comprehensive source for foundation information in both print and electronic form. The Directory contains the most current and thoroughly researched foundation profiles and grant information on over 1,600 foundations that are actively granting in Canada. To help you succeed at foundation fund raising, your Directory includes a free copy of *Building Foundation Partnerships,* their best-selling foundation fund-raising resource manual.

Chronicle Guide to Grants

1255 Twenty-Third Street NW, Washington, DC 20037
Tel: 800-287-6072
WWW: http://philanthropy.com/grants/

▶ This is an electronic database of all corporate and foundation grants listed in *The Chronicle of Philanthropy* since 1995. Subscriptions are available for periods of one week to one year. There is a significant discount if you are also a subscriber to *The Chronicle of Philanthropy.*

IDI Magic Valley Technologies Corporation

P.O. Box 97655, Las Vegas, NV 89193-7655
Tel: 800-804-5270; FAX: 800-390-1315 (Purchase Orders)
E-mail: emil@idimagic.com (Emil S. Sotirov), fmr-info@fed
money.com; WWW: http://www.idimagic.com

▶ IDI is the distributor of Federal Money Retriever (FMR), a software package that helps people and organizations looking for federal grants and funding in general. It offers the most current information on 1,324 federal funding programs worth more than one trillion dollars in grants, loans, and other forms of assistance. FMR includes four components: FMR Pre-Application Wizard (easy step-by-step preparation and printout of professionally formatted preapplication documents); *FMR Guide to Federal Funding* (specific and easy-to-follow instructions on how to prepare your grant application); FMR Database (always up-to-date information on over 1,400 grant, loan, and other assistance programs offered by the U.S. federal government); and FMR Search and Report Tools (fully integrated graphical point-and-click set of searching and reporting instruments custom developed to correspond to the information in the FMR database). Registered users receive database updates as often as the government updates this type of information (usually twice yearly). The package comes complete with a printed manual that has useful chapters covering the basics of grant writing and federal grant application procedures and terminology. Easy-Help offers extensive explanation of federal funding terminology and procedures; names, phone numbers, and addresses for additional information; and a preview of the latest programs of special interest. Five smart indexes identify all funding sources matching your search criteria. You can search by applicants, beneficiaries, functional, or agencies. You can also enter your own keywords for a search.

Metasoft Systems

Suite 203, 1080 Howe Street, Vancouver, BC V6Z 2T1, Canada
Tel: 888-638-2763, 604-683-6711; FAX: 604-683-6704
E-mail: sales@bigdatabase.com; WWW: http://www.bigdata
base.com/bigonline.nsf/publish/welcome/

▶ Producer of BigOnline, a comprehensive and current source of Canadian and American fund-raising information for nonprofits and charities, providing critical information about more than 5,000 available funding sources. This resource that helps you find *new* sources of funding by providing in-depth corporate and foundation profiles, grant histories, government programs, executive biographies, contact information, sample winning proposals, daily news updates, and more.

Third Sector Innovations, Inc.

480 3¼ Road, Grand Junction, CO 81504
Tel: 800-406-7274, 970-434-7621; FAX: 970-434-0955
E-mail: thirdsec@gj.net; WWW: http://www.gj.net/~thirdsec/

▶ This company distributes the Grantmaster software package, which includes Windows disk, instructional manual, and toll-free computer support. In addition, they offer the Grantmaster Subscriber Service. This service is designed to maximize your effectiveness and success beyond writing the grant proposal. It includes the Grantmaster software package; quarterly newsletter with information on grant writing, grantsmanship, and other fund raising; and three hours each quarter of grant editing/critique or other selected technical assistance.

Grant Writing

Education Daily

Corporate headquarters: 200 Orchard Ridge Drive,
Gaithersburg, MD 20878
Tel: 301-417-7500; FAX: 301-695-7931

Distribution center: 7201 McKinney Circle, Frederick, MD 21701
Tel: 800-234-1660 or 800-638-8437, 301-698-7100 or
301-417-7543; FAX: 301-417-7650
E-mail: customer.service@aspenpubl.com;
WWW: http://www.educationdaily.com/pages/catalog/otherstuff.html,
http://www.educationdaily.com/pages/catalog/grantwrite.html,
http://www.educationdaily.com/pages/catalog/budgetwrite.html

▶ Education Daily distributes GrantWrite: A Step-by-Step System for Writing Grant Proposals that Win. This software program leads you step by step through each section of a proposal, explains its purpose, and tells you how to compose it. You get quick help to link various sections together to make a smooth, flowing document; express project budgets clearly and accurately; organize several proposals at the same time; copy elements of one proposal into another; train others to write winning proposals; and streamline every phase of the proposal-writing process, in Windows, DOS, or Mac versions. It also distributes BudgetWrite: A Comprehensive System for Developing Effective Project Budgets, a software program helps you prepare project budgets more quickly and easily. It's designed with built-in formulas and spreadsheets, so all you do is fill in the numbers and let the program do the calculations for you. You get a proven budget format that complies with federal grant application requirements and can be adapted for private-sector proposals too. You save time and avoid errors: copy information rather than rekey it, manage deadlines and schedules with the special calendar feature, save valuable notes and reminders for help with future budgets, and budget into the future with the five-year planner, in DOS, Windows, or Mac.

Grantmaster.com

8721 Oak Avenue, Orangevale, CA 95662
E-mail: Support@GrantMaster.com;
WWW: http://www.grantmaster.com/

▶ Grantmaster.com provides the tools you need to help yourself write quality proposals. They offer free grant/proposal resources; GrantMaster Guidebook with 3.5″ companion disk; subscriptions to the GrantWizard for Windows; On-line GrantMaster Wizard, a web-based proposal writer that teaches you as you enter data about your proposal; and complete four-hour reviews to ensure you get the most out of your proposal.

GrantWrite: A Step-by-Step System for Writing Grant Proposals that Win

Aspen Publishers, 200 Orchard Ridge Drive,
Gaithersburg, MD 20878
Tel: 800-847-7772, 301-417-7500; FAX: 301-417-7650
E-mail: customer.service@aspenpubl.com;
WWW: http://www.educationdaily.com/pages/catalog/grantwrite.html

▶ This software program leads you step by step through each section of a proposal, explains its purpose, and tells you how to compose it. You get quick help to link various sections together to make a smooth, flowing document, express project budgets clearly and accurately, organize several proposals at the same time, copy elements of one proposal into another, train others to write winning proposals, and streamline every phase of the proposal-writing process. It comes in Windows, DOS, and Mac versions. Highlights include: convert GrantWrite DOS proposals to the Windows format; copy and rename an entire proposal; search and replace text in a proposal section, including global replacement; print the Help text for "Using GrantWrite" and "Proposal Sections"; and print a draft copy of the compiled proposal before exporting it into a word processing program. Convert GrantWrite DOS proposals to the Windows format. It is based on the how-to book, *Writing Grant Proposals That Win!* In addition to proposal-writing instructions and examples found in the software package, the book explains the federal and private-sector grant review processes, the differences between them, and many other grant-seeking issues.

GrantWriter Professional

155 Calle Ojo Feliz, Suite W, Santa Fe, NM 87505
Tel: 505-983-1525; FAX: 505-983-0658
E-mail: admin@gwusa.net

▶ GrantWriter Pro is an affordable proposal planning and writing tool developed by professional grant writers to enable you to write fundable proposals. GrantWriter Pro was developed specifically for small to medium-sized nonprofits so that they have cost-effective means to write competitive proposals. GrantWriter Pro provides guidelines, examples, and outlines that illustrate each proposal component. The software is organized so you can choose which components to use to meet the criteria of each prospective donor. An extensive background section helps you to assemble the information needed to plan and document a successful proposal. A demonstration version of the package can be downloaded from the vendor's Web site.

Research Associates

P.O. Box 1755, Irmo, SC 29063-1755
Tel: 803-750-9759
E-mail: contact@grantexperts.com;
WWW: http://www.researchassociatesco.com/grant_software.htm

▶ This firm is the developer of GW Computer Express, a computerized grant-writing software. This computerized version of grant writing will take you through a series of detailed steps such as the problem statement, evaluation, and much more to help develop your grant proposal. Each part will start off with a brief description of the section and will then provide you with a series of questions and comments to guide your grant writing and keep you focused.

USCCCN International

P.O. Box 663, South Plainfield, NJ 07080-0663
E-mail: iaso@aol.com or uscccn@home.com;
WWW: http://hometown.aol.com/IASO/fgmr.index.html

▶ USCCCN is the distributor of *Grantwriting: A Hands-On Approach,* a grant proposal software writing tool complete with online manual for successful grant proposals for use on DOS, Windows, and Macintosh (hypertext included) computers. This electronic tutorial guides you step-by-step through the entire grant-writing process and helps you compose a persuasive, powerful proposal that introduces your agency or organization and its history to the prospective donor or grantor; clarifies the social need or problem; addresses the population(s) it will serve; defines outcomes you are aiming for upon completion of the proposed project within a specific time frame; outlines the plan of work, activities and staff

proposed, clarifying methods and, time-lining task; describes and summarizes program evaluation; illustrates the total project budget, in-kind donations, and grant amount request; outlines plans for future funding; and more. It is organized by eight proposal components, vital information that grantors and donors look for: Introduction; Social Problem Statement; Project Objectives; Methods and Work Plan; Evaluation Methods; Future Funding Plans; Budget; and Project Timeline. Each component has three sections: tutorial screens with specific guidelines on how to write that component; a "fill-the-blanks" template screen with a heading where you can write your proposal component; and checklists to proofread your writing.

Grants Management

Bromelkamp Company

106 East 24th Street, Minneapolis, MN 55404
Tel: 888-290-9087, 612-870-9087; FAX: 612-870-9616
E-mail: info@bromelkamp.com, henry@bromelkamp.com (Henry Bromelkamp, President); WWW: http://www.bromelkamp.com/ index.html, http://www.egrant.org/

▶ This is an information systems consulting firm for grant-giving organizations. They write and support integrated database and accounting software. They also help clients design and use our software to accomplish their goals. Bromelkamp is the developer of Egrant, which provides grant applicants an option to fill out an electronic application and submit the results via email or on diskette. A stand-alone Windows application, Egrant allows the applicant to complete a customized application from the grant maker and provides help and instruction throughout the process. Egrant can be sent to an applicant on a diskette, via e-mail, or as a download from your Web site. A slide show demonstration can be downloaded for further information about Egrant.

Easygrants

E-mail: info@easygrants.com;
WWW: https://www.easygrants.com/eg/grantseeker/gs_home.asp

▶ This tool makes it easy to apply for grants and fellowships. With easygrants.com, you can search and apply for multiple funding opportunities using one application. You can also set up a grant-seeker profile about yourself or your organization that will be made available to grant makers looking to invite candidates.

Grant Tracker®

E-mail: kendric@stanford.edu (Kendric C. Smith, PhD);
WWW: http://www.stanford.edu/~kendric/GT/

▶ It is a simple, commonsense bookkeeping program that allows grant recipients to keep track of the financial status of their grants, with up-to-the-minute displays of funds awarded, expense-to-date, commitments, balances, and personnel. The manual teaches how to set up the accounts and how to reconcile the accounts with the expenditure statement from your institution. Grant Tracker is free. This includes the Grant Tracker Manual and the Grant Tracker Software, which includes a sample data file for learning purposes, and empty preprogrammed files that are ready for you to enter the data for your grants. The current version of Grant Tracker works with Quicken 2000 (Intuit Inc.), a popular bookkeeping program, and is available for both Macintosh and Windows 95/98 and NT4.

Grant Proposal Tracking Software

CharityChannel, LLC, 30021 Tomas Street, Suite 300,
Rancho Santa Margarita, CA 92688
WWW: http://charitychannel.com/softshare/grant_download.htm

▶ This shareware application that runs in Access 97 and 2000 was developed by Andrew Grant for small offices specializing in foundation and corporate work. This software simplifies the process of tracking proposals. The application is on an "as-is" basis with no warranties, expressed or implied, by Andrew Grant and *American Philanthropy Review*. Users are allowed to modify the application to fit their individual needs. The use of the application is supported by a discussion forum on CharityChannel called GuestSoft. The application can be downloaded from the vendor's Web site. The shareware fee for Grant Proposal Tracking Software is $20. This fee is charged to support the CharityChannel discussion lists maintained by *American Philanthropy Review*.

PeopleSoft

6903 Rockledge Drive, Suite 1100, Bethesda, MD 20817
Tel: 301-571-5922; FAX: 301-581-2133
E-mail: rachel_cayelli@peoplesoft.com;
WWW: http://www.peoplesoft.com

4460 Hacienda Drive, Pleasanton, CA 94588-8618
Tel: 925-694-4010

▶ PeopleSoft Grants provides an integrated solution that organizes the entire scope of grants accounting and sponsored research administration—from proposal creation and submission to the seamless conversion of proposals to awards. Grants provides powerful award tracking, sophisticated facilities and administration processing, comprehensive bill generation, and the ability to create financial reports. Created in collaboration with a consortium of public and private universities, PeopleSoft Grants begins with real-world knowledge of the grants process, then applies PeopleSoft's expertise in creating integrated, easy-to-use management tools.

Grant Seeking

Easygrants

E-mail: info@easygrants.com;
WWW: https://www.easygrants.com/eg/grantseeker/gs_home.asp

▶ This tool makes it easy to apply for grants and fellowships. With easygrants.com, you can search and apply for multiple funding opportunities using one application. You can also set up a grant-seeker profile about yourself or your organization that will be made available to grant makers looking to invite candidates.

Major Gifts

(See also Planned Giving; Prospect Research)

Institute for Charitable Giving *(See Donor Management)*

Institutional Memory, Inc.

559 Solon Road, Chagrin Falls, OH 44022-3334
Tel: 440-247-2957; FAX: 440-247-7056
E-mail: lange@giftedmemory.com (Scott R. Lange, President);
WWW: http://www.giftedmemory.com

▶ This company is the developer of Gifted Memory software, an intuitive prospect management system to organize, track, and manage major gift donors, volunteers, and staff. It is available for Windows 32-bit operating systems. Clients include arts, civic, and cultural organizations; independent schools; universities; colleges; postgraduate schools; community colleges; and other nonprofit organizations. Features include: improves prospect research; provides on-line research profiles; aids solicitation planning; identifies relationships; tracks prospects, staff, and volunteers; increases productivity; enhances management capabilities; improves communication; and develops institutional memory. It is built for personal computers and networks. It is available for stand-alone (single computer, limited use); network (variable license agreements available); or remote (a synchronized database system for laptop computers and regional offices).

Matching Gifts

Blackbaud, Inc.

2000 Daniel Island Drive, Charleston, SC 29492-7541
Tel: 800-443-9441; FAX: 843-216-6100
E-mail: sales@blackbaud.com; WWW: http://www.blackbaud.com/products/showproduct.asp?F=FRPG&P=WMF

▶ This company is the distributor of MatchFinder software, which provides you with immediate online access to comprehensive information about corporate matching gift programs. MatchFinder's extensive database of matching gift companies, combined with the user-friendliness of the Windows interface, works with your prospect and donor records to help maximize your institution's potential for increasing matching gift dollars. More than just a database, MatchFinder allows you to determine which companies in your fund-raising database match gifts. You don't have to use other Blackbaud products to use MatchFinder. It works with any standard database.

Membership

Advanced Data Solutions

P.O. Box 714, Luray, VA 22835
Tel: 540-743-4910
E-mail: adv_data@shentel.net;
WWW: http://www.ads-software.com/mem_dir.htm

▶ Advanced Data Solutions is the developer of Membership Director, an application to track information about members of any type of association.

Linked Software

78 Lake Frankston, Frankston, TX 75763
Tel: 800-546-5966 (Sales), 903-876-2224 (Support);
FAX: 903-876-2860
E-mail: linksoft@flash.net;
WWW: http://www.linkedsoftware.com/mms.html

▶ Membership Management System version 5 by Linked Software is a full-featured, 32-bit program designed for maximum flexibility and user customization in managing membership and fund-raising information. Some of the features are unlimited funds and pledges, scheduled pledges, contribution statements, letters, postcards, honor/memorial processing, e-mail with embedded values, labels, phone dialer, attendance, appointments, automatic dues billing, accounts receivable statements and reports, automated bank drafts, spell checking (including e-mail), two easy-to-use report generators, unlimited member demographics and dates, and much more. No word processor is required for letters, postcards, and labels. The program is designed for maximum flexibility and user customization. A free demonstration copy of the software can be downloaded from the Linked Software Web site. The Membership Management System (MMS) from Linked Software is a universal membership and fund-raising software program for all nonprofits, clubs, churches, professional and trade associations, museums, country clubs, yacht clubs, health clubs, chambers of commerce, political organizations, fraternities and sororities, zoos, and many more.

Morant Information Systems

3343 Duke Street, Alexandria, VA 22314
FAX: 703-212-8244
E-mail: morant.com (Nonie Stages), bob@morant.com
(Bob Mossadeghi, President and CEO);
WWW: http://www.morant.com/master.html

▶ The company is primarily engaged in selling, installing, and supporting computer software to trade and professional associations, and other membership organizations throughout North America and Canada. Morant has developed and copyrighted an integrated suite of comprehensive software applications entitled AMPAC for operating and managing membership organizations. The company produces and sells these products directly to associations without distributors or other retailers. Strategic partnerships have been formed with industry-leading consultants, manufacturers, and developers of related products and services to provide total integrated systems for its clients. The AMPAC System is Morant's copyrighted association management software and the heart of each of Morant's client systems. Today, there are over 30 separate software application modules, completely integrated and available to associations, from which to select. Each module operates independently and provides stand-alone functionality, yet is integrated to operate with all other AMPAC modules through a single relational database. Of the separate modules, most are membership based and designed by Morant. The remaining modules are accounting modules and are integrated with your most popular accounting software systems. Morant maintains satellite offices in New York and Chicago.

Planned Giving

(See also Major Gifts; Prospect Research)

Crescendo Software—Planned Giving Marketing Software

Comdel, Inc., 1601 Carmen Drive, Suite 103,
Camarillo, CA 93010
Tel: 800-858-9154; FAX: 805-388-2483
E-mail: crescendosoft@hotmail.com, ardis@hotmail.com (Ardis
C. Schultz, Vice President/Marketing);
WWW: http://www.crescendosoft.com/

▶ Crescendo Interactive provides a full line of products and services to the planned giving professional that enhance productivity, create dynamic gift proposal presentations, and deliver donor and advisor gift options and explanations: Crescendo Pro for Windows 95/98/2000/NT is the most comprehensive system available. Complete with persuasive graphs, charts, calculations, and detailed explanations, Crescendo Lite is designed for the individual or

organization whose planned giving needs are less extensive than the comprehensive gift plan options of Crescendo Pro; Crescendo Plus helps you to create dynamic seminar presentations. Crescendo Estate focuses on the charitable tax planning concerns of the advisor (i.e., attorney, CPA, financial planner, or underwriter). Crescendo Presents software lets even the novice gift planning professional deliver compelling presentations. Crescendo Admin. helps you to organize and simplify administration of gift annuities. Its fully integrated tracking system produces checks to annuitants, year-end 1099Rs, numerous detailed reports, and more. Crescendo provides training seminars.

PG Calc, Inc.

129 Mount Auburn Street, Cambridge, MA 02138
Tel: 888-497-4970, 617-497-4970; FAX: 617-497-4974
E-mail: info@pgcalc.com; WWW: http://www.pgcalc.com/

▶ A major provider of software and services to the gift planning community in the United States. Their products include: Planned Giving Calculations (Planned Giving Manager and Mini Manager); Gift Administration (GiftWrap), Pooled Funds (Pooled Fund Organizer). Services include: Call-In Service for Gift Proposals; Annuity Reserves Report Services; FASB 116/117 Liabilities Report Service. They also offer seminars and list Internet resources on their website.

PhilanthroTec

10800-F Independence Pointe Parkway, Matthews, NC 28105
Tel: 800-332-7832; FAX: 704-845-5528
E-mail: info@ptec.com; WWW: http://www.ptec.com/

▶ This software company, founded in 1983, provides planned giving software and Internet solutions to the nonprofit and financial services sector. Products include PhilanthroCalc for Windows and PhilanthroCalc for the Web.

PlanGiv

Kingston, Ontario
Tel: 800-463-4854, 704-845-5527
E-mail: Service@PlanGiv.com; WWW: http://www.plangiv.com

▶ This company was founded in 1994 to provide resource materials for use in the marketing of planned giving programs. Their products include Gift Planning Assistant software, designed for use in preparing financial illustrations for donors of planned gifts; copy for educational brochures, newsletters, and other marketing pieces, which can be purchased by institutions and organizations that design and print their own materials; and *printed booklets* that organizations can purchase for distribution to clients and prospective donors.

Prairie Dog Software, LLC

6100 West 52nd Street, Sioux Falls, SD 57106
Tel: 605-376-5361
E-mail: PGSS1997@aol.com (Kirk Evenson, Operating
Manager); WWW: http://www.PrairieDogSoftware.com

▶ The Planned Giving Companion Calculation and report software for planned gifts.

Prospect Research

(See also Major Gifts; Planned Giving)

Institute for Charitable Giving *(See Donor Management)*

Prospect Information Network

501 North Grandview Avenue, Suite 203, Daytona Beach, FL 32118
Tel: 888-557-1326; FAX: 904-226-1154
E-mail: info@prospectinfo.com, dlawson@prospectinfo.com
(David Lawson); WWW: http://www.prospectinfo.com
▶ This organization founded by David Lawson in 1997 to create a service that would enable fund raisers to more efficiently identify and profile their share of today's new wealth. Products include Prospect ID and ProfileBuilder 2.5. They also offer training. Check their schedule at *http://www.prospectinfo.com/training/index.html.*

SunGard BSR Inc.

1000 Winter Street, Suite 1200, Waltham, MA 02451
Tel: 781-890-2105; FAX: 781-890-4099
E-mail: sales@sungardbsr.com; WWW: http://www.sungardbsr.com/
▶ SunGard BSR, Inc., supports the advancement efforts of higher education and other not-for-profit organizations. For more than 25 years, SunGard BSR has been dedicated to supporting the advancement efforts of educational and other nonprofit institutions in health care, religion, social services, and the arts. Their best-of-breed software and services help their clients create and sustain the relationships that make it possible to reach ambitious fund-raising goals. Their client list numbers more than 140 major institutions worldwide.

Target America

10560 Main Street, Suite LL17-19, Fairfax, VA 22030
Tel: 703-383-6905; FAX: 703-383-6907
E-mail: info@tgtam.com; WWW: http://www.tgtam.com/products.html
▶ Founded in 1995 to meet the rapidly changing needs of fund-raising professionals, the Target America database contains more than 4 million records of the wealthiest and most generous people in the nation, the top 5 percent in terms of income, assets, and philanthropic history. Ninety-four percent of the individuals on the database give more than $5,000 a year to charities. This exclusive database includes philanthropists, foundation trustees, private investors, individuals with income-producing assets of $250,000 to over $5 million, professionals with large private pension plans, executives of private companies with company financials, SEC insiders of publicly traded companies, luxury and estate property owners; and many more. You can access and use this data in several ways: screening programs; Prospect Management; and etarget (EasiTarget, Sherlock, Wealthknowledge).

Telephone Fund-Raising Software/Automated Calling Systems

Digisoft Computers, Inc.

369 Lexington Avenue, New York, NY 10017
Tel: 800-423-8862, 212-687-1810; FAX: 212-687-1781
E-mail: adavidson@digisoft.com; WWW: http://www.digtel.com/
▶ Founded in 1983, they are developers of Telescript, a call center management software. It uses graphical scripting, detailed real-time reporting, powerful predictive/super dialing, and an *open database design* featuring links to Access, SQL Server, Oracle, and many other ODBC-compliant databases. Clients include those in the areas of sales, political action, market research, telemarketing, collections, fund raising, lead generation, direct marketing, order entry, and more.

MoonFire Corporation

131 Hunters Cove Road, Mead, CO 80542
Tel: 970-535-9500; FAX: 970-535-0351
E-mail: tracyj@dialvision.com (Tracy Jones);
WWW: http://www.dialvision.com/,
http://www.dialvision.com/np_features.htm
▶ MoonFire developed the DialVision® Phonathon software in 1994 for nonprofit organizations such as colleges and universities. The software has also been implemented by traditional nonprofits. Organizations can use the software through traditional licensing, or they can rent the software over the Internet. It is being used for fund raising, student recruiting, alumni surveys, student retention, and random polling. They provide on-site planning and training services, as well as ongoing 24-hour 365-day support.

Portal Connect (Formerly EIS International Inc.)

555 Herndon Parkway, Herndon, VA 20170
Tel: 800-274-5676; FAX: 703-767-6720
E-mail: info@portal-connect.com; WWW: http://www.eisi.com/
▶ Portal Connect is the new company formed by EIS International, a leading provider of telephony contact center solutions, and SER Systems AG of Germany, a world-class supplier of knowledge management and e-business process automation. Portal Connect synergizes the EIS contact center expertise with the SER Internet and knowledge technology to deliver the next generation of business interaction management solutions. Their solutions anticipate customer needs and incorporate best practices from more than a decade of contact center and e-business experience, enabling organizations to seamlessly and intelligently manage their customer interactions by providing sophisticated contact management, workflow, and analytic software and hardware that add insight to every interaction.

Ruffalo CODY

221 Third Avenue SE, Suite 10, Cedar Rapids, IA 52401
Tel: 800-756-7483
E-mail: bshowalter@ruffalocody.com;
WWW: http://www.ruffalocody.com/
▶ They provide software, phonathon management, and telemarketing solutions for nonprofit organizations. They have combined the SUMMIT system for fund raising with their CAMPUSCALL® telemarketing system to create systems available to institutions of any size. They combine their suite of software products with their direct-marketing services and telemarketing management expertise. All software applications are backed by their 24/7 support services. They also provide both on-site and off-site telemarketing programs for nonprofit organizations. They make calls for over 250 institutions per year from one of their 15 call center locations.

Workplace Campaigns

BeechMere Associates, Inc.
3880 Ellendale Road, Moreland Hills, OH 44022-1124
Tel: 216-247-4392; FAX: 800-386-1042
E-mail: dlcobb@beechmere.com (David L. Cobb);
WWW: http://www.beechmere.com/

▶ BeechMere Associates, Inc., has developed a program specifically designed to support workplace campaigns for United Way, Community Share, or other charities. A DOS-based demonstration version of Workplace Campaign Manager can be downloaded from the vendor's site. Features of Workplace Campaign Manager include: supports multiple charities and donor choice; creates and tracks multiple report envelopes; tracks special events, agency speakers, and agency tours; tracks multilevel leadership giving; tracks up to five years of information; imports employee information from payroll or human resources systems; exports deduction information for payroll; optionally transfers donor choice and employee pledge information to United Way or charity funds; all functions are invoked from menus or pick lists; no codes or IDs are needed to access and update activities; provides 22 different reports that can be customized; supports local area networks.

Young-Preston Associates
P.O. Box 280, Cloverdale, VA 24077
Tel: 800-344-5701
WWW: http://www.youngpreston.com/

▶ Publishers of planned giving newsletters, booklets, brochures, and books for your own reading and for you to give to your donors.

GENERAL RESOURCES

General Interest (Strategies and Evaluation)

Achieving Excellence in Fund Raising: A Comprehensive Guide to Principles, Strategies, and Methods

HENRY A. ROSSO (THE JOSSEY-BASS NONPROFIT SECTOR SERIES, 1991)

▶ Rosso's essential guide for every successful fund raiser—covers the key elements of fund raising and explains the profession's major principles, concepts, and techniques. A comprehensive, authoritative volume written by and under the direction of Hank Rosso, one of America's most distinguished fund-raising professionals, this book provides a detailed guide to successful fund raising, explaining the profession's major principles, concepts, and techniques. The author demonstrates why fund raising is a strategic management discipline, and elucidates each step in the fund-raising cycle: assessing human and societal needs, setting goals, selecting gift markets and fund-raising techniques, soliciting new gifts, and encouraging renewals. It provides a conceptual foundation for the fund-raising profession, thoroughly examining its principles, strategies, and methods. Using practical examples, the author explains the reasoning behind the planning and selection of strategies for all fund-raising activities. In twenty-three original chapters, fund-raising professionals and faculty of the Fund Raising School bring to life the principles and techniques of the fund-raising profession. Resources including gift range charts, special solicitation tips, and readiness tests will help the student of fund raising convert abstract concepts into workable tools for effective fund raising. *Hardcover, 346 pages, $45.95*

Ask and You Shall Receive

KIM KLEIN (JOSSEY-BASS, 2000)

▶ Fund-raising expert Kim Klein has trained thousands of groups and individuals to cultivate assets that make good works possible. The *Ask and You Shall Receive* training package is a do-it-yourself, start-to-finish program on jump-starting fund-raising efforts. An essential component to this practical training package, the *Participant Manual* assumes no prior fund-raising experience from users and presents the easy-to-learn core competencies of fund-raising without specialized jargon. Participants will find worksheets and other hands-on instruments for developing and implementing a full-fledged fund-raising strategy for their organization or congregation. No mission-driven organization should be without this unique tool. This set of five Participant Manuals is now available at a discounted rate. *Softcover, 1 Leader's Guide (120 pages) + 1 Participant's Workbook (72 pages), $29.95*

Beyond Fund Raising: New Strategies for Nonprofit Innovation and Investment

KAY SPRINKEL GRACE (JOHN WILEY & SONS, 1997)

▶ Nonprofit fund raisers and managers are discovering that they need to develop fresh new visions of their nonprofits' missions and new strategies for connecting with a dedicated base of donors and volunteers. This book shows them how: by presenting a fund-raising model that links philanthropy, development, and fund raising. This book is a blueprint for building new donor organization relationships and explains how organizations can integrate fund-raising practices into the far more dynamic, comprehensive, and rewarding process of development. This book examines the common concerns of many nonprofits and presents model for fund raising that establishes a relationship between philanthropy, development, and fund raising. It includes forms, checklists, and flow charts to help readers better understand, visualize, and incorporate this new philosophy into their own nonprofit organizations. The author demonstrates that technique, no matter how sophisticated, is not enough. Too often, explains Grace, organizations persist in trying new fund-raising practices but fail to see they still lack the development framework to create a lasting base of donors. *Hardcover, 228 pages, $34.95*

The Board Member's Guide to Fund Raising: What Every Trustee Needs to Know About Raising Money (Jossey-Bass Nonprofit Sector Series)

FISHER HOWE (JOSSEY-BASS, 1991)

▶ This is a concise yet comprehensive resource for the entire fund-raising process. It shows why board members must take the lead in fund-raising efforts, and how this role can be personally satisfying. *Hardcover, 166 pages, $27.95*

Born to Raise

JEROLD PANAS (BONUS BOOKS, 1998)

▶ Fifty of the most respected fund raisers in the country share their secrets to success. Jerry Panas interviews and analyzes the traits and skills of great fund raisers—the best in the business. These interviews, along with a comprehensive survey of over 3,000 fund raisers, produce the most in-depth study of fund raising ever done. It shows you which qualities in fund raising are innate, which can be learned, and how to use this information right away. The findings are inspirational and controversial. A self-appraisal test helps you determine your fund-raising strengths and weaknesses (a self-test so unique we had it registered). Best of all, this test is an effective tool for CEOs and administrators when evaluating fund-raising programs and staff. *Hardcover, 228 pages, $40*

Building and Managing an Asset Base: Information and Advice for Nonprofit Organizations (New Directions for Philanthropic Fundraising #14)

JIMMIE R. ALFORD (JOSSEY-BASS, 1996) (SPONSORED BY THE INDIANA CENTER ON PHILANTHROPY)

▶ For any nonprofit organization, building and managing an asset base is a continual process that demands hard work and creative leadership rather than mere luck. The authors of this volume—nonprofit directors and fund raisers, as well as accountants, lawyers, and consultants who assist nonprofits—offer insightful, practical recommendations and real world examples of how to build and manage an asset base. Learn how any organization can develop a planned and deferred giving program and successfully present that program to potential donors. Get expert advice on the technical side of building and managing assets with updates on tax issues and investment strategies for maximizing income from endowment growth. Discover how to work effectively with intermediary agents such as trust and private banking officers, legal counselors, and community trusts to secure planned and major gift support. This sourcebook will serve as an invaluable tool for any nonprofit organization, whether it is an established institution with a multimillion-dollar budget or a grassroots agency looking to grow. *Softcover, 130 pages, $25.00*

CPR for Nonprofits: Creating Strategies for Successful Fundraising, Marketing, Communications and Management

ALVIN H. REISS (JOSSEY-BASS, 2000)

▶ In this practical guide, Alvin H. Reiss shows how dozens of organizations have developed creative strategies for tackling the real-life fund-raising, marketing, and management challenges that nonprofits face every day. This practical first aid kit for nonprofits shows how to use "CPR"—Challenge, Plan, Result—to find creative solutions to the challenges they face everyday. Reiss introduces a real challenge faced by a nonprofit, guides readers through the steps the organization took in developing a plan to meet the challenge, and then presents the result of the organization's plan. The book offers accessible, adaptable strategies for dealing with a broad spectrum of nonprofit concerns, such as increasing attendance at special events, stepping up board involvement in fund raising, and handling negative press. Throughout the book, Reiss poses the practical questions readers need to answer in order to apply the case study strategies to their own organizations' experience. *Softcover, 240 pages, $23.95*

The Complete Guide to Fund-Raising Management (Book & Disk Edition)

STANLEY WEINSTEIN (NSFRE/WILEY FUND DEVELOPMENT SERIES)

▶ A practical how-to book tailored specifically to the needs of professional and volunteer fund raisers, it moves beyond theory to address the day-to-day problems faced in these organizations, and offers sound advice and proven solutions. Stressing the importance of high-payoff, cost-effective fund-raising strategies, this book provides straightforward guidelines and step-by-step instructions on how to strengthen your not-for-profit organization and garner the resources needed to carry out its mission. Along with helpful suggestions on board development, institutional advancement, and volunteer involvement, this complete resource includes a disk that contains innovative prospect rating, call report, prospect tracking, and various other essential forms; sample fund-raising reports that focus on trends and emphasize the importance of monitoring net contributed income and other critical success factors; as well as innovative time management and board nominating grids. With incisive explanations of basic fund-raising principles and practices, as well as the fundamentals of strategic management, it shows how to oversee a comprehensive resource development program that focuses on planning, self-assessment, and continual improvement. Covering all the bases, it has complete details on managing the resource development function (analysis and planning, setting goals, and monitoring the budget); prospect ratings and evaluations

(determining the "ideal" volunteer solicitor, the capacity to give, and the request amount); grantsmanship (government contracts, foundations, project development, and foundation research); and capital and endowment campaigns (chronological steps for success, including prestudy, advancement, intermediate, and public phases). *Hardcover, 272 pages, $48.28*

Conducting a Successful Fundraising Program: A Comprehensive Guide and Resource

KENT E. DOVE (JOSSEY-BASS, 2001)

▶ Using the techniques that made his *Conducting a Successful Capital Campaign* so popular, Kent Dove, one of the nation's most successful and respected fund raisers, presents what is certain to become the standard handbook for the field. This must-have resource covers all the traditional elements of fund raising—including major gifts, direct mail, and donor appreciation—as well as the latest issues such as gift administration, technology, and the use of consultants in the solicitation process. *Hardcover, 720 pages, $69.95*

Coping with Cutbacks: The Nonprofit Guide to Success When Times Are Tight

EMIL ANGELICA AND VINCENT HYMAN (AMHERST H. WILDER FOUNDATION, 1997)

▶ Devolution—the shifting of money and power from federal to local governments—is here, it's real, and it's BIG. Estimates are that cuts to nonprofits may add up to $250 billion by the year 2002. This guide can help you deal with funding problems in a new way. It shows you how (and why) to shift your thinking from "How do we get more money to keep our nonprofit in business?" to "How do we involve other segments of the community to address community issues?" *Coping with Cutbacks* also includes a list of 185 short-term solutions collected from a variety of nonprofits. These strategies can be put to use right away to help you overcome short-term crises, manage change, and use your resources effectively. *Softcover, 128 pages, $20*

Critical Issues in Fund Raising (NSFRE/Wiley Fund Development Series)

DWIGHT F. BURLINGAME, ED. (JOHN WILEY & SONS, 1997)

▶ Many forces—from demographics to politics to business trends—shape the nonprofit sector and the practice of fund raising, but little attention has been given to the premises underlying many of the decisions fund raisers make in their daily professional lives. This book examines the impact of different factors on this growing and changing field. In *Critical Issues in Fund Raising*, highly respected practitioners and researchers address these issues and premises head-on. These contributors bring their vision, insight, study findings, and hard-won wisdom to bear in answering pivotal questions about the profession's future and revisiting some of its ongoing dilemmas. They examine hard data and reach well founded, often surprising conclusions on controversial topics such as formula versus nonformula fund raising, fund-raising cost ratios as a measure of efficacy, and the perceived scarcity of minority donors. They explore myriad topics of both immediate and long-term concern to the profession. Based on a think tank sponsored by the NSFRE in collaboration with the Counsel for the Advancement and Support of Education, the Association for Research on Nonprofit Organizations and Voluntary Action, and the Indiana University Center on Philanthropy, *Critical Issues in Fund Raising* offers up-to-date research on important issues, numerous ideas for improving and expanding fund-raising operations, and a generous portion of food for thought. *Hardcover, 256 pages, $45*

The Donor Bond
BARRY J. MCLEISH (THE TAFT GROUP, 1991)

▶ Apply these proven marketing and selling concepts to your fund raising efforts and watch your donor relationships flourish. A pro in the field details specialized strategies in direct marketing, public relations, and relationship marketing in easy-to-understand language. It covers the need for market research, the role of the CEO, and the importance of building strategies based on the needs of donors. *Hardcover, 173 pages, $12*

Earning More Funds: Effective, Proven Fundraising Strategies for All Non-Profit Groups, 3rd Revised Edition
CHIP BLASIUS AND RALFIE BLASIUS (BC CREATIONS, 1995)

▶ This practical, inspirational guide for nonprofit fund raisers covers dozens of topics from car washes to newsletters to grant-writing. It gives the reader a complete brainstorm-to-cleanup approach to fund raising as well as guidelines for successfully managing nonprofit organizations and volunteers. It provides the reader with the nuts and bolts of planning, managing, and marketing fund raisers and promoting their nonprofit organization. It provides the reader with proven techniques and strategies to manage all aspects of a nonprofit organization's fund-raising activities; develop your group's marketing skills (publicizing fund raisers, profiting from telemarketing, producing budgets and projections, cut costs with nonprofit and bulk mail permits, create newsletters with ads that can pay the bills, design compelling brochures, posters, etc.); discover little-known funding sources; pick lucrative fund-raising sales events; stage fun and profitable service fund raisers; and create fun and special events for money. Complete with 45 photocopiable worksheets and forms. *Softcover, $19.95*

The Five Strategies for Fundraising Success: A Mission-Based Guide to Achieving Your Goals
(Jossey-Bass Nonprofit and Public Management Series)
MAL WARWICK (JOSSEY-BASS, 1999)

▶ This entirely new approach to fund-raising strategy shows non-profits how to make mission-based decisions on what their fund-raising goals should be, and how to select, implement, and stick to the right strategies to meet those goals. Warwick introduces his revolutionary "Five Fundamental Fundraising Strategies" approach. The five strategies—growth, involvement, visibility, efficiency, and stability (GIVES)—are directly linked to specific fund-raising goals. This book shows readers how to choose a primary strategy that will drive both long-term fund-raising planning and day-to-day fund-raising activities. In this practical guide, fund-raising consultant Mal Warwick introduces an entirely new and revolutionary approach to fund-raising strategy and planning. He shows nonprofit organizations how to set fund-raising goals based on mission and how to select, implement, and stay with the right strategies to meet those goals. His five fundamental fund-raising strategies link directly to specific and appropriate fund-raising goals. The decision as to which strategy to use springs from the organization's mission, and all fund-raising activities are focused on fulfilling that mission. *Hardcover, 208 pages, $28.95*

Fund Raising 101 Deskbook
(SINCLAIR & TOWNES)

▶ This deskbook provides the ABCs for most areas of fund raising, including annual funds, capital campaigns, proposal writing, planned giving, prospect research, volunteer development, and more. For those new to the fund-raising field, this deskbook will help you gain the knowledge to be successful. *Fund Raising 101* will help strengthen your development program and your abilities as a development officer. In turn, you will be able to deal more confidently with your staff, volunteers, and donors. *Softcover, $95*

Fundraise Painlessly: How to Earn More Funds
CHIP BLASIUS AND RALPHIE BLASIUS (SAGE CREEK PRESS, 1999)

▶ *Fundraise Painlessly* takes a hands-on approach to the basics of fund raising, from organizing events to coordinating volunteers to seeking media coverage and publicity. Chip and Ralfie Blasius have compiled their own experiences in the field into a useful basic resource book for grassroots nonprofit management and fund raising.

With a focus on grassroots programs, they offer numerous sample pages and worksheets, including budget sheets, Form 990 samples, a 501(c)(3) exemption application and other helpful tools for beginners.

Covering the wide range of fund raising options, they offer an introduction to the elements of direct mail, telemarketing, grant writing, events, and even planned giving. Most coverage is cursory, but they do offer some handy basic advice and useful inserts such as application for bulk third-class mailing rates, sample pledge sheets, and recipes to make your bake sales even more tasty.

The book also includes a compendium of fund-raising ideas and, for each idea, includes a description of the event, as well as supplies and equipment, and the human resources required to make it a success.

Fundraising Painlessly is a good basic primer for grassroots organizations in need of fresh ideas, or those that want a basic introduction to the wide array of fund-raising options available. *Softcover, 192 pages, $19.95*

Fund Raising & Marketing in the One-Person Shop: Achieving Success with Limited Resources
MICHAEL J. HENLEY AND DIANE L. HODIAK (DEVELOPMENT RESOURCE CENTER, 1997)

▶ The suggestions offered by most fund-raising strategists often cannot be utilized by smaller organizations with limited financial and personnel resources. With this thorough and well-organized guide, they target the "one-person shop," stressing the need for smaller organizations to be selective in setting priorities. They show how to get others involved by taking advantage of volunteers, interns, and well-placed board members and offer up hundreds of useful tips. Always with an eye to cost effectiveness and savings, the authors detail how to identify potential donors, utilize technology, put together a strategic plan, garner publicity, solicit major gifts, and acknowledge and recognize donors. They have purposely designed a "how-to" resource that provides hundreds of ideas to help nonprofit managers to raise more money in cost-effective ways. Additionally, managers will learn many new ideas for cost-effective public relations, including techniques for donors, volunteers, community partners, and other key constituencies. Learn how to use technology to help you work smarter, how to cut costs in marketing, and how to secure donated services and supplies. It contains hundreds of practical tips and 19 case examples, along with sample marketing and planning documents, to help you improve results in fund raising, marketing, and nonprofit management. *Softcover, 204 pages, $29.95*

Fund Raising Basics: A Complete Guide

BARBARA KUSHNER CICONTE AND JEANNE G. JACOB (ASPEN PUBLISHERS, 1997)

► This primer helps new fund raisers learn the basics, from the vocabulary of fund raising to the nuances of major trends affecting nonprofit fund raising today. With up-to-date case studies and real-life examples, this practical guide will provide an overview of the field and give development staff, managers, and directors a platform from which to operate their fund-raising programs. This guide is a must-have for anyone new to the fund-raising arena. *Softcover, 336 pages, $64*

Fund-Raising Cost Effectiveness: A Self-Assessment Workbook (Book & Disk)

JAMES D. GREENFIELD (JOHN WILEY & SONS, 1996)

► A leading fund-raising professional presents a comprehensive, step-by-step guide that will help others in the profession ensure that their department and campaigns are as efficient and cost-effective as possible. This book combines a thorough explanation of the issues critical to fund-raising self-assessment with easy-to-use worksheets and practical advice. It explores, in detail, the key areas of fund-raising analysis: environmental, department, and program audits; feasibility study; and productivity evaluation. The accompanying disk contains all the sample worksheets plus software for downloading a nonprofit's fund-raising data from major software products into charts, graphs, and P&L-like spreadsheet templates. *Softcover, 333 pages, $64.95*

Fundraising for Dummies

JOHN MUTZ AND KATHERINE MURRAY (IDG BOOKS WORLDWIDE, 2000)

► Fund raisers, here are the tricks that get the cash! *Fundraising for Dummies* is the complete, fun-to-read guide to the art and science of raising money for nonprofit endeavors, from Little League to big foundations. *Fundraising for Dummies* helps you to find the secrets of writing grants that get the green; conduct effective grassroots campaigns, phone and mail solicitations, events, and more; discover tips on starting a nonprofit organization from scratch; and put the "fun" in fund raising. *Softcover, 359 pages, $19.99*

Fund Raising: Evaluating and Managing the Fund Development Process, 2nd Edition

JAMES M. GREENFIELD (JOHN WILEY & SONS, 1999)

► Designed for fund-raising executives of organizations both large and small, this resource covers initial preparation and 15 areas of fund raising, as well as discusses the ongoing management of the process. Included are numerous examples, case studies, checklists, and a unique evaluation of the audit environment of nonprofit organizations. Now revised and expanded, this practical resource provides an accessible game plan for not only raising funds, but also developing them effectively for increased productivity and profitability. Written by James M. Greenfield, a leading authority in the field, *Fund Raising* takes you step-by-step through the entire fund development process, from planning and marketing to community relations and donor management. Along with an added, in-depth discussion of ethics, the second edition introduces new best practices that have developed over the past few years and features updated data, useful worksheets, such as economic statistics, demographics, and reports from the American Association of Fund-Raising Council. *Hardcover, 428 pages, $49.95*

Fundraising for Non-Profit Groups: How to Get Money from Corporations Foundations and Government (Self-Counsel Business Series), 5th Edition

JOYCE YOUNG AND KEN WYMAN (SELF-COUNSEL PRESS, 2001)

► Explaining in detail the process of fund raising, this comprehensive book has been recently expanded and updated to explore fund raising through telemarketing and to provide excellent strategies for procuring long-term corporate sponsorships. With samples and examples, this book covers determining who to approach, motivating volunteers, and developing a fund-raising campaign. *Softcover, 256 pages, $15.95*

Fundraising for the Long Haul

KIM KLEIN (CHARDON PRESS, 2000)

► This book helps readers assess the health of their nonprofit organization and take the necessary steps to create a more dynamic, effective, and sustainable fund-raising program. Klein outlines the characteristics of healthy fund-raising programs and provides checklists and benchmarks to evaluate your organization's progress. Using real-life examples, she explains that lack of money is often a symptom of a deeper problem and offers specific solutions for overcoming the obstacles that nonprofit organizations most commonly face. *Fundraising for the Long Haul* reminds nonprofits that engaging in frequent self-examination through planning and evaluation, welcoming new ideas and people, and taking risks are the hallmarks of vibrant and dynamic organizations. *Fundraising for the Long Haul* provides a road map, grounded in Klein's vast experience as a fund raiser, trainer, and writer, for organizations wanting a long and healthy life. *Softcover, 176 pages, $20*

Fundraising for Non-Profits

P. BURKE KEEGAN (HARPERCOLLINS, 1994)

► Fund raising is central to all nonprofit organizations, yet few do it well, primarily because they see themselves and the communities they serve as adversaries rather than partners. This book shows these groups how to establish better relations with their communities and raise more money for their causes. *Softcover, 240 pages, $18*

The Fund Raising Game

(KEN WYMAN & ASSOCIATES—PUBLISHED/PRODUCED BY TV ONTARIO, 1994) (VIDEO)

► This video education tool for volunteers, board, and staff in all kinds of charities and nonprofit groups provides eight half-hour programs on the basics and intricacies of fund raising. Host Ken Wyman takes a practical and entertaining approach, offering his own expert advice, while tips and strategies from experienced fund raisers reinforce key fund-raising principles. The programs include: (1) the fund-raising pyramid; (2) making people want to give; (3) designing direct mail—when and how to mail; (4) special events that raise more money; (5) upgrading gifts to major individual levels; (6) corporate and institutional gifts: money, in-kind, and sponsorships; (7) recruiting volunteers for fund raising; and (8) creating workable action plans: realistic deadlines and do-able tasks. A 270-page workbook offers exercises to help you test your knowledge, activities to help you put new ideas to work fast, and case studies of nonprofits in actions. *2 Videotapes (eight half-hour video programs) plus 270-page spiral-bound workbook: $90 (includes shipping)*

Fundraising: Hands-On Tactics for Nonprofit Groups
PETER L. EDLES (MCGRAW-HILL, 1993)

▶ This hands-on operations manual remedies the funding crisis by showing nonprofit professionals and volunteers how to design and run successful fund-raising campaigns for their organizations. It combines sound, cost-effective strategies for building better organizational, management, sales, and marketing practice along with insider tips for training solicitors, cultivating donors, and organizing small and large gift drives that capture the emotions and imaginations of potential supporters. Sample letters, scripts, invitations, pledge cards, acknowledgment letters, press releases, budgets, grant proposals, and action checklists guide readers every step of the way toward fund-raising success. *Softcover, 288 pages, $16.95*

The Fundraising Planner: A Working Model for Raising the Dollars You Need (Jossey-Bass Nonprofit and Public Management Series)
TERRY SCHAFF AND DOUGLAS SCHAFF (JOSSEY-BASS, 1999)

▶ Missed deadlines and forgotten follow-ups are a thing of the past with these guided exercises for creating campaigns that bring in the funds nonprofit groups need, when they need them. This plan covers everything from recruiting volunteers to writing mailings, cultivating prospects, targeting financial goals, launching fundraising efforts, and monitoring their progress. This workbook will take new fund-raising professionals through the process of creating and implementing a detailed annual fund-raising plan for their organizations, one that they can use to navigate any fund-raising environment. The process of fund raising is made up of many smaller pieces such as special events, the annual fund, capital campaigns, and foundation and corporate support, just to name a few. At small and medium-sized nonprofits, usually one development officer is in charge of all these tasks and many more. By completing this book, the reader will have a fund-raising plan for the entire year, covering every aspect of fund raising. This plan will provide the reader with a map, calendar, and itinerary—along with reports, schedules, worksheets, and other exercises that readers complete in each chapter. *Softcover, 240 pages, $27.95*

Fundraising Skills for Health Care Executives
JOYCE J. FITZPATRICK AND SANDRA S. DELLER, EDS. (SPRINGER PUBLISHING, 2000)

▶ A former dean and a director of major gifts of a renowned nursing institution, with a combined 50 years in the profession, present an explicit, hands-on guide to successful fund raising among individuals, foundations, and corporations. From the basic principles of development to the specifics of tax regulations and the sometimes delicate matter of stewardship, this book articulates strategies for success. Case studies, extensive support materials, and illustrative tables make this an accessible and indispensable tool for health care executives. *Hardcover, 193 pages, $38.95*

Getting Started in Fundraising
MICHAEL NORTON AND MURRAY CULSHAW (SAGE PUBLICATIONS, 2000)

▶ The need for efficient and regular fund raising has become a necessity among nongovernmental organizations. Many NGOs have to devote considerable time and energy toward raising funds for their activities, so it is important to be able to do this effectively. This book is a practical guide to getting started in fund raising. It is aimed primarily at small and medium-sized voluntary organizations. The book is replete with case studies and real-life examples that illustrate the practical advice that the authors give. There are also exercises and checklists to help the reader relate the advice in the book to the specific situation of their own organization. The book concludes with an appendix, which provides information on useful organizations and networks in India and a list of publications for further reading. *Softcover, 168 pages, $24.95*

Grants, Etc., 2nd Edition
ARMAND LAUFFER (SAGE PUBLICATIONS, 1997)

▶ Has your program suffered from a lack of funding? Do you find that your fund-raising efforts are not yielding a healthy share of the resource pie? In *Grants, Etc., 2nd Edition* (originally published as *Grantmanship and Fund Raising*), Armand Lauffer offers concrete evidence that the resources are out there. You just have to know where to find them and how. He emphasizes methods of expanding what has been viewed as a finite pool of resources by detailing innovative ways of targeting markets and aligning program goals. He also provides specific guidelines for writing grant proposals, designing sound programs, developing and nurturing resources, and other key aspects of winning in the game of fund raising. Through case illustrations, Lauffer spotlights grant seekers who share inspirational wisdom and the nuts and bolts of their success. Through scores of examples he spotlights the innovations in funding and fund raising that are likely to characterize funding patterns in the early part of the twenty-first century. *Grants, Etc.* includes a step-by-step checklist of project design essentials as well as a new section on Internet access filled with key Web site links and information on creating your own Web page. *Softcover, 414 pages, $37*

Growing from Good to Great
JUDITH E. NICHOLS (BONUS BOOKS, 1995)

▶ In a changing world, development programs that just plod along demand a wake-up call. Dr. Judith Nichols shows how today's "changing paradigms" of audience and technologies are revolutionizing fund-raising strategies. Dr. Nichols offers specific guides to dramatically increase traditional benchmarks of growth. Are dollar increases of 5 to 25 percent no longer enough for your organization? Dr. Nichols shows you how to reorganize your development program to accommodate exponential increases of 50 percent, 100 percent, or more annually. She tackles the question of how to pull miraculous gains out of an already overworked staff, volunteers, and fixed budget. This book gives you the secrets to dramatically increase your fund-raising revenue. Topics include: Interpreting Organizational "Vision"; The Move to Aftermarketing; How to Double Your Results in One Year; Changing Roles of the Board; The Role of the Executive Director; and Determining Realistic, Yet Challenging, Goals and Objectives. *Hardcover, 210 pages, $40 (plus $4.50 shipping)*

Hand in Hand: Funding Strategies for Human Service Agencies
WILLIAM MENGERINK (THE TAFT GROUP, 1992)

▶ This is a practical guide, written in nontechnical language, for directors of medium-sized to small social service and health care agencies and cultural organizations on creating a strong fundraising program with limited resources. Learn how to develop a board of directors who donate annual gifts (not just time and talent), put together a simple wills and estates endowment, conduct a capital campaign, and more. *Hardcover, 115 pages, $35 (includes shipping)*

The Hands-On Guide to Fundraising Strategy & Evaluation

MAL WARWICK, STEPHEN HITCHCOCK, JOAN FLANAGAN, AND ROBERT H. FRANK (STRATHMOOR PRESS, 1997)

▶ This workbook gives you everything you need to assess the strengths and weaknesses of your fund-raising program. Mal Warwick guides you step by step through 10 benchmarks for evaluating everything from revenue growth to donor upgrades. Easy-to-use forms and checklists enable you to gain a quick and accurate picture of what you're already doing. Arrangement of this handbook is in five parts. The first provides an introduction for those new to fund raising or needing a refresher. The second details what's needed for a successful program, including how to assess costs and track results. A section containing 44 forms, checklists, and other tools is followed by discussion of how to explain what things to boards, staff, donors, and the public. The resources section gathers guidelines, standards, and codes of ethics developed by top fund-raising organizations, as well as information about state requirements, the ways and means of using consultants, and a reading list. Then with Warwick's expert guidance, you can choose the best course of action. *Loose-leaf manual, 452 pages, $45.95; Book and PC or Mac diskette, $60.95*

Hidden Assets: Revolutionize your Development Program with a Volunteer-Driven Approach

DIANE HODIAK AND JOHN RYAN (JOSSEY-BASS, 2001)

▶ While many nonprofits have significant volunteer resources, few know how to direct those resources strategically and systematically into their all-important development programs. Written by two fund-raising experts, *Hidden Assets* shows you how, introducing a unique, proven formula for volunteer development that aims at enhancing fund raising, public relations, and marketing results through the strategic use of volunteers. Volunteers play a key role in a powerful new technique—affinity fund raising—that teaches step-by-step how to cultivate the donors who have the greatest affinity for an organization's work and mission. Brimming with real-life examples of how organizations have incorporated volunteers into their development programs, this hands-on guide comes with a wealth of worksheets, sample dialogues with donors, and practical tips on recruiting, retaining, and motivating volunteers.

Volunteers map the route to incredible riches for libraries and nonprofit organizations, according to fund-raising veterans Hodiak and Ryan. The treasure map, complete with sample agendas, forms, helpful hints, and assessment and training tools, are included in this book. This how-to book is based on the success stories of some 2000 nonprofit organizations, spanning a period of 20 years. The case studies are sure to inspire staff and volunteers at any organization. They will learn that the philanthropist is everywhere, not just residing in the wealthiest neighborhoods. One case example describes the "church organist who makes a $14 million gift to his beloved charity." An assessment chart, included in the contents, helps nonprofit staff to determine their level of success with the easy-to-use affinity fund-raising method described in detail by the authors. Sample questions from the assessment chart include: Does the organization's donors involve family and friends in the work of the organization? To what extent do volunteers contribute to the organization? What is the level of support for the organization from key community leaders? To what extent do volunteers want to become involved in additional projects, or suggest other potential projects that might benefit the organization? Are there many volunteers who have a long history of involvement with the organization?

Libraries, religious and educational institutions, and political groups, as well as environmental, arts, human services organizations, and nonprofits of all shapes and sizes are expected to benefit from the book. "It is never too early to begin," state the authors. Best of all, if your organization is characterized as "high affinity," you may be able to surface large gifts in as little time as 60 days. Even "low-affinity" organizations, nonprofit entities whose programs are very new, unknown, and who might have few donors and volunteers, are provided with specific steps for involving board members, volunteers, and friends of the organization. The techniques are simple. In as few as four meetings, volunteers and staff are ready to "visit" with the closest friends of the organization. Technical training is not necessary. Readers learn how to interpret the results of their prospect visits as well as how to identify the best candidates for various types of giving projects: annual giving, capital campaign, and special project–type donors. A sample "affinity grid" is included, which indicates how to identify the right volunteers for the project. *Softcover, 128 pages, $27.95*

Hidden Gold: How Monthly Giving Will Build Donor Loyalty, Boost Your Organization's Income, and Increase Financial Stability

HARVEY MCKINNON (BONUS BOOKS, 1999)

▶ While it has proven enormously successful for tens of thousands of organizations, the golden days of direct mail are over. Soon there may even be a reduction in the volume of donor acquisition mailings, as organizations begin to find large-scale prospecting increasingly expensive. This is due partly to increased costs, but an equally pertinent factor is that response rates continue to decline. For most established organizations, donor lists are not growing. Many, if not most, are shrinking. Therefore, to increase income or even maintain current income levels, organizations must generate an increasing amount of money from existing donors. Harvey McKinnon argues that monthly giving is a perfect way to raise more money from your current donor base (whether it is composed of 100,000 or 100 donors).

If your nonprofit organization does not operate a monthly giving program, this book will tell you everything you need to know to get one started. If your organization already has a monthly giving program, you're bound to gain new insights about a topic that most nonprofits discuss only behind closed doors. Monthly giving appeals to younger donors, who find it convenient and easy. But it also appeals to older donors, who tend to live on a budget. Regardless of their age, monthly donors are far more likely to leave bequests than are occasional or even reliable annual donors. There are, according to McKinnon, seven compelling reasons to start your monthly giving program: (1) You'll dramatically increase your annual income; (2) you'll build a better relationship with your donors; (3) donors will stay with your organization longer; (4) monthly giving revenue is predictable; (5) you'll lower your fund-raising costs; (6) your income will continue to grow over time; and (7) monthly giving is convenient. You'll understand why monthly giving programs are one of the fastest-growing, highest-potential techniques in fund raising today. This book will help you learn which kinds of people are most likely to join a monthly giving program and how to find them; discover which arguments appeal most effectively to prospective monthly donors; gain appreciation for a wide range of options open to you in designing a monthly giving program and how to choose among them; learn how to promote loyalty and sustain giving over the long term; find out how to encourage more and bigger gifts from monthly donors; and discover how to expand a successful monthly giving program. Included are scores of real-world examples drawn from successful monthly giving programs. *Softcover, 300 pages, $39.95*

How to Ask for Money Without Fainting: A Guide to Help NonProfit Staff and Volunteers Raise More Money!, 4th Edition

SUSAN SCRIBNER (SCRIBNER & ASSOCIATES, 1996)

▶ The basic "guide to help your staff and volunteers raise money" walks the staff and board through the difficult process of raising money the most effective way—by teaching them how to ask for it. It includes tips on how to clearly articulate your agency's need, determine your best prospects, learn how to use your strengths, exercises to use *How to Ask* without dropping dead, and what to do when meeting face-to-face with a prospective funder. It includes a special Recession Funding Guide. *Softcover, 44 pages, $12 (plus shipping and handling)*

How to Raise More Money for Your Healthcare Organization

BETH-ANN KERBER (HEALTH RESOURCES PUBLISHING, 1996)

▶ This book provides valuable information to help prepare future fund-raising strategies. It includes tips from today's most successful fund raisers and leading fund-raising consulting firms. You'll find out how to judge whether you're ready to launch a capital campaign and how to sustain fund-raising momentum after that campaign is over. Find out how to thank volunteers; who your best prospects are for corporate funding and how to reach them; how to select top volunteer campaign leadership; and how to run a successful special event. Plus, you'll get some real-life suggestions for dealing with tough situations in soliciting a planned gift and for soliciting funds from foundations. *Ring bound, 182 pages, $79 (plus $7.00 shipping)*

It's a Great Day to Fundraise: A Veteran Campaigner Reveals the Development Tips and Techniques That Will Work for You

TONY PODERIS (FUNDAMERICA PRESS, 1998)

▶ In this publication, Poderis has condensed his nearly three decades of fund-raising experience to provide a concise step-by-step guide to help all volunteers and professionals be as successful as possible as they carry out their fund-raising responsibilities for their respective nonprofit institutions. He states that the process is a combination of common sense, hard work, preparation, courtesy, commitment, enthusiasm, understanding, and a belief in what you are selling. The book starts with goal setting and leadership. Chapter 1 covers the Nine Basic Truths of Fund-Raising. After Chapter 1, he moves methodically through what it takes to succeed. Chapter 2, on goal setting and leadership, is quickly followed by an admonition to "know your organization" (Chapter 3); creation of a general development plan (Chapter 4); funding sources (Chapter 5); prospecting for donors (Chapter 6); rating and evaluating prospects (Chapter 7); annual campaigns (Chapter 8); endowment campaigns (Chapter 9); capital campaigns (Chapter 10); sponsorships and underwriting campaigns (Chapter 11); developing a campaign plan (Chapter 12); preparing for a campaign (Chapter 13); managing a campaign (Chapter 14); assessing and reviewing a campaign once it's over (Chapter 15); and developing the development team (Chapter 16). *Softcover, 115 pages, $22.95 (plus $5.50 shipping and handling)*

Marketing the NonProfit: The Challenge of Fundraising in a Consumer Culture

MARGARET M. MAXWELL, INDIANA UNIVERSITY CENTER ON PHILANTHROPY (JOSSEY-BASS, 1998)

▶ This volume of New Directions for Philanthropic Fundraising offers sound advice on how nonprofits can make their message heard and become more savvy in their efforts to attract donors, participants, and, ultimately, greater revenue to support the programs that fulfill their mission. The authors illustrate how partnerships with for-profit businesses can be an effective marketing technique and suggest practical steps for attracting and maintaining corporate sponsorships. They explain the importance of developing a brand identity and recommend a number of brand-building strategies. The authors also discuss how to develop relationships with individual donors by treating them as customers, and report on successful, innovative marketing programs that have been implemented by nonprofits. (For more information on the series, please see the Journals and Periodicals section.) *Softcover, 122 pages, $25*

Maximum Dollars: The 12 Rules of Fundraising (Workbook)

ROBERT ZIMMERMAN (ZIMMERMAN LEHMAN, 2000)

▶ How do I raise funds for my organization? What are the different ways organizations fund raise? How can I get my board to fund raise? How can I create some enthusiasm for fund raising? These and other questions are answered in this book intended to alert nonprofit organizations of all shapes and sizes to the rules that guarantee fund-raising success. While the techniques available to nonprofits to raise funds are quite well known, the rules that should underpin every fund-raising effort are rarely understood. Far too much fund-raising is poorly conceived, episodic, and unimaginative. Even worse, nonprofit administrators shoot themselves in the foot time and again by viewing fund raising as genteel begging. As explained in this workbook, fund raising means something very different: the creation of opportunities for citizens to "invest" in successful nonprofit enterprises through philanthropic contributions. *Softcover, 30 pages, $19.95*

The NSFRE Fund-Raising Dictionary

R.L. CHERRY AND BARBARA R. LEVY, EDS. (JOHN WILEY & SONS/THE NATIONAL SOCIETY OF FUND-RAISING EXECUTIVES, 1996)

▶ Unlike many other areas of not-for-profit management, fund raising has no direct corollary in the for-profit sector. While it draws upon the strategies and techniques of the business world, it invariably applies them in significantly different ways because it draws its impetus from philanthropy, public service, and donors' charitable intent. Consequently, over the years, fund raising has developed a distinct vocabulary all its own. The only complete reference of its kind, *The NSFRE Fund-Raising Dictionary* offers instant access to nearly 1,400 essential fund-raising and not-for-profit terms. It is fully cross-referenced and includes terms used by fund-raising professionals throughout the English-speaking world. Terms included span a wide range of topics, from development and accounting to marketing and public relations. Some terms are drawn from federal and regulatory agencies like the IRS and the Financial Accounting Standards Board; others emerge from the for-profit sector. Most of the vocabulary stems, however, from the unique circumstances of charitable fund raising. The definitive culmination of a project that began 25 years ago by members, staff, and consultants from the National Society of Fund-Raising Executives and other professional associations, this concise, comprehensive guide reflects the latest trends in this rapidly expanding field. It is the only dictionary that provides definitions exclusively from the fund-raising perspective. The dictionary is cross-referenced and contains a bibliography and three appendices that outline the NSFRE's fund-raising principles and its "Donor Bill of Rights." *Hardcover, 201 pages, $29.95*

No Strings Attached: Untangling the Risks of Fundraising and Collaborations

MELANIE L. HERMAN AND DENNIS M. KIRSCHBAUM (NONPROFIT RISK MANAGEMENT CENTER, 1999)

► This publication provides a practical framework through which nonprofit CEOs, boards, and others engaged in fund raising can address the risks and pursue fund raising responsibly. The authors address the risks associated with budgeting, raising money from foundations, soliciting individual donors, obtaining corporate support, negotiating collaborations and partnerships, and the challenge of restricted funding. *Softcover, 70 pages, $15*

The Nonprofit Handbook, Second Edition, Fund Raising

JAMES M. GREENFIELD, ED. (JOHN WILEY & SONS, 2001)

► You have to know all you can about the driving need behind every nonprofit organization—fund raising. Volume 2 of *The Nonprofit Handbook* guides you through the maze to help you raise the money you need to advance your organization's cause. In this volume, more than 40 field leaders share their fund-raising expertise with you. From grassroots to international groups, you'll get practical, hands-on guidance for instituting basic preparations, market research, and financial requirements; understanding demographics, donor motivation, and prospect research; increasing direct mail and volunteer solicitation; improving corporate donation and grant seeking; and finding support systems and consultants. This book can serve both as a supplement to the main volume edition or on its own as a resource on current developments in the fund-raising industry. Topics covered include a not-for-profit ethics program, cause-related marketing and sponsorship, and fund-raising software, as well as an appendix updating material to the main volume. This title is free with the purchase of the main volume. The revised and expanded format provides more coverage to both "sides" of the nonprofit equation; management and fund raising. In practice, these two aspects of a nonprofit's organizational structure each keep to themselves. *The Nonprofit Handbook: Management* offers proven advice, from experts in the field, on every facet of a nonprofit's daily operations: management and leadership, human resources, benefits, compensation, financial management, marketing and communications, and law and regulations. *The Nonprofit Handbook: Fund-Raising* covers every aspect of the practice from preparatory, organizational, and managerial issues, to both annual and major giving to specialized types of nonprofit organizations. It is supplemented annually. *Hardcover, 730 pages, $105.00*

1001 Fundraising Ideas and Strategies

JIM HAWKINS (FITZHENRY & WHITESIDE, 1998)

► From Internet solicitation to chili parties, from fall fairs to fashion shows, from dream homes to raffles and red nose days, veteran fund raiser Jim Hawkins covers all the bases, condensing over 30 years of fund-raising expertise into this comprehensive and easy-to-use guide. Though written for Canadian nonprofits, the information is universally pertinent and useful. *Softcover, $22.36*

Official Fundraising Almanac: Facts, Figures, and Anecdotes from and for Fund Raisers, Reissue Edition

JEROLD PANAS (PRECEPT PRESS, 1998)

► If you're interested in increasing your company's fund-raising potential or simply looking for some fresh new ideas to spruce up your speeches, presentations, and promotional material, this book is a necessity. Written exclusively for fund raisers, this resource and reference material contains hard data to chart, plan, and compare with your own fund-raising plans, including over 100 graphs and tables; also quotes and anecdotes that add punch to your speeches, helpful promotional materials, and hundreds of facts and figures to keep your fund raising fresh, effective, easier, more enjoyable, and productive. It covers everything you ever wanted to know about fund raising, including its history, who the largest donors are and where they are giving the money, and a glossary of the 100 most important and effective fund-raising words and terms. *Softcover, 424 pages, $50 (plus $4 shipping)*

Planning Successful Fundraising Programs

KEN WYMAN (CANADIAN CENTRE FOR PHILANTHROPY/KEN WYMAN & ASSOCIATES, 1990)

► Planning is a systematic process of setting measurable goals in relation to needs and abilities; researching relevant data; comparing options; minimizing risks; balancing resources; taking appropriate action; and evaluating results so you can make changes for the next plan. But how do you do it? When should you start? Who should you involve? And how do you find the time to plan? In this informative and practical book, Ken Wyman takes you through all the stages of planning. You'll learn what research you should do, how to do it, what the key elements are to a successful plan, how to select the fund-raising strategy appropriate to your organization, and how to conduct evaluations that help you build for the future. It includes homework exercises and checklists that you can use to improve your planning process now to help nonprofits of all sizes and interests get started in fund raising. *Softcover, 175 pages, $40 (including shipping)*

Power Funding

DR. DAVID EMENHISER (THE TAFT GROUP, 1992)

► In *Power Funding*, Dr. David Emenhiser offers revolutionary ideas on how to identify the civic and business leaders who make funding decisions at the grassroots level in American communities. Here is sound, practical advice for fund raisers on how to identify members of the local power structure; understand how they attained their positions and the mentor–protege relationships among them, and how to involve their financial and human resources in the fund raiser's organization. *Hardcover, 189 pages, $18*

Principles of Professional Fundraising: Useful Foundations for Successful Practice

JOSEPH R. MIXER (JOSSEY-BASS PUBLISHERS, 1993)

► This book applies concepts and theories of psychology, organizational development and behavior, and management to the practice of professional fund raising. It goes beyond the traditional nuts-and-bolts approach to provide a comprehensive conceptual framework that underlies basic fund-raising techniques and practices; offers practical models for soliciting donations, from individuals and both large and small organizations. The book describes tools that can help fund-raising professionals discern the attitudes, influences, and values of potential donors. It outlines a framework of management and organizational theories and concepts specifically for the fund-raising profession; details strategic planning guidelines and offers practical information (illustrative strategic planning charts, criteria for selecting fund-raising methods, and key elements in the organization of fund-raising activities) to help fund raisers develop a strategic plan specifically targeted to their organizational needs; and furnishes an analysis of shifting market resources and offers an assessment of alternative revenue strategies. *Hardcover, 299 pages, $30 (plus $4.50 shipping)*

Raising More Money: A Step by Step Guide to Building Lifelong Donors

TERRY S. AXELROD (BOYLSTON BOOKS, LIMITED, 2000)

▶ Nonprofit staff, board members, and volunteers who are passionate about the mission of their organizations but tired of the old model of raising funds will be inspired by *Raising More Money®: A Step-by-Step Guide to Building Lifelong Donors*. This incisive and practical manual by fund-raising veteran Terry Axelrod teaches how nonprofit organizations—regardless of size, location, or mission—can become financially self-sustaining. It provides you with a painless, state-of-the-art system for growing exponentially your organization's base of individual donors. It provides a simple, usable road map for getting off the treadmill of annual appeals and special events and thriving in today's individual-centered fund-raising environment. This book was written for every fund raiser who has ever said, "There must be a better way to do this." *Hardcover, 252 pages, $36.95*

Raise More Money for Your NonProfit Organization: A Guide to Evaluating and Improving Your Fundraising

ANNE L. NEW AND WILSON C. LEVIS (THE FOUNDATION CENTER, 1991)

▶ Anne L. New sets guidelines for fund-raising programs that will benefit the new as well as the established nonprofit organization. The author delineates the necessary steps a nonprofit must take before launching a development campaign, encourages organizational self-analysis, and points the way to an effective program involving many sources of funding. It is divided into three sections: "The Basics," which delineates the necessary steps a nonprofit must take before launching a development campaign; "Fundraising Methods," which encourages organizational self-analysis and points the way to an effective program involving many sources of funding; and "Fundraising Resources," a 20-page bibliography that highlights the most useful research and funding directories. *Softcover, 51 pages, $14.95 (plus $4.50 shipping and handling)*

The Raising of Money: 35 Essentials Every Trustee Should Know (See Governance—Roles and Responsibilities for full description)

Reinventing Fundraising: Realizing the Potential of Women's Philanthropy

SONDRA C. SHAW AND MARTHA A. TAYLOR (JOSSEY-BASS, 1995)

▶ This book reveals the reasons women have not been taken seriously as philanthropists, identifies model programs focusing on women's giving that have been developed, and outlines new program models that organizations can tailor to their own female constituents. The practical advice offered shows volunteer and professional fund raisers, consultants, and other nonprofit staff members how to develop a gender-sensitive fund-raising program by using an innovative eight-step process, better communicate with women using advertising strategies, understand how and why women give and identify their characteristics as donors, recognize and overcome barriers to women's giving, improve communications with women, and develop and implement a multiyear com-

prehensive program to attract more women as leaders and major donors. *Hardcover, 304 pages, $28 (plus $4.50 shipping)*

Relationship Fundraising: A Donor-Based Approach to the Business of Raising Money

KEN BURNETT (PRECEPT PRESS, 1996)

▶ The most popular fund-raising book in recent years in Europe is now being distributed in the United States by Bonus Books. Ken Burnett takes the reader through his prize-winning, and money-raising, strategies for creating strong donor base. Burnett focuses on fund-raising management that not only benefits the nonprofit organization but the donor as well. You will learn about people, not technology. What makes the philanthropist tick? What are the donor's needs and interests? Burnett walks you through with a passionate point of view that is easily adaptable to your existing program. With all the hype about the "information superhighway," it's easy to forget that fund raising is all about people, not technology; everything you do should make donors feel important, valued, and considered as it is your only route to generating more funds per donor in the long term. Use the case histories, donor profiles, and action points to quickly and conveniently convert theory into practical relationship fund raising. It will teach you: (1) what relationship fund raising can do, (2) a deeper understanding of your donors, (3) what donors will allow, (4) how to find new donors, (5) how to avoid errors and pitfalls, (6) how to build a relationship database, (7) a better way to communicate with donors, (8) new opportunities, and more. It is illustrated with case histories, donor profiles, and 160 practical "action points." *Hardcover, 332 pages, $28*

The Relentlessly Practical Guide to Raising Serious Money

DAVID LANSDOWNE (EMERSON & CHURCH, 1997)

▶ Lansdowne is concerned first and foremost with the actual practice of raising money, what you specifically need to do, using each fund-raising method, to raise the maximum amount of capital. This is a thorough, step-by-step book (hence the word *relentless*). In comprehensive fashion, he addresses every relevant aspect: major gifts, fund-raising leadership, personal solicitation, gift clubs, donor cultivation, prospect research, direct mail, special events, telemarketing, writing grant proposals, attracting corporate support, planned giving, and more. Two additional standout chapters include, "The 16 Best Pieces of Fund Raising Advice," in which the author presents the collective wisdom of 50 years of fund raising, and "Fund Raising's 20 Biggest and Costliest Mistakes," where Lansdowne cautions against possible pitfalls that can waylay you. *Softcover, 268 pages, $34.95*

Secrets of Successful Fundraising: The Best from the Non-Profit Pros

CAROL WEISMAN (F.E. ROBBINS & SONS PRESS, 2000)

▶ Nineteen nonprofit gurus share their fund-raising secrets. Chapters include board involvement, feasibility studies, generating multiple revenue streams, hiring consultants, special events, direct mail, planned giving, grants, major gifts, cause-related marketing, corporate giving, Internet fund raising, social entrepreneurism, newsletters, accounting 101, strategic alliances, and donor recognition. *Softcover, 352 pages, $25*

Secrets of Successful Grantsmanship: A Guerrilla Guide to Raising Money

(JOSSEY-BASS NONPROFIT SECTOR SERIES) SUSAN L. GOLDEN (JOSSEY-BASS, 1997)

▶ Based on the provocative premise that people—not proposals—secure grants, Golden's innovative approach concentrates on investing time, energy, and resources into building and maintaining solid relationships between grant makers and seekers. Golden reveals how the grant-making process really works and arms fund raisers with the skills they need to be successful. Directed at local nonprofits, such as a rape crisis center and a dance company, Golden's fund-raising advice differs from standard counsel on grant proposal writing. Drawing on more than 20 years of experience with more than 100 organizations, Golden arms fund raisers with the grantsmanship skills they need to successfully navigate the grant-making process. From conducting effective prospect research and making initial conversations count to preparing, submitting, and following up on grant proposals, Susan Golden offers a focused, step-by-step method for reliably achieving success in any fund-raising activity. She believes creating that thick document is a time waster and the lowest priority on a leader's task list. A better place to start is to systematically consider how foundations and governments make grants: Some respond to emergencies, some to a chronically unmet need, and some to ongoing requirements, such as operating expenses. Golden gives a pep talk—replete with aphorisms from Mao Tse-tung and Che Guevara (neither noted for sympathy with capitalist philanthropy)—on thoroughly preparing oneself and one's organization for the initial contacts and meetings, and for sustaining the personal relationships made thereby for the future health of the nonprofit. *Softcover, 192 pages, $25.95*

Securing Your Organization's Future: A Complete Guide to Fundraising Strategies
MICHAEL SELTZER (FOUNDATION CENTER, 1987)

▶ Author Michael Seltzer acts as your personal fund-raising consultant. Beginners get bottom-line facts and easy-to-follow worksheets that guarantee success. Fund raisers benefit from a complete review of the basics, money-making strategies, and ideas for meeting the challenges of increased competition for limited philanthropic dollars. *Softcover, 514 pages, $24.95*

Small Nonprofits: Strategies for Fundraising Success
(New Directions for Philanthropic Fundraising #20)
MARY LOUISE MUSSOLINE (JOSSEY-BASS, 1998)

▶ As advocates for the poor, builders of community, and guardians of the environment, small organizations are big players in the work of the not-for-profit world. This volume of *New Directions for Philanthropic Fundraising* was written to help people within these small organizations approach fund raising in the same way they approach their programs—with pride, determination, and passion. The authors consider areas of special importance for small organizations: diversity of income sources, strength of the board of directors, involvement of diverse constituencies in fund raising—issues that all small nonprofits face today. They also discuss more focused topics important to small organizations, such as the conversion of special events donors to annual fund donors and the important human aspects of working with volunteers. This is the twentieth issue of the quarterly journal *New Directions for Philanthropic Fundraising*. For more information on the series, see Periodicals. *Softcover, 109 pages, $25.00*

Solicitation Skills Builder
(STEVENSON CONSULTANTS, 1999)

▶ This book offers effective training methods to improve your "prospect calls" success rate and tried-and-true techniques to help

you better manage your "asking" time. Some of the "hands-on" information covered includes: how to eliminate fund-raising anxiety; what motivates donors to give; how to turn volunteers and board members into effective fund raisers; how to effectively track prospect calls; tips for writing effective appeals; ways to manage and protect your fund-raising time; how to close the gift; ways to solicit first-time gifts; how a winning attitude can improve your success rate; techniques for soliciting businesses and corporations; closing gifts by phone; when and how to use a solicitation team; ways to deal with unresponsive prospects; how to use a camcorder to train staff and volunteers; and forms to help track prospect activities. It is filled with easy-to-understand charts and forms for tracking and soliciting prospects; examples of effective call reports, letters and more; ready-to-use worksheets to help solicitors put their training into action; and dozens of tips, techniques, and solicitation strategies you can use now. *Softcover, 48 pages, $64*

Start-to-Finish Fund Raising: How a Professional Organizes and Conducts a Successful Campaign
WILLIAM R. CUMERFORD (PRECEPT PRESS, 1998)

▶ This course for professional fund raisers covers in depth all stages of a campaign effort, starting with the precampaign survey. Each step is explained so that the campaign will avoid embarrassing and expensive oversights. *Hardcover, 340 pages, $50 (plus $4 shipping)*

Strategic Fund Development: Building Reliable Relationships That Last
SIMONE P. JOYAUX (ASPEN PUBLISHER, 1997)

▶ Discover a unique new relationship strategy for successful fund raising and how to implement it using specific methods. Learn to conduct strategic planning, market to donors, develop a constituency, and empower volunteers to be effective fund raisers. Charts, case studies, and expected results help guide the way. This is an essential book for anyone looking for a new, comprehensive approach to fund raising in nonprofit organizations. *Softcover, 213 pages, $62*

Strategic Planning for Fund Raising: How to Bring in More Money Using Strategic Resource Allocation
WESLEY E. LINDAHL (JOSSEY-BASS, 1992)

▶ This book offers a detailed, strategic planning methodology that nonprofits can use to get the best results for their fund-raising dollars. Lindahl shows how nonprofit organizations, including health care providers, colleges and universities, and others, can optimize gift income by strategically allocating fund-raising resources. The book explains how to analyze such programs as major gifts, planned giving, annual campaigns, direct mail, and phone-a-thons, and how to distribute resources among them most effectively. The strategies and methods outlined in the book will help nonprofit institutions, large and small, plan for successful, long-term development programs. *Hardcover, 152 pages, $37.95*

Successful Fundraising: A Complete Handbook for Volunteers and Professionals, 2nd Edition
JOAN FLANAGAN (NTC PUBLISHING GROUP, 1999)

▶ Today's fund raisers are facing the toughest competition in years and an uncertain economy. Flanagan provides volunteers and professionals with proven methods for landing major donors, organizing direct-mail solicitations and community-wide campaigns, and more. Flanagan gives readers the information they need to capture a fair share of available fund-raising dollars. Community volunteers and professional fund raisers alike will find helpful tips and advice on time-proven fund-raising techniques and the most profitable new ways to successfully raise money. Packed with real-life examples from the author's extensive fund-raising experience, this essential handbook is complete with planning guidelines, sample worksheets, and timetables, plus all new information on using the Internet, e-mail, Web sites, and online auctions as fund-raising tools, and expanded coverage of working with celebrities to raise funds and how to win corporate dollars. *Softcover, 336 pages, $18.95*

Successful Fundraising for Arts and Cultural Organizations

CAROLYN L. STOLPER AND KAREN BROOKS HOPKINS (ORYX PRESS, 1989)

▶ Here's the ideal "how-to" book on fund raising specifically for arts and cultural groups. It provides guidelines for all types of fund-raising campaigns. Material is divided into sections covering major sources of funds and possible methods of fund raising. You will find not only valuable advice and suggestions on raising money, but also practical tips on writing proposals, personal soliciting, government funding, using telemarketing and direct mail, and more. Included are step-by-step instructions, charts, examples of letters, reports, direct-mail packages that really work, and planning and monitoring tools. *Softcover, 208 pages, $27 (plus $2.65 shipping)*

Targeted Fund Raising: Defining and Refining Your Development Strategy

JUDITH E. NICHOLS (PRECEPT PRESS, 1994)

▶ This book focuses on the development strategies that make sense today and tomorrow. It suggests a demographically driven, commonsense approach to working smarter, not harder. It serves as a companion to Changing Demographics (see separate listing) and, based on a series of workshops given by the author, it is aimed at the seasoned development professional looking for new ideas and motivation. It will also be of value to senior- and midlevel fund raisers who are new to their current position and want to accelerate the progress of their development program and those new to the profession desiring an overview of how the components of fund raising fit together. It will help those with an established program needing evaluation in terms of potential. It organizes your projects, focusing on the development strategies that make sense today and tomorrow. Key topics include making sure you know who your current contributors are, demographically and psychographically; finding the donors of the future; evaluating the potential of your fund-raising program and concentrating your efforts where the pay-offs are greatest; reviewing your solicitation techniques; and more. *Hardcover, 229 pages, $40 (plus $4 shipping)*

Team-Based Fundraising Step-by-Step: A Practical Guide to Improving Results Through Teamwork

MIM CARLSON AND CHERYL CLARKE (JOSSEY-BASS, 2000)

▶ If you are a development officer, you have no doubt experienced the lonely challenge of being the identified fund raiser for an organization and felt the heavy burden of bringing in donor dollars single-handedly. Many nonprofits rely on a lone staff member or volunteer to raise the money they need to sustain or grow their programs. In this insightful resource, leading fund raiser Mim Carlson presents a practical approach to involving the entire organization in fund raising. In doing so, she helps board members, executive directors, and development directors turn their staff and volunteers into a cohesive team with clearly defined goals, specific roles, joint accountability, diverse talents and skills, and strong leadership. In *Team-Based Fundraising Step-by-Step,* Carlson draws on popular team-building theory and successful techniques—as well as on her years of fund-raising experience—to offer a fresh framework for helping teams become more unified in their fund development activities. She argues that individuals who act alone cannot make the most of fund-raising strategies and instead advises readers to include the board of directors, the executive director, staff, and other volunteers in strategic planning and development. This practical, step-by-step guide shows readers how to develop and implement a whole-organization approach. Providing both a rationale for this novel approach and illustrations of how it has produced successful results, Carlson offers important tools for effective collaboration: detailed implementation strategies, sample forms, checklists, worksheets, and summaries of roles and responsibilities.

The author presents a practical and step-by-step approach to involving the entire organization in fund raising, the ultimate goal being to unite board members, staff, and volunteers into a cohesive team with clearly defined goals, specific roles, joint accountability, diverse talents and skills, and strong leadership. Part One describes the steps necessary to build your fund-raising team. Part Two brings the team into focus with a vision, mandate, and plan of action. It also describes a process to train your team effectively to raise money. Part Three contains the steps for putting the team into action. It discusses the major tasks of fund raising and presents a picture of who does what on the team. Part Four concludes discussion of the step-by-step approach with strategies to evaluate fund-raising success as a team. *Softcover, 200 pages, $26.95*

Transforming Fund Raising: A Practical Guide to Evaluating and Strengthening Fund Raising

JUDITH NICHOLS (JOSSEY-BASS, 1999)

▶ In this practical and straightforward guide, Judith E. Nichols, an internationally renowned fund-raising expert, introduces a proven method of fund-raising evaluation: the Development Assessment Process. This formula will fundamentally transform the way nonprofit organizations approach evaluation and help them improve fund-raising strategies to not only achieve their mission, but to keep pace with a changing world. Nichols's revolutionary Development Assessment Process is a unique evaluation tool that combines traditional internal evaluation practices with a method for appraising shifting philanthropic and demographic trends. Proven successful in a wide variety of nonprofit organizations, this innovative process creates opportunities for open dialogue among audiences inside and outside the organization, encourages useful feedback, and provides practical recommendations that can be seamlessly incorporated into current operations. *Transforming Fundraising* walks readers step by step through the process of evaluating current fund-raising programs, assessing their potential for improvement, and planning for change. Readers will also find a real-life, in-depth case that clearly demonstrates—from the first step through the last—how the Development Assessment Process works. Written in clear, accessible language and designed to be a hands-on guide and workbook, *Transforming Fundraising* is filled with easy-to-use worksheets, checklists, exhibits, and a resource guide. By using Nichols's groundbreaking Development Assessment Process, nonprofit organizations—of all sizes—will dramatically increase their fund-raising results.

Part One reviews the rationale for conducting an assessment, why it helps to maximize your fund development efforts, who the key players must be, the components of the assessment, and various sample forms you'll need to get started. Part Two scans the current philanthropic climate, reviews methods for fund raising, and examines how changes in the donor marketplace force you to make changes in the way you raise money. Part Three offers a full-scale sample report that puts all the elements together. *Softcover, 192 pages, $28.95*

Understanding and Improving the Language of Fundraising (New Directions for Philanthropic Fundraising #22)
TIMOTHY L. SEILER (JOSSEY-BASS, 1999)

▶ The language of fund raising is laden with combative and unsavory terms—*suspects, prospects, acquisition, campaign, target.* This volume of *New Directions for Philanthropic Fundraising* challenges fund raisers to be more aware of language and its effect both on the users and the audience. Fund raisers and linguists offer practical analyses of how language is used in fund-raising appeals. Chapters provide case studies of writing grant proposals, illuminating how writers shape their language to fit their audience; content analyses of fund-raising letters, considering what persuades donors to give; and guidelines for developing successful visual rhetoric for both print and online formats. This is the twenty-second issue of the quarterly journal *New Directions for Philanthropic Fundraising.* For more information on the series, see Periodicals. *Softcover, 122 pages, $25.00*

Women as Fundraisers: Their Experience in and Influence on an Emerging Profession (New Directions for Philanthropic Fundraising #19)
JULIE C. CONRY (JOSSEY-BASS, 1998)

▶ Within the last decade, one of the most striking changes in fund raising has been the composition of the workforce itself—the dramatic increase in the numbers of women pursuing fund-raising careers. This issue of *New Directions for Philanthropic Fundraising* addresses the opportunities and challenges created by these marked shifts in the gender makeup and workplace culture of fund raising. Using personal histories, demographic trends, statistical data, and life and work experiences, the authors highlight the significant ways the nonprofit sector is being shaped by women's leadership in fund raising and greater participation in the professional ranks. They outline a number of professional development strategies for women in fund raising; examine the current status of women in fund raising as measured by compensation rates and organizational position; and analyze the impact of women's changing socioeconomic role on the organizational structures and policies of traditional fundraising institutions, such as religious organizations and the YWCA. This is the nineteenth issue of the quarterly journal *New Directions for Philanthropic Fundraising.* For more information on the series, see Periodicals. *Softcover, 139 pages, $25.00*

Annual Giving

Donor-Focused Strategies for Annual Giving
KARLA WILLIAMS (ASPEN PUBLISHERS, 1997)

▶ This book takes a fresh look at annual giving from the donor's perspective, which will enable you to better match donor interests to your organization's needs. Most important, you'll learn how to implement an important new model, the annual integrated development program, today's most donor-sensitive, effective fund-raising strategy for the long term. *Softcover, 287 pages, $62*

Fund-Raising Fundamentals: A Guide to Annual Giving for Professionals and Volunteers (Nonprofit Law, Finance, and Management)
JAMES M. GREENFIELD (JOHN WILEY & SONS, 1994)

▶ A step-by-step, hands-on guide to the basic techniques of annual giving campaigns, this book covers direct-mail solicitation (including when to mail, to whom, and how often); membership drives; gift renewals; groups, guilds, and support organizations; benefits, activities, and special events; volunteer fund raising (including how to recruit and train volunteer solicitors); premiums, advertising, and coupons; cause-related marketing and affinity cards; gambling and games of chance; door-to-door and on-street solicitation; multimedia options and telemarketing; and television and telethon solicitation. *Fund-Raising Fundamentals* shows you how to create a total annual giving strategy that uses these different methods in conjunction with each other and maximizes your success. Throughout this practical guide, you will find sample letters and documents, charts, and checklists that illustrate principles and help you put these proven methods into action. Written by a top fund-raising executive with 30 years' experience, *Fund-Raising Fundamentals* not only details each of the methods and how it functions, but also explains how each builds upon the others. Annual giving is essential to your nonprofit organization not simply to raise money, but also to help you market your mission to a wide audience, increase the number of friends and donors your organization can rely upon year after year, and inspire active public participation in accomplishing your good works. *Softcover, 432 pages, $25.56*

Keep the Money Coming: A Step-by-Step Strategic Guide to Annual Fundraising
CHRISTINE GRAHAM (PINEAPPLE PRESS, 1993)

▶ It is a "how-to" book on getting the most from your annual giving program. Divided into four major parts, it opens with "Understanding Annual Funds." Here, Graham explores the direct and indirect benefits of a robust annual fund, how the mission of your organization, and your phrasing of that mission, affects your success, and the underlying reasons why people contribute. Especially helpful is the chapter, "Are You Ready?," which offers a valuable list of three dozen questions to ask before embarking on annual giving—everything from financial matters to mission and goals to public relations to staff and volunteers. What a superb tool this could be for a board evaluating its overall performance. Next, in "Planning the Annual Fund Campaign," Graham turns her attention to pressing, specific matters such as gauging how much you can raise annually, the challenging task of setting goals that inspire (rather than intimidate) volunteers, and on which prospects to concentrate for best results. "Proven Fund Raising Methods" are the focus of section three. In these pages, Graham examines the approaches that work best for annual fund raising, namely, personal solicitation, direct mail, special events, membership programs, and fund raising by phone. For anyone who's ever been frustrated with a board that hems and haws about its responsibility for fund raising, *Keep the Money Coming* concludes with an inspired treatment on countering board reluctance. Graham offers 15 common board excuses, ranging from "I'll do anything except raise money" to "I give my time, that should be enough" to "I don't know the right people" to "I don't have the time"—and convincingly shatters each excuse. Those who have heretofore felt tongue-tied in such situations will relish this chapter. *Softcover, 124 pages, $17*

Profitable Annual Gift Strategies

(STEVENSON CONSULTANTS, 1999)

▶ Features include dozens of ways to dramatically increase annual gifts (or memberships) for your organization; step-by-step methods for generating bigger and greater numbers of gifts from your constituency; strategies used by others to increase annual gifts and memberships; charts, forms, and examples to make your annual gifts program more successful; dozens of tips and techniques you can use right away to dramatically increase annual gifts, get bigger gifts (or membership), more gifts, involve volunteers, and more; how direct mail can increase annual gifts; ways to generate big gifts for your annual fund; 20 tried-and-tested strategies used by other nonprofits. Sample of topics include how to make matching gifts work for you; how a sponsorship menu can help generate greater support from businesses; why annual giving should include restricted gift options; how bouncebacks can increase your direct-mail response rate; ways to solicit donations on the Internet; how a museum's party successfully targeted new members; how to use telemarketing to improve pledge fulfillment; ways to generate more annual gifts of $1,000-plus; how a raffle can help encourage pledge payments; why it can help to compare your charity with the competition; how to pinpoint new prospects; how a university's $1 campaign reached out to nondonors; why it pays to evaluate your mailing list; strategies that generate first-time gifts; 15 ways to improve employee giving; and ways to bolster year-end gifts. *Spiral bound, 48 pages, $67*

Capital Campaigns

Blueprint for a Capital Campaign: An Introduction for Board Members, Volunteers, and Staff

CHRISTINE GRAHAM (CPG ENTERPRISES)

▶ A straightforward and systematic description of capital campaign fund raising, from planning to completion. This booklet will demystify the process and help each participant understand their role. It includes a chronological checklist and tips on how to maintain campaign momentum, with timeline, charts, and a basic description of the process. *Softcover, 24 pages, $12 (plus shipping and handling)*

Capital Campaigns Deskbook

(SINCLAIR TOWNES)

▶ This deskbook will help guide you through a successful endowment or capital campaign, from preplanning to the victory celebration. If your institution or organization is considering a capital or endowment campaign, large or small, this deskbook will help you in the most critical phase: before the campaign ever kicks off and before the first dollar is even solicited. *Softcover, $95*

Capital Campaign Implementation: Are You Ready?

PAUL J. STRAWHECKER (PAUL J. STRAWHECKER, INC., 1998)

▶ This book contains helpful hints about planning and managing a campaign. *"Campaign-style"* fund raising is understood by most people, but it is an underutilized methodology that organizations can employ with success to achieve a number of objectives. Traditionally, capital campaigns have been relied upon to provide financial support for construction needs. Today, they are also used to increase endowments and generate fund dollars. Occasionally, the campaign methodology is used to secure planned gifts as well. The concepts provided in this publication should be helpful for

most organizations. While the publication was not written to provide every detail of a campaign, it can be used as a helpful manual in designing a campaign for an organization. The publication describes the role of the staff, volunteers, and consultants. The material in the book covers such areas as analysis of the project to be funded, how to prepare your organization for a campaign, the use of a consultant, feasibility study, campaign overview and plan, organizing the campaign, and the solicitation process. *Softcover, 109 pages, $25*

Capital Campaigns: Realizing Their Power and Potential (New Directions for Philanthropic Fundraising #21)

ANDREA KIHLSTEDT AND ROBERT PIERPONT (JOSSEY BASS, 1999)

▶ Capital campaigns are the most cost-efficient means of raising funds. A well-executed campaign has even further advantages—focusing the public's attention on an organization, uniting its constituencies in a common cause, strengthening staff morale, and developing new annual fund prospects. This issue of *New Directions for Philanthropic Fundraising* explores both the technical aspects of conducting a capital campaign and the powerful transformational impact of campaigns on an organization's long-term development. Topics include creating the right conditions for achieving leadership gifts, setting and resetting realistic campaign goals; using computer systems to manage the information generated during a campaign; and developing an effective challenge grant strategy. This is the twenty-first issue of the quarterly journal *New Directions for Philanthropic Fundraising*. For more information on the series, please see Journals and Periodicals. *Softcover, 125 pages, $25.00*

Capital Campaigns: Strategies that Work

ANDREA KIHLSTEDT AND CATHERINE SCHWARTZ (ASPEN PUBLISHERS, 1997)

▶ The authoritative work on developing plans, strategies, and tactics that will work to raise funds for capital projects. Step-by-step instructions guide the inexperienced and smooth the way for anyone planning this major fund-raising activity. Full of charts, graphs, checklists, and case studies that illustrate each step of the process, this book will direct you to success. In addition, valuable troubleshooting advice will help you avoid the pitfalls of planning and executing a capital campaign. The first of the 14 chapters shows how you can gauge your readiness for a major gifts drive. Succeeding chapters explore feasibility studies, prospect research, building the campaign team, methods of soliciting, campaign materials, and more. There are chapters on the roles of direct mail and special events in capital campaigns. There's an especially helpful section entitled, "Troubleshooting Guide to Capital Campaigns," that sets forth more than two dozen problems that can, and usually do, arise during campaigns and shows you how to overcome them. *Softcover, 256 pages, $64*

Conducting a Successful Capital Campaign, 2nd Edition

KENT E. DOVE (JOSSEY-BASS, 1999)

▶ *Conducting a Successful Capital Campaign*, the updated, revised, and substantially enlarged version of his late 1980s classic of the same name, assembles, in one source, the primary ideas and techniques central to all modern capital campaigns. In an all-new handbook format, Dove presents a systematic guide to every aspect of a capital campaign. He provides new discussions on such important topics as linking strategic planning to fund raising, conducting external market surveys, defining leadership roles, establishing a campaign and solicitation process, and much more. It sets forth the principles that govern any successful capital campaign. It is a comprehensive, systematic guide, filled with practical tools and advice for planning and managing a successful campaign. The expanded resource section offers samples of key elements of a capital campaign, including a complete volunteer kit, sample budget report, program brochures, newsletters, a strategic plan, and market survey questionnaires, among other invaluable tools. It is a well-organized book, and one that generously supplies the collateral material of a capital campaign (i.e., sample case statement, volunteer kit, campaign plan, newsletter, pledge form, and more). *Hardcover, 504 page, $49.95*

The Nonprofit Entrepreneur: Creating Ventures to Earn Income

EDWARD E. SKLOOT, ED. (THE FOUNDATION CENTER, 1988)

▶ This well-organized, topic-by-topic analytical approach to nonprofit business venturing demonstrates how nonprofits can launch successful earned income enterprises without compromising their mission. Each chapter is written by a different expert on topics including legal issues, marketing techniques, business planning, avoiding the pitfalls of venturing for smaller nonprofits, and a special section on museums and their retail operations. It includes case studies, practical "how-to" information, and insights from the experiences of nonprofit executives. *Softcover, 170 pages, $19.95 (plus $4.50 shipping)*

Preparing Your Capital Campaign (Excellence in Fundraising Workbook Series)

MARILYN BANCEL, THE FUND RAISING SCHOOL, AND TIMOTHY L. SEILER (JOSSEY-BASS, 2000)

▶ In this hands-on workbook, fund-raising expert Marilyn Bancel shows you how to prepare your organization to embark on a successful capital campaign, detailing each step that must be taken before the launch. It breaks down the preparation stage into practical, manageable parts, outlining in straightforward language such essentials as creating a campaign timetable, setting up the campaign committee, determining a campaign goal, and getting the whole organization ready for a fund-raising drive. Packed with useful resources, this nuts-and-bolts workbook includes a campaign skills checklist, strategies for estimating fund-raising costs, a sample campaign budget, and a list of Web sites tailored to the specific needs of fund raisers. If you are brand new to fund raising, the book offers a concise introductory chapter that lays out the basics and answers the key questions about capital campaigns. More experienced fund raisers will benefit from a wealth of reminders for avoiding common mistakes and a framework for staying focused on the factors that are most important for success. *Softcover, 192 pages, $25.95*

The Successful Capital Campaign: From Planning to Victory Celebration

H. GERALD QUIGG, ED. (CASE PUBLICATIONS, 1986)

▶ Ensure the survival of your institution with a successful capital campaign; build the friendships and raise the money you need to prosper. This book describes the roles of each participant in a capital campaign. Twenty-one experts show how to involve the entire institutional community, identify and train new leadership, motivate trustees and volunteers, create documents that state your case, build momentum to put you over the top, and administer for maximum productivity. It is an invaluable tool for the campaign manag-

er as well as others (president, trustees, staff, and volunteers) who have major responsibilities in the capital campaign. It helps key players understand their role and how they can contribute to the success of the capital campaign effort. *Softcover, 188 pages, $41.50 (Nonmember), $31 (Member)*

Successful Capital Campaigns: From Start to Finish (Manual)

(STEVENSON CONSULTANTS)

▶ This book provides a step-by-step process you can follow to plan and execute your next successful capital campaign, and helpful and easy-to-use resources such as charts, formulas, examples, and more for you to use throughout the campaign process. A sampling of topics covered includes prioritizing funding projects before launching a campaign; measuring your constituency's gift potential; how to go about prioritizing your prospects; preparing your board for campaign success; six ways to make your case statement more compelling; how to track your prospects' readiness; how to prepare your solicitation team; ways to express gratitude to major donors; making the most of your capital campaign announcement; how naming opportunities encourage gifts; why and how to conduct a feasibility study; tips for closing major gifts; how to use campaign planning to leverage gifts; groundbreaking ceremonies with pizzazz; how to determine a prospect's gift capability; how to test the campaign waters; how to conduct a peer screening program; why your board should understand "sacrificial" giving; why the postcampaign period is important; and how to develop a scale-of-giving model for your campaign. *Softcover, $69*

Corporate Philanthropy and Funding Resources

Corporate Social Investing

CURT WEEDEN, PAUL NEWMAN, AND PETER LYNCH (BERRETT-KOEHLER PUBLISHERS, INC., 1998)

▶ According to Weeden, corporate philanthropy is on its way out. A new concept called *corporate social investing*—which requires that every commitment of money and/or product/equipment/land that a company makes must have a significant business reason—is taking its place. The transition has implications to every business and nonprofit organization in America. This book provides the strategic plan for making the transition to corporate social investing. By following the practical steps described here, businesses and nonprofits can forge creative alliances that can boost corporate profits while at the same time providing added resources for schools, colleges, cultural organizations, civic groups, and other important charities. Weeden's breakthrough plan, based on his innovative concept of corporate social investing, has the potential to dramatically change the way businesses and nonprofits interact. If widely implemented, it could substantially increase corporate support for nonprofits, turning the tide against cutbacks, offering profound benefits to businesses, and revitalizing the essential services nonprofits provide.

The 10-step program outlines how to transform corporate gifts into corporate social investments, forging creative alliances with nonprofit organizations that will bolster or maintain profits while at the same time providing needed resources for schools, colleges, civic groups, cultural organizations, and other charities. It explains why corporations should be concerned about social investing and how such philanthropy is changing. It tells how to research and make company-appropriate investments and which ones to avoid. It provides staffing and management designs for different types of organizations and gives suggestions for nonprofits seeking corporate investors as they face increased cutbacks in public funding. *Hardcover, 250 pages, $29.95*

Corporate Foundation Profiles (See Grant Seeking)

Corporate Giving Directory (See Grant Seeking)

Dollars for Doers: A Guide to Employee Volunteer Grant-Matching Programs

DIANE J. GINGOLD (DIANE GINGOLD & ASSOCIATES, 1999)

▶ The first directory devoted exclusively to grants given by corporations to nonprofit organizations where employees volunteer. The grants, which range from $10 to $10,000, provide direct support to community organizations where employees commit volunteer time ranging from an hour a week to hundreds of hours per year. More than 109 million people volunteer in the United States—the largest army of volunteers in the world. As part of their community service efforts, many corporations match employees' and retirees' volunteer hours with a cash donation to the nonprofit organization that they serve. *Dollars for Doers: A Guide to Employee Volunteer Matching Grant Programs,* the first directory of these grant opportunities, will help volunteers increase their contributions to the nonprofit organizations they support, and help nonprofits identify additional funding sources. Each corporate entry provides contact information, eligibility requirements, application process, and grant amounts. *Spiral bound, 35 pages, $15.00 (plus shipping and handling); $12.00 (plus shipping and handling) for Nonprofit Organizations*

Giving by Industry: A Reference Guide to the New Corporate Philanthropy, 2000–2001 Edition

(ASPEN NONPROFIT FUND RAISING & ADMINISTRATIVE DEVELOPMENT GROUP, 2000)

▶ The only national directory that analyzes these new giving practices on an industry-by-industry basis, it's designed to give you the insightful information you need to adjust your strategies, reevaluate your major prospects, and spend your energies where they will pay off in this new philanthropic era. Key general information is provided in each industry profile to help you spot partnership synergies and plan your strategy. Profiles outline industry challenges, philanthropic history of the industry, how and why the current industry giving philosophy has developed, opportunities nonprofits might find in the industry for partnering, case histories of specific corporate giving programs that work, and how the industry giving structure is expected to change in the foreseeable future. More than 300 corporate listings highlight the top corporations in each specific industry. You'll get a true picture of a company's corporate giving program and philosophy, how much they give, and the types of nonprofits they get involved with. Each listing also contains full contact information. *Softcover, 464 pages, $149*

Successful Corporate Fund Raising: Effective Strategies for Today's Nonprofits

K. SCOTT SHELDON (JOHN WILEY & SONS, 2000)

▶ This book provides simple steps to help increase your organization's access to the corporate philanthropic dollar. Approximately 10 percent of all dollars contributed to nonprofits in the United States today come from corporations. *Successful Corporate Fund Raising* shows nonprofits how to tap into this money with very little effort. Corporate fund raising is one of the core activities in a nonprofit's fund-raising program, and this book reveals simple, practical, easy-to-follow corporate fund-raising strategies. It shows fund raisers and executives at nonprofits of all sizes how to take advantage of the current corporate funding opportunities. It walks the reader step-by-step through the entire corporate fund-raising process. Each section of the book provides in-depth information on a certain aspect of corporate giving (research, cultivation, solicitation, evaluation, recognition, and more) and offers a range of cost-effective strategies that can be used to increase your share of today's corporate support dollar. Sheldon, a seasoned Director of Development himself, also illuminates the ways in which technology is having a profound impact on the sector, and ways you can use this technology to your advantage. Near the end of the book, in addition to a sample corporate proposal and a sample online proposal form, Sheldon provides a case study highlighting employee matching gifts and how to maximize success in this area. *Hardcover, 208 pages, $34.95*

Corporate Sponsorship

IEG's Complete Guide to Sponsorship, 2nd Edition

LESA UKMAN, ED. (INTERNATIONAL EVENTS GROUP, 1999)

▶ This is a detailed, practical book for corporate sponsors, sponsees, and sponsorship agencies. It provides a basic understanding of the concepts and terms related to sponsorship, as well as a working knowledge of how to apply them. In addition to giving you the essential building blocks, *IEG's Complete Guide to Sponsorship* goes a step further and shows you how to apply them, with checklists for you to use and real-life examples that illustrate the principles in practice. Included are an explanation of what sponsorship is and how it fits in the marketing mix; why sponsorship is the fastest-growing marketing medium and who's using it; what companies sponsor and why they sponsor; the decision-making process for sponsorship selection; how to determine what a sponsorship is worth; how to maximize sponsorship's value through leveraging; how to measure sponsorship's results; why sponsorships fail; and how sponsorship agencies work. *IEG's Complete Guide to Sponsorship* also contains the IEG Sponsorship Glossary; checklist of sponsorship rights and benefits; menu of promotional ideas to extend sponsorship's value; case studies of successful sponsorship measurement; and charts detailing sponsorship spending, projected growth, and comparison to other media. It serves as a valuable training manual for colleagues and staff, as well as support documentation for executives, board members, and volunteers. It is useful as a daily reference to answer specific questions that arise. *Softcover, 43 page, $69*

The Sponsorship Seeker's Toolkit (Book and Disk)

ANNE-MARIE GREY AND KIM SKILDUM-REID (MCGRAW-HILL, 1999)

▶ This is a how-to guide to getting funding by speaking to organizations in corporate language—using the right tools to open the money box. It also ensures that the sponsor gets value return for their investment. The two savvy authors walk you through every step of the process and provide checklists and templates for planning, proposals, and presentations, backed up by the diskette that comes with the book. The beauty of this book is that strategies for obtaining sponsorship by providing competitive benefits have been built into the instructions for structuring, negotiating, and managing a sponsorship proposal. Whether you represent a small local group or a large nonprofit organization, this toolkit will equip you to achieve your funding goals. It shows how to find sponsors, how to secure them, and, most important, how to keep them. It is attractively designed and clearly set out, and full of easy-to-use tools, techniques, and exercises that can be undertaken individually or collaboratively. There are detailed checklists, forms, sample letters, and templates, and as a bonus, 15 of the book's key documents are also available electronically on the accompanying floppy disk. Sponsorship has come into its own as the most powerful of all marketing media. This step-by-step, no-nonsense "how-to" workbook explains how to secure sponsorships and build highly innovative win–win partnerships that will last. The Sponsorship Seeker's Toolkit and accompanying disk provide a step-by-step, no-nonsense approach to securing, retaining, and managing sponsorship. The Toolkit is full of easy-to-use tools, techniques, resources, and templates, creating a straightforward framework for people just starting out in sponsorship, and enhancing the skills of seasoned professionals. *The Sponsorship Seeker's Toolkit* takes you through all the steps of setting up a sponsorship program, from creating and packaging your property to developing promotional plans to developing hit lists and proposals to negotiating contracts. Simple checklists, question-and-answer worksheets, and templates give you everything you need to make your sponsorship program a success. *Softcover, 203 pages, $27.95*

Direct Mail and Direct Response

The Complete Book of Model Fund-Raising Letters
ROLAND KUNIHOLM (PRENTICE HALL, 1995)

▶ This book provides hundreds of samples and models of every possible type of fund-raising letter, ready to generate higher donations for any nonprofit organization. It includes new donor acquisition requests, special appeals, lapsed-donor letters, corporate and foundation requests, letters recruiting volunteers, and more. They're persuasive, well-written appeals that cover the gamut from acquiring new donors, to reactivating lapsed donors, to building memberships, to soliciting gifts in kind, to increasing the average gift of your largest mail donors. Whether yours is an established institution or a grassroots group, there are model letters that will be applicable to your needs. In addition to the model letters, he provides sample letters from actual organizations to illustrate how others put into practice the elements of which he speaks. Not only does Kuniholm provide a storehouse of well-crafted letters, but you'll also find plenty of envelope "teasers" to get your letter opened, pointers for writing strong copy, tips for asking for the right amount, as well as pointers for designing your direct mail package, and producing cost-effective mailings. *Hardcover, 365 pages, $39.95*

Direct Mail Testing for Fund Raisers
JOSEPH P. KACHOREK (BONUS BOOKS, 1998)

▶ Nervous about marketing your campaigns? Not testing is a bad idea. Improper testing is worse. *Direct Mail Testing for Fund Raisers* examines what to test, from components to concepts. It tells you how to establish proper test structures so that results can be acted upon. You can never be certain the package you are currently mailing is the most effective if you don't test against it. Things change. Makes sure you can change too, profitably and pragmatically. *Hardcover, 185 pages, $40*

Direct Response Fund Raising: Mastering New Trends for Results (Book and CD-ROM)
MICHAEL JOHNSON, ED. (JOHN WILEY & SONS, 2000)

▶ Nonprofits can boost donor and membership response rates with these exciting examples and tips guaranteed to reinvigorate direct-mail campaigns. The success of a nonprofit direct-mail program requires staying on top of recent trends in the field. These trends include appealing to aging baby boomers as well as tapping into powerful new databases, the Internet, CD-ROMs, diskettes, and videos. Dealing directly with new trends, this indispensable guide gives fund raisers, nonprofit managers, and volunteers an excellent understanding of how to plan bold and successful direct mail campaigns guaranteed to revitalize a fund-raising program. Scores of examples reconnect readers with the latest in the medium. Features include real-life results related to response percentages, costs, and average dollar return, and a CD-ROM with checklists to help organizations implement ideas and 30 fund-raising models searchable by theme, type, and subject matter. Representing a broad spectrum from seasoned veterans like Mal Warwick to up-and-comers like Jason Potts, Johnston has brought together some of the best-known practitioners in the field and asked them to provide insight, examples, and expertise on a wide range of direct-response fund-raising issues. Everything from predicting the future to taking advantage of the synergy between different fund-raising media, to recognizing the profile of tomorrow's donor, to manipulating your database to increase giving, to the new techniques of online fund-raising, to an examination of what works today and will continue to work tomorrow and plentiful other issues are explored in this estimable new book. *Hardcover, 188 pages, $39.95*

Eighty-six Tutorials on Creating Fundraising Letters and Packages
JERRY HUNTSINGER (EMERSON PUBLISHERS, 2000)

▶ Direct-mail guru Jerry Huntsinger offers tutorials on a wide range of subjects, including "Pavlov's Dog and Fundraising Letters," "Whatever Happened to Real Stories About Real People?," "20 Dangerous Ways to Get Your Letter Off to a Good Start," and many other provocative subjects. This is a limited edition, published personally by Jerry Huntsinger through Emerson Publishers, for professional direct-mail fund raisers only. *Three-ring binder, 520 pages, $130.00 to ad agencies and consultants; $95.00 to nonprofit organizations (includes shipping and handling)*

Everything You Need to Know to Get Started in Direct Mail Fundraising
KEN WYMAN (KEN WYMAN & ASSOCIATES, 1995)

▶ This complete how-to guide for succeeding with direct mail answers all these questions and more: Is direct-mail fund raising for you? What results can you expect? Who gives through the mail? How do you build lists? Will the envelope be opened? Why is the reply everything? Is donor fatigue a problem? Can you recover lapsed donors? When are the seasons to be mailing? What is a winning package? How do you write letters that work? How long should a letter be? How do you test the real winners? How often should you mail? How can you make money saying thank you? *Spiral bound, 270 pages, $40 (including shipping)*

How to Write Powerful Fund-Raising Letters
HERSCHELL GORDON LEWIS (BONUS BOOKS, 1998)

▶ This book tells you what to write, how to write, and how to tailor your message to a specific, targeted audience. Herschell

Gordon Lewis covers a variety of organizations—from politics to the ecology to your cause. Mistakes are often our best teachers; in this book, you'll meet some of the best teachers around. Filled with examples, each letter is followed by Mr. Lewis's commentary discussing its strong and weak points. It provides the rules and guidelines professionals can put to work right away. With it, you'll simply never write a weak, ineffective fund-raising letter. *Hardcover, 206 pages, $40 (plus $4 shipping and handling)*

How to Write Successful Fundraising Letters
MAL WARWICK (STRATHMOOR PRESS, 1996)

▶ According to this practical handbook, a "fundraising letter is like a personal visit." Writing from extensive experience in guiding companies and organizations through fund-raising efforts, Warwick offers detailed advice and analysis along with copious examples and instructive case studies. Warwick, who is both personal and hard-hitting, suggesting a cross between a preacher and a salesman, views fund raising by mail as a three-stage process. "First, donors are acquired. Then, they are converted into repeat donors. Finally donors may be upgraded into higher levels of generosity and commitment." The well-organized instructions include the planning of whole campaigns, the phrasing of appeals, composition and punctuation, information packets, and follow-up. In a time when fund raising is perquisite to nearly all professions and organizations, library managers of all types as well as library users should find this both fascinating and worthwhile.

Divided into three parts, *How to Write Successful Fundraising Letters* opens with 10 "how-to" chapters. Here, Warwick covers everything from the 23 reasons why people respond to fund-raising appeals to the cardinal rules of writing fund-raising letters. Along the way, he discusses literally dozens of topics. Among the most intriguing are how people decide whether to open fund-raising letters; how writing for results is different than literary writing; and how the first 20 seconds in your letter's life determine its fate, what to do before you write a single word, and how some of the country's top organizations (profitably) thank their donors. In Part Two, Warwick serves up real-world examples of fund-raising letters written to achieve seven different goals, with one chapter devoted to each letter. Here, the emphasis is on identifying new donors, appealing for special gifts, soliciting high-dollar gifts, asking for year-end contributions, and building long-term loyalty among your donors. Especially helpful are the "before" and "after" versions of letters that Warwick presents. Part Three wraps up the story with a look at outer envelope "teasers," strong leads for fund-raising letters, powerful endings, outstanding ways to use the word *you,* and a variety of ways to start a direct-mail program. *Softcover, 242 pages, $19.95*

Making Direct Response Fund Raising Pay Off: Outstanding Fund Raising Letters and Tips
JERRY HUNTSINGER (PRECEPT PRESS, 1994)

▶ As the author states, "There is absolutely no shortage of money for your organization. The only shortage is creative ideas to raise that money." This book is designed to help fund raisers do a better job of writing direct-mail letters. It includes specific examples of language, style, approach, content, and usage, as well as diagrams of dozens of outstanding fund-raising letters. It analyzes actual fund-raising letters to show what works and what does not. *Hardcover, 232 pages, $49.95 (plus $4 shipping)*

Many Happy Returns: A Comprehensive Q. & A. Guide to Mastering the Art of Direct Mail Fund Raising (Disk)
STEPHEN HITCHCOCK (AVAILABLE FROM THE COMPLEAT PROFESSIONAL'S LIBRARY)

▶ In *Many Happy Returns: A Comprehensive Q. & A. Guide to Mastering the Art of Direct Mail Fund Raising,* Hitchcock shares his broad knowledge of all elements of direct mail, addressing a broad range of questions that touch upon everything from proven techniques to questionable practices, to the "terrible truths" of direct mail, and much more. *$39 (plus $4.95 shipping and handling)*

Maximum Gifts by Return Mail: An Expert Tells How to Write Highly Profitable Fund Raising Letters
ROLAND KUNIHOLM (THE TAFT GROUP, 1989)

▶ The author asserts that the key element in creating a great direct response mailing usually comes before you even put a single word on paper. This skilled teacher shows you how to get the creative process started. He discusses the best methods for writing solicitation letters and emphasizes the preparation that should take place before fund raisers begin their solicitation letter. He also discusses how to start the creative process involved in developing a direct-mail piece, how to find the writing approach that works best for a particular cause, how to test new creations, and how to duplicate the success of nine letters that raised large amounts of money. Learn the 16 questions to ask before you write. *Softcover, 261 pages, $42 (includes shipping)*

999 Tips, Trends, and Guidelines for Successful Direct Mail and Telephone Fundraising
MAL WARWICK (STRATHMOOR PRESS, 1993)

▶ This book offers guidelines to help the new fund-raising practitioner walk the minefield of direct-response fund raising and a refresher course to prod the veteran professional to maintain a link with the basics as well as to develop new ideas in direct-mail and telephone fund raising; and hundreds of tips for those seeking guidance in defining a mail campaign, selecting lists, writing powerful letters, designing effective mail packages, and formulating winning telephone strategies. Some of the 109 individually written articles include: seven questions to ask before launching a direct-mail fund-raising program, how to start your letter with a bang, seven copy-writing mistakes that kill your mailings, twelve tips for envelope teasers, fourteen ways to cut design and production costs, how to use personalization to raise more money, six ways the telephone can improve your fund-raising results, twelve tips for choosing prospect lists, how small nonprofits can build donor lists, market research for big budgets and small, new ways to build your donor list, raising the capital to seed a direct-mail fund-raising program, scheduling your mailings for maximum advantage, fourteen things to know about every one of your donors, how to renew your lapsed donors, using newsletters effectively, ten things you need from your computer system, the basic facts about direct-mail premiums, and seven ways to encourage your donors to give more. It includes actual statistical reports you can use as models when tracking mailing results. *Softcover, 316 pages, $35 (plus $3 shipping)*

The One to One Future: Building Relationships One Customer at a Time
DON PEPPERS AND MARTHA ROGERS (CURRENCYDOUBLEDAY, 1997)

▶ This completely revised and updated edition—with an all-new User's Guide—takes readers step by step through the latest strategies needed for any organization to compete, and succeed, in the Interactive Age. Traditional direct-mail fund raisers try to pitch their appeals to the greatest number of people, but, with current technologies, securing larger gifts from fewer people is actually more efficient and more profitable. This book presents a radically new paradigm that focuses on "share of customer" (one customer at a time, rather than just share of market). It teaches you how to find the customers and prospects that are most loyal and offer the greatest opportunity for future profit, how to collaborate with them individually through a variety of media, and how to structure your organization to deal with these new realities. *Softcover, 446 pages, $17.95 (plus $4.50 shipping)*

Open Me Now!
HERSCHELL GORDON LEWIS (BONUS BOOKS, 1995)

▶ "Open Me Now!" is more than a command; the three words are a sales imperative for any envelope that wants to get itself opened. Every year, half a billion pieces of worthwhile direct mail are tossed into the wastebasket because whoever designed their envelopes didn't know how to convince the recipient to Open Me Now! In this book you have, for the first time ever, absolute rules for direct-mail envelope copy. Why? Because the envelope is a salesperson; in fact, it's the first—and, if defective, the only salesperson your target sees. The author describes various types of envelope treatment psychology and gives us sample after sample of each type. Covered in detail are ways to be sure your envelope catches the reader's eye. Did you know that as a mailer you have a wealth of sizes from which to choose—sizes envelope manufacturers regard as "standard" but recipients will notice because they demand to be noticed in the day's stack of mail? Did you know that using a post office box as a return address can damage response? You'll find lots of answers to "Did you know. . .?" questions in this clear, tightly written, no-nonsense guide to envelope use. If you use the mails, this book is more than an eye-opener—it can be the key to profit. *Hardcover, 260 pages, $40*

Raising Money By Mail: Strategies for Growth and Financial Stability, Revised Edition
MAL WARWICK (STRATHMOOR PRESS, 1996)

▶ This newly revised edition of *Revolution in the Mailbox* provides information on direct-mail fund raising. The book now focuses exclusively on nonprofit groups, with new text and illustrations, updated facts and statistics, and modified layout and typography. Learn how to find the names of potential donors, how much one should pay for a mailing to recruit new contributors, and the most important points to include in a fund-raising letter. *Raising Money by Mail* will help lay the foundation for your organization's direct-mail success. Mal Warwick believes in a creative, no-holds-barred entrepreneurial approach, one that makes use of the newest insights and the latest technologies. *Softcover, 126 pages, $19.95 (plus $3 shipping)*

Raising Money by Mail: Strategies for Growth and Financial Stability
MAL WARWICK (BONUS BOOKS, 1996)

▶ Learn all you need to know about boosting your organization's revenue through direct mail in this fund-raising classic. It places direct mail in the context of a total, forward-looking fund-raising strategy and shows how to use letter writing to lay the foundation

for your organization's continuing success. Warwick believes in a creative, no-holds-barred entrepreneurial approach—one that makes use of the newest insights and the latest technologies. Clearly written examples and case histories help you strategize and create direct-mail campaigns that work. Features include hundreds of practical tips to teach you how to save money while increasing donations; easy-to-understand graphs and tables illustrating everything from how to calculate a donor's "long-term value" to how to select mailing lists; and reproductions of actual letters, envelopes, inserts, and reply devices showing you what works—and what doesn't. *Softcover, 126 pages, $19.95*

Teach Yourself to Write Irresistible Fund-Raising Letters (Workbook)
CONRAD SQUIRES, THE NATIONAL COPY CLINIC (PRECEPT PRESS, 1994)

▶ As "The Copy Corner" columnist for *Fund Raising Management* magazine (see separate listing under Periodicals) and president of the National Copy Clinic, the author has spent 20 years teaching professional copywriters how to write better letters. Twenty study units make up the heart of this workbook. It offers a step-by-step approach to writing a fund-raising letter, including tips on defining objectives, choosing a theme, creating a lead, developing the argument, and selecting an appropriate suggested gift. The introductory chapter takes you through every key step in planning a fund-raising letter; picking a strong theme; slanting your letter toward prospects, donors, lapsed donors, and other segments; creating powerful leads; building your case in believable but compelling terms; creating an "ask" appropriate for each segment (crucial to your response); and a powerful close, adding a PS encouraging a response, evaluating and editing your letter to build on its strong points while eliminating the weak ones, and how to get past the approval process. This is followed by 20 self-teaching units. Each contains a sample fund-raising letter, highlighting segments that affect reader response, an essay explaining why the letter works (or why it doesn't), and several exercises that prompt you to dissect and modify each letter. Each letter is "scored" with the author's exclusive CopyRater™, an invaluable tool for you to use on all of your own fund-raising letters. It is an ideal letter-writing workbook for the one-person marketing department. The chapters are full of ideas and examples on creating powerful leads (more than 50 given), constructing your "ask" to fit the donor, and ideas for many enclosures that help you build response. *Softcover, 215 pages, $50*

Type & Layout: How Typography and Design Can Get Your Message Across or Get in the Way
COLIN WHEILDON (STRATHMOORE PRESS, 1996)

▶ It's not just what you say, it's how you say it—and, more important, how you print it! In this book, based on nine years of scientific research, Colin Wheildon reveals how typesetting and design techniques can improve reading comprehension or kill a reader's interest almost immediately. *Type & Layout* shows you how following a few simple and proven rules can help you drastically increase your readership. *Softcover, 264 pages, $24.95*

You Don't Always Get What You Ask For: Using Direct Mail Tests to Raise More Money for Your Organization
MAL WARWICK (STRATHMOOR PRESS, 1992)

▶ This book explains the advantages and pitfalls of direct-mail tests for nonprofit fund raisers through real-life examples; topics covered include what is important to test and what isn't, whether "teasers" still work, whether brochures improve direct-mail response, whether window envelopes will scare away your donors, whether direct mail donors are environmentally conscious, and testing tips from the pros. *Softcover, 129 pages, $20 (plus $2.50 shipping)*

Foundation Funding Sources *(See also Federal Funding; Funding; Grants; Grant Seeking)*

America's New Foundations *(See Grant Seeking)*

Building and Equipment Grants, 5th Edition
(RESEARCH GRANT GUIDES)

► This book profiles 800 foundations that award grants for building and equipment. It features an article on "Successful Strategies for Winning Building and Equipment Grants." Subject index categories include Community Development, Culture, Disabled, Education, Elderly, Health, Higher Education, Hospitals, Libraries, Recreation, Religion, Renovation, Social Service, Women/Girls, and Youth. It includes 200 more foundations than the previous edition and has a state-by-state arrangement. *Softcover, $59.50*

Directory of Computer and High Technology Grants: A Reference Directory Identifying Computer, Software, and High-Tech Grants Available to Nonprofit Organizations, 4th Edition
RICHARD M. ECKSTEIN, ED. (RESEARCH GRANT GUIDES, 1998)

► This book profiles 750 foundations that award grants for computers and technology. Subject index categories include Community Development, Culture, Disabled, Education, Elderly, Health, Higher Education, Hospitals, Libraries, Recreation, Religion, Renovation, Social Service, Women/Girls, and Youth. It includes 250 more foundations than the previous edition and has a state-by-state arrangement. *Softcover, $59.50*

Directory of Grants for Organizations Serving People with Disabilities: A Reference Directory Identifying Grants Available to Nonprofit Organizations, 10th Edition
RICHARD M. ECKSTEIN AND ANDREW J. GRANT, EDS. (RESEARCH GRANT GUIDES, 1997)

► This book profiles 800 foundations that award grants to organizations serving individuals with disabilities. Index categories include Accessibility Projects, Blind, Cultural Programs, Deaf/Hard-of-Hearing, Developmentally Disabled, Education, Independent Living Programs, Learning Disabilities, Mental Health, Mentally Disabled, Physically Disabled, Recreation, Rehabilitation, Research, Speech Impaired, Vocational Training, and Youth. *Softcover, $59.50*

Directory of Health Grants, 2nd Edition
(RESEARCH GRANT GUIDES)

► This book profiles 1,000 foundations that award health grants pertaining to education and youth, among others. Subject index categories include AIDS, Alzheimer's Disease, Cancer, Cardiovascular, Clinics, Diabetes, Education, Health Organizations, Hospices, Hospitals, Medical Equipment, Medical Research, Nursing Services, and Youth. It has a state-by-state arrangement. *Softcover, $59.50*

Directory of Internet Guide to Grants
(RESEARCH ASSOCIATES, 2000)

► Includes the following specialized directories: *Funding for Recreation Programs* (outlines 100+ foundations with assets up to $1 million); *Funding for Mental Health and Hospitals* (includes 100+ foundations with assets between $1 and $10 million); *Funding for Aging and Senior Services* (lists 64 large foundations supporting aging and senior programs); *Funding for Colleges and Universities* (includes 100+ foundations with assets over $1 million); *Funding for Private, Nonprofit Operating Expenses* (contains 100+ foundations with assets up to $1 million); *International Funding* (outlines 98 foundations supporting international projects); *Funding for Day Care and Child Development Programs* (includes 118 foundations); *Women's Issues and Programs* (contains 100+ foundations supporting women's programs); *Environmental and Wildlife Grants* (lists 100+ foundations for environmental and wildlife issues); *Funding for Economically Disadvantaged* (includes foundations supporting the economically disadvantaged); *Funding for Community and Neighborhood Development* (outlines 100+ foundations); *Funding for Youth* (includes 100+ grants for youth programs); Violence Prevention Funding (lists 109 grant funding sources); *Funding for Minority Issues and Programs* (includes 104 grants supporting minority-related programs); *Computer Technology Funding* (includes 110 grants for computers, software, and other technology); *Christian and Jewish Organizations* (over 160 sources for churches and synagogues); *Funding for Alcohol, Tobacco, and Other Drug Abuse* (lists over 148 grant programs); *Grants for the Healthcare Field* (includes 100 national foundations with a history of funding healthcare); *Funding for Law Enforcement (PALS) and Criminal Justice* (grants from 125 foundations and corporations); *Grants for the Classroom Teacher K–12* (contains 150 small government and private grants); *Art, Music, Dance, and Drama Funding* (includes 142 grants for nonprofits, government, and education); *Special Education and Developmental Disabilities* (includes 100+ grant sources); *Internet Guide to Grants* (clears out the "junk" Web sites and identifies the 100 quality, major sites); *HIV/AIDS/STD Funding* (includes 107 national grant sources); *Building, Renovation, and Construction* (includes 152 funding sources). *All directories are $44.95 each (includes shipping and handling). Purchase five of any combination of the directories and receive any three additional directory/software selections free. All 62 directories on CD-ROM: $499*

The Directory of Oklahoma Foundations, 6th Edition
(FOUNDATION RESEARCH PROJECT, 1997) (BIENNIAL)

► Based on information from the latest IRS 990-PF forms on file at the State Attorney General's Office, this directory provides information on Oklahoma foundations and profiles more than 240 foundations that filed tax returns with the state Attorney General. The Directory lists foundation assets, income, total grants made, board of trustees, and funding interests/restrictions. *Softcover, $30*

Directory of Operating Grants, 5th Edition
(RESEARCH GRANT GUIDES)

► This book profiles 850 foundations that award grants for overhead expenses. Three articles target the strategies needed to win operating grants. Operating grants are not restricted to a specified project or a set of activities. They can support general operating expenses that sustain an organization's usual activities. Operating grants can underwrite salaries, rent, mortgage payments, utilities, office supplies, and additional overhead expenses. Each profile lists the verified areas of support and address. Geographic restrictions, grant range, and previously awarded grants are included when available. Subject index categories include: Animal Welfare, Community Development, Cultural Organizations, Disabled, Education, Elderly, Environment, Health Organizations, Higher Education, Hospitals, Minorities, Recreation, Religion Organizations, Social Service, Women, and Youth. It has a state-by-state arrangement. *Softcover, $59.50*

Directory of Pennsylvania Foundations, 7th Edition

S. DAMON KLETZIEN, ED. (TRIADVOCATES PRESS, 2001)

▶ Long considered Pennsylvania's "fundraisers' bible," it includes exceedingly detailed information about the Commonwealth's large and diverse foundation "community." All Pennsylvania foundations having $150,000+ in assets and/or awarding $7,500 or more in grants annually on a discretionary basis are fully profiled. It includes 1,509 profiled foundation entries. Each of these exceptionally detailed profile entries includes the following data: (1) All grants awarded to Pennsylvania organizations—down to at least the $1,000 level and listed in descending order of size (with purpose of grant, when known); also selected, significant out-of-state grants; (2) up to 24 giving interest categories for each foundation are coded and fully indexed; (3) financial data includes assets at market value, fiscal year, gifts received, number of grants awarded, and their total; (4) name of contact person (with telephone number) as well as all officers, directors, trustees, and donors, including out-of-state residents, and all fully indexed; (5) corporate affiliations, if any, and now fully indexed; (6) year created and Employer ID Number; (7) availability of published annual reports, guidelines, or other foundation publications; and (8) grant application guidelines, deadlines, and required background documentation, if the foundation has established policies. An additional 2,100+ Pennsylvania foundations are listed with summary data (name, address, and status code). These did not meet criteria to be profiled for one of the following: (1) Limited Assets/Giving—market value of assets is under $150,000 and total grants under $7,500; (2) Operating Foundation—does not award grants; (3) Restricted Trust—no discretionary giving; (4) Inactive—assets under $5,000 and no recent grants; (5) Moved out-of-state; (6) Terminated; and (7) Undetermined Status—no recent information available. In addition, about three-fourths of the profiles are supplemented with data on giving priorities/policies and application guidelines that foundation administrators supplied directly. Finally, all profile entries were sent to all foundation administrators within weeks of publication for last-minute verification/updating of their profile entry. This edition has the following indexes: foundation name (all profiled and nonprofiled foundations); officer, directors, trustees, and contact persons (over 9,000 listed); corporate connection (400+ corporate foundations or corporate-related); major interest (giving) codes—up to 24 for every foundation; application deadlines, by month; Pennsylvania county of location; and foundations that give to Pennsylvania organizations outside their primary region. It is also available on CD-ROM (contains the full text of all 1,509 foundation profiles as published in the print edition, plus about two dozen new foundation profiles and many address/telephone updates). The CD-ROM is shipped with a free copy of the *Directory of Pennsylvania Foundations,* book edition. *Print Edition: $73.50 postpaid (plus 6% Pennsylvania sales tax, unless exempt); CD-ROM: $150 for nonprofit organizations; $300 for consultants and other for-profit businesses (plus $7.00 postage);*

each interim update/releases will be $50 plus ($3.00 postage) for those customers who originally bought the Directory DATABASE at the full purchase price

Directory of Program Grants

(RESEARCH GRANT GUIDES)

▶ This book profiles 775 foundations that award grants in the areas of: Animal Welfare, Community Development, Cultural Organizations, Disabled, Education, Elderly, Environment, Health Organizations, Higher Education, Hospitals, Minorities, Recreation, Religion Organizations, Social Service, Women/Girls, and Youth. It has a state-by-state arrangement. *Softcover, $59.50*

Directory of Social Service Grants: A Reference Directory Listing Social Service, Child Welfare, Family Service, and Related Grants Available to Nonprofit Organizations, 2nd Edition

RICHARD M. ECKSTEIN, ED. (RESEARCH GRANT GUIDES, 1998)

▶ This book profiles 1,100 foundations that award grants pertaining to social services, including child welfare, disabled, family services, homeless, minorities, and substance abuse. It has a state-by-state arrangement. *Softcover, $59.50*

Directory of Texas Foundations 2001, 20th Edition

(NONPROFIT RESOURCE CENTER)

▶ This book provides the most complete and up-to-date information on more than 2,200 private and community foundations in Texas. Highlights include: helps identify the best funding prospects, features over 100 newly listed foundations each year; summarizes foundations by grants, assets, and grant distribution; allows research by areas of interest, city, foundation name, trustees and officers, and types of support; tracks giving interests and grant distributions patterns of the top 100 foundations in Texas; lists assets and grants by major cities and regions in Texas; and identifies foundations by city, size, and grant dollars awarded. See also the Directory of Texas Foundations Online at *http://www.nprc.org/advanced/contents.html. Softcover, 601 pages, $160*

The Directory of Virginia Foundations: 2000–2001

(THE GRANTS CONNECTION, 2000)

▶ The Directory includes profiles on 992 foundations whose combined assets exceed $3.5 billion, details on the $235 million in grants awarded by Virginia foundations, listings of 14,533 specific awards, and application guidelines for those foundations that publish them. It is available in CD-ROM, print, and diskette formats. *Print: $150 (Shipping $10 each); CD-ROM, $250 (Shipping $5 each); Diskette, Windows Version, $195 (Shipping $4 each); Diskette, LAN (for up to 6 networked users) $350 (Shipping $4 each)*

The Effective Grant Office: Streamlining Grants Development and Management

JACQUELINE FERGUSON (ASPEN PUBLISHERS, 1999)

▶ Implement a well-organized grants development and management system, and you'll win more grants. *The Effective Grant Office* helps you do just that, as it reveals practical strategies to improve every step of the process: create effective policies and procedures, build an efficient grants team, train others to handle grants tasks, oversee the preparation and filing of reports, stimulate interest in grants development, streamline your office procedures in other areas of your institution, and much more. Sharpen the grant-seeking skills of your office, identify and eliminate weak links, and build on your staff members' strengths. Let *The Effective Grant Office* help you make the most of your available resources and efforts. *Hardcover, 94 pages, $68*

The Foundation Directory *(See Grant seeking)*

Foundation Grants Index *(See Grant seeking)*

The Foundation 1,000 *(See Grant seeking)*

Foundations in Wisconsin: A Directory, 18th Edition *(Annual)*
(MARQUETTE UNIVERSITY FUNDING INFORMATION CENTER, 1999) (ANNUAL)

▶ This book covers every active, grant-making foundation in the state of Wisconsin. One thousand sixty-five foundations are profiled, including contact information, total assets, grants paid, and areas of interest. The directory is available in print and electronic editions. The electronic edition is an application for Microsoft Windows 95 or later and is available on CD-ROM. This program will perform keyword and subject searches of the directory profiles. Foundation profiles include: Foundation Name; Address and Telephone Number; Contact Person; Officers and Directors; Fiscal Year Reporting; Total Asset Value; Total Grants Paid; Grant Range and Median; Areas of Interest; Purpose Statement; Application Procedures; Limitations; Geographic Focus; Sample Grants List; and Web Address. Electronic edition features include: searches can be made in any category or across multiple categories; no previous database experience is needed; automated construction of queries makes searching easy; advanced searching allows experienced users to formulate their own queries; the foundation profiles can be printed or saved as an ASCII text file; and fast searches through the 1,065 foundations in the database. *Print: $63.36 ($45 Nonprofit) (plus $2 shipping); Stand-alone PC: $158.40 ($105 Nonprofit) (plus $3.50); Networked Access: $369.60 ($245 Nonprofit) (plus $3.50)*

Guide to U.S. Foundations, Their Trustees, Officers, and Donors *(See Grant seeking)*

The Insider's Guide to Grantmaking: How Foundations Find, Fund, and Manage Effective Programs
JOEL OROSZ (JOSSEY-BASS, 2000)

▶ Written for program officers and of considerable value to grant seekers, this volume is the first and only practical guide to making foundation grants and developing essential skills for effective and ethical grantmaking. Author Joel J. Orosz not only introduces readers to the history, structure, and function of foundations in society but also explores the complex role that program officers play in their day-to-day activities. He takes you behind the scenes and into the thought processes of grant makers' philanthropy. Ostensibly written for foundation program officers teaching the whys, wherefores, and do's and don'ts of grant making to program officers, simultaneously he's presenting to grant seekers the blueprint for successfully approaching funders. A selection of the topics that will reveal these secrets to grantseekers include: the eight rules grant makers follow when meeting with applicants; 12 characteristics of a good proposal, from the grant maker's perspective; four reasons to decline a proposal; traps for the unwary program officer; grant

seeker complaints, grant maker responses; site visits, why and how grantmakers decide; to renew or not to renew and how grant makers decide; the grant maker's seven deadly sins of philanthropy. For the serious grant seeker, *The Insider's Guide to Grantmaking* is a "code-breaking" book that could very well transform the way you approach foundations. *Hardcover, 276 pages, $32.95*

How Foundations Work: What Grant Seekers Need to Know about the Many Faces of Foundations
DENNIS P. MCILNAY (JOSSEY-BASS, 1998)

▶ Dennis McIlnay offers a unique and remarkable look inside foundations—exploring the complex workings of the mysterious and often misunderstood organizations that so often determine the success or failure of a nonprofit's fund-raising ventures. Based on his extensive research and on insights from foundations themselves, Dennis P. McIlnay reveals the underlying principles and philosophies that guide grant making. He gives the grant seeker an edge in the highly competitive world of foundation grants both by debunking many of the myths and misconceptions surrounding foundations and by including more productive strategies for dealing with them. Structured around six perceptions of foundations—judges, editors, citizens, activists, entrepreneurs, and partners—this book provides a thorough understanding of what makes foundations tick and how this affects their interactions with nonprofits. He suggests that foundations have unique organizational personalities with unique values, languages, cultures, rituals, and behaviors. Understanding these personalities is the key to grant seekers' success. *Hardcover, 240 pages, $29.95*

Federal Funding

Catalog of Federal Domestic Assistance
(SUPERINTENDENT OF DOCUMENTS)

▶ This is a government-wide compendium of federal programs, projects, services, and activities that provide assistance or benefits to the American public. It contains financial and nonfinancial assistance programs administered by departments and establishments of the federal government. It details every federal grant, including description, eligibility, deadlines, and award procedures. As the basic reference source of federal programs, the primary purpose of the Catalog is to assist users in identifying programs that meet specific objectives of the potential applicant, and to obtain general information on federal assistance programs. In addition, the intent of the Catalog is to improve coordination and communication between the federal government and state and local governments. The Catalog provides the user with access to programs administered by federal departments and agencies in a single publication. Program information is cross-referenced by functional classification (Functional Index), subject (Subject Index), applicant (Applicant Index), deadline(s) for program application submission (Deadlines Index), and authorizing legislation (Authorization Index). These are valuable resource tools that, if used carefully, can make it easier to identify specific areas of program interest more efficiently. Other sections of the Catalog provide users with information on programs added and deleted since the last edition of the Catalog, a crosswalk of program numbers and title changes, regional and local offices, intergovernmental review requirements, definitions of the types of assistance under which programs are administered, proposal writing, grant application procedures, and additional sources of information on federal programs and services. Also included are two charts on how to use the Catalog to locate programs of interest. Programs selected for inclusion in the federal assistance database are defined as any function of a federal agency that provides assistance or benefits for a state or states, territorial possession, county, city, other political subdivision, grouping, or instrumentality thereof; any domestic profit or nonprofit corporation, institution, or individual, other than an agency of the federal government. It is available in print, CD-ROM, and diskette formats. *Hard copy: $87 (includes midyear supplement); CD-ROM (issued semiannually): $45 for single copy or an annual subscription (complete editions in June and December) for $75; Diskette (issued semiannually): $85*

Federal (Grant) Money Retriever *(See Products and Services—Software, Grant Research)*

Government Assistance Almanac 1999–2000, 14th Edition

J. ROBERT DUMOUCHEL, ED. (OMNIGRAPHICS, 1999)

▶ This book provides updated information on all 1,424 federal domestic assistance programs available. These programs represent more than $1 trillion worth of federal assistance earmarked for distribution to consumers, children, parents, veterans, senior citizens, students, businesses, civic groups, state and local agencies, and others. The book covers every program described in the *Catalog of Federal Domestic Assistance* (CFDA), but in a format that is much more understandable and accessible to the general reader. It condenses the information in the federal catalog's more than 2,000 pages to the essentials needed by those seeking federal assistance. It describes federal assistance programs, including research grants, business assistance, loans, and aid to individuals as well as organizations. Features include: Master Index with extensive referencing and cross-referencing. For ease of use, programs providing financial assistance are italicized; Agency Index lists all federal administrative units and subunits. While still incorporated in the Master Index, this new feature helps expedite user searches specifically for administrative entities; Summary Tables provide four-year comparisons of federal assistance by agency, department, and administrative unit, with details on the 50 largest and the 50 smallest programs in the current year; Field Office Contacts provides addresses and telephone numbers for more than 3,000 field offices. Also included are references to legislation authorizing government assistance. *Hardcover, 1,000 pages, $195*

Guide to Federal Funding for Education

(THOMPSON PUBLISHING GROUP)

▶ The *Guide to Federal Funding for Education* keeps educators, state and local educational officials, community organizations, and service providers abreast of funding opportunities for more than 550 education-related programs available from the federal government. A source of grants and funding information, the *Guide to Federal Funding for Education* describes hundreds of programs in the U.S. Department of Education and scores of other federal agencies in one easy-to-use reference. The Guide provides clear, timely explanations of grants for schools, libraries, colleges and universities, nonprofits, and social service agencies, and the unique 5-Star Funding Opportunity Index™ shows what your chances are for winning funds. Plus, three indexes make grant-finding easier. Quarterly newsletters provide news on recent legislative and regulatory developments, appropriations action, and funding opportunities. Quarterly Guide updates include new and updated program descriptions. Also provided is a semimonthly Federal Grant

Deadline Calendar and access to their subscriber-only web page. A one-year subscription to the *Guide to Federal Funding for Education* includes a two-volume loose-leaf manual with quarterly updates, twice monthly Federal Grant Deadline Calendars, and access to the subscriber-only Web site. *Loose-leaf, $297 (plus $14.50 shipping and handling)*

Guide to Federal Funding for Governments and Nonprofits

(THOMPSON PUBLISHING GROUP)

▶ This guide helps state and local governments, communities, and nonprofits win thousands of federal grants and other aid. In one easy-to-use reference, the Guide gives you the key facts and insider tips for tapping more than 750 federal aid programs offering funds for: housing and homelessness; law enforcement and juvenile justice; environmental protection and recovery; parks and museums; child care and social services; fire and emergency services; community facilities; job training and business development; highways and mass transit; sewers, roads, and other public works; services for the elderly; telecommunications; public health; and many more critical functions. With the Guide's special indexes, you'll identify the programs that are best for you. With the Guide's explanations, you'll compare different programs in terms of eligibility requirements and uses of funds. Finally, with the help of the exclusive 5-Star Funding Opportunity Index™, you'll decide which programs offer you the best shot of winning, so you can focus your efforts. Quarterly Updates include new and updated program descriptions, as well as articles detailing new legislation and regulations, budget action, and funding trends. You also get twice-monthly Federal Grant Deadline Calendars, along with subscriber-only access to their continually updated list of new grant announcements. A one-year subscription to the *Guide to Federal Funding for Governments and Nonprofits* includes the two-volume loose-leaf manual with twice-monthly Federal Grant Deadline Calendars, quarterly updates and newsletters, and access to the subscriber-only Web site. *Loose-leaf binder, 2 volumes, 2,156 pages, $339 (plus $14.50 shipping and handling)*

The "How To" Grants Manual: Successful Grantseeking Techniques for Obtaining Public and Private Grants, Fourth Edition

DAVID G. BAUER (ORYX PRESS, 1999)

▶ The author shares valuable insight into the grant-seeking process while providing a helpful "get organized" book. Additionally, the fourth edition has been updated to include advice on ways to use the Internet when seeking grants. This useful guide puts grant seekers on the right track using a simple, three-part approach that offers advice on: Part 1: Funding differences between private and public sectors, and which tools and methods are most useful; Part 2: The best ways to win a federal grant; Part 3: Funding differences between foundations and corporations, and how to approach the private sector. *The "How To" Grants Manual* packages its proven methods together with worksheets, sample letters, an extensive list of resources, and a practical step-by-step outline on preparing a proposal—all in one helpful "get organized" book. *Hardcover, 264 pages, $34.95*

Winning Federal Grants: A Guide to the Government's Grant-Making Process

PHALE HALE JR. AND LESLIE A. RAMSEY (ASPEN PUBLISHERS, 1996)

▶ Don't miss out on thousands of grant opportunities worth millions of dollars. Winning Federal Grants reveals what areas and issues are funded by various agencies of the federal government; how Congress creates grant programs, and how you can monitor their activities to track programs that interest you; how agencies review proposals and make grant awards; and how to manage a grant once you receive the funds, including federal rules you must follow and reports to file. You get practical tools to help you win more grants, including copies of standard federal grant application forms, a list of federal agencies and their grant-making offices, a glossary of federal grant terms, and expert advice on how to locate federal funding sources beyond the obvious agencies. *Softcover, 96 pages, $62*

Funding

The Changing World of Foundation Fundraising: New Challenges and Opportunities (New Directions for Philanthropic Fundraising #23)
SANDRA A. GLASS (JOSSEY-BASS, 1999)

► There are over 40,000 unique private foundations in the United States, with total assets of approximately $300 billion. As these foundations grow in number and size, it is increasingly important for grant seekers to understand their missions and modes of operation. This volume of *New Directions for Philanthropic Fundraising* offers insights into the changes taking place in different types of foundations, including special-purpose, regional, community, and international foundations. The authors suggest practical ways that grant seekers can improve relations with foundations, and show how grant makers and other foundation staff enhance their effectiveness—and better serve their constituents' needs—through strategic planning and alliance building. This is the twenty-third issue of the quarterly journal *New Directions for Philanthropic Fundraising*. For more information on the series, see Journals and Periodicals. *Softcover, 96 pages, $25.00*

The Complete Guide to Corporate Fund Raising
JOSEPH DERMER AND STEPHEN NERTHEIMER, EDS. (THE TAFT GROUP, 1991)

► Nine of the nation's most distinguished fund-raising counselors reveal the secrets of their success at getting grants from corporate sources in this fascinating reference. *The Complete Guide to Corporate Fund Raising* includes a witty, penetrating essay by the manager of a contributions program at a major corporation. You'll be surprised at the holes he pokes in common misconceptions of corporate giving. *Softcover, 112 pages, $10*

Corporate and Foundation Fund Raising: A Complete Guide from the Inside
EUGENE A. SCANLAN (ASPEN PUBLISHERS, 1997)

► If you truly want to be successful in raising money from foundations and corporations, there are many steps you must take before a proposal goes out the door. And there are many things you must do after it is in the hands of the potential funder. That's why you should have a copy of *Corporate and Foundation Fund Raising: A Compete Guide from the Inside*. It's the only step-by-step guide that provides a total and comprehensive strategic approach to fund raising. You'll get a wealth of hands-on techniques, strategy tips, real-life examples, war stories, time-saving forms, suggested readings, a glossary, and an extensive bibliography. As those who regularly seek corporate or foundation money know, you don't win grants simply by sending proposals. If that's all you do, your proposal will

rest among countless others representing the same approach. To be successful in raising money from foundations and corporations, there are a wealth of things you must do before you send your proposal, and others to tend to once your proposal is in the hands of the potential funder. It is this entire grant-seeking process—from understanding what drives funders to maintaining a productive relationship once you've received a grant—that Eugene Scanlan illuminates in this book. Similarly, Scanlan explains how to penetrate various barriers (he calls them filters) by asking specific questions of the foundation or corporation. *Softcover, 304 pages, $64*

From Idea to Funded Project, 4th Edition
JANE C. BELCHER AND JULIA M. JACOBSEN (ORYX PRESS, 1992)

► This expanded edition shows you exactly how to cultivate an idea to its total funding potential and garner support from within your organization. The authors demonstrate how to develop and refine the project to ensure success and how to plan for successful implementation and administration of awarded funds. They also share proven methods to help protect the best ideas from being lost, ignored, or improperly developed. Helpful appendices identify additional reference materials and information sources as well as feature examples of application forms and other materials. *Softcover, 144 pages, $26.50*

Fund-Raising Law and Regulations

First Legal Answer Book for Fund Raisers
BRUCE HOPKINS (JOHN WILEY & SONS, 2000)

► As the competition for dollars grows increasingly intense, managers and fund raisers need to know how to work with business law. This book looks at different legal strategies that fund raisers can use to optimize their return without jeopardizing their exempt status or donors' goodwill. *Softcover, 320 pages, $49.95*

Fund-Raising Regulation: A State-by-State Handbook of Registration Forms, Requirements, and Procedures
SETH PERLMAN, BETSY HILLS BUSH (JOHN WILEY & SONS, 1996)

► Using an easy-to-follow format, this invaluable resource presents all the necessary fund-raising registration information for nonprofit organizations, fund-raising counsel, and professional solicitors in every state. It contains a complete set of forms for each state that can easily be photocopied and an "exceptions" packet for nonstandard forms. It includes material on what, where, and when to file; annual reporting requirements; essential definitions; exemptions for specific categories of exempt organizations; requirements for cause-related marketing, and much more. It includes a free annual supplement. *Hardcover, 1,024 pages, $370*

The Law of Fund Raising, 2nd Edition
BRUCE R. HOPKINS (JOHN WILEY & SONS, 1995)

► One of the few legal experts on fund-raising laws pertaining to nonprofit organizations, Hopkins provides the tools to spot and address the issues that will affect the lifeblood of charitable enterprises' existence during the coming years. He details federal and state laws, emphasizing administrative, tax, and constitutional law. He explains state and federal rules affecting the responsibilities of fund-raising professionals. He explores compliance issues, prospective laws, and regulatory trends, and features summaries of every state's Charitable Contribution Solicitation Act. The book includes scores of tables of cases, IRS rulings and pronouncements, an 82-item IRS checklist for monitoring charitable fund raising, and sample IRS forms. *Softcover, 762 pages, $160*

Retirement Assets and Charitable Gifts: A Guide for Planned Giving Professionals, Financial Planners, and Donors *(See Planned Giving)*

Tax Law of Charitable Giving, 2nd Edition

BRUCE R. HOPKINS (JOHN WILEY & SONS, 2000)

▶ Charitable giving involves a complex set of rules and regulations with high monetary stakes. This book provides comprehensive information on the laws, definitions, and forms of various charitable gifts, ranging from art to real estate and beyond. All of the effective vehicles for gift giving available to nonprofits are explained in this comprehensive guide. There are discussions of the structure and timing considerations for one-time gifts, as well as planned giving programs. Learn the best opportunities for tax savings, depending on donor type, tax circumstances, and gift-giving desire. *Hardcover, 816 pages, $150*

For-Profit Ventures

Complete Guide to Money Making Ventures for Nonprofit Organizations

(THE TAFT GROUP, 1996)

▶ Generate more earned income for your nonprofit with this self-help guide. This workbook leads you through the stages of identifying and structuring money-making ventures, organizing board and staff commitment, developing a business plan, and avoiding costly mistakes—all while contributing directly to your group's nonprofit mission. It includes actual planning documents of four nonprofits' quests for earned income. *Softcover, 235 pages, $20*

Gifts-in-Kind

Gifts-in-Kind

DONALD T. NELSON AND PAUL H. SCHNEITER (THE TAFT GROUP, 1991)

▶ Two veteran development officers take you through the steps of acquiring, managing, and selling charitable contributions in this interesting guide. Learn how to evaluate real estate, set up a trust file, understand planned giving devices, and more. *Softcover, 178 pages, $11.98*

Grant Writing/Proposal Writing

The Complete Guide to Getting a Grant, Revised Edition

LAURIE BLUM (JOHN WILEY & SONS, 1996)

▶ Best-selling author and professional fund raiser Blum discloses proven strategies for recognizing and developing a good idea, choosing the appropriate funder, writing the proposal, and following up. She lists the most current sources, sample budgets and proposals, and do's and don'ts of working with a sponsor. With clear explanations and proven strategies for success, her indispensable guide will help you develop a game plan to get the grant you need.

Here's where you'll find complete details on: shaping your idea to attract funding; preparing your funding campaign—from research and organization to budgeting and marketing; finding the right resource—building a prospect list, using basic references, and keeping data sheets; writing your proposal; and following up on responses—what to do if you receive a grant and what steps to take if your request is turned down. *Softcover, 368 pages, $19.95*

Designing Successful Grant Proposals

DONALD C. ORLICH (ASSOCIATION FOR SUPERVISION & CURRICULUM DEVELOPMENT, 1996)

▶ This book offers proven guidelines for compiling successful grant proposals. It includes suggestions on how to organize ideas and establish needs, information on monitoring funding sources, a model of a successful proposal, and an extensive list of sources that award both public and private grants. *Softcover, 135 pages, $20.95*

The Elements of Grant Writing

(THE GRANT DOCTORS)

▶ A step-by-step guide to creating new programs and writing grant proposals to private/corporate foundations. The handbook includes an introduction to grants; an organizational assessment guide; program development tips; proposal writing techniques; work plan, evaluation, and budget templates; and a loose-leaf copy for reproduction. *Softcover, $21*

Finding Funding: Grantwriting and Project Management from Start to Finish, Including Project Management and Internet Use, 3rd Edition

ERNEST W. BREWER, CHARLES M. ACHILLES, AND JAY R. FUHRIMAN (CORWIN PRESS/SAGE PUBLICATIONS, 1998)

▶ This book provides helpful assistance from the beginning of the process of identifying funding sources, through the grant writing process, to the actual management of the program. *Softcover, 320 pages, $49.95*

Finding Funding: The Comprehensive Guide to Grant Writing *(Book and Disk)*

DANIEL M. BARBER (BOND STREET PUBLISHERS, 1994)

▶ This is a step-by-step handbook for writing winning proposals. Building on over three decades of experience, the author has organized a foolproof guide for experienced and novice grant writers. It includes a document diskette that features more than 500 funding sources, sample letters, forms, budgets, timetables, PERT charts, and other valuable "boilerplate" that will help you work smarter, not harder. This book has been adopted by scores of colleges and universities across the country and is in the libraries of major foundations and community-based organizations. *Softcover, 212 pages, $24.95 (plus $4 shipping and handling); Diskette only: $9.95 (plus $2.00 shipping & handling)*

From Idea to Funded Project: Grant Proposals That Work, 4th Edition

JANE C. BELCHER AND JULIA M. JACOBSEN (ORYX PRESS, 1992)

▶ This latest edition of *A Process for the Development of Ideas* has more than a new title—it has been expanded to show you exactly how to cultivate an idea to its total funding potential and garner support from within your organization. The authors demonstrate how to develop and refine the project to ensure success and how to plan for successful implementation and administration of awarded funds. They also share proven methods to help protect the best ideas from being lost, ignored, or improperly developed. Helpful appendices identify additional reference materials and information sources as well as feature examples of application forms and other materials. *Softcover, 144 pages, $26.50*

"Fundraising with the Corporate Letter Request—A 30-Minute Audio Book

BEV BROWNING (BEV BROWING & ASSOCIATES, 2000)

▶ This "all details included" 30-minute audio training tape teaches everyone from fund-raising newcomers to successful fund-raising veterans how to research business prospects, refine a mailing list to the "most likely to give" funding sources, and write a results-oriented corporate letter request in just 30 minutes. This tape is for anyone who wants to learn and try new letter-writing approaches when asking for money or gifts for nonprofit organizations. The tape's author, Bev Browning, has raised more than $45 million in grants and gifts—half using the corporate letter format she developed. On the tape, Bev answers questions from A to Z on corporate letter solicitation for listeners. *$19.95*

Getting Funded: A Complete Guide to Proposal Writing

MARY HALL (CONTINUING EDUCATION PRESS, 1988)

▶ In the face of shrinking grant funds and increasing competition, a good proposal is more critical than ever. But a good proposal requires more than good writing. It also calls for a useful idea, careful research, and proper selection of potential funding sources. *Getting Funded* shows you step by step how to test the appeal of your idea; how to measure your organization's capability to carry out what it proposes; how to research and develop your idea; how to select the most promising funding sources; how to construct your proposal, from abstract to budget, using proven management planning procedures; how to present and negotiate your proposal; and how to prepare for a subsequent round of funding. Now in a new, easier-to-use format, this guide has been expanded to include current information on funding trends, more information on funding sources and databases, and a broader range of examples and cases: both how to and how not to go about grant writing. The book covers not only project and operating grants, but also research and capital funding. It applies to science, the arts, health, education, social services, and many other fields. As an aid to building your proposal, it offers dozens of critical checklists, sample formats, and models. It is the only book to treat proposal writing as a form of management planning. It contains more information on funding sources than any comparable book on the market, including sections on unions and associations as well as government agencies, foundations, and corporations. *Softcover, 206 pages, $23.95*

Getting Grants Funded in Your Community: A Workbook for Grantseekers, Large Print Edition

BEVERLY A. BROWNING (BEV BROWNING & ASSOCIATES, 1999)

▶ This comprehensive grant-writing workbook offers current, relevant information for novice grant seekers and essential writing and funding-related tips. It has eight chapters, beginning with "Encouragement" and ending with "Thoroughness and Expectations." The appendices contain information on national funding contacts, examples of funded federal, state, and foundation grants and proposals, and other helpful resource links. The author takes the mystique out of grantwriting and grantseeking by showing how to identify funding sources, conduct strategic planning for community projects, by providing guidelines for working with a grantwriting consultant, showing the reader how to write a

complete proposal narrative, and provides supportive encouragement throughout. The appendices are filled to the brim with sample foundation, state, and federal grant applications, and a sample of a regional writing format and the National Network of Grantmaker's writing format. Electronic and print resources are listed throughout. The workbook comes with an IBM-formatted computer disk with templates for both the regional and national funding source format. The disk is a 1.44-MB floppy, Windows 95, Word 97 format. The book's step-by-step, commonsense approach is useful for anyone planning to train community members to form a grant-writing team, schools planning to train teachers to form a team, or the individual exploratory grant-seeker. *Hardcover, 265 pages, $99 (includes shipping and handling); $79 (Web price)*

Grant Application Writers Handbook

LIANE REIF-LEHRER (JONES & BARTLETT, 1995)

▶ The ideal companion to the videocassettes, the Handbook follows the same organization and includes appendices on oral presentations, expository writing, foundation grants, examples of summary statements, and Reviewer's Reports for NIH and NSF applications (highlighted to show you what reviewers look for), and an extensive glossary. *Softcover, 496 pages, $42.95*

Grant Proposals That Succeeded

VIRGINIA WHITE, ED. (PLENUM PUBLISHING, 1983)

▶ This book offers testimony, examples, and evaluations from people in real-life grant-writing experiences. It is a guide to presenting your program's goals effectively and professionally. It provides examples of requests that won $5,500 to $450,000 for a wide range of purposes; illustrates how the project was conceived, how the initial search for funding sources was done, and the negotiations that took place before applications were made; presents proposals originally appearing in *Grants* magazine; and covers research grants, training grants, arts applications, humanities (describing the grant-making process of the National Endowment for the Humanities), and a response to a request for proposal. *Hardcover, 256 pages, $56*

Grant Seeker's Budget Toolkit: How to Get It Right! (Book and CD-ROM)

JAMES A. QUICK AND CHERYL C. NEW (JOHN WILEY & SONS, 2000)

▶ Step-by-step guidance, insider tips, and all the tools needed to create the kind of budgets and financial plans that win grants—this book tells you how to develop your project budget and proposal budget and narrative or justification in a step-by-step manner. It tells you what words like *overhead, in-kind,* and *direct* and *indirect costs* mean. Grants are a major source of funding in the nonprofit sector, and nonprofits invest considerable time, effort, and resources into obtaining them. A key aspect of any successful grant application initiative is budgeting and financial planning. Unfortunately, many nonprofit professionals lack the know-how required to create budgets that instill grantors with confidence. This book gives it to them, and much more. Authors James Aaron Quick and Cheryl Carter New walk readers through the entire budgeting process, providing invaluable insider tips, guidelines, and rules of thumb. It includes a computer disk containing the full range of budget forms accepted by federal agencies in Word for Windows format. *Hardcover, 352 pages, $39.95 (plus $3 shipping)*

Grant Writing: A Hands-On Approach

PATRICIA RIFE (RIFE & ASSOCIATES, 1998)

▶ A guide for step-by-step writing of professional grant proposals, this book contains clear, concise explanations of each component of a standard proposal and samples from successful grants, including budget formats. *Softcover, 50 pages, $12.95*

Grant Writing for Dummies

BEV BROWING (HUNGRY MINDS, INC, 2001)

▶ Tap into deep government, foundation, and corporate pockets to fulfill your nonprofit organization's needs for funding. An expert tells you how to successfully target these institutions and get them to put their money behind your organization's cause. This step-by-step guide to writing a winning grant proposal delivers an overview of what types of grants are available and how to apply for them; strategies for cutting through red tape; a guide to the grant-writing terminology; an explanation of why some proposals succeed while others fail; samples of successful grant proposals; and the proper etiquette for following up a proposal and getting a response. *Softcover, 360 pages, $19.99*

Grant Writing for Teachers: If You Can Write a Lesson Plan You Can Write a Grant

DR. LINDA KARGES-BONE (GOOD APPLE RESOURCE BOOKS, 1994)

▶ This step-by-step workbook includes tips from a "pro," Grant Writer's Glossary, and 200 Hot Topics for grants. *Softcover, 144 pages, $14.99*

Grant Writing: Strategies for Developing Winning Proposals

PATRICK W. MILLER (MILLER & ASSOCIATES, 2000)

▶ Designed to walk the funding seeker through the major phases of grant development, this book represents more than nine years of ideas and techniques used in the development of grant proposals. It includes seven chapters with more than 50 exhibits. A series of review questions and exercises are presented at the end of each chapter to reinforce the reader's learning. Exercises in this book were developed to teach proposal writing and budget development skills to new and experienced grant writers. The book also includes a glossary, selected funding resources, and comprehensive review questions. The author believes that funding seekers who win grants on a consistent basis usually follow a series of comprehensive proposal development activities. It presents six fundamental phases of grant development: (1) activities before the RFP/RFA is released; (2) prewriting activities after the RFP/RFA is released; (3) writing, reviewing, rewriting, and editing the narrative; (4) preparing the budget; (5) producing, reproducing, packaging, and delivering the proposal; and (6) postsubmission activities. It focuses on organizing, writing, and submitting grant proposals and budgets. Topics include making smart bidding decisions, following appropriate bidding strategies, writing convincing themes, using compliance checklists, determining sound budgets, submitting appropriate and complete documents, and preparing for postsubmission activities such as responding to questions and negotiating with governmental personnel. Features include more than 50 illustrations and examples, 12 grant preparation exercises, 70 up-to-date resources, and 140 comprehensive review questions to stimulate learning. *Softcover, 170 pages, $39.95*

"Grant Your Wish: Learn from the Professionals How to Write a Successful Grant Proposal" (Videotape)

TOM EZELL AND RHONDA RITCHIE (SUCCESSFUL IMAGES, 1998)

▶ This video takes potential grant applicants through 12 elements that the scriptwriters believe are components of a winning proposal. Tom Ezell, president of Ezell & Company, a consulting company in Miami, and Rhonda Ritchie, a freelance consultant who works in southern Florida, discuss what they consider to be tried-and-true tenets of grant-proposal writing. For example, they suggest building an argument that the proposed project could survive without future support. A computer-animated pen points to relevant information on sample title pages and budget outlines. Other topics that are discussed include cover letters, appendices, and project timelines. Creed C. Black, former president of the John S. and James L. Knight Foundation in Miami, serves as narrator and offers the cardinal rule of proposal writing in the videotape's second minute: Be concise and easy to understand. "Contrary to the popular impression, foundations do not weigh proposals, they read them," he says. The Florida Association of Nonprofit Organizations in Miami provided guidance and advice to the videotape's producers. *30 minutes, $35.95 (plus $6 postage and handling)*

Grants for Nonprofit Organizations: A Guide to Funding and Grant Writing

ELEANOR GILPATRICK (PRAEGER BOOKS, 1989)

▶ Written especially for professionals in nonprofit organizations, this is a comprehensive, step-by-step guide to finding funds for programs and writing effective grant proposals. The author bases her work on 10 years of experience in successful funding and teaching in the nonprofit sector. She takes the reader through every phase of the funding and grant-writing process. Notable for its comprehensive coverage and practical "hands-on" orientation to the subject, the book is also distinguished by its coverage of the specific areas of program planning and evaluation, topics usually ignored in other works on grant writing. Following an overview of the basic funding strategies, Gilpatrick moves to a sequential discussion of the various aspects of the grant-writing process. Of particular help are detailed case examples showing the application of the manual's principles in real situations. The author follows five project ideas, taken from a broad range of nonprofit organizations, from the initial idea to the final proposal. She presents strategies on finding funding sources and writing proposals and includes a set of cumulative writing steps that build toward the final application for funding. In addition, the Guide provides, for the first time, a coherent, underlying intellectual/theoretical structure for the funding and grant-writing process, making this an ideal text for students in public administration programs as well as an indispensable resource for practicing professionals in nonprofit organizations. *Hardcover, 213 pages, $55.00*

The Grantseeker's Guide to Project Evaluation, 2nd Edition

JACQUELINE FERGUSON, ED. (EDUCATION DAILY/ASPEN PUBLISHERS, 1999)

▶ Design your own evaluation plan, or judge the credibility of evaluations conducted by others. Here are step-by-step strategies for evaluating grant-funded projects. You get easy-to-follow instructions, examples, and statistical formulas to help you collect evaluation information, select sampling methods, analyze evaluation data, write an evaluation report, and more. *Softcover, 82 pages, $49*

Grantseeker's Toolkit: A Comprehensive Guide to Finding Funding (Book and CD-ROM)
CHERYL CARTER NEW AND JAMES AARON QUICK OF POLARIS CORPORATION (JOHN WILEY & SONS, 1998)

▶ Grants are a key source of support for most nonprofit organizations, particularly new organizations or those starting new programs. This guide, developed out of a series of seminars, helps grantseekers develop a strategic plan for finding funds for their programs. It outlines how to develop a program that will receive funding, provides the best methods for writing a grant proposal, and includes a disk that allows organizations to customize the forms and exercises in the book. *Softcover, 256 pages, $39.95*

Grantseeking: A Step-by-Step Approach (Workbook)
ROBERT M. ZIMMERMAN (ZIMMERMAN LEHMAN, 1998)

▶ How do you write a foundation proposal and letter of intent? How much should you ask for? How do you research foundations to ask the right ones to fund your project? How much information is available on the Internet? What role does the board of directors play in the grant-seeking process? These and other questions are answered in this workbook, which is filled with hands-on information, user-friendly task lists, sample letters of intent, foundation profiles, an online research chapter, and other valuable material to guide you step-by-step from project to completed grant proposal and follow-up. This reference book explains in easy-to-understand language how to research and write a proposal to a foundation, corporation, government agency, or religious donor, with an emphasis on private foundation grant writing and exploration. It includes details of what funders want in a letter of intent, how to write a successful proposal, how to design a budget for all you need and how to follow up with grantors, and a section on the role of the board of directors in the grant-seeking process. This easy-to-follow and informative book will ensure that your proposals are expertly researched, formatted, and written using tried and proven methods. *Softcover, 50 pages, $24.95*

The Grant Writer's Guide: How to Become an Expert Grant Writer for Schools and Nonprofit Groups
DR. LINDA KARGES-BONE (GOOD APPLE, 2000)

▶ This companion resource to the highly successful *Grant Writing for Teachers* offers a comprehensive sampling of grants and letters of intent, and an extensive directory of grant resources. There are questions and answers for grant writers, ranging from how to deal with ethical situations involving grants to how to use the Web to do dissemination. *Softcover, 128 pages, $14.99*

The Grant Writer's Guide to Internet Resources
(ONDINE PUBLICATIONS)

▶ This complete list of grant-writing and funding links to make your web searching easier includes government funding links, corporate donors, foundation resources, grantsmanship resources, conferences and training, consultants, nonprofit management, newsletters, freebies, and more. *Softcover, $15.99*

Grants for School Technology: A Guide to Federal and Private Funding, 3rd Edition (See Grant Seeking)

GrantWrite: A Step-by-Step System for Writing Grant Proposals That Win (Software)
(EDUCATION DAILY/ASPEN PUBLISHERS)

▶ This easy-to-use software package guides you through each section of a grant proposal, explaining its purpose and how to compose it. Based on the best-selling book, *Writing Grant Proposals That Win* (see separate listing under Publications), this program allows you to actually write proposals on your computer screen. It is compatible with Macintosh and DOS-based PCs. All instructions appear right on screen as well as in a comprehensive user manual. *$149 (Single user), $199 (Multiple user) (plus $4 shipping)*

The Grantwriter's Internet Companion: A Resource for Educators and Others Seeking Grants and Funding
SUSAN LOUISE PETERSON (CORWIN PRESS, 2000)

▶ This book is designed to assist educators and others interested in grant writing in using the Internet as a resource to help locate funding sources and other sites that may prove useful when seeking funding. After reading Chapter 2's preliminary information on search engines, prospective grant writers can learn about U.S. as well as state Departments of Education, foundations, and educational organizations and associations, and more. The author also covers mailing lists, discussion groups, and the most efficient ways to use e-mail addresses. Contents include: Introduction; The Internet Advantage; Learning to Look: The World of Search Engines; Finding the Big Bucks: U.S. Department of Education; Other Federal Agencies; All About Foundations; Numbers, Numbers Everywhere: Other Useful Sites; Make the Most of What You've Got: Educational Organizations and Associations; On-Line Booksellers, Journals, and Publishing Companies; On the Home Front: State Departments of Education; Other Internet Applications; and When the Pencil Meets the Paper: On-Line Grant Writing Tips. *Hardcover, $24.95 ($3.50 plus shipping and handling)*

The Grantwriter's Start-Up Kit (Workbook)
SUCCESSFUL IMAGES, INC. (JOSSEY-BASS, 1999)

▶ Fund raisers are often intimidated by the prospect of writing grant proposals. But missing a grant opportunity can mean losing important programs and essential services. For the fund raiser in need of practical skills and guidance, *The Grantwriter's Start-Up Kit* shows how to prepare for the process of writing a successful grant proposal. The video (see separate listing) and companion workbook are specifically designed to help you streamline your efforts and avoid common mistakes. This workbook is organized into two sections: I. Start-Up Exercises (these exercises will help you translate your organization's mission into language that speaks to grantmakers. Each exercise consists of three logical parts: (1) Getting Started, (2) Thinking About Next Steps, and (3) When You Are Ready to Move On); II. Resource Guide (this section is filled with video highlights, samples of proposal elements, and tips on the strategy and structure of each element). These easy-to-use tools allow you to apply different lessons to any number of objectives. *Softcover, 80 pages, $10.95*

The Grantwriter's Start-Up Kit: A Beginner's Guide to Grant Proposals (Video)
SUCCESSFUL IMAGES, INC. (JOSSEY-BASS, 1999)

▶ This video makes the basics of grant writing easy to understand. The many examples scattered throughout the video make the abstract ideas more concrete. The graphics are well done, and the pace gives the viewer time to absorb the material and even take notes. Anyone should be able to write a simple grant proposal after watching this video. Fund raisers are often intimidated by the prospect of writing grant proposals. But missing a grant opportunity can mean losing important programs and essential services. For the fund raiser in need of practical skills and guidance, *The Grantwriter's Start-Up Kit* shows how to prepare for the process of writing a successful grant proposal. The video and companion workbook are specifically designed to help you streamline your efforts and avoid common mistakes. *$59.95*

Grantwriting, Fundraising, and Partnerships: Strategies That Work!
KAREN B. RUSKIN AND CHARLES M. ACHILLES (CORWIN PRESS/SAGE PUBLICATIONS, 1996)

▶ This comprehensive guide contains specific and practical information that will help you negotiate the often-confusing world of private-sector grant writing. It's a "how-to" book that will make it easier for you to get more money for your school. Every aspect of grant writing is thoroughly discussed, from questions to ask before you begin to resources for grants available to educators. Ruskin and Achilles help you understand the private funding process so that you will be more likely to write a successful proposal. You'll find out how to identify a funder for your project and coordinate your goals with theirs, describe your school setting using catchwords that elicit positive responses, market your grant proposal and develop partnerships between your school and community businesses. If you've ever wished for more money to support innovative programs or to augment your school's budget, then *Grantwriting, Fundraising, and Partnerships* was written with you in mind. It has the facts and the tips you need to complete your successful grant-writing project. *Softcover, 200 pages, $27.95*

Grassroots Grants: An Activist's Guide to Proposal
ANDY ROBINSON AND KIM KLEIN (CHARDON PRESS, 1996)

▶ This book was written for grassroots organizations working for social change. Author and activist Andy Robinson describes just what it takes to win grants, including how grants fit into your complete fund-raising program, using your grant proposal as an organizing plan, designing fundable projects, building your proposal piece by piece, and more. It contains an analysis of four complete proposals, plus suggestions from 40 foundation staff who fund groups working for social, economic, and environmental justice. *Softcover, 194 pages, $25*

The "How To" Grants Manual: Successful Grantseeking Techniques for Obtaining Public and Private Grants, 4th Edition
DAVID G. BAUER (ORYX PRESS, 1999)

▶ At the beginning of the 1980s, available grants from federal and private sources totaled around $80 billion. In 1999, it is estimated that figure will have increased by more than three times, to nearly $250 billion. David Bauer's new edition of *The "How To" Grants Manual* is an essential guide for grant seekers who want to successfully navigate recent changes in the marketplace. Additionally, the fourth edition has been updated to include advice on ways to use the Internet when seeking grants. This useful guide puts grant seekers on the right track using a simple, three-part approach that offers advice on: Part 1: Funding differences between private and public sectors, and which tools and methods are most useful; Part 2: The best ways to win a federal grant; Part 3: Funding differences between foundations and corporations, and how to approach the private sector. *The "How To" Grants Manual* packages its proven methods together with worksheets, sample letters, an extensive list of resources, and a practical step-by-step outline on preparing a

proposal—all in one helpful "get organized" book. This classic offers suggestions for applying for private funds with a single letter proposal; shows proposal writers and their organizations how to find funding sources that share their missions; illustrates how to organize a grant-seeking effort and includes important advice about how to develop a proposal that links the needs of the institution to the priorities of the funder; and the process for researching the various funding sources is described along with information about the differences between seeking government and private support. It includes chapters on developing and evaluating proposal ideas, redefining proposal ideas to find more funding sources, and a checklist for government proposal preparation. There is also an informative section covering computer databases and electronic search and retrieval systems, including the Internet; worksheets and sample letters are also included to help grant seekers write better proposals in less time. *Hardcover, 264 pages, $34.95*

How to Write Proposals That Produce
JOEL P. BOWMAN AND BERNADINE P. BRANCHAW (ORYX PRESS, 1992)

▶ Whether a proposal is a solicitation for funds, a project bid, or an internal call for action, the techniques for creating it are the same. This book takes a thorough look at what makes these documents work and the steps involved in putting together a winning proposal—from in-house memos to voluminous bids for government contracts. Authors Joel P. Bowman and Bernadine P. Branchaw, acknowledged experts on business writing and communication, explain exactly what an effective proposal is and what it should do. They even discuss how to prepare for the oral presentations that are often required in the final evaluation process. The authors describe the variety of proposal audiences and their communication styles, outline strategies, and recount the writing process from a proposal's beginning to end. Nearly 50 examples of sample documents, abstracts, tables of contents, formats, and headings complement their clear and concise text. *Softcover, 242 pages, $23.50*

How to Write Successful Corporate Appeals
JAMES P. SINCLAIR (THE TAFT GROUP, 1982)

▶ Grab the competitive edge for your organization with this primer on corporate grantsmanship—a resource that can save you hundreds of hours of trial-and-error effort. This book gives you actual examples of grant-winning letters and proposals, plus pointers and tips that will make your proposal writing easier, clearer, and more successful. *Softcover, 107 pages, $17.50*

How to Write Successful Foundation Presentations
JOSEPH DERMER (THE TAFT GROUP, 1977)

▶ Here's an opportunity to read and study presentations that have secured grants from $5,000 to $200,000. Learn why they worked and how you can create a winner. Discover the finer points of crafting a general-purpose appeal; the do's and don'ts of special project presentations; specific strategies for building proposals, and more. This book could be the key to clinching your next grant. *Softcover, 80 pages, $17.50*

I'll Grant You That: A Step-by-Step Guide to Finding Funds, Designing Winning Projects, and Writing Powerful Proposals (Book and CD-ROM)
JIM BURKE AND CAROL ANN PRATER (HEINEMANN, 2000)

▶ Part book, part CD-ROM, part Web site, *I'll Grant You That* is an all-in-one resource for finding funds, designing winning projects, and writing powerful proposals. The book itself offers everything you need to write a successful proposal. Not only does it walk you step by step through the process, it provides a series of workshops in those areas you might need a little help, including writing, organizing, presenting, and being creative. On the CD-ROM, you'll find annotated sample grants that explain what works—and what doesn't—in writing a winning grant, links to a host of Internet resources for grants and grant writing, and self-assessment tools to help you write the best grant possible. Plus, the accompanying Web site (www.grantwriterstoolkit.com) offers even more support, featuring an extensive, up-to-date directory of the many organizations that offer either grants or funds. *Softcover, 288 pages, $25*

Program Planning and Proposal Writing: Introductory & Expanded Version (Guide)
NORTON J. KIRITZ AND JERRY MUNDEL (THE GRANTSMANSHIP CENTER, 1988)

▶ For two decades, the Grantsmanship Center's PP&W has been the most widely used proposal writing format in the world. It shows how to: (1) establish your credibility, (2) conceptualize and state your objectives, (3) lay the groundwork for future funding, (4) assess needs, (5) design an evaluation, (6) define methods, and (7) formulate a budget. The introductory version lays out the seven-step process in clear, concise language. The expanded version examines each of the steps in greater detail and illustrates them with concrete examples, and the checklist and evaluation form lists the points to consider in proposal writing. This is an indispensable tool for anyone involved in researching, writing, or evaluating grant proposals. *Introductory version, 12 pages, $3; Expanded version, 48 pages, $4; Proposal checklist and evaluation form (set of ten), $3 (plus $2 shipping)*

Proposal Planning and Writing, 2nd Edition
LYNN E. MINER, JEREMY T. MINER, AND JERRY GRIFFITH (ORYX PRESS, 1998)

▶ Now newly revised and expanded, this self-help book is designed for first-time proposal writers and planners. The authors use a concise, straightforward approach, offering specific examples of how to find grants and how to plan, write, and submit proposals that get results. They also share their streamlining techniques for submitting more proposals in less time. Each of the techniques presented in the book has been extensively field-tested. The authors offer greatly expanded coverage of computerized grant seeking, covering such topics as sources of public and private funding information on the World Wide Web, search engines, award information, online editorial advice, and access to forms and policy manuals. Also updated is the chapter on the basics of effective technical writing that includes helpful tips on document design, computer editing, and improving proposal readability.

The book is divided into three main sections: (1) the process of getting started, describing how to find out what public and private grants are available and what grantmakers ("sponsors") are really looking for in a proposal; also explains how to find a sponsor who shares your interests and the different ways to write your proposal so as to appeal to a broader base of sponsors; (2) the "how to's" of writing proposals for both public and private sponsors; presents a model of an effective two- to three-page proposal with many examples taken from real proposals including samples of early drafts of proposals and how they could be strengthened; the examples cited are all from proposals that were actually funded; the chapters on public proposals analyze the major proposal components and offer definitions, examples, tips and reasons why specific proposals were

turned down; and (3) addresses the principles of document design and suggests ways to make a proposal more attractive by considering such things as type style, binding, and the use of headers; the latest electronic resources are described, and outlines, charts, and examples help establish a procedure for each step of the process. *Softcover, 184 pages, $34.50*

Proposal Writer's Swipe File: Fifteen Winning Fund-Raising Proposals . . . Prototypes of Approaches, Styles, and Structures, 3rd Edition
SUSAN EZELL KALISH, ED. (THE TAFT GROUP, 1984)

▶ Six professional proposal writers invite you to steal ideas from their grant-getting works. Read (and borrow from) these outstanding examples—covering grants in such areas as education, the arts, the elderly, youth services, and others. The proposals are presented just as they were submitted to corporate and foundation funding officers. *Softcover, 162 pages, $8.78*

Proposal Writing, 2nd Edition
SORAYA M. COLEY AND CYNTHIA A. SCHEINBERG (SAGE PUBLICATIONS, 2000)

▶ In this second edition of Soraya M. Coley and Cynthia A. Scheinberg's book, *Proposal Writing,* the authors have broadened their scope while still maintaining the aspects that made the first edition a bestseller. They have added a chapter on program development; updated the material to reflect changes in service delivery, such as collaborations; and addressed the use of technology in proposal writing. As in the first edition, this book is written primarily for students or beginning-to-moderately experienced grantwriters working in nonprofit corporations, school districts, or city or county agencies, and provides a step-by-step guide to writing a successful grant proposal. *Softcover, 128 pages, $23.95*

A Proposal Writing Workshop CD
ROGER H. PLOTHOW (HENRY DEAN PUBLISHING, 2000)

▶ This resource contains highly competent researched and field-tested writing principles. You will be taught how to research, write, and submit successful proposals; questions answered by e-mail; receive critiques by the author; research federal agency Web sites; research 60,000 foundations nationally; and make notes on electronic notepad. Samples of successful grants are included. *$95*

Six Easy Steps to Millions in Grants: A Grant-Writing Manual
DEBRA M. WINN (MALDON ENTERPRISE, 1993)

▶ This grant-writing manual is an introduction into the world of proposal writing (asking for funding, for services provided to the community), in addition to resource links for scholarships and financial aid. Fortunately, more and more grant makers are also viewing various churches and community organizations as tools to alleviate poverty and urban distress, by utilizing their ministries and programs for neighborhood revitalization, senior services, youth and children, food programs, and the like. The electronic version of *Six Easy Steps to Millions in Grants* is a no-nonsense approach to understanding and writing the grant request from beginning to end. This manual is a preferred, practical guide for anyone with little or no experience. *Softcover, $19.95*

Successful Grant Writing: Strategies for Health and Human Services Professionals
LAURA N. GITLIN AND KEVIN J. LYONS (SPRINGER PUBLISHING, 1996)

▶ Tailored for both academics and direct-service providers, this book provides a general overview of grantsmanship for inexperienced grant seekers and those who are looking to sharpen or brush up on their skills. The authors, instructors at the College of Allied Health Sciences at Thomas Jefferson University, examine the perspectives of both the grant maker and the recipient, and advise how to find the appropriate foundation or government agency. They suggest what to say to program officers, how to prepare a budget, and how to avoid jargon and imprecise language in the proposal. They also dissect the proposal into different components and offer a case study of hypothetical "Mrs. L," who needs money for an educational program to team medical students with homeless people. Information specific for grant seekers in the health and human services fields includes a list of "what is hot, what is not" among grant makers, and how to shape a proposal involving research on human subjects. Appendices list key acronyms, guidelines for collaborating on a project with one's institution, and sample budget sheets and time frames for proposals. *Softcover, 243 pages, $34.95*

The User-Friendly Guide to Writing Grant Proposals (Software)

GARY S. MESSINGER (ORCA KNOWLEDGE SYSTEMS—AVAILABLE FROM RICHARD J. CONDON & ASSOCIATES)

▶ One of the primary keys to resource development success is effective proposal writing. *The User-Friendly Guide to Writing Grant Proposals* helps you do just that with instruction and 31 easy-to-follow, step-by-step prompts that result in ready-to-submit grant proposals. The Guide's computerized format is the most effective and efficient way to write winning grant proposals. You'll see examples of model federal, foundation, and corporate proposals that went from average in quality to superior after these 31 prompts were applied. It includes: Section I (essential information, with strategies that work for writing proposals to government agencies, foundations, and corporations), Section II (exhibits and exercises that expand on basic principles in Section I: tools to sharpen your basic skills, specific examples of erroneous and corrected grants, and a model proposal in the three different formats), and Section III: The Proposal Writer's Kit (31 essential questions that all grant-making organizations ask). It is available for DOS, Windows, and Macintosh. *$69.95 (plus $5 shipping)*

Winning Grant Proposals: Eleven Successful Appeals by American Nonprofits to Corporations, Foundations, Individuals, and Government Agencies

GORDON JAY FROST, ED. (THE TAFT GROUP, 1993)

▶ This book offers a look at an array of successful proposals, representing a diverse body of institutions, grant makers, projects, and gift sizes. The full text of more than a dozen proposals is reprinted, each resulting in full funding. An essay by editor Gordon Jay Frost introduces common elements that contributed to the proposals' success and the stories behind them. *Hardcover, 160 pages, $27*

Winning Grant Proposals Online

(THE GRANTSMANSHIP CENTER, 2001)

▶ This resource is designed to help nonprofit organizations and government agencies write better grant proposals and develop better programs. It consists entirely of recently funded, top-ranked grant proposals in a wide variety of subject areas, including education, arts and humanities, health, housing, law enforcement, substance abuse, disabilities and rehabilitation, and minorities. It provides a wealth of useful information, examples, and insights. Your organizations can use these top-ranked grant proposals as examples of effective proposal writing, models for designing cutting-edge programs, examples of today's best practices in your field or illustrations of how to construct a program budget. All the proposals in this continuously expanding collection have been selected by major government funders from among their highest-rated grant applications. You may also read, browse, or search the entire collection of over 600 proposal abstracts absolutely free at *http://www.tgcigrantproposals.com. Multiple-proposal CD-ROM sets: $99; Custom-made CD-ROM: the first proposal of your choice is $29; each additional proposal is $20*

Winning Grants Step by Step: Support Centers of America's Complete Workbook for Planning, Developing, and Writing Successful Proposals

MIM CARLSON (JOSSEY-BASS, 1995)

▶ Carlson structures *Winning Grants Step by Step* to follow the process normally used when preparing a proposal. Naturally, she begins with "Developing the Proposal Idea." The aim here is to help you determine which projects in your organization are most likely to be funded through a grant. Rather than put you through an exhaustive (and unrealistic) exercise, Carlson merely asks you to address six fundamental questions, the answers to which will identify which of your projects are most appealing to a prospective funder. This "cut to the bone" approach is Carlson's hallmark and is in evidence throughout the book. Next, the author, in Steps Two through Nine, guides you through the process of developing your idea into an effective proposal. In a presentation that is simultaneously clear and pleasing to the eye, Carlson explores each individual component of the grant proposal. These include writing a compelling need statement, defining clear goals and objectives, developing your methods, preparing the evaluation component, developing future funding strategies, preparing the program budget, and writing the introduction to the proposal, and writing the proposal summary. Throughout these nine steps, the author presents "insider" tips to strengthen your proposals and catch the attention of funders. She also provides worksheets that are well conceived and genuinely helpful. The final two steps are concerned with putting the proposal package together. Carlson pays due attention to the vital role of the cover letter, then discusses the appendices and how to present the entire package once it's completed. The author, in summing up, provides a final proposal checklist to help ensure that you've followed each of the preceding 11 steps. As well, she outlines how you should follow up with funders once your proposal is submitted. *Hardcover, 128 pages, $26.95*

Winning Strategies for Developing Grant Proposals

DON HOFFMAN AND DENISE LAMOREAUX LISA HAYES (THOMPSON PUBLISHING GROUP, 1999)

▶ Intended to help local governments, educational agencies, community-based nonprofit groups, and other organizations develop well-written grant proposals, this book takes you through the grantseeking process, offering advice and information from grantseeking experts on researching potential funders, writing a project narrative, and approaching federal and private sector grant makers. It includes samples of award-winning proposals, discusses why some proposals fail, and explains common mistakes made by grant seekers. Copies of the federal government's standard application and a sample of a common grant proposal form used by private foundations are also included. Featured topics include: Do's and

Don'ts of Writing a Grant Proposal; Creating a Grant Proposal Library; Basics of Good Proposal Writing; Standard Elements of a Proposal; What Kind of Federal Funding Is Available; and Common Concerns About Project Management. *Softcover, 96 pages, $59*

Writing for a Good Cause: The Complete Guide to Crafting Proposals and Other Persuasive Pieces for Nonprofits

JOSEPH BARBATO, DANIELLE S. FURLICH (FIRESIDE/SIMON & SCHUSTER, 2000)

▶ Filled with tips and survival skills from writers and fund-raising officers at nonprofits of all sizes, *Writing for a Good Cause* is the first book to explain how to use words well to win your cause the money it needs. Whether you work for a storefront social action agency or a leading university, the authors' knowledgeable, practical advice will help you write the perfect proposal—from the initial research and interviews to the final product; draft, revise, and polish a "beguiling, exciting, can't-put-it-down and surely can't-turn-it-down" request for funds; create case statements and other big money materials; write, design, and print newsletters, and use the World Wide Web effectively; and survive last-minute proposals and other crises—with the Down-and-Dirty Proposal Kit!

Writing for nonprofits is a juggling act. One's job might entail writing grant proposals, newsletters, thank-you notes, case statements, and Web site material—each for a different boss. The most successful development writers take the time to both experience their causes firsthand (sleep in the shelter, go to rehearsals, visit the wilderness) and cultivate personal relationships with their donors ("people give to people"). You'll give yourself an amazing head start when applying for a grant, say Joseph Barbato and Danielle Furlich, just by following an organization's guidelines and getting your math right—it's surprising how many fund raisers do neither. Make your point once, clearly, and don't forget the human element. "You aren't just asking for money," say the authors of *Writing for a Good Cause,* "you are asking to help people." Barbato and Furlich, both veteran fund raisers, interviewed both grants administrators and development writers for this guide. The result is an inside view of the arcane workings of the world of fund raising that would make any novice feel more proficient immediately. Their "gotta-get-it-out-right-now, how-late-is-FedEx-open? Down-and-dirty proposal kit" is a terrific tool when there isn't time to write the "knockout, beguiling, exciting, can't-put-it-down, and surely can't-turn-it-down fundraising proposal." And keep in mind: when a donor gives your proposal the nod, say thank you. Twice. In fact, say Barbato and Furlich, "It is almost impossible to thank a donor too much."

The authors define fund raising ("Once, it was called begging") and offer a quick view of the nonprofit universe. They carry the reader through proposal writing, case statements, newsletters, and all of their myriad parts, from executive summaries and cover letters to budgets and appendices, enlivening an already lively text with model sidebars. Pages are liberally peppered with boxes called "Hot Tip" and "Writer Beware!." The advice on organizing material, interviewing people, and sitting down to write would serve any writer. They even provide a special section, "the down-and-dirty proposal kit," for those times when you have two days in which to cram two weeks of work. Underlying it all is the energy that comes from working for a good cause and using your words to make the world better. *Softcover, 332 pages, $15*

Writing Grant Proposals That Win!

(EDUCATION DAILY)

▶ Nationally known grants expert Phale Hale Jr. gives you step-by-step instructions and practical examples of how to write winning grant proposals. The second edition of his best-selling *Writing Grant Proposals That Win* has been updated and expanded to include significant new proposal-writing help, including easy-to-use flowcharts to quickly organize proposals logically; a new "Helpful Hints" feature that provides expert tips and advice on all phases of the grant-writing process; and new information about fund raising on the Internet. *$75*

Writing the Winning Grant Proposal, 1999 Edition

(QUINLAN, 1999)

▶ This handy and informative book will show you step-by-step how to research the right grants to apply for, write a cover letter to grab the imagination, prepare your proposal's introduction to capture the essence of who you are, describe your needs and problems so you get noticed, communicate your plans effectively and clearly, and develop an accurate budget. Plus, it contains excerpts from other proposals that you may use to frame yours in addition to useful do's and don'ts in every step of your grant-writing process and a handy glossary of terms you need to know. *Softcover, $59.95*

Grants Management

Administering Grants, Contracts, and Funds: Evaluating and Improving Your Grants System

DAVID G. BAUER (ORYX PRESS, 1998)

▶ David Bauer provides valuable guidance in effectively administering a sponsored project within any size institution or organization. Beyond contacting funding sources and submitting proposals are the critical functions of developing ethical guidelines and practical management procedures. This guide supplies the methods and the process to create or more effectively administer a grants office that works to ensure continued support. From budgets and records to personnel management, the detailed text is further enhanced by examples of planning materials, forms, and documents. *Softcover, 248 pages, $36.95*

Federal Grants Management Handbook

(THOMPSON PUBLISHING GROUP)

▶ This guide provides extensive practical and management information on financial and compliance issues related to grant requirements once you have received a federal grant. It covers regulations, executive orders, and administrative and court decisions affecting federal grants management. The Handbook explains everything from setting up financial management systems to purchasing procedures to record keeping and reporting to audits. Learn how to comply with a wide array of laws and directives, such as nondiscrimination, environmental impact, lobbying restrictions, and more. From submitting grant proposals to setting up financial management systems for payment and reporting to audits and grant close-out, the Handbook covers every aspect of the grants award and management life cycle and is thoroughly indexed and cross-referenced for easy use. All of the primary source documents grant recipients need are included—OMB circulars, Treasury regulations, and other government-wide policies such as lobbying restrictions, debarment, and nondiscrimination. Throughout the Handbook, you'll find helpful compliance tools such as checklists, sample forms, and proven methods of grant management compliance. Monthly newsletters and Handbook updates provide timely news and analysis. Also available are 23 separate Federal Agency Reference Chapters, which include detailed information about each federal agency's grant programs, agency- and program-specific regulatory citations, and key grants personnel. Features include: Steps to Take in Applying for a Federal Grant; Managing Accounting and Financial Systems; Developing and Negotiating Indirect Cost Rates; Purchasing and Procurement Using Federal Funds; Complying with Federal "Cross-Cutting" Rules; Strategies for Reporting and Recordkeeping; Audit Requirements; and Disputes, Appeals, and Remedies. *Print: Loose-leaf, 2 volumes, 269; Online: $269; Print and online: $368*

Grant Winner's Toolkit: Project Management & Evaluation (Book and Disk)

JAMES A. QUICK AND CHERYL C. NEW (JOHN WILEY & SONS, 2000)

▶ This book provides guidance for managing a grants process after the grant has been won. It covers the key topics to securing future grants, and helps nonprofits make sure that they have responded to the priorities of the grant maker, those they serve, and their organization and its mission. The authors also show grant winners how to respond to the higher levels of accountability, entrepreneurship, and efficacy that today's funders demand. It includes a disk with customizable forms to help organizations use the methods outlined in the book. *Softcover, 371 pages, $39.95 (plus $3 shipping)*

Successful Grants Program Management

DAVID G. BAUER (JOSSEY-BASS, 1999)

▶ As school districts struggle with decentralized management, the need to coordinate grant proposal development has grown dramatically. This indispensable resource contains all the practical tools that districts need to manage cross-curricular proposals for all their schools. It describes the key elements of a successful grants system; explains the legal, ethical, and financial requirements of grant-seeking programs; and offers worksheets and checklists to help organize every aspect of grants promotion and administration. Grants expert David Bauer shares sound advice and such important instruments as a planning matrix for refining goals and objectives, a systems analysis spreadsheet for reviewing budget and staff resources, and a step-by-step outline for developing a grants procedure manual. This comprehensive guide also shows how to provide grant seekers with computer-based research tools. Timely and practical, *Successful Grants Program Management* focuses on the district's role in winning corporate, federal, and foundation grants. *Softcover, 288 pages, $29.95*

Grant-Seeking Sources

The 2001 Alaska Funding Guide: Directory to Alaska Foundations and Corporate Giving Programs (Annual)

CYNTHIA M. ADAMS (FUNDING EXCHANGE, INC., 2001)

▶ This book contains entries for foundations and corporation giving programs that are located or fund projects in the state of Alaska. The Guide contains over 120 entries describing giving programs benefiting nonprofit organizations in Alaska. It is also available on CD-ROM. There is also an online database of grant makers customized for individual states available for the Pacific Northwest. It includes national, regional, and local foundations and corporations that fund in the Northwest. *Softcover, $64*

America's New Foundations 2000, 14th Edition

(THE TAFT GROUP, 1999)

▶ The new, fully updated edition identifies, describes, and provides current contact information on nearly 3,000 private, corporate, and community foundations created since 1989, including about 350 funding organizations never before profiled in *America's New Foundations*. Profiles include contact information, gifts received, giving histories, typical recipients, officers and directors, application information, and the top 10 grants made by the foundation. With individual assets or annual giving of $100,000 or more, the funding organizations profiled here total more than $9.1 billion in assets and $825.8 million in total giving. *America's New Foundations* helps smaller, less established nonprofit organizations secure a lasting, beneficial relationship with emerging philanthropies. *Softcover, approx. 1,300 pages, $195*

Arizona Guide to Giving, 5th Edition (Annual)

MARILYN M. BOESS, ED. (ARIZONA HUMAN SERVICES, 2000)

▶ This resource profiles more than 800 corporations and foundations with a history of making grants in Arizona. It is also available in electronic format. *Print version $55; Electronic version (CD-ROM or diskette, IBM-compatible): $75 (includes shipping and handling)*

Arkansas Funding Directory 2001–2003, 3rd Edition (Biennial)

CAROLINE PROCTOR, ED. (NONPROFIT RESOURCES INC., 2001)

▶ This book includes information about all Arkansas-based foundations as well as government and other funders in the state. *Softcover, 250 pages, $70*

Big Book of Library Grant Money 1998–99: Profiles of Private and Corporate Foundations

(THE TAFT GROUP, FOR ALA EDITIONS, 1998)

▶ With more than four times the number of library-friendly givers than in any other directory, the Big Book is a must for libraries seeking a share of the more than seven billion dollars in this category of giving. Providing targeted access to the most promising major givers, the Big Book of Library Grant Money 1998–99 is an indispensable tool for library development in today's competitive grant-seeking environment. This latest edition lists nearly 2,200 profiles—nearly 500 of which are brand new to this edition. *Softcover, 1,464 pages, $235; ALA Members: $211.50*

California Grants Guide

(GRANT GUIDES PLUS, 2000)

▶ This is a desk reference for nonprofits, schools, local governments, and any organization looking for grants. It is five guides in one, including foundations and philanthropic trusts, corporations and businesses, state government departments and agencies, religious institutions, and a Tool Kit. It has more resources than before, including $8.3 billion in total giving, 800 profiles of funding sources, 628 foundations, 128 corporate giving programs, 27 religious funders, and 95 state government programs.

It provides comprehensive details on areas of funding interest, financial data on assets and giving, amount of California giving, examples of recent grants, application procedures/deadlines, contact names, how much to apply for, types of support, and officers and trustees. It is indexed in 120 ways, including areas of funding interest, financial data on assets and giving, amount of California giving, examples of recent grants, application procedures/deadlines, contact names, how much to apply for, types of support, and officers and trustees. The Tool Kit section gives you all the information you need to raise money successfully, including strategies, tips, and "how to's" on fund raising from successful grant writers; how to write a winning proposal; how to prepare a budget as part of the proposal; how to work with corporations—marketing versus philanthropic donations; how to develop a fund-raising plan; how to involve your board in fund raising; how to research funders online; and how to work with the media. *Softcover, $179*

Charitable Foundations Directory of Ohio, 12th Edition

(OHIO ATTORNEY GENERAL'S OFFICE, CHARITABLE LAW SECTION, 1999)

▶ This directory is assembled and published as a public service by the Ohio Attorney General's Office. It is compiled from information submitted to the office by more than 18,000 registered charitable organizations in Ohio. The directory lists all of the grant-making charitable foundations in the state. It provides the address, contact person, telephone number, charitable purpose, and assets of each foundation. The foundations can also be referenced by both county and type of foundation. A total of 2,517 grant-making charitable foundations are listed in this edition. Combined, these organizations held assets totaling $9.3 billion and awarded grants totaling $666 million in fiscal year 1998. The directory is published every other year and contains information for the years previous to its release. Therefore, the 1999–2000 edition is scheduled for release in the summer or fall of 2001. *Softcover, $7.50*

Church Philanthropy for Native Americans and Other Minorities: A Guide to Multicultural Funding from Religious Sources

(CRC PUBLISHING)

▶ This reference is the only comprehensive directory of funding to document funds available *from* mainstream religious bodies *for* minority projects. The Guide contains 67 grant programs and 34 loan programs available from Judeo-Christian sources for Native American and other multicultural secular and/or religious nonprofit organizations. Eleven denominations with national and statewide programs of philanthropy for issues of self-determination, social justice, and economic development are represented. Indexed both by geographic and subject areas, the work presents previously unknown alternative sources of funding for multicultural projects. *Softcover, 280 pages, $118.95*

The Cincinnati Area Foundation Directory: 2000, 5th Edition

(MR & COMPANY, 2000)

▶ This book contains profiles of approximately 100 foundations and charitable trusts located in Cincinnati and the northern Kentucky region. *Softcover, 108 pages, $65*

Colorado Grants Guide 2001–2002 (Biannual)

(COMMUNITY RESOURCE CENTER, INC., 1999)

▶ This is a comprehensive funding guide for nonprofit and community-based organizations in Colorado. It provides information about more than 250 public and private sources of nonprofit support in the state of Colorado. This comprehensive resource guide contains hundreds of profiles on local foundations and trusts, corporations, national funders, government agencies, and religious organizations that support Colorado nonprofit organizations. Each

profile details the funder's purpose and mission, areas of interest, geographic focus, application guidelines, financial information, board of trustees, recent grants, and more. This new edition features a Technical Assistance Section that includes articles about budgeting, working with fund-raising consultants, and future trends in the nonprofit sector. It is also published in CD-ROM format. By purchasing a subscription to the online version, grant seekers can conduct targeted, time-saving research via the Internet. The online version will provide you with an easy-to-use search screen; a quick way to find funders who are interested in your funding needs; searches that can take minutes rather than hours; immediate access to a foundation's Web site (when available); regularly updated profiles; a new feature that will allow you to select "favorite" funders for instant recall; and e-mail updates when changes are made to "favorite" funder profiles. *Spiral bound, 740 pages, $135.00; one-year online subscription: $200; one-year online subscription and printed version: $295*

The Complete Grants SourceBook for Higher Education, 3rd Edition

DAVID G. BAUER (ORYX PRESS, 1995)

▶ This is a resource for faculty and administrators who are seeking funding for research or other projects. Part I is a concise primer of grantsmanship. Parts II, III, and IV are the heart of the volume and include detailed profiles of grant-funding sources. This updated edition adds two new appendices: a list of all five locations of the Foundation Center and libraries throughout the country that carry Foundation Center materials; and additional grant searching resources, including computer research services. The *Sourcebook* contains all of the information needed for higher education faculty and administrators to conduct effective grant-seeking campaigns. Detailed descriptions of more than 250 foundations, corporations, and government agencies that contribute regularly to higher education are provided in an easily accessible format. David Bauer reveals his own proven fund-raising system to show exactly how to develop and implement time- and money-saving strategies. *Softcover, 352 pages, $65*

The Complete Guide to Florida Foundations, 12th Edition

FRANCES PASSANNANTE, ED. (FLORIDA FUNDING PUBLICATIONS)

▶ This annual guide is the only complete directory of private grant-making foundations in Florida. Profiles are provided for more than 2,200 foundations incorporated in Florida. This annual guide is the only complete directory of private grant-making foundations in Florida. Profiles are provided for more than 2,000 foundations incorporated in Florida that provide over $550 million in grant awards annually and $5.5 billion in assets. Foundations are thoroughly researched and indexed to provide all the information needed to create a realistic target list for funding requests. The guide also includes a section devoted to step-by-step instructions for preparing a successful proposal. Updated annually, *The Complete Guide to Florida Foundations* has helped hundreds of nonprofit organizations, educational institutions, and government entities reach their funding goals. *Softcover, 350+ pages, $90*

Corporate and Foundation Fundraising Manual for Native Americans, 3rd Edition

(CRC PUBLISHING, 1996)

▶ This resource presents its proven fund development system, a step-by-step process for securing private sector grants. The primer focuses on the fund-raising needs of American Indian projects.

Activities such as nonprofit incorporation, proposal writing, prospect research, and Internet fund-raising sites are covered in detail. Sample forms and guidelines may be duplicated, providing unlimited access to tools essential for every fund-raising office. *Spiral bound, 288 pages, $129.95*

Corporate Foundation Profiles, 11th Edition

(THE FOUNDATION CENTER, 2000)

▶ Through multipage profiles, this completely updated volume brings you reliable information on 207 of the largest corporate foundations in the United States, grantmakers that each give at least $1.2 million annually. Each profile offers comprehensive, practical data. Grant-maker portraits feature the essential facts you need when writing a proposal, including the grant maker's address and contact person; purpose and giving limitations statements, application guidelines, and key officials; and an analysis of its parent company. In addition, comprehensive grants analyses, available in no other corporate directory, let you discover the subject areas favored by the foundation (if the foundation funds education, you'll immediately see how much grant money is earmarked for higher education, for scholarships and student services, and for elementary education); learn what kinds of recipient organizations have received grants (if you're looking for a health-related grant, you can quickly see how much money a foundation gives to hospitals, public health organizations, disease-specific associations, and research institutes); and ascertain which population groups a grant maker targets for support (each profile shows the amount of grant money a foundation directs to specific population groups such as children and youth, minorities, or the elderly—important information that many grant descriptions don't include. *Corporate Foundation Profiles* also breaks down grant makers' philanthropic activities by geographic area and types of support awarded. The volume includes a special appendix that lists quick-reference financial data on an additional 1,300 smaller corporate grant makers. *Softcover, 724 pages, $155*

Corporate Foundations in Illinois, 6th Edition

ELLEN DICK (ILLINOIS ASSOCIATION OF NON-PROFIT ORGANIZATIONS, 1998)

▶ This book profiles 120 corporate foundations and corporate-giving programs that support projects in Illinois. Each entry contains contact information, grant-making interests, geographic limitations, financial information, names of key officials, and whether or not the company provides operating support. *Softcover, 130 pages, $40 (includes shipping and handling)*

Corporate Giving Directory 2001, 22nd Edition

(THE TAFT GROUP, 1999)

▶ This book highlights, indexes, and expands coverage of the top 10 corporate givers for the previous year to arts and humanities, civic and public affairs, education, environment, international, social services, health, and the top five givers in science. In addition, you'll find listings of Top 10 givers mentioned in the introduction to this volume. To match corporate foundations and direct givers to fund raisers, they have added new analytical features of Corporate Giving Directory, information previously only available to subscribers of Taft's *Corporate Giving Watch* (see listing under Periodicals). Included in this edition are more than 100 new corporate foundation profiles. It offers expanded coverage of the 100 biggest givers and more, including: top 100 companies (pie charts for each of the top 100 givers display their giving priorities. These pie charts are also feature separately in a larger format so customers can easily compare and contrast companies; the top 100 givers are also indicated with a star in the master index); and preselected giving lists (*Corporate Giving Directory* now lists all companies that support preselected organizations in the front for easy reference, but also profiles these companies in case organizations decide to network in other ways. It also includes fully updated profiles of more than 1,000 of the largest corporate foundations and corporate direct-giving programs in the United States. Arranged alphabetically by company name, each entry contains: Master Index of Corporations/Foundations; full contact information, including more than 800 Web and e-mail addresses; corporate revenue figures and *Fortune* 500 ranking; cash, nonmonetary, and corporate sponsorship giving information; details about corporate matching gift and company-sponsored volunteer programs; analysis of the corporation's giving priorities and typical recipients; an enhanced list of corporate operating locations; geographic giving preferences; application procedures and evaluative criteria; and biographical data on corporate and foundation officers and directors (more than 600 have been newly researched for this edition). Indexes guide researchers to: Companies by Headquarters; Companies by Operating Location; Companies by Location of Grant Recipient; Companies by Grant Type; Companies by Nonmonetary Support Type; Companies by Recipient Type; Companies by Application Deadline; Officers and Directors by Name; Officers and Directors by Place of Birth; Officers and Directors by Alma Mater; Officers and Directors by Corporate Affiliation; and Officers and Directors by Nonprofit Affiliation; Officers and Directors by Club Affiliation. *Softcover, approx. 1,850 pages, $465*

Corporate Giving Yellow Pages 2000, 15th Edition

(THE TAFT GROUP, 1999)

▶ This guide to identifying and contacting the people who make grant decisions for the leading corporate giving programs and corporate foundations in America provides nearly 3,500 listings that provide contact name, title, address, phone number, and FAX number. *Softcover, 350 pages, $115*

Directory of Biomedical and Health Care Grants 2001, 15th Edition

(ORYX PRESS, 2000)

▶ The latest edition has added almost 500 new sources, now offering information on over 3,000 funding programs. It includes the most comprehensive list on funding sources from all levels of government, corporations, foundations, and others. Concise, accurate, and updated, grant seekers will find the Directory the best source when tracking down funding programs for research; faculty development; dissertations; internships, scholarships, and assistantships; facilities and organizational support; conferences; and more. *Softcover, 700 pages, $84.50*

Directory of Charitable Funds in New Hampshire, 7th Edition

(DEPARTMENT OF JUSTICE, CHARITABLE TRUST DIVISION, OFFICE OF THE ATTORNEY GENERAL, 2000)

▶ The newest edition of the Directory is available on-line at the Department's Web page (*http://www.state.nh.us/nhdoj/CHARITABLE/directory/directory-main.html*) and will be updated at least every other month. The Charitable Trusts Unit oversees approximately 5,000 charitable organizations and trusts, including trust funds held by municipal trustees. The latest financial reports filed by these trustees indicate that approximately $35 billion

($35,002,434,077) in assets is being held by charities conducting business in the state of New Hampshire. The Directory includes 318 of the largest New Hampshire charitable grant-making foundations. In most cases, funds are not listed unless their asset value is at least $25,000. The Directory is indexed by name, by geographic region, and by purpose. [*The Charitable Trusts Unit will no longer produce hard copies of the Directory.*]

Directory of Charitable Trusts and Foundations for Hawaii's Non-Profit Organizations, 1999–2000

ALBERTA FREIDUS-FLAGG, ED. (HELPING HANDS HAWAII, 1999)

▶ This directory contains listings about trusts and foundations in the state and on the mainland that give grants to Hawaii's charitable organizations and individuals in need.

The Directory of Corporate and Foundation Givers 2000, 10th Edition

(THE TAFT GROUP, 1999)

▶ This directory puts you in touch with more than 8,000 funding sources, including full contact information, including more than 2,000 Web and e-mail addresses; 4,500 private foundations that have assets of at least $1.8 million or distribute a minimum of $250,000 in grants annually; approximately 3,500 corporate giving programs, including more than 1,475 corporate foundations and 2,000 corporate direct givers; identifies and indexes top 10 givers in nine recipient type areas: Arts and Humanities, Civic and Public Affairs, Education, Environment, Health, International, Religion, Science, and Social Services; and details on more than 45,000 actual grants. Features include biographical data (includes data on more than 34,000 foundation officers, directors, trustees, and corporate officers. You'll find essential background information for uncovering important links and relationships between foundations and corporations and the members of your board of directors and constituency. When available, profiles of individuals include titles; place and year of birth; alma mater and year of graduation; current employer; and corporate, nonprofit, and philanthropic affiliations. Includes Index of Officers and Directors by Name); recent grants (lists the top 10 grants recently disbursed. These top grants take most of the guesswork out of your prospect research by listing the actual organizations receiving major support, how much they received, and where they're located); historical data (almost all of the profiles list assets, giving figures and contributions received for three years. You can track the increases or decreases in the level of contributions and assets, then rate philanthropic programs according to their financial potential and giving trends, identify new potential donors, and predict future giving patterns); comprehensive scope and arrangement (profiles are listed in a single two-volume directory and organized in an easy-to-use alphabetical series that lists the most active foundation and corporation grant makers. You'll find detailed information on whom to contact and application procedures, current financial activity, biographical data, and major products/industries, enabling you to evaluate your chances for receiving funding and determine the best approach for soliciting potential donors); and nine easy-to-use indexes (speed access to information on location of operation, fields of interest, and relationships that will help you target and refine your prospect research in order to find the best potential donors). *Softcover, 2 volumes, 3,960 pages, $270*

Directory of Delaware Grantmakers

(DELAWARE COMMUNITY FOUNDATION, 1998)

▶ The directory is designed to aid fund-raising professionals, volunteers, and individuals in their search for funding. The Directory lists the names and addresses of more than 450 grant-making organizations in Delaware; provides detailed information on more than 65 foundations and corporations; and defines each grant maker's areas of interest, types of support, and application guidelines and procedures. Also included are tips on proposal writing and a list of resource centers and publications that contain basic information on the grant-making process and how to develop successful development programs. *Softcover, $25.00 (plus $3.00 shipping and handling)*

Directory of Grants in the Humanities, 2000/2001, 14th Edition

(ORYX PRESS, 2000)

▶ This book provides current data on funds available to individuals and organizations from corporations, foundations, and professional associations as well as from the NEA, NEH, and state and local arts and humanities councils. Completely updated facts are presented on more than 4,000 funding sources (corporations, foundations, and professional associations as well as local, state, and federal arts and humanities councils), including more than 400 programs identified for the first time. Programs listed include funding for research, travel, internships, fellowships, dissertation support, conferences, exhibitions, and performances, primarily in the United States and Canada, as well as in other countries. Among the disciplines covered are literature, language, history, anthropology, philosophy, ethics, religion, painting, dance, photography, sculpture, music, drama, crafts, and folklore. *Softcover, 888 pages, $84.50*

Directory of Idaho Foundations, 9th Edition

ELAINE C. LEPPERT, ED. (CALDWELL PUBLIC LIBRARY, 1999)

▶ This directory is based on 990-PF returns filed with the IRS by foundations and corporations either headquartered in Idaho or with a history of giving in Idaho.

Directory of Illinois Foundations, 6th Edition

VALERIE S. LIES AND SIU YUIN PANG, EDS. (DONORS FORUM OF CHICAGO, 2000)

▶ This biannual publication provides detailed information on more than 2,200 Illinois foundations and corporate giving programs (including over 400 newly established foundations, 25% more foundation listings than the 1998 edition). With extensive profiles of foundations and corporate giving programs, eight indexes for targeted research efforts, and detailed tables on the top 100 Illinois foundations, this is the most comprehensive resource of its kind and should be part of every Illinois nonprofit's reference collection. Profiles contain address, phone, and fax numbers; contact person and staff and trustee listings; total assets and grants; principal funding areas; geographic focus; complete application procedures and deadlines; and financial data. The Directory also features eight indexes for targeted research efforts and detailed tables on the top 100 Illinois foundations. In addition, it includes extensive profiles of 465 foundations and 29 corporate giving programs that make more than $50,000 in grants annually. *Print edition: Softcover, 411 pages, $85 ($65 for Donors Forum Members, Associate Members, and Forum Partners); Electronic edition: $150 ($120 for Donors Forum Members, Associate Members, and Forum Partners)*

Directory of Indiana Grantmakers 1999–2000

SUSAN R. WILSON, ED. (INDIANA DONORS ALLIANCE, 1999)

▶ This directory features private foundations, corporate giving programs and foundations, family foundations, community foundations, and grantmaking public charities; a series of appendices in which foundations are listed by asset size, grants paid, program interests, contact person, and county where headquartered; a section on other resources for individuals and nonprofits seeking to learn more about grant writing and fund raising; a listing of libraries with significant collections of fund-raising materials; and more. Grant-maker profiles include organization name, contact, address, phone and FAX numbers, and e-mail and Web site addresses; listings of the grant maker's donors, officers, and staff; financial information, including fixed assets, amount and number of grants paid, largest and smallest grant paid; information concerning funding interests, types of support, geographic preferences, and specific limitations; deadlines for grant proposals; and the method of approaching given grant makers. It includes 1,629 grant makers located in Indiana with assets of more than $12.83 billion and more than $451 million in grants; and 659 grantmakers headquartered in other states with giving of more than 95,000 grants and nearly $5 billion. A CD-ROM version is also available (Mac or Windows). *Softcover, 650 pages, $35 (print); $50 (CD-ROM); $70 (print and CD-ROM)*

Directory of International Corporate Giving in America and Abroad 2000, 11th Edition

(THE TAFT GROUP, 1999)

▶ This directory profiles and tracks the charitable giving activities of 650 companies with international connections. It emphasizes coverage of corporations that specialize in direct giving (75% of the companies profiled in the new edition engage in this elusive form of grant making). Highlights include histories of contributions, assets, and gifts going back three years; biographies of corporate and contributions officers that include alma mater, affiliations, place of birth, and more; company data, including lines of business, markets, plant locations, sales offices, and number of countries in which it operates; international outlook, describing expansion plans, product launches, joint ventures, and more for up to two years; key financial data for *Forbes* 100 companies; details on more than 10,000 operating locations for U.S. companies; and up to 50 recent grant recipients for the most recent year data is available. Divided into two independently indexed sections, covering U.S.-based and foreign-based firms, *International Corporate Giving* can be used for broad-based research or to focus on company headquarters location, products/industry, grant type, director name, grant recipient location, or type. *Softcover, approx. 900 pages, $220*

The Directory of Kansas Foundations, 2000–2001

(KANSAS NON PROFIT ASSOCIATION, 2000)

▶ This directory provides information on 669 foundations.

Directory of Kentucky Foundations, 1999–2000

(INDIANA DONORS ALLIANCE, 1999)

▶ The Directory features private foundations, corporate giving programs and foundations, family foundations, community foundations, and grant-making public charities; a series of appendices in which foundations are listed by asset size, grants paid, program interests, contact person, and county where headquartered; a section on other resources for individuals and nonprofits seeking to learn more about grant writing and fund raising; a listing of libraries with significant collections of fund-raising materials; and more. Grant-maker profiles include organization name, contact, address, phone and FAX numbers, and e-mail and Web site addresses; listings of the grant maker's donors, officers, and staff;

financial information, including fixed assets, amount and number of grants paid, largest and smallest grant paid; information concerning funding interests, types of support, geographic preferences, and specific limitations; deadlines for grant proposals; and the method of approaching given grant makers. It includes 754 grantmakers located in Kentucky with assets of more than $1.97 billion and nearly $67 million in grants; and 749 grant makers headquartered in other states with giving of more than 90,000 grants and $4.9 billion. A CD-ROM version is also available (Mac or Windows). *Softcover, 400+ pages, $35 (print); CD-ROM: $50; $70 (print and CD-ROM)*

Directory of Maine Grantmakers, 2nd Edition

PRISCILLA MILLER AND FRANCES L. RICE (MAINE GRANTS INFORMATION CENTER, 1998)

▶ This directory gives brief profiles of all Maine foundations and corporations, scholarship funds that file IRS 990-PFs, and out-of-state foundations that give in Maine (more than 600 entries). It is also available in electronic format for members only (updates e-mailed periodically). *Softcover, 105 pages, $20 (Nonmember), $15 (Member)*

The Directory of Missouri Foundations 1988–1999, 6th Edition

WILDA H. SWIFT AND ANNE BORMAN, EDS. (SWIFT ASSOCIATES, 1998)

▶ This directory is based on 990-PF returns and questionnaires of 1,114 foundations. It profiles 381 private, corporate, and community foundations registered in Missouri. According to the compilers, the Directory includes all foundations in Missouri that report to the Internal Revenue Service. Each entry provides contact information, a list of trustees, total assets, types of support provided, grant-making interests, total amounts of grants awarded, and giving restrictions. Listings contain data from the informational tax return most recently filed with the IRS, as well as information supplied by foundation officials. *Softcover, 168 pages, $50 (plus $3.50 postage and handling)*

Directory of Missouri Grantmakers, 3rd Edition

(THE FOUNDATION CENTER, 1999)

▶ This directory provides a comprehensive guide to grant makers in the state—approximately 1,000 foundations, corporate giving programs, and public charities, from the largest grant makers to local family foundations. The *Directory of Missouri Grantmakers* facilitates your funding research with information-filled entries that list giving amounts, fields of interest, purpose statements, sample grants, and much more. In addition, the volume's indexes help you target potential funders by subject interest, types of support, and names of key personnel. *Softcover, 159 pages, $75*

Directory of Pennsylvania Foundations, 6th Edition

S. DAMON KLETZIEN, ED. (TRIADVOCATES PRESS, 1998)

▶ This directory includes 1,510 profiles of Pennsylvania foundations with assets of $150,000 or more and/or annual grants of at least $7,500. In addition to financial data, each profile contains contact information, staff and board listings, year created and employer ID number, application deadlines, and guidelines. *Softcover, 550+ pages, $73.50*

Directory of Research Grants 2000

(ORYX PRESS, 1999)

▶ This directory provides current data on funds available from foundations, corporations, and state and local organizations, as well as from federal sources, for research projects in medicine, the physical and social sciences, the arts and humanities, and education. The latest information is presented on more than 6,200 funding sources, including 600 programs identified for the first time. All major disciplines and subject areas are covered. Included in applicable program profiles are *Catalog of Federal Domestic Assistance* program numbers and National Science Foundation announcement numbers. Programs listed include funding for such categories as basic research, materials and equipment, acquisition, research centers, training programs and internships, graduate assistantships, fellowships, faculty development, symposiums, and dissertation research. *Softcover, 1,264 pages, $135*

Directory of Texas Foundations, 20th Edition

(NONPROFIT RESOURCE CENTER OF TEXAS, 2001)

▶ This directory provides the most complete and up-to-date information on more than 2,200 private and community foundations in Texas. Features include: helps identify the best funding prospects; features over 100 newly listed foundations each year (377 new this edition); summarizes foundations by grants, assets, and grant distribution, and allows research by areas of interest, city, foundation name, trustees and officers, and types of support; tracks giving interests and grant distributions patterns of the top 100 foundations in Texas; lists assets and grants by major cities and regions in Texas; and identifies foundations by city, size, and grant dollars awarded. The Directory as well as the new online database includes current information on all private and community foundations in Texas. Featuring newly listed foundations each year, it allows you to research foundations by areas of interest, city, foundation name, trustees and officers, and types of support. Texas foundations are also summarized by 1999 (or latest tax information available) total assets, total grants, and grant distribution. Also available online (for further information, go to *http://www.nprc.org/advanced/public/#online*). *Softcover, 601 pages, $160*

Education Grants Directory 2000

(QUINLAN PUBLISHING GROUP, 1999)

▶ This directory includes hundreds of concise, information-packed profiles of grant opportunities, organized both by subject and by eligibility in separate federal and private groupings; a detailed appendix listing all state education agencies, regional resource centers, relevant Web sites, and a glossary of helpful funding terminology; and a special section on block grants that are available through your state. The Subject Indexes include such categories as arts and humanities, athletics, at-risk youth, bilingual education, disabled students, literacy programs, math and science, professional development, reading and writing, school safety, and technology. Let's say you're looking for new computers for your school. All you do is go to the "Technology" section in the two Subject Indexes (Federal and Private) and find the complete list of grants available for computers in each section. The Eligibility Indexes save you even more time by focusing on grants available to specific categories of institutions or types of education—public school systems, elementary and/or secondary schools, colleges and/or universities, educational organizations and associations, individuals, special education programs, and so on. Here you'll find a complete list of grants available to suit your particular needs. *Softcover, $149.99 (plus shipping and handling)*

Effective Evaluation: A Systematic Approach for Grantseekers and Project Managers

(EDUCATION DAILY)

▶ This strategic approach to project evaluation focuses on four major aspects of project evaluation: conceptual, managerial, technical, and political. You'll see how to combine all four aspects into a practical, effective evaluation plan to impress funders and capture the information you need to strengthen your project. *$59*

Environmental Grantmaking Foundations, 5th Edition

(RESOURCES FOR GLOBAL SUSTAINABILITY, INC.)

▶ This is a guide to the most significant independent, community and company-sponsored foundations that fund environmental projects. These foundations give over $600 million for environmental purposes annually. It profiles 889 foundations that give environmental grants, including 213 members of the Environmental Grantmakers Association. Each profile gives you the data you need to target your most likely sources of support. Multiple indexes help you narrow your search to the grant makers that fund your topics or your geographic focus. The Directory is available in print and CD-ROM formats. Directory features include officers, directors, and key personnel; environmental programs in depth; analyses drawn from RGS's databases; and listing of recent grants. Indexes list foundations by recipient and activity region, environmental topics and activities, emphases and limitations, location, issues, and deadlines. *Print directory: $105; CD-ROM version: $115*

FC Search: The Foundation Center's Database on CD-ROM (Version 4.0)

▶ This resource gives you access to the Foundation Center's exclusive database of foundation and corporate grant makers, as well as their associated grants. Its fully searchable database in CD-ROM format includes data found in: *The Foundation Directory, The Foundation Directory Part 2, The Foundation Directory Supplement,* the *Guide to U.S. Foundations, Their Trustees, Officers, and Donors,* the *National Directory of Corporate Giving,* and *The Foundation Grants Index.* Features include: covers every known U.S. grant maker—over 53,000 foundations, corporate givers, and, new to this edition, hundreds of grant-making public charities. It includes associated grants file of 210,000 grants, linked to the largest U.S. funders. It features a searchable index of more than 200,000 trustees, officers, and donors; in-depth program descriptions and enhanced application guidelines for select funders; links to over 1,000 grant-maker Web sites and 500+ *Fortune* 500 corporate Web sites; link to special *FC Search* subscribers-only home page with value-added links and e-mail list sign-up; free update disk; includes extensive Help file and printed User Manual; allows users to create customized prospect lists by selecting from among 21 search fields: Grantmaker Name; Grantmaker State; Grantmaker City; Grantmaker Type; Geographic Focus; Establishment Date; Fields of Interest; Types of Support; Total Assets; Total Giving; Corporate Name; Corporate Location; Text Search; Trustees, Officers, and Donors; Recipient Name; Recipient State; Recipient City; Recipient Type; Subjects; Grant Amount; and Authorization Year. Prices include two disks and one User Manual. Larger local area network versions (nine or more users in one location) and wide area network versions are also available. It is compatible with Microsoft Windows™ 2000, Microsoft Windows™ 98, Microsoft Windows™ 95, or Windows™ NT. *Stand-alone (single user) version: $1,195; Network (two to eight users in one* *building) version: $1,895; Additional copies of User Manual: $19.95 each*

F.I.N.D. Database
(FLORIDA FUNDING PUBLICATIONS)

▶ This IBM-compatible program includes detailed profiles of over 3,800 federal, state, and private grant programs available, collectively representing over $250 billion in grants. It is a comprehensive program that drastically reduces research time and allows the user to take full advantage of a wide range of available grant programs through area-of-interest searches. Little computer experience is necessary to successfully operate this program and to access information about related grants programs. It includes semiannual updates. Site licenses are also available for multiple installations. *Full version: $395.00*

Florida State Grant Programs 2000–2001, 14th Edition
JOHN L. ADAMS AND FRANCES S. PASSANNANTE, EDS. (FLORIDA FUNDING PUBLICATIONS, 1997)

▶ This book is an annual directory that is the only available comprehensive summary of state programs plus federal grant programs administered by the state of Florida. This guide provides detailed profiles of over 200 government grant programs representing more than $2.1 billion in funding programs. It is an essential tool for Florida government entities, nonprofit organizations, and educational institutions. *Softcover, 250+ pages, $80*

The Foundation 1000, 2000/2001 Edition
(THE FOUNDATION CENTER, 2000)

▶ This book delivers the comprehensive information available on the 1,000 wealthiest foundations in the country. The grant makers covered in this edition hold more than $234 billion in assets and award close to 250,000 grants worth $10 billion to nonprofit organizations each year. If you plan to seek grants from these major funders, you can't afford to be without this singularly effective resource. *The Foundation 1000* contains 3,000+ pages of meticulously researched, easy-to-read profiles that answer the questions you need to ask when targeting major funders: Which major foundations support projects like mine in my geographic area? What kinds of projects have they funded recently? How much of their budget have they earmarked for my subject area? What are the names and affiliations of their key personnel? *The Foundation 1000* helps you answer these questions by providing profiles including grant-maker contact information, reviews of program interests, purpose and giving limitations statements, application guidelines, names of key officials, and much more; in-depth analyses of grant programs (tables document funding patterns by subject, recipient type, population group, type of support, and geographic area); extensive lists of sample grants (profiles list up to 50 or more recent grants, often the best indication of a grant maker's funding interests); and easy-to-use indexes (you can target potential funders by donor, officer, and trustee names; by subject area; by types of support awarded; and by geographic area). A separate index tracks foundations that award international grants. *Softcover, 3,030 pages, $295*

The Foundation Center's User-Friendly Guide: A Grantseeker's Guide to Resources, 4th Edition
(THE FOUNDATION CENTER, 1996)

▶ This book leads you through the maze of unfamiliar jargon and the wide range of resources used effectively by professional fund raisers. You'll learn about securing tax exemption, how to research potential funders with the most recent fund-raising directories, using online services and CD-ROMs to gather data on potential grantmakers, writing grant proposals, seeking grants as an individual, and much more. *Softcover, 40 pages, $14.95*

FoundationDataBook
(C&D PUBLISHING)

▶ There is a *Foundation DataBook* available for Washington, Oregon, and California. A Colorado edition will be available soon. Each *Foundation DataBook* is a state-specific, comprehensive, up-to-date directory and database of grant-making foundations with a categorical listing of all the grants they made for the most recent year on record, including the Foundation's stated purpose for awarding each grant. It includes grant purpose and restrictions; geographic focus; granting interests and priorities; deadlines; and largest, smallest, and average size of grants awarded—by foundation and by grant category. They also provide each foundation's name and address, contact person to whom grant requests and questions should be directed, trustees, income and expense, and more. For the most recent year available via IRS records, every single grant is listed, along with the grant recipient's name, city, state, the dollar amount of the grant, the statement of purpose for the grant, and its classification according to the National Taxonomy of Exempt Entities classification system. This taxonomy was developed specifically to track the funding activities of nonprofit organizations and can be used to improve the effectiveness of your grant requests. Print and CD-ROM (Mac and Windows) versions are available. *Print: $100 (California: $150); CD-ROM: $250 (includes postage and handling)*

The Foundation Directory, The Foundation Directory Part 2, The Foundation Directory Supplement (Annual)
(THE FOUNDATION CENTER, 2000)

▶ The new edition of the Directory features current data on the nation's most influential funders, those that hold assets of at least $3 million or distribute $200,000 or more in grants each year. The volume includes key facts on over 10,000 of these important foundations, more than 1,700 of which did not appear in the last edition. Directory foundations hold assets in excess of $358 billion and donate well over $17 billion each year. With over 35,000 descriptions of recently awarded grants, the Directory provides fund raisers with unique insights into foundations' giving priorities.

The *Directory Part 2* is designed specifically for nonprofit organizations that want to broaden their funding base to include midsized foundations—those that hold between $1 million and $3 million in assets or have annual grant programs from $50,000 to $200,000. The new edition features more than 8,700 of these important foundations, over 3,800 of which are covered for the first time. These grant makers contribute hundreds of millions of dollars to nonprofits each year, providing crucial support for organizations on both the local and national level. The *Directory Part 2* includes descriptions of over 22,000 grant descriptions, often the best indication of a grant maker's giving interests.

The *Supplement* provides the latest-breaking news on *Foundation Directory* and *Directory Part 2* grant makers in updated entries that keep you abreast of recently altered giving interests, new staff, and more.

These data-packed volumes enable you to identify funders by subject field; geographic region; donors, officers, and trustees; types of support; grant makers new to the volume; and foundation name. They are also available online and on CD-ROM (see separate listings in this section and Internet Resources, respectively). *The Foundation Directory: Hardcover, 2,686 pages, $215; The Foundation Directory, Part 2: Softcover, 1,800 pages, $185; The Foundation Directory Supplement: Softcover, 902 pages, $125*

The Foundation Directory on CD-ROM

(THE FOUNDATION CENTER)

▶ You can search for funding prospects from among the same set of *Foundation Directory*-size foundations that appear in their print *Directory* (see separate listing in this section). The powerful search engine enables you to select multiple criteria and quickly create customized prospect lists. The database contains authoritative information on 10,000+ of the largest foundations in the United States. Featured grant makers each hold assets of $3 million or more, or distribute $200,000 or more in grants each year. Together, these foundations hold total assets in excess of $358 billion and donate over $17 billion yearly. It covers over 10,000 of the nation's largest foundations. Features: Over 3,800 foundation records include a list of approximately 10 sample grants; features searchable index of 62,000 trustees, officers, and donors; links to close to 800 foundation Web sites and the Foundation Center's Web site; free update disk; includes extensive Help file and printed user guide; allows users to create customized prospect lists by selecting from 12 search fields: Grantmaker Name; Grantmaker State; Grantmaker City; Fields of Interest; Types of Support; Trustees, Officers, and Donors; Geographic Focus; Grantmaker Type Total Giving; Total Assets; Establishment Date; Text Search. It is compatible with Microsoft Windows™ 2000, Microsoft Windows™ 98, Microsoft Windows™ 95, or Windows™ NT. Prices include two update disks. Discounts are available if purchased with print version of *The Foundation Directory. Stand-alone (single-user) version: $295; Local area network version (two to eight users in one building: $595*

Foundation Fundamentals, 6th Edition

(THE FOUNDATION CENTER, 1999)

▶ It teaches you the skills you need to target the most receptive funders, and it provides a definitive response to that oft-repeated question: "What is a foundation?" The sixth edition shows you how to use print and electronic funding research directories and databases to develop your prospect list; how to use the Internet's World Wide Web to locate information on potential funders; how to target grant makers by subject interest, types of support, and geographic area; how to shape your proposal to reflect the special concerns of corporate funders; and much more! It is fully revised, with up-to-date charts and worksheets to help you manage your fund-raising program. *Softcover, 222 pages, $24.95*

The Foundation Grants Index, 2001 Edition

(THE FOUNDATION CENTER, 2000)

▶ A foundation's recently awarded grants provide an excellent indication of its future funding priorities. It is a current and accurate source of information on recent grant-maker awards. The *Grants Index* covers the grantmaking programs of more than 1,000 of the largest independent, corporate, and community foundations in the United States and features over 97,000 grant descriptions in all. The *Grants Index* is designed for quick, effective, grants-based research. Grant descriptions are divided into 28 broad subject areas such as health, higher education, and arts and culture. Within each of these broad fields, grants are listed geographically by state and alphabetically by name. The 97,000+ grants of $10,000 or more

featured in this edition will help you to locate potential funding sources by helping you locate grant makers that have funded projects within your specific field (the subject index targets grant makers by thousands of key words. If you need a grant for a museum, for example, you can track awards made for natural history [capital campaigns], ethnic/folk arts [Native American], and a variety of other subcategories); discover the foundations that favor your geographic area (the type of support/geographic index directs you to foundations that have made the kind of grant you need in your geographic area); and target foundations by grants made to nonprofits similar to your own (the recipient category index points you toward foundations that have supported your type of organization. The recipient name index helps you uncover foundations that have funded specific nonprofits that share your goals). *Softcover, 2,130 pages, $165*

Foundation Reporter 2001, 31st Edition

(TAFT GROUP, 1999)

▶ This comprehensive resource contains detailed information on more than 1,000 of the leading private foundations that have at least $10 million in assets or have made $500,000 in charitable giving. The combined assets for the foundations in this edition total more than $216 billion and charitable giving adds up to more than $8 billion. It gives you the important contact information, financial and grant information, as well as extensive biographical data on the people who make the grant decisions (donors and their families, foundation officers, directors and trustees). Each foundation profile contains full contact information, giving philosophy, history of donors, geographic preferences, application procedures and restrictions, biographical data on foundation officers and directors, typical recipients, and recently awarded grants. It identifies and indexes "Top Ten" foundation givers in their nine Recipient Type areas: Arts and Humanities, Civic and Public Affairs; Education; Environment; Health; International; Religion; Science; and Social Services. Using 13 indexes, you can easily zero in on a specific type of foundation: Foundations by State; Foundations by Location of Grant Recipient; Foundations by Grant Type; Foundations by Recipient Type; Foundations by Donors; Foundations by Application Deadline; Officers and Directors by Name; Officers and Directors by Alma Mater; Officers and Directors by Corporate Affiliation; Officers and Directors by Nonprofit Affiliation; Officers and Directors by Club Affiliation; Officers and Directors by Place of Birth; and Master Index of Foundations. *Softcover, approx. 2,000 pages, $425*

Foundations in Wisconsin: A Directory 2000, 19th Edition

JOHN MUENZBERG, ED. (MARQUETTE UNIVERSITY FUNDING INFORMATION CENTER, 2000)

▶ This resource covers every active grant-making foundation in the state of Wisconsin. One thousand sixty-five foundations are profiled, including contact information, total assets, grants paid, and areas of interest. The directory is available in print and electronic editions. The electronic edition is an application for Microsoft Windows 95 or later and is available on CD-ROM. This program will perform keyword and subject searches of the directory profiles in *Foundations in Wisconsin*. Foundation profiles include: Foundation Name; Address and Telephone Number; Contact Person; Officers and Directors; Fiscal Year Reporting; Total Asset Value; Total Grants Paid; Grant Range and Median; Areas of Interest; Purpose Statement; Application Procedures; Limitations; Geographic Focus; Sample Grants List; and Web

Address. The electronic edition features include: searches can be made in any category or across multiple categories; no previous database experience is needed; automated construction of queries makes searching easy; advanced searching allows experienced users to formulate their own queries; the foundation profiles can be printed or saved as an ASCII text file; and fast searches through the 1,065 foundations in the database. *Print: $63.36 ($45 Nonprofit); Stand-alone PC: $158.40 ($105 Nonprofit); Networked access: $369.60 ($245 Nonprofit)*

Foundations Today Series

(THE FOUNDATION CENTER, 2000)

▶ Successor to the Foundation Center's *Foundation Giving* report, the *Foundations Today Series* provides the latest information on foundation growth and trends in foundation giving. Subscribe to the 2000 edition of the *Foundations Today Series* and receive copies of all four reports and the estimates update (as they are published) for one price (available as subscription only). Included are: Foundation Giving Trends: Update on Funding Priorities (examines 1998 grant-making patterns of a sample of more than 1,000 larger U.S. foundations and compares current giving priorities with trends since 1980) (2000, 96 pp.); Foundation Growth and Giving Estimates: 1999 Preview (provides a first look at estimates of foundation giving for 1999 and final statistics on actual giving and assets for 1998. Presents new top 100 foundation lists) (2000, 12 pp.); Foundation Yearbook: Facts and Figures on Private and Community Foundations (documents the growth in number, giving, and assets of all active U.S. foundations from 1975 through 1998) (2000, 92 pp.); Foundation Staffing: Update on Staffing Trends of Private and Community Foundations (examines changes in the staffing patterns of U.S. foundations through mid-2000, based on an annual survey of nearly 3,000 staffed foundations) (2000, 24 pp.); Foundation Reporting: Update on Public Reporting Trends of Private and Community Foundations (documents changes in voluntary reporting patterns of U.S. foundations through mid-2000, based on an annual survey of more than 3,000 foundations that issued publications) (2000, 24 pp.). *Softcover, $95 (includes shipping and handling)*

Fund Raiser's Guide to Human Service Funding 2000, 11th Edition

(THE TAFT GROUP, 1999)

▶ This book lists organizations that fund programs in child welfare, aiding the homeless, spouse abuse shelters, or volunteer services. The Guide identifies and describes in detail more than 1,900 private and corporate foundations, including hundreds of corporate direct givers not covered in any other source. It provides three years of financial history for each funding organization, including foundation assets, total giving, and gifts received. Features include: entries provide detail on up to 50 recent grants; foundations and corporate givers are indexed under 33 distinct recipient type categories to help you quickly find the organization you need; biographical data on the officers and directors of the grant maker is included; profiles contain a listing of nonmonetary support offered by a corporate giver; the geographic preference and types of human service agencies supported are highlighted to help you focus your search; contact information includes FAX numbers and the foundation's employer identification number; a special section details programs, activities, or organizations not supported by the profiled company or foundation, so you can concentrate on only the best prospects. Eight indexes help you to quickly focus your search: Funders by Headquarters State; Funders by Grant Type; Funders by

Nonmonetary Support Type; Funders by Recipient Type; Funders by Location of Grant Recipient; Grant Recipients by State and City; Officers and Directors by Name; and Master Index of Funding Organizations. *Softcover, 1,420 pages, $145*

Fund Raiser's Guide to Religious Philanthropy 2000, 13th Edition

(THE TAFT GROUP, 1999)

▶ This focused directory provides detailed profiles and giving histories of philanthropic grant makers responsible for donating more than $800 million annually to religious causes. The new edition of the *Fund Raiser's Guide to Religious Philanthropy* will help churches, synagogues, sectarian colleges, hospitals, health and human services programs, and other religious organizations focus on America's top religious funding prospects. Highlights include: nearly 90 percent of the listees donated more than $100,000 to religious organizations, and all contributed at least $50,000; entries provide a list of up to the top 20 recent religious grants and 20 historical grants, plus valuable information on foundation donors, denominational and geographic preferences, funding priorities and much more; get key financial information on each grantmaker, including religious contributions, assets, and gifts received; the foundation grant makers profiled in this volume have combined assets of more than $95 billion, total giving of more than $4.8 billion, and total religious support of nearly $751 million. Other features include profiles of 20 church-affiliated donors to nonprofit organizations and an appendix listing more than 2,000 foundations and corporations that contributed at least $10,000 to religious organizations in their most recent reporting period. Eight indexes lead fund raisers to: Foundation by Headquarters State; Denominational Preference; Geographical Preference; Grant Type; Recipient Type; Officers and Directors; Grant Recipients by Location; and Master Index. *Softcover, approx. 1,000 pages, $175*

Funding Sources for Community and Economic Development 2000: A Guide to Current Sources for Local Programs and Projects, 6th Edition

JEREMY T. MINER AND LYNN E. MINER, EDS. (ORYX PRESS, 2000)

▶ This newly updated edition offers individuals, organizations, and government agencies instant access to the latest information on funding sources for social service programs and economic development projects at the local level. Over 700 new entries have been added. Created from The Oryx GRANTS Database, GrantSelect (see separate listing), the directory now features more than 3,200 funding opportunities for health care administration, equipment acquisitions, public policy research, special school programs, business development, capital construction projects, cultural outreach, and general operating support. The Guide includes nearly 100 funding sources for Canadian programs and projects. Each entry features the information needed to target the best sources, anticipate deadlines, and plan proposal strategies, including the sponsoring organization's name and address, a program description, grant amount, application date(s), contact name and phone number, Web site address, and sample listings of grants previously awarded. Indexes by program type, subject, sponsoring organization, and geographic location make searching the directory fast and easy. *Softcover, 704 pages, $64.95*

Funding Sources for K–12 Education 1999

(ORYX PRESS, 1999)

▶ This volume contains over 1,500 grants focusing on curriculum development, teacher training/development, arts-in-education, museum programs, special education, and other discipline-enrichment programs, as well as materials and equipment acquisition, building construction/renovation, and general operations grants. More than 450 new funding opportunities for 1999 are included in this updated edition. Each entry includes all of the information needed to submit grant proposals to the right people at the right time, including grant title, program description, sponsor name and address, and contact name. Also included when available are applicable restrictions/requirements; amount of grant, deadline/renewal dates, Catalog of Federal Domestic Assistance (CFDA) program number (for federal programs); contact phone and FAX numbers along with e-mail and Web page addresses, and samples of recently awarded grants. The directory is thoroughly cross-referenced for ease of use. Four indexes—subject, sponsoring organization, program type, and geographic restriction—speed the search for appropriate funding opportunities. Also included is the excellent resource "Guide to Proposal Planning and Writing" by leading grants experts Lynn E. Miner and Jeremy T. Miner. *Softcover, 760 pages, $34.50*

Georgia Foundation Directory and Service (Annual)

(SINCLAIR, TOWNES AND CO., 2001)

▶ This book provides comprehensive profiles of more than 900 foundations located in Georgia with multiple years of grant history, in alphabetical order by name and a geographic index by region and city. Your annual subscription includes a two-volume directory, quarterly updates for one year, four valuable indices, and more. *Softcover, $350*

Georgia Giving: The Directory of the State's Foundations

(CAPITAL DEVELOPMENT SERVICES, 2000)

▶ This comprehensive, up-to-date, and easy-to-use directory of the state's 836 foundations is now available. This vital resource will save you countless hours of research by telling you where foundations are located, who makes the decisions, what nonprofits received grants, what geographic areas the foundations favor, and what special interests the foundations fund. Highlights include an overview of the Georgia foundation sector, including the total number of foundations, their assets, where they are located, to whom they give, staffing, and much more; up-to-date and comprehensive profiles of Georgia's 836 independent, corporate, and community foundations; over 100 categories of giving indexed for fast, effective research; index of foundations by city; Index of Georgia foundations funding programs in surrounding states; index of foundation directors and trustees; foundation application guidelines and deadlines; and chapters on grant writing and donor research by fund-raising experts. *Print Directory or disk: $55; Print Directory and disk: $85*

Grant Funding for Elderly Health Services, 3rd Edition

EDWARD MILES, ED. (HEALTH RESOURCES PUBLISHING, 1999)

▶ Reports on foundation, corporate, and government giving for senior services. It points you in the direction of millions of dollars in grant funds from federal agencies, charitable foundations, and corporations for senior services. You'll get a detailed overview of how your organization can find success for your grant-seeking efforts by writing the right proposal and presenting it to the right grant makers. You'll also get the hard-to-find information such as details of the leading foundations' funding priorities for programs just like yours and expert tips on how to improve your chances of grant success. It also contains a directory of funding information

sources. *Spiral bound, 222 pages, $91.50 (plus $6.50 for shipping and handling)*

Grant Guides, 2000/2001 Editions

(THE FOUNDATION CENTER, 2000)

▶ These guides provides you with up-to-date information on the grants recently awarded in your field. With descriptions of hundreds—often thousands—of foundation grants of $10,000 or more recently awarded in your subject area, *Grant Guides* can help you: locate funders for your specific project (the subject index lets you search for grant makers by hundreds of key words); discover the grant makers that favor your geographical area (the geographic index directs you to foundations that have funded projects in your state or country); target foundations by grants awarded to other nonprofits (the recipient index lets you track grants awarded to organizations like yours). Available guides include: *Aging* (grants for legal rights, housing, education, employment, health and medical care, recreation, arts and culture, volunteer services, and social research) (112 pp.); *Arts, Culture, & the Humanities* (grants to arts and cultural organizations, historical societies and historic preservation, media, visual arts, performing arts, music, and museums) (452 pp.); *Children & Youth* (grants to support neonatal care, child welfare, adoption, foster care, services for abused children, research on child development, pregnancy counseling and adolescent pregnancy prevention, rehabilitation of juvenile delinquency, and youth clubs) (554 pp.); *Community/Economic Development, Housing & Employment* (grants to community organizations, government agencies, and universities for a wide range of social services, housing and urban development programs, including business services and federated giving programs) (443 pp.); *Elementary & Secondary Education* (grants to elementary and secondary schools for academic programs, scholarships, counseling, educational testing, drop-out prevention, teacher training and education, salary support, student activities, and school libraries) (318 pp.); *Environmental Protection & Animal Welfare* (grants to environmental protection and legal agencies; for pollution abatement and control, conservation, and environmental education; and for animal protection and welfare, wildlife preservation, zoos, botanical gardens, and aquariums) (232 pp.); *Film, Media & Communications* (grants for film, video, documentaries, radio, television, printing, publishing, and censorship issues) (136 pp.); *Foreign & International Programs* (grants to organizations in foreign countries and domestic recipients for international activities, for development and relief, peace and security, arms control, human rights, and conferences and research) (345 pp.); *Health Programs for Children & Youth* (grants to hospitals, social service agencies, and educational institutions; and for research, program development, general operating support, education programs, treatment for drug and alcohol abuse, pregnancy, and handicapped children) (183 pp.); *Higher Education* (grants to higher education and graduate/professional schools for programs in all disciplines, as well as to academic libraries and student services and organizations) (450 pp.); *Hospitals, Medical Care, & Research* (grants for hospitals, clinics, nursing homes, health care facilities, public health programs, reproductive health care, and medical research); *Information Technology* (grants for engineering and technology; computer science; data processing; telecommunications services; e-mail and the Internet; and computer hardware, software, and CD-ROMs) (120 pp.); *Libraries & Information Services* (grants for public, academic, research, special, and school libraries; for archives and information centers; and for consumer information and philanthropy information centers) (111 pp.); *Literacy, Reading & Adult/Continuing Education* (grants to organizations supporting literacy, reading, and adult basic education and continuing education programs) (68 pp.); *Mental Health, Addictions & Crisis Services* (grants to hospitals, health centers, residential treatment facilities, group homes and mental health associations; for addiction prevention and treatment; for hotline/crisis intervention services; and for public education and research) (162 pp.); *Minorities* (grants for minority populations, including African Americans, Hispanics, Asian Americans, Native Americans, gays and lesbians, and immigrants and refugees) (344 pp.); *Physically & Mentally Disabled* (grants to hospitals, schools, and primary care facilities for research, medical and dental care, employment and vocational training, education, diagnosis and evaluation, recreation and rehabilitation, legal aid, and scholarships) (174 pp.); *Program Evaluation* (grants to nonprofit organizations to establish formal measures of the impact and efficacy of their programs) (70 pp.); *Public Health & Diseases* (grants for public health programs and diseases, including genetic diseases, birth defects, cancer, AIDS, diseases of specific organs, allergies, and other specific named diseases; for prevention of STDs; and for epidemiology) (192 pp.); *Recreation, Sports, & Athletics* (grants to clubs, leagues, camps, parks, scouting, social service agencies, community organizations, and secondary educational institutions for recreation, athletics, and physical fitness) (161 pp.); *Religion, Religious Welfare, & Religious Education* (grants to churches, synagogues, missionary societies, and religious orders; and to associations and organizations concerned with religious welfare and education) (278 pp.); *Scholarships, Student Aid, & Loans* (grants for scholarships and student aid, to colleges and universities, medical and dental schools, law schools, nursing schools, music and art schools, vocational/technical schools, and social service organizations) (134 pp.); *Social Services* (grants to human service organizations for a broad range of services, including children's and youth services, family services, personal social services, emergency assistance, residential/custodial care; and services to promote the independence of specific population groups such as the homeless and developmentally disabled) (460 pp.); *Technical Assistance/Management Support* (grants to technical assistance and nonprofit management providers, and other agencies and organizations for operational and management assistance including fundraising, accounting, budgeting and financial planning, strategic and long-range planning, program planning, legal advice, developing marketing plans, and hiring and training) (116 pp.); *Women & Girls* (grants for education, career guidance, vocational training, equal rights, rape prevention, shelter programs for victims of domestic violence, health programs, abortion rights, pregnancy programs, athletics and recreation, arts programs, and social research) (270 pp.). *Softcover, $75 each*

Grant Seekers Guide: Foundations That Support Social and Economic Justice, 5th Edition

JAMES MCGRATH MORRIS AND LAURA ADLER, EDS. (MOYER BELL, 1998)

▶ The definitive listing of corporations and foundations funding social change projects, with how-to chapters on fund raising. *Softcover, 624 pages, $39.95*

The Grant Seeker's Primer: A Guide to Applying for Federal, Foundation & Corporate Grants, 2nd Revised Edition

EDWARD A. TUREEN AND HEATHER A. WEAVER (SEK PUBLICATIONS, 1999)

▶ A source of information to those applying for federal, foundation, or corporate grants, this valuable resource provides tips on the entire grant-seeking process. It is written in an easy-to-use style that simplifies the whole process of grant seeking, from finding potential funders to the writing of the proposal itself. *The Grant Seeker's Primer* includes advice and insights from federal and foundation grant officials that will improve your grant applications. In this book, you will learn what grant makers really look for in a grant proposal and how to avoid potential pitfalls that cause proposals to fail. The book provides step-by-step instructions into how to research and apply for grants. *Softcover, 112 pages, $15.25*

The Grant Seeker's Resource Guide: A List of Resources for Those Seeking Private or Federal Grants

EDWARD A. TUREEN, ED. (SEK PUBLICATIONS, 1997)

▶ This book provides grant seekers with names, phone numbers, addresses, and Internet sites of use in grant research. The book is designed to show you where to go for help in seeking grants. In addition, it will teach you how to find and use 990-PF forms and the *Catalog of Federal Domestic Assistance* to gain valuable information in your search for funding. This valuable publication puts a myriad of grant resources at your fingertips. It will show you where to look on the Internet, who to call in your area, what national resources are available to help you find grants, write proposals and applications, and win funding. If you are trying to find additional resources of funding or improve your grant applications, this book will show you where to look to achieve your goal. *Spiral bound, 77 pages, $8.95*

Grantmaker's Directory 2000–2001, 6th Edition

(NATIONAL NETWORK OF GRANTMAKERS, 2001)

▶ The number one source for social change funding serves as a reference tool and a working document for members of the National Network of Grantmakers, an organization of progressive fund raisers, as well as for their grant-making programs and grant seekers. This edition provides information on 200 grant-making institutions. Grant-maker categories include: Anti-Oppression, Anti-Poverty Programs, AIDS/HIV, Arts and Culture, Civil Rights, Communications, Community Organizing, Criminal Justice, Disability Issues, Economic & Community Development, Education, Elderly, Environmental Issues, Farmworkers Issues, Fighting the Right/Building the Left, Free Press, Government Accountability, Health Care, Housing, Immigration and Refugee Issues, Labor Issues, Lesbian and Gay Issues, Parenting and Family, Peace Issues, People of Color Programs, Population, Public Policy Advocacy, Research, Spirituality, Technical Assistance, Women's and Girls' Issues, Youth, and Other. There are also indexes by geographic areas and target populations. Target populations include: African Americans, Arab Americans, Asian Americans, Children, Differently Abled, Elderly, Immigrants and Refugees, Indigenous Peoples of America, Jewish Americans, Latinos/Latinas, Lesbians/Gays, Low-Income Communities, Native Americans, Pacific Islanders, People of Color, Women, and Youth. It includes a Tool Kit for writing effective proposals, developing fund-raising strategies, and finding Internet resources; specifics on contacts, guidelines, grant sizes, and areas of interest; and indexing by program/issue areas, geography, and target populations. *Softcover, 336 pages, $50.00 (plus shipping and handling)*

Grants and Awards for Teachers: A Guide to Federal and Private Funding, Third Edition

JACQUELINE FERGUSON, ED. (ASPEN PUBLISHERS, INC, 1997)

▶ This is a guide to federal and private funding for classroom teachers. Find funding for professional development and education projects with this invaluable resource. It includes advice and examples on researching and identifying appropriate funding sources, understanding the ins and outs of federal agencies, developing project proposals, and details on more than 260 actual funding and recognition opportunities, complete with purpose deadlines, award amounts, eligibility requirements and contact information, and more. *Softcover, 270 pages, $64*

Grants: Corporate Grantmaking for Racial and Ethnic Communities

NATIONAL COMMITTEE FOR RESPONSIVE PHILANTHROPY (MOYER BELL, 2001)

▶ African Americans, Hispanics and Latinos, Native Americans, and Asian Pacific Americans are the fastest growing population segments in the United States, according to the U.S. Census Bureau. By 2025, most of the children born in the United States will be from one of these communities. They are among the fastest-growing economic segments as well, which is the link this book makes between the enlightened self-interest of corporate giving and the communities these corporations serve. This is the only comprehensive listing of 124 corporations and over 10,000 grants they offer each year to benefit minorities. This thorough guide was compiled from information on 72,000 grants made by the corporations in 1995, the most recent year for which data is available. The 124 companies included collectively had revenues of $2 trillion dollars in 1995 and their grants of $1.3 billion made up 22 percent of all grant making from American corporations. Many of the companies are among the largest employers of minorities. The book has compiled a wealth of statistics on the ethnic groups it covers, as well as corporate giving patterns by company and location. Six cross-referenced indices provide grant seekers with access to a multitude of information on thousands of grants available. *Softcover, 736 pages, $89.95*

Grants for Schools: How to Find and Win Funds for K–12 Programs (Grantscape Annual Guidebook), 4th Edition

JACQUELINE FERGUSON, ED. (EDUCATION DAILY/ASPEN PUBLISHERS, 2000)

▶ This newly updated and expanded funding directory helps education grant seekers find grants for their schools or districts. It provides more than 570 federal and private funding opportunities for elementary and secondary education. Funder profiles include information on giving restrictions, application procedures, giving priorities, and recent grants (when available). Profiles also include contact information and lists of funders' officers and directors. Jacqueline Ferguson, the book's author and national fund-raising consultant, imparts tips and strategies for finding and approaching funders, writing and submitting grant proposals, and managing your grant funds. Ferguson also provides insights on the changes in the federal government's grant procedures and technology's increasing role in prospect research. *Softcover, 270 pages, $119*

Grants for Special Education and Rehabilitation: How to Find and Win Funds for Services, Research and Training, 3rd Edition

(EDUCATION DAILY)

▶ Here are more than 200 federal, private, and corporate funding opportunities in the field of special education. Each funding profile includes contact information; geographic restrictions; giving priorities; financial information about the funding institution; examples of recent grants awarded; application guidelines and deadlines; and

names of directors, officers, and trustees when available. You get an in-depth introduction on how to find and win special education funds, expert advice specifically tailored to the unique needs of special education grant seekers, and additional tips and information on funding available from the federal government. *$99*

Grants for Technology (formerly Grants for School Technology: A Guide to Federal and Private Funding), 3rd Edition

(ASPEN PUBLISHERS, 2000)

▶ This one-stop resource helps school administrators identify and win funds to support school technology programs. It includes state-by-state contact information for more than 200 private, corporate, and federal funders, including contact information, types of grants available, eligibility and use requirements, application guidelines and deadlines, and examples of recent grants funded. You'll also discover dozens of funders who donate computer equipment and other technology products, plus helpful advice on how to write more effective proposals. *Softcover, 310 pages, $125*

Grantscape: Electronic Fundraising Database, Version 3.0 (CD-ROM)

ASPEN STAFF (ASPEN PUBLISHERS, 2000)

▶ Filled with profiles of nearly 15,000 private, community, and corporate foundations plus information on hundreds of direct corporate givers, GrantScape Electronic Fundraising Database helps you quickly, easily, and cost effectively locate prospective funders. Each profile includes: Geographic Restrictions; Eligibility Restrictions; Giving Priorities; Application Information and Guidelines, Grant Types; Financial Information; Recent Grants; Directors, Officers and Trustees; and more. *$595.00*

Grantscape: Electronic Fundraising Database, On-line, Version 3.0 On-Line

MOLLIE MUDD, AND ASPEN HEALTH & ADMINISTRATION DEVELOPMENT GROUP (ASPEN PUBLISHERS, 2000)

▶ Filled with profiles of nearly 15,000 private, community and corporate foundations plus information on hundreds of direct corporate givers, GrantScape Electronic Fundraising Database helps you quickly, easily, and cost effectively locate prospective funders. Each profile includes: Funder Contact Information; Employer Identification Numbers; Source Date; Geographic Restrictions; Eligibility Restrictions; Giving Priorities; Application Information and Guidelines, Grant Types; Financial Information; Recent Grants; Directors, Officers and Trustees; and more. *$715.00*

GrantSelect (Online Database)

(ORYX PRESS)

▶ This database offers more than 10,000 funding opportunities in the largest collection of sponsored research opportunities on the Web. The E-mail Alert Service delivers funding information right to your e-mail inbox, including funding from state and federal governments, corporations, foundations, and associations, as well as from Canadian and other non-U.S. organizations. This extensive database is updated daily to provide complete information on more than 10,000 current funding opportunities in the U.S. and Canada. Subscribe to the entire research grants database or to any of the five special segments offered: *Arts and Humanities; Children and Youth; Health Care and Biomedical; K–12 Schools and Adult Basic Education; Community Development; International Programs; Operating Grants.* The E-mail Alert Service notifies you immediately of any new funding opportunities within your area of interest. *Full database: $1,000; E-Mail Alert Service Only: $1,000; Full database Plus E-Mail Alert Service: $1,500; Database segments: Single segment: $350; Single segment E-Mail Alert Service Only: $350; Single segment Plus E-Mail Alert Service: $500*

The Grantseeker's Answer Book: Grants Experts Respond to the Most Commonly Asked Questions, 2nd Edition
LAUREL DRAKE-MAJOR, JACQUELINE FERGUSON, AND MICHAEL V. GERSHOWITZ (ASPEN PUBLISHERS, 1999)

▶ This newly updated edition provides detailed answers to more than 100 commonly asked questions about searching for grants, written by a trio of experienced fund-raising consultants with more than 50 years' combined experience. Wouldn't you like to have a consultant you could turn to with questions whenever you wanted, without paying hefty fees? Get straight answers from grants experts about proposal-writing strategies, staffing and operations management in your grants office, financial management, media involvement in grant-seeking efforts, and many other questions regarding the federal and private-sector funding arenas. *Softcover, 267 page, $88 (plus $6 shipping, sales tax to Virginia and DC residents)*

Grantseeker's Desk Reference
(POLARIS, 1992)

▶ This comprehensive reference to grant-seeking and grant-writing resources, is a directory of critical resources and sources including Internet addresses of organizations publishing information about grant makers; federal, foundation, corporation, state, and regional grants resources contact information; CD-ROM and disk aides; and more. Learn more about grant seeking, access newsletters and other periodicals with grant-seeking information, and much more. It includes profiles and contact information useful to grant seekers. Includes: Grant Seeker's Internet Sites; Funding Source Directories; Grants Support Organizations; Grant and Fundraising Books in Print; Periodicals with Funding Sources and other Grant Seeking Information; Clearinghouses; Databases; CD-ROM Resources; Foundation, Corporate, and Federal Resources; Statistic Sources; Field Reader Opportunities; Federal Divisions and Departments; and more. It is updated quarterly. It is also available on disk for PC or Mac. *Softcover, 250+ pages, $35 (plus $3 shipping)*

The Grantseeker's Handbook of Essential Internet Sites 2000-2001, 4th Edition
MOLLIE MUDD, ED. GAITHERSBERG (ASPEN PUBLISHERS, 2000)

▶ What sources of funding are out there? And how does one go about finding them? Search engines can be useful, but who has time to wade through all those results? When looking for funding, one either finds too much (and usually irrelevant) information, or none at all. The fourth edition of *The Grantseeker's Handbook of Essential Internet Sites* attempts to create order out of chaos and answers these as well as other questions. Senior editor Mollie Mudd, a contributing writer to *Corporate Philanthropy Report,* has added 250 new sites to the 500 sites listed in the third edition, bringing the total number of "essential" sites in the fourth edition to more than 750. The new edition also drops sites that had either declined in quality or disappeared completely. Site entries include the name of the grant-making organization, the organization's URL, an abstract giving an overview of the site's features and highlights, and a "giving category (ies)" that classifies the grant maker by subject or giving area. The book's entries are organized into five categories:

(1) Corporations, (2) Foundations and Associations, (3) Government, (4) Research, and (5) Resources. Within each category, entries are arranged alphabetically. Although the entries themselves are rather short and, in many instances, are missing important details, they provide a nice introduction to the Web sites to which they refer. The book also includes two indexes: a simple alphabetical list of all the sites listed and a more useful index that provides subject access, by major category of giving, to the corporate and foundation sections. (The categories used include arts, civic, education, environment, health, humanities, international, religion, science, social services, and youth). An online version is also available. *Softcover, 243 pages, $95; Online version: $99*

Grantseeker's Toolkit: A Comprehensive Guide to Finding Funding (Book and Disk)
CHERYL CARTER NEW AND JAMES AARON QUICK (JOHN WILEY & SONS, 1998)

▶ This guide, developed out of a series of seminars, helps grant seekers develop a strategic plan for finding funds for their programs. It outlines how to develop a program that will receive funding, provides the best methods for writing a grant proposal, and includes a disk that will allow organizations to customize the forms and exercises in the book. Cheryl Carter New and James Aaron Quick have laid out, in easy-to-follow steps, the complete grant-writing process. They have generously shared their own specific techniques that begins with formulating ideas for fundable projects to the actual writing of grants and ultimately to finding appropriate funders. It is a realistic and throrough approach that teaches readers how to prepare proposals that meet the requirements of funding sources. *Grantseeker's Toolkit* is divided into parts. Part I covers the designing of fundable projects that includes the development and refining of ideas, grant-seeking strategies, and designing and organizing the projects. Part II covers finding suitable funders for projects. This section explains federal, state, foundation, and corporate funders and their general proposal requirements. Part III includes the development of the final project, explaining how to meet the grantor's guidelines and the actual writing of proposals. Part IV takes readers through each step of writing proposals. The procedure teaches readers how to write problem statements, determine the operation of the project, laying out budgets, and also shows readers how to prepare the final package for submission. *Grantseeker's Toolkit* provides an all-inclusive method to follow for grant writing and thoroughly prepares readers for completing successful proposals. *Softcover, 325 pages, $39.95*

Guide to California Foundations, 11th Edition
(NORTHERN CALIFORNIA GRANTMAKERS)

▶ This guide lists more than 900 California foundations with total grants of $40,000 or more. This new edition of the Guide covers more than 1,380 grantmakers, a 25 percent increase from the previous edition. These foundations contribute more than $2 billion in grants annually to support a range of organizations and programs which are working to improve the quality of life in our state. A joint venture of the Northern California Grantmakers and the Southern California Association for Philanthropy, the Guide is the only California foundation directory that is published by grant makers themselves. Listings include the basic information you need to identify your best foundation prospects, the appropriate contact person at each, and how and when to apply. It contains a how-to-use section, helpful information about the grant-seeking process, profiles on each foundation, and indexes to help you find information quickly. The brand new CD-ROM version is a searchable database that allows users to easily conduct basic and advanced searches based on such features as foundation name, location, areas of interest, types of support, geographic focus, assets, grants made, and much more. The new edition is available for the first time in both print form (directory) and electronic form (CD-ROM). It is compatible with Windows 95, Windows 98, or Windows NT 4.0 (or greater). *Book/CD-ROM set(s), $70.10 each (includes tax, shipping, and handling); Book(s) only, $34.84 each (includes tax, shipping and handling)*

Guide to Connecticut Grantmakers 1999

(CONNECTICUT COUNCIL FOR PHILANTHROPY, 1999)

▶ This book gives profiles on 1,600 foundations, corporate giving programs, and charitable trusts located or giving in Connecticut. The print edition features include profiles on over 1,500 grant makers; seven indispensable indexes, including grant makers by areas of interest, target populations, and staff and trustees; an extensive introductory section on the basics of grant making and grant seeking, including a glossary of terms, copies of the Common Grant Application form and the Common Report form, and more. The CD-ROM edition features detailed profiles on 700 grant makers that accept unsolicited requests; automatic searching for grant makers based on areas of interest, types of support, grant-maker name, and more; automatic sorting of your search results by grants paid, total assets, grant range, city, or zip code. Your results can be printed or downloaded in text format. Grant-maker profiles include such valuable information as key contacts; key financial data; program priorities, limitations, and restrictions; geographic priorities; grant ranges; sample grants; application deadlines and procedures; and staff and trustees. *$75, one 1999 book and 2001 updated CD licensed for one stand-alone PC, plus $4.50 shipping; $130, one 1999 book and 2001 updated CD licensed for a local area network in one building; nonprofit rate (see Software License for details), plus $4.50 shipping; $250, one 1999 book and 2001 updated CD licensed for a local area network in one building; for-profit rate (see Software License for details) plus $4.50 shipping; $30, 2001 Updated CD (available only if nonprofit previously purchased Guide), plus $2.00 shipping. Quantity discounts are available for purchases of five or more book/CD sets. Contact the Council for details. $4 per book/CD set (shipping and handling)*

Guide to Funding for International and Foreign Programs, 5th Edition (Directory)

(FOUNDATION CENTER, 2000)

▶ Each year, the grant makers featured in this volume award millions of dollars to international nonprofit institutions and projects. This edition covers all the facts you need to bolster your target list of funding prospects: grantmaker portraits (more than 1,000 up-to-date entries with the data you need about potential funding sources—addresses, financial data, giving priorities, application procedures, and the names of key officials); Sample Grants (8,900+ descriptions of recently awarded grants provide additional insights into foundations' funding priorities); a range of indexes (the volume helps you find the funders that support your subject field, award grants in your geographic area, and make the type of grant you need). The grant makers included have supported a wide range of projects with an international focus, both in this country and abroad—programs concerned with international relief, conferences, disaster assistance, human rights, civil liberties, community development, education, and many other subjects. *Softcover, 358 pages, $125 (plus $4.50 shipping)*

The Guide to Grantmakers in the Rochester Area 1999–2001, 9th Edition

(ROCHESTER GRANTMAKERS FORUM)

▶ Its listings describe the giving programs of 165 corporations, foundations, trusts, and other funders distributing charitable dollars to nonprofit organizations in the six-county Greater Rochester region. It includes the first edition of the new *Directory of Evaluators* in upstate New York; the new Common Application Form and Common Report Form, with a list of funders accepting them; The Rochester Area Logic Model, which is the core of the new Common Application and Report Forms, with guidelines for developing logic models and samples of completed logic models; new listings of funders who have never appeared in previous editions; and information on some out-of-town funders that have given in this region. *Softcover, 350 pages, 58.00 + a tax-exempt number OR $4.64 tax for current dues-paying members of the Rochester Grantmakers Forum; $64.00 + a tax-exempt number OR $5.12 tax for nonmembers*

Guide to Greater Washington DC Grantmakers on CD-ROM

(THE FOUNDATION CENTER, 2000)

▶ Developed by The Foundation Center and the Washington Regional Association, you can use the CD-ROM's powerful search engine to explore this comprehensive source of information on funders in the District and surrounding counties. Compiled with WRAG's assistance and unique local perspective on the dynamics of DC grant making, this CD-ROM covers funders that dispense millions of dollars nationally each year as well as smaller institutions that focus their giving within the DC area. Grant-maker portraits feature crucial information: address, phone number, contact name, financial data, giving limitations, and names of key officials. For the large foundations—those that give at least $50,000 in grants per year—the volume provides even more data, including application procedures and giving interest statements. Highlights include: covers over 1,500 foundations, corporate giving programs, and grant-making public charities that are located in the greater Washington, DC, region or that have an interest in DC-area nonprofits; includes 300 funders outside of the DC region, representing more than 30 states; contains close to 1,800 selected grants; features searchable index of 8,000+ trustees, officers, and donors and their grant-maker affiliations; links to more than 150 grant-maker Web sites; connects to special Web page with resources of value to DC grant seekers; flexible printing and saving options and ability to mark records; and includes online Help file and printed user guide. Choose from 12 search fields (Grantmaker Name; Grantmaker State; Grantmaker City; Fields of Interest; Types of Support; Trustees, Officers, and Donors; Geographic Focus; Grantmaker Type; Total Giving; Total Assets; Establishment Date; Text Search). *Single User: $75; Local Area Network (LAN): $125*

The Guide to Minnesota Foundations and Corporate Giving Programs 1999–2000

(MINNESOTA COUNCIL ON FOUNDATIONS, 1999)

▶ This comprehensive directory is available in both print and a first-ever CD-ROM version. Both the print and CD-ROM editions feature: 863 grant-maker listings; 326 detailed grant-maker profiles that include such valuable information as key contacts, key financial data, areas funded, program limitations and restrictions, geographic priorities, targeted populations, grant ranges, sample grants, application deadlines and procedures, and staff and trustees. The CD-ROM edition features automatic searching for grant makers based on geography, areas of interest, types of support, targeted populations, grant-maker name, grant-maker city, and more; and automatic sorting of your search results by grants paid, total assets, grant range, city or zip code. Your results can be printed or downloaded in text format. The print edition features eight indexes, including indexes of grant makers by areas of interest, geography and target populations, and indexes of staff and trustees; and an extensive introductory section on the basics of grant making and grant seeking, including the popular article "How to Write a Successful Grant Proposal." IBM-compatible PC (no Mac version available). Windows 95 or later version (including Windows NT). *$40 for print version only (plus shipping and handling); $100 for CD-ROM—Stand-Alone PC*; $200 for CD-ROM—Networked Access*; (*1 copy of the print edition included with every CD-ROM order)*

Guide to Orange County and Los Angeles County Foundations, 2000 Edition
(NONPROFIT RESOURCE CENTER, 1999)

▶ Updated annually this comprehensive guide is an invaluable funding research resource for nonprofit professionals. The Guide contains over 800 detailed entries on private and corporate foundations in Los Angeles and Orange County. Listings include contact names, phone numbers, addresses, giving limitations, application guidelines, and sample grants. It includes tips on funding research and a brief overview of grant proposal writing (*http://www.volunteercenter.org/nrc/library.htm#publications*). *Orange County Edition: $25.00 (Member); $30.00 (Nonmember); Los Angeles County Edition: $55.00 (Member); $60.00 (Nonmember); Combined County Edition: $70.00 (Member); $85.00 (Nonmember)*

The Guide to Oregon Foundations, 10th Edition
GEIL, JULIA, ED. (GUIDE LINE, 2000)

▶ Contains entries for selected grant making foundations with a history of giving in Oregon. *$25*

Guide to U.S. Foundations, Their Trustees, Officers, and Donors
(THE FOUNDATION CENTER, 2001)

▶ The new edition of this essential reference book, the only published source of data on all active grant-making foundations and the individuals who run them, provides current information on 47,500 foundations. Featuring a master list of the decision makers who direct America's foundations, the *Guide to U.S. Foundations* is a powerful fund-raising reference source that will facilitate your grant seeking in several crucial ways: Discover your own donors' philanthropic connections (the comprehensive Trustee, Officer, and Donor Index will help you discover the foundation affiliations of your board members, donors, and volunteers, allowing you to quickly see whether they or their families are connected to foundations. Think how useful the name index can be when networking for grant prospects); target local funding prospects that appear in no other funding directory (the *Guide to U.S. Foundations* should be the first stop in your search for local grant dollars. Arranged by state and total giving, it helps you identify both large and small foundations in your geographic area. And you can also check trustee, officer, and donor names to learn more about the giving choices of local families); learn more about the sources of small gifts you have received (you can follow up giving leads by checking for individual names in the Trustee, Officer, and Donor Index or by tracking a grant-maker contribution in the Foundation Name Index and

Locator. Each entry lists current assets and grants to help you determine a grant-maker's giving potential); locate additional information (the *Guide to U.S. Foundations* uses codes to show you whether other Foundation Center directories include more detailed information on the grant maker you're researching). It is divided into two volumes: Volume 1: The Foundations; and Volume 2: Foundation Trustee, Officer, and Donor Index and Foundation Locator. *Softcover, 2 volumes, 4,235 pages, $215*

The Health Funds Grants Resources Yearbook, 9th Edition
BETH-ANN KERBER, ED. (HEALTH RESOURCES PUBLISHING, 1999)

▶ Learn more about the funding priorities of government agencies, foundations, and corporations. Study the information on health grant priorities of major foundations, to find the funding sources for your program. Learn from the case studies of other organizations' grant-seeking success stories to generate new ideas to get your programs funded. This resource gives you dollar amounts, descriptions of previous grant recipients and the programs that attracted funding, and details of future funding trends. It is divided into practical subject categories to make your search easy: trends in foundation grants for health; AIDS research and health services; funding for cancer; elderly health services; and child, maternal, and adolescent health care, just to name a few. It includes step-by-step instructions on application procedures, deadlines, and funding interests for some of the top health care grant makers in the country; and an expanded section overflowing with essential development strategies and tips for successful grant seeking. Plus, you'll get the latest information available on cultivating corporations, federal funding, and trends in philanthropy today. *Softcover, $165 (plus $8.00 shipping)*

How to Evaluate and Improve Your Grants Effort
DAVID G. BAUER (ORYX PRESS, 2001)

▶ The author states that in his 30 years of experience in the field of grants, most institutions do not invest enough time, effort, or money into making the grant-seeking effort and grants administration more efficient and successful. Bauer seeks to provide grant seekers with a dynamic, flexible, and ever-adapting system for the procurement and administration of external funds. He offers techniques for improving grants systems and examines how the functions of an academic grants office will change in the future. Including information that helps the user develop the ability to assess the grants system, gather feedback on a routine basis, and accept change as an inevitable part of the process involved in pre- and post-award grants administration, this book helps the user move from the development of a logical, efficient system to improving and changing such procedures as needed. Arranged into 17 chapters, each chapter provides an explanation of the different functions of a grants office; the rationale for including these functions in a grants and contracts system; assessment tools, including survey questions to help the user evaluate how effectively his or her office provides each of these functions; and strategies for improving, initiating, and implementing the differing functions that help the user meet his or her office's goals and objectives. To further aid the user in evaluating his or her grants system, a disk is included that contains Eastern Michigan University's Client Satisfaction Survey, another survey that contains all of the survey questions at the end of each chapter, and the PDF version of both surveys to assist in creating tailored e-mail client-satisfaction surveys. It also provides suggestions on how to systemize your grants effort through standardized worksheets and forms, sample letters to grantors, step-by-step information on preparing a proposal, and an extensive list of grant-seeking resources. *Hardcover, 248 pages, $36.95*

The "How To" Grants Manual: Successful Grantseeking Techniques for Obtaining Public and Private Grants, 4th Edition
DAVID G. BAUER (ORYX PRESS, 1999)

▶ The new edition incorporates changes and trends over the past five years in seeking and landing funding for education-based projects and institutions. It reflects the growing number of foundations with Web pages, using the Internet, the government trend toward online applications, recent statistics, and new resources. It includes worksheets, forms, sample letters, and examples. Since it was first published in 1984, Bauer's manual has become a standard in its field. In this new edition, he has updated the examples, added some new strategies, and expanded the information about online resources. Bauer offers many suggestions and tips (as well as encouragement) to help grant seekers become proactive. The first section does a good job of helping grant seekers see the grant proposal from the grantor's perspective. It also provides information on how to develop and document a proposal, write and refine it, and find the right venue for it. The second and third sections cover the process of identifying and applying for government and private grants. In addition to clarifying the differences between public and private funding, these sections detail the planning, research, and submission of grants, as well as how to follow up on them. The book includes tables, charts, and worksheets that summarize the information and help grant seekers focus their thinking. If a library can purchase only one book on developing grant proposals, this one should be at or very near the top of the list. *Hardcover, 264 pages, $34.95*

Illinois Foundation Directory
(FOUNDATION DATA CENTER)

▶ This directory provides complete giving data (including itemization of every grant awarded) on all Illinois foundations and corporate giving programs, based on the most current 990-PF and -AR returns and annual foundation questionnaires, various indices include donors, trustees and administrators, guidelines and deadlines, and banks and trust companies as corporate trustees of foundations. It is updated quarterly. *$675 (Initial purchase includes one year of update service), $225 (Annual service thereafter)*

I'll Grant You That: A Step-by-Step Guide to Finding Funds, Designing Winning Projects, and Writing Powerful Proposals *(See Grant Writing/Proposal Writing)*

Massachusetts Grantmakers Directory, 1999–2000 Edition
GRACELAW SIMMONS, ED. (ASSOCIATED GRANTMAKERS OF MASSACHUSETTS, 1999)

▶ This directory profiles the funding interests and application procedures of nearly 500 corporate giving programs, corporate foundations, community foundations, private foundations, bank trust departments, and grant-making public charities. The directory questionnaire was sent to almost all of the giving programs in Massachusetts and is supplemented by descriptions derived from the IRS 990-PF tax forms. This method ensures the inclusion of virtually all Massachusetts-based foundations with assets valued at $2 million or more, or with annual giving in excess of $200,000.

Designed to help make foundation and grants research more efficient and accurate, the *Massachusetts Grantmakers Directory* also includes "Quest for Funds," an indispensable "how-to" fund-raising guide and comprehensive indexing by areas of funding interest, as well as population and geographic focus. *Softcover, $50.00 (Nonmember), $45 (Member)*

Michigan Foundation Directory, 12th Edition
(Biennial)
(COUNCIL OF MICHIGAN FOUNDATIONS/FOUNDATION CENTER/MICHIGAN LEAGUE FOR HUMAN SERVICES, 2000)

▶ Features of the new directory include information on more than 1900 Michigan grant makers, and approximately 162 out-of-state grant makers with a giving interest in Michigan. Based on information compiled from foundations, the Foundation Center, and IRS 990 returns, the *Michigan Foundation Directory* is designed to help simplify the process of identifying potential sources of funding for grant seekers and to inform the public about foundations and corporate giving programs in Michigan. Section 1 is mainly an alphabetical listing of Michigan foundations having assets of $200,000 or more or making annual awards of $25,000 or more. Entries for these larger foundations are quite detailed, including statement of purpose, contacts, geographic priorities, limitations, application procedures, and grant analysis. The *Michigan Foundation Directory* provides much briefer information on Special Purpose Foundations and foundations making grants of less than $25,000. It also identifies corporate giving programs and corporate foundations; public foundations that redistribute funds usually raised through a fund-raising campaign; and foundations that have terminated since the previous edition. It is also noted for an in-depth analysis of Michigan grant making in general as well as tips on seeking grants. The Directory provides a listing of foundations by geographic areas—the Detroit metropolitan area is kept separate from the out-state areas. Separate indexes provide subject, officer, and foundation name approaches. It is also available in CD-ROM format. *Softcover, $30*

Minnesota Foundation Directory
(FOUNDATION DATA CENTER)

▶ This directory includes every foundation registered in the state of Minnesota and on file with the United States Internal Revenue Service. (There are presently over 800 foundations listed.) Included in the directory are the following sections: How-to-Use-the-Directory—details on the research process and types of foundations; Summary Reports—overviews on foundations with assets under $300,000 and total grants of less than $75,000; Major Reports—comprising the largest section, showing financial information, type of foundation, areas of interest, geographic range, officers, trustees and donors, and a complete detailing of every gift: the recipient, state of residence, grant amount and type of gift (if this information is available); Index of Donors, Trustees, and Administrators—kept up to date by the foundations; Index of Banks and Trust Companies Acting as Corporate Trustees—updated regularly; Areas of Interest—makes researching specific types of grant prospects easier for you; and, Foundation Guidelines and Deadlines—if the foundation publishes guidelines, they are reproduced. It provides complete giving data, including itemization of every grant awarded by all Minnesota foundation and corporate giving programs, based on the most current 990-PF and -AR returns and annual foundation questionnaires. Indices include donors, trustees and administrators, bank and trust companies as corporate (foundation) trustees, guidelines, and deadlines of Minnesota foundations. Initial purchase includes major directory, one-year update service, and annual seminar. It is updated quarterly (monthly FAX updates are included in the service). *Directory: $375; Subscription service: $475; Update service: $230 (annually)*

The Mitchell Guide: A Directory of New Jersey Foundations, 9th Edition

(MITCHELL GUIDE, 1999)

▶ This guide profiles 574 foundations that have made total grants of $15,000 or more annually and/or have assets of $150,000 or more.

Montana Foundation Directory 2000, 12th Edition

ALLYSON AND GIERKE AND MELISSA STREICHER, EDS. (GRANTS DEVELOPMENT OFFICE, 2000)

▶ Contains entries for foundations active in Montana. *Softcover, $15*

National Directory of Corporate Giving, 6th Edition

(THE FOUNDATION CENTER, 1999)

▶ This book provides up-to-date entries on approximately 3,000 corporate foundations and direct-giving programs. Corporate funders often make grants that reflect the interests of their parent companies, and it benefits grant seekers to discover these funding priorities before submitting proposals. The new edition of the *National Directory of Corporate Giving* provides an efficient and effective way to get the inside track on your corporate prospects. It will save you research time and effort by helping you to access crucial data on approximately 3,000 corporate funders (detailed portraits of close to 1,900 corporate foundations and an additional 1,000+ direct-giving programs include such essential information as the names of key personnel, types of support generally awarded, giving limitations, financial data, purpose and activities statements, and application procedures); determine grant-maker giving interests (many entries include descriptions of recently awarded grants, an excellent indication of a grant maker's funding priorities. Many entries also include program analyses to further indicate the grant maker's interests); and research the business concerns of the sponsoring companies. The new sixth edition includes data on the companies behind the philanthropies—essential background information for corporate grant searches. Entries give the parent company's name and address, a review of its businesses, financial data, and plant and subsidiary locations. In addition, seven indexes help you target the best funding prospects for your program. *Softcover, 1,095 pages, $195*

National Directory of Corporate Philanthropy for Native Americans

PHYLLIS A. MEINERS, ED. (CRC PUBLISHING, 2001)

▶ A sourcebook of private-sector grants for Native American Studies programs, tribes, and Indian nonprofit organizations, this work has been widely acclaimed as the definitive reference guide of funding for Native programs. The Directory contains information on 39 mainstream grant makers, 24 foundations, 12 corporations and corporate foundations, and three religious institutions considered to be the most prominent funders of American Indian programs. Indexes compile grant makers by subject and geographic priorities, permitting quick identification of the most likely funding prospects. Profiles include contact persons, sample grants, application deadlines, geographic limitations, special interests, and sample grants. *Softcover, 260 pages, $98.95*

National Directory of Corporate Public Affairs, 19th Edition (Annual Directory)

ARTHUR C. CLOSE, J. VALERIE STEELE, AND MICHAEL E. BUCKNER, EDS. (COLUMBIA BOOKS, 2001)

▶ This directory tracks the public/government affairs programs of about 1,700 major U.S. corporations and lists the 12,000 people who run them. It also lists Washington area offices, corporate foundations and giving programs, corporate PACs, and federal lobbyists. It is indexed by subject and geographic area and includes a membership directory of the Public Affairs Council. It is an authoritative source of information on "who's who" and "who's doing what" in corporate public affairs. It also provides a complete state-by-state listing of contract lobbyists and their clients. Since philanthropy is often tied to a company's overall public relations effort, this directory is a good source for pinpointing the logical officials to approach within many corporate hierarchies; it provides information on more than 1,900 major U.S. corporations and contains the names and titles of approximately 16,000 corporate personnel who handle community and public affairs (as well as government relations, lobbying, and policy planning). In addition, the book features concise descriptions of corporate foundations and charitable trusts For firms that have an active foundation or corporate giving program, recent recipients of major gifts are also listed. *Softcover, 1,200+ pages, $129 (plus $5 shipping)*

National Directory of Foundation Grants for Native Americans

PHYLLIS A. MEINERS, ED. (CRC PUBLISHING, 1998)

▶ This reference documents the philanthropy of 55 private foundations considered to be the most prominent funders of Native American programs. Mainstream foundations who target self-help and self-determination in American Indian communities and those who earmark Native American studies are featured. Grants for other indigenous projects are also included. Profiles include key contact persons, foundation assets and grantmaking budgets, sample grants, deadlines, geographic and subject preferences, and detailed application procedures for each grant maker. The Directory contains detailed subject and geographic indexes. *Softcover, 190 pages, $99.95*

National Directory of Philanthropy for Native Americans

PHYLLIS A. MEINERS, GREG A. SANFORD, AND HILARY HENRI TUN-ATZ, EDS. (CRC PUBLISHING, 1992)

▶ Derived from grant-maker annual reports, guidelines, interviews, and IRS 990s, this directory lists 39 private-sector grant makers (24 foundations, 12 corporations and corporate foundations, and three religious institutions) considered to be the most prominent supporters of programs for Native Americans. It includes family foundations, corporate foundations and direct giving programs, and religious institutions. It also includes contact persons, assets and revenues, sample grants, application deadlines and procedures, special-interest categories, and geographic preferences. Indexes compile grant makers by subject and geographic priorities, permitting quick identification of the most likely funding prospects. *Softcover, 139 pages, $69.95 (plus $5 shipping)*

National Directory of Seed Money Grants for American Indian Projects

PHYLLIS A. MEINERS CFRE (CRC PUBLISHING COMPANY-EAGLEROCK BOOKS, 2000)

► This is a new sourcebook of private-sector seed money grants for startup and innovative programs managed by Native Americans. Small "alternative" grant makers who focus on projects of self-determination and social change are featured. The Directory contains profiles of some 40 single and multistate private grant makers. In addition, a section devoted to American Indian foundations (grants *from* American Indians *to* American Indians) is included. Indexes compile grant makers by subject and geographic priorities. Profiles include contact persons, sample grants, application deadlines, geographic limitations, special interests, and application procedures. *Softcover, 280 pages, $109.95*

National Guide to Funding for Children, Youth and Families, 5th Edition

(THE FOUNDATION CENTER, 1999)

► This book features current data on more than 5,100 foundations and corporate giving programs—all with an interest in funding nonprofit organizations that serve these special populations. The grant makers covered in this volume award millions of dollars each year to programs involved with child development and welfare, family planning, family services, delinquency prevention, youth centers, and hundreds of other subject areas. Features include fact-filled portraits that provide easy access to grant-maker addresses and contact names; financial data to help you determine giving potential; giving priorities and limitations; application guidelines; the names of key officials; and descriptions of recent grants (over 9,000 in all), often the surest indication of a funder's giving priorities for projects in the field. Over 19,100 sample grants give you special insight into grant-maker priorities; and a range of helpful indexes that match your funding needs with the most appropriate grant makers. You can target potential funders by the names of donors, officers, and trustees; subject area; geographic focus; and types of support. The six indexes help grant makers target appropriate sources of funding by the: (1) names of donors, officers, and trustees; (2) geographic area; (3) types of support; (4) subject area preferred; (5) grants awarded by subject; and (6) name of the foundation or corporate giver. A bibliography facilitates further research in the field. *Softcover, 1,664 pages, $145 (plus $4.50 shipping)*

National Guide to Funding for Community Development, 2nd Edition

(THE FOUNDATION CENTER, 1998)

► With more than 2,600 foundations and corporate direct-giving programs and public charities covered, this volume offers fund raisers in the field an excellent opportunity to increase their funding base. The grant makers covered in this volume have supported community improvement projects; economic development; business promotion (including chambers of commerce); community funds and federated giving programs; community service clubs; housing development, construction, and rehabilitation; low-cost temporary housing and homeless shelters; employment and vocational training; and more. Entries feature crucial information: addresses and contact names, giving interest statements, current financial data, application guidelines, and, in many cases, examples of recently awarded grants—10,000+ grant descriptions provide unique insight into foundation funding priorities. A range of indexes help you find the most appropriate funders by subject area, geographic focus, and types of support. *Softcover, 808 pages, $135*

National Guide to Funding for Elementary and Secondary Education, 5th Edition

(THE FOUNDATION CENTER, 1999)

► This volume provides essential facts on more than 3,300 grant makers, each with a history of awarding grant dollars to projects and institutions related to elementary and secondary education. It is designed to help you get the facts you need to bolster your target list of funding prospects. Each entry provides crucial data—address, financial data, giving priorities statement, application procedures, contact names, and key officials. Many entries also include descriptions of recently awarded grants, often the best indication of a grant maker's funding priorities. The volume includes over 8,800 sample grants, often the best indication of a grant maker's particular funding interests. Six indexes help you target potential funders by subject and geographic area, types of grants generally awarded, foundation name, and the names of key personnel. The grant makers included in the *National Guide to Funding for Elementary and Secondary Education* have supported a wide range of organizations, from the smallest schools to nationwide research initiatives, as well as bilingual programs, cooperative/community education, dropout prevention, educational testing, programs for gifted children, remedial reading/math initiatives, and vocational/trade schools. *Softcover, 725 pages, $135 (plus $4.50 shipping)*

National Guide to Funding for Information Technology, 2nd Edition

(THE FOUNDATION CENTER, 1999)

► This book provides essential facts on over 700 foundations and corporate direct giving programs, each with a history of awarding grant dollars to projects involving information technology. Imagine the time you'll save by having in a single convenient source a list of grant makers already interested in this field. Features include grant-maker portraits (over 700 entries with the data you need to decide to pursue the funding source—address, financial data, giving priorities, application procedures, contact names, and the names of key officials); sample grants (over 2,400 descriptions of recently awarded grants provide insight into foundation giving interests); and a range of indexes (to help you target funders by specific program areas favored and geographic areas preferred by grant makers). Each year, the grant makers featured in this volume award millions of grant dollars to a wide range of institutions and projects, from the smallest public libraries to major research facilities. Grant recipients include academic, law, art, and medical libraries, as well as other nonprofit information clearinghouses, databases, and public service centers. *Softcover, 336 pages, $115*

National Guide to Funding for Libraries and Information Services, 5th Edition (Directory)

THE FOUNDATION CENTER, 1999

► This completely revised edition provides essential data on over 880 grant makers, each with a history of awarding grant dollars to libraries and other information centers. Features include: grant-maker portraits (each entry provides crucial data, including address and contact name, financial data, giving priorities, application procedures, and the names of key officials); sample grants (many entries include descriptions of recently awarded grants, often the best indication of a grant maker's particular funding interests. The fifth edition includes close to 1,600 sample grants); and a range of indexes (the volume's indexes help you target potential funders by the names of donors, officers, and trustees; geographic area; types of support; subject area; and grant-maker name). *Softcover, 234 pages, $95 (plus $4.50 shipping and handling)*

National Guide to Funding for the Environment and Animal Welfare, 5th Edition
(THE FOUNDATION CENTER, 2000)

► It covers over 2,900 foundations, corporate direct-giving programs, and grant-making public charities with an interest in the field, providing you immediate access to crucial fund-raising information: grant-maker addresses, financial data, giving priorities, contact names, and key officials; lists of sample grants; and a range of indexes. To show you the grant makers' demonstrated giving interests, the volume includes over 7,200 descriptions of grants recently awarded to projects and organizations involved in international conservation, ecological research, litigation and advocacy, waste reduction, animal welfare, and many other related projects. *Softcover, 527 pages, $115*

National Guide to Funding for Women and Girls, 5th Edition
(THE FOUNDATION CENTER, 1999)

► This book provides essential information on more than 1,200 foundations and corporate direct-giving programs, all with a specific interest in the field of women and girls. The grant makers listed in this edition of the *Guide to Funding for Women and Girls* have funded child care, health care, civil rights, homeless and abuse shelters, education efforts, legal defense, employment programs, rape prevention programs, family planning clinics, and many other subject categories. Each entry includes the grant maker's address and contact name, financial data, giving priorities, application guidelines, and names of key officials. Many entries also feature descriptions of recently awarded grants (the volume includes more than 5,400), often the best indication of a grant maker's particular funding interests. *Softcover, 414 pages, $115*

National Guide to Funding in Aging, 6th Edition
(THE FOUNDATION CENTER, 2000)

► This volume provides essential facts on over 1,200 grant makers with a specific interest in the field of aging. Each year, the grant makers featured in this volume award millions of grant dollars to senior citizen programs and institutions such as hospitals, community centers, nursing homes, and continuing education facilities, as well as organizations that concentrate on legal rights, housing, employment, health, veterans, cultural affairs, nutrition, and much more. Features include: grant-maker portraits (entries feature updated addresses, financial data, giving priorities statements, application procedures, contact names, and key officials); and sample grants (nearly 500 foundation entries include descriptions of over 2,100 recent grants, the best indication of grant-maker funding interests. *Softcover, 294 pages, $115*

National Guide to Funding in AIDS
(THE FOUNDATION CENTER, 1999)

► All 600+ grant makers featured in this crucial directory have stated or demonstrated a commitment to AIDS-related services and research. *National Guide to Funding in AIDS* (formerly *AIDS Funding, 5th Edition*) includes current information on the grant-making programs of foundations and corporate giving programs as well as public charities. Most entries list recently awarded grants to show you the kind of AIDS-related projects the grant maker has funded. Over 760 sample grants are included. It is valuable if you raise funds for direct relief, medical research, legal aid, preventative education, or any other program that empowers people with AIDS or helps them combat the disease. *Softcover, 206 pages, $75*

National Guide to Funding in Arts and Culture, 6th Edition
ELIZABETH H. RICH, ED. (THE FOUNDATION CENTER, 2000)

► The new sixth edition of the *National Guide to Funding in Arts and Culture* provides essential facts on over 7,500 foundations, corporate direct-giving programs, and public charities, each with a history of awarding grant dollars to arts and culture-related projects and organizations. Imagine the time you'll save by having, in a single convenient source, a list of thousands of U.S. grant makers that support arts and culture. Features include: grant-maker portraits (over 7,500 up-to-date entries feature the information you need to decide whether or not to pursue a funding source, including financial data, giving priorities, application procedures, the names of key officials, and contact names and addresses); sample grants (16,500 descriptions of recently awarded grants provide additional insights into foundation funding priorities); and a range of indexes (the volume is indexed by subject area, geographic area, and types of support to help you target the most appropriate funders for your organization). *Softcover, 1,138 pages, $155.00*

National Guide to Funding in Health, 6th Edition
(THE FOUNDATION CENTER, 1999)

► This book features current data on 7,700+ foundations, corporate giving programs, and grant-making public charities, all with an interest in funding health-related programs and institutions. The grant makers covered in this volume award millions of dollars each year to hospitals, universities, research institutes, health care associations, and a variety of other organizations and projects. Features include: fact-filled grant-maker portraits that provide easy access to address and contact name; financial data to help you determine giving potential; giving priorities and limitations; application guidelines; the names of key officials; and descriptions of recent grants, often the best indication of a grant-maker's funding priorities. More than 16,900 sample grants give you additional insights into grant-maker priorities; and a range of helpful indexes that match your funding needs with the most appropriate grant makers. You can target potential funders by names of donors, officers, and trustees; subject area; geographic focus; and types of support. *Softcover, 2,032 pages, $150*

National Guide to Funding in Higher Education, 6th Edition
(THE FOUNDATION CENTER, 2000)

► This guide provides essential facts on more than 7,200 foundations, corporate direct-giving programs, and public charities, each with a history of awarding grant dollars to higher-education projects and institutions. Imagine the time you'll save by having, in a single convenient source, a list of thousands of U.S. grant makers that support higher education. Each year, the grant makers featured in this volume award millions of dollars to colleges, universities, professional and technical schools, scholarship funds, and a range of other related programs and projects. The *National Guide to Funding in Higher Education* covers all the facts you need to bolster your target list of funding prospects: grant-maker portraits (more than 7,200 grant-maker entries with the data you need to decide whether to pursue potential funding sources—addresses, financial data, giving priorities, application procedures, contact names, and the names of key officials); sample grants (more than 18,000 descriptions of recently awarded grants provide additional insights into foundations' proven giving interests); and a range of indexes (to help you target funders by specific program areas and geographic area preferred by grant makers). *Softcover, 1,275 pages, $175*

National Guide to Funding in Religion, 5th Edition
(THE FOUNDATION CENTER, 1999)

▶ This guide provides detailed fund-raising information in your specific field. This essential directory brings together a group of more than 6,700 foundations, corporate direct-giving programs, and grant-making public charities, all of which have proven their commitment to the field by funding churches, synagogues, and mosques, as well as by providing support for building preservation, humanitarian aid, missionary societies, religious schools, welfare, youth groups, and many other religious-affiliated programs. Included are grant-maker addresses and contact names, financial data, giving interest statements, application guidelines, and the names of key officials. Many entries also feature descriptions of recently awarded grants (the volume includes more than 8,000), often the best indication of a grantmaker's funding priorities. *Softcover, 1,448 pages, $140*

National Guide to Funding in Substance Abuse, 2nd Edition
(THE FOUNDATION CENTER)

▶ This book provides easy access to grant-maker addresses, financial data, giving priorities, contact names and key officials; lists of sample grants; and a range of indexes to help you target potential funders. Many entries include a list of recent grants, providing additional insight into a grant maker's funding priorities. The volume includes over 680 sample grants. The 580+ foundations and corporate direct-giving programs included in this volume have supported a wide range of projects and organizations. Search for prospects among grant makers that fund counseling, preventative education, treatment, medical research, residential care, and halfway houses, as well as programs that address alcohol and drug abuse, smoking addiction, and drunk driving. *Softcover, 238 pages, $95*

New Hampshire Directory of Foundations, 1st Edition
CHRISTINE GRAHAM (CPG ENTERPRISES, INC., 2001)

▶ This directory lists all foundations incorporated in New Hampshire plus foundations incorporated elsewhere with giving or guidelines that include New Hampshire. Information includes names, addresses, phone, and other contact information; assets and typical grant ranges; application guidelines; areas of interest; restrictions and limitations; and lists of recent New Hampshire grantees. *Softcover, $45*

New Jersey Grants Guide, 2000–2001
(GRANT GUIDES PLUS)

▶ Published in association with the Center for Non-Profit Corporations, this directory combines profiles of grant makers with tutorials for grant seekers. The foundations, corporate-giving programs, and government agencies listed are either based in New Jersey or support projects within that states' borders. The compilers of the guide—who use informational tax returns, foundations' annual reports, and their own surveys—list foundations whose total giving was $50,000 or more annually in New Jersey. The guide begins with lists of the top 25 foundations and top 25 corporate grant makers, ranked by giving within their states and by total giving nationwide, respectively. It continues with a "tool kit" for grant seekers. This section runs at least 50 pages in each guide and provides information on writing proposals, developing budgets, drafting board members and volunteers for fund raising, creating news media coverage, and other topics. Profiles of grant makers follow,

and they are divided into sections that list state-based foundations and trusts, national grant makers, corporate grant makers, state government units, and religious organizations. Each entry provides contact information, total assets, the number of grants made in the state, types of support given, geographic areas of interest, sample grants, and a roster of trustees. For government grant makers, most of the information above is supplanted by more detailed summaries of the programs operated by the agency. Appendices include alphabetical lists of the grant makers, as well as lists by county, types of support given, and an index of trustees. It contains a wall calendar that notes the deadlines for grant proposals for more than 100 foundations in the state. *Softcover, 738 pages, $149*

The New Mexico Funding Directory, 5th Edition
(Biannual)

DENISE A. WALLEN AND AMY ELDER, EDS. (UNIVERSITY OF NEW MEXICO, 1998)

▶ This directory contains information on more than 300 funding sources located in New Mexico as well as out-of-state funding sources that focus on New Mexico and the Southwest, including private, community, and corporate foundations; state government grant programs; associations and organizations; corporate direct-giving programs; and competitive award programs at the University of New Mexico. The fifth edition contains over 50 new funders. All listings include a program profile, eligibility requirements, application information, fiscal information, deadlines, and sample grants. The directory also contains a time-saving subject index for easy access to information and a selected bibliography of general funding literature and other important directories. A searchable version is also available online at *http://www.unm.edu/~ors/public. Softcover, $40*

New York State Foundations: A Comprehensive Directory, 6th Edition
(THE FOUNDATION CENTER, 1999)

▶ Since many grant makers consider their commitment to a particular city, region, county, or state to be their first priority in awarding grants, this volume represents an invaluable resource for New York nonprofits. It provides current facts on every foundation in the state. *New York State Foundations* will help you tap into the most active grantmaker community in the United States—this volume covers over 7,000 foundations that fund New York state nonprofits. Close to 5,900 of these foundations are located in New York and an additional 1,200 are out-of-state grant makers with a documented interest in the state. These grant makers award over one-fifth of all foundation grant dollars in the United States, a total of more than $2 billion to nonprofits each year; track down local support—organized by county, the volume is especially useful for targeting potential grant sources in your specific region. You can scan through sections of the book that cover your county and use the geographic index to immediately find the grant makers located in your city; match giving interests to your grant request—whether you raise funds for organizations involved with arts and culture, higher education, health, or many other subjects, the subject index directs you to foundations that support your specific field. The grant maker portraits feature crucial information: application addresses, financial data, giving limitations, and key officials. For the large foundations—those that give at least $50,000 in grants per year—the volume provides even more data, including application procedures and purpose and activities statements. Many entries also include descriptions of recently awarded grants, which provide unique insight into funding priorities. The volume includes over 12,600 sample grants. *Softcover, 1,095 pages, $180.00*

The New York State Grants Guide

MANDY RIGG, ED. (GRANT GUIDES PLUS, 2000)

▶ This desk reference is for nonprofits, schools, local governments, and any organization looking for grants. It is five guides in one, including foundations and philanthropic trusts; corporations and businesses; state government departments and agencies; religious institutions; and a Tool Kit. It has more resources than before, including almost $5 billion in total giving, 697 profiles of funding sources, 473 foundations, 62 corporate giving programs, 28 religious funders, and more than 100 state government programs. It provides comprehensive details on areas of funding interest, financial data on assets and giving, amount of New York giving, examples of recent grants, application procedures/deadlines, contact names, how much to apply for, types of support, and officers and trustees. It is indexed in 120 ways, including alphabetical, by areas of interest, by geographic location, by trustees, and by county. The Tool Kit section gives you all the information you need to raise money successfully, including strategies, tips, and "how to's" on fund raising from successful grant writers; how to write a winning proposal; how to prepare a budget as part of the proposal; how to work with corporations—marketing versus philanthropic donations; how to develop a fund-raising plan; how to involve your board in fund raising; how to research funders online; and how to work with the media. *Softcover, $199*

North Carolina Giving: The Directory of the State's Foundations, 4th Edition

(CAPITAL DEVELOPMENT SERVICES, 1999)

▶ Based on information taken from 990-PF tax returns filed with the North Carolina Attorney General's Office and the Internal Revenue Service, this directory contains profiles on more than 950 foundations. It offers an overview of North Carolina's nonprofit sector, including the total number of foundations, their assets (more than $8 billion!), where they are located, to whom they give (more than $387 million in grants), staffing, and more; up-to-date and comprehensive profiles of North Carolina's 997 independent, corporate, and community foundations; 130 categories of giving indexed for fast, effective research; index of foundations by county; index of North Carolina foundations' funding programs in surrounding states; index of foundation directors and trustees; foundation application guidelines and deadlines; and chapters on grant writing and donor research by fund-raising experts. It is also available online (see Internet Resources—Funding Sources). *Softcover, 899 pages, $120*

The Ohio Grants Guide 1999–2001, 2nd Edition

(GRANT GUIDES PLUS/OHIO ASSOCIATION OF NONPROFIT ORGANIZATIONS, 2000)

▶ This desk reference is for nonprofits, schools, local governments, and any organization looking for grants. *The Ohio Grants Guide* is the only comprehensive resource for organizations seeking grant funding in Ohio. It is five guides in one, including foundations and philanthropic trusts, corporations and businesses, state government departments and agencies, religious institutions, and a Tool Kit. It has more resources than before, including almost $5 billion in total giving, 697 profiles of funding sources, 473 foundations, 62 corporate giving programs, 28 religious funders, and more than 100 state government programs. It provides comprehensive details on areas of funding interest, financial data on assets and giving, amount of Ohio giving, examples of recent grants, application procedures/deadlines, contact names, how much to apply for, types of support, and officers and trustees. It is indexed in 120 ways,

including alphabetical, by areas of interest, by geographic location, by trustees, and by county. The Tool Kit section gives you all the information you need to raise money successfully, including strategies, tips, and "how to's" on fund raising from successful grant writers; how to write a winning proposal; how to prepare a budget as part of the proposal; how to work with corporations—marketing versus philanthropic donations; how to develop a fund-raising plan; how to involve your board in fund raising; how to research funders online; and how to work with the media.

This guide features more than 600 profiles of funders, 8,000 sample grants, and more than $3 billion in grants. It provides critical information on Ohio foundations, trusts, corporations, state governments, and religious institutions that give grants to all types of organizations throughout Ohio. It offers step-by-step advice, from that first call to the grant maker through turning it into a proposal. Features include 200+ corporations and businesses, 500+ foundations and philanthropic trusts, state government departments and agencies, religious institutions, and national funders giving in Ohio. It provides details on financial data on assets, amount of Ohio giving, examples of recent grants, application deadlines, contact names, and how much to apply for. It is indexed in 120 ways, including areas of interest, geographic location, funding levels, types of support, and officers and trustees. A "tools" section gives strategies, tips, "politics" of fund raising from seasoned grant writers. It includes free biannual updates. *Softcover, 1000+ pages, $147 (plus shipping and handling)*

Operating Grants for Nonprofit Organizations

(ORYX PRESS, 2000)

▶ This is a guide to foundations, corporations, and government agencies that offer operating support. It is the ideal resource for nonprofit organizations seeking scarce operating funds. More than 1,100 grants for all types of nonprofits are listed, including arts and humanities, community development, health care, science, children and youth, and education. Contains more than 1,000 listings for current funding programs that offer support for some or all general operating expenses of nonprofits and other institutions. The main section is organized alphabetically by state, with indexes organized by subject, sponsoring organizations, and geographic location. Most current information can be accessed on the companion Web site. Three user-friendly indexes (subject, sponsors, and geographic restrictions) let users quickly locate the right funding for their organization. Each entry includes grant title; sponsor name and address; contact information (name and title, phone and FAX numbers, e-mail and Web site addresses); requirements and restrictions (when available); samples of operating grants (when available); and sponsor's areas of interest. *Softcover, 296 pages, $29.95*

The Pennsylvania Grants Guide 1998–2000

(GRANT GUIDES PLUS, 2000)

▶ Desk reference for nonprofits, schools, local governments, and any organization looking for grants. It is five guides in one, including foundations and philanthropic trusts, corporations and businesses, state government departments and agencies, religious institutions, and a Tool Kit. It has two-thirds more resources than before, including almost $6 billion in total giving, 772 profiles of funding sources, 509 foundations, 86 corporate giving programs, 43 religious funders, and more than 100 state government programs. It provides comprehensive details on areas of funding interest, financial data on assets and giving, amount of Pennsylvania giving, examples of recent grants, application procedures/deadlines, contact names, how much to apply for, types of support, and officers and trustees. It is indexed in 120 ways, including alphabetical; by areas of interest; by geographic location, by trustees, and by county. The Tool Kit section gives you all the information you need to raise money successfully, including strategies, tips, and "how to's" on fund raising from successful grant writers; how to write a winning proposal; how to prepare a budget as part of the proposal; how to work with corporations—marketing versus philanthropic donations; how to develop a fund-raising plan; how to involve your board in fund raising; how to research funders online; and how to work with the media. *Softcover, $350*

Philanthropic Foundations of Utah Directory, 2000
(Biannual)
(HENRY DEAN PUBLISHING, INC., 2000)

▶ This directory provides information on more than 404 private foundations located in the state. Features include alternate years addendum; $99.8 million dollars in awards annually, address and telephone numbers, names of officers and managers, purposes and interests, fiscal data, and lists of grants. It is also available on CD-ROM. *Softcover, $54*

Philanthropy Northwest Member Directory 2000–2001, 4th Edition
(PHILANTHROPY NORTHWEST, 2000)

▶ Every two years, Philanthropy Northwest (formerly the Pacific Northwest Grantmakers Forum) publishes its *Member Directory*. This directory serves two purposes: It allows grant makers to publish information (in their own words) about their foundations or giving programs, and it serves as a comprehensive resource for grant seekers to use in identifying funding options. The *Member Directory* facilitates more appropriate grant requests, which saves time for grant writers as well as grant makers. The 2000–2001 edition of this valuable reference includes individual listings of over 143 grant-making organizations, including community foundations, corporate foundations, corporate giving programs, private foundation, and public foundations. The directory allows grant seekers to search by type of support (e.g., capital building funds, start-up funding, multiple-year awards) and funding areas (e.g., arts, literacy/ESL, programs for women and girls). Sections on preparing grant proposals and sources of technical assistance for nonprofits are included. Members fund programs in the states of Washington, Oregon, Idaho, Montana, and/or Alaska. This resource is searchable by funding area, grant amount, or keyword. If you order a subscription to the online, searchable database, you will have immediate access once you fill out the order form and submit it. The other advantage of the online version over the print version is that it is constantly updated and can be used by up to five people in the organization. Subscriptions are for one year, and users will be notified in time to renew. *12-month subscription plus one printed Directory, $162.75; 12-month subscription, $119.75*

Profiles of South Florida Donors: 1999–2000, 7th Edition
(DONORS FORUM, 1999)

▶ This book profiles the giving philosophy and criteria of some 125 companies and foundations who fund in South Florida, and provides contact information for each grant maker. Included is other information useful to grant seekers, such as sections on how to write strong proposals, how funders evaluate proposals, Web sites of use to nonprofits, and other resources for fund raisers. *Softcover, $60 (plus $5 shipping and handling)*

Religious Funding Resource Guide
ELLEN PAUL AND LINDA CLEMENTS (RESOURCEWOMEN/CHARDON PRESS, 2000)

▶ This is a guide to 38 faith-based grant and loan programs supporting social service and social change work. It includes guidelines, application forms, and information on the previous year's funding; with an introduction on how to approach and address religious funding sources. It helps community-based and nonprofit organizations find religious organizations interested in financing social justice and social service work. It includes guidelines and application forms for 37 ecumenical sources, an introduction explaining the process of seeking funds from these sources, and a deadline calendar. It is updated annually. *Softcover, 520 pages, $85 (plus $5 shipping)*

Silicon Valley Funders
(SUPPORT CENTER/NDC, 1999)

▶ This guide to foundations and corporate giving programs serving Silicon Valley nonprofit organizations lists nearly 200 funders headquartered in Santa Clara or Monterey counties or that contribute in that area. It is also available free online as a searchable database at *http://www.supportcenter.org/resources/svf. Softcover, $19.95*

South Carolina Foundation Directory, 7th Edition
KAREN D. MCMULLEN AND MARY R. BULL, EDS. (SOUTH CAROLINA STATE LIBRARY, 2000)

▶ The seventh edition of the *South Carolina Foundation Directory* contains 399 active private foundations, community foundations, and grant-making public charities located in the state of South Carolina. The *South Carolina Foundation Directory* is published every three years. It is designed to be a starting point for grant seekers in their search for funds to support nonprofit organizations' programs and projects. Information in the Directory is based on the foundation's most recent federal income tax returns. In some cases, additional information was taken from annual reports or newsletters. Each foundation entry includes the name, address, telephone number, officers, program interests, assets, dollar amount of grants awarded, sample grants, geographic interests, employer identification number (EIN), and when available, application and giving restrictions. *Softcover, 506 pages, $15 (includes shipping and handling)*

The South Dakota Grant Directory *(See Resource Development—Internet Resources, Funding Sources)*

Tennessee Directory of Foundations and Corporate Giving Programs
(CENTER FOR NONPROFIT MANAGEMENT)

▶ Profiles over 390 foundations and corporate giving programs. *Softcover, 200 pages, $69 (includes shipping)*

The Vermont Directory of Foundations, 10th Edition, 2000–2001
CHRISTINE GRAHAM, ED. (CPG ENTERPRISES, 2000)

▶ The only complete source of information on foundations incorporated in Vermont, and regular funders of Vermont projects incorporated out of state. *$48*

Washington State Charitable Trust Directory, 1999–2000 Edition

(CHARITIES DIVISION, SECRETARY OF STATE OFFICE)

▶ This directory lists about 900 grant-making and grant-seeking organizations registered in the state of Washington. The listings are brief, showing the organization's purpose, assets, distributions, limitations, geographic guidelines, and application procedures. This edition also contains a number of indexes, which allows you to search for specific information. Not all information is listed for every organization. *Softcover, $20 (includes postage)*

Wyoming Foundations Directory, 8th Edition

M. ANN MILLER, ED. (LARAMIE COUNTY COMMUNITY COLLEGE, 2001)

▶ Profiles Wyoming foundations and out-of-state funders with an interest in Wyoming. *Softcover, $8*

Grassroots Fund Raising

The Brown Bag Papers

KEN WYMAN & ASSOCIATES (1985–1990)

▶ This is the complete collection (five years of *The Brown Bag Papers* newsletters). You'll receive concise answers to many questions that face grassroots fund raisers, such as: How can I get my group in the publicity spotlight? Is phone fund raising going to bother or attract donors?

How can I ask someone for a really large donation? How can I build a more productive board? How can I find and keep great volunteers? How can I get our message across to the media? Plus hot tips on dozens of topics. *Softcover, 200+ pages, $40 (including shipping)*

Fundraising for Social Change, 3rd Edition

KIM KLEIN (CHARDON PRESS, 1996)

▶ The purpose of this book is to provide low-budget organizations—those with budgets under $500,000—with the information they need to establish, maintain, and expand successful community-based fund-raising programs. Successful grassroots fund raising will allow them to move away from reliance on foundations, corporations, and government assistance. Low-budget groups need to keep in mind that their fund-raising efforts take place in a context different from those of more traditional community service organizations in the following ways: (1) many people will not agree with or even understand what your group is trying to do; (2) you probably have little or no front money and not enough staff; therefore, you cannot afford to invest in large-scale fund-raising strategies; and (3) your board, volunteers, and staff are likely to be unfamiliar with fund-raising strategies and may not be comfortable with even the idea of fund raising. Traditional fund-raising strategies need to be rethought with these three premises in mind and translated into workable terms for grassroots groups. It presents detailed descriptions of how to carry out strategies to acquire, retain, and upgrade donors to your organization. These proceed from the most impersonal—direct-mail appeals and special events—to the most personal—solicitation by telephone and in person. Special attention is given to the difficulties most people have asking for money, offering concrete ways to overcome them. Finally, the book covers the rudiments of setting up a fund-raising office, record keeping, and hiring fund-raising staff or consultants.

Special circumstances are also covered, such as raising money in rural communities, for coalitions, in times of financial crisis, and so forth. *Softcover, 346 pages, $25*

Fundraising Ideas That Work for Grassroots Groups

(KEN WYMAN & ASSOCIATES, 1994)

▶ This is meant to be, literally, a *guide*book, pointing directions and suggesting options. Some points are touched on only briefly. Others had to be left out completely, and may form the ground for a future work. Where possible, a few selected resources are suggested to help you go further. It will help you get solid advice on good ideas for fund raising and on how to avoid major errors; find suggestions for sources of help on most topics, so you can do additional research if you need to; and discover techniques that have been outlined with grassroots and disabled persons' self-help groups in mind. Methods are adapted to help you raise money whether you are in a small community far from corporate headquarters and foundation offices, or are in the heart of a metropolis, feeling unable to compete with the multimillion-dollar charity drives that surround you; share the experiences of professional fund raisers (and professional fund*givers*) who work regularly with grassroots organizations that are committed to self-help and social change. Emphasis is placed on essential basic information for which there are no other readily available sources. Where other first-rate sources were available, reference is made to them rather than duplicating their content. It is also available for free online at *http://www.pch.gc.ca/cp-pc/ComPartnE/pub_list.htm. Softcover, 156 pages, $40 (including shipping)*

Grantmakers Directory, 2000 Edition (See Grant Seeking)

The Grass Roots Fundraising Book: How to Raise Money in Your Community, 3rd Edition

JOAN FLANAGAN (NTC/CONTEMPORARY PUBLISHING, 1996)

▶ Practical, comprehensive, and readable, this new updated edition offers an indispensable resource for novice community fund raisers. Professional fund raiser Joan Flanagan includes foolproof money-making strategies already tested by hundreds of successful fund raisers, the basics of organizing special events, advice on approaching philanthropists, a step-by-step guide to direct mailing, the how-tos of door-to-door canvassing, and more. For the organization that does not enjoy a guaranteed annual income, this manual includes the mechanics of raising money and resource information on sources in each state in the country. It provides the nuts and bolts of raising money for good causes, presenting innovative ideas on choosing the right fund-raising method, organizing special events, and making the most money in the least time. It contains specific information on how to raise money from members, supporters, the general public, businesses, and philanthropists. It tells how to use direct mail, door-to-door canvassing, and special events to raise big money; also how to manage taxes and legal affairs and how to publicize your events and your image. Learn how to keep on making money for your organization and how to plan ahead. *Softcover, 352 pages, $15 (plus $2.50 shipping); Nonprofit organizations, $11.25 (plus $2.50 shipping)*

Grassroots Grants: An Activist's Guide to Proposal Writing (See Grant Writing/Proposal Writing)

Major Gifts

The Artful Journey: Cultivating and Soliciting the Major Gift
WILLIAM T. STURTEVANT (BONUS BOOKS, 1997)

▶ Here is the first really practical book on major gift fund raising. It is a step-by-step guide to ensuring a successful ask. Low on philosophy, high on nuts-and-bolts, the book is an extensive review of strategic cultivation that moves a prospect to higher and higher levels. The methodology is failproof and makes certain you keep on track. *Hardcover, 250 pages, $40*

Asking: A Hands-on Guide to Gift Solicitation
CHRISTINE GRAHAM (CPG ENTERPRISES)

▶ This booklet gives down-to-earth advice for successful solicitation of charitable contributions, based on understanding donors' motivations and solicitors' fears, in a booklet for askers, with accompanying training guide. It covers the hows and whys of giving and asking, courage and sensitivity, basic skills, and practice scenarios. The set includes booklet and facilitator's manual. *Softcover, 24 pages, $37 (plus shipping and handling)*

Big Gifts: How to Maximize Gifts from Individuals, With or Without a Capital Campaign
M. JANE WILLIAMS (THE TAFT GROUP, 1993)

▶ Cultivate the big donors who can make a real difference to your organization's future with this step-by-step guide. Discover ways to find major donors, establish relationships, and ask for contributions. Learn how to organize a major gifts program and launch a successful capital campaign. The book includes 400 sample charts, brochures, and reports. *Softcover, 330 pages, $42.50*

Breaking the Major Gift Barrier: Impelling the Ultimate Gift (Videotapes)
DAVID DUNLOP (EMERSON & CHURCH)

▶ A half century ago fund raising was simple—and almost always personal. You felt strongly enough about a cause that you went out and asked your neighbor, friend, or colleague to join you in supporting the effort. Then sophistication crept in—demographics, psychographics, market studies, response rates. And with sophistication came carefully honed techniques. It wasn't long before technique itself dominated, overshadowing the flesh, blood, bones, and passion that truly is at the heart of successful fund raising. People with money to give weren't nearly as important as deciphering just the right tactic to extract it from them. This trio of videotapes delivers the same message, from one of the country's most distinguished names in the field of major gifts. David Dunlop, a recipient of many of fund raising's most prestigious awards, advocates a concept called "nurturing fund raising." Dunlop takes you on a journey from "regular" gifts to "special" gifts to "ultimate" gifts— showing you precisely how to make nurturing fund raising—and its extraordinary benefits—part of the fabric and culture of your own organization. *Three videotapes, $179*

Developing Major Gifts (New Directions for Philanthropic Fundraising #16)
DWIGHT F. BURLINGAME AND JAMES M. HODGE (JOSSEY-BASS, 1997)

▶ This book addresses the following topics: Profiling Major Gift Fundraisers: What Qualifies Them for Success; Meshing Development Efforts with Major Gift Fundraising; Managing a Successful Major Gifts Program; Ethics and Major Gifts; Women as Philanthropists: Leading the Transformation in Major Gift Fundraising; CEOs and Trustees: The Key Forces in Securing Major Gift Fundraising; Major Donors, Major Motives: The People and Purposes Behind Major Gifts. *Softcover, 116 pages, $25.00*

Developing Major Gifts: Turning Small Donors into Big Contributors
LAURA FREDRICKS (ASPEN PUBLISHERS, 2000)

▶ Don't let staff shortages or tight marketing budgets stand in your way when it comes to doing what it takes to court your "low" givers and make them big spenders with your organization. *Developing Major Gifts* has the insightful answers and cost-effective techniques you can use today—that will deliver tremendous returns for years to come. For example, the book reveals the success strategies that made one donor move from giving a $2,500 gift to a $50,000 gift and another donor from giving between $250 and $500 a year to a gift of $5 million. Rely on *Developing Major Gifts* to provide strategies for turning any gift into $1,000 checks—or bigger; today's most successful "ice-breakers" with potential givers; easy-to-use formulas to help you determine and target your best prospects; insight on how to "make the ask" with donor prospects; and specific gift proposals you can use for your organization. Content highlights include: What Is a Major Gift? The Essentials to Starting a Major Gifts Program; Getting in the Door; Meeting Your New Best Friends; Preparing the Right Gifts Proposal; Asking for Major Gifts; Thanking and Recognizing Your Major Donors; Stewarding Your Donors for Their Next Enhanced Gift; Tracking Prospect Activities and Gifts; and The Success Stories. *Softcover, 248 pages, $64*

Ethics in Fundraising: Putting Values into Practice
(New Directions for Philanthropic Fundraising #6)
(Sponsored by the Indiana Center on Philanthropy)
MARIANNE G. BRISCOE (JOSSEY-BASS, 1994)

▶ This groundbreaking sourcebook takes a major step toward developing a code of professional ethics for fund raisers. The examination of the fund-raising profession in the moral life of a civil society is the topic of the first three chapters. These chapters are meant to give fund raisers a better and more elevated view of their work as much as to help their donors, bosses, and friends understand that fund raising may be difficult work, but it is certainly not *dirty* work. The remaining five chapters deal with ethics and the practical issues of fund raising, such as personal and professional decision making, the nonprofit board of directors, compensation methods, research, and fund-raising management. This is the sixth issue of the quarterly journal *New Directions for Philanthropic Fundraising*. (For more information on the series, see the Journals and Periodicals.) *Softcover, 134 pages, $25.00*

Face to Face: How to Get Bigger Donations from Very Generous People
KEN WYMAN (KEN WYMAN & ASSOCIATES, 1993)

▶ This is a complete how-to guide for succeeding with big gifts from major donors. More than 80 percent of the donations come from 20 percent of the donors. This guide answers all these questions and more: What are the six secrets of big gifts? Who are the right donors for you? Is face-to-face fund raising for you? How do you recruit and train the right volunteers? How do you overcome the fear of fund raising? It is also available for free online at *http://www.pch.gc.ca/cp-pc/ComPartnE/pub_list.htm. Softcover, 196 pages, $40 (including shipping)*

Fund Raising Realities Every Board Member Must Face: A 1-Hour Crash Course on Raising Major Gifts for Nonprofit Organizations

DAVID LANSDOWNE (EMERSON & CHURCH, 1996)

▶ David Lansdowne has distilled the essence of major gifts fund raising, put it in the context of 47 "realities," and delivered it in exceptionally clear prose. Nothing about this book will intimidate board members. It is brief, concise, easy to read, and free of all jargon. Further, it is a work that motivates, showing as it does just how do-able raising big money is. The appeal of *Fund Raising Realities* is that Lansdowne addresses every important principle and technique of fund raising, and explains them in a succinct way board members will grasp immediately. In other words, *Fund Raising Realities* puts everyone on a level playing field—board member with board member, and board member with staff. *Softcover, 112 pages, $24.95*

Finders Keepers

JEROLD PANAS (BONUS BOOKS, 1999)

▶ One of the nation's best writers on the art of motivating gifts now offers a behind-the-scenes look at the strategies and skills that lead to successful fund raising. Each chapter is full of instructive anecdotes, case histories, and interviews with a message. An award-winning writer, Jerold Panas directs this book to professional and aspiring fund raisers, but board members and volunteers will find his message just as useful. Whether readers are seasoned professionals or just starting out, Panas will help fund raisers advance their skills in the most pleasant way imaginable—by reading about actual case histories. *Hardcover, 280 pages, $39.95*

Getting Major Gifts, 3rd Edition

(CHARDON PRESS, 2000)

▶ In a healthy nonprofit organization, 60 percent of the money comes from 10 percent of the donors. These are the *Grassroots Fundraising Journal*'s 10 best articles on how to develop a major gifts program, find prospects and ask them for money, then ask them for more money—putting the most lucrative fund-raising strategy within reach of small nonprofits. Articles include: Getting Major Gifts: The Basics; Getting Over the Fear of Asking; The Fine Art of Asking for the Gift; Responding to Put-Offs; Twenty Common Questions; Conducting a Major Gifts Campaign; Keeping in Touch with Major Donors; Going Back to Major Donors; Moving Up to the Big Gift; and Stop Looking for Wealth. *Softcover, 40 pages, $12*

How to Ask for Money Without Fainting: A Guide to Help NonProfit Staff and Volunteers Raise More Money! 4th Edition

SUSAN SCRIBNER (SCRIBNER & ASSOCIATES, 1996)

▶ The basic "guide to help your staff and volunteers raise money" walks the staff and board through the difficult process of raising money the most effective way— by teaching them how to ask for it. It includes tips on how to clearly articulate your agency's need, determine your best prospects, learn how to use your strengths, exercises to use *How to Ask* without dropping dead, and what to do when meeting face to face with a prospective funder. It includes a special Recession Funding Guide. *Softcover, 44 pages, $12 (plus shipping and handling)*

How to Get Million Dollar Gifts and Have Donors Thank You!

ROBERT HARTSOOK (ASR PHILANTHROPIC PUBLISHING, 1999)

▶ Filled with interesting and thought-provoking strategies for securing million-dollar gifts as illustrated through real-life examples of extraordinary gifts made by average Americans, this book is presented in a modified textbook fashion. Each chapter begins with a fund-raising principle, followed by the story, and concludes with the lesson learned. Part practical instruction, part effective motivation, Bob Hartsook's new book, *How to Get Million Dollar Gifts and Have Donors Thank You!* covers a lot of ground. Fund raisers, board members, trustees, staff, volunteers, prospects, and donors—every philanthropic relationship is examined from an insider's angle. The foundation of his philosophy on fund raising is that there's always enough to go around. He sees our limitations as self-imposed. Limited outlook equals limited outcome. With each new strategy he takes on another issue, but it's his ineffable conviction that "You can receive million dollar gifts!" that has the most persuasive and influential effect on the reader. The book is a synthesis of the prevailing strategies and techniques of major gifts fund raising. Hartsook identifies every important element, from identifying prospects to securing their commitment, and presents them as 101 strategies. There are all those intervening steps such as research, cultivation, knowing what interests the donor, how to earn trust, how to present your project, how to meet the donor's expectations, and many more. All of these carefully orchestrated steps, which form the core of *How to Get Million Dollar Gifts*, undergird successful development programs and in large measure determine whether the person appealing for the gift walks away with a substantial commitment or none at all. *Softcover, 281 pages, $39.95*

Major Donors: The Key to Successful Fundraising

ROBERT M. ZIMMERMAN (ZIMMERMAN LEHMAN, 1998)

▶ How do you find major donors? How much should you ask for? Whom should you ask? How do you conduct a major donor campaign? How do you research a major donor's net worth? Can it be done online? These and other questions are answered in Bob Zimmerman's workbook filled with hands-on information, user-friendly task lists, scripts of typical major donor requests, donor research tips, and other valuable material to help prepare you and your volunteers for a major donor campaign or request. This easy-to-follow guidebook is designed for board members and volunteers of nonprofits who want to help solicit funds through a major donor effort but don't have a lot of experience or time. It is also available as an e-published book (you print it off the Web yourself for only $10.00). *Softcover, 30 pages, $12.95*

Mega Gifts: Who Gives Them, Who Gets Them, Reissue Edition

JEROLD PANAS (BONUS BOOKS, 1998)

▶ This book was first published in 1984. Panas calls up the experiences of well-known philanthropists, volunteers, educators, religious leaders, fund-raising experts, and others to underscore a primary principle of successful fund raising: Technique is no substitute for a committed heart. The second step (after reading this book) to getting $100,000+ donations is to understand how donors with large resources think. It provides the inside story from 25 prominent donors who tell why they gave a million dollars or more to a variety of institutions. Learn how to get an appointment and which "hot buttons" to push to get large gifts; includes intensive interviews with some of the most articulate and noteworthy givers in the history of American philanthropy. Leaders from the health care field, education, religious institutions, the YMCA, and the Salvation Army, along with consultants and professional fund raisers, rate 22 major factors that motivate giving. These analyses are then compared against evaluations made by the men and women who actually gave the $1 million gifts. The book explains how to understand and put to work the motivations and incentives behind large gifts. There are 17 insightful chapters, including: Why People Give, You Win With Bold Plans, Seize the Magic Moment, and Tax Incentive Is Little Incentive. It also provides 65 tenets for fund-raising success which will provide the road map, the signs and signals that help you secure major gifts for your institution. It is filled with detailed case histories. *Hardcover, 229 pages, $40 (plus $4 shipping)*

Model Major Gift Policy Manual, 7th Edition
(Manual & Disk)
STEPHEN C. NILL (AMERICAN PHILANTHROPY REVIEW, 1997)

▶ This edition has been extensively revised to reflect sweeping charitable giving changes imposed on U.S. nonprofit organizations by the *Taxpayer Relief Act of 1997*. This edition also contains a newly revised section on compliance with the often misunderstood provisions of the Philanthropy Protection Act. With the recent changes in tax, securities, and other laws, it is more important than ever for U.S. nonprofit organizations to protect themselves—and their board members, officers, staff members, and benefactors—by ensuring that gift policies and procedures comply with IRS guidelines and other laws, industry practices, and ethical standards. Even if a nonprofit organization has a gift policy manual, it would take hours for its legal counsel to research and draft the necessary revisions to bring it into conformity with recent changes in the law that the *Model Major Gift Policy Manual*™ already tracks. It ships on a 3.5″ diskette as 59-page word processing document, available in Word® and WordPerfect® formats. The Manual has been designed to be easily customized to the needs of your organization. It is in use at colleges and universities, hospitals and other health care organizations, performing and visual arts centers, public television stations, and many other types of nonprofit organizations throughout the United States. The author makes extensive use of the "comments" feature available in the latest versions of Word and WordPerfect to guide you through each step in customizing the Manual for your organization. It's almost like having the author sitting right there with you, giving you hints and suggestions as you work. The Manual automatically renumbers articles, sections, and paragraphs as you make changes. Its Table of Contents and extensive Index are already coded in as fields, enabling you to generate updated tables in seconds; the Table of Contents is hyperlinked to each article and section of the Manual, enabling you to navigate around the document easily. There is also a document hyperlink mapping feature that eliminates endless scrolling as you look for the topic you need. *Manual and software; $189*

Moves Management Prospect Management System
(Software)
(INSTITUTE FOR CHARITABLE GIVING)

▶ This is a prospect tracking and management system for major-gift fund raising. It structures and monitors your cultivation and solicitation activities. The Moves Management™ template is designed to help fund raisers manage and improve the relationship-building activities that are the basis of successful major and planned gift programs. In addition to the comprehensive "contact management" screen, there are eight screens designed precisely to apply Moves Management principles to any fund-raising program. It is guaranteed to improve the effectiveness and efficiency of generalists, as well as those who specialize in major and planned gifts. The system includes a comprehensive planning module for both culti-

vation initiatives and solicitation visits. Additionally, there are planned giving donor recognition and corporate/foundation information elements. You will be reminded of upcoming "moves," necessary strategies, and essential next actions. It gives you lists of your prospects and complete summaries of your activities. Features include: contact and action planning; strategic tracking for all your donors and prospects (individuals, corporations, and foundations); fail-proof coordination of individual, corporate, and foundation prospects and donors; call reports; tickler alerts and warning signals; prospect ratings; a design for donor upgrading; prospect and donor classifications; activity and results review; fund raiser–friendly reports by prospect, worker, classification, capability, or any combination; works with all popular word processing systems to produce letters, notes, and other donor-winning communications; and assures you of asking for the "right" gift, at the right time, by the right person, and getting it. Windows 95/98/NT version, includes software, manual, and support for one year. It is appropriate for any size development office. *$895 ($725.00 for Moves Management software if you already own ACT! 4+) (includes shipping)*

Pinpointing Affluence: Increasing Your Share of Major Donor Dollars
JUDITH NICHOLS (BONUS BOOKS, 1994)

▶ Strengthen your fund raising by rethinking who your best prospects and donors really are—persons of affluence, not persons of wealth. Unfortunately, most fund raisers spend precious time and effort dreaming of catching the attention of the wealthiest individuals. This book shows you how to restructure your development program to discover who has the money and is willing to give. You can't rely solely on the once-in-a-lifetime million-dollar gift. It makes much more sense to try to identify, cultivate, and form charitable partnerships with the nearly 19 million people capable of giving gifts of $1,000 to $10,000 annually. With these tools, you can open the door to a much wider audience of prospects—prospects who are able and willing to provide not-for-profits with support. First, understand the distinction between those who are wealthy and those who are affluent. The former are prospects who can make million-dollar gifts; the latter are those capable of giving anywhere from $1,000 to $100,000. Since there were only 350 reported gifts of $1 million in 1992, contrasted with 19 million prospects capable of giving $1,000 to $100,000, it's only logical, argues Judith Nichols in her new book, to try to identify, cultivate, and form charitable partnerships with the much larger affluent group. To do this, you must clearly understand how to find these prospects, interpret their needs, analyze their past giving behavior, and know how to reach them. This is precisely what this book attempts to do, to empower you to switch your focus from the small, oversolicited base of wealthy persons to the broader, often ignored base of affluent prospects. Sections include: I. Meet Today's and Tomorrow's Donors: Understanding Demographics and Psychographics; II. Working Smarter, Not Harder: Focusing Where the Donors and Dollars Are Found; III. Fund-Raising Strategies That Make Sense: Targeting Your Development Efforts; IV. Creating Donor and Prospect Involvement; V. Targeting Affluent Prospects Demographically and Psychographically. *Hardcover, 293 pages, $39.95 (plus $4 shipping and handling)*

Secrets of Major Gift Fund Raising
CHARLES F. MAI (THE TAFT GROUP, 1987)

▶ The author shares lessons he has learned in his 25 years of securing major gifts for organizations such as the American Cancer

Society, the Kansas City Art Institute, The Boy Scouts, and many others. Learn how "cultivation" really works and how to plan your call, how to tell when it's time to ask for the gift, how to use mail to uncover big prospects, when to mention the deferred gift idea and when not to, how to bring up real estate as a viable method of giving, and more. *Hardcover, 170 pages, $14 (includes shipping)*

The Seven Faces of Philanthropy: A New Approach to Cultivating Major Donors

RUSS ALAN PRINCE AND KAREN MARU FILE (JOSSEY-BASS PUBLISHERS, 1994)

▶ This groundbreaking publication in the field of fund raising provides development professionals with the Seven Faces approach, a powerful new tool to enable them to maximize their effectiveness when approaching major donors for gifts; using this framework, the authors identify and profile seven types of major donors that emerged from a detailed, comprehensive study of wealthy donors and offer detailed strategies on how to approach them. The seven types of major donors include the communitarian (give to improve the community), devout (give for religious reasons), investor (give with one eye on the cause and one eye on tax and estate benefits), socialite (throw social functions for charity and have a good time doing it), altruist (contribute out of generosity and empathy), repayer (have typically benefited from charities they support), and dynast (have family tradition of charitable giving). The authors explain why each type requires a different strategy when approached for gifts, and show how fund-raising professionals can identify and understand the motivations of each type of donor in order to build successful and sustaining relationships with major donors. They go on to show how to act on this knowledge, providing a coherent, step-by-step system to implement the Seven Faces framework. Detailed examples illustrate how to attract prospective donors, motivate the donor to support a cause, position the giving strategy, and ultimately empower the philanthropist. *Hardcover, 247 pages, $28 (plus $4.50 shipping)*

Shaking the Money Tree: What Motivates Donors
(Videocassette)

LED BY JERRY PANAS (INSTITUTE FOR CHARITABLE GIVING)

▶ The author of America's most popular book on major gifts presents a probing revelation of the factors that motivate men and women to make gifts to your organization. This video explores the critical role of listening, emotion, and integrity, and how to combine them for proven results. The presentation is based on market research with over 3,000 fund-raising executives and interviews with 40 men and women whose individual gifts were $1 million or more. *53 minutes, $59.99 (plus $2 shipping)*

Smart and Caring: A Donor's Guide to Major Gifting

RICHARD LIVINGSTON AND LINDA LIVINGSTON (RDL PUBLISHING, 1999—ALSO AVAILABLE FROM THE COUNCIL ON FOUNDATIONS, ASSOCIATION OF FUNDRAISING PROFESSIONALS)

▶ This is a book written by donors for donors. Richard and Linda Livingston bring a commonsense directness to a subject that often gets bogged down in detail and complexity. They address the issues, actions, and rewards of major gifting from a fresh perspective—that of the donors themselves. The Livingstons have done us all a favor by partnering with their estate attorney, Kathleen Hammond, and their CPA, William Rogers, to ensure that their discussions remain technically accurate while staying in the comfort zone of the lay reader. In *Smart and Caring,* the Livingstons have divided the issues of major gifting into three general categories.

The first is the personal side, where they share the process that they have gone through in moving from being detached citizens of the community to becoming deeply involved donors and volunteers. Second, they look at the technical side of becoming a donor, bringing structure and insight to the choices available for tax-efficient gifting. Last, they tackle the financial side of major gifting, providing analysis tools that allow donors to put gifting in the context of their own lifetime net worth, income, asset growth, and tax situation. *Softcover, 214 pages, $15*

The Successful Ask, Winning the Gift: Part I
(Videocassette)

LED BY BILL STURTEVANT (INSTITUTE FOR CHARITABLE GIVING)

▶ Designed for volunteers and staff of institutions seeking grants. Includes an exercise to help fund raisers and volunteers learn from objections and build on them for greater success. Makes clear who should ask for the gift and for how much, who should be present, and at what location; learn how to determine when the precise moment has arrived to make the ask; learn all the critical determinants of successful solicitation; understand how to allay anxiety and capitalize on confidence. *1 hour, 26 minutes, $79.99 (plus $2 shipping)*

The Successful Ask, Winning the Gift: Part II
(Videocassette)

LED BY BILL STURTEVANT (INSTITUTE FOR CHARITABLE GIVING)

▶ This video takes a practical and confidence-building look at such specific issues as "planned" spontaneity, solicitor flexibility, and donor roadblocks. Find out when a "no" is only a "maybe" or not just yet. Find out to what extent a solicitation should be orchestrated and scripted. Learn how to prepare for surprises. It also covers handling objections, short-circuits, and side issues without stress. It includes a personal exercise to help fund raisers and volunteers learn from objections and build on negatives for greater success. *86 minutes, $79.99 (plus $2 shipping)*

Take the Fear Out of Asking for Major Gifts

JAMES A. DONOVAN (DONOVAN MANAGEMENT, 1993)

▶ Now you have the "quick cure" for the leading cause of failure in every fund-raising program: the ugly truth that most board members, and many staffers, suffer from "cold feet" when the time comes to ask for a major gift. Based on 20 years of asking for big gifts, and field-tested on thousands of nonprofit executives, this book gives you the actual words you need to: (1) build confidence for asking, (2) overcome the four most common fears of asking, (3) prepare and state the strongest case to your potential donors, (4) welcome the objections and use them to your advantage, (5) use the "double-it" tactic to double your major gifts, and (6) master the three most effective closings. It includes checklists, charts, graphs, and actual letters and case statements that you can modify for your own use and to train your volunteer solicitors. *Softcover, 110 pages, $24.95 (plus $4 shipping)*

Ten (x 20) Things: Recreating the Principles & Techniques of Major Gifts Fund Raising (Disk)

KAY SPRINKEL GRACE (EMERSON & CHURCH)

▶ When she isn't breaking new ground, as in her illuminating chapters on: Transformational Gifts, The New Realities of Capital Campaigning, and Positioning Your Organization as a Solid Investment, Grace is recasting the principles of major gifts fund raising for twenty-first-century practitioners, people who operate in a climate far different from their predecessors. Topics include overcoming your board's objections to fund raising, understanding your donors' motivations, keeping your pipeline full of prospects, and a wide range of other pertinent matters. *Note: The publisher permits you to output appropriate chapters of this work to create handouts at trainings. $39*

Online Fund Raising

Direct Connection's Guide to Fundraising on the Internet
HOWARD LAKE (AURELIAN INFORMATION LTD)

▶ The first book to be published on the subject in any language draws together and places at your disposal the experiences and advice of fund raisers working in many different not-for-profit environments. Via a multitude of listed Internet addresses, you can shortcut the experience of many years and get to work right away, in support of your activities, or in striking out in new fields. Author Howard Lake, himself an experienced fund raiser, confronts the key issues, but in everyday language. How do I raise funds? How do I get help and exchange ideas? How can I find online donors and keep them? Should I set up a Web site? What looks effective on screen, and how should I present our group on it? What's going on in Internet fund raising? Where do I find lists of donors, other fund raisers, and useful publications? Can I use e-mail to raise funds? How can money be moved across the Internet? How can the Internet support existing fund-raising activities, and how can they be transferred across? How can the Internet help my research? This down-to-earth, practical book answers all these questions and a host of others, many through its extensive Internet addresses giving free information and help in exchanging ideas with other people working in your field in other parts of the world.

The Foundation Center's Guide to Grantseeking on the Web (Book and CD-ROM)
(THE FOUNDATION CENTER, 2000)

▶ Learn how to maximize use of the World Wide Web for your funding research. Packed with a wealth of information, *The Foundation Center's Guide to Grantseeking on the Web* provides both novice and experienced Web users with a gateway to the numerous online resources available to grant seekers. Foundation Center staff experts have team-authored this guide, contributing their extensive knowledge of Web content as well as their tips and strategies on how to evaluate and use Web-based funding materials. Presented in a concise, "how-to" style and filled with sample Web sites, the *Guide to Grantseeking on the Web* will structure your research with a toolkit of resources: abstracts of hundreds of grantmaker Web sites; abstracts of a variety of related nonprofit sites; corporate grant-making information; government funding sources; profiles of searchable databases (both free and fee-based); online journals, periodicals, and newsletters on philanthropy; and interactive services: bulletin boards, discussion groups, and mailing lists. *Softcover, 548 pages, $19.95; CD-ROM, $19.95; Book and CD-ROM, $29.95*

The Fund Raiser's Guide to the Internet (Book and Disk)
MICHAEL JOHNSTON (JOHN WILEY & SONS, 1998)

▶ *The Fund Raiser's Guide to the Internet* presents the issues, technology, and resources involved in online fund raising and donor relations. It is a "how-to" book that presents the real-world best practices that the author's consulting firm has developed as they raised measurable dollars for their clients. Each chapter has a case study, background, analysis, conclusion, and study area, which provide warnings, guidance, and inspiration to nonprofits learning to develop this new fund-raising technique. It covers areas such as determining your market, finding out about your donors, grant seeking, online solicitation pieces, setting up your web site, security issues, campaigning, marketing, and finalizing the donation. An accompanying disk includes online bookmarks of successful nonprofit sites. Michael Johnston (Toronto, Ontario) has set up several successful fund-raising sites on the Web as a consultant with Hewitt Johnston Consulting. *Softcover, 235 pages, $34.95*

Fundraising and Friend-Raising on the Web (Book and CD-ROM)
ADAM D. CORSON-FINNERTY AND LAURA BLANCHARD (AMERICAN LIBRARY ASSOCIATION, 1998)

▶ This book shows you how to weave a Web strategy—whether you're a small library with a fledging friends group or already have a structure in place for major development campaigns. Adam Corson-Finnerty and Laura Blanchard, innovators from the Development Office of the University of Pennsylvania Libraries, share resources, strategies from nonprofit fund raisers of all types, and advice on such topics as donor recognition on cyberspace, future prospects for collecting micro-donations with digital cash, and learning from pioneering Web fund raisers. The Web-enabled CD-ROM for Macintosh and Windows shows in-depth examples and links you to live fund-raising sites. Corson-Finnerty and Blanchard, of the University of Pennsylvania libraries development staff, advise on using the World Wide Web to expand a development program that should serve excellently any nonprofit organizations, not just libraries. In addition to detailed advice on developing and using a Web site, they offer a case study of their institution's production of a CD-ROM version of its Web site for those lacking online access to it. Indeed, a CD-ROM containing examples of Web sites discussed, which can function as a gateway to those sites online, comes with the book. Appendices list some of the sites Corson-Finnerty and Blanchard consider cool and online sites for helping new users get started at creating and mounting a Web site. *Softcover, 152 pages, $50.00*

Fundraising on the Internet: Recruiting and Renewing Donors Online
NICK ALLEN, MAL WARWICK, AND MICHAEL STEIN, EDS. (STRATHMOOR PRESS, 1996)

▶ The first book on using e-mail and the Internet to find and cultivate donors, *Fundraising on the Internet* gives you practical information on who's raising money online and how they're doing it. The Internet won't replace traditional fund-raising methods, but it will play an increasing role in the fund-raising strategies of many organizations. This book focuses on acquiring new donors. The editors believe even greater opportunities are available right now for organizations to work with substantial numbers of their existing donors who are comfortable, even enthusiastic, about communicating electronically. *Softcover, 168 pages, $24.95*

The Nonprofit Organization's Guide to E-Commerce
GARY M. GROBMAN (WHITE HAT COMMUNICATIONS, 2000)

▶ This book is a guidebook at any and all aspects of e-commerce for nonprofit executives who want to use the Internet for generating revenues. From determining if launching an e-commerce program is right for your organization to identifying where to get free or low-cost tools to facilitate your program, to learning what works in nonprofit e-commerce and what doesn't, you will find virtually everything you need to know to gain secure footing in this arena. For example, after reading *The Nonprofit Organization's Guide to E-Commerce,* you should, among other things, have the confidence to sell your products, handle Internet payments, fulfill orders, and provide customer service; add an e-commerce site to your Web site; set up an online shopping mall, charitable online auction, or online community; address security, privacy, copyright, and other legal issues; and effectively market your Web site. You will also be exposed to a wealth of Web sites that will further enhance your understanding of the e-commerce phenomenon. This book also includes capsule site reviews of more than 150 World Wide Web sites where you can obtain free e-commerce software, tools for your Web page, partner with online retailers, and much more; practical advice about for-profit providers of e-commerce solutions; and what nonprofit organizations should know about e-commerce. *Softcover, 182 pages, $19.95*

300 Top Websites for Fundraisers (Diskette)

MARILYN GROSS (EDUCATIONAL FUNDING STRATEGIES, LTD.)

▶ If you've ever spent an afternoon flailing about the Internet, searching for fund-raising information, and concluded that: (1) there are simply too many sites to choose from, (2) the information is too scattered to be of real use, and (3) specific data you were seeking couldn't be found anywhere on the Internet, then *300 Top Websites for Fundraisers* is for you. Internet veteran Marilyn Gross has spent literally hundreds of hours scouring the Internet, uncovering some of the best, most useful, and almost always free sites a fund raiser could ever ask for. Gross has arranged the disk by 14 broad categories, making *300 Top Websites* as convenient as possible. The categories include: capital and annual campaigns; corporate giving and sponsorship; foundations; fund raising and development; grant resources and funding; grant seeking; international grant seeking; proposal writing; prospect research; online fund raising; online periodicals, alerts, and publications; online discussions, listservs, and forums; small donors; and training opportunities. Many of these sites are among the most difficult to find, with most of them "buried" deep within the home pages of major and not-so-major organizations. With your Web browser open at the same time as your disk drive, you can either click on the links and go directly to the sites, or "cut and paste" the Web addresses into your browser. *Print or disk version: $39; Print/disk combination: $65*

Top 300 E-Commerce Websites for Nonprofit Organizations (Disk)

GARY M. GROBMAN (EMERSON & CHURCH)

▶ Whether your aim is to use the Internet to generate additional donations, increase membership, or market your products and services, you'll find here the most complete and up-to-date information yet produced on scores and scores of e-commerce and related Web sites. Grobman, one of America's premier Internet guides, reviews each of the 300 sites, allowing you to identify and select the best and most appropriate for your purposes (thereby saving you a measurable amount of time and effort). Receiving Grobman's scrutiny are online shopping malls, click-to-give sites, fund-raising portals, merchant service sites, site development software providers, sites with free or low-cost tools for developing your e-commerce program, and many more, including a handful of organizational sites that have optimized the Internet to significantly enhance their operations. (With your Web browser open at the same time as your disk drive, you can click on any of the links and go directly to the sites.) *$39*

The Wilder NonProfit Field Guide to Fundraising on the Internet

GARY M. GROBMAN, GARY B. GRANT, AND STEVE ROLLER (AMHERST H. WILDER FOUNDATION, 1999)

▶ Your quick road map to using the Internet as a new fund-raising channel. This guide gives you practical tips on how to prospect for donors, find funders and download grant applications, get listed on sites that direct donors to organizations, use e-mail to collect grant information, and more. It also shows you how to use the Internet to increase your fundraising *skills.* You'll find specifics on how to network with other fund raisers, search out creative ideas, and keep up with fund-raising news. Whether you want to attract new donors, troll for grants, or get listed on sites that assist donors, this concise guide will help. You'll find practical tips on how to prospect for potential donors; find funders who fit your profile and download grant applications; increase your visibility by getting listed on sites that direct donors to organizations; use e-mail to collect grant information *automatically;* attract support using "e-zines"—electronic newsletters; and effectively use your Web site to ask for donations. *Fundraising on the Internet* also provides scores of Internet addresses, showing you where to get information on all kinds of fund raising. Better still, the authors provide detailed reviews of 77 Web sites useful to fund raisers, including foundation-related sites, charity sites, prospect research sites, and sites that assist donors. Even if you don't intend to raise a dime on the Internet, you can use it to learn more about the art of fund raising. *Fundraising on the Internet* provides the online solution to getting the information you need in a way that's easy to search, convenient, and low-cost. You'll get specifics on how to network with other professional fund raisers using online mailing lists; search out creative new fund-raising ideas, books, and courses; visit other organizations' Web sites to see what they're offering; keep up with fund-raising news by visiting Web sites for philanthropy publications; and join online "newsgroups" on foundation relations, fund raising, and planned giving. *Softcover, 69 pages, $15*

Outcome Funding

Outcome Funding: A New Approach to Targeted Grantmaking, 3rd Edition

HAROLD S. WILLIAMS, ARTHUR Y. WEBB, AND WILLIAM J. PHILLIPS (THE RENSSELAERVILLE INSTITUTE, 1996)

▶ Based on the premise that grant makers are really investors in human gain, *Outcome Funding* addresses the key questions that the funder as investor should ask: What am I buying? What is the probability I will get it? *Outcome Funding* begins with an abrupt and timely challenge to the standard wisdom of the request for proposal process. The authors make the point that very little of the traditional proposal content addresses results favoring explanations of process instead. Grant making by governments at all levels is a multibillion-dollar business. As often as not, public agencies fund other groups (nonprofits, local governments, and businesses) to carry out social programs. The cornerstone of this business is a document called "The Proposal." From needs statement to the evaluation section, its content and review process have changed little over many years.

The typical copy under "measurable objectives" is more likely to focus on how many workshops are held than on gains by people attending them. And the connection between a great needs statement and a great project is doubtful at best. (There is a correlation between the 20-point needs statement and the presence of a grants writer, but supporting the grantsmanship profession is, presumably, not the investor's intent.) The book is not only persuasive in the need for change, but also practical on how to achieve it. Unlike so many management books, which are long on theory but short on tactics, it offers chapter and verse on proven new tools. And this second edition is strengthened by reader comments and applications. This book offers as much to grant recipients as to grant makers. With conventional proposals, the applicant must write one paper to get money and another to spend it. With a results focus, one document serves both purposes. It also covers budgeting, in which the same principles apply. *Softcover, 250 pages, $21*

Planned Giving

The Art of Planned Giving: Understanding Donors and the Culture of Giving

DOUGLAS E. WHITE (JOHN WILEY & SONS, 1998)

▶ Planned giving is a vital yet complicated segment of fund raising and charitable giving. It can include gifts of cash, stocks, insurance, art and antiques, real estate, gift annuities, and trusts. This book addresses the human side of planned giving as opposed to the tax and management subjects, and examines the psychological and professional challenges involved in the process. Based on the author's expertise and interviews with planned giving officers, this book provides an inside look at the human side of this important segment of fund raising and charitable giving. It traces the process of acquiring a planned gift; examines the psychological and professional challenges involved; and explains the culture within which a planned giving program functions. It includes practical advice on dealing with donors and their professional advisors and suggests effective approaches to becoming a successful planned giving officer. *Softcover, 384 pages, $27.95*

Charitable Planning Primer

(CCH, INC., 1999)

▶ This combines the best of legal explanations plus advice for professionals working with clients making all types of planned gifts. It deals with all the different aspects of charitable giving. It discusses when to consider charitable giving as part of an estate plan, integrating the charitable gift into the client's estate plan, outright gifts, bargain sales, charitable remainder trusts, lead trusts, gift annuities and pooled income funds, working with residence and farm property, planning for wealth replacement, liability concerns, and more. It examines all the possible tax ramifications—income tax, gift tax, estate tax, and the generation-skipping transfer tax. The Primer is written in straightforward, practical language, taking the mystery out of this challenging planning area. Each chapter begins with an overview of the topic and then is broken into bite-size portions, clearly organized so readers can quickly and effectively grasp the material. Each chapter also includes a conclusion and quiz section to help users reinforce their understanding of the subjects covered. The *Charitable Planning Primer* comes complete with sample documents and related tax forms and tables. *Hardcover, 505 pages, $99*

The Complete Guide to Planned Giving: Everything You Need to Know to Compete Successfully for Major Gifts, Revised 3rd Edition

DEBRA ASHTON (ASHTON ASSOCIATES, 2000)

▶ You will learn how to start and run a successful planned giving program from scratch, even if you are an alien who dropped off the moon having no knowledge of fund raising, development, or U.S. federal taxation; deal effectively with your board of trustees so that its members will be on your side, or if not, how to work around them; recruit, train, and work with volunteers to substantially increase the success of your program without going into therapy in the process; develop a master plan, a budget, and a set of goals and objectives that will see you through the next 12 months; evaluate which planned giving vehicles or gift types to offer and set up the procedures to make them all run smoothly; integrate planned giving into a campaign for maximum result; generate inquiries from marketing and direct mail so you can keep the gifts coming in; work with annual giving, major gifts, principal gifts, and other fund-raising departments in a partnership to increase all gift categories in harmony with yours; start a bequest program in 60 days; run a planned giving program in a one-person shop and get results all by yourself; cultivate potential donors and then effectively solicit them for gifts without caving; and more. *Softcover, 407 pages, $49.95*

Doing Planned Giving Better: Improve Your Program with Powerful Ideas from the Pages of Planned Giving Today

G. ROGER SCHOENHALS, ED. (PLANNED GIVING TODAY, 1997)

▶ Powerful, effective planned giving doesn't happen overnight. This book helps you build on a solid foundation by suggesting program ideas, gift strategies, and advice on working with professional advisers. Ideal for the program that has been operating for a year or more. Whether you are a veteran gift planner or a newcomer to the field, *Doing Planned Giving Better* will serve you well. Use it for personal development, staff training, board awareness, and committee enrichment. *Softcover, 60 pages, $39*

First Steps in Planned Giving: Practical Ideas from the Pages of Planned Giving Today

G. ROGER SCHOENHALS, ED. (PLANNED GIVING TODAY, 1999)

▶ *First Steps* combines the know-how of more than 25 planned giving professionals. Together, they share their methods and advice in 30 different articles. You will learn how to launch a successful planned giving program. You'll also discover some pitfalls to avoid. Whether you're just considering planned giving or are ready to get your feet wet, this book will give you practical suggestions on how to take those "first steps" with confidence. This book is excellent for new planned giving officers, support staff, and volunteers who serve on the board or on the planned giving committee. *Softcover, 60 pages, $39*

Gaining More Planned Gifts (How-To Series—Book 3)

G. ROGER SCHOENHALS, ED. (PLANNED GIVING TODAY, 1997)

▶ This book is full of marketing ideas, including the use of focus groups, target marketing, visitation techniques, seminar planning, donor cultivation, and solicitation. This book overflows with practical ideas from gift planners who practice what they preach. *Softcover, 60 pages, $39*

Getting Going in Planned Giving: Launch Your Program with Powerful Ideas from the Pages of Planned Giving Today (How-To Series—Book 1)

G. ROGER SCHOENHALS, ED. (PLANNED GIVING TODAY, 1997)

▶ An impressive list of veteran gift planners make the case for planned giving. This book outlines specific steps for starting a new program. It provides guidance regarding bequests and gift annuities and offers insights on ethical matters. It is an excellent resource for the first-year planned giving program. *Softcover, 60 pages, $39*

A Guide to Starting a Planned Giving Program for Nonprofit Executives and Volunteer Trustees

(NATIONAL COMMITTEE ON PLANNED GIVING) (RESOURCE KIT)

▶ A planned giving program is a vital part of the asset development efforts of a charitable organization and, in order to be successful, the organization must have a well-communicated, important charitable purpose and need for long-term financial resources. This kit was developed in response to frequent requests for assistance in initiating a planned giving program. It covers basic issues to be considered in starting a planned giving program, outlines a phased approach to implementing a full gift planning program, and provides advice for assessing organizational readiness and outlines the relationship between gift planning and the general development process. A complete glossary of planned giving terms is included. Member Kit includes: A Guide to Starting a Planned Giving Program for Nonprofit Executives and Volunteer Trustees, Order Form, Model Standards of Practice for the Charitable Gift Planner, Directory of Councils, and NCPG Brochure. Nonmember Kit includes all Member Kit materials plus Training Opportunities Calendar, Bibliography & Resource Guide, and Syllabus for Gift Planners. *$10 (Member), $30 (Nonmember)*

Harnessing the Power of the Charitable Remainder Trust, 5th Edition

MARC D. HOFFMAN AND LELAND E. HOFFMAN (PHILANTHROTEC, 1999)

▶ Today, charitable remainder trusts are playing an increasingly important role in helping individuals and corporations accomplish their financial and philanthropic planning objectives. This is a learning guide for those individuals interested in charitable planning. This book, authored by Marc D. Hoffman and Leland E. Hoffman Jr., is an in-depth look at the complexities of the charitable remainder trust. It not only tells you what to do, but when and why. The text, legally edited by Douglas K. Freeman, JD, LLM, and Fred J. Marcus, JD, LLM, contains an 11-page Table of Authorities listing hundreds of Internal Revenue Codes, Treasury Regulations, Revenue Rulings, Revenue Procedures, General Counsel Memoranda, Private Letter Rulings, and IRS Notices. Originally published in 1992 by two of the nation's leading professionals, the fifth edition is well organized and up to the minute, covering all the issues that surround the effective creation and operation of this powerful financial, estate, and philanthropic planning tool. Discover who candidates for charitable remainder trusts are and what motivates them; how CRTs are used to convert assets to income on a tax-favored basis; comprehensive technical discussions of qualification requirements and design variables; review of new laws and final regulations, including: (1) 50 percent payout and 10 percent present value limitations, "Flip" unitrusts: when to use them and how to reform existing trusts, (2) restrictions on allocating capital gains to trust income, (3) new distribution timing rules, (4) valuation of "unmarketable" assets, (5) gift tax valuation of income interests; income, gift, and estate tax deduction rules and

how they apply; the best assets to contribute, and ones to avoid; how to comply with all tax and operational requirements; developing a trust investment policy; cash flow planning and income deferral; and more. *Spiral bound, 227 pages, $69.95 (plus $5.00 shipping and handling)*

Planned Giving: A Board Member's Perspective

GRANT THORNTON (NATIONAL CENTER FOR NONPROFIT BOARDS, 1999)

▶ The responsibility for asking for major gifts belongs with the board—and planned giving campaigns are no exception. Understanding the complexities of deferred giving and cultivating relationships with donors is key to the campaign's success. Unlike most fund-raising efforts, which often raise immediate cash, results from planned giving campaigns are seen over the long term. Written by the accounting and management consulting firm of Grant Thornton, this booklet explains in clear terms the different planned giving options available to donors. Board members will learn about present and deferred gifts, bequests, charitable trusts, or annuities. A planned giving campaign requires the commitment of time, effort, and proper management on the part of both board and staff. Find out if planned giving is right for your organization and for your donor base. *Softcover, 24 pages, $9.00 (Member); $12.00 (Nonmember)*

Planned Giving Essentials: A Step by Step Guide to Success (Aspen's Fund Raising Series for the 21st Century)

RICHARD BARRETT & MOLLY WARE (ASPEN PUBLISHERS, 1997)

▶ Planned giving is perhaps the most intimidating component in the fund-raising arena. But you don't need to be an attorney or have a large staff to incorporate this component into your organization's fund-raising program. This book provides the instructions and tools needed to both begin a successful planned giving program and expand it later. In addition, a glossary of terms, models, letters, and policies; sample advertisements; and other tools help make planned giving manageable. If you're not familiar with planned giving—the techniques, the terminology, and the role it can play in your organization's overall development program—then *Planned Giving Essentials: A Step by Step Guide to Success* will serve you well. Written by Richard Barrett and Molly Ware, the book is divided into two parts. Part One sets forth the basic elements of planned giving and planned gifts, defines key terms, describes types of gifts, and discusses the importance of planned giving for maintaining an organization's viability. Part Two provides detailed advice on starting a planned giving program from scratch. The book shows you how planned giving fits into a total fund-raising plan; how a planned giving program can be started easily and for minimal costs; gives you practical suggestions for implementing the activities required to start a planned giving program; and offers tips on what to do and what to avoid. Contents include: Planned Giving Defined; Philanthropy and the Philanthropist; Planning Giving and Fund Raising; First Steps; Not-for-Profit Organizations; The Business of Philanthropy and the Practice of Planned Giving; Planned Gifts; Communication: Letting Your World Know About Your Program; International Planned Giving; Preparing Your Action Plan; Organizing to Begin the Planned Giving Program; Marketing Planned Giving; Managing the Gifts; Avoiding Pitfalls; and Glossary. *Softcover, 192 pages, $64*

Planned Giving for the One-Person Development Office: Taking the First Steps, 2nd Edition

DAVID G. SCHMELING (DEFERRED GIVING SERVICES, 2000)

▶ This book is a how-to introduction to planned giving for the fund raiser who has a limited budget and is short on time. It details the eight steps in starting a successful program and how to make planned giving an integral part of the overall development process. It includes chapters on the "tools of the trade," how to talk with donors and how to write a gift proposal, policy and procedures for receiving gifts and for the endowment fund, gift plan models, a glossary of terms, and more. It was written with the fund raiser in mind who often has more responsibilities than time. It doesn't deal with the technicalities of the various gifting arrangements. Rather, it speaks in plain language about what the average work-a-day fund raiser needs to do in order to let donors know that the charitable organization would really appreciate receiving charitable gifts through financial and estate plans. The first few years of the planned giving program are usually just positioning the charity in the donor's mind as wanting these types of gifts, so the fund raiser responsible for the program does have time in which to grow with the program. The second edition has two new chapters that should be very helpful, especially for the fund raisers who are new to the field of planned giving. The chapter on gift planning language (Chapter 30) should help you to better understand the concepts. The chapter on gift models (Chapter 26) will give some valuable insights on how charitable gift planning can actually help your donors solve their personal problems by making a planned gift. Periodic updates and electronic version are also available. *Print: Loose-leaf three-ring binder, 217 pages, $44 (plus shipping and handling); Electronic version, $69 ($4 shipping and handling); Both: $87 ($6 shipping and handling)*

Planned Giving Made Easy: What Every Fundraiser Needs to Know (Videocassette)

LED BY BILL STURTEVANT (INSTITUTE FOR CHARITABLE GIVING)

▶ This video helps you seize planned giving opportunities without the need for specialization or technical jargon. It is an easy way to understand the road map for those who don't want or need to be tax experts, but who seek a threshold or knowledge to secure the gift. Discover how to achieve the highest potential with prospects at all levels; a working, practical foundation of knowledge that leads to expanded avenues of giving for your organization. It is useful for novice and advanced fund raisers. *65 minutes, $59.99 (plus $2 shipping)*

Planned Giving: Management, Marketing, and the Law, 2nd Edition (Book & Disk)

RONALD R. JORDAN, KATELYN L. QUYNN, AND CAROLYN M. OSTEEN (JOHN WILEY & SONS, 1999)

▶ This book covers most everything a development officer needs to know to develop, market, and manage a successful planned giving program. It also discusses technical topics, such as types of gifts, estate and financial planning, retirement planning, and investment strategies; It instructs how to administer a planned giving program, from record keeping and donor relations to strategic planning and training. This book will help you develop these valuable strategies: (1) launching, managing, and expanding a planned giving program; (2) marketing a planned giving program; (3) better managing prospects and donors; (4) meeting both the donor's and the nonprofit's needs; (5) promoting the financial advantages of planned

gifts to philanthropic donors; (6) establishing a bequest program; and (7) attracting new business to new and established planned giving programs.

Part One of their instructive book examines the goals of a planned giving program, how it functions most effectively within the development office, where to find planned giving prospects, and how to work with them once you've located them. In Part Two, the authors turn their attention to marketing the program. Not only do they discuss the promotional materials you'll need, but—and here is where the diskette's value is immeasurable—they provide model forms for everything from brochures, advertisements, slip notes, newsletters, even columns for local papers or in-house publications on subjects ranging from real estate gifts to gifts of insurance, to life income gifts, to gifts of appreciated securities. The focus of Part Three centers on the assets donors can use to make planned gifts. And, rather than inundate the reader with minute details, Jordan and Quynn cover the essential ins, outs, ups, and downs of gifts of tangible personal property, gifts of securities, real estate, and life insurance. Part Four is devoted to the heart of planned giving, namely, the gift vehicles: pooled income funds, gift annuities, lead trusts, and bequests. Here, again, the diskette is invaluable, providing three dozen model letters to prospects, and agreements that outline the terms of the gift vehicles. Part Five discusses the tax consequences of charitable giving and, for development officers, offers a refresher course on estate planning, financial planning, and retirement planning. Part Six concludes with a discussion of coping with and changing, if necessary, management's perception of the role of planned giving. It includes a 3.5-inch IBM-compatible computer diskette with more than 140 actual marketing documents, newsletters, brochures, sample agreements, checklists, IRS-approved tax forms, and more. It is supplemented annually. *Hardcover, 576 pages, $165*

Planned Giving Simplified: The Gift, the Giver and the Gift Planner

ROBERT F. SHARPE (JOHN WILEY & SONS, 1998)

▶ In this book, charitable gift planning expert Robert F. Sharpe Sr. demystifies the complex world of planned giving for not-for-profit managers. He provides a detailed blueprint for starting and building a successful planned giving program, and develops a rational framework for managing the subtle interplay of legal, administrative, and interpersonal factors involved in the planned giving process. Central to Sharpe's proven approach is his controversial definition of the effective charitable gift planner as being not so much a fund raiser as an expert at helping potential benefactors satisfy a deeply felt emotional need. Rather than soliciting or closing on planned gifts, the planner's primary focus should be on forming relationships with donors and providing them with the means and opportunity to fulfill their desire to do good. *Hardcover, 210 pages, $34.95*

Planned Giving: Starting, Marketing, Administering

CONRAD TEITELL (TAXWISE GIVING)

▶ A basic yet comprehensive overview, this volume complements *Deferred Giving, Lead Trust and Outright Charitable Gifts* (see separate listings under Publications in Financial Management, Taxes section). You have to know the tax rules when promoting charitable gifts but that isn't enough. It takes you by the hand and shows you how to start, market, and administer planned giving programs. It includes: Introduction (explains tax rules for outright and deferred gifts and tells how a planned giving program relates to your overall development program); How to Establish a New Program or Improve a Present One; Promotion (individualized proposal, prospects, advertising, direct mail, booklets and other publications, volunteers); Seminars (conducting planned giving seminars for professional advisors, volunteers, and constituents); Investment Guidelines (different investment strategies for various plans); and Administration (administering charitable remainder unitrusts, annuity trusts, pooled income funds, charitable gift annuities). It is supplemented and revised as needed. *Loose-leaf binder, $175 (plus $7 shipping)*

The Portable Planned Giving Manual, 8th Edition

CONRAD TEITELL (TAXWISE GIVING/PHILANTHROPY TAX INSTITUTE, 2000)

▶ This book lays out what you need to know about planned giving in one handy volume. It covers life income gifts; lead trusts; outright charitable gifts; and starting, marketing, and administering planned giving programs. For more detailed information, see Teitell's volumes on *Outright Charitable Gifts, Planned Giving, Deferred Giving,* and *Charitable Lead Trusts. Softcover, 700 pages, $195 (plus $7 shipping and handling)*

Practical Guide to Planned Giving 2000, 8th Edition

LEONARD G. CLOUGH, DAVID G. CLOUGH, EDNALOU C. BALLARD, AND A. B. TUELLER (THE TAFT GROUP, 1999)

▶ *Practical Guide to Planned Giving* presents the finer points of a planned giving program's marketing and management efforts. Use it to help you decipher the confusing legal, tax, and marketing problems that often arise when soliciting a planned gift. To maximize tax benefits for your donors, you need the kind of current, accurate information supplied by this valuable reference. Fully updated with the most recent information and advice, *Practical Guide to Planned Giving* provides you with the following: extensive information on the "nuts and bolts" of marketing and running a planned giving program—from creating and budgeting a successful program to winning board approval; detailed chapters devoted to the principal planned giving options—revocable gifts, irrevocable trust gifts, irrevocable nontrust gifts—with clear explanations of the advantages and disadvantages of each gift option for donors and recipients; timely, essential information that is updated annually to reflect the changes in tax laws; and useful chapters on establishing and running a planned giving program for the small, "one-person" development office. *Softcover, 930 pages, $140*

Retirement Assets and Charitable Gifts: A Guide for Planned Giving Professionals, Financial Planners, and Donors

CHRISTOPHER R. HOYT AND BRUCE R. HOPKINS (JOHN WILEY & SONS, 2001)

▶ This book explains, in plain language, the complex rules and regulations governing charitable gifts made from retirement accounts. The gifts are becoming the *preferred* option for charities, donors, the donor's heirs, and the donor's financial advisors. The book clearly lays out an advantageous tax strategy for charities and donors, and addresses the elements that make the best charitable and estate plan. This book will provide solutions to such issues as the higher distributions that accompany naming a charity as a beneficiary, how the nonprofit can avoid the "trapping distribution" of pooled-income funds that is to neither their benefit nor that of the donor, and how to address the concerns of the donor's heirs. *Hardcover, 300 pages, $55*

Sample Planned Giving Policy Manual for Promoting and Accepting Non-Cash Gifts
(Manual or Disk)

T. JOSEPH MCKAY AND DANIEL G. WORTHINGTON (PLANNEDGIVING.COM)

▶ The PlannedGiving.Com software is a desk manual document that includes suggested policies and procedures, marketing concepts, tax issues, and graphic or pictorial illustrations for each type of planned gift. These features are combined in one policy manual in order to place each gift vehicle in proper perspective for board members, volunteers, staff, and others. It is available on 3.5-inch diskettes as a word-processing document (in either Word or WordPerfect formats for Windows—either Microsoft Word 6.0 for Windows, or WordPerfect 6.1 for Windows (or later versions) is required to edit and print the manual.). The document can be easily personalized throughout with the name of your nonprofit organization, and readily adapted to the needs of each charity. *Softcover, 50 pages, $49; MS Word or WordPerfect: $189.00*

Smart and Caring: A Donor's Guide to Major Gifting

RICHARD LIVINGSTON AND LINDA LIVINGSTON (RLD PUBLISHING, 1999)

▶ This is a book written by donors for donors. The authors bring a commonsense directness to a subject that often gets bogged down in detail and complexity. They address the issues, actions, and rewards of major gifting from a fresh perspective—that of the donors themselves. The Livingstons have done us all a favor by partnering with their estate attorney, Kathleen Hammond, and their CPA, William Rogers, to ensure that their discussions remain technically accurate while staying in the comfort zone of the layman reader.

In *Smart and Caring,* the Livingstons have divided the issues of major gifting into three general categories. The first is the personal side, where they share the process that they have gone through in moving from being detached citizens of the community to becoming deeply involved donors and volunteers. Second, they look at the technical side of becoming a donor, bringing structure and insight to the choices available for tax-efficient gifting. Last, they tackle the financial side of major gifting, providing analysis tools that allow donors to put gifting in the context of their own lifetime net worth, income, asset growth, and tax situation. *Softcover, 214 pages, $15*

Start at Square One: Starting and Managing the Planned Gift Program

LYNDA S. MOERSCHBAECHER (PRECEPT PRESS, 1998)

▶ The world of not-for-profit fund raising can be one of high-cost special events and persistent lobbying, while other types of fund raising can provide a much higher reward at a lower cost without the nagging frustration and weary disappointment. The most successful nonprofit organizations and institutions rely on seasoned know-how, faithful preparation, and a fervent commitment to the "process." For many years, Lynda S. Moerschbaecher has unlocked and outlined the simple secrets of this tried-and-true process in nationally recognized seminars designed for fund-raising professionals. Now, this esteemed specialist in the field of planned giving shares her practiced expertise in this enlightening new book. Because creating or even revitalizing a planned giving program is much like starting a new business, it too must move through several important stages before becoming profitable. *Start at Square One* effectively demonstrates that the road to long-term success depends on a sophisticated strategy, defined roles, a thorough business plan, effective marketing, and more. *Hardcover, 222 pages, $40*

Taxwise Giving Booklets
CONRAD TEITELL (TAXWISE GIVING)

▶ This is a series of booklets for donors on tax-encouraged giving with up-to-the-minute information on the latest tax laws. All booklets can be imprinted with your institution's name and address. The Series includes these titles: *Planning Your Estate, Making Your Will, God's Will Is Not Subject to Probate, Personal and Financial Records, Taxwise Charitable Giving, You Can Be a Philanthropist, The Joys of Giving, The Charitable Remainder Trust, The Charitable Remander Annuity Trust, The Charitable Gift Annuity, The Deferred Payment Gift Annuity, Pooled Income Fund Gifts, Counsellor's Tax Guide to Charitable Contributions, Women's Financial Planner, The Charitable Lead Trust,* and *A Guide to Living Wills.* Bulk discounts are available. *$.93 each (12-page booklets), $1.01 each (24-page booklets), $1.05 each (32-page booklets), $4.95 (The Charitable Lead Trust) (plus $4.50 shipping)*

Values-Based Estate Planning: A Step-by-Step Approach to Wealth Transfer for Professional Advisors
SCOTT C. FITHIAN (JOHN WILEY & SONS, 2000)

▶ This is the estate advisor's guide to helping baby boomers explore values-based estate planning. Baby boomers have amassed fortunes through their innovation, work, and investments. They are also the beneficiaries of the largest intergenerational transfer of wealth in history. Boomers who will receive this wealth are wondering how it will affect them and their families' lives and are beginning to seek the advice of competent professionals to help them achieve their highest financial and philanthropic aspirations. Author Scott Fithian shows advisors how to help wealth holders of all levels use their personal values to simplify the planning process, ensure lifetime financial independence, and control their ultimate family and social capital legacies. Featuring a step-by-step system, this book shows advisors how to motivate clients to develop clear, concise objectives, particularly when it comes to "soft" issues such as philanthropy and values. *Hardcover, 272 pages, $39.95*

Program-Related Investments

The PRI Directory: Charitable Loans and Other Program-Related Investments by Foundations
(FOUNDATION CENTER, 2001)

▶ Certain foundations have developed an alternative financing approach, known as program-related investing, for supplying capital to the nonprofit sector. PRIs have been used to support community revitalization, low-income housing, microenterprise development, historic preservation, human services, and more. This directory lists leading PRI providers and includes tips on how to seek out and manage PRIs. Foundation listings include funder name and state; recipient name, city, and state (or country); and a description of the project funded. There are several helpful indexes to guide PRI seekers to records by foundation/recipient location, subject/type of support, and recipient name, as well as an index to officers, donors, and trustees. *Softcover, approx. 250 pages, $75*

The PRI Index: 500 Recent Foundation Charitable Loans and Investments
(FOUNDATION CENTER, 1997)

▶ This guide features crucial facts on loans and other charitable investments made by the growing community of foundations that make PRIs. Listings of some 500 recent PRIs made by 125 foundations include funder name and state; recipient name, city, and state (or country); PRI amount; year of authorization or payment; and a description of the project funded. Four indexes guide PRI-seekers to records by foundation location, subject/type of support, recipient name, and recipient location. *Softcover, 65 pages, $75*

Program-Related Investments: A Guide to Funders and Trends
(FOUNDATION CENTER, 1995)

▶ Foundations have developed an alternative financing approach, known as program-related investing, for supplying capital to the nonprofit sector. PRIs have been used to support community revitalization, low-income housing, microenterprise development, historic preservation, human services, and more. *Program-Related Investments* includes sections that cover current perspectives from providers and recipients; crucial tips on how to seek out and manage PRIs; a directory of leading PRI providers; and examples of over 550 PRIs. *Softcover, 189 pages, $45*

Program-Related Investments: A Primer
(COUNCIL ON FOUNDATIONS, 1993)

▶ Program-related investments (PRIs) are fast becoming an invaluable philanthropic tool. Tap into this innovative funding strategy to meet your charitable goals with *Program-Related Investment Primer.* By outlining the laws that govern program-related investments, this book teaches you how to preserve your charitable assets while expanding the reach of your programs. *Softcover, $25 (Nonmember), $15 (Member) (plus $2 shipping)*

Proposal Writing

The Foundation Center's Guide to Proposal Writing, 2nd Edition
(THE FOUNDATION CENTER, 1997)

▶ This book provides an up-to-date and comprehensive manual on the basics and finer points of this crucial nonprofit skill. Incorporating recent interviews with the people who review your proposals, the volume furnishes current and valuable "insider information"—candid tips from grant makers who clue you into the best proposal strategies. It guides you through the entire grant-writing process, from preproposal planning to the writing itself, to the essential post-grant follow-up: sample proposals—you'll learn about all the necessary components of the grant proposal package and how to develop and fine-tune each part. This edition includes new examples of actual proposals—cover letters, project descriptions, budgets, and more—to provide you with models of well-constructed grant proposals that have recently won support; grant-maker guidance—the revised edition reflects findings from a recent survey of 20 grant makers. You'll learn about new trends in grant making and the proposal review process—the behind-the-scenes decisions that will affect your proposal. You'll get straight answers to questions on proposal formats, follow-up strategies, how to resubmit a rejected request, and much more; preproposal planning tips—the first section of the Guide emphasizes the work you must accomplish before you start to write. It helps you to decide when your nonprofit is ready to raise funds and to define the project for which you plan to submit proposals. An updated bibliography of other readings on the topic is also included. *Softcover, 191 pages, $34.95*

Prospect Research

(See also Grant Writing/Proposal Writing; Grant Seeking)

FRI Prospect Research Resource Directory, 2nd Edition

ALEX NORSWORTHY, ED. (THE TAFT GROUP, 1991)

▶ This handy desktop reference points prospect researchers to hundreds of resources that will help identify and gather information on potential funding sources, including 850 directories in print; 220 newsletters; nearly 500 databases tracking major corporate events; stock ownership and public policies; 250 consultants who specialize in information management; and more than 600 publishers of electronic information sources. *Softcover, 491 pages, $34*

Marquis Who's Who in America, 55th Edition

(MARQUIS WHO'S WHO, 2001)

▶ In one reference source you'll get current biographical information on careers, education, personal accomplishments, addresses, and so much more. The 2001 edition chronicles American leadership with over 131,000 achievers; 68,000 updated entries; 34,000 brand new listings; free indexes: Geographic, Professional, Retiree, and Necrology; and over 100 years of biographical expertise and experience. Compiled by the Marquis *Who's Who* editors using more than 80 proprietary standards developed in a century of biographical reference publishing, *Who's Who in America* provides information on up to 20 different biographical categories per individual. With personal and career details unavailable in any other source, it's the ultimate networking, prospecting, fact-checking biographical reference tool. *Hardcover, three-volume set, 6,000 pages, $575.00*

Prospect Research Fundamentals

(STEVENSON CONSULTANTS)

▶ This book contains proven methods and strategies to help you uncover major gifts from individuals, foundations, private companies, public corporations, and more. Features include easy-to-understand charts and forms to better manage research and information; examples of effective rating and screening forms, charts to determine prospects' giving capability, prospect profile forms, and more; lists of resources to point you in the right direction; dozens of tips, techniques, and research strategies; practical prospecting tips and techniques; research strategies anyone can use; and helpful ways to track prospects and manage information. Some of the "hands-on" information covered includes researching individuals' assets; ways to rate and screen prospects; uncovering information on private companies; how to effectively track prospect calls; free resources for researching prospects; ways to find lost constituents; building a mailing list from scratch; researching foundations and companies; analyze your board's connections; methods to research land holdings; the role of technology in prospect research; how to manage prospect information effectively; ethical issues in prospect research; ways to generate new prospects; forms to help track prospect activities; research strategies for small nonprofits; selecting database software methodically; ways to prioritize prospects; and hiring research staff. *Softcover, 46 pages, $64*

Prospect Researcher's Guide to Biographical Research Collections (Directory)

JANE KOKERNAK, ED. (THE TAFT GROUP, 1992)

▶ This book gives researchers a powerful new tool with its geographical arrangement of more than 1,000 genealogical, biographical, business, fund-raising, newspaper, foundation, historical, and other special libraries that maintain files on individuals, public and private companies, funds, and philanthropy in the United States, whether they are organized based on a common theme (e.g., health care) or geographical area. It also tells how to gain access to the collections. Detailed entries provide up to 25 points of information on libraries and their collections, including subjects covered, contact information (names, phone numbers, FAX numbers, etc.), special collections, both content and quantities, subscription services, computerized information services, networks and consortia, special catalogs and indexes, remarks and additional descriptions, and more. *Softcover, 339 pages, $34 (includes shipping)*

Prospector's Choice 2000 (CD-ROM)

(THE TAFT GROUP, 1999)

▶ This resource gives you key financial information on foundations and corporate giving programs. You'll find detailed funder profiles covering nearly 10,000 foundations and corporate giving programs—providing information on up to 50 grants per profile, as well as total giving figures and helpful directions for making contacts and completing applications. Grant analysis is also provided, as well as each organization's application requirements. Search features enable you to identify funders, recipients, and grants in a number of ways: (1) search funders by: name (view all foundations and corporate giving programs in the database in alphabetical order); location (choose the state, or city and state, to find funders); officer name (scan the names of all foundation officers in alphabetical order); officer alma mater (links all 1,650 colleges and universities to officers who attended them); (2) search recipients by: location (choose the state, or city and state, to find funders who issued grants to recipients in that area; type (an alphabetical menu lists recipients by 228 subjects, from adolescent health issues to zoos); (3) search grants by: type (see what types of grants are available. Scroll through topics such as art and history, environment, community, religion, research, social politics and more); (4) extended search—combine any or all of the above search functions. Helpful data each entry provides: contact information (identify the name, title, and address of the key decision makers); financial summary (analyze the organization's key financial data); contributions summary (Does this organization typically contribute to causes like yours? Find out here); giving officers (Who are the decision makers? What are their titles? Their other interests?); application information (in this section, you will find clear instructions on how to get an application, how to apply, what to include, deadlines, and more); grant analysis (hone your request based on total dollar amount, number of grants, the highest grant, average grant, typical range and disclosure period); and recent grants (scan the most recent grants and their recipients). Windows™ version. *Windows version; $849.00 (annual subscription); allows up to eight simultaneous users, plus $50 for each additional user*

Top 300 Web Sites for Prospect Researchers (Disk)

SUSAN RUDERMAN (EMERSON & CHURCH)

▶ Have you ever wondered: How much money your top prospect received in an IPO? Where the wealthiest zip codes are? What the estimated sales of a private company are? How large a gift your top prospect made to another organization? Answers to these questions and scores of others can be found on the Internet, as Susan Ruderman expertly demonstrates on the *Top 300 Websites for Prospect Researchers*. With this disk loaded into your computer, you will be instantly transported to the right Web site to answer your particular research needs. Ruderman, who cut her teeth on prospect research at MIT and Harvard, has sifted through the multitude of existing sites and selected only those proven to be uncommonly useful to prospect research. Her commentary and interpretation of each proves invaluable. It is divided into 12 categories—from Individual Wealth Information to Public and Private Company Information to Donor Lists, and nine more. *$49*

Where the Money Is: A Fund Raiser's Guide to the Rich, 2nd Edition

HELEN BERGAN (BIOGUIDE PRESS, 1992)

▶ Put a private research librarian on your side. Here is the definitive guide to prospect and donor search. It provides a complete overview of prospect and donor research, giving both the basics and the finer points. It teaches you how to: (1) bolster your prospect list by locating wealthy individuals, (2) find the net worth of anyone, (3) use your local library to search out sources of wealth in your community, (4) locate essential biographical facts using a wide range of reference books and computerized services, (5) research public and private companies and their executives, and (6) solicit the gift after you have targeted the donor. *Softcover, 257 pages, $30 (plus $2 shipping)*

Who's Wealthy in America 2000, 10th Edition

(THE TAFT GROUP, 1999)

▶ The only source available whose listings are based solely on wealth, it profiles nearly 100,000 of America's most prosperous people. It contains information on thousands of new prospects, plus new information on previous listings, such as address changes, new political contributions, and stock holdings. Biographical entries provide name, phone number, address, plus critical data on political contributions, education, and lifestyle indicators (Rolls Royce owners, art collectors, yacht owners, etc.). Features include: (1) the only biographical directory whose listings are based solely on the criteria of inferred wealth, allowing users access to affluent prospects previously available only through list brokers and marketing consultants, at a fraction of the cost; (2) includes valuable prospecting information, such as insider stock holdings and political contributions of listees, not found in most electronic "affluent" databases; (3) stockholder data is derived from CDA/InvestNet, a company well respected by prospect researchers for accurate and current information on insider stockholders; (4) indicates the number of corporate boards upon which these wealth holders hold seats; and (5) four indexes (Insider Stock/Security Index, Political Contributions Index, Alma Mater Index and Geographic Index) allow users myriad ways to target those wealth holders who are most likely to give to their organization. Volume One contains listings of more than 112,600 wealthy individuals. Volume Two provides information on the insider stock holdings of individuals listed in Volume One. *Hardcover, approx. 2,500 pages in two volumes, $470 (includes shipping and handling)*

Special Events

Aspen's Guide to 60 Successful Special Events: How to Plan, Organize and Conduct Outstanding Fund Raisers

CINDY HAUSER (ASPEN PUBLISHERS, 1996)

▶ This book gives a simple straightforward "recipe" for planning a wide variety of fund-raising special events. With 60 events of varying complexity featured, every nonprofit is sure to find fund raisers that meet its needs. Each entry contains a description of a successful event and one organization's history of hosting it; how much money must be spent and can be raised, and suggestions for securing underwriting or in-kind donations; how much time and effort is needed for successful planning; the community participation required to make the event a success; and how many staff members and volunteers will be needed. Every event has its own countdown timeline listing each step of the planning process and when it should be completed, and additional forms and checklists are provided (also on diskette). In addition, this unique book contains helpful tips for maximizing effectiveness—as well as identifying pitfalls to avoid—from the people who have successfully hosted the event for their own organization. *Loose-leaf, 256 pages, $80*

Best Ever Directory of Special Events

(STEVENSON CONSULTANTS, INC., 1998)

▶ This booklet features a wide assortment (more than 60 in all) of tried-and-tested fund-raising events you can put to immediate use in addition to tips and techniques to make your fund raiser more profitable and well attended. Each event will share the amount of revenue generated, costs, sources of revenue, how many attended, how the event was implemented and marketed, any unique aspects, and more. Highlights include descriptions of more than 60 successful (and widely different) special events; examples of revenue-producing features: auctions, raffle, sponsorships, ad journals, and more; examples of how volunteers and board members can make your event successful and self-sustaining; 60-plus profitable events to choose from; fun and unique ideas to spice up existing events; practical, step-by-step description of each event from start to finish. *Softcover, 46 pages, $63*

Black Tie Optional

HARRY A. FREEDMAN (TAFT GROUP, 1991)

▶ Discover the basic ingredients needed to make any special event a money-making success with this first-rate guide from Harry A. Freedman, who is nationally recognized for producing large-scale special events, often featuring big-name celebrities. Learn how to choose the right time and place for a successful event, how to reach and book celebrities, get media publicity, develop budgets, set ticket prices, organize committees, and promote an event. *Softcover, 247 pages, $35*

The Business of Special Events: Fundraising Strategies for Changing Times

HARRY A. FREEDMAN AND KAREN FELDMAN (PINEAPPLE PRESS, 1998)

▶ Nowhere else will you find such a wealth of practical, experiential advice along with plenty of worksheets, checklists, samples, examples, and anecdotes from the authors' years in nonprofit management. With wisdom, know-how, and an eye on detail, the authors show you how to produce a special event, whether a sidewalk sale or a glamorous gala, to make money and friends in the name of your cause. Harry Freedman is nationally recognized as a leader in nonprofit fund raising. He has produced hundreds of large-scale special events, often featuring celebrities. A member of the National Society for Fundraising Executives, he speaks and writes on topics such as special events marketing for charities, major donor fund raising, and the cultivation of volunteers. *Softcover, 160 pages, $17.56*

Dynamic Fund-Raising Projects

RICK ARLEDGE WITH DAVID FRIEDMAN (BONUS BOOKS, 1998)

▶ Add $500 to $50,000 to your bottom line. Not once, not twice, but every year. Create a new tradition in your community by sponsoring an event. You choose the amount of money that your organization needs and select the appropriate projects. Over a dozen events are listed in detail in this reader-friendly, lay-flat instruction manual. Projects include direct-mail campaigns, generic 300 Club, carnivals, movie premieres, concert promotions, haunted houses, rummage sales, t-shirt sales, concession stands, Secret Santas, auctions, and an automobile party. *Loose-leaf, 153 pages, $50*

Event Planning: The Ultimate Guide to Successful Meetings, Corporate Events, Fundraising Galas, Conferences, Conventions, and Other SP

JUDY ALLEN (JOHN WILEY & SONS, 2000)

▶ A detailed blueprint for planning and executing special events with flair and without unexpected surprises and expenses. Special events such as fund-raising galas, conferences, and product launches are complicated, fraught with thousands of details, and have to come off without a hitch. This book gives readers practical advice on every aspect of organizing and managing special events, such as how to choose the best venue; preparing and managing the budget; scheduling; coordinating food and beverages; selecting decor, themes, and entertainment; media; and staffing. It includes many forms, checklists, and tips for planning and managing events. It features examples of events where things went right and wrong and provides techniques to maximize savings and avoid surprises. *Hardcover, 288 pages, $29.95*

Fundraising Ideas: Over 225 Money Making Events for Community Groups, With a Resource Directory

JANELL SHRIDE AMOS (MCFARLAND & COMPANY, 1995)

▶ From "-athons" (e.g., bikeathons, walkathons) to yard booths, over 225 proven fund raisers are included in this essential reference work. Each entry contains a brief description of the event, the type of workers and tools needed to ensure its success and a reference to the resource directory. Hints for organizing fund raisers are augmented by a section of "success stories" that further emphasize the basics. It offers suggestions and directions for special events to raise money, plus tips on planning events, promotion, honoring the law, and dealing with problems. Alphabetical entries on crowd pleasers such as men-only beauty contests, tearooms, cakewalks, and kissing booths describe events and the workers and tools needed. A resource directory provides vendor information. *Softcover, 160 pages, $33*

The Fundraising Manual: A Step-by-Step Guide to Creating the Perfect Event

MICKI GORDON (FIG PRESS, 1997)

▶ This book will serve as an all-in-one resource guide for fundraising professionals and volunteers. In addition, it lists vendors,

telephone numbers, FAX numbers, philanthropy publications, and lots more. It's all in here. *Softcover, 184 pages, $19.95*

Going...Going...Gone!: Successful Auctions for Non-Profit Institutions, 2nd Edition

ANNE CONNELLY AND MAUREEN WINTER (TARGET FUNDING GROUP, 1999)

▶ In terms of special events, a smartly conceived and well-executed benefit auction is one of the most efficient methods of raising substantial money. This book illuminates the entire process from the initial steps of identifying volunteers to the actual auction event. Connelly and Winter provide 22 chapters in all, each focusing on a single auction element. There's a chapter on the committees you'll need and the responsibilities of each. There's a chapter on acquiring items for your auction, which includes sample merchant letters, telephone scripts, and even a solicitation packet. There's a chapter on putting your auction catalog together, including matters of design, content, solicitation of ads, and format. In this comprehensive book, there are also individual chapters on food, decorations, entertainment, invitations, advertising, publicity, raffles, preview parties, silent auctions, live auctions, and evaluations. There are even chapters on organizing a software system for your auction and codes, taxes, and insurance. *Softcover, 226 pages, $45*

Guide to Special Event Fundraising

KEN WYMAN (KEN WYMAN & ASSOCIATES, 1995)

▶ Special events are probably the most widely used fund-raising technique. Yet some groups still dive into disaster while others really do well and make substantial gains. Designed to guide the beginner and help the expert discover new ideas and rediscover basic principles, this is a complete how-to guide for succeeding with special events. It answers all these questions and more: Winners or losers: how do you know before you start? What's my best choice given my budget, staff, and volunteers? More than money? What else can I gain from special events? How can I reduce my costs to nearly zero? How do I set the right admission prices and recruit an all-star ticket sales team? It includes chapters on nine ways a souvenir program increases effectiveness; getting musicians and celebrities to give their time happily; recruiting enough good volunteers; getting bigger bucks from any crowd; and hidden gold: extra income after events end. It also has an Event-Ability Quiz, a self-scoring quiz to evaluate your experience, your team, your expected guests and supporters, your public profile, the costs and income, the type of event you've chosen, and your planning. This publication is also available free online at *http://www.pch.gc.ca/cp-pc/ComPartnE/pub_list.htm. Softcover, 170 pages, $40 (including shipping)*

How to Produce Fabulous Fundraising Events: Reap Remarkable Returns with Minimal Effort

(Book & Disk)

BETTY STALLINGS AND DONNA MCMILLION (BUILDING BETTER SKILLS, 1999)

▶ This book on fund raising emphasizes the importance of volunteers and the principles of volunteer management. Tapping their many successes in raising money through special events, the authors generously share their blueprint for selecting, planning, and running a profitable fund raiser—whether yours is a grassroots organization or a major institution. You also have the option of buying the accompanying computer disk (Windows or Mac) giving you all the forms you'll need to put on a fabulous fund-raising event:

templates for letters and invitations, checklists, timelines, budget worksheets, and more—all fully adaptable to your unique organization and event. The book includes all the essential elements for effective fund raising: setting goals and choosing, staffing, planning, promoting, staging, and evaluating the event. In addition, step-by-step guides are provided for different events and different steps in the fund-raising process. Even more time and effort can be saved with the computer disk (Windows or Mac) that contains event forms, letters, lists, budgets, and more needed by fund-raising organizations. *Softcover, 168 pages, $30 (book only, $20)*

Make Your Events Special: How to Plan and Organize Successful Special Events Programs for Nonprofit Organizations, 2nd Edition
TED GEIER, CAUSE EFFECTIVE (FOLKWORKS, 1986)

▶ Ideal for any executive director, development director, public relations specialist, board member, community organizer, or volunteer for a nonprofit organization looking for ways to achieve their organization's fund raising, promotion, enlistment, morale, and program goals, this user-friendly, soup-to-nuts guide helps both experienced and special events organizers and novices save time, money, and worry while increasing the effectiveness of their special events. It provides a practical, 10-step approach to developing and implementing your organization's special events programs, including setting objectives, selecting activities, budgeting, fund raising, programming, promotion and marketing, execution, administration, personnel, and evaluation. It provides you with case studies, checklists, and worksheets. This revised edition includes updated guidance and tools. *Softcover, 127 pages, $24.95 (bulk discounts available)*

Money Makers: A Guide to Special Events Fund Raising
(WHITCOMB ASSOCIATES, 1982)

▶ This definitive, easy-to-use guide gives you step-by-step directions for each of 18 different events. Golf Classics, spaghetti dinners, garden walks—all are there, ready for your use. Three supplements have been published with three to four additional events included. Subsequent supplements, $25 each, cover three or more additional events. The entire book is published in a three-ring binder, making it easy to copy timelines, job descriptions, and other key elements for volunteers and staff. *Three-ring binder, $80, $25 per supplement (plus $6.95 shipping and handling) (Prepaid books or supplements get free shipping and handling)*

Organizing Special Events and Conferences: A Practical Guide for Busy Volunteers and Staff
(See Marketing and Communications—Special Events for full description)

Raising Money and Cultivating Donors Through Special Events
APRIL HARRIS (CASE PUBLICATIONS, 1991)

▶ Events deliver your message personally to target audiences by showcasing your organization and its achievements in time-effective and creative ways. Learn how to plan and hold fund-raising events that raise money and cultivate friends for your institution. Concrete how-to information covers the basics for the beginner while the experienced professional can work on fine-tuning traditional or new events. *Softcover, 57 pages, $16*

Raising Big Bucks: The Complete Guide to Producing Pledge-Based Special Events
CINDY R. KAITCER (BONUS BOOKS, 1996)

▶ This book gives step-by-step directions on how to raise a lot of money through events, including how to create a budget, how to recruit participants, and how to make your cause compelling. The information in the book could apply to almost any event. With *Raising Big Bucks,* the challenges are simplified, the risks are eliminated, and the pledges are collected, all while participation is simulated. Whether you are a newcomer to event management or a veteran fund raiser, this book is for you—it's a formula for success. As you study it, you will learn to launch aggressive promotional campaigns; recruit new and train past participants; attract more *cash* sponsorships; utilize the Internet to reduce advertising costs; increase pledge-per-participant average; garner media attention and support; write and design *compelling* communication pieces; plan a budget and keep it on track; recruit, structure, and manage committees and volunteers—from 10 to 1,000; design routes and expand sites; build loyalty and increase name recognition; identify new markets; and more. It offers more than 200 pages of trenchant advice and counsel on virtually every aspect of pledge-based sporting events. Add to these the fact that participants can and do come from every income and age bracket of society and the makings are there for a blockbuster event (not to mention profit). Pricing, budgeting, recruiting, training, job descriptions, timelines, worksheets, corporate sponsorships, incentives, promotion— you'll find field-tested advice on these and scores of other matters in this unique book. *Hardcover, 240 pages, $39.95*

Special Events: Planning for Success, Second Edition
APRIL HARRIS (CASE BOOKS, 1998)

▶ Every savvy advancement professional knows that special events can make or break your program. They can draw your audiences closer to your organization or turn them away. They send messages that can be more powerful than your slickest publication. In the 10-plus years since CASE first published *Special Events: Planning for Success,* special events have become integral aspects of advancement. The updated edition includes new information and examples that reflect how the field of special event planning has evolved, plus specific how-to guides for the most common campus events. Chapters cover creative suggestions to delight attendees and make each event a successful marketing vehicle; tips on incorporating technology into events management; seasoned advice on insurance, liability, tax laws, and other issues that can influence event success; how events fit into fund raising; suggestions on contracting with outside vendors and hiring independent event planners; early planning and strategy; invitations, tickets, and publicity; location selection and logistics; making guests feel welcome; giving your program impact; working with volunteers; budgets and contracts; follow-up and follow-through; details that make the difference; and basic event checklists. *Spiral bound, $52 (Nonmember), $35 (Member)*

Special Events: Proven Strategies for Nonprofit Fund Raising (Book and Disk)
ALAN L. WENDROFF (JOHN WILEY & SONS, 1999)

▶ If carefully planned, special events can be a monetary and marketing bonanza for nonprofits. However, many organizations end up running into the red because of poor budget planning, insufficient volunteers, mediocre media attention, badly negotiated service contracts with caterers and hotels, or careless oversight of other essential elements. In this practical and comprehensive guide, Alan L. Wendroff, CFRE, shows you how to sidestep potential mistakes by covering the do's and don'ts of running a successful special event. *Special Events: Proven Strategies for Nonprofit Fund Raising* presents the essential knowledge necessary for organizing and holding events that will meet your objectives. It starts by helping you determine your particular goals, from raising money, marketing and public relations, and building and expanding a donor base to building and motivating a volunteer pool, training the board to solicit funds, educating the public about your mission, and gathering endorsements. It then provides the fundamentals necessary for achieving your organization's multidimensional goals. The Master Event Time Table, the ultimate special event tool, will walk you step by step through each stage of the process, and this 26-week checklist can be abridged or modified based on your organization's needs. Packed with practical insights and planning tips, as well as common misconceptions, pitfalls to avoid, and warning flags, this invaluable resource also includes sample worksheets and checklists, both as illustrations and on an IBM-compatible disk. Some of the need-to-have information that you will find in this book includes: models for a special event (auctions, theater and gallery openings, sports tournaments, testimonial events); monetary goals and budgets (calculating revenue sources and expenses, estimating attendance, figuring gross revenue); recruiting volunteer leadership (stakeholders, agency governing boards, honorary chairpersons, event chairs); administration (choosing a location, contract negotiations, staffing, postal and financial matters, insurance); final preparation (documents, reception, guest seating, the PDQ checklist); and post-event duties (how and when to say "thank you," evaluating outcomes). *Hardcover, 214 pages, $39.95*

Successful Special Events: Planning, Hosting, and Evaluating

BARBARA LEVY AND BARBARA MARION (ASPEN PUBLISHERS, 1997)

▶ To help you realize the greatest potential from special events and steer clear of a multitude of obstacles, Barbara Levy and Barbara Marion in their new book, *Successful Special Events: Planning,*

Hosting, and Evaluating, propose a systematic way of approaching special events so that they take an appropriate, productive role in your overall development program. The book is a veritable workshop on conducting special events, with instruction on every relevant topic. There are the requisite chapters on budgeting, committees, timelines, site and theme selection, publicity, and logistics—each of which is thorough and generous with forms, suggestions, and checklists. But the authors don't stop there. Drawing upon their experience of conducting events over the past two decades, they offer especially helpful chapters on keeping your volunteers involved, on avoiding pitfalls and disasters with a series of checkpoints, even precautionary measures to take to ensure a worry-free event. *Softcover, 233 pages, $62*

Telefundraising

Reach Out and Raise More Funds: Phonathon Training Videotape

(CASE PUBLICATIONS, 1986)

▶ Developed by the CASE Independent Schools Department and AT&T, this package can improve your phonathon results by showing this video to all of your volunteer callers. The video takes callers through all the steps, from greeting to closing. Volunteers will learn what to say and what not to say, appropriate attitude and tone, how to establish a rapport with the prospective donor, how to ask for the gift, how to show appreciation for a pledge, and how to handle rejection politely. The guide will help you set goals, develop a strategy, prepare prospects with advance mailings, recruit volunteers, and prepare for opening night. The package includes one 15-minute videotape, one administrative guide, and 10 tent cards. *Complete package: $25, Additional guides ($8), Additional tent cards ($6 for set of ten) (includes shipping)*

MicroMarketing: How to Attract Donors, Clients, Volunteers and Publicity *(See Marketing and Communications—General for full description)*

JOURNALS AND PERIODICALS

Advancing Philanthropy (Monthly Magazine)
Association of Fund Raising Professionals (formerly National Society of Fund Raising Executives), 1101 King Street, Suite 700, Alexandria, VA 22314-2967
Tel: 800-666-FUND; FAX: 703-684-0540
E-mail: ap@nsfre.org; WWW: http://www.nsfre.org

▶ This magazine provides practical information, useful tools, and other resources to help fund raisers at every practice level to do their jobs and advance professionally. It includes articles on practices, theories, and research in the field of fund raising. It also offers expert analyses of trends and issues affecting the practice of fund raising. Subjects covered include management, technical information, and philanthropy. Sections include Book Reviews, Employment Changes, and Developments. *$75/year (Individual), $125 (Organization)*

Aging News Alert (24 Issues)
CD Publications, 8204 Fenton Street, Silver Spring, MD 20910
Tel: 800-666-6380, 301-588-6380; FAX: 301-588-6385
E-mail: subscriptions@cdpublications.com, cdpubs@clark.net;
WWW: http://www.cdpublications.com/seniors/ana.htm

▶ This resource reports on successful senior programs, funding opportunities, and federal actions affecting the elderly. It covers the Older Americans Act, long-term care, Social Security and Medicare, transportation, health and nutrition, senior law, elder abuse, and much more. Every issue provides an independent outlook on congressional legislation and agency regulation, with inside news from the Administration on Aging, Social Security Administration, the National Institute on Aging, the Department of Health and Human Services, the Health Care Financing Administration, and the Department of Housing and Urban Development. It also contains interviews with government officials and association representatives and details how state and local governments provide critical services cost effectively. It also describes grants available from federal agencies such as the National Institutes of Health, the National Institute on Disability and Rehabilitation, and the Health Resources and Services Administration. In addition, *Aging News Alert* highlights corporate and foundation grants. *12–14 pages, $287/year*

Aid for Education Report (Twice-Monthly Newsletter)
CD Publications, 8204 Fenton Street, Silver Spring, MD 20910
Tel: 800-666-6380, 301-588-6380; FAX: 301-588-6385
E-mail: subscriptions@cdpublications.com, cdpubs@clark.net;
WWW: http://www.cdpublications.com/funding/afe.htm

▶ This newsletter provides the latest federal and private grant information and funding opportunities for all levels of education, including grants for special education, bilingual education, literacy, minorities, general education, higher education, at-risk youth, math and science education, technology, and curriculum development, with updates on application deadlines and eligibility criteria for forthcoming programs, financing levels, and budget trend. It also contains proposal writing tips and innovative fund-raising strategies. Regular features include Highlights, Washington Watch, Education in General, Grants & Notices, Higher Education, State & Local News, Funding Tips, Private Funding, Grant Update, and Publications. *14–18 pages, $319/year*

AIDS/STD News Report (Merged into Community Health Funding Report—see separate listing)

Arts & Culture Funding Report (Monthly Newsletter)
Capitol City Publishers, 1408 North Fillmore Street, Suite 3, Arlington, VA 22201-3819
Tel: 703-525-3080; 703-525-3044
E-mail: inquiry@capitolcitypublishers.com;
WWW: http://capitolcitypublishers.com/pubs/arts/index.html

▶ This newsletter covers federal, state, and private- and nonprofit-sector funding and financial assistance to arts and cultural organizations. Subscribers include grant seekers in museums, schools, art councils, libraries, or government organizations with responsibility for programs in dance, theater, music, visual arts, creative writing, or any other art form. Features include federal budget news, art education news, grants for artists, business–arts partnerships, and funding trends in the arts. Grant Alert section highlights upcoming grant application deadlines for federal and private-sector aid from the federal government, foundations, and corporations. *$178/year ($158 Web price)*

Canadian Fundraiser (Biweekly Newsletter)
Hilborn Communications Ltd., 109 Vanderhoof Avenue, Suite 205, Toronto, ON M4G 2H7, Canada
Tel: 800-461-1489, 416-696-8816; FAX: 416-424-3016
E-mail: circulation@hilborn.com, jimhilborn@hilborn.com
(James Hilborn, Publisher and Editor);
WWW: http://www.charityvillage.com/charityvillage/cfr.html

▶ This is the only independent newsletter for Canadian nonprofit managers. Each issue is filled with information regarding corporate giving, postal matters, accountability, planned giving, media, and PR. Regular features include short articles, Coming Events, In Brief, People, Letters to the Editor, and more. *8 pages, $197 CDN/year*

Case Currents (Monthly Magazine)
Council for Advancement and Support of Education, 1307 New York Avenue NW, Suite 1000, Washington, DC 20005-4701
Tel: 800-554-8536, 301-604-2068, 202-478-5662;
FAX: 202-387-4973
E-mail: membership@case.org, kent@case.org (Erica Kent);
WWW: http://www.case.org/CURRENTS/,
http://www.case.org/CURRENTS/archives.htm

▶ Features include: Public Relations, Alumni Relations, Student Recruitment. Columns include: Talking Points, Manager's Portfolio, Campaign Strategies, Tech Support, Closing Remarks. Departments include: Advance Work, In CASE. *$50/year (Member), $100 (Nonmember)*

Charitable Gift Planning News (Monthly Newsletter)

Moerschbaecher, McCoy & Simmons, P.O. Box 214373,
Dallas, TX 75221
Tel: 214-978-3325, 214-328-4244
E-mail: carolcgpn@aol.com (Carol Stone)

▶ You will benefit from this newsletter if you are advising clients on charitable transfers; advising charitable institutions; in development or planned giving; or an executive needing updates on latest charitable gift developments. Features include: Planner's Forum (monthly in-depth analysis of a topic of vital interest to charitable planners); IRS in the News (late-breaking developments from the Internal Revenue Service); Revenue Rulings and Private Letter Rulings of interest; Washington Report (new laws and proposed legislation); and Reader's Guide (books and articles on charitable subjects). *$168/year*

Children and Youth Funding Report (24 Issues)

CD Publications, 8204 Fenton Street, Silver Spring, MD 20910
Tel: 800-666-6380, 301-588-6380; FAX: 301-588-6385
E-mail: subscriptions@cdpublications.com, cdpubs@clark.net;
WWW: http://www.cdpublications.com/funding/cyf.htm

▶ This report contains detailed coverage of federal, foundation, and private grant opportunities for programs in such vital areas as public assistance, child welfare, juvenile justice, education, mental health, substance abuse, job training, disability services, health care, and other children-, youth-, and family-related areas. Plus, you'll find valuable advice from public and private officials on how to prepare winning proposals and case studies of successful fundraising activities, ranging from special events to direct-mail campaigns. It covers every department and agency in the field, including the Department of Health and Human Services, the Department of Justice, and the Centers for Disease Control and Prevention. It highlights funding from foundations such as the David and Lucille Packard Foundation, the Kellogg Foundation, and the Hazen Foundation. It provides updates on national and local news, with in-depth reports on welfare, the federal budget, and entitlement programs. It also features program ideas from around the country, to help children and youth service providers learn about innovative new strategies they can implement in their communities. *14–18 pages, $329/year*

The Chronicle of Philanthropy (Biweekly Newspaper)

Circulation Department, 1255 Twenty-Third Street NW,
Washington, DC 20037
Tel: 800-728-2819; FAX: 202-223-6292
E-mail: subscriptions@philanthropy.com,
editor@philanthropy.com; WWW: http://philanthropy.com

▶ This is the newspaper of the nonprofit world. Published every other week, it is the No. 1 news source for charity leaders, fund raisers, grant makers, and other people involved in the philanthropic enterprise. In print, *The Chronicle* is published biweekly except the last two weeks in June and the last two weeks in December (a total of 24 issues a year). A subscription includes full access to this Web site and news updates by e-mail, all at no extra charge. The Web site offers the complete contents of the new issue, an archive of articles from the past two years, and more than four years' worth of grant listings, all fully searchable. Some of this material is available only to *Chronicle* subscribers. The Guide to Grants is an electronic database of all foundation and corporate grants listed in *The Chronicle* since 1995. *Chronicle* subscribers can search grants from the two most recent issues. Complete access to the *Guide to Grants* requires a separate subscription. It offers free e-mail updates for nonsubscribers and e-mail newsletter especially for subscribers. *$67.50/year (print and online); Guide to Grants: $199/year*

Community Health Funding Report (24 Issues)

CD Publications, 8204 Fenton Street, Silver Spring, MD 20910
Tel: 800-666-6380, 301-588-6380; FAX: 301-588-6385
E-mail: subscriptions@cdpublications.com, cdpubs@clark.net;
WWW: http://www.cdpublications.com/funding/chf.htm

▶ This report helps nonprofit executive directors, program coordinators, and development directors maximize their fund-raising and grant-seeking effectiveness. It highlights funding sources for a wide range of health care concerns, including substance abuse, teen pregnancy, minority health care, maternal/child health, chronic illness, mental health, and AIDS programs. Each issue contains public and private grant announcements, interviews with grant officials, practical tips on preparing winning grant applications, case studies of effective fund-raising techniques, and updates on federal budget allocations. It also keeps health care professionals informed about federal agency actions and congressional developments that could affect funding for community programs. Examines how managed care and other changes in health care have affected the delivery of services at the local level. In-depth reports of model programs from around the country show administrators more effective ways to use limited resources. *14–18 pages, $319/year*

Computer Grants Alert (Monthly Newsletter)

Aspen Publishers
Corporate headquarters: 200 Orchard Ridge Drive,
Gaithersburg, MD 20878
Tel: 301-417-7500; FAX: 301-695-7931

Distribution center: 7201 McKinney Circle, Frederick, MD 21701
Tel: 800-234-1660, 301-698-7100; FAX: 301-695-7931
E-mail: customer.service@aspenpubl.com;
WWW: http://www.aspenpub.com, http://www.grantscape.com

▶ This publication helps you find and win computer-related funds for services and equipment for your organization. It reveals the grants you need for networks, hardware software, wiring, training, the Internet, and more. Each issue includes everything you need to apply for and win computer-related grants, including complete contact information, the scope of the grant, deadlines, eligibility requirements, and more. Each issue is also filled with grantwinning tips and strategies. *12 pages, $205/year*

Contributions (Magazine—Six Issues)

Emerson & Church Publishers, P.O. Box 338, Medfield, MA 02052
Tel: 508-359-0019; FAX: 508-359-8084
E-mail: contrib.@ziplink.net;
WWW: http://www.contributionsmagazine.com

▶ This magazine provides advice on fund raising and nonprofit management. Selected articles from the current and back issues of *Contributions* are available on the magazine's Web site. Other Web site features include Marketplace (Wise Buyer's Guide), Bookstore (The Compleat Professional's Library), and WOW (Who Offers What). *$36/year*

Corporate Giving Watch (Monthly Newsletter)

Street address: The Taft Group, Gale Communications,
27500 Drake Road, Farmington, MI 48331

Mailing address: P.O. Box 9187, Farmington Hills, MI 48333-9187
Tel: 800-877-8238
E-mail: referencedesk@galegroup.com;
WWW: http://www.taftgroup.com

▶ This monthly newsletter profiles corporate funding and provides tips on obtaining corporate grants. Each issue brings you news, analysis, and statistics on the people, organizations, and events that affect the industry and its relationship with the nonprofit sector. Each issue includes: FunderSearch: complimentary customized searches in different key program and geographic areas each month; highlights companies and their foundations who have given in the chosen subject area; Looking Further: uncovering little-known and underutilized funding opportunities; Recent Grants: Tracking trends by reporting on the "who" and "how-much" of specific grants; Corporate Giving Profiles: detailed analysis of six newly updated corporate givers; Quick Takes: informative news column—when Microsoft gives away millions, we know about it; and annual "Top Ten" listings: exclusive, detailed ratings of the year's top corporate givers. *20 pages, $149/year*

Corporate Philanthropy Report (Monthly Newsletter)

Aspen Publishers
Corporate headquarters: 200 Orchard Ridge Drive,
Gaithersburg, MD 20878
Tel: 301-417-7500; FAX: 301-695-7931

Distribution center: 7201 McKinney Circle, Frederick, MD 21701
Tel: 800-234-1660, 301-698-7100; FAX: 301-695-7931
E-mail: customer.service@aspenpubl.com;
WWW: http://www.aspenpub.com, http://www.grantscape.com

▶ This publication is devoted to the development of strategic alliances between the business and nonprofit worlds. It discloses exclusive, hard-to-find information that would be expensive and time consuming—if not impossible—to research yourself. It helps you find out which companies are setting corporate giving pace. Discover which industries are aligning themselves with specific causes, why they are doing so, and how you can successfully approach them; discover how to take advantage of opportunities for donations that go beyond cash, such as sponsorships, technology and equipment, use of corporate personnel and resources, and more. Identify and respond to trends in corporate philanthropy so you can position your programs for future success. Improve your image in the community and promote support for your programs. You get the corporate as well as the nonprofit view, so you can see how both sides partner to create successful, long-term alliances. Plus, every issue analyzes giving patterns in specific industries. Each article contains contact names and phone numbers so you can follow up. *$238/year*

Criminal Justice Funding Report (Biweekly Newsletter)

Capitol City Publishers, 1408 North Fillmore Street, Suite 3,
Arlington, VA 22201-3819
Tel: 703-525-3080; FAX: 703-525-3044
E-mail: inquiry@capitolcitypublishers.com;
WWW: http://capitolcitypublishers.com/pubs/crime/index.html

▶ This newsletter covers federal and private-sector funding and financial assistance for law enforcement, courts, and correctional institutions. Subscribers include grant seekers in police or sheriff departments, correctional institutions, state and local governments, public agencies, community and victim-assistance groups, and youth and nonprofit organizations. Features include new and proposed federal grant programs, federal budget news, key legislation, funding trends and priorities, and appropriations for law enforcement and criminal justice grants. Grant & Regulation Alert section highlights upcoming grant application deadlines for receiving financial and technical assistance from the federal government, foundations, and corporations. It also includes a conference calendar and profiles of private funding sources. *$258/year ($218 Web price)*

Development Director's Letter (Monthly Newsletter)

CD Publications, 8204 Fenton Street, Silver Spring, MD 20910
Tel: 800-666-6380, 301-588-6380; FAX: 301-588-6385
E-mail: subscriptions@cdpublications.com,
DDL@cdpublications.com (Mark Sherman, Editor);
WWW: http://www.cdpublications.com/funding/ddl.htm

▶ This newsletter offers grant-seeking tips and fund-raising strategies to help nonprofit and government administrators win additional support for programs in health care, education, family services, child welfare, crime prevention, and other critical areas. It includes grant application critiques, how-to advice, interviews with grant reviewers, and timely updates on private and federal funding trends. It also highlights Washington news that could have an impact on nonprofit fund raising, including congressional legislation, IRS regulations, and Postal Service proposals. It is specifically geared toward nonprofits who seek *both* federal assistance and private fund-raising support, and is an excellent complement to any of our newsletters on private and public grant opportunities. *8–10 pages, $199/year*

Direct Marketing (Monthly Magazine)

Hoke Communications, Inc., 224 Seventh Street,
Garden City, NY 11530-5771
Tel: 800-229-6700, 516-746-6700; FAX: 516-294-8141

▶ Since 1938, this trade magazine has covered all facets of direct marketing. This includes the use of direct mail, telephone marketing, lists and databases, creative strategies, computer software, plus other timely issues and trends affecting today's direct marketers. Each issue brings you the best in direct marketing. Each monthly issue features case studies, up-close analysis of issues, and solution-savvy articles, like "Opening Doors to Retail Stores: Infomercials with Shelf Space for Your Products"; "Selling Art Through Catalogs"; "Copy Talk: Learn Habits that Make You a Better Direct Marketer"; and "Cataloging for Entrepreneurs." Issues frequently cover: Internet marketing; database marketing; direct-mail writing; marketing strategies; catalog marketing; and direct response. It is read by top catalogers, retailers, manufacturers, ad agency executives, list brokers, and other professionals whose business depends on staying up-to-date on issues in direct response advertising. In addition to breaking industry news, case histories, and profiles, a typical year of *Direct Marketing* features subjects like mail order, telemarketing, Internet marketing, alternate delivery, creative lead generation, computer software, and Infomercials, plus forecasting and a review of the year's trendsetting direct-response ad campaigns. In addition to *Direct Marketing* magazine, Hoke Communications also publishes a weekly newsletter for the direct marketing profession: *Friday Report.* Written by the editors of *Direct Marketing, Friday Report* keeps you up to the minute on postal issues, legislation, and new ideas in direct-response advertising. It mails Friday evening to be on your desk Monday morning. A one-year subscription (51 issues) is $165.

Disability Funding News (24 Issues)

CD Publications, 8204 Fenton Street, Silver Spring, MD 20910
Tel: 800-666-6380, 301-588-6380; FAX: 301-588-6385
E-mail: subscriptions@cdpublications.com, cdpubs@clark.net;
WWW: http://www.cdpublications.com/funding/dfn.htm

▶ This publication provides details on public and private funding opportunities for a wide range of programs, in areas such as emotional disabilities, physical handicaps, learning disabilities, visual impairment, autism, speech impairment, multiple handicaps, and many others. There are grants for housing, transportation, rehabilitation, research, special education, and more. In addition to tips from grant officials and fund-raising consultants, case studies reveal what works and doesn't work for other nonprofit and agency executives. It also reports on congressional legislation and agency actions that might affect programs for the disabled, and covers the work of major advocacy groups, such as the National Organization on Disability and the Easter Seal Society. It highlights significant legal developments nationwide and summarizes state and local news stories. *14–18 pages, $319/year*

Drug Abuse Funding Monitor (Monthly Newsletter)

Capitol City Publishers, 1408 North Fillmore Street, Suite 3, Arlington, VA 22201-3819
Tel: 703-525-3080; FAX: 703-525-3044
E-mail: inquiry@capitolcitypublishers.com;
WWW: http://capitolcitypublishers.com/pubs/drug/index.html

▶ This newsletter covers federal and private-sector funding and financial assistance for drug and alcohol programs, law enforcement agencies, and drug courts. Subscribers include grant seekers in state and local governments, public housing agencies, schools, law enforcement agencies, treatment and rehabilitation centers, outreach programs, hospitals, halfway houses, and community youth and nonprofit groups. Features include new and proposed federal grant programs, federal budget news, key legislation, funding trends and priorities, and appropriations for drug treatment and prevention grants. Grant & Regulation Alert section highlights upcoming grant application deadlines for receiving financial and technical assistance from the federal government, foundations, and corporations. It also includes a conference calendar and profiles of private funding sources. *$257/year ($217 Web price)*

EGA Updates (Quarterly Newsletter)

Environmental Grantmakers Association,
437 Madison Ave, 37th Floor, New York, NY 10022
Tel: 212-812-4260; FAX: 212-812-4299
E-mail: ega@rffund.org; WWW: http://www.ega.org/aboutus.html

▶ This newsletter provides Association news, updates on member foundations, and lists of recent environmental grants made by EGA participants.

Education Daily (Newsletter, 245 Issues)

Corporate headquarters: 200 Orchard Ridge Drive, Gaithersburg, MD 20878
Tel: 301-417-7500; FAX: 301-695-7931

Distribution center: 7201 McKinney Circle, Frederick, MD 21701
Tel: 800-234-1660, 800-638-8437, 301-698-7100;
FAX: 301-695-7931
E-mail: customer.service@aspenpubl.com;
WWW: http://www.aspenpub.com, http://www.grantscape.com, http://www.educationdaily.com/pages/catalog/dailycopy.html

▶ This independent daily publication is for educational professionals and policy makers. Devoted to covering the news on national education policy, *Education Daily* helps you keep your schools in compliance with federal laws and regulations, protect your schools from legal challenges, and use practical techniques to manage your schools and maximize learning. *Education Daily* helps you prepare in advance for changes to general laws and regulations that affect your programs, shape federal education policy, protect your eligibility for federal funding, keep your schools out of legal hot water, get early alerts to grant opportunities, including scope of the grant, eligibility, deadline, funding amount and contact, and more. Also available online and via e-mail. *$599/year*

Education Funding News (Weekly Newsletter)

Headquarters office: Thompson Publishing Group, Inc., Government Information Services, Education Funding Research Council, 1725 K Street NW, Suite 700, Washington, DC 20006
Tel: 800-876-0226, 202-872-4000

Thompson Fulfillment Services: 5201 W. Kennedy Boulevard, Suite 905, Tampa, FL 33609-1823
Tel: 813-282-8807

E-mail: service@thompson.com; WWW: http://www.thompson.com/libraries/grantseeking/knew/index.html

▶ Provides information on educational funding from federal, corporate, and foundation sources; legislation; and regulations. It guides readers through the world of education funding, legislation and regulation. *Education Funding News* includes a wealth of information on federal and foundation funding opportunities, analysis of education-related programs, funding news, and grant deadline calendars. Subscribers are kept up to date on the latest program and regulatory changes from the U.S. Department of Education, as well as information about lesser known education programs operated by other federal agencies. Of special interest to grant seekers and program managers are the grant and regulation alerts, which offer readers time-saving summaries of regulatory notices affecting grant-in-aid programs and notices of funding availability that appear in the *Federal Register*. Subscribers may receive e-mail versions of the grant and regulation alerts, which will arrive days before the printed version, as well as access to online calendars of application deadlines for federal funding. A quarterly newsletter index is also provided. *$298/year*

Education Grants Alert (Newsletter, 50 Issues)

Aspen Publishers
Corporate headquarters: 200 Orchard Ridge Drive, Gaithersburg, MD 20878
Tel: 301-417-7500; FAX: 301-695-7931

Distribution center: 7201 McKinney Circle, Frederick, MD 21701
Tel: 800-234-1660, 301-698-7100; FAX: 301-695-7931
E-mail: customer.service@aspenpubl.com;
WWW: http://www.aspenpub.com, http://www.grantscape.com, http://www.educationdaily.com/pages/catalog/egasamp.html

▶ This newsletter helps elementary and secondary school grant seekers win more money for their schools by saving research time, providing tips to maximize their chance of success, and alerting them to new funding opportunities and spelling out the details needed to apply for a grant. It provides information on federal and nonfederal funding available for K–12 programs, application deadlines, and tips on how to prepare better proposals. Win more grants with this comprehensive source of funding opportunities for K–12 grant seekers. *Education Grants Alert* reveals the grants you need for every kind of program: math and science education, technology education, special education, vocational education, crime prevention, teacher training, computers and other technology, and other K–12 programs! You'll get early notice of federal funding opportunities—weeks or even months before the formal application notice appears elsewhere—including all the details necessary to apply funding priorities, grant amounts, deadlines, eligibility requirements, and the primary contact's name and telephone number. Plus, you'll get regular updates on hard-to-find sources of private funding, including those specially tailored to your geographic region. *Education Grants Alert* features regular columns from top education grants consultants, which give you inside advice and expert strategies on how to maximize your chances of success. *$329/year*

Education USA (Biweekly Newsletter)

Aspen Publishers
Corporate headquarters: 200 Orchard Ridge Drive,
Gaithersburg, MD 20878
Tel: 301-417-7500; FAX: 301-695-7931

Distribution Center: 7201 McKinney Circle, Frederick, MD 21701
Tel: 800-234-1660, 301-698-7100; FAX: 301-695-7931
E-mail: customer.service@aspenpubl.com;
WWW: http://www.aspenpub.com, http://www.grantscape.com

▶ This newsletter provides information on U.S. Department of Education policies on special education, bilingual education, Title I programs, and drug-free schools. It includes legislative updates and federal grant funding available. It gives you a concise, easy-to-read overview of everything you need to know in education, from effective classroom practices and avoiding liability to general funding and regulation. *Education USA* helps school administrators stay in compliance with federal laws and regulations, set and meet high academic standards, make your schools safer places, enhance teachers' content knowledge and classroom skills, maximize your share of federal funding, and more. *$195/year*

Events: Ideas & Resources for Fundraising Events (Bimonthly Newsletter)

P.O. Box 3206, University City, MO 63130-0606
Tel: 314-726-0651
E-mail: events@sprintmail.com (Michael Donovan, Publisher and Editor)

▶ This newsletter is dedicated to providing bottom-line ideas and to-the-point resources for the special event fund raiser. It will give you the edge you need to stay ahead in this competitive field. Filled with news, it covers successful special events, tips on managing volunteers, resources for getting sponsors, and how to maximize both publicity and profits. Regular features include: Event$ Reports (six executive reports on successful event fund raisers from around the country); Event$ Worksheet (a ready-to-copy worksheet that will make your event planning more efficient and effective); Event$ File (a swipe file of ideas and resources you can use); Ask Event$ (submit your toughest problems to the question-and-answer forum); Event$ To Do List (an action list of professional tasks designed to keep you focused and productive); Event$ Index (indexed annually, Event$ will become an easy-to-use reference). *16 pages, $45*

501(c)(3) Monthly Letter (Monthly Newsletter)

Great Oaks Communication Services, 400 Chestnut Street,
P.O. Box 192, Atlantic, IA 50022
Tel: 712-243-5257; FAX: 712-243-2775
E-mail: jkenney@nishna.net;
WWW: http://www.nishna.net/501c3/index.html

▶ This newsletter features articles by leaders in the nonprofit world on such varied topics as fund raising, grants, computerization, communication, special events, working with volunteers, selecting board members, attracting media attention, postal rate savings, and more. Regular features include The Grant Doctor by Dr. Donald Levitan, Suffolk University: Book Reviews and a Calendar of Events featuring nonprofit association conferences across the nation. *12 pages, $46/year*

FRM Weekly (Newsletter)

Hoke Communications, Inc., 224 Seventh Street,
Garden City, NY 11530-5771
Tel: 800-229-6700, 516-746-6700; FAX: 516-294-8141

▶ Written by the editors of *Fund Raising Management* magazine (see separate listing), it is the timeliest source of fund-raising information available. This weekly alert service is designed to keep professional development directors fully informed about late breaking news in the fund-raising field. It provides news of significant campaigns and techniques being used by successful institutions, up-to-the-minute notice of meetings to attend, moves of development directors, and current legislation and regulation of concern to nonprofit institutions. It includes access to "Direct Marketing on Grayfire," an interactive fax-on-demand database by dialing 800-866-2435 and entering your personal identification number. *$115/year*

Family Services Report (24 Issues)

CD Publications, 8204 Fenton Street, Silver Spring, MD 20910
Tel: 800-666-6380, 301-588-6380; FAX: 301-588-6385
E-mail: subscriptions@cdpublications.com, cdpubs@clark.net;
WWW: http://www.cdpublications.com/funding/fsr.htm

▶ This twice-monthly publication contains federal, foundation, and corporate grants for family service programs. It covers the impact of welfare reform on state/local efforts to prevent child abuse and neglect and provide transitional housing and job training, plus details on successful family service programs. It provides the latest on shifting state and federal family policies, comprehensive grant information, and practical proposal-writing tips, all in one convenient source. It contains federal and private grant opportunities for programs in domestic violence, transitional housing, child abuse and neglect, mental health, and substance abuse. There are grants from the Department of Health and Human Services, Department of Education, Department of Labor, and the National Institute of Justice, as well as funding announcements from foundations such as the Robert Wood Johnson Foundation and the Pew Charitable Trusts. It also analyzes the impact that new legislation, such as the welfare reform bill, has on family service programs, including funding for child care, abstinence education, and employment placement. Case studies of successful model programs detail how family service providers are responding to changes in the political environment. *14–18 pages, $319/year*

Federal Assistance Monitor (24 Issues)

CD Publications, 8204 Fenton Street, Silver Spring, MD 20910
Tel: 800-666-6380, 301-588-6380; FAX: 301-588-6385
E-mail: subscriptions@cdpublications.com, cdpubs@clark.net;
WWW: http://www.cdpublications.com/funding/fam.htm

▶ This twice-monthly publication provides a comprehensive review of federal funding announcements, private grants, rule changes, and legislative actions affecting social services, education, health, housing, and other community programs. It also contains

537

grant tips, budget analyses, program previews, and funding trends. It features a comprehensive review of federal funding announcements, private grants, and legislative actions affecting community programs, including education, economic development, housing, children and youth services, substance abuse, and health care. Each grant notice is categorized by subject matter. For foundations it indicates areas of interest and projected grant awards, as well as funding priorities for both national and regional organizations. In addition, each issue contains proposal-writing tips to help grant coordinators and development professionals write more successful applications. It also offers advice from grant officials on exactly what funders are looking for, and details key points from fund-raising workshops sponsored by the Foundation Center, the Support Center, and other public and private agencies. It includes reports on congressional legislation, with insightful analysis of what might happen to specific programs as a result of policy shifts and changes in budget appropriations. It frequently obtains advance notice of proposed regulations, agency memoranda, and other items unavailable elsewhere. *16–18 pages, $329/year*

Federal Grants & Contracts Weekly (Newsletter, 50 Issues)

Aspen Publishers
Corporate headquarters: 200 Orchard Ridge Drive,
Gaithersburg, MD 20878
Tel: 301-417-7500; FAX: 301-695-7931

Distribution center: 7201 McKinney Circle, Frederick, MD 21701
Tel: 800-234-1660, 301-698-7100; FAX: 301-695-7931
E-mail: customer.service@aspenpubl.com;
WWW: http://www.aspenpub.com, http://www.grantscape.com,
http://www.educationdaily.com/pages/catalog/fgcwsamp.html

▶ *Federal Grants & Contracts Weekly* helps readers find and win federal grants and contracts. It flags the latest funding opportunities in all areas across all agencies and tells how to pursue them. The newsletter alerts readers early to future funding, signaling specific solicitations often months in advance, unveiling agency grant plans in progress, tracking trends, and forecasting areas of funding growth. Articles pass on advice from the experts and help readers calculate their chances and locate key prospecting resources. This comprehensive weekly newsletter brings you early alerts to the newest funding opportunities from all federal agencies—at least a dozen grant announcements in every issue (they'll tip you off to competitions that haven't been published); a broad spectrum of funding opportunities—including education, scientific and social research, community development, health, criminal justice, and more; insider tips on the details of federal grant programs and what the agencies are looking for in proposals and how to make your applications stand out from the crowd; up-to-the minute news analysis on what the administration, legislators, and regulators are up to; foundation and private grant opportunities that you might be eligible for—you'll find them in a special monthly supplement, *Foundation Grants Alert.* Regular features include: Congressional Action, Community Services, Education, Research, Private Giving, Special Report, What Works, Resources/Reports, Grant Update. Additional services include: (1) "Grant Tips," a grant seeker's primer offering proposal-writing advice from leading professionals that can help ensure your applications have the best chance of success, (2) Application Advisor Service (free grant application critique), (3) Grants Hotline, and (4) Document Service (fee-based, access to hard-to-find regulations, agency memos, and *Federal Register* notes within 24 hours). *$398/year*

Federal Register (Daily, except federal government holidays)

Office of the Federal Register, National Archives and Records Administration, Washington, DC 20408
Tel: 202-783-3238

Superintendent of Documents, New Orders (Subscription),
P.O. Box 371954, Pittsburgh, PA 15250
Tel: 202-512-1800; FAX: 2020512-2250
E-mail: info@fedreg.nara.gov; WWW: http://www.nara.gov/fedreg/

▶ This is a legal newspaper published every business day by the National Archives and Records Administration (NARA). It contains federal agency regulations; proposed rules and notices; and executive orders, proclamations, and other Presidential documents. The *Federal Register* informs citizens of their rights and obligations and provides access to a wide range of federal benefits and opportunities for funding. NARA's Office of the *Federal Register* prepares the Federal Register for publication in partnership with the Government Printing Office (GPO), which distributes it on paper, on microfiche, and on the World Wide Web. It provides information about newly announced federal funding opportunities, making it an essential resource for keeping abreast of new grant programs and new competitions of established grant programs (see also *Catalog of Federal Domestic Assistance* listing under Publications). Search by federal agency, date of issue, or subject category. Free access to the online *Federal Register* and Code of Federal Regulations (CFR) is available at GPO Access: *http://www.access.gpo.gov/nara.* *$340/year*

Florida Funding Newsletter (Monthly Newsletter)

Florida Funding Publications, P.O. Box 561565, Miami, FL 33256
Tel: 305-251-2203; FAX: 305-251-2773
E-mail: Info@FloridaFunding.com;
WWW: http://www.floridafunding.com

▶ Each month, the newsletter provides you with thorough, up-to-date information about federal, state, foundation, and corporate grant programs. These programs are available for Florida nonprofit, educational, and governmental entities. Regular newsletter categories include Announcement of Awards, New Programs, Legislative Information, Deadlines, and much more. Not only will it help you find grants, it will also help you win them with monthly feature articles that focus on increasing the skills of Florida grant seekers. Along with the feature article, the newsletter includes program descriptions, deadlines, grant awards, conference information, profiles of Florida's corporate giving programs, and details about recent grant recipients. *8 pages, $142*

Foundation & Corporate Grants Alert (Monthly Newsletter)

Aspen Publishers
Corporate headquarters: 200 Orchard Ridge Drive,
Gaithersburg, MD 20878
Tel: 301-417-7500; FAX: 301-695-7931

Distribution center: 7201 McKinney Circle, Frederick, MD 21701
Tel: 800-234-1660, 301-698-7100; FAX: 301-695-7931
E-mail: customer.service@aspenpubl.com;
WWW: http://www.aspenpub.com, http://www.grantscape.com

▶ This newsletter helps grant seekers find and win private and corporate support. It provides comprehensive coverage of available national and local funding well in advance of deadlines, and reveals proven techniques and inside information on how to win more money. With *Foundation & Corporate Grants Alert,* you'll get the details you need concerning the exact foundation or corporation most likely to fund your projects. Every month, you'll uncover information on funding opportunities, new foundations, and hard-to-find regional funders. You'll also get to know foundation and corporate funders from the inside, with foundation profiles and interviews with program officers. Detailed grant notices alert you to upcoming proposal deadlines, funding levels, funders' priorities, and the program officer's name and phone number. In addition, subscribers can contact the publisher with grant-seeking questions, to be answered each month by an expert in private grant seeking. *$318/year*

Foundation Giving Watch (Monthly Newsletter)

Street address: The Taft Group, Gale Communications, 27500 Drake Road, Farmington, MI 48331

Mailing address: P.O. Box 9187, Farmington Hills, MI 48333-9187
Tel: 800-877-8238
E-mail: referencedesk@galegroup.com;
WWW: http://www.taftgroup.com,
http://www.taftgroup.com/taft/newsltrs.html#fgw

▶ Each issue carries timely news and analysis on the individuals, organizations, and events that make a difference in achieving goals. It includes detailed profiles of new sources of funding, biographies of decision makers, notes on organizational changes, specifics of recent grants, and unique sources for specific types of grants. Regular columns include: FunderSearch: complimentary customized searches in different key program and geographic areas each month; highlights foundations who have given in the chosen subject area; Recent Grants: details on who gives what to whom; Foundation Hotline: up-to-the-minute changes of address, personnel, and operations; New Foundations: Profiles of newly created foundations; Annual "Top Ten" list: Eagerly awaited, exclusive ranking of private giving. *20 pages, $149/year*

Foundation & Corporate Funding Advantage (Monthly Newsletter)

Progressive Business Publications, 370 Technology Drive, Malvern, PA 19355-9863
Tel: 800-220-8600, 610-695-8600; FAX: 610-647-8089
E-mail: Customer_Service@pbp.com;
WWW: http://www.pbp.com/np.html

▶ This newsletter uncovers national and regional grant opportunities for private funds and provides busy nonprofit fund raisers with inside information for getting foundation and corporate grants. The newsletter not only provides a current listing of leads and new grant opportunities, it offers methods for handling and managing pressure associated with raising funds, including examples of how smart nonprofits position themselves as strong candidates for private funds. Every issue is filled with information about finding grant makers that have a matching cause, getting grants for seed or new projects, and developing long-term relationships with donors or grant makers. Regular sections include: Applying for a Grant, New Grant Announcements, Regional Grant Opportunities, What Worked for Other Grant-Seekers, and Hottest Current Source. *8 pages, $240/year*

The Foundation Grants Index Quarterly

The Foundation Center, 79 Fifth Avenue, New York, NY 10003-3076
Tel: 800-424-9836, 212-620-4230; FAX: 212-807-3677
WWW: http://fdncenter.org/marketplace/catalog/giq.html

▶ This subscription service provides the most current information on new grant-making programs and trends on foundation funding

every three months; updated supplement to *The Foundation Grants Index* and the subject-specific guides from the Foundation Center (see separate listings under Publications) listing more than 5,000 grants of $10,000 or more awarded by about 840 of the largest independent, corporate, and community foundations per issue, arranged by state. Grants are listed by donor foundation, and indexed by subject keyword and recipient. It contains updates on grant makers that note changes in foundation address, personnel, program interests, and application procedures, and more. Also included is a list of grant makers' new annual reports, information brochures, grants lists, newsletters, and other publications issued by foundations. A discount is available when ordering with *The Foundation Grants Index*. *Approx. 200 pages per issue, $95/year (includes shipping and handling)*

Foundation News & Commentary (Bimonthly Magazine)

Council on Foundations, Inc., 1828 L Street NW, Washington, DC 20036
Tel: 800-771-8187, 202-466-6512
E-mail: fnceditor@cof.org;
WWW: http://www.cof.org/foundationnews/1100/index.htm

▶ This publication is for foundation grant seekers. It includes articles on grant writing, exploring new technologies, management and planning, and issues and trends of foundations. Regular departments include: At Issue, Feedback, Of All Things, Clips, Affinities, RAGs, Great Grants, People, Releases, and Givers. An abridged version is available online. *$48 (Member), $88 (Nonmember)*

Fund Raising Management (Monthly Magazine)

Hoke Communications, Inc., 224 Seventh Street, Garden City, NY 11530-5771
Tel: 800-229-6700 (outside New York), 516-746-6700; FAX: 516-294-8141

▶ This magazine presents articles of interest to fund raisers, including special reports related to capital campaigns, direct mail and telemarketing, entrepreneurship, communications, computers, and legal issues. It includes a calendar of events and current topics and strategies in fund raising. Special feature articles provide helpful management and practical information for the fund-raising executive. Conference reports keep readers up to date on issues and trends. Every issue includes a development section, calendar of events, club news, newsmakers, marketplace, cassettes, fund-raising directory, and a classified section. It is geared toward the low-budget organization, with how-to articles on all aspects of fund raising and reports on successful campaigns and methods. It covers the people, issues, and events in fund raising, as well as the services, products, and techniques useful to fund raisers. Every issue focuses on one or more major aspects of fund raising, including direct mail techniques and ideas, planned giving for your future, telemarketing without tears, finding and dealing with donors, how to plan and use special events, back to fund-raising basics, computer software for nonprofits (annual review offers advice for selecting the best programs available), recruiting and using volunteers, capital campaigns, ethics and financial disclosure issues, selecting and using consultants, year's best nonprofit campaigns, and more. It features the "Copy Corner" column by Con Squires, and includes access to fund-raising information, the HCI Book, and audio and video libraries. *$58/year*

Funding Alert Newsletter (Monthly Newsletter)

Research Associates, P.O. Box 1755, Irmo, SC 29063-1755
Tel: 803-750-9759
E-mail: contact@grantexperts.com (Mike Dubose, President and Publisher); WWW: http://www.researchassociatesco.com/ funding_alert_newsletter.htm

▶ This nationally focused grants newsletter identifies 80+ new funding sources every 30 days from the federal government, large corporations, and foundations. It also includes employment opportunities for grant writers. *20 pages, $119/year*

Fundraiser's Guide (Monthly Newsletter)

Arkansas Support Network, Inc., 3380 North Par Court, Fayetteville, AR 72703
Tel: 800-748-9768, 501-587-1636
E-mail: subs@fundraisers-guide.com;
WWW: http://www.fundraisers-guide.com/articles.htm

▶ A fund-raising newsletter made specifically for the small nonprofit, the *Fundraiser's Guide* provides the latest information on these important topics: special-events fund raising: a powerful public relations tool; includes: Planned giving: It can work for the small nonprofit; How to increase your income through effective grant proposal writing; Should you ever hire an outside fundraiser? How the small nonprofit can succeed with direct mail fundraising; Unrelated business income: When is fund raising subject to taxation? Select articles and an archive are available online. *$32/year*

The Grant Advisor (11 issues, monthly except July)

P.O. Box 650518, Potomac Falls, VA 20165
Tel: 703-421-6061; FAX: 815361-2971
E-mail: kit@grantadvisor.com (Christopher "Kit" Watkins, Publisher and Editor); WWW: http://www.grantadvisor.com

▶ Since 1983, *The Grant Advisor* has been a leading source of information on grant and fellowship opportunities for U.S. institutions of higher education and their faculty. It covers grant opportunities from federal agencies (except NIH) as well as many independent organizations and foundations. Published monthly (except July), each issue contains 20 to 25 program reviews with descriptions, eligibility requirements, special criteria, funding amounts, and contact information (including phone and FAX numbers, e-mail and Web addresses). The remainder of the newsletter is composed of the *Deadline Memo,* with more than 300 listings of grant and fellowship programs for the coming four months, organized into eight academic divisions (fine arts, humanities, sciences, social sciences, education, international, health related, and unrestricted/other). It is available online in both PDF (Adobe Acrobat®) and TXT (ASCII text) formats. Additional electronic services are also offered (see Internet Resources section). *$198/year*

Grants for School Districts (Biweekly Newsletter)

Quinlan Publishing Group, 23 Drydock Avenue, Boston, MA 02210-2387
Tel: 800-229-2084, 617-542-0048; FAX: 617-345-9646
E-mail: info@quinlan.com; WWW: http://www.quinlan.com/, http://www.schoollaw-funding.com/gsd.html

▶ This newsletter provides current listings of available grants, foundations, school programs, and business partnerships. It also includes important deadlines from the *Federal Register,* online resource listings, and regional grants update, plus an inside track on the U.S. Department of Education. *$149/year*

Grantseekers Horizon (Ten-Issue Newsletter)

Nonprofit Resources, Inc., 500 Broadway, Suite 403, Little Rock, AR 72201-3342
Tel: 501-374-8515; FAX: 501-374-6548
E-mail: bjohnson@nonprofitarkansas.org (Bonnie Johnson); WWW: http://www.nonprofitarkansas.org/

▶ This newsletter provides information on philanthropy from foundations, corporations, and government sources plus the latest news and tools for nonprofit organizations. Each issue contains listings of grants available from governments, foundations, and other sources; tips for successful grant seeking; tools of the trade: publications, workshops, conferences, Web sites; and information on nonprofit governance and management. It includes information about government and private grant makers; current RFPs; nonprofit governance and management; and resources for nonprofits. The content is somewhat focused on the state of Arkansas, but 80 to 90 percent of it is relevant to other states. *12 pages, $75/year*

Grant$line Monthly (Monthly Newsletter)

Bev Browning & Associates, 1990 North Alma School Road, P.O. Box 3020-504, Chandler, AZ 85244
Tel: 480-786-9465; FAX: 480-899-0233
E-mail: grantsline@home.com;
WWW: http://www.grantsconsulting.com/

▶ Each issue features local, state, federal, and foundation funding opportunities. Information includes dollars available, category, eligibility, source contact person and address, and deadline. Information is provided about grants-related workshops and other significant funding information important to your organization. *$99/year*

The Grantsmanship Center Magazine

1125 W. Sixth Street, Fifth Floor, P.O. Box 17220, Los Angeles, CA 90017
Tel: 213-482-9860; FAX: 213-482-9863
E-mail: susan@tgci.com (Subscriptions);
WWW: http://www.tgci.com/publications/magazine.htm

▶ Filled with information on how to plan, manage, staff, and fund the programs of nonprofit organizations and government agencies. You may access articles from recent issues on agency management; proposal writing/grant seeking; foundation/corporate funding; government funding; fund raising; nonprofit business ventures; Internet issues; consulting; nonprofit law; and international funding. Both the current and back issues of *The Grantsmanship Center Magazine,* a quarterly newspaper on nonprofit management and fund raising, are available on the Grantsmanship Center's Web site.

Grassroots Fundraising Journal (Bimonthly Magazine)

Chardon Press, 3781 Broadway, Oakland, CA 94611
Tel: 888-458-8588, 510-596-8160
E-mail: chardon@chardonpress.com;
WWW: http://www.chardonpress.com

▶ This publication will help you raise money from community-based sources. Learn how to increase your income and diversify your sources of funding using proven, practical strategies, including special events, direct mail, major donor programs, membership campaigns, and more. *$32/year*

Health Grants Funding Alert (Monthly Newsletter)

Health Resources Publishing, 1913 Atlantic Avenue, Suite F-4,
Manasquan, NJ 08376
Tel: 732-292-1100; FAX: 732-292-1111
E-mail: hrp@healthrespubs.com

Customer Service: P.O. Box 456, Allenwood, NJ 08720
Tel: 888-843-6242; FAX: 888-329-6242
WWW: http://www.healthrespubs.com/

▶ Published monthly since 1978, it identifies opportunities for federal, corporate, and foundation support of health care. In addition to alerting development professionals as to requests for proposals and upcoming application deadlines, it tracks where health care grant making has been and in which areas there is likely to be growth and future opportunities. It also provides proven tips for grant-seeking success and in-depth profiles of health care grant makers. In each issue you'll learn the latest funding interests of the nation's leading health granting foundations. You'll discover what types of projects are being funded. You'll get descriptions of specific health funding programs. You'll have at your fingertips details including the number of grants that may be funded for a certain program, dollar amounts of grants, and ranges of grant funds that each of the major foundations has awarded. *$237/year*

Health Grants & Contracts Weekly (Weekly Newsletter)

Aspen Publishers
Corporate headquarters: 200 Orchard Ridge Drive,
Gaithersburg, MD 20878
Tel: 301-417-7500; FAX: 301-695-7931

Distribution center: 7201 McKinney Circle, Frederick, MD 21701
Tel: 800-234-1660, 301-698-7100; FAX: 301-695-7931
E-mail: customer.service@aspenpubl.com;
WWW: http://www.aspenpub.com, http://www.grantscape.com

▶ This newsletter helps you uncover funding opportunities in every health-related area: aging, AIDS, maternal and child health, substance abuse, disease and injury prevention, basic biology, disabilities, Alzheimer's disease and related disorders, family violence, social sciences, biotechnology, environmental health, health education, health services for the homeless, nutrition research and education, biomedical research and equipment, health professionals training, and more! *Health Grants & Contracts Weekly* reveals every health-related grant competition issued each week from all federal agencies: National Institutes of Health, Substance Abuse and Mental Health Services Administration, as well as many agencies not normally associated with funding in the health arena. Weekly issues bring you early alerts on funding opportunities, insights on what the agencies are looking for in a winning proposal, and tips and strategies to maximize your chance of success. Each grant alert is divided into six parts so you can scan it quickly and decide if it's an opportunity for which you can apply. You'll know the scope of the project, deadline, funding amount, eligibility requirements, specific areas of interest, and the name and telephone number of the primary contract. *$399/year*

Healthcare Fund Raising Newsletter (Monthly Newsletter)

Health Resources Publishing, 1913 Atlantic Avenue, Suite F-4,
Manasquan, NJ 08376
Tel: 732-292-1100; FAX: 732-292-1111
E-mail: hrp@healthrespubs.com

Customer Service: P.O. Box 456, Allenwood, NJ 08720
Tel: 888-843-6242; FAX: 888-329-6242
WWW: http://www.healthrespubs.com/

▶ For nearly two decades, it has been showing fund-raising professionals at health care organizations how to develop new ways to generate larger charitable gifts. Tackling such issues as annual giving and capital campaigns, grant seeking, prospect cultivation, special-event planning, and planned giving, it provides proven techniques for successful health care fund raising, from the traditional to the innovative. You can keep up with current trends, helpful tips, how other health care fund-raising professionals are raising money and government actions that could affect your plans. In each monthly issue, you'll benefit from detailed reports on new capital campaigns and approaches to annual giving efforts that have proven successful for other organizations. You'll find new ways of getting your fair share of the corporate giving money and learn how to meet the challenges of physician solicitation. By reporting on activities in fund-raising departments of health care organizations throughout the nation and including the name of a contact person at the end of each article, it also serves as an exchange medium and promotes networking among health care development professionals. *$197/year*

The Journal of Gift Planning (Quarterly Magazine)

National Committee on Planned Giving, 233 McCrea Street,
Suite 400, Indianapolis, IN 46225
Tel: 317-269-6274; FAX: 317-269-6276, 317-269-6272
(Nonmember Subscriptions)
E-mail: ncpg@iupui.edu WWW: http://www.ncpg.org/journal.html

▶ This magazine provides its readers with timely, advanced, and comprehensive information on all aspects of planned giving. Articles on planned giving ranging from how to give, why to give, legalities of giving, who gives, etc. Original articles and columns appear in each issue of the journal. Every issue includes an article in each of the following subject areas: technical, advanced gift planning, marketing/sales, and how-to/basics. Also included are legislative and tax updates, educational opportunities, panel discussions, letters to the editor, and more. *$22.50/year (Member),* *$45/year (Nonmember)*

Justice Technology Monitor (Monthly Newsletter)

Capitol City Publishers, 1408 North Fillmore Street, Suite 3,
Arlington, VA 22201-3819
Tel: 703-525-3080; FAX: 703-525-3044
E-mail: inquiry@capitolcitypublishers.com;
WWW: http://capitolcitypublishers.com/pubs/jtech/index.html

▶ This newsletter covers technology news, programs, and funding for law enforcement, courts, and corrections. Subscribers include grant seekers and administrators with responsibility for implementing or operating new technologies in police or sheriff departments, correctional institutions, state and local governments, public agencies, community and victim assistance groups, and youth and nonprofit organizations. The newsletter reports on the latest news, model programs, and developments in new and emerging technologies; covers new and proposed federal grant programs, federal budget news, key legislation, funding trends and priorities, and appropriations for law enforcement and criminal justice grants; highlights upcoming grant application deadlines for receiving financial and technical assistance from the federal government, foundations and corporations; and includes a conference calendar and profiles of private funding sources. *$277/year ($247 Web price)*

Local/State Funding Report (Weekly Newsletter)

Headquarters office: Thompson Publishing Group, Inc.,
Government Information Services, Education Funding Research
Council, 1725 K Street NW, Suite 700, Washington, DC 20006
Tel: 800-876-0226, 202-872-4000

Thompson Fulfillment Services: 5201 W. Kennedy Boulevard,
Suite 905, Tampa, FL 33609-1823
Tel: 813-282-8807
E-mail: service@thompson.com; WWW: http://www.thompson.com/
libraries/grantseeking/stat/index.html

▶ This newsletter provides grant seekers in state and local governments, nonprofit organizations, and community groups with the information they need to find federal, corporate, and foundation funding for their programs and projects. Each week, the *Local/State Funding Report* includes alerts to funding opportunities for social services, law enforcement, health care, community development, jobs, housing, transportation, and many other programs. The weekly newsletter includes all regulatory changes issued by the federal agencies, as well as updates on congressional initiatives to create new, or amend existing, grant programs. Of special interest to grant seekers and program managers is the weekly feature, "Local/State Grant & Regulation Alert," which is a compilation of all regulatory notices affecting grant-in-aid programs and funding announcements appearing in the *Federal Register.* Newsletters are indexed quarterly. Subscribers may receive e-mail versions of the grant and regulation alerts that arrive days before the printed version, as well as access to online calendars of application deadlines for federal funding. *$279/year*

The Major Gifts Report (Monthly Newsletter)

Stevenson Consultants, Inc., P.O. Box 4528, Sioux City, IA 51104
Tel: 712-239-3010; FAX: 712-239-2166
E-mail: subscribe@stevensoninc.com (Subscriptions),
inquiry@stevensoninc.com (Inquiries);
WWW: http://www.stevensoninc.com

▶ Filled with concisely written articles, this monthly newsletter offers practical tips and techniques that will enhance all your fund-raising efforts. You will be linked with thousands of professionals who are sharing their success stories in each monthly issue. It will answer these important questions: How can I use my charity's uniqueness to attract a $12 million gift? Can using e-mail really help me secure a million-dollar gift? How can I easily discover who lives in our wealthiest neighborhoods? What methods can I use to uncover prospects' salaries? How can I grab the attention of those who have made major gifts to other nonprofits, but not ours? What proven strategies can I use to land huge endowment gifts? How can a nonprofit with no history of major gifts get started? And more. *8 pages, $149/year*

Mal Warwick's Newsletter: Successful Direct Mail, Telephone & Online Fundraising (Bimonthly Newsletter)

Mal Warwick & Associates, Inc., 2550 Ninth St., Suite 103,
Berkeley, California 94710
Tel: 510-843-8888; FAX: 510-843-0142
E-mail: info@malwarwick.com;
Web: http://www.malwarwick.com/subscribe.html

▶ This newsletter offers you money-saving tips, no-nonsense analysis of fund raising, many mail samples, plus advice from top pros. *$69/year*

National Fund Raiser (Monthly Newsletter)

Barnes Associates, Inc., 909 15th Street, Suite 9,
Modesto, CA 95354-1130
Tel: 800-231-4157; FAX: 209-523-3368

▶ This newsletter provides "how-to" instructions for new and basic fund-raising methods. It includes step-by-step procedures and a monthly calendar that suggests specific tasks for assuring your success, as well as working-tool forms for planning, budgeting, and analyzing your development program. Each issue includes a "working tool" supplement to aid in planning a fund-raising campaign. Subscriptions also include access to a toll-free consulting hotline, which provides professional advice from fund-raising experts. It also provides Fast Fax response to requests for forms, directions, statistics, and detailed suggestions. It includes a toll-free Consulting Hotline and "How to Meet Today's Fund Raising Challenges." *$95/year*

New Directions for Philanthropic Fundraising (Quarterly Journal)

Jossey-Bass Publishers, Inc., 350 Sansome Street,
San Francisco, CA 94104
Tel: 415-433-1740; FAX: 415-433-0499
WWW: http://www.josseybass.com/JBJournals/ndpf.html

▶ This journal was created to strengthen voluntary giving by addressing how the concepts of philanthropy pertain to fund-raising practice. In each quarterly paperback, authors address themes related to fund-raising management and technique, always keeping in mind the values of voluntarism and public benefit that characterize philanthropic organizations. It is sponsored by the Indiana University Center on Philanthropy. *$67/year (Individual),* *$115/year (Institution)*

New Directions in Philanthropy (Bimonthly Newsletter)

2327 NW Northrup Street, Suite 7, Portland OR 97210 USA
Tel/FAX: 503-478-9631
E-mail: judnich@aol.com (Judith E. Nichols, PhD, CFRE)

▶ This newsletter helps astute fund-raising professionals to shape and validate their fund-raising strategy by providing them with concise information on new trends in giving, marketing, demographics, and psychographics. For each of the six issues yearly, Judith Nichols, author of *Pinpointing Affluence* (see listing under Major Donors) and other well-received fund-raising books, sifts through business magazines and books, fund-raising publications, demographic and psychographic surveys, and public and government information to uncover the latest—and most important—research and trends affecting fund raising today. *$99/year*

Non-Profit Nuts & Bolts (Monthly Newsletter)

Nuts & Bolts Publishing, 4623 Tiffany Woods Circle,
Oviedo, FL 32765
Tel: 407-677-6564; FAX: 407-677-5645
E-mail: info@nutsbolts.com (Lisa Beach, Editor),
csr@nutsbolts.com (Customer Service);
WWW: http://www.nutsbolts.com/, http://www.nutsbolts.com/
Non-Profit%20Freebies.htm, http://www.nutsbolts.com/Non-
Profit%20Resources.htm (Non-Profit Resource Center)

▶ This newsletter provides practical tips for building nonprofit professionals. It covers fund raising, volunteer management, public relations, special events, team building, board relations, committees, leadership, time management, marketing, media relations, technology, meetings, staff management, budget-stretching ideas, and more. Each issue contains approximately 30 to 35 articles on a variety of key nonprofit management topics. *8 pages, $49/year ($41.65 Web price)*

The Nonprofit Times (Biweekly Newspaper)

Executive offices: 120 Littleton Road, Suite 120,
Parsippany, NJ 07054-1803
Tel: 973-394-1800, 973-394-1800 (Subscriptions);
FAX: 973-394-2888
E-mail: ednchief@nptimes.com (Editor-in-Chief, Paul Clolery);
WWW: http://www.nptimes.com/

▶ The focus of this publication is on nonprofit management and fund-raising techniques. Sections may include news/features, computer software, technology, management and finance, commentary on current issues, and other areas of interest. Job opportunities are listed in the Employment Marketplace, and the Resource Directory lists providers of products and services. Subscriptions include the Direct Marketing Edition (6 issues per year) and the Financial Management Edition (6 issues per year), in addition to special report issues, The NPT 100 and the NPT Salary Survey. It is free to subscribers who meet certain qualifications; check with the publisher.

Nonprofit Vermont (Bimonthly Newsletter)

CPG Enterprises, P.O. Box 199, Shaftsbury VT 05262
Tel: 802-862-0327; FAX: 802-862-0327
E-mail: graham@lemming.uvm.edu (Christine Graham)

▶ This newsletter covers Vermont and national news, fund-raising skills and opportunities, nonprofit management and political issues that would be of interest to Vermont organizations, book reviews, workshops, and more. *$24/year*

Nonprofit World (Bimonthly Magazine)

Society for Nonprofit Organizations, 6314 Odana Road, Suite 1,
Madison, WI 53719-1141
Tel: 800-424-7367, 608-274-9777; FAX: 608-274-9978
E-mail: snpo@danenet.org; WWW: http://danenet.wicip.org/snpo/

▶ This is a comprehensive national leadership, management, and governance-focused magazine for the nonprofit sector. It contains articles on all aspects of running an effective nonprofit organization, including fund raising, income generation, and legal advice. *Free (Member), $79/year (Nonmember)*

Nonprofit World Funding Alert (Monthly Newsletter)

The Society for Nonprofit Organizations, 6314 Odana Road,
Suite 1, Madison, WI 53719-1141
Tel: 800-424-7367, 608-274-9777; FAX: 608-274-9978
E-mail: snpo@danenet.org; WWW: http://danenet.wicip.org/snpo/

▶ This newsletter provides updates on current grant and fundraising opportunities for nonprofit organizations. Here, readers will find the latest information on national and regional funding opportunities from across the country, categorized by type (i.e., civic, educational, health, etc.). Included, too, are in-depth profiles on various foundations. Society members receive a copy of the *Alert* as part of their memberships. The publication is not available to nonmembers.

The Planned Gifts Counselor (Monthly Newsletter)

Practical Publishing, 1602 West 1050 North, Provo, UT 84604-3062
Tel: 888-58-TRUST (588-7878), 801-802-8930
E-mail: pschneit@inquo.net (Paul Schneiter);
WWW: http://premieradministration.com/pgc.htm

▶ This newsletter covers the latest news on changes in tax laws (as well as practical strategies to help your donors take advantage of these tax laws while helping your organization), regulation, and pending legislation that affects your planned giving program. It also offers insight into managing and marketing a planned giving program, researching, cultivating and soliciting donors, board relations, ensuring that your planned gifts program complements your other fund-raising efforts, and more. It focuses on news, analysis, announcements, and successful strategies. Easily scanned and quickly read, it offers wide-ranging and pertinent information targeted toward your success. *8 pages, $150.00/year*

Planned Giving Today

100 Second Avenue South, Suite 180, Edmonds, WA 98020-3551
Tel: 800-KALL-PGT (525-5748), 425-744-3837 (PG-4EVER);
FAX: 425-744-3838
E-mail: roger@pgtoday.com (G. Roger Schoenhals, Publisher and Editor); WWW: http://www.pgtoday.com/

▶ Launched in September 1990, the publication serves the charitable gift planning community as a practical resource for education, information, inspiration, and professional linkage. It is dedicated to helping gift planners enable others to give generously, prudently, and joyfully. Subscribers receive a resource supplement, The PGT Marketplace, containing news about services, products and employment opportunities of interest to the charitable gift planner. *The PGT Marketplace* also includes a comprehensive listing of current training events for gift planners. In addition, subscribers receive a handy "Rate of the Month" card for easy access to the Applicable Federal Mid-Term Rate (AFR). PGT-CD 2000 is an electronic library containing the first 10 years of *Planned Giving Today* (1,112 issues). It includes more than 1,000 articles from 400 authors, fully indexed for fast and easy access, and Adobe Acrobat®Reader 4.05b. *12 pages, $179/year; PGT-CD 2000: $129 (Subscriber), $279 (Nonsubscriber)*

Right on the Money (Monthly Newsletter)

Grants Link, Inc., P.O. Box 10140, 601 West Nifong Boulevard,
Suite 4B, Columbia, MO 65203
Tel: 800-396-8829
E-mail: info@grantslink.com, drutter@grantslink.com (David Rutter, Business Manager); WWW: http://www.grantslink.com/newslet.htm

▶ Provides essential information on grants from federal, private, foundation, and corporate funding sources. With it, you will learn who is making grants, what they're for, whom to contact, and what the deadlines are in time to write and submit your proposal for funding. It does the homework for you, locating grants for agriculture, crime prevention, cultural programs, education, health services, housing, human services, youth, and dozens of other areas. *$89/year*

Special Education Report (Biweekly Newsletter)

Aspen Publishers
Corporate headquarters: 200 Orchard Ridge Drive,
Gaithersburg, MD 20878
Tel: 301-417-7500; FAX: 301-695-7931

Distribution center: 7201 McKinney Circle, Frederick, MD 21701
Tel: 800-234-1660, 301-698-7100; FAX: 301-695-7931
E-mail: customer.service@aspenpubl.com;
WWW: http://www.aspenpub.com, http://www.grantscape.com

▶ This newsletter helps special educators ensure compliance with federal regulations, improve the quality and outcome of educational programs, and protect your sources of funding. It shows special education directors and advocates how to take advantage of opportunities and protect against challenges their programs may face as Congress rewrites special education law; develop placement policies and curricula that best serve students' needs; keep the pressure on Congress to increase federal funding by providing the names, phone numbers, and FAX numbers of the key committee members; create and implement the best possible individualized education programs; and more. It includes legislative updates, litigation updates nationwide, and federal grant funding available for special education. *$317/year*

School Administrator's Title I Hotline (Monthly Newsletter)

Quinlan Publishing Group, 23 Drydock Avenue,
Boston, MA 02210-2387
Tel: 800-229-2084, 617-542-0048; FAX: 617-345-9646
E-mail: info@quinlan.com; WWW: http://www.quinlan.com/,
http://www.schoollaw-funding.com/t1.html

▶ This newsletter offers how-to advice from Title I experts and consultants, online help, and notice of funding opportunities. A resource for school administrators, Title I coordinators, teachers, and consultants, *Title I Hotline* covers grant application tips, legislative updates, needs assessment, compliance with IASA and the new IDEA, GOALS 2000, how-to advice from experts in the field, and much more. It is an authoritative source to help you deal with the legal, educational, and financial challenges of Title I programs. *$139/year*

Substance Abuse Funding News (24 Issues)

CD Publications, 8204 Fenton Street, Silver Spring, MD 20910
Tel: 800-666-6380, 301-588-6380; FAX: 301-588-6385
E-mail: subscriptions@cdpublications.com, cdpubs@clark.net;
WWW: http://www.cdpublications.com/funding/saf.htm

▶ This resource provides public and private grant announcements of alcohol, tobacco, and drug abuse programs. Teenagers, the homeless, and other special populations are highlighted. It offers advice on grant seeking and proposal writing, along with tips from funding officials on what they look for in grant applications. Each issue concisely summarizes corporate and foundation grant opportunities as well as federal funding notices from such agencies as the Substance Abuse and Mental Health Services Administration, the National Institute on Alcohol Abuse and Alcoholism, the Office of National Drug Control Policy, the Bureau of Prisons, the Department of Housing and Urban Development, the Labor Department, the Department of Education, and the Department of Veterans Affairs. It also covers the latest federal and state initiatives to prevent drug abuse and highlights innovative programs being implemented nationwide to cost-effectively address substance abuse and related concerns. *14–18 pages, $319/year*

Successful Fund Raising (Monthly Newsletter)

Stevenson Consultants, Inc., P.O. Box 4528, Sioux City, IA 51104
Tel: 712-239-3010; FAX: 712-239-2166
E-mail: subscribe@stevensoninc.com (Subscriptions),
inquiry@stevensoninc.com (Inquiries);
WWW: http://www.stevensoninc.com

▶ Filled with concisely written articles, this monthly newsletter offers practical tips and techniques that will enhance all your fundraising efforts. You will be linked with thousands of professionals who are sharing their success stories in each monthly issue. Each issue of *Successful Fund Raising* covers topics including major gifts, prospect research, solicitation techniques, annual gifts, capital campaigns, telemarketing, special events, direct mail, planned gifts, strategic planning, training and motivating volunteers, board recruitment and relations, and more. *8 pages, $120/year*

The Welfare Reporter

Capitol City Publishers, 1408 North Fillmore Street, Suite 3,
Arlington, VA 22201-3819
Tel: 703-525-3080; FAX: 703-525-3044
E-mail: inquiry@capitolcitypublishers.com;
WWW: http://capitolcitypublishers.com/pubs/welfare/index.html

▶ This resource covers welfare, welfare reform, and welfare-to-work for state and local governments. Subscribers include welfare and social service professionals, health care providers and grant seekers in state and local governments, welfare agencies, private industry councils, public housing authorities, one-stop employment service agencies, child care centers, health care organizations, and job creation/training/placement agencies. Features include new and proposed federal grant programs, federal budget news, key legislation, funding trends and priorities, and appropriations and regulations for all issues affecting welfare and work, including TANF, food stamps, housing, job training, child care, children and families, child support and collection, transportation, and Medicaid. It also includes state news, model programs, and private funding initiatives. *$279/year ($249 Web price)*

Youth Crime Alert (Monthly Newsletter)

CD Publications, 8204 Fenton Street, Silver Spring, MD 20910
Tel: 800-666-6380, 301-588-6380; FAX: 301-588-6385
E-mail: subscriptions@cdpublications.com, cdpubs@clark.net;
WWW: http://www.cdpublications.com/funding/yca.htm

▶ This newsletter reports on successful programs, legislation, and funding to reduce school violence, gang activity, teenage drug abuse, and juvenile delinquency. Upcoming issues will cover innovative programs to combat gangs and reach out to at-risk youth. It also covers grants available from public and private sources, such as the Department of Education, the Substance Abuse and Mental Health Services Administration, the Department of Justice, and dozens of national and regional foundations. *18 pages, $235/year*

INTERNET RESOURCES

General Development and Fund-Raising Information

Advice at Chardon Online
▶ *http://www.chardonpress.com/newsletter/advice.html*

Advancement Services Pages—R.I. Arlington
▶ *http://www.riarlington.com/*

Association of Fundraising Professionals Resource Center
▶ *http://www.nsfre.org/resource_center*

Big Online
▶ This comprehensive and current source of Canadian and American fund-raising information for nonprofits and charities provides critical information about more than 6,000 available funding sources representing billions in annual funding. *http://www.big-database.com/bigonline.nsf/publish/welcome*

CDS Resources and Links—Custom Development Solutions
▶ A fund-raising directory of foundations, fund-raising and philanthropy articles, industry journals, nonprofit organizations, and philanthropy resources. *Updated frequently. http://www.cdsfunds.com/resources.htm*

DANA Answer Center: Fundraising—Delaware Association of Nonprofit Agencies
▶ *http://www.delawarenonprofit.org/fundfaq.htm*

Development Resource Center
▶ Consultants Henley and Hodiak offer marketing, public relations, and fund-raising tips for smaller organizations. *http://www.drcharity.com/*

Findit.org—Fund Raising
▶ *http://www.findit.org/html/fund_raising.html*

The Foundation Center's Electronic Reference Desk
▶ The Foundation Center in New York City has added an "Electronic Reference Desk" to its Web site. The free service allows people to send questions about foundations, management, fund rais-ing, and other topics to one of the Foundation Center's librarians, who promise to return an answer by e-mail within two business days. For more information, contact Beth Lewitzky, Online Librarian, Foundation Center, 79 Fifth Avenue, Eighth Floor, New York, NY 10003; 212-807-3675; E-mail: *library@fdncenter.org. http://fdncenter.org/onlib/librarian.html*

Fundraiser.org
▶ *http://www.fundraiser.org*

The Fundraiser's Guide Online
▶ *http://www.fundraisers-guide.com/articles.htm*

Fund Raising—The Nonprofit Zone
▶ *http://www.nonprofitzone.com/fndrsg.htm*

Fund-Raising and Grant-Writing Resources
▶ *http://www.fundsnetservices.com/grantwri.htm*

Fund Raising for Small Nonprofits
▶ *http://www.resolveinc.com/NEWS.htm*

Fund Raising Forum Library—Tony Poderis
▶ Features monthly discussions on such topics as identifying prospective donors. *http://www.raise-funds.com/library.html*

Fund-Raising Innovations for Nonprofits
▶ *http://www.nonprofit-innovations.com/*

Fund-Raising Library—Philanthropic Service for Institutions
▶ *http://www.philanthropicservice.com/library.html*

Fund Raising Online
▶ Links, interviews, and news about fund raising. Recent topics include using e-mail to fund raise. It also includes listing of workshops on online fund raising around the world. *http://www.fundraising-online.com*

Fund-Raising Page—from The Nonprofit Resource Center
▶ This page provides links to the Web sites of specific individual fund-raising consultants, as well as larger or broader organization sites, such as "Catholic Stewards," "Successful Auctions for

Nonprofits," and "The Fundraising Bazaar"—not to mention others less known, such as "Surfree.com," "WorldxChange," and even "Scratch 'N' Give Fund Raising System." *http://not-for-profit.org/fund.htm*

Fund-Raising Productivity Series—Internet Nonprofit Center

▶ Sponsored by the Evergreen State Society, a Seattle charity that promotes civic involvement, this site includes a series of essays by Bill Levis, a professor at the City University of New York, that discuss how the cost and efficiency of fund-raising efforts are measured, the importance of investing in fund raising, and accountability to donors. *http://www.nonprofit-info.org/misc/fps/fps.html*

Fund-Raising Resources Data—Philanthropic Service for Institutions

▶ *http://www.philanthropicservice.com/resources/resources.html*

Fund-Raising Resources—Paul Bowerman's Web Index

▶ *http://www.non-profit-services.com/resources.htm*

Fund-Raising Resources on the Internet

▶ *http://www.iugm.org/dev-trak/links.html*

Fund-Raising Resources and Other Information Links for Libraries

▶ *http://members.nbci.com/sdcheckitout/fundraise.html*

FundraisingInfo.com

▶ *http://www.fundraisinginfo.com/*

Fund-Raising.com

▶ A service of NicheNET, Fund-Raising.com provides nonprofits with information about creative ways to generate contributions. Resources include fund-raising–oriented products, a Web-based fund-raising competition, related links, and an "Idea Bank" that features suggestions from site visitors. *http://www.fund-raising.com/*

Fundsnet Services Online

▶ *http://www.fundsnetservices.com/*

Gill Foundation: OutGiving

▶ Developed by the Gill Foundation in Denver, this Web site provides information on fund raising and management for nonprofit organizations. The site includes interactive audits that groups can use to assess their fund-raising and management practices, a sample fund-raising plan, and advice on making a fund-raising pitch at a special event. *http://www.gillfoundation.org/outgiv/og01hh01.htm*

Grant Resources—Polaris

▶ *http://www.polarisgrantscentral.net/resources.html*

Grants and Grant Writing—United Cerebral Palsy Association, Greater Utica (New York) Area

▶ *http://www.ucp-utica.org/uwlinks/grants.html*

GrantScape.com—A Web Site for Nonprofit Professionals

▶ Target audience: nonprofit professionals of all types—grant seekers, fund raisers, nonprofit managers, and prospect researchers. Web site features include Funder of the Day, a Nonprofit Forum for discussion, a searchable archive of five newsletters and a reprint order form, Links, a Meetings Calendar, and Tips for Grant-seekers. A searchable catalog of publications includes newsletters (complete sample issues available), books, software, electronic databases (demo downloads available), and an easy-to-use feature for completing secure orders online. The Web site also has several areas for customer feedback, including a registration form that allows users to tell the GrantScape staff what they want from the Web site. *http://www.grantscape.com*

Grants and Related Resources

▶ This bibliography lists books and videos available in the Michigan State University library collections. It is intended as a starting point for those who are interested in learning more about foundations, fund raising, proposal writing, nonprofit organizations, nonprofit organization administration, philanthropy and philanthropists, corporate philanthropy, international philanthropy, government funding, planned giving, prospect research, and voluntarism. *http://www.lib.msu.edu/harris23/grants/4fc_h.htm*

GRANTS, ETC.

▶ This site is designed to enable both experienced and novice grant seekers and fund raisers to access information on the Internet by providing annotated links to a variety of funding sources, including corporate, foundation, nonprofit, government, individual, and international sources. This site also provides information about related learning resources, such as workshops, associations, journals, and libraries. Grant seekers will also discover proposal-writing suggestions and supportive data sources, such as statistical information, from this site. *http://www.ssw.umich.edu/grantsetc*

Helping.org

▶ This AOL-sponsored site is designed as a one-stop online resource to help people find volunteer and giving opportunities in their local communities and beyond. The site also provides online resources and tools to help nonprofits utilize the Internet in their strategic planning, recruiting, and fund raising. *http://www.helping.org/*

ICD Fund Raising Online Resources

▶ *http://www.goidc.com/help.htm*

InnoNet's Workstation for Innovative Nonprofits

▶ Created by InnoNet, a nonprofit consulting organization in Washington that helps charities plan and evaluate programs, this Web site offers interactive worksheets that nonprofit staff members can use to plan new programs and develop budgets, grant applications, and evaluation and fund-raising plans. InnoNet offers to review users' completed plans free. The site also explains how to conduct focus group discussions, interviews, and surveys, and provides sample evaluation tools. *http://www.innonet.org/*

Internet Fundraising Central

▶ *http://www.internet-fundraising.com/home.html*

Internet Nonprofit Center: The Nonprofit FAQ

▶ Formerly titled "Information for Nonprofits," this site includes information on fund raising, nonprofit management, and resources for nonprofit organizations. The information was compiled from the soc.org.nonprofit newsgroup, an online discussion about the nonprofit world. The site is sponsored by the Evergreen State Society, a Seattle charity that promotes civic involvement. *http://www.nonprofits.org/npofaq*

The Maine Philanthropy Center Index of Philanthropy & Nonprofit Web Resources

▶ This well-maintained site as an excellent resource for a multitude of different fund development sites. *http://www.megrants.org/bookmk98.html*

National Society of Fund Raising Executives

▶ Renamed the Association of Fundraising Professionals, it is the professional association for individuals responsible for generating philanthropic support for a wide variety of not-for-profit, charitable organizations. The site includes a searchable directory of fundraising consultants. *http://www.nsfre.org/welcome/index.html*

Nonprofit Charitable Orgs—About.com

▶ *http://nonprofit.about.com/careers/ nonprofit/mbody.htm.* See also the Nonprofit Charitable Orgs Forum at *http://www.delphi.com/ab-nonprofit/start/.*

Nonprofit Fundraising and Grantwriting—Free Management Library

▶ *http://www.mapnp.org/library/fndrsng/np_raise/np_raise.htm*

Nonprofit Universe—Aspen Publishers/Grantscape

▶ *http://www.grantscape.com/*

One-Stop Info for Starting a Nonprofit

▶ If you're thinking of starting a nonprofit organization, this is the place to begin. You'll find links to basic information such as planning, legal resources, and fund raising. *http://nonprofit.about.com/careers/nonprofit/library/weekly/blonestart.htm*

Raising More Money—Terry Axelrod

▶ *http://www.raisingmoremoney.com/*

Successful Fundraising Online—Mal Warwick & Associates, Inc.

▶ *http://www.malwarwick.com/success0010.html*

Techportal.org

▶ Search for funding and grants, in-kind donations, training, volunteers, or more. For nonprofits with needs in technology. From TeamTech in San Francisco (a program from AmeriCorps). *http://www.techportal.org*

Tony Poderis—Your Nonprofit Fundraising Resource

▶ *http://www.raise-funds.com*

Wired Development Office

▶ *http://www.nsfremass.org/wired.htm*

Zimmerman Lehman

▶ Maintained by Zimmerman Lehman, a fund-raising consulting company in San Francisco, this Web site provides articles about fund raising. Topics discussed include how to determine if an organization is ready for a capital campaign, stage a special fund-raising event, and use the Internet to gather information about donors, foundations, and businesses. *http://www.zimmerman-lehman.com/articles.htm*

Direct Mail

All About Direct Mail Fundraising—Mal Warwick & Associates

▶ *http://www.malwarwick.com/direct.html*

Direct Mail Response Rate Calculator

▶ Developed by Moore Corporation Limited, a communications company in Lincolnshire, Illinois, this Web site includes forms that help fund raisers determine how large a test mailing is necessary to test a new direct-mail fund-raising appeal, calculate how many recipients must make a gift for a mailing to cover its costs, and test whether the results are statistically significant. The site also allows fund raisers to calculate how large the full-scale mailing should be to match the response rate to the test mailing and to figure out how large a variance to expect between the results of the test mailing and the full-scale mailing. *http://www.moore.com/products/integrated/dirmarket/dmarketCalc/dmarketCalc.html*

Learning Center—L.W. Robbins

▶ *http://www.lwra.com/Learning/learn.htm*

Mal Warwick and Associates

▶ Maintained by Mal Warwick and Associates, a fund-raising consulting company in Berkeley, California, this site provides articles on direct-mail and Internet fund raising. Topics include how to start a direct-mail program, choose the right mailing lists, write effective fund-raising letters, build monthly donor programs, attract visitors to a charity's Web site, and use e-mail to raise money. *http://www.malwarwick.com*

Successful Fundraising Online—Mal Warwick & Associates, Inc.

▶ *http://www.malwarwick.com/success0010.html*

Excess Inventory

Excess Access, LLC

▶ An Internet and toll-free number database that matches business and individual donations with nonprofit wish lists. *http://www.Excess Access.com*

Federal Funding

Catalog of Federal Domestic Assistance

▶ Searchable index of federal programs, projects, services, and activities. *http://www.cfda.gov/*

Deborah Kluge—Independent Consultant

▶ This site describes not only this consultant's services but also includes an FAQ section as well as Proposal Writing and Government Contracting Links. *http://www.proposalwriter.com/about.html*

Federal Commons

▶ Federal grant applicants can access all of the information they need to act on federal government grant opportunities. Federal Commons, an Internet grants management portal serving the grantee organization community, has joined with the General Services Administration's Catalog of Federal Domestic Assistance to offer online access to information about Federal Grants Programs. *http://www.cfda.gov/federalcommons/*

Nonprofit Gateway—Grants and Nonfinancial Support

▶ Links to government agency home pages for information on grants and nonfinancial support. *http://www.nonprofit.gov/resource/support.html#agencies*

Notices of Funding Availability (Empowerment Zone/Enterprise Communities Community Toolbox)

▶ NOFAs are announcements that appear in the *Federal Register,* which is printed each business day by the U.S. government. The site allows users to generate customized listings. *http://ocd.usda.gov/nofa.htm*

Funding Sources

The Art Deadlines List

▶ Primarily a fee-based service, the site offers a free selection of listings as well as a free monthly newsletter providing information

about juried exhibitions and competitions; poetry and other writing contests; jobs and internships; scholarships and fellowships; casting calls, auditions, and tryouts; grants, funding, and financial aid; and other opportunities for artists, art educators, and art students. *http://custwww.xensei.com/adl*

CSC Non-Profit Resource Center (formerly Campaign Service Consultants)

▶ *http://people.ne.mediaone.net/cscunningham/Foundation.htm*

Catalog of Federal Domestic Assistance

▶ The Catalog of Federal Domestic Assistance Programs (CFDA) is a government-wide compendium of all 1,381 federal programs, projects, services, and activities that provide assistance or benefits to the American public. These programs provide grants, loans, loan guarantees, services, information, scholarships, training, insurance, etc., to millions of Americans every day. *http://www.cfda.gov/*

Community Resource Institute's Grant Funding Resources

▶ *http://www.granted.org/grants.html*

Council on Foundations' Community Foundation Locator

▶ This is a searchable database of community foundations across the United States. The Council site also has a list of their member foundations and corporate giving programs with Web sites. *http://www.cof.org/links/memberindex.htm*, *http://www.cof.org/applications/Locators/main.cfm*

Directory of Texas Foundations Online

▶ *http://www.nprc.org/advanced/directory/*

Federal Register

▶ *http://www.access.gpo.gov/su_docs/aces/aces140.html*, *http://www.ed.gov/legislation/FedRegister/announcements/*, *http://www.nara.gov/fedreg/*

The Foundation Center

▶ At their Web site, there are links to grant-maker Web sites, information on the top U.S. funders, funding trends and analysis, an online library, *Philanthropy News Digest,* and Foundation Finder, a search tool that provides basic facts on more than 48,000 U.S. foundations. This site also provides links to the home pages of nearly 900 grant makers, including private foundations, corporate grant makers, community foundations, and grant-making charities. The center's database of information on more than 10,000 foundations is available for a monthly subscription fee. In addition, the site also lists the top grant makers, by both assets and total giving. The "Online Library" section of the site provides information about the grant-seeking process, corporate philanthropy, nonprofit management, and nonprofit resources. Users who have additional questions can send e-mail to the "Online Librarian" and receive an answer within three to four business days. The reference section also includes annotated links to other Web sites of interest to nonprofit organizations. *http://fdncenter.org*

Foundation Center: Grantmaker Info

▶ This site provides rankings of the largest private, corporate, and community foundations, both by assets held and amount of total giving. It also includes excerpts from the center's publications that discuss trends in grant making and information about the National Taxonomy of Exempt Organizations, a system that classifies charities by the type of work they do. *http://fdncenter.org/grantmaker/index.html*

Foundation Center Search Zone

▶ This page brings together all of the searching options offered on the Foundation Center's Web site. The site's "Grantmaker Web Search" feature allows users to conduct a search for keywords on more than 1,000 Web sites run by grant makers. The page also takes visitors to the center's collection of annotated links to grant makers' Web sites; the "Foundation Finder," a database that includes basic contact information for more than 50,000 grant makers; and "The Literature of the Nonprofit Sector," a database of books, articles, and reports on philanthropy. For a monthly fee, visitors can also gain access to the center's database of detailed information about the 10,000 largest foundations in the United States. *http://fdncenter.org/searchzone*

Foundations On-Line

▶ A directory of charitable grant makers. *http://www.foundations.org/*

The Foundation Center's User-Friendly Guide to Funding Research & Resources

▶ *http://fdncenter.org/onlib/ufg/index.html*

FoundationDataBook.com

▶ There is a Foundation DataBook available for Washington, Oregon, and California. A Colorado edition will be available soon. Each Foundation DataBook is a state-specific, comprehensive, up-to-date directory and database of grant-making foundations with a categorical listing of all the grants they made for the most recent year on record, including the Foundation's stated purpose for awarding each grant. *http://www.foundationdatabook.com*

Fund-Raising and Foundation Research

▶ A set of links from the University of Southern California. *http://www.usc.edu/advancement/webster/found.htm*

Fundsnet Online Services

▶ This site is a comprehensive, somewhat randomly organized directory of funders and funding resources on the World Wide Web. It has lots of links, some annotated, arranged alphabetically and/or by subject area. It also offers a section, organized by subject area, in Spanish. *http://www.fundsnetservices.com/*

The Grant Advisor Plus

▶ Information on grant and fellowship opportunities for U.S. institutions of higher education and their faculty. *http://www.grantadvisor.com/*

Grant Giver of the Week—EducationDaily (Aspen Publishers)

▶ *http://www.educationdaily.com/FTP/giver.html*

GrantMatch.com

▶ GrantMatch.com is an Internet portal assisting grant seekers and grant makers in finding pertinent information about one another. Through GrantMatch, both funders and nonprofit organizations can access an online database that will identify and provide links to specific funders or programs. GrantMatch also maintains a listing of consultants, including program evaluators, grantwriters, accountants, lawyers, and others. Use of the GrantMatch database and consultant registry is free and does not require registration. Registration currently costs $120/year for both grant seekers and grant makers. Once registered, users can post specific proposals or funding interests. Intended to extend the ways in which donors and nonprofit organizations communicate with one another, GrantMatch enables organizations to list grant proposals and requests for donations by specific category, while donors may list their funding interests by category to avoid inapplicable proposal submissions. Donors may also create an RFP. GrantMatch gives philanthropists the option of keeping their identities hidden. Searching may be conducted by key words or NTEE Codes (National Taxonomy of Exempt Entities Codes). One special feature of the site is "Rosie the Robot," an automated search feature that is easily programmed to conduct highly tailored searches for registered users. Rosie "remembers" user-specified parameters and instantly returns results and highlights new information, saving regular users from having to repeatedly set parameters for each search. *http://www.grantmatch.com/index.html-ssi*

Grants Link Funders Online

▶ Comprehensive corporate and foundation giving information. *http://208.141.107.238/funder/*

Grants Resources: A Selected Bibliography

▶ Provided by the Galen Web site at the University of California at San Francisco (the UC medical school), this site includes a bibliography of especially significant printed materials and a list of e-mail lists for discussions of grant-related issues. It emphasizes health and/or science information. It is well organized with good links. *http://www.library.ucsf.edu/ref/path/grants/*

GrantsDirect.com

▶ GrantsDirect.com was designed to help fund raisers research Washington, D.C., and Maryland grant makers and their grant lists. For a $499 single-user annual subscription, grant seekers gain access to a searchable database of over 32,000 grants and a companion guide to the funders entitled *The Maryland/DC Foundation Directory Online*. The database is easily searchable by subject, name, or specific text. Visitors to the site can "test drive" a reduced database to get a sense of the services. *http://www.grantsdirect.com/*

The Grantsmanship Center

▶ This site includes links to federal government, state government, community foundations, and international funding. *http://www.tgci.com/*

Grantsnet

▶ A project of the Howard Hughes Medical Institute (HHMI) and the American Association for the Advancement in Science (AAAS), this free searchable database offers hundreds of funding opportunities in the biological and medical sciences. *http://www.grantsnet.org*

GrantsNet (U.S. Dept. of HHS)

▶ This is a tool for finding and exchanging information about HHS and selected other U.S. federal grant programs. It includes a tutorial on how to find grant information as well as a powerful search tool. *http://www.hhs.gov/grantsnet/*

Grantseeker

▶ This site offers comprehensive research data identifying billions of dollars available to organizations looking for funding in California, Ohio, New Jersey, Pennsylvania, New York, and Texas. *http://www.grantseeker.com*

GrantSpring.com

▶ Developed by GrantSpring, a grant-seeking consulting company in Phoenix, this Web site provides links to corporate grant makers and to state and federal agencies that award grants to charities. The links are organized by the grant makers' areas of interest: the arts, education, the environment, health care, and social services. *http://www.grantspring.com*

GrantStation.com

▶ *http://www.grantstation.com*

The Guide to Grants

▶ This is an electronic database of all foundation and corporate grants listed in *The Chronicle* since 1995. *Chronicle* subscribers can search grants from the two most recent issues. Complete access to the Guide to Grants requires a separate subscription. *http://philanthropy.com/grants/*

HUD Nonprofit Home Page

▶ *http://www.hud.gov/nonproft.html*

The IRIS Alert Service

▶ Use the IRIS Alert Service to receive funding alerts automatically. You can modify your Alert Service profile at any time. *http://carousel.lis.uiuc.edu/~iris/profiles/start.html*

The IRIS Database

▶ Search the IRIS Database for funding opportunities in every field from agriculture to zoology, or view upcoming deadlines in 25 subject areas; also, the OPS Database of selected items from the *Commerce Business Daily* and *Federal Register*. *http://carousel.lis.uiuc.edu/~iris/databases.html*

Just Grants Arizona

▶ This site includes a fully searchable database, much like the Foundation Center. If interested in using the search function, just send an e-mail to *mboess@azgrants.com*. It includes a free biweekly e-mail grants newsletter, Tips and Tools, Great Grants Links, and a Consultants Directory. *http://www.azgrants.com*

Links to Sites for Funding Searches

▶ *http://www.grantresults.com/grant_results/Funding%20Searches1.htm*

Mickey's Place in the Sun Fundraising Resources

▶ *http://people.delphi.com/mickjyoung/funding.html*

Minnesota Foundation Directory Online—Foundation Data Center, Inc.

▶ *http://www.capriotti.com/fdc/mfdinfo.htm*

Nonprofit Gateway—Grants and Nonfinancial Support

▶ Links to government agency home pages for information on grants and nonfinancial support. *http://www.nonprofit.gov/resource/support.html#agencies*

North Carolina Giving Online—Capital Development Services

▶ *http://www.capdev.com/online/index.htm*

Notices of Funding Availability (Empowerment Zone/Enterprise Communities Community Toolbox)

▶ NOFAs are announcements that appear in the *Federal Register*, which is printed each business day by the U.S. government. The site allows users to generate customized listings. *http://ocd.usda.gov/nofa.htm*

ProgressivePubs.com

▶ The site also allows users to post anonymous comments about their experiences dealing with the foundations that are profiled. *http://www.progressivepubs.com*

Progressive Foundation Database

▶ A service of Progressive Resources Publications, a Washington company that sells books and other materials produced by public-policy organizations, this Web site profiles more than 300 grant makers that support progressive projects. It includes their addresses, phone numbers, program officers, giving priorities, average grant size, and deadlines. (Free registration required.) *http://www.progressivepubs.com/foundations*

South Dakota Grant Directory

▶ *http://www.sdstatelibrary.com/grants/introduction.htm*

State and Local Funding Directories: A Bibliography—The Foundation Center

▶ *http://fdncenter.org/onlib/topical/sl_dir.html*

Thompson & Thompson's Community Foundations Directory

▶ State-by-state listing. *http://www.t-tlaw.com/resource.shtml*

TRAM Search

▶ Database includes government and private funding opportunities. *http://tram.east.asu.edu/*

U.S. Government Notices of Funding Availability

▶ The U.S. government published all notices of funding availability in the *Federal Register,* which is published each business day. This is a keyword searchable database. *http://ocd.usda.gov/nofa.htm*

Fund-Raising Consultants

Choosing and Using a Fund-Raising Consultant: A Bibliography

▶ *http://www.utsystem.edu/Dev/ConsultantGuidePart2.htm*

Grants and Grant Seeking

ASU ResearchNet Funding Information

▶ *http://researchnet.asu.edu/resources/*

Chronicle Guide to Grants

▶ This is an electronic database of all corporate and foundation grants listed in *The Chronicle of Philanthropy* since 1995. Subscriptions are available for periods of one week to one year. There is a significant discount if you are also a subscriber to *The Chronicle of Philanthropy. http://philanthropy.com/grants*

CyberGrants, Inc.

▶ CyberGrants is a business-to-business portal for nonprofit organizations seeking grants and private and corporate foundations wishing to provide funding to the nonprofit community. CyberGrants allows nonprofits to research grant guidelines of member grant makers and flag proposals that fit, and write proposals online and submit them to multiple, flagged grant makers. It can be used by nonprofit organizations free of charge. An online demonstration of available. *http://www.cybergrants.com/contact.htm*

CyberGrants—Grant Seekers—Apply Online

▶ *http://www.cybergrants.com/gsapply.htm*

Easygrants

▶ This tool makes it easy to apply for grants and fellowships. With easygrants.com, you can search and apply for multiple funding opportunities using one application. You can also set up a grant seeker profile about yourself or your organization that will be made available to grant makers looking to invite candidates. *http://www.easygrants.com/eg/grantseeker/gs_home.asp*

eGrant

▶ Developed by the *Center for Arts Management and Technology* at Carnegie Mellon University, it is a fast and secure method for submitting your grant application. *http://demo.egrant.org*

The Foundation Center Online

▶ Includes Grantmaker Info, Online Library, Marketplace, and Philanthropy News Digest. *http://fdncenter.org/about*

Foundations On-Line

▶ This is a directory of charitable grant makers. You can browse the foundation directory, pick a listed foundation, search any foundation's information page, or search any foundation's home page. Foundation home pages may contain downloadable information such as grant applications, periodical and financial reports, and e-mail capabilities. *http://www.foundations.org/*

The Grant Seeker's Guide to the Internet: Revised and Revisited

▶ *http://www.nonprofit.net/info/guide.html*

Grant Seeker's Resources—Polaris

▶ *http://www.polarisgrantscentral.net/resources.html#GS%20Re sources*

Grant Tracker®

▶ *http://www.granttracker.com/, http://www.stanford.edu/~kendric/ GT/*

Grant Update

▶ This site was designed to inform grant seekers of the latest information regarding new grant announcements, insider tips, and innovative fund-raising ideas through use of the Internet. It also serves as an index to hundreds of funding sources and to other Web sites that provide useful information and tools to aid grant seekers. *http://www.grantupdate.com/*

Grantmaster.com

▶ *http://www.grantmaster.com/FreeResources.asp, http://www.grant-master.com/FundingSources.asp*

Grantmatch.com

▶ This for-profit company allows charities and nonprofit organizations to inform potential donors about their work and match donations to specific projects. Grant seekers can post grant proposals or donation requests by category. *http://www.grantmatch.com/index.html-ssi*

Grants and Other Funding Sources—University of Tennessee

▶ *http://www.lib.utk.edu/refs/grants.html*

Grants and Related Resources

▶ *http://www.lib.msu.edu/harris23/grants/fraisers.htm*

Grants, Etc.

▶ Enables novice and advanced grant seekers, funders, fund raisers, and donors to access relevant information throughout the Internet. *http://www.ssw.umich.edu/resources/index2.html?collection=grants*

Grants Information Center—University of Wisconsin

▶ *http://www.library.wisc.edu/libraries/Memorial/grants/non-prof.htm*

The GrantSAT (the Grant Proposal Self-Assessment Tool)

▶ This site provides assessment criteria for many aspects of a proposal; a good complement to a proposal library. *http://www.orsp.cmich.edu/hbappen_f.htm*

GrantsDirect.com

▶ *http://www.grantsdirect.com/Resources.htm*

GrantsInfo.com—Academic Research Information System

▶ *http://www.arisnet.com/*

Grant$eeker

▶ *http://www.regis.edu/grants/search.htm*

The Grantsmanship Center

▶ The Center, a clearinghouse of fund-raising information and training for the nonprofit sector, provides links to the Center's online magazine and a listing of publications for fund raisers, daily grant announcements, and news from federal government agencies. An online subscription service featuring current grant opportunities on the Internet is in development. *http://www.tgci.com/*

GrantSmart.org

▶ A project of Canyon Research with support from the J.C. Downing Foundation, GrantSmart.org serves grant seekers, philanthropic organizations, and individual donors, providing a searchable database of 990-PFs (IRS tax returns) filed by private foundations. (The site will eventually include tax forms filed by public foundations and charitable organizations as well.) Also featured are news and press releases, frequently asked questions, blank tax forms and instructions, and an online discussion forum. *http://www.grantsmart.org/*

GrantStation

▶ *http://www.grantstation.com/*

GrantsWeb

▶ *infoserv.rttonet.psu.edu/gweb.htm, www.research.sunysb.edu/research/kirby.html, www.msue.msu.edu/msue/resources/grantweb.html, www.usc.edu/hsc/nml/e-resources/info/grantsweb.html*

Maine Grants Information Center Index of Web Resources

▶ *http://www.megrants.org/bookmk98.html*

National Network of Grantmakers

▶ The National Network of Grantmakers is a 20-year-old organization of 400 members concerned about funding organizations working toward social change and economic justice. Composed of individual donors, foundation staff, board, and grant-making committee members, NNG offers services to funders, practitioners, and grant seekers. Grant seekers visiting this site will be most interested in the sections containing NNG's members, the Grantmaker Directory, working groups, upcoming conferences, publications, research, job listings, and NNG's "Common Grant Application." *http://www.nng.org/*

Polaris

▶ Check out the following sections: Tips and Hints; Funding Sources; Ideas and Resources; Grant Seeker's Resources. *http://www.polarisgrantscentral*

SRA Guide to Resources—Society of Research Administrators

▶ *http://www.srainternational.org/cws/sra/restrict/rguide1.htm*

Seliger & Associates—Free Grant Information

▶ Seliger & Associates, a grant-writing consulting firm, provides access to two types of free grant availability information: the online Seliger Funding Report, which lists available federal, state, local, foundation, and corporate giving grant opportunities, and e-mail Grant Alerts. Registration is required.

Six Easy Steps to Millions in Grants Additional Resources and Links—Maldon Enterprise

▶ *http://members.aol.com/Grantbook/link.htm*

Grant Writing/Proposal Writing

Basic Elements of Grant Writing

▶ *http://www.cpb.org/grants/grantwriting.html*

Best of the Web for Grant Writers

▶ *http://www.usc.edu/dept/source/grantsweb.htm*

Deborah Kluge—Independent Consultant

▶ This site describes not only this consultant's services but also includes an FAQ section as well as proposal writing and government contracting links. *http://www.proposalwriter.com/about.html*

EPA Grant-Writing Tutorial

▶ *http://www.epa.gov/seahome/grants/src/grant.htm*

Elements of a Grant Proposal

▶ A proposal must convince the prospective donor of two things: that a problem or need of significant magnitude exists, and that the applicant agency has the means and the imagination to solve the problem or meet the need. *http://www.silcom.com/~paladin/promaster.html*

Fund Raiser/Grant-Writing Consultants—Grants and Related Resources

▶ *http://www.lib.msu.edu/harris23/grants/fraisers.htm*

Fund-Raising and Grant-Writing Resources

▶ *http://www.fundsnetservices.com/grantwri.htm*

Grant Proposal Writing course

▶ Online courses from American River College. *http://trfn.clpgh.org/nonprofits/grants.html*

Granthelp

▶ Developed by grant-proposal writer Frank Evangelisti, in Binghamton, New York, this Web site provides advice on how to write grant proposals, a glossary of grant-seeking terms, and a list of commonly used acronyms. *http://granthelp.clarityconnect.com*

Grant Writer's Guide and Related Resources

▶ *http://www.tandl.leon.k12.fl.us/grants/grant-resources.htm*

Grant Writing—Education World Grants Center

▶ *http://www.education-world.com/grants/writing/index.shtml*

Grant-Writing Help and Research Materials—University of Nebraska at Omaha

▶ *http://www.unomaha.edu/~wwwspr/writing.htm*

Grant-Writing Tips

▶ *http://www.seanet.com/~sylvie/grants.htm*

Grants and Grant Proposal–Writing Manual, 2nd Edition—Education for Entrepreneurship, St. Louis University

▶ *http://www.slu.edu/eweb/grants.htm*

Grants and Grant Writing—United Cerebral Palsy Association, Greater Utica (New York) Area

▶ *http://www.ucp-utica.org/uwlinks/grants.html*

Grants and Letters—Ondine Publications

▶ *http://www.grantsandletters.bigstep.com/*

The GrantSAT (the Grant Proposal Self-Assessment Tool)

▶ Provides assessment criteria for many aspects of a proposal. A good complement to a proposal library. *http://www.orsp.cmich.edu/hbappen_f.htm*

Grantwriters.com

▶ *http://www.grantwriters.com*

Grantwriting Basics and Tips—Maine Grant Information Center

▶ *http://www.megrants.org/grantwriting.html*

Guide for Writing a Funding Proposal

▶ Created to provide both instructions on how to write a funding proposal and actual examples of a completed proposal; from S. Joseph Levine, PhD (levine@msue.msu.edu), Department of Agricultural and Extension Education, Michigan State University, East Lansing, Michigan. *http://trfn.clpgh.org/nonprofits/grants.html*

Guide to Grant Proposal Writing

▶ *http://www2.njstatelib.org/njlib/grhdtoc.htm*

A Guide to Proposal Planning and Writing—Oryx Press

▶ Condensed version of the 1998 book, *Proposal Planning and Writing*. *http://www.oryxpress.com/miner.htm, http://www.uvm.edu/~reshmpg/miners~1.htm*

How to Write a Grant for Funding—Especially Non-Profits Consulting

▶ *http://especiallynonprofits.com/grants.htm*

Innonet

▶ A recent "gift" to the nonprofit community is this Workstation for Innovative Nonprofits. This interactive Web tool enables nonprofit organizations to create top quality program plans, budgets, evaluation plans, and grant proposals. It even offers a free review and critique of those plans once completed. *http://www.innonet.org/*

Introduction to Proposal Writing—The Foundation Center

▶ *http://fdncenter.org/onlib/orient/prop1.html*

Mickey's Place in the Sun Grant and Grant Writing Resources

▶ *http://people.delphi.com/mickjyoung/grants.html*

National Certification Directory—Certified Grants Specialists and Reviewers by State (Research Associates)

▶ *http://www.researchassociatesco.com/national_directory.htm*

Proposal Tracking Software

▶ Andrew Grant created an Access software program some time back for the purpose of tracking grant proposals. It is easy to go in and change the headers to allow for the tracking of volunteers instead. The software can be downloaded for free with a $20 contribution to Charity Channel suggested. *http://www.charitychannel.com/softshare/grant_download.htm*

Proposal Writing Short Course—The Foundation

▶ *http://fdncenter.org/onlib/shortcourse/prop1.html*

Proposals for Funding—Phil Bartle

▶ *http://www.scn.org/ip/cds/cmp/proposal.htm#SIntro*

SchoolGrants: Grant Writing Links

▶ *http://www.schoolgrants.org/Links/grant_writing.htm*

Steer Your Way to a Winning Grant

▶ *http://www.ag.org/acts/perspectives/9910_winninggrant.cfm*

Step-by-Step Online Grant Writing Proposal Workshop

▶ *http://www.cyberworkshops.com/syllabus.htm*

Tips for Writing Grant Proposals

▶ *http://www.kinesisinc.com/resource_article_granttips.html*

Tips for Writing Grants

▶ *http://www.ncsa.uiuc.edu/people/bievenue/gw.html*

Top 10 Grant Writing Tips (and Other Links)

▶ *http://www.grantresults.com/grant_results/Tips1.htm*

In-Kind Donations/Excess Inventory

Excess Access

▶ A site where donors of furniture, computers, and just about anything else can meet up with nonprofits that can use the equipment. *http://www.excessaccess.com/*

Purchasing Services Agency

▶ This nonprofit organization negotiates with vendors for preferential pricing of goods and services on behalf of their member agencies and simplifies the ordering process for individual agencies. *http://www.psagency.org/index.cfm*

Matching Gifts

MatchingGifts.com

▶ An online resource dedicated to the understanding, promotion, and tracking of matching gifts. *http://www.matchinggifts.com*

Online Fund Raising

Affinity Resources

▶ *http://www.affinityresources.com/awz5.html*

"A Brave New World of Giving" (Chronicle of Philanthropy)

▶ *http://www.philanthropy.com/free/articles/v12/i17/17000101.htm*

CMSi Study of Socially Engaged Internet Users

▶ Conducted by the Mellman Group for Craver, Matthews, Smith, & Company, this 1999 study explores the potential for growth in online fund raising. According to the report, nearly 50 million Americans over the age of 18 have Internet access and currently donate their time and/or money to charitable causes. Of these, however, most have never visited the Web site of a charity, and only 3.5 million say they have given online. *http://www.craveronline.com/*

Exploring Online Fund Raising for Nonprofit Arts Organizations

▶ *http://www.idealist.org/beth.html*

Fund Raising on the Internet: Acquiring and Cultivating Donors with E-Mail and the Web

▶ *http://www.malwarwick.com/fundnet.html*

Guidestar

▶ *http://www.guidestar.org/*

Internet Nonprofit Center's "How Can We Use the Internet for Fundraising?"

▶ This comprehensive 1998 report by Eric Mercer was designed to provide "an introduction and a classification scheme to help readers learn to effectively evaluate alternative methods of online fundraising." *http://www.nonprofits.org/misc/981027em.html*

NPTalk: Technology Funding and Fundraising Resources

▶ *http://www.ombwatch.org/npt/nptalk/may2000/funding.html*

National Federation of Nonprofits' "Nonprofits and the Internet"

▶ Provides links to several full-text reports covering online fundraising regulation and related issues. *http://www.federationofnonprofits.org/net.htm*

Nonprofit Charitable Orgs' Donate Online

▶ This list of online fund-raising Web sites is provided by Stan Hutton, the About.com guide for Nonprofit Charitable Orgs. The related site, *Information About Online Fundaising (http://nonprofit.about.com/careers/nonprofit/msubonl.htm)* includes articles and relevant online resources for those interested in learning more about the subject. *http://nonprofit.about.com/business/nonprofit/msubdonl.htm*

Online Fundraising Mailing List

▶ The Gilbert Center's mailing list for online fund raising provides a learning environment for fund raisers at all levels of experience. *http://www.gilbert.org/fundraising/*

Online Fundraising Resources Center

▶ This site offers a sampling of chapters from the book *Fundraising and Friend-Raising on the Web,* with updates and a good set of successful Web site examples. *http://www.fund-online.com/*

Online Donations: Sorting Out the Chaos—ONE/Northwest

▶ *http://www.onenw.org/toolkit/online-donations.html*

Philanthropy News Digest Special Issue: Nonprofits & the Internet

▶ *http://fdncenter.org/pnd/19991221/index.html*

RE:NetDonors for Online Fund-Raising—Blackbaud

▶ Blackbaud has released RE:NetSolutions, a new suite of tools that empowers nonprofits to use the Internet to enhance communication with donors. These Web-based services offer a direct link to The Raiser's Edge®, the world's most widely used fund-raising management system. Blackbaud hosts the hardware and components that drive these services, freeing nonprofits from having to invest in secure servers and address technical issues. RE:NetDonors, which enables nonprofits to implement a secure donation page on their Web sites, is the core offering in the RE:NetSolutions suite. The components of RE:NetSolutions are: RE:NetDonors for Online Fund-Raising (a nonprofit organization can add a secure donation feature to its Web site and transfer gift information to The Raiser's Edge without manual data entry); RE:NetMail for Online Communication and Appeals (create personalized mass e-mails with links to online giving pages, send e-mail newsletters, and much more. Measure the success of each e-mail communication by tracking click-throughs to the online giving page, the number of donations, and the total amount donated online); RE:NetEvents for Online Event Registration (organizations can offer online event registration and fee payment to their constituents and easily record online event information in The Raiser's Edge); RE:NetDirectories for Online People Search (an organization can add alumni, professional, member, and other types of directories to its Web site. Visitors can search the directories for classmates, members, and more using a variety of powerful search options); Consulting Services (Blackbaud consultants can help organizations create, implement, and execute an Internet fund-raising strategy that is consistent with their overall development goals); and Educational Opportunities (to make the most of a Blackbaud solution, educational opportunities are available on the use of RE:NetSolutions and Internet fund-raising strategy). *http://netsolutions.blackbaud.com*

Resources for Fundraising Online

▶ Compiled by Putnam Barber of the Internet Nonprofit Center, this comprehensive list includes annotated links to a wide range of online fund-raising sites. *http://www.nonprofits.org/npofaq/ misc/990804olfr.html, http://beamus.com/resources_for_fundraising_online.htm*

Social Ecology Online Fundraising Resources

▶ *http://www.socialecology.com/resources.html*

Some Legal Implications of Soliciting Online Using Third-Party Hosting Agents

▶ *http://www.nonprofits.org/npofaq/16/21.html*

Online Learning

FundClass—Online Fundraising School

▶ FundClass is a free e-mail list used for teaching fund-raising lessons in an informal online classroom in which veteran fund raisers share their knowledge on a chosen topic with those who are new to fund raising. *http://www.fundraiser-software.com/fundclass.html*

Fundwell.com—Online Certificate in Fund Raising

▶ *http://www.fundwell.com/*

Internet Fund-Raising Classes—Online Fundraising Resources Center

▶ *http://www.fund-online.com/classes/index.html*

Planned Giving Resources

American College of Trust and Estate Counsel

▶ Run by the American College of Trust and Estate Counsel, a professional association of lawyers who specialize in trust and estate law, this Web site provides information on legal decisions and legislation that affect estate planning and has links to other legal and estate-planning resources. *http://www.actec.org*

American Philanthropy Review: Model Gift Policy Manual

▶ Developed by the American Philanthropy Review, a company that reviews and sells books on fund raising and nonprofit management, this site provides a sample policy manual for planned giving programs. The manual outlines deferred-giving options, gift-acceptance procedures, and appraisal and reporting requirements. It also describes the advantages and disadvantages of different planned giving approaches, including annuities, unitrusts, pooled-income funds, and charitable gift annuities and provides a glossary. *http://CharityChannel.com/Manual*

Ashton Associates Planned Giving Links

▶ *http://www.debraashton.com/links.html*

Canadian Association of Gift Planners

▶ The association, based in Edmonton, Alberta, is a professional organization for planned giving officers and others who advise donors on deferred gifts. *http://www.cam.org/~cagp*

CharityVillage.Com Library

▶ Articles on planned giving gathered by this great mega site of nonprofit resources. *http://www.charityvillage.com/charityvillage/research/rpg.html*

GiftLaw

▶ The free public service by Crescendo software and Comdel, Inc. helps attorneys, CPAs, financial planners, CLUs, trust officers, and other gift planning professionals work together with charities. GiftLaw includes Web pages for the Washington Hotline, Revenue Rulings, Private Letter Rulings, the Article of the Month, and the Case of the Week. The GiftLaw content may be accessed through "Portal Pages" on the Web sites of participating charities. Each professional will first select the GiftLaw Portal Page on the Web site of the charity and then may access the GiftLaw site. When a charity subscribes to the free GiftLaw service, a Web page may be downloaded by the charity. The charity agrees that it will include that page in its Web site. Each charity is permitted to use the upper part of the charity's GiftLaw Web page for local content. *http://www.giftlaw.com/*

Gift Planning Resources Centre

▶ Created by the Quebec Roundtable, an affiliate of the Canadian Association of Gift Planners, GPIC-Plus, a planned giving newsletter on the Internet published in French, and Charity Village, a Web site for Canadian nonprofit professionals, this site provides links to Internet resources of interest to planned giving officials in Canada and the United States and has links to charities that present planned giving information on their Web sites. *http://www.cam.org/~gprc*

Glossary of Planned Giving Terms

▶ *http://www.premieradministration.com/glossary.htm*

Innovations in Planned Giving—California Community Foundation

▶ *http://www.calfund.org/html/giving.html*

Kaspick & Company

▶ Under a new rule issued by the Internal Revenue Service in December 1998, and in effect until June 30, 2000, certain charitable remainder trusts in which donors' payments are based on the income generated by the trusts may now be "flipped" to provide a payment based on a fixed percentage of what the assets are worth each year. The investment advisory company Kaspick & Company, in Boston and Palo Alto, California, has posted copies of the new IRS rules, a summary of the pros and cons of converting the trusts for both donors and charities, sample letters alerting donors about the "flip" provision, and a summary of the risks involved in converting trusts. *http://www.kaspick.com*

Law & Estate Planning Sites on the Internet

▶ Commercial site connecting to technical information on estate planning, trusts, wills, case law, and related topics. *http://www.caprobate.com/links.htm*

Learning About Trusts

▶ *http://www.premieradministration.com/Learn.htm*

National Committee on Planned Giving

▶ Run by the National Committee on Planned Giving, an organization in Indianapolis for people who specialize in arranging deferred gifts, this Web site provides links to sites that provide information on planned giving. *http://www.ncpg.org*

PG Calc

▶ Maintained by PG Calc, a planned giving software company in Cambridge, Massachusetts, this Web site lists the monthly Internal Revenue Service discount rates since 1983, offers advice on how to pick the best discount rate for deferred gifts, and describes different planned giving vehicles. It also provides information on periodicals, books, consulting companies, and Internet resources of interest to planned giving officials and has links to charities that present planned giving information on their Web sites. *http://www.pgcalc.com*

PhilanthroTec: The Charitable Remainder Calculator

Run by PhilanthroTec, a planned giving software company in Matthews, North Carolina, this Web site offers free software that allows fund raisers to calculate the payout rate that will generate a remainder interest of a specified percentage for unitrusts, annuity trusts, pooled income funds, and charitable gift annuities. The software can be downloaded from the company's Web site. *http://www.ptec.com/ptec/rwf-20001017134254*, *http://www.ptec.com/html/free_crt_software_news.html*

Philanthropy Information—Web sites Useful for Gift Planners (Crescendo Software)

▶ *http://www.crescendosoft.com/phil.asp*

Planned Giving at Lawrenceville

▶ *http://www.lawrenceville.org/plannedgiving/*

PlannedGiving.Com

▶ This is a commercial site to sell their planned giving policy manual. Sample chapters are included. Free feature is a list of other planned giving sites and resources. *http://www.plannedgiving.com*

Planned Giving Design Center

▶ The Planned Giving Design Center is the world's largest Web site on the subject of planned giving. You may register with the PGDC for free. When you register with the PGDC, you will be taken to either the PGDC USA site or a locally hosted PGDC. The PGDC is a network of Web sites throughout the country that are hosted by a charitable organization in your community, or sponsored by a corporate sponsor for the entire community. These organizations have made a financial commitment to delivering the highest-quality planned giving information to you at no cost. The Planned Giving Design Center provides free news and information on planned gifts and related topics. Subscribers receive e-mail alerts that describe and analyze new regulatory actions affecting planned gifts, detailed information on specific types of gifts, and weekly articles by experts. *http://www.pgdc.net/pub/*

Planned Giving for Beginners—Crescendo Interactive

▶ *http://www.crescendosoft.com/beginner.asp*

Planned Giving for the One-Person Office—David Schmeling

▶ *http://www.thecuttingedge.com/Consult/D_Schmeling/planned_giving_foreword.htm*

Planned Giving Online

▶ *http://www.plannedgift.com/pgo/*

Planned Giving Resource for Nonprofit and Charitable Organizations—Premier Administration

▶ *http://www.premieradministration.com/profres.htm*

Planned Giving Resources

Developed by James B. Potter, a planned giving consultant in Alexandria, Virginia, this Web site lists the state regulations that govern charitable gift annuities—a type of planned gift that allows donors to contribute cash, securities, property, or other assets to a charity in exchange for fixed payments—as well as sources in each state that can provide more information. *http://www.pgresources.com*

Planned Giving Today

▶ This site provides selected articles from *Planned Giving Today,* a monthly newsletter published by G. Roger Schoenhals, a planned giving consultant, that discusses such topics as how to establish and promote a planned giving program, build relationships with donors, and deal with the technical aspects of planned giving. It also explains what planned gifts are and how they differ from other charitable donations and describes the role of the planned giving officer. *http://www.pgtoday.com*

Planning Links and Resources—Henry & Associates Gift & Estate Planning Services

▶ *http://www.gift-estate.com/crt.html#links, http://www.gift-estate.com/crt.html#resources*

Robert F. Sharpe & Company

▶ This company is a commercial vendor of planned gift information products and services. The Web site features communication tools about estate and gift planning ideas for organizational use in working with its donors. *http://www.rfsco.com/home.html*

Seniors in Cyberspace

▶ Created by Natasha van Bentum, director of planned giving at Greenpeace Canada, in Vancouver, this Web site discusses how older people are using the Internet. The site is designed to help fund raisers create planned giving sites that appeal to elderly donors. *http://www.seniorsincyberspace.org*

Web Sites Useful for Gift Planners

▶ *http://www.crescendosoft.com/phil.asp*

Prospect Research

David Lamb's Prospect Research Page

▶ A list of helpful resources compiled by a University of Washington prospect researcher. *http://www.lambresearch.com/*

Dorry Kelley's Favorite Prospect Research Links

▶ *http://web.syr.edu/~dekelley/hotlist.html*

Estate/Wealth/Gift Statistics Personal Wealth

▶ *http://www.irs.ustreas.gov/prod/tax_stats/soi/est_pw.html*

Fund Raising: Prospect Research—CASE Advancement Link Center

▶ *http://web.case.org/links/frprspct.htm*

Grants and Related Sources—Prospect Research Resources

▶ *http://www.lib.msu.edu/harris23/grants/prospect.htm*

Internet Prospector

▶ From the Association of Professional Researchers for Advancement, a site intended primarily for professional nonprofit fund raisers, this site provides not only links to foundations/grants but also advice on using the Internet more efficiently, information on business ethics (see Reference Section) and other useful information. You'll find an online newsletter and archives of past issues, a directory of U.S. Secretary of State incorporation records, search engine prospecting and test results, and tips for foundation searches. The APRA also maintains a free electronic discussion group. You can subscribe at this site. *http://www.internet-prospector.org/*

Links Prospect Research

▶ *http://129.8.21.20/links/prospect_research.htm*

NETSource@USC

▶ *http://www.usc.edu/dept/source/*

Princeton University Development Research Links

▶ *http://www.princeton.edu/One/research/netlinks.html*

Prospect Research

▶ *http://oia.mines.edu/advancement_resources/research/default.htm*

Prospect Research and Reference Tools—University of Vermont

▶ *http://www.uvm.edu/~prospect/research.html*

Prospect Research Bookmarks—Northwestern University Development Research Office

▶ *http://pubweb.acns.nwu.edu/~cap440/bookmark.html*

Prospect Research Links from Veritas Information Services

▶ *http://www.veritasinfo.com/training.htm*

Prospect Research Online

▶ *http://wwwrpbooks.com*

Prospect Research Tips from Waltman Associates

▶ Somewhat similar to David Lamb's site but with many different useful sites. *http://www.tc.umn.edu/~bergq003/wa/rsrchtips.html*, *http://www.tc.umn.edu/nlhome/g248/bergq003/wa/rsrchtips.html*

University of Virginia Prospect Research

▶ *http://www.people.virginia.edu/~dev-pros/*

Virtual Prospect Research

▶ *http://www.butler.edu/~mmurphy/index.htmlx*

Solicitation Regulations

State Charitable Solicitations Requirements— Raffa & Associates

▶ Developed by Raffa & Associates, an accounting firm in Washington, this Web site explains each state's registration requirements for charities that want to raise money from state residents. The site provides contact information for the agencies that regulate fund raising and links to the text of the state laws that govern charitable solicitation. The site also discusses the Uniform Registration Statement, an effort to standardize registration requirements among states. *http://www.raffa.com/Interior/s_frame.htm*

The Unified Registration Statement

▶ This Web site explains the Uniform Registration Statement, an effort to standardize the registration process in states that require charities to register before soliciting their residents. Organizations can use the statement—which is available on the site—to register in 32 states and the District of Columbia, although six of the states require additional information. *http://nonprofits.org/library/gov/urs*

Special Events

WorldofEvents.net—Directory for Professionals, Educators, Students, and Researchers

▶ Check out the fund-raising link as well as others. *http://www.world ofevents.net/*

E-Mail Discussion Lists

ABA-PTL

▶ The American Bar Association's discussion list for estate planners and administrators. *listserv@home.ease.lsoft.com.* To subscribe, send e-mail leaving the subject line blank, with the message SUBSCRIBE ABA-PTL. Archives are at *http://206.241.12.9/archives/aba-ptl.html.*

ADVANCE-L

▶ This site is for senior advancement professionals. To subscribe, send an e-mail message to *listserv@hermes.case.org.* Leave the subject line blank. Type in the body of the message: *Subscribe ADVANCE-L <your name>.* Send the message. From this site you can also subscribe to the following lists: ALUMNI-L; CFRNET; FUNDLIST; FUNDSVCS; GIFT-PL; PRSPCT-L; SCHOOLS-L; STEWARDSHIPLIST; TWOYEAR-L. *http://www.case.org/info/groups.htm*

ALUMNI-L

▶ This site covers alumni relations. To subscribe, send this e-mail message: *subscribe ALUMNI-L [YOUR FIRST AND LAST NAME]* to *listserv@brownvm.brown.edu.*

Annual Giving

▶ This is an online forum to discuss annual giving, maintained by T. Greg Prince, associate director for annual giving at the University of North Carolina at Chapel Hill. To subscribe, send an e-mail message to *listserv@unc.edu* that states in the body of the message *subscribe annfund Your Name.* Leave the subject blank, and do not include e-mail addresses in the body of the message.

ARTS_GIFT

▶ This is a discussion list from American Philanthropy Review dedicated to the challenges of raising funds for the performing and visual arts. It is open to any person who is responsible for any aspect of fund raising in the arts. There are two methods to subscribe:

1. Send an e-mail to *listserv@CharityChannel.com* with *SUBSCRIBE ARTS_GIFT YourFirstname YourLastname* as the message. Leave the subject line blank.

2. Visit the CharityChannel Web site at *CharityChannel.com/forums* and click on the subscription information for ARTS_GIFT.

CAPTALK

▶ This site is for discussion of all aspects of capital campaign fund raising. These are two methods to subscribe:

1. Send e-mail to *listserv@CharityChannel.com* with *SUBSCRIBE CAPTALK YourFirstname YourLastname* as the message. Leave the subject line blank.

2. Visit the CharityChannel Web site at *CharityChannel.com/forums* and click on the subscription information for CAPTALK.

CFRNET (Corporation and Foundation Fund Raising for Educational organizations)

▶ To subscribe, send e-mail, leaving the subject line blank, with the message *subscribe cfrnet Your Name. cfrnet-request@medicine.wustl.edu*

Consult-I

▶ This is an online discussion group for fund-raising consultants. Topics include relations with clients, collection of fees, ethics, marketing, strategies for working on campaigns, and other topics. To subscribe, send an e-mail message to *listserv@jtsa.edu* that states in the body of the message *"sub consult-l Your Name."* Leave the subject blank, and do not include e-mail addresses in the body of the message.

Corporate and Foundation Relations (CFRNET)

▶ This site covers corporate and foundation fund raising. To subscribe, send this e-mail message: *subscribe CFRNET [YOUR FIRST AND LAST NAME]* to *listserv@unc.edu.*

ACCOUNTABILITY

▶ Covers all aspects of accountability, ethics, and nonprofit organizations, both online and off. *http://www.charitychannel.com/ forums/forums-a.htm*

ADVANCEMENT

▶ Covers all aspects of college and university advancement. *http://www.charitychannel.com/forums/ADVANCEMENT.htm*

ALUMNI

▶ All aspects of higher education alumni relations. *http://www.charitychannel.com/forums/ALUMNI.htm*

ANNUAL_FUND

▶ Covers all aspects of the annual fund form of fund raising. *http://www.charitychannel.com/forums/Annual_Fund.htm*

APRA-MO-KAN

▶ Discussion forum for members of the Missouri–Kansas chapter of the Association of Professional Researchers for Advancement. *(Must be a chapter member to join.) http://www.charitychannel. com/forums/APRA-MO-KAN.htm*

ARTS_GIFT

▶ Covers fund raising for arts and cultural organizations. *http://www.charitychannel.com/forums/Arts_gift.htm*

CAPTALK

▶ Covers all aspects of the capital campaign for nonprofit/NGO organizations. *http://www.charitychannel.com/forums/CapTalk.htm*

CHARITYBOOKS

▶ Covers all aspects of writing, publishing, marketing, and review of nonprofit-sector books. *http://www.charitychannel.com/ forums/CHARITYBOOKS.htm*

CHARITYLAW

▶ Covers all aspects of the U.S. law of tax-exempt organizations. *http://www.charitychannel.com/forums/CharityLaw.htm*

CHARITYLAW-CANADA

▶ Covers all aspects of the Canadian law of tax-exempt organizations. *http://www.charitychannel.com/forums/CHARITYLAW-CANA-DA.htm*

CHARITY-PR

▶ All aspects of nonprofits and public relations; open to anyone interested in the subject. *http://www.charitychannel.com/forums/ CHARITY-PR.HTM*

CHARITYSOFT

▶ Covers software, the Internet, and charities. *http://www.charity-channel.com/forums/CharitySoft.htm*

CHARITYTALK

▶ This is the "Big Tent" Internet discussion list of the nonprofit world (their flagship list that discusses literally any topic in the nonprofit sector, with the emphasis on philanthropy). It is open to anyone in the nonprofit sector, anywhere in the world. *http://www.charitychannel.com/forums/CHARITYTALK.htm*

CHRISTIANDEV

▶ This site is open to any person who shares the Christian faith and an interest in the topic of development of churches, ministries, and organizations such as Christian schools, colleges, universities, and hospitals. Discussion is expected to focus on North America, but is open to Christians from all parts of the world. *http://www.charitychannel.com/forums/CHRISTIANDEV.htm*

CONSULTANTS

▶ This site focuses on all aspects of consulting to nonprofit/NGO organizations. Business aspects, ethics, law, etc. of interest to consultants are discussed. *http://www.charitychannel.com/forums/ CONSULTANTS.htm*

CYBERGIFTS

▶ This site is open to any person who shares an interest in any aspect of charitable fund raising over the Internet. It will be particularly of interest to officers, directors, and staff of nonprofit organizations; Internet consultants and other professionals who advise nonprofit organizations; and those who have developed for-profit fund-raising sites for the nonprofit community. It will further be of interest to those with an interest in the law and ethics of tax-exempt organizations as these topics relate to interstate, interprovincial, and/or international fund raising over the Internet. To subscribe, go to *http://charitychannel.com/Forums* or send an e-mail message to *Listserv@CharityChannel.com.* In the body of the message, type the words: *subscribe cybergifts Your Name. http://www.charity-channel.com/forums/CYBERGIFTS.htm*

DCMETRO

▶ Online communication among governments, nonprofits, community organizations, foundations, and businesses in the D.C. metropolitan area about partnerships, resource development, and grants. *http://www.charitychannel.com/forums/DCMETRO.htm*

DEV-WRITING

▶ Development writing takes many forms and crosses many disciplines within the development arena. This is the first forum dedicated to all aspects of development writing. *http://www.charity channel.com/forums/DEV-WRITING.htm*

EVENTS

▶ Focuses on the special-events form of fund raising. *http://www.charitychannel.com/forums/EVENTS.htm*

FUNDLIST

▶ To Subscribe to fundlist, send a message to *listproc@listproc.hcf.jhu.edu* that says: *SUB FUNDLIST Firstname M. Lastname. Stephen.A.Hirby@Lawrence.Edu* (Steve Hirby, listowner)

GIFTMANAGE

▶ Covers all aspects of the management of endowment, charitable trust, and foundation funds. *http://www.charitychannel.com/forums/GiftManage.htm*

GIFTPLAN

▶ Planned giving forum, focusing on issues of interest to U.S. gift planners. *http://www.charitychannel.com/forums/GIFTPLAN.htm*

GIFTPLAN-CANADA

▶ Planned giving forum, focusing on issues of interest to Canadian gift planners. *http://www.charitychannel.com/forums/GIFTPLAN-CANADA.htm*

GIFTPROSPECTING

▶ Focuses on all aspects of prospect research, including techniques, privacy, legal aspects, and ethics. *http://www.charitychannel.com/forums/GiftProspecting.htm*

GRANTS

▶ This discussion list from American Philanthropy Review focuses on all aspects of grants and foundations. Grant seeking, foundation formation, foundation funding, and foundation administration in education, health care, human services, arts/humanities, public/society benefit, environment, animals, science, technology, international affairs, social science, and religion are permissible topics. There are two methods to subscribe:

1. Send e-mail to *listserv@CharityChannel.com* with *SUBSCRIBE GRANTS YourFirstname YourLastname* as the message. Leave the subject line blank.

2. Visit the CharityChannel Web site at *CharityChannel.com/forums* and click on the subscription information for GRANTS.

HEALTH_GIFT

▶ Focuses on all aspects of health care philanthropy. *http://www.charitychannel.com/forums/Health_Gift.htm*

K–12

▶ All aspects of development of K–12 schools, public and private. *http://www.charitychannel.com/forums/K-12.htm*

NSFRE-ALASKA

▶ Discussion list of the Alaska Chapter of the National Society of Fundraising Executives (NSFRE). *http://www.charitychannel.com/forums/NSFRE-ALASKA.htm*

NSFRE-VA

▶ Discussion list of the Virginia chapters of the National Society of Fundraising Executives (NSFRE). *(Must be a chapter member to join.)* *http://www.charitychannel.com/forums/NSFRE-VA.htm*

PRACTAC

▶ This site brings together nonprofit-sector practitioners and academic researchers. One of the biggest challenges for practitioners is having ready access to the best that the academic world has to offer—books, research, theory, and perspective. Practitioners, such as nonprofit officers, directors, and staff, as well as those in specialized fields such as fund development, will benefit from interacting with their academic colleagues. Academic researchers can often benefit from direct and easy access to practitioners, as well; PractAc (pronounced "Pract-Ack") will facilitate such collaborations. *http://www.charitychannel.com/forums/practac.htm*

RECOGNITION

▶ Donor recognition is a topic that every nonprofit organization that accepts charitable contributions must handle, and handle well. This forum discusses all aspects of donor recognition. *http://www.charitychannel.com/forums/recognition.htm*

SPONSORSHIP

▶ SPONSORSHIP is a place for people who raise sponsorship funds for sports, arts, charities, events, and more. SPONSORSHIP is also for those companies and others that provide that funding. *http://www.charitychannel.com/forums/sponsorship.htm*

TECHNOLOGY

▶ Leading-edge Internet and other technology is being harnessed by nonprofit organizations to raise funds, manage and mine donor databases, communicate with supporters, and run more efficiently. The sheer pace of technological advances raises new questions concerning online accountability, ethics, privacy, law, and more. TECHNOLOGY is focused on the broader voluntary-sector social, management, strategic, legal, policy, privacy, and other issues brought about by the ever-increasing pace of technology—especially Internet technology. Despite its name, it is not a "technogeek" forum and welcomes individuals with little or no technical background, those who have a sweeping and in-depth knowledge of the Internet and other technologies, and everyone in between. *http://www.charitychannel.com/forums/technology.htm*

UNITED_WAY

▶ Open to anyone with interest in any aspect of the United Way of America and its affiliates, including fund raising and fund seeking, management and governance, policies, and strategic direction. *http://www.charitychannel.com/forums/united_way.htm*

CDN-GIFTPL-L

▶ This is an online forum for discussion of planned giving in Canada. To subscribe, send an e-mail message to *listproc@listserv.mcmaster.ca* that states in the body of the message *subscribe cdn-giftpl-l Your Name*. Leave the subject blank, and do not include e-mail addresses in the body of the message.

CONSULT-L

▶ This listserv is for fund-raising consultants or those persons interested in consulting. The purpose of CONSULT-L is to discuss issues related to philanthropy and its associated services. The list is open to independent consultants as well as those employed by firms. Points of discussion may include such business aspects of consulting to nonprofit organizations as marketing, client/consultant relations, fees and collection, ethics, standards, strategies, and resources. Although some discussions about philanthropy in general will take place, these issues are covered adequately by other lists. It is for anyone with an interest in consulting, either because they do it full or part time or because they may be thinking about offering their services as a consultant. It may also be of interest to institutions considering using consultants. How to evaluate consultants and how to work with them are questions that will provide stimulating discussion. It is *not* a list through which business is solicited. People can join by sending a message to *LISTSERV@JTSA.EDU*. The message should read *SUB CONSULT-L yourfirstname yourlastname*.

DEADLINES

▶ Competitions, contests, calls for entries/papers, grants, scholarships, fellowships, jobs, internships, etc. in the arts or related areas. To subscribe, send the message: *SUBSCRIBE DEADLINES. adl@rtuh.com*

DEVELOPMENT-WRITING

▶ This site focuses on all aspects of development writing, including grant proposal writing, letter writing to prospective donors, and more. There are two methods to subscribe:

1. Send e-mail to *listserv@CharityChannel.com* with *SUBSCRIBE DEVELOPMENT-WRITING YourFirstname YourLastname* as the message. Leave the subject line blank.
2. Visit the CharityChannel Web site at *CharityChannel.com/forums* and click on the subscription information for DEVELOPMENT-WRITING.

EVENTS

▶ This site is for discussion of all aspects of special event planning and execution. Two methods to subscribe:

1. Send e-mail to *listserv@CharityChannel.com* with *SUBSCRIBE EVENTS YourFirstname YourLastname* as the message. Leave the subject line blank.
2. Visit the CharityChannel Web site at *CharityChannel.com/forums* and click on the subscription information for EVENT.

ESTPLAN-L (Estate Planning List, Planned Giving)

▶ To subscribe, send e-mail, leaving the subject line blank, with the message *SUBSCRIBE ESTPLAN-L YOUR NAME. listserv@netcom.com*

FOUNDATION-L

▶ This is an "announcement only" listserv, providing information about foundations. To subscribe, send this e-mail message: *Subscribe Foundation-L [YOUR FIRST AND LAST NAME]* to *majordomo@fallingrock.com*.

CANADIAN FUND RAISING AND ALUMNI AFFAIRS

▶ To subscribe to FUNDCAN, send an e-mail message to *LISTSERV@QUCDN.QUEENSU.CA*. The message should read *SUBSCRIBE FUNDCAN firstname lastname*.

FundClass: Online Fundraising School

▶ Sponsored by Professional Support Software but moderated by volunteers, this list is a forum for discussion of fund raising. Each month, the list focuses on a different topic. Previous topics have included direct mail, annual campaigns, and special events. To subscribe, send an e-mail message to *fundclass-request@fundraiser-software.com* that states in the body of the message *subscribe*. Leave the subject blank, and do not include e-mail addresses in the body of the message. More information about the list and its archived discussions are available at *http://www.fundraiser-software.com/fundclass.html*.

Fundlist

▶ This online forum for discussion of fund raising is maintained by Steve Hirby, director of development at Lawrence University, and administered by the Johns Hopkins University. To subscribe, send an e-mail message to *listproc@listproc.hcf.jhu.edu* that states in the body of the message *subscribe fundlist Your Name*. Leave the subject blank, and do not include e-mail addresses in the body of the message.

Fundraising

▶ This site is for "anyone remotely interested in this field, and anything related to fundraising." To subscribe, head to the OneList Web site (*http://www.egroups.com/subscribe.cgi/fundraising*) and follow the subscription instructions.

FUNDRAISNG

▶ A list about raising money. *fundraising@capcon.net*

FundRaisingFriends Discussion List

▶ This moderated list is provided as a forum for those who raise money through charity and nonprofit fund raisers. They discuss fund-raising issues in order to help each other achieve the highest possible level of success with their upcoming events. Issues for discussion can include, but are not limited to, fund-raising practices, software, ethics, training, vacancies, research, management, and volunteers. All types of fund-raising disciplines may be covered, including direct marketing, trading, events, tax-efficient giving, collections, corporate, statutory, etc. *E-mail: FundRaisingFriends-subscribe@egroups.com* (list owner), *http://www.egroups.com/group/FundRaisingFriends*

Fundsvcs

▶ This is an online forum for discussing technical details of fund raising, as well as the use of technology in fund raising. Topics of discussion include hardware and software issues, accounting rules, and Internal Revenue Service regulations. The list is maintained by John H. Taylor, director of Duke University's Office of Alumni & Development Records. To subscribe, send an e-mail message to *majordomo@acpub.duke.edu* that states in the body of the message *subscribe fundsvcs.* Leave the subject blank, and do not include e-mail addresses in the body of the message.

FUNDSVCS (Fundraising Software and Technology)

▶ To subscribe, send e-mail, leaving the subject line blank, with the message *SUBSCRIBE FUNDSVCS. majordomo@acpub. duke.edu*

GiftManage

▶ This site covers all aspects of the management of endowment, charitable trust, and foundation funds. There are two methods to subscribe:

1. Send e-mail to *listserv@CharityChannel.com* with *SUBSCRIBE GiftManage YourFirstname YourLastname* as the message. Leave the subject line blank.

2. Visit the CharityChannel Web site at *CharityChannel.com/ forums* and click on the subscription information for GiftManage.

Gift-Mgt

▶ This site covers planned giving issues after the gift has been made—investment issues, administration, reporting, etc. To subscribe, send this e-mail message: *subscribe GIFT-MGT [YOUR FIRST AND LAST NAME]* to *listserv@netcom.com*

Gift-PL

▶ This is an online forum for discussion of planned giving, maintained by the National Committee on Planned Giving. To subscribe, send an e-mail message to *listserv@listserv.iupui.edu* that states in the body of the message *subscribe gift-pl Your Name.* Leave the subject blank, and do not include e-mail addresses in the body of the message.

GIFT-PL

▶ This site is for discussion of planned giving topics. To subscribe, send e-mail, leaving the subject line blank, with the message *SUBSCRIBE GIFT-PL YOUR NAME. listserv@indycms.iupui.edu*

GIFT-PL@LISTSERV.IUPUI.EDU

▶ List owners: *GIFT-PL-request@LISTSERV.IUPUI.EDU.* To search the GIFT-PL archives online, go to *www.listserv.iupui.edu/ archives/gift-pl.html.*

GIFTPLAN

▶ This site is for discussion of U.S. and Canadian issues of gift planners. There are two methods to subscribe:

1. Send e-mail to *listserv@CharityChannel.com* with *SUBSCRIBE GIFTPLAN YourFirstname YourLastname* as the message. Leave the subject line blank.

2. Visit the CharityChannel Web site at *CharityChannel.com/ forums* and click on the subscription information for GIFTPLAN.

GiftProspecting

▶ This site focuses on all aspects of prospect research, including techniques, privacy, legal aspects, and ethics. There are two methods to subscribe:

1. Send e-mail to *listserv@CharityChannel.com* with *SUBSCRIBE GiftProspecting YourFirstname YourLastname* as the message. Leave the subject line blank.

2. Visit the CharityChannel Web site at *CharityChannel.com/ forums* and click on the subscription information for GiftProspecting.

GIVING

▶ This is a forum for donor's discussion. To subscribe, send an e-mail to *listpro@envirolink.org,* with the message *subscribe giving (firstname lastname).*

Giving

▶ This site covers fund raising and giving, aimed at donors and volunteers. To subscribe, send this e-mail message: *subscribe giving [YOUR FIRST AND LAST NAME]* to *listproc@envirolink.org.*

GNET-L

▶ U.S. Dept. of HHS: GrantsNet Info and Updates. *GNET-L@LIST.NIH.GOV*

GRANTS

▶ This is a discussion list from American Philanthropy Review that focuses on all aspects of grants and foundations. Grant seeking, foundation formation, foundation funding, and foundation administration in education, health care, human services, arts/humanities, public/society benefit, environment, animals, science, technology, international affairs, social science, and religion are permissible topics. There are two methods to subscribe:

1. Send an e-mail to *listserv@CharityChannel.com* with *SUBSCRIBE GRANTS YourFirstname YourLastname* as the message. Leave the subject line blank.

2. Visit the CharityChannel Web site at *CharityChannel.com/ forums* and click on the subscription information for GRANTS.

GRANTS-L

▶ A joint initiative of the Regents' Global Center of the University System of Georgia and Valdosta State University, and serves to promote external funding for international education and research. The listserv is intended to provide a forum for sharing experience, ideas, thoughts, comments, and sources of information on the preparation and administration of contracts and grants. Specific topics include, but are not limited to, proposal writing and editing; federal/state laws and regulations; campus policies and procedures; animal care and use; misconduct in science; procurement integrity; consulting; cost sharing; publication rights; budget development; direct and indirect costs; grant/contract administration; client relations;

Internet resources; electronic editing and software; and so on. To subscribe, send an e-mail message to *listproc@.gsu.edu*. Leave the subject line blank. In the body of your e-mail message, write: *sub grants-L yourfirstname yourlastname* (replacing yourfirstname and yourlastname with your own first and last name). *http://www.uwex.edu/disted/grantsl.html*

listserv@gsuvml.gsu.edu

▶ The list's owners are: *ibcjfp@gsusgi2.Gsu.EDU, mwatson@grits.valdosta.peachnet.edu, hcsdar@panther.Gsu.EDU.*

GRANTWRK

▶ This site is for discussion of the grants process by people working in the public and private sectors. To subscribe, send an e-mail with *subscribe grantwrk YourFirstName YourLast Name* as the message. Leave the subject line blank. *listserv@iubvm.ucs.indiana.edu*

Hilaros

▶ An online forum to discuss fund raising for Christian organizations and the Christian perspective on fund raising, maintained by Cliff Glovier, Director of the Geneva Fund at Geneva College. To subscribe, go to *http://stewardship.org/Hilarosform.html* or send an e-mail message to *majordomo@mark.geneva.edu* that states in the body of the message *subscribe hilaros*. Leave the subject blank, and do not include e-mail addresses in the body of the message.

INTFUND

▶ This site covers international fund-raising issues. To subscribe, send this e-mail message: *subscribe INTFUND [YOUR FIRST AND LAST NAME]* to *listserv@vm1.mcgill.ca.*

MATCHLIST-L

▶ Listserv for nonprofit and corporate matching gift professionals. *MATCHLIST-L@HERMES.CASE.ORG*

MICHFUND

▶ This site is for fund-raising professionals in Michigan. To subscribe, send e-mail, leaving the subject line blank, with the message *SUBSCRIBE MICHFUND YOUR NAME. listserv@cms.cc.wayne.edu*

NONPROFIT-NET

▶ This site covers nonprofit- and Internet-related topics. To subscribe, send this e-mail message: *SUB NONPROFIT-NET* to *listproc@lists.nonprofit.net.*

Online Fundraising Mailing List

▶ This site is open to anyone who is doing online fund raising or who would like to. A noncommercial forum for discussing the challenges of raising money online. To subscribe, send e-mail, leaving the subject line blank, with the message: *sub fundraising. autoshare@gilbert.org*

PG-USA

▶ This list focuses on all aspects of planned giving in the United States. To subscribe, send this e-mail message: *subscribe pg_usa [YOUR FIRST AND LAST NAME]* to *listserve@Philanthropy-Review.com.*

PRSPCT-L

▶ PRSPCT-L (pronounced "prospect el") is an electronic mail list provided as a forum for discussion of prospect research issues. More generally, PRSPCT-L is a collection of individuals INTERNET e-mail addresses that allows subscribers to instantaneously (well practically) send and receive messages between hundreds of their colleagues. The electronic nature allows discussions to take place in "real-time" and thus serves as an important conduit of information in the Prospect Research field. Joseph Boeke (*BOEKE@bucknell.edu*) founded the list at the University of California, Irvine in 1992. To subscribe, send this e-mail message: *subscribe PRSPCT-L [YOUR FIRST AND LAST NAME]* to *listserv@bucknell.edu. http://www.egroups.com/group/PRSPCT-L*

Raiser's Edge Users Group

▶ The Raiser's Edge Users Group is an independent e-mail discussion list for people who use the Blackbaud fund-raising software program. The new e-mail forum was started by a charity fund raiser who wishes to remain anonymous, who said that he was frustrated that the company's official e-mail forum did not allow him or others to openly discuss problems they encounter with the software. Blackbaud denies that its employees modify or delete clients' messages to its discussion lists. *http://reusers.listbot.com*

STEWARDSHIPLIST

▶ This site covers donor cultivation and stewardship. To subscribe, send this e-mail message: *subscribe to: majordomo@ocaxpl.cc.oberlin.edu.*

Online Charity Shopping Malls

4charity.com

▶ This online shopping site includes more than 140 stores, and all the commissions from the retailers—which generally range from 1 to 25 percent of the purchase price—go to participating charities. Organizations that have received tax-exempt status from the Internal Revenue Service can sign up with the site or be recommended by shoppers. The company signs contracts with all participating organizations and sends checks out monthly. 4charity.com was founded by Scott Dunlop and Tracey Pettingill, two recent graduates of Stanford Business School, and is located in San Francisco. *http://4charity.com*

4myCommunity.com

▶ The purpose of this site is to help members of local communities raise money for nonprofits via Web shopping through negotiated partnerships with popular Web merchants. Every time a purchase is made at a designated site, a percentage of it goes to an organization of the visitor's choosing. Site visitors may search for potential recipient organizations by performing a zip code search on the initial screen. This shopping site features more than 130 retailers, with commissions that range from 1.5 to 20 percent of the purchase price—although the average commission is 7 percent. Shoppers may choose from a list of more than 5,000 schools, churches, temples, and community organizations. Once a user chooses an organization, about 82 percent of the commission from goods purchased will be passed on to that organization. Participating organizations receive checks quarterly, as long as they have raised $5 during that quarter. Organizations are not required to have tax-exempt status from the Internal Revenue Service to participate. Participating organizations can gain access to their account information online. They also receive money every time a user chooses a link to one of several search engines— each click earns 3 to 5 cents for the participating organization. 4myCommunity.com is located in Redmond, Washington. *http://www.4mycommunity.com*

AllCharities.com

▶ A searchable database of charities and nonprofits that channels 100 percent of online donations to recipient organizations, the site also sells Web-based services to nonprofits and provides a mechanism for organizations to securely receive donations. *http://www.allcharities.com/servlet/home*

CharityCounts.com

▶ CharityCounts offers visitors the opportunity to make contributions to nonprofit organizations through auctions, a "charity mall," or by direct donation. Organizations can publicize upcoming fundraising activities through the Community Event Calendar. Donors can suggest nonprofits for inclusion as a "Nonprofit Partner." CharityCounts does not receive a commission for any of these services. CharityCounts.com passes 60 percent of the commissions it receives from the 36 stores on its site to participating charities. Commissions range from 2 to 25 percent of the purchase price, and are sent to charities monthly. Shoppers can choose their beneficiary from the more than 50 charities that have signed up with the site. In addition to shopping at retail stores, visitors may also make online donations or bid on items that are being auctioned. The company keeps 2 to 6 percent of each donation to cover expenses, while 95 to 99 percent of auction sales, depending on the final price, go to the charity that has been selected. Sellers may either determine which charity will benefit from the sale, recommend a charity, or allow the buyer to choose the beneficiary. CharityCounts.com is located in New York. *http://charitycounts.com*

Charitygift

▶ Charitygift channels 100 percent of a visitor's donation to the charity of his choice. The site generates revenue through the sale of gift cards, which users can design and modify. The home page also features a top 10 donors section and a list of the most popular charity recipients. *http://www.charitygift.com/*

CharityMall.com

▶ CharityMall.com features more than 100 retailers, and all of the commissions earned from the retailers go to participating organizations. Commissions range from 3 to 30 percent, but most are between 3 and 5 percent. More than 100 charities have signed up for the service. To qualify for inclusion, organizations must be classified as charities by the Internal Revenue Service. The company sends checks to participating groups quarterly. Tim Kunin and Greg

Hesterberg bought the company—which is now located in Ann Arbor, Michigan—in 1999 to expand their publishing and advertising business. *http://charitymall.com*

CharityWave

▶ CharityWave provides an online donation service for selected charities. The selection process includes nonprofit status, a Web site that lists the organization's program and budget, a readily available 990, and recommendation by CharityWave's Board of Advisors. Organizations are listed alphabetically, and by category. Profiles of the organizations are also available, to help the donor make informed decisions. An annual audit is conducted, to ensure that 100 percent of every donation goes to the charity for which it was intended. *http://www.charitywave.com/*

CharityWeb

▶ An online marketplace that receives a commission from e-tailers for each sale made through the site. CharityWeb provides an online donation site for nonprofits with incomes of $2 million or more. Participating nonprofits pay a one-time starting fee and then monthly charges after that. Ninety percent of the commission goes into a pool that is then split equally among participating charities at the end of each quarter. CharityWeb is also exploring adding an online shopping mall option. *http://www.charityweb.com/*

ConsumerSaints

▶ *www.consumersaints.com*

CyberCares.com

▶ CyberCares.com includes more than 60 stores, with commissions that range from 3 to 30 percent. The company splits the commissions with participating charities fifty-fifty. Charities can register on the site, but they do not need to do so to receive donations. Shoppers must gain access to the stores' Web sites through CyberCares.com, and then forward the electronic receipts they receive from the retailer to CyberCares.com, along with their choice of charity beneficiary. CyberCares.com is run by the London Company in New York. *http://CyberCares.com*

eCHARGE

▶ The eCHARGE billing system allows Internet users to "charge" items, such as charitable donations, to their local phone bills. *http://www.echarge.com*

DonorNet

▶ DonorNet provides a wide range of Internet- and e-commerce-based–solutions to nonprofit organizations that enable them to function and fund raise more effectively. Tools include a collection of fund-raising modules, e-mail fulfillment, database administration, customization services, e-commerce capabilities, and general Web services. The site includes an overview of DonorNet and its offerings, an online demonstration of the DonorNet system, a list of members, links to free plug-ins and utilities for viewing Web content, links to relevant online periodicals, frequently asked questions, and press clippings and releases. *http://www.donornet.com/*

eDonate

▶ eDonate is devising a corporate giving program that includes payroll deduction and corporate matching. It plans to work through a company's intranet to process payroll deductions that are electronically designated for approved nonprofit organizations. *www.edonate.com*

eGrants.org

▶ eGrants is a forward-looking nonprofit which works to help progressive nonprofits increase their financial support by fund raising online. Special software applications allow individuals, organizations, and businesses to donate money through online transactions. The site encourages interested organizations to contact eGrants to either establish an online presence or add their tool to an existing site. Visitors can find answers regarding how giving online compares with traditional means and how eGrants can assist different audiences. A section of the site features the group's first project.

Entango

▶ This site brings online donation capability to nonprofit organizations with no out-of-pocket cost by providing custom Web pages that integrate fully into an organization's existing Web site. *http://www.entango.com*

4myCommunity.com

▶ This shopping site features more than 130 retailers, with commissions that range from 1.5 to 20 percent of the purchase price—although the average commission is 7 percent. Shoppers may choose from a list of more than 5,000 schools, churches, temples, and community organizations. Once a user chooses an organization, about 82 percent of the commission from goods purchased will be passed on to that organization. Participating organizations receive checks quarterly, as long as they have raised $5 during that quarter. Organizations are not required to have tax-exempt status from the Internal Revenue Service to participate. Participating organizations can gain access to their account information online. They also receive money every time a user chooses a link to one of several search engines—each click earns 3 to 5 cents for the participating organization. 4myCommunity.com is located in Redmond, Washington. *http://www.4mycommunity.com*

FundraisingAuctions.com

▶ FundraisingAuctions.com, the nonprofit sector's answer to eBay, capitalizes on the popularity of online auctions to help nonprofit organizations raise money. Sellers donate the proceeds of their items to a nonprofit of their choice; additionally, nonprofits that wish to convert in-kind gifts received to cash can use FundraisingAuctions.com to do so. Product listing is free, and for a limited time, auction-closing fees will be waived. *http://www.fundraisingauctions.com/*

Givetocharity.com

▶ This international secure online donation service works from the nonprofit organization's Web site. *www.givetocharity.com*

TheGivingNetwork.com

▶ An online service that simplifies and enhances giving to charity by empowering people with choice and information. At no cost, we provide your organization with significant technological and marketing advantages to promote your organization and raise more funds. *http://www.thegivingnetwork.com/*

Givingshop.com

▶ Givingshop.com passes 75 percent of all commissions earned—which range from 1 to 40 percent of the purchase price, with an average commission of 7.5 percent—to participating charities. The site features more than 100 stores, and shoppers can choose their nonprofit beneficiary from a list of more than 900 participating charities. Givingshop.com verifies the nonprofit status of all organizations that sign up to participate. Checks are sent to participating organizations monthly, after organizations have raised $20. The company is located in Cambridge, Massachusetts. *http://givingshop.com*

GoodCause.com

▶ *http://www.goodcause.com*

GreaterGood.com

▶ GreaterGood.com features more than 70 stores, and gives half the commissions it receives from retailers—which range from 6 to 30 percent of the purchase price—to participating charities. The company sends organizations the commissions in quarterly checks. Charities do not need to sign up to participate, since customers may designate any charity they wish to support on their receipts. To qualify, however, organizations must be classified as charities by the Internal Revenue Service, and organizations that do register must sign a contract with the company. The company, located in Seattle, was started by Paul Goodrich, chairman of the Madrona Investment Group. *http://greatergood.com*

Guidestar

▶ Guidestar, the donor's guide to the nonprofit universe, provides a free searchable database of reports on the programs and finances of over 600,000 U.S. charities. The site also features news on the nonprofit world, profiles on charities, and short articles on giving. Though technically not an e-commerce site, it does serve the purpose of informing potential donors about charities/nonprofit organizations to which they may wish to make donations. *http://www.guidestar.com*

Help by Shopping

▶ *www.helpbyshopping.com*

HelpYourCause.com

▶ *www.helpyourcause.com*

Helping.org

▶ This AOL-sponsored site is designed as a one-stop online resource to help people find volunteer and giving opportunities in their local communities and beyond. The site also provides online resources and tools to help nonprofits utilize the Internet in their strategic planning, recruiting, and fund raising. It also serves as a one-stop online resource designed to help people find volunteer and giving opportunities in their own communities and beyond. *http://www.helping.org/*

I-Charity

▶ I-Charity provides support services to nonprofit organizations for a fee. These services include online giving opportunities, e-mail information campaigns, and fund-raising campaigns. I-Charity also offers services and information to philanthropists, companies, students and youth, and private citizens, including partnering with a charity, free online petitions, the ability to set up an e-commerce site, and advertising opportunities. *http://www.i-charity.net*

iGive.com

▶ iGive.com passes up to 90 percent of the commissions paid by the 195 stores on its site to charity—usually 3 to 12 percent of the purchase price. Participating organizations receive payment monthly, provided they have raised at least $10. iGive.com allows both shoppers and participating charities to see how much money has been raised for their organizations and track the checks that have been sent to the organization. Any "worthy cause" or nonprofit group specified by the shopper—not limited to organizations classified as charities by the Internal Revenue Service—can participate. iGive donates $10 to each new member's specified charity, and members can earn additional money for their charity by viewing advertisements. iGive, which is located in Evanston, Illinois, was founded by Robert Grosshandler, who also founded eCharity, an online donation site. *http://www.iGive.com*

Independent Charities of America

▶ A nonprofit organization that prescreens and certifies the charities it presents to potential donors via Web-based giving, workplace giving programs, and other low-cost fund-raising methods. Charities are reviewed and certified annually. *http://www.independentcharities.org/*

Independent Givers of America

▶ The Independent Givers of America Web site is a "nonprofit tax-exempt charitable organization whose mission is to bring together generous people and deserving causes, principally but not exclusively by developing workplace-based and internet-based systems that reduce the cost and increase the productivity of charitable solicitation." It also gives philanthropists the opportunity to set up a personal, private online foundation, make contributions at any time, and subsequently contribute to any IRS-recognized charity, church, or school. *http://www.givedirect.org/welcome.asp*

iPledge

▶ This site features 16 merchants, with commissions that range from 2 to 20 percent of the purchase price, although the average is about 6 percent. Charities receive 50 to 66 percent of the commissions. Shoppers can select their beneficiary from 25 charities in the United Kingdom. Participating charities must be in the United Kingdom, and have an annual budget of less than £5 million. Checks are sent to charities quarterly, regardless of the amount raised. Charities may look at their account records with iPledge upon request. iPledge is located in Harrogate, North Yorkshire, and

was founded by Adam Atkinson, a businessman with a background in advertising and technology. *http://www.ipledge.net*

iReachOut.com

▶ Formerly called Shop4Charity.com, this Los Altos, California–based shopping site features more than 140 stores. Commissions from these stores range from 1 to 50 percent, although the average commission is about 8 percent. Users can select one of more than 150 participating charities to receive the commissions from their purchases. Additionally, charities earn 10 cents every time a user sends an e-mail greeting card from the iReachOut.com site, with a limit of $40,000 per charity per year. Checks are sent to charities on a quarterly basis, if the charity has raised at least $10. If a charity has not raised the minimum, but still wants its commissions, it can request a check from the site. Organizations that have been classified as charities by the Internal Revenue Service are eligible to sign up with the site. *http://www.ireachout.com*

KickStart.com

▶ KickStart.com includes approximately 160 stores, and more than 1,700 participating organizations. The company splits commissions fifty-fifty with the organizations. In addition to earning money through shopping commissions—which range from 2 to 25 percent—organizations earn one to one-and-a-half cents each time one of their supporters clicks on their start page, conducts an Internet search, or uses free KickStart.com e-mail. Groups can sign up for free, but KickStart.com will begin charging an annual fee of $100 in February 2001. Revenues that organizations raise on the site will be used to pay the fee, and after they raise the $100 annual fee, they will begin receiving commissions and other revenue. If a group does not raise $100 by the end of the year, the company will wave the remainder of the fee. Checks are sent out monthly, as long as the group has raised at least $50. Organizations may sign up on the Web site, and they do not need to be recognized by the IRS as a tax-exempt charity. KickStart.com is located in Denver. *http://kickstart.com*

Local Independent Charities of America

▶ Local Independent Charities of America is a federation of more than 500 local nonprofit organizations in 19 states. The Web site provides an online giving service. Potential donors can conduct a keyword search to access information on member charitable organizations. Information provided includes the mission statements, programs offered, and links to the Web sites of various nonprofit charitable organizations. *http://www.lic.org/*

LocalVoice.com

▶ LocalVoice.com offers Web-based solutions enabling nonprofits to accept donations directly from their Web sites, deploy e-mail marketing strategies, and utilize membership and event registration solutions. Rented for a flat monthly fee, these applications are easily and seamlessly deployed and provide the highest-level security and scalability. *www.localvoice.com*

Mrgoodbucks.com

▶ Mrgoodbucks.com passes 50 percent of commissions from more than 150 stores to participating nonprofit organizations.

Commissions at the site range from 2 to 15 percent of the purchase price, although the average commission is about 10 percent. More than 300 organizations are listed on the site, as well as 60 partner organizations that have signed contracts with Mrgoodbucks.com. Charities may sign up—or be recommended by a shopper—by filling out a form at the site. The company contacts organizations that have been recommended to make sure that they want to participate, and asks them to sign a partner agreement. Partner charities may create their own malls, which they work with the company to promote. Partners can also track the amount of money they have raised online. Checks are sent to all charities on the site quarterly. Mrgoodbucks.com also has a section that allows businesses to shop for office supplies online while donating their commission to the charity of their choice. The company's headquarters are in Charlottesville, Virginia. *http://www.mrgoodbucks.com*

MyCause.com

▶ MyCause.com passes 60 to 100 percent of the commisions it receives from the seven stores on its site to charity. Shoppers can choose their charity beneficiary from a list of 275,000 nonprofit organizations. The list has been compiled from the Internal Revenue Service database and shoppers' requests. Each organization has its own page that lists the amount that the organization has received between checks. Checks are sent out quarterly, as long as an organization has raised at least $10. MyCause.com, located in Ithaca, New York, was started by Brendan Wyly, a reference librarian at Cornell University, Frank Adelstein, a computer-science researcher, and Kristen Grace, a graduate student. *http://mycause.com*

Non-Profit Shopping Mall

▶ Seventy percent of the commissions paid by the 70 stores on this site goes to participating nonprofit organizations. Shoppers can select their beneficiary from the more than 75 charities that have registered and signed agreements with the site. Checks are sent quarterly. The Non-Profit Shopping Mall is operated by Samson Marketing, an Internet company in Paoli, Pennsylvania. *http://www.npsmall.com*

Public Spirit

▶ Public Spirit is an online store that sells computer-related products. Shoppers can designate one of the site's more than 20 participating charities to receive 50 percent of the company's profit on the items that they purchase. Organizations that have received tax-exempt status from the Internal Revenue Service are eligible to sign up. This Walnut Creek, California, company is owned by David Hodges and Chris Smith, co-founders of National Identifications Systems, a company which ran driver's license photo systems and is now owned by AT&T. *http://www.publicspirit.com*

ShopForChange.com

▶ An online initiative of Working Assets Long Distance, ShopForChange.com donates 5 percent of the revenue from its products to "progressive causes." Past recipient organizations include Human Rights Watch, Friends of the Earth, and Stand for Children. *http://www.workingforchange.com/shop/index.cfm*

Shop2Give

▶ Shop2Give passes to charity 50 to 100 percent of the commissions it receives from the more than 70 retailers on its site.

Shoppers can select the charity that will benefit from their purchases from a list of the more than 640,000 organizations that the Internal Revenue Service has classified as charities. The company sends out checks quarterly, unless a charity has earned over $75, in which case a check is sent at the end of the month. The site is registered in California to raise money for nonprofit organizations. Shop2Give was started by Ami Kassar, a former sales and marketing executive at a manufacturing company. *http://www.shop2give.com*

VirtualGiving.com

▶ VirtualGiving.com specializes in the development of planned giving Web sites that are tailored to the needs of the nonprofits they serve, integrating each organization's "look and feel" with enhanced marketing/promotional and information dissemination capabilities online. *http://www.virtualgiving.com/*

Web Charity

▶ WebCharity is a Web site where nonprofit organizations can transform in-kind gift donations to cash. Individuals or companies can "pledge" new or used items to one of the several hundred WebCharity members, which will then be sold via an auction or retail sale format, with 100 percent of the donation going to the nonprofit organization. The list of member organizations is very well organized into categories, with a description of each charity, including contact information. *http://www.webcharity.com/*

News Services and Online Publications

Abe's Grant Report

▶ This free daily e-mail grants newsletter lists the basic contents of grant RFPs listed in the *Federal Register,* state registers, and foundation information. The e-mail newsletter, delivered every weekday to over 3,500 subscribers, focuses on federal grants listed in the *Federal Register* and includes requests from states and private foundations. To subscribe, send an e-mail message to *abes-grant-reports-subscribe@egroups.com.* E-mail: *abeperlstein@mindspring.com* (Abraham J. Perlstein, Esq.), *grant_report@excite.com*

Case Currents Online—Council for Advancement and Support of Education

▶ *http://www.case.org/currents/, http://www.case.org/CURRENTS/archives.htm*

Chardon Press Electronic Newsletter

▶ A free bimonthly e-mail newsletter, with the "Dear Kim Klein" grassroots fund-raising advice column, the latest grassroots fund-raising tips, new publication announcements, and workshop opportunity alerts from Chardon Press. *http://www.chardonpress.com/newsletter/index.html*

Charity Auction Newsletter

▶ This is a monthly newsletter on charity auctions. *Charity Auction Newsletter* is a free monthly e-mail offering tips, reviews, and resources to help you produce, grow, and manage your nonprofit auction. To subscribe, or receive past issues, please send e-mail to: *mwinter@flite.net.*

The Chronicle of Higher Education

▶ Published weekly, the online version of *The Chronicle* is a source of news and information for college and university faculty and administrators and includes lists of recent gifts and grants to higher education, new software titles, and appointments and promotions in the academic world. "Academe Today," a free online service available to subscribers of the print version of *The Chronicle,* provides daily updates on federal grant opportunities in addition to other features. Limited grant and award deadline information is available to nonsubscribers. *http://chronicle.com*

The Chronicle of Philanthropy

▶ The full text of *The Chronicle,* the national newspaper of the nonprofit world, is available to subscribers on its Web site—including more than two years of back issues, all of which are fully searchable. For an additional fee, users can search the *Guide to Grants,* an electronic database of all foundation and corporate grants listed in *The Chronicle* since 1995. The site also contains a wealth of free materials. The Internet Resources section of the site features an extensive collection of annotated links to Web sites and e-mail discussion lists of interest to nonprofit professionals. The site also posts hundreds of job opportunities in the nonprofit world, updated every two weeks and fully searchable. In addition, forthcoming conferences, workshops, and deadlines for grants and awards are listed. A free e-mail newsletter is available to alert people to new additions made to the site. Some of this material is available only to *Chronicle* subscribers. For information on which portions of the site are free and which are restricted to subscribers, see their site map. Stories from the new issue are posted every other week, at 9 A.M. U.S. Eastern time, on the Monday preceding *The Chronicle's* issue date. The job announcements are updated on the Monday following the issue date. *http://philanthropy.com*

Chronicle of Philanthropy: Deadlines

▶ *http://www.philanthropy.com/deadlines/*

Contributions Magazine

▶ Lots of interesting articles and resources. *http://www.contributionsmagazine.com/*

Development Resource Center News

▶ Free newsletter at *http://www.drcharity.com/newslet.html.*

Donor Digital.com—Mal Warwick & Associates

▶ Free e-mail newsletter on fund raising and marketing on the Internet. *http://www.fundraisingonline.com/newsletter.html*

Donorwall

▶ Short articles about fund raising, donor walls, and donor recognition, by a company that can lend a hand. *http://www.donorwall.com/*

ENewsletter—Donovan Management Inc.

▶ Published electronically and in print, this recource covers a wide range of issues, topics, and trends in philanthropy in Florida and the Caribbean. Readers enjoy the easy-to-read/scan how-to articles and interviews with the experts. It is available free for registered subscribers and e-mailed monthly. *http://www.donovanmanagement.com/Publications.htm, http://www.donovanmanagement.com/Tips%20Free.htm*

E-Philanthropy Hotsheet

▶ This twice-monthly e-letter includes the latest news about online fund raising and original articles designed to help you understand this rapidly changing area. The latest news on online fund raising for nonprofits by Allison Schwein, AMS Consulting. *http://www.internet-fundraising.com/*

Federal Funding Reports

▶ The online *Federal Funding Report* is a weekly compilation of items published in the *Federal Register* that affect Federal Domestic Assistance Programs. It makes no attempt to include *Federal Register* notices not directly related to Grants and Loans programs. The summary consists of three parts: (1) *Federal Register* Summary, (2) Early Warning Grants Report, and (3) Disaster Loan Applications. Courtesy of Congressman Nick Lampson (Texas). *http://www.house.gov/ffr/*

Federal Register

▶ The *Federal Register* is a legal newspaper published every business day by the National Archives and Records Administration (NARA). It contains federal agency regulations; proposed rules and notices (including notices for grant applications); and executive orders, proclamations, and other presidential documents. An online search of the *Federal Register* is available at this site. *http://www.nara.gov/fedreg/*

Foundation Center RFP Bulletin

▶ The Foundation Center's *RFP* (Request for Proposals) *Bulletin* is published every Friday afternoon in conjunction with the posting of the Digest to the Web and is also sent out in a listserv format. Each RFP listing provides a brief overview of a current funding opportunity offered by a foundation or other grant-making organization. Interested applicants should read the full RFP at the grant maker's Web site or contact the grant maker directly for complete program guidelines and eligibility requirements before submitting a proposal to that grant maker. Topics vary. Sample topics may include: Arts/Humanities, Athletics, Community, Education, Environment, Health, International, Journalism, Leadership, Libraries, Medical Research, Miscellaneous, Nonprofit Sector, Science, Social Science, Technology, Substance Abuse, Voluntarism, Women, and Youth/Families. *http://fdncenter.org/pnd/rfp/index.html*

For Us Women Grants Newsletter

▶ Highlights funding resources for women and people of all ethnic backgrounds. *http://www.grantlady.com/grants_newsletter.htm*

Fund$Raiser Cyberzine

▶ This free online magazine for fund raisers covers news items, reviews of new products and fund raising ideas for small, locally based nonprofit groups, all with a how-to, hands-on approach. They target small to medium-sized groups looking to raise money (booster clubs, scout groups, school clubs, civic groups, sports teams, fraternal organizations, church groups, libraries, humane societies, arts groups—any and all kinds of nonprofit organizations). They give those readers loads of information, news, reviews, feature articles, and much more. They publish monthly, and access to the current issue is always free. *http://www.fundsraiser.com*

Fundraiser's Guide Online (Selected Articles Full Text)—Arkansas Support Network, Inc.

▶ The Guide is an electronic newsletter that targets smaller nonprofits and offers funding guidance through articles and archives.

With *The Fundraiser's Guide,* you'll always have the latest information on these important topics: special-events fund raising: a powerful public relations tool; planned giving: it can work for the small nonprofit; how to increase your income through effective grant proposal writing; should you ever hire an outside fund raiser?; how the small nonprofit can succeed with direct-mail fund raising; and unrelated business income: when is fundraising subject to taxation? Subcriptions are available online for $32/year. *http://www.fundraisers-guide.com/articles.htm*

Fundraising for Small Groups Newsletter

▶ This newsletter is designed for small groups with volunteer fund raisers that don't normally consider themselves nonprofits. Examples of groups that will find this newsletter helpful are booster clubs, scout groups, school clubs, civic groups, day care centers, sports teams, fraternal organizations, and church groups. Free, AOL friendly. *http://www.fundraising-newsletters.com/small.html*

Fundraising Free Press Newsletter—Custom Development Solutions

▶ *http://cdsfunds.com/cgi-bin/newsletter.pl*

Giving Forum Online

▶ The Newspaper of Minnesota Grantmaking. *Giving Forum* is a quarterly newspaper providing readers in the nonprofit community with a wide range of news and information on Minnesota grant making. *Giving Forum* publishes original in-depth articles that explore current giving issues, educate readers on philanthropy, and report on grant-making research. The newspaper's regular departments report on the people, organizations, and events making news in Minnesota grant making. Many of the articles will be of interest to those outside Minnesota as well. *http://www.mcf.org/mcf/forum/index.html*

The Grant Advisor Plus

▶ This is the online information service for grantspersons and faculty in higher education. Subscriptions include: (1) *The Grant Advisor Newsletter* (covers grant opportunities from federal agencies, except NIH, as well as many independent organizations and foundations). Published monthly (except July), each issue contains 20 to 25 program reviews with descriptions, eligibility requirements, special criteria, funding amounts, and contact information (including phone and FAX numbers, e-mail and web addresses). The remainder of the newsletter is composed of the *Deadline Memo* with more than 300 listings of grant and fellowship programs for the coming four months, organized into eight academic divisions (fine arts, humanities, sciences, social sciences, education, international, health related, unrestricted/other). It is available online in both PDF (Adobe Acrobat®) and TXT (ASCII text) formats; (2) Deadline Memo Hyperlinks (include links directly to the following (all where applicable): (a) Web site of the funding agency or organization; (b) abstracts and program reviews from *The Grant Advisor* newsletter; (c) complete text from all current *Federal Register* grant listings; (d) National Science Foundation online documents; and (e) e-mail addresses); (3) Database and Article Searches (allows you to enter your own search criteria (such as funding agency, keywords, academic division, and more). Results are displayed in the same powerful table format as the Deadline Memo Hyperlinks); (4) 200+ Useful Links to Funding Sources (full access to their ever-expanding list of links to funding sources, sep-

arated into two categories: Federal and Related Sources, and Foundation and Independent Sources); (5) *The Grant Works* (the electronic book of the entire series of articles by Robert J. Toft, PhD, presented here in Acrobat® PDF format. Included are hundreds of essays providing useful advice and tips for the grantsperson in higher education. Chapter titles include Proposal Development, Running the Grants Office, Budget Considerations, Tips on Writing, Grants Office Policy, and more). *http://www.grantadvisor.com/about.htm*

Grant Update

▶ Designed to inform grant seekers of the latest information regarding new grant announcements, insider tips, and innovative fund-raising ideas through use of the Internet, it also serves as an index to hundreds of funding sources and to other Web sites that provide useful information and tools to aid grant seekers. Access insider tips to securing grant money, fund raising on the Internet, fellowship listings, and more. For more, send e-mail to newgrant@wt.net. *Note:* full access requires a paid subscription. Includes New Grant Announcements; Government, Corporate, Foundation Sources; Cash for College, Nonprofit, Small Business; Insider Tips; Internet Fundraising; Grantwriting for Beginners; Resource Sites; Foundation Sites; and Free Newsletter. *http://www.grantupdate.com/*

Grantmakers in Health (GIH) Bulletin

▶ This biweekly newsletter contains breaking news in health philanthropy on grants, people, surveys and studies, and upcoming conferences. Once a month, the Bulletin features a Grantmaker Focus spotlighting the activities and accomplishments of one of GIH's funding partners. This feature alternates with Issue Focus, an in-depth look at a single health issue, its implications for health grant makers, and examples of what grant makers are doing to make a difference. *http://www.gih.org/info-url2678/info-url.htm*

Grants Action News

▶ This resource primarily lists funding opportunities from the state of New York, but also lists federal funding opportunities as well. Courtesy of the New York State Assembly. January 1999 to date. *http://assembly.state.ny.us/Reports/Gans/*

GrantsHotline: Grants and Funding Information for Schools, Cites, Towns, and Police Departments—Quinlan Publishing

▶ *http://www.grantshotline.com/*

The Grantsmanship Center Magazine

▶ Both the current and back issues of *The Grantsmanship Center Magazine,* a quarterly newspaper on nonprofit management and fund raising, are available on the Grantsmanship Center's Web site. *http://www.tgci.com/publications/magazine.htm*

GrantVine

▶ An e-mail newsletter with important grant deadlines, conferences, and links for community development, youth programs, and small businesses. *http://www.grantsandletters.bigstep.com/*

Grants On-line Digest (GOLD)

▶ GOLD is the free monthly e-mail publication of The Grant Doctors. It's a newsletter, a column, a discussion of issues related to grants for novices and experts alike. In it, you will find tips and techniques for writing proposals and searching for grants; new grant announcements; answers to frequently asked questions; and questions and answers to/from GOLD subscribers. *http://www.the-grantdoctors.com/GOLD.htm*

GrantSpring.com

▶ Developed by GrantSpring, a grant-seeking consulting company in Phoenix, this Web site provides links to corporate grant makers and to state and federal agencies that award grants to charities. The links are organized by the grant makers' areas of interest: the arts, education, the environment, health care, and social services. You can also sign up for their free e-mail newsletter, *GrantSpring News* at *http://www.grantspring.com/gsnews.htm*. *http://www.grantspring.com*

Grassroots Fundraising Journal

▶ Selected articles from the current and past issues of the *Grassroots Fundraising Journal,* a magazine on fund raising for small and medium-sized charities that is published six times a year, are available on its Web site. *http://www.chardonpress.com*

Internet Insider

▶ This free e-mail newsletter, published twice a month, profiles Web sites and e-mail discussion lists of interest to nonprofit professionals. Each issue includes (at least) five useful sites, many of which would be difficult to locate. It is provided by Marilyn Gross and Education Fundraising Strategies, a company that provides online fund-raising courses. To subscribe, send an e-mail message to *mlgross@aol.com* and in the body type *subscribe insider.* *http://www.efsinternet.com/*

Internet Prospector

▶ This free online and e-mail newsletter offers news, advice, and links to Web sites that help fund raisers use the Internet to gather information about foundations, corporations, and individuals in the United States and abroad. An archive of newsletters and a reference desk are available on the site. A virtual reference desk for prospect researchers and other information professionals in the nonprofit fund-raising arena. *http://www.internet-prospector.org/index.html*

Join Together Online

▶ A project of the Boston University School of Public Health, Join Together offers frequently updated funding information, including RFPs, in the fields of substance abuse, gun violence, and related topics. It includes the Funding Finder, which lets users search archived news items. It is also available in an e-mail format. *http://www.jointogether.org*

Just Grants Arizona

▶ This site includes a fully searchable database, much like the Foundation Center. If interested in using the search function, just send an e-mail to *mboess@azgrants.com*. It includes a free biweekly e-mail grants newsletter, Tips and Tools, Great Grants Links, and a Consultants Directory. *http://www.azgrants.com*

Nonprofitxpress

▶ A project of the A. J. Fletcher Foundation, in Raleigh, North Carolina, Nonprofitxpress provides news about fund raising, management, giving, and volunteerism. The site also includes a section that focuses on nonprofit news in North Carolina. *http://www.npxpress.com*

The NonProfit Times

▶ Both the current and back issues of *The NonProfit Times,* a monthly newspaper on nonprofit management and fund raising, are available on its Web site. *http://www.nptimes.com*

Online Fund Raising Report

▶ Tracks the use of the Internet for fund raising. Using newspaper accounts of Web use, Online Publishers Inc. of New York prepares a trend line that measures the growth of Internet fund raising. Many brand name nonprofits are benefiting from Internet-based fund raising. For more information, contact them at *INFO@Online FundraisingRpt.com*. *http://onlinefundraisingrpt.com*

Philanthropy in Texas Online

▶ This resource informs and educates fund-raising executives, board members, and potential donors about charitable giving as it relates to Texas. *http://www.philanthropyintexas.com/*

Philanthropy News Digest—The Foundation Center

▶ This weekly online news service provided by the Foundation Center summarizes philanthropy-related articles and feature topics in the U.S. media. It also contains a search engine. *http://fdncenter.org/pnd/current/index.html*

Philanthropy News Digest RFP Bulletin—The Foundation Center

▶ *http://fdncenter.org/pnd/rfp/index.html*

Philanthropy News Network Online

▶ Produced by the Philanthropy News Network, this site offers daily updates on news events that affect nonprofit organizations in categories such as giving, fund raising, technology, and volunteerism. *http://www.pnnonline.org*

Planned Giving Today

▶ The practical newsletter for planned giving professionals provides selected articles from *Planned Giving Today,* a monthly newsletter published by G. Roger Schoenhals, a planned giving consultant, that discusses such topics as how to establish and promote a planned giving program, build relationships with donors, and deal with the technical aspects of planned giving. It also explains what planned gifts are and how they differ from other charitable donations and describes the role of the planned giving officer. The Web site provides the table of contents from the current issue, selected articles from other issues, and links to other resources of interest to planned giving professionals. *http://www.pgtoday.com/*

Planned Giving Web Letter

▶ This Web-based newsletter targets the planned giving and estate planning informational needs of nonprofit executives. It is a monthly cyber-newsletter written in plain English since August 1996 by the Recer Companies. *http://www.recer.com/news*, *http://4nonprofits.4anything.com/network-frame/0,1855,5251-69882,00.html*

Research Associates Funding Alert Newsletter

▶ This nationally focused grants newsletter identifies 80+ new funding sources every 30 days from the federal government, large corporations, and foundations. It also includes employment opportunities for grant writers. A sample newsletter and ordering information are available at this site. *http://www.grantexperts.com/funding_alert_newsletter.htm*

Seliger & Associates—Free Grant Information

▶ Seliger & Associates, a grant-writing consulting firm, provides access to two types of free grant availability information: the online *Seliger Funding Report*, which lists available federal, state, local, foundation, and corporate giving grant opportunities, and e-mail Grant Alerts. Registration is required. It provides funding announcements broken out into the following categories: Community Development, Economic Development, Education/Youth Services, Family Services, Health Services, Miscellaneous, Native Americans, and State/Local. *http://www.seliger.com/freeservices.cfm*

Show Me the Money

▶ This is an online newsletter with fund-raising tips from 4 Paws Fundraising, a company specializing in animal welfare organizations. Many of the tips would be helpful to any nonprofit organization. Copies of the January through September 2000 newsletters are available on the web site. *http://www.4pawsfundraising.com/Show_Me.html*

TrustWise E-letter

▶ This electronic newsletter is for the busy financial professional, attorney, CPA, or planned giving professional who is too busy to wade through newsletter after newsletter, just to stay abreast of the latest issues related to tax exempt trusts and other planned giving issues. *http://trustnews.listbot.com/*

ZimNotes—Zimmerman Lehman

▶ Sign up for this electronic newsletter, which provides information, articles, and news on fund raising, marketing, boards, and planning published by Zimmerman Lehman, a fund-raising consulting firm based in San Francisco. It is sent to your e-mail address once or twice a month. For recent *Zimnotes* articles, visit their Free Articles page at: *http://www.zimmerman-lehman.com/articles.htm, http://www.mediate.com/zl/zimnotes.htm*

Workplace Fund-Raising Coalitions

America's Charities

▶ This is a coalition of more than 90 health, education, environment, human services, and civil and human rights charities. Its headquarters is in Chantilly, Virginia. *http://www.charities.org*

Animal Funds of America

▶ This is a coalition of more than 30 animal protection organizations and charities that train animals to assist disabled people. Its headquarters is in Corte Madera, California. *http://www.animalfunds.org*

Children's Charities of America

▶ This is a coalition of more than 115 children's organizations. Its headquarters is in Corte Madera, California. *http://www.childrenscharities.org*

Community Health Charities

▶ Formed by the 1999 merger of National Voluntary Health Agencies and the Combined Health Appeal of America, Community Health Charities is a coalition of more than 60 national health organizations. Its headquarters is in Washington. *http://www.healthcharities.org/*

Conservation and Preservation Charities of America

▶ This is a coalition of more than 45 historic preservation and environmental organizations. Its headquarters is in Corte Madera, California. *http://www.conservenow.org*

Do Unto Others

▶ This is a coalition of more than 55 emergency relief and international development organizations. Its headquarters is in Corte Madera, California. *http://www.duo.org*

Earth Share

▶ This is a coalition of more than 40 environmental organizations. Its headquarters is in Washington. *http://www.earthshare.org*

Educate America: The Education, School Support, and Scholarship Fund Coalition

▶ This is a coalition of more than 35 educational organizations. Its headquarters is in Corte Madera, California. *http://www.educateamerica.org*

Independent Charities of America

▶ This is a coalition of more than 450 animal welfare, children's, education, environmental, health, international, medical research, military, and women's charities. Its headquarters is in Corte Madera, California. *http://www.independentcharities.org*

International Service Agencies

▶ This is a coalition of more than 50 international human-services charities. Its headquarters is in Alexandria, Virginia. *http://www.charity.org*

Military, Veterans, & Patriotic Service Organizations of America

▶ This is a coalition of more than 30 organizations that serve veterans and their families and provide scholarships for the children of military personnel, as well as memorials and museums that honor veterans and military service. Its headquarters is in Corte Madera, California. *http://www.mvpsoa.org*

National Black United Federation of Charities

▶ This is a coalition of more than 40 charities that serve blacks. Its headquarters is in Washington. *http://www.usbol.com/nbufc*

United States Office of Personnel Management: Combined Federal Campaign

▶ Maintained by the U.S. Office of Personnel Management, this Web site provides information on the Combined Federal Campaign, the federal government's annual charity drive. *http://www.opm.gov/cfc*

United Way of America

▶ This is an association of more than 1,300 United Ways that run local charity fund-raising drives. Its headquarters is in Alexandria, Virginia. *http://www.unitedway.org*

Women, Children, and Family Service Charities of America

▶ This is a coalition of more than 50 policy and social-services organizations that serve women, children, and families. Its headquarters is in Corte Madera, California. *http://www.womenandchildren.org*

Using the Internet to Seek Donations

(See also Online Fund Raising)

"Charity Shopping Portals"

▶ Written by Allison Schwein, a nonprofit consultant in Sunnyvale, California, this report lists and compares more than 20 online shopping sites that allow shoppers to designate a portion of their purchases for charity. The report explains how each site splits the affiliate fees it receives from retailers with participating charities and lists additional features that the sites offer. *http://www.internet-fundraising.com/charitymalls/introduction.htm*

Craver, Mathews, Smith and Company: "Socially Engaged Internet Users: Prospects for Online Philanthropy and Activism"

▶ This survey asked 800 adults who spend time on the Internet and who donate their time or money to charities or public interest groups about their attitudes toward online giving and advocacy. The survey was commissioned by marketing and fund-raising consultants Craver, Mathews, Smith and Company, in Arlington, Virginia, and conducted by the Mellman Group, in Washington. *http://www.craveronline.com*

"Exploring Online Fundraising for Nonprofit Arts Organizations"

▶ Written by Beth Kanter, education coordinator for Arts Wire, a program of the New York Foundation for the Arts, this article explains how charities can use the Internet to raise money. It discusses online shopping malls that allow customers to donate a portion of their purchases to charity, Web sites that collect donations for charities, and e-commerce systems that allow charities to accept donations on their own sites. Although the site uses arts organizations as examples, most of the information provided would apply to any nonprofit group. *http://www.artswire.org/kanter/cyberfundraising/index.html*

Fundraising Online

▶ Sponsored by Mal Warwick & Associates, a fund-raising and marketing company in Berkeley, California, this site shows nonprofit organizations how to use e-mail and the Internet in fund raising. *http://www.fundraisingonline.com*

Internet Nonprofit Center: Resources for Fundraising Online

▶ Operated by the Evergreen State Society, a Seattle charity that promotes civic involvement, this site provides short descriptions of and links to shopping Web sites that allow customers to designate a portion of their purchases to charity, Web sites that let visitors make online donations to nonprofit organizations, and companies that provide technology services to help charities with their online fund-raising efforts. The site also offers links to articles and Web sites on Internet fund raising. *http://www.nonprofits.org/npofaq/misc/990804olfr.html*

Nonprofit Genie: "Elementary E-Philanthropy"

▶ "Elementary E-Philanthropy" explains the workings of shopping sites that allow customers to donate a portion of their purchases to charity, Web sites that accept donations on behalf of many charities, and payment processing services that allow charities to accept online donation on their own sites—and offers charities advice on how to make a selection from among the many choices. The article was written by Michael Stein, an Internet manager at CompassPoint, a nonprofit group in San Francisco that provides training and consulting services to other charities. *http://www.genie.org/hottopic_pages/e_philanthropy.htm*

"Ringing Up a New Way to Give: Growth of On-Line Shopping Malls Raises Cash, Questions for Charities" (*The Chronicle*, December 16, 1999).

▶ *http://philanthropy.com/free/articles/v12/i05/05000101.htm*

UK Fundraising

▶ Run by Howard Lake, a fund-raising consultant in Great Britain, this Web site includes information on how charities in Europe and North America are using the Internet to seek donations and provides links to articles on Internet fund raising and to examples of charities using their World Wide Web sites to raise money. *http://www.fundraising.co.uk*

"Using the Internet for Fundraising"

▶ This report discusses the advantages and disadvantages of using the Internet for fund raising, legal issues related to soliciting charitable contributions over the Internet, and mechanisms for accepting pledges and donations online. It also describes techniques charities can use to raise money online, including corporate sponsorships, charity auctions, merchandise sales on their Web site, and e-mail solicitations. The report includes links to examples of the fund-raising approaches discussed. *http://www.nonprofit-info.org/misc/981027em.html*

W.K. Kellogg Foundation: "E-Philanthropy, Volunteerism, and Social Changemaking: A New Landscape of Resources, Issues, and Opportunities"

▶ This report, published by the W.K. Kellogg Foundation, provides summaries of and links to more than 140 Web sites of interest to nonprofit organizations. The sites are organized into eight categories. Four of the categories involve online fund raising: shopping sites that allow consumers to donate a portion of their purchases to charity, sites that allow visitors to make charitable contributions online, sites that offer information for donors, and online fund-raising events. The other four types of sites included are those that focus on nonprofit news, volunteerism, and advocacy, as well as sites that provide multiple services. *http://www.wkkf.org/Publications/e-phil.pdf*

PART IX

Strategic Planning

Organizations

(See also Evaluation and Assessment; Financial Management; General Management; Organizational Development; Marketing and Communications; Resource Development)

Innovation Network, Inc. (InnoNet)
1001 Connecticut Avenue NW, Suite 900, Washington, DC 20036
Tel: 202-728-0727; FAX: 202-728-0136
E-mail: info@innonet.org; WWW: http://www.innonet.org/

▶ Innovation Network, Inc. (InnoNet) is a 501(c)(3) organization dedicated to enabling public and nonprofit organizations to better plan, execute, and evaluate their structure, operations, and services. It offers two programs: Information Search Service (provides an information service that surveys the country for successful model programs [usually three to five existing models] that can be adopted by client organizations; it then produces a jargon-free written report with analysis and works with clients to identify components and ideas from these models that can be adapted by the client organization; the resulting program combines best practices from around the country with the unique strengths of the client community); and a Participatory Evaluation Service (involves all of the major stakeholders in planning and implementing the evaluation. Both services are built on InnoNet's core principles of participation, empowerment, ongoing learning, and continuous improvement. InnoNet conducts research, provides consultations, conducts trainings, conducts workshops, and provides Internet technical assistance. Together, InnoNet and its clients develop a framework to conduct a program evaluation and establish a system of accountability for staff, directors, and funders; also ensures that clients have the tools to continue to evaluate their programs in the future.).

National Center for Strategic Nonprofit Planning and Community Leadership (NPCL)
2000 L Street NW, Suite 815, Washington, DC 20036
Tel: 202-822-6725; FAX: 202-822-5699
E-mail: info@npcl.org; WWW: http://www.npcl.org/

▶ NPCL was formed in 1996 to offer one-step expertise in all facets of building and running a successful small to medium-sized nonprofit organization. Its mission is to improve the governance and administration of nonprofit, tax-exempt organizations. Services are geared to staff and volunteers of small and medium-sized nonprofit organizations with annual operating budgets of between $5,000 and $1 million. Additionally, they assist community-based nonprofit organizations that work with families, fathers, and neighborhoods to solve community problems. They provide guidance in the areas of: evaluation and technical assistance (conduct evaluations of and for nonprofit organizations; provide documentation services, management information system development, and organizational assessments including board and staff, evaluation design, and process and impact evaluation); training and technical assistance (offer expert assistance in the areas of board development, community collaboration, financial management, fund raising, human resource planning, leadership development, management information systems, marketing, program development, and strategic planning supervisory skills).

OMG Center for Collaborative Learning
1528 Walnut Street, Suite 805, Philadelphia, PA 19102
Tel: 215-732-2200; FAX: 215-732-8123
WWW: http://www.omgcenter.org/

▶ The mission of the OMG Center for Collaborative Learning is to support organizational learning and problem solving through consultation, applied research, and professional education. Center staff draw upon recent and established theory within the paradigms of systems thinking, action research, and organization behavior. The Center works with individual organizations and inter-organizational partnerships, primarily in the nonprofit and philanthropic sectors. OMG staff are skilled in delivering strategic planning and organizational development support that help organizations create their futures and adapt to changes in their environments. Through strategic planning, they work interactively with executives, staff, and boards of organizations in a process of identifying challenges and opportunities, reframing missions, setting goals and priorities, shaping teams and decision-making structures, and designing program responses.

The Performance Institute *(See Organizational Design, Structure and Development)*

Rensselaerville Institute
Pond Hill Road, Rensselaerville, NY 12147
Tel: 518-797-3783; FAX: 518-797-5270
E-mail: info@tricampus.org; WWW: http://www.tricampus.org/

▶ TRI helps grow high-performing communities and organizations. They do so by providing the tools and mindsets for leading change, solving problems, and seizing opportunities. Founded in 1963, they are an independent and nonprofit development center that works with individuals and organizations to build and test solutions to social, economic, and educational problems and help charities focus on ways they can be more entrepreneurial and effective. They publish the quarterly journal, *Innovating* (see separate listing under Periodicals), and *Outcome Funding* (see separate listing under Publications in Social Entrepreneurship section).

Amherst H. Wilder Foundation
919 LaFond Avenue, St. Paul, MN 55104-2198
Tel: 612-642-4000; FAX: 612-642-4068
E-mail: webmaster@wilder.org; WWW: http://www.wilder.org/

▶ This Foundation provides consultation to nonprofit, government, and community organizations in the Twin Cities area, with emphasis on the central urban communities of St. Paul. They provide training to nonprofit and community leaders locally, nationally, and internationally. They have expertise in collaboration planning and development, including cross-sector collaboration; community capacity building; community planning; conflict management and mediation; convening large groups of people for a specific purpose; training; leadership development; meeting facilitation; organizational planning; strategic planning; board development; team building; and specialized subject-area technical assistance, such as community organizing, economic development, housing, and urban planning. They also produce publications on planning, marketing, collaboration, and other issues. They publish the *Strategic Planning Workbook for Nonprofit Organizations* and the *Marketing Workbook for Nonprofit Organizations* (see separate listings under Publications), both step-by-step guides with worksheets and examples.

PRODUCT AND SERVICE PROVIDERS

Advocacy and Philanthropy
180 Mansion Drive, Newtown Square, PA 19073-3407
Tel: 610-356-5507; FAX: 610-353-8860
E-mail: advocon@juno.com (John P. Wilwol Sr.);
WWW: http://www.advanthropy.org/

▶ Founded in 1992, it offers the services of four consultants in the areas of charitable gift planning and documentation, strategic planning, fund raising, and professional search. It works exclusively with nonprofits located or headquartered in Pennsylvania, New Jersey, or Delaware.

The Alford Group, Inc.
7660 Gross Point Road, Skokie, IL 60077
Tel: 847-966-6670; FAX: 847-966-6782
E-mail: info@alford.com; WWW: http://www.alford.com/home.html

▶ This organization was founded in 1979 to provide leadership in improving the quality of life by serving not-for-profits. It maintains regional offices in Seattle and Washington, D.C., an area office in San Diego, and a nationwide network of local strategic partners. The firm has worked with over 430 organizations whose budgets and missions span the range of the not-for-profit sector.

Association Works—Consultants to Nonprofits
(See Organizational Development)

Brody & Weiser
250 West Main Street, Suite 110, Branford, CT 06405
Tel: 203-481-4199; FAX: 203-481-9536
E-mail: suzannec@brodyweiser.com (Suzanne Calise);
WWW: http://www.brodyweiser.com/Frames/index.html

▶ This firm helps nonprofit organizations accomplish their missions. They work with all types of nonprofits, helping them succeed through strategic planning, research, board development, and organizational capacity building. To help nonprofits accomplish their missions, Brody & Weiser can facilitate board and staff planning processes; assess management and organizational systems; analyze mechanisms and costs of service delivery; examine financial history, capacity, and trends; conduct environmental scan, market research, and analysis; facilitate action on new strategic directions, structures, roles, and responsibilities; and evaluate program impact.

Cause & Effect, LLC
178 Ninth Street, Providence, RI 02906
Tel: 401-331-2272; FAX: 401-621-9572
E-mail: CEffect@aol.com

▶ This firm helps nonprofit and public-sector agencies effect strategic change and build their constituencies. Their services include board and organization development, strategic planning, fund development, and communications for grassroots to international organizations. Gayle L. Gifford, CFRE, and Jonathan W. Howard, APR are the General Partners of Cause & Effect, LLC.

Center for Simplified Strategic Planning, Inc.
P.O. Box 851, Southport, CT 06490-0851
Tel: 203-255-8080; FAX: 203-255-9191
E-mail: grayson@cssp.com (Justine Grayson), simmonds@cssp.com;
WWW: http://www.cssp.com/index.asp

▶ Since 1981, the Center for Simplified Strategic Planning has provided client companies the tools and leadership required to obtain superior strategic results. It is a consulting firm with a strict focus on strategic planning services for the small to mid-sized organization. Their work with client companies is built around the simplified strategic planning process. It is a streamlined, hands-on methodology designed to ensure that course and direction are well thought out, and that the limited resources of the organization are sharply focused in support of that course and direction. Their consultants provide process leadership that will stimulate good strategic thinking, challenge subjective thinking, draw out balanced input from the team, build consensus, and develop commitment.

The Conservation Company
50 East 42nd Street, 19th Floor, New York, NY 10017
Tel: 212-949-0990; FAX: 212-949-1672
E-mail: info@consco.com; WWW: www.consco.com

One Penn Center, Suite 1550, Philadelphia, PA 19103
Tel: 215-568-0399; FAX: 215-568-2619

▶ From offices in Philadelphia and New York, the firm works with clients nationally and, increasingly, globally. Services include strategic planning, organizational assessment and development, feasibility studies, program and organizational evaluation, board development, restructuring, and repositioning, as well as grant program design, evaluation, and facilitation.

The Dini Partners, Inc.
2727 Allen Parkway, Suite 700, Houston, TX 77019
Tel: 713-942-8110; FAX: 713-942-8708
E-mail: dinipart@dinipartners.com;
WWW: http://www.dinipartners.com/

▶ Strategic direction services include long-term planning, building commitment to strategic plans, developing vision and mission statements, setting goals and objectives, and facilitating board retreats and meetings. They also maintain offices in Dallas and Austin.

Doug Eadie Presents!

1 Spyglass Court, Frisco, TX 75034
Tel: 800-209-7652; FAX: 469-384-1441
E-mail: Doug@dougeadie.com; WWW: http://www.dougeadie.com/

▶ Doug Eadie Presents! offers presentations and workshops, as well as planning and development retreats.

Hayes Briscoe Associates

322 West Bellevue Avenue, San Mateo, CA 94402
Tel: 650-344-8883; FAX: 650-344 3387
E-mail: hbaconsult@aol.com; WWW: http://www.hbaconsult.com/

6671 Southwest 70th Terrace, Miami, FL 33143
Tel: 305-667-2795; FAX: 305-667-3195

▶ This firm offers full-service consulting to nonprofit organizations throughout the United States and abroad. Their clients include national and international organizations and their state and local affiliates, universities, colleges and schools, churches and religious organizations, arts organizations, museums, membership and advocacy organizations, civic organizations, professional associations, government agencies, foundations, corporate giving programs, health and human service agencies, and hospitals. Planning services include executive coaching, strategic planning, mission development, goals/objectives, internal audits, budgeting, data system audits, staffing needs, personnel policies, program expansion, government relations, interim management, organization capacity building, and accreditation preparation.

Hiller Associates, Inc.

Corporate office: 6 Water Street/Long Wharf,
Mattapoisett, MA 02739
Tel: 800-482-4498, 508-758-3436; FAX: 508-758-6975

Regional office: 406 Farmington Avenue, Farmington, CT 06032
Tel: 860-676-7711
E-mail: tom@hiller.com (Thomas P. Hiller, President);
WWW: http://www.hiller.com

▶ Hiller Associates, Inc., senior staff analyze your organization's mission, services, and programs and work your board and management team to structure a planning process. They help your organization understand and articulate its vision through an honest assessment of current trends and future programs. Through the strategic planning process, they help to create a plan that serves as a road map for the organization, with goals, objectives, and a timeline for implementation.

JBK Group, Inc.

107 North Main Street, Farmville, VA 23901
Tel: 804-391-3737, ext. 102; FAX: 804-391-3730
E-mail: julia@jbkgroup.com (Julia Kurdt, President/CEO);
WWW: http://jbkgroup.com/

▶ JBK Group is an Association Management Company (AMC). AMCs provide professionally trained staff and suitably equipped headquarters for nonprofit organizations that do not want to maintain their own management staff. They provide strategic planning consulting and membership surveys.

Lawrence-Leiter and Company

4400 Shawnee Mission Parkway, Suite 204,
Shawnee Mission, KS 66205
Tel: 800-821-7812, 913-677-5500; FAX: 913-677-1975
E-mail: lleiter@sky.net (David R. Bywaters, President);
WWW: http://www.lawrence-leiter.com/1.htm

▶ Established in 1950, the firm conducts an international practice centered on organization strategy. Key services supporting solid strategy development and execution include people selection and development, a wide variety of research, organization design, and futures studies.

The Metanoia Group

Saint Mary's University of Minnesota, 700 Terrace Heights #3,
Winona, MN 55987-1399
Tel: 507-457-1750; FAX: 507-457-1722
E-mail: metanoia@smumn.edu (Tim Burchill, CFRE, President);
WWW: http://www.smumn.edu/academics/affiliation/metanoia.
html#areas

▶ The service areas provided include organizational analysis (articulation of mission, clarification of vision, strategic planning, tactical planning, governance, climate studies, needs assessment surveys, development function audits, leadership audits) and organizational effectiveness (organizational assessment, programmatic assessment, structure and decision making, team building and skill development, board/trustee development, training and orientation, retreats, and in-service).

Mirenda & Associates

360 South Monroe Street, Suite 270, Denver, CO 80209
Tel: 303-377-3389; FAX: 303-322-1445
E-mail: info@mirenda.com; WWW: http://www.mirenda.com

▶ Their comprehensive, strategic approach helps their clients focus on solutions that strengthen long-term financial viability. As a starting point, they review your mission and case for support. When necessary, they help you refine them. With these clear guidelines and an understanding of your market, they help you define short-term and long-term fund-raising goals and strategies to meet them. They customize those strategies to meet the unique needs of every organization. And they provide continuing counsel to senior leaders and monitor progress toward goals.

Mollenhauer & Associates

14 Langmuir Crescent, Toronto, ON M6S 2A7, Canada
Tel: 416-767-4059; FAX: 416-767-3065
E-mail: mollenhauerl@home.com (Linda Mollenhauer)

▶ Linda Mollenhauer is a consultant working with nonprofit organizations in strategic planning and organizational development. She helps your organization to achieve greater performance by delivering facilitation services, guiding your planning or organizational review, and offering training. You also benefit from *Benchmarks of Excellence* for the Voluntary Sector, an educational, evaluation, and planning tool designed to teach you the critical ingredients of excellent organizations and/or identify areas of strength/weakness. Linda Mollenhauer has 23 years of sector experience, including as former CEO of the Canadian Centre for Philanthropy.

Nonprofit Management Solutions, Inc.

P.O. Box 7536, Hollywood, FL 33081
Tel: 954-985-9489; FAX: 954-989-3442
E-mail: terriet@nonprofitmgtsolutions.com (Terrie Temkin);
WWW: http://www.nonprofitmgtsolutions.com

▶ Services include board development, defining roles and responsibilities, enhancing communication, facilitating change, facilitating retreats, facilitating training, mission-based planning, needs assessments, organizational audits, policy development, staff development, team building, visioning, and volunteer program development.

Nonprofit Works

10 Gibbs Street, Suite 250, Rochester, NY 14604
Tel: 716-546-2420; FAX: 716-546-2423
E-mail: mail@nonprofitworks.com;
WWW: http://www.nonprofitworks.com/about/team.asp

▶ Nonprofit Works provides the following planning services: strategic planning, feasibility studies, program development, outcome measurement and evaluation, and marketing and communication plans. It also provides course, computer training, grant-writing services, Web development, and Web hosting.

The Oram Group, Inc.

275 Madison Avenue, New York, NY 10016
Tel: 212-889-2244; FAX: 212-986-2731
E-mail:hankus@juno.com

44 Page Street, Suite 604C, San Francisco, CA 94102
Tel: 415-864-7567; FAX: 415-621-2533
E-mail: mbancel@aol.com; WWW: http://www.oramgroup.com

▶ A viable, effective nonprofit organization results from the successful interaction of four critical elements: a clear sense of mission and identity; congruent long- and short-range goals, understood and embraced throughout the organization; inspired board leadership, which fully understands and accepts its policy-making governance, and funding responsibilities; and professional staff management dedicated to effective and efficient fulfillment of the organization's charitable purpose. The Oram Group helps clients achieve this interaction through advice and guidance in strategic planning, board development, staff training, effective management, program evaluation, and institutional assessment. The Oram Group, Inc., has recently formed an alliance with Raybin Associates, Inc.

Phillips & Associates

10877 Wilshire Boulevard, Suite 708, Los Angeles, CA 90024
Tel: 310-208-7772
E-mail: contact@phillipsontheweb.com;
WWW: http://phillipsontheweb.com/pa

▶ Established in 1971, this is a professional management consulting firm specializing in organizational planning, financial planning, and fund-raising counsel for not-for-profit institutions and organizations. Strategic planning services include evaluation of fundraising programs and methodologies within the context of overall organizational goals and fund-raising needs; facilitation and guidance in strategic planning; and development of "action-step" plans specifically designed to meet near-term as well as long-term fundraising goals. Since the firm's founding, Phillips & Associates has

served over 316 nonprofit organizations—89 percent within California, Arizona, Hawaii, Oregon, and Washington. They have and will continue to selectively accept special client assignments in other areas of the United States. They maintain offices in Fullerton, San Francisco, and Los Osos, CA.

RPA, Inc.

951 Westminster Drive, Williamsport, PA 17701
Tel: 800-992-9277; FAX: 570-321-7160
E-mail: rpainc@suscom.net; WWW: http://www.rpainc.org/

▶ RPA assists managers in making the most of their capital and human resources in order to operate financially secure and more efficient organizations. They can identify operational and strategic planning opportunities, share insights and experience, and recommend a plan that maximizes your organization's strengths while minimizing any weaknesses.

Raffa & Associates, PC

1899 L Street NW, Suite 600, Washington, DC 20036
Tel: 202-822-5000; FAX: 202-822-0669
E-mail: raffa@raffa.com; WWW: http://www.raffa.com,
http://www.iknow.org

▶ Management consulting services include the following: financial projections and forecasts; budgeting and cash management; strategic planning; due diligence procedures; investment analysis; evaluation and structuring of business transactions and mergers; evaluation and structuring of dispositions and reorganizations; establishment of new organizations, charter organizations, and affiliates; establishment of for-profit and nonprofit subsidiaries; grant and contract applications and administration; applications for the combined federal and United Way campaigns; assistance in audits by granting, contracting, and taxing authorities; establishing and reevaluating indirect cost rates; establishment and compliance reviews of employee benefit programs; temporary assistance as the acting CFO or other accounting positions; interviews of potential candidates for their clients' staff; litigation support; annual membership surveys; establishing or expanding banking relationships; developing policies and procedures manuals; assistance in establishment of endowments and capital campaigns; assistance with lease negotiations; implementing systems that deal effectively with foreign banks and currency translations; enhancing membership dues billing process; establishing the membership dues allocation to comply with lobbying regulations; structuring the financial operations among subsidiaries and affiliates; and serving on the board of directors.

Raybin Associates, Inc.

275 Madison Avenue, Suite 1811, New York, NY 10016
Tel: 212-490-0590; FAX: 212-986-2731
E-mail: information@rabyinassociates.com;
WWW: http://www.raybinassociates.com/flash/index-flash.html

▶ Consisting exclusively of senior professionals with over 80 years of combined experience, the partners of Raybin Associates have developed an exclusive process to help clients achieve and move beyond their goals. Founded in 1973, the firm has assisted more than 500 organizations that provide services for the overall benefit of society, including education; religion and spiritual development; arts, culture, and humanities; environment and conservation; health, research, and disease prevention; legal services; youth development; human services; civil and human rights; and philanthropy. Raybin Associates works in affiliation with the Oram Group on selected client assignments. Raybin is a member of AAFRC.

Rebecca Leet & Associates (RL&A)

2501 North Quantico Street, Arlington, VA 22207-1053
Tel: 703-533-8966; FAX: 703-533-8971
WWW: http://www.leetassociates.com/

▶ Since its founding in 1985, Rebecca Leet & Associates has helped organizations develop clear strategic directions, solve management and marketing problems successfully, and create effective communications. Throughout its history, RL&A has emphasized targeting resources at market sectors that are most likely to provide high mission return on resources invested. Services include strategic planning, meeting and retreat facilitation, strategic marketing planning, message development, program and communication audits, communication planning, and corporate charitable involvement: assessment and planning.

Results Group International

230 West 41st Street, Suite 1602, New York, NY 10036
Tel: 212-869-3373; FAX: 212-869-5535
E-mail: get@resultsg.com; WWW: http://www.resultsg.com

▶ Full-service planning capabilities include board and staff retreats, strategic planning, feasibility studies, staff and trustee training, deficit reduction planning, program audits, management counsel, results assessment, planning process management, and organization audits.

Ruotolo Associates

Horizon Square, 29 Broadway, Suite 210, Cresskill, NJ 07626
Tel: 201-568-3898; FAX: 201-568-8783
E-mail: info@ruotoloassoc.com;
WWW: http://www.ruotoloassoc.com/

▶ Strategic planning has become an essential process for any organization or institution. Planning provides an opportunity for the organization to influence its future rather than be influenced by it. Effective planning further enables the organization to stimulate forward thinking; measure fulfillment of its mission; build ownership; determine strategies and unique opportunities; evaluate programs; create an inclusive process; respond to needs, immediate and long-range; consider redefining the institution or segments of the institution; improve performance; adjust to changing demographics; and chart its future course. Ruotolo Associates provides counsel on initiating, conducting, and implementing planning processes. They also maintain New England, Midwest, and Baltimore/Washington Divisions.

Tecker Consultants, LLC

427 River View Executive Park, Trenton, NJ 08611
Tel: 609-396-7998; FAX: 609-396-6260
E-mail: info@tecker.com, gtecker@tecker.com
(Glenn H. Tecker, President and CEO);
WWW: http://www.tecker.com/tecker/web/ index.htm

▶ This is an international consulting practice focused on meeting the special needs of organizations managing through change. Using a portfolio of techniques and tools carefully selected for each assignment, their partners provide a combination of consultation, facilitation, and education to address key areas like leadership and governance, organizational design, staff development, and marketing. Services include research, evaluation, planning, education, facilitation, consultation, and strategy.

Transitions in Leadership, LLC (TIL)

1129 Lorien Court, St. Louis, MO 63131-4611
Tel: 314-822-4868; FAX: 314-966-6973
E-mail: info@tilnonprof.com; WWW: www.tilnonprof.com

▶ TIL will work with board and staff in planning the process. They facilitate the planning process, resulting in a document that will assist the board and staff in defining the organization's future. TIL will specifically design the planning process to meet your organization's needs. The outcomes of the planning process are intended to clarify the environment in which the organization functions; identify opportunities for positioning of the organization to be fiscally sound; strengthen board cohesion by developing a shared sense of direction; provide a sense of stability for the organization's stakeholders; and define methods for measuring the efficacy of the organization in relation to its stated mission, vision, and values through strategic goals and objectives.

Trustee Leadership Development, Inc.

719 Indiana Avenue, Suite 370, Indianapolis, IN 46202
Tel: 877-564-6853
E-mail: info@tld.org; WWW: http://www.tld.org

▶ A national leadership education and resource center whose mission is to educate and assist a variety of leaders in diverse settings to bring about significant and constructive changes and transformation in themselves, others, their organizations, and their communities. They provide annual leadership education workshops, institutes, and forums; organizational consultation, assessment, and development; board leadership development; executive coaching and mentoring; customized, skill-based workshops; training of professional educators to work with the not-for-profit sector; consultation and training; change management; design and development of leadership programs; and development and dissemination of research-based, practitioner-oriented educational resources.

The Whelan Group

155 West 19th Street, New York, NY 10011
Tel: 212-727-7332; FAX: 212-727-7578
E-mail @ twg@whelangroup.com;
WWW: http://www.whelangroup.com/strat/strat.htm

▶ The Whelan Group's strategic planning and financial planning services are tailored to the needs of organizations interested in charting the course for growth over a period of three to five years. These services are employed most frequently by successful organizations seeking to expand the reach of their work and by organizations requiring a "turnaround intervention." Other organizations utilize their planning services to examine the operating and financial implications of expanding an existing program, launching a new initiative, or building a new facility. These services include organization-wide strategic planning; organization-wide financial planning; strategic fund raising and development planning; new venture/new initiative planning; and financial needs assessments.

Work-Volf Consultants

3 Gamecock Avenue, Suite 304 A, Charleston, SC 29407
Tel: 843-766-7989; FAX: 843-766-7990
E-mail: info@workvolf.com;
WWW: http://www.workvolf.com/developmentfeedback.htm

▶ Planning is really rehearsing your future. Sound plans are critical in this rapidly changing world. Work-Volf helps clients build solid plans that prepare for the months and years ahead. Work-Volf Consultants can help your organization define and achieve its goals. It assists organizations in the following areas: revisit/create a mission, vision, and values so they are clear to all employees; guidance in identifying their strengths and weaknesses; how to benefit from best practices research; assistance in identifying their strategic issues; and developing a planning process that builds an action-oriented team eager to put their plans to work.

Zimmerman Lehman & Associates

582 Market Street, Suite 1112, San Francisco, CA 94104
Tel: 800-886-8330 (outside the San Francisco Bay Area),
415-986-8330; FAX: 415-986-2048
E-mail: zl@zimmerman-lehman.com;
WWW: http://www.zimmerman-lehman.com

▶ Fund raising, marketing, executive recruitment, planning, and facilitation—Zimmerman Lehman has served the nonprofit community since 1988, offering a broad range of services to help nonprofit organizations maximize their financial, board, volunteer, and staff resources. They strengthen organizations by examining their planning needs and identifying areas that require attention by working with boards and staff to evaluate the entire organization and make recommendations for improvement; developing a strategic plan to address deficiencies and maximize opportunities; assisting the organization to develop, design, fund, and implement new programs; and facilitating retreats and planning meetings.

GENERAL RESOURCES

(See also Assessment and Evaluation; Financial Management; General Management; Governance; Information Technology; Marketing and Communications; Organizational Development; Resource Development)

Applied Strategic Planning: How to Develop a Plan That Really Works

LEONARD GOODSTEIN, TIMOTHY NOLAN, AND J. WILLIAM PFEIFFER (MCGRAW-HILL, 1992)

▶ Written by three top consultants and trainers, *Applied Strategic Planning* shows managers and CEOs a clear, totally effective way to identify and implement strategic objectives. It surpasses other strategic planning models in many key areas, including its emphasis on organizational culture, the integration of business and functional plans, the performance audit, and gap analysis. Plus, values clarification is explicitly confronted in a systematic way early in the process. Goodstein, Nolan, and Pfeiffer take managers through all phases of the strategic planning process, including how to determine if an organization is ready for strategic planing, effectively communicate a corporate vision, recognize the role of culture in changing strategic direction, understand the various roles of a consultant, write effective mission statements, and create contingency plans. Charts, diagrams, and checklists make the book especially helpful. Along with illuminating examples from the authors, extensive consulting experience, and even cartoons that convey important points, *Applied Strategic Planning* lets managers at the helm navigate expertly through today's unpredictable business climate. *Hardcover, 379 pages, $27.95*

Beyond Strategic Planning: How to Involve Nonprofit Boards in Growth and Change

DOUGLAS C. EADIE (NATIONAL CENTER FOR NONPROFIT BOARDS, 1993)

▶ Although strategic planning has gained wide acceptance among board members and executives, many nonprofit organizations have found their excursions into strategic planning to be unproductive and disillusioning. *Beyond Strategic Planning* focuses on the practical step boards can take to lay a meaningful role in the process, helping you identify key strategic issues and implementing a plan to ensure that each issue is fully developed and addressed. *Softcover, 24 pages, $12.00 (Nonmember), $9.00 (Member)*

Blueprint for Success: A Guide to Strategic Planning for Nonprofit Board Members (Video)

HOSTED BY MARIA SHRIVER (NATIONAL CENTER FOR NONPROFIT BOARDS, 1997)

▶ A strategic plan can help a nonprofit organization involve key stakeholders, increase its effectiveness at meeting community needs, and create a vision for the future. While methods and plans vary, one component is essential to creating a successful strategic plan: the commitment and participation of the board. NBC News broadcast journalist Maria Shriver, also a board member of Special Olympics International, guides an exploration of how two nonprofit organizations carry out strategic planning. The Mid-America Chapter of the American Red Cross and the Levine School of Music are two very different organizations that provide excellent models of strategic plans in action. Board and staff leaders from each organization explain why planning is important, why the board must be involved, and the benefits and challenges of the strategic planning process. This video is the perfect motivational tool for nonprofit boards considering a strategic plan, for board members who are unfamiliar with strategic planning, or as inspiration for boards about to embark on the process. Your board can view the video as a group or individually. A user's guide written by noted consultant Kay Sprinkel Grace includes guidelines and discussion questions that will make the video a starting point for in-depth discussion. *$62.00 (Nonmember), $46.50 (Member)*

The Board Member's Guide to Strategic Planning: A Practical Approach to Strengthening Nonprofit Organizations

FISHER HOWE AND ALAN SHRADER (JOSSEY-BASS, 1997)

▶ This is a quick, compact guide for busy nonprofit board members by a veteran board member and sought-after consultant to nonprofits. Presenting illustrative examples and straightforward action steps, the book guides board members through each step of strategic planning, including planning meetings, using consultants and facilitators, and determining visions and values. *Hardcover, 144 pages, $22.95*

Board Basics: Understanding the Planning Process

RAYMOND M. HAAS (ASSOCIATION OF GOVERNING BOARDS OF UNIVERSITIES AND COLLEGES, 1997)

▶ Members of governing boards should (1) ensure that planning takes place and (2) insist that plans are used regularly for decision making. In carrying out these basic responsibilities, boards should attend to the following: recognize and promote the usefulness of planning in higher education and support its use; review and approve a planning process for the institution; hold the chief executive accountable for the planning function; participate in certain steps in the planning process; and use the institution's plans to make decisions, especially those that involve setting priorities and allocating resources. *Softcover, 12 pages, $9.95 (Nonmember), $5.95 (Member)*

The Board's Role in Strategic Planning

KAY SPRINKEL GRACE (NATIONAL CENTER FOR NONPROFIT BOARDS, 1996)

▶ This best-selling, 24-page booklet from the governance series explains the importance of strategic planning and why board involvement is essential. It discusses types of planning, defines key planning terms, and outlines a sample process. The lesson discusses the importance of ongoing monitoring, evaluation, and revision once the plan is in place. Use this booklet as a valuable primer for board members and executives who are beginning a planning process and a perfect companion to NCNB's video, *Blueprint for Success* (see separate listing). This publication is also available on audiotape. *Softcover, 24 pages, $12 (Nonmember), $9 (Member)*

The Board's Role in Strategic Planning: NCNB Governance Series (Booklet and Audiotape)
KAY SPRINKEL GRACE (NATIONAL CENTER FOR NONPROFIT BOARDS, 1996)

▶ This kit includes the14-page booklet and 30-minute audio program from the governance series. This set explains the importance of strategic planning and why board involvement is essential. It discusses types of planning, defines key planning terms, and outlines a sample process. The lesson discusses the importance of ongoing monitoring, evaluation, and revision once the plan is in place. Components of strategic plans (vision, mission, goals, objectives, and action steps) are defined. The types of planning processes (staff-driven versus participatory) are outlined. A brief list of suggested resources is included. Use this set as a valuable primer for board members and executives who are beginning a planning process. Good companion to our NCNB's video, *Blueprint for Success* (see separate listing). *Softcover, 24 pages, $20 (Nonmember), $15 (Member)*

Changing by Design: A Practical Approach to Leading Innovation in Nonprofit Organizations (Jossey-Bass Nonprofit Sector Series)
DOUGLAS C. EADIE AND ALAN SHRADER (JOSSEY-BASS, 1997)

▶ *Changing by Design* offers a proactive approach to both designing and implementing change initiatives within nonprofit organizations. By addressing three key areas—coordinated leadership on the part of the chief executive and the board, creative innovation in deciding what needs to change and how to change it, and effective implementation of new ideas and programs—this book presents a balanced, comprehensive model for successfully managing change in today's nonprofit. Illustrated by real-life case studies, *Changing by Design* shows how to design and manage a change plan—from initial analysis through implementation, partner effectively with the board in leading change, encourage and unleash creativity and innovation in developing change initiatives, effectively involve staff in designing and implementing change, protect change initiatives from becoming sidetracked by day-to-day pressures, and recognize and deal with barriers to change. *Hardcover, 304 pages, $29.95*

The Complete Guide to Nonprofit Management, Second Edition
ROBERT H. WILBUR, ED., SMITH, BUCKLIN & ASSOCIATES, INC. (JOHN WILEY & SONS, 2000)

▶ This is the complete nuts-and-bolts guide to managing today's bottom-line oriented nonprofit organizations. This significantly revised and expanded second edition of the highly popular how-to book identifies and addresses the unique concerns of nonprofit organizations. Cutting through the morass of mere theory, the experts at Smith, Bucklin & Associates, Inc., a leading nonprofit

management firm, get right to actual practice with dozens of real-world examples and case studies, and up-to-date, vital, "combat-tested" strategies and techniques for dealing with virtually every nonprofit business management issue, including the daily role of boards of directors; fund development and marketing; public and government relations; educational programs and certification; information services; human resources management; and using the Internet. In addition, featured here is a refocused strategic planning chapter that presents an ongoing, organic form of planning, as well as updated discussions of the importance of mission statements, planning publicity campaigns and coordinating special conventions, developing and marketing education programs, and much more. *Hardcover, 374 pages, $29.95*

Creating and Implementing Your Strategic Plan: A Workbook for Public and Nonprofit Organizations, 2nd Edition
JOHN M. BRYSON AND FARNUM K. ALSTON (JOSSEY-BASS, 1995)

▶ An updated companion to John M. Bryson's *Strategic Planning for Public and Nonprofit Organizations* (see separate listing), this hands-on workbook is a step-by-step guide to conducting strategic planning in public and nonprofit organizations. The second edition is filled with useful tools, including illustrative examples, detailed questionnaires, and easy-to-understand worksheets. It takes users through every step of creating a strategic plan. It is a simple and easy way to heighten interest and broaden participation in strategic planning within any organization. This workbook shows you how to create and implement a strategic plan in the public and nonprofit sector including charts, checklists, suggestions, and tricks for the practitioner. *Hardcover, 140 pages, $26.95*

The Drucker Foundation Self-Assessment Tool, 2nd Edition *(See Assessment and Evaluation for complete description)*

The Executive Guide to Strategic Planning
PATRICK J. BELOW, GEORGE L. MORRISEY, AND BETTY L. ACOMB (JOSSEY-BASS, 1987)

▶ This book offers executives and senior staff a comprehensive, straightforward, and practical approach to strategic planning. It explains in detail how to formulate strategic plans that will develop the company's strengths, be responsive to changing business conditions, and serve to chart a productive and profitable future. In presenting steps for developing down-to-earth strategic plans, the authors describe how to identify team goals and define the role of each member, develop a clear mission statement, choose attainable long-term objectives, prepare realistic financial projections, and evaluate the effectiveness of your efforts. *Hardcover, 159 pages, $32*

Financial & Strategic Management for Nonprofit Organizations *(See Management—General for full description)*

Forging Nonprofit Alliances: A Comprehensive Guide to Enhancing Your Mission Through Joint Ventures & Partnerships, Management Service Organizations, Parent Corporations, and Mergers
JANE ARSENAULT (JOSSEY-BASS, 1998)

▶ This insightful guide shows how, by joining forces, nonprofits can use consolidation as a strategic tool to enhance rather than undermine mission. As nonprofits find ways to increase effectiveness in services and fund raising and face the growing competition for limited resources, they can focus on their real goal—serving their constituents. Arsenault explores the various options for consolidation—including joint ventures and partnerships, management service organizations, parent corporations, and mergers. She also details the negotiation process and demonstrates how to design and frame the consolidation process in a positive and constructive way for staff, donors, and constituents. Written for nonprofit managers and boards, *Forging Nonprofit Alliances* determines which options are right for an organization and clearly defines the roles and responsibilities of all members of nonprofit board and staff in planning and implementing an alliance. *Hardcover, 224 pages, $27.95*

Guidebook of Best Practices for Nonprofit Strategic Planning Facilitators

CARTER MCNAMARA (THE MANAGEMENT ASSISTANCE PROGRAM, 1997)

▶ This book provides concise yet comprehensive directions to facilitating strategic planning for nonprofit organizations. It is one of the few guidebooks, if any, focused on the facilitation of strategic planning. The Guidebook includes suggested best practices from 20 experienced nonprofit strategic planning facilitators. The Guidebook is structured to be comprehensive, yet concise and easy to reference. The Guidebook provides specific advice about planning phases in which facilitators seem to experience the most problems, including setting a sound foundation for planning, understanding the unique needs of nonprofits, and dealing with resistance. It is highly useful to facilitators with some planning experience or nonprofits that want a concise overview of the typical planning process. It is also available in PDF format (see Internet Resources). *Softcover, 30 pages, $25*

Handbook of Strategic Planning for Nonprofit Organizations

SIRI N. ESPY (PRAEGER PUBLISHERS, 1986)

▶ This is the first practical step-by-step guide to strategic planning specifically written for managers of all types of nonprofit organizations, large and small. Born out of one such manager's own successful planning efforts, it details the key techniques involved in strategy planning, such as identifying organizational needs, guiding goal development, targeting markets, and developing marketing plans. Discussing a broad range of nonprofit organizations, *Strategic Planning for Nonprofit Organizations* provides the nonprofit manager with the basic planning and implementation tools essential to the success of his or her organization. *Hardcover, 143 pages, $57.95*

High Impact Tools and Activities for Strategic Planning: Creative Techniques for Facilitating Your Organization's Planning Process

ROD NAPIER, PATRICK SANAGHAN, CLINT SIDLE, AND PATRICK SARAGHAN (MCGRAW-HILL, 1998)

▶ Not just another book on the theory of strategic planning, here are dozens of recipes for creative group activities to facilitate strategic planning in any organization. Designed for use by consultants, facilitators, and management team leaders, step-by-step instructions guide you through exercises for gaining employee and management participation; gathering feedback from management about the current state of the organization; creating an organized mission, vision, and values statement; and planning so that the vision becomes reality. Ready-to-use reproducible materials and handouts are also included. Get management and employee support

for your organization's new strategic direction with these electrifying group activities. Strategic plans are successfully implemented only when the planning process itself engages every stakeholder and gives everyone a genuine sense of "ownership" of the new organizational strategy. *High Impact Tools and Activities for Strategic Planning* offers you all the practical resources to generate that passionate involvement, with dozens of radical group activities to help you facilitate the planning process for a team or an entire organization. This unique handbook for consultants, trainers, and managers brings you 40 creative, field-tested activities that jumpstart strategic planning meetings, inspire new ways of thinking, and build the momentum critical to any change effort. Unlike most books on strategic planning, *High Impact Tools and Activities for Strategic Planning* gives you step-by-step instructions for targeted activities to help an organization kick off planning efforts that create energy, hope, and clarity of purpose; turn "data gathering" from employees and management into a forum for open communication; clarify and create its core values, mission, and vision statements; monitor and assess planning efforts to ensure accountability; and establish ongoing planning to allow proactive—not reactive—responses to changing environments and organizational priorities. Featuring case studies that detail how the book's activities galvanize planning efforts of various sizes and complexity, *High Impact Tools and Activities for Strategic Planning* enables you to pump new blood into even the most anemic planning process and build a greater sense of empowerment and commitment throughout an organization. *Hardcover, 424 pages, $149*

Implementing Your Strategic Plan: How to Turn 'Intent' into Effective Action for Sustainable Change

C. DAVIS FOGG (AMACOM, 1998)

▶ Planning is easy, but implementing a plan is tough—often involving the coordination and direction of numerous people, resources, programs, and actions over a sustained period of time and across many organizational boundaries. *Implementing Your Strategic Plan* is packed with action-oriented principles, tools, and techniques designed to help CEOs, managers, consultants, or anyone who needs to make a strategic plan a reality—not just a pipe dream. It shows how to turn strategic priority issues into assigned, measurable actions; foster creative leadership; overcome resistance to change; provide an environment in which people can excel; fix broken core processes, and more. *Implementing Your Strategic Plan* is packed with practical, action-oriented principles, tools, and techniques for making your strategic plan a reality. At its core, the book pinpoints and explains the 18 keys to strategy implementation. Derived from both the author's extensive experience and in-depth interviews with CEOs, these are the essential steps for developing and enacting the strategic plan tasks and for successfully achieving sustained organizational change. Specifically, you'll learn how to design an accountability system that aligns actions throughout the organization with the corporate plan and uses interlocking scorecards for teams, departments, and individuals; turn strategic priority issues into assigned, measurable action plans; make sure that your organization's structure follows its strategy, and swiftly changes it if it doesn't; put people with the skills you really need in the tough jobs; foster creative leadership and the mental rigor to make timely, risky decisions; use cross-functional teams effectively, without succumbing to "teamitis"; define your current cultural values and norms and those you want in the future; allocate your resources effectively, putting your money and people where your future is; fix broken core processes, the essential channels for delivering what the customer wants; and design a balanced compensation package that rewards both long-term strategic accomplishments and ongoing results, plus eight other implementation keys. *Hardcover, 360 pages, $65*

Long-Range Planning Manual for Board Members
DARLA STRUCK, ED. (ASPEN PUBLISHERS, 1998)

▶ Long-range planning should be one of your board's top priorities. A quality plan gives direction, prevents problems, and makes decision making a whole lot easier. The *Long-Range Planning Manual* provides your board with the skills and tools to do the job right. Handing each of your board members a personal copy of this hands-on workbook shows them your concern for long-range planning. This guide is packed with practical hints, worksheets, and forms your board will use. This book defines why long-range planning is important to the board, why board members should be involved, the components of a strategic plan, and how to set aside time during board retreats for planning functions. Sample forms and worksheets are included. *Softcover spiral edition, 44 pages, $32*

Management & Planning, Leadership Series, Volume I *(See Management—General for full description)*

Management & Planning, Leadership Series, Volume II *(See Management—General for full description)*

Managing a Nonprofit Organization: Staffing, Fundraising, Choosing Trustees, Financing, Marketing, Computerizing, Planning, Succeeding
(See Management—General for full description)

Managing for Impact in Nonprofit Organizations: Corporate Planning Techniques and Applications
(See Management—General for full description)

Market Analysis: Assessing Your Business Opportunities
ROBERT E. STEVENS, PHILIP K. SHERWOOD, AND PAUL DUNN (HAWORTH PRESS, 1993)

▶ Planning is a critical process when starting a new business or introducing a new product. *Market Analysis* shows readers how to execute a feasibility study for more effective planning. A step-by-step approach leads the reader through the feasibility analysis process and describes what needs to be done and how to do it. Techniques and tools used in preparing a feasibility study are emphasized and can easily be applied directly from the book to real situations. Three sample feasibility studies are included to demonstrate the application of tools in manufacturing, service, and nonprofit settings. *Market Analysis* contains all the information needed to complete a feasibility study and a complete outline of a business plan. It covers such important topics as strategic management and planning, determining market size for a product or business, analyzing costs and returns on investment for new products and services, sources of capital for new ventures, and analysis of competition. An annotated bibliography of sources of data used for feasibility studies is included for quick reference. *Market Analysis* is the ideal guide for all strategic planners, market analysts, and marketing researchers. *Softcover, 240 pages, $34.95*

Market-Driven Management: Lessons Learned From 20 Successful Associations
DONALD M. MORRIS (AMERICAN SOCIETY OF ASSOCIATION EXECUTIVES FOUNDATION, 1990)

▶ Use the tools of marketing to anticipate and meet the needs of your members. In this book, you will see how other organizations used marketing-supported strategic planning and program redesign, based on an assessment of client needs, aggressive entrepreneurialism, and other types of market-influenced behavior, to move toward a more prosperous future. Also included are critical success factors for becoming market driven, checklists to help you enhance your organization's market-driven orientation, important future issues organizations, and an annotated bibliography. *Softcover, 154 pages, $45 (Nonmember), $18.95 (Member)*

Marketing Planning Guide *(See Marketing and Communications—General for full description)*

The Nonprofit Management Handbook: Operating Policies and Procedures *(See Management—General for full description)*

Nonprofit Mergers and Alliances: A Strategic Planning Guide (Nonprofit Law, Finance and Management Series) (Book and Disk)
THOMAS A. MCLAUGHLIN (JOHN WILEY & SONS, 1998)

▶ In *Nonprofit Mergers and Alliances*, Thomas McLaughlin describes a context for nonprofit mergers and discusses the forces that shape their use. He demonstrates that nonprofit mergers are fundamentally different from corporate mergers, that they can be of immense benefit to the community as well as the merging organizations, and that failure to merge can be disastrous for everyone. McLaughlin focuses on the concerns of the nonprofit sector: achieving the mission, retaining tax-exempt status, and behaving responsibly in the community. He shows nonprofit managers and board members how to make their way through the merger process without repeating Wall Street misbehavior. Using real-world examples and case studies, *Nonprofit Mergers and Alliances* offers clear, practical, step-by-step guidance through the merger process from preliminary considerations to actual implementation, pointing out pitfalls and offering insightful commentary along the way. This helpful volume provides a penetrating discussion of the reasons to collaborate; the C.O.R.E.™ model, a merger/alliance analysis framework; advice on partner selection; structure choice analyses; step-by-step guidance through merger and alliance processes; and a disk with forms and worksheets that any nonprofit can customize for its own needs. Supplemented with easy-to-use checklists and analytical tables, *Nonprofit Mergers and Alliances* helps nonprofit board members and managers make the right decisions, monitor the entire process, anticipate problems, and find solutions quickly. *Hardcover, 256 pages, $55*

The Nonprofit Mergers Workbook: The Leader's Guide to Considering, Negotiating, and Executing a Merger
DAVID LA PIANA (AMHERST H. WILDER FOUNDATION, 2000)

▶ The result of nearly two years of work, drawing on the author's 20 years in the sector, the Workbook takes a thoroughly practical approach to the topic of mergers. This practical guide walks you through the entire merger process from assessing your reasons and readiness, to finding a partner, negotiating the deal, and completing the merger. *Softcover, 240 pages, $28*

Nonprofit Organization: Essential Readings *(See Management—General for full description)*

A Nonprofit Organization Operating Manual (See Management—General for full description)

Nonprofit Strategic Alliances Project Materials
(PHILADELPHIA HEALTH MANAGEMENT CORPORATION)

▶ These materials were developed with funding from The Pew Charitable Trusts to assist nonprofit executives and board members in exploring strategic alliances. The project addressed the areas of finance, nonprofit law, organizational effectiveness, and strategic alliances to create seven case studies and 12 quick-reference directories. *Softcover, $40*

Nonprofit Strategic Planning for Quick Results
SHEA SMITH (SHEA SMITH, 1997)

▶ Be guided through the long-range strategic planning process in the most time-effective manner possible. Some 22 real-life examples illustrate how the seven steps in the process lead to identifying key issues and how to decide what to do about them. In addition, learn how to manage the planning effort, how to ensure that the plan will be used through planning control, and how to handle the two most prevalent problems. *Softcover, 196 pages, $16.95*

The Planning Committee: Shaping Your Organization's Future
JUDITH O'CONNOR (NATIONAL CENTER FOR NONPROFIT BOARDS, 1997)

▶ Rapid-fire changes in the economy, culture, and government are making the need for effective strategic planning for nonprofit organizations even more evident. Planning is an important board function—and the planning committee guides the process. What is the role of the board during strategic planning? Who should be involved? How can the board devise an effective planning process? This booklet answers these questions and defines the committee's responsibilities, outlines how the committee and full board relate to staff and constituents during strategic planning, and provides guidance in conducting the planning process. *Softcover, 20 pages, $12.00 (Nonmember), $9.00 (Member)*

Private Sector Strategies for Social Sector Success: The Guide to Strategy and Planning for Public and Nonprofit Organizations
KEVIN P. KEARNS (JOHN WILEY & SONS, 2000)

▶ This practical guide offers a realistic approach to strategic management, while borrowing from the most helpful and relevant business ideas, and allows the public or nonprofit organization to achieve success without compromising its unique mission or constituency. Executives, managers, and policy makers will find key principles for everyday application, including how to identify trends that will most affect programs and services, assess the organization's core strengths and competencies, select strategies that advance the mission while building operational success, explore opportunities for collaborations with other organizations, and encourage a culture of strategic thought and action. Throughout this innovative guide, there are numerous illustrations and examples of how to apply the most appropriate technique to a particular need or goal. At last, public and nonprofit organizations have a real-world guide to finding lasting success. *Hardcover, 384 pages, $26.95*

Redesigning the Nonprofit Organization: How Vision, Leadership, and Planning Helped One Nonprofit Redefine Itself (See Organizational Dynamics and Design for full description)

Reengineering Your Nonprofit Organization: A Guide to Strategic Transformation
ALCESTE T. PAPPAS (JOHN WILEY & SONS, 1995)

▶ To stay alive and compete in today's business world, a nonprofit needs to be willing and able to start from scratch and reinvent itself. A former Big Six partner with 25 years of experience in advising nonprofits on management presents the best practice of the nonprofit sector and describes innovative strategies for effecting change including establishing partnerships and alliances, sharing resources, and expanding the organization and means of delivering services. Reengineering is the radical redesign of an organization's processes, structure, and culture; the realities of the nonprofit world are not all that different from those of the corporate world, what with shrinking budgets, changing societal needs, and scandals forcing nonprofits to heed the call of reengineering. In order to survive and remain "competitive," nonprofits must reexamine their raisons d'etre, how they carry out their missions, their organizational structures, and their business processes. Those involved in strategic planning and reengineering a nonprofit range from paid staff to volunteer board members. To better achieve these goals, this book takes a new "zero-base" look at strategic planning (more than merely updating a mission statement and calling it change, a nonprofit needs to be willing and able to start from scratch and reinvent itself); examines innovative strategies for effecting change, including the establishment of partnerships and alliances, both with other nonprofits and for-profits, for sharing resources; and presents the "best practices" of the nonprofit world that are designed to improve performance in establishing cost-effective systems and structures. Targeted at the nonprofit market, it is intended for executives and directors, board of director members, managers, fund-raising professionals, and consultants. *Hardcover, 224 pages, $34.95*

The Self-Sustaining Nonprofit: Planning for Success
E. JANE RUTTER (GRANTS LINK, 1997)

▶ Written from the perspective of an executive director, this important resource features strategies and planning guides designed to help leaders transition a volunteer organization to a formal organizational structure. *The Self-Sustaining Nonprofit* concentrates on start-up through year three, highlighting incorporation, image, client service, the business plan, the marketing plan, IRS 501(c)(3) status, budgets, case studies, board development, team building, fund raising, training, mission statements, personnel, and accountability. *Softcover, 117 pages, $50*

Simplified Strategic Planning: A No-Nonsense Guide for Busy People Who Want Results Fast! Revised Edition
ROBERT W. BRADFORD, PETER DUNCAN, AND BRIAN TARCY (CHANDLER HOUSE, 2001)

▶ This book is about how to devise an appropriate strategy for your organization. The contributors all share tips and tricks with each other on a regular basis, trying to find the best answers to these questions: (1) What strategies assure the greatest growth in profitability? (2) What is the fastest way to assure you have a good strategy? (3) What will create sustainable success over a longer period of time? *Softcover, 240 pages, $22.95*

Strategic Management for Nonprofit Organizations: Theory and Cases
SHARON M. OSTER (OXFORD UNIVERSITY PRESS, 1995)

▶ *Strategic Management for Nonprofit Organizations* applies powerful concepts of strategic management developed originally in the for-profit sector to the management of nonprofits. It describes the preparation of a strategic plan consistent with the resources available, analyzes the operational tasks in executing the plan, and describes the ways in which nonprofits need to change in order to remain competitive. Drawing on literature in the fields of economics, management, accounting, and organizational theory, Sharon Oster explores a wide range of topics including a discussion of the role and mission of the nonprofit—from fund raising to accounting and from evaluation to the treatment of volunteers and the board of directors. Examples are taken from all parts of the nonprofit arena, including the arts, health care, education, social services, foundations, and economic development. This is the first book to bring modern strategic management concepts to the problems of managing nonprofit organizations. It draws clear distinctions between the different industries and offers practical solutions to the challenges confronting managers of nonprofits. *Hardcover, 360 pages, $45*

Strategic Management in Public and Nonprofit Organizations: Managing Public Concerns in an Era of Limits, 2nd Edition
JACK KOTEEN (GREENWOOD PUBLISHING GROUP, 1997)

▶ This new edition captures and blends the essence of new ways of managing public and nonprofit organizations to better serve the client given the new realities that are drastically altering the ways in which these organizations do business. Pioneering, but applicable, private-sector management behavior is identified and explained along with time-tested management fundamentals and numerous practices developed over the last several decades. This edition retains the comprehensive coverage of the earlier edition while including the cutting edge of management technology. *Softcover, 332 pages, $30.95*

Strategic Management of Public and Third Sector Organizations *(See Management—General for full description)*

Strategic Planning for Fund Raising: How to Bring in More Money Using Strategic Resource Allocation *(See Resource Development—General for full description)*

Strategic Planning for Nonprofit Organizations: A Practical Guide and Workbook (Book & Disk)
MICHAEL ALLISON AND JUDE KAYE (JOHN WILEY & SONS, 1997)

▶ Designed to be accessible and practical, this workbook takes the fear out of planning for nonprofit managers. It breaks strategic planning into six steps, and uses field-tested worksheets, checklists, and tables—both in print and on disk. The book also carries a real-life case study through the entire process. Acknowledging that different organizations have different needs and resources, this clear, concise guide presents a process that can be adjusted to work for a 1- to 2-day planning retreat or for a longer, 6- to 12-month planning cycle. Aimed primarily at small and medium-sized nonprofit organizations of all kinds, it takes a no-nonsense approach to an organization's most vital management activity. This comprehensive book–disk set shows you how to create and implement an effective strategic plan using a simple, seven-phase process that covers everything from defining your mission and setting your course to initiating, monitoring, and streamlining your plan. The workbook is designed for nonprofits of all shapes, sizes, and budgets, and can be easily adapted to fit any time frame. The package comes with field-tested worksheets, checklists, and tables in both print and disk formats, plus a sample case study that demonstrates strategic planning in action from start to finish. Filled with real-world insights, planning tips, and useful pointers, this accessible guide is a must for every forward-thinking nonprofit professional. Topics covered include how to construct clear mission and vision statements; how to conduct SWOT (Strengths, Weaknesses, Opportunities, Threats) analyses and program evaluations; how to assess client needs and determine stakeholder concerns; how to set priorities and develop core strategies, goals, and objectives; how to write and adopt a solid strategic plan; how to develop a user-friendly annual work plan; and how to establish planning cycles, evaluate progress, and update strategies. *Softcover, 320 pages, $39.95*

Strategic Planning for Not-For-Profit Organizations
R. HENRY MIGLIORE, ROBERT E. STEVENS, AND DAVID L. LOUDON (HAWORTH PRESS, 1995)

▶ This book describes a strategic planning process for bringing direction and unity to not-for-profit organizations. It covers writing a mission statement, setting goals, evaluation and control procedures, and situational analysis, and offers worksheets, case examples, and a strategic plan outline. *Strategic Planning for Not-for-Profit Organizations* covers all the steps involved in developing a strategic plan for a not-for-profit organization. Strategic planning has become a critical issue for not-for-profit organizations as they strive for direction and orderly adjustment to a changing environment. In this book, the authors describe a strategic planning process that will help readers bring direction and unity to their organizations and help create a sense of enthusiasm and anticipation as organizations' visions of what they can be begin to unfold. *Strategic Planning for Not-for-Profit Organizations* is both a tutorial and an easily accessible reference. It is packed with user-friendly information to help readers prepare their own strategic plans and evaluate plans created by others. The book presents essential concepts and techniques in a concise, readily usable form that readers can immediately use in decision making. Worksheets and real-life examples throughout the book help readers in the step-by-step development of strategic plans for their own organizations. A set of appendices includes a strategic plan outline and presents sample strategic plans so readers can see what one actually looks like and get a head start on theirs. A complete guide to strategic planning for not-for-profit organizations, this book covers everything from writing purpose or mission statements and setting goals to strategy development and evaluation and control procedures. Managers and administrators of not-for-profit organizations will find *Strategic Planning for Not-for-Profit Organizations* an extremely helpful guide for their planning duties. The book also serves as a valuable text or supplemental reading for college courses on managing not-for-profit organizations. *Hardcover, 200 pages, $69.95*

Strategic Planning for Public and Nonprofit Organizations: A Guide to Strengthening and Sustaining Organizational Achievement, Revised Edition
JOHN M. BRYSON (JOSSEY-BASS, 1995)

▶ This book shows leaders and managers of public and nonprofit organizations both how and why they should use strategic planning to improve the performance of their organizations. This expanded edition includes many examples to illustrate both successful and unsuccessful planning efforts, while new chapters address planning implementation, strategy evaluation and reassessment, and key leadership roles vital to effective strategic planning. In addition, the author presents a planning process used successfully by many public and nonprofit organizations, the Strategy Change Cycle, along with detailed guidance on its application. This cycle is based on a 10-step strategic planning process that contains the basic components of many planning approaches. However, the cycle as presented "is typically very fluid, iterative, and dynamic in practice, but it nonetheless allows for a reasonably orderly, participative, and effective approach to determining how to achieve what is best for an organization."

According to John Bryson, "strategic thinking and acting are more important than any particular approach to strategic planning." He stresses "that strategic planning is ultimately about purpose, meaning, value, and virtue, and therefore, it is philosophical at its base." Leadership is a key component in planning because it recognizes that this is a people process imbued with the values of individuals, customers, stakeholders, and the organizational culture. Consequently, it is essential that the organizational leaders guide, monitor, and manage the process to ensure success. Bryson stresses the critical role of leadership in the initiation of planning and implementation of action plans. Leaders can serve in one or more of three roles: as sponsors, champions, and/or facilitators. Sponsors are typically in top positions in organizations. They are therefore able to commit the organization to strategic planning and hold people accountable for outcomes. While not involved in the daily details of planning, they provide resources and make commitments needed for success. In contrast, the champions are those who have the responsibility for managing the day-to-day strategic planning process. They monitor progress and details. Finally, facilitators handle the management of the group processes needed for planning so the champions can focus on substantive discussions. Skilled facilitators help build the partnerships among all participants.

Bryson's book is not a recipe for planning but rather a menu of strategy choices to be selected as appropriate. He does not prescribe a one-size-fits-all mechanistic approach but stresses instead the importance of customizing strategies to fit the culture of the organization, the values of the people involved, the complexity of the issues being addressed, the needs of stakeholders and customers, the resources available, and a wide variety of other factors. In addition, the text continually stresses that unexpected outcomes, both successes and failures, are normal results of the dynamics of the process. The author also includes an annotated list of important points about group processes developed in each chapter, which are summarized in sections called "process guidelines." In addition, the book includes an excellent bibliography for reference on topics of interest. This thoroughly revised and updated edition offers new information on leadership, strategic planning, and tools that can help leaders and followers enhance organization achievement. It includes many new examples of successful and unsuccessful strategic planning practices, along with entirely new chapters on how to implement strategies, how to reassess strategies and the strategic planning process, and how to fulfill the key leadership roles that must be undertaken if strategic planning is to be effective; gain innovative strategic planning skills designed specifically for public and nonprofit organizations; provides detailed practical guidance on how to initiate and implement each phase of the strategic planning process, from forming planning committees and developing mission statements to formulating strategies that address key issues; and can help you improve agency performance, fulfill your mission, and satisfy constituents. *Hardcover, 348 pages, $34.95*

Strategic Planning: The ASTD Trainer's Sourcebook
JOHN WILLS (MCGRAW-HILL, 1997)

▶ Here's the easy way to assemble and run effective workshops on the hottest topics in training today. Fast, flexible, and developed by top experts, The ASTD Trainer's Sourcebook Series provides the step-by-step resources you need to conduct a complete full-day, half-day, or one-hour session—including background information, facilitator notes, training designs, participant handouts, games and activities, instruments, assessments, overheads, and flipcharts. And because all components are fully reproducible, you're welcome to photocopy and customize them to your needs without cost or permission. In addition to the titles you see here, forthcoming contributions to the series include tools on coaching, quality, supervision, team building, leadership, customer service, facilitation skills, project management, strategic planning, and creativity. Each can help you achieve maximal training benefits with minimal training expense and preparation time. *Softcover, 252 pages, $39.95*

Strategic Planning: What Every Manager Must Know
GEORGE ALBERT STEINER (TOUCHSTONE/SIMON & SCHUSTER, 1997)

▶ In today's complex business world, strategic planning is indispensable to achieving superior management. George A. Steiner's classic work, known as the bible of business planning, provides practical advice for organizing the planning system, acquiring and using information, and translating strategic plans into decisive action. An invaluable resource for top and middle-level executives, *Strategic Planning* continues to be the foremost guide to this vital area of business management. *Softcover, 400 pages, $16*

Strategic Planning Workbook for Nonprofit Organizations, Revised Edition
BRYAN W. BARRY (AMHERST H. WILDER FOUNDATION, 1997)

▶ How do you reach your goals and make an impact when you're faced with funding cuts and increased competition? You'll find the answer in the *Strategic Planning Workbook,* Revised and Updated. With practical, step-by-step guidance and worksheets to develop your own plan, you'll gain a sense of direction that will guide your choices, build teamwork, and stimulate forward thinking and refocus your mission. You'll gain a sense of direction that will guide your choices about which opportunities to pursue and which to avoid. Written by national strategic planning expert Bryan Barry, this updated edition builds on the original and adds new sections so that you get step-by-step guidance through the five planning phases; critical ingredients of a sound plan; information on how to create a shared vision of your nonprofit's future to guide staff in making everyday choices; strategies to address problems and opportunities that the nonprofit sector now faces; a new, more detailed sample of one nonprofit's actual three-year plan including goals, strategies, staffing, financial, and implementation plans; new suggestions on how to format your plan; additional tips for implementing and updating your plan; examples of how multiple organizations, coalitions, and communities can use strategic planning; and easy-to-complete, detachable worksheets to help you develop your own plan, sell it to your colleagues, and measure results. *Softcover, 129 pages, $28*

Strategic Readiness: The Making of the Learning Organization
JOHN C. REDDING AND RALPH C. CATALANELLO (JOSSEY-BASS, 1994)

▶ This book shows executives or anyone concerned with making change happen how to move beyond the limitations of fixed strategic planning processes and programs to a creative, flexible, responsive organization that thrives in today's climate of uncertainty: the learning organization. It draws from an extensive study of 200 change-oriented organizations. *Hardcover, 222 pages, $34.95*

Successful Strategic Planning: A Guide for Nonprofit Agencies and Organizations

PATRICK J. J. BURKHART AND SUZANNE REUSS (SAGE PUBLICATIONS, 1993)

▶ Strategic planning is often considered a complex and difficult task and is frequently avoided because of perceived lack of time, resources, or expertise. This step-by-step guide aims to demystify the process of strategic planning for nonprofit agencies and organizations by using case examples to illustrate major concepts. It explains how to get started, conduct internal assessments and external assessments, identify key issues and opportunities, build consensus, set goals and objectives, complete the plan, implement the plan, and use the plan for evaluation. *Softcover, 152 pages, $16.95*

Sustaining Innovation: Creating Nonprofit and Government Organizations That Innovate Naturally (Jossey-Bass Nonprofit Sector Series)

PAUL CHARLES LIGHT (JOSSEY-BASS, 1998)

▶ Any organization can innovate once. The challenge is to innovate twice, thrice, and more to make innovation a part of daily good practice. This book shows how nonprofit and government organizations can transform the single, occasional act of innovating into an everyday occurrence by forging a culture of natural innovation. Filled with real success stories and practical lessons learned, *Sustaining Innovation* offers examples of how organizations can

take the first step toward innovativeness, advice on how to survive the inevitable mistakes along the way, and tools for keeping the edge once the journey is complete. Light also provides a set of simple suggestions for fitting the lessons to the different management pressures facing the government and nonprofit sector. Unlike the private sector, where innovation needs only to be profitable to be worth doing, government and nonprofit innovation must be about doing something worthwhile. It must challenge the prevailing wisdom and advance the public good. *Sustaining Innovation* gives nonprofit and government managers a coherent, easily understood model for making this kind of innovation a natural reality. *Hardcover, 350 pages, $26.95*

Team-Based Strategic Planning: A Complete Guide to Structuring, Facilitating and Implementing the Process

C. DAVIS FOGG (AMACOM, 1994)

▶ Strategic planning is a critical part of running an organization, but when you get a team of people together to plan, it can often become a confused exercise in grand visions without a clear process for establishing workable goals. This book is unique in providing both guidance for the actual content of strategic plans and techniques for how to plan in a team context. Readers will discover how to structure the process so it custom-fits their organization's needs; effectively facilitate the process (keep meetings on track, train others in planning skills, document decisions made at meetings, present and communicate the plan); and use teams and teamwork smoothly and productively to create a far-reaching plan and then to implement it. It features detailed guidelines for each step, dozens of flowcharts, and three self-contained "facilitator's guides" to follow. *Hardcover, 337 pages, $65*

PERIODICALS

Innovating (Quarterly Journal)
The Rensselaerville Institute, 63 Huyck Road,
Rensselaerville, NY 12147
Tel: 518-797-3783; FAX: 518-797 5270
WWW: http://www.tricampus.org/publications.htm

▶ This journal is for people who practice innovation in public- and private-sector organizations. It is good for agency heads, direct-line workers, and their supervisors. This quarterly publication instructs on how to trigger change through example by using small projects to test new thinking in immediate ways. Names and phone numbers are included for follow-up, personal accounts of innovators, and a timely digest of innovations in government, schools, and businesses. It presents experiences and viewpoints of innovative scholars and in public- and private-sector organizations. *$30/year*

INTERNET RESOURCES

Answer Center: Strategic Planning—Delaware Association of Nonprofit Agencies

▶ *http://www.delawarenonprofit.org/StrPlanFaq.html*

Center for Simplified Strategic Planning

▶ *http://www.cssp.com/*

Developing Your Strategic Plan—Free Management Library

▶ *http://www.managementhelp.org/np_progs/sp_mod/str_plan.htm*

Echoing Green

▶ This site contains information on a variety of topics including strategic planning, public relations and marketing, defining mission vision and values, and corporate partnerships. *http://www.echoinggreen.org/resource/orgdev/index.html*

***Facilitators' Guide to Nonprofit Strategic Planning*—Management Assistance Program**

▶ Concise, yet comprehensive directions to facilitating strategic planning for nonprofit organizations. One of the few guidebooks, if any, focused on the facilitation of strategic planning. *http://www.mapnp.org/library/docs/plng_gde.pdf*

InnoNet's Workstation for Innovative Nonprofits

▶ Created by InnoNet, a nonprofit consulting organization in Washington that helps charities plan and evaluate programs, this Web site offers interactive worksheets that nonprofit staff members can use to plan new programs and develop budgets, grant applications, and evaluation and fund-raising plans. InnoNet offers to review users' completed plans free. The site also explains how to conduct focus-group discussions, interviews, and surveys, and provides sample evaluation tools. *http://www.inetwork.org/index.html, http://www.innonet.org/strategic.html*

Interactive Knowledge for Nonprofits Worldwide: Strategic Planning

▶ *http://www.iknow.org/StrategicPlan.html*

Lessons Learned: A Planning Toolsite for the World Wide Web—National Endowment for the Arts

▶ Developed for the National Endowment for the Arts, the government agency that oversees federal support of the arts,

this Web site offers 25 essays on strategic planning. The site also includes several checklists and worksheets, a list of recommended reading, and links to Web sites on planning. Although the site uses arts organizations as examples, the information provided applies to planning at all types of charities. *http://arts.endow.gov/pub/Lessons/index.html*

Nonprofit GENIE: Strategic Planning

▶ *http://search.genie.org/genie/ans_result.lasso?cat=Strategic+Planning*

Practical Suggestions for Strategic and Operational Planning

▶ *http://www.u.arizona.edu/~sexasslt/arpedep/planning.html*

Starting a Nonprofit Organization: A-Stop Answer Page

▶ If you're thinking of starting a nonprofit organization, this is the place to begin. You'll find links to basic information such as planning, board of directors, legal resources, and fund raising. *http://nonprofit.about.com/careers/nonprofit/library/weekly/blonestart.htm*

Strategic Planning: A Ten Step Method

▶ *http://www.improve.org/stratpln.html*

Strategic Planning—Nonprofit Management Solutions, Inc.

▶ *http://www.nonprofitmgtsolutions.com/index.htm*

Strategic Planning FAQ—Alliance for Nonprofit Management

▶ *http://www.allianceonline.org/faqs/spfaq1.html*

Strategic Planning for Non-Profit Organizations: New Plans for New Times—Ginsler & Associates

▶ A hands-on workbook for steering your organization through the changing demands of the new nonprofit environment. *http://www.ginsler.com/html/free.htp*

Strategic Planning for Nonprofits—About.com

▶ *http://www.nonprofit.about.com/careers/nonprofit/library/weekly/aa030998.htm*

Strategic Planning in Nonprofit and Public Sector Organizations

▶ *http://www.uwex.edu/li/learner/martinellidoc.html*

Strategic Planning (in Nonprofit or For-Profit Organizations) Free Management Library

▶ *http://www.mapnp.org/library/plan_dec/str_plan/str_plan.htm*

Strategic Planning in Smaller Nonprofit Organizations: A Practical Guide for the Process— Western Michigan University

▶ *http://www.wmich.edu/nonprofit/Guide/guide7.htm*

Strategic Solutions: Tips, Testimonials, and Solutions—La Piana Associates

▶ *http://www.lapiana.org/tips/index.html*

Strategy—Internet Nonprofit Center FAQ

▶ *http://www.nonprofits.org/npofaq/keywords/1o.html*

StrategyWeb

▶ *http://www.strategyweb.net/*

What Are the Steps of a Strategic Planning Process?

▶ *http://www.nonprofits.org/npofaq/03/24.html*

PART X

Volunteerism

Organizations & Governmental Agencies

Civic Participation and Volunteerism
(See also Community Service and Volunteering Opportunities; Service Learning)

Association for Research on Nonprofit Organizations and Voluntary Action (ARNOVA)
(See Philanthropy—Organizations for full description)

The Grantmaker Forum on Community & National Service *(See Support and Advocacy)*

Independent Sector (IS)
1200 Eighteenth Street, Suite 200, Washington, DC 20036
Tel: 202-467-6100, 888-860-8118 (Publications);
FAX: 202-467-6101
E-mail: info@IndependentSector.org;
WWW: http://www.independentsector.org/
▶ IS is a nonprofit organization whose mission is to promote giving, volunteering, not-for-profit initiative, and citizen action. It is a nonprofit coalition of 800 corporations, foundations, and voluntary organizations that have a national interest in philanthropy and voluntary action. The organization's mission is to create a national forum capable of encouraging the giving, volunteering, and not-for-profit initiatives that better serve people, communities, and causes. Since 1980, IS has fought legislative battles, published research data, and worked for better management in the nonprofit world. In addition, the organization launched a major national campaign in 1986, "Give Five," to encourage all Americans to volunteer five hours of their time a week and to give 5 percent of their annual income to causes they care about. IS also publishes informative materials, including "Giving and Volunteering in the United States—Findings from a National Survey" (this is the largest study ever taken, providing the fullest assessment to date about patterns, motivations, and satisfactions of giving and volunteering). (See also separate listing in The Nonprofit Sector—Support and Advocacy Organizations for more detailed description.)

Indiana University Center on Philanthropy
(See Philanthropy—Education and Research Centers for full description)

The Institute for the Study of Civic Values
1218 Chestnut Street, Suite 702, Philadelphia, PA 19107
Tel: 215-238-1434; FAX: 215-238-0530
E-mail: edcivic@libertynet.org (Ed Schwartz);
WWW: http://www.libertynet.org/edcivic/iscvhome.html
▶ The Institute for the Study of Civic Values is a nonprofit organization established in Philadelphia in 1973 to promote the fulfillment of America's historic civic ideals. The Institute has conducted a wide range of seminars, workshops, and public forums aimed at applying America's civic values to contemporary issues and problems. In the process, they have helped thousands of people and grassroots organizations in the knowledge and skills needed for effective participation in the community and politics. In order to address the serious problems facing America today, they follow these basic principles: civic values, community, civic literacy, and democracy. The Institute has been collaborating with the Center for Civic Networking to create an online Civic Network in America. You can join this network by subscribing to one of their e-mail lists: Civic-Values, Build-Com, and Neighbors-Online (see separate listing under Volunteerism—Internet Sites).

Institute on Philanthropy and Voluntary Service
(See Service Learning, Youth and Young Adult Volunteering)

Nonprofit Sector Research Fund *(See the Nonprofit Sector—Organizations for full description)*

Community Service and Volunteering Opportunities (National, International)

National

AFS Info Center *(See International)*

Action Without Borders, Inc. *(See International)*

American Friends Service Committee *(See International)*

American Red Cross
431 18th Street NW, Washington, DC 20006
Tel: 800-HELP-NOW
E-mail: info@usa.redcross.org; WWW: http://www.redcross.org/

▶ As the largest humanitarian organization in the United States, the Red Cross depends on volunteers to accomplish the organization's mission: providing relief to victims of disasters and helping people prevent, prepare for, and respond to emergencies. To prepare volunteers to participate in this vital mission, the Red Cross provides training for most volunteer positions; the level of training varies according to the requirements of the position. Volunteers serve at all levels of the Red Cross, including governance, management, direct service, support services, and advisory. If you are interested in volunteering for your local Red Cross, go to their volunteer form at: *http://www.redcross.org/volunteer/volform.html.* For more information, look up your local Red Cross office in the phone book or browse their Web site at *http://www.redcross.org/where/where.html.*

Association of Community Organizations for Reform Now (ACORN)

88 Third Avenue, 3rd Floor, Brooklyn, NY 11217
Tel: 718-246-7900; FAX: 718-279-7939
E-mail: fielddirect@acorn.org; WWW: http://www.acorn.org/

▶ ACORN is a multiracial, grassroots, membership organization composed of community groups made up of low- and moderate-income families. Founded in Little Rock, Arkansas, in 1970, ACORN has grown to a membership of 100,000 families over 26 states and the District of Columbia. ACORN's goal is to organize to win a fairer share and a greater voice for low and moderate Americans in what happens in neighborhoods, cities, states, and the nation. Volunteers work as grassroots neighborhood organizers through the 35+ offices in the United States and must commit to one year of service. A working knowledge of Spanish and previous organizing experience is preferred but not required. A modest salary is provided.

Association of Junior Leagues International (AJLI)

132 West 31st Street, 11th Floor, New York, NY 10001-3406
Tel: 212-683-1515; FAX: 212-481-7196
E-mail: info@ajli.org; WWW: http://www.ajli.org/contact.html

▶ AJLI is an international organization of women committed to promoting volunteerism and to improving the community through the effective action of trained volunteers. AJLI reaches out to women of all races, religions, and national origins who demonstrate a commitment to volunteerism. It represents more than 193,000 women working together toward a common mission represented by 295 Junior Leagues in Canada, Great Britain, Mexico, and the United States. The Junior League works on implementing changes and improving conditions in almost every sector of our society. Junior Leagues provide hundreds of thousands of volunteer hours every year to address issues in their local communities, including health (adolescent health, child health, HIV/AIDS, infant mortality, violence prevention, women's health); education (adult education, early childhood education, elementary education, financing, literacy, middle school/high school, school readiness); child care (before- and after-school care, center-based care, family child care); youth services (community service, dropout prevention, leadership, pregnant and parenting teens, substance abuse prevention, violence prevention); family support services (abuse prevention, counseling, housing, parent education and support, services for the homeless, welfare-to-work services); child welfare (adoption, child abuse and neglect, domestic violence, foster care, parental leave, permanency planning); aging (day care, foster grandparents, nursing homes);

community development (gender equity, public safety, transportation, voluntarism, women's leadership development, work and family); culture (arts education, children's theater, dance, historic preservation, museums, libraries); and environment (conservation, recycling, education).

Big Brothers Big Sisters of America (BBBSA)

230 N. 13th Street, Philadelphia, PA 19107
Tel: 215-567-7000; FAX: 215-567-0394
E-mail:national@bbbsa.org; WWW:http://www.bbbsa.org/

▶ Big Brothers Big Sisters of America has remained the expert in youth mentoring since its founding in 1904. In 1977, the Big Brothers and Big Sisters organizations merged into Big Brothers Big Sisters of America and the national headquarters was established in Philadelphia. Today, BBBSA provides one-to-one mentoring relationships between adult volunteers and children primarily from single-parent families in over 500 programs throughout the United States.

Camp Fire Boys and Girls

4601 Madison Avenue, Kansas City, MO 64112
Tel: 800-669-6884, 816-474-9407; FAX: 816-756-0258
E-mail: info@campfire.org; WWW: http://www.campfire.org

▶ This is a national youth agency serving boys and girls from kindergarten through high school. It is a prevention-based program targeting high-risk, inner-city children developed to address the issues of child isolation, boredom, and negative behaviors in the nonschool hours. It allows youth a safe place to practice positive alternatives. Volunteers and staff help the kids develop self-reliance and self-confidence through a program of informal education and activities. Self-confidence and responsibility is what Camp Fire's Self-Reliance courses are all about. Exciting programs teach young people how to handle threats to their safety and security, take care of themselves in different situations, and provide service to their communities. Youth leadership opportunities are abundant in all of Camp Fire's activities. Several opportunities exist for teens: National Youth Forums, Teens in Action, Counselor-in-Training, and Youth Leadership.

Catholic Network of Volunteer Service

1410 Q Street NW, Washington, DC 20009
Tel: 800-543-5046, 202-332-6000
E-mail: volunteer@cnvs.org; WWW: http://www.cnvs.org

▶ This is a catholic network of lay-mission programs in the United States and other countries. Their annual directory, *Response,* includes 173 programs for all ages: summer, short-term, long-term (see Internet Sites—Voluntary Opportunity Databases for full description).

Church World Service *(See International)*

The Corporation for National Service

1201 New York Avenue NW, Washington, DC 20525
Tel: 800-94-ACORPS (for interested national service participants)
or 800-942-2677, 202-606-5000
E-mail: ncss_recruting@cns.gov, webmaster@cns.gov;
WWW: http://www.cns.gov, http://www.nationalservice.org/,
http://www.cns.gov/about/family/commissions.html,
http://www.cns.gov/about/family/state_offices.html

▶ Established in 1993, the Corporation for National Service engages more than a million Americans each year in service to their communities—helping to solve community problems. It offers a variety of programs for individuals wishing to provide service directly addressing the nation's education, human, public safety, and environmental needs at the community level. It offers opportunities for Americans age 17 or older to make a substantial commitment to serve their country and to earn education awards for college or vocational training in return. The Corporation for National Service matches talented, motivated people with opportunities to serve their community and the nation. It works with governor-appointed state commissions, nonprofits, faith-based groups, schools, and other civic organizations to provide opportunities for Americans of all ages to serve their communities. The Corporation's three major service initiatives are AmeriCorps, Learn and Serve America, and the National Senior Service Corps. Their Web site includes links to other Internet sites about volunteering and about ways that education and service can be integrated. Discussion mailing lists of interest include: ACList, AmericaReads, NSCCTalk (see separate listings under Volunteerism—Internet Sites).

Earthwatch (See International)

Habitat for Humanity (See International)

ImpactOnline

385 Grove Street, San Francisco, CA 94102
Tel: 415-241-6868, 415-241-6872 (Nonprofit or Volunteer Questions); FAX: 415-241-6869
E-mail: respond@impactonline.org;
WWW: http://www.impactonline.org/,
http://www.volunteermatch.org/citymatch/

▶ ImpactOnline is a nonprofit organization investing in the development of public interest Internet applications. Since its founding in 1994, ImpactOnline has been providing innovative public services on the Web. VolunteerMatch, the organization's premier service, utilizes the power of the Internet to help individuals nationwide find volunteer opportunities posted by local nonprofit and public-sector organizations.

Jesuit Volunteer Corps (See International)

Jewish Volunteer Corps (See International)

Lutheran Volunteer Corps

1226 Vermont Avenue NW, Washington, DC 20005
Tel: 202-387-3222; FAX: 202-667-0037
E-mail: staff@lvchome.org; WWW: http://www.hers.com./lvc,
http://www.lvchome.org/placemnt2000.htm

▶ This one- to two-year program places volunteers (minimum age: 21) in nonprofit, social justice organizations. Placements include shelters, community health centers, legal assistance centers, hospice care, advocacy, housing assistance, and more. Emphasis is on simplified living, intentional community, and social justice. No specific skills or experience are needed, but maturity, commitment, and a good sense of humor are required. They provide a subsistence allowance, covering expenses for food, housing, utilities, medical insurance, transportation, and a small stipend. Terms begin/end in August.

National Mentoring Partnership (See Support and Advocacy)

National Urban League, Inc.

120 Wall Street, New York, NY 10005
Tel: 212-558-5300
E-mail: info@nul.org; WWW: http://www.nul.org/,
http://www.nul.org/affiliat.html

▶ Founded in 1910, the National Urban League is a premier social service and civil rights organization in America. The League is a nonprofit, community-based organization, with 115 Urban League Affiliates in 34 states and the District of Columbia. It provides program services to more than 2 million people in need. It works to secure equal opportunities for African Americans and other minorities, working on social and economic empowerment and justice, and educational opportunity issues. Volunteers are an active part of these programs, and they are needed to help with programs concerning career training and summer youth employment, tutoring and educational assistance, crime prevention, mentoring and guidance for at-risk young people, teen pregnancy prevention, AIDS prevention, and services (including meals) for senior citizens and people with disabilities. There are many other effective campaigns, services, and programs initiated by the Urban League, all of which need support. Join (*http://www.nul.org/mlist.html*) if you would like to be involved in a virtual community of leaders who share resources and solve problems related to the development of inner-city youth, families, and communities. You can also now search (*http://www.nul.org/architext/AT-mlistsquery.html*) Urban Leaders via the Web, subscribe and unsubscribe via the Web, and visit the archives (*http://www.nul.org/mlists/urban-leaders*). You can utilize the National Urban League's portable professional development resource, the Leadership Network on America Online. Use keyword *urban league* or *nul* to get management and community leadership best practices, speeches from Hugh B. Price, and to see a pictorial history of the National Urban League.

Presbyterian Church Mission Service Recruitment (See International)

Prisoner Visitation and Support (PVS)

1520 Race Street Building, Philadelphia, PA 19102
Tel: 215-241-7117 (Eric Corson, Director); FAX: 215-241-7227

▶ This nationwide program for federal and military prisoners is the only nationwide, interfaith program authorized by the Federal Bureau of Prisons and the Department of Defense to visit any prisoner in the federal and military prison systems (not state prisons). More than 260 volunteers visit 75 federal and military prisons across the United States. They are authorized by the Federal Bureau of Prisons and the Department of Defense. Sponsored by 35 national groups, PVS has volunteers across the United States who regularly visit prisoners. These volunteers live near a particular prison and have access to any prisoners in that facility. PVS visitors do not do any legal work or military counseling. They simply offer friendship and trust to prisoners and communication with the outside world.

Quaker Information Center *(See International)*

Rotary International *(See International)*

United Way of America (UWA)
701 North Fairfax Street, Alexandria, VA 22314
Tel: 800-411-UWAY (8929), 703-836-7100
WWW: http://national.unitedway.org, http://www.unitedway.org/
▶ The national service and training center supports member United Ways by helping them pursue dual strategies of adding value to the community and conducting cost-effective, donor-oriented fund raising to increase financial resources. In 1998, nearly 1,400 United Way organizations were members of UWA.

Unitarian Universalist Service Committee (UUSC)
Human Resources, Unitarian Universalist Service Committee,
130 Prospect Street, Cambridge, MA 02139
Tel: 800-388-3920, 617-868-6600, ext. 216; FAX: 617-868-7102
E-mail: jobs@uusc.org;
WWW: http://www.uusc.org/involved/index.html,
http://www.uusc.org/involved/workcamps.html
▶ Grounded in Unitarian Universalist principles that affirm the worth, dignity, and human rights of every person, and the interdependence of all life, the UUSC is a voluntary, tax-exempt, independent, nonsectarian organization working to advance justice throughout the world. The UUSC confronts injustice by combining human rights education and advocacy in the United States with direct support for grassroots initiatives in other countries. Short- and long-term volunteer opportunities for adults and older youth are available through the nationwide Just Works program, within Unitarian Universalist congregations, and (rarely) in the headquarters office. There are no overseas opportunities. Except for the positions in congregations, there are no faith requirements.

United Church Board for Homeland Ministries
United Church of Christ, 700 Prospect Avenue,
Cleveland, OH 44115-1100
Tel: 216-736-3266; FAX: 216-736-3263
E-mail: rooneys@ucc.org, sanderss@ucc.org (Susan Sanders);
WWW: http://www.ucc.org
▶ This organization provides volunteer opportunities within the United States and Puerto Rico. Age for various programs: 17+ for summer service; 19+ for three months to one year of volunteer service; there is no upper age limit. The placement site provides: (1) room and board for those doing community summer service; (2) room and board for short-term volunteers (commitment of at least three months); and (3) room and board, a small monthly stipend, and return transportation for those performing one year of voluntary service.

United Methodist Volunteers in Mission
(See International)

Volunteer America!
E-mail: rbs@volunteeramerica.net;
WWW: http://www.volunteeramerica.com/

▶ Volunteer America! connects individuals, families, and groups with volunteer opportunities and volunteer vacations on public lands all across America. They list opportunities by agencies, such as the National Park and U.S. Forest Service, as well as state parks. Additionally, they link the sites of organizations that provide volunteer activities on public lands, like the Student Conservation Association, to their site. From time to time, they publish an electronic newsletter to keep you up-to-date on the activities of Volunteer America! You can subscribe for free.

Volunteers in Mission Office
National Ministries, American Baptist Churches USA,
P.O. Box 851, Valley Forge, PA 19482-0851
Tel: 800-ABC-3USA, ext. 2449, 610-768-2449;
FAX: 610-768-2453
E-mail: carole.dieciedue@abc-usa.org (Carole L. Dieciedue,
Director); WWW: http://www.nationalministries.org/mission/VIM/
▶ This organization facilitates individual volunteer missionary appointments, summer service opportunities, group mission experiences, specialized service projects, and disaster response. It provides opportunities for caring people to give freely of their valuable time and talents to meet needs in the United States and Puerto Rico. There are over 100 mission settings available where people can serve through Volunteers in Mission. Volunteers in Mission administers a variety of placement options: one-year appointment with option to extend service, short-term experiences, summer service opportunities, specialized service projects, disaster response, and rebuilding of burned churches. Volunteer opportunities include: community development through Christian centers in the inner city; emergency food and shelter ministries; services for the elderly; summer camp counselors; advocacy; teaching Native American children; teaching English as a second language in a variety of settings; and providing administrative service at an American Baptist college or seminary, and more. Appointed volunteers must be age 18 or older, have sound physical and mental health, have a high school education, have a responsible attitude and be open to personal growth and change, and have the ability to live and work with others, possibly in a different cultural environment. Volunteers must pay travel costs to and from the place of assignment and all living expenses while there. Housing, if needed, is provided by the on-site organization. Volunteers must provide their own hospitalization and medical plan. National Ministries provides travel/accident insurance protection. Consideration is given to special needs.

Volunteers in Prevention, Probation and Prisons, Inc. (VIP)
1020 Michigan Building, 220 Bagley Street, Detroit, MI 48226
Tel: 313-964-1110; FAX: 313-946-1145
E-mail: staff@vipmentoring.org; WWW: http://vipmentoring.org/
▶ The mission of Volunteers in Prevention, Probation and Prisons, Inc. (VIP) is to reduce recidivism in the juvenile and criminal justice system. VIP carries out its mission by encouraging and supporting the development of community justice programs, which include one-to-one mentoring of offenders with trained volunteers. VIP supports programs that include the mentoring of juvenile and adult offenders with volunteers because of their proven results in curbing recidivism in individuals served, thereby enabling them to become more educated, productive, and self-sufficient members of the community. It is VIP's goal to see these cost-effective models grow within all court systems and other justice-related agencies,

thereby providing benefits to all communities. VIP offers the following programs and services: a professional affiliate program; training and networking institutes; the *VIP Examiner* quarterly publication; and a National Information and Resource Clearinghouse.

Volunteers of America

110 South Union Street, Alexandria, Virginia 22314
Tel: 800-899-0089, 703-548-2288
E-mail: voa@voa.org; WWW: http://voa.org/

▶ Founded in 1896 by Christian social reformers, it is a national, nonprofit, spiritually based organization providing local human service programs and the opportunity for individual and community involvement. Its locally administered and governed 54 community-based service organizations offer more than 400 programs in more than 300 communities across the United States. From rural America to inner-city neighborhoods, Volunteers of America engages its professional staff and volunteers in designing and operating innovative programs that deal with today's most pressing social problems. It provides meals to elderly and homebound persons; day care for children and adults with disabilities; emotional and support services for people with AIDS; suicide prevention, programs and support; emergency shelter for the homeless, youth, families in crisis, abused and neglected children, and ex-offenders returning to society; and many other programs and services. Their work can be classified under three primary headings: human services (shelters for homeless individuals and families, adoption agencies, day care centers, food banks, meals-on-wheels services, foster care for abused and neglected children, senior citizen centers, drug and alcohol recovery, and job training and rehabilitation for ex-offenders); housing (it is the nation's largest nonprofit provider of quality, affordable housing for low-income families and the elderly); and health care.

YMCA of the USA

Association Advancement, 101 North Wacker Drive,
Chicago, IL 60606
Tel: 312-977-0031
WWW: http://www.ymca.net/

▶ As a YMCA volunteer, you can lead an exercise class, read to a preschool class, coach a basketball team, cook for a bake sale, design a program brochure, greet people at the front desk, find items for an auction, serve as a role model for young people, help out in the office or at a special event, or be part of a group or committee working on a neighborhood problem. To learn more about volunteering, check out these helpful links: *http://www.ymca.net/get_involved/youngvol.htm* (what kinds of volunteer activities can young people participate in?) and *http://www.ymca.net/kfc/volunteer.htm* (volunteers: how you can be a champion for kids, families, and communities).

YWCA of the USA

WWW: www.ywca.org

▶ The nation's oldest and largest women's membership movement empowers women and girls and eliminates racism through its child care, domestic violence, violence prevention, shelter, fitness, and social justice programs.

International

AFS Info Center

310 SW 4th Avenue, Suite 630, Portland, OR 97204-2608
Tel: 800-AFS-INFO (237-4636) (International Opportunities),
800-876-2377 (Domestic Opportunities); FAX: 503-241-1653
E-mail: afsinfo@afs.org; WWW: http://www.afs.org/usa/border.html

▶ Tens of thousands of volunteers in the United States and around the world ensure that the intercultural experience is valuable to all participants.

Action Without Borders (formerly the Contact Center)

350 Fifth Avenue, Suite 6614, New York, NY 10118
Tel: 212-843-3973; FAX: 212-564-3377
E-mail: info@idealist.org; WWW: http://www.idealist.org

▶ Action Without Borders is a global coalition of individuals and organizations working to build a world where all people can live free, dignified, and productive lives. Action Without Borders focuses on five goals from which everyone can benefit and to which anyone can contribute: promoting action and participation around the world; sharing ideas, experience, and information; expanding the pool of resources available for good work; facilitating collaboration among individuals, organizations, schools, businesses, and other institutions; and promoting the freedom to do all this. Action Without Borders is independent of any government, political ideology, or religious creed. Its work is guided by the common desire of its members and supporters to find practical solutions to social and environmental problems, in a spirit of generosity and mutual respect. First called the Contact Center Network, Action Without Borders was founded in 1995 to build a network of neighborhood contact centers that would provide a one-stop shop for volunteer opportunities and nonprofit services in communities around the world. Idealist is the most comprehensive directory of nonprofit and volunteering resources on the Web (see Volunteerism—Internet Sites).

AHEAD, Inc. (Adventures in Health, Education and Agricultural Development, Inc.)

P.O. Box 2049, Rockville, MD 20852
Tel: 301-530-3697; FAX: 301-530-3532
E-mail: aheadinc@erols.com;
WWW: http://users.erols.com/aheadinc/

▶ This nonprofit, private organization was developed to address the problems of developing countries. AHEAD was founded as a people-to-people exchange between African Americans and other people of goodwill living in the United States with those in developing countries. Since 1985, AHEAD has provided a unique opportunity for professionals as well as undergraduate and graduate students to work side by side with their African counterparts in community projects in rural Africa. Volunteers spend from one month to one year working with development projects. Volunteers are challenged physically as well as intellectually as they work with projects in health care, agriculture, construction, renovation, water, engineering, and education.

American Friends Service Committee (AFSC)

1501 Cherry Street, Philadelphia, PA 19102
Tel: 215-241-7000; FAX: 215-241-7275
E-mail: afscinfo@afsc.org, mexsummer@afsc.org;
WWW: http://www.afsc.org/jobs.htm,
http://www.afsc.org/emap/help/volunteer.htm,
http://www.afsc.org/wwopp.htm

Quaker Information Center, 1501 Cherry Street,
Philadelphia, PA 19102
FAX: 215-567-2096
E-mail: quakerinfo@afsc.org;
WWW: http://www.afsc.org/qic/oportnty.htm

▶ The American Friends Service Committee (AFSC) is a Quaker organization that includes people of various faiths who are committed to social justice, peace, and humanitarian service. Its work is based on the Religious Society of Friends (Quaker) belief in the worth of every person, and faith in the power of love to overcome violence and injustice. AFSC has programs that focus on issues related to economic justice, peace building and demilitarization, social justice, and youth, in the United States, and in Africa, Asia, Latin America, and the Middle East.

Amigos de las Americas *(See Service Learning, Youth and Young Adult Volunteerism)*

Catholic Network of Volunteer Service *(See National)*

Church World Service (CWS)

Resource Development and Service Center: 28606 Phillips Street,
P.O. Box 968, Elkhart, IN 46515
Hotline: 888-CWS-CROP (888-297-2767); Pledge line: 800-297-1516, ext. 222; FAX: 219-262-0966

Administrative offices: 475 Riverside Drive, Room 678,
New York, NY 10115
Tel: 212-870-2257; FAX: 212-870-3523
E-mail: cws@ncccusa.org; WWW: http://bruno.ncccusa.org/cws/,
http://www.churchworldservice.org/contactregional.html

▶ Church World Service is a part of the Church World Service and Witness Unit of the National Council of Churches of Christ in the United States. Born in the aftermath of World War II, today Church World Service is 36 Protestant, Anglican, and Orthodox communions in the United States, cooperating worldwide (in more than 80 countries) in programs of long-term development, emergency response, and assistance to refugees. Within the United States, CWS assists communities in responding to disasters, resettles refugees, promotes fair national and international policies, provides educational resources, and offers opportunities to join a people-to-people network of local and global caring through participation in CROP WALKS, the CWS Tools of Hope/Blanket, and the Gift of the Heart Kit Program. Church World Service responds to natural and human-caused disasters throughout the world through local partners it supports via counsel, technical assistance, training, funds, and material resources. The volunteers who do the work for CWS-ERP (CWS Emergency Response Program) in the field are provided by the denominational member organizations of the CWS Emergency Response Committee; they are not recruited directly by CWS-ERP. To explore how you may become a volunteer in the field, contact the denominational member organizations listed at *http://www.cwserp.org/committees.* To learn more about the

Emergency Response Program, in general, and to investigate becoming a trained CWS Volunteer Disaster Consultant, contact Bob Arnold, Associate Director, Church World Service Emergency Response Program, 475 Riverside Drive (#606), New York, NY 10115. Tel: 212-870-3151; FAX: 212-870-2236; e-mail: *boba@ncccusa.org;* WWW: *http://www.cwserp.org.*

Coordinating Committee for International Voluntary Service

Resource Centre, CCIVS, UNESCO House, 1, reu Miollis, 75 732,
Paris, Cedex 15, France
Tel: (33 1) 45 68 49 36; FAX: (33 1) 42 73 05 21
E-mail: ccivs@unesco.org;
WWW: http://www.unesco.org/ccivs/address.htm

▶ In 1948, under the aegis of the United Nations Educational, Scientific and Cultural Organisation (UNESCO), the Coordinating Committee for International Voluntary Services (CCIVS) was created. CCIVS gradually extended its sphere of activities to include organizations in Eastern Europe, North America, Africa, Asia, and Latin America. It was created as an international non-governmental organization responsible for the coordination of voluntary service. It is today one of the main international structures that acts as a coordinating link between voluntary organizations that run workcamps and medium- and long-term activities. CCIVS has currently over 140 member organizations all across the world, among which some of them are international organizations having their own national branches in over 100 countries. The activities and programs of these organizations are carried out by groups of national and international volunteers over a period ranging from a few weeks (e.g., international workcamps) to more than a year. CCIVS functions essentially with the aim of coordinating and developing voluntary service all over the world. For instance, it contributes to the setting up of new organizations in regions where voluntary service is not yet developed. CCIVS as a coordinating body does not recruit volunteers. Those who are interested in volunteering must directly contact CCIVS member organizations in their own country that propose activities within the country and abroad. (To receive a list of CCIVS members in your country, please address your request to CCIVS together with two International Reply Coupons, which can be obtained from the post office). It publishes *CCIVS NEWS* (published three times a year) and *Volunteer's Handbook,* a guide with useful addresses, among other publications.

Council International Volunteer Programs

CIEE, 205 East 42nd Street, New York, NY 10017-5706
Tel: 888-COUNCIL, 212-822-2600; FAX: 212-822-2779
E-mail: info@ciee.org; WWW: www.ciee.org

▶ They sponsor over 600 projects a year in over 30 different countries. A directory of projects is listed on their Web site at *www.councilexchanges.org/vol/index.htm.*

Earthwatch

3 Clock Tower Place, Suite 100, Box 75, Maynard, MA 01754
Tel: 800-776-0188, 978-461-0081; FAX: 978-461-2332
E-mail: info@earthwatch.org; WWW: http://www.earthwatch.org

▶ This nonprofit organization, founded in 1971, supports scientific field research worldwide to improve our understanding and management of the Earth by matching some 4,000 paying volunteers each year with scientists on expeditions in 24 states and 52 countries. The Institute's mission is to promote sustainable conservation of our natural resources and cultural heritage by creating partnerships between scientists, educators, and the general public. The Earthwatch Institute's goals are to support scientific research, to provide experiential education, and to inspire global citizenship. Once volunteers locate projects that fit their schedules, interests, and budget, they can send for a detailed Expedition Briefing Kit containing maps, background information, biographies, goals and scenarios, and requirements. Volunteer opportunities are available year-round, many in summer. Participants pay travel costs to the site and back, as well as the shared costs of the modest accommodations and food during the project. Many of the expenses are tax deductible. Some financial aid is available to teachers and students to cover expedition costs.

Global Volunteers

375 East Little Canada Road, St. Paul, MN 55117
Tel: 800-487-1074, 651-407-6100; FAX: 651-482-0915
E-mail: e-mail@globalvlntrs.org, info@globalvolunteers.org;
WWW: http://www.globalvlntrs.org,
http://www.globalvolunteers.org/regions.htm

▶ Founded in 1984, Global Volunteers is a private, nonprofit U.S. corporation with the goal of helping to establish a foundation for peace through mutual international understanding. At the request of local leaders and indigenous host organizations, Global Volunteers sends teams of volunteers to live and work with local people on human and economic development projects identified by the community as important to its long-term development. One-, two-, or three-week volunteer experiences are in rural communities in Africa, Asia, the Caribbean, the Americas, and Europe. Costs range from $350 to $2,395, depending on the country, plus airfare. There is no age limit, except that minors must be with an adult family member or guardian.

Habitat for Humanity International

121 Habitat Street, Americus, GA 31709
Tel: 800-HABITAT, 229-924-6935, ext. 2551 or 2552;
FAX: 229-924-6541
E-mail: public_info@habitat.org; WWW: http://www.habitat.org/,
http://www.habitat.org/local/

▶ This nonprofit, ecumenical Christian housing ministry seeks to eliminate poverty housing and homelessness from the world. Habitat invites people from all walks of life to work together in partnership to help build houses with families in need. Habitat for Humanity International has over 1,700 affiliates in more than 55 countries around the world, including affiliates in every U.S. state. In 1994, Habitat for Humanity International and the AmeriCorps National Service Program entered into a partnership aimed at mobilizing more volunteers in the fight against poverty housing. Through AmeriCorps, individuals of all ages and backgrounds can help address the nation's needs through service. In return, they receive education awards to help finance their college education or vocational training or to pay back student loans. While there is no typical AmeriCorps member, all people selected for the program will demonstrate an interest in serving the community while learning new skills. To volunteer in your local area, use the search engine on their Web site at *http://www.habitat.org/local* to find contact information for a Habitat affiliate near you.

InterAction (American Council for Voluntary International Action)

1717 Massachusetts Avenue NW, 8th Floor,
Washington, DC 20036
Tel: 202-667-8227; FAX: 202-667-8236
E-mail: ia@interaction.org; WWW: http://www.interaction.org,
http://www.interaction.org/volunteer.html,
http://www.interaction.org/jobs/

▶ This coalition of more than 150 U.S.-based nonprofit, private, and voluntary organizations works to promote human dignity and development in 165 countries around the world. InterAction member organizations engage in international humanitarian efforts, including disaster relief; sustainable development; refugee protection, assistance, and resettlement; public policy; and public awareness of international development issues. Volunteer opportunities are available as office support. InterAction also offers resources that are useful to people seeking paid or volunteer positions, in the United States and abroad, with international relief and development agencies. These include: *Monday Developments*, a biweekly newsletter available to the public by subscription, which lists dozens of job opportunities at international organizations in each issue; *InterAction Member Profiles, 2000–2001*, a 425-page directory that gives detailed information about over 150 U.S.-based nonprofits working internationally; and *Global Work*, a 98-page publication of volunteer, internship, and fellowship opportunities with 68 organizations in 120 countries.

International Association for Volunteer Effort
(See Support and Advocacy)

International Jewish College Corps *(See Service Learning and Youth Volunteerism)*

International Volunteer Program

210 Post Street, Suite 502, San Francisco, CA 94108
Tel: 415-477-3667; FAX: 415-477-3669
E-mail: rjewell@ivpsf.com;
WWW: http://www.ivpsf.com/Contact.htm

▶ This project aims at promoting volunteerism in Europe and the United States. For six weeks, through daily cooperation with staffs of overseas organizations, volunteers learn how others live and view the world. The International Volunteer Program was instituted in 1991 by La Société Française de Bienfaisance Mutuelle with the assistance and cooperation of the French Consulate in San Francisco, the University of California at Irvine, and le Comité des Jumelages de Troyes. The International Volunteer Program links cultural frontiers by allowing visitors to act as important volunteers and colleagues. This complete cultural immersion helps to open new horizons and foster philanthropy on both community and global levels. In Europe and in the United States, the International Volunteer Program has facilitated this firsthand cultural understanding for hundreds of volunteers and provided volunteer staffing for more than 100 not-for-profit organizations.

International Volunteer Programs Association

(See Support and Advocacy)

Jesuit Volunteer Corps (JVC)

P.O. Box 25478, Washington, DC 20007
Tel: 202-687-1132
E-mail: jvi@gunet.georgetown.edu;
WWW: http://www.jesuitvolunteers.org/,
http://www.jesuitvolunteercorps.org/

▶ Hundreds of grassroots organizations across the country count on Jesuit Volunteers to provide essential services to low-income people and those who live on the margins of our society. Jesuit Volunteers serve the homeless, the unemployed, refugees, people with AIDS, the elderly, street youth, abused women and children, the mentally ill, and the developmentally disabled. JVC has become the largest Catholic lay volunteer program in the country. Some job placements require specific credentials or licenses, but most JVC jobs can be done by people who have a general educational background and a willingness to learn new skills. Jesuit Volunteers working outside the United States are supported by an in-country coordinator, usually a Jesuit, who helps volunteers adjust to a new culture and reflect on their experiences. JVC offers men and women, aged 21 and over, an opportunity to work full time for justice and peace throughout the United States by serving the poor directly and by working for structural change. This is a one-year (renewable) term of service, starting mid-August. JVs also accompany people of great need in several other countries, assisting in human development primarily through education. International placements require a minimum commitment of two years. Volunteers live together in communities of three to eight and are committed to the cornerstone ideas of JVC: community, spirituality, simple living, and service. Applicants to JVC may choose from a wide field of positions of interest in both urban and rural areas. Volunteers are provided with a stipend, room and board, and health insurance, plus transportation home at the end of term of service: all international travel is provided. Applications are accepted on a rolling basis through July, with priority given to applications postmarked by March 1 of each year.

Jewish Volunteer Corps

American Jewish World Service, 989 Avenue of the Americas,
10th Floor, New York, NY 10018
Tel: 800-889-7146, 212-736-2597; FAX: 212-736-3463
E-mail: jvcol@jws.org, jws@jws.org;
WWW: http://www.ajws.org/jvcdoc.html

▶ American Jewish World Service is an independent nonprofit organization founded in 1985 to help alleviate poverty, hunger, and disease among the people of the world regardless of race, religion, or nationality. It provides humanitarian aid, technical support, emergency relief, and skilled volunteers to grassroots project partners that are implementing small-scale, self-sustaining development projects in the areas of health care, education, economic development, and agriculture reform. Founded in 1993, the Jewish Volunteer Corps successfully continues to provide humanitarian relief in the form of technical assistance to grassroots, nongovernmental organizations. It enables Jewish men and women to renew and strengthen their bonds to Judaism by giving them the opportunity to fulfill the ethical imperative of *tikkun olam,* and communicate to the world the Jewish commitment to the well-being and dignity of all people.

Operation Crossroads Africa, Inc.

475 Riverside Drive, Suite 1366, New York, NY 10027
Tel: 212-870-2106; FAX: 212-870-2644
E-mail:oca@igc.apc.org,
International_Programs@Juno.Com,ocainc@aol.com;
WWW: http://www.igc.org/oca/

▶ Founded in 1958, Operation Crossroads Africa is a nonprofit, nongovernmental organization that promotes cross-cultural sharing and understanding. It sponsors two programs: the Africa Program (in Benin, Cote d'Ivoire, Eritrea, Ethiopia, Gambia, Ghana, Guinea Bissau, Kenya, Malawi, Mali, Namibia, Senegal, South Africa, Tanzania, Uganda, Zambia, and Zimbabwe) and the Diaspora Program based in Brazil. Crossroads volunteers spend three orientation days, six work weeks, and one travel week as part of an international team composed of one leader and 8 to 10 women and men of various racial, cultural, and educational backgrounds, living and working with African or Brazilian hosts at a workcamp project designed to provide maximum interaction, learning opportunities, and cultural awareness. All projects involve a component of physical work, and most are located in rural areas. Types of projects include community construction/development, community health/medical, environmental/agricultural, and educational/training. This is designed as a post–high school experience; although most Crossroaders are college students and young professionals, there are no set age or occupation requirements. Fee: $3,500. Group leaders are also sought (must be at least 26). Applications will be reviewed on an ongoing basis until all spaces are filled.

Oxfam America

26 West Street, Boston, MA 02111-1206
Tel: 800-77-OXFAM, 617-482-1211; FAX: 617-728-2594
E-mail: info@oxfamamerica.org

733 15th Street NW, Suite 340, Washington, DC 20005
Tel: 202-393-3544; FAX: 202-783-8739
E-mail: dc@oxfamamerica.org;
WWW: http://www.oxfamamerica.org, http://www.oxfam.org

▶ This development and relief agency works to put an end to poverty worldwide. Internship and volunteer opportunities are available in the Boston headquarters or in the advocacy office in Washington, D.C. It also offers volunteer and study trips lasting seven to nine days in the United States and Africa. These trips are for high school and college students, teachers, and organizers; they take place during the spring break and cost $315 to $575, plus airfare.

Peace Corps

1111 20th Street NW, Washington, DC 20526
Tel: 800-424-8580
WWW: http://www.peacecorps.gov,
http://www.peacecorps.gov/volunteer/index.html

▶ Since 1961, the Peace Corps has been providing opportunities for American citizens to share with developing countries their skills in education, agriculture, environment, business, and health. You must be a U.S. citizen, be over 18 years of age, and have a degree or three to five years of work experience in a skill area. There is a 27-month commitment (3 months of training plus 2 years of service). All expenses are paid, including full medical/dental coverage and a $5,400 readjustment allowance upon completion.

Presbyterian Church (USA) Mission Service Recruitment

100 Witherspoon Street, Louisville, KY 40202
Tel: 800-779-6779
WWW: http://www.pcusa.org/pcusa/msr,
http://www.pcusa.org/pcusa/msr/vol_opps.htm,
http://www.pcusa.org/pcusa/msr/yav.htm

▶ This organization offers numerous possibilities for mission service, both within the United States and international for individuals of all ages. Length of service is variable, depending on program.

Quaker Information Center (QIC)

1501 Cherry Street, Philadelphia, PA 19102
Tel: 215-241-7024; FAX: 215-567-2096
E-mail: quakerinfo@afsc.org; WWW: http://www.afsc.org/qic.htm,
http://www.afsc.org/qic/oportnty.htm

▶ In response to numerous requests, the QIC has developed an extensive list of volunteer and service opportunities, workcamp experiences, and internships concerned with peace and social issues, education, and community development. The list currently comprises more than 300 options—short, medium, and long term, Quaker and non-Quaker, domestic and international.

Rotary International

1560 Sherman Avenue, Evanston, IL 60201
Tel: 847-866-4600; FAX: 847-866-3276
E-mail: krahlr@rotaryintl.org; WWW: http://www.rotary.org/

▶ Rotary is an organization of business and professional leaders united worldwide, who provide humanitarian service, encourage high ethical standards in all vocations, and help build goodwill and peace in the world. There are approximately 1.2 million Rotarians, members of more than 29,000 Rotary clubs in 161 countries. Community service includes the scope of activities that Rotarians undertake to improve the quality of life in their community. Many official Rotary programs are intended to meet community needs, whether it be to promote literacy, help the elderly or disabled, combat urban violence, or provide opportunities for local youth. International service describes the activities that Rotarians undertake to advance international understanding, goodwill, and peace. The Rotary Volunteers Program is the embodiment of Rotary's ideal of "Service Above Self." It provides opportunities for Rotarians and other skilled professionals to offer their services and expertise to local, national, and international projects in need of assistance. Descriptions of its many and varied programs, both domestic and international, can be found on its Web site at *http://www.rotary.org/programs/index.htm.* Several Rotary programs help young people continue Rotary's tradition of volunteerism. Interact (for high school students) and Rotaract (for young adults 18 to 30) are Rotary-sponsored service clubs that provide opportunities for service and leadership development. Many Rotaract and Interact service projects focus on issues of importance to young people such as AIDS, the environment, homelessness, urban peace, and drug abuse prevention. Rotarians initiate community projects that address many of today's most critical issues, such as violence, drug abuse, AIDS, hunger, the environment, and illiteracy.

The Rotary Volunteers International Volunteers List, published twice annually, contains information about Rotarians, Rotaractors, Rotary Foundation alumni, and non-Rotarians who are willing to volunteer their services on projects in other countries. Coordinators of Rotary-sponsored projects directly contact those on the list who appear to meet their projects' needs. *The Rotary Volunteers International Site List,* also published semiannually, includes a list of Rotary and Rotaract club service projects requesting volunteers from abroad. Potential volunteers can contact project coordinators and explore possibilities for service. The *Rotary Volunteers Resource List* lists other organizations that place, train, support, or fund volunteers.

SCI International Voluntary Service

Workcamp Volunteers: 814 NE 40th Street, Seattle, WA 98105
Tel/FAX: 206-545-6585
E-mail: sciinfo@sci-ivs.org; WWW: http://www.sci-ivs.org/

Long-Term Volunteers: 205 North Plain Road,
Great Barrington, MA 01230
Tel: 413-528-1307; FAX: 801-906-7716
E-mail: ltv@sci-ivs.org

▶ Through various nonprofit partner organizations worldwide and through SCI international, national, and regional branch development, the U.S. branch of SCI participates in the SCI network, which exchanges over 5,000 volunteers each year in short-term two- to four-week international group workcamps and in long-term three- to 12-month volunteer postings in over 50 countries. It is a secular organization depending on the general public for funding and support.

Service Civil International (SCI)

St-Jacobsmarkt 82, B-2000 Antwerpen, Belgium
Tel: 32.3.2265727; FAX: 32.3.2320344
E-mail: sciint@sciint.org (general correspondence),
sciisa@sciint.org (International Coordinator)

▶ SCI is a voluntary service organization with 33 branches and groups worldwide. The aims are to promote peace, international understanding and solidarity, social justice, sustainable development, and respect for the environment. SCI believes that all people are capable of living together with mutual respect and without recourse to any form of violence to solve conflicts. The organization was founded in 1920. SCI has consultative status with UNESCO and the Council of Europe and it is a member of CCIVS (Coordinating Committee of International Voluntary Service Organisations); YFJ (European Youth Forum); and AVSO (Association of Voluntary Service Organisations). (SCI offers online *IS Newsletter* and maintains several e-mail lists.

United Methodist Volunteers in Mission (UMVIM)

315 West Ponce de Leon Avenue, Suite 750, Decatur, GA 30030
Tel: 404-377-7424; FAX: 404-377-8182
E-mail: sejumvim@compuserve.com;
WWW: http://www.gbgmumc.org/volunteers,
http://www.gbgm-umc.org/volunteers/usopps.html,
http://www.gbgm-umc.org/volunteers/intteams.html

▶ UMVIM facilitates placement of short-term volunteer teams (one to three weeks) and individual volunteers for periods of two months to two years. Opportunities exist for youth and adults and for a wide variety of skills and experience. Their Web site is very complete, with opportunities for individuals and teams, youth and adults, national and international options, as well as information about UMVIM Disaster Response volunteer needs, connection to their Medical Fellowship, and a current list of urgent needs.

United Nations Volunteers

Peace Corps, 1111 20th Street NW, Washington, DC 20526
Tel: 800-424-8580, ext. 2243, 202-606-3370; FAX: 202-606-3627
E-mail: unvolunteer@peacecorps.gov; WWW: http://www.unv.org,
http://www.unv.org/unvols/index.htm

▶ This organization was created by the General Assembly of the United Nations in 1970 to serve as an operational partner in development cooperation at the request of UN member states. It reports to the United Nations Development Programme (UNDP) and works through UNDP's country offices around the world. U.S. citizens apply to be United Nations Volunteers through the Peace Corps. There are more than 4,500 qualified and experienced women and men of over 140 nationalities annually serving in developing countries as volunteer specialists and field workers. Since 1971, more than 20,000 UN Volunteers from some 150 developing and industrialized nations have worked in about 140 countries. Currently, 70 percent are citizens of developing countries while 30 percent come from the industrialized world. They work in technical, economic, and social fields, under four main headings: in technical cooperation with skills-short governments; with community-based initiatives for self-reliance; in humanitarian relief and rehabilitation; and in support of human rights, electoral, and peace-building processes. They are professionals who work on a peer basis. The UNV program involves a wide variety of sectors: It maintains a roster covering more than 100 professional categories. Agriculture, health, and education feature prominently, as do human rights promotion, information and communication technology, community development, vocational training, industry, and population.

Visions in Action—Volunteers in International Development

2710 Ontario Road NW, Washington DC 20009
Tel: 202-625-7403
E-mail: visions@igc.org; WWW: http://www.visionsinaction.org,
http://www.igc.org/visions/

▶ This international development organization offers long-term volunteer positions in five African countries and Mexico. Visions offers six- and 12-month positions in Zimbabwe, South Africa, Tanzania, Uganda, Burkina Faso, and Mexico. Positions are available with nonprofit development organizations, research institutes, health clinics, community groups, and the news media in a wide variety of fields, including social work, public health, environment, refugee relief, human rights, and journalism.

Visions International, Inc. *(See Service Learning, Youth and Young Adult Volunteerism)*

Volunteers for Peace (VFP) International Workcamps

1034 Tiffany Road, Belmont, VT 05730-0202
Tel: 802-259-2759; FAX: 802-259-2922
E-mail: vfp@vfp.org, WWW: http://www.vfp.org/index.html,
http://www.vfp.org/DirectoryIntro.htm,
http://www.vfp.org/links/links.htm

▶ This nonprofit membership corporation has been coordinating International Workcamps since 1982. VFP is a member of the Coordinating Committee for International Voluntary Service (CCIVS) at UNESCO and works in cooperation with Service Civil International (SCI), the Alliance of European Voluntary Service Organizations, and the International Youth Action for Peace (YAP). Services include providing consultation and a placement service for workcamp hosts and volunteers, linking people with programs. Their programs foster international education, voluntary service, and friendship.

Volunteers in Asia (VIA)

Haas Center for Public Service, 3rd Floor, 562 Salvatierra Walk, Stanford, CA 94305

P.O. Box 20266, Stanford, CA 94309
Tel: 650-725-1803; FAX: 650-725-1805
E-mail: volasia@volasia.org; WWW: http://www.volasia.org

▶ Volunteers in Asia is a private, nonprofit, nonsectarian organization dedicated to increased understanding between the United States and Asia. Since 1963, its Volunteer Program has provided young Americans with an opportunity to work and live within an Asia culture while meeting the needs of Asian host institutions. VIA's Trans-Pacific Exchange designs and offers a wide range of short-term, international study programs between the United States and Asia and among various Asian nations.

WorldTeach

c/o Center for International Development, Harvard University, 79 JFK Street, Cambridge, MA 02138
Tel: 800-4-TEACH-0, 617-495-5527; FAX: 617-495-1599
E-mail: info@worldteach.org; WWW: http://www.worldteach.org/

▶ WorldTeach is a nonprofit, nongovernmental organization based at the Harvard Institute for International Development, which provides opportunities for individuals to make a meaningful contribution to international education by living and working as volunteer teachers in developing countries. Since its inception, WorldTeach has placed thousands of volunteer educators in communities throughout Asia, Latin America, Africa, and Eastern Europe. It sends volunteers overseas to teach for a school year, which requires a BA, but not teaching experience or knowledge of a foreign language. There are programs in China, Costa Rica, Ecuador, Namibia, Poland, Thailand, Russia, and South Africa.

Youth for Understanding *(See Service Learning, Youth and Young Adult Volunteerism)*

Youth Service International *(See Service Learning, Youth and Young Adult Volunteerism)*

Insurance, Liability, and Risk Management

Nonprofit Risk Management Center *(See Financial Management—Organizations; Legal—Organizations)*

Professional Associations and Acccrediting Organizations

American Society of Directors of Volunteer Services (ASDVS)

American Hospital Association, One North Franklin, 27th Floor, Chicago, IL 60606
Tel: 312-422-3939; FAX: 312-422-4575
P.O. Box 92247, Chicago, IL 60675-2247
E-mail: nbrown1@aha.org (Nancy Brown, Executive Director); WWW: http://www.asdvs.org

▶ ASDVS is the only national professional organization for directors of volunteer services in health care institutions. As a society, it endeavors to promote and enhance the profession of volunteer administration; assess the needs and interest of its members; provide needed services, information, programs, and resources; facilitate the exchange of ideas and networking among members; advance the personal career objectives of members through professional development programs and other opportunities; and network with other organizations involved in the management of volunteer services programs. ASDVS holds the Annual Meeting and Educational Conference, in addition to regional conferences, workshops, and courses. It publishes the bimonthly newsletter, *Volunteer Services Administration* (for ASDVS members), *Volunteer Leader, ASDVS Resource Guide,* and other publications.

Association for Volunteer Administration

P.O. Box 32092, 3108 North Parham Road, Richmond, VA 23294
Tel: 804-346-2266; FAX: 804-346-3318
E-mail: avaintl@mindspring.com; WWW: http://www.avaintl.org/

▶ Founded in 1960, it is the international professional membership association for individuals working in the field of volunteer management. Membership is open to salaried and nonsalaried individuals in public, nonprofit, and for-profit organizations. Continually building relationships with other organizations that share their commitment to excellence and competence in volunteer leadership, it currently partners with American Humanics, Inc.; American Society of Directors of Volunteer Services of the American Hospital Association; and Points of Light Foundation. Programs/services include a credentialing program, a competency-based process through which you can earn the CVA (Certified in Volunteer Administration) designation; a job bank of current opportunities in the field, plus links to additional sites; and a cumulative index of articles from *The Journal of Volunteer Administration,* to assist in locating those that may pertain to your area of research or interest. A Bibliography of Resources on Volunteer Program Management is also available on the Web site at *http://www.avaintl.org/resources/bibliography.html.* It provides a list of books and publications that will help anybody working with volunteers and nonprofit organizations. Areas covered are: Volunteerism & Citizen Engagement, Volunteer Resources Management, Corporate Volunteerism, Fundraising, Governance, and Risk Management. The Web site also offers a list of trainers and consultants in the profession at *http://www.avaintl.org/resources/candt.html.* A select list of volunteer management software is available on the Web site at *http://www.avaintl.org/resources/software.html.* A calendar of events and important dates is provided on the Web at *http://www.avaintl.org/news/calendar.html.*

Service Learning, Youth and Young Adult Volunteerism

American Red Cross

WWW: www.redcross.org/youth

▶ One of the nation's largest humanitarian organizations, it provides relief to disaster victims and helps people prevent, prepare for, and respond to emergencies. The American Red Cross provides more than half the nation's blood supply and is the largest provider of blood, plasma, and tissue products in the United States. The organization has 1.2 million volunteers, and is guided by its Congressional Charter and the Fundamental Principles of the International Red Cross Movement.

America's Promise—The Alliance for Youth

(See Support and Advocacy)

Amigos de las Americas

International Office, 5618 Star Lane, Houston, TX 77057
Tel: 800-231-7796 or 888-AMIGOSL, 713-782-5290;
FAX: 713-782-9267
E-mail: info@amigoslink.org;
WWW: http://www.amigoslink.org/getinvolved/get_involved.html

▶ This is an international, voluntary, not-for-profit organization that, through service, provides leadership development opportunities for young people, promotes community health for the people of Latin America, and facilitates cross-cultural understanding for the people of the Americas. After completing an extensive training program, high school and college students are assigned to ongoing health projects of sponsoring agencies in the host countries. They usually live with families in small communities in rural and urban areas and are supervised by more experienced volunteers and officials of the host agency. Volunteers must be at least 16, have successfully completed at least one year of high school Spanish or Portuguese or one semester of college-level Spanish or Portuguese or the equivalent before entering the training program, demonstrate a commitment to developing their leadership skills through participation in the summer AMIGOS training program and organization of fund-raising activities, and agree to comply with all health and safety policies set forth by AMIGOS.

BREAK AWAY: The Alternative Break Connection

(See Support and Advocacy)

Camp Fire Boys and Girls *(See Community Service—National)*

Campus Compact: The Project for Public and Community Service *(See Support and Advocacy)*

Campus Outreach Opportunity League *(See Support and Advocacy)*

City Year-AmeriCorps

285 Columbus Avenue, Boston, MA 02116
Tel: 617-927-2613; FAX: 617-927-2687
E-mail: sfr aser@cityyear.org (Steve Fraser, National Director);
WWW: http://www.city-year.org,
http://www.city-year.org/joinus/volunteer.html

▶ City Year, part of the AmeriCorps National Service Network, is a national service program that unites young adults, ages 17 to 23, from diverse racial, cultural, and socioeconomic backgrounds for a demanding year of full-time community service, leadership development, and civic engagement. City Year is a private–public partnership supported by the AmeriCorps National Service Network, corporations, foundations, individuals, states, and localities. Corporate partners develop unique partnerships with City Year that include collaborative service activities, career mentoring, and opportunities to experience their industry. Through these partnerships, City Year seeks to address unmet community needs, break down barriers of race and class, and demonstrate that service is the single idea most capable of strengthening the bonds of the community. Service is provided in areas of education, public safety, and human needs, and the comprehensive educational program provides GED course work, CPR certification, college and career counseling, and focused leadership training. Corps members receive a weekly stipend of $135, and upon completion of their terms of service earn a post-service education award of $4,725. Programs currently exist in Boston, Massachusetts; Chicago, Illinois; Cleveland and Columbus, Ohio; Columbia, South Carolina; Philadelphia, Pennsylvania; Providence, Rhode Island; San Antonio, Texas; New Hampshire; Washington, D.C.; and San Jose, California.

The Civic Literacy Project (CLP)

1100 East Seventh Street, Woodburn Hall #210,
Bloomington, IN 47405
Tel: 812-856-4677; FAX: 812-856-7137
E-mail: clpadmin@indiana.edu, wdmorgan@indiana.edu
(William Morgan, Director); WWW: http://serve.indiana.edu/,
http://serve.indiana.edu/publications/journal.htm

▶ The Civic Literacy Project is part of the Center for the Study of Participation and Citizenship at Indiana University, Bloomington. Housed in the Political Science Department, the Civic Literacy Project works to advance civic education and participation through academic service-learning. The CLP works primarily with K–12 students, teachers, and administrators, and they are currently a comprehensive school reform initiative, STAR Schools, that fully integrates service-learning into academic curriculum. Founded in 1997, they provide young people with a positive way to be involved in their communities—through academic service-learning that addresses locally defined community needs. CLP publishes the journal *The Review of Service and Volunteer Programs*.

Communities in Schools

277 South Washington Street, Suite 210, Alexandria, VA 22314
Tel: 800-CIS-4KIDS, 703-519-8999; FAX: 703-519-7213
E-mail cis@cisnet.org; WWW: http://www.cisnet.org/index.html

▶ The nation's largest network of independent, not-for-profit, community-school partnerships, it gives students in need access to mentors, tutors, safe environments, essential health and human services, marketable skills, and opportunities to give back to their community.

Do Something *(See Support and Advocacy)*

Earth Force

1908 Mount Vernon, 2nd Floor, Alexandria, VA 22301
Tel: 703-299-9400; FAX: 703-299-9485
E-mail: earthforce@earthforce.org;
WWW: http://www.earthforce.org/

▶ Through Earth Force, youth discover and implement lasting solutions to environmental issues in their community. In the process, they develop lifelong habits of active citizenship and environmental stewardship. Educators turn to Earth Force for innovative tools to engage young people in community problem solving.

Global Works, Inc.

RD2, Box 356-B, Huntingdon, PA 16652
Tel: 814-667-2411
E-mail: info@globalworksinc.com;
WWW: http://www.globalworksinc.com

▶ Global Works offers summer service programs for high school students. Programs include service, cultural immersion, language learning, travel, and adventure. Programs range three to four weeks in length. Projects include rebuilding habitats; construction of community centers, playgrounds, and water systems; reforestation; castle restoration; and more. During nonproject time, the group plays together snorkeling, scuba diving, hiking, swimming, biking, rock climbing, or visiting cultural and historic sites. Costs range from $2,550 to $3,475, depending on length of time and location.

Habitat for Humanity Campus Chapters and Youth Programs *(See Habitat for Humanity—Community Service, International)*

Institute on Philanthropy and Voluntary Service

The Center on Philanthropy at Indiana University,
Indianapolis, IN 46202-3272
Tel: 317-684-8959
E-mail: mkplumme@iupui.edu (Martel Plummer, Associate Director of Academic Programs); WWW: http://www.ipvs.org/

The Fund for American Studies, IU Summer Institute on Philanthropy and Voluntary Service, 1706 New Hampshire Avenue NW, Washington, DC 20009
Tel: 800-741-6964; FAX: 801-697-8329
E-mail: philanthropy@tfas.org; WWW: http://www.tfas.org

▶ Presented by The Fund for American Studies, in partnership with Indiana University Center on Philanthropy, the Institute is an intensive seven-week residential program for college undergraduates from across the nation who are engaged in tutoring, mentoring, and other kinds of service programs on and off their campuses, and who are interested in exploring careers in the nonprofit sector. It will enable students to deepen their understanding of the history and ethics of philanthropy and volunteering; explore the role of the nonprofit sector as an alternative to government in solving social, economic, and other social problems; gain practical experience through an internship with a leading nonprofit organization; meet nationally prominent leaders in philanthropy and voluntary service; and identify opportunities for fulfilling careers in nonprofits, particularly in foundation and corporate contribution programs.

International Jewish College Corps

American Jewish World Service, 989 Avenue of the Americas,
10th Floor, New York, NY 10018
Tel: 800-889-7146, 212-736-AJWS; FAX: 212-736-3463
E-mail: ijcc@ajws.org; WWW: http://www.ajws.org/ijccdoc.html

▶ College students and recent graduates explore international development, study social justice within a Jewish context, and serve on hands-on volunteer projects in the developing world and Israel with the International Jewish College Corps (IJCC), a seven-week immersion experience. Following the summer, participants continue in the IJCC domestic program that includes educational seminars, retreats, public speaking engagements, article writing, and volunteer service.

The International Partnership for Service-Learning (IPS-L)

815 Second Avenue, Suite 3155, New York, NY 10017
Tel: 212-986-0989; FAX: 212-986-5039
E-mail: pslny@aol.com; WWW: http://www.ipsl.org

▶ The International Partnership for Service-Learning, founded in 1982, is an incorporated not-for-profit organization serving colleges, universities, service agencies, and related organizations around the world by fostering programs that link community service and academic study. IPS-L also organizes conferences on the development of service-learning, promotes the principles and practice of service-learning by encouraging partnership relationships, and publishes materials related to service-learning. Volunteers study at an overseas university and volunteer in a community for a summer, semester, or year. Programs are available in Latin America, the Caribbean, the United Kingdom, Asia, Europe, and the Middle East.

JustAct (formerly Overseas Development Network)

333 Valencia Street, Suite 101, San Francisco, CA 94103
Tel: 415-431-4204; FAX: 415-431-5953
E-mail: info@justact.org; WWW: http://www.justact.org

▶ JustAct works to develop lifelong commitments to social and economic justice. Their programs link students and youth in the United States to organizations and grassroots movements working for sustainable and self-reliant communities around the world. Their Alternative Opportunities Clearinghouse was designed for individuals who are interested in volunteering or interning internationally and want to know what options are available to them. JustAct does not have an international program in which volunteers participate directly, but rather is a resource and referral center where you may discover the various opportunities that exist. The Clearinghouse offers publications and research referral service.

National 4-H Council

7100 Connecticut Avenue, Chevy Chase, MD 20815
Tel: 888-77-YOUTH, 301-961-2800
E-mail: info@fourhcouncil.edu;
WWW: http://www.fourhcouncil.edu

▶ National 4-H Council's mission is to advance the 4-H youth development movement to build a world in which youth and adults learn, grow, and work together as catalysts for positive change. Council partners with 4-H at all levels—national, state, and local. If you would like to get involved, you can volunteer by contacting your state extension office, become involved in one of their many programs, or find a career or internship at National 4-H Council.

The National Society for Experiential Education (NSEE)

1703 North Beauregard Street, Suite 400,
Alexandria, VA 22311-1714
Tel: 703-933-0017; FAX: 703-933-1053
E-mail: info@nsee.org; WWW: http://www.nsee.org/

▶ This is a nonprofit membership association of educators, businesses, and community leaders. Founded in 1971, NSEE also serves as a national resource center for the development and improvement of experiential education programs nationwide. NSEE supports the use of learning through experience for intellectual development, cross-cultural and global awareness, civic and social responsibility, ethical development, career exploration, and personal growth. NSEE is nationally recognized for serving over 2,000 members and an extended network of over 15,000 nonmembers who are teachers, professors, principals, deans, directors of service-learning programs, professionals in career development and youth employment, counselors, directors of internships and cooperative education programs, school-to-work coordinators, superintendents, college presidents, researchers, and policy makers; taking leadership in developing and disseminating principles of good practice and innovations in experienced-based learning; providing a forum for discussion of state-of-the-art ideas, practices, and innovations at the National Conference; keeping practitioners up to date through the *NSEE Quarterly;* informing educators about critical issues, program models and practices, theory, and research through books and resource papers on experiential education; assisting with a variety of needs in starting or strengthening experience-based learning programs through consulting services provided by a trained network of NSEE members; providing information and referrals about research, theory, and high-quality programs through NSEE's National Resource Center for Experiential and Service Learning; and collaborating with hundreds of other national, regional, and local organizations to strengthen and advance experiential education.

National Institute for Work and Learning (NIWL)

1875 Connecticut Avenue NW, Washington, DC 20009-5721
Tel: 202-884-8186; FAX: 202-884-8422
E-mail: NIWL@aed.org; WWW: http://www.niwl.org/

▶ The full development of our human resource demands that education and work be treated as lifelong pursuits. The National Institute for Work and Learning (NIWL), an Institute of the Academy for Educational Development, seeks to promote active collaboration among the institutions of work, learning, and community to achieve this end. NIWL accomplishes its mission through basic research and policy analysis, action and development projects, program evaluations, technical assistance, and information networking. The Institute targets the millions of Americans who could profit from a better integration of the traditionally separate worlds of work and education. The National School-to-Work Learning and Information Center provides information, assistance, and training to build school-to-work opportunities in the United States. The Center utilizes the latest information technology to help increase the capacity of professionals, and to develop and implement school-to-work systems across the nation. Its services are available to state and local school-to-work offices, employers, schools, labor, parents, students, and the general public.

The Center functions as the national hub for synthesizing, communicating, and disseminating information that is essential to creating school-to-work opportunities across the country. Operating under the School-to-Work Opportunities Act, the Center services as a broker of technical assistance expertise in the fields of School-to-Work system building, school-based learning, work-based learning, and connecting activities. Guided by experts in the field, the Center offers customers access through six distinct services: a resource bank of select technical assistance providers; an 800-number "Answer Line" (800-251-7236); an Internet home page/ Information Network (*http://www.stw.ed.gov*); databases on key school-to-work contacts, organizations, and practices; relevant publications; and meetings, conferences, and training sessions.

National Youth Leadership Council *(See Support and Advocacy)*

Operation Crossroads Africa *(See Community Service— International)*

Oxfam America *(See Community Service—International)*

Presbyterian Church Mission Service Recruitment
(See Community Service—International)

Public Allies
633 West Wisconsin Avenue, Suite 610, Milwaukee, WI 53203
Tel: 414-273-0533; FAX: 414-273-0543
E-mail: PANational@publicallies.org,
PANational@publicallies.org; WWW: http://www.publicallies.org/

▶ This nonprofit organization works to identify young people (ages 18 to 30) from a broad range of backgrounds and experiences in order to provide them with the opportunities and tools they need to develop into community service leaders. They create full-time professional apprenticeships in nonprofit and public agencies where allies take responsibility for projects in areas such as youth development, health, education, economic development, and public safety. They provide rigorous training from community leaders, nonprofit and business executives, and professional consultants that helps Allies develop cutting-edge skills, knowledge, and personal insight necessary for them to practice leadership in today's changing communities: diversity, communication, critical thinking, conflict resolution, identifying community assets, responsibility, and accountability. They place Allies in charge of creating innovative responses to local challenges through Team Service Projects— teaching them to mobilize resources in a community and work productively with people from all walks of life. They encourage these individuals to be public-spirited through a 10-month Apprenticeship Program and an awards ceremony called "Tomorrow's Leaders Today." They maintain programs in Washington, D.C.; Chicago; Wilmington, Delaware; Milwaukee, Wisconsin; Durham, North Carolina; New York; Cincinnati; Los Angeles; and San Jose, California.

Rotary International *(See Community Service—International)*

UREP: University Research Expeditions Program
University of California, One Shields Avenue, Davis, CA 95616
Tel: 530-752-0692; FAX: 530-752-0681
E-mail: urep@ucdavis; WWW: http://urep.ucdavis.edu/

▶ The mission of the University Research Expeditions Program (UREP) is to improve our understanding of life on earth through partnerships between University of California researchers and members of the general public. Established in 1976, UREP has supported hundreds of research teams and provided opportunities for students, teachers, and other members of the public to join UC scientists on research projects investigating critical issues of environmental, human, and economic importance worldwide.

Visions International, Inc.
110 North Second Street, P.O. Box 220, Newport, PA 17074-0220
Tel: 800-813-9283, 717-567-7313; FAX: 717-567-7853
E-mail: visions@pa.net; WWW: http://www.visions-adventure.org

▶ This nonprofit, nonsectarian summer program offers community service experiences in cross-cultural settings for students between the ages of 11 and 13 (for Northwest Passage) and 14 to 18 (other programs). It is a co-ed summer program for teenagers combining construction-based community service, outdoor exploration and adventure, and intercultural living. Programs operate during July and August in Australia, Peru, Alaska, Montana, South Carolina, the Dominican Republic, British Virgin Islands, Guadeloupe, and Dominica. Most programs last about a month and cost between $2,300 and $3,400, depending on location and length of time.

The Washington Center for Internships and Academic Seminars
2000 M Street NW, Suite 750, Washington, DC 20036
Tel: 800-486-8921; FAX: 202-336-7609
E-mail: info@twc.edu, GARYA@TWC.ED;
WWW: http://www.twc.edu

▶ Since 1975, The Washington Center for Internships and Academic Seminars has provided over 24,000 students with a comprehensive, participatory learning experience in Washington, D.C. The unique format of The Washington Center's program promotes future leadership for the public, private, and nonprofit sectors of society. By combining experiential learning components to their academically based structure, students have the opportunity to experience and explore various career paths while sampling the intellectual and cultural diversity of our nation's capital. The goal of The Washington Center's program is to prepare students for the challenges they will face as they enter the working community. By providing a comprehensive, educational environment, they strive to assist in the continued development and success of our future leaders.

YMCA Earth Service Corps
National Resource Center, 909 Fourth Avenue, Seattle, WA 98104
E-mail: info@yesc.org; WWW: http://www.yesc.org/

▶ YMCA Earth Service Corps is a service-learning program for teens ready to make a difference in their communities. Grounded on the building blocks of leadership development, environmental education and action, and cross-cultural awareness, this proven program works in diverse communities and allows teens to use their talents, develop new skills, and learn more about themselves and their surroundings. Most importantly, young people in Earth Service Corps are recognized as valuable resources who work hand in hand with others to solve important issues. Founded in 1989, YMCA Earth Service Corps is operating in 111 YMCAs in 30 states and continues to be a fast-growing national program for the YMCA. In its 10-year history, the program has involved close to 20,000 young people in well over a million hours of service. Each year, participants (almost half of whom are from low-income families) contribute 200,000 hours of service. By running recycling projects, planting trees, adopting streams, and writing elected officials, these young people learn science as they become future volunteers and leaders.

YouthAction

P.O. Box 12372, Albuquerque, NM 87195
1001 East Yale Boulevard SE, Albuquerque, NM 87106
Tel: 505-873-3343; FAX: 505-873-3245
E-mail: youth-action@usa.net;
WWW: http://youthaction.net/Home.html
► Developing young people into community leaders, Youth-Action's vision is to prepare the new wave of youth who are, and will continue to be, the lifeblood of community improvement efforts for the coming decades. Founded in 1987, it is a national nonprofit organization that works in partnership with community-based organizations in low-income communities and communities of color to develop opportunities for young people in social, environmental, and economic justice efforts. Programs include political education, organizer training, technical assistance, and regional networking opportunities for their participating organizations. Our programs take the form of three-day long weekend trainings. YouthAction utilizes popular education methodology to incorporate the strengths of participating organizations at these events.

Youth Corps

National Association of Service and Conservation Corps,
666 11th Street NW, Suite 1000, Washington, DC 20001-4542
Tel: 202-737-6272; FAX: 202-737-6277
E-mail: nascc@nascc.org; WWW: http://www.nascc.org/
► The National Association of Service and Conservation Corps (NASCC) unites and supports youth corps as a preeminent strategy for achieving the nation's youth development, community service, and environmental restoration goals.

Youth Corps are conservation and service corps programs that harness the energy and idealism of young people to meet the needs of communities, states, and the nation. Corps programs engage young people, generally 16 to 25 years old, in paid, productive, full-time work that benefits both the young people and their communities. Participants in corps programs most often work in crews or teams of 8 to 12 with a paid adult supervisor who sets and models clear standards of behavior. Youth Corps crews undertake a wide range of work projects. Some are similar to the forestry and parks projects of the Civilian Conservation Corps of the 1930s; others fill gaps in the services of urban parks, renovate housing, and assist human service agencies. Most corpsmembers receive at least minimum wage for their work. Corpsmembers devote part of each week to improving their basic education skills and to preparing for future employment. Most corps not only offer pre-/GED, GED, and college credit courses, but also offer classes focusing on essential life skills, such as budgeting, parenting, and personal health and well-being. Corps programs also encourage corpsmembers to engage in tangible acts of citizenship, such as voting. Some corps offer educational scholarships or cash bonuses to corpsmembers who complete their term of service. More than 100 Youth Corps operate in 38 states and the District of Columbia. Some of these programs are statewide; the majority are locally based. Most corps operate year-round, although some operate only during the summer.

Youth for Understanding (YFU)

3501 Newark Street NW, Washington, DC 20016-3199
Tel: 800-TEENAGE, 202-966-6800; FAX: 202-895-1104
E-mail: pio@us.yfu.org; WWW: http://www.yfu.org/, http://www.youth forunderstanding.org/mission_control/volunteering.htm
► This is a worldwide movement of committed individuals and organizations working together to prepare young people for their responsibilities and challenges in a changing, interdependent global community. Established in 1951, YFU conducts exchanges with more than 50 countries around the world.

Youth on Board *(See Support and Advocacy)*

Youth Service America *(See Support and Advocacy)*

Youth Service International (YSI)

3024 Tilden Street NW, Washington, DC 20008
Tel: 202-966-5461; FAX: 202-966-8450
E-mail: ysintl@aol.com (Roger Landrum);
WWW: http://www.ysideal.org/
► YSI places young people aged 17 to 24 in three-month voluntary service projects overseas. It focuses on scientific research and community service projects. Youth Service International is an entrepreneurial nonprofit organization developing opportunities for every young person to devote a year or more to intensive community or national service. YSI is based on the belief that participatory citizenship by young people, combating local environmental, educational, and social problems, is the most powerful element for building civil society in emerging democracies.

Senior Volunteerism

American Association of Retired Persons (AARP)

601 E Street NW, Washington, DC 20049
Tel: 800-424-3410
E-mail: member@aarp.org; WWW: http://www.aarp.org/vol
► AARP is a nonprofit, nonpartisan association dedicated to shaping and enriching the experience of aging for its members and for all Americans. Founded in 1958 by retired educator Dr. Ethel Percy Andrus, they are today the nation's largest organization of midlife and older persons, with more than 30 million members. AARP has four primary areas of expertise and proven success: information and education; community service; legislative, judicial, and consumer advocacy; and member services. Local community service and fellowship activities are carried out by members and volunteers, including those who belong to 4,000 AARP chapters and 2,700 Retired Teachers Association units across the country. Community programs include Tax-Aide, 55 ALIVE/Mature Driving, Women's Financial Information Program, Money After 50, National Legal Assistance Training Program, Senior Community Service Employment Program, Widowed Persons Service, Connections for Independent Living, and a variety of other activities that serve the needs and interests of members where they live.

National Retiree Volunteer Coalition (NRVC)
(Merged with Volunteers of America—See Separate Listing)
1660 Duke Street, Alexandria, VA 22314
Tel: 800-899-0089, 703-341-5000
E-mail: jhough@voa.org (Jeffrey Hough);
WWW: http://www.nrvc.org

▶ Created in 1979, NRVC is a nonprofit organization that serves as the catalyst in creating a national movement of corporate retiree volunteer leadership and service. It brings together retirees, their former employers, and community agencies to form dynamic partnerships to address critical community issues, and offers corporations a blueprint for initiating and implementing Corporate Retiree Volunteer Programs (CRVP). Currently, there are 71 CRVPs in 55 corporations, hospitals, and universities in 35 cities and 18 states in the United States, and four cities and three provinces in Canada. Through a team of on-site program specialists, it assists and facilitates the CRVP management team in developing the leadership and collaborative skills necessary to recruit and train retiree volunteers, and to form partnerships with community agencies. It provides ongoing evaluation, support, and consultation to ensure continued CRVP growth and success. It publishes the quarterly newsletter, *NRVC Roundtable.*

The National Senior Service Corps
Corporation for National Service, 1201 New York Avenue NW, Washington, DC 20525
Tel: 202-606-5000
E-mail: nssc_recruting@cns.gov;
WWW: http://www.seniorcorps.org/

▶ Through the Senior Corps, nearly half a million Americans age 55 and older share their time and talents to help solve local problems. The National Senior Service Corps has a 30-year history of leadership in senior volunteer service. The Senior Corps is a national network of projects that place older volunteers in volunteer assignments in their communities. There are actually three national programs under its umbrella. One is the Foster Grandparent Program, which links senior volunteers to children who need their help. Another is the Senior Companion Program, which places its volunteers with adults needing extra assistance to live in the community, such as frail older persons. Finally, the Retired and Senior Volunteer Program (RSVP) is "one-stop shopping" for senior volunteers. Senior Corps programs operate in local communities throughout the United States.

Support and Advocacy

Alliance for National Renewal (ANR)
National Civic League, 1445 Market Street, Suite 300, Denver, CO 80202-1728
Tel: 303-571-4343; FAX: 303-571-4404
E-mail: ncl@ncl.org; WWW: http://www.ncl.org/ANR/index.htm,
http://www.ncl.org/ANR/director.htm,
http://www.ncl.org/ANR/pubs.htm

▶ Created in 1993 by the National Civic League, it is a coalition of over 200 national and local organizations dedicated to the principles of community renewal. A catalyst for inspiring and helping citizens work together to improve their communities and thus our nation, ANR offers assistance to communities that want to start community renewal alliances; access to a network of people who believe in taking back our nation, neighborhood by neighborhood; a collection of stories on successful community renewal efforts; and inspiration, ideas, tools, and collaborative processes shared through conferences, publications, technical assistance, and the World Wide Web. ANR publishes *National Civic Review* (see separate listing under Volunteerism—Periodicals), a quarterly publication for civic leaders, public officials, and collaborative community problem solving, as well as the *ANR Community Resource Manual, The Community Visioning and Strategic Handbook,* and *Guide to Alliance for National Renewal,* among others.

America's Promise—The Alliance for Youth
909 North Washington Street, Suite 400, Alexandria, VA 22314-1556
Tel: 888-55-YOUTH, 703-684-4500; FAX: 703-535-3900
E-mail: webmaster@americaspromise.org,
commit@americaspromise.org, local@americaspromise.org;
WWW: http://www.americaspromise.org

▶ America's Promise was founded after the Presidents' Summit for America's Future, April 27–29, 1997, in Philadelphia. The Summit was co-sponsored by the Points of Light Foundation and the Corporation for National Service. It mobilizes people from every sector of American life to build the character and competence of our nation's youth by fulfilling five promises for young people: ongoing relationships with caring adults in their lives—parents, mentors, tutors, or coaches; safe places with structured activities during nonschool hours; healthy start and future; marketable skills through effective education; and opportunities to give back through community service. America's Promise has created a diverse and growing alliance of nearly 500 national organizations called Commitment Makers, which make large-scale national commitments to fulfill one or more of the five promises. These organizations agree to expand existing youth programs or create new ones and hold themselves accountable by measuring their progress. Spanning all sectors of society, these groups include corporations, not-for-profits, higher education and faith-based groups, associations and federal agencies, and arts and culture organizations. It distributes publications by e-mail.

BREAK AWAY: The Alternative Break Connection
Box 6026, Station B, Nashville, TN 37235
Tel: 615-343-0385; FAX: 615-343-3255
E-mail: breakaway@alternativebreaks.com;
WWW: http://www.alternativebreaks.com/

▶ Founded in 1991, it is a nonprofit organization that serves as a national resource of information on alternative break programs. They provide key information on planning and running a quality break program to schools and community organizations in the BREAK AWAY network. BREAK AWAY'S programs and services include training and special events, publications, membership opportunities, networking, and access to the *SiteBank Catalog* (*http://www.vanderbilt.edu/breakaway/sitebank*), a directory of community organizations that host alternative break programs across the country. Its mission is to promote service on the local, regional, national, and international levels through break-oriented programs that immerse students in often vastly different cultures, heighten social awareness, and advocate lifelong social action. It places teams of college or high school students in communities to engage in community service and experiential learning during their summer, fall, winter, or spring breaks. Students perform short-term projects for community agencies and learn about issues such as literacy, poverty, racism, hunger, homelessness, and the environment. The objectives of an alternative break program are to involve college students in community-based service projects and to give students opportunities to learn about the problems faced by members of communities with whom they otherwise may have had little or no direct contact. It envisions a not too distant future, where quality alternative breaks will be as much a part of the college experience as going to class. Students will walk away with a redefined sense of community and a lifetime commitment to social action. BREAK AWAY publishes *Connections,* its quarterly newsletter, among other publications. It holds an annual conference.

Campus Compact: The Project for Public and Community Service

Box 1975, Brown University, Providence, RI 02912-1975
Tel: 401-863-1119; FAX: 401-863-3779
E-mail: campus@compact.org; WWW: http://www.compact.org/

▶ Campus Compact was founded in 1985 by the presidents of Brown, Georgetown, and Stanford universities, and the president of the Education Commission of the States. It maintains network offices in 23 states, and has a rapidly growing membership of 620 public and private two- and four-year colleges and universities, located in 41 states and the District of Columbia. In addition to the work done at the national level, these affiliates serve as key liaisons to school systems, and higher education, community-based, and government organizations, as well as provide area member colleges and universities with hands-on assistance, workshops, and conferences.

Campus Compact is an organization actively engaged both on and off campus in community service. To fulfill their mission, they create supportive academic environments for community service; assist in federal and national legislation promoting public and community service; form partnerships with business, community, and government leaders; provide timely, vital information to our members; provide timely, vital information to their members; award grants to member schools and state affiliates; provide funding and awards for outstanding service work; and organize conferences, forums, and meetings.

It publishes a number of publications, including: *Service Matters: A Sourcebook for Community Service in Higher Education; Guidelines for Developing a State Campus Compact* (also available online at *http://www.compact.org/resources/guidelines.html*); and *Compact Current,* their bimonthly newsletter, among other publications.

Campus Outreach Opportunity League (COOL)

37 Temple Place, Suite 401, Boston, MA 02111
Tel: 617-695-COOL (2665); FAX: 617-695-0022
E-mail: inquiry@cool2serve.org;
WWW: http://www.cool2serve.org/,
http://www.cool2serve.org/programs/programs.htm

▶ Founded in 1984, COOL is a national nonprofit organization working to encourage, support, and expand campus-based community service efforts. COOL's mission is to educate and empower students to strengthen our nation through service. It works to encourage, support, and help improve college student service programs. Among the many things they sponsor is the National Conference on Student Community Service every spring in which approximately 2,000 student leaders and administrators and nonprofit professionals meet in a focused three days of sharing their

thoughts and experiences. Additionally, staff members visit hundreds of college campuses giving workshops encouraging, promoting, and initiating programs that get students involved in service. COOL Press publishes resource books and technical assistance manuals designed to help students organize for effective community service. The COOL Leaders program is an intensive leadership training and development program for college students who are actively involved in campus-based community service and service-learning programs. The primary purpose of the program is to help strengthen and expand campus-based community service programs through the increased training and support of emerging student leaders. Its Web site includes COOL Tools, an online, searchable database that contains resources for enhancing, improving, and strengthening campus community service programs and projects and many excellent links to its nonprofit affiliates. It maintains a listserv for members and affiliates. It publishes *What's COOL!,* a quarterly newsletter (during the academic year) and resource with advice and tips for COOL members, and *On Your Mark, Go!, Get Set: From Campus Ideals to Community Involvement.*

Center for Youth as Resources (CYAR)

1000 Connecticut Avenue NW, 13th Floor, Washington, DC 20036
Tel: 202-261-4131
E-mail: yar@ncpc.org; WWW: http://www.yar.org/

▶ The Center for Youth as Resources (CYAR) serves as the national and international umbrella organization for Youth as Resources (YAR), and, as such, promotes the YAR philosophy and program. CYAR's headquarters are in Washington, D.C., with the first of four planned regional offices located in Indianapolis, Indiana. Local YAR programs, governed by boards composed of youth and adults, provide grants for youth-initiated, youth-led community projects. Through instructional materials, technical assistance, and training conducted by experienced youth and adults, CYAR helps local YAR programs start, develop, and expand.

City Cares, Inc.

1605 Peachtree Street, Suite 100, Atlanta, GA 30309
Tel: 404-875-7334; FAX: 404-253-1020
E-mail: info@citycares.org; WWW: www.citycares.org,
http://www.citycares.org/national/network.asp?

▶ This nonprofit organization provides technical assistance to the local City Cares organizations (and helps people who want to start a program in their community); these organizations are in major cities nationwide, and they organize volunteer projects for people who are extremely busy. Volunteers usually get together as a group on weekends (and, sometimes, early in the morning before work or late in the afternoon after work) to help with a variety of activities, including serving meals in soup kitchens, participating in environmental projects (like park clean-ups and tree plantings), taking a group of children with disabilities on a picnic or to the park or the zoo, delivering meals to homebound seniors, renovating housing for low-income families, reading to people who are blind, tutoring at-risk children, and more; volunteer opportunities vary from city to city. City Cares of America (CCA) was formed in 1992 to serve as the national umbrella organization for these local Cares organizations. The primary mission of CCA is to provide support for and strengthen the existing Cares network and to foster the development of new Cares organizations. In cities large and small, Cares groups have been established, and many more are currently being formed. It holds an annual conference. It is an America's Promise (see separate listing for full description) Alliance Member.

City Cares organizations, known as "Cares" or "Hands On" groups, engage over 100,000 individuals in direct, hands-on service within their local communities each year. A pull-down menu on their Web site permits you to locate a Junior League in your area by selecting state/province/country. Local affiliates currently operate in the following cities: Baltimore; Atlanta; Birmingham, Alabama; Boston; Charlotte; Chicago; Greenville, South Carolina; Kansas City, Kansas; Los Angeles; Memphis; Miami; Morristown, New Jersey; Nashville; New Orleans; New York; Philadelphia; Pittsburgh; Phoenix; Portland, Oregon; San Diego; San Francisco, SF Bay Area; Seattle; Southfield, Missouri; and Washington, D.C. Cares organizations help you find projects that fit your schedule. Projects typically occur before or after regular work hours, or on weekends, to complement busy work schedules. Search for your local network affiliate at *http://cares.org/national/network.asp.* America Cares™ is a national corporate program for companies seeking to fulfill President's Summit commitments while making direct contributions to the community. The Cares model of service is an ideal one for companies who seek to engage their employees in meaningful volunteer service in areas that they support, both geographically and philanthropically. CCA's Corporate Partners Program, in partnership with *CCA affiliates* offer a wealth of resources, including knowledgeable staff who are sensitive to corporate cultures; a wide range of hands-on projects that address different community needs; team volunteer opportunities for large or small groups; team-building and leadership opportunities; access to a network of affiliates across the country; and flexible scheduling and commitment levels that need not interfere with the workday.

Council on International Education Exchange

633 Third Avenue, 20th Floor, New York, NY 10017
FAX: 212-822-2779
WWW: http://www.ciee.org/

▶ Council is one of the largest international education organizations in the world, with almost 800 professionals and support staff working in more than 30 countries. Over a million students come to them for services every year. Council is divided into three interrelated but very independent operating entities: Council-International Study Programs, Council Exchanges, and Council Travel.

Do Something

423 West 55th Street, 8th Floor, New York, NY 10019
Tel: 212-523-1175; FAX: 212-582-1307
E-mail: mail@dosomething.org; AOL: Keyword Do Something;
WWW: http://www.dosomething.org/

▶ This national nonprofit organization inspires young people to believe that change is possible, and trains, funds, and mobilizes them to be leaders who measurably strengthen their communities. It was founded, developed, and managed by young people working to inspire young Americans from all backgrounds and from every part of the country to take problem-solving action in their communities. It believes that young people should be social artists, blending their creativity and entrepreneurial spirit in pursuit of novel solutions to community problems. With an eye toward long-term change, Do Something strives to promote tangible and quantifiable results, and Do Something strongly believes that change must come from within the community. While undertaking its media campaign and fund-raising efforts on a national level, Do Something is work-

ing to catalyze problem solving on a local level. Programs include: The Do Something BRICK Award for Community Leadership; The Do Something Kindness & Justice Challenge; The Do Something League; and The Do Something Community Connections Campaign. While Do Something does not directly provide volunteering in local communities or give information about volunteering in a particular community, they do offer grants nationally for projects already designed. Visit their online volunteering information center: The Community Connections Campaign at *http://www.dosomething.org/dosomething/shared/c3page.cfm.*

The Grantmaker Forum on Community & National Service (GFCNS)

2550 9th Street, Suite 113, Berkeley, CA 94710
Tel: 510-665-6130; FAX: 510-665-6129
E-mail: web@gfcns.org; WWW: http://www.gfcns.org

▶ This is an affinity group of foundation and corporate-giving programs nationwide committed to expanding opportunities for people of all ages and backgrounds to serve their community and their country. The Grantmaker Forum encourages private and philanthropic support and investment in service and volunteer programs and opportunities. Convened in 1993 by a small group of foundation and corporate grantmakers, GFCNS organizes regional and national events, conferences, and dialogues, and produces publications and public relations strategies to promote the value of citizen service, volunteerism, and civic engagement. The work of the Grantmaker Forum is directed by its foundation and corporate members through their participation on task forces and working groups. Professional staff implement the plans and vision articulated by its members. GFCNS works closely with partners who share an interest in or commitment to citizen service, volunteerism, and civic engagement.

International Association for Volunteer Effort (IAVE)

1400 Eye Street NW, Suite 800, Washington, DC 20005
Tel: 202-729-8250; FAX: 202-729-8103
E-mail: IAVE@pointsoflight.org; WWW: http://www.iave.org/

▶ IAVE was created in 1970 by a small group of women throughout the world who shared a common vision of how volunteers can contribute to the solution of human and social problems and to the development of bridges of understanding among people of all nations. They recognized the importance of international exchange of information, best practices, and mutual support as a way of encouraging and strengthening volunteering worldwide.

International Volunteer Programs Association (IVPA)

P.O. Box 381161, Cambridge, MA 02238
Tel: 617-496-8414; FAX: 617-495-1599
E-mail: ivpa@volunteerinternational.org;
WWW: www.volunteerinternational.org,
http://www.volunteerinternational.org/index-res.html

▶ This alliance of nonprofit, nongovernmental organizations based in the Americas is involved in international volunteer and internship exchanges. IVPA encourages excellence and responsibility in the field of international voluntarism and promotes public awareness of and greater access to international volunteer programs. IVPA offers a forum for international volunteer program representatives (staff, board members, etc.) to share information and resources, develop new skills, and collaborate on cost-saving initiatives. IVPA distributes the *Volunteer International News,* a bimonthly e-mail newsletter.

The National Association of Volunteer Programs in Local Government (NAVPLG)

Marion County, 100 High Street NE, Salem, OR 97301
Tel: 503-588-7990; FAX: 503-588-5237

City of Coral Springs, FL
Tel: 954-346-4430
E-mail: kms@ci.coral-springs.fl.us (Kim Sanecki, President),
navplg@open.org, gchapin@open.org (Glenis Chapin, Volunteer
Coordinator); WWW: http://www.naco.org/affils/navplg/

▶ This is an association of administrators, coordinators, and directors of volunteer programs in local governments. Its purpose is to strengthen volunteer programs in local government through leadership, advocacy, networking, and information exchange. NAVPLG is an affiliate of both the Association for Volunteer Administration and the National Association of Counties. Members receive resource and networking opportunities, a quarterly newsletter, discount membership when joining AVA, and a reduced fee for AVA- and NAVPLG-sponsored workshops and conferences.

National Mentoring Partnership

1600 Duke Street, Suite 300, Alexandria, VA 22314
Tel: 703-224-2200; FAX: 703-226-2581
E-mail: NMP@mentoring.org; WWW: www.mentoring.org

▶ The National Mentoring Partnership is an advocate for the expansion of mentoring and a resource for mentors and mentoring initiatives nationwide. They work to help entire communities and states work together to sustain and expand mentoring opportunities for young people; schools, businesses, civic associations, faith communities, and youth-serving organizations build or strengthen their mentoring programs; educators and workforce preparation leaders integrate mentoring into programs; and individuals learn about mentoring opportunities and become the mentors young people want and need. They deliver leadership and support to a national network of community and state leaders who have formed mentoring partnerships to bring mentoring to scale; standards—"Mentoring: Elements of Effective Practice" for developing responsible mentoring programs in any setting; *www.mentoring.org*—immediate access to the latest information and resources on mentoring as well as online networking and training events for practitioners and mentors; training for mentors and organizations via local mentor training institutes and the *How to Be a Great Mentor* guide and interactive Web site (produced with Kaplan Educational Centers and Newsweek); response line to answer questions about mentoring and help organizations start or expand mentoring programs; Technical Assistance Corps—mentoring experts who are available to consult and train on all aspects of mentoring, including workplace-based, faith-based, and school-based programs; state and local mentoring partnerships and mentor training institutes; public awareness campaigns via partnerships with America's Promise, The Harvard Mentoring Project, ABC television network, and other media and mentoring initiatives; Public Policy Council—composed of the nation's leading practitioners, to generate public support, funding, and action to expand mentoring opportunities for young people; and membership in a national network of individuals who care deeply about the future of young people and mentoring.

The National Society for Experiential Education (NSEE) *(See also Service Learning, Youth and Young Adult Volunteerism)*

1703 North Beauregard Street, Suite 400,
Alexandria, VA 22311-1714
Tel: 703-933-0017; FAX: 703-933-1053
E-mail: info@nsee.org; WWW: http://www.nsee.org/

▶ This is a nonprofit membership association of educators, businesses, and community leaders. Founded in 1971, NSEE also serves as a national resource center for the development and improvement of experiential education programs nationwide. NSEE supports the use of learning through experience for: intellectual development; cross-cultural and global awareness; civic and social responsibility; ethical development; career exploration; and personal growth. NSEE is nationally recognized for serving over 2,000 members and an extended network of over 15,000 nonmembers who are teachers, professors, principals, deans, directors of service-learning programs, professionals in career development and youth employment, counselors, directors of internships and cooperative education programs, school-to-work coordinators, superintendents, college presidents, researchers, and policy makers; taking leadership in developing and disseminating principles of good practice and innovations in experienced-based learning; providing a forum for discussion of state-of-the-art ideas, practices, and innovations at the National Conference; keeping practitioners up to date through the *NSEE Quarterly;* informing educators about critical issues, program models and practices, theory, and research through books and resource papers on experiential education; assisting with a variety of needs in starting or strengthening experience-based learning programs through consulting services provided by a trained network of NSEE members; providing information and referrals about research, theory, and high-quality programs through NSEE's National Resource Center for Experiential and Service Learning; and collaborating with hundreds of other national, regional, and local organizations to strengthen and advance experiential education.

National Youth Leadership Council (NYLC)

1910 West County Road B, St. Paul, MN 55113
Tel: 800-808-SERV (National Service-Learning Clearinghouse),
651-631-3672; FAX: 651-631-2955
E-mail: nylcinfo@nylc.org; WWW: http://www.nylc.org/

▶ NYLC's mission is to engage young people in their communities and schools through innovation in learning, service, leadership, and public policy. As one of America's most prominent advocates of service-learning and youth service, the NYLC is at the forefront of efforts to reform education and guide youth-oriented public policy. It accomplishes its mission through several related strategies: developing innovative model programs in schools across America; creating curricula and training programs for educators and youth; advocating educational reform and progressive youth policy; conducting ongoing research in youth issues; and maintaining extensive networks in support of these measures. It sponsors the National Youth Leadership Camp (*nylccamp@nylc.org*), an experiential high-adventure curriculum that trains young people as active problem solvers in their communities. Since 1983, this intensive 8- to 10-day summer program has emphasized personal development through a carefully planned series of physical, social, and artistic challenges. In partnership with the National 4-H Council, the Points of Light Foundation, the Corporation for National Service, America's Promise, and the W.K. Kellogg Foundation, the National

Youth Leadership Council is supporting follow-up efforts of young people to the Presidents Summit for America's Future. Strategies of the movement include developing and disseminating Principles of Youth Involvement, and planning for a National Youth Summit (*youthlead@pointsoflight.org*). It holds the annual National Service-Learning Conference (*conference@nylc.org*), which highlights and promotes service-learning as a way of teaching and learning that builds academic and citizenship skills while renewing communities. It is the only major national education conference that provides service-learning professional development to a diverse audience of K–12 educators, administrators, preservice teacher education staff and faculty, researchers, youth leaders, parents, program coordinators, AmeriCorps members, community-based organization staffs, and corporate and foundation officers.

Points of Light Foundation

1400 I Street NW, Suite 800, Washington, DC 20005
Tel: 800-VOLUNTEER, 800-879-5400 (Volunteer Placement
Service), 202-729-8000; FAX: 202-729-8100
E-mail: volnet@pointsoflight.org;
WWW: http://www.pointsoflight.org

▶ This nonpartisan nonprofit organization is devoted to promoting volunteerism. Founded in 1990, the Foundation's mission is to engage more people more effectively in volunteer community service to help solve serious social problems. The Foundation works in communities throughout the United States through more than 450 volunteer centers. The Points of Light Foundation has developed a number of ongoing programs, initiatives, and partnerships designed to promote volunteerism. Services/programs include: training and consulting to enhance your volunteer program and meet your critical business needs; innovative, short courses that include practical, use-it-now tools for corporations, volunteer centers, nonprofit and government agencies, youth organizations, educational institutions, individuals, and community groups; services and products geared toward volunteer program managers in every type organization; seminars and courses; and customized trainings and consultations. It holds the annual National Community Service Conference in partnership with the Corporation for National Service, the premier training event for volunteer management, community volunteering, and national service leaders in nonprofit organizations, businesses, government agencies, and volunteer centers. The National Community Service Conference offers a large selection of workshops, critical issues forums, and exhibits. Its Volunteer Marketplace Catalog of publications and promotional items is available both in print and online at *http://www.pointsoflight.org/volunteermarketplace/TableOfContents.cfm*. It includes volunteer management, board issues, building community, changing the paradigm, communications and marketing, corporate citizenship and employee volunteering, faith-based volunteering, fund raising, mentoring, resources and references, strategic planning and leadership, youth volunteer management, and promotional items.

Project America

1520 West Main Street, Suite 102, Richmond, VA 23220
Tel: 800-880-3352, 804-358-1605; FAX: 804-355-9701
E-mail: project@project.org; WWW: http://www.project.org/

▶ Project America, founded in 1993 by three college students, believes in the power of the individual to make an impact on his or her community. A nonprofit organization, Project America inspires and teaches people to take positive steps in their communities, and creates partnerships between volunteers and organizations that need them. Project America works with companies, large member organizations, national and local nonprofits, and communities to design service initiatives that involve people of all ages in volunteer efforts. Throughout the year, Project America offers a variety of programs and services that educate and empower individuals to make a difference in their community. Project America also designs specific service initiatives for companies and organizations to involve their employees and members in positive community action. Services include program design (designs and helps implement service programs created specifically for companies and large member organizations to involve their employees/members in positive community development on the local and national level); partnership creation (achieves its goals through linking other national nonprofit and corporate partners to maximize the power of people); volunteer referral (in partnership with Impact Online, Project America works to bring together volunteers and the organizations that need them); volunteer education (Project America's *Action Guide to Community Service* provides all the resources needed to plan and implement a service project. The *Action Guide to Community Service* educates the project leader on every aspect of service from team building strategies and motivation to organizing, budgeting, and publicizing the event; *The Navigator,* Project America's quarterly newsletter provides up-to-date information on volunteering and innovative service ideas for volunteer leaders. *The Navigator* is circulated to over 1,500 volunteers, companies, and organizations, and is available to volunteers at no cost); technical assistance (Project America's volunteer education resources, project implementation assistance, and volunteer referral assistance program are all available online and via e-mail at *project@project.org*).

Volunteer Support Project

6500 SW Pacific Boulevard, Albany, OR 97321
Tel: 541-917-4478; FAX: 541-917-4838

▶ The Volunteer Support Project was formed in 1993 to assist nonprofits needing help in developing materials to run successful volunteer programs. It publishes materials designed to strengthen volunteer organizations. The Project's first book, *The Generic Volunteer Orientation Manual: Your Guide to Developing an Orientation,* is available.

Youth Service America (YSA)

1101 15th Street, Suite 200, Washington, DC 20005
Tel: 202-296-2992; FAX: 202-296-4030
E-mail: info@ysa.org; WWW: http://www.ysa.org

▶ Founded in 1986, it is a resource center and alliance of 200 organizations that are increasing the quality and quantity of opportunities for young Americans to serve locally, nationally, or globally. YSA's mission is to strengthen the effectiveness, sustainability, and scale of the youth service movement. YSA envisions a powerful network of organizations committed to making service the common experience and expectation of all young Americans. A strong youth service movement will create healthy communities, and foster citizenship, knowledge, and the personal development of young people. The Network provides youth service organizations and the media with key information and research on best practices, resources, and opportunities in the youth service field. The National Service Affiliates Program is the largest network of youth service organizations in the United States, representing over 30 million young Americans. The Affiliates program provides its members with the weekly National Service Briefing, service-related information, issue papers, discounts on a broad array of goods and services, and convenes the field around key issues through the monthly Working Group on National and Community Service. To make it easier for people to volunteer, Youth Service America has developed SERVEnet, an online matching service for volunteers and nonprofits (see Internet Sites—Voluntary Opportunity Databases for full). YSA sponsors National Youth Service Day, the President's Student Service Awards, and the Institute for Leadership Training.

Youth on Board

58 Day Street, P.O. Box 440322, Somerville, MA 02144
Tel: 617-623-9900, ext.# 1242
WWW: http://www.youthonboard.org/

▶ A Project of YouthBuild USA, Youth on Board helps young people and adults think differently about each other so that they can work together to change their communities. They don't just build skills, but mutually respectful relationships between young people and adults that allow youth to move from the margins of their communities into the center. Their services can be offered as is, in any combination, or customized to fit your specific needs. They work with mixed groups of young people and adults, or either group separately, and all trainings are facilitated by a team of young people and adults in a highly interactive format. Among the established training topics for young people and adult audiences are: training young people for their roles as board, committee members, or community leaders; determining your model for youth involvement; legal issues about including young people in decision making; involving the next generation in philanthropy; developing and communicating your project or organizational message; understanding adultism—looking at barriers that inhibit youth involvement; conflict resolution: using appreciations as a tool to resolve conflict; recruiting young people for your project; building close relationships between young people and adults; and making mentoring work. They offer customized assistance to further involve young people in your organization or community. Individualized assistance can be either long or short term, and participants can work separately in age groups, and together during intergenerational sessions. Youth on Board works with organizations such as The Nathan Cummings Foundation to find ways to involve the next generation of family members in the work of the foundation. Youth on Board assists foundations with building a base of leadership so that the succession of leadership is effective and rewarding for all involved. Youth on Board has consulted with several organizations on philanthropic issues, including work with the Ewing Marion Kauffman Foundation on how to involve young people in grant-making roles.

Virtual Volunteering

(See Internet Resources)

Workplace Volunteerism

Business Volunteers Unlimited (BVU) (formerly Business Volunteerism Council)

Tower City Center, Suite 950, 50 Public Square,
Cleveland, OH 44113-2204
Tel: 216-736-7711; FAX: 216-736-7710
WWW: http://www.businessvolunteers.org/

▶ Established in 1983, it has developed and refined a unique and powerful model to engage volunteers from businesses in productive and rewarding leadership and volunteer activities. BVU prepares and refers business volunteers for service on nonprofit boards of trustees; involves professionals in providing volunteer management assistance to nonprofits; and channels thousands of employees and their families to a variety of well-organized direct service volunteer activities. It provides training and consulting services to business and community leaders from cities throughout the United States seeking to replicate successful BVU programs and services. BVU makes compelling and informative presentations regarding effective strategies to engage businesses, and assists other cities in exploring the feasibility of establishing programs to facilitate corporate community involvement on a large scale in their communities. BVU assists other cities in determining what is involved in making their effort successful, and provides training to organizations seeking to involve business executives on nonprofit boards and provide corporate community involvement consulting services in their own communities.

National Council on Workplace Volunteerism (NCWV)

Points of Light Foundation, 1400 I Street NW, Suite 800,
Washington, DC 20005
Tel: 800-272-8306, 202-729-8000; FAX: 202-729-8100
E-mail: SHeiler@PointsofLight.org, volnet@pointsoflight.org;
WWW: http://www.pointsoflight.org/
assistance/assistance_corporate.html

▶ NCWV leads and supports the development of employee volunteer programs and Corporate Volunteer Councils by promoting volunteerism in the business community on behalf of the Points of Light Foundation. To receive e-mail updates on corporate volunteerism and the work of the Points of Light Foundation, go to *http://www.pointsoflight.org/assistance/assistance_corporate_requ est99.html*.

Products and Service Providers

Consultants

Blue Vision Training

P.O. Box 15118, Fort Wayne, IN 46885-5118
Tel: 219-485-9081; FAX: 219-485-5847
*E-mail: georgeanjc@aol.com (Georgean C. Johnson-Coffey,
MEd); WWW: http://www.bluevisiontraining.com/*

▶ Blue Vision provides volunteer management development consulting services, including: Building an Effective Service Program; Orientation of Volunteers; Implemented Volunteer Service Programs in Public School; Developing Meaningful Volunteer Positions; Effective Training of Volunteers; How to Supervise Volunteers; Building the Government Volunteer Program: Federal, State, and Local; Government Staff and Citizen Volunteers: Building Healthy Relations; How to Get Your Hands on Resources When Tax Dollars Are Hands Off; Trends in Volunteerism; Volunteer Recognition; Staff/Volunteer Relations; Fundamentals of Volunteer Management; Dynamics of Managing Short-Term, Long-Term, and Required-Term Volunteers; How to Supervise Volunteers; The Future of Volunteer Management; How to Organize Volunteers for Veterinary Service; When Volunteers Grieve; and Effective Volunteer Recruitment. Clients include local, regional, and national organizations representing education, government, health care, libraries and nonprofits. Topics include: Team Building, Conflict Management, Train-the-Trainer, Staff/Volunteer Relations, Fundamentals of Volunteer Management, Family Volunteering, Trends in Volunteerism, and other aspects of volunteer management. Johnson-Coffey is also a certified VolunteerWorks software trainer.

Cornerstone Consulting Associates, LLC

1100 Pepperidge Court, Midland, MI 48640
Tel: 517-631-3380
*E-mail: cornrstn@concentric. net (Sue Waechter, Principal);
WWW: www.peopleprocessproduct.com*

▶ Through consulting or training services, learn to build strategic partnerships, create a client-focused culture, establish best leadership practices, plan strategically, assess and manage quality volunteer programs, manage change, communicate for effectiveness, resolve conflict, charter effective teams, and others. Sue and her partners, Deb Kocsis and Lee Rouse, are all qualified to administer and interpret the Myers-Briggs Type Indicator.

Energize, Inc.

5450 Wissahickon Avenue, Box C-13, Philadelphia, PA 19144
*Tel: 800-395-9800 (Book Orders), 215-438-8342;
FAX: 215-438-0434*
*E-mail: energize@energizeinc.com, info@energizeinc.com,
susan@energizeinc.com (Susan J. Ellis, President);
WWW: http://www.energizeinc.com,
http://www.energizeinc.com/prof.html,
http://www.energizeinc.com/art.html*

▶ This is an international training, consulting, and publishing firm specializing in volunteerism. If these words are in your vocabulary—community service, membership development, auxiliary, community organizing, service learning, lay ministry, pro bono work, supporter, friends group, political activist, service club—they can help. Founded in 1977, Energize has assisted organizations of all types with their volunteer efforts, whether they are health and human service organizations, cultural arts groups, professional associations, or schools. Their Web site includes a compilation of articles and excerpts, listing of conferences/classes, online bookstore, job bank, and many other services. The *Volunteer Energy Resource Catalog* offers over 65 books, training materials, and software from 38 sources in the United States, Canada, and the United Kingdom. They provide a free monthly electronic update describing new features on the Energize web site and other items of interest to the volunteer field. To receive it, send a blank e-mail to *join-energize@sparklist.com*. Check out articles, excerpts, and electronic books on volunteer program development and management, plus special resource lists including a comprehensive bibliography on volunteerism. You'll find the Virtual Appendix (*http://www.energizeinc.com/supervising.html*) for *Supervising Volunteers* here as well. The online version (Bookstore) is available at *http://www.energizeinc.com/bkstore.html*.

Bobby Finch & Associates, Inc.

3400 Fairlane Drive, Des Moines, IA 50315
Tel: 515-282-5014 (40); FAX: 515-883-2016
E-mail: Bfinch@dwx.com

▶ A nationally recognized trainer and presenter with over 18 years experience in the field of volunteerism and aging issues, she has served as Director of the Iowa Governor's Office on Volunteerism under two governors and as the Executive Director of the Iowa Commission on Volunteer Service. Areas of expertise include fund raising and resource development, volunteer program development and management, working with AmeriCorps and Commissions on Volunteer Service, and ethics and character building. Other presentations and workshops are available on request.

Arlene Grubbs

21 Briar Cliff Road, Pittsburgh, PA 15202
Tel/FAX: 412-766-6528
E-mail: briar21@aol.com

▶ Arlene Grubbs has worked in the field of volunteer management for 25 years, first as a manager of volunteer programs and in the last 15 years as a consultant and trainer in volunteer management. She conducts workshops on all aspects of volunteer management from planning a volunteer program to recognition activities and almost everything in between. She consults with organizations who are initiating volunteer programs or who need to restructure their volunteer system. Since boards of nonprofits are an organization's most important volunteers, Arlene conducts board retreats and works with organizations to strengthen their board's functioning. Her skills in training and facilitation have been widely praised by the organizations she has worked with. Arlene has worked in the field of volunteer management for 25 years, the last decade as a consultant to volunteer programs and nonprofit organizations. She is particularly interested in developing effective boards of directors, building teams, and improving communication skills.

Anne S. Honer

419 Normandy Road, Mooresville, NC 28117
Tel: 704-663-5129
E-mail: ashoner@aol.com

▶ Anne has over 30 years experience with nonprofits, in both volunteer (including board) and staff positions. With a master's degree in adult education, she offers training in fund development and volunteer management: capital campaigns, annual giving, volunteers in fund raising, recruiting volunteers, volunteer overview, and more.

JRB Associates, Inc.

2462 Lake George Drive NW, Cedar, MN 55011
Tel/FAX: 612-753-4636
E-mail: AgriFolks@aol.com (Juanita J. Reed-Boniface, Principal)

▶ JRB offers specialized programs in volunteer development and management; group leadership, adult education, and contract services in education and organizational management. Each program is designed to meet the specific needs of the client by providing positive and practical learning experiences. Workshops are highly interactive and experiential, combining group and individual challenges, lectures, and personal assessment tools to achieve successful results. Private consultations can assist organizations in program planning, development, and evaluation.

Ann Jacobson & Associates

400 West 49th Terrace, Suite 2068, Kansas City, MO 64112
E-mail: annrj5@aol.com

▶ Ann consults on an individual and organizational level in volunteer administration, career development, life coaching, boardsmanship, curriculum development and older adult volunteering. She formerly taught at the University of Kansas, Rockhurst, and comunity colleges. She is a former vice president of United Way, and has 20 years' experience with nonprofits, including volunteerism, aging issues, and information and referral. She is past chair of AVA curriculum development committee and author and publisher of hands-on, low-cost publications: *Volunteer Management Handbook, Self-Study Guide for Volunteer Programs,* and *Principles for the Field of Volunteerism.*

KM Consulting & Training Connection

7303 Fire Oak Drive, Austin, TX 78759
Tel: 512-219-7058; FAX: 512-219-1395
E-mail: kmccleskey@aol.com

▶ For over a decade, Kathy McCleskey has developed curriculum and conducted workshops and program evaluations for-profit and nonprofit organizations in the United States and in five foreign countries. A sampling of workshop titles includes, but is not limited to: Volunteer Management, Problem Solving, Team Building, Communication, Motivation, and Situational Leadership.

Leipper Management Group

P.O. Box 21481, Reno, NV 89515
Tel/FAX: 775-972-5011
E-mail: Nvassoc@attglobal.net

▶ Diane Leipper has over 20 years' experience in volunteer management. She has been a program director, trainer, board member, and volunteer for a variety of nonprofit organizations. Diane has provided management consulting, presentations, training workshops, and informational meetings to various volunteer programs and service organizations. Topics include volunteers' role in disaster and public relations plans, technology planning, and building inclusive volunteer programs.

Macduff/Bunt Associates

821 Lincoln Street, Walla Walla, WA 99362
Tel: 509-529-0244; FAX: 509-529-8865
E-Mail: mba@bmi.net, mba@volunteertoday.com;
WWW: http://www.volunteertoday.com/publish.html

▶ This firm provides training on volunteer management and administration, as well as books and kits on all aspects of volunteerism and consulting services on volunteer management, training, and organizational change. Publications on volunteerism include the electronic newsletter *Volunteer Today* (see separate listing under Volunteerism—Internet Sites).

McKinley Professional Development

1555 Sherman Avenue, Suite 180, Evanston, IL
Tel: 773-509-6435

▶ Connie McKinley, MS, CVA, is the principal of McKinley Professional Development. She works with individuals, organizations, and businesses to increase their effectiveness through career management, improving performance, and organizational consulting. As a trainer, she leads sessions covering topics of managerial productivity, communication, motivation, networking, stress management, and problem solving. Connie teaches diversity awareness in Harper College's Certificate in Volunteer Management program, facilitates certification planning workshops for AVA, and has taught at Harold Washington College.

Merrill Associates

101 Orchard Lane, Columbus, OH 43214
Tel/FAX: 614-262-8219
E-mail: mmerrill@merrillassoc.com (Mary Merrill);
WWW: http://www.merrillassoc.com/

▶ This firm provides consultation and training services nationally and internationally for nonprofit boards of trustees, corporate employee volunteer programs, and nonprofit volunteer programs.

Merrill's extensive background in board development and volunteer management ranges from grassroots volunteer organizations to arts organizations, to communities of faith, to sophisticated statewide organizations with extensive staff. Focus areas include: strategic planning; nonprofit board development; volunteer management services; leadership/change management; communication/team building/collaborations; and corporate volunteerism. Merrill also offers workshops (see Workshops, Seminars, and Training).

Nonprofit Management Solutions, Inc.

P.O. Box 7536, Hollywood, FL 33081
Tel: 954-985-9489; FAX: 954-989-3442
E-mail: terriet@nonprofitmgtsolutions.com (Terrie Temkin, Principal); WWW: www.nonprofitmgtsolutions.com

▶ This firm specializes in enhancing the efficiency and effectiveness of nonprofits through board, staff, and organizational development. Our services include board development, defining roles and responsibilities, enhancing communication, facilitating change, facilitating retreats, mission-based planning, needs assessments, organizational audits, policy development, staff development, team building, visioning, and volunteer program development.

Frank Pomata

35 Satellite Drive, Islip Terrace, NY 11752
Tel: 631-277-7365, 631-277-7365; FAX: 631-277-7365 (must call first)
E-mail: Beacon006@aol.com

▶ Frank Pomata is a nonprofit and volunteer management consultant. He can assist your organization in a variety of areas, including staff and volunteer training, conference planning, and program development. Areas of expertise include establishing and enhancing volunteer programs in nonprofit agencies, schools, government, and corporate settings; developing partnerships and collaborative ventures between nonprofit organizations, government, and corporations; implementing "customer service"-oriented practices in nonprofit settings; and developing publicity and marketing strategies for nonprofit entities. He is available for on-site, telephone, and online consulting assignments.

Stallings & Associates

1717 Courtney Avenue, Suite 201, Pleasanton, CA 94588
Tel: 925-426-8335; FAX: 925-426-8335
E-mail: bettystall@aol.com

▶ Betty Stallings, President, Building Better Skills, is an international trainer, keynote speaker, and consultant specializing in management of volunteer programs, fund raising, and board development. She has authored five books in the areas of volunteer management and fund development. Betty is known for her vitality, inspiring message, engaging humor, practical presentations, and valuable resources. She teaches at universities and is a popular trainer for state, national, and international conferences. She received the 1999 Harriet Naylor Distinguished Member Award from AVA. Services include consultation (volunteer management, board development, fund raising, planning, team building, start-up organizations), facilitation (board and/or staff retreats, long-range planning, team building), training (volunteer management, fund development, corporate partnerships, fund-raising events and volunteers, board/staff development, team building [utilizing Performax's Personal Profile]),

materials development (volunteer programs, fund raising, foundation/corporate grants), and keynote talks (available for regional, state, national conference meetings on the above topics). She is the author of *Getting to Yes Fund Raising, Volunteer Program Assessment Guide, Resource Kit for Managers of Volunteers,* and *Building Staff Commitment and Competence in Utilizing Volunteers.*

Strategic Nonprofit Resources

2939 Van Ness Street NW, Suite 1248, Washington, DC 20008
Tel: 202-966-0859; FAX: 202-966-3301
E-mail: cpirtle@compuserve.com (Connie Pirtle);
WWW: www.volunteertoday.com/Connie.html

▶ This firm provides guidance and assistance to nonprofit organizations in the areas of board/staff development and volunteer program management. Services include volunteer program management (assessments of volunteer programs—either one or more elements or the entire program; customized training workshops for small and large groups tailored to meet the needs of the group; executive coaching for volunteer officers, volunteer program managers, senior staff, and executive directors; management of volunteers for special events; public speaking on all elements of volunteer program management); boards of directors (one- or two-day retreats customized to meet the needs of the board; self-assessment tools; executive coaching for board presidents and executive directors; resources to strengthen board committees; public speaking on the roles and responsibilities of boards).

Trudy Seita Associates

907 51st Street, Vienna, WV 26105
Tel: 304-295-6527; FAX: 304-295-8719
E-mail: ctseita@citynet.net (Trudy Seita, Principal)

▶ A noted trainer and author with 15 years of experience, Trudy provides seminars, workshops, keynotes, organizational consulting, and meeting planning and facilitation to organizations across the United States and Canada. Areas of expertise include organizational change, strategic planning, leadership skills, basic volunteer program management, marketing, communications, public relations, resource development, stress management, and training skills. Trudy is the author of *Leadership Skills for the New Age of Nonprofits, Communications: A Positive Message From You,* and *Change: Meet It and Greet It* (with Sue Waechter).

Don R. Simmons, PhD

Leadership Training Network, Golden Gate Baptist Theological Seminary, 201 Seminary Drive Mill Valley, CA 94941
Tel: 415-380-1468; FAX: 415-380-1452
E-mail: donsimmons@ggbts.edu; WWW: http://www.ggbts.edu

▶ Don's areas of expertise include team development, conflict management, grant writing, collegiate volunteer administration, and creative collaborations. His work focuses on mobilizing church and other religious volunteers in systematic, organization-wide volunteering. He is experienced with college volunteers, church volunteers, volunteer centers, United Way, and arts organizations.

Stevenson Consultants, Inc.

P.O. Box 4528, Sioux City, IA 51104
Tel: 712-239-3010; FAX: 712-239-2166
E-mail: ssteven105@aol.com (Scott C. Stevenson, Principal), inquiry@stevensoninc.com; WWW: http://www.stevensoninc.com

▶ Stevenson Consultants, Inc. publishes the monthly newsletter, *The Volunteer Management Report*. In addition, they publish the monthly newsletter, *Successful Fund Raising*. They have also published several "hands-on" manuals including: *The Best Ever Directory of Special Events, Solicitation Skills Builder, Prospect Research Fundamentals, Successful Capital Campaigns: From Start to Finish*, and *Profitable Annual Gift Strategies*.

Volunteer Management Associates

320 South Cedar Brook Road, Boulder, CO 80304
Tel: 800-944-1470, 303-447-0558; FAX: 303-447-1749
E-mail: marlene@volunteermanagement.com,
rosemaryw@compuserve.com;
WWW: http://www.volunteermanagement.com/

▶ Founded in 1975 by Marlene Wilson, Volunteer Management Associates (VMA) is a consulting and publishing company dedicated to providing quality volunteer management training and resources for organizations and churches that utilize volunteers. They present workshops, specialized training, or lectures on a variety of topics relating to volunteerism. The *Volunteer Resource Catalog* lists books, audiotapes, and videotapes available for sale.

Insurance, Liability, and Risk Management

CIMA Companies, Inc./Volunteers Insurance Service (VIS)

Corporate Insurance Management Assistance, 216 South Peyton Street, Alexandria, VA 22314-2892
Tel: 800-468-4200; FAX: 703-739-0761

250 South President Street, Baltimore, MD 21202
Tel: 410-752- 2350
E-mail: inbox@cimaworld.com (Vicki Brooks, Account Executive); WWW: http://www.cimaworld.com

▶ The CIMA Companies' Volunteers Insurance Service (VIS) program, in operation over 30 years, provides low-cost insurance protection for nonprofit organizations, their boards, and volunteers. This program to insure volunteers is unique. For only a few dollars a year per volunteer, you can protect them in the event they are injured, or injure someone else, during their volunteer duty—rather than insuring the volunteers on your general liability policy. They also provide accident insurance for participants in alternative sentencing and work release programs. They serve over 5,000 nonprofits nationwide. VIS provides the following services to members: publishing *VIS Connections* newsletter; maintaining for members' use a library of information relating to management of risks in the nonprofit organization; researching available and appropriate insurance relating to volunteer activities; designing and administering insurance programs and compiling underwriting information; providing consultation on risk management issues at no charge to their members, via a toll-free line (800-468-4200); and assisting members, on request, with matters relating to insurance. Also useful is the FAQ (frequently asked questions) for Nonprofits—Volunteer Insurance section on their Web site, accessible at *http://www.cimaworld.com/htdocs/faq.cfm.*

Recognition Products

Baudville

Putting Applause on Paper, 5380 52nd Street SE,
Grand Rapids, MI 495-9765
Tel: 800-728-0888
E-mail: DebraS@baudville.com (Debra Sikanas, President);
WWW: http://www.baudville.com

▶ Items for recognition, team building, and special events.

C.D.&M., Inc.

P.O. Box 970115, Boca Raton, FL 33497
Tel: 561-487-5684; FAX: 561-487-1439
E-mail: cdm9@aol.com; WWW: http://www.volunteergifts.com/

▶ Recognition gifts for volunteers since 1981.

CAHHS Volunteer Sales Center

California Hospitals & Health Systems, P.O. Box 340100,
Sacramento CA 95834-0100
Tel: 916-928-3950; FAX: 916-928-1733
E-mail: gcaruso@calhealth.org

▶ Volunteer recognitions and gifts. CAHHS offers a free catalog that also includes descriptions of a choice of books and newsletters specifically written for the volunteer sector.

Cup of Kindness

International Incu-Idea, Inc., PMB 301, 829 Shields Street,
Fort Collins, CO 80521
Tel: 800-949-2799; FAX: 970-490-1680
E-mail: sara@cupofkindness.com;
WWW: http://www.cupofkindness.com/

▶ This organization offers acknowledgment gifts for donors, contributors, volunteers, family, or friends—anyone who has shown you kindness or generosity. Use the Cup of Kindness™ in nonprofit fund raisers, in school or charity events, or as employee recognition gifts or incentives.

Dinn Bros.

68 Winter Street, P.O. Box 111, Holyoke, MA 01041
Tel: 800-628-9657/828-3466, 413-536-3902; FAX: 800-876-7497
E-mail: sales@DinnTrophy.com; WWW: http://www.dinntrophy.com/

▶ Free 32-page catalog of recognition awards, plaques, and trophies at wholesale prices.

Emblem & Badge, Inc.

P.O. Box 6226, 859 North Main Street, Providence, RI 02940-6226
Tel: 800-875-5444, 401-331-5444; FAX: 401-421-7941
WWW: http://www.recognition.com

▶ This firm is a manufacturer of specialty items for awards, recognition, and advertising (glassware, trophies, medals, laminations, certificates, and more). A free catalog is available.

Great Events

135 Dupont Street, P. O. Box 760, Plainview, NY 11803-0760
Tel: 888-433-8368
E-mail: Events4You@aol.com

▶ Great Events offers a free brochure, "How to Plan a Great Event." It is ideal for meetings, conferences, fairs, trade shows, and other special events. Include your name, company name, mail address, and e-mail address.

Harrison Promotions, Inc.

7926 Queen Street, Wyndmoor, PA 19038-8037
Tel: 800-929-2271, 215-233-6101; FAX: 888-826-9926, 215-233-6102
E-mail: HarsnPromo@aol.com;
WWW: http://www.promo-web.com/harrisonpromo

▶ Distributor of promotional products, specializing in recognition items for volunteers, staff and board members, as well as for program promotion, organizational awareness, and products for resale; representing more than 2,500 manufacturers of imprinted promotional and advertising products, the company specializes in working with nonprofit organizations to help them find products that meet their special needs. They will help you create gifts that appeal to volunteers of all ages, both sexes, and in all types of roles. Their "sampler" product catalogs contain more than 300 items, and they maintain 370,000 additional items on a CD-ROM. They carry more than 15,000 different types of products.

Main Event Advertising

10379 W. Fair Avenue, Apt. B, Littleton, CO 80127-5536
Tel: 303-973-2866
E-mail: mainevent@promotionalproducts.com;
WWW: http://www.promotionalproducts.com/distrib/dist/pp306/main.htm

▶ Recognitions, promotional items.

The March Company

2815 Academy Parkway North NE, Albuquerque, NM 87509-4408
Tel: 800-33MARCH (336-2724), 505-345-2521; FAX: 505-345-0407
WWW: http://www.marchco.com

▶ The March Company has been a leading supplier of custom emblematic jewelry and embroidered patches for 20 years. They design pins/patches of your design/logo, plus over 2,000 in-stock products, including commemorative postage stamp related products (1,500 jewelry items, award plaques, Christmas ornaments). A free color catalog is available.

Media Specs and Promotions, Inc.

P.O. Box 36367, Denver, CO 80236
Tel: 303-986-5926
E-mail: mediaspec@promotionalproducts.com;
WWW: http://www.promotionalproducts.com/distrib/dist/pp298/main.htm

▶ Recognitions, promotional items.

Midnight Oil Printing & Promotions

P. O. Box 9851, Colorado Springs, CO 80932
Tel: 719-573-4363
E-mail: midniteoil@promotionalproducts.com;
WWW: http://www.promotionalproducts.com/distrib/dist/pp294/main.htm

▶ Recognitions, promotional items.

Modlich Engraving

301 North Hague Avenue, Columbus, OH 43204
Tel: 877-844-4101, 614-276-1439; FAX: 614-279-4594
E-mail: sales@modlichs.com; WWW: http://www.modlichs.com

▶ Engraved bricks and tile since 1936.

Multiple Choice

P. O. Box 2592, Greeley, CO 80632-2592
Tel: 303-353-7448
E-mail: multchoic@promotionalproducts.com;
WWW: http://www.promotionalproducts.com/distrib/dist/pp303/main.htm

▶ Recognitions, promotional items.

Philanthropic Service for Institutions/Philanthropic GIFT

12501 Old Columbia Pike, Silver Spring MD 20904-6600
Tel: 800-622-1662, 301-680-6131; FAX: 301-680-6137
E-mail: clientservice@philanthropicservice.com;
WWW: http://www.philanthropicgift.com/

▶ Donor and volunteer recognition products.

Points of Light Foundation

Catalog Services, P.O. Box 79110, Baltimore, MD 21279-0110
Tel: 800-272-8306; FAX: 703-803-9291

Points of Light Foundation, 1400 I Street NW, Suite 800 Washington, DC 20006

Tel: 202-729-8000; FAX: 202-729-8100

E-mail: volnet@pointsoflight.org;
WWW: http://www.pointsoflight.org/volunteermarketplace/

▶ Volunteer catalog listing recognition items.

Positive Promotions

40-01 168th Street, Flushing, NY 11358
Tel: 800-635-2666

▶ Distributes catalog for "Volunteer Appreciation Week."

Recognition Enterprises

214 Woodford Avenue, Plainville, CT 06062
Tel: 800-960-2677; FAX: 860-793-8794
WWW: http://www.recognition-gifts.com/

▶ Recognition Enterprises provides quality products to corporations for many purposes such as employee recognition or reward, new client welcome or thank you, general token of appreciation, or seasonal/calendar events.

Sanford White Company, Inc.

P.O. Box 157, Pawtucket, RI 02862-0157
Tel: 800-245-7825, 401-726-2310; FAX: 401-728-3080
E-mail: Information@Sanfordwhitecompany.com, SWCO2310@aol.com; WWW: www.sanfordwhitecompany.com

▶ They manufacture a wide range of items, both stock and custom, for religious denominations and nonprofit organizations such as schools, hospitals, colleges, youth groups, service organizations, and the like. Established in 1953, it is a manufacturer of custom recognition items to donors and volunteers for annual campaigns, major gift clubs, capital campaigns, special events, and planned giving programs; discounts available to members of NSFRE, CASE, AHP, NAIS, NCDC, or NCSC. A free catalog is available.

Shaw-Barton, Inc.

4218 Senneth Street, McFarland, WI 53558
Tel: 608-838-9051
E-mail: Alden@itis.com

▶ Shaw-Barton is the nation's largest manufacturer of advertising specialties, including calendars, direct mail, greeting cards, foil certificates, plaques, and more. A free catalog is available.

Successories

2520 Diehl Rd, Aurora, IL 60504
Tel: 800-535-2773; FAX: 800-932-9673
WWW: http://www.successories.com/

▶ Successories carries items to motivate, inspire, and reward. Their collection of themed merchandise is designed to promote a positive outlook, celebrate human achievement, and inspire excellence in your career, your business, and your life.

The Thanks Company

136 Woodberry Drive, P.O. Box 220, Cherryville NC 28021-0220
Tel/FAX: 888-875-0903, 704-435-8828
E-mail: CustomerService@thankscompany.com;
WWW: http://www.thankscompany.com/

▶ Cards and recognition gifts are designed to help you express appreciation to your volunteers and to other special people who deserve your recognition.

VolunCheer.com

1139 Doon Court, Sunnyvale, CA 94087
Tel: 510-339-0810; FAX: 510-339-2587
E-mail: info@VolunCHEER.com, john@voluncheer.com (John L. Lipp), LippVCCA@aol.com; WWW: http://www.voluncheer.com/

▶ Established in 1999, it is a national firm offering a full line of recognition products and publications designed to enhance volunteerism in the nonprofit, public, and private sectors.

Software Vendors

Aspen Software

1019 Juniper Street, Quakertown, PA 18951
Tel: 215-536-7648; FAX: 800-446-1373
E-mail: aspensof@ptd.net, gordonr@ptd.net (Gordon S. Roeder Jr., President); WWW: http://www.aspen-sftwre.com/

▶ Aspen is the developer of Trail Blazer®, a fully integrated campaign management software package. Trail Blazer provides nearly unlimited features and capabilities in the areas of supporter tracking, financial management, and a voter database. Features include easy installation; integrated (seamless) accounting; voter database; mail merge; voter polling and phone banking; fully PAC compatible; auto dial feature; rapid data entry; volunteer tracking (search for volunteers quickly by name or other criteria; match needs with qualifications and availability; generate thank you letters; automatically dial volunteers with the click of a mouse); import/export compare; excellent for *any* size campaign or PAC. Trail Blazer also

features approved reporting, online FEC guides, and electronic forms filing.

BWB Associates, Ltd.

10-A South 7th Street, Akron, PA 17501-1331
Tel: 800-234-4846, 717-859-6642; FAX: 717-859-6643
E-mail: BruceBech@aol.com (Bruce W. Bechtold, President);
WWW: http://members.aol.com/BruceBech/index.html

▶ BWB is the distributor of Basic V.I.M., designed for volunteer agencies that track and manage their own volunteers. The V.I.M. program was started in January 1989 and has undergone many revisions and enhancements since that time. They listen to their clients and give them what they want and need to better manage their volunteer programs. They have hundreds of satisfied clients all over the United States and Canada; and V.I.M.-RSVP&VO Edition, designed for the retired and senior volunteer program and other volunteer outplacement programs, such as colleges/universities, corporate volunteer programs, and volunteer referral agencies. This program currently meets the reporting requirements for the RSVP/Corporation for National & Community Service. They will be coming out with a major upgrade of this program by the end of 1996. Many new features are specifically developed for university/school-based volunteer programs in which the volunteers are placed in other agencies in the community to serve. Some of the new features are designed to help track "service-learning" and other course-related volunteering.

Enscribe Technologies, Inc.

Tel: 905-689-8926
E-mail: info@enscribe.net; WWW: http://www.servus.org/

▶ Enscribe is the distributor of Servus Volunteer Software Database. Features include: any information you need to know about the people associated with your organization is stored on one of seven different Notecards (each person—whether a volunteer, an interested volunteer, a project director, a community contact, or anyone else—has his or her own set of Notecards. Each of the Notecards is used to store a different category of information about the people in your organization. They store schedules, addresses, contacts made, awards won, attributes, how you can get in touch with your volunteers, when they are available, what their skills and interests are, and in which projects they're involved); view several records simultaneously (if you want to see all of your people or projects at once, you can press the "List" button on any Notecard); track project addresses, schedules, needs, and more; match volunteers with projects; print personalized letters and labels; print many useful reports. They also offer the Servus "WebWorker" program if you want to attract more volunteers, offer higher-quality service, and post your lastest volunteer opportunities.

Futures Program

P.O. Box 16355, Golden, CO 80401
Tel: 800-467-5871
E-mail: fp2001@worldnet.att.net;
WWW: http://www.schoolvolunteer.org/

▶ Futures Program is a system designed to recruit and manage volunteers at the elementary, middle, and high school levels. It is a platform that links a volunteer core together for an entire school district. The Golden Futures Foundation became a reality as a nonprofit organization in 1989, four years following its initial development of the Futures Program at Golden High School, Golden, Colorado. Since that time, the program has been offered to hundreds of communities across North America. Today, the Futures Program is being used in nearly 150 high schools in 31 states and two countries. It is estimated that the Futures Program has served in excess of 250,000 high school students since its origin. It is a systematic approach to develop, staff, and manage a high school volunteer program.

GCi Management Systems

221 Bedford Road, Suite 108, Bedford, TX 76022
Tel: 800-889-9356, 817-590-9582; FAX: 817-280-9838
E-mail: GCI@npyp.net; WWW: http://www.npyp.net/GCI

▶ GCi has been providing management software to nonprofit organizations since 1983. The company's primary software designers have over 40 years of professional fund-raising and volunteer management experience with national nonprofit organizations. They develop software products to meet the unique fund-raising, donor, membership, and volunteer management requirements of nonprofit organizations. They distribute The Consultant, a system used by nonprofit organizations (associations, health care, educational, museums, arts, theater, youth, political, religious, zoos) in the United States, Canada, Europe, and Asia. The Volunteer Management component tracks the value of donated time and volunteer availability by date and tasks; driver license or insurance renewal management; and generates numerous volunteer activity reports.

Granite Consulting

401 11215 Jasper Avenue, Edmonton, Alberta, Canada, T5K 0L5
Tel:780-853-8308; FAX: 780-853-4724
E-mail: ttoews@agt.net (Tony Toews);
WWW: http://www.granite.ab.ca

▶ Granite is the developer of VolStar, the complete tracking system to manage hundreds or thousands of volunteers for major special events. Planning a major event that involves hundreds or thousands of volunteers is no easy task. You want to get the best use of your valued volunteers, and make sure important details don't slip through the cracks. VolStar helps you cover all the bases! VolStar is the software solution for sporting, cultural, or other events that involve 500 or more volunteers. VolStar simplifies the planning and paperwork, so you can help your event managers and volunteers perform at their best. Features of VolStar include: builds a detailed structure of each committee/component and its needs for volunteers; allows volunteers to enter their information, including availability and preferences, via the Internet; produces information on volunteer availability, preferences, and scheduling; matches volunteers' preferences with committee needs; schedules volunteers, including pre/post-event times, for preparatory, event, and winddown activities; generates a wide variety of management reports and statistics to let you easily see where volunteers are still needed; prints mailing labels and identification tags and eliminates duplicate mailings to households, saving on postage, materials, and envelope stuffing time; monitors positions requiring special security clearance; generates "to-do" items and checklists by volunteer; and tracks your unique requirements such as clothing issued, fees paid, languages spoken, or security access codes.

Magic Application Software

2160 17th Street NE, Rochester, MN 55906
Tel: 507-282-2642

▶ This company distributes VolMagic computer software, designed to help small or mid-size volunteer centers, student placement offices, and other volunteer clearinghouses manage their volunteer referral system. Features include: an agency/job database than can be searched to locate volunteer jobs that match the skills and interests of volunteers; a skills bank to locate volunteers who have the skills and availability to match with community needs; a referrals database to follow up with volunteers already referred and to report volunteer referral information to the agencies being served; a reporting system that generates statistics on agencies, volunteers, volunteer jobs, and referrals (labels can also be created); and the ability to run in a single-user or multiuser environment; IBM-compatible; free demo disk available; multiuser capability, data conversion, unlimited phone support, and on-site training also available at additional charge.

Performance Masters, Inc.

2969 Euclid Heights Boulevard, Cleveland Heights, OH 44118

P.O. Box 40180, Cleveland, OH 44140-0180
Tel: 800-745-5204, 216-835-5204; FAX: 216-371-1694
E-mail: support@performancemasters.com (Mark E. Wernet, President), sales@performancemasters.com;
WWW: http://www.performancemasters.com

▶ Since 1992 Performance Masters has provided software and related services solely to the nonprofit sector. They have been the distributor of *TDS Volunteer File*™ since 1988, an integrated volunteer management software program designed exclusively to meet the needs of volunteer service organizations and other organizations using volunteer workers; maintains complete personnel records, easily generates all reports, tracks required tests, hours, skills, assignments, availability, and community service. The software comes in three versions: TDS Volunteer File Basic, TDS Volunteer File Version 3, and TDS Volunteer File Version 4. It consists of Volunteer File Data Management System Hours Reporter, Scheduler & Calendars, Trainings/Requirements Recorder, Comprehensive Community Service Maintenance, Award Calculator, Workstation Sign In/Out, Skills & Assignment Tracker, Client Database, Report Generator, Mailing Label Generator, Membership Rosters (Trainings/Requirements Recorder, Report Generator, and Mailing Label Generator not included in Basic program). It operates on any IBM compatible microcomputer that operates under the MS or PC DOS operating system version 3.3 or higher. Toll-free technical support and comprehensive user's manual are provided. A working demo is available.

Polytheoretics

P.O. Box 1825, Wake Forest, NC 27588
Tel: 800-853-5056, 919-554-0388; FAX: 919-554-9231
E-mail: polyt@mindspring.com;
WWW: http://polyt.home.mindspring.com/polyt/polytheoretics.htm

▶ Polytheoretics distributes ProVelle™, which is a fully relational database keeping records and tracking volunteer availability and activities. The basic version of the program has an easy-to-use interface; keeps records of personal data, work, orientation, PPD/Lat tests, dues, and other items; tracks volunteer availability; produces labels with optional bar-coding, mail lists, and automated mail merge for work statements, letters, and postcards; produces volunteer award alerts; includes preformatted reports and unlimited custom reports; and has an optional touch-screen time clock system available. ProVelle is available in two editions. The ProVelle

Professional Edition comes prepared to manage volunteer activities, communications, and records. The ProVelle Healthcare Edition contains all of the features of the Professional Edition, but was developed specifically for hospitals, in collaboration with several large, high-visibility accredited institutions.

Red Ridge Software Company

205 North Morton Street, Bloomington, IN 47404
Tel: 800-245-4413, 812-336-3300; FAX: 812-336-4495
E-mail: sales@redridge.com; WWW: http://www.redridge.com/

▶ Red Ridge is the developer of VolunteerWorks, software for volunteer leaders. It runs on nearly any computer or network that has the Microsoft® Windows® operating system. It's designed to make day-to-day volunteer record keeping easy: clearly organized tabs make it easy to find or add information; it uses popular Windows features like the clipboard, help, and tool bars; plus, it's easy to set up and maintain—even for those with little or no computer experience. It is complete with features like prospective volunteer tracking, applicant processing automatic reminders, volunteer–job matching, recognition queuing, automatic status management, and much more, all in addition to basic record-keeping features. It comes with common volunteer office reports already set up (like lists, labels, letters, hour reports, job profiles, and more), plus a Report Builder you can use to adapt the sample reports or create new reports of your own. Their "Filters" enable users to query the database for special sets of volunteers. Comprehensive set-up tools enable you to customize VolunteerWorks to a wide variety of volunteer program settings.

SP Extreme

E-mail: info@spextreme.com;
WWW: http://www.spextreme.com/voltrack/

▶ SP Extreme distributes Vol-Track, an easy-to-use system that enables a user to track volunteers by hours they work and by the different organizations where they volunteer. This system will allow the user to better manage volunteer information by using reports that can be generated at any time. In addition, Vol-Track has input cards that can be printed and distributed to volunteers and organizations to obtain all personal or hour information. These input cards are designed to match the data fields in the system exactly, which allows for ease of data entry. Features include predesigned input cards; agency and volunteer reports; customizable toolbar; detail information handling; import/export of data; generate reports over a specific time period; and multiple report styles.

Salmon Falls Software

1561 Hidden Bridge Road, El Dorado Hills, CA 95762
Tel: 916-933-2035
E-mail: infotraker@aol.com;
WWW: http://members.aol.com/infotraker/volunter.htm

▶ Salmon Falls is the developer of Volunteer Info Tracker, a Windows software program. Implementation possibilities include: volunteer agencies use the Volunteer Info Tracker software to refer volunteers to agencies with projects having matching needs; hospitals and courts use the Volunteer Info Tracker software to refer and track volunteers that are volunteering for specific court and hospital duties and projects; businesses are using the Volunteer Info Tracker software to track the needs of and place employee mentors into the regional school districts to support curriculum; and schools are using the Volunteer Info Tracker software to match students with specific businesses which are working with the education system to provide school to career opportunities.

Samaritan Software

4885 South 900 East, Suite 304-A, Salt Lake City, UT 84117
Tel: 888-904-6060, 801-262-3969; FAX: 801-262-3966
E-mail: info@samaritan.com; WWW: http://www.samaritan.com/

▶ Samaritan distributes the Recruiter and Coordinator volunteer management software packages. Recruiter is a Web-based program that works in the background of your Web site. The functions that Recruiter adds to your site are: for volunteers (searching for service opportunities by zip code and personal attributes [up to 20 categories]; Intelli-Match. Recruiter will make suggestions to the volunteers about the best opportunities; registration for selected service opportunities); for you (automatic synchronization with your coordinator database. This allows your day-to-day changes to be automatically uploaded to your Web site. Additionally, all volunteers who register online are transferred directly into your local database. For organizations you contract with: security verification that they can access your Web systems; registration of their organization and opportunity data; editing of their organization and opportunity data; transferring of their profiles to online fund-raising systems [optional]). Coordinator is a software application that works on either your PC or directly from the Internet (Coordinator/ASP). It is very flexible, allowing you to choose everything from matching attributes to which functions you wish to use on a daily basis. Everything you don't want gets "turned off." Features include: volunteer, organization, and opportunity registration; Intelli-Match (makes suggestions for the best placement of volunteers); scheduling; tracking; impact analysis (evaluates the impact volunteers have on community objectives); and reporting (including custom report building).

Selston Volunteer Management Systems

1366 Cape Cod Drive, Parksville, BC V9P 2T5 Canada
Tel: 250-954-1921
E-mail: selston@home.com; WWW: http://www.selston.ca/

▶ Since 1991, they have worked with hundreds of nonprofit organizations throughout Canada, the United States, the United Kingdom, and Australia to develop a series of relational database computer programs. These programs have been designed to assist administrators, directors, and coordinators of volunteers in the effective management of their volunteer resources to enable the daily scheduling of their dependent clients and Association members. They are developers of the Selston Series M software package, designed to enable a community-based nonprofit organization to effectively schedule volunteers for in-house volunteer services such as seniors' activity centers, municipal sports facilities, and hospital volunteer departments. The program provides a method for in-house volunteer coordinators to schedule and maintain an ongoing record of the facility's work requirements, the volunteer's availability and skills, and the scheduling of work assignments and temporary volunteer replacements. The program will record and monitor all demographic, availability, and skills data relating to all volunteers. It will record volunteer hours worked, courses and/or workshops taken, birthday and seniority lists, and all current and outstanding assignments between any two dates. It will provide comprehensive reports for analysis, schedule work assignments, search work categories and availability lists for a volunteer, print a selection of lists and address labels of all or selected lists of volunteers, and allow customization for local area and interests of organizations.

They are also developers of The Selston Series P software package, designed to enable a community-based nonprofit organization to effectively schedule volunteers to meet the requirements of community-dependent clients. The program will record and monitor all demographic and operational data relating to volunteers and clients, marry service calls made by clients with volunteer's availability and skills, then record each volunteers' activities in response to the client's needs. It will record volunteer hours worked, mileage, expenses, courses and/or workshops taken, birthday and seniority lists, and all current and outstanding services between any two dates. It will provide comprehensive reports for analysis, schedule work activities, search work categories and availability lists for a volunteer, print a selection of lists and address labels of all or selected lists of clients and volunteers, and allow customization for local area and interests of organizations.

TechRocks

One Penn Center, 1617 John F. Kennedy Boulevard, Philadelphia, PA 19103
Tel: 215-561-3608
E-mail: info@techrocks.org;
WWW: http://www.techrocks.org/ebase/index.lasso

▶ TechRocks is the distributor of ebase™, a free software that enables nonprofit organizations to manage their most important resources: their relationships with their members, donors, activists, and volunteers. ebase is also a technical support model that helps nonprofit staff develop relationships with other organizations, building a self-help community where novice and experienced data managers can exchange ideas about building communities while building better databases. Using a license derived from the "Open Source" model, ebase source code and passwords are available to anyone who owns a copy of Filemaker, and the data dictionary is distributed freely: Anyone who wants to copy the logic of the program on any other database platform can do so without restriction.

Technology Resource Assistance Center (TRAC)

610 Cowper Avenue, Palo Alto, CA 94301
Tel: 800-676-5831; FAX: 650-853-1677
E-mail: info@tracworld.com; WWW: http://www.tracworld.com/

▶ TRAC has been producing software programs for nonprofit organizations since 1986. TRAC currently distributes programs for both the Windows environment as well as Macintosh. TRAC is the developer of Exceed! Written in Microsoft's Visual FoxPro for Windows, the Exceed! program, combined with modules, includes the following features: donor tracking, gift management, electronic funds transfer, online gifts, volunteer scheduling, grant tracking, grant giving, mailing list management, contact management, intuitive reporting, automated mail merge, and export. MacTRAC remains one of the most widely used fund-raising programs for the Macintosh. MacTRAC also gives you the ability to track donors, prospects, and volunteers.

Volunteer Information Control Tracking & Analysis (VICTA)

1717 Comox Street, Suite 102, Vancouver, BC V6G 1P5 Canada
Tel: 604-681-7775; FAX: 604-681-9907
E-mail: instanet@istar.ca ((Michael Corber);
WWW: www.victasystem.com

▶ Especially designed for volunteer centers, VICTA's main purpose is to help volunteer referral organizations to match potential volunteers with requests from various agencies. At the same time, VICTA fills many of the volunteer centers' other needs.

Volunteer Software

628 South Second Street, West Missoula, MT 59801-1830
Tel: 800-391-9446, 406-721-0113; FAX: 303-265-9288
E-mail: Info@volsoft.com; WWW: http://www.volsoft.com/

▶ This company is the developer of RSVP Reporter, designed for retired and senior volunteer programs and volunteer centers, and Volunteer Reporter Professional, designed for hospitals, parks, libraries, and other organizations that use volunteers in-house and need to schedule their volunteers. RSVP Reporter allows you to place volunteers in suitable positions around your community and keep track of their hours. It prints dozens of different reports including quarterly reports, project profile, hours served, and mailing labels. Features include: fully Windows 95/98/NT compatible; data protection prevents silly mistakes; customizable skills bank; quick and easy data entry; online help; optional password protection; filters for limiting chosen records; cut and paste; easily see skills and groups for any volunteer; visual display of volunteers' placements and hours; multiuser for any network—no additional costs no matter how big your network; and backups are made as industry-standard Zip files, which can easily be sent over the Internet. A DOS version of the program is available to run under Windows 3.x systems. Volunteer Reporter Professional is the Windows version of the popular Volunteer Reporter Professional. It is designed to help you manage, schedule, and track all of the volunteers you use within your organization. This program differs from the RSVP Reporter in that it tracks volunteers serving within your own organization, not placed in other organizations as the RSVP Reporter tracks. It still enables you to match volunteers with suitable positions by using the user-defined skills bank, but you can also print schedules for both your volunteers and job supervisors so everyone knows who's serving when. It prints dozens of different reports including quarterly reports, project profile, hours served, and mailing labels.

Workshops, Seminars, and Training

Knowledge Transfer

3932 Cielo Place, Fullerton, CA 92835
Tel: 714-525-5469; FAX: 714-525-9352
E-mail: knowtrans@aol.com; WWW: http://www.volunteerpro.com/,
http://www.volunteerpro.com/seminars_dates.htm

▶ This organization facilitates learning by conducting training for leaders in nonprofits, government, and education. Their training events are common sense, down-to-earth, and easy to apply once you get back home. Their niche is volunteer leadership, and they are focused on the development of excellent volunteer programs. They offer seminars nationwide and on-site. Topics include: encouraging the heart; recruitment; retaining; recognition; leadership skills for volunteer programs; coaching; team building; empowering your volunteers; motivating your volunteers; evaluating volunteers; minimizing the risks in your volunteer program; develop a risk management system; screening; and legal analysis of volunteer programs.

Merrill Associates

101 Orchard Lane, Columbus, OH 43214
Tel/FAX: 614-262-8219
E-mail: Mary Merrill (mmerrill@merrillassoc.com);
WWW: http://www.merrillassoc.com/

▶ This firm provides consultation and training services nationally and internationally for nonprofit boards of trustees, corporate employee volunteer programs, and nonprofit volunteer programs. Workshop topics include: Contemporary Trends and the Growth of Family Volunteering; Developing Family Volunteer Opportunities; Ten Trends Shaping the Future of Volunteerism; Strengthening Corporate and Employee Volunteer Programs; Generational Differences: Generation X and Baby Boomers; Five Barriers to Volunteer Retention; Understanding Volunteer Motivations; New Frontiers in Measuring Inputs; Evaluating Outcomes and Assessing Program Impact; A High Stakes Affair: Managing Risks in Volunteer Programs; Challenges of the Volunteer Marketplace; Walking the Management Tightrope Without a Net: Making Ethical Decisions in Volunteer and Service Programs; Effective Strategic Planning for Volunteer Organizations: Linking Shared Vision with Planned Action; and Volunteer Program Administration.

Volunteer Management Associates

320 South Cedar Brook Road, Boulder, CO 80304
Tel: 800-944-1470, 303-447-0558; FAX: 303-447-1749
E-mail: volunteer@rmi.net (Marlene Wilson),
marlene@volunteermanagement.com,
rosemaryw@compuserve.com,
WWW: http://www.volunteermanagement.com/,
http://www.volunteermanagement.com/catalog.htm

▶ Founded in 1975 by Marlene Wilson, Volunteer Management Associates (VMA) is a consulting and publishing company dedicated to providing quality volunteer management training and resources for organizations and churches that utilize volunteers. VMA presents workshops, specialized training or lectures on a variety of topics relating to volunteerism. Most requested workshop topics include: Influencing Outcomes You Care About in a Changing World; Leading Volunteer Programs with Soul and Vision; Musings of a Chronologically Gifted Crone; Building Collaborative Volunteer/Staff Teams; How to Mobilize Church Volunteers; How to Motivate Volunteers and Staff: Matching Right People with Right Jobs; Delegating to Today's Volunteers; The 3 R's of Effective Volunteer Management: Recruitment–Retention–Recognition; Group Projects Made Simple; The Essential Skills of Interviewing and Placing Volunteers Effectively; Stress and Time Management; and You Can Make a Difference! (based on book of the same title—see separate listing under Publications).

GENERAL RESOURCES

(See also Financial Management [Risk Management and Insurance]; Human Resource Management [Interpersonal Communications, Recruitment and Retention, Training, Workplace Structure]; Internet Sites [Bibliography]; Leadership; Legal [Liability]; The Nonprofit Sector [Philanthropy]; Professional Development)

Committees/Boards

Building Effective Volunteer Committees, 2nd Edition
NANCY MACDUFF, ED. (MACDUFF/BUNT PUBLISHING, 1998)

▶ The backbone of volunteer efforts is provided by functioning committees. This book outlines the steps to build effective committees. Detailed explanations are given for recruiting the right people, writing guidelines, establishing annual work plans, holding members accountable for their responsibilities, and evaluating individuals and committee work. Each chapter is followed by forms suitable for copying that can be used at your next committee meeting. New and revised. *Spiral bound, 107 pages, $23.70*

Corporate and Workplace Volunteerism

Best Practices in Employee Volunteer Programs
SUE VINEYARD (THE POINTS OF LIGHT FOUNDATION, 1996)

▶ This book shares the best practices of large, medium, and small company employee volunteer programs as they effectively serve the needs of their communities. It includes hundreds of benchmarking ideas; involvement at all levels; building strategic alliances; recruitment; selecting efforts to support; evaluation; project ideas; governance and management; communications and recognition; principles of excellence; plus a Directory of Best Practices Companies. *Softcover, 36 pages, $11.95 (Nonmember), $9.95 (Member)*

Developing a Corporate Volunteer Program: Guidelines for Success
(THE POINTS OF LIGHT FOUNDATION, 1992)

▶ This book is a how-to publication for you, the manager of a corporate volunteer program. It is designed to help you make community service and volunteering part of your company's business operations. *Softcover, 40 pages, $25 (Nonmember), $20 (Member)*

Heroes After Hours: Extraordinary Acts of Employee Volunteerism
DAVID C. FORWARD (A JOINT PUBLICATION OF THE JOSSEY-BASS NONPROFIT SERIES AND THE JOSSEY-BASS MANAGEMENT, 1994)

▶ This book describes the remarkable efforts of "everyday" employees to make a difference in their communities, their cities, and their world. The author, a long-time consultant on employee volunteerism and vice president of Phoenix Financial Services, details numerous examples of people at all levels of the corporate ladder who saw a need and then initiated an activity to meet it. Based on interviews with employee volunteers, their co-workers, and managers at 14 *Fortune* 100 companies, their inspirational stories demonstrate how one person can make a difference in the lives of others, whether in a one-person project or in motivating dozens of co-workers to participate. It shows that not only do the individual employees gain personal satisfaction from their efforts, but companies inherit a workforce with increased morale and productivity, as well as recognition from their customers for being good corporate citizens. It includes samples of corporate-driven programs and a special resource section that highlights practical steps for participating in community service. *Hardcover, 291 pages, $23 (plus $4.50 shipping)*

Building Value: The Corporate Volunteer Program as a Strategic Resource for Business
MELANIE HOFFMAN (THE POINTS OF LIGHT FOUNDATION, 1999)

▶ Corporate volunteer programs are increasingly valued for their role in meeting today's strategic business goals. Analyze the purpose of your company's volunteer programs. Learn proven strategies to help manage corporate volunteering during organizational change; examine methods used, and get answers from leaders in the field. *Softcover, $42 (Nonmember), $33 (Member)*

Development and Orientation
(See also Recruitment and Retention; Volunteer Management)

Focus on Volunteering KOPY KIT: Ready-to-Print Resources for Volunteer Organizations, 2nd Edition
SUSAN J. ELLIS (ENERGIZE, INC./PARLAY INTERNATIONAL, 1998)

▶ Each page is a stand-alone document on a single volunteer-related subject, all ready for the copier or printer—perfect for newsletters, training handouts, flyers, and more. Susan J. Ellis has included a range of over 100 informative and practical themes for different audiences, including: Traditions of Volunteering in the United States; Welcoming Diversity; Ideas for Volunteer Recruitment; The Controversy of Mandated Service; and What Is a Volunteer? (you may be surprised!). It also includes an all new and updated ready-to-use graphics section, which includes "thank you" and "we miss you" letters, certificates and awards, recruitment flyers, and even greeting cards. *Loose-leaf binder, 120 pages, $69*

The Generic Volunteer Orientation Manual: Your Guide to Developing an Orientation Manual for Volunteers, Revised Edition

(VOLUNTEER SUPPORT PROJECT, 2000)

▶ Covering everything from parking to telephone usage and scheduling, this loose-leaf notebook is accompanied by a disk (either IBM or Macintosh). It includes a broad selection of policies and procedures for volunteers; samples of mission statements, program histories, guidelines, and standards for volunteers; examples for scheduling and tracking volunteers, grievance procedures, emergency plans, safety regulations, and the like; an index of the included information; a plan to easily develop customized orientation manuals using the enclosed disk copy of the materials; and access to low-cost technical assistance. This orientation manual and the trainings developed from its materials build volunteer commitment, improve morale, and increase productivity. Included with the manual at no additional charge is a disk copy of the materials in either PC or Macintosh format. *Loose-leaf, $25.00 (includes shipping and handling)*

Hidden Assets: Involving Volunteers to Revolutionize Your Development Program

DIANE HODIAK (JOHN WILEY & SONS, 2001)

▶ Although their volunteers are some of their richest resources and their development programs some of their highest priorities, most nonprofits fail to tap the power of these two elements to support each other. In this book, Diane Hodiak shows nonprofit managers how volunteer development can help organizations meet their marketing and fund-raising needs. In addition to boosting volunteers' effectiveness in the day-to-day activities of the development office, Hodiak presents ways to convert volunteers into donors and to inspire donors to become volunteers. *Softcover, 128 pages, $27.95*

Leadership Skills: Developing Volunteers for Organizational Success

EMILY KITTLE MORRISON (FISHER BOOKS, 1994)

▶ This is a comprehensive guide, packed with invaluable information and easy-to-use worksheets and forms. Any nonprofit organization, volunteer group, board, auxiliary, fraternal organization, social-service agency, or club can use and adapt these forms to help their group achieve goals successfully. Starting with the basics of leadership for management positions, you'll learn to achieve your goals and to inspire the best, most productive work from volunteers. It discusses trends in voluntarism, who volunteers and why, community resources for training, guidelines, and contacts. Learn how to conduct an effective meeting, establish goals, manage time, set priorities, create publicity, and develop your career, as well as how to create unity within committees, enhance motivation, solve problems, communicate effectively, identify nonproductive behavior, evaluate the group's effectiveness, delegate responsibility, and develop commitment and involvement. *Softcover, 240 pages, $17.95*

The Seven Rs of Volunteer Development: A YMCA Resource Kit

CELESTE J. WROBLEWSKI (HUMAN KINETICS PUB YMCA OF THE USA, 1994—AVAILABLE FROM ENERGIZE)

▶ Reflection, research, readiness, recruitment, retention, recognition and resources—it's all here. This multimedia tool gives you everything you need to create and run a great volunteer program. No matter what your setting, this YMCA presentation synthesizes some of the best thinking in volunteerism today and is excellent for training others in volunteer management. It includes worksheets, training modules, and guidance to develop firm plans and targeted strategies for any volunteer program. It also includes a videotape on the benefits of volunteering, plus an audiotape by trainer Nora Silver on "Breaking Down the Barriers to Volunteer Involvement." *Loose-leaf, 286 pages, 76-minute audiotape and 9-minute videotape, $55*

Training Volunteers for Community Service: The Step-by-Step Guide of the Shanti National Training Institute

CHARLES GARFIELD AND CAROL KLEINMAIER (JOSSEY-BASS, 2000)

▶ Techniques presented in this manual are based on expertise gained over 25 years of training, managing, and retaining 12,000 volunteers at San Francisco's Shanti, an internationally recognized provider of volunteer training and direct services to those with chronic and life-threatening illness. Sixteen program modules enable volunteer managers to train their volunteers to provide high-quality, compassionate service while increasing volunteer retention. Comprehensive and flexible, *Training Volunteers for Community Service* is a step-by-step guide for creating a training program that is sourced in an understanding of volunteers' primary motivations and offers trainees a uniquely rewarding training experience. The *Trainer's Guide* and *Participant's Workbook* provide methods for instructing volunteers in critical issues such as listening and communication, psychosocial issues, the volunteer–client relationship, and cultural diversity and offers the tools and information agencies need to train, motivate, and retain volunteers. *Ring bound, 336 pages, $149.95*

Grant Assistance

Dollars for Doers: A Guide to Employee Volunteer Matching Grants

DIANE J. GINGOLD (DIANE GINGOLD & ASSOCIATES, 1999)

▶ This is the first directory exclusively devoted to grants given by corporations to nonprofit organizations where employees volunteer. The grants, which range from $10 to $10,000, provide direct support to community organizations where employees commit volunteer time ranging from an hour a week to hundreds of hours per year. *Dollars for Doers,* one of several terms created to describe these programs, is a growing phenomenon as companies seek ways to support their employees and the issues and organizations that are most meaningful to them and their communities. Recent studies show that there is higher job satisfaction and employee retention in companies with organized employee volunteer programs. Consumers are also increasingly judging companies by their social responsibility. It is an invaluable resource for nonprofit organizations seeking to identify new sources of funding. Each of the entries includes details about employee eligibility for grants, volunteer requirements, nonprofit organization eligibility, grant amounts, and grant restrictions. The alphabetical listing of entries is supplemented by a geographical index. Diane Gingold & Associates is a Washington, D.C., consulting firm that assists corporate donors and nonprofit organizations in developing innovative solutions for corporate and nonprofit partnerships. *Dollars for Doers* will be updated on a biannual basis. *Spiral bound, $15.00 (plus $3.50 shipping and handling); $12.00 (plus $3.50 shipping and handling) for nonprofit organizations*

Insurance, Liability, and Risk Management

(See also Recruitment and Retention)

Beyond Police Checks: The Definitive Volunteer and Employees Screening Guidebook

LINDA GRAFF (VOLUNTEER VANCOUVER, 1999)

▶ Screening volunteers (and employees) was always an important part of the volunteer coordinator's job, but in today's climate of risk and liability, the stakes have risen considerably. In a clear, practical, and compelling way, Linda provides the reader with the rationale for initial screening and ongoing credential checks, models for developing screening processes, and a variety of screening tools—everything to raise your comfort level in dealing with applicants. It is a comprehensive "how-to" manual on volunteer and employee screening you have been waiting for! Loaded with practical tips, helpful cautions, and fully reproducible checklists and assessment tools, this guidebook will lead you step by step to increased screening effectiveness and program safety. Written in Canada, the book is truly applicable to any location because its emphasis is on protecting program participants rather than simply on meeting legal requirements. *Softcover, 150 pages, $25*

Child Abuse Prevention Primer for Your Organization

JOHN PATTERSON WITH CHARLES TREMPER AND PAM RYPKEMA (NONPROFIT RISK MANAGEMENT CENTER, 1995—AVAILABLE FROM ENERGIZE)

▶ Any organization working with youth knows both the seriousness of child abuse and also the damage even an allegation of abuse could do to its reputation, yet often this issue is so sensitive or frightening that it becomes difficult to design a comprehensive child abuse prevention program. This primer provides a workable and easy-to-use approach for developing policies and procedures to protect children in your program. The authors do not limit themselves to the most obvious forms of abuse, but look at how to identify and manage the risks of all forms of child maltreatment. Highlights include defining and identifying signs of child abuse, describing traits common among individuals who abuse children as well as circumstances that trigger abuse, actual examples of effective prevention programs, and a plan for training volunteers and staff. *Softcover, 87 pages, $7.50 (plus $3.25 shipping)*

Kidding Around? Be Serious! A Commitment to Safe Service Opportunities for Young People

ANN SEIDMAN AND JOHN PATTERSON (NONPROFIT RISK MANAGEMENT CENTER, 1996)

▶ This book deals with the issue of managing the risks of programs that use young people in volunteer and service-learning projects. It addresses issues that are often ignored when organizations and schools seek to involve young people in community service work. It answers critical questions about collaborations between organizations and schools on youth service projects. The authors assert that young people can be a valuable resource for communities while they gain important knowledge about the communities in which they live. Accomplishing these goals, however, requires that those organizations providing the young people and those receiving their services be serious about managing the risks associated with service assignments. The book points out that youths are not "little adults" and that organizations must take the development characteristics of each young volunteer into consideration when making

an assignment. A section of the book describes the necessity of negotiating clear lines of responsibility when service projects involve more than one organization. Another section of the book addresses specific risk management areas such as compliance with child labor laws and transportation. In addition, information is provided concerning the influence of violence, youth gangs, and drugs and alcohol as they affect volunteer programs for young people. *Softcover, 100 pages, $10 (plus $3 shipping)*

A Legal Handbook for Nonprofit Corporation Volunteers, 6th Edition

JAMES D. DEWITT (VOLUNTEER ACTION CENTER, UNITED WAY OF THE TANANA VALLEY—ALSO AVAILABLE FROM THE ALASKA BAR ASSOCIATION, 2000)

▶ This manual is intended for and dedicated to all volunteers, including volunteer managers, directors of nonprofit corporations, and officers of nonprofit corporations. These materials should also help executive directors of nonprofit corporations and their paid staff. The focus of the manual is risk management, but to understand risk management, you must be able to evaluate risk and, in today's society, that means understanding the law. The manual opens with some common kinds of risks associated with operating a nonprofit corporation, and asks some pointed questions. That is followed by a long discussion of the law and the legal risks facing nonprofit corporations today. Not all of the discussion of law is relevant to all nonprofit corporations, and a considerable portion involves issues of Alaska law, which are probably only marginally helpful to non-Alaska organizations. The second major section of the manual is a discussion of risk management for nonprofit corporations. There is no such thing as a risk-free nonprofit corporation, but there are certainly ways of minimizing the risks and even managing them. The final sections of the manual are resources for nonprofit corporations. An online version is also available at *http://iciclesoftware.com/vlh*. *Softcover, $15 (plus $3 shipping and handling)*

Managing Legal Liability and Insurance for Corporate Volunteer Programs (Booklet)

CHARLES TREMPER AND JEFFREY D. KAHN (UNITED WAY OF AMERICA/NONPROFIT RISK MANAGEMENT CENTER, 1992—AVAILABLE FROM ENERGIZE)

▶ Written for managers of corporate employee volunteer programs, this is a practical guide to reducing uncertainty about liability and insurance when businesses become involved in volunteer programs. With a minimum of "legalese," it clarifies the liability risk of corporate volunteer programs and suggests strategies for controlling those risks and helps managers recognize volunteer program risks and related insurance issues, ask the right questions of company lawyers (including waivers and releases), ensure that the company and individual volunteers have adequate insurance, and take appropriate programmatic steps to control risks. Major concerns of top management and front-line company volunteers, as well as the nonprofit or government agency putting those volunteers to work, are addressed. Much of the information is relevant to noncorporate volunteers. It includes a reference guide on specific insurance issues. *Softcover, 30 pages, $10*

No Surprises: Controlling Risks in Volunteer Programs

CHARLES TREMPER AND GWYNNE KOSTIN (NONPROFIT RISK MANAGEMENT CENTER, 1993)

▶ A collaboration of the Center and the American Bar Association, this is an easy-to-use, step-by-step guide to risk management (preventing lawsuits and other unpleasant surprises). It demystifies "risk management." It is filled with practical, realistic pointers and gives volunteer program managers the guidance they need to keep harm and related costs to a minimum without diverting organizations from their missions. It is applicable to volunteer efforts in any type setting. It shows how proper planning and procedures can make a safer environment for clients and volunteers, while limiting the potential for problems. It compares risk management for volunteers with the issues equally important for employees. It includes sections on limiting financial risks in handling money and some of the basic risk management issues related to boards of directors (themselves volunteers); presents the tasks of volunteer program management and explains how to limit the risks at each stage (staff selection and service, volunteer job design, application and screening process, board functions, ongoing training and supervision, finances, abuse, emergencies and information management) arising from volunteer program management; and aids in dealing with agency lawyers and insurance agents. *Softcover, 60 pages, $10 (plus $3 shipping)*

Risk Management: Strategies For Managing Volunteer Programs

SARAH HENSON AND BRUCE LARSON (MACDUFF/BUNT PUBLISHING, 1988)

▶ This book, written by a volunteer program manager and an attorney, covers the area of risk management. Written in lay language, the book covers tort claims; liability management; risk reduction strategies; the importance of bylaws, policies, and procedures; and how to create a "paper trail." Each chapter is followed by worksheets that can be used by a risk management team and samples of documents that are used in well-managed programs. *Softcover, $31*

Screening Volunteers to Prevent Child Sexual Abuse Organizational Kit

THE NATIONAL COLLABORATION FOR YOUTH (NONPROFIT RISK MANAGEMENT CENTER, 1997)

▶ This is a set of publications for assisting organizations serving children and youth to determine the screening requirements for volunteers based on an assessment of the elements of risk in the role of the volunteer. Rather than focus on information from each volunteer, the Guides provide a rational basis for organizations to decide what kind of screening is needed for each position. The key to the recommended process is an 11-factor risk matrix organizations can use to focus on program elements that either contribute to the risk of child sexual abuse or can serve to lessen or mitigate those risks. The kit includes: *Screening Volunteers to Prevent Child Sexual Abuse: A Community Guide for Youth Organizations* (presents the detailed rationale supporting the recommended process); and *Screening Volunteers to Prevent Child Sexual Abuse: A Three-Step Action Guide* (summarizes the information in an easy-to-read, "user-friendly" format). *Community Action Guide: 34 pages, $15; Action Guide: 8 pages, $5*

Staff Screening Tool Kit: Keeping Bad Apples Out of Your Organization, 2nd Edition

JOHN PATTERSON WITH CHARLES TREMPER AND PAM RYPKEMA (NONPROFIT RISK MANAGEMENT CENTER, 1998)

▶ This is a guidebook for how to screen and select appropriate employees and volunteers, particularly in situations in which an organization needs to protect vulnerable clients. It covers legal and ethical issues. Since the original Tool Kit was first published, changes have taken place that influence the screening process and govern access to records. Besides these issues, the second edition addresses the increased focus on official agency records as tools for staff screening, and features a state-by-state directory of agencies that maintain records useful for screening. *Softcover, 135 pages, $30*

Yes You Can!: Discipline and Dismissal of Volunteers (An Audio Workshop)

LINDA L. GRAFF (VOLUNTEER VANCOUVER)

▶ Hear Linda Graff and experience the energy of live presentation in this spirited and pragmatic treatment of one of our toughest management issues. Discover the elements of rightful dismissal, master the steps and principles of progressive discipline, and learn how to decrease both personal and organizational risks in all your dismissal actions. She tackles this tough management issue with a discussion of the elements of rightful dismissal, the principles of progressive discipline, and how to decrease both organizational and personal risks. *$17*

Marketing Skills

Marketing for Volunteer Managers: Mastering Its Magic in a New Millennium

SUE VINEYARD (POINTS OF LIGHT FOUNDATION, 1998)

▶ This text brings marketing skills into the next century. It teaches readers the basics of marketing: its components, its rewards, its process, trends that impact our recruitment and support efforts, marketing plans and strategies, the art of asking, "friend-raising," positioning, public perceptions, promotions, and removing reasons to say no. It is complete with dozens of tips, forms, and tools, plus a bibliography to help volunteer managers use this vital tool to their program's success. *Softcover, 72 pages, $19.95 (Nonmember), $15.95 (Member)*

Marketing Nonprofit Programs and Services: Proven and Practical Strategies to Get More Customers, Members and Donors

DOUGLASS B. HERRON (JOSSEY-BASS, 1996)

▶ This is a reader-friendly guide to expanding your programs; developing your staff and volunteers, and balancing your budget. Learn how to evaluate the effectiveness of your promotion efforts, especially if your organization relies on a mixed base of fees and contributions for support. Chapters worth a second look include: "Strategies for Recruiting the Volunteers You Want Most" and "Your Marketing Strategy: 15 Steps for Putting It All Together." *Hardcover, 302 pages, $32.95*

Marketing Workbook for Nonprofit Organizations Volume II: Mobilize People for Marketing Success

GARY J. STERN (AMHERST H. WILDER FOUNDATION, 1997)

▶ You have been told to organize a comprehensive plan to mobilize the community around your mission and must form a people-based promotion campaign. But how? Use this new guide to put together a successful promotional campaign based on the most persuasive tool of all: personal contact. It showcases a logical, 10-step approach to the practical solutions for creating a people-based promotional campaign. Whether your goal is raising funds, recruiting volunteers, or selling tickets, the old saying, "people buy from people," is as true as ever. *Mobilize People for Marketing Success* shows you how to mobilize your entire organization, its staff, volunteers, and supporters in a focused, one-to-one marketing campaign. This unique guide gives you complete instructions, real-life examples, and detailed worksheets to create an effective campaign. It includes such useful items as training guides, case studies, reproducible worksheets, and a 48-page marketing booklet, the "Pocket Guide for Marketing Representations," a pocket guide available for all your representatives. In it, they can record key campaign messages and find motivational reminders. *Softcover, 208 pages, $25.00*

Online Volunteering

The Virtual Volunteering Guidebook (pdf file): How to Apply the Principles of Real-World Volunteer Management to Online Service

SUSAN J. ELLIS AND JAYNE CRAVENS (ENERGIZE, 1999)

▶ Detailed information on the basics of setting up and managing a successful virtual volunteering program. This publication compiles several years of research and experiences in online volunteering, presented by two volunteerism leaders: one among the best-respected authors in the field and the other the field's leading expert on virtual volunteering. It is available at no charge on the Energize Web site at *www.energizeinc.com.*

Senior Volunteers

Older Volunteers: A Guide to Research and Practice

LUCY ROSE FISCHER AND KAY BANISTER SCHAFFER (SAGE PUBLICATIONS, 1993)

▶ Based on comprehensive research of volunteerism and outstanding volunteer programs, this book makes these findings available to those who develop, implement, or participate in volunteer programs with seniors. It provides a wealth of information about effective ways to recruit, retain, and work with older volunteers, so that their time and gifts can be better utilized. A broad range of issues is examined and addressed, including motivations for volunteering, research on minority seniors, and the potential for exploitation of older volunteers. Although written with the older volunteer in mind, it addresses such universal volunteer management questions as: What makes certain recruitment techniques more effective? and Why do some volunteers stay while others leave? What motivates people to do volunteer work? What are the most effective ways of maintaining commitment in volunteers? What problems are confronted in working with volunteers—especially older volunteers—and what are the solutions to these problems? How can organizations avoid exploiting older volunteers? Answering these and a host of other questions, *Older Volunteers* offers a comprehensive review of current research and case studies to provide a synthesis of "best practices" for those who plan, implement, and participate in volunteer programs. The authors examine the range of volunteer roles and organizations, multiple motivations for volunteering, techniques of recruiting and keeping volunteers, and managerial issues. They also examine and discuss research on minority elderly and address such formidable issues as bias from paid staff and the potential for exploitation. This book is of value to anyone wishing to tap the senior community and to understand the differences and similarities of older volunteers and other ages. *Softcover, 272 pages, $31*

Service Learning, Youth and Young Adult Volunteerism

(See also Insurance, Liability, and Risk Management; Recruitment and Retention)

160 Ways to Help the World: Community Service Projects for Young People

LINDA LEEB DUPER (CHECKMARK BOOKS, 1996)

▶ This is a valuable book for mentoring programs, schools, local neighborhood communities, church groups, and after-school programs (or even regular school curriculums). Clearly written and well formatted, it contains information about how to get started on community projects to help others and keep kids interested and stimulated beyond the modern TV- and video-watching activities, with or without adult supervision, or even how to start to get the adult support kids need to be able to do the projects mentioned. Descriptive outlines of what you need to do are extremely helpful and easy to follow—the author seems to know how to connect to a young audience and keep the older ones interested, too, using contemporary language and tidbits of her own experiences in some cases. It is a great resource for teachers, community leaders, churches, and neighborhood activists who want to get their kids more involved and active with services to others. This excellent reference book features step-by-step project instructions and extensive resource listings of helpful organizations and publications to contact, and suggests projects young people can pursue to benefit their communities. The volume offers advice on how to plan and execute a project, obtaining support from businesses and individuals, creating publicity, conducting drives, handling money, and volunteering. *Softcover, 144 pages, $9.95*

Children as Volunteers: Preparing for Community Service, Revised Edition

SUSAN J. ELLIS, ANNE WEISBORD, AND KATHERINE H. NOYES (ENERGIZE, 1991)

▶ Designed both for leaders of volunteer programs and leaders of children, this book focuses on how to adapt volunteer management principles to work effectively with children as volunteers, and enthusiastically endorses the growing trend of children under the age of 14 becoming volunteers. Recognizing the many benefits of children volunteering, the authors provide practical and fun suggestions for incorporating children into an adult volunteer program and how to solicit and use their input. It includes examples of actual volunteer projects accomplished by children, models of child–adult teams, how to design assignments, and recruiting and training for this age group. It includes a special section on mandated school-based community service, plus up-to-date information on legal issues and insurance-related concerns, as well as tips on family volunteering. *Softcover, 68 pages, $14.75 (plus $3.25 shipping)*

Combining Service and Learning: A Resource Book for Community and Public Service (3 volumes)

JANE KENDALL, ED. (NATIONAL SOCIETY OF EXPERIENTIAL EDUCATION)

▶ This book is published by NSEE with 93 other national and regional organizations, for faculty, administrators, policy makers, and students in colleges, universities, and K–12 schools; leaders in government, community or corporate settings; lawmakers; foundations; and others interested in community and public service, youth service, volunteerism, leadership, civic awareness, or cross-cultural learning. Volume I (principles of good practice; rationales; theories; research; public policy and institutional issues plus strategies for gaining support; education for civic and social responsibility, cross-cultural awareness, and intellectual, moral, ethical, career and leadership development); Volume II (practical issues and ideas for programs and courses—integration into the curriculum, recruitment, orientation, supervision, evaluation, school/community relations, legal issues, monitoring and assessing both service and learning outcomes); Volume III (a fully annotated bibliography of the literature for combining service and learning and other resources). *Volume I: 693 pages, $32.50 ($12.50 NSEE members); Volume II: 528 pages, $32.50 ($12.50 NSEE members); Volume III: 81 pages, $6.00 ($4.00 NSEE members)*

Community Service and Social Responsibility in Youth

JAMES YOUNISS AND MIRANDA YATES (CONTRIBUTOR) (UNIVERSITY OF CHICAGO PRESS, 1997)

▶ James Youniss and Miranda Yates present a sophisticated analysis of community service's beneficial effects on adolescents' political and moral identity. Using a case study from a predominantly black, urban high school in Washington, D.C., Youniss and Yates build on the insights of Erik Erikson on the social and historical nature of identity development. They show that service at a soup kitchen as part of a course on social justice gives youth the opportunity to reflect on their status in society, on how society is organized, on how government should use its power, and on moral principles related to homelessness and poverty. Developing a sense of social responsibility and a civic commitment, youth come to see themselves as active agents in society. The most authoritative work to date on the subject, this book challenges negative stereotypes of contemporary adolescents and illustrates how youth, when given the opportunity, can use their talents for social good. It will interest readers concerned with the development of today's youth and tomorrow's society. *Softcover, 176 pages, $13*

Growing Hope: A Sourcebook on Integrating Youth Service into the School Curriculum

RICH WILLITS CAIRN AND JAMES C. KIELSMEIER, EDS. (NATIONAL YOUTH LEADERSHIP COUNCIL, 1993—AVAILABLE FROM THE POINTS OF LIGHT FOUNDATION)

▶ For educators beginning or expanding curriculum-based youth service programs, this is one of the most widely used resources in the youth services/service-learning field. This workbook offers background, comprehensive definitions, rationale, nuts-and-bolts implementation help, and sample program materials and resource contacts to assist in developing or improving youth service and service-learning programs, with special attention paid to combining service with learning in the classroom. It includes stories and case studies on local programs, contact information, and an annotated bibliography of youth service publications and descriptions of key state and national youth service organizations. *Softcover, 260 pages, $29*

The Kid's Guide to Service Projects: Over 500 Service Ideas for Young People Who Want to Make a Difference

BARBARA A. LEWIS AND PAMELA ESPELAND (FREE SPIRIT PUBLISHING, 1995)

▶ This guide has something for everyone who wants to make a difference, from simple projects to large-scale commitments. Kids can choose from a variety of topics, including animals, crime fighting,

the environment, friendship, hunger, literacy, politics and government, and transformation. This book contains more than 500 service ideas for young people of all ages. They range from simple projects (running an errand for a friend) to complex projects (working for a state law to create stronger penalties against graffiti). *Softcover, 184 pages, $12.95*

A Kid's Guide to Social Action: How to Solve the Social Problems You Choose—and Turn Creative Thinking into Positive Action, Revised Edition

BARBARA A. LEWIS, PAMELA ESPELAND, AND CARYN PERNU (FREE SPIRIT PUBLISHING, 1998)

▶ Exciting, empowering, and packed with information, this is the ultimate guide for kids who want to make a difference in the world. Step-by-step instructions show how to write letters, do interviews, make speeches, take surveys, raise funds, get media coverage, and more. Reproducible forms make it easy to circulate petitions, initiate proclamations, and prepare news releases. This book provides real stories about real kids who are doing great things to let readers know that they're not too young to solve problems in their neighborhood, community, and nation. Resources point the way toward government offices, groups, organizations, Web sites, and books. Designed for kids to use on their own, this inspiring book is also ideal for schools, clubs, groups, troops, and youth organizations. It includes 25 reproducible handout masters. This book teaches the skills necessary for kids and adults to implement service-learning in their schools and communities. *Softcover, 232 pages, $16.95*

Learning by Giving: K–8 Service-Learning Curriculum Guide

RICH CAIRN WITH THERESA COBLE (NATIONAL YOUTH LEADERSHIP COUNCIL—AVAILABLE FROM THE POINTS OF LIGHT FOUNDATION, 1993)

▶ This resource guide is for anyone starting a K–8 service-learning program. The first chapters focus on what service-learning is, why it's important, and how to begin. Later chapters give classroom examples of service-learning activities at the K–2, 3–5, and 6–8 levels. Utilizing current practices for educational excellence such as cooperative learning, student-centered curriculum, outcome-based education and experiential activities, this user-friendly guide is the most complete service-learning resource for elementary and middle schools available. Service-learning is an educational method by which students gain social and academic skills through addressing community needs. This user-friendly guide gives basic background in service-learning methodologies, provides 15 sample service activities based on projects submitted by teachers nationwide, and offers a framework and resources for teachers to develop their own activities. It contributes to the paradigm shift that children learn by interacting with their communities, rather than being "educated" within the confines of four walls. It contributes to the growing understanding that students must be involved in meaningful projects, working together cooperatively to achieve a goal, contributing insights on engaging students in thoughtful reflection, as the critical piece of any authentic assessment process. *Loose-leaf notebook, 260 pages, $45*

Learning to Care: Elementary Kindness in an Age of Indifference

ROBERT WUTHNOW (OXFORD UNIVERSITY PRESS, 1996)

▶ A sequel to *Acts of Compassion*, this is a probing look at how we can nurture caring in our young people. Drawing on deeply moving personal accounts from young people who have become involved in community service, as well as on data from recent national surveys, this book looks at why teenagers become involved in volunteer work, what problems and pressures they face, and what we can do to nurture caring in our youth. Robert Wuthnow's intimate interviews bring to life the stories of high school student volunteers, teenagers such as Tanika Lane, a freshman who works with Literacy Education and Direction (LEAD), a job-training program for inner-city kids, and Amy Stone, a homecoming queen and student body president at a suburban southern school who organizes rallies for AIDS awareness. Through these profiles, Wuthnow shows that caring is not innate but learned, in part from the spontaneous warmth of family life, and in part from finding the right kind of volunteer work. He contends that a volunteer's sense of service is shaped by what he or she finds in school service clubs, in shelters for the homeless, in working with AIDS victims, or in tutoring inner-city children. Wuthnow also argues that the best environment to nurture the helping impulse is the religious setting, where in fact the great bulk of volunteering in America takes place. In these organizations, as well as in schools and community agencies, teenagers can find the role models and moral incentives that will instill a sense of service that they can then carry into their adult life. *Hardcover, 304 pages, $27.50 (plus shipping and handling)*

No Kidding Around! America's Young Activists Are Changing Our World and You Can Too
WENDY SCHAETZEL LESKO (ACTIVISM 2000 PROJECT, 1992—ALSO AVAILABLE FROM THE POINTS OF LIGHT FOUNDATION)

▶ This book explains how young people can form their own community service efforts, equipping themselves to take on serious social problems and work toward solutions. This guide addresses every aspect of launching a service campaign from gathering information and building a team to developing an action plan, getting the word out, and garnering contributions. It relates true-life success stories of young people's efforts to save wetland areas, create a community center, and more. This handbook on civic activism features 10 full-length oral histories of people not old enough to vote but who score political homeruns in city halls, school boards, and statehouses across the country. These true stories have been used in the classroom by many social studies teachers and community service-learning resource coordinators. It also contains a comprehensive road map describing how young people can launch their own campaign and make a lasting difference. *Softcover, 263 pages, $18.95 (includes shipping and handling)*

Service Opportunities for Youths (Pamphlet)
ADOLESCENT PREGNANCY PREVENTION CLEARINGHOUSE (CHILDREN'S DEFENSE FUND, 1989)

▶ This pamphlet supports the belief that young people can contribute to the well-being of their communities by engaging in service activities. Disadvantaged youths providing service can also improve their skills and their self-esteem. *16 pages, $5.50 (includes shipping)*

A Student's Guide to Volunteering
THERESA FOY DIGERONIMO (CAREER PRESS, 1995—AVAILABLE FROM ENERGIZE, INC.)

▶ Especially for teenagers, this book presents a road map for the who, what, where, when, why, and how of getting involved. It shares the real-life experiences of teens who have done it and sup-

plies a directory of national organization resources and a list of local volunteer centers. Beyond developing marketable and useful abilities, volunteers have the opportunity to touch people, showing that they care. And caring itself is something to be learned. The first part of the book covers some general principles, then discusses opportunities in six major areas open to teens. The second part is a listing of resources in the six areas, then volunteer organizations by state (in the United States). The chapters include story examples of what volunteering in various jobs is like. One chapter discusses how to set up a youth volunteer organization. *Softcover, 187 pages, $10.99*

What Do You Stand For?
BARBARA A. LEWIS (FREE SPIRIT, 1997)

▶ This book presents 26 character traits—including caring, empathy, citizenship, leadership, and respect—that are essential for children to develop in order to become their best selves. It provides a wealth of ideas for training young volunteers. Inspirational background material, thought-provoking scenarios, learning activities, and stories about real children challenge the reader to identify, explore, and build each character trait. *Softcover, 284 pages, $18.95*

Youth Service: A Guidebook for Developing and Operating Effective Programs (Report)
DAN CONRAD AND DIANE HEDIN (INDEPENDENT SECTOR, 1987)

▶ *Youth Service* provides step-by-step advice on developing and operating programs that get youth involved in community service. You'll get advice for working with existing projects, starting your own project, doing a community survey to uncover the community needs, recruiting youth participation, and evaluating the program. The book also includes a section on how to help young people learn life skills from their service activities. Topics such as liability and transportation are also covered. Sample parental approval forms, volunteer agreements and evaluations, and other forms complete this road map for effective youth service programs. *Softcover, 70 pages, $8.50 (Nonmember), $5.95 (Member)*

Volunteer Recognition

Beyond Banquets, Plaques and Pins: Creative Ways to Recognize Volunteers and Staff!, Revised Edition
SUE VINEYARD (HERITAGE ARTS PUBLISHING, 1994)

▶ This is a guide to the different motivations of volunteers and how recognition should match individual needs. It includes lists of ideas for showing appreciation. *Softcover, 24 pages, $10*

Recognizing Volunteers Right from the Start
NAN HAWTHORNE (MBA PUBLISHING)

▶ A really fun training to give, this is far more than a workshop on volunteer recognition! Redefining volunteer recognition as a complete relationship rather than a single generic event, it presents participants, through acquaintance with four distinct and well-defined individuals, with a chance to consider how each volunteer's personal "measuring stick" for success can shape how one designs volunteer jobs, whom one recruits and how, what supervision styles work best, and then and only then, how to design a relationship of recognition that strengthens the agency–volunteer team. The kit contains an instruction manual, handouts, transparencies, exercise tools, announcement flyer, and diskette. You can customize the handouts by going to Nan Hawthorne's Web site at *http://www.cybervpm.com/*.

The Volunteer Recognition Skit Kit
ARLENE GRUBBS AND EVELYN LEVINE (ENERGIZE, INC., 1992)

▶ This kit contains seven ready-to-produce skits created for volunteer recognition events, with full scripts and reworked lyrics to well-known songs. *Loose-leaf, 124 pages, $24.95*

Volunteerism, Citizen Participation, and Community Building

Altruists and Volunteers: Life Histories
WILLIAM N. STEPHENS (MACDUFF BUNT ASSOCIATES, 1991)

▶ This book is a study of altruism and volunteering reported through the eyes and ears of active volunteers. The focus is on what we can learn about them from their life history and in the context of altruism research. Learn about the influence of organizations in shaping volunteer careers. *Softcover, $27*

Better Than Money Can Buy: The NEW Volunteers
JOSEPH KILPATRICK AND SANFORD DANZIGER, COMPILERS (INNERSEARCH PUBLISHING, 1996)

▶ This book demonstrates how all-volunteer groups like Human Service Alliance provide impeccable services at no charge with "new volunteers," ordinary people discovering meaning and purpose through hands-on service. *Softcover, 168 pages, $10.95 (plus $2.50 shipping and handling)*

The Business of Heart: How Everyday Americans Are Changing the World
MICHAEL GLAUSER (DESERET BOOK COMPANY, 1999)

▶ Share our strength. Community Hope Center. Camp Mak-A-Dream. All of these nonprofit organizations are thriving, altruistic causes that bring a better way of life to people around the world. And they all began with people who saw a need—heroes with big hearts and a big idea. Michael J. Glauser tells the inspiring stories of these and other great servants of the community. Glauser shows how service can be a rewarding way of life and reveals strategies for readers who want to start service organizations. Chapters include "Serving Our Children," "Teaching Our Youth," "Healing Our Infirm," "Feeding Our Hungry," and "Aiding Our Needy." From identifying needs to underwriting and fund raising to getting volunteers, *The Business of Heart* chronicles 25 success stories that will inspire and motivate readers to make a difference. *Hardcover, 272 pages, $19.95*

The Call to Service: A Witness to Idealism
ROBERT COLES (HOUGHTON MIFFLIN, 1994)

▶ The author examines not only what those who serve mean to us and what their actions mean to them—most of his subjects emphatically resist the "idealist" designation—but also his own part in the equation (as volunteer and witness) and his enduring sources of inspiration: the examples of his own parents, of novelists whose ideas he finds edifying; and of mentors familiar from earlier works. Mixing autobiographical reminiscence, analysis, and oral testimony, the book doubles as a record of many conversations about the nature of voluntary service, and as an account of Coles's own reflections on his work. The book's central message is that volunteer work can have a transformative influence on those who heed the "call of service," even though they frequently experience doubts, misgivings, depression, and even a sense of futility and despair. According to Coles, the satisfactions of service are plentiful and sustaining, conferring importance on small interactions and providing affirmation to those involved—often in place of lasting social or political change. The volunteers who are most successful, he finds, are those who genuinely like the people they meet, who quickly lose the sense that they are martyrs making a sacrifice, and, most importantly, who realize that they are getting something in return. Again and again, the stories affirm that service is not a hierarchy but a reciprocity in which the distinctions between teacher and pupil, giver and receiver, helper and helped constantly dissolve. Throughout the book, Coles quotes his own teachers and mentors, people such as Dorothy Day, William Carlos Williams, and Anna Freud, whom he feels are important role models for service. *Softcover, 334 pages, $12.95*

Care and Community in Modern Society: Passing on the Tradition of Service to Future Generations
PAUL SCHERVISH, VIRGINIA A. HODGKINSON, AND MARGARET GATERS, EDS. (JOSSEY-BASS, 1995)

▶ This is an extension of Independent Sector's 1993 Research Forum, which examined the role people, institutions, and public policy play in promoting or inhibiting the development of a caring society. Expert contributors explore how individuals become involved in and dedicated to caring for others, and the role such care plays in providing a foundation for our civic, ethical, and spiritual traditions. A well-balanced combination of theory and practice, the chapters collected in this book were written by scholars from a variety of disciplines, including psychology, religious studies, and public policy, and by leaders of community organizations, youth groups, and federal government agencies. Comprehensive in scope, the book offers theories and practical models of what constitutes and defines a caring community and reveals how care is delivered by families, schools, communities, and society. The editors examine six key topics, including how family upbringing influences the development of individuals who provide service to their communities; the types of institutions most likely to teach and transmit caring traditions; and the kinds of public policies that promote caring, service, and generosity. The book offers an insightful analysis of how these factors interrelate and affect the ability of members of society to transmit caring traditions. Sections of the book include: The Role of Family and Community in Transmitting the Tradition of Care, Children as Givers and Receivers of Care, Civic and Religious Traditions of Care, Social and Political Environments of Care, and Mobilizing Care Through Mutual Self Interest. *Hardcover, 535 pages, $$39.95 (plus shipping)*

The Cathedral Within: Transforming Your Life by Giving Something Back
WILLIAM H. SHORE (RANDOM HOUSE, 1999)

▶ *The Cathedral Within* uses the metaphor of architecture to look at the way individuals allocate their resources to improve public life. Just as the enduring magnificence of a cathedral is not erected overnight, so, too, the transformation of a society takes many, many years to complete. And just as the construction of a cathedral is less a reflection of its builders' interest in masonry than a testament to the soaring reach of the human spirit, philanthropy is not so much a response to need as to a basic human requirement to give something meaningful back to society. *Hardcover, 292 pages, $21.95*

Community Works: The Revival of Civil Society in America
E.J. DIONNE, ED. (BROOKINGS INSTITUTE, 1998)

▶ America is experiencing a boom of voluntarism and civic mindedness. Community groups are working together to clean up their cities and neighborhoods. People are rejoining churches, civic associations, and Little Leagues. And, at every opportunity, local and national leaders are exhorting citizens to pitch in and do their part. Why has the concept of a civil society—an entire nation of communities, associations, civic and religious groups, and individuals all working toward the common good—become so popular? Why is so much hope being invested in the voluntary sector? Why is a civil society so important to us? This book looks at the growing debate over the rise, importance, and consequences of civil society. E.J. Dionne puts the issues of the debate in perspective and explains the deep-rooted developments that are reflected in civil society's revival. Alan Wolfe and Jean Bethke Elshtain discuss reasons why the idea of a civil society is important today. Theda Skocpol and William A. Schambra offer two opposing viewpoints on where successful voluntary civic action originates—nationally or at the local grass roots. John J. DiIulio Jr. shines a light on the success of faith-based programs in the inner city, and Bruce Katz studies the problems caused by concentrated poverty in those same neighborhoods. Jane Eisner underscores the extent to which the volunteer sector needs organization and support to effectively complete its work. Other contributors include Bill Bradley, William A. Galston, and Gertrude Himmelfarb. An online version is available at *http://brookings.nap.edu/books/0815718675/html/index.html. Hardcover, 180 pages, $24.95*

The Halo Effect: How Volunteering Can Lead to a More Fulfilling Life—and a Better Career

JOHN REYNOLDS (GOLDEN BOOKS, 1998)

▶ A "business book with a heart," *The Halo Effect* illustrates how inspiration in careers and in lives can be renewed by service to others. Volunteer work can help you learn new skills, meet new people, and develop a whole new perspective on your goals. A complete resource that outlines everything you need to know about volunteer work, *The Halo Effect* includes an appendix that lists and describes the best volunteer organizations that need your help today. *Hardcover, 224 pages, $21.95*

Ignite the Community Spirit: 301 Ways to Turn Caring into Action

JOY J. GOLLIVER AND RUTH HAYES-ARISTA (IGNITE THE COMMUNITY SPIRIT, 1997)

▶ This book is the best of the first three years of the *I CAN* Newsletter collected in book form. This book educates, motivates, and encourages more people to be involved in their community. If you are already involved, the book sparks your creativity and gives you new ideas to add to your volunteer experience. Celebrate the good news about people helping people. *Softcover, 82 pages, $18.00*

Pass It On: Outreach to Minority Communities, Revised

CHARYN D. SUTTON (BIG BROTHERS/BIG SISTERS OF AMERICA, 2000)

▶ Want to recruit a racially and ethnically diverse volunteer corps including African Americans, Latinos, Asian Americans, and Native Americans? Each minority group is presented in historical, geographical, and cultural context, which helps readers in any setting become more aware and accepting of diverse cultural characteristics. It covers cultural awareness and sensitivity training networks and establishing credibility. *Softcover, $35.00*

Passionate Volunteerism

JEANNE BRADNER (CONVERSATION PRESS)

▶ This book tells you what volunteers are really worth to society and why this worth is too seldom recognized. It shows you the vision that guides volunteer involvement and activity, and it outlines what government, nonprofits, and individuals can do to make volunteerism even more beneficial to all of society. *Softcover, 80 pages, $3.95 (plus shipping and handling)*

The Quickening of America: Rebuilding Our Nation, Remaking Our Lives

FRANCES MOORE LAPPE AND PAUL MARTIN DU BOIS (JOSSEY-BASS 1994)

▶ From national political campaigns to local community action groups, a grassroots approach to change is taking hold of America. Driven by a desire to go beyond rhetoric and ideology and address problems in a direct, practical way, "ordinary" citizens are changing the way we live, work, and govern ourselves. The book brings to light an invisible revolution taking place in communities across the nation. It reveals how this new approach to solving our problems is working in local government, education, the workplace, human services, and the media. Exploding the popular myths about public life, power, and self-interest that stop individuals from discovering the rewards of public involvement, it offers practical advice on how to get more involved and details specific guidelines that anyone can use in mastering the "arts of democracy" (strengthening the skills of speaking, listening, conflict resolution, and more) and how to bring our country alive again. *Softcover, 353 pages, $18 (plus $3.50 shipping)*

Rediscovering Community: The Cultural Potential of Caring Behavior and Voluntary Service

(See Philanthropy—The Nonprofit Sector for full description)

Remaking America: How the Benevolent Traditions of Many Cultures Are Transforming Our National Life

JAMES A. JOSEPH (JOSSEY-BASS, 1995)

▶ Native Americans, African Americans, Asian Americans, and Latinos all have distinctive legacies of self-help and volunteerism. This landmark book examines the long history and rich charitable traditions and customs among people of color. It offers a new vision of a larger American community with shared values and universal compassion. *Hardcover, 278 pages, $27.95*

Soul of a Citizen: Living with Conviction in a Cynical Time

PAUL ROGAT LOEB (ST. MARTINS PRESS, 1999)

▶ How can ordinary people make their voices heard and actions count in a time when they're told neither matter? *Soul of a Citizen: Living with Conviction in a Cynical Time* tells wonderful stories and offers powerful lessons about how citizens of all ages have engaged themselves in their communities and worked for a more just world in a variety of ways. Based on 30 years of Loeb's work examining the psychology of involvement (including his earlier study of current students, *Generation at the Crossroads*), *Soul of a Citizen* explores how people engage themselves in critical public issues and what stops them from getting involved; what makes the difference between burning out in exhaustion or maintaining commitment for the long haul; and how involvement can give a rare sense of connection and purpose. The book helps us think through what it takes to get more people involved and to keep them involved, and to keep on ourselves, despite inevitable doubts and frustrations. *Softcover, 376 pages, $15.95*

Virtuous Giving: Philanthropy, Voluntary Service, and Caring *(See Philanthropy—The Nonprofit Sector for full description)*

Voices from the Heart: A Compassionate Call for Responsibility
EDDIE SHAPIRO AND DEBBIE SHAPIRO, EDS. (J. P. TARCHER, 1998)

▶ Some of the world's most renowned leaders and visionaries— Archbishop Desmond Tutu, Marianne Williamson, Mikhail Gorbachev, Rachel Naomi Remen, MD—offer original essays and ruminations about taking one's spirituality to task. The editors' premise here is singular and straightforward: It is not enough to pursue one's bliss; one must apply the lessons of spiritual wisdom to healing the world. Yet these essays are anything but singular in voice and solutions. Author Stephen Levine, who spent 20 years counseling the terminally ill, vows to address our "confused and confusing world" by embracing "the qualities of the opening heart rather than the rusted machinations of the ever-defensive mind." John Bird, editor-in-chief of London's *Big Issue* street magazine for the homeless, writes about his determination to replace despair with a belief that "It's possible; whatever it is, it's possible." Sheila Cassidy, a physician who was tortured in Chile for helping a wounded soldier, writes about her ongoing commitment to helping those in pain. In their introduction, editors Debbie and Eddie Shapiro state that "every change that each individual makes creates a chain reaction that is a benefit to all." One can't help but believe that this expertly edited collection will ignite exactly this mighty of a chain reaction. *Softcover, 362 pages, $14.95*

Voices from the Heart: In Celebration of America's Volunteers
BRIAN O'CONNELL (JOSSEY-BASS, 1998)

▶ "There's something wonderfully rewarding in being part of an effort that makes a difference," O'Connell (founding president of Independent Sector, now a professor of public service) declares in his introduction to this collection of commentaries by and photographs of 25 of the nearly 100 million Americans who volunteer. The 25 range in age from 13 to 84 and represent various ethnic groups. Many volunteer by sharing their expertise—in yoga, film and video, computers, math and science, self-defense, farming techniques, or legal research. Other volunteers draw on painful experiences (e.g., with breast cancer or HIV) to teach or counsel others. Hobbies such as dancing, hiking, and singing are the basis for some volunteer work; more traditional services (e.g., food, shelter, and medical care) are provided by other volunteers through groups or one on one. *Voices from the Heart* is a tribute to this spirit of giving and the ideal of community. Author Brian O'Connell and editor Rebecca Buffam Taylor present a moving portrait of compassion at work. We meet volunteers from across the country and hear their passionate voices speak about what they do and why. Compelling images by leading photojournalists add to the story of each volunteer's work and its rich rewards. A nonprofit joint endeavor by Chronicle Books, Jossey-Bass Publishers, and major national foundations, profits from the sale of *Voices from the Heart* will go to Independent Sector, a nonprofit group dedicated to America's volunteer organizations. *Softcover, 160 pages, $19.95*

Volunteering: 101 Ways You Can Improve the World and Your Life
DOUGLAS M. LAWSON (ALTI PUBLICATIONS, 1998)

▶ This handy guide presents 101 ways to help others and yourself by volunteering. It is written for today's volunteers who are already working to make the world a better place and for those who have not yet experienced the joy of volunteering. For those who are active volunteers, the book answers many questions that confront them every day. *Softcover, 144 pages, $7.95*

Volunteers in Action
BRIAN O'CONNELL AND ANNE BROWN O'CONNELL (THE FOUNDATION CENTER, 1988)

▶ Essential reading for all who write, study, speak about or participate in voluntary activities, this inspiring book offers insights into the voluntary sector and captures the spirit of a cross-section of the 98 million volunteers in America today. Through case histories, citations, and testimonials, the authors illustrate the roles and impact of ordinary citizens and how their dedication enriches and empowers themselves, their communities, and their nation. Learn who in such fields as health, education, religion, recreation, and the arts are positively affected by the kinds of jobs volunteers perform every day, and you will find out how to encourage future voluntarism in adults and youth. The book provides both insights into vast dimensions of the voluntary sector and offers concrete direction for initiating and developing volunteer activities. This indispensable book serves as a call to arms, urging every citizen to get involved in this unique example of participatory democracy. It offers a comprehensive look at hundreds of volunteers and volunteer efforts in a very readable format, concluding with a solid case for developing a base of volunteers among young people. *Softcover, 346 pages, $19.95 (Nonmember), $13.95 (Member) (plus $3.50 shipping)*

The Volunteer's Survival Manual: The Only Practical Guide to Giving Your Time and Money
DARCY CAMPION DEVNEY (THE PRACTICAL PRESS, 1992)

▶ This volunteer's consumer guide shows how to choose a volunteer organization, custom-design a volunteer position, turn volunteer experience into a paying job, and solve group problems. It also explores the ethics of fund raising, corporate philanthropy, and cause-related marketing. Sections include: (1) Where Do You Fit? 1001 Ways to Volunteer; (2) Join Today, Job Tomorrow; (3) Savvy Networking: People & Politics; (4) What Do You Give, What Do You Get?; (5) A Volunteer's Dilemmas: Evaluations & Ethics; and (6) Resources: Organizations & Publications. *Softcover, 192 pages, $16 (plus $2 shipping)*

You Can Make a Difference!
MARLENE WILSON (VOLUNTEER MANAGEMENT ASSOCIATES, 1993)

▶ This inspirational, step-by-step guide has been called a "self-help book with a twist"—improve your own life by helping others. Volunteer opportunities, reasons for volunteering, and inspirational stories of people who are volunteering and making a difference are highlighted. This timely book is a celebration of the spirit of giving and a guide for those who want to take a step toward a more fulfilling life. *Softcover, 210 pages, $12.95*

Volunteer Management
(See also Development and Orientation; Insurance, Liability, and Risk Management; Recruitment and Retention)

101 Ideas for Volunteer Programs

STEVE MCCURLEY AND SUE VINEYARD (HERITAGE ARTS, 1986)

▶ First in the popular "Brainstorm Series," this timeless, easy-to-read reference contains nearly 1,000 practical suggestions for planning and administering your volunteer program. Discover an array of creative ideas and innovative tips, presented with the wit and wisdom of two of volunteerism's most respected trainers. It is based on conversations with over 20,000 leaders in the field. *Softcover, 72 pages, $11.95*

Building Better Relations with Volunteers

NAN HAWTHORNE (MBA PUBLISHING)

▶ This training kit has all you need to bolster positive relationships between staff and volunteers within your organization: a step-by-step training manual, handout masters, transparencies, and a flyer announcing the training. Help staff understand why people volunteer, and use this information to enhance both the work and their own jobs. You can customize the handouts by going to Nan Hawthorne's Web site at *http://www.cybervpm.com/. $28.70*

Building Staff/Volunteer Relations

IVAN H. SCHEIER (ENERGIZE, INC., 1993)

▶ This is a discussion of how and why volunteer/employee relationships can deteriorate and what to do to build teamwork. It offers practical suggestions for analyzing paid and volunteer work in order to develop the best volunteer assignments. It helps employees and volunteers work together successfully by exploring the reasons for conflict between volunteers and employees. Scheier eases the all-too-common stresses of this relationship with a step-by-step process for analyzing tasks and work preferences for both paid and unpaid staff. It offers a great number of creative and practical solutions and contains lots of useful planning guides. *Softcover, 70 pages, $16.95*

By Definition: Policies for Volunteer Programs, 2nd Edition

LINDA L. GRAFF (GRAFF AND ASSOCIATES/VOLUNTEER ONTARIO, 1997)

▶ Policies are critical in reducing risks and ensuring safe and satisfying volunteer involvement. This is a step-by-step manual on developing policies specifically for volunteer programs. The manual provides clear definitions of policies and procedures; outlines how managers of volunteers, boards of directors, and senior staff can work together on policy design; and includes working samples of policies in over 70 different topic areas. It is a key resource that will crucially inform the process of making policies for your program. *Spiral bound, 90 pages, $24.95*

The Effective Management of Volunteer Programs

MARLENE WILSON (VOLUNTEER MANAGEMENT ASSOCIATES, 1996)

▶ This book is a gold mine of practical strategies and proven ideas: a one-stop source for information on volunteer attitudes and philosophies, developing volunteer training programs, management roles and techniques, motivating volunteers, goal setting, planning and evaluation, creative job design, volunteer recruitment essentials, interviewing techniques, and more. It includes many worksheets, exercises, and diagrams. *Softcover, 197 pages, $11.95*

From the Top Down: The Executive Role in Volunteer Program Success, Revised Edition

SUSAN J. ELLIS (ENERGIZE, INC., 1996)

▶ This book is addressed to the top decision makers of an organization and covering the things necessary to lay a foundation for successful volunteer involvement. It includes budgeting and resource allocation, employee/volunteer relationships, liability, and legal issues. It clearly illuminates the issues necessary to facilitate volunteer program success, including developing a vision for volunteer involvement, addressing questions of policy, budgeting funds and other resources, staffing the volunteer program, assessing the impact of volunteer contributions, and dealing with legal, risk management, and insurance issues. It also includes the revised FASB regulations on accounting practices regarding donated time. *Softcover, 210 pages, $24.95*

Handling Problem Volunteers

SUE VINEYARD AND STEVE MCCURLEY (HERITAGE ARTS PUBLISHING, 2000)

▶ Are your volunteers' problems causing you problems? Not sure what to do next? Steve and Sue take a lighthearted look at some of the most common volunteer performance problems and deliver some serious solutions. It helps you to assess the extent and root causes of problems. Examples range from "Annoying Volunteers" with poor interpersonal skills to "Dangerously Dysfunctional" ones, posing risk concerns. Sample volunteer policies directly related to the handling of problematic volunteer situations are also included. *Softcover, 60 pages, $18*

The (Help!) I-Don't-Have-Enough-Time Guide to Volunteer Management

KATHERINE NOYES CAMPBELL AND SUSAN J. ELLIS (ENERGIZE, INC., 1995)

▶ This book presents a step-by-step framework for creating a team approach to volunteer management. With this realistic, no-nonsense book, you'll learn how to map the boundaries of your job and clarify expectations; find administrative volunteers and put them to work in vital ways; and share ownership and the work of the volunteer program with everyone in your organization. It includes an appendix of electronic volunteerism resources. *Softcover, 120 pages, $14.95*

Leadership and Management of Volunteer Programs: A Guide for Volunteer Administrators

JAMES C. FISHER AND KATHLEEN M. COLE (JOSSEY-BASS 1993)

▶ Based on the "Certification Competencies" developed by the Association for Volunteer Administration, it details the professional knowledge, skills, and abilities managers need to involve volunteers in the work of an organization; each chapter offers insight into a particular functional area within volunteer administration, including establishing an organizational climate for volunteers, staffing, recruiting volunteers from a marketing approach, motivation, managing relationships between paid and volunteer staff, and training, supervising, and evaluating volunteers. It explains the volunteer administrator's role as both a manager and leader of volunteers, drawing upon general management references as well as volunteerism sources to make its points. Many case study examples from real life illustrate the principles presented. It is an excellent tool for new volunteer administrators or those reviewing their own professional development. *Hardcover, 228 pages, $24.95 (plus $4.50 shipping)*

Leading Volunteers for Results: Building Communities Today

JEANNE H. BRADNER (CONVERSATION PRESS, INC., 1999)

▶ This book shows you that some volunteer efforts fall short because the people in leadership positions don't understand the principles of volunteer management. In other cases, those in charge are so concerned about administrative management that they fail to exercise leadership. *Leading Volunteers for Results* focuses on the important marriage of leadership and management skills that inspires results-oriented volunteer efforts. It will give the 10 crucial steps needed to lead volunteers successfully; save you from "I wish I had known" hindsight; show you how to apply human resource management skills to the volunteer world; teach you that leadership is mission driven and that generic management formulas will not work; help you make volunteer service by others rewarding, worthwhile, and productive; revitalize your enthusiasm for the programs in which you lead or are involved; and prepare you to cope with change in the volunteer world. *Softcover, 128 pages, $11.95 (plus $2.00 shipping and handling)*

Managing Volunteers in Record Time
NAN HAWTHORNE (MBA PUBLISHING)

▶ Tired of time management books and training obviously written for business executives with paid staff to help them? Here's an interactive workshop that covers how to set priorities and recognize typical barriers to "getting it all done." It even builds teamwork, a common goal, and a sense of success through an exercise in which participants solve one chosen time-crunch problem before they even walk out the door. The kit contains an instruction manual, handouts, transparencies, exercise tools, announcement flyer, and diskette. You can customize the handouts by going to Nan Hawthorne's Web site at *http://www.cybervpm.com/*. It is perfect for DOVIA or volunteer managers training session. *$28.70*

Policy Development for Volunteer Services Audio Workshop
LINDA L. GRAFF (GRAFF & ASSOCIATES/ENERGIZE, INC., 1996)

▶ A follow-up piece to *By Definition,* this audiotape and accompanying guide provide more in-depth discussion of how to develop policies for volunteer programs. It offers step-by-step guidance on the rules of policy writing, gaining board support, ensuring policy compliance, and reducing risk and liability through volunteer program policies. It includes examples and real-life stories. Follow along with the accompanying workbook. *90-minute audiotape and 16-page workbook, $14.95*

Proof Positive: Developing Significant Volunteer Recordkeeping Systems, Revised Edition
(Workbook/Manual)
SUSAN ELLIS & KATHERINE NOYES (ENERGIZE, INC., 1990)

▶ This revised edition presents the basic elements of a volunteer record-keeping system and guidelines for developing forms and procedures to suit individual programs. It discusses everything needed to organize your record keeping into a valuable management tool, such as application forms, volunteer fact cards, assignment logs, time and activity report-sheets, and assignment tracking. Though the focus is on designing a workable manual system, there is a chapter on computers, helping you to decide whether to computerize and what to look for in volunteer program software. It explains how to develop a manual record-keeping system to track and manage volunteer efforts. It includes many sample forms and information on hard-to-keep record situations. *Softcover, 60 pages, $12.75 (plus $3.25 shipping)*

Stop Managing Volunteers! New Competencies for Volunteer Administrators
SUE VINEYARD (HERITAGE ARTS PUBLISHING, 1996)

▶ This is a teaching workbook that explains the competencies needed by volunteer administrators in our new century, including "leadershift," inspiring creativity, new forms of recognition, being a change agent, handling conflict, dealing with problem volunteers, leading in a healthy climate, working with staff, thinking entrepreneurially, broadening the resource base, and reinventing the organization! It even explains why volunteer administrators cannot afford to spend all their time directly managing volunteers. It includes many worksheets and tools to use today. *Softcover, 109 pages, $18.95*

Virtual Volunteering Guidebook *(See Online Volunteerism)*

The Volunteer Management Audit
SUSAN J. ELLIS (UNITED WAY OF AMERICA, 1992—AVAILABLE FROM ENERGIZE)

▶ Originally produced as a consultation tool for volunteer centers, it is ideal for developing and evaluating an agency's volunteer program. It has a self-contained, self-administered checklist for analyzing an organization's effectiveness in supporting volunteers. Containing a set of 25 booklets and an instruction guide, the book allows teams of employees and volunteers to each complete an assessment and then gather together to discuss their results. It covers the 13 elements of a successful volunteer program (planning, recruiting, employee/volunteer relationships, etc.). While basic standards are presented, it encourages each agency to evaluate itself against its own objectives. It can be facilitated by a volunteer center or a consultant. DOVIAS can use the booklets in a session in which members consider the basic standards for themselves. *Set of 25 AUDIT booklets and one Instruction booklet, $20 (plus $4.75 shipping)*

The Volunteer Management Handbook
TRACY DANIEL CONNORS, ED. (JOHN WILEY & SONS, 1999)

▶ National authorities offer a wealth of practical, how-to information in the art and science of volunteer development, administration, and law-related areas. Particular attention is given to pointing out the similarities and differences in volunteer policy and law in various states. This handy desktop reference contains all the information a nonprofit manager needs in order to establish and maintain an active volunteer program. It provides crucial material on legal issues ranging from standard employment law to risk management and such management practices as recruiting, training, and integrating volunteers into the general organizational structure. It features guidelines, suggestions, checklists, and sample forms plus proven strategies and techniques from experts in the nonprofit sector. *Softcover, 407 pages, $34.95*

Volunteer Management: Mobilizing All the Resources of the Community
STEVE MCCURLEY AND RICK LYNCH (HERITAGE ARTS PUBLISHING, 1996)

▶ This book offers a thorough examination of every facet of a successful volunteer program, from planning and organizing through measuring effectiveness. Highlighted throughout this manual are insightful quotes by practitioners and consultants in the field. It includes an extensive bibliography, a list of organizations and Web sites, sample volunteer management policies, and numerous sample forms and worksheets, as well as a comprehensive discussion of each of the functions of volunteer program development and management. Also included is an extensive appendix with hundreds of books and organizational resources. *Softcover, 236 pages, $25*

Universal Volunteering: A Practical Workbook for Nonprofit Organizations, Volunteers, and Corporations (Book and Disk)

WALTER P. PIDGEON JR. (JOHN WILEY & SONS, 1997)

▶ With its unique ability to fulfill personal and professional goals, social needs, and corporate objectives, volunteering is much more than its own reward. But just how much more depends on the thought and planning that go into the process. That's why, as more and more nonprofits and for-profits pool their resources in volunteering partnerships, the development of an effective approach to the design and management of these programs is essential. This comprehensive book–disk set provides not-for-profit leaders, for-profit business executives, individual volunteers, community leaders, and others with the systematic, hands-on guidance they need to maximize the benefits of volunteering for everyone involved, from front-line volunteers to community members. Focusing on the crucial concept of "return value," the workbook offers solid practical advice on recruiting, training, and retaining today's volunteers. It examines volunteer program planning and implementation for both not-for-profit and for-profit organizations. And, most importantly, it explores how these entities can forge strategic alliances that match the nonprofit need for motivated, business-wise volunteers to the corporate desire to boost staff teamwork, time management, and other key skills. The workbook comes complete with easy-to-follow procedures and checklists, plus worksheets and sample documents that are also included on the IBM-compatible disk. Simple to use and ready to implement, *Universal Volunteering* is an invaluable how-to tool for tackling a full range of volunteering challenges. *Hardcover, 256 pages, $39.95*

What We Learned (the Hard Way) About Supervising Volunteers: An Action Guide for Making Your Job Easier

JARENE FRANCES LEE WITH JULIA M. CATAGNUS (ENERGIZE, INC., 1999)

▶ Whether supervising volunteers is just one of your many responsibilities or your sole job is to coordinate your agency's volunteers, this new book by Jarene Lee with Julia Catagnus offers a comprehensive understanding of what it means to be a supervisor, and provides a wealth of practical tips on how to perform at your best and most efficient. Packed with the advice, wisdom, and experience of over 85 real-life, on-the-job supervisors of volunteers, this guide offers a crystal clear analysis of what works and what doesn't in supervision. It also includes comments from volunteers about what they need from those who supervise them, as well as excerpts from classic articles and books by experts in the field and a self-assessment survey covering the attitudes and actions necessary to be an effective supervisor. Every relevant subject is explored: defining expectations, training and providing support, communicating effectively, coaching your team, solving performance problems, conducting formal evaluations, and assessing your own skills. Aided by a cadre of experts, Lee and Catagnus demonstrate what works and what doesn't—always taking pains to explain why. They share their challenges and tell you how they met them. Among

other things, you'll learn how to define volunteer job expectations and establish the goals to meet them; train new volunteers and provide ongoing education to all volunteers; resolve performance problems promptly and satisfactorily; motivate volunteers through recognition and feedback; build successful relationships with volunteers; and evaluate your program to determine its strengths and weaknesses. A Virtual Interactive Appendix is available at *http://www.energizeinc.com/supervising.html*. *Softcover, 155 pages, $21.95*

When Everyone's a Volunteer: The Effective Functioning of All-Volunteer Groups

IVAN H. SCHEIER (ENERGIZE, INC. 1992)

▶ This book challenges conventional wisdom about managing an all-volunteer effort (or one with very few paid staff) and provides an innovative framework for change; examines member participation in setting achievable goals, facing the challenges of leadership, distributing work fairly, continuity on a bare bones budget, and preventing burnout; and introduces creative concepts such as feasible fund raising, time tithing, co-promotion campaigns, and cultivating a "network attitude" within the group. The last section gives full instructions on several outstanding networking exercises (one initiates a sign-up process for connecting with other volunteers who have common interests; another encourages people to think about their talents and skills and how they can best utilize them to accomplish the group's goals) and points out that "it is in all-volunteer effort that risk can be taken on behalf of the quality of life." *Softcover, 63 pages, $15.75 (plus $3.25 shipping)*

Yes You Can!: Discipline and Dismissal of Volunteers (An Audio Workshop)

LINDA L. GRAFF (GRAFF AND ASSOCIATES/VOLUNTEER VANCOUVER, 1999)

▶ *Yes You Can* tackles this tough management issue with a discussion of the elements of rightful dismissal, the principles of progressive discipline, and how to decrease both organizational and personal risks. Experience the energy of a live presentation in Linda Graff's spirited and pragmatic treatment of one of our toughest management issues: discipline and dismissal of volunteers. This audiocassette workshop will help you to discover the elements of rightful dismissal, master the steps and principles of progressive discipline, and learn how to decrease both personal and organizational risks in all of your discipline and dismissal actions. Gain both the confidence and skills to do what needs to be done. *95 minutes, $12*

Volunteer Opportunities

Alternatives to the Peace Corps: A Directory of Third World and U.S. Volunteer Opportunities, 8th Edition

FILOMENA GEISE AND MARILYN BORCHARDT, EDS. (FOOD FIRST BOOKS, 1999)

▶ This is a guide to voluntary service, study, and alternative travel overseas and in the United States with organizations that "address the political and economic causes of poverty." It offers options other than the Peace Corps for people wishing to gain international experience. Exciting possibilities for working abroad can be designed independently according to your interests and beliefs. This resourceful guide provides essential information on voluntary service organizations, technical service programs, work brigades, and study tours, as well as alternative travel in the Third World. This is a valuable starting point to explore the options for volunteering. It has an excellent bibliography. *Softcover, 96 pages, $9.95*

The Back Door Guide to Short Term Job Adventures: Internships, Extraordinary Experiences, Seasonal Jobs, Volunteering, Work Abroad, Revised Edition

MICHAEL LANDES (TEN SPEED PRESS, 2000)

▶ This book offers in-depth reviews of thousands of perennially unique internships, seasonal jobs, overseas work, volunteer vacations, and other extraordinary short-term job opportunities. Whether you're just graduating, considering a midlife change of scenery, or planning an adventurous sabbatical, *The Back Door Guide* has something for everybody. Opportunities range from mountaineering to museums, work camps to wildlife, and each listing is complete with detailed and up-to-date information, including who to talk to, what it pays, where it's located, helpful insider tips on getting hired, and Internet sites for the Web savvy. This revised edition features 150 new listings for internships, seasonal work, volunteer opportunities, and overseas jobs. Numerous tips, quotes, features, and stories from other *Back Door* readers enlighten and amuse you, and five indexes make it all totally accessible. *Softcover, 336 pages, $19.95*

Council International Volunteer Projects

(COUNCIL ON INTERNATIONAL EDUCATIONAL EXCHANGE)

▶ This free brochure is available from the Council. It describes over 600 short-term summer voluntary service options available through the Council in 23 countries of Europe, Africa, and North America.

Council International Volunteer Projects Directory

(COUNCIL ON INTERNATIONAL EDUCATIONAL EXCHANGE)

▶ Available each April, it describes the workcamps in depth. *Softcover, 82 pages, $12*

Global Works 2000/2001 (Interaction)

▶ This guide lists volunteer, internship, and fellowship opportunities in international development abroad. It provides extensive volunteer opportunities from nearly 70 organizations working in 120 countries, including the United States. The guide also lists contact information for more information on volunteer work. A geographic and program index helps guide readers with specific interests. *$10 (Nonmember), $8 (Member)*

Going Places

JOANNE WOODS, ED. (NATIONAL STUDENT CAMPAIGN AGAINST HUNGER AND HOMELESSNESS, 1997)

▶ A collaborative effort between COOL and NSCAHH, it is a catalog of domestic and international internship, volunteer, travel, and career opportunities in the fields of hunger, housing, homelessness, and grassroots development. It includes descriptions of 98 organizations. *Softcover, 49 pages, $6.25 (plus shipping and handling)*

Helping Out in the Outdoors

(AMERICAN HIKING SOCIETY)

▶ Whether you're looking for a one-week or one-year volunteer position, you'll find it in *Helping Out in the Outdoors,* American Hiking Society's national listing of internships and volunteer opportunities. It is an annual directory of over 2,000 volunteer jobs at national parks, forests, and other public lands in all states. To view *Helping Out in the Outdoors* opportunities online, check out the *Hiker's Info Center* at *http://www.americanhiking.org/infocenter/index.html. Softcover, $10*

International Directory of Voluntary Work, 8th Edition

LOUISE WHETTER AND VICTORIA PHYBUS, EDS. (VACATION WORK, 2000—AVAILABLE FROM PETERSON'S)

▶ This directory contains details of over 700 organizations that are looking for voluntary help from all types of people for all kinds of work. It covers short-, medium-, and long-term residential opportunities in Europe and around the world in addition to nonresidential opportunities in the United Kingdom. Both skilled and unskilled people are needed, whether to help for a few hours or a few years. Help a development project in Mozambique, a steam railway in Yorkshire, a street clinic in Calcutta, sea turtles in Mexico, or orphanages in Romania. *Softcover, 272 pages, $12.76*

International Workcamp Directory

(SERVICE CIVIL INTERNATIONAL)

▶ Every April the U.S. Group of Service Civil International (SCI) publishes its directory of hundreds of workcamp opportunities in North America, eastern and western Europe, sub-Saharan Africa, South Asia, and Latin America. *Magazine format, 56 pages, free on request*

Invest Yourself: The Catalogue of Volunteer Opportunities

SUSAN G. ANGUS, ED. (THE COMMISSION ON VOLUNTARY SERVICE AND ACTION, 1999)

▶ This comprehensive directory of nongovernmental international and domestic voluntary service opportunities through North American–based organizations includes sections written by current and former volunteers and a discussion of voluntarism as a way of life. *Softcover, 282 pages, $8*

The Peace Corps and More: 175 Ways to Work, Study, and Travel at Home and Abroad

MEDEA BENJAMIN AND MIYA RODOLFO-SIOSON, EDS. (GLOBAL EXCHANGE, 1997)

▶ This book contains almost 200 organizations that allow you to gain development experience while promoting ideas of social justice and sustainable development. *Softcover, 127 pages, $8.95*

Response: Volunteer Opportunities Directory of the Catholic Network of Volunteer Service

(CATHOLIC NETWORK OF VOLUNTEER SERVICE)

▶ This is a directory of lay mission opportunities in the United States and abroad, most of which have an activist, nonproselytizing approach. Listings include some non-Catholic religious organizations. It includes indexes by type of placement, location, length of time, couples, parents with dependents, and so on, and is updated annually. *Softcover, 90 pages, free*

Service-Learning & Business/Education Partnerships: A Guide for Service-Learning Coordinators

JIM PITOFSKY (NATIONAL ASSOCIATION OF PARTNERS IN EDUCATION, 1994))

▶ Formerly titled *Creating and Managing Partnerships for Service-Learning Integration: A Guide for Service-Learning*

Coordinators, this revised, self-guiding manual takes you through Partners in Education's 12-Step Process for Program Development, and it includes more lessons learned from partnerships around the country. It gives you the information and guidance you need to develop and implement quality partnerships. After using the manual, you will be able to identify the key players and how to recruit and manage their involvement for integrating service into school curricula. Based on NAPE's service-learning model, IDEALS (Innovative Democratic Education And Learning through Service) Project, this self-guiding manual takes you through Awareness, Needs Assessment, Potential Resources, Goals & Objectives, Program Design, Partnership Management, Recruitment, Orientation, Training, Retention & Recognition, and Monitoring & Evaluation. *$40 (Nonmember) (Professional and institutional member discounts available) (plus $7.50 shipping)*

VFP International Workcamp Directory
(VOLUNTEERS FOR PEACE)

▶ Available each April, it describes over 800 short-term service placements in over 40 countries throughout western and eastern Europe, Russia, North and West Africa, Asia, and the Americas available through VFP for the summer and fall of the year of publication. *Softcover, $12*

Vacation Study Abroad 2000/2001 (Annual)
(INSTITUTE OF INTERNATIONAL EDUCATION)

▶ This book lists and describes over 2,200 programs offered in over 70 countries by U.S. and foreign universities, schools, museums, associations and organizations—on land and sea, in western and eastern Europe, Asia, Africa, the Middle East, Oceania, and the Americas. It covers U.S. education abroad for precollege students, graduate students, teachers, professionals, senior citizens, and other adult learners,—as well as U.S. undergraduates. Learning options range from class work and intensive language immersion to work-study, internships, student teaching, field research, and volunteer service. *Softcover, $42.95*

Volunteer!: The Comprehensive Guide to Voluntary Service in the U.S. and Abroad
RICHARD CHRISTIANO, ED. (COUNCIL ON INTERNATIONAL EDUCATIONAL EXCHANGE, 1995)

▶ This book lists nearly 200 voluntary service organizations recruiting volunteers for work in the United States and abroad. It is organized by short-term and long-term opportunities, with indexes by country and type of work. It is a good place to start exploring volunteer options, though becoming dated. *Softcover, 188 pages, $12.95*

Volunteer Vacations: Short-Term Adventures That Will Benefit You and Others, 6th Edition
BILL MCMILLON (CHICAGO REVIEW PRESS, 1999)

▶ Fully updated and revised, the sixth edition of this classic adventure travel guide profiles more than 250 charitable organizations and 2,000 projects in the United States and abroad that need volunteers. It is indexed by cost, length of time, location, type of project, and season. Opportunities range from one weekend to six weeks. *Softcover, 453 pages, $16.95*

Work Abroad 2001: The Complete Guide to Finding a Job Overseas, 3rd Edition
CLAYTON A. HUBBS, SUSAN GRIFFITH, AND WILLIAM NOLTING, EDS. (TRANSITIONS ABROAD, 2000)

▶ This is the first comprehensive guide to all aspects of international work, including work permits, short-term jobs, teaching English, volunteer opportunities, planning out an international career, starting your own business, and much more. It is essential reading for anyone who wants to find a job overseas. *Softcover, 252 pages, $19.95 (includes shipping and handling)*

Working for Global Justice Directory
(YOUTH ACTION FOR GLOBAL JUSTICE, 1999)

▶ This is a handbook of volunteer, internship, educational travel, or career opportunities in the United States and abroad, which focus on global justice. *Softcover, $8*

Volunteer Recruitment and Retention
(See also Insurance, Liability, and Risk Management)

101 Tips for Volunteer Recruitment
STEVE MCCURLEY AND SUE VINEYARD (HERITAGE ARTS, 1988)

▶ This third part of the timeless "Brainstorm Series" covers all aspects of recruiting. It examines both targeted and general recruitment, as well as tips on recruiting for difficult-to-fill volunteer positions. It explores trends, motivation, benefits, interviews, and much more. It covers all aspects of recruiting for volunteers, board members, and organization membership in an easy-to-read format, from planning the general recruitment campaign to specific advice on recruiting seniors and youth. It has hundreds of effective ideas to help recruit individuals for every possible volunteer job. It even suggests ways to recruit for the most impossible or difficult volunteer positions. It is a complete and informative guidebook to finding the volunteers you need in the quantities you have to have. *Softcover, 72 pages, $10 (plus $4.25 shipping)*

Beyond Banquets, Plaques and Pins: Creative Ways to Recognize Volunteers and Staff!, 2nd Edition
SUE VINEYARD (HERITAGE ARTS, 1994)

▶ Written from the viewpoint that the people to be recognized are our most priceless resource and deserving of our most creative and sensitive thinking, this updated edition of the best-selling book helps you offer meaningful recognition to the modern volunteer. It details the hows and whys of recognition, examining traditions, trends, climate, motivation, management, and what recognition is and is not. It presents more than 400 low-cost and no-cost ways ideas for honoring different volunteers (youth, working, senior, professional, church, hospital, low-income, and others) and provides the basics to create long-lasting recognition programs. *Softcover, 23 pages, $7 (plus $4.25 shipping)*

Beyond Police Checks: The Definitive Volunteer & Employee Screening Guidebook
LINDA L. GRAFF (GRAFF & ASSOCIATES, 1999)

▶ This is a comprehensive "how-to" manual on volunteer employee screening. Loaded with practical tips, helpful cautions, and fully reproducible checklists and assessment tools, this comprehensive guidebook will lead you step-by-step to increased screening awareness and program safety. Don't wake up one morning to a tragedy and find yourself wishing you had paid more attention to the escalating liabilities and higher standards of employee and volunteer screening. *Softcover, 150 pages, $25*

The Care and Feeding of Volunteers: Recruiting, Retaining & Rewarding Volunteers

BILL WITTICH (KNOWLEDGE TRANSFER, 2000)

▶ This book challenges the reader to consider applying many of the leadership strategies that are working in corporate America to how nonprofits manage volunteers. In this book, the author presents unorthodox ways of working with volunteers. It attempts to change the paradigm of how America thinks about managing volunteers. In *The Care & Feeding of Volunteers,* the author challenges you to consider applying many of the leadership strategies that are working in corporate America to your nonprofit place. This publication suggests, in an out-of-the-box way, that organizations should not be recruiting volunteers in a 1970 fashion. It's a new millennium and tomorrow's volunteers will not respond to yesterday's management thinking, but will be looking for an agency that respects their energy, passion, and talents. This publication is a part of Bill Wittich's training seminars on the Care and Feeding of Volunteers. *$17.95 (plus $4.00 shipping)*

Designing Programs for the Volunteer Sector

NANCY MACDUFF (HERITAGE ARTS—AVAILABLE THROUGH MBA PUBLISHING)

▶ Exciting programs attract excited and committed volunteers. This short book outlines a five-step process to design programs that are guaranteed to attract volunteers. Learn how to conduct a program needs assessment, set program objectives, arrange and plan activities, develop an administrative plan to support the new program, and evaluate the overall program. *Softcover, $11*

Episodic Volunteering: Building the Short-Term Volunteer Program

NANCY MACDUFF (MBA PUBLISHING, 1991)

▶ Many of today's volunteers want assignments of short duration. This book provides strategies to determine your readiness for this type of program, techniques to recruit, and ways to sustain the episodic volunteer. *Softcover, 27 pages, $10.95*

Secrets of Motivation: How to Get and Keep Volunteers & Paid Staff!

SUE VINEYARD (HERITAGE ARTS, 1991)

▶ This booklet examines motivation that turns people on to work that needs to be done and describes how to get and keep volunteers and paid staff members. It takes a look at today's volunteers, trends, theories, expectations, recognition, climate, retention, and satisfaction. It includes 42 "secrets," plus a section of more than 300 ideas for motivating specific types of people. *Softcover, 36 pages, $12.95*

Volunteer Recruiting And Retention: A Marketing Approach, 2nd Edition

NANCY MACDUFF (MBA PUBLISHING, 1996)

▶ Designed for volunteer program managers who have skills in one aspect of volunteer management but need a whole array of skills, this manual is divided into specific areas of volunteer program management. It outlines a step-by-step approach to the recruiting and retention of volunteers. The first seven steps explain a marketing approach to the recruitment of volunteers. Topics include conducting needs assessments, strategic planning, program promotion, developing job descriptions, and the use of volunteer recruiting teams. Explanations of the elements that contribute to volunteer retention are covered, including interviewing, motivation, supervision, volunteer evaluation, recognition, programs, and training. *Spiral bound, 251 pages, $40.50*

The Volunteer Recruitment Book, 2nd Edition

SUSAN J. ELLIS (ENERGIZE, INC., 1996)

▶ The author first shows how to design the best assignments for volunteers as the initial step to finding the most qualified people. What follows is a wealth of information on topics ranging from how your organization's image affects your success in recruitment to where to look for new volunteers, including your own backyard. Ellis shows how to analyze what you want volunteers to do, how to increase your recruitment effectiveness by designing the right jobs for volunteers, how to present your organization's image (something that can dramatically affect your success in recruitment), and how to identify the right recruiting technique for each group of volunteers you seek. As Ellis knows, however, recruitment doesn't exist in a vacuum, so she makes it a point to focus as well on preparing your organization for volunteer involvement; how to develop teamwork between volunteers and employees; orientation and training for volunteers; techniques of volunteer supervision; evaluation; and recognition. All of these must be in place or your recruitment will be hollow. It has a complete chapter on membership development for all volunteer groups. The book offers a fresh approach to the important management function of volunteer recruitment, presenting a recruitment strategy that breaks the process down into logical, manageable, and successful steps. It helps you analyze what you want volunteers to do and emphasizes the importance of developing job assignments before active recruitment begins. It includes suggestions on targeting sources for volunteers, evaluating the most effective techniques for recruiting, how to handle the media, how to handle one-to-one recruiting and many other topics. Learn about: (1) where to look for new volunteers (fresh ideas about sources of volunteers; looking in your own backyard with "The Proximity Chart," and such strategies as piggybacking); (2) why some people volunteer and why others do not, and what you can do about it; (3) the many techniques of recruitment (giving speeches, using electronic bulletin boards, etc.; gives pros and cons of almost any technique, plus tips to make better exhibits, speeches, flyers, and personal pitches); (4) recruiting for diversity (identify what "diversity" means to your organization and how you can find volunteers who expand your current membership); (5) how designing the best jobs for volunteers leads directly to more effective recruitment (develop the widest range of options, including work for evening volunteers and those seeking short-term assignments); and (6) how your organization's image affects your success in recruitment, plus the trends and issues in volunteering that influence you. It includes a chapter on membership development for all-volunteer organizations, including how to find new members, get current members "off the rolls and on their feet," and how to encourage people to accept leadership positions. It includes checklists and illustrations. *Softcover, 144 pages, $18.75 (plus $3.25 shipping)*

Volunteer Screening: An Audio Workbook

NANCY MACDUFF (MBA PUBLISHING)

▶ Selecting the right volunteer for the right job is both art and science. This electronic book, on cassette tape, includes forms to accompany the tape. Listen to Nancy Macduff review the important strategies to screen volunteers: job descriptions, applications, interviews, and contracts. There is a special section on recruiting and interviewing for large volunteer programs. *$23*

Volunteers: How to Get Them, How to Keep Them, 2nd Edition

HELEN LITTLE (PANACEA PRESS, INC., 1999)

▶ This practical, down-to-earth guide offers real advice on solving your volunteer shortage. Whether yours is a large international association or a local food pantry, volunteers are the lifeblood of your organization. You rely on volunteers to carry out projects, head up task forces, coordinate events, and eventually become the future leaders of your organization. It outlines 12 basic needs of volunteers and volunteer leaders and clearly explains how to meet those needs. Find out how to compete for volunteers, recruit the best person for the job, ensure that projects are completed on time, equip new volunteers to hit the ground running, manage volunteers (versus managing employees), fire a volunteer, keep your best volunteers coming back, and more. It is especially focused on all-volunteer organizations. *Softcover, 128 pages, $24.95*

Volunteer–Staff Relations

Building Staff/Volunteer Relations

IVAN H. SCHEIER (ENERGIZE, 1993)

▶ Revised edition of the *Staff/Volunteer Relations Collection,* this creative and practical book deals directly with one of the major challenges in volunteer management: helping employees and volunteers work together successfully. It advises a step-by-step process for analyzing tasks and work preferences for both paid and unpaid staff. It demonstrates how concern for clear and desirable job descriptions avoids the pitfalls of blurry lines of responsibility, and defuses the tension inherent in this subject, exploring the reasons for conflict between volunteers and employees and offering a great number of useful solutions. It incorporates and updates three previous publications on staff relations. It includes many useful planning guides. *Softcover, 70 pages, $17*

PERIODICALS

ARNOVA News *(See The Nonprofit Sector for full description)*

GRAPEVINE: A Volunteerism Newsletter (Bimonthly Newsletter)

Heritage Arts Publishing (Editorial), Sue Vineyard, 8493 Chicory Court, Darien, IL 60561
Tel: 630-910-0095

Volunteer Sales Center, California Association of Hospitals and Health Systems (CAHHS), P.O. Box 340100, Sacramento, CA 95834-0100
Tel: 800-272-8306, 916-928-3950

▶ This newsletter keeps you up to date on all aspects of volunteerism, including volunteer management, current affairs, nonprofit management, and facts and figures on relevant trends. It is a source of latest volunteer news, articles, research information, resources, legal and legislative issues, trends, recruitment and training tips, recognition suggestions, calendar of events, and more to help volunteer leaders manage activities effectively, providing useful "how-to" tools and instruction. Regular features include: "News to Use," the latest information you should have; "Along the Vine," news about people, places, and things in the field; "Management," in-depth, how-to articles on people and program management, "Resources," a look at new products; "Vintage Vineyard," comments and insights from founding editor, Sue Vineyard; and "DOVIA (Directors of Volunteers in Agencies) Exchange," news for local groups; also Statistics, Research, Training & Management Tools, Liability Issues, Legislative Updates, Jobs, Grant Application Instructions, Guides, etc. *16 pages, $25/year*

The Journal of Volunteer Administration (Quarterly)

Association for Volunteer Administration, P.O. 32092, Richmond, VA 23294
Tel: 804-346-2266; FAX: 804-346-3318
E-mail: avaintl@mindspring.com; WWW: http://www.avaintl.org/

▶ This is a professional journal written by people in the field of volunteer administration. *The Journal* features in-depth articles on program management, model projects, tested techniques for successful volunteer involvement representing a wide diversity of volunteer program types, settings, and location; also articles on professional career development, practical concerns, and philosophical issues, as well as significant research related to the management of volunteers. The spring edition is traditionally utilized as a format for speeches, workshops, seminars, and consultations given at the annual conference. *$45/year*

Nonprofit and Voluntary Sector Quarterly *(See The Nonprofit Sector for full description)*

The Review of Service and Volunteer Programs (Quarterly Journal)

Civic Literacy Project, Center for the Study of Participation and Citizenship, Indiana University, Woodburn Hall #210, 1100 East Seventh Street, Bloomington, IN 47405
Tel: 812-856-4677; FAX: 812-856-7137
E-mail: wdmorgan@indiana.edu (William Morgan), clpadmin@indiana.edu; WWW: http://serve.indiana.edu

▶ This journal brings together peer-reviewed research articles written in an accessible style with book reviews and feature articles. This will allow program directors and nonprofit professionals to benefit from the growing research and evaluation that examines the elements that help make programs more effective. Further, it will build the research base that supports the use of community service and service learning. *The Review of Service and Volunteer Programs* will provide an excellent forum for all professionals involved in service-related pursuits. Research will not only further the integration of the service community, but it will also help to illuminate successful trends and pitfalls experienced by others. *48 pages, $40/year*

Transitions Abroad: The Guide to Learning, Living, and Working Abroad (Bimonthly Magazine)

Dept. TRA, Box 3000, Denville, NJ 07834
Tel: 800-293-0373
E-mail: trabroad@aol.com, business@TransitionsAbroad.com; WWW: http://www.transabroad.com

▶ This is a guide to practical information on affordable alternatives to mass tourism: living, working, studying, volunteering, or vacationing alongside the people of the host country. It is a very helpful resource, with new information every two months, complete with Web addresses for hundreds of sponsoring organizations. *$24.95/year*

Volunteer Leadership (Quarterly Magazine)

Points of Light Foundation (Editorial), 1400 I Street NW, Suite 800, Washington, DC 20005
Tel: 202-729-8000; FAX: 202-729-8100
E-mail: info@pointsoflight.org

Volunteer Leadership Circulation, P.O. Box 79246 (Circulation), Baltimore, MD 21279-0246
Tel: 800-272-8306/879-5400

▶ For leaders in volunteer management, regular features include Leader to Leader (short takes on leadership skills and working styles, board trends, travel tips, and more); Workshop (a series of articles that focus on a specific aspect of volunteer management and nonprofit administration, such as nonprofit risk management, strategic planning, board development, fund raising, recruitment, recognition, training, record keeping, interviewing); Board Primer (nuts and bolts of volunteer leadership: skills in leading a board, fiduciary responsibilities, volunteer protection, leading committees to productive outcomes, succeeding as a spokesperson); Program Profiles of innovative volunteer programs and leaders, such as teen mentoring, volunteering in other countries, intergenerational volunteer programs, volunteers as social entrepreneurs, and more; Points of View from nonprofit, government, and business leaders on current issues affecting the volunteer community); Legislative Updates on congressional bills that affect the volunteer field; and Tool Box, a resource listing of inexpensive or complimentary publications/resource materials (books, booklets, periodicals, videotapes and films, and more). It also includes a special "networking directory" of members in your area of volunteer management. *40 pages, $30/year*

Volunteer Management Report (Monthly Newsletter)

Stevenson Consultants, Inc., P.O. Box 4528, Sioux City, IA 51104
Tel: 712-239-3010; FAX: 712-239-2166
E-mail: subscribe@stevensoninc.com (Subscriptions),
inquiry@stevensoninc.com (Inquires), ideas@stevensoninc.com (General Comments and Ideas); WWW: www.stevensoninc.com/usefulconnect.htm

▶ Filled with concisely written articles, this monthly newsletter offers practical tips and techniques that will strengthen all your volunteer efforts. You'll be linked with thousands of professionals like yourself who are sharing their success stories in each monthly issue. Each issue of the *Volunteer Management Report* covers topics including volunteer/board recruitment, motivation techniques, training volunteers, screening procedures, special events, recognition ideas, grants for volunteer programs, volunteer telemarketing, retention strategies, nurturing leadership, managing meetings, successful programs, board relations, effective communication, roles and responsibilities, increasing membership, effective committees, volunteer profiles, enlisting a "can-do" chairperson, and more. The last page of the newsletter, Volunteer Insider, will be written to reproduce for your volunteers. *8 pages, $119/year*

INTERNET SITES

General Information

Amizade Volunteer Links

▶ *http://amizade.org/links.htm#Volunteer*

Ask Connie

▶ A feature of *Volunteer Today* where readers ask questions about volunteer management and administration. *http://www.volunteerto-day.com/Connie.html*

Association for Volunteer Administration Links

▶ Valuable connections for volunteer administration professionals. *http://www.avaintl.org/resources/links.html*

CyberVPM.com

▶ Maintained by Nan Hawthorne, a consultant on volunteer management, this site has two sections. One is for volunteers and contains information about service opportunities and links to Internet sites. The other is intended for managers of volunteers and has articles and links to Internet sites that deal with such topics as volunteer–staff relations and how to recruit and screen volunteers. CyberVPM concentrates entirely on Internet-related services regarding volunteer resource management and volunteerism. Users can sign up for a free monthly e-mail newsletter on volunteer program management and view resources on volunteerism. *http://www.cybervpm.com/*

Energize

▶ Maintained by Energize, a Philadelphia consulting and publishing company that specializes in volunteerism, this site allows people to debate controversial topics in the management of volunteers and includes a bibliography of more than 1,000 books, articles, and reports on volunteer–management issues. It also contains articles on volunteerism, a section that allows users to contribute their favorite quotations on volunteering and giving, a schedule of forthcoming conferences on volunteerism and volunteer management, and links to other Internet sites on volunteerism. *http://www.ener-gizeinc.com*

Give Five—Independent Sector

▶ Give Five works to raise public awareness about the important role that giving and volunteering play in our communities. Another place to post volunteer opportunities online, with some general information about volunteerism. *http://www.indepsec.org/give5/g5volunteer.html*

Internet Resources for Volunteer Programs

▶ *http://www.cybervpm.com/kits.htm*

Merrill Associates

▶ This site features a "Topic of the Month" focusing on a helpful tip relating to volunteer management, strategic planning, board development, leadership/change management, communication, collaborations, or corporate volunteerism. *http://www.merrillas-soc.com*

Nonprofit Frequently Asked Questions (FAQs)— Volunteerism (Internet Nonprofit Center)

▶ This site features frequently asked questions and their answers, compiled from posts by nonprofit professionals to NONPROFIT (list) and soc.org.nonprofit (USENET group), as well as from information posted to other nonprofit-related Internet discussion groups. It is comprehensive, with information or links to information on volunteering from both a volunteer's and an agency's point of view. It includes information on setting up an all-volunteer program, program development strategy, training, and screening volunteers. *http://www.nonprofit-info.org/npofaq/04/index.html*

Online Book List for Volunteer Managers— Directors of Volunteers in Agencies of Denver

▶ This is an online book list with over 700 resources of printed resources available for nonprofit professionals and volunteer managers. It includes categories such as aged volunteers, boards, communication, conflict, directory, diversity, education, fund raising, history, internet, leadership, liability, management, marketing, mentor, motivation, newsletters, organization, periodicals, recognition, recruitment, retention, service-learning, software, staff–volunteer relations, teams, training, videos, vocations, volunteer management, and youth. *http://www.regis.edu/spsmnm/dovia/do04001.htm*

Volunteer Center of Dallas County—Nonprofit Links

▶ *http://www.nonprofits.org/Agencies/nonprofit_links.htm*

Resources for the Volunteer Management Professional

▶ *http://www.voluncheer.com/vmt.html*

Volunteers—The Nonprofit Zone

▶ *http://www.nonprofitzone.com/voluntr.htm*

Web Sites Promoting Volunteerism/Community Service

▶ This site is for those looking for information about volunteerism (why do it, who is doing it, tips for doing it, etc.) and organizations that sponsor national or international volunteering efforts of their own. This site also provides links to service-learning resources. *http://www.serviceleader.org/vv/vonline4.html*

Web Sites Related to Philanthropy and Voluntarism (An Index)

▶ This comprehensive list is compiled by David James of the Center for the Study of Philanthropy and Voluntarism. *http://www.pubpol.duke.edu/courses/pps280s/index.html*

Bibliography

Check out the following comprehensive lists of books and other resources on volunteerism and related issues:

http://www.energizeinc.com/art.html
http://energizeinc.com/bkstore.html
http://www.caresource.com/volunteer.htm
http://www.vancouver.volunteer.ca/resources/resource_library. asp
http://www.regis.edu/spsmnm/dovia/Library/search.htm
http://www.nonprofits.org/library/bib3.html
http://www.volunteermanagement.com/catalog.htm
http://www.umich.edu/~icenter/overseas/work/volunteer3.html
http://www.davidson.edu/administrative/careers/serbooks.htm
http://www.backdoorjobs.com/books.html
http://www.transabroad.com/resources/work/resources/index.shtml
http://www.cybervpm.com/resource.htm
http://www.charityvillage.com/charityvillage/books10a.html
http://www.servenet.org/cont/control_cont_item_view.cfm?cont entTypeId=10
http://www.thecuttingedge.com/Np/NP_BookLists/NP_Volunteer Mgmnt.asp
http://www.nfpaccounting.com/books_volunteers.htm
http://www.regis.edu/spsmnm/dovia/do04001.htm
http://www.volunteerpro.com/resources_books.htm
http://www.avaintl.org/resources/bibliography.html
http://www.main.org/dovia/tools/print.htm
http://www.volunteertoday.com/bookstore.html
http://www.pointsoflight.org/volunteermarketplace/TableOfCon tents.cfm

Education and Professional Development

Courses in Volunteer Management at Institutions of Higher Education

▶ *http://www.serviceleader.org/training/courses.html*

Training and Education (Classes, Certificate Programs, and Institutes)—Energize

▶ *http://www.energizeinc.com/prof/class.html*

Washington State University's Volunteer Management Certificate Program

▶ The Volunteer Management Certificate Program is a Web-based learning opportunity encompassing the training, recruiting, man-

agement, and recognition of volunteers. Prospective students visiting the site will find program and enrollment information, a description of program instructors, and a skills assessment self-test. Registered students have their own point of entry into the site, and have easy access to online help and support as needed. *http://vmcp.wsu.edu/*

E-Mail Discussion Lists and Newsgroups

ARNOVA-L (Nonprofit and Voluntary Action Discussion Group)

▶ This list was established as an international electronic forum for anyone using or interested in nonprofit organizations, voluntary action, or philanthropy, to facilitate the rapid sharing of concerns, interests, problems, and solutions among interested scholars and practitioners. ARNOVA was one of the first social science research associations to establish an ongoing discussion list, and ARNOVA-L has been an interesting and lively forum throughout its nearly nine-year history. Roger A. Lohmann, PhD, Professor of Social Work and Director of the Nonprofit Management Academy at West Virginia University, created the list and continues to operate it for the benefit of the Association for Research on Nonprofit Organizations and Voluntary Action (ARNOVA) and the international research and practitioner community interested in nonprofit organizations, voluntary action, and philanthropy. To join ARNOVA-L, send the following one line e-mail message (please do not use commas): *SUBSCRIBE ARNOVA-L FirstName LastName* to: *LISTSERV@WVU.EDU.* The result will be automatically referred to the list owner. *http://www.arnova.org/arnova_l.htm*

CharityVillage Online Resources: Online Discussions

▶ *http://www.charityvillage.com/charityvillage/stand.html*

Cybervpm

▶ Maintained by Nan Hawthorne, a consultant on volunteer management, CyberVPM is an online discussion group for managers of volunteer programs. To subscribe, send an e-mail message to *listserv@listserv.aol.com* that says in the body of the message *Subscribe cybervpm Your Name.* Leave the subject blank, and do not include e-mail addresses in the body of the message. The CyberVPM discussion group is sponsored by CyberVPM.com Resources for Volunteer Program Managers. Register at the site and receive a free monthly subscription to the CyberVPM.com Update. Just follow the link to the Update on the home page. To unsubscribe from this listserv, send *UNSUBSCRIBE CYBERVPM* to *listserv@listserv.aol.com.* For more info on your subscription options, including setting digests, etc., see *http://www.cybervpm.com/ cybervpm.htm. http://www.cybervpm.com*

Distance Voluntary Work

▶ Billed as primarily for volunteers but has a fair amount of focus on program development. Contact *distance-voluntarism@onelist.com.*

GIVING (For Donors and Volunteers)

▶ To subscribe, send e-mail, leaving the subject line blank, with the message *SUBSCRIBE GIVING YOUR NAME. listproc@envirolink.org*

GOV-VPM

▶ Sponsored by the Points of Light Foundation in Washington and maintained by Nan Hawthorne and Nancy Macduff, consultants on volunteer management, GOV-VPM is an online discussion group for managers of volunteer programs at government agencies. An online application to join the list is available at *http://www.pointso flight.org/government/government.html* for those who manage volunteers in government. Each day or two, you will receive e-mail messages from other people on the list. There might be questions about ways to recognize volunteers, how to solve personality conflicts, or ideas on software to record the work of volunteers. Membership in the GOV-VPM online discussion group is limited to those persons working with volunteers in programs in government settings or those academics concerned with this topic. You must apply for membership to the list administrator who will approve and effect your enrollment. Use the online form (*http://pointsof light.org/government/gov-join_b.html*) or send the following information to the listmaster (*hawthorne@cybervmp.com*): *Your name; Your position; Your program; Your phone number* (in case your subscription doesn't "take"); whether you are a government program, academic doing research, or other (please specify if other); the government organization in which it is based; whether you want individual posts or a daily digest; and where you heard about GOV-VPM. If you have questions or problems, contact the list administrator, Nan Hawthorne, at *hawthorne@cybervpm.com.*

INTVOL Discussion List—International Volunteer Programs Association

▶ This is an e-mail discussion group for staff of international volunteer programs to share ideas and ask for advice from peers in the field of international volunteer exchanges. The listserv was created in direct response to the recommendation of the 20 organizations present at the Community Service Around the World 1997 Conference, who saw the listserv as a first step to continuing the dialogue begun at the conference. A listserv seemed like a great way to do things like coordinate calendars of events and training, exchange strategies for recruitment and fund raising, make specific requests for advice and support from staff members of other organizations, talk about diversifying program participation, share information about visas and immigration issues, and propose ways to collaborate. This listserv is for people who work and volunteer with organizations that place volunteers internationally, are involved in promoting the field of international volunteerism in general, or are involved in supporting individuals volunteering internationally independently (outside of a formal placement organization). This listserv is *not* for people looking for international volunteer opportunities. To receive more information, or to subscribe to the listserv, please contact the moderator at *ivpa@lafetra.org* or call 510-763-9206.

K–12 Service Learning (Learn & Serve America)

▶ "The NSLCK-12 Listserv is an electronic forum for the discussion of service-learning among administrators, practitioners, researchers, and students. By subscribing to the listserv, members have a wealth of knowledge to tap into in the form of like-minded individuals" (from the NSLC website). This list is hosted by the National Service-Learning Clearinghouse at the University of Minnesota. To join by e-mail, send a message to *listserv@ tc.umn.edu* with this text in the body: *subscribe nslck-12.*

NSCCTalk

▶ NSSCtalk is an unmoderated e-mail discussion group, created primarily for the 500,000+ participants in the National Senior Service Corps, a program of the Corporation for National Service. Anyone with related concerns, however, is invited to join in. To subscribe by e-mail, send a blank message to *join-nssctalk@ lists.etr.org.*

NSLC K–12 Service-Learning List Serve

▶ This is a forum for K–12 service-learning discussion and info sharing. You need only an e-mail address to use this. To subscribe, send an e-mail message to *listserv@tc.umn.edu* Skip the "subject" area (or if you have to put in a message, write "hello"). In the body, or where you write your message, type: *sub nslck-12 Yourfirstname Yourlastname.* You can also follow your name with a 15-character organization name if you want. But type nothing else; then send your message. You will receive a confirmation that you have been subscribed and directions for posting messages to the whole list.

National Youth Service Affiliates—Youth Service America

▶ This Weekly National Service Briefing contains the most up-to-date service news, calendar events, and employment opportunities. Send an e-mail to *macjordomo@ysa.org* with the following command in the body of your e-mail. Please leave the subject line blank. *SUB nsb Your_FirstName Your_LastName.* Brainstorm with membership of over 175 organizations about volunteering, fund raising, collaborating, or technology. E-mail Shannon Maynard for more information about becoming an affiliate or joining this listserv.

Online Discussion Groups for Volunteer Managers & Volunteers

▶ USENET newsgroups, e-mail groups, and updates via e-mail for and by volunteer managers and service leaders. Great places to interact with other volunteer/service managers of various types of organizations, get suggestions and feedback, and ask questions. *http://www.serviceleader.org/vv/vonline3.html*

Service Civil International Listservs

▶ *http://www.sciint.org/subscribe_lists.htm*

Service-Learning

▶ The primary focus of this mailing list is service-learning in higher education; however, anyone with an interest in service-learning is welcome to subscribe and participate in discussions. This list is hosted by the Communications for a Sustainable Future program at the University of Colorado at Boulder. To join by e-mail, send a message to *listproc@csf.colorado.edu* with this text in the body: *subscribe service-learning.*

Service Learning and Social Change

▶ This is an e-mail group to facilitate discussion of service learning and social change. To join this list, send e-mail to *service_learning-subscribe@egroups.com.*

Service-Learning Listserv for Community-Based Organizations

▶ The listserv is a national, electronic mailing list for individuals at community-based organizations who are engaged in service-learning activities. The listserv is an open list, with the intention that it will include a diverse group of practitioners from local CBOs, organizations that are assisting CBOs (volunteer centers, state commissions), and national organizations with an interest in community-based service-learning. Send an e-mail to *listserv@listserv.pointsoflight.org*. In the body of the e-mail message, type: *subscribe cbo-sl city state firstname lastname*. Additional questions can be directed to *youth@pointsoflight.org*

Virtualvols Discussion Group for Online Volunteers

▶ Maintained by the Virtual Volunteering Project at the Charles A. Dana Center at the University of Texas at Austin, Virtualvols is an e-mail discussion list for volunteers who do their charity work via the Internet. To subscribe; send an e-mail message to *listproc@lists.cc.utexas.edu* that states in the body of the message "subscribe virtualvols Your Name." Leave the subject blank, and do not include e-mail addresses in the body of the message. *http://www.serviceleader.org/vv/volslist.html*

VISTAnet

▶ VISTAnet is an ongoing discussion group for VISTAs, former VISTAs, AmeriCorps folks, and anyone interested in national service and social issues. Special thanks to St. Johns University, Dr. Zenhausern and Paul Kariangelis, for hosting this discussion group. The entire archives of discussion on VISTAnet is available online (*http://maelstrom.stjohns.edu/archives/vistanet.html*). You can search the entire archive or browse by month. To join in, address an e-mail message to: *listserv@maelstrom.stjohns.edu*. Leave the subject field blank (or "none"). Type the following in the body of the message: *subscribe VISTAnet (Your Name)*. Visit the VISTAnet FAQ at *http://www.friendsofvista.org/vistanet*. *http://www.friendsofvista.org/living/h.html*

VOLU-Volunteers · VOLU—Global Volunteers to Ghana and to Dozens of African Countries

▶ Projects focus on HIV/AIDS, public health, medicine, education, tutoring, building schools and clinics, farming, husbandry, reforestation, environment and conservation, youth work, sports, social services, wildlife conservation, computer training, and distance education. *http://groups.yahoo.com/group/VOLU-Volunteers/files/*

Volunteer-Issues—CharityChannel.com

▶ This site focuses on all aspects of volunteers in the nonprofit sector. This is a topic that cuts across nearly every form of nonprofit management, administration, fund raising, leadership, and function. You can subscribe to Volunteer-Issues either via e-mail or from the CharityChannel.com web site. Via e-mail; send an e-mail message to *Listserv@CharityChannel.com*. The "subject" or "re" is ignored. In the body of your message, type: *SUBSCRIBE VOLUNTEER-ISSUES yourFirstname yourLastname*. *http://www.Charity-Channel.com/Forums*

Volunteers

▶ To subscribe, send an e-mail, leaving the subject line blank, with the message *SUBSCRIBE VOLUNTEERS YOUR NAME* to: *listserv@listserv.aol.com*. Online discussion for those dedicated to voluntary service to their communities.

Yahoo's Volunteer Manager Corner

▶ An electronic club for volunteer managers; can network and chat on the Web site. *http://clubs.yahoo.com/clubs/volunteermanagerscorner*

Insurance, Liability, and Risk Management

Insurance Issues for Volunteers—Costello & Sons

▶ Information on general liability, workers' compensation, auto, and injuries, from the volunteer's point of view, the nonprofit's point of view, and the corporate point of view. By Costello & Sons Insurance Brokers. *http://www.costelloandsons.com/nonprofit/volunteers.shtml*

The Three Top Reasons Volunteers Get Sued—The Internet Site for Tax-Exempt Organizations

▶ *http://www.nonprofitlaw.com/volrisk/*

Volunteer Legal Handbook

▶ This is the online version of *A Legal Handbook for Nonprofit Corporation Volunteers,* written for the Volunteer Action Center of the United Way of Tanana Valley, Alaska. While Alaska users may find this the most helpful, the Handbook has some general application for outside users. The Handbook, aimed at volunteers for non-profits as well as their supervisors, summarizes what volunteers and nonprofits can do to protect themselves against legal action. A useful bibliography of additional resources is provided at the end. For more information, contact Jim DeWitt. *http://iciclesoftware.com/vlh/*

International Volunteering

(See also Virtual Volunteering; Volunteer Opportunity Databases and Search Engines; Volunteerism, Organizations—Community Service and Volunteering Opportunities [National]; International)

European Volunteer Centre

▶ *http://corporate3.skynet.be/cev/*

International Volunteer Programs Association—Other Websites on Volunteering Abroad

▶ *http://www.volunteerinternational.org/index-res.html*

National Service

Epicenter (Effective Practices Information Center)

▶ This is an online database of effective practices for national service programs (AmeriCorps, VISTA, SeniorCorps, etc.). Search the database over the Web to find what is working for others in national service. Epicenter also allows you to contribute your own effective practices to the database. Explore this resource on the Web site of the Corporation for National Service at *http://www.nationalservice.org/resources/epicenter/.* If you have questions about the site, contact the epicenter Webmaster: *webmaster@etr.org,* Voice: 800-860-2684 ext. 130, TDD: 831-461-0205, AOL Instant Messenger Screen Name: NSRC TA

Online Periodicals, Updates, and Alerts

CyberVPM.com Update

▶ Published once a month, this e-letter covers topics of interest to those working with volunteers in a wide variety of settings. Archived issues are also available. A weekly e-zine accompanies the CyberVPM.com Update and is published every Monday other than weeks the Update is published. It covers topics of interest to those working with volunteers in a wide variety of settings. It is sent to all CyberVPM.com Update subscribers on the 15th of each month. *http://www.cybervpm.com/update.htm*

Energize's Volunteer Management Web Update

▶ At the beginning of each month, they will send you an e-mail announcing changes to their Web site and new additions to their Online Bookstore. The Update includes a volunteer management "tip of the month"—available only via the Update. *http://www.energizeinc.com/fillin/e-mail.html*

E-Volunteerism—The Electronic Journal of the Volunteer Community

▶ This is a quarterly "publication," in which a table of contents is posted at the start of each quarter, with a few items "ready" from the first day of the quarter. More items will be posted until, at the end of three months, the entire issue is hot-linked and available. Every item in the publication will be interactive, inviting you to contribute comments and additional materials. At the end of each quarter, that issue will be made permanent and archived—its major articles and features continuing to be accessible and interactive. In addition to several quality articles each quarter, regular features for each issue include commentaries by volunteerism experts, Steve McCurley and Susan J. Ellis (the editorial team); sections expressly for the leaders of DOVIAs, and for the leaders of all-volunteer organizations; an "international perspectives" feature inviting colleagues from around the world to comment on a specific topic; a "tools you can use" section with sample forms, bylaws, certificates, and more; a training design feature; and a "Research for Practitioners" feature to interpret scholarly research for nonacademics. Instructions on subscriptions are at *http://www.e-volunteerism.com/subscribe.html.* For more information, contact Energize, Inc., at 215-438-0342 or *info@energizeinc.com.*

I CAN Newsletter

▶ *http://www.ICSpirit.org/newsletter.html*

Ideas in Action

▶ An e-mail newsletter that every month or two brings you a brief selection of news and pointers to useful resources. *http://www.idealist.org/newsletter.html*

Impact Online's Electronic Update

▶ *http://www.volunteermatch.org/mail/newsletter.gsp*

The Journal of Volunteer Administration Index— Association for Volunteer Administration

▶ *http://www.avaintl.org/resources/journal.html*

Volunteer International News—International Volunteer Programs Association

▶ This is a bimonthly newsletter on international volunteer opportunities. To subscribe to the newsletter, send a blank e-mail to: *volintnews-subscribe@igc.topica.com.* To unsubscribe to the newsletter, send a blank e-mail to: *volintnews-unsubscribe@igc.topica.com.* For more information, send an e-mail to: *ivpa@lafetra.org. http://www.volunteerinternational.org*

VolunteerMatch's Volunteer Newsletter

▶ To subscribe, send an e-mail with *subscribe volunteer* in the subject or body to *listserv@volunteermatch.org. www.volunteermatch.org*

Service Learning Quarterly—Close Up Foundation

▶ *http://www.closeup.org/servlern.htm*

VIRTUAL VERVE—Virtual Volunteering News and Updates

▶ To subscribe, send an e-mail to: *listproc@lists.cc.utexas.edu* and in the body of the e-mail, type: *subscribe vverve Yourfirstname Yourlastname.* For example: subscribe vverve Jane Doe. (Please note: The list processor, will reject requests that do not contain a first and last name.)

Volunteer Today

▶ The Electronic Gazette for Volunteerism. Compiled and maintained in Walla Walla, Washington, this site provides current news and conference information, tips on recruiting and retaining volunteers, book reviews, and links to additional resources of interest, including a calendar of events. *http://www.volunteertoday.com/*

Volunteering Online

▶ This is an electronic newsletter produced on a free voluntary basis, which aims to encourage the participation and involvement in all forms of voluntary work through the media and in particular by the direct use of the Internet. If you wish to subscribe/unsubscribe to this newsletter, please send an e-mail and write *subscribe* or *unsubscribe* (as the case may be) to *teddy@vol.net.mt.*

Yahoo News: Philanthropy and Volunteerism

▶ Maintained by the search engine Yahoo, this Web site provides links to articles about philanthropy and volunteerism in newspapers and magazines, as well as from various news services. The site also provides links to other sources of nonprofit news. *http://headlines.yahoo.com/Full_Coverage/World/Philanthropy_and_Volunteerism*

Publications

Giving and Volunteering in the United States— 1999 National Survey (Independent Sector)

▶ http://www.independentsector.org/GandV/default.htm

How to Reach Youth Volunteers—Ad Council, MTV

▶ There is a huge untapped pool of potential volunteers in the United States today: the 26 million young adults between the ages of 18 and 24, but reaching them requires nonprofits to rethink the messages they use, their recruiting methods and vehicles, and their expectations for volunteers. So says a new 40-page study conducted by the Ad Council and MTV: Music Television, and funded by a grant from the Pew Charitable Trusts. The report aims to help non-profits effectively reach the young adult market (ages 18 to 24) by providing data, important insights, successful case histories, and strategies for developing relevant messages and media programs. You can download the full report in a PDF file. *www.adcouncil.org/fr_research.html*

The New Volunteerism Project—The Archival Collection of Ivan Henry Scheier

▶ http://www.regis.edu/spsmnm/dovia/ivan/

"A Summary of E-Sites for Philanthropy, Volunteerism, and Social Change"(PDF)

▶ http://www.independentsector.org/give5/E-Philanthropy.pdf

The Virtual Volunteering Guidebook: How to Apply the Principles of Real-World Volunteer Management to Online Service

▶ Written by Susan J. Ellis, a volunteer-management consultant, and Jayne Cravens, manager of the Virtual Volunteering Project, this 133-page book explains how to recruit, manage, and evaluate volunteers who do their charity work on the Internet. It also includes a chapter on how nonprofit organizations can involve people with disabilities in their online volunteer programs. *http://www.energizeinc.com/art/elecbooks.html*

Recognition

Sources for Volunteer Recognition Materials

▶ http://www.avaintl.org/resources/recog.html

Senior Volunteering

Senior Corps

▶ http://www.cns.gov/senior

Service Learning, Youth and Young Adult Volunteerism

Capella University

▶ Offers on-line learning and certificate programs in service-learning. *http://www.capellauniversity.edu/*

Community Engagement and Volunteerism—The Texas Education Network (TENET)

▶ http://www.tenet.edu/volunteer/

The Declaration of Principles (PDF File)

▶ http://www.nylc.org/pdf/declaration.pdf

How to Reach Youth Volunteers—Ad Council, MTV

▶ There is a huge untapped pool of potential volunteers in the United States today: the 26 million young adults between the ages of 18 and 24, but reaching them requires nonprofits to rethink the messages they use, their recruiting methods and vehicles, and their expectations for volunteers. So says a new 40-page study conduct-ed by the Ad Council and MTV: Music Television, and funded by a grant from the Pew Charitable Trusts. The report aims to help non-profits effectively reach the young adult market (ages 18 to 24) by providing data, important insights, successful case histories, and strategies for developing relevant messages and media programs. You can download the full report in a PDF file. *www.adcouncil.org/fr_research.html*

The Learn and Serve America Exchange

▶ Supports service-learning programs in schools, colleges, universi-ties, and community organizations across the country through peer-based training and technical assistance. *http://www.lsaexchange.org/*

The Learn & Serve America National Service-Learning Clearinghouse

▶ A comprehensive information system that focuses on all dimen-sions of service-learning, covering kindergarten through higher education, school-based as well as community-based initiatives. *http://www.cns.gov/learn/index.html*

Learning in Deed

▶ Sponsored by the W.K. Kellogg Foundation, this is a national initiative to increase the likelihood that service-learning will become the common experience of students across the nation. *http://www.learningindeed.org/*

National Association of Service and Conservation Corps (NASCC)

▶ This site provides updates on dealing with common or "hot" issues that many service programs face: member management, member development, member motivation, multisite supervision, partner relations, service versus work, staff development, retention issues, recruitment issues, understaffed programs, and "How State Commissions Can Work Closer With AmeriCorps Programs in their State." *http://www.nascc.org/ttahotissues2.shtml*

The National Commission on Service-Learning

▶ Composed of 20 high-profile thought leaders and innovators from sectors that influence education and public opinion, this site brings a new level of public commitment to service-learning by (1) developing recommendations and an action plan to make qual-ity service-learning available to all K–12 students and (2) encour-aging adoption of service-learning among target audiences. *http://www.servicelearningcommission.org/*

The National Service-Learning Cooperative Clearinghouse

▶ Funded by Learn and Serve America, the National Service-Learning Cooperative Clearinghouse serves as a national resource on service learning. It assists Learn and Serve America–funded programs, educators, and community agencies and provides a range of information about and offers a variety of services to support service-learning projects. It contains databases (events, listserv search, literature, programs, and add event and add program features), resources (FAQs [*http://www.nicsl.coled.umn.edu*], listservs, bibliographies, monographs, newsletters, state reports, videos, publications list), and links. The Center of the Clearinghouse is located at the University of Minnesota, Department of Work, Community and Family Education, with collaboration from a consortium of 12 other institutions and organizations. *http://www.nicsl.coled.umn.edu, http://nicsl.jaws.umn.edu/*

National Service-Learning Leader Schools— Corporation for National Service

▶ *http://www.learnandserve.org/leaderschools*

Service Learning

▶ *http://ase.tufts.edu/cte/occasional_papers/service.htm*

Service-Learning and Community Service in K–12 Public Schools Report (PDF File)

▶ *http://www.nylc.org/resources_k-12report.cfm*

Service Learning Quarterly—Close Up Foundation

▶ *http://www.closeup.org/servlern.htm*

Service-Learning—The Home of Service-Learning on the World Wide Web

▶ *http://csf.colorado.edu/sl*

Students.gov—Student Gateway to the U.S. Government: Community Service

▶ *http://www.students.gov/link_search/listsubs.cfm?Topic=0500*

Volunteerism and Community Engagement for K–12 Schools

▶ *http://www.tenet.edu/volunteer/*

Web Sites Promoting Volunteerism/Community Service

▶ This site is for those looking for information about volunteerism (why do it, who is doing it, tips for doing it, etc.) and organizations that sponsor national or international volunteering efforts of their own. This site also provides links to service-learning resources. *http://www.serviceleader.org/vv/vonline4.html*

Youth on Board

▶ This organization envisions a world where young people are fully respected and treated as valued and active members of their families, communities, and society. *http://www.youthonboard.org/*

Youth Service America

▶ This is a resource center and the premier alliance of 200+ organizations committed to increasing the quantity and quality of opportunities for young Americans to serve locally, nationally, or globally. *http://www.ysa.org/*

State Volunteerism

ServeWeb: State Service Web Sites

▶ Developed by nonprofit consultant Anne M. Ostberg as part of a Corporation for National Service fellowship to study how state community-service networks use the Internet to collaborate, this Web site includes links to state agencies on volunteerism. *http://www.ostberg.org/serveweb/list.htm*

Virtual Volunteering

(See also Volunteer Opportunity Databases and Search Engines)

The Beacon Project

▶ Their two programs are the e-corps and the Virtual Resource Campus (VRC). The e-corps is a volunteer program that matches teams of volunteers expert in management disciplines with nonprofit organizations to consult and to assist with project work. All e-corps activities are conducted online. The volunteers assist with strategic planning, board development, fund-raising planning, and various other projects that help the nonprofit organizations to better improve their client focus. *http://www.beaconproject.org/*

CompuMentor

▶ Matches volunteers who have strong computer skills with schools and nonprofit groups across the country. *http://www.compumentor.org/*

Geekcorps

▶ *http://www.geekcorps.org/closetohome.html, http://www.geekcorps.org/getinvolved.html*

GuideStar

▶ This site is an initiative of Philanthropic Research, whose mission is to provide information about charities to donors and others. In addition to its information to help donors of money, equipment, and time monitor the programs and performance of charities, GuideStar also features a "classifieds" section of volunteer opportunities at agencies around the United States. Onsite volunteer opportunities are listed at *http://nonprofit.guidestar.org/classifieds/#2*. Web development (online) opportunities are listed at *http://nonprofit.guidestar.org/classifieds/ms_sbn.cfm*. *http://nonprofit.guidestar.org*

Idealist

▶ *http://www.idealist.org .*

Impact Online's Virtual Volunteering

▶ This site offers volunteer opportunities for individuals, including those with disabilities, who wish to contribute time via e-mail. The site's VolunteerMatch service (*http://www.volunteermatch.org/*) helps individuals nationwide find on-site volunteer opportunities posted by local nonprofit and public-sector organizations. *http://www.volunteermatch.org/virtual*

Impact Online

▶ This site includes listings of short-term and remote (online) volunteer opportunities, and advice for volunteers. *http://www.impactonline.org/*

InterConnection Virtual Volunteer Program

▶ Help a developing community without leaving your home. As a Virtual Volunteer, you'll create Web sites for organizations dedicated to benefiting the local community or environment. By developing an Internet presence for these organizations, you'll also empower them by allowing them direct access to global markets and international support. *http://www.interconnection.org/volunteer/index.htm*

International Telementor Center

▶ A program at the Center for Science, Mathematics & Technology Education at Colorado State University (*www.csmate.colostate.edu*), facilitates electronic mentoring relationships between professional adults and students worldwide. *http://www.telementor.org/*

NetAction

▶ A project of The Tides Center, this site has information on a variety of resources for "Virtual Activists," and organizations that want to use such activists via the Internet in grassroots campaigns. *http://www.netaction.org*

Netaid.org

▶ People from around the world are able to peruse online volunteer opportunities submitted by nongovernmental organizations to serve as volunteers and submit their applications. Many of the current assignments are in the areas of publications development (articles, design, promotional material) and teaching. Other activities taken up by online volunteers include research, promotion, Web-related work, translation, information technology, professional advice/consultancies, fund-raising, and administration. For more information, contact Georg Eichhorn or Andrea Goetzke: Tel: +49 (228) 815 2224; E-mail: *netaid@unv.org,* or Klas Bergman: Tel: +49 (228) 815 2511 E-mail: *Klas.Bergman@unv.org. http://www.netaid.org/OV*

Nonprofit Volunteers on the Web—Nonprofit Charitable Organizations (Mining Company)

▶ *http://nonprofit.miningco.com/careers/nonprofit/library/weekly/aa120298.htm*

TechSoup

▶ *http://www.techsoup.org/*

The Virtual Volunteering Guidebook: How to Apply the Principles of Real-World Volunteer Management to Online Service

▶ Written by Susan J. Ellis, a volunteer-management consultant, and Jayne Cravens, manager of the Virtual Volunteering Project, this 133-page book explains how to recruit, manage, and evaluate volunteers who do their charity work on the Internet. It also includes a chapter on how nonprofit organizations can involve people with disabilities in their online volunteer programs. *http://www.energizeinc.com/art/elecbooks.html*

Virtual Volunteering Project

▶ Launched in 1996, the Virtual Volunteering Project works to encourage and assist in the development of volunteer activities that can be completed off-site via the Internet. It publishes *Virtual Verve,* a monthly electronic newsletter on virtual volunteering. *www.serviceleader.org*

Voluntary Opportunity Databases and Search Engines

(See also Virtual Volunteering)

Action Without Borders (See Idealist)

Alternative Opportunities Database—Just Act

▶ *http://www.justact.org/volunteer/alt_opps.html*

American Hiking Society: Events and Volunteer Opportunities

▶ *http://www.americanhiking.org/events/index.html*

Amizade Volunteer Links

▶ *http://amizade.org/links.htm#Volunteer*

Backdoor Jobs

▶ *http://www.backdoorjobs.com/*

Best Bets for Volunteering Abroad

▶ This University of California at Irvine site is the most complete collection of links to organizations that provide voluntary service opportunities abroad. Click here for links to organizations from Amigos de las Americas to Habitat for Humanity to the Peace Corps, essential to your volunteer abroad search. This site also includes Best Bets for Internships Abroad. *http://www.cie.uci.edu/iop/voluntee.html*

Campusaccess.com—Database of Internship and Volunteer Organizations

▶ There are abundant internships and volunteer work possibilities, but usually these internships are hard to find since it is hard to know where to start looking. Furthermore, there are so many internships to choose from, with work available in so many different fields, countries (Canada, United States, and international), and organizations that it is hard to choose what internship or volunteer opportunity is right for you. What you will find here is a categorized list of Canadian internships, American internships and international internships, and organizations. Each organization details their particular internship and volunteer opportunities (mission statements as well as contact address, e-mail and Web site address). *http://www.campusaccess.com/campus_web/intern/i2int.htm*

CharityVillage (Canada)—Volunteer/Donate

▶ *http://www.charityvillage.com/charityvillage/volbb.asp*

CompuMentor

▶ This site gives information as well as listings of volunteer opportunities for computer help with programs and projects of nonprofits and schools. *http://www.compumentor.org/mentor/default.html*

Connections—Pallotti Center

▶ This is a directory of over 100 domestic and international faith-based (90 percent Catholic) volunteer programs. The Connections directory profiles over 100 volunteer programs, which need volunteers to work in education, community outreach, campus ministry, advocacy, construction, medicine, homeless ministry, and ministry to the elderly, the sick, and the poor. These are faith-based programs (90 percent of which are Catholic), but they are not inappropriately proseletyzing. Connections gives a detailed profile of each program including deadlines, benefits, requirements and more! Scroll through the volunteer program profiles and contact the organizations in which you may be interested. Visit home pages and e-mail them directly from their profile. Some hints to keep in mind as you read: Red Programs are Domestic; Blue Programs are International; Purple Programs are both Domestic and International. *http://pallotti.cua.edu/content/fr_connections.htm*

Directory on International Voluntary Service

▶ This is a valuable website resource on myriad short-term volunteer opportunities within the United States and abroad. It is particularly useful for European sources. *http://www.avso.org/en/links/dirinVS.html*

Do-it

▶ For people looking to volunteer in the United Kingdom, the do-it Web site provides a detailed database of volunteer opportunities. Search the database for loads of fantastic opportunities that suit your time frame, your interests, and your skills. *http://www.do-it.org.uk*

EarthWise Journeys

▶ An independent resource and clearinghouse for responsible travel worldwide. *http://www.teleport.com/~earthwyz/index.htm, http://www.teleport.com/~earthwyz/volunt.htm*

Ecovolunteer

▶ *http://www.ecovolunteer.org/*

Energize

▶ Energize is an international training, consulting, and publishing firm specializing in volunteerism. They have a great list of volunteer opportunities throughout the world and links to other volunteer opportunity sites. *http://www.energizeinc.com* Volunteer link: *http://www.energizeinc.com/prof/volop.html*

eVolunteer:

▶ A great Web site for volunteers with all the useful tools of a Web portal. They have a searchable database, and best of all, their system is supported by open source software, which means it is a Web site for volunteers, run by volunteers, on software developed by volunteers. *http://evolunteer.co.uk, http://www.evolunteer.co.uk/search.php3*

Explorations in Travel, Inc.

▶ *http://www.volunteertravel.com/*

GuideStar

▶ This site is an initiative of Philanthropic Research, whose mission is to provide information about charities to donors and others. In addition to its information to help donors of money, equipment, and time monitor the programs and performance of charities, this site offers a searchable database of more than 640,000 nonprofit organizations in the United States with a section devoted to volunteering. On-site volunteer opportunities are listed at *http://nonprofit.guidestar.org/classifieds/#2*. Web development (online) opportunities are listed at *http://nonprofit.guidestar.org/classifieds/ms_sbn.cfm. http://nonprofit.guidestar.org*

Hearts and Minds—Volunteering Opportunities, Links and Resources

▶ *http://www.heartsandminds.org/links/vol.htm*

Helping.Org—America Online

▶ Helping.org is a one-stop online resource designed to help people find volunteer and giving opportunities in their own communities and beyond. Created by the AOL Foundation, in Dulles, Virginia, this Web site allows visitors to learn about the activities of more than 650,000 charities, and to make online contributions to them. Visitors can also search for volunteer opportunities—and sign up for them on line. Nonprofit organizations will find information that explains ways that they can better use technology in their programs. In addition, the site provides details on how charities can increase access to technology in poor communities. *http://www.helping.org*

Idealist: Action Without Borders

▶ Idealist: Action without Borders is "the global clearinghouse of nonprofit and volunteering resources." Click on "Volunteer Opportunities" for a listing by country of volunteer and internship opportunities. It is the most comprehensive directory of nonprofit and volunteering resources on the Web. The site includes 20,000 nonprofit and community organizations in 140 countries, which you can search or browse by name, location, or mission; volunteer opportunities in your community and around the world, and a list of organizations that can help you volunteer abroad; a directory of companies and consultants that provide products and services to nonprofit organizations; a Nonprofit Career Center with listings of jobs and internships, both with nonprofit organizations and with companies and consultants that serve the sector; links to the most useful resources we have found on the Web for managing and funding a nonprofit organization; a collection of the most informative and frequently updated Nonprofit News Sites on the Web; a global directory of Public Internet Access Points in hundreds of schools, libraries, community centers, and Internet cafes. You can choose from 45 areas of interest at Idealist, and you can also specify the skills you offer—from carpentry, graphic design, and medical to public speaking—and the country, city, and zip code where you want to volunteer. Find volunteer opportunities in your community and around the world on its opening volunteer Web page at *http://www.idealist.org/IS/vol_search.html*. You can also browse all volunteer opportunities in North America (*http://www.idealist.org/browse/vol/north_america.html*) and worldwide (*http://www.idealist.org/browse/vol/countries.html*). Finally, it includes NEW: Organizations that Can Help You Volunteer Abroad (*http://www.idealist.org/travel.html*). *http://www.idealist.org* Volunteer link: *http://www.idealist.org/IS/vol_search.html*

India Development Information Network

▶ Visitors to this site will find a wealth of information related to development in India. The site contains a search engine of development organizations that can be used to find volunteer opportunities. *http://www.indev.nic.in* Volunteer link: *http://www.indev.nic.in/indevdb/ngos/ngo_search.cfm*

InterAction

▶ *http://www.interaction.org*, *http://www.interaction.pair.com/volunteer.html*

InterAction

▶ This is an excellent site for major international volunteer organizations, especially those working in development and relief. It includes a partial list of agencies that employ volunteers internationally. Created by the American Council for Voluntary International Action, a coalition of over 150 U.S.-based nonprofits and worldwide nonprofit organizations. Of the links, the "InterAction Guide to Volunteer Opportunities," which is divided by type of opportunity (i.e., "share your medical skills" or "participate in a citizen exchange program") is particularly useful. Sections include Advocacy, Development, Refugees, Disasters, a Members listing, and Publications. It has news items, legislation updates, job and volunteer site, and links to other sites with similar missions. *http://www.interaction.org/jobs/*

The Interchange

▶ A clearinghouse of information for mission sponsoring groups and those wishing to serve in some capacity, it collects and collates data on groups who need and sponsor people in mission. While groups are primarily Catholic, ecumenical and humanitarian placements are also covered. It seeks to address the needs of those who wish to serve in various capacities, as well as listing groups, projects, and the like, that need personnel. It addresses the needs by channeling information on the various opportunities, at home and abroad, to those seeking them. The information offered is determined by the Personal Profile the individual fills in and returns to the office. The individual can then pursue their search with the organizations in which they are interested. The Interchange is not a placement agency, it is a "go-between." Work, volunteer, or find an internship abroad. Use this database as a tool to assist you in your research. Simply type in a keyword or search term below and follow the links to some programs that they have found through their research. This database contains roughly 150 opportunities to volunteer in developing countries and eastern Europe. After performing a search, you will obtain a description of each program and further contact information. *http://www.web.net/~interchg*

International Directory of Voluntary Work

▶ *http://www.voluntarywork.org/go.htm*

International Study and Travel Center Work Options Search

▶ *http://www.istc.umn.edu/work/search.html*

International Volunteer Programs Association

▶ Search by world region, country, type of work, or project duration. *http://www.volunteerinternational.org/* *http://www.volunteer-international.org/what_next.html*

International Volunteer Projects—Council on International Educational Exchange

▶ *http://www.councilexchanges.org/us/18plus/int_vol/index.html*

Internet Volunteer Initiative

▶ Connects volunteers with service opportunities. *http://www.4LaborsOfLove.org*

International Networked Volunteering— Involvement Volunteers Association, Inc.

▶ This site operates to identify suitable volunteer placements for individual people wishing to participate in volunteer activities around the world. It has volunteer placements in this country, all months of the year. Please see Worldwide for their main entry. *http://www.volunteering.org.au/*

Liaison Centre for Ecumenical Services for Justice, Peace and the Integrity of Creation—World Council of Churches

▶ *http://www.wcc-coe.org/liaison/*

Make a Difference Day

▶ Each October, sponsored by USA Weekend. Includes a database of volunteer opportunities for the Day. *http://www.usaweekend.com/diffday/*

Oneworld.net

▶ The famous news and NGO site has a section devoted to volunteer posts in human rights, environment and sustainable development. *http://www.oneworld.net* Volunteer link: *http://www.oneworld.net/action/volunteers/index.html*

Quaker Information Center—American Friends Service Committee

▶ This site offers 16 different lists/categories of volunteer and service opportunities, including workcamps, internships, other potentially transformational experiences, and some perennial jobs—Quaker and non-Quaker; short, medium, and long term; domestic and international. *http://www.afsc.org/qic.htm*, *http://www.afsc.org/qic/oportnty.htm*

Response Directory—Catholic Network of Volunteer Service

▶ This is a database of thousands of full-time volunteer opportunities available through over 200 member programs. This database can help you find a volunteer program that fits your skills and interests. You can search this database by type of placement, region/state/country, length of service, financial arrangements, living arrangements, size of program, and special categories. A free print version is also available by calling 800-543-5046 or e-mailing *volunteer@cnvs.org. http://www.cnvs.org/cf/programs.cfm*

The Riley Guide: Volunteer Opportunities

▶ *http://www.dbm.com/jobguide/intern.html#vol*

SCI-IVS List for M-/LVT Opportunites—Service Civil International

▶ *http://www.sci-ivs.org/ltv/listing.html*

SERVENet—Youth Service America

▶ Users can search for or post volunteer positions on this site, which also provides service-related news. SERVEnet is a project of Youth Service America. YSA is a resource center and the premier alliance of 200+ organizations committed to increasing the quantity and quality of opportunities for young Americans to serve locally, nationally, or globally. Through SERVEnet, users can enter their zip code, city, state, skills, interests, and availability and be matched with organizations needing help. Through SERVEnet, Affiliates reach potential volunteers by posting opportunities on the Volunteer Now! locator, the nation's first local database for matching volunteers of all ages. SERVEnet is also a place to search for calendar events, job openings, service news, recommended books, and best practices. *http://www.servenet.org/*

SiteBank Catalog Online—Break Away

▶ This continuously updated directory is a comprehensive list of potential alternative break work sites. Designed to fit the needs of any group, the SiteBank Catalog allows you to spend less time searching for places to work and more time planning other aspects of your break. The SiteBank Catalog provides site descriptions and contact information. Students can go directly from working with the SiteBank Catalog to working directly with the community organization on the details of the alternative break. *http://www.alternativebreaks.com/sitebank/*

Student Conservation Association

▶ More than 1,200 expense-paid conservation internships, available year-round, in America's most spectacular national parks, wildlife refuges, national forests, and state and local conservation areas. *http://www.sca-inc.org/*

Transitions Abroad

▶ Descriptions of the following programs were supplied by the organizers. Contact the program directors to confirm costs, dates, and other details, and make sure you tell them you heard about them from Transitions Abroad. If you do not see the program you want in the country of your choice, look under "Worldwide" for programs located in several different regions. This is a companion site to *Transitions Abroad* magazine, a bimonthly guide to living, working, and studying abroad. You can access their work abroad–related publications, resources, program listings, and articles here. *http://www.transitionsabroad.com/resources/work/volunteer/index.shtml, http://www.transabroad.com/resources/work/resources/index.shtml*

United Nations Volunteers—Other Volunteer Organizations

▶ The following list of links is for those looking for a short-term volunteering activity or those whose qualifications do not meet UNV requirements as stated in our pages "Becoming a UN Volunteer" (*http://www.unv.org/unvols/index.htm*). *http://www.unv.org/unvols/volhelp.htm*

University of Michigan International Center

▶ This is the University of Michigan's extremely comprehensive Web site on international opportunities for students. It includes an excellent listing of publications and directories related to volunteering abroad, as well as information on fund raising, grants, and scholarships related to volunteering abroad. *http://www.umich.edu/~icenter/overseas/work/volunteer2.html*

University of Minnesota International Study and Travel Center

▶ This is a searchable site from the University of Minnesota International Study and Travel Center. To find it, select the "volunteer database" under the "Work Abroad" section on their home page. The database allows you to search by program name, country and work type, and also provides a list of all of its volunteer programs. This site has several searchable databases. Each one produces lots of listings by using the term *volunteer*. Searches are possible by country and many other variables. *http://www.istc.umn.edu/work/search.html*

VFP International Workcamp Directory—Volunteers for Peace

▶ *http://www.vfp.org/director.htm, http://www.vfp.org/DirectoryIntro.htm*

Virtual Volunteering—ImpactOnline

▶ With Virtual Volunteering, you can volunteer from "virtually" anywhere using your computer. *http://www.volunteermatch.org/virtual/*

Virtual Volunteering Project

▶ Virtual Volunteering allows anyone to contribute time and expertise to not-for-profit organizations, schools, government offices, and other agencies that utilize volunteer services without leaving home or the office. This site provides resources and information on virtual volunteerism. The project is part of the Volunteerism and Community Engagement Initiatives of the Charles A. Dana Center at the University of Texas–Austin. *www.serviceleader.org*

Volunteer Abroad

▶ This is a new online source for international volunteer positions, teaching positions around the world, jobs abroad, study abroad, etc. This is a sub-site of *www.goabroad.com,* which offers travel services, travel gear, and travel insurance. *http://www.volunteerabroad.com/*

Volunteer America

▶ *http://www.volunteeramerica.net/*

Volunteer America!

▶ *http://www.geocities.com/RainForest/2958/vol.html*

Volunteer Classifieds—The Nonprofit Zone

▶ *http://www.nonprofitzone.com/volcl/volins.asp*

Volunteer Connections—Volunteer Center National Network (Points of Light Foundation)

▶ *http://www.volunteerconnections.org/, http://www.1800volunteer.org/1800VolunteerCenterMap.cfm*

Volunteer for Change—Working Assets

▶ *http://www.workingforchange.com/volunteer/*

Volunteer Opportunities from Coolworks

▶ *http://www.coolworks.com/vlnteer.htm*

Volunteer Opportunities Organization Listing— Seeds of Hope

▶ *http://seedspublishers.org/volopp.html*

Volunteer Organizations—A List of Organizations

▶ *http://alumni.aitec.edu.au/~bwechner/Documents/Travel/Lists/VolunteerOrgs.html*

The Volunteer Resource Center (Minneapolis)

▶ The Volunteer Center works to strengthen the Twin Cities community through volunteerism. At the Center's site you can browse a database of volunteer opportunities, and order a free copy of the Twin Cities Volunteer's Handbook. *http://www.thevolunteercenter.org*

Volunteer Solutions

▶ Volunteer Solutions promotes volunteerism across all sectors of society. The site features a comprehensive online database of volunteer opportunities; the database currently lists opportunities in Austin, Boston, Detroit, Los Angeles, Omaha, and San Francisco. Volunteer Solutions has three main constituencies: individual volunteers, nonprofit agencies, and universities. *http://www.volunteersolutions.org*

Volunteer Vacations: Sources of Information— Chronicle of Philanthropy

▶ *http://philanthropy.com/free/articles/v12/i20/20003401.htm*

Volunteer Web—Epic Productions

▶ Another place to post volunteer opportunities online, with some general information about volunteerism. *http://www.epicbc.com/volunteer/*

Volunteer Work Information Service and Working Abroad

▶ VWIS is a Swiss-based, independent, nonprofit organization providing information on voluntary work opportunities in over 150 countries worldwide, principally in the environmental and humanitarian fields, for people of all ages and nationalities. It is the international networking service for volunteers, workers, and travelers. *http://www.workingabroad.com/*

Volunteerism Resources by Area or Type of Service

▶ *http://www.txserve.org/national/select.html*

VolunteerMatch—ImpactOnline

▶ This is a free online matching service for volunteers and non-profits. The premier service of ImpactOnline, it helps individuals nationwide find volunteer opportunities posted by local nonprofit and public sector organizations. Their online database allows volunteers to search thousands of one-time and ongoing opportunities by zip code, category, and date. Then sign up automatically by e-mail for those that fit their interest and schedule. Contributing organizations post their own opportunities, giving volunteers easy access to an accurate and diverse source of activities including, walk-a-thons, beach day cleanups, tutoring, home building, meal deliveries, and more. *http://www.volunteermatch. org/, http://www.volunteermatch.org/citymatch/, http://www.volunteermatch.org/directory/, http://www.volunteermatch.org/virtual/*

Web Sites to Find Volunteer Opportunities

▶ This site is for agencies looking for a place to post volunteer opportunities online and for individuals looking for a place to volunteer. This is an index of links to major regional and nationwide sites in the United States that provide updated lists of volunteer opportunities at various different organizations. Many of these are third-party volunteer databases (they provide information about other organization's volunteer opportunities). Also included are links to indices of local sites, such as volunteer centers and community networks/freenets. *http://www.serviceleader.org/vv/vonline2.html*

World Wide Wander's Central America Volunteer Guide

▶ A listing of small, grassroots projects that serve the needs of the local populations of Central America. More often than not, these projects are understaffed and cash-strapped, most of them running on budgets far less than the average American's yearly salary. It is for such projects as the ones to be listed here that one good volunteer could make a world of difference—perhaps you are precisely the person they need. There are thousands of these little projects throughout Central America, but presently, they are essentially invisible to the world. They work from day to day, perhaps occasionally helped by an outside volunteer or donor who chances upon them. However, for the most part, due to their remoteness and lack of communication infrastructure, these small projects remain a sight unseen by the rest of us elsewhere in the world. *http://www.tmn.com/wwwanderer/Volguide/WWWvolhome.html*

Volunteer Centers

Volunteer Connections: Volunteer Center National Network—Points of Light Foundation

▶ *http://www.volunteerconnections.org/*

Volunteer Management

Answer Center: Volunteer Management— Delaware Association of Nonprofit Agnecies

▶ *http://www.delawarenonprofit.org/VolFaq.html*

Ask Connie

▶ A feature of *Volunteer Today* where readers ask questions about volunteer management and administration. *http://www.volunteertoday.com/Connie.html*

Association of Volunteer Administration

▶ *www.avaintl.org*

Energize, Inc.

▶ *www.energizeinc.com*

The DOVIA Directory for North America

▶ *http://www.energizeinc.com/prof/dovia.html*

GOV-VPM Networking Resources for Government-Based Volunteer Programs

▶ *www.pointsoflight.org/government/government.html*

Grants and Related Resources: Volunteer Program Management

▶ *http://www.lib.msu.edu/harris23/grants/volunteer.htm*

ImpactOnline

▶ *www.impactonline.org*

Index of Websites Featuring Volunteer Management Information and Resources—Virtual Volunteering Project

▶ *http://www.serviceleader.org/vv/vonline1.html*

Managing Volunteer Programs

▶ *www.mapnp.org/library/staffing/outsrcng/volnteer/volnteer.htm*

National Service Resource Center

▶ Resource center to access training, technical assistance providers, and other support for all national service programs. *http://www.volunteertoday.com/Connie.html*

The New Volunteer

▶ This site provides a basic introduction to all aspects of volunteer management, discussing in brief a variety of topics, from who volunteers to ensuring good staff–volunteer relations. By Lester Schick, County Extension Director in Jackson County, Michigan. *http://www.canr.msu.edu/jackson/Community%20Dev/Volunteer/new_volunteer.htm*

Nonprofit Frequently Asked Questions (FAQs)—Volunteerism (Internet Nonprofit Center)

▶ Frequently Asked Questions and their answers, compiled from posts by nonprofit professionals to NONPROFIT (list) and soc.org.nonprofit (USENET group), as well as from information posted to other nonprofit-related Internet discussion groups. It is comprehensive, with information or links to information on volunteering from both a volunteer's and an agency's point of view. It includes information on setting up an all-volunteer program, program development strategy, training, and screening volunteers. *http://www.nonprofit-info.org/npofaq/04/index.html*

Points of Light Foundation

▶ *www.pointsoflight.org*

Professional Networks—Association for Volunteer Administration

▶ *http://www.avaintl.org/networks/index.html*

Resources for Volunteers

▶ *www.cybervpm.com*

ServiceLeader.org—Volunteer Management and Volunteerism Resources (Charles A. Dana Center, University of Texas Austin)

▶ *http://www.serviceleader.org/*

TxServe—Texas Commission on Volunteerism and Community Service

▶ This is a Texas-based project to serve the leaders and managers of volunteer and community service initiatives, and looked at as a model Web site by other statewide initiatives across the United States. It is a project in collaboration with Texas Commission of Volunteerism and Community Services. *http://www.txserve.org*

The Virtual Volunteering Guidebook: How to Apply the Principles of Real-World Volunteer Management to Online Service

▶ Written by Susan J. Ellis, a volunteer-management consultant, and Jayne Cravens, manager of the Virtual Volunteering Project, this 133-page book explains how to recruit, manage, and evaluate volunteers who do their charity work on the Internet. It also includes a chapter on how nonprofit organizations can involve people with disabilities in their online volunteer programs. *http://www.energizeinc.com/art/elecbooks.html*

Volunteer Center of Memphis Resources

▶ An index of Web sites featuring nonprofit management/volunteer management information and resources. *http://www.volunteer-memphis.com/resources.html*

Volunteer Management—501Click

▶ *http://www.501click.com/mt_vm_main.html*

Volunteer Management Library—Energize

▶ *http://www.energizeinc.com/art.html*

Volunteer Management for Program Directors

▶ Hosted by the Court Appointed Special Advocate (CASA), *http://www.casanet.org/,* and Guardian ad Litem (GAL) programs, this site includes information on volunteer retention, supervision, sample volunteer management policies, how to fire a volunteer, and volunteer interviewing techniques, many written by Steve McCurley and Rick Lynch. An Envoy Plug In is necessary to view this information; the Web page has a link to more information about this download. *http://www.casanet.org/program-management/volunteer-manage/index.htm*

Volunteer Management Reference Guide: A Annotated Bibliographic Resource

▶ This is an online booklist searchable database with over 700 references. You can choose your category of reference that including

topics such as recruitment, recognition, advocacy, disability, liability, management, leadership, retention, boards, communication, videos, service-learning, and much more. *http://www.regis.edu/spsmnm/dovia/do04001.htm*

Volunteer Management/Service Leadership Online Resources

▶ Information on volunteer screening, matching, record keeping and evaluation, legal issues/risk management, volunteer/staff relations, online activism by volunteers, volunteer management software, using the Internet to recruit volunteers, university and college level courses in volunteer management (including distance learning information), national conferences, and more. *http://www.service-leader.org/manage/index.html*

Volunteer Management/Service Leadership Online Resources—The Texas Education Network (TENET)

▶ *http://www.tenet.edu/volunteer/manage/*

Volunteer Manager's Corner

▶ *http://clubs.yahoo.com/clubs/volunteermanagerscorner*

Volunteer Organizations

The World of Volunteers

▶ *http://www.iyv2001.org/iyv_eng/world/world.htm*

Workplace Volunteerism

Resources for Employee Volunteer Program Managers—Points of Light Foundation

▶ *http://www.pointsoflight.org/assistance/assistance_corporate_resources.html*

ABOUT THE CD-ROM

INTRODUCTION

The files on the enclosed CD-ROM are saved in Microsoft Word for Windows version 7.0. In order to use the forms, you will need to have word processing software capable of reading Microsoft Word for Windows version 7.0 files.

SYSTEM REQUIREMENTS

- IBM PC or compatible computer
- CD-ROM drive
- Windows 95 or later
- Microsoft Word for Windows version 7.0 (including the Microsoft converter*) or later or other word processing software capable of reading Microsoft Word for Windows 7.0 files.

NOTE: Many popular word processing programs are capable of reading Microsoft Word for Windows 7.0 files. However, users should be aware that a slight amount of formatting might be lost when using a program other than Microsoft Word.

USING THE FILES

Loading the Files

The use the word processing files, launch your word processing program. Select **File, Open** from the pull-down menu. Select the appropriate drive and directory. A list of files should appear. If you do not see a list of files in the directory, you need to select **WORD DOCUMENT (*.DOC)** under **Files of Type.** Double click on the file you want to open.

Printing Files

If you want to print the files, select **File, Print** from the pull-down menu.

USER ASSISTANCE

If you need assistance of if you have a damaged CD-ROM, please contact Wiley Technical Support at:

Phone: (212) 850-6753

Fax: (212) 850-6800 (Attention: Wiley Technical Support)

URL: *www.wiley.com/techsupport*

---

*Word 7.0 needs the Microsoft converter file installed in order to view and edit all enclosed files. If you have trouble viewing the files, download the free converter from the Microsoft web site. The URL for the converter is: *http://office.microsoft.com/downloads/2000/wrd97cnv.aspx*
Microsoft also has a viewer that can be downloaded, which allows you to view, but not edit documents. This viewer can be downloaded at: *http://office.microsoft.com/downloads/9798/wd97vwr32.aspx*

For information about the CD-ROM see the **About the CD-ROM** section on page 659.

WILEY

Publishers Since 1807